The American Democracy

BY THE SAME AUTHOR

FAITH, REASON, AND CIVILIZATION

REFLECTIONS ON THE REVOLUTION OF OUR TIME

WHERE DO WE GO FROM HERE?

THE AMERICAN PRESIDENCY

THE DANGER OF BEING A GENTLEMAN AND OTHER ESSAYS

PARLIAMENTARY GOVERNMENT IN ENGLAND

THE STATE IN THEORY AND PRACTICE

A GRAMMAR OF POLITICS

THE FOUNDATIONS OF SOVEREIGNTY AND OTHER ESSAYS

STUDIES IN LAW AND POLITICS

AN INTRODUCTION TO POLITICS

DEMOCRACY IN CRISIS

THE RISE OF EUROPEAN LIBERALISM

KARL MARX

THE SOCIALIST TRADITION IN THE FRENCH REVOLUTION

AUTHORITY IN THE MODERN STATE

THE PROBLEM OF SOVEREIGNTY

POLITICAL THOUGHT IN ENGLAND FROM LOCKE TO BENTHAM

COMMUNISM

THE DANGERS OF OBEDIENCE AND OTHER ESSAYS

HAROLD J. LASKI

THE

American

Democracy

A COMMENTARY AND

AN INTERPRETATION

1948

NEW YORK · THE VIKING PRESS

PRINTED IN U.S.A. BY THE HADDON CRAFTSMEN, INC., SCRANTON, PA.

BY ARRANGEMENT WITH THE VIKING PRESS

1

For Frida
with my love and devotion

The Contents

	Preface	ix
I	The Traditions of America	3
II	The Spirit of America	39
III	American Political Institutions: Federal	72
IV	American Political Institutions: State and Local	138
V	American Business Enterprise	165
VI	American Labour	200
VII	Religion in America	264
VIII	American Education	323
IX	American Culture	393
X	America and Its Minority Problems	452
XI	America as a World Power	495
XII	The Professions in America	564
XIII	Press, Cinema, and Radio in America	615
XIV	Americanism as a Principle of Civilization	714
	Index	763

Preface

IN A sense this book has been a generation in the making; for when I first began to teach at Harvard thirty years ago, I realized that, as a European, I had entered upon an experience wholly different in character from anything I had known. I first began to think about writing it when I was in America in 1937; and, three years later, during the Battle of Britain, I began to try and put it into organized form. No one, I venture to believe, knows its defects more fully than I do. As it has got written, I have realized more and more how disproportionate is the fulfilment to the task I had set myself. There is so much more in America than any one man can know. There is so much in it, both of beauty and ugliness, of good and evil, that he cannot put into words. I can plead only two things in defence of the result; first, that this book is written out of deep love of America, and, second, that I have done my best to make intelligible to Europeans, and, above all, to Englishmen, why America arouses that deep love.

America is in large part Americans; and my debts to them are quite beyond repayment. First of all, I owe much to my friends, Mr. Justice Frankfurter and Dr. Alfred E. Cohn, with whom I have discussed these matters for more than half my life; and, in a younger generation, to Max Lerner, from whom I have learned much. I do not know how to express the thanks I feel that a happy fortune gave me the high privilege of intimacy with those great judges, Oliver Wendell Holmes and Louis Brandeis; nor can I forget the magnanimity with which the late Franklin D. Roosevelt allowed me to see the working of the presidential system from within. I know, too, that I have been, in a real sense, the pupil of Professor Morris R. Cohen, and that I owe many insights to the fact that I taught at Harvard when Turner and Channing and S. E. Morison were interpreting for me, in their different ways, what I myself was experiencing. I owe much, too, to the first of my American friends, B. W. Huebsch, to Max Lowenthal, Roger Baldwin, Harlow Shapley, E. R. Murrow, Robert and Helen Lynd, Samuel Berger, Frank Buxton, Merle Curti, Thomas Reed Powell, and Charles and Mary Beard, and, far from

ix

least, to the care and generosity of Miss J. R. Heringman of the Viking Press. I wish I could recall the countless others, students, taxi-drivers, railroad conductors, lawyers and doctors, engineers and business men, who have helped me to form the generalizations I have ventured to make here. But a book of this kind is always the product, really, of many people's thinking, and I can only hope that I have not omitted anyone whose name ought to be here. For the result, of course, I only am responsible; most of whatever merit it has it owes to those who, consciously or unconsciously, have helped me to shape it.

I owe debts, also, to English friends, above all to my colleague H. L. Beales, and to my former colleague, Professor D. W. Brogan of Cambridge, upon whose unique fund of Americana I have been able to rely for years. From Sydney Herbert of University College, Aberystwyth, I have had much assistance by discussion; and, though I knew him only in his last years, from talk with Lord Bryce about his hopes of America in the eighties of the last century, and his fears for it after the First World War. My gratitude to R. T. Clark and C. A. Furth is very great, not least for their infinite patience.

I have been much helped, also, by books; and I must especially emphasize what I owe to the writings of Professor Schlesinger of Harvard University, to Professor Commons and his colleagues for their *Documentary History of American Industrial Society,* to Professor E. S. Corwin, Professor Perry Miller, Professor C. E. Merriam, to Professor R. B. Perry for his great work on William James, to Professor Bernhard J. Stern for his remarkable writings on American technology and medicine, to Dr. W. E. B. DuBois and to Professor G. Myrdal, and to Professor M. L. Hansen. I must record, too, my gratitude to Professor M. Rostovtzev whose monumental *Social and Economic History of the Hellenistic World* has been a continuous source of illumination. Like all students of American history, I have learned a great deal from the writings of the great Adams dynasty, above all from that unique *Diary* of John Quincy Adams of which a modern reprint is so badly needed. I owe many insights, especially on the American Revolution, to the writings of my friend Louis B. Hacker, and, on American Literature, to Professor F. O. Matthiessen's *American Renaissance.* Other debts, I have, I hope, sufficiently acknowledged in the notes to this work.

I add that the dedication of this book means far more than its words imply. But there is gratitude too intimate even to search for expression.

Little Bardfield,   H. J. L.
Essex.

The American Democracy

I

The Traditions of America

I

MOST of the heritage of past civilizations has gone into the making of American democracy. Europe and the Far East have alike nourished its rise and development; it has strains from the African continent which lie deep in its foundations. In the four and a half centuries since it emerged into the historic consciousness, it has passed from the epoch in which it was an object of colonial ambition to the epoch where it stands, independent, at the summit of political power. And in that momentous period there can be no sort of doubt but that its impact has changed the outlook of mankind wherever there has been the power to reflect on the meaning of human affairs. No state, until our own day, has done so much to make the idea of progress a part of the mental make-up of man. No state, either, has done more to make freedom a dream which overcame the claims both of birth and of wealth. It has been, in an impressive way, a refuge for the oppressed, alike in the political and in the religious field, for at least the period since the Pilgrim Fathers landed on the rocky shores of New England. It has offered to the common man an opportunity of self-advancement such as he has never known elsewhere until the Russian Revolution of 1917. Few countries have ever developed material resources on so vast a scale. Few countries have ever been able to move so swiftly from the circumference to the centre in their impact upon civilization. If it has often been hated and even more often envied, there has always been a perception, even in the hatred and the envy, that it occupied a unique position among the nations of the world. Now it stands close to the zenith of its fortunes. For something like the next generation it is difficult to doubt that world politics will be set in the context of American purposes. Upon the use it decides to make of its overwhelming productive power, no small part of the fate of Europe and Asia, perhaps of Africa as well, is bound overwhelmingly to depend.

There is hardly a type of European humanity which has not contributed its quota to the shaping of American tradition. The Spaniard made his mark on California; the Dutchman on New York; the English-

3

man on the Atlantic coast; the German in Pennsylvania; the Swedes in the Northwest; the Irish in New York and Chicago; the French in Louisiana and, for a period, in the Mississippi Valley. And as America developed economically, the call of the West and the endless spaces which craved for settlement brought Poles and Ruthenians, Serbs and Croats, Italians and Greeks. Already, by the time that independence had been won in 1783, the United States was a microcosm to which almost every European adventurer contributed his quota; after independence it was like a vast pit into which was poured whatever there was in Europe of the spirit of enterprise and adventure. Possibly it is true that until some such time as the Civil War the predominant mould into which this immense variety was poured in endless succession was shaped by the English tradition. The way of thought, in institutions, in religion, in science, and in literature, was perhaps more fully English than any other outlook. The language made for that primacy; so, also, did the pattern of the political framework.

But it was always English with a difference. Even the first generation of emigrants from the British Isles wore their Englishry with a difference. That is obvious in the case of men like Tom Paine, and it is still more obvious when the American is native-born. If it be true that it is not very difficult to think of George Washington as in temperament and habit a wealthy English squire, no one can doubt that Samuel Adams and Jefferson, Franklin and John Jay, are Americans in a sense which makes their English inheritance an element only in the final character they displayed. No one can read the literature of America, even up to the outbreak of the War of Independence, without seeing that a new national type has emerged upon the historic stage. He has an experimentalism in temper, a passion for making his own way in life, a zeal for self-assertion which were all of a world removed from the England he had defeated. The environment in which he functions breaks the cake of custom, which, had the English connection remained, he would doubtless have been eager to preserve. The conservatism of Alexander Hamilton was probably as profound as that of Lord Eldon in England; but it is very obviously an American conservatism. The radicalism of Thomas Jefferson goes back to foundations which Charles James Fox would have been proud to accept; but it is already a radicalism which has grown in a very different direction from any which Fox would have found it easy to follow. Chief Justice Marshall defended the claims of property with a zeal that must have made the members of the English bench feel that here was a spiritual partner in their legal effort; but there are elements in the method by which he defends his approach which would have been hardly intelligible to an English judge of his time. John Adams may analyse the weaknesses of democracy with a zeal that William Windham would have applauded had he been aware of it; but it is difficult to think that he would have grasped the basis upon which Adams approached his problems.

And if, by 1783, the peaks of the mountain ranges have already become so different, it is natural that the valleys are even more different. What is outstanding in the ordinary American, by the time the Peace of Versailles was signed in that year, is that he does not assume the duty to remain in the position in which he was born. Most English radicals of the time look backwards for their inspiration; as late even as Dickens it is goodwill and generosity that will solve the social problem. The English thinker who desires to reorganize the foundations of his community upon a new basis, like Robert Owen, or his disciple William Thompson, is not only rare; it is even suspected that he is a little mad. The average radical, O'Connor, Hunt, or Cobbett, is not only a man whose ideals are of the pre-Industrial Revolution; he is tempted to think that the ideal England means a recovery of the past rather than a search for the future.

That is in no sense true of the analogous American type. He is confident that he is in himself a person of social significance. He is rarely interested in his past because he is so certain that his future will bear no relation to it. The tradition that he has inherited is that of a dynamic civilization in which he is assured that whatever was yesterday, it will be different again tomorrow. He assumes as a part of his inheritance that he will have the right continually to go forward. He does not accept the postulates of a society where, as in the Europe from which he largely came, birth or inherited wealth may make all the difference to the hopes he may venture to form. No doubt it is true that there has been in American history that craving for the recognition of a special status, the desire to possess the inherent right to command, of which the remains lingered on in the South until they were broken to pieces in the Civil War. No doubt, also, the formulation of hope has been different in the level towards which it might reach in special groups like the Negroes and the American citizens of Oriental origin, in the Jews, and, to some degree and in some places, the Roman Catholics. But even when these exceptions have been made the dynamic quality of the American tradition is as notable as it is unmistakable. From the very outset the psychological roots of the American idea have been built upon the foundation of expansionism. There was expansion territorially; there was expansion in the power to utilize the vast resources which, until 1929, seemed to have no limit. There was, too, a cultural expansion symbolized, perhaps, above all, in the faith in education and the intensity with which applied science has been accepted as a normal part of living.

The very bigness of America has an importance in the formation of its tradition which it is not easy to overestimate. It creates the belief that America is different, is somehow exceptional, that there is reserved for its citizens another destiny from that which is to befall the Old World. The spaciousness of the United States as a physical entity makes the idea of unlimited horizons, of constant discovery, of novelty that is always imminent, part of the background against which each American is set. However much the colonial period may be dependent upon European ways of thought, their adaptation to American use always involves some change of greater or lesser profundity. This is, I think, because at the base of the tradition is, even when unconsciously, the thought in every man that he is somehow a pioneer, and, therefore, the growth of a conviction that there is no problem he cannot tackle. If he is an immigrant he is a pioneer because he has made the break with the Old World; if he is the child of an immigrant he is a pioneer because he is affirming in his own person the finality of the break; and if he is an American, like the remarkable Adams family, of long standing, he is a pioneer because he belongs to the small group of men who have shaped the contours of the New World.

This concept of the pioneer penetrates every nook and cranny of the American tradition. It explains why the ordinary American rarely assumes that any career upon which he embarks is, outside such special professions as medicine and the churches, the final career in which he will end. Thomas Jefferson is a polymath who attains distinction in every subject he touches; Benjamin Franklin is only less eminent as a diplomat and statesman than as a scientist; when Charles Carroll wishes to build himself a house in Baltimore, he does not send for an architect but for books on architecture, out of which he composes one of the loveliest houses in the New World. Almost as a boy, Alexander Hamilton is a distinguished officer on Washington's staff; he is then, within four years, as brilliant a political philosopher as the party of property has produced in the United States; he is as brilliant an administrator as the Treasury Department has known; and few advocates have won for themselves a higher position at the American Bar. Or there is Andrew Jackson, farmer, merchant, lawyer, soldier, congressman, and, finally, president of the United States. Towering above all is the majestic figure of Abraham Lincoln, lonely, aloof, tragic, who grows from the illiteracy of a home where there is little but failure and poverty to impose himself not merely on the mind of America, but on the mind of all civilization, as the supreme figure in the democratic tradition of the nineteenth century. As one examines the significance of these men, it is impossible not to conclude that they represent a new category in the conventional distribution of the human beings who search for the means to rule their fellow-citizens.

For, if we compare them with their European analogues, the characteristics they display are utterly different. Washington, perhaps, and the Adams dynasty are of the type that in the England or France of the early nineteenth century might have attained political distinction. Of all the others, I think it is true to say that either they would not have dreamed of a political career, or, had they dreamed of it, there is little likelihood that there would have been any avenue through which they could have passed to positions of authority. Here again, there is inherent in the American tradition the spaciousness of hope and the exhilaration that hope conveys; and it is the greatness of this quality that it brings out in so many the zest for adventure, the sense of ambition, the willingness to break the routines in which they have been enclosed. Indeed, it is notable that where the routine is over-valued it tends to become an object of satire or of indignation; one has the conviction of this in the inter-relations between what is old-established convention in Boston or Philadelphia or Charleston, and the challenge which seeks to adapt it to new claims.

The American tradition is, in essence, an individualistic tradition which has tended to look upon the State with doubt or suspicion. In part, of course, this attitude stems from the religious background of the seventeenth century; the pioneers were men and women seeking to escape from a persecuting government to which their truths were unacceptable. That does not mean for a moment that the pioneers were generally in favour of toleration; the attitude of Massachusetts to Anne Hutchinson and Roger Williams and the first group of Quaker missionaries is sufficient evidence that the growth of toleration was alike slow and painful. But its growth was called for by the conditions which Americans confronted. There was a common danger from the Indian tribes; there was the variety of national origin of the settlers themselves, and the impossibility, in its light, of maintaining for long any rigid form of orthodoxy. No doubt the general basis of the American tradition was the Christian heritage from Europe; and no doubt, also, the clergy occupied a specially important place in its making. But it was rarely possible for any of the thirteen colonies to maintain for very long the union of some given Church with the State. And the outcome of this tendency to separation was to emphasize the idea that the individual should find his own pathway to salvation. The release this effected in the sphere of belief had inevitable repercussions far beyond its boundaries.

The first object of the settler on American soil was to be the master of his environment. He had to build his house, to sow his crops; and his wife had to provide the largest part of those needs which could only slowly come to count upon the results of the division of labour. The consequence of this was that few Americans, comparatively, lived by owning merely; and this fact conferred upon the idea of toil a claim to dignity, a sense of self-reliance, which gave the idea of individualism a special sanctity. By the War of Independence about one American in ten lived in a town. This meant that most of them assumed that they must depend upon themselves for the provision of services we now regard as a normal function of the government. And from this it followed that the individual citizen became what he could make himself, so that he tended to think of any restraint placed by authority upon his power to develop his fortunes as in itself a harmful thing. The tradition, therefore, looked upon the government as, above all, an organ of defence and order. And this attitude was even intensified by the colonial experience of restraints imposed upon the economic prospects of American citizens by the restrictive legislation of the mother-country. No doubt Great

Britain was a safeguard as long as the government of France left it uncertain whether the civilization of the New World was to owe allegiance to London or to Versailles. But once the Seven Years' War had drawn to its victorious close, the sovereignty of Parliament became a clear restraint of opportunity, the more deeply resented the more vigorously it was applied. It is not fanciful to argue that no small part of the ease with which the doctrine of natural rights obtained acceptance in the eighteenth century arose from the fact that it seemed to restrain the exercise of an authority which was obviously a factor limiting the fulfilment of opportunities men like the merchants and farmers saw in front of them. To urge, therefore, that the government was best which governed least was to open gates which seemed to colonial America closed for no other reason than the protection of vested interests, and to limit the field of government action became almost a religious act when it was attained by victory in a revolutionary war.

This individualistic tradition is reinforced in a number of ways. It is democratic in the sense that, despite all pride of ancestry and wealth, the sheer abundance of land made it impossible to keep the planter aristocracy a closed caste. And, in any case, it was rare even for the wealthy planter to succeed unless he himself had a pretty shrewd judgment of men and the capacity to handle the details of his commerce. The outcome of this was to give trade a status which it never achieved in a society in which, as in France or England, the ruling class was composed of gentlemen of leisure, soldiers and sailors, eminent churchmen, and an occasional lawyer of the type of Lord Mansfield, a great advocate and a greater judge. It was democratic, too, in that the rise of the educational system was not accompanied by that suspicion that learning might "make servants insubordinate to their masters" which, even now, is not wholly extinct in Britain. The eighteenth century gave a general and intense impetus to the idea of self-help; and the fame of men like Nathaniel Ames and Benjamin Franklin proved the practical value of this virtue.

Self-help, moreover, in a frontier civilization necessarily meant versatility. The farmer was coping, as he settled down to life, with new land, new plants and animals, and a climate which required inventiveness as almost its first demand. If, in general, the intellectual life out of which the American tradition was founded was more narrow than most of its historians are ready to admit, it was still a life in which the spread of new ideas was extraordinarily rapid and the growth of a sense that the future was bright remarkably widespread. The belief in progress was practically universal; even sour John Adams did not doubt that America was destined "for the illumination and the emancipation of the slavish part of mankind all over the earth." That is the theme, also, of Joel Barlow's epic, *The Vision of Columbus,* written in 1787. Countless ballads tell the same story. In America man and woman reach a stature that comports with the dignity inherent in human nature. There is a sense of self-confidence, a conviction that the world is theirs for the taking, which are both unmistakable.

The American War of Independence coincided with, is, indeed, a part of, the Age of Enlightenment. It therefore is natural to find that there is a new faith in reason, a growth in the humanitarian temper, a sense of initiative and exertion, all of which have had an important role to play in the shaping of the tradition. If the war dealt a heavy blow to the cultural life of America, it also evoked an energy and effort among humble men which was of the first importance for the future. The very fact that men like Thomas Paine could exercise so profound an influence both on the character and the purpose of the struggle meant that natural rights, hostility to monarchy, and faith in the validity of freedom became a part of the mental constitution of Americans. The influence of the greatest of the figures in the Virginian dynasty, Thomas Jefferson, was directed to the formal separation of Church and State; and this, in its turn, not only made for religious toleration, but also laid the basis for that faith in education for the common people which Americans have never lost. No doubt it is true that conservatives like John Adams and Fisher Ames had no thought of an America in which the common man would play a vital part; they desired the rule of "gentlemen" on the ground, as Adams said, that "the people of all nations are naturally divided into two sorts, the gentlemen and the simple men." Fisher Ames wrote bitterly of the pretensions of the poor to positions for which the well-born and the rich were the proper candidates; and the *Diary* of Gouverneur Morris is full of contempt for the ordinary folk who, without careful discipline, would drift into insubordination and shiftlessness. It was notable that he was even prepared to leave Paine to perish in a French prison when he was ambassador of the new republic to Paris.

But neither the well-born nor the rich defined the ideology of the American tradition. By 1800, it is beyond all doubt that it was to be shaped by ordinary men. The lawyers, the clergy, the rich merchants, and the great landowners might feel, like Hamilton, that the people was "a great beast"; but the victory of Jefferson in the great election of 1800 meant that the idea of an America would triumph in which the notion of an *élite* to whom government was confided would have no place. And with the victory of Jeffersonian democracy there begins to mature a cultural democracy that is indigenous and not foreign in its origin. The sense that this would be the case is already present in books like those of Crève-cœur and Chastellux. It is announced with passion by poets like Philip Freneau, and by the eminent lexicographer Noah Webster. They think of America as young and Europe as old, of America as a country with a mighty future, and Europe as a decrepit continent which is bound to decline. Even though there is a recognition that it will be far from easy to build an independent American culture, they have the conviction that it must and can be done. Books like Jefferson's *Notes on Virginia*, indeed, are nothing so much as a stone deliberately laid in the edifice he sought to build; and it is significant that, as the nineteenth century began, Americans were already insisting that its history and geography should be the basis upon which its educational system should be built. Joel Barlow may have exaggerated the level of American achievement in his poems, but it is important that, as early as the year in which the Federal Convention met, he was claiming the cultural, as well as the political, independence of the United States.

What is important in these years of the Enlightenment is the conviction that Americans will first free themselves and then set an example to the rest of the world. The power of the moneyed class was very great; and pamphlets like those of Timothy Dwight of Yale University show that events like Shays' Rebellion and the French Revolution struck terror into the minds of the men of property. But the Federalists were beaten on the political field and Paine's *Age of Reason* swept through every element in the population from students in the colleges to the small farmers in Massachusetts and Georgia. Men like Paine and Volney prepared the ground which, on the one hand, made possible the remarkable influence of the British reformers Robert Owen and Frances Wright, and, on the other, made theological principles like those of Universalism and Unitarianism replace the rigid Presbyterian orthodoxy of Jonathan Edwards. There is a passionate advocacy of new ideas, feminism, humanitarianism, and scientific analysis. The American tradition rarely goes beyond the limits of the Deist principle; but it is natural, as the nineteenth century dawns, to see any novelty in ideas receive a welcome far more profound than any it was likely to secure in Europe.

Not, indeed, that the tradition is wholly democratic or radical. There are elements in it of a deep conservative strain. In one sense, it is difficult to deny that the French Revolution threw the men of solid property into a panic as great as any upon the European continent, and the deposit of its influences is traceable right down to our own day. The men who had not hesitated to throw off their British chains by war explain with passion the evil of violence and the nobility of order and property. There emerges the hostility between the little men, the debtors who lined up behind the appeal of Shays' Rebellion, and the creditor class whom Hamilton defended as the true source of civilized life. He, and the great Chief Justice, John Marshall, are the authors of an American tradition which venerates the men of property and birth as eagerly as do Burke and Joseph de Maistre. William Ellery Channing was in a profound sense a liberal, with a keen sense of the rights of labour, but even he insists that the "French Revolution had diseased the imagination and unsettled the understanding of man everywhere." If there is a revolutionary principle in the American tradition, based upon the rights of man, there is also a counter-revolutionary principle based upon the rights of property; and it is difficult not to feel that the shield which safeguards the counter-revolutionary principle was, in Jefferson's time, as it is a century and a half later, the revival of religious orthodoxy. It is interesting and significant that James Fenimore Cooper should urge the possession of piety as the quality most valuable in a husband. It is equally significant that President Dwight of Yale University appointed Benjamin Silliman to his chair in that university in order that the students might see that science and Christianity are the twin sides of a single outlook.

There is, indeed, a middle way within this bifurcated tradition. Until, at least, the Civil War, the main outlines of American civilization are set in terms of an aristocratic leadership. But these terms do not exclude a popularization of culture, whether in education, in science, in literature, or in religion. If the intellectual leaders of America tended to look to Europe for their inspiration, the masses, on the other hand, sought to build an America free from the trammels of the Old World. And this antithesis is, after all, natural enough. The Brahmins of Boston, for example, had leisure and security; their cosmopolitan outlook was the expression of the self-confidence these implied. But the masses of America, whether the native-born workers or the immigrants from Europe, were naturally eager to prove their Americanism by drawing their inspiration, whether in thought or act, from the soil they were turning from a wilderness into a settlement. One finds, accordingly, within the American tradition a dependence upon the European heritage at the apex of the social pyramid, and, at its base, a proud insistence upon the American right to see things with their own eyes and in their own way. The rich American must obtain his letters of credit in Paris or in Rome, in Naples or Madrid; the poor American emphasizes above all his freedom from the rigidity of the European scheme. So long as the resources of America seem infinite, there is little difficulty in arriving at a compromise between the two ways of looking at life. There is room alike for a patrician cosmopolitanism and a plebeian nationalism; and both of these outlooks reveal, on examination, a deep conviction that the American idea has somehow come to include all the discoveries of civilized living. It is because all types of American, both rich and poor, native and foreign-born, knew in their inner being that the promise of American life was certain of fulfilment that they had the faith which is vital to building a nation.

2

AMERICA inherited most of what the Old World had to offer; but it has been central to the American tradition that it has been unfettered by old methods. In part, that was because it confronted problems that were either in their essence new or that called for techniques with which the Old World was unacquainted. Adaptability is inherent in the personality of the American, and, with it, there has gone a zeal for what is new merely because it is new. From the outset of its history, the American people has had the sense that it was conquering a wilderness, that it was, as it were, wresting from Nature an unlimited area of virgin soil. This meant that, in general, the human qualities most valued were those of the practical man, rather than of the theorist. What was required was the man or woman who could meet an immediate situation with a solution that fitted the problem. Abstraction, philosophizing, these tended to delay the mastery of Nature, and this is why, I think, that theory developed comparatively late in the evolution of the American mind, and when it did develop assumed very characteristically that form of empiricism which rejected absolutes in favour of concrete solutions that worked in the particular instance. Wherever an American philosophy has been non-empiric in character, it has always, also, like Hegelian idealism, been non-American in origin.

It is this pragmatism in the tradition which explains why the American mind tends to give so emphatic a priority to the man of action over the man of theory. Throughout American history there has been a zest, an admiration, for the concrete and the particular. Abstraction, the faculty of large-scale generalization, tends, on the whole, to be regarded as sterile. For the environment has called for men who can do things, whether it is to clear a forest, or build a house, or construct a railroad. The contemplative mind is, in the tradition, associated very largely with the idea of a leisured class; and that idea, in its turn, has always had about it a suspicion of the aristocratic idea of which American civilization, above all after 1776, has been a living denial. And this priority of the practical has meant the supremacy, in American life, of the executive type, of the man who can organize, of the person who sees his way through an immediate problem. Even outstanding "intellectuals" in American history are notable, like Franklin and Thomas Jefferson, for their power to get things done. Not only does the "gentleman," in the English sense of that complex term, arrive relatively late in American history; it is hardly until Eli Whitney had made the ownership of slaves a profitable enterprise that the planters of the South accepted the notion that leisure was itself a career.

Even in our own day the tradition tends to look askance at the man whose business is ideas. Woodrow Wilson is held, partially at least, to have failed because he was a college professor; and it is the assumption of his critics that he therefore lacked the practical common sense that is expected from a lawyer or a business man. It is natural enough to an American that a successful general should, like Jackson or Taylor, Harrison or Grant, go to the White House; and it is equally natural that a melancholy scholar like Henry Adams, who aims, above all, at the achievement of a philosophy of history, should be regarded as a decorative ornament for whom there is no use in practical affairs. The men who arouse admiration are those who, like Edison or Ford, can apply with exceptional brilliance ideas that other men have conceived. The successful politician is, almost invariably, what Bagehot recognized in Sir Robert

Peel as the "uncommon man of common opinions." Jefferson and Lincoln, no doubt, are partial exceptions to this rule; but both of them united to profound political insight a skill in the management of men which has a recognizable kinship with the executive type in great business enterprise.

Certain other features of this American tradition need to be emphasized. It has always been difficult to persuade Americans to take long views in matters of social constitution. The changes in the character of its economic life have been so swift that, until practically the other day, a long-term plan was out of date almost before it sought acceptance from the people. What was the West in Jefferson's day was already a part of the East when Jackson entered the White House; and the West that Jackson knew had little relevance to the frontier by the time of the Civil War. Nor must we forget the layer upon layer of immigration, each with a new source in the Old World, and each bringing some new element into the tradition. The one constant feature of the social landscape is the virtually universal passion for physical prosperity. The speed with which this passion spread had never previously been equalled; and it was built at once upon the possession of massive physical resources and an inventiveness in their use which has made the idea of mass production a typically American conception. The character and extent of this idea has made the United States a civilization in essence different from anything known in the Old World until the Russian Revolution of 1917.

Its influence has been overwhelming. In the first place, it developed in almost every citizen the idea of a dynamic career. He could not believe that he would remain where he began. He could not escape, until some such time as the Great Depression of 1929, from the conviction that he would better his condition in a material way. The result has been that almost every element in American life has been shaped by this conviction. It has had enormous influence on all the forms of religious life; no church which urged the desirability of asceticism had any hope of influence or much hope of survival. It has been responsible for the amazing range of American philanthropy. Suffering, even in foreign countries, seemed like nothing so much as a contradiction of the American idea; and the price of success has always been the obligation of the man who has obtained it to find the ways and means of proving his goodwill to his fellow-creatures. It has enormously influenced the habits of American education; there have been few colleges which did not assume that the character of their training should be ultimately controlled by the successful business man. It is, indeed, tempting to argue that, the Negro and the sharecropper apart, all Americans regard themselves as middle class in character. That is why socialism has made such little progress in the United States; and it is perhaps the most solid reason for the absence of a doctrinal trade-unionism which found permanent expression in a political party. There are few Americans, in fact, who do not set great store on the chance of accumulating private property; and it is this attitude, more than any other, which explains why the revolutionary ideas of the European continent have found it so difficult to get a hold upon the American mind.

The zeal for accumulation by the individual sets the background for some important elements in the American tradition. It has been, at least since the Civil War, a whole-time job. The result has been that few American men could announce that they were functionless in the sense of an aristocrat in England or France or Tsarist Russia. They gave all their energies to work; they were, indeed, expected to do so. This has evolved an American ruling class with little knowledge of how to spend their leisure when they had it. In general, they were not certain that leisure was not a kind of sinful waste; and the great collectors, Morgan, or Frick, or Huntington, brought together their superb books and pictures and *objets d'art* not so much as amateurs to whom selection was a source of pleasure, but, rather, as professionals who sought, in the particular sphere they made their own, at once to outbid any rival who might appear upon the scene, and, after their death, to leave a permanent memorial which would satisfy the national passion for philanthropic effort.

The zeal for material well-being has had a profound effect, also, upon the American tradition in politics and literature. No foreign observer can watch the political process without noting how temporary and casual is, in general, the hold of the elected person on the constituents he represents. An occasional figure, like Senator Borah, may make a permanent career at Washington, but the real high road for the average member of a legislative assembly is less the quality of his contribution to the state or to the nation than his ability to gratify his supporters with a constant succession of small favours. That is, of course, the secret of the success of the machines like Tammany; its leaders bind their followers to them not by the doctrines they profess but by the favours they confer. No doubt there comes a time, after an interval, when some city boss steps beyond the permitted line and is replaced by a reform administration; but it rarely lasts for long simply because the reformers lack that gift of personal kindliness which no boss ever omits to display. And the average American, in the long run, finds it difficult not to believe that the bankers and financiers are merely doing for themselves on a great scale what the city boss and his henchmen do with relative moderation, accompanied by a kindly interest in the fortunes of their constituents, not least if these latter be the first generation of Americans.

And with, of course, remarkable exceptions, the same is true of literature in the American tradition. It is, unless it seeks deliberately to imitate some European examplar, experimental rather than imitative in character. Its emphasis is usually on substance rather than on form. It is, above all, a middle-class literature in the important sense that it finds its power of appeal in its representation of ordinary American life as a vast and romantic adventure. Where, as with Henry James, the roots of its tradition lie in Europe rather than in America, the main impression one derives from reading it is that the author, in drawing his Americans, is remote from the mainstream of American life. His American, man or woman, is divorced from the tradition that gives America its peculiar character; and he becomes a stranger to his native land who sees his fellow-countrymen through the eyes of one who has deliberately chosen a foreign mirror through which to look at them. But Emerson, Thoreau, Mark Twain, Hawthorne, and Melville, while they may be deeply influenced by the central stream of civilized intelligence, are always profoundly American, not least in the sense that, wherever their imagination may roam, it is always in the American tradition that they put their ultimate allegiance. And once an American writer fails in that allegiance, it is difficult not to feel that the pseudo-European style through which he finds expression is really a mask which he wears like one who hides behind a domino at a ball.

At the centre of the American tradition is the idea of enlightened self-interest. It is assumed that with energy and determination every man can not only look after himself, but is part of a world in which the capacity to advance is universal. That outlook lies at the core of the thought of men so different in temperament and training as Abraham Lincoln and Woodrow Wilson; and there is an important sense in which it is the main principle of Franklin Roosevelt's policies. The consequence of this outlook is far-reaching. On the one hand, it creates a suspicion of all action taken by the government on behalf of the individual. It is argued that this limits his capacity for enterprise and responsibility, and it is widely held, sometimes in the most unexpected quarters, that what a man does for himself is almost certain to be better done than what is done on his behalf. Enlightened self-interest is regarded as the parent of experimentalism; and it is insisted that an accumulation of small acts of self-denial enables any energetic citizen to advance his fortunes. This is perhaps why it seems to take a great crisis—world war, for example—to evoke great sacrifices from Americans; the drama needs to be staged on a vast scale before the average man thinks far beyond the cultivation of his own garden. He can be kind and hospitable and friendly; but the limits of his imagination are more narrow than one would expect from the scale of the civilization in which he is involved. Nor do I think it is fanciful to connect this attitude with the priority of the practical man over the thinker.

Few Americans find it easy to be happy unless they are doing something. The gospel of hard work which they have inherited, in part from the impact of the physical environment and in part from the Puritan tradition, makes it difficult for them not to equate contemplation with laziness. That is why they find the creative use of leisure a more difficult art than any other nation with which I am acquainted. That is why, also, even when they play, there is a seriousness in the amenities of life which is unparalleled elsewhere. To the rich man, for instance, golf is less a game than a pursuit in which, with the aid of the club professional, he gives an almost religious attention to the reduction of his handicap. That is why, again, the intercollegiate athletic contests, whether they are base-ball or track-running or even debating, make so important a difference to the status of an academic institution. I have heard a president of Prince-ton University address its football team before a game with Harvard in terms not very different from Haig's famous "Backs to the Wall" order of March 1918. And athletic eminence may easily result in the kind of solid career which brings the player comfort for the rest of his days. The American is rare who knows how to play merely for the pleasure of play-ing. He finds it hard to be lazy; so that even in a relatively small town an indifferent bridge-player will take lessons from a professional teacher rather than be looked upon as a failure. A surprising number of Amer-icans do not think it strange that the author of a system of card-playing should turn his attention, in the grim years of the Second World War, to the development of methods by which permanent peace may be secured.

It may well be that so striking a change as the emergence of a special-ist in bridge into a specialist in international affairs is merely one expres-sion of that pioneering tradition which has made Americans so apt to specialize in omnicompetence. It may well be, also, that it is the Puritan element in the American tradition which makes them not only take their play so seriously, but assume that they will be open to criticism if their way of earning a livelihood is out of accord with the call of the times. For few peoples, save, possibly, the Japanese, are more sensitive to praise or blame than the Americans. They have none of the Englishman's ca-pacity for assuming that his own judgment about himself is final. They have little of that power of moral and intellectual self-sufficiency which is rooted in the French habit of mind. They never seek, like the Germans since the era of Bismarck, to give a universal character to their national standard of conduct; and they cannot, like the Japanese, enfold them-selves with a veil of mystery which the outsider is forbidden to pene-trate. In a sense, the American outlook resembles that of the Russian to a remarkable degree. Each is eager to know what is thought about him; and each is as elevated by eulogy as he suffers from blame. This is why, I think, *The American Commonwealth* of Lord Bryce was a real event in the history of the relations between Great Britain and the United States. For Bryce's was the first book by a British writer in which the greatness of America was acknowledged in its due proportions. It atoned for the contempt and dislike which had been poured upon Americans by writers like Captain Basil Hall and Mrs. Trollope and even Charles Dickens. It was the recognition that the United States had reached its historic majority; and it is not, I think, unfair or inaccurate to date the decline of that "inferiority complex"—which emerges in the pages of N. P. Willis and was symbolized with genius by Dickens in the character of Jefferson Brick—from the publication of Bryce's book. And this is true even though, half a century before, Tocqueville had seen the sig-nificance of America far more profoundly than Bryce; for Tocqueville was really writing a book on French civilization, and the United States crept into its pages as a source of illustration rather than as the central theme.

3

EVER since its emergence as an independent political community America has been a political democracy; and the idea of majority rule through representative institutions has been deeply embedded in its tradition. But we must be careful not to embody in the idea of this political democracy more than it in fact implies. It is essentially a democracy of the middle class, which assumes, though it does not announce, the authority of wealth, and has been careful, throughout its history, not to permit its informing idea to jeopardize the claims that men of property invariably put forward as the boundaries beyond which democracy may not pass. No one can scrutinize the political history of the democratic tradition in America without seeing that those boundaries are in fact more narrow than might be inferred either from a classic utterance like the Gettysburg speech or from the myriad orations which are evoked on each Fourth of July. They are restrained quite deliberately by the Constitution itself; they are still more restrained by the masterful construction John Marshall, and most of his colleagues and successors, have employed as their method of interpreting its purpose. They are restrained by the difficulty of absorbing into an effective unity the countless immigrants from so many nations of whom America is composed. And they are restrained by the fact that, despite passing phases of passionate anger, the effective organization of the working class into trade-unions began only in the eighties of the last century and has not yet begun to attain an adequate political expression.

But that is not all. There is an important sense in which the very vastness of the opportunity America offered its citizens was inimical to the fulfilment of what a democratic community implies. For, first, until the frontier was exhausted there were few Americans who expected to stay on the bottom rung of the ladder, and fewer still who ever expected that their children would stay there. They mostly took it for granted that the revised edition of Jeffersonian democracy which Woodrow Wilson called the "new freedom" was open to them; and, save in moments of panic or crisis, they rarely dreamed of attacking property, because they expected so soon to own it themselves. That the history of the United States would, despite everything, follow the general pattern of capitalist democracy in Europe occurred only to a few men of special insight like John Taylor of Caroline. In the result, until at least the outbreak of the Great Depression in 1929, the American was rare who recognized that the European pattern was emerging; and if he urged this conclusion in terms of socialism, it was relatively easy to push him aside on the ground that socialistic ideas were a European product with no relevance to the special conditions of American civilization.

So that, in the years, especially after the Civil War, the walls which protected property from democratic invasion grew increasingly high. The farmer was increasingly driven from ownership to tenantry. The worker in industry increasingly found that machine technology called for a scale of investment which only the great corporations could hope to attempt. The professional man, whether lawyer or doctor, engineer or architect, found that economic comfort was rarely attainable unless he was willing to be a dependent of the economic masters of America. And since the political parties were, in their turn, the means through which those masters did their will, it followed that the successful politician, whatever might be the rhetoric of his perorations, was successful because, somehow, he had come to an understanding with men like Mark Hanna or Nelson Aldrich, who were nothing so much as the agents of Wall Street and State Street. It seemed obvious to President Coolidge, whose mind was that of the average successful resident of Main Street, that Mr. Andrew Mellon should be his Secretary of the Treasury since few fortunes rivalled the Mellon fortune in the United States. It would have been interesting to hear the judgment of Jefferson or John Taylor upon that conclusion.

The American Constitution established a political democracy ; and the circumstances in which it operated involved a large measure of social equality. The traditions which have been evoked by the history of the last three centuries have given opportunities for individual advancement which, save for Russia since 1917, have been unparalleled in their scale in modern times. It is, moreover, probably true to say that nowhere was the social ascent more easy nor the belief in its validity more profound. Until, at any rate, the Civil War, it would be broadly fair to argue that the proportion of immigrants who failed to better the position they had held in the Old World was relatively small. There are dramatic careers in the industrial field, as there are dramatic careers in the political. Men force their way to success by reason of their own energy and ability. The absence of barriers in their way made the individualism of the Gilded Age seem the mental climate most appropriate to achievement. If the battle was hard, the rewards were magnificent, and most of the social theorists of the time, from William Graham Sumner at Yale to John Bates Clark at Columbia, were emphatic in their conviction that a government which confines itself to police, defence, and the opportunity of education is doing not only most of what it may legitimately do, but is also assuring the survival of the fittest. There are, no doubt, real problems, like the railroads, the growth of trusts, depression among the farmers, the danger lest, as in the great forests of the Northwest, inadequate measures of conservation should be adopted to safeguard the interests of the future. But, in general, the faith in *laissez-faire* was widespread and profound ; the growth in population and productive capacity not less than the rise in the standard of life seemed to suggest that the American system reproduced the order of nature. Certainly until the

Great Depression of 1929, it did not seem to the vast majority of Americans that a positive state meant more than the protection of the lazy and the inefficient against the consequences of their own inadequacies.

Yet it may be argued, I think, without unfairness, that once the main incidence of American economic effort became industrial rather than agrarian in character, they were too few in the United States who realized that the complexity of relations in the great society made it urgent that there should be a rapid increase in the power of government to regulate. The forms of political democracy obscured, but did not conceal, the fact that they were being based on an economic foundation which was growingly oligarchical in character. The great business man of the eighteen forties and fifties became the great corporation of the eighties and nineties. Montana might display all the typical organs of a democratic state; but behind those organs the effective power which moved them was in the hands of the Anaconda Copper Mining Company. The electors of Delaware might send their two representatives to the Senate; but everyone knew that their real principal was the great Du Pont family. No doubt there are states, like New York and Massachusetts, or California and Washington, the population of which is too big to be dominated by a single interest; and, no doubt, also, there are epochs when the depth of national feeling has reached an intensity so great that, as in 1932, all habits of traditional allegiance are swept on one side. But it is important to note that in all normal circumstances no relation is more significant in American politics than that between the party machine, whether in state or city, and the great corporations, and that there are areas, like Imperial Valley in California, or Jersey City in New Jersey, in which the meaning of political democracy is hardly known. Nor is it irrelevant that when the first Senator La Follette was seeking to make Republicanism progressive in Wisconsin, he had to build up a machine to carry out his purpose. In the American tradition, in brief, the forces which bind men together generally are interests rather than ideas; and those who give their support to the successful candidate almost assume that they have made an implied contract enforceable by reason of the consideration upon which it is built.

To two other elements in the pattern of the political tradition I must draw attention. The first is the judicial element. It is, of course, true that the United States has had many great judges, whether in the federal courts, like Marshall and Holmes, Brandeis and Cardozo, or in the state courts, like Shaw of Massachusetts or Kent of New York. But it is also true that among their functions not the least the courts have performed is to act as a brake on the democratic habits of legislatures. Anyone who reads either the address to the court by Mr. Choate in the Income Tax cases, or the decision of the court itself, or examines some of the utterances of Mr. Justice McReynolds during the springtime of the New Deal, or analyses the injunctions granted against trade-unions in strike cases, will have no difficulty in understanding why Mr. Justice Holmes was insistent that judges do in fact legislate.[1] They are, in a word, a third chamber of the legislature in the area of their operation; and it is difficult not to argue that in all major political matters they find it extremely difficult to avoid the temptation to substitute their own ideas of what is politically wise or reasonable for the conclusions at which the elected members of the legislature have arrived. Certainly it is hard not to feel that the vital difference between the decision of the Supreme Court in *Abrams* v. *United States*,[2] and what would have been found by a court in Nazi Germany was less in the actual result arrived at than in the noble phrasing of the famous dissent of Mr. Justice Holmes. But when the courts in a political system cross the tenuous boundary which separates legal issues from political conclusions it will usually be found that they are acting, however unconsciously, as counsel against the purposes of democracy.

The other element of importance is that of the Civil Service. No doubt there are departments of the American government, the Geological Survey, for example, and the Bureau of Standards, which it would be very difficult to overpraise. No doubt, also, there are periods of great crisis when the Executive attracts to itself men and women of brilliant capacity and remarkable initiative. But I think it is broadly true to say that the American Civil Service, both in the federal and in the state governments, has been the Cinderella of the American democracy to which no prince appears at midnight with a glass slipper. For since the highest posts are political, it is rare to find among their occupants either men or women with the time to work out a great programme on an ample scale; there have been exceptions, of course, but it is rare to discover them. And when one moves down the hierarchy, it is difficult to find, outside exceptional men like Mr. Joseph B. Eastman of the Interstate Commerce Commission, or that Mr. Edward Mosely to whom the United States owes so much of the legislation that protects safety on the railroads, officials who have either the status or the authority to do creative work of the quality a democracy requires. It is true, indeed, that in the period of the New Deal there developed a new sense of the significance of government; it did much to restore that confidence in democratic principles which business men did so much to destroy in the first years of the Great Depression. But, apart from a small number of men in each Department, it is pretty true to say that the posts available were not likely to attract men of first-rate talent whose qualities had a marketable value elsewhere. And when to this difficulty there is added the continuous, often profound hostility of Congress to the idea of positive administration, it was pretty inevitable that, below the highest grade of officials, not many men of outstanding capacity would suffer the humiliation it was the special delight of Congress, both in the Senate and the House of Representatives, to in-

[1] *Southern Pacific Company* v. *Jensen*, 244 U.S. 205 (1916).
[2] *Abrams* v. *United States*, 250 U.S. 616 (1919). See Z. Chafee, *Free Speech in the United States* (Cambridge: Harvard University Press, 1941), Chap. III.

flict upon them. The abolition of the National Resources Planning Board, and the determined efforts made to arrest the development of the T.V.A., which is one of the outstanding American achievements of modern times, equal, if they do not surpass, the attempt of the State Department to bolster up the Vichy regime and to support, through men like Giraud and Peyrouton, the France which in the opinion of many people betrayed its own citizens in the summer of 1940. It is little short of amazing that the propertied interests of the United States, with all their heavy responsibility for the Great Depression, should have been able to depict creative administration as the equivalent of bureaucracy when it was by that creative administration that it was saved in 1933. The one objective of property was to maintain, in the second and third terms of President Roosevelt, the belief in a system of "free enterprise" which had long ceased to have relevance to the conditions of American economic life.

4

IT is interesting to realize the methods by which this belief has been maintained. It is interesting because, alongside the political democracy so deeply rooted in the American tradition, most of the instruments through which the picture of the scene to be interpreted to the American is painted have become a branch of Big Business. That is true of the cinema; it is true of the radio, it is true of the overwhelming proportion of the press. Even if, here and there, a source of doubt whether the habits of Big Business fit into the habits of a democratic way of life, find means of expression, in some of Mr. Chaplin's films, for instance, in the remarkable use to which President Roosevelt put the radio, in a small number of weeklies whose total circulation does not add up to the influence of a single publication like the *Saturday Evening Post,* or in the occasional columns of an eminent though small-town journalist, like the late William Allen White, the incidence of the whole picture is enormously and continuously tilted towards the support of vested interests against the democratic tradition for which America came into being as an independent nation. And the immense influence of advertising moves in the same direction. In general, too, that is the end which the theatre serves; only an occasional play raises doubts about the validity of the "economic royalists' " claim to rule. If it is different with the printed book, as when Mr. Steinbeck's *Grapes of Wrath* brings home so vividly the tragedy of the migrant unemployed, or Mr. and Mrs. Lynd's remarkable studies in *Middletown* draw an impressive contrast between democracy as an idea and democracy in action, the number of Americans to whom these criticisms of the actual situation penetrate is gravely small compared to those who live by the ordinary newspaper, the ordinary film, or those trade journals which spend so much of their space in explaining that American democracy involves a government which leaves unfettered the activities of business men. It is not, I think, an exaggeration to say that Mr. Sinclair Lewis's *Babbitt* is an accurate composite photograph of the mind produced by these instruments of propaganda.

Mr. Babbitt is kindly, he is hospitable, he has moments when he dreams that he can break away from the conventions by which he is mastered. He is an honourable husband and a father with an eager desire to spoil his children. He is proud of his house and his car, and he is anxious that his wife shall be at least equal in spending power to any of her average neighbours. He rarely reads, and still more rarely thinks. Surrounding him is a vast miasma of what he thinks good fellowship, but which, in fact, hides from him the sight of that actuality he uncomfortably suspects is near at hand. He is capable of a temporary indignation. But as soon as he begins to count the cost of its translation into action, he realizes that he is in fact a prisoner who dare not take the risk of attempting to escape. So that he settles down to the acceptance of conventions which he is persuaded to identify with the American tradition even while he is oppressed by the uncomfortable suspicion that they are in fact its antithesis.

And to the immense weight of these influences must be added the power of Big Business in the educational world as well as in the realm of scientific research. The schools, where they are publicly controlled by the state governments, are almost wholly devoted to the exposition of a faith which makes "getting on in the world" practically an article in a religious creed; and, where they are private institutions, they do not even question the validity of the traditional economic system. In the field of higher education the power of wealth is almost overwhelming. Where the university or college is maintained by the state, it is difficult for radical theory to express itself in any subject which may endanger the rights of property; it is typical that the University of Montana should have dismissed a distinguished professor of economics for proving that, over long years, the great copper companies had evaded their fiscal obligations. The university or college which depends on private endowment is, in some ways, more liberal in outlook than the university or college dependent upon state funds; but in any field of study which raises the issue of property it is rare indeed to find that the challenging mind is sure of a welcome. It was, after all, a great New York newspaper which practically invited Columbia University to dismiss the eminent historian, Charles Beard, for examining in a realistic way the origins of the Federal Constitution; and when, in 1919, the police of Boston, under great provocation, went on strike, the immediate reaction of the president and corporation of Harvard University was to offer its services to the governor of Massachusetts though they were wholly unaware of the grievances through which the strike had arisen. Nor is it unimportant that investigation has established the payment to professors of economics of not inconsiderable sums by trade associations to argue in their textbooks against the dangers of public ownership.

The simple fact is that the American educational system reflects the character of the economic system within which it functions. It could hardly, indeed, be otherwise. One could no more expect a capitalist society to permit its teachers generally to undermine the foundations of private property than one could expect the schools and universities of the Soviet Union to admit teachers whose energies are devoted to expounding the fallacies of Marxism, or the authorities in the academic institutions of Vatican City to exhibit an eager tolerance for scholars who think more highly of Strauss and of Bauer, of Loisy and of George Foot Moore, than of the representatives of the official outlook. No society ever permits the foundations of its system to be called into question unless it is certain that it will triumph overwhelmingly in the reply.

What is of interest in the working of the American educational system is less its subordination to the effective sources of sovereignty than the immense mythology it has contributed to the shaping of the American tradition. Few aspects of its life have done so much to persuade the masses not only to believe that the path from log cabin to White House is direct and universally open, but also to accept the faith that every man has a full opportunity to climb to the apex of the social pyramid. If Napoleon persuaded the common soldier to believe that he carried a marshal's baton in his knapsack, the American school has made it difficult for any able and ambitious boy not to dream of the day when his name will be mentioned with those of Rockefeller and Astor, of Vanderbilt and Henry Ford. And, after all, until quite recent times the chances in the economic field were so immense, the examples of remarkable achievement so numerous, that it was far from easy for the sceptic not to be doubtful about the validity of his own scepticism. The hope of the White House for the politically ambitious young man might, in truth, be far more imaginary than real. The innumerable books and speeches which have eulogized the almost self-educated Abraham Lincoln as the symbol of the common people of America have usually failed to note that Lincoln was that symbol essentially because he was a very extraordinary man. A vast legion, no doubt, has set out on the road to the White House, but it is only a small platoon that has ever had real hope of arriving there.

And yet, when this has been said, we are bound to remember that the political careeer has been more fully open to ordinary people in the United States than in any other country in the world right down to our own day. It has been easier for the poor and the humble to attain membership of either House of Congress or of the state legislatures than in any country save the Soviet Union. Nor is that all. The absence of a monarchical system has meant the absence of a court, and the absence of a court has meant the absence of that special atmosphere of "deference" which Bagehot noted in England as typical of the Victorian Age. There is no career that is closed to any American, save on the ground of colour, and, perhaps, also, of creed. The embassies and legations of the United States are not what John Bright called the Foreign Office of Great Britain—the "outdoor relief department of the aristocracy." Lawyer, doctor, engineer, university professor, there is a wide highway along which the humblest may pass to the summit of professions such as these. While it is no doubt true that there are some half-dozen American universities in which the student has advantages either by reason of birth or wealth, there are scores of other universities in which there is no such advantage. Even the long years of depression and war have done relatively little to destroy that fundamental element in the American tradition—the belief that a man makes himself and that his best chance of self-fulfilment comes from opening to him as widely as possible the gates of education. There are, indeed, narrow boundaries set to his hopes if he is of Negro descent. The experience of Governor Smith, in 1928, makes it clear that the time has not yet come when a Roman Catholic may count on entering the White House. Save in the world of industry and finance, there are many invisible barriers to the upward progress of the Jew, universities where he may not teach, hospitals where he may not practise, clubs which he cannot join, even areas in cities where he cannot rent a house or spend a night in an hotel.

We must not underestimate the price that is paid by these minorities, whether on racial or religious grounds, for their exclusion from a full participation in the American tradition. It is a high price materially; that is shown by the wage differential in the South, to take one example only, as between white and coloured labour. And, not less, it is a high price spiritually, for the sense of psychological frustration imposed on these minorities is often as ugly and as brutal as the characteristic habits of Nazi or of Fascist. It breeds in large numbers of American citizens an unnnecessary inferiority complex, and this, in its turn, finds expression in excessive arrogance or undue humility.

Yet even when this price is entered on the debit side of the American tradition—and it is a heavy addition to that side—what remains in amplitude of opportunity is remarkable. The ordinary man has the conviction that no gates may be barred to his entry. He feels that he has the right to experiment with himself. He feels the elbow-room that comes from membership in a community that is dynamic in quality. Not only can he lift up his eyes to the hills, the community expects him to lift them up. That he has made his way forward gives him a title to pride; there is no assumption that he is moving outside the boundaries to which, by his origins, he ought to be confined. For the ordinary American citizen no trace has remained of that feudal heritage which still has deep influence on the social relationships of most European countries. There is an equality between citizen and citizen which one finds widespread in France and Scandinavia, but very partially in England, and hardly at all in Central or Southeastern Europe. The English workman may speak frankly to his employer, but he stands, as it were, with his cap in his hand. He expects always to be a workman; he cannot forget his dependence on his employer. There is no such habit of deference in the American workman. He is aware of an economic distinction of class between himself and his employer. But he does not easily regard that economic distinction as entailing a social consequence; and he may well feel convinced, especially if he is young, that he will in any case transcend the economic distinction in course of time. I do not say that the conviction is likely to be realized; on the contrary, the development of the economic pattern in the age of giant industry reduces the likelihood in each decade. But it is important that the incentive to the conviction is inherent in the environment. It means that the static relations of the Old World have been banished from the New.

This difference in expectation is so vital to the understanding of the difference between the American tradition and that of Europe that it is worth while for a moment to illustrate its consequence. It is significant, for example, that it is difficult to find an American who can perform the duties of a butler or a valet as they are performed in a great English house by a trained English servant; indeed, the rich American who has arrived at the level where he desires to be conspicuous by domestic ostentation is likely to engage an English butler or valet, as his wife is likely to employ an English or a French maid. It is seen, again, in the relation between the officer class and the rank and file of the armies; the kind of disciplinary relationship which is imposed between the two grades in the historic European armies would provoke a riot if its imposition was sought in an American regiment. The European officer belongs to an organ which, historically, has usually been the instrument of aristocratic purposes; his regiment is the country in which he is a nobleman. But no such military tradition has ever existed in the United States, nor could it easily be formed. For though Washington was a Virginia gentleman, and, perhaps, the richest American of his time, his army was built, like Cromwell's New Model, of small farmers and independent working men who enlisted, not because they were pressed, nor because they had no alternative means of life, but because they believed in the greatness of the cause for which they fought. And this has set the background of the American discipline in all branches of the service of defence. It has made impossible the growth of a caste spirit which could prevail against the notion that the soldier is in essence a civilian who, for temporary and democratic purposes, has taken up arms.

One final instance may be quoted. The Londoner is rare, the English citizen rarer still, who has been inside the palace of his king or knows the historic residence of the prime minister as more than a name. But few Americans visit Washington without going to see the White House, and there are days when it is crowded, not with some specially invited guests of high social status, but with ordinary citizens who wish to see for themselves how their president lives. And I have myself seen, in Albany, New York, and Olympia, Washington, a teacher taking in his class of boys and girls for a talk with the governor of the state after a visit to the legislative assembly. The psychological significance of all this is the absence it implies in the tradition of the hierarchical structure which surrounds so much of the process of government in Europe and Asia. Scandinavia and in a less degree Holland apart, there is nothing on either of those continents which can rival the decisive simplicity the American tradition has effected. It has not come without opposition; John Adams' conception of what the presidency should be in its public expression is sufficient proof of that. President or senator, governor or judge of the Supreme Court, the American has given his chosen representatives a stature of ample dignity without himself having to go down on his knees. That is an achievement of which the impact on the democratic idea is more profound than it is easy to recognize.

5

THERE is a religious element in the American tradition the nature of which it is obviously easy to mistake. The dramatic history of the colonies of New England in the seventeenth century, the almost theatrical exploits of the remarkable Mather dynasty in Massachusetts, the struggle between Puritan orthodoxy and the antinomianism of Anne Hutchinson, the defiant plea of Roger Williams for separation between State and Church, the social prestige of the clergy until some such time as that of William Ellery Channing and Emerson, these factors, together with the admittedly great influence in forming the climate of the Revolution of ministers like Jonathan Mayhew and Charles Chauncy, has led, I think, to a misapprehension of the part played by this religious element. For perhaps fifty or sixty years after the landing of the *Mayflower,* there is no reason to doubt that the influence of Puritanism in New England was extensive and profound. There is no reason to doubt, either, that a considerable number of the early settlers left England for conscience' sake, and that they approved the imposition of a rigorous code of conduct and belief upon all whom they were able to influence.

But it is important not to exaggerate either the influence of Puritanism on the American scene or the degree to which it expressed itself in a gloomy outlook even among the most faithful of its votaries. The full rigour of Puritan orthodoxy was, after all, challenged almost from the outset of the settlement of New England. What it contributed of importance to the life about it was far less a dogmatic theology than a sense of the urgency of effort and a will to be saved in heaven by attaining first to comfort and safety upon earth. That the party of theocracy was persistent and influential there is no reason at all to doubt; but it was already prepared to compromise by the middle of the seventeenth century, and, by its end, a liberal outlook had developed, as in the writings of John Wise, which was fatal to its claims. By the middle of the eighteenth century Puritan orthodoxy was already at a discount; and by the time when the obstinacy of George III and the folly of his ministers were preparing the ground for independence, it was already ceasing to be possible to make the profession of a Christian creed the basis of citizenship.

That is why the separation of Church and State was so easily accomplished in 1787. The religious logic of Jonathan Edwards, and the passionate emotionalism of the Great Awakening, are far less authoritative than the demands of a life that is continually calling for experiment and makes the very concept of the frontier a perpetual source of the obligation to recognize novelty and adapt it to experience.

That is why what begins as a theocratic principle ends by becoming a tradition that it is not very easy to distinguish from utilitarianism. It may well be that there were many to whom this utilitarian outlook was framed in a religious background. To work hard, to live an orderly life, to have a name for integrity and fair dealing, not to spend one's substance in reckless display, to have the resolution to carry out the purposes you undertake—it is, roughly, to an ethic such as this that the religion of America had been shaped when the basic tradition was formed. Many who followed it, as in the case of Jefferson, were Deists; many others found it helpful to support this view by attaching divine sanction to its validity. What it is important to stress is the fact that, as so notably shown in both the life and the works of Benjamin Franklin, the environment of America shaped traditional religions to its needs much more than the traditional religions shaped the American environment to their claims.

And the outcome is, I think, not easily to be mistaken. The churches must aid men in their struggle to be citizens; religion is of social value as a means of keeping order and stirring men to make the exertions that life requires. That is what Nathaniel Hawthorne meant when he wrote that "the entire system of man's affairs, as at present established, is built up purposely to exclude the careless and happy soul. The very children would upbraid the wretched individual who should endeavour to take life and the world as—what we might naturally suppose them meant for —a place and opportunity for enjoyment." [3] The vast continent needed men and women who had this faith if they were to subdue it to their purposes. And since to some of those whose faith was equalled by their capacity or their skill there came an immense reward, it became natural to think of that reward as God's favour to the man of grace; more, to think that worldly failure was the outcome of sin. The relation between man and his Maker then becomes an individual matter between them, interference with which is resented. This outlook at once encourages individualism in politics, since it urges a man to depend upon his own effort, and discourages the notion of churches as institutions with a part to play upon the political scene.

It is in its encouragement of individual effort that religion found its place in the American tradition. And that power was intensified by the influence upon it of frontier conditions and frontier psychology. For these brought out all the drive to independence that was inherent in the Protestant idea. Mostly, the doctrines which developed were evangelical,

[3] *Cf.* Lloyd R. Morris, *The Rebellious Puritan* (New York: Harcourt, Brace, 1927), p. 331.

and they emphasized the right of the individual to salvation. They were far more successful in terms of an emotional appeal than they were in terms of their intellectual content. They were in large part built upon the faith of their possessor in an inner light which it was beyond the power of scholarship even to reach, much less to destroy. For the dwellers of the frontier areas this inner light had the immense value of conferring upon them an unbreakable self-confidence which was easily capable of suffusing the whole of their personalities and thus provided them with armour against the physical and economic difficulties of frontier life. Not seldom, the character of the doctrines accepted seems to us to reproduce the wilder fanaticisms of the English Civil Wars; and a new Thomas Edwards would have had no difficulty in writing a new *Gangraena* about the Muggletonians, Come-Outers, Shakers, Rappites, and so on. It is true that a number of these sects, like the Moravians of Pennsylvania or the Brotherhood of Perfection, began with communist ideals; but it was rare for them to endure. The very nature of the physical environment made for individualism in economic matters. Outside the Mormons, indeed, and the Shakers, the persistence of the co-operative spirit in religion for any length of time and on any considerable scale was very exceptional.

The impact of this frontier religion was to intensify the idea of equality, and this, in its turn, had profound influence upon the idea of democracy in politics. It made for universal suffrage; it was impossible to exclude the self-confident pioneer of Kentucky or Tennessee from the right to determine how he would be governed. Nor must we forget that none of the emotional satisfaction which the multiplicity of religious sects afforded ever interfered with the growing secularization of American life. From the first third of the eighteenth century, at any rate, acceptance of the supernatural, often in the most fantastic forms, developed at an equal pace with an interest in science and philosophy. That secularization is shown, among other things, by the greater variety of the professions on which university graduates embarked between 1750 and 1800, as compared with 1700 to 1750, and the decrease in the proportion of those who desired the clerical career. It is shown by the widening interest in science and literature, and by the rapid growth of newspapers and pamphlets the basis of which was devotion to non-religious matters.

By the time of the American Revolution a large part of the character which religion has contributed to the tradition had begun to take the form it has ever since assumed. Everywhere the established Churches were losing ground, not least because colonies like Rhode Island and Pennsylvania were showing that religious toleration is closely connected with commercial prosperity. And it is significant that a propagandist of genius like Samuel Adams thought it worth his while to warn his correspondents against the dangers of prelacy. On the evidence, it seems clear beyond dispute that the experience of religious freedom begat an impatience of constraint in political matters. Perhaps that is one of the reasons why the prohibition of any religious test as a qualification for federal office went through so easily at Philadelphia in 1787. By 1833 even Massachusetts had accepted the separation of Church and State as part of its Constitution. There still remained a small number of states in which a faith in the teachings of Christianity was necessary to public office; and Tocqueville was present in court when the testimony of a witness was refused on the ground of atheism. The case of Abner Kneeland, again, shows that half a century after the making of the Federal Constitution a man could still be imprisoned for blasphemy, in the face of protest from men like Emerson, Theodore Parker, and Channing. And laws against blasphemy continue on the statute books of a number of states.

The tradition that has emerged has something of the character that Tocqueville predicted for it in the great classic that was the outcome of his famous visit to the United States. He had left a Europe in which it was broadly true that it was rare indeed to hold democratic and religious opinions at one and the same time. He had read in the literature of the French Age of Reason that faith would decline as understanding developed. He found, to his surprise, that Americans believed in the close connection between religion and democracy. When he sought for the cause of this unexpected conception, he believed that it was because, with the separation of Church and State, the clergy did not concern themselves with political issues. The inference has followed that religion, in itself, is a mainstay of the social order, with the result that, with minor qualifications, all property devoted to religious purposes is exempt from taxation.

That inference is a living part, it may even be said, perhaps, a growing part, of the American tradition. Particular faiths may be unpopular at some given time, as the Roman Catholic Church was unpopular with the Know-Nothing party in the fifties of the last century, or the Ku Klux Klan after the First World War. On issues by which the country is passionately divided, as on slavery, for instance, or the treatment of the Negro people today, the Churches will, as a rule, be careful to insist that the issue is outside their competence. No politician would think of running for office on the basis of an announcement of his atheism; certainly he would not be elected if he did. And no party which is seeking to win elections in a great centre of population, like New York or Chicago or Boston, would think of adopting candidates without regard to the distribution of religious opinions among the voters. Congress has its chaplains, as have the armed forces of the republic; and it is, on the whole, unusual for the president or the governor of a state not to offer the historic courtesies to the Church into which he was born. And, on the whole again, it is pretty accurate to say that the main impact of the Churches is to show a vague interest in mild reforms, but a deep antagonism to any radical social philosophy. Certainly it would be true to argue that it is the combined influence of religious institutions, including Jewish, that has dug the main abyss between the United States and the Soviet Union. The constant insistence by President Roosevelt on the duty of the Soviet government to make possible freedom of religious worship to its citizens has been of extraordinary interest. What it is not easy to discover is whether the power of religion in the American tradition is due to the individualism it clothed in garments of respectability in the past, or to the hope, in its ruling class, that the leaders of the Churches will moderate any popular zeal for reform in the years to come.

6

THE famous phrase of the Massachusetts Constitution which sought to establish "a government of laws and not of men" expresses a vital element in the American tradition which is of peculiar interest both for what it has achieved and for the cross-currents it has encountered in the historic environment. Part of its strength is due, no doubt, to the fact that the maxims of popular government enshrined in the Common Law seemed, as indeed they were, a safeguard against tyranny whether in Church or State. The tyrant might be a monarch like George III, or a Tory governor like Andros or Hutchinson, or a vested interest like that of British mercantilists; one can detect in the growth of esteem for, and power among, the lawyers in the eighteenth, as compared with the seventeenth century, a sense of respect for objective rules which cannot be twisted to anyone's favour. Nor is it possible to mistake the enhanced prestige of the idea of law as soon as the debate began with Parliament which grew into the War of Independence. The need to state a case that was logically convincing against the claim of the House of Commons meant a new regard for the lawyer who could show from Coke and Locke and Blackstone the right of Americans to self-government. And, once the Constitution had been ratified, the Supreme Court attained a status in public respect which not even the poorest of its members have permitted it to lose. For the Supreme Court has been, in a very especial sense, the guardian of property against the power of numbers. From the days when Chief Justice Marshall gave it this character—despite the presence of occasional members on the court like Justices Holmes and Brandeis and Cardozo, with their view that legislative experiments "must be considered in the light of our whole experience and not merely in that of what was said a hundred years ago"—to protect the property of the few against the will of the people has remained the function of the lawyer in most American courts and, above all, on the Supreme Court of the United States. This has been, broadly speaking, clear beyond mistake.

That function has been to arrest the pace of the dynamism inherent in American society. It is not merely that it has arrested obvious techniques like the income tax or the prohibition of child labour. It is not merely that the courts have regarded "due process" not, as Judge Learned Hand so aptly described it, as an expression of "the English sporting idea of fair play," but rather as though the Fifth and the Fourteenth Amendments were, in Mr. Justice Holmes' famous jibe, the enactment of "Mr. Herbert Spencer's *Social Statics.*" The courts have been hostile to trade-unionism almost throughout its history. They have used the idea of liberty of contract to strike down measure after measure which a legislative assembly believed, after careful examination of the evidence, to be necessary to the social welfare. And, from the time of the Sedition Laws of 1798, they have not hesitated to admit appeals to freedom which were, in fact, what Mr. Justice Cardozo called "the masquerade of privilege or inequality seeking to intrench itself behind the catchword of a principle." Their hostility to the development of an effective administrative law has been nothing so much as a method by which they could strike into impotence the first efforts to develop in the great society of the United States the obvious implications of the positive State. American courts, in general, have used the power of judicial review to replace the expert's inference from social and economic fact, which he examines in the spirit of scientific inquiry, by criteria which derive both their content and their standard from an America which hardly knew what the great society involved.

Yet, in general, the rule of law, as lawyers think of that rule, has seemed to Americans an essential part of their tradition and the outstanding guarantee of their freedom. Living under a written constitution, trained, therefore, to think of the lawyer, in his capacity of judge, as the natural source of its final interpretation, they did not easily see that, in general, the man appointed to the bench was fairly certain to be a successful lawyer, and that few people could be successful lawyers unless they possessed as clients the prosperous class in the American community. Or, alternatively, the men nominated to the bench were usually receiving the reward of service to their political party; and it was then at least equally unlikely that they would have opinions which differed at all widely from the party norm. It is only necessary to read the enormous volume in which the Judiciary Committee of the Senate reported its hearings on the fitness of Mr. Justice Brandeis for the Supreme Court, or, from a different angle, the correspondence between Theodore Roosevelt and Senator Henry Cabot Lodge on the desirability of nominating Mr. Justice Holmes to the court of which he was for a generation the greatest member, to realize that the normal criteria of judicial fitness have been an eager acceptance of the American past rather than an eager interest in the American future.

And this attitude of acceptance of these criteria is, I suggest, remarkable because the American tradition is one in which veneration for law is at least equalled by the widespread habit of a violence which disregards the habits of law. Partly, that violence is the inevitable accompaniment of a frontier civilization; where the settled habits of law are absent, it is not surprising that men should take its making, as in the Gold Rush of 1849, into their own hands. Partly, also, the violence derives from the mixture of races and philosophies out of which, at so swift a pace, America has emerged. It is connected very directly with the fact that it was so easy, if the law was put aside, to make one's way to wealth on so immense a scale. That led to the corruption of courts and legislatures of a type comparable in intensity with the normal habits of Southeastern Europe. But it is important to remember that "graft" cannot become endemic in a society without creating a class of men who live by their power to flout the law. The business man who buys the political machine, whether he be big or small in his ambitions, is bound to beget the "boss"; and since the boss can survive only by his power to deliver to business the favours it is purchasing, gangsterism is the necessary corollary of the boss system. And once this technique is accepted at the apex of the economic pyramid, it is bound to be accepted at its base as well. Senator Penrose belongs to the same species as such a boss as Platt of New York or Pendergast of Kansas City; and their species is part of the same genus as that of which a gangster like Capone is likely to remain the supreme symbol for the first half of this century. For once men seek to by-pass the law, they are bound to call into being not merely those who will evade it if they can, but those who will break it with savage indifference if they know no other road to power and fortune.

Two other factors in this aspect of the American tradition require emphasis. There is a real sense in which the American respect for law has of itself begotten lawlessness. For the effort to control every field of human conduct by statute—an obvious deposit of the Puritan heritage— with the result that the sale of tobacco and liquor can be prohibited, meant that a group of men would arise to supply these wants to which the law refused satisfaction. The more widespread the want, the greater would be the profit in supplying it, and the more earnest would be the zeal of those responsible for applying the law to see that it was enforced. Out of this there developed quite naturally a sense of satisfaction in outwitting the law-makers. And once there is that kind of tension in the social environment, which this generation has witnessed in the conflict between those who regarded prohibition as almost an article of religious faith and those to whom it was a wanton interference with personal freedom, the stage is set for the breeding of violence by the attempt to compel obedience to the law. No one can read the history of the methods by which Mr. Rockefeller established his supremacy in the oil industry without seeing that the long trail of bribery and corruption, thuggery and suicide, that accompanied it gave birth inevitably to a world in which the law was not a principle to respect, but an obstacle to evade. And Mr. Rockefeller is only an outstanding figure in a vast procession of men prepared to hack their way to power remorselessly. The methods by which Texas became American, the domination of the farmers by the railroads, the habits of the lumber and the cattle millionaires—all these must be set in the framework of a community which wants at once the advantages of settled rules without allowing them to impede their march to fortune.

The other factor of importance is the need to realize that the primitive values of the pioneer, which loom so large in the American tradition, are psychological as well as geographical in character. It is not merely on the frontier that men seize the opportunity before their eyes; they seize it also in that settled realm where, in a new industry or a new method of organization, there is the big chance present for the taking. Capitalist industrialism presented to men like Astor and Vanderbilt, Jay Gould and Rockefeller, exactly the same chance in kind as virgin America presented to the Puritan settlers of the seventeenth century. Just as the Red Indian was the enemy in one generation, so was a strong trade-union in the later period; and the same satisfaction that was felt when an Indian attack was beaten off was felt when a strike was broken. The central ideal in the perspective of which all values are set is the lure of vast and sudden wealth. Its influence on every aspect of American life is hardly capable of over-estimation. It infects the politician, the lawyer, the priest, even the teacher. And it infects them while they are troubled in their consciences by that American dream of equal opportunity which is always challenging the values of a business civilization.

This, I think, is why so large a proportion of American millionaires have sought to achieve goodwill in the community by the generosity of their public gifts. The men whom Theodore Roosevelt attacked as "male-factors of great wealth" sought thereby to prove, perhaps as much to themselves as to their fellow-citizens, that they followed a path which was not merely a selfish one. They might act in their business life with the remorseless cruelty of a Cæsar Borgia; but, like the latter, they craved the reputation of being benefactors of the society they dominated. They erected great buildings, they founded universities, they bought rare pictures and manuscripts and books, they endowed great researches in science and medicine, in archæology and exploration. The condition they exacted was the admission of their right to shape the power of the State to their own interests. But this condition made the idea of a rule of law which bore equally upon all citizens a myth by which they were hardly even themselves deceived. And it meant, also, that most of those who sought to challenge their supremacy had to fight their way to wealth by themselves insisting that the rule of law was a myth. Later, the new-comers, too, would pay the price of their insistence by a similar generosity. What all of them omitted to notice was that the habit of mind they engendered did profound and widespread injury to that respect for law upon which so much of the future of the American tradition depended.

7

THE power of a tradition to endure depends upon its capacity to command a continuing faith; and this, in its turn, depends upon its power to evoke hope and exhilaration from the masses. A ruling class is usually safe so long as the system it controls is able to secure this evocation.

For so long as men have the sense that the road is open, they do not feel that they must take to jungle paths. No student of American history can fail to observe that, the Negro problem alone apart, its mental climate is one of discovery, expansion, optimism. There are periods, no doubt, of crisis; but the vitality of the scene is so abundant that it is rare for men to be unable to overcome them rapidly. The legend of America is of unlimited spaces, of endless opportunities, of resources which know no bounds. All that is valid in the Old World it has inherited; to that it has added a chance of personal fulfilment which the Old World has never known. And to these immense benefits there was added a virtual freedom, for over a century, from the dangers of military attack, the power, accordingly, to emphasize the primacy of civil life as the context in which political effort was set. If the successful soldier has been rewarded four times with the presidency of the United States, it is as a person in civil life that he has received his reward.

The United States, moreover, has been free from all the limitations of a feudal tradition. It has had no permanent ruling class either in a personal or in a geographical sense. If it has been essentially a bourgeois civilization, its middle class has never, as in Europe, had to share the possession of the state power with the survivors, whether the landowners or a military caste, of an earlier regime. No doubt it suffered the terrible anguish of a civil war, the marks of which can still be seen in the mind and habits of the South and in its relative place in the social economy of America; and it is even true that though the Civil War formally abolished Negro slavery, it did not solve the problem of the Negro's status in the social and economic life of the nation. But, apart from this exception, the hindrances which in the Old World have stood in the way of the rise of the common man have been in principle absent. Nor is there any other nation with such natural resources to explore which has explored them so profoundly. No other nation, either, has been so little the prisoner of its past, or so apt to technological invention and its use to ease the burden of toil. No other nation has placed less emphasis upon birth, or regarded with greater honour the task of earning one's daily bread. No other nation has made the road to knowledge more accessible to the mass of its people. Nor is there any other nation in which the faith in progress has been more deep or universal, the confidence in the ability of the ordinary man to solve for himself the problems by which he is confronted more abiding.

For something over three hundred years after its emergence into world history these have been the elements out of which the American tradition was built. It was rarely called into question; and some of the outstanding figures in the American record, Jefferson, for example, and Walt Whitman, believed in it with a fervour that was almost religious in its intensity. If, on occasion, the tradition was challenged, if, sometimes, men feared for its preservation, or could not, like Henry James, accept the inference it implied, it is difficult to doubt that, until the end of the First World War, the acceptance of the framework it provided for life in the United States was the postulate on which the overwhelming majority of its citizens organized their daily activities. They might be poor; they would not remain poor. They might be out of work; a job was waiting round the corner. They might be half-literate; their children would go to college. They might be foreign-born; in the fullest sense of the term their children born in America would inherit the tradition in all its amplitude. It may even be said that, after 1919, the tradition enjoyed an Indian summer which lasted for a decade. It was as nothing so much as the fulfilment of the tradition that, in his inaugural address on March 4, 1929, President Hoover could announce to the world that the problem of poverty had been solved in the United States.

It was within eight months after that ardent declaration had been made that the United States was caught in the greatest depression of its history. The unemployed were counted by millions; men who had been accounted wealthy were bankrupt paupers; perhaps a third of the productive capacity of America remained unused; something between a quarter and a third of its population was dependent upon public relief; scores of thousands of farmers were in the hands of creditors; hundreds of banks were compelled to close their doors; and a dollar based on the largest gold reserve in the history of the world had to be revalued and cut loose from gold.

On that momentous day when President Franklin Roosevelt took office it was no longer possible to pretend that the American tradition held the same high place even among the citizens of the United States that it had held when President Hoover entered so confidently upon his task. New winds of doctrine were blowing from East and West, some of them cold winds, cheerless and harsh. If the next years were to show that Adam Smith was right indeed when he said that there "is a great deal of ruin in a nation," the three terms—this fact alone was a startling development of the tradition—were to open a new epoch in American history, to force its people to ask themselves new questions, even to compel them to answer some of the old in a new way. Americans became aware, in part, at least, to their chagrin, that they were, with all their power, still a unit only in a larger and more complicated whole from whose fate they could not separate themselves. A new meaning emerged for California and Oregon and Washington when Pearl Harbor emphasized the significance of being a Pacific power; and there was a portent of unmistakable urgency when it became obvious, with the fall of France, that the occupation of North Africa by a hostile power might challenge the safety of the United States from the Caribbean to the North Atlantic. Much that, until then, had been little more than rhetoric became almost overnight a stark reality; for the Japanese menace bound up the fate of the United States with Australia and Canada, as the German menace bound it up with that of Canada and Great Britain and the future of the Middle East. There is a sense in which the United States had taken the

First World War almost in its stride; there was hardly a moment in its course when American citizens felt that they had to think out afresh the historic principles by which they had prospered in the first century and a half of their existence as an independent national community.

But the epoch from March 4, 1933, down to the catastrophe of Pearl Harbor shook the United States to its foundations. Not only did it become obvious that its enemies were striking at the roots of its civilization; more important were the facts, first, that the organization of recovery and of victory would require a total mobilization of all its resources, for its own safety not less than for that of its allies, but it was clear, in the second place, that the validity of the American tradition would be tested not by the victory over its enemies so much as by the purposes that victory was made to serve when it was won. No doubt there were millions among the men and women called into national service by America's entrance into the Second World War who thought of little beyond the central fact of powerful enemies upon whose defeat depended the independence of the United States in the future. But among those millions, and, not least, among the younger generations of Americans, there were many who had vital questions to ask to which they would demand an answer. Most of them were filled with a passionate devotion to the American dream; but most of them, also, were going to insist that the time had come to make the dream come true. They had grown up with the clarion call of American promises ringing in their ears; and they had watched, in the years since 1929, a mass of misery and suffering and poverty which contrasted strangely with the tradition of which they had been told.

The years from the Great Depression to the liberation of civilized life from the threat of nazism and the militarists of Japan were years in which Americans were perhaps more confused in their thinking than at any time since the Civil War. Though Franklin Roosevelt and his supporters strove hard to adapt the historic tradition to the new conditions it confronted, the antagonism he encountered went, perhaps, deeper than any president had met in the second seventy-five years of the republic's history. Property was everywhere on the defensive. The hatred of the Soviet Union was intense. Business men emphasized that adventure and security were antithetic ideals, and they sought to prove that where the federal government took the initiative, instead of leaving it in private hands, there was bound to be the decay of civilization. The little man sought everywhere for an escape from problems which he felt beyond his power to solve. Sometimes he took refuge in forms of religious revival which, like the Buchmanite movement, sought to liberate him from fear by an emotional revival of self-confidence. Sometimes he began to doubt the validity of the democratic idea; and he followed with enthusiasm the gospel of men like Father Coughlin who spoke to him, indeed, in a terminology that was formally Catholic, but upon the basis of an attitude not easily distinguishable from that of Hitlerism. The cinema became, with a mass of magazines whose reading matter sought to shut out the real world, a vital method of consolation. Though the tragedy of persecution in more than half of Europe brought to America a mass of refugees, some of them, like Einstein and Thomas Mann, among the outstanding intellectuals of the Old World, most Americans, save for a relatively small group of liberals, were too preoccupied with their domestic problems to appreciate the scale of the tragedy. And even the liberals were divided; for there were not a few who vigorously insisted that America could best help Europe by the fulfilment of democracy at home, while there were others who argued that, in essence, there was no real difference between the ends of Hitler and Japan, on the one hand, and those of the Soviet Union on the other. And when, from September 1939 to May 1940, the leaders in Europe rather manœuvred for position than fought on the scale of 1914, there was a growing tendency to think that the war abroad was nothing more than a new stage in the evil power politics of the Old World with which America need not concern itself.

The scene began to change with Hitler's conquest of the Low Countries, of Norway and of France; and the sight of Britain at bay alone in the summer of 1940 began to suggest that between the American tradition and Nazi totalitarianism there was an antithesis it was difficult to overlook. That suggestion was reinforced when Hitler struck at the Soviet Union; and, inevitably, it became a living part of every citizen's thoughts after Pearl Harbor and the sweeping conquests of the Japanese forces. There were then few Americans who failed to understand how profound was the challenge to all for which the United States stood, how necessary was the decisive defeat of nazism in all its forms, European or Asiatic, if the American dream was to possess reality in the history of the future.

The recognition that the challenge was profound did not, indeed, answer the central question of how much vitality the American tradition still retained. The United States showed courage and initiative, resolution in plan and skill in execution. In common with its allies, it moved forward, stage by stage, to a victory that was obviously bound to be formally overwhelming. But it was careful not to put to itself in the period of conflict the questions it was urgent to ask, much less attempt to answer them. No doubt all its leaders, from the president downwards, paid formal tribute to the ideas of democracy and freedom. No doubt, also, the United States displayed an unequalled power of organizing its resources for the struggle. Its youth went to their rendezvous with destiny in a mood of sublime courage which, if it was equalled in Britain and the Soviet Union, and in the marvellous endurance of a half-armed China, was nowhere surpassed. But the war was not, for the overwhelming mass of Americans, a renewal of faith in the historic tradition. Their mood was one of conviction that the enemy must be overthrown, but of doubt and hesitation about the consequence of his defeat. There was little sense, among those who planned the direction of the war, that they were engaged in a crusade for the renovation of the American tradition. On the contrary, it was sometimes a little difficult not to question whether they were certain that it ought to be renewed. As almost always in a crisis, they showed a power of improvisation on a scale that it is legitimate to equate with genius. As always they made their war to win their war; they did not engage in its agonies for any end other than the complete overthrow of their opponents.

But they did not discuss what they were fighting for, nor how those ends could be achieved. They did not suddenly awaken to a renewed sense of the splendour of the American dream. Before they entered the war, indeed, President Roosevelt spoke with impressive eloquence of the Four Freedoms and indicated with incisiveness that they could be fulfilled in our own generation. Mr. Henry Wallace, the vice-president of the United States during Roosevelt's third term, made a series of addresses of which the main theme was the urgency of so using the victory over totalitarianism that the next age would become what he termed the "century of the common man"; but the significant thing about the impact of Mr. Wallace's approach is that he was not renominated by his party and was replaced by one of those professional politicians who was unlikely to disturb the voter who did not like inconvenient questions to be posed.

So that I do not think it is unfair to argue that Americans have refused to ask themselves whether the historic principles of their tradition can be adapted to the environment of a new time. They had—and not least President Roosevelt had—a sense that their power was very great, that the influence they could exert would be greater, in the next generation, than that of any other people. In both these conclusions they were probably justified. But there were too few thoughtful Americans who were willing to inquire for what their power would be used, or what effect their influence would have upon a civilization that is in the melting pot. And, to the outsider, that refusal to inquire was something it was hard not to connect with the character of the answers they were suspicious they might receive. For they were deeply aware not only of the increasing tensions of our society; even more, they were aware that when, in a period of crisis, increasing tensions demand new formulas, we must move from one set of social idealisms to another set, and adapt to the claims of these the form of economic and political organization which is proving obsolete, and even dangerous. For it is not less true today than it was when Lincoln was building his claim to the allegiance of all civilized men nearly ninety years ago that a house divided against itself cannot stand. The issue which the guardians of the American tradition today seem to me to be evading is whether there is that division, and, if so, what will be its outcome. Until that question is answered with the confidence of Jefferson and his followers, it seems to me quite certain that the historic American tradition, for all its great achievements, will be viewed with uncertainty and even suspicion by those who should be its beneficiaries.

II

The Spirit of America

I

AMERICANS are optimistic, friendly, inquisitive, practical-minded. They find it difficult to believe that progress is not inevitable. They do not easily accept the right to reserve and privacy; they assume that if two men meet the natural thing is for them to exchange experiences. They have a distrust of theory. What interests them is the ability to apply an idea to the solution of a problem; and they reserve their supreme respect for men of the type of Ford rather than for men of the type of Theodore Richards. This is why there is an important sense in which the supreme symbol of the American spirit is Benjamin Franklin, for he made a success of all that he attempted. He met kings and statesmen, merchants and workmen, on equal terms. He always wanted to know the how and, if possible, the why of anything he encountered; and if he is a great figure in the history of physics, his invention of the cooking stove enabled him greatly to improve the domestic amenities of his time. There was nothing in him of that remoteness which is characteristic of George Washington, nothing, either, of that inner and ultimate melancholy which makes Lincoln so untypical an American. In his shrewdness, his sagacity, his devotion to making this world the thing that a kindly and benevolent soul would wish it to be, Franklin seems to summarize in a remarkable way the American idea of a good citizen.

From the outset, almost, of his history, the American has been accustomed to scan a vast horizon, and this has tempted him to equate bigness with grandeur. It has made him a restless person, anxious rather to do than to be. For, until quite recent times, there has always been, for him, the frontier beyond the frontier, and his amazing vitality has been the secret by which he has conquered the continent. And the very fact of that immense space to which, once Jefferson had completed the Louisiana purchase, he has been in fact the unchallenged heir, has made him approach the issues of life very differently than did his European ancestors. He never needed to assume, as the Englishmen did, that there was some allotted station in life that was his, and others that were, almost *a priori,* beyond his reach. He never accepted the Frenchman's ideal of achieving an adequate competence as early as possible that he might devote his time, preferably in some provincial countryside, to cultivating his garden. History never imposed upon him the tragedy of the German citizen who was not of noble birth—the need to realize that the great careers, whether of politics or of the army, were only too likely to be closed to him. Nor did he suffer from the human contradiction of being either a nobleman without the means to live the noble life, or being a merchant or a peasant, and finding, even if he was successful, that these circles of social life to which he might aspire were beyond his hope of entry.

There is a real sense in which every American belongs to a self-made generation; he is full of the consciousness that he may both begin anew and climb upwards without the fear that he will encounter some barrier laid by history in his road. It is even, I think, broadly true to say that the Americans most certain to fail in satisfying their needs of the spirit are those who expect the past they have inherited to determine the future upon which they can enter. It is difficult to think of a more complete example of this truth than Henry Adams. He had a mind of the first order, he was a man of profound cultivation, he knew almost everyone in the America of his time whom it was worth while to know, and he had an intimate experience of the forces by which the civilization of his time was shaped. Yet no one can read his autobiography without the conviction that, from the time he returned to America with his father after the Civil War, he was a profoundly unhappy man. And that unhappiness was not the outcome merely of the personal tragedy of his married life. Some of the things he achieved might well have left him with the conviction of a fulfilled personality. In his academic days at Harvard University, it is clear that he swiftly conquered a significant place among scholars. The books that he wrote before he had passed the milestone of middle age secured for him the admiring recognition of all who were capable of judging. He had friends of outstanding quality who gave him instant and abiding affection. Wherever he heard of beauty, in nature, in art, in architecture, he would travel to see it. When he settled in Washington, few visitors of distinction but sought the chance of his acquaintance. Yet not all the quasi-scientific alibis by which he sought to ward off despair can conceal the fact that there was in his most intimate self a black sense of frustration.

Henry Adams yearned, like the three generations of his family before him, to play a pivotal part on the political stage. But he could not stoop to conquer. There was something in his disposition which made him seek the palm without the dust. And since he chose to mask his passionate ambition in the role of a spectator to whom descent into the arena was unthinkable, no one thought of asking him to enter the battle. He spent the crucial years of his life preparing to be the general of an army in which some quality of his nature prevented him from enlisting. He saw far smaller men than himself, Henry Cabot Lodge, for example, and John Hay, move to the forefront of the political stage. He could not bring himself to take the steps which might have organized for him the opportunities he desired. It was not that his nature was too precious for him to do so. Partly, I think, he was weighed down by the fear of failure if he made the attempt; partly he assumed that a man of his position and connections would be sought after; an Adams in the United States was the moral equivalent of a Cecil or a Stanley in England. What he did not see, and what, I suspect, he never understood, was that the American spirit compelled the citizen to build for himself the ladder on which he could mount in politics. So that when he became conscious of a failure for which, mainly, great historian though he was, his own lack of historical insight was largely responsible, he spent almost a generation of his life in building himself, as compensation, into a legend, and writing those books of his later years in which, behind the appearance of an historical cosmology, there is in reality an apologia for his failure, large parts of which are no more than a method of concealing his angry contempt for an age which did not call upon him to lead it.

It would be interesting to compare the symbols of the American spirit which Franklin epitomized in the eighteenth century with the judgment implicitly passed upon them by Henry Adams in the nineteenth. But that would sacrifice the larger issues of this theme to a single variation upon it. I can only summarize the argument by saying that what emerges, as the United States emerges from the thirteen colonies, is the conviction that the successful man is the happy man, and that the criterion of success is either the utilitarian one of power—most easily measured by wealth and the influence it commands—or the judgment of one's fellows that one has achieved significance. John Jacob Astor and Abbott Lawrence are happy because their success in material terms is beyond denial, just as Henry Wadsworth Longfellow and Bronson Alcott are happy because the world about them accords them the crown of that genius for which they longed. The happy American is thus, on my view, the American who is deemed successful in the relevant environment in which he moves. So that, when one reads the history of New England in the early part of the nineteenth century, Miss Peabody may be happy in her little bookshop because her friends regard her judgment as important in the same way as the textile manufacturers of New England regard the judgment of Abbott Lawrence as important. The vital roots of the American spirit are either the building of a fortune or the building of a reputation which makes you held in esteem by your neighbours. And for either of these things it is important to be doing something, until some such epoch as the presidency of General Grant, to be doing something oneself. It is not easy, therefore, for most of his contemporaries to understand why Thoreau can be happy; they almost need the assurance of Emerson, who is at once successful and a seer, that the queer contemplative spirit of Walden finds ecstasy so great in the observation of nature that his massive acquiescence is itself a form of action. And if practically nothing material that Bronson Alcott undertakes seems able to keep poverty from his door, he is yet successful because he is so incredibly energetic in discovering, almost every other week, the inner secret of the universe.

No attempt to grasp the nature of the American spirit can be complete which does not emphasize the degree to which action is of its essence. Americans are always doing things or trying things; more, they are always seeking a shorter way of getting things done. And with that search there goes the desire, first, to discover the shorter road for oneself, and, second, so to discover it that others want to follow where the pioneer has led. It is, I think, significant that, until that remarkable springtime of New England in the first half of the nineteenth century, what is important in American life is related either to the amenities of practical living, architecture for example, or to the writings of jurists and political pamphleteers. Early American theology is sometimes persuasive, and even, as with Jonathan Edwards, of amazing logical power, but it is rarely an innovating literature. And polite letters, until this New England springtime, are rarely much more than what the scholar is driven to read to see how the winter burgeoned into that spring. Law and politics, and, to some degree, economics also, are from the outset different. There the writer is conscious that the word is the deed. He is writing, whether it be Thomas Hooker or Cotton Mather in one century, or John Wise or Thomas Jefferson in the next, to make people act one way rather than another way. His aim is not to fill an idle hour, but to push his generation in a direction of which he approves.

It thus becomes tempting to argue that the American spirit, in its main outlines, has been until quite recent times the quintessence of a secularized puritanism. The regard for effort, the belief that success attends upon it, the suspicion that failure is due to some defect of character, the justification of wealth as a stewardship the obligations of which the public may expect to see fulfilled, the dislike of radical doctrines as a social form of antinomianism, the fear of any ideas which may bring into jeopardy the unity of the commonwealth, all of these seem little more than an adaptation of the religious principles with which the seventeenth century was familiar. And because the Puritan gospel was operative in a society which almost until our own day was still engaged in pioneering, it is natural enough that, as it became secularized, it should regard with praise the qualities that enable the pioneer to succeed. To take a risk, to show courage, to display the capacity to organize, even more, to show that talent for leadership which imposes law and order in a community fighting primitive conditions, whether physical or social, all of these are elements in the character of man which shape the American spirit. It is not a spirit which easily accepts the notion of a social hierarchy. It is not the spirit of a civilization which emphasizes either perfection of technique or refinement of manner. It is more concerned with getting the thing done, with shaping the tools which can do the job, with saying bluntly what needs to be said, than with method or with convention, whether of craftsmanship or speech.

Since the American spirit works in an environment that is constantly changing, it lays great stress on the power to innovate and adapt. It has a veneration for the past; there are few countries in the world where the past is so religiously commemorated as in the United States. But this veneration is wholly compatible not only with the right of each generation to experiment with itself, but, more, with the right of each individual to make his own bargain with fate. Because America has been a land of adventurers, its spirit has put a high value on self-reliance. This high value, in its turn, has begotten an impatience with constraint, an assumption, accordingly, that the less the interference with the individual's action, the more fully he will be a whole man. It is not wholly fanciful to argue that American individualism is the secularized form of American puritanism, that it leaves the individual face to face with his fate, as the chief forms of puritanism left the individual face to face with his God. The American, moreover, as he watched the toughening of fibre, the assurance of success, the inventiveness developed, by this kind of experience, came almost unconsciously to think that a state power which did more than organize external defence and internal police was going beyond its proper function. The "rugged individualism" of Mr. Herbert Hoover has deep links with the foundations of the American spirit. It assumes the validity of that social order which, violence apart, permits a man to make the best of himself that he can.

And it urges, very intelligibly in the light of American history, that a man makes the best of himself where he is free to learn from experience by what acts he is most likely to succeed. It is certain that a man is likely to be the best judge of his own interests. It is doubtful whether anything done on the citizen's behalf by government is as well done as when the citizen does it on his own behalf for himself. It is, indeed, suspicious of government, partly because it associates the ruler with tyranny and constraint, and partly because it has a profound regard for freedom, by which it means letting a man go his own way. Where government intervenes, it doubts whether there is likely to be an equal incidence of action upon all. The shadow of government is still set for great numbers of Americans in the habit of the European monarchies of the eighteenth century. The generation which was taught by Paine that that government is best which governs least has left a deep impact on the American spirit. It is not very sure that the citizen who needs to be helped is really fit to be helped, still less to be a member of the sovereign people. It fears that once some single road is barred, all roads will be barred. It suspects the politician in a way rather akin to the author's suspicion of the critic; the politician has taken to living off the public because he has failed to make a living elsewhere, just as the critic is the man who attacks the picture he cannot paint, or the symphony he cannot compose, or the book he cannot write.

It is upon this foundation that the American spirit has been built, from these sources that it has found its habits of life, conscious and unconscious. Far more of it than Americans are usually aware is due to the special environment in which the United States grew to maturity. It could not have become what it is had there not been so boundless a territory to explore. It could not have become what it is, either, had it not been virtually free from any fear of serious aggression from the age of Chatham to the age of the aeroplane. Nor must one omit the immense part played in its making by the fact of the break-down of the plantation economy built on slavery and its final destruction in a terrible civil war. The effect of this dual event was a revolution perhaps more profound than any other in the nineteenth century. For, in the first place, the South recovered from the Civil War only by submitting to being transformed into what was virtually a colony of the North, exploited by the North very much at its will. And, in the second place there emerged from the Civil War what Myrdal has termed the "American dilemma." For, once the South was compelled by force to give up its "peculiar institution," it gave up with that surrender its belief in equality. To keep the Negro "in his place," it found itself, perhaps only half-consciously, compelled to keep the poor white man in his place. But to do that with any effectiveness, it had to take its stand against those influences in the North which sought to protect the worker from exploitation by his employer. And that meant, under normal conditions, not merely that the "Solid South" was an unchanging appendage of the Democratic party; it meant also that, the greater the social character of legislation in the North, the more likely was it that the South could attract capital investment simply by the promise of safeguards against social legislation. The revenge taken by the South for its defeat in the Civil War has been not merely to punish the Negro by enforcing an inferiority upon him; it has also enforced a kindred inferiority upon the poor whites. For whatever aspect of political activity one takes, whether it is education or public health, factory laws or the level of public services, the South is at a lower level than the North or the West. And the outcome of that lower level is, first, that it loses the Negro with ability or self-respect to the North, and, second, that the white labour it retains has neither the skill nor the efficiency of white labour in the North. The poverty of the poor Southern white is associated with a determination not to be classed with the Negro, and, therefore, with an hostility to him. The outcome of this hostility is division by race where economic interest should build a unity. There enters into the American spirit that poison of inequality of which all that is most reactionary in the United States has rarely failed to take advantage.

It is interesting to note that what I have termed the secularization of puritanism has not yet developed in the United States a genuinely indigenous philosophy. Until some such period as the First World War the cultural inspiration of America was centred in Europe rather than in the United States. While it is, of course, true that until the death of Emerson the creativeness of New England remained noteworthy, and that, in Whitman and Melville, America produced two of the giant figures of nineteenth-century literature, it is also true that the position of the creative artist in this period was always difficult and sometimes tragic. The American was not, so to say, culturally sure of himself until the final end of colonialism with the First World War. He was not quite convinced that literature was a valid occupation for a man like farming or building or engineering. He tended to think of the writer, the painter, the sculptor, the musician, as someone available to fill in his scanty hours of leisure when he rested from his labours of conquering the continent. He was not even sure that the arts were not an aspect of life more suitably left to women with time on their hands. It is, I think, this attitude which explains why the artist in America was, almost until yesterday, self-conscious, so much so that the practical man found it difficult to take him seriously. He was the proof that the new civilization was reaching the stage where it could afford to pay attention to culture. To the solid business man on Wall Street and State Street the artist was always a little esoteric. If he was Edgar Allan Poe, he seemed hardly to be American at all. If he was Fenimore Cooper or Washington Irving, his reputation was a reflection, in large part, of what was reported as seen in the mirror of European judgment. Much could be pardoned to Oliver Wendell Holmes, Sr., since he was a famous professor at the Harvard Medical School. James Russell Lowell, Francis Parkman, John Lothrop Motley, William Prescott, had all of them positions in life which rendered them independent of the arts. Where that status of independence was absent, as with Hawthorne or Howells, a minor diplomatic appointment seemed a suitable recognition of their gifts.

The Gilded Age might shake with laughter at the humour of Mark Twain, but it saw him merely as a superb entertainer. It never knew what to make of Walt Whitman, though it was clear that a man who openly employed some of the terms he used was unfit to hold a minor post in a government department. Not until 1866 did Melville secure that post of district inspector of customs in New York which was the mainstay of his security for the next nineteen years. There is little music of importance; a good deal of the architecture is less the expression of the American genius for building than the translation into brick and stone of the flamboyant plunderers displaying in New York and Washington, in Chicago and Philadelphia, their power, as Veblen put it, to waste conspicuously. There are few painters of anything beyond mediocre significance, though Mr. F. O. Matthiessen has reminded us how high was the level of that photographic art achieved in the portraits of Mathew Brady. The wealthy man who wants to indulge in self-display becomes the patron of the great European dead rather than of the significant Americans of his own generation. Art in most of its forms is superimposed on the American spirit; and the test that it is really great art, in almost all its forms, is recognition by Europe rather than acclaim by America. When President Coolidge said, with his typical Yankee phlegm, that the "business of America is business," he was summarizing a principle in the American approach which was only beginning to be questioned when he became president. Where culture had sought a full American expression, as, above all, in New England, and, predominantly, in Boston, it had an unmistakable tendency to preen itself on its fine feathers, as though it were in fancy dress. Certainly it is difficult not to infer that the Brahmins of Beacon Hill and Brattle Street felt that they were the aristocratic *élite* guarding a precious heritage that otherwise might well be in danger of disappearance.

What Santayana has called the "genteel tradition" is, in fact, a very small element in the American tradition. The men who were cultivating what had been, as it were the day before, a wilderness, who were bridging the continent with their railways, who were making their level of technological achievement something which, when width and quality are taken together, the world had never known before, were almost bound to think of culture as a by-product of their effort which could either be left to their womenfolk or be developed by men who lacked the ruthless drive involved in taming a continent. The sprawling, clumsy, merciless builders of a new civilization had no time to substitute philosophy for pioneering. They may have vaguely heard that, dotted all over the United States, were queer experiments like Brook Farm or the Oneida and Shaker communities. They may even have heard, though still more vaguely, that all sorts of curious doctrines—Fourierite socialism, Swedenborgian supernaturalism, that intense zest of Emerson for half-digested versions of Oriental faiths—were claiming here and there their votaries. The spirit they deemed important had neither the time nor the interest to dwell upon these things. They paid, of course, lip-service to the democratic principle. They experienced to the full the flavour of its romance. They knew the intense excitement of fighting for political and economic power, and the perhaps even more intense excitement of fighting to stay at the top when they had got to the top. They were, nearly all of them, convinced that they had built a society in which opportunity was equal and each man counted for what he was in himself. They listened with rapture to the men who, like Daniel Webster and Henry Clay and John C. Calhoun, put their thoughts into orations as remarkable as their own achievements in the mercantile field. Now and again they had their moments of discomfort about things like slavery, though they could either comfort themselves with Jefferson's faith in its inevitable disappearance, or with Fitzhugh's discovery in his *Sociology for the South* that Aristotle had no sort of use for abolitionists. But the moments of discomfort, as the American spirit was formed, were not only rare, but intelligibly rare.

For it was broadly true, until the administration of General Grant, that the energetic man of ability, whatever his origin, was pretty certain to find his reward. It was broadly true that such a man, whether he was English by origin, or German, or Scandinavian, had a genuine chance of moving upwards all the time. After all, they saw in front of their eyes the fulfilment of careers that looked more like a story from a fairy-tale book than an actual piece of life. The self-schooled railsplitter from Illinois becomes President of the United States ; the distance that separated his status from that of Washington or Adams was surely proof that the foundations of the American commonwealth were even more broad in spirit. What would have been the chances of such a career in Europe? The swiftness with which a man like Patrick Tracy Jackson, apprenticed to a Massachusetts merchant at fifteen, a sea-captain when barely twenty, the founder and manager, with Francis Lowell, of the Waltham Factory in his thirties, and within a decade the real organizer of New England railroads, is surely a swiftness with something of epic quality about it. So, also, has the tale of Harnden and Adams and their apotheosis in the firm of Wells Fargo, of which, as early as 1869, Samuel Bowles, the editor of the *Springfield Republican,* could write that "the first three establishments set up in a mining town were a restaurant, a billiard saloon, and a Wells Fargo office."

An American born in 1790 would have seen the population of his country in 1860, when he was seventy years old, grow from just on four millions to nearly thirty-two millions. He could have noted that whereas in 1790 all but five per cent of the people lived in the thirteen colonies of the original federation, by 1850 more than half the population lived west of the Alleghenies. While, at his birth, there were only five towns with more than eight thousand inhabitants, by 1860 there were one hundred and forty-one towns of a greater size than eight thousand. The discovery of gold, the possibilities of free land, the growth of the conviction that public education was by all odds the best means to counter crime and pauperism and to safeguard the implications of Jackson's democracy, all these were elements in the making of the American spirit. Nor is it without great significance that while there were twenty-four colleges in the United States in 1800, in 1860 there were at least ten times as many. Most of them, of course, were denominational institutions, small in size and unlikely to have attained a high academic standard. But they are the proof of a faith in the value of learning, and their constant tendency was to an increasing emphasis upon its secular character. Nor is it unimportant that in these years the influence of the constant stream of immigrants and of the frontier was to weaken the power of institutional religion whatever may have been its effect upon the individual faith. The very size of the country meant that, while it was being settled, even the outstanding Churches had to depend upon missionary effort among a widely scattered population, few of whose communities could support a resident clergyman. And since, in most cases, the pioneer was rarely likely to be a man of cultivation, American religion developed in the period before the Civil War that tendency to emotional revivalism which it has never lost. The result of this, too little emphasized, is that the faith accepted by Americans outside the great cities was less a code of rules which permeated the daily behaviour of the believer than a temporary mode, in between the daily round of toil, of satisfying the passion for self-expression. And even in the great cities the rigidity of doctrine became increasingly hard to maintain. After all, it was Emerson who won his battle with orthodoxy; and the address which shocked the Harvard Divinity School is one of its chief claims to being historically remembered.

Nor must anyone who seeks to understand the American spirit forget how important has been the growth of devices and inventions to lessen the burden of domestic toil. Tin utensils instead of copper, the enclosed stove, the rapid development of a piped water supply in all the large cities, even the development of agricultural machinery, made for an easier way of living. Street lighting was immensely improved by the forties; and the cheap postage introduced in 1845 and 1851 was hardly less valuable than the growth of railroads and canals in breaking down the barriers of isolation. And by 1840 the birth of the penny press had not only contributed enormously to the decline of parochialism, but had begun to grow into that thirst for information about everything which has made the news-getting power of the American journalist something that is different in the character of its scale from the habits of any other nation in the world. The hunger for news is a quality of the American spirit which remains insatiable. Even when the novel medium of radio developed, it was evident from the broadcasting programmes in the United States that the appetite grew by what it fed on.

The Americans, in the first epoch of their history, were not easily tempted into ease and play. Tocqueville is only the most outstanding of the early commentators who emphasized the intensity of their application to business. It is true that there was built around the churches a fairly eager social life; and the itinerant lecturer, as the experience of Emerson shows, was always welcome when it was thought that he had something to say. The proportionate place in American habits of institutions like the drama, the opera, the ballet, was relatively small, its significance hard to distinguish, before the Civil War. It may be true that in the South dancing and horse-racing, gambling and hunting, had, all of them, a conspicuous place in the life of the plantation; and a few weeks in Charleston or New Orleans in the winter was as natural to the rich landowner as a London season to a country family of position in England. American hospitality was amazing; and even the slightest acquaintance with American literature reveals how deep are the roots of that dry humour of which Artemus Ward, Mark Twain, and Finley Peter Dunne were only the outstanding exponents.

Yet it is the degree of seriousness in the American spirit which is its main characteristic until the Civil War. It is as though Americans realized that the challenge of Nature over that vast continent could not be taken with gaiety or light-heartedness. The American lives hard, works hard, even plays hard; he seems to feel that only intense living will make him the master. It is notable, for instance, that not until a comparatively late period did there develop a literature of irony in America, and irony is the instrument of a people who can watch their own effort with a high degree of amusement. There is wit and satire and invective in plenty; but each of these is intense in its quality. And the intensity seems proportionate to the pace of life. They are moving at such a speed that they are almost afraid, perhaps a little ashamed, of the slow contemplative mind; they are not quite sure that to rest on their oars, so to say, is not a denial of progress. And as intensity is proportionate to pace, so it is proportionate to size. The American seeks not merely, in Matthew Arnold's phrase, to affirm himself; he wants to affirm himself as bigger and part of a bigger whole this year than he was in the year that has passed.

That, I suspect, is why there has been a suspicion of the unconventional throughout the history of the United States. An American can be a "character"; its civilization is incredibly rich in the number of characters it has possessed. But an American is not wholly comfortable, even at the present day, with the "character" who does not conform to the central habits of the American spirit. He does not easily find a place for a weird genius like Edgar Allan Poe; he can welcome with enthusiasm a great American like William James; he is puzzled by a great American like Henry James whose frame of reference is only partly American. He did not buy many of Emerson's books while he was alive; and he was half-bewildered and half-dismayed by Walt Whitman. Most American oratory that has remained classical—the Gettysburg speech is a shining and remarkable exception—whether it be Webster or Clay, whether it be Jackson or Calhoun, is florid, as though the orator feels it urgent to leave his audience with the conviction that he accepts with a heart full almost to bursting the traditional American ethos. The American orator, indeed, has to be a very exceptional man if what he has to say is not to read in cold print rather like a secularized sermon; in this context, it is of the highest interest to compare the oration at Gettysburg of Edward Everett—which was what the audience anticipated—with what Lincoln said, and to remember that many of the most important newspapers of the time did not even bother to print an utterance which history has agreed to put alongside the Funeral Speech of Pericles.

One is led to the conclusion that, at least until recent times, there was a deep conviction, perhaps only half-conscious, in the American mind that an intense team-work was the condition upon which alone it had the hope of fulfilling its destiny. And that team-work meant that while there might be an individualism in economic matters as remarkable as the habits of Rockefeller or Vanderbilt or the elder Morgan, the American spirit required that the limits of uniformity be drawn with a certain tautness. It is not wholly accident that one Main Street is all Main Streets, that if Harvard has "houses," Yale must have "colleges" of a similar model. Nor is it accident that "keeping up with the Joneses," whether it be in the equipment of a house, or the number of cars in a family, or the books that one ought to have read, or the magazines to which one subscribes, is a fundamental principle of American living. The uniformity of values which has been the outcome of the American conquest of the continent is far more startling than even that remarkable observer, Tocqueville, predicted it would be. For it is at least doubtful whether there is any capitalist democracy in the world where Marx's famous aphorism that "the ruling ideas of an age are the ideas of its ruling class" has become more profoundly true than in the United States. The spiritual values which secure universal acceptance are the same in New York as in Chicago, and the same in Chicago as in Los Angeles.

And that is true with two additions each of which is in a high degree remarkable. It is not, perhaps, surprising that great cities like New York and Chicago should have similar criteria of action; but it is surprising that the same criteria should seem valid in relatively small provincial cities like Worcester, Massachusetts, or Bloomington, Indiana. St. Paul and Minneapolis may laugh at one another as Manchester and Liverpool do; but the central difference between them is in geographical position and not in ideas. When Professor and Mrs. Lynd painted their remarkable picture of Muncie, Indiana, they were, if on a small scale, painting what might easily have been a miniature of any great metropolitan area. Boston and Philadelphia may have had their special differential as recently as a century ago; those special conditions have so largely disappeared that it has ceased to be possible to deny the fundamental uniformities. The great city will have its university, its symphony orchestra, its picture gallery, all similarly patterned like its hotels and department stores and movie theatres. Now one and now another may be more interesting; just as Howells thought that Boston was the cultural centre of the United States after the Civil War, as New York seemed to emerge into the performance of that function after the war with Spain, though Chicago trod, and treads, upon its heels. And just as provincial writers like Mark Twain or Hamlin Garland would lay stress in the last century on their freedom from the great metropolitan "wen," so, in this century, Sherwood Anderson or William Faulkner would renew that emphasis. Federalism, which began by seeking to maintain variety in unity, has ended by succumbing to the influence of giant capitalism, which is, by its inherent nature, unfavourable to the variety which federalism seeks to maintain. If there has remained an interesting and significant regional literature, in the Middle West, in the Far West, in the South, the central result of economic development has been to emphasize the obsolescence of the federal idea.

The other addition that is remarkable is the amazing degree to which the *mores* of the business man have penetrated the overwhelming proportion of those elements in the United States which might have been expected at least to prepare the basis of opposition to them. Nowhere, in any society of major economic importance, have what President Roosevelt has called the "underprivileged" so fully accepted the assumptions upon which successful men have made their way to power. Even if we measure the radical movements which, from Shays' Rebellion onwards, have sought to give some real foundation to the idea of equality in economic life, the outstanding result has been their inability to remain more than a passing phenomenon. Some of them, like the Populist movement, have been deeply interesting; and they may one day come to have an historical perspective as interesting as that of Lilburne and the Levellers in the Cromwellian epoch. No one can belie the fascination of the communal experiments like Brook Farm; and it is obvious that men like the early Orestes Brownson or William Ellery Channing or Theodore Parker understood a good deal of the implicit dangers of American development. Here and there, too, the union of a great personality, like Henry George, with the advent of depression, has caused a momentary arrest in the completeness of the business man's hold upon the predominant American habit. But it is vital to remember that no radical movement has for long endured in the United States except as a thin thread in the total pattern of the whole. It is vital, also, to remember that after John Taylor and Orestes Brownson even the chief radical movements of the United States have, in the main, accepted that faith in progress and that confident optimism which are, as I have suggested, integral elements of the American spirit. The trade-unions, after the period, at any rate, of Andrew Jackson, were suffused with the spirit of successful capitalism. They asked for better conditions; they never sought for political power. The Socialist party has had, as in Daniel de Leon and Eugene Debs, men of noble character and deep moral insight whom it could run for the presidency, or use, as with De Leon, to define an alternative to the business man's philosophy. There have been violent strikes, like Ludlow and Paterson and Gastonia; and the "Molly Maguires" have shown that a violent attack upon the habits of American business has been at least possible over a fairly lengthy period. But, in the end, the pattern which has prevailed, even easily prevailed, has been that which assumed the validity of the business man's outlook.[1] Farmers might be told to "raise less corn and more hell"; there may have been moments when a particular conflict resulted in concessions from the employers to the workers; but there has never, as yet, been a time when the character of the American state power has been shaped by a philosophy which the owning class has not been able to define. American radicalism has always been a phenomenon capable only of temporary and partial successes; and it is not, I think, unfair to suggest that, so far, the radicals themselves have assumed that this was the fortune which awaited them.

[1] See Samuel Yellen, *American Labor Struggles* (New York: Harcourt, Brace, 1936), *passim.*

2

THE significance of this is obvious enough. The problem of the American spirit was the problem foreseen by Tocqueville over a hundred years ago. The more amply political democracy was organized, the more powerful, at least until the Great Depression of 1929, was the authority of the industrial oligarchy. What Senator Elihu Root called the "invisible government" secured a power which decade by decade grew greater as it grew more irresponsible. Ownership and control in business became even more concentrated; and no political device, from the direct primary through the short ballot, to the referendum, initiative, and recall, seemed able to limit that concentration. Scholars like J. Allen Smith and Parrington and Beard might make into a philosophy of politics the solid inquiries into business habits which were conducted by Henry Demarest Lloyd or Ida Tarbell, to take two instances only. Beard might write with vigour that "the real state is not the juristic state, but it is that group of persons able to work together effectively for the accomplishment of their joint aims, and overcome all opposition on the particular point at issue at a particular time." Realism of this kind reached, relatively, but a little way. Perhaps it influenced a small group of intellectuals, and an occasional trade-union organization. Perhaps as early as the eighties of the nineteenth century there were many scattered people who felt, as William Dean Howells wrote to Henry James, that "after fifty years of optimistic content with 'Civilization,' and its ability to come out all right in the end, I now abhor it, and feel that it is coming out all wrong in the end unless it bases itself anew on a real equality." Ed Howe and Hamlin Garland might write of the faded hopes of agricultural life. Edith Wharton, Frank Norris, Theodore Dreiser, and Robert Herrick might grimly, though in Mrs. Wharton's case elegantly, deflate the bubble of American hopefulness. Henry James, at three thousand miles' distance, might, however labyrinthine his approach, still indicate with characteristic indirectness that a civilization of bourgeois *nouveaux riches* leads in the end to revolution. The important point was that the legend of American fulfilment transcended all the criticisms that were brought against it from the time of the Civil War. It was believed, despite everything, that America was different, that her destiny was special, that her hopes were on a higher plane than those of any other country in the world.

It was from the persistence of this remarkable piece of mythopoesis that the American spirit was compounded. For it was mythopoesis despite its overwhelming success. Even though there was always an escape, so long as free land was available, from the slavery of the wage system as Europe knew it in all its hopelessness, the position of the worker was not a very enviable one. Even Harriet Martineau, who wrote of it with enthusiasm, admitted that the working week was about seventy hours. Child labour was widespread. Factories were mostly unsanitary. And after the great crisis of 1837 there was a progressive deterioration in the standard of the workers' life generally. Wages were reduced; attempts at union organization resulted in the blacklisting of any active radical; and housing conditions were as bad as in the cotton towns of the North of England. And the larger the number of immigrants, the greater was the employers' power, not least because differences in nationality and language made unity on any serious scale a matter of quite special difficulty. We who look at the end result of the Industrial Revolution in the United States are able to see how immense were its consequences, and how overwhelming was the productive capacity that it had created by the time of the Civil War. But we know all too little of the psychical costs entailed. We can imagine that they were heavy, not only from the working-class journals of the period before 1860, but also from the impact made by the growth of industry on generous minds like those of Channing and Theodore Parker. We can see it, also, in the attraction of communist experiments for some of the most generous minds in the first half of the nineteenth century; they may all have failed lamentably, but their significance lies not so much in their failure as in the sense of passionate idealism which led to their being undertaken. And we can see the profundity of the myth in the conviction, before 1861, in the South, that it contributed, by reason of its peculiar institution, a life in which the chivalrous and cultivated gentleman preserved that ideal for a United States in which, otherwise, it would have been lost by the hard materialism of the North and the West. That conviction, indeed, is still far from dead, and its power to permeate the politics of the South is still distressingly profound.

What has been essential in the formation of the American spirit is a threefold factor, no part of which can easily be separated from the others. The first is the dramatic aspect, which almost no one could escape, of a vast continent, from which were absent alike the panoply and the hierarchy of the Old World, not only being subdued by the hands of men, but being subdued by men many of whom, in that Old World, would have been the victims of its panoply and its hierarchy. And, on any showing, it is a remarkable drama, whether one looks at it from the angle of the speed of its development, or from the angle of the sheer size of the success achieved. Anyone who sets it over against the parallel developments of Canada or of Australia ought not to find it hard to understand American self-confidence, the scale of American energy, the driving power of its endless ingenuity.

The second aspect is the fact that in the conquest of the American continent what was naturally remembered was not the tradition of failure and of sorrow, but the tradition of success and of joy. Men who started with nothing but their ability and their energy end as presidents, or judges of the Supreme Court, as senators or governors of their states, in the political field; in the industrial, they accumulate fortunes which the wealthy aristocrats of the Old World are almost bound to regard with envy. And in all this the successful man, whether he be politician or industrialist, never finds in front of him a barrier he cannot break down. There is always a climate of hope; if he fails today, he may win through tomorrow. So that he rarely gives up and always assumes that it is worth his while to go on trying. This climate of hope produces that amazing American vitality which triumphs over tropical heat and arctic cold. The basis from which, in the nineteenth century, Americans started was that, if they were immigrants, they had chances they could not dare to dream of, while, if they were native-born, the fulfilment that came to Jackson or to Lincoln, to John Jacob Astor or to Nicholas Biddle, might just as easily come to them. In this regard, the history of the United States is like a vast competitive examination in which, at least until our own day, every competitor believes that he has a chance of a prize, and, with that belief, the knowledge that some of the prizes are of epic proportions.

The third aspect which gives its special character to the American spirit is that, just as the thirteen colonies began their effective life in the seventeenth century, the supreme age of scientific discovery, so the United States began its effective life in the nineteenth century when science begins, in a full way, to attain technological maturity. From this it is, I think, legitimate to draw the inference that the American temper is adventurous and experimental, I am almost tempted to say revolutionary, in the psychological context in which it is set. And this temper, at least until the frontier was reached, was intensified by the fact that the American had no alternative but to pioneer if he was to make his country his own. He was, therefore, rarely weighed down by the burden of an inherited tradition which he hardly dared to examine, much less to alter. And, though piece by piece there is built up the idea of a unified America, there enter into its making thoughts and emotions to which all the world contributes. It is a society in which the categories are never fixed, in which the search for security is in itself almost an admission of failure, because security is always half-regarded as stagnation. One can see that attitude in the faded splendour of New England after the West begins to be opened. Most of its young men with a life to live move on to the new areas where there are new opportunities; those who remain are concerned to protect a position won against the immigrant challenge so that, even if they remain wealthy, they have to see State Street accept a position inferior to what New York or Chicago, St. Louis or Denver or Minneapolis, Seattle or San Francisco, can offer. In one way, perhaps, nothing is so revealing, as a portrait of American adventurousness, as the large number of New England spinsters in the second half of the nineteenth century. They come from good families; not seldom they have substantial means. But New England has begun to accept an almost European hierarchy of caste, with the result that, if they cannot marry their own kind, at least they must refrain from disgracing their pedigree by alliance with the son of an Irish or a Jewish immigrant. So that Emily Dickinson, the Elizabeth Barrett of New England, stays almost like a nun in the house that her father has made her convent; the American Browning who might have persuaded her to break down its doors is in Iowa or Idaho or California. We hardly know what dreams may have passed across that remarkable mind as it lay hidden in its conventual cell. We can, I think, be sure only that Emily Dickinson was never more than half of what she might have been because she did not dare, in the true American tradition, to defy the life in which she was imprisoned.

If we look, therefore, at the American spirit in the middle fifty years of its making when above all it received its essential habits, certain things emerge beyond mistake. It is bold to the point of audacity and even recklessness. With all its formal veneration for the law, its decisive end is to reach its objective; and if that means going round the law, or, at the margins, ignoring it even with violence, it has rarely displayed any hesitation in doing so. Its vigour is abounding and its endurance of heroic proportions; anyone who reads the detailed story of the founding of the state of Utah will understand the kind of strength of will and purpose that was brought to the making of this tradition. And it is a spirit which has a power of persistence not less remarkable. The supreme example of that power is perhaps best seen in the career of Abraham Lincoln with its relentless movement to the goal he set before himself. Indeed, there is a real sense in which General Grant's famous remark, "I shall fight it out on this line if it takes all summer," is symbolic of the history of the United States. The American in this critical middle epoch knows what he wants, and he cannot be turned from the struggle to attain it, whatever the cost.

He cannot be turned from the struggle; there is a great significance in the fact that, mostly, it is struggle which has shaped the American spirit. Sometimes he is fighting Nature; sometimes he is fighting the Indian; twice he has fought Great Britain, and once he has overwhelmed the relics of ancient Spain with a speed that made the battle against the military enemy far less difficult than the battle against disease among his own troops. I speak only of the nineteenth century. I do not know which is more fully American, the relentless drive to fortune of the first head of the Rockefeller dynasty, or the eager tasting of everything that the world's philosophy can offer that emerges in Emerson's pages. And here, perhaps, it is worth while to point out that the half-mystic transcendentalist of Concord has an interesting kinship of manner and method with a man whose interests and character were widely separated from his own—I mean Benjamin Franklin. For while Emerson may hitch his wagon to a star, two of the most striking features of his effort to interpret life are, first, a brilliant power of conveying truth by an aphorism, which is very like the memorable technique of Franklin's almanacs; and, second, a passion for the examination of ethical and metaphysical systems, which is very like Franklin's zest for peering into the secrets of nature. And in them both there is a power at once to be among their fellows and yet aloof from them that is of extraordinary interest.

The American spirit is active; it is rare to find among Americans the zeal for or gift of contemplation. Where they do have it, as Thoreau had it, for example, the tendency of their neighbours is to regard them as eccentric. Contemplation, for the American, is the luxury an old man may enjoy as the price for life spent in action. To be is to do; and to do is to overcome the difficulties that are in one's path. That is the inner ethos of the American spirit. It makes the victory an individual responsibility, an effort which the citizen must engage in by himself, without expecting that he can look to the community for aid. This is, I think, why the Darwinian concept of the struggle for existence made so rapid a conquest of the American mind; and why, to take an instance which it would not otherwise be easy to explain, so wise and acute an observer as Mr. Justice Holmes retained to the very end of his long life a deep sense of gratitude to Herbert Spencer as the thinker who, above all others in his youth, had released that generation from philosophies set in a quasi-theological context and made it understand that there was an ultimate conflict between the individual and the state power which no amount of Hegelian moonshine could reconcile.

Nor must we fail to notice that activity as in itself a virtue is combined with shrewdness and a natural liking for the solution which meets a political problem quickly, rather than the solution which, though more æsthetically adequate, takes longer to apply. The American spirit is a pragmatic spirit; it looks more closely to the results it requires than to the methods by which those results are obtained. It is relatively uninterested in the formalism to which the British, for example, attach so much importance. A man is chosen because he is "available" for the particular job he is asked to perform; and it is interesting to compare this with the British conception of fitness for a post, into which there still enter birth and training as well as capacity. And the passion in the American for quick results is revealed in a habit of inventiveness which is in almost all its aspects remarkable. One can see that passion in the American zest for domestic "gadgets" which save time and labour. It is seen in the organization of mass production. It appears again in the growth of standardization in commodities of general use. The difference, to take a simple example, between the making of men's clothing in America and in Great Britain is the difference between a spirit which, once a level of style and efficiency is reached, does not bother itself much about the importance of differentiation, and a spirit which is disturbed by any large-scale similarity of output. Even in the dress of women something of the same contrast appears, if in a lesser degree. Uniqueness tends to be confined in the United States to the wife of a very wealthy man who, at any rate before 1939, could afford to do her shopping in the Rue de la Paix.

I have noted the friendliness of the American spirit. It is a quality of which it is difficult to exaggerate the intensity. An American puts his house at your disposal. He asks whom you want to meet and arranges that you should meet them. If his wife entertains upon a modest scale, it is more than likely that the dinner that she serves you is one that the wives of her guests will have helped her to prepare, and, before they leave her house, they have more than probably assisted her to clear away the dishes. Where the English housewife is above all anxious to create the impression that she is, however admirable a hostess, utterly remote from the rota of domestic work, the American housewife takes a pride in her personal relation to it. And while the British entertain at home at the point where acquaintance has passed into friendship, the Ameriicans offer an hospitality that is so swift, after acquaintance has begun, that most Englishmen feel embarrassed by the degree of intimacy to which they are at once admitted. Even more is this the case where the Frenchman is concerned; with the latter, domestic hospitality is the end result of a long acquaintance that is almost invariably so rare an occurrence as to be an event even in the relations between close friends. A bock at a café, a causerie when dinner is over, an invitation to the monthly Thursdays of Madame, these are the French equivalents of the American friendliness which have almost the air of assuming that one moves in a straight line direct from an introduction to something that only barely falls short of actual relationship.

I think this attitude of mind has its roots in two great characteristics of American life. The first, and perhaps the most important, was, until the end of the nineteenth century at any rate, the idea that democracy meant equality, and that it was not easy for equality to be real where fraternity was absent. Domestic service, on any considerable scale, was rarely achieved except by the really rich, and it was either a very highly paid vocation or else a part-time function in which the housewife thought herself fortunate if she could engage a cook or housemaid—who might easily be a girl seeking to pay her way through college—for two or three hours in the day. And to this there must be added the innumerable American families who belong to small towns and know in detail every item of their neighbours' lives; alongside this must be set the fact that few Englishmen know their neighbours, and fewer still are anxious to cultivate relations with them. One has only to compare the habits of Americans in the smoking car of a train with those of Englishmen in a railway carriage to recognize that the former would know each other's business and history before an hour had passed, while few Englishmen would consider that anything short of a fatal accident could possibly justify conversation between strangers. This was true even during the Second World War, when a degree of mutual understanding was an essential element in victory.

The second factor, I think, is the influence of the frontier. The stranger who has come from miles away, and has, it may be, miles still to travel, expects to find, and does find, kindness at most places where he stops upon his journey. He has news to give of interest, and he receives information which he is entitled to think will help him on his road. It is, of course, true that the more fully settled the area, the less likely is this friendliness. It is improbable that a traveller will receive in Vermont the kindness he will receive in California. It is certain that New York will be far less interested in the man who comes to settle there than the citizens of Fargo, North Dakota, or Fort Wayne in Indiana. A stranger in Chicago is merely an item in a statistical table unless he is of exceptional standing; but a stranger in Pullman, Washington, is an event in the life of the town. Wherever the settlements of the United States have either remained relatively small in size or are off the railroad track of the main lines, there is in the United States a community temper which it is impossible not to note as a significant element in its spirit. It is not the same in its expression in every state. It depends, in some degree, upon the race or religion or even the opinions of the new settler. There will be more friendliness shown to a Scandinavian in a Minnesotan township than is likely to be received by an English settler; just as there will be more kindliness for a Welshman in the anthracite region of Pennsylvania than is likely to be shown to a French Canadian who decides to settle in some part of Tennessee. But the essential point I am anxious to make is that American democracy has bred, outside the great metropolitan areas, a personal magnanimity which it is difficult not to recognize as the spirit of that fraternity upon which the period of the French Revolution laid such stress. It is only in quite recent times that its expression has come to be regarded as an absence of that temper of sophistication which the contemporary citizen is bidden to regard as proof of a modern outlook.

This attitude of friendliness is notable for another reason. It breaks down not a few of those barriers of class which, in most European countries, have remained high and forbidding. A small American farmer who barely scratches a living from the soil is still profoundly conscious that he is a citizen of the United States; he does not merely live by the reception of orders which he is practically compelled to obey, like the peasant of Hungary or the rack-rented peasant of Spain. From time to time he makes his will known in a fashion which no government may dare to neglect; and if he has been in no small degree the victim of the swift process of settlement and industrialization, he is profoundly conscious of his own individuality. There is, indeed, a sense in which it is tempting to argue that, despite his mortgages and bad harvests, the small farmer in Vermont or Iowa has been made a man by the climate of the American spirit, in Matthew Arnold's sense that he forms his own views in his own way in the light of an experience that he insists upon interpreting for himself. This attitude emerged with vigour both in the Jeffersonian revolt against Federalist domination, and, once again, in that remarkable Populist movement which maintained for over a generation its abiding loyalty to William Jennings Bryan. It was not very skilful in its capacity to organize; it was usually beaten when the votes were counted. But it never admitted its defeats; and when one campaign was over, it usually assumed the democratic right to begin all over again its preparations for the next. It watched its officials very narrowly; and it judged their performance less in terms of their efficiency than upon the basis of experience that they were good fellows who did not get above themselves. From a senator like Mr. Borah to the sheriff of a county, whatever the importance of the political ideas they represented, it was far more important for the man who sought elective office to know his constituents as well as if they were members of one immense family. Nor was it frequent to find the sense, at least in the native-born American, that political office was something beyond the reach of the average man.

It is difficult not to assume that, in this regard, the election of Andrew Jackson to the presidency contributed an element to the American spirit which has still considerable importance. It broke the hold upon office of the great dynasties of Virginia and New England; after 1828, it was rarely an advantage to be a member of an ancient and wealthy American family until the election of Franklin D. Roosevelt. For though Theodore Roosevelt may seem an exception to this rule, it must be remembered that he went to the White House as the result of McKinley's assassination; and he had been nominated to the vice-presidency in order to stifle his presidential ambitions. Anyone who goes through the list of elected persons in the post-Jacksonian period will realize at once that it is the uncommon man of common stock who reaches the places of importance. Not until quite recent times do we find in the record names like those of Vanderbilt or Saltonstall. It is even pretty accurate to say that, despite the remarkable opportunities for higher education in the United States, the man who can claim to have educated himself starts with a significant advantage over the man whose path to the university has been the result of parental care. Harvard and Yale and Princeton play nothing like the part in American politics before 1933 that Oxford and Cambridge have played in British politics, or even the Ecole Normale in the politics of the Third Republic. When an ex-president of Princeton did become first governor of New Jersey and then president of the United States, it was usual to attribute his mistakes to the fact that his career had separated him for too long from the experience of practical life.

The common man did not have, in the century after Andrew Jackson's election, a monopoly of the political field; but he was far more likely than the wealthy or the well-born to find the road to it an accessible one. This fact has a close connection with the remarkable power of the machines of the different parties in each state. For if the wealthy or the well-born were an exceptional element in politics, they were nevertheless, and naturally, anxious to see that their privileges were not invaded. They had, therefore, to form alliances with the men who could safeguard them against this danger; and since the boss, both in city and country, was master of the votes through his domination of the machine, there grew up inevitably an undercover relation between the machine, on the one hand, and big business or large-scale agriculture, on the other. But this, in its turn, had unexpected results. The boss could organize his cohorts in an efficient way only by his ability to manipulate the police and the judiciary, the civil service and the legislature. The outcome was that the great industrialists, like those of Chicago and Pittsburgh, the great timber barons, like those of Colorado and the Pacific coast, and the great cattle owners, like those of Texas, were always in close relations with men whose habits they were compelled to denounce in public. There were, so to speak, three governments in power in any area at a given time. There were the elected officials who, though they might be proud New Englanders like Henry Cabot Lodge, would never dare to forget their dependence upon a vote like that of the Boston Irish Catholics. There were the machine politicians, from a vital figure like the Grand Sachem of Tammany in New York, or men, for example, like Boss Croker, down to the humblest ward heeler, who, whatever their overt profession, devoted their main energies to keeping the voters attached to their parties and expected, quite naturally, to be paid for the time and trouble they spent in the effort. And there were the aristocrats of industry or agriculture who, though they had no time for politics, arranged, so far as they could, with the party machines to be protected against the reformer manias which, from time to time, would seem to threaten them with danger.

No country could have afforded this complicated and, mostly, negative extemporization of its policies that did not seem capable of infinite expansion and therefore able to offer an almost boundless hope. But these are the characteristics of the life of the United States until the dawn of the second third of the twentieth century. There were panics; they were always overcome. There were unemployed; but few people believed, including the unemployed themselves, that they were condemned to the permanent position of the poor. There were the familiar phenomena of the trade cycle; but all the successful men and most of the economists assured public opinion that these were merely the growing pains of a new civilization. From time to time there would be a sudden doubt whether the system of free enterprise, with its ever-growing monopolies and its faith in the tariff and the gold standard, was really going to fulfil the American dream. From time to time, also, the violent magnificence of men like Vanderbilt and Gould, Renaissance bravos so curiously projected into the nineteenth century, represented what America was intended to be; but most people, as they watched the incredible spectacle these presented, were not quite sure that these bravos were not a price it was necessary to pay, and were impressed by the impact of this magnificence upon a Europe which was obviously divided between desire to share in the spoils and ardent envy of their immense scale. Certainly by the time the elder Morgan had attained his amazing primacy in the world of finance, it was a relatively small minority which insisted that America was denying the purposes of its origin. Most people felt a confidence that was unbreakable in the permanently progressive character of the system. Most people felt, also, that those who refused to show this confidence were themselves a source of danger to this progress.

3

No SMALL part of the American spirit has been formed by reaction against what its citizens believed—sometimes not without justice—to be the spirit of Europe. In part, at least, that explains why Americans have been so sensitive to the criticism of foreigners, and why, in return, the immense development of the United States has evoked in most parts of Europe, above all among its ruling classes, a certain *Schadenfreude* at American failures or mistakes. The American has believed that he is simple where the European is complex, democratic where he is an aristocrat, egalitarian where his system is built on the notion that only a social hierarchy can preserve order. He is shocked at European poverty, at its narrow opportunities, at its relative unwillingness to take a man at his own worth. He is contemptuous of the large number of Europeans who had privilege without function, and inclined to a sense of amazement at the habit of deference to "one's betters" that he regards as endemic in European society. He is appalled by the weight of tradition throughout the European scene, the slow pace at which change proceeds, the fear of innovation, the basic assumption that each citizen has his allotted place beyond which he may not hope to go. And he is disturbed by the lack of political unity in Europe, the relatively small scale on which it is able to produce, the immense volume of its illiteracy, its refusal to accept the implications of technological change. He thinks of Europe as a civilization that has already passed its zenith, that lacks the capacity to renew its foundations. He dislikes the reverence for outmoded habits, the zest for the old merely because it is old.

Nor can he help remembering that, until some such time as the publication of Lord Bryce's famous book, it was the exception rather than the rule for Europeans to write politely of American civilization. Perhaps the best index to this temper emerged during the course of the Civil War; and nothing is so revealing of the European approach as the conversations recorded by Nassau Senior during his visits to France, or the attitude of the British and French press to the Northern cause in general and to President Lincoln in particular.[2] It is reasonably clear that the ruling classes in England and France hoped for a breach in the Union that would be permanent; and most of its members clung eagerly to every straw in the wind which indicated the prospect of Southern success. It is, of course, both true and important that the working classes did not take this view; and it is always worth remembering that one

---

[2] Nassau W. Senior, *Conversations with . . . Distinguished Persons during the Second Empire* (London: Hurst & Blackett, 1878).

of the early acts of the First International was to send a warm letter of good wishes to President Lincoln. But the general impression was that the European aristocracy, whether of wealth or of birth—Tsarist Russia is a curious but significant exception—cared less about the issues which were in dispute on American battlefields than they did about the need to prevent the rise of so formidable a power as the United States on the new continent. It was not merely that Louis Napoleon sought to take advantage of American difficulties to establish an imperial quasi-dependency in Mexico. It was not merely even that men like Mr. Gladstone and Lord Acton could be grievously mistaken about the nature of the war. The thing that was dismaying was the fact that Lord Palmerston and Lord John Russell quite obviously confronted the possibility of war with the North with a considerable degree of complacency; and only the resolution of Charles Francis Adams, the American Minister in London, and the skill of Lincoln, as revealed in the alterations he made in the dispatches of Secretary Seward, averted what was on several occasions a grave danger that European intervention would break the unity of the United States. It was small consolation for those difficulties that men like Bright and John Stuart Mill and Cairnes, in the older generation, and Leslie Stephen in the newer one, understood from the outset the things that were involved.

But an American could be pardoned if, in the years up to the presidency of General Grant, he had assumed that the central principle of American life was almost a direct contradiction of the central principle of the European idea. The American might easily have reminded himself of the deep suspicion of the European purpose which runs through so much of Jefferson's writings. The European was told that Americans were materialistic, loud, barbaric, ungenerous; that so far as they approximated to civilized living, it was in the habits of the South rather than of the North that a culture worth preserving was to be found. The men and women who compiled this legend did so, with occasional exceptions, partly because of a widespread European fear of the influence of America, both in power and in ideas, upon a world which still distrusted the democratic principle, and partly because there were few Europeans who understood the ethos of an American still engaged in the adventure of pioneering. For, after all, if one compares the sins laid at the American door with the evils of European life, it is obvious enough that the real difference was merely between American crudity and European sophistication. The England and the France of the sixties were not unanxious to make money; the writings of Carlyle and Matthew Arnold, of Flaubert and Renan, suggest that there was in the European bourgeoisie a loudness and a barbarism at least as great as that of the United States; and it was in these years that Bismarck was developing that policy of "blood and iron" which it is not easy to reconcile with the habits of civilization. And few people who compare the South with the North in the generation before the Civil War will be able to discover in the former any superior virtue but elegance of manner. In courage, in ideas, in energy, in the power of discovery, the superiority of the North was beyond all question.

But in the epoch from the foundation of the United States until the publication of Bryce's *American Commonwealth* in 1888, it is, I think, an accurate generalization to say that Americans had an inferiority complex in the face of Europe. Though they were developing a remarkable and indigenous literature, they assumed that the criteria of literary merit were set by European and not by American standards. Though they displayed a technological genius at least comparable with that of Europe, they did not doubt that they must set their course by the European star. Though their soldiers and sailors and statesmen compared at least favourably, certainly with those of England and France, and, on the military side, even with the skill of the German General Staff, they assumed that the Old World set the standards of the New. Though the fulfilment of the Industrial Revolution in Europe was almost child's play compared to the achievement of Americans in the same period, they accepted, hardly with reserve, the view that they followed and did not initiate. When their entrepreneurs grew rich, it was Europe they visited, European treasures they sought to amass, European writers and craftsmen they sought to patronize. I think it is true that in music and poetry, in painting and in sculpture, the quality of the European product was greatly superior to anything that America could show. I think that is true, also, in the realm of philosophy, and in pure science in contrast with applied science. But the result of it all was that Americans had an inferiority complex about Europe which lasted until well into the twentieth century. There was a colonialism about their attitude. They did not feel that they had really succeeded until they had received their due meed of European eulogy. And, like all peoples with an inferiority complex, their habits displayed a curious mingling of arrogance and of servility. The outcome of this dual response was a sentiment of sensitiveness which did not begin to subside into a normal attitude until Lord Bryce told his fellow-countrymen that there had arisen a new and creative civilization in the Western Hemisphere which had at least as much to teach as it had to learn.

Lord Bryce's book was a masterly piece of description, even though it lacked the philosophical profundity of Tocqueville's work of a half century earlier. Its importance was that it bridged the gap between Europe and America in a way that no earlier work had been able to do. And its effect upon the American spirit was, therefore, the very important effect that it began the process of enabling Americans to free themselves from dependence on Europe, and to approach their problems in terms of their own conditions. It began the process; it did not complete it. The German university, and the European literary technique, were still, for some thirty years, to control the habits of the United States. That is evident from the influence of Johns Hopkins; it is evident from the assumption of Henry James that he must set the American scene in the context of European travel. But, after Bryce, there emerges not only the immensely important thesis of F. J. Turner, which interprets American evolution in terms of the frontier; [3] there begins, on a massive scale, the judgment of Europe by America instead of the other way round; American literature and American science begin, in a vital way, to have a frame of reference that is able to assume equal importance with European achievement. One can see in the nineties of the last century that the American spirit is beginning to be domesticated in American soil.

But this domestication is a far slower process than is usually imagined. Until almost the end of the First World War, the cultural centre of America is in Europe. Until almost that same period, work in fundamental science—that of Willard Gibbs, for example—achieves recognition in Europe before it achieves recognition in America. And when the First World War comes to an end, the generation that has fought it and triumphed in it has a bad attack of *Weltschmerz;* it wants to find in Paris and London, in Berlin and Capri, the values that it cannot find in the thousand Main Streets of the United States. It tries to make of Greenwich Village in New York a Latin Quarter, where the sophisticated *demimonde* of the artistic world can tell one another how hopeless it is for an American to seek either for peace or recognition in the United States where, it avers, Eddie Guest is a well-known poet, Henry Ford the symbol of its dreams, and Harold Bell Wright the novelist with the largest audience. It almost seems as though the disillusion of the post-war years made Americans think of themselves in much the same way as Europeans had written of them before Bryce wrote his book. There is a breakdown in the confidence of America in itself; and there is little compensation for that break-down in the easy prosperity of the Coolidge era, which can regard the social ideas of an inspired and wealthy mechanic like Henry Ford as of vital importance.

The truth, I think, is that American participation in three great wars and a minor one—the Civil War and the wars with Germany and Spain—precipitated it on to the theatre of world affairs before it had achieved a real maturity for its own inherent ethos. That, I take it, is the explanation of the mean and tawdry splendour of the Gilded Age, with its fantastic architecture, its lavish, even reckless spending, its willingness to be represented by figures like Blaine and Mark Hanna in politics, like "Bet a Million" Gates and Vanderbilt in finance, its inability to recognize the greatness of Walt Whitman, its angry refusal to recognize trade-unions, its fantastic sacrifice of the Chicago anarchists on the altar of its fears. And that evolution has a parallel in the nineteen-twenties when Daugherty and Mellon can be members of the American government, when its rulers are willing to ignore events like the massacre at Centralia, when the Van Sweringen brothers are princes in financial operations, and even as brilliant a critical historian as Parrington fails to see that James

---

[3] See his *The Frontier in American History* (New York: Holt, 1921), pp. 1–38.

Branch Cabell is wholly devoid of importance. Only such a period could have assumed that Gertrude Stein was important and that the "learning" of Ezra Pound was real.

Yet if one compares the nature of the American spirit after the Civil War with its nature after the First World War, it is impossible not to realize how immense is the difference in creativeness. The first period is self-confident, but its habits are loud and raucous; from the death of Lincoln to the election of Theodore Roosevelt there is not a single occupant of the White House who is worthy of the first traditions of the Republic. Immense fortunes are being made, but few of those who make them have any sense of the responsibility of great wealth, and most of those who make them either want money merely for the power it brings, or seek to waste it conspicuously in the hope of obtaining notoriety. The second period is self-confident too, but it is, all the time, coolly scrutinizing itself, and in men like the elder La Follette, George Norris, and Louis D. Brandeis, it is insisting that there are certain standards of political conduct to which a decent American must conform. Not less significant is the contrast between the literary character of the earlier period and of the later. John Dos Passos, Sinclair Lewis, Ernest Hemingway, William Faulkner, all of them have a love for America at least as great as that of their predecessors. But all of them are insistent that self-examination is not inconsistent with their love. They have rid America of that "genteel tradition" which made even William Dean Howells insist that there were certain subjects, sex, for example, upon which one ought not to dwell.

One has the sense, in the American novel of this period, that while it has learned the lessons implicit in the great European masters, it is also independent of them in both the subject matter it selects and the technique upon which it relies. I do not think that it is a period of great poets, at least in the sense that Walt Whitman was a great poet; but it is an age which knows that it must take poetry with profound seriousness, and whether it is Robert Frost or Carl Sandburg, Robinson Jeffers or Archibald MacLeish, it has that attitude to the poet as legislator which is an invitation to creativeness. Nor is the change in criticism less important. Irving Babbitt and Paul Elmer More represent in the period before the First World War the settled conviction that America has made its bargain with fate, and that truth ends where Beacon Street or Brattle Street or the upper sixties off Fifth Avenue end. They are sure that they know; they look upon the man who has not yet made up his mind as only a degree nearer destruction than the man who indulges in radical experiment. But the newer critics who take their function seriously, Edmund Wilson, for example, use their instrument to probe into the vitals of American civilization. They are prepared to praise what is great in the achievement of America; but, not less, they are prepared to call into question principles and ideals which, a generation before, most Americans would have taken for granted.

Nor is it less interesting to compare the scholarship of the earlier period with that of the later. The difference lies, I think, partly in the immensely wider range that the second covers, and partly in the insistence that the criteria of truth must be more rigorous, the standards of assessment more severe. It is true, of course, that the earlier period produced certain works of scholarship—Moses Coit Tyler's *History of American Literature,* for example—which have not been surpassed, and perhaps not equalled, in the later. And no doubt works like those of Parkman and Prescott will always retain, as perhaps, the Dutch history of Motley, a classic value. But the central difference between the scholarship of the Gilded Age, and the scholarship of the period after some such year as 1914, is that it does not argue after 1914 that the test of worth is set by that American standard of achievement which thought Cleveland a great man and admired Mark Hanna because he combined wealth with the power of king-making. The reader of works like those of Haskins on the medieval renaissance, or of Ferguson on Hellenistic Athens, to take scholars who deal with non-American themes, or of Alvord and Carl Becker, of Charles Beard and Arthur Schlesinger, to select examples only from the field of American history, has the sense not only that the whole evidence has been sifted with both delicacy and accuracy, but also of an ability to do something more than stand alongside the subject matter and cheer for the glory of American achievement. A book like Carl Becker's *Declaration of Independence,* or Charles and Mary Beard's *Rise of American Civilization,* has a width of outlook and a maturity of spirit which were rare indeed in the nineteenth century.

And what is true of the world of letters, as between the two periods, is true also, in perhaps a lesser degree, of the world of science. It is still true that American science tends to specialize on the applied rather than on the pure side; and American philosophy, where it is not some species of instrumentalism, tends still to do little more than adapt, with minor variations, the main categories of European philosophy. But the development of American jurisprudence has far outstripped in realistic understanding that of most European countries, and very certainly that of England, which still does little more than ring the changes on the ideas of Jeremy Bentham and Sir Henry Maine. Perhaps no American lawyer has had a genius for historical insight as brilliant as that of Maitland, though the *Common Law* of Mr. Justice Holmes hardly yields in quality to that insight; but in relating law to the totality of social relationships it is difficult to feel that America has now any rival, and though it has had few economists of first-rate standing in analytic power, in the application of economics to industry and agriculture, I think it could be claimed that the United States has, in the last generation, outstripped all rivals; an achievement the more remarkable when it is remembered that little American work in this field had any significant importance before the Civil War.

Nor can one omit to note that, despite its patchiness, the American educational system, at its best, is as good as anything in the world. It is true that it is, for the most part, poor in quality, and even poor in the mark at which it aims in the South; but anyone who compares even the Harvard or Yale or Princeton before the Civil War, or shortly there-after, with what they have become since 1919 both in aim and in standard of achievement, cannot, I think, doubt that the degree of improvement has been immense. It is, of course, true that there are innumerable col-leges in the United States which it would be hard to defend on any grounds, above all the colleges with a denominational connection; and while there are many schools of the first quality, there are still more of which both staff and buildings seem the expression of a standstill agree-ment. Not least, it is true that while Negro education has advanced since the late sixties, it has not advanced in anything like the proportion in which the education of white American citizens has advanced; and the opposition to the educated Negro still leaves his race the hewers of wood and drawers of water for their white masters. But, despite this important lacuna, the contrast between American education in the two eras is over-whelming. With all that remains to be done, no other country (the West-ern states in particular), except the Soviet Union, has so fully committed itself to the principle that the education of the citizen is the condition of democracy's survival, nor has any other country, again with the same exception, so remarkably transcended the fear, far from dead in Europe in general and in England especially, that the education of the masses is a threat to the privileges of the few.

4

WHAT has been the meaning of this contrast in its influence upon the spirit of America? Above all, I think, it has encouraged the advent of a maturity of mind and heart which it was not always easy to detect, save in the most outstanding Americans, Franklin, for instance, or Jefferson, in the history of the United States before the epoch of Woodrow Wilson. For national maturity is marked not merely by the ability to play a sig-nificant role on the stage of world history; it is marked, also, by the capacity of a people to recognize that it must be able to laugh at itself, and to re-examine, if necessary, the basic principles on which it is founded. It would be going too far to say that Americans in general have reached out to that second quality with any enthusiasm. But I do not think it is going too far to argue that, in the years between the two world wars, and especially in the years since the Great Depression, a significant group of Americans, growing ever larger, has become aware that it would be necessary to undertake the task.

They realized that the simple formula of "no entangling alliances," with which Jefferson provided Washington, has no serious meaning in an interdependent world. They realized, too, with the advent of men like Huey Long and Gerald K. Smith and Father Coughlin, that where any considerable portion of a people is unemployed or underprivileged, then, whatever the original tradition, the power of democracy to survive is in real danger. The America of the inter-war years maintained a good deal of its optimism, most of its faith in progress, its ardent and widespread conviction that a destiny was reserved for it different from that of all other nations. A small group of its citizens might find its inspiration in the Soviet Union; but to the overwhelming mass of Americans, bolshevism was a direct, even evil contradiction of the American idea. Another group might plead that America was ripe for socialist development; but the presidential returns, after 1920, made it pretty clear that this was not a view which was able, at least to the period of the Second World War, to make any widespread appeal. Even those who thought it possible that the era of expansion was over still retained a belief that they themselves would somehow escape the results of its termination. And the overwhelming majority retained the opinion that whatever was done by government was less well done than when it was undertaken by private enterprise. They were held in the grip of economic individualism as in a vice. They thought of private property as something in a higher moral category than property which belonged to the public. The gospel of success had a hold of almost legendary proportions. Even President Franklin Roosevelt, who had to cope with the greatest economic crisis in American history, was nevertheless emphatic that the American system was fully adequate to the well-being of the people; he attributed the break-down less to principles inherent in it than to their deliberate perversion by men intent on their own prosperity without regard to the interest of their neighbours.

It is, indeed, a striking fact that although many of the measures put on the statute book during the New Deal were in direct antithesis to the historic principles of the American economy, nevertheless it was always argued, after the first flush of enthusiasm over the beginnings of recovery faded, either that the New Deal was in fact the natural outcome of the American spirit, as by the Democrats, or that, by running counter to the American spirit, the New Deal was jeopardizing the chance of its fulfilment. Only two groups in America remained solidly attached to the New Deal: the main body of the trade-unions, and the administrators, mainly academic, whom President Roosevelt brought to Washington. The wealthy and the privileged, the main body of lawyers and professional men, and most of the great figures in business life were continuously and relentlessly hostile. It was, indeed, remarkable that President Roosevelt was almost as bitterly opposed by some members of his own party, among whom were numbered important and influential members of the Senate, as by members of the Republican party. He was exposed to a criticism more bitter than any president had encountered since Lincoln in the Civil War, and Jefferson when he overthrew the Federalist party. And the essence of the criticism he encountered was the accusation that his policy was "un-American."

It is important to be clear what his critics meant by this charge. The New Deal sought to check the ravages of unemployment by bringing into being what was virtually a limited edition of the social service state. It was argued that this would erode the individual's sense of responsibility, that it would weaken the creativeness of the American adventure, that it would intensify bureaucracy to the point of nauseation, that it would destroy the citizen's incentive to effort. The critics, in short, were seeking to discredit the New Deal by setting over against it the pattern of that pioneering America which was in fact already extinct by the beginning of the twentieth century. What is remarkable in the New Deal is the degree in which it is, in fact, simply the completion of a continuous development of discontent with traditional individualism which goes back, in one sense, to Shays' Rebellion, and, in another, at least to the Populism of the period after the Civil War. In these aspects, the struggle waged by Jefferson and Jackson against the financial interests embodied first in the Federalist movement, and then in the Bank of the United States, must be regarded as in the direct line of its ancestry. So, too, if from a somewhat different approach, was the tradition of the Republican Progressive movement which Theodore Roosevelt offered to take to Armageddon. All this is on the federal plane; if the experience of the states is examined, the Wisconsin of the elder La Follette is only the most advanced development of a mass of social experiments from which very few of the forty-eight states can be wholly excluded.

Yet the spirit of America found it difficult to accept what was in fact no more than a new emphasis of an old experience. It was as though, in the period between Grant and Cleveland, there had been formulated what Mr. Walter Lippmann has admirably called a "stereotype" of what American policy ought to be, and anything which savoured of an approach to the positive state was, almost *a priori,* a denial of it. That "stereotype" has become a living part of the thought of the ordinary American. He learns it in school; it is the framework in which his college teaching is set; and there are few, indeed, of the journals, whether daily or weekly, which do not seek to drive it home. In the result, he finds it difficult to escape from the pattern it imposes upon him. If he starts a business, he is quickly convinced that the less connection he has with government the better. If he practises law, his main chances of an effective career depend upon his ability to build connections with business men. If he is a teacher of the social sciences, the record, for example, of the American Association of University Professors indicates the danger of departing from the traditional path; and, in any case, the rulers of the institutions of higher learning are drawn, in overwhelming proportion, from the men to whom the "stereotype" is almost an article of religious faith. If he is a professional man, an engineer, for example, or a chemist, his opportunity to advance in his career is likely to be dependent upon the great corporations which, as the Senate Banking and Currency Committee saw so clearly in 1933, make the translations of the "stereotype" into practical terms almost the law of their being. And, generally speaking, if he has political ambitions, he will find that either party, Republican or Democrat, in any period unmarked by special crisis, expects from him the acceptance of the "stereotype" as the condition of his availability.

All of this goes to say that the idea upon which the spirit of America is founded is something like thirty to forty years behind the actual facts of American social and economic life. The theoretical equality of opportunity has somehow to relate itself to the picture drawn by F. W. Taussig and C. S. Joslyn of the growing nepotism in industrial enterprise.[4] The expanding economic universe has to be squared with a world in which there are normally at least four million American unemployed,[5] and in which, if government orders ceased, there might, at the level of production in 1940, be something like sixteen million unemployed. The ardent faith in the prospects of education must be fitted into a pattern in which, during the single year of 1942, one hundred thousand teachers in the South left their profession to become munition workers to obtain the higher level of wages.[6] The eager faith in progress is in part offset by the growing conviction of the owning class that capitalism and democracy do not easily exist on the same plane; and while there is an immense growth in the centralization of economic power, there is an increasing dislike of the parallel effort of the workers to organize in trade-unions. The American spirit eulogizes with passion the rule of law; but it is difficult to see that it receives its due respect in Gastonia and Paterson, in the cases of Mooney in California and Sacco and Vanzetti in Massachusetts. The theory of the politician's progress from log cabin to White House is an attractive one; but it is increasingly evident that men of wealth or birth tend to secure the vital positions that the process of government can offer. Mr. Roosevelt was the chosen nominee of a people in revolt against the power of wealth over its life; but it is doubtful whether the State Department has ever had a diplomatic service so largely staffed by wealthy men as in his time. The American spirit is hostile to the idea of a hierarchy in social organization; but few modern countries have given a power so great or an authority so wide to men who have been successful in business or in law.

It is true that, except in the great days of New England, the literature of protest against the turn taken by the American spirit has rarely been so widespread. In the novel, the essay, the poem, almost all the outstanding figures are of the Left; and in American philosophy the outstanding figures, John Dewey and Morris Cohen, are of a progressive temper, as is the greatest figure in the social sciences of the last half-century. Thorstein Veblen drew up a vast, if complex, indictment against the epoch

---

[4] See their *American Business Leaders* (New York: Macmillan, 1932).

[5] Chester Bowles, *Tomorrow Without Fear* (New York: Simon and Schuster, 1946).

[6] Nor is it likely that a large number of them thought of returning to a teaching career.

in which he lived. On the other hand, it must be remembered that the main emphasis of jurisprudence and religion in America has been in the direction of a support to the traditional American spirit. Even if, as notably in American religious writing, the trend has been towards the utterance of noble thoughts, the actual practice of the Churches—Episcopal, Baptist, Methodist, Roman Catholic—has rarely sought to translate those noble thoughts into action. The American spirit sought to make of the United States a refuge for the oppressed of other lands; the immigration laws of the United States have, since the twenties, made that tradition a faded memory which disappointed innumerable hopes in the most bitter epoch of modern times. There have been, of course, not least on the Supreme Court, a number of men who embodied with distinguished ability the great tradition for which America was founded; and when President Roosevelt enunciated, in 1941, the noble framework of the Four Freedoms as a present possibility at which to aim, he showed that there was a living reality in the American dream.

But no honest observer could analyse the operation of the spirit of America in the nineteen-forties without some hesitation about its outcome. It was not merely that there was a growth of anti-Semitism and of bitter hostility to the Negro advance. It was, even more, the fact that the ruling class of the United States employed the traditional American spirit to prevent the adaptation of the purpose of American life to the facts that it encountered. The reader of the Lynds' *Middletown in Transition* (1937) who compared the landscape they painted so effectively with the hopes of men like Emerson and Thoreau, the great affirmations of Jefferson and Lincoln, would have found it difficult to discover in the contemporary scene the fulfilment of the spirit America had sought to embody. There was a wide abyss between the dream and the reality. There was a contradiction between the simple faith of men like Jefferson and Lincoln and the grim reality of an America in which the South was, despite increased industrialization, in large part an economic tragedy, and the North, outside the agrarian states like Vermont and Maine, was beginning to approach the European position. And, not least of all, it was significant that wealthy America was so related to the habits of the European aristocracy that it had lost no small part of its simplicity and an even larger part of its direct and eager insight. The American spirit, as the Second World War showed clearly, retained in all its vigour its original vitality, but it was far from obvious that it was still directed to the ends which had made the United States a source of hope and comfort to the poor and the oppressed. Yet that, after all, was the supreme justification of the American adventure.

III

American Political Institutions: Federal

I

FEW POLITICAL systems have changed in form so little as the Constitution which the Philadelphia Convention drafted in 1787. Congressional elections are still held every two years, presidential elections every four, whether in peace or war. The elaborate farce of the Electoral College is still enacted even though all the world knows that it has lost any meaning. Voters are still born into the Republican and Democratic parties, even though it is difficult to distinguish between them and uncertain whether they are parties at all in either a national or an ideological sense. Every state is still able to produce a "favourite son" at a presidential convention, and to retain a faint hope that the clash of other antagonisms will give him a significance he would not otherwise possess. Nearly every vice-president is either forgotten or a music-hall joke; if he is a person of political significance, the outstanding fact about him is that, like Mr. Henry Wallace, he is unlikely to be nominated a second time. The Senate and the Supreme Court retain their hold on the respect of American citizens, though there have been moments in the history of each when that hold seemed likely to fail. The House of Representatives has always been the least successful of federal institutions, and it retains that unenviable characteristic. The federal Civil Service remains, on its quasi-permanent side, less a body for building the materials out of which policy is made than a corps of mostly second-rate administrators who execute a policy they have little desire to formulate.

The greatest change in the federal system is in the significance of the presidential office. It is not merely that the election of 1940 put an end to the second-term tradition. Much more important is the fact that the initiative of the president is of ever-increasing influence, and that the eyes of the nation are focused upon his actions in a degree that has become normal instead of exceptional. Almost his thoughts have become news. The difference between a good Congress and a bad one is largely the difference between a Congress which accepts his leadership and one which seeks to refuse the initiative he tries to communicate. A stage, moreover, has been reached in the evolution of America where its citizens can no more risk the direction of a president like Harding than Great Britain could risk a prime minister like Lord Goderich. For America can no longer afford the kind of negation in the White House which took the place of a policy with both Harding and Coolidge. The futility of negation in a president is not merely the consequence of the Great Depression and the resultant New Deal. At least from the turn of the century, it has been obvious that the quality of the man who is president determines the general quality of federal politics.

I do not mean that a great president means a great Congress; there is even evidence that the more outstanding the president, the more likely he is, granted the effect of the division of powers, to have a Congress in which there is hostility to him, even when he is possessed of a formal majority in either or both Houses. Partly, I think, that is because a period in which the president has a great policy to put forward is a period in which public opinion is deeply interested in politics; and even if the president is in conflict with Congress, like Mr. Roosevelt over his proposed court reforms, the drama of political warfare elicits a public attention of great importance. That is an end it is highly desirable to achieve, since it has too often been the weakness of federal politics in America that, pressure groups apart, it is able to awaken public attention only in election years. A great president gives his people a supreme lesson in adult education. He fixes their minds on great objectives. He is a safeguard against that banal dullness which makes the democracy no more than a mass of private persons. The significance of a great president, therefore, lies not only in the measures he is able to carry out, but in the width of public interest he is able to evoke. He gives to the democratic process a vividness and a reality which it lacks when a weak president is in office.

It is notable that only the president is able to achieve this result. The members of his cabinet, even when they are men of remarkable ability, do not seem able to evoke that continuity of political interest which a democracy requires. Partly, of course, this is the outcome of the fact that an American cabinet minister operates in a relatively confined sphere of action; what he says and does is, therefore, more likely to interest a special than the general public. Partly, also, the very fact that he is an adviser to the president, upon whose authority he pretty completely depends, means that it is only in the presidential context that he is likely to have significance. Partly, further, the character of the federal system in America tends to confine the activities of a cabinet minister pretty closely to his department; it is the elected, rather than the appointed, person who tends to make the kind of general political commentary to which English people are accustomed by the parliamentary system. Englishmen are not surprised if Mr. Herbert Morrison or Mr. Anthony Eden makes the kind of general political speech which we expect from the Prime Minister; but an American audience would have been amazed if, for example, Mr. H. L. Stimson, when Secretary of War, had discussed in public the methods by which a system of international security could be organized in the era of peace. For that is assumed either to fall within the special sphere occupied by the Secretary of State, or to be a matter of general policy which, on the executive side, is a problem with which the president is expected to deal.

In the result, there is no aspect of policy, and, therefore, no aspect of action which does not, in the federal sphere, ultimately come back to the president. It may be a matter of minor ceremonial; it may be a matter as vital as the establishment of Lend-Lease or the building of Coulee Dam. From one end of the scale to the other it is the presidential attitude which, on the government side, can alone make a universal impact on public opinion. The president is the one man in the United States the expression of whose opinions is certain to receive attention. But it is obvious that the quality of the attention he receives depends upon the significance of what he has to say. If, like Buchanan, presidents evade every issue by which they are confronted, or, like Coolidge, merely pile commonplace on commonplace, it is natural enough that they should fail to interest the masses in the objectives they have in view. A dull president may, indeed, create that interest by being unable to agree with his Congress, in which case the drama of the conflict may arouse the electors to watch the fight between them. But this is, on the whole, rare; for the main object a dull president is likely to have in view is to reach the end of his term with the minimum of disturbance.

No one can survey the record of American history without the conviction that its quality depends, in an ever-increasing degree, on great leadership, and no one can pretend that great leadership can achieve its objective save as it is associated with the presidential office. Men of eminence can sit in the cabinet or the Senate, like Webster or Clay or Calhoun before the Civil War, or like La Follette or Borah or Norris after it. But they cannot, save from the White House, either conceive a great programme or carry it into execution. They may touch important aspects of American life in an important way; the development of the Tennessee Valley Authority will for long be associated with the name of Senator Norris. But unless leadership is presidential in character, it is usually more likely to be negative than positive, and still more likely to lack coherence and continuity. A president with ideas has, obviously, supreme opportunities that no one can rival while he is in office. The eyes of the whole nation are turned to him; whatever may be the voice it does not hear, his voice, at least, is certain to be heard. The very fact that he is president leads to the assumption that he will point to the direction in which the nation should move. He has an authority that no other democratically elected person can rival, for the very nature of his position is an invitation to the initiative which no other person can rival. That is why so much of the political fortune of the United States turns upon the man who is chosen for this office. If he is anxious to do nothing, little can be done anywhere on the federal plane. If he is urgent about the programme he has in mind, he can be certain that public opinion will discuss little else. And even if he is defeated in his aims, the very fact that the discussion is widespread will mean politics that are vivid and attractive. It is not accidental that it is the positive presidents in American history who have, almost always, brought people with brains and vision to Washington.

Not, indeed, that American presidents have always been men with positive aims to pursue. Party rivalry has brought dull men to the office because they were deemed more "available" than exciting men; and death or assassination has too frequently elevated to the presidency men whom the party conventions have chosen as much because their delegates wanted to get home as for any other reason. Nor must it be overlooked that the character of federal institutions in the United States almost starts from the assumption that an active president must be checked. From the early days of George Washington the anxiety of both Houses of Congress has been to prevent the president, if they could, from exercising either an unrivalled or an unlimited leadership. It was a wise remark of Calvin Coolidge that, as a rule, there are ninety-six men at the other end of Pennsylvania Avenue who not only think that they could do most things as well as the president, but also have an ardent conviction either that they could do the particular thing he is trying to do better than he is doing it or, alternatively, are anxious to prevent him from doing it at all. And even when he has been skilful enough to manage the Senate—and it is not easy to exaggerate the skill this requires—he has also to manage the House of Representatives, and to watch, with some care, the tendencies of the men, sometimes his own nominees, on the Supreme Court. While it is true that the Congress, somewhat curiously, has provided only a single president in the twentieth century, it has provided a very large number of men whose one objective has been the frustration of his policies. No man is likely to remain many weeks in the White House without learning abundantly both their number and their influence.

For the historical background in which the Constitution was set has meant that the legislature of the United States has always watched the Executive with a careful, and not seldom with an hostile, eye. The special association of the Senate both with foreign affairs and appointment to high office, the fixed period of tenure in both branches of the legislature, the fact that so much of the work of both chambers is done in the secret recesses of committee rooms, the fantastic rule which gives not only membership of the main committees, but what may often be the vital post of their chairmen, to men whose main qualification may merely be their length of legislative service, all of these things tend to drive even a strong president to compromise, and are responsible for a kind of pre-natal control in policy of which every president must take account. It is hardly an exaggeration to say that there have been chairmen of vital committees, like Foreign Relations in the Senate, or Appropriations in the House of Representatives, and, until quite recently at least, the Speaker of the House, who, if they have not been rivals to the president, have been able to exercise a kind of half-veto upon his policy. That has been the case, for all major purposes, with Senator Vandenberg since 1946 in foreign affairs. Even President Coolidge, at the height of his popularity, had to accept the humiliation of a refusal on the part of the Senate Judiciary Committee to accept his nominee as attorney-general. Mr. Hoover was elected President in 1928 by an overwhelming majority; but he could not get his concept of the tariff accepted by Congress. Mr. Roosevelt was re-elected triumphantly in 1936; but very shortly afterwards his proposals for the reorganization of the federal courts were decisively rejected.

There is a sense, indeed, in which the president and his cabinet colleagues are confronted by a quasi-executive built from the chairmen of legislative committees. This quasi-executive is less a body directly initiating policy than relating the aims of the president to what is found acceptable in the stresses and strains of legislative opinion. No president can hope to have the whole of his way; even Washington learned that. The presidential problem is so to organize his forces that he has enough of his way not merely to retain his normal followers but, still more, to convince that part of the electorate which is not directly connected with any party that he is a successful president.

That conviction is a function of many variables. Partly, it depends on the condition of the country; nothing could have re-elected Mr. Hoover in 1932. Partly, it depends upon the power of the candidate to secure a full and ardent support from the forty-eight state machines in each party; Justice Hughes lost the election of 1916 through his failure to win that support from the Republican machine in California. Partly, again, it depends upon the sense in the unattached voter that the candidate is "available"; and, so far, he is unlikely to be regarded as "available" if he is a Roman Catholic, or a Jew, or an atheist, in the field of religious opinion, or eccentric in economic matters like currency, or only a first-born generation of American. It is possible, as President Franklin Roosevelt has shown, to be re-elected even when the press is overwhelmingly opposed to him, though it is at least probable that he must be able to offset the influence of the press by his skill in broadcasting. Certainly, though it is largely true that Hitler gave Mr. Roosevelt his third term in 1940, the course of the campaign suggests that Mr. Willkie was at least a very close rival until Mr. Roosevelt, in the last weeks of October, summoned to his aid the remarkable magic of his radio personality.

Anyone who looks at all closely at the history of the presidency will be tempted, I think, to conclude that, with exceptions due specifically to the circumstances of war, it has gone, roughly speaking, through three periods. There is the epoch from the foundation of the republic to the end of Jackson's second term; in this period the presidents are all of them exceptional men, they mostly serve for two terms, and there is some positive element in the presidential tradition which is traceable to them. From Jackson's second term to the arrival of Woodrow Wilson in the White House there is a second epoch in which, Lincoln apart, there is no president who has a positive policy to put forward. Cleveland may have been a president of strong character; but there is nothing in the record of his two terms in Washington that is notable except his hostility to organized labour and his devotion to the gold standard. Theodore Roosevelt was a colourful and romantic figure with something like a genius for publicity; yet as one looks back upon his years of office they seem more full of sound and fury than of enduring significance. It is possibly true that Woodrow Wilson, had he been free to choose, would have differed but little from a Southern Democrat of the ancient vintage; but the circumstances of his time forced him to play a positive role, in his Federal Reserve Act as well as in foreign policy. And while it is true that, in the reaction from the aftermath of the European war, the years from 1920 to 1932 seem almost like a revival of the epoch after the Civil War, it is important to note that the hostility to the negativism of Coolidge and of Hoover was built upon the recognition that the presidential office must be active and not passive in character.

That recognition reached its full expression in the first term of the New Deal, and that recognition means nothing so much as the acceptance by public opinion that the initiative of the president is the keystone of the whole arch of the federal structure. If it be said that this acceptance was the result of the Great Depression, and that nothing less would have made it possible, the answer, I think, is the simple one; first, that the Great Depression was itself the outcome of an attempt by three presidents to return to an inactive role; and, second, that the main critics of the New Deal offered an alternative programme which differed from it less in the methods it proposed than in the persons through whom it was to be carried out. Republican party leaders may have hated the New Deal and all its works; but, alike in 1936 and 1944, they really asked for power on the assumption that they could give better and more efficient expression to its central principles. And, once the United States was sucked into the vortex of the Second World War, no one with an atom of imagination could suppose that the president could surrender his right to a vital initiative without making the American federal system an inchoate and incoherent muddle from which there would be no escape. The era of the positive state had arrived in America as decisively as in Europe; and with the arrival of the positive state there was no room for negativism in the White House any more than in Downing Street or in the Kremlin.

2

FEW things are more curious to the foreign observer than the character of political parties in the United States. In one sense they are only national in extent at election times; in another, they are far more effectively local organizations which cohere about persons rather than about ideas. They hardly represent even interests in the sense that one can distinguish between the purposes they serve. It is, indeed, difficult to find criteria by which to lay down permanent ideas which are Republican in contrast to permanent ideas which are Democratic. It is, of course, true that the attitude of the Democrats to the Negro problem differs from the attitude of the Republicans; but that is an attitude which derives rather from geographical distribution than from any basis in ideological approach. On all other matters, each party overlaps the other in all matters of doctrine. On the whole, the Republicans derive their main strength from industrial, and the Democrats from agrarian, interests; but Maine and Vermont are both overwhelmingly Republican and, at the same time, overwhelmingly agrarian. On the whole, again, the main incidence of finance-capitalism is probably Republican rather than Democratic. Yet, from time to time, the Democrats have attracted to their support some of the wealthiest members of the financial aristocracy. It would not be an easy thing to distinguish, except from the angle of electoral history, the platforms of either party. And the change in the personnel of each can be made, as it seems, without undue effort. For Mr. Henry A. Wallace, the son of a Republican Secretary of Agriculture, was first the holder of that position in the cabinet of Franklin Roosevelt and later his vice-president; while Mr. Wendell Willkie, the Republican candidate of 1940, was a warm supporter of Mr. Roosevelt in 1932. Mr. Harold Ickes, the Secretary of the Interior in Mr. Roosevelt's cabinet after 1933, was a Progressive Republican in 1912, and an ardent enthusiast for the elder Roosevelt in that famous campaign.

This kind of confusion is the natural outcome of the party system in America. For no party has a permanent leader; the president, while he is in office, has a transcendent influence upon the party which has nominated him, and it is usual for ex-presidents, and even ex-presidential candidates, to play an important role in their party—yet it is never quite clear what the role will be. Ex-Governor Landon of Kansas and ex-President Hoover are content to be "regular" Republicans who support whatever the National Convention of their party has decided; but it is far from clear whether Mr. Willkie would have been content with that kind of regularity. Former Senator Burton Wheeler has been the Progressive candidate for the vice-presidency; but there are few Republicans who have spent more energies in fighting President Roosevelt. In a formal sense, too, men like former Representative Dies of Texas, or Senator Byrd of Virginia, are members of the Democratic party; but it would have been impossible for President Roosevelt to place any reliance upon their support of the kind that he could place upon the late Senator Robinson of Arkansas, or Senator Wagner of New York. An American political party has far less continuity of principle than an English political party; it is rather a group of supporters gathered round a temporary leader who imposes upon them what influence he can. The unity of the two major parties arises less from the principles they apply to the issues before them than from the quality of the personality in the leader each chooses for the time being. And if the leader, on defeat, is replaced by another leader, as Mr. Willkie in 1940 was replaced by Mr. Dewey in 1944, the whole incidence of party emphasis may change because the outlook of the leader has changed.

The fact is that political parties in the United States, because they are the parties of a continent, are rarely unified in a European sense of the term. They are much more like a bloc of interests than a system of principles. They are, as it were, a sum of numbers added together the different integers of which may never be the same in any two presidential years. The machine in each state may have the same composition over a long period; but that does not mean that it defines the national objective in the same way or that it will appeal to the electors by the same methods. It has only one unchanging aim, the attainment of office and, therewith, the power that office confers. Within either of the major parties, there may be every shade of opinion from far to the Left to the extreme Right. Senator Norris of Nebraska was for most of his career a member of the Republican party; but it would have been very difficult to discover any principle of action that he held in common with either Senator Lodge or Senator Mark Hanna, who were also Republicans. The opinions of Senator "Cotton Ed" Smith or Senator George had nothing in common with those of Senator Cutting or Senator Black; but all of them were members of the Democratic party. The truth is that a continent so vast makes almost all parties a federation of interests between which such a compromise can be arrived at as is judged likely to be compatible either with keeping or with attaining political office.

The life of the party has the character that might be expected from the immense variety in the life of the American nation. And in each part of the continent the party adjusts itself to the historical and economic conditions of the area in which it is operating. Neither Republican nor Democrat would venture to forget the significance of the Scandinavian settlements in Minnesota either in choosing its candidates or in expounding its programme. Nor would either attack the Roman Catholic Church or Eire in New York or Massachusetts, as neither would attack Fundamentalism in Kentucky or Tennessee. Each has to consider a mass of special interests, sometimes racial, sometimes religious, sometimes economic, which it is rarely easy to arrange in a single pattern. That is why a presidential election will flank a nominee from one section of the country by a nominee from another section. That is why, also, it is difficult to know whether an outstanding personality is more helpful or more harmful to the fortunes of a party than a candidate who is likely to arouse the minimum of resentment. It is, of course, true that for practically half a century the Democrats had to bear the burden of the defeat of the South in the Civil War; there is a real sense in which it is true to say that it took the First World War to purge the Republican party of the conviction that Appomattox conferred upon it a title to the permanent government of the nation so that a Democratic victory might be regarded as inherently unnatural. That a man as honest and upright as Andrew D. White, the first president of Cornell University, could force himself to vote for James G. Blaine in 1884, even while he was aware that Blaine was both corrupt and untruthful is an interesting relic of that conviction. What really restored the balance was the realization that the outcome of merely "waving the bloody shirt" was to sacrifice agriculture and the West to industry and eastern finance. The critical date was the rejection by the Republicans of Theodore Roosevelt as their candidate in 1912. For that was an announcement that, under the colour of a great mass of patriotic rhetoric, the Republican party was content to be merely the instrument of Big Business. The assumed radicalism of Theodore Roosevelt was, in fact, far more a matter of striking postures than of actual deeds. But the fact that he was regarded as dangerous by that senatorial oligarchy which hardly concealed the manœuvres of Wall Street and State Street deprived the Republican party of a pretension to a national outlook which a little more skill would have enabled it to exploit for many more years.

What is now clear about the character of political parties on the federal plane is that the Second World War will compel them to make an adjustment that is likely to be far deeper than either is now ready to concede. The New Deal has already thrown a number of ancient traditions into the melting pot, of which not the least important is that whatever the lip-service paid to "rugged individualism," however deep the formal protest against the growth of federal power, both parties know that American democracy will find it hard to survive a second great depression of the scale of 1929. That means that it is highly unlikely that the main foundations of the New Deal can be undone without the loss not merely of that trade-union vote which is being increasingly organized, but the loss, also, of millions of votes of men and women who know that it is in the power of the federal government to prevent mass unemployment. And to this knowledge there must be added the expectation of many millions of Americans, which no party dare evade attempting to fulfil, that they will be suitably rewarded for the part they have played—and it is a great part—in achieving victory over the enemy in the Second World War.

On a superficial view, it is striking not merely that so little headway has been made by socialism or communism in the United States, but, even more, that the trade-unions should have rested content with the working of a party system which has offered them so little of the power they have been able to achieve on the European continent. All efforts so far at the creation of a mass-voting third party have failed dismally. The Socialist party of the United States has decreased in strength since 1933. The American Communist party has never even seemed to be more than a branch of the Soviet Foreign Office *in partibus infidelium*. The party of the elder La Follette, which polled some four million votes in the presidential election of 1924, was rather the expiring convulsions of the old Progressive movement than the birth of a really new force; and though Farmer-Labor parties have had brief epochs of success in North Dakota and Minnesota, their victories have been rather an episode than a creation. There was a long epoch of municipal socialism in Milwaukee, though it hardly went as far as the normal governmental commitments of Manchester or of Glasgow; and a reformist Socialist mayor has long been elected to office by the voters of Bridgeport, Connecticut. Distinguished philosophers, like John Dewey, have, from time to time, sponsored national committees, like the Committee of Forty-Eight, which they fondly hoped might become something more than a pale flicker of transient dissatisfaction with the two historic parties. But, so far, no movement has had the strength or the drive of that Progressive movement which Theodore Roosevelt proposed should march out to Armageddon in the name of the Lord; and no one, looking back at the Progressive movement, can see in it anything more than a means of enabling the older parties to take account of issues they were seeking to evade. The striking thing of the past dozen years is that, using an instrument which had little relation to the ends he encompassed, President Franklin Roosevelt brought into being a positive federal state in America even though he was never seeking deliberately to serve a social philosophy of which that state was the expression. The most brilliant empiricist American politics has ever known was driven on by large and impersonal forces which he rarely stayed to examine.

It is tolerably certain, I think, that when the Democratic party nominated Franklin Roosevelt in 1932, it had not the remotest conception of the consequences of its decision; and it is not less certain that he himself had little more than a vague sense that the state power should be used to help the underprivileged. Yet his election marks an epoch in the history of the United States of which the impact on political parties is certain to be as deep as that of the Civil War. It is one of those rare cases in which the sweep of events carries its main figure an immense distance beyond the point he had intended to go. And the outcome of this journey is pretty certain to be that the America of the next generation will either have to adapt its party structure to a far more positive democracy than any it has so far known, and that whether Republicans or Democrats be in power; or else it will move rapidly to some American form of corporate state which will prove incompatible with the traditions of political democracy in the United States. It is important to remember that those traditions go very deep in American history, and it will not be easy to abandon them without what may prove, if the attempt be made, as decisive an event as the Russian Revolution.

For the factor that is going to alter the whole basis of the party system in America is the twofold coincidence that the conclusion of its pioneering age is accompanied by its need to accept the responsibilities of leadership in an interdependent world. Whatever the rhetoric beneath which American parties go forward to the work of adapting the United States to its new tasks, it is, I think, certain that it will become altogether a society which tries to fulfil the democratic ideal or a society which tries wholly to deny it. It can no more survive as a plutodemocracy than it could, before the Civil War, survive half slave and half free. It is unnecessary to deny that in both the major American parties there are forces, not without considerable influence, which will do all they can to arrest, if not to prevent, the fulfilment of democracy—forces that are, in their ultimate nature, economic, but which receive expression now as religious reaction, now as racial prejudice, now as gangsterism and racketeering on a scale large enough, as in places like Jersey City, to corrupt the administration and the courts of law. But it is significant that an America which sought to preserve the power of plutodemocracy would have to make the grave choice between a profound diminution in its standard of living and an embarkation on a policy of economic imperialism which would in the end almost certainly unite against America forces which her citizens could not hope to overcome. And it is probable that before it was well advanced in either of these directions the whole basis of its party system would be challenged successfully. In the party evolution of the United States in the next generation there will, no doubt, be reaction as well as advance. But it is hardly possible, on the evidence, not to feel that the impersonal forces of the world are shaping American destiny in a democratic direction which no party can deny and yet survive. Here is the real promise of American life.

3

THE Congress of the United States has, of course, derived its character in part from the circumstances in which it was born, and in part from the impact upon it of the history it has encountered. This is true of any legislative assembly; and the special problems to which Congress gives rise, in both of its Houses, are due to features in the working of each which are special to the American environment. It is fundamental to the character of Congress that, whatever its party complexion, at some stage the doctrine of the separation of powers will bring it, if not into direct conflict with, at least towards a suspicion of, the habits of the Executive. Since it lacks executive direction, such as that of the British cabinet over the House of Commons, and is rather the president's rival than his colleague, it has no inherent need to discover a unity of which he will approve. The character of American political parties is reflected in the habits of Congress. Since each of them is a federation of sectional groups, it is not easy to evoke from their activities, save in crises of outstanding magnitude, an emphasis upon the interest of the nation as a whole. Few members of either House are likely to see that interest as vividly as the interest of the section from which they come, and most are uneasily aware that a deficient zeal for sectionalism may evoke defeat in the next party primary. There is all the difference in the world between the modest life of a small-town lawyer in the deep South, and the exciting contact with great events at Washington. It is the latter that most members of either House are likely to choose.

The House of Representatives suffers from three major weaknesses which seem rather to have grown than to have diminished with time. The first is the outcome of the custom that requires a member to be a resident of the district he represents, although the Constitution demands only that he be an inhabitant of the state. The result of this rule is a twofold one. It deprives the House of the services of many able men, and tends to make the elected person not the man most fit to be in Washington but the man regarded as most "available"; and since "availability" means that the candidate has no extreme opinions and can be relied upon not to offend any powerful interests in his district, most members of the House are mediocre men and women who do not differ greatly from one another and try to maintain their places by rendering as wide a number of small services locally as will act as a safeguard of their position. Only once since the twentieth century opened has a member of either House of Congress been nominated as a presidential candidate. A president will usually take one or two men with experience of, and influence in, Congress into his cabinet; but that is less because of the help they can give him in the fields of their departments than from the knowledge that their intimacies at the other end of Pennsylvania Avenue will smooth a relationship that is always tending to go awry.

It is exceptional for the House of Representatives to win the ear of the nation for its debates; and it must be said in frankness that the House takes all possible steps to prevent itself from being successful in what should be among the most important of its functions. For the fact that most of its major decisions are taken in the private sessions of its committees means that the public can rarely follow the argument on which they are based, while even the full-dress discussions of the whole House tend to be a series of formal speeches so mechanically arranged by time-table that the House is ready to agree that a member who did not get a chance to speak in the debate shall nevertheless print—the speech he would have made as an appendix to the *Congressional Record* of the day. A skilful anthologist, moreover, could make an unsurpassable treasury of American humour by selecting the varied matter, from a prize poem recited at the local high school commencement to an obituary oration on almost anyone from President Washington to an eminent football coach, the reprint of which in the *Record* is thought likely to give pleasure

to the congressman's constituents when he distributes free copies under
the privilege of his postal frank. No House of Representatives is ever
lacking in a number of really able and experienced men who give devoted
service in its committees. But no House ever uses them to the full level
of their ability and experience; and it is rare, indeed, that the House is not
ready to aid men like ex-Congressman Dies of Texas, or Eugene Cox of
Georgia, to utilize its power of special investigation for ends the means to
which have often been deeply deplored by many fair-minded Americans
of eminence. Every House of Representatives gets an enormous mass of
business done; but no House, save in moments of the gravest crisis, offers
in its procedure anything like an adequate assurance either that it will
be the right business or will be done in the right way. The chamber in
which the House of Representatives sits is, in any case, at once too big
and wrongly arranged for debate to be either intense or intimate, or for
any save the most outstanding occasion to be able to engage the interest
of much more than a handful of members.

The congressman generally has two centres of operations where he
seeks to be effective. If he is an important member of his party he may
hope for influence on the committees for which he is chosen; and, on the
great committees, like Ways and Means, or Appropriations, or Armed
Services, an important congressman is never a person to be overlooked.
And every member of the House has his own office, with the free provision of a small secretarial staff; and in that room he can be interviewed
by any of the innumerable pressure groups which keep their special lobbyists in Washington. There is a real sense in which these pressure groups,
despite their seeming incoherence, are a kind of Congress behind the
Congress whose authority must not be minimized. They can do a great
deal for a member of the House, not least for the unimportant or the new
member. They can help him with his speeches. They can organize for him
a publicity back home or in his state which he himself might not so
easily secure. They can see that he meets important people, not least upon
important occasions. And since the lobbyists have usually the closest relations both with the great press agencies and the remarkable corps of
special correspondents which the great metropolitan newspapers maintain
in Washington, they can, if he is helpful to them, do something to build
him up, if that is possible, into a national figure. At the least, if he is co-
operative, they can make his constituents feel that their representative in
the House is something more than the local boy who has made good. If he
wins the support of the right lobbyist at the right time, that may well be
a decisive factor in his political career.

The House of Representatives, in short, has gravely failed to fulfil the
functions it might have been expected to perform; the functions, indeed,
that, in no small degree, it did perform in the days when men like Henry
Clay presided over its discussions. It fails to elicit the interest of the politically minded section of the nation not because it is deficient in power,
but because it is never so organized as to use its power for great ends.

It makes the headlines by the antagonism it arouses and not by the creation for which it is responsible. It is notable, for example, that its best-known members in the last generation have been men for whom a sense of respect in the nation at large has almost always been rare. Congressman James M. Beck made loud noises in the House, but no one can seriously pretend that they were significant noises. I suspect that more people respected Congressman Hamilton Fish in his capacity of a one-time football player at Harvard than in his capacity as a legislator. Congressman Bruce Barton is more likely to be remembered as the author of a unique approach to the interpretation of the life of Jesus Christ, whom he seems to have regarded as the permanent president of the National Advertising Association, than as a congressman of high eminence. When Connecticut sent Clare Boothe Luce to the House, the real result of her work was less significant in politics than that it was a new episode in her career as a figure in the American theatre; and it is a pretty fair guess that if her husband had not been a great magazine proprietor she would have made no more mark than Miss Jessie Sumner of Illinois, who, without her backing, at least equals her in shrillness and acidity.

4

ON THE legislative side of the federal government, indeed, it is the Senate that has mattered and to which the attention of the American public has been directed. Some of the reasons for this distinction are inherent in the functions it performs. The fact that it shares with the president the treaty-making power—he must win a two-thirds majority if his treaty is to become the law—and that it must confirm all the main appointments, political, judicial, and diplomatic as well as administrative, that he seeks to make, would, in all circumstances, make it a chamber that is bound to arouse the public interest. But, in addition, it has many advantages over the other House. It is small in size; its ninety-six members are sufficient to assure it variety of outlook without depriving it of that temper of intimacy which exists between the two front benches in the House of Commons. The senator's length of term gives him time to emerge, if he has the ability, as a person who can elicit nation-wide interest; and the fact that he now—though only since 1913—is elected by the vote of the whole of his state means not only that more people are interested in what he does, but also that he can afford to think in far wider terms than the average member of the House of Representatives.

No doubt it is true that every Congress contains a number of senators whose election is hard to explain, and still more difficult to justify. It cannot be denied that, as a general rule, the Senators from Delaware have represented less its voters than the powerful DuPont Corporation, as the senators from Montana have, somehow, had to arrive at a *modus vivendi* with the great copper interests of that state. There have been senators from Pennsylvania who ought to have been in jail instead of in

Washington, as there have been senators from Kentucky and Illinois whose proper home was the music-hall stage. To the foreign observer it seems little less than fantastic that a state like New York should have the same representation as Nevada with rather less than one-hundredth of its population. A majority of the Senate, indeed, as Professor Lindsay Rogers has pointed out in his admirable treatise,[1] is returned by less than one-fifth of the American people; and the agricultural "bloc" there has a power out of all proportion to its numerical weight in the population. Its zeal for authority in terms of years of service not seldom gives to men for whom it is difficult not to feel contempt a position to which they are not entitled either by character or intelligence. And it is undoubtedly true that some of the most important experiments in American life—the Missouri Compromise of 1820, for example—were driven through by senators from states which represented a minority of the electors. It is even reasonable to emphasize, as President Coolidge did, that the Senate, in general, is convinced that it is better than the president; it is pretty clear, on the evidence, that the Senate thought far more of Lincoln after his assassination than before it.

But despite the weaknesses of the Senate, it still remains a remarkably successful assembly in which, at any given time, there are pretty certain to be men of outstanding ability and character. If Ohio sent Harding there, it also once sent John Sherman; if South Carolina sent "Cotton Ed" Smith, Nebraska sent George Norris—the John Bright of American politics—and Alabama sent Hugo Black. If in its composition there is a clear tendency to equate antiquity with wisdom, especially in the inter-war years, the election of men like Senator Lister Hill and Senator Claude Pepper shows that the tendency is capable of correction. No student of American history can fail to note how often among the half-dozen outstanding figures in its life a member of the Senate is to be found. It may be Daniel Webster or the elder La Follette, John C. Calhoun or William E. Borah; there is hardly a presidential term in which the man in the White House is not approached in influence and authority by some member of the Senate. And it is difficult not to conclude that the change to popular election by the Seventeenth Amendment, though it has had the result of sending some weird persons to Washington, has also gone far towards destroying its character as predominantly a rich man's club. Certainly it is far less accessible today than it was at the turn of the century to the influence of Big Business; and certainly, also, popular election has meant that membership of the Senate is far less akin to something like tenure for life than it was when senators were chosen by the state legislatures.

As an assembly intended to deliberate upon great issues the Senate, with all its faults, has the immense merit of being able to interest the American people. No doubt the faults are grave: the refusal, except under practically impossible conditions, to accept the closure in debate; the

[1] *The American Senate* (New York: Knopf, 1926), p. 92.

consequential power of a minority so to filibuster that majority rule ceases to have any meaning; the principle of senatorial "courtesy," which really means that the president must bow the knee in any appointments in the state where the senator is of his own party so that the wheels of the senator's machine there may be oiled at the expense of competence or even decency; the attempt, sometimes successful, to prevent the presidential power of removal; the deliberate interference with finance, not for the sake of efficiency, but to protect the vested interests on which senators so often depend; the reckless attitude to the tariff based on similar considerations; the use of the power of investigation not merely where a clear case for inquiry exists, but also in the hope of hamstringing the president in his policy; despite all these grave faults in the functioning of the Senate, it remains, without exception, the most successful second chamber in the world. It may, indeed, be rather termed a first chamber since, though financial legislation must originate in the House of Representatives, the real incidence of final authority remains, subject to the president's veto, in the Senate.

The most dramatic aspect of the Senate's power is, of course, in the realm of foreign policy. The famous remark of John Hay to Henry Adams that "I have told you many times that I did not believe another important treaty would ever pass the Senate," [2] has been the basis of endless discussion, especially since Senator Lodge torpedoed the Treaty of Versailles in 1919. The necessity of a two-thirds majority for the approval of a treaty means, of course, that a single recalcitrant senator may destroy the work of months. And it is perhaps true to say that, since the First World War, no power of the Senate has been more bitterly criticized or resented. It is argued that the result is to persuade a few members of the Senate to try to compel the president, especially if he is of the opposite party, to accept their judgment in place of his own even though, as Jefferson insisted, the negotiation of treaties is "executive altogether."

Ever since the defeat of President Wilson's plans in 1919, commentators on the treaty-making power have, outside the Senate itself, devoted long and passionate attention to preventing the repetition of that famous debacle. Sometimes it is suggested that a simple majority ought to suffice for ratification; sometimes, it is proposed that, just as the two Houses of Congress declare war, so they should combine to make peace; sometimes, again, it is proposed to safeguard presidential policy in this field by organizing for him a special "Foreign Policy Cabinet" which will give him the assurance that what he accepts in conjunction with it will have a smooth passage through the Senate. We are reminded of the indignation of foreign statesmen, who, after long negotiations with the executive, are dismayed to find that the Senate either insists on amendments to the agreement arrived at, or rejects it altogether.

I must frankly say that, in my own judgment, most of the criticism

[2] W. R. Thayer, *Life and Letters of John Hay* (Boston: Houghton Mifflin, 1915), Vol. II, p. 170.

which has been poured upon the treaty-making power of the Senate seems to me singularly ill-conceived. If the test taken is that of time, the normal period before action is little more than two months. If the test is substance, then most of the amendments introduced will be found, on analysis, to secure additional benefits to the American people. The rejection of the Treaty of Versailles was, no doubt, a tragedy for the world; but subsequent electoral history has made it clear that it anticipated, if on different grounds, the verdict of the American people. And the answer to the indignation of foreign statesmen is surely the simple answer that when they negotiate with the United States they must, or ought to be, aware of the conditions upon which ratification is possible.

Nor is that all. A president who knows his job has the fullest opportunity of formal or informal consultation before he has the treaty ready for submission to the Senate. There is a large realm, also, in which he can achieve the end he has in view by executive agreements which fall short of actual treaties; the exchange of the fifty destroyers with Great Britain in 1940 simultaneously with British concession of bases, as in the Caribbean, is a good example of this type of understanding. And anyone who examines the treaty-making power of the British Crown, as exemplified, for instance, in the Hoare-Laval Treaty of 1935, or the Munich Agreement of 1938, will, I suggest, be led to the conclusion that the existence of a check upon the Executive which is real, has a good deal to be said for it. A British government which makes a treaty as momentous as that of Versailles, and allows one day to the discussion, with the knowledge on all sides of the House of Commons that either amendment or rejection means a dissolution, is really penalizing dissent of any kind. I think myself that the motives which led Senator Lodge to the action he took in 1919 were mean and unworthy. But one's judgment of senatorial power in this realm ought not to be based on a single instance, however important. Englishmen who remember how Lord Salisbury made a treaty with Germany in 1898, by which we agreed to press Portugal to sell Angola to Germany, without a word of discussion in Parliament; or the agreement on naval strength behind the back of France with Hitler Germany in 1935; or the discussion, abortive it is true, between Herr Wohlthat and Mr. Robert Hudson in the summer of 1939—all of them negotiations of which Parliament never heard at all, or heard only, as in the Hoare-Laval Treaty, by an accidental leakage— will, I believe, find it reasonable to conclude that there is a great deal to be said for organizing a careful legislative examination of executive decisions.

It is no doubt true that there is wisdom in the privacy of negotiation; but it is surely true also that its results ought not only to be public, but submitted to an examination that is more than the formality, under sanction of dissolution, which obtains in Britain. If that is the case, the American Senate is safeguarding the interest of the people of the United States in a way, and to a degree, that Britain has never known. And while I am inclined to the view that the special two-thirds majority is an excessive protection against executive error, it seems to me all to the good that the president should be aware that he is not the sole master of foreign policy. I think that the more when I remember the methods adopted by presidents in the last thirty or forty years to arrive at results which they were pretty sure the Senate, and perhaps the people, of the United States would not approve. The policy of Theodore Roosevelt in Colombia; that of Woodrow Wilson in Mexico; that of Calvin Coolidge in Nicaragua; and that of Franklin Roosevelt in the civil war in Spain on the one hand, and in his handling of North Africa in the Darlan-Peyrouton-Giraud period on the other; all these, not to go further back in American history, suggest that the need of the Executive to satisfy the Senate is a valuable protection against the kind of diplomacy which conceals power politics altogether, or else covers it in a fine show of rhetoric. And it is worth remembering, in this context, that there has rarely been an English statesman in the last thirty years who has not urged with vigour the desirability of a House of Commons Committee on Foreign Affairs. Particularly, it is worth noting that the most successful of our Foreign Secretaries in modern times, Mr. Henderson, decided to submit all treaties for approval to the House of Commons. He did not desire a special majority; but he did at least recognize the wisdom of approval by the legislature of executive action. That, after all, is the central principle upon which the power of the American Senate is based.

The Senate does not merely debate; it also conducts massive investigations. Granted the principle of the separation of powers, it is of high importance that this function should be performed. Anyone who examines the way in which a Senate Committee dug down into the habits of Mr. Harry Daugherty, or the Teapot Dome scandal, or the methods of Wall Street in the period before the crash of 1929, cannot, I think, doubt that this is a vital function of the Senate. It may be incredibly expensive; it may be, also, that it drags on interminably; and no doubt there are occasions when very grave injustice is done to particular individuals. It may even be admitted that time and again senators use the system for party ends or for the exploitation of personal rancour. It remains the case that the method is the main guarantee against dishonesty or inefficient administration. After all, a system which drove three cabinet members to resign in 1924 and resulted in imprisonment and two suicides may reasonably claim to have a measurable public value.

It is a value which is increased by the fact that cabinet ministers in the United States have neither collective responsibility nor continuity of contact with Congress. The investigating power, however much it may be resented by presidents and their cabinet colleagues, is the only effective way in which the quality of their administrative efforts may be properly assessed. And it has the additional merit that where the investigation touches an issue of importance—as in Senator Black's careful probe in 1933 of the habits of Wall Street during the Depression of 1929

—it not only awakens widespread public interest, but it eases the road to desirable legislation. Few reasonable people now doubt the value of the Securities and Exchange Commission; but it would hardly have come into being if it had not been preceded by the Senate Banking and Currency Committee's dissection of Wall Street. The method combines something of the value of a Royal Commission in Britain with the illumination afforded by question-time in the House of Commons. It is superior to the former in that the minister is not in a position to "pack" it with distinguished nonentities; and it is at least equal to the latter in that its use of experts as advisers—like Judge Pecora in the Wall Street inquiry—makes it probable that the information secured will go pretty near to the roots of the problem. Mr. Charles Mitchell was regarded as a great pillar of American finance until Mr. Pecora dragged his habits out into the light of day. And even so powerful an organization as the House of Morgan emerged from the inquiry with a diminished status from which it is hard to feel that it has recovered.

The central fact is that the Senate of the United States is the one constitutional expedient that provides the American public with the material upon which it can make an effective judgment of presidential policy. And this is so whether, as with Mr. Wilson or both of the Roosevelts, the president seeks to set the political direction in which America is to move, or, as with Harding and Coolidge, he avoids the responsibility of leadership. It has been able to elicit the interest of the people practically continuously from the birth of the republic. Unless it had functioned in this fashion, it is obvious that, with a strong president, effective power would have been centralized in him, or, with a weak president, there would have been a drift toward bureaucracy. While it is, of course, true that an effective president can elicit an interest with which no other institution can compete, it is also true that the Senate is able to compel attention to every aspect of its activities. It is the master of the House of Representatives; it is even able to make the House give way on matters like finance and the tariff. And while it would be an exaggeration to say that the Senate is the master of the president, it is reasonable to argue that no president dare neglect the drift of senatorial opinion.

This position, I think, is derived from two factors. In the first place the senator is there long enough for his personality to make an impact on the nation. In the second place, the amazing freedom of debate has the result of eliciting a public opinion which does not emerge in the House of Representatives because, when discussion begins, it is little more than the outcome of argument which has already reached a decision in the committees of the House. While it is true to say that the press is unlikely to devote much attention to debates in the House, it is almost bound to discuss what happens in the Senate. Discussion in the House is formal and static; discussion in the Senate is living and dynamic. The Senate makes politics interesting. It is interesting because of its relation to foreign affairs; it is interesting because of its relation to major political appointments; and it is interesting because, even if it contains—like all legislative assemblies—a considerable number of dull men, it always contains a number of politicians who know how to dramatize the issues in which they are interested.

That becomes obvious as soon as one looks at its history. Debates like those between Webster and Hayne aroused the attention of the whole nation. Figures like Calhoun and Borah and the elder La Follette dramatized ideas in a fashion which made it impossible to neglect their significance. No doubt it is true that the Senate has often abused its power; the attitude of Senator Lodge to President Wilson was obviously the outcome of personal prejudice and not of intellectual difference. But the important thing is that whenever an important issue arises in the United States, it is sooner or later bound to be set in the context of action by the Senate. It may act wrongly; it may act unwisely; it may act with incredible folly. But the point is that it has to act, and that the whole country will watch to see its action. It is the one institution in the federal system where the members feel untrammelled and unrepressed. A congressman, unless he is a vital figure, passes unnoticed by the mass of the public; a senator is a person by the mere fact that he is a senator. A congressman, with two years at Washington, is bound to think of his re-election from the moment he arrives at the capital; a senator can seek the time and energy to become a figure hardly less than the president and usually more than a member of the cabinet. He has almost certainly seen presidents come and go; he rarely feels any responsibility to the man who seems to him a temporary incumbent. He may respect a president in the period while the patronage is being distributed; once that period is passed, he is mostly conscious that he is approaching the presidential level. He has access to the White House whenever he wishes. He is confident that almost any pronouncement he makes is national news. He is the effective source of criticism of the executive. He can usually, emergency apart, secure amendments upon which he has made up his mind.

The Senate is, of course, open to profound criticism. Few legislative assemblies waste so much time. Still fewer have made logrolling so perfect an art. It has no responsibility to the executive, and it knows quite precisely when it will be judged by the voters. It is a body which is eager to act as a unity wherever appointments are in question; "courtesy of the Senate" is one of the supreme methods by which it asserts itself against presidential authority. It is quite impossible to defend the concept of "senatorial courtesy." It is nothing more than a means of enabling a senator from the president's party to strengthen his hold upon the electors of his state by co-operating in the exercise of patronage. And whether the post be judicial or administrative, the history of its exercise makes it abundantly clear that the senator is far more interested in rewarding his friends than in the capacity they may bring to the post for which they are chosen.

Yet when all is said against the Senate that can be said, it remains one of the outstanding successes of the American political system. It has the immense merit of being able to interest the ordinary citizen; and it has the special virtue of being an object of ambition which few are able to resist. No doubt bad men have been senators; no doubt the Senate itself has been ready on too many occasions to abuse its power. It suffers, too, though in a less degree than before the Seventeenth Amendment, from an excessive tenderness for its corporate privileges. There have been periods in its history when its main objective has been less the well-being of the United States than the desire to wreck some presidential policy. And the fact that it is decreasingly regarded as the natural avenue to the White House tends to make its members anxious to define a policy on most matters which makes plain their difference from the president; few senators are willing, like Mr. Robinson of Arkansas, to be out and out the president's man. There is even a tendency, sometimes a corporate tendency, to act irresponsibly in order to prove that it is independent. When the extension of the Tennessee Valley Authority is held up in deference to Senator McKellar's objection to its chairman, Mr. David Lilienthal, it becomes evident that an assembly pays heavily, and makes the country pay heavily, for the lack of executive direction. The Senate, in short, has an inherent desire to please its own members whatever the cost, whether they are tired old men like the late Senator Reed Smoot, or dangerous young men like the late Senator Huey Long.

Nevertheless, the Senate is an outstanding success. It is perhaps the most vital check upon the despotism an ambitious president could so easily develop. If it sometimes contains members with a narrowly parochial outlook, as a legislative assembly it transcends the sectionalism which pervades every nook and cranny of the House of Representatives. If it irritates most presidents and their cabinet colleagues, it is astonishing how often its irritation is supported by the electoral opinion of the American people. All in all, the level of its big debates is remarkably high; and the general quality of the investigations it undertakes is quite equal to that of Select Committees of the House of Commons. Nor must one forget that it respects its minorities, even men whose difference from its main stream of thought has been profound. It says a good deal for a legislature that, to take the last generation only, it made men like the elder La Follette and George W. Norris into figures of national significance. It respects independence and gives it a full opportunity of expression. By so doing it gives a vivid reality to political democracy in the United States which no other institution so fully or so gladly supplies.

5

THE president's cabinet is unknown to the Constitution as such, and it is difficult to feel that it has been an outstanding success in American history. While it is true that it has attracted men of the first eminence, like Jefferson and Hamilton, into its ranks, it has rarely been an effective team, and its formal subordination to the president has meant that it has never been, in a really continuous way, a policy-making body. The president may or may not consult it, as he chooses; he may or may not compose it of men of national standing. The only permanent features by which it is distinguished are, first, that it usually requires at least one member whose previous presence in Congress enables him to aid the president in handling that body, and that the office of postmaster-general is usually held by the party specialist in patronage; it is still an important truth in the United States that, despite the growing increase in a classified civil service, the victors expect (and will receive) the spoils.

The American cabinet is not a body with the collective responsibility of the British cabinet. It is a collection of departmental heads who carry out the orders of the president. They are responsible to him and he can always dismiss any of them without any peril to his own position. There is no relation between them and him like that of Lord John Russell and Lord Palmerston in 1851, or Mr. Asquith and Mr. Lloyd George in 1916, or Mr. Chamberlain and Mr. Churchill in the early summer of 1940. President Wilson's Secretary of War, Mr. Garrison, desired, in 1916, to embark on great military preparations. Mr. Wilson refused and Mr. Garrison resigned. Mr. Wilson then appointed Mr. Newton D. Baker to this office, and, in a brief time, Mr. Baker had begun military preparations upon a scale which went far beyond anything Mr. Garrison had proposed. President Franklin Roosevelt put into his cabinet in 1933 two former Progressive Republicans, Mr. Henry A. Wallace and Mr. Harold Ickes; and it is said that the President did not know Mr. Ickes, a Chicago lawyer, personally until he visited Hyde Park to urge on Mr. Roosevelt the appointment of his partner, Mr. Donald Richberg, to the post he himself was offered and accepted.

Inevitably, of course, the president's cabinet is a body which seeks to embody certain features of the American nation. If there are officers from the East, there must be officers from the West; if there is a Northerner, it is usual to balance him by some nominee from the South. Until Mr. Roosevelt made Miss Frances Perkins the first woman member of the cabinet as Secretary of Labor, that post was usually occupied by a trade-union official who held a high place in the American Federation of Labor. Most presidents, at least since the Civil War, have given some attention to the religious composition of the cabinet; a Methodist, a Roman Catholic, and an Episcopalian have been almost necessary choices. As a rule, the average American cabinet has been well on in years; and, as a rule, also, the Secretary of the Treasury has been a man who was *persona grata* to the important banking interests of the country. It is notable that cabinet office, since the Civil War, has made the reputation (or destroyed it) of the men the president has chosen; in the earlier period, its officers were most of them men who might, like Clay and Calhoun, have reached the White House, or, like Jefferson and Madison, actually did so. But in the second period of the republic's history Mr. Taft and Mr.

Hoover alone attained that eminence; and in each case there are special circumstances which explain their choice.

An American cabinet minister may be a very important man, but there is no reason in the world why a very important man should be an American cabinet minister. He cannot make his own policy with any real independence. For, first, he must accept the wishes of the president, whose servant he really is, and, second, since the separation of powers excludes him from Congress, he must persuade not only the president but the appropriate chairmen of the committees in each of its Houses before he can hope to have his way. Nor is this all. It is unlikely that more than two or three cabinet officers will have had any intimate experience of politics before they take their posts. They are not, like the vast majority of cabinet ministers in Great Britain, people who have made a profession of politics. Mr. Ramsay MacDonald first took office when he became prime minister in 1924; but he was already by that time an old parliamentary hand. Lord Haldane took office for the first time as Secretary of War in 1906; but at that date he had already been in the House of Commons for some twenty years. Mr. Arthur Henderson's outstanding success as Foreign Secretary from 1929 to 1931 was built not merely on many years of parliamentary experience, including cabinet office; he had also for over a score of years been an outstanding figure at the Congress of the Second International.

That kind of apprenticeship is rare in an American cabinet minister. Senator John Sherman went to the Treasury as Mr. Blaine went to the Department of State. But Mr. Ickes went to Washington directly from his law office in Chicago as Mr. Newton D. Baker went from his law office and municipal politics in Cleveland. Mr. Hoover went from mining engineering in China to food relief in Belgium, and thence to the Department of Commerce under Presidents Harding and Coolidge without any first-hand acquaintance with the Congress. Mr. Andrew Mellon was made Secretary of the Treasury solely because he was an incredibly rich man under a president who seemed to assume that all really rich men are in a state of grace. Mr. Henry Morgenthau, Jr., became the Secretary of the Treasury under President Roosevelt not because he was either a specialist in finance or a professional politician, but because he was a near neighbour of the President in Dutchess County, New York, and one of the rare enthusiasts for the New Deal in that area. Miss Perkins, indeed, had won her spurs as Commissioner of Labor in New York when President Roosevelt was its governor; and Mr. Henry A. Wallace, as the editor of a farmer's paper and the son of a Republican Secretary of Agriculture may be said to have seen a good deal of political life from close at hand. But, if we take the last half-century of American history and omit the two or three figures in each cabinet who have sat in Congress, there is little experience of first-rate administration on the grand scale among the men whom the various presidents have chosen for office. It is, indeed, not seldom difficult to explain a particular choice except on grounds of personal friendship between the president and the man he nominates.

The cabinet is a body of persons administering their departments and advising the president. He need not take their advice; he need not even ask for it. Anyone who reads the diaries of cabinet ministers like Gideon Welles under Lincoln, or Franklin Lane or Robert Lansing in the Wilson era, will see at once that their relation to the making of policy was always interstitial. They did not always know what the president had decided to do; they did not even know whom the president had decided to appoint; and they might easily find that an important senator had a relationship far closer to the president than any they could seek to claim. Nor is that all. There may be "king-makers" in the Senate like Mark Hanna; but there may also be "king-makers" outside the Senate, like Colonel House under Mr. Wilson; and there may be men like Mr. Harry Hopkins who are far closer to the president than any of his official advisers. And from the time of the "Kitchen Cabinet" of Andrew Jackson, there have been few presidents who have not relied for advice and counsel upon men who held no official position at all. President Franklin Roosevelt had, in his "Brain Trust," a body of advisers not one of whom held cabinet rank, and not one of whom it was likely that he would have attempted to put into the cabinet. It is not even certain that the president will give his full confidence to the cabinet officer whom he has chosen; certainly Amos Kendall had more influence with Andrew Jackson than any cabinet official, and there were periods when Raymond Moley and Sumner Welles had more influence with Mr. Roosevelt than their formal superiors even though they did not attend any cabinet meetings.

An American cabinet officer may be, like Mr. Elihu Root, a man of outstanding importance; he may even be groomed for the presidency by reason of his cabinet experience, like Mr. Taft or Mr. Hoover. But it is a reasonable generalization that such significance as he has depends upon the context in which the president puts him, and that, in the result, he may have no significance at all. Certainly it is true that a senator of long standing has far more importance than any save the most exceptional of cabinet ministers; and the fact that Mr. Fall, as Secretary of the Interior under Harding, went to jail, and that Mr. Harry Daugherty ought to have gone there, without in either case making any impact on the status of their colleagues, is a significant thing. The inference is the obvious one that the cabinet discusses no more than the president wishes it to discuss; and where there is no discussion it is to be assumed that there is no responsibility. For it is at least a striking thing that Mr. Fall should have carried through his criminal intrigue over Teapot Dome without in any way influencing the reputation of Mr. Hoover or Mr. Charles Evans Hughes.

The real fact is that an American cabinet officer is more akin to the permanent secretary of a government department in England than he is to a British cabinet minister; with the difference that he makes speeches and has certain ceremonial functions to perform. He has no way, save in the quality of his argument, of influencing either the president or Congress; and his disappearance from office is unlikely to affect the position of either. His speeches, no doubt, will be reported; but his status is likely to be greater abroad than it is at home. He may find that one or more of his subordinates has more influence in the White House than he has himself; and his only remedy against the emergence of such a position is either to secure an influence in Congress, of which the president must take account, or else to resign. It is clear, for example, that there was a considerable period during which Mr. Sumner Welles had more influence with the President than the Secretary of State, Mr. Cordell Hull; but it is clear, also, that when the latter insisted upon a showdown, his influence in Congress made it necessary for Mr. Roosevelt to part with Mr. Welles; the President could not risk the loss of Mr. Hull's influence in a Congress where he was rarely certain, after 1940, that he could hope to have his way.

To the foreign observer, therefore, the American cabinet is one of the least successful of American federal institutions. It can never be more than the president makes it; and the president is rarely likely to make it an outstanding body. Even if he did, the separation of powers means that its standing is dependent upon the goodwill of both Houses of Congress; and it finds there a dual antithesis which is anxious to prevent it from achieving too great a credit. Even an eminent cabinet minister may find that his career moves relentlessly to a dead end; there is no assurance, however distinguished his achievement, that his period of office will be more than an interlude in his life. Since, at least from the Civil War, he is unlikely to be president, and even unlikely to be a member of either House of Congress, a cabinet post is hardly more, for most of its holders, than a temporary achievement which leads nowhere in particular. It is the president who matters. It is the president whose decisions will count. It is the president whose vote will carry the day even against the unanimous opinion of his colleagues. He need not consult them; they may even find that he has decided not to consult them. He may rely upon advisers who have no political position in his party but simply a personal relation that he values. So that while a cabinet officer may be a figure of importance, he has no assurance that he will be one. This depends for the most part on the president, and, in a less degree, upon his relations with Congress. He may find that he has to resign for political reasons or for personal reasons. He may be working with a president who is exceptional in his loyalty and eager for his advice; or he may be working under a president who has no sense of loyalty to him and is largely uninterested in his counsel. The cabinet minister in the United States embarks upon a gamble when he accepts office; and it is not until he has felt out his president and the Congress that he can hope for awareness of what he may achieve.

The president, in recent times, has not relied only upon his cabinet.

He has had a group of advisers some of whom have held official positions, and some of whom have had no official status of any kind. Colonel House, Mr. Norman Davis, Professor (now Mr. Justice) Frankfurter, Mr. Louis D. Brandeis (later Mr. Justice Brandeis), are examples of the latter type; in the last few years, Mr. Dean Acheson, Mr. Adolf Berle, and Mr. T. G. Corcoran are examples of the former. Most of them were consulted upon issues of outstanding importance; and it is hardly excessive to say that few cabinet ministers have ever exercised an influence of comparable importance. Certainly no reader of the House Papers can doubt that, in the epoch of Woodrow Wilson, Colonel House was second only to the President himself in his influence upon affairs. And in the early days of the "New Deal" the counsel of some half-dozen young men probably counted for more in the formation of presidential decisions than all the cabinet put together.

On the other hand, it is important to notice one feature of this extra-cabinet advice. Whether the counsellor be on the level at which Colonel House operated, or on the level of Mr. Corcoran's influence, his authority depended upon his ability to keep the friendship of the president. Once Mr. Wilson had made up his mind that Colonel House was acting beyond the power confided in him, he ceased to have any influence of any kind; so, too, with Mr. Corcoran. It is, indeed, true to say of these non-cabinet advisers that they rarely survived a difference of opinion with the president. He used them as an assurance for opinions he was seeking to form; when they were hostile to those opinions it was rare for him to use them in a confidential capacity. Even of Colonel House, perhaps the supreme *éminence grise* of American history, it is probably true to say that he took the most careful pains to find out what was in Mr. Wilson's mind before he offered him advice; and, where he ventured to differ from him, it was invariably upon minute issues rather than upon big principles. That is even more true of lesser figures than Colonel House. Either they dug out information of which the president was in need, or they acted on his behalf in some circle he wished to influence. It is broadly true to say that their utility for him ended when they found that they could not reconcile their opinions with his. For it is always vital that the executive power of the United States is centred in the president; and those who cannot accept his decisions must surrender the hope of influencing his mind.

The mortality rate of presidents in office is high, so that the post of vice-president, though it normally implies no more than the semiformal function of presiding over the Senate, has, in fact, a significance that cannot be overlooked. It is, no doubt, true that most vice-presidents have been little more than objects of commiseration; they become significant only if the president dies. But it is also true that certain vice-presidents have changed from objects of commiseration into men of character and determination. This is true of Tyler and Andrew Johnson, of Theodore Roosevelt and, in his own special way, of Calvin Coolidge. It is curious that so little interest is taken in the office; and it is still more curious that so few presidents have attempted to acquaint their possible successors with the functions they might be called upon to perform. President Harding, indeed, sought to associate Vice-President Coolidge with the working of his cabinet; but Mr. Coolidge rapidly formed the impression that he was wasting his time. President Franklin Roosevelt called upon his vice-president, Mr. Henry A. Wallace to perform certain domestic and international functions. But, as a general rule, the vice-president has been little more than a faint wraith on the American political horizon. It is not, indeed, an exaggeration to say that, as a general rule, a nomination to the vice-presidency is either intended to serve a geographical purpose so that an eastern candidate may get western votes, and vice versa, or else, as in the famous choice of Theodore Roosevelt, it is a technique by which the party machine hopes to end the career of an aspirant for the nomination to the presidency whose character or principles seem to its members too positive to make for his availability.

The result is the curious one that a man who has one chance in five of being president of the United States is rarely known to the multitude, and, where he is known, is usually an object of ridicule. His choice is frequently so casual that it is difficult to persuade the delegates to the convention to remain while he is being selected. Where he is chosen by the active will of the presidential candidate, as Mr. Henry A. Wallace was chosen by Mr. Roosevelt in 1940, there is a sense that he is being given an importance which is beyond his due. It appears to be the general view that if a vice-president should be seen, he should at least not be heard; and few things in recent American history have been more interesting than the surprise, even the resentment, when it was discovered that Mr. Wallace not only had strong views, but was prepared to voice them strongly. It is, in fact, something more than a possibility that Mr. Roosevelt was able to hold his party together in the Democratic convention of 1944 only by offering up Mr. Wallace as a sacrifice upon the altar of the city bosses. For though Senator Truman was honest, he was at least "regular," and he had entered political life as a nominee of the boss of Kansas City. With his choice, therefore, nicely balanced by that of Governor Bricker of Ohio by the Republican party, there was a renewed hope that the vice-president would retire into that obscurity which, so curiously, Americans considered his proper place.

So curiously, I suggest, because it is obvious that the president's *métier* is not something that can be learned overnight. And that is especially the case as the United States emerges, inevitably, into the era of the positive State. Whether the next era of its history be Democratic or Republican, it is quite obvious that it will not return to the age of *laissez-faire*. Certain changes in the New Deal epoch have become an accepted part of the American tradition. No federal government will attempt to repeal the legislation dealing with social security. No federal government will attempt to alter more than the details of the machinery of the

Securities and Exchange Commission. No federal government will even hope to withdraw from international arrangements which seek to prevent aggression by one State against another. No federal government even will dare, unless it seeks deliberately to embark upon a fascist policy, to allow mass unemployment to develop upon the scale of the Great Depression. I am deliberately limiting here the range of federal activities to the minimum involved in the situation of the United States; I shall attempt, in later chapters, to show that the policies of Washington, whichever party be in power, will inevitably go beyond this minimum. And if this view of the minimum be correct, it seems to me clear that the type of vice-president the United States will require will be far more like that of Mr. Henry A. Wallace than like that, to take an example merely, of Mr. Thomas R. Marshall. For though it is no doubt true that Mr. Marshall added what is almost a proverb to the stock of American folk-lore, when he defined the American need as a "good five-cent cigar," it is pretty obvious that if he had been compelled to take over the White House in the era of Woodrow Wilson he would have been utterly inadquate to the tasks he would have confronted. One has only to think for a moment of Mr. Marshall grappling with the problems of Versailles to realize how dangerous it is to think of Mr. Throttlebottom as the president of the United States.

6

THE great change in the federal government—independently of the Second World War—is the growth in the number of federal jobs. It was just over 6000 in 1816; it was slightly over 49,000 in 1861; it was 562,000 in 1921; and 920,000 in June 1939. Where some 13,800 positions were classified for competitive examination in 1884, nearly 623,000 positions were similarly classified in 1939. Where 3542 candidates were examined in 1884, of whom 57.7 per cent were passed, 556,573 were examined in 1939, of whom 45.7 per cent were passed; and whereas 489 were appointed in 1884 to the classified Civil Service, 72,198 were so appointed in 1939. The growth, in part, is obviously due to the growth of the United States itself; but the major factor in this expansion has been the assumption by the federal government of functions which the founders of the American commonwealth would not have dreamed of as a possible public enterprise in 1787.

The classified Civil Service of America is in some ways like, and in some ways unlike, its British analogue. There is a resemblance in that the vast majority of the posts in both are now the result of examination; but whereas the British system is built on competitive examination, the American system is built on a qualifying examination. The real distinction, however, emerges at the apex of the administrative pyramid. In the British system, it has been very rare, wartime apart, for the chief officials to enter except through the narrow gate of the competitive examination. Broadly, a method has been built which corresponds roughly with the educational system of the country; and the overwhelming proportion of the highest civil servants have taken an examination which fits in with university examinations, and particularly those of Oxford and Cambridge. A British official in the administrative class—the highest class—expects, in normal circumstances, to have embarked upon a life career. He will usually enter between the ages of twenty-two and twenty-four and retire at sixty. He may enter the Ministry of Education as a junior Principal and leave the service as the Permanent Secretary of the Board of Trade. The examination by which he enters is intended to test his general intelligence and has no relation to the work he may subsequently be called upon to do. The outstanding civil servant in Great Britain in modern times was Sir Robert Morant. He took a first-class degree in theology at Oxford; he then became tutor to the Crown Prince of Siam; a palace revolution there resulted in his dismissal and his return to London. He was then appointed to the Board of Education, where he was largely responsible for the Education Act of 1902. When Mr. Lloyd George embarked upon his Health Insurance Scheme of 1911, Sir Robert was his principal administrative architect. In 1918–19 he was mainly responsible for the transformation of the old Local Government Board into the present Ministry of Health. Save that Sir Robert entered the service by nomination instead of examination, his was the typical career of an imaginative civil servant in Great Britain, aware of the main currents of his time and skilled by his education to the views of the ministers he served.

The contrast with the highest ranges of American government officials is very striking. It is rare for most of them to act as officials throughout their careers. They tend to come in with a particular administration and to depart with it when a new one takes over. They very infrequently change from one department to another. All under-secretaries and assistant-secretaries are, with three exceptions, appointed by the president with the advice and consent of the Senate. No doubt he frequently consults the cabinet officers whom they are to serve. But he need not do so, and quite frequently does not do so. He has to bear in mind the need to reward the men who have assisted his party to victory, and aided him in his own personal triumph. He must not forget the importance of sectionalism in a federal community; and he may well need to remember that a wise appointment may usefully placate some hostile element in his party. Below the assistant-secretary is, as a rule, the chief clerk. A good example of this type of official is Mr. W. H. McReynolds, who served as administrative assistant to the president from 1939 to 1945. Mr. McReynolds had only an elementary education before he became a hand on a ranch. He then went to Michigan where he took a commercial training as a preparation for the Civil Service. In 1906 he became a Post-Office clerk at nine hundred dollars a year. In 1913 he went to the Bureau of Efficiency as an investigator and later became assistant chief. In 1930 he became Director of the Classification Board; after a brief experience as assistant to the Director of the Budget, he returned to the Bureau of Efficiency. This body was abolished in March 1933, and Mr. McReynolds then went to the Farm Credit Administration as its director of personnel. When Mr. Morgenthau, the head of F.C.A., was made Under-Secretary of the Treasury, he took Mr. McReynolds with him as his assistant. In that capacity, Mr. McReynolds was the channel through which all issues reached Mr. Morgenthau while he was at the Treasury.

Other officials of his rank have had similar careers. An Assistant-Secretary of the Interior has been, before he entered the service of the government, an employee of a bank, a railway, and a publishing business. Mr. Paul H. Appleby, the Executive Assistant to the Secretary of Agriculture from 1933 to 1940, worked on a fruit farm after he had been graduated from college; he then became an employee in department stores in Tacoma, from which he moved to an Iowa newspaper. Later he was able to purchase some weekly newspapers in Virginia, and thereby became acquainted with Mr. Henry A. Wallace, under whom he served in the Department of Agriculture. Mr. Appleby's main task was to see to it that his chief had no papers before him for decision which had not been properly considered and he acted as what might be termed the personal relations officer to Mr. Wallace. Another example of the same type was Mr. Joseph Stewart who, after being an insurance clerk and a bank clerk, took a law degree and practised law in Kansas City. In 1890 he entered the Post Office by competitive examination. By 1908 he was Second Assistant Postmaster-General. In 1915 he was made a Special Assistant to the Attorney-General and assigned to the Post Office where he continued to serve until his death in 1929.

Each of these examples is of a man who has made himself generally indispensable to a cabinet officer and has fulfilled much the same function as an under-secretary in a British government department. The real differences emerge in the fact that, the cabinet minister apart, few officials in the higher ranks have been in office, except in the Post Office, for longer than three years, and few, except specialists, remain in office for more than four or five years. Partly, no doubt, this is due to the sectional claims to which all parties in office must respond; but I suspect that, far more often, it is due to the fact that an official who has risen to one of the three or four highest posts in his department has opportunities in American business which, if they are offered, are very rarely taken in British business by British civil servants of comparable status.

It is worth noting that, where the merit system applies in the American Civil Service, the age of appointment to leading posts is about ten years less than when political considerations enter. And it is worth noting, also, that the great majority of the scientific bureaus of the American Civil Service—the Geological Survey, the Bureau of Standards, the Smithsonian Institution, the Coast and Geodetic Survey—though they have paid salaries that are low by almost any standards, have been astonishingly rich in scientific achievement. And it is of special interest that when, in 1933, Secretary Wallace had to make an appointment to the headship of the Weather Bureau he acted upon the advice of a committee of scientists one of whom was a Nobel prize man and two of whom were men eminent for their services to the sciences in which they specialized. Nor must we fail to notice the selection of Elwood Mead as head of the Reclamation Service just at the time when the United States began the construction of Boulder Dam. The scientific and technological services of the federal government have been, almost throughout their history, fortunate in the quality of the men and women they have been able to attract.

In the general Civil Service of the United States there are certain contrasts with British methods which are almost startling in their magnitude. Where examination is the road to entry, the contrast is usually remarkable. The British, at every level, attempt to test the general intelligence of the candidate; the Americans have tried to work out an examination system which is directly relevant to the post to which the candidate seeks appointment. In this aspect of the Civil Service problem, I find it very difficult to believe that the American method has any real validity after the stage at which a candidate normally embarks upon a university career. There is, indeed, a sense in which this is admitted by Americans themselves, since it is rare for the highest posts in a Department to go to candidates who have entered by examination. What one usually finds in Washington is a minister surrounded by a small team of his own choosing, while the routine work of the department is run by middle-aged men and women who have rarely had experience either of using their imagination or of the need to take important decisions. This method, no doubt, has its advantages if and when the minister and his team have a great policy for which, at all costs, they are prepared to fight. But if one examines the history of the method since, say, the Civil War, its success has been both rare and interstitial.

On the other hand, it must be borne in mind that while the British method brings a considerable number of really first-rate officials to Whitehall in each generation, it exacts a dual price for their ability. It tends, in the first place, to create a departmental tradition from which only the very exceptional minister departs, and from which only the still more exceptional official will persuade him to depart; and, in the second place, since a departmental mistake may so easily have important consequences for a government, it tends to make the official averse from action and anxious to dwell upon familiar ground. No honest observer could deny to the British Civil Service merits of the first importance. It is broadly incorruptible, it knows its job from beginning to end, and it is capable of what is, in the circumstances of its history, a quite remarkable political detachment. But these very virtues result in an absence of audacity and imagination, as well as a tendency to urge on the minister the inherent undesirability of any large-scale change. The good civil servant in Britain will always tend to look backwards rather than forwards for his inspiration. He will be tempted to think of the problems with which he has to deal very much on the assumption that the proper way to handle them is the way in which a gentleman might handle them. There is implicit in almost all his actions that philosophy which Mr. Sidney Webb so happily termed the "inevitability of gradualness." He hopes that tomorrow will be the same as today. He thinks that it is ungenerous not to take a man, even if he is Adolf Hitler, at his word. He refrains from examining into the foundations of the social philosophy he applies at the instance of his various ministers. He is part of an upper-class caste in British society which rarely looks at the living strata below itself, and finds it hard to believe that those strata have thoughts and emotions as deep as its own. Trained over long years to a habit of ironic deference, it is never really certain that anything save minutiæ are really important, or that anything save the events of tomorrow are worthy of its attention. It produces eminent essayists and great novelists, writers of verse and history, and experts in medieval Latin or the different brands of Burgundy. But, with all its merits, it is important to note that, in the realm of social ideas, Jeremy Bentham penetrated both wider and more deeply than any group of British civil servants in any decade since his time.

Until quite modern times the American Civil Service was a disappointing institution. Now and then there emerged from among its members remarkable men, like John Bassett Moore, the great international lawyer, or Elwood Mead, who did such excellent work in forest reclamation. Yet, the essential services apart, I do not think it can be said that the federal Civil Service has, so far as its permanent members are concerned, been proportionate to the problems it has confronted. Since most of its members have been, where they entered by competitive examination, confined to routine duties, it has been rare for men of ambition or energy to look to an official career as a source of life tenure. The general rule has been either that the official occupies a high place in some department as a political reward, or he occupies it as the result of special competence which is tested by grounds other than those of competitive examination. While it cannot yet be said that the spoils system has really disappeared, outside the Post Office, the Treasury, and the State Department the range of reward at the party's disposal when it is in office is hardly greater than that at the disposal of the prime minister in Great Britain. As Professor Brogan has rightly said, "The whole spoils system is today but the shadow of a great name, and the Civil Service of the United States is in the main like the Civil Service of most countries." [3]

Yet that generalization also serves to conceal a truth of great importance. While the overwhelming majority of minor federal officials are as much engaged in a life career as civil servants in London or in Paris, the making of major policy is less in their hands than it is in the hands of their

[3] D. W. Brogan, *The American Political System* (London: Hamilton, 1943), p. 203.

opposite numbers in London or in Paris. While there is no department without a career official who is likely to have considerable influence and even, like Mr. Harry Slattery,[4] real and effective power, the turnover at the top of each is far greater than it is in most other countries. Under-secretaries and assistant-secretaries tend to be, in an increasing degree, personal presidential appointments, and they hold their positions for part or for the whole of a presidential term. In the result, each cabinet officer tends to be surrounded by what the French term a *cabinet particulier,* a body of officials who share common principles of action and help their political chiefs to give them operative effectiveness. For them, this ad-ministrative experience is little more than an interlude, no doubt an important interlude, in their main careers. They may be university pro-fessors, lawyers, bankers, or journalists, or even business men. The es-sence of their position is that they work at the highest level of policy, and that they regard their position as entirely temporary in character. They may even, like Mr. Dean Acheson, go into a department for a time, return to their normal vocation, and accept a call back to official life. There is little or no resemblance between the character of their function and the generation of services which is characteristic of the permanent secretary of a government department in Great Britain, with very rare exceptions. They accept the post to which they are called because they agree with the direction in which the president or some minister in his cabinet has decided that its policy should go. No doubt they have to put a good deal of reliance upon the officials in the department who are accustomed to handling its papers and can steer them safely through the innumerable rocks which every group in Washington will put in the way of any high official. But the permanent official is a routineer; the business of a presidential appointee is invention. And the latter may find that invention involves anything from the drafting of a presidential speech, through the "fixing" of an inconvenient member of Congress, to the preparation of a bill which they will assist the chairmen of the appropriate committee in each House to see safely through to the statute book. They are concerned not only with administration; they have also to protect both their minister and the president against the possible hos-tility of the journalists and the innumerable pressure groups in Washing-ton. When Mr. Corcoran and Mr. Benjamin Cohen worked in the offices of the Department of the Interior in Mr. Franklin Roosevelt's second term, it was difficult not to describe them as maids of all work to the President. They prepared the drafts of speeches for him to work upon; they drew up the outlines of congressional bills; they "lobbied" not only among the members of both Houses but among the bodies which sought to influence those members; it is hardly too much to say that they acted as the eyes and ears for the President and gave him much of the material out of

---

[4] In his capacities as personal assistant to Secretary of Interior Ickes, assistant to administrator of the Federal Emergency Administration of Public Works, 1933–1938, and as Under-Secretary of Interior, 1938–39.

which his policies were formed. Both of them were lawyers with no previous experience of administration. What is important in their work is the realization that they retained their value just so long as they were likely, in the judgment of the President, to help in securing the results he desired. When, in his opinion, that terminal had been reached, they left in the same way as Mr. Sumner Welles did when he was unable to see eye to eye with Mr. Cordell Hull. Their value was in their ability to "put over" a policy they no doubt shared in making; but they ceased to have any value the moment when they differed from the policy it was their business to approve.

There is another sense in which the American Civil Service is very different from that of Great Britain. Though it is true that, from time to time, men of political distinction, Lord Derby, Lord Lothian, Lord Halifax, for example, who have had no formal training, have been called upon to occupy important diplomatic posts, it is the general rule that these are mainly filled by members of the Diplomatic Service. Since 1919, entrance into that service has, subject to the approval of the Foreign Secretary, been dependent upon the same examination as is taken by the ordinary entrant to the Civil Service; the only distinction of importance has been the special weight placed on a knowledge of languages by those who compete. The American attitude has been remarkably different. Though it is true that the lesser ranks in the service are filled by "career" men, the posts of the first significance, London, Paris, Berlin, Moscow, are usually the rewards of men who have assisted the president, by financial contributions to his campaign or otherwise, to reach the White House.

Among the American ambassadors to London, for example, have been, since 1920, Colonel Harvey, Mr. Houghton, Mr. Dawes, Mr. Mellon, Mr. Joseph P. Kennedy, Mr. John G. Winant, and Mr. W. A. Harriman. Of these only Mr. Houghton could be regarded as a professional diplomat. Colonel Harvey was a newspaper proprietor; Mr. Dawes was a banker from Chicago; Mr. Mellon was one of the three or four richest Americans of his time; Mr. Kennedy was a successful speculator on the stock exchange; and though Mr. Winant had long administrative experience, including periods in which he was governor of New Hampshire and director-general of the International Labour Office, he had not previously specialized in foreign affairs. Mr. Roosevelt sent a Chicago professor of history to Berlin, and a millionaire-lawyer to Moscow; to Paris, at the start of his period of office, he sent the head of a great New York department store, later replaced by a rich Philadelphian who had become a kind of playboy in the politics of the Democratic party. To Spain, he sent first a wealthy New Yorker and, later, an ardent Catholic professor of history from Columbia University. To the Vatican, he sent an eminent figure in the United States Steel Corporation. And he gave a kind of roving diplomatic commission to Mr. Norman Davis, a distinguished New York lawyer of whom it is not an exaggeration to say that he picked up his knowledge of international affairs as he went along.

What is striking in this technique is that while there were, no doubt, failures among those he chose, they were in general at least as valuable to him as were the professionally trained diplomats to the Foreign Secretary of Great Britain. Anyone, for instance, who compares the *Diary* of Ambassador Dodd with Sir Nevile Henderson's *Failure of a Mission* will find it very difficult not to conclude that Mr. Dodd's sterling common sense penetrated much further into the nature of nazism than the sterile pages of the British expert. And few people can read Mr. Joseph E. Davies' *Mission to Moscow* without the conviction that he understood the Soviet Union more thoroughly and more swiftly than any British ambassador who was sent there before June 22, 1941. It is, I think, true that Lord Lothian was a success in his brief period as ambassador in Washington; but it is at least equally true that Mr. Winant was an overwhelming success as American ambassador in London. If one has to pick out the failures among Americans, they would be found, for the most part, among the professional diplomats, Mr. Robert Murphy, for example, whom Mr. Roosevelt sent to France.

What is the explanation of this contrast? I do not think it is in any sense an easy matter to decide. Partly, no doubt, the range from which the British Diplomatic Service has been drawn has been pretty small; it was not without reason that the Foreign Office has remained the kingdom of the "elect." But, alongside this, there must be set the fact that a considerable proportion of the American Diplomatic Service is, its ambassadors apart, composed of men with an inherited income who more or less correspond to their opposite numbers in the British service. The main reason, I suspect, is to be found in the character of the president at any given time. Where he is a man of real quality, whether intellectual or moral, he tends to attract similar people to the offices in his disposal. Men like Jefferson, John Quincy Adams, Gallatin, Charles Francis Adams, go naturally into office under a great leader; just as men like Colonel George Harvey or Mr. Andrew W. Mellon typify the president whom they represent. It is, of course, true that many of the presidents who belong to the first rank have had officials both in the State Department and in American embassies abroad for whom it has been difficult to have any feeling but contempt; but most of those cases are explicable by the need of the president concerned to pay a supporter for the assistance he has been given. Few people, I imagine, suppose that President Wilson chose Mr. William Jennings Bryan as his Secretary of State out of a natural eagerness for his diplomatic knowledge; and his judgment of Mr. Walter Hines Page was sufficiently expressed by the mass of unopened dispatches from London which were found when the President died. All in all, there are two things that are, I think, worth saying. The average American who reaches a high position in the foreign service of his country is likely to have had a much wider experience of life than his opposite number in the British service;

though, beyond doubt, this is not the case if the series of American Secretaries of State is compared with the series of British Foreign Secretaries. And the second generalization that I would hazard is that the average member of the foreign service in Great Britain confines his relations to a far smaller number of persons, whether at home or abroad, than is the case with the American diplomat. It happens that the first labour attachés were appointed in London and Washington during the Second World War. I doubt whether there were a dozen people in Great Britain who knew every side of its labour movement as intimately as Mr. Roosevelt's nominee; and I do not think it is an unfair judgment to say that the British representative whose business was the study of American labour knew little more of its habits than could be gained from the limited perspective that Washington afforded.

It is exceedingly difficult to make any fair comparison between the American Civil Service and that of the other great powers. Until some such time as the presidency of Theodore Roosevelt, it was pretty rare for an able man to adopt official life as a career; the opportunities elsewhere were far too great. From the time of Theodore Roosevelt there began, at first slowly, and, after the entrance into the White House of Woodrow Wilson, fairly rapidly, to be a growing interest in the federal administration. Partly, that was the outcome of the growing range of federal power; it is not excessive to say that after 1900 the states ceased to have anything like the influence or authority they had possessed in the nineteenth century, and they became, first slowly, and after the First World War pretty rapidly, dependent upon federal aid. I venture to doubt whether the important American official had generally that zest for perfection and infallibility which, for something like half a century, has been characteristic of important British officials. I am pretty sure that he lacked the exquisite culture which the high French *fonctionnaire* brought to his work. If he was set alongside the comparable German civil servant, he probably lacked the precision of mind and deference of manner by which the latter was distinguished. But he was less hampered by tradition and authority and caste than any of these. He was capable of audacity and innovation on a scale which was rivalled only by exceptional men in the Civil Services of Europe. Perhaps that was the case because he did not expect to stay in Washington; and he assumed that the post to which he would go when his career there ended would in large part be decided by his work as a federal official. I think it was the case also, because, the president apart, it was rare for an important American civil servant to have the deferential habit which even the majority of permanent secretaries in Britain will show to their ministers. And not a little of this difference must be attributed to the operation of the division of powers. An eminent British official who makes a bad mistake knows that he may not only ruin his minister, but may even bring down the government to which his minister belongs. An American civil servant of importance has no such fears. Once his minister is on good terms with the

president, and he himself is on good terms with his minister, he has little
to fear from criticism or investigation. The result is to urge him to use
his position for all it is worth. Anyone who compares for example, the
work of Mr. Felix Frankfurter as chairman of the War Labor Policies
Board and, later, as secretary of the President's Mediation Commission
during the First World War, will be inclined to doubt whether anyone,
except Sir Robert Morant, in the British Civil Service would have shown
an equal public determination. It is obvious that Lord Vansittart, in whom
shyness is not his most notable quality, nevertheless held himself bound
by that rule of silence to which British civil servants traditionally adhere;
he never sought, therefore, to reveal his differences either with Lord Halifax or Mr. Neville Chamberlain on vital matters of foreign policy until
he had left the Foreign Office and had been given the House of Lords
as a platform from which to expound his views. And by that time he had
become, so to speak, an elder statesman, wielding an influence hardly
greater than he would have exercised by writing letters to the London
Times.

The scale of official influence, moreover, has grown by leaps and bounds
since Franklin Roosevelt became president in 1933. I do not suggest that
it has been all to the good. It is not easy to understand when one is a
foreign observer, why the Secretary of the Treasury under the New Deal
should have depended upon the advice of two economists to whom, quite
obviously, the New Deal and all its works, were anathema. It is not easy
to understand why so many of the more important officials of the State
Department supported Franco in Spain and Mussolini in Italy and
showed so curious a tenderness to Marshal Pétain and Vichy France. It
is not easy, either, to understand why there was a censorship of news and
books which cut off the American Army abroad from the essential information they required to vote wisely in the election of 1944. The volume of contradictions in the American political scene covers an area
wider than is easily accountable. There is no Treasury control to give
any primacy to the financial context of proposals. There is no basis upon
which the cabinet can achieve an executive unity, either because its members have not had long years of work together or because their chief officials do not share a common tradition which is built out of a similar experience. There is no doctrine of common responsibility which assures
any clear direction in policy; one has only to read a diary like that of
Gideon Welles, Lincoln's Secretary of the Navy, or the memoirs of
Robert Lansing, Woodrow Wilson's second Secretary of State, to realize
how full is the reliance on presidential direction for the making of administrative unity, how unlikely is its achievement when the president has
not made up his mind.

The foreign observer is tempted, as he examines the history of the
American Civil Service, to two conclusions. The first is the reasonably
obvious one that it takes great policies to attract great officials to Washington, and that great policies are almost always formulated by great

presidents. The second is that the federal Civil Service is more likely in the future than in the past to play an increasing part in the shaping of policy. The reason for this is the quite simple one that the area of federal administration grows wider year by year; and the result of this expansion is to make a career in Washington at once more appealing and more significant than at any previous period. An official who is near to his minister has the chance in his generation of that influence which, despite the famous maxim of Washington, it becomes increasingly difficult to differentiate from power. Few people who had the choice between the chairmanship of the Tennessee Valley Authority and the presidency of the American Tobacco Company would hesitate in their choice, granted that they had imagination and a sense of public spirit.

Few people, indeed, are likely to make the federal service, at the apex, a career in which they pass their lives. They think of it as an interlude, no doubt of exceptional interest, but still fundamentally an interlude. That is, I think, the outcome of a characteristic of American life. For its citizens, politics and the political career are still on the plane of federal matters, a temporary concern and not a permanent interest.

That is why they do not know what to do with ex-presidents; John Quincy Adams apart, no president except Mr. Chief Justice Taft has overcome the handicap of having had the supreme office in the gift of the American people. Few cabinet officers have been able to serve more than a single president; and few of them have utilized the experience of their chief officials for more than at most a presidential term. There is a sense, no doubt, in which this is the outcome of the relatively low salaries that are paid to civil servants; and the attraction of a great career in law, or banking, or industry, becomes almost irresistible in a community in which the possession of a great fortune means the exercise of a great influence. Carnegie, Frick, Rockefeller, Astor, Gould, men like these did not need office to emphasize their authority; their wealth assured them of an influence which few cabinet officials could rival. It is intelligible that a relatively young man, or, in a real crisis like a war, an old man, should accept an office from the president; it is even intelligible that men like John Hay or Secretary Hamilton Fish should be willing to assist in shaping the whisper of the presidential throne even in ordinary times. But, in general, the politician who wants a career in the realm of federal affairs will think first of the Senate, and then, *longo intervallo,* of the House of Representatives. In either of these he can become a person whose thoughts and acts are his own; and the longer he stays in Congress, the more significant is his personality. A cabinet officer under a great president is almost bound to be a mere echo of his master's voice; if he refuses to accept that status he is very likely to cease to be a cabinet minister. Where he serves a president of poor calibre, he is grimly likely to find that policy is shaped mainly at the other end of Pennsylvania Avenue, and he finds that, if he has status, he is lacking in authority. And the lower one goes in the scale of federal officials, the more true will it be

either that the president is all in all, or that the effective centre of power
is in Congress. In the result, it is wholly natural for an American to think
of his career as a political official not in Congress as an experience that
is likely to help him rather by the connections it enables him to form than
as a means of putting into practice principles for whose victory he is
deeply concerned. Most high civil servants are surprised when they are
chosen for the posts they occupy; and they are still more surprised when
they discover that their post enables them to carry out to its conclusion a
coherent body of ideas in which they are interested. Washington is a place
through which they pass on their way elsewhere; and its main importance
for them is likely to lie in the contribution it makes to their careers when
they have ceased to be federal officials.

7

IN NO country in the world today has the lawyer a standing remotely
comparable with his place in American politics. The respect in which the
federal courts and, above all, the Supreme Court are held is hardly surpassed by the influence they exert on the life of the United States. If it
is excessive to say that American history could be written in terms of its
federal decisions, it is not excessive to say that American history would
be incomplete without a careful consideration of them. The presidency
apart, no position is more eagerly canvassed than that of a justice of the
Supreme Court of the United States. And while it is true that there have
been judges of poor quality in each of the three tiers of the federal courts,
it is also true that they have been able to attract into their service men
whose ability, taken as a whole, rivals that of the men who have sought
to win the ultimate prize of the presidency. Cabinet officers and senators
have gladly exchanged their places for a position on the Supreme Court;
and from Marshall, in the first generation of its history, to Chief Justice
Vinson in the present age, it is not an exaggeration to say that the influence of the Court has been second to that of no other American institution.

It is, of course, a hierarchy of courts the main part of whose business
is concerned with private law. Session by session, the judges in the District Courts, in the Circuit Courts of Appeal, in the Supreme Court of the
United States itself, deal with issues of equity and the Common Law in
nowise different from the ordinary work of the courts in England. It may
be a matter of contract or tort or testamentary disposition; the judiciary
at each level deals with them much as they would deal with them in London. Where the difference arises is in the fact that the American Constitution is a written constitution and there is no authority, whether private
or executive or legislative, which can, since Marshall's great decision in
McCulloch v. *Maryland*,[5] which made the Supreme Court the effective
source of constitutional interpretation, venture upon an action that, subject to the complex amending power of the Constitution, seeks to over-

[5] 4 *Wheat.* 316 (1819).

ride it. The issue may be a decision taken by a body like the Public Service Commission of New York; it may be a statute passed with enthusiasm by a state legislature or by Congress itself; the action to be tested may be the policy of a trade-union or an employers' association. The problem may arise, as in the famous Frank case, because a man who has been found guilty insists that in terms of the American Constitution he has not been given a fair trial. A Negro law student in Missouri may seek to compel the academic authorities of a university in that state to admit him to a school of law on the same terms as white students. The children of that peculiar sect, Jehovah's Witnesses, may insist that their exclusion from the public schools on the ground that they refuse to salute the American flag is an example of the religious intolerance forbidden by the Constitution. A Russian-born American may argue that his plea to the citizens of New York in 1919 to "keep their hands off the Soviet Union" cannot be validly regarded as a violation of the Espionage Act of 1918.[6] The effort of the District of Columbia to prohibit the employment of child labour may be put to the courts as a reasonable exercise of the police power of the state. The legislature of New York may argue that, if its Assembly decides to prohibit the baking of bread at night, it is entitled to do so.[7] An ancient college like Dartmouth may urge, through the persuasive genius of Daniel Webster, that once New Hampshire has made it a grant, the contract is inviolable. And the eminent lawyer, Mr. Choate, may ask the Court to announce that an attempt to impose a tax upon incomes not merely violates the constitutional clause which guarantees equal distribution of taxation, but risks the danger of imposing upon the people of the United States the horrific principles of that socialist democracy against which the Founding Fathers sought, in 1787, to erect a permanent barrier. In these, and a thousand other cases, it is the ultimate decision of the Supreme Court, it may well be five out of nine middle-aged or even ageing men, which determines, subject only to the overriding amending power, just precisely what the American Constitution means at a given time.

The inference is the unmistakable one that, in the last analysis, the Supreme Court, by exercising this power of judicial review, is, in fact, a third chamber in the United States. No doubt it is a chamber the will of which depends, as Mr. Justice Miller remarked, upon the concurring will of the Executive if it is to be operative; but this inference that it is therefore a weak body does not seem logically to follow. On the contrary, so long as the Supreme Court is careful not to outrage public opinion, it may be pretty justifiably claimed that, constitutional amendment apart, the Court sets the framework, both negatively and positively, within which both the states, on the one hand, and the federal government, on the other, do their work. It is, of course, true that its power to define this framework is not an initiative that it can undertake of its own volition;

[6] *Abrams* v. *United States.*
[7] *Lochner* v. *New York,* 198 U.S. 45 (1905).

some outside body, whether a private citizen or a public person, must invoke the exercise of its powers. But there is no modern community in which respect for the principle of judicial review goes deeper than it does in the United States, with the result that acceptance of the Court's authority by all persons or institutions affected is taken for granted. Where that acceptance is called into question, as over the Dred Scott case before the Civil War, or, rather less emphatically, in the generation from the election of McKinley to the second election of Franklin D. Roosevelt, it is legitimate to assume that the Court has lost the support of that public upon which its status depends; and there will then follow either a change in the postulates upon which its policy is built or, sooner or later, such changes in its membership as will lead to a change in those postulates.

It is inherent in this view of the place of the federal courts, and especially of the Supreme Court, in the American political system that its judges who have made a real mark on the history of American life have been not less notable for their political wisdom than they have been for their legal learning. John Marshall, after all, was hardly a great lawyer in the sense that he was the equal in technical equipment of Coke or Blackstone or Mansfield; his greatness was the outcome of a mind powerful enough to see what the new republic required, and a character determined enough to see that the new republic received what it required from the Court. Holmes and Cardozo had a quality of legal scholarship unsurpassed in any contemporary court of the Common Law; but what made them great judges was not the depth of their learning in the law, but the combination of power and grace with which they expressed what they perceived to be needed by the period in which they sat on the Court. And, in a sense, given the implications of judicial review, there is a good deal to be said for the argument that the greatest of Marshall's successors was Mr. Justice Brandeis in that his decisions were the consummate expression of a legal philosophy which he tried to fit, with a coherent amplitude, into the needs of his time.

The power of judicial review is a very great power; but it is, after all, a power which must be exercised by men. It is never automatic in its application; there enter into the use of this power all the habits and thoughts and experience which make each judge regard its meaning in the special sense he attaches to it. Because the final determination is the work of a court, the result is summarized as a legal finding. But the legal finding which is the result is never logically separable from all the forces that are at work in the American community. So the courts are what presidents have made them with the approval of a majority of the Senate in the case of each particular judge. But as the courts are made by presidents, so presidents are made by the electoral forces which enable now the Republican party to beat the Democratic party, and now the Democratic party to beat the Republican.

But the chain of causation does not end there. Every court is shaped in at least some degree by the members of the Bar who plead before it; and members of the Bar are what all the forces they encounter tend to make of them. A New York barrister whose father was an Iowa farmer and who was deeply influenced by his courses in the Harvard Law School in the days of Ames and Thayer is not very likely to try to influence the Supreme Court in the same way as that curious embodiment of rhetoric from Pennsylvania, Mr. James M. Beck, or as Professor William D. Guthrie of Columbia University, at once an ardent Roman Catholic and an eager exponent of conservatism in the manner of Nicholas Murray Butler. Anyone who examines, for example, Professor Guthrie's explanation of Magna Charta will realize without much difficulty why even an eminent lawyer can look upon a thirteenth-century feudal statute with the mind and, even more, with the heart of an eighteenth-century natural rights philosopher, and so be blind to all the research into its meaning that was attempted about the time when, at the height of the Victorian era, Bishop Stubbs set the mental climate of medieval constitutional inquiry. No one can examine the mind of Mr. Justice Peckham, as it was revealed in his opinion in *Lochner* v. *New York,* or note the long years in which Mr. Justice Field maintained that the Court prevents "dangerous changes in the good society," without concluding that, by substituting their private social philosophies for that of the legislatures whose statutes they sought to strike down, both of them were confusing the function of a judge with that of a legislator. For it is, frankly, impossible for the Court to divide on vital issues of political or economic policy by five to four or even six to three without making the student of the doctrine of judicial review a little more apprehensive about its complexities and limitations than has been customary with, say, men like Mr. Choate, or the famous John G. Johnson, of Philadelphia, or, in our own day, Mr. John W. Davis or Mr. Justice McReynolds. And when, as in the Jehovah's Witnesses cases, the Court divides eight to one in the first hearing, and listens, in the second, to an apology from two of its members for having been found with the majority on the first occasion, it is not unreasonable to infer that judicial review is vitally related to judicial personalities, and that much goes to the shaping of the latter of which Marshall made no mention in *Marbury* v. *Madison.*

What Marshall omitted to mention is that the doctrine of judicial review is a complex of several things. In part, it enables the Supreme Court to declare unconstitutional any act which, in the words of Mr. Justice Holmes, "violates the plain letter of the Constitution"; I think it should be added that, on the whole, such cases have been rare, or that, alternatively, where they do occur—in *ex parte Milligan,* a Civil War issue, or in *Abrams* v. *United States,* a legacy from the war of 1914–18— either it is too late to correct the mischief, or the judges tend to agree by a majority to approve the wrong which the executive power has inflicted for the simple reason that they share the same climate of opinion which led the executive power to act in that particular way. Or judicial review may be an important method at once of maintaining the supremacy of the Federal Constitution in that area where it must be kept supreme, or of preventing some state authority from violating principles to the observance of which all Americans are committed. An obvious example of the first is safeguarding the supremacy of the treaty-making power as federal in its nature; but the second method is much more difficult to define because there is no agreement about the principles which all Americans ought to observe. A foreign observer would be tempted to insist that the "Jim Crow" laws of the South are an obvious violation of those principles; but when Mr. Justice Black wrote the decision of the Court in the St. Louis law school case, there was a flood of enthusiastic comment about his courage in so doing in the light of his Southern origin.

But there is a sense in which the importance of the doctrine of judicial review comes not from any of these sources but from the far more important fact that for a century and a half of its history it has enabled the Court to see that the power of a majority, whether in Congress or in a state legislature, does not disturb the rights of property.

It is important to remember that the doctrines of the Court took their predominant shape in the age of the negative state; it is not an accident that the Declaration of Independence and the *Wealth of Nations* both date from the same year. Nor is it accident that the doctrines of the Court were the expression of an expanding America in the age of individualism, in the period, that is, of the "simple system of natural liberty," in which the more uninhibited were the rights of property by state action, the more amply was it supposed that social well-being would be secured. It is improbable that the business men who so largely determined the character of American civilization after 1787, and, still more, after 1860, had any conscious sense that the political philosophy of Locke and natural rights would provide them with a legal theory needed to protect their privileges from the invasion of majority rule. But it is in a high degree significant that, from the work of the Founding Fathers, the Court was able to infer the necessity for the payment of debts in a sound currency, the sanctity of contracts, the distinction between legislation which directly, and legislation which indirectly, affects interstate commerce, the invalidity of an income tax, and the prohibition of statutes which sought to settle the terms upon which a citizen could sell his or her labour. It is still more significant that the most widely read books on American Constitutional Law in the nineteenth century, like T. M. Cooley's *Constitutional Limitations,* should have been based on an outlook which assumed the undesirability of government interference. And when the "due process" clauses come to be used as a weapon by which the Court strikes down all legislation which interferes with vested property rights, the concept of liberty becomes so closely identified with the concept of property in the mind of the judges that legislative action which touches property becomes regarded as inherently action which is hostile to freedom.

The title, indeed, of Herbert Spencer's famous polemic—*The Man versus the State*—is no bad summary of the first century and a quarter of the legal philosophy of the American Constitution. The overwhelming mass of judges thought in those terms; so, too, did the overwhelming mass of those lawyers who defended the great vested interests in the United States from attack. It is the fact that this is so which gives its point to Mr. Justice Holmes' famous insistence to the Supreme Court that the "Fourteenth Amendment does not enact Mr. Herbert Spencer's *Social Statics.*" [8] The fact is that, until his dissent, there were few judges on the Bench to whom it would have occurred to suppose that the Fourteenth Amendment had some alternative purpose. For almost all of them, "due process" was not a road but a gate; and the thing that it barred was any attempt to transform political democracy in the United States into social democracy. Where any effort of that kind was made, as in the Populist movement, for example, it was pretty speedily obvious to both Bench and Bar that this was exactly one of those blows at the root of American well-being which the Constitution had been brought into being to prevent.

The mental climate of America was remarkably favourable to this view until some such time as the rise of the Progressive movement, a time, it is worth noting, in which the majority decision in the Lochner case evoked from Mr. Justice Holmes his historic protest. After its rise, it became increasingly difficult to maintain the view that a negative state fulfilled the historic purposes of the American tradition. A stage then arrived in the working of the Supreme Court where "due process of law" began to mean what a majority of the Court happened to regard as reasonable at any given time. But the basis of "reasonableness" was not a concept it was possible to determine by any simple and objective legal criteria; this was clear from the fact that what appeared "unreasonable" to a majority of the judges of the Supreme Court appeared in a quite different light to the minority; and there was not always agreement among the majority about the grounds upon which they arrived at their decisions. When the Court arrived at the stage where, in the first term of the New Deal, it fought passionately and strenuously against the policies of the president, it was abundantly clear that it was a wholly unsuitable agency to control the governmental process with any effectiveness. Its movement was too interstitial; it was far too slow for the tempo with which it sought to grapple; and it was so costly that it was pretty obviously the case that only wealthy interests could take advantage of such controls as the Court might be willing to impose. At this stage the one "reasonable" conclusion about "reasonableness" was that wherever the determination of wisdom in legislation might be placed, no resi-

[8] *Lochner* v. *New York*, 198 U.S. 45, 74.

dence was less suitable than the Supreme Court of the United States. For almost a century and a half, so to say, the judges had their day in Court, and what emerged from the way they used it was the impossibility of reconciling the judicial function with the power to solve the problems of modern government. Once that is admitted, it follows that the only ultimate source of authority must be in that rule of the majority which the judges sought to limit. On a long view, it became clear that the main ground upon which they sought to limit it was, however carefully they might seek to obscure it, a theory of what was to the economic advantage of the United States; and, again on a long view, it became not less clear that they acted mostly upon a theory which assumed the identity of that economic welfare with the protection of business interests. That theory might work in the Gilded Age of Mark Twain, or in the golden days when Calvin Coolidge watched Mr. Mellon make his refunds of income and corporation taxes with unmitigated admiration. It could not possibly work either in the epoch of the Great Depression or when, as under Franklin Roosevelt, the rebirth of hope among the masses depended upon the acceptance of New Deal policies which business men denounced with furious indignation. The positive state, in a world, cannot depend upon a procedure so cumbrous as the combination of judicial review and the American process of constitutional amendment. Wherever its essential shape was to be derived, its artificers would have to look in a different direction.

8

IN WHAT direction should they look for leadership in the making of policy? Once it be granted that the American system is unlikely to change its presidential for a parliamentary character, it seems to me inescapable that the residence of effective leadership must be in the White House and cannot with wisdom be placed elsewhere. I have given reasons for my view that judicial review is a wholly inadequate instrument for policy-making in a positive state. It is unlikely that either House of Congress can assume that role. The House of Representatives is necessarily sectional in outlook by the method by which it is chosen; and few men can learn the art of lawmaking in a term of office which may not last longer than two years. The claim of the Senate to leadership is stronger. It is composed of members most of whom represent an area large enough to make it possible for them to transcend a sectionalist obscurantism; and the six-year term, which is, more often than not, renewed, enables its members to develop a coherent view of American problems.

Both of these are strong arguments, but they are unconvincing because the Senate, while it may amend or frustrate, cannot itself actually operate the necessary administrative power. It can debate, it can investigate, it can ventilate the issues which are before the United States. But it lacks the foundation of strength which comes from an origin by choice of the whole nation. The manner of its election makes it always less than fully representative of the mood of the nation. Its internal relationships make it a body more suited to judge policy than to initiate it. Nor could a body in which relations are as intimate as they are in the Senate hope to act in an executive capacity unless it handed over the making of policy to what was virtually a committee of its own members; otherwise it could not attain coherency of outlook, nor could it devote itself to the daily oversight of administration. But once such a committee came into being, the Senate would become a matrix upon which the character of parliamentary government was impressed. It would then be bound to alter the nature of the presidency on the one hand, and of the House of Representatives on the other. The alteration, indeed, would be so massive in its implications that it would amount to a constitutional revolution. And implicit in that revolution would be the danger that senators representing a minority of the population should govern a majority of the electorate. That there are limits to the authority a majority may seek to exercise was shown unmistakably by the aftermath of the Civil War. It is not an exaggeration to suggest that the limits to the authority a minority may seek to impose render it impossible to hope for constitutional or democratic government from minority control.

It is obviously impossible to make the president's cabinet the essential policy-making organ. For, in the first place, it has no elective authority behind it, and, in the second, such unity of direction as it possesses is derived from the impulse to unity which the president is able to communicate to its members. No one who examines at all carefully the history of the American cabinet will be inclined to believe that this has been the function the president has been able most successfully to perform. For it is rare indeed that an average cabinet persists unchanged even through a single administration; it is still more rare for it to develop any genuine sense of collective responsibility. Its members are rarely operating on the same plane of thought, or even with the same purposes in mind. Some cabinet officers are professional politicians who are thinking mainly of their party's future, or, as with men like Salmon P. Chase under Lincoln, of their own careers. Others are essentially personal nominees of the president, and their political status is wholly the outcome of his decision to put them in the cabinet. Others attain that dignity because of the nexus they establish with an important interest, sometimes religious, sometimes economic, sometimes geographical, over which the president hopes to establish or to maintain an influence. Others, again, are being rewarded for their services to the man who has won his place in the White House; and, not infrequently, they are his unsuccessful rivals for the nomination whom the President thinks it will be useful or gracious to placate. The point is that the American cabinet can be made into a team only by the president and that its standing as an organ of government is very largely dependent on the use he chooses to make of it. The one thing a cabinet has never done in American history is to act as a unit against its leader; and that it cannot do for the very simple reason that the president alone is in a position to make it the kind of unit which is capable of organizing a policy and carrying it to a successful conclusion.

From all this, it seems to me to follow logically that political leadership in the United States is bound, in the federal sphere, to reside in the president. But it is bound to be a very difficult thing to give effectiveness to that leadership. It is bound to be difficult for a number of reasons. In the first place, in the absence of grave crisis, there is an almost inherent antagonism between president and Congress. In the degree that the policies are of his patterning, Congress loses the capacity to enhance its prestige with public opinion; in the degree that it wrecks his policies, Congress deprives the president not only of the ability to lead effectively but also of the prestige he requires to build a coherent policy. It is this antagonism which makes the presidential control of the patronage so important; without it, he would be deprived of the assets which are the real basis of his bargaining power. Anyone who examines a presidential term of office will find that, as a normal rule, it is fairly divisible into three periods. There is the period in which the president has not yet decided how to dispose of what is in his gift; this is generally that "honeymoon" period in which his influence is at its highest; there is the middle period when the parties are doing nothing so much as deploying for position in terms of the general balance of social forces in American society; and there is the final period in which the strategy of the next presidential election is being shaped on every plane to which its result is relevant.

There is an implication in this analysis which bears with great importance on the power of the president to be a great leader. The choice of a candidate is only too often the outcome of a parallelogram of social forces which makes availability if not the supreme, at any rate an important, criterion in his selection. Alfred E. Smith was not "available" in 1932 because it was clear that the Solid South would not remain solid if it was asked to support a Roman Catholic Democrat again. Wendell Willkie was not available in 1944 because the machine politicians of the Republican party suspected that they could not be sure where they would be taken if he was elected. Men of the calibre of Clay and Calhoun have seen themselves beaten by candidates of the second order on the principle that "availability" means the minimum degree of offensiveness. The system, to put it briefly, makes for the emergence of the good pack-horse who will tread the wanted path without seeking to reach his goal in his own way. That is shown clearly in the political goodwill that accrues to men like Grover Cleveland and William McKinley. Neither possessed any special qualities of leadership; each had that party virtue of solid regularity, which meant that they would always do the expected thing in the expected way. In the outcome, what happens to the American presidency is that it attracts a series of routineers to its occupation until the historical position is obviously one in which routine and regularity would be fatal. There then supervenes a crisis president during whose activities to meet the crisis one can almost see the party machine holding its breath in mingled fear and indignation. And as the crisis president begins to overcome the situation he encounters, there emerges the professional fatigue at innovations which are outside the rules, and the preparation, within the party, of the conditions which make possible a speedy return to the wonted ways. Even the electorate is tempted into the belief that it is, in some mysterious fashion, safer if the man in the White House follows the historic presidential chart and does not venture upon innovation.

Nothing shows this more clearly than the influence of Franklin Roosevelt on the American party system. That he was able to break the tradition against a third term for the president was, despite all the special circumstances which made it possible, a very remarkable achievement. No doubt he owed this possibility to the scale and the intensity of the Second World War; but the fact remains that a tradition which neither Grant nor Theodore Roosevelt, neither Woodrow Wilson nor Calvin Coolidge, was able to overcome ceased, in 1940, to be the unstated postulate of the presidency for the first time. And therefore, again for the first time, a major political party was led by one man for more than a decade. The price of that leadership, indeed, was higher than appears to a merely superficial view. Franklin Roosevelt's second term lacked something of the incisive *élan* of the first; his third term was so overshadowed by the war that it is not excessive to argue that he sacrificed most of the principles of the New Deal to securing the unity of the nation in the war effort. Nor is that all. It is significant that, whereas in 1940, he could insist on the choice of the leading progressive in his cabinet, Mr. Henry A. Wallace, for the vice-presidential nomination, in 1944 he surrendered Mr. Wallace to the demands of the party machine. No doubt Mr. Roosevelt could have insisted on Mr. Wallace's renomination; but it is difficult not to feel that even with the war there was so great a strain on his decision to run for a fourth term, that he thought it wiser to leave the choice to the party convention.

Nor is this the whole price. Anyone who examines the personnel of the administration as it was organized by President Roosevelt for war purposes can hardly avoid the conclusion that it is deliberately characterized by three important features. The first is the fact that the administration progressives were increasingly pushed into the background. Mr. Wallace ceased, early in 1944, to play the active part he had been asked to play after Pearl Harbor. Big Business got rid of men who, like Mr. Leon Henderson of the Office of Price Administration, were associated with criticism of its habits; and Mr. Thurman Arnold who, as assistant attorney-general, had been engaged in a vigorous assault upon the growing trustification of American industry, disappeared into the quiet eminence of a Circuit Court of Appeals; while his successor, Mr. Berge, confined his attacks to the realm of words rather than of suits, even though the words contained the threat of post-war action.[9] The chief advisers of the President on the domestic side were conservative Democrats like ex-Justice Byrnes, who had gone to the Supreme Court from the Senate, or Mr. Baruch, a distinguished stock-exchange speculator of great wealth, who had been chairman of the War Industries Board under Woodrow Wilson in the First World War. The direction of finance and manufactures for war purposes were mainly entrusted to men like Mr. Donald Nelson and Mr. Charles E. Wilson and Mr. Leo Crowley outside, and Mr. Jesse Jones inside, the cabinet—men, that is to say, who had the confidence of Big Business. Miss Perkins remained Secretary of Labor, and a well-known trade-unionist, Mr. Sidney Hillman, had functions of some importance in industrial relations; but neither had either the influence or the prestige which was theirs in the New Deal epoch of Mr. Roosevelt's presidency.

Two vital things, in fact, suggest that not even the war could prevent American politics, despite the superficially revolutionary appearance of a nomination for a fourth term, from swinging back from the creative excitement of a crisis presidency to the normal routines which the party system seeks to preserve. The first was the fact that, in 1944, the Republicans nominated Mr. Thomas E. Dewey, the governor of New York, as their presidential candidate. It is not, I think, ungenerous or erroneous to insist, first, that Governor Dewey, the choice of the Republican machine, was a kind of stream-lined edition of ex-President Hoover, whose main virtues in the eyes of his supporters were, first, that he was not Franklin D. Roosevelt and, second, that unlike his main rival for the Republican nomination, the late Mr. Wendell Willkie, there was no sort of danger that, if elected, he would do anything outside the expectations of the machine. And, second, it is important that President Roosevelt had the warm backing of the great city machines of the Democratic party, Mayor Kelly's in Chicago, Mayor Hague's in Jersey City, the inheritors of the Pendergast organization in Kansas City and that of Butler in St. Louis. But by the fact that he secured this support, the President in truth checked the progress in social matters of which the New Deal was symbolic. For the city boss is not interested in the "forgotten man." He is interested in the power to be attained by the possession of a majority. And power means jobs, contracts, franchises; the city boss and his henchmen are, for all practical purposes, simply the affiliates of Big Business, acting as their agents in municipal affairs. To command their support is to announce in other terms a boundary beyond which the president does not propose to go. Their alliance is an indirect assurance to the existing interests in society that the epoch of invention has given place to the epoch of routine. And routine, of course, is a prophecy that business need have no fear.

[9] Mr. Berge resigned, as of May 1, 1942, owing to congressional refusal of adequate appropriations for his department.

The more closely this argument is examined, the more does it seem to indicate one general, and one specific, conclusion. Granted the need for creative leadership in the positive state; granted, also, on the grounds I have here urged, that this task of leadership can be performed with real adequacy only by the president, the general conclusion is that the institutional apparatus of American federalism maximizes the difficulty of this performance. For underlying each of the postulates on which this institutional apparatus is built is a belief in the validity of the negative state, a general distrust of power, and its division by a system of checks and balances which weights it particularly against the exercise of power by the chief executive. To get the authority he needs, it is a delicate and complicated task for the president to act either simply or directly. Some of it he gets from national support of public opinion; some of it he gets through his temporary leadership of his party; some of it he gets through the skilful use of patronage. In a critical period the main emphasis is likely to be on the first of these sources; in the absence of crisis it is likely to be on the third. But in either kind of climate the president is bound to remember—what, in any case, his opponents will never allow him to forget—that his leadership is a passing phase in the history of the United States, that he must use all the capacity at his disposal if he wants to keep it. It is worth remembering that in the hundred years which elapsed between the retirement of Andrew Jackson, and the first re-election of Franklin Roosevelt only seven presidents were able to keep that power for a second term, and of these seven, Lincoln and McKinley were assassinated early in their second period of office.

The specific conclusion was foreseen over a century ago by Tocqueville in what remains the most superb discussion of the American idea. Once a president, he argued, desires to serve a second term, he must sacrifice a good deal of his independence to the need to purchase the support requisite to that end. Where there is this desire, the president "no longer governs for the interest of the State, but for that of his re-election; he does homage to the majority, and instead of checking its passions, as his duty commands, he frequently courts its worse caprices." It is at least legitimate to argue that, for all normal purposes, what Tocqueville here describes as the "majority" is, in fact, never anything of the kind. Save in such exceptional circumstances as led to the quite untraditional nomination of Wendell Willkie by the Republican convention in 1940, that to which a president who desires to keep in the White House for another term pays homage is that body of vested interests in his party which has the means of insuring his renomination. When Theodore Roosevelt desired a third term of office, it was not to the elder La Follette that he turned to enable him to appear at Armageddon, but to George W. Perkins, a partner in the firm of J. P. Morgan and Company, who does not fit quite so easily into the natural role of protector of the "forgotten man." It is not easy to be certain whether President Coolidge's famous "I do not choose to run" did or did not conceal a desire to be "drafted" by the Republicans in 1928; but it is at least clear that whether one takes his veto of the McNary-Haugen farm relief bill, the visitors whose reappearance at the White House he encouraged, or his curious failure to lend his support to any of the contenders for the succession to himself, he was seeking to organize an atmosphere in which the possibility of his being drafted would not be ruled out by conflict with any important element of strength in his party. Mrs. Eleanor Roosevelt has confronted what Professor Myrdal has called the "American dilemma" with a straightforward courage that is beyond all praise; but in the twelve years since 1932, whatever may have been the President's opinions on the Negro question, he never forgot the place of the South in the organization of the Democratic party.

The right inference, I think, to be drawn from all this experience is that presidential leadership, the character of the individual occupant of the White House apart, depends upon the power of the president to be really independent. That he cannot be in full measure if he desires a second term, or a third, or a fourth. Once he desires renomination he has, in Tocqueville's phrase, as a matter of necessity to "court the caprices" of those interests in his party which may prevent it, and those elements in the nation whose strength is important. He would be a remarkable Republican president who announced that he preferred the support of the Congress of Industrial Organizations to that of the National Association of Manufacturers; just as it was a great risk for a Democratic president to make a speech of greeting at the annual meeting of the National Association for the Advancement of Colored People. It is not easy to dissociate President Roosevelt's acceptance of the principle of non-intervention in the days of the ill-fated Spanish Republic from his sense that he might, otherwise, jeopardize his hold on the great mass of Roman Catholic voters who normally support the Democratic party. It is tempting to compare the first Roosevelt's public and passionate denunciation of "malefactors of great wealth" with his actual tenderness towards the great business corporations; the conservative President Taft indulged in far fewer flights of rhetoric, but his record in this regard is far better than that of his "progressive" rival. When President Woodrow Wilson was elected for the second time in 1916, his claim that he had kept the United States out of the First World War was probably as powerful a weapon as he had in his armoury; yet even when he made it he was aware, as all his close supporters were aware, that only a miracle could prevent American intervention during his second term of office. And, on the other side, the policy of Tyler, after he succeeded to the presidency, was as certain, by reason of foreign affairs alone, to limit his period of office to a single term as was the inherent inability of John Quincy Adams, when he was in the White House, to treat even his supporters on a basis which did not assume that the world was broadly divided into Adamses and other people.

On this basis, assuming once again that it is to the presidential, and not to some model of parliamentary, government that the American people has decided to entrust its fate, I think the case for a single term of six or seven years, with re-eligibility ruled out by constitutional provision, is likely to result in a more effective and independent leadership than is attainable under the present system. A president with some such period at his disposal can work out a real policy ample enough in scope to cover an important field of activity. The fact that he is not re-eligible would make him far less concerned than he must today be concerned to placate the critics and vested interests he will encounter. It will also enable him to use his appointing power without that excessive deference that he now must pay to such indefensible principles as that of "senatorial courtesy." He has in such a scheme a method of protection against the kind of internal intrigue in his own cabinet which Lincoln had to suffer from Chase. The fact that he could not be re-elected would mean that he could put before the voters of America a policy for which his responsibility would be as clear and direct as the responsibility of Congress in amending or rejecting it. He would be free, in a way that he cannot now be free, from the influence of pressure groups which seek, only too often under threat, to make every item of his measures move in one direction rather than in another. And if, as would obviously be wise, the presidential term were made to coincide with the senatorial term, the habits of the latter body, in treaty-making, for example, or the confirmation of proposed appointments, would enable the electorate to thread its way clearly through the present maze to a clear definition of respective spheres of action. The political parties would be saved from the tortuous and often indefensible intrigues by which a president seeks to secure more terms than one. The president would be saved the strain he now suffers in endeavouring, usually through the patronage, to placate one interest or another in either of the two Houses. He would be given the means to stand up to the claims of sectionalism in a way that is now hardly open to him.

That is not all. The very fact of a term of office ample enough to give him elbow-room for large-scale thinking would mean that he could call upon citizens to serve him—periods of crisis apart—in the knowledge that their posts would not be in jeopardy just as they had become accustomed to their operation. He could learn whom to retain and whom to reject in the confidence that if he rejected this colleague or that he could offer his successor a spaciousness of opportunity that is now largely absent. Such a president would not suffer from the knowledge that to most senators of first-rate ability an administrative post offers few attractions in comparison with their legislative office; for it is at least probable that an administrator who did a first-rate job for the president would establish the kind of reputation out of which there would grow the demand that he be used still longer—whether in administration or in a branch of the legislature is relatively unimportant. The president would not suffer, as he now usually suffers, from the fact that his first two years of office are in large part devoted to preparing for the mid-term congressional elections, and no small part of the second two years in organizing his renomination by his party, where he desires it. Not least, in the realm of international policy, the president, with such a reform as this, would have the time at his disposal to mobilize an Executive public opinion in his support, where he is right, just as the Senate would not suffer from the inhibition that it is jeopardizing its members' chances of re-election where it is convinced that the president's proposals are mistaken.

It is worth noting that, the unique experience of President Franklin Roosevelt apart, a single term of seven years would give any president almost as vast an opportunity to prove himself as most presidents have enjoyed since the time of Andrew Jackson. He would be as long in office as Theodore Roosevelt, as long as Woodrow Wilson was physically able to operate the presidency, longer than Abraham Lincoln, and almost as long as Grover Cleveland in his two separate terms. I suggest, indeed, that a single term of seven years offers far greater opportunities to a really able man than two terms of four years which are divided by an interval. If it be said that a period of seven years is too long a period for a president whose unfitness for the office becomes obvious pretty soon, there are, I think, two decisive answers. The first is that the political parties are likely to be more careful in their nomination of a candidate if they are to live for seven years under his direction; and the political party which chooses as its nominee a second-rate candidate is much less likely than under the present scheme of the Constitution to be able to conceal from the public the fact that he is second-rate. I believe, too, that a term of this length would make the choice of candidates for the vice-presidency something taken as a matter of importance instead of being, only too often, the mechanical selection of Mr. Throttlebottom. And I suspect that there might well grow up a belief that an outgoing president ought to be succeeded by a man who has had important experience in the work of administration. In perhaps half the cases since the Civil War, the succession has fallen to a man the choice of whom was a pure gamble. And while it may be true that what was a good deal of a gamble resulted in both Abraham Lincoln and Franklin D. Roosevelt, that is no effective answer to Bagehot's famous remark that success in a lottery is no argument for lotteries.

It may be said that the long years in office of President Roosevelt are the proof that it is foolish to end at a definite period the term of a great president when he has been found. I have no doubt at all that Mr. Roosevelt belongs to the small group of presidents of the very first order; Thomas Jefferson and Lincoln apart, I venture to doubt, so far as a foreigner may express an opinion, whether the quality of his record has been surpassed. But President Roosevelt, so to say, was given his period of office after his second term by Hitler and, in a less degree, by Mussolini, rather than by the positive determination of the American people.

It was the crisis of world war that made the electorate accept Lincoln's famous maxim that one ought not to swap horses while crossing a stream. Had it not been for the dark and ugly phenomena of nazism in its various forms, the end of Mr. Roosevelt's second term would unquestionably have seen the end of his presidency. I venture, also, the opinion that, had it not been for the war and its implications, much of the domestic policy of Mr. Roosevelt, something, even, of his international policy, would have been more audacious than it was. I suspect, again, that some of the administrators who were sacrificed on the altar of congressional relationships, administrators whose success was hardly a matter of discussion, would still be in office. It is no doubt both true and important that the vital impulse contributed by Franklin Roosevelt to American affairs has been an element of outstanding importance not merely in the education of the United States, but even in the history of the world. We could ill have spared the impact that impulse created in the thought of mankind. But, again, I am bound to emphasize that, since 1940, the grounds for the retention of that impulse have been in Germany and Italy and Japan and not in the United States.

I do not deny the folly of those who worked themselves up into a fury of passionate excitement over the third term. That, until 1940, presidents were never permitted a third term is, after all, an historical accident due almost wholly to Washington's ill health and fatigue and irritation in the last months of his second term. And any detached observer would be bound to note that to the two terms of Washington's presidency, there ought, on any rational basis, to be added the seven years of passionate strain during which he was commander-in-chief of the American Armies during the War of Independence. Against President Roosevelt's period of office there ought, therefore, in all logic, to be set the fifteen years in which George Washington was the vital figure in American administration; and there is then little to choose between the two records. If more than one term is accepted as reasonable, there is no argument save that of tradition to distinguish a second term from a third, or a third from a fourth, save the quality of the incumbent's performance and his ability, especially under modern conditions, to bear the strain of the responsibility, and not least its range, that he has to bear. Washington, after all, was the president of a predominantly agrarian republic of which the population was less than three millions, and in which the very idea of the positive state had not yet come to the birth; Franklin Roosevelt was the president of a predominantly industrial society of nearly one hundred and forty millions whose interests have become positive and range over the five continents of the world. A comparison between their burdens belongs more to the realm of the poet's imagination than to that of the sober estimate of a political scientist.

9

IN THE next decade, it is inevitable that the United States should play a leading part in the world authority which will be seeking, in the next phase of history, to safeguard the world from the catastrophe of a third world war; and it is likely that the Pan-American Union, perhaps reinforced in importance by the membership of Canada, will develop into the regional organization of the Americas under that authority, and charged by it with functions both of a legislative and executive kind. If American leadership in the international realm is to be effective, two things are, I think, pretty obvious. The first is that the treaty-making power of the Senate becomes set in a very different perspective than in the past. The second is that it is at the least questionable whether American leadership can be proportionate to its power if, as in the last, bitter years of Woodrow Wilson, the president and the Senate have different party outlooks. For it is clear that if the machinery of the world authority is to function smoothly, it must have the means, especially where it is seeking to arrest aggression, to act swiftly; and, whatever the merits of the present powers which the Senate possesses, swiftness is not, nor is it likely to be, amongst them. Nor could a world authority hope to work smoothly if its decisions were always at the hazard of the winds of doctrine that blow through the Senate from time to time. And the wider the powers of that authority, the more important, especially, the agencies of economic control related to it, the more difficult would be its power to function if the United States could be committed to an agreement only after the Senate had approved.

If we assume that the immense authority of the United States is, this time, to operate as part of the world order, especially for the purpose of maintaining the peace, it seems to me beyond question that the relation of the Senate to that body will have to be put on a quite different footing from that of the eighteenth-century habits it has, thus far, consistently maintained. There is no escape from Jefferson's conclusion that diplomatic negotiations are "executive altogether." It is obvious that the American representative on any international agency must be responsible to the president alone, and act in terms of whatever policy the president may approve. Granted the tradition of senatorial power in this field, it is, obviously, in a high degree unlikely that the Senate would be prepared to part with its present power of examination and, in the case of treaties, approval by a two-thirds majority. But I venture to suggest that, if the world authority is really to work, an adaptation of the Senate's power to the conditions of our age is of the first importance. There are two categories of decision to be considered. In the first place, there is the action to be taken by states against one of their number which threatens, or embarks upon, aggression. In a world like ours where the aggressor state acts almost as it announces its declaration of war, like Germany over Poland in 1939 and over the Low Countries in 1940, or, as with Japan at Pearl Harbor, without even making the gesture of such a declaration, control by the world authority may be a matter of hours, and there is no time to wait, first, for investigation by the Foreign Relations Committee of the Senate, and then for the approval of its findings by a two-thirds majority of the whole body. The urgent principle in this realm is that if sanctions are to be invoked against an aggressor, there should be no delay in their application.

I suggest, therefore, that an amendment to the American Constitution is desirable which would permit the president alone to commit the United States to any action which a world authority to which it belonged decided to take against an imminent or actual peace-breaker. There is no serious reason to suppose that the president would abuse this power; if he did, the remedy, granted the magnitude of the offence, seems to me to be impeachment. But it is urgent to realize that time lost in this realm of policy can never be fully recovered. It is at least possible that, had Hitler known in 1939 that his attack on Poland would mobilize against him all the world save the Axis powers and the few small neutrals who were able to keep outside the conflict, he would not have unleashed the Second World War. But sanctions which have to wait while a legislature makes up its mind whether the action of its Executive should be approved are in a high degree unlikely to obtain their end. They put a premium on the side of that gambler's policy which is inherent in a gangster system like that of Hitler or of Japan. It is, indeed, not unreasonable to prophesy that, a generation from now, the great power which embarks upon aggression will attack the main industrial centres of any other power it fears without a declaration of war and without even the preliminary hypocrisies of Japan before Pearl Harbor. And to this must be added the high probability that the range of the aeroplane and its speed will have increased as greatly as the destructive power of the explosives chemists will be making. The Hitler of 1975, were he to emerge, might make New York into a shambles while the world authority was discussing his claim; and he might do so, not because of any direct quarrel with the United States, but because it was obvious to him that only the sudden paralysis of its power would afford him the gambler's chance of victory. That, after all, is the real lesson of Pearl Harbor and the atomic bomb. If the United States is to play its part in a living system of collective security, the Senate must apply a self-denying ordinance in the realm of sanctions; and to make sure of its application, when that body may contain men like Senator Nye or Senator Chandler, it is wisest to make constitutional provision for it. Granted the techniques of modern warfare, the present procedure is a relic, no longer even pleasant, of the horse-and-buggy age.

Quite different considerations, of course, apply to those areas of action with which a world authority may concern itself in which there is ample time for a full discussion of the policy proposed. Here, it is obvious, the president must carry with him the opinion of the Senate in support of the international conventions that he desires to sign. The ratification of long-term policy ought not to rest upon the judgment of a single man, however eminent the office he holds. But if this view be accepted, it follows, I think logically, that the two-thirds rule in the Senate ought to be replaced by the simple majority principle; for it may, otherwise, happen that the vote of a single senator may prevent the fulfilment of the two-thirds rule, and there is no more reason for giving a senator the right to prevent approval than there is for giving the president alone the right of confirmation. I would myself, indeed, go further than this. Since it is now possible, even though it be rare, for the president to belong to one party and the majority of the Senate to another, an international convention may be rejected by the Senate not on grounds related to its substance at all, but as part of the general domestic struggle of parties in the United States. And that rejection might easily relate to some matter in which it was highly desirable to secure uniform international action; it might be safety rules in civil aviation, or a uniform minimum standard for seamen, or the conditions upon which land is acquired by white men in Africa or Polynesia. In cases of this character, it would be a grievous thing to sacrifice the achievement of an international standard because members of the Senate are naturally anxious to discredit a president who belongs to an opposing party. And this is more definitely the case since the prospect of its rejection by the Senate may either halt an important project before it is born, or encourage other states to refuse ratification lest its rejection by Washington operate to their disadvantage.

Where the Senate refuses to confirm action taken by the president on behalf of the United States in the world authority, I suggest that the proper course of action is an appeal to the people. Obviously such a decisive procedure must be used with caution. A president ought not to have what might easily become a method of penal dissolution. He ought not to be able to exercise it in the first year of a Senate's life, which should, like the president's term, be seven years without the rule of partial elections; nor in its last; for in each of these cases the Senate is near enough to the electorate from which it receives its power, in the first case to make its decision binding, and, in the second, to have judgment passed upon it in the light of its decision within twelve months. But in the middle years of the Senate's life it is only just that the electorate should resolve the conflict. Without some such remedy as this, there is the real danger that the United States, which is essential to the status of the world authority, may be a deterrent to action of which its own citizens approve. No doubt the right to dissolve the Senate, on this kind of basis, gives the president a much larger authority than in the past. But this is not only important to give his leadership the perspective which is so urgent in the modern state; it is also important to encourage the United States to accept its full responsibility in the international order. It is difficult to exaggerate the importance of that responsibility. The history of the world between the two world wars is sufficient evidence of the price that is paid when this responsibility is absent.

10

No SMALL part of the future of federal institutions in the United States depends upon the development, above all on the plane of ideas, of its political parties. If, in a sense, there are four political parties of importance in America—the Democrats, the Republicans, the Socialists, and the Communists—the real barrier of theory lies between the first two and the second two. A distinction between the Republicans and the Democrats is far from easy to draw. In part it is geographical. No one, for instance, expects Maine or Vermont to go Democratic, as no one expects Georgia or Mississippi to go Republican. There is a slight tendency in the Democratic party to be more agrarian than industrial, though it has great influence in the big cities, more inclined to a low than a high tariff, more interested, for historical reasons, in the problems of the debtor class than of the creditor class, than its rival. But the tendency is no more than slight; and if great bankers like J. P. Morgan have been mostly Republican, great manufacturers like Myron C. Taylor, and hereditary millionaires like Vincent Astor and Marshall Field III, supported Mr. Roosevelt. It is still more important to note that leading industrialists have admitted without embarrassment that, at the time of a presidential election, they subscribed to both major parties in order to exercise a proportionate influence on either should it win at the polls. No one seriously supposes that either the Republicans or the Democrats have a clear and coherent political philosophy. Their platforms, as formulated at the presidential conventions, are little more than a *cri de cœur* of quite temporary significance, in which the attack upon their opponents is far more genuine than their promises of measures which will accompany their victory. It is, indeed, hardly an exaggeration to say that what gives the major parties their character is, above everything, the character of the candidate they adopt for president. For, at least until the election is decided, it is what their nominee has to say that makes the unattached voter decide the direction in which he will cast his ballot.

This appears quite unmistakably if one compares the outlook of Democrats and Republicans in the period of the New Deal. There have been men of an ardent progressive outlook in each; and each has contained reactionaries not less ardent. If the Democratic party has had Senator Wagner of New York, it has also had Senator Reynolds of North Carolina. If the Republicans have had the younger La Follette as senator from Wisconsin, they have also had Congressman Hamilton Fish of New York. The problem for the American voter is the very real problem that the dividing line between parties, whether as to persons or as to principles, is never clear and never straight. In the election of 1944, a Republican, Senator Ball of Minnesota, announced that he would support the candidature of President Roosevelt on international grounds; and a voter in Virginia might have been pardoned if he found it difficult to understand why Senator Byrd, of Virginia, did not decide to "bolt" his party and vote the Republican ticket during the course of the campaign.

The ideology of the two great parties, in short, is less a function of their purposes than of the person for whom they are fighting. No doubt a Republican will never make a speech without seeking to invoke the shade of Abraham Lincoln; just as every Democratic oration reminds the audience that the party is linked to the memories of Jefferson and Jackson. But all this is by-play which the speaker's hearers will take for granted. The real truth is that, since the Civil War at any rate, no candidate of any party would have found any intellectual difficulty in being the nominee of the opposing party. There are millions of voters who support the one or the other on grounds of historic connection. One expects the grandson of one of Lincoln's veterans to find a body of reasons why he should vote Republican, just as one expects the grandson of a Confederate soldier to argue that American salvation depends upon the victory of the Democratic party. But the attitude of each is an emotional rationalization which refuses to confront the vital fact that, unless there is a remarkable president in office, it is in a high degree unlikely that a Republican policy will differ in any marked degree from a Democratic policy. If one follows, for example, the speeches of the candidates in the election of 1944, it is not an unfair description of Governor Dewey's campaign to describe it as a promise to maintain the New Deal of President Roosevelt but to administer its principles more efficiently than his rival. And that has been broadly true of the conflict between American parties with a real prospect of power ever since General Grant entered the White House. The only exception to this experience was the candidature of William Jennings Bryan. He gave the Democratic party, from 1896 until his withdrawal in 1912, a Populist perspective that it did not possess under Cleveland or Woodrow Wilson; and it is reasonable to argue that, while crisis imposed it on President Roosevelt until some such period as 1936, thereafter the erosion of this attitude was an outstanding feature of his administration.

I am assuming that one digs beneath the promises to the performance. On that assumption, it is difficult to argue that a presidential election in America is, with all its excitement, very different from a choice by the voters between the two wings of a single Conservative party. The emphasis may differ at different times; but that is the reality of the choice. No doubt there are variations in the pattern of the choice; the Democratic party when led by Grover Cleveland is different from the Democratic party when led by Franklin Roosevelt, just as the Republican Party was not the same under Calvin Coolidge as it was in the brief months when Wendell Willkie was its standard bearer. But the vital fact is that the two major American parties do not seriously differ from each other in outlook and philosophy. They are more easily distinguished by the men who lead them than by the doctrines they profess.

Nor must one omit the significance of the fact that the parties on the

Left have very little hold on the electoral mind. The American Socialist party consists of a few hundred thousand people among sixty million voters; and they speak to one another without being heard, or, at least, without being taken seriously, by the public at large. The American Communist party has that remarkable zeal and energy which the Soviet Union seems able to stimulate among its devotees; and it has that almost fantastic ingenuity which enables it to appear in a variety of guises and shapes through men who form its contacts in almost every sort and kind of organization, especially among the trade-unions. But, though it has succeeded in becoming one of the bogies with which American politicians, like Mayor Hague, or, as in the election of 1944, Governor Bricker, hope to frighten the ordinary American into an acceptance of traditional habits, no one can seriously claim that the Communist party in the United States is regarded anywhere as an obvious alternative to the major parties. The very fact that it did not even run a candidate in 1944 is an illuminating illustration of the degree to which it really still remains a branch of the Soviet Foreign Office.

Other parties have from time to time developed on the Left. There was the unique La Follette machine in Wisconsin; there has been the Farmer-Labor party which, for a brief period, captured Minnesota and North Dakota. Groups have arisen, like the "End Poverty in California" movement of Mr. Upton Sinclair, or the Commonwealth Federation in the state of Washington, which revealed the incapacity of the historic parties to satisfy, in any permanent way, voters of a progressive outlook. A Liberal party, with men as various as the progressive educator, Professor Childs, or Columbia University, Professor Alvin Hansen, whose economic outlook roughly corresponds to that of Lord Keynes, and Mr. Matthew Woll, who combines a vice-presidency of the American Federation of Labor with social views compared to which Mr. Winston Churchill's may not unfairly be termed Bolshevik, announced its desire to lunch and discuss the issues of the time. But it is true to say that, since the Civil War, no third party has been able to establish itself as at once a permanent and profound influence in the politics of America. Even the Progressive party of Theodore Roosevelt in 1912, though it aroused deep passions among its members, was no more, in essence, than a temporary split in the Republican party, caused by the conviction that the Roosevelt delegates to the Republican convention of that year had not been given an honest deal by the Credentials Committee; that is shown decisively by the fact that, in 1916, Theodore Roosevelt urged his supporters to press for the nomination of Senator Henry Cabot Lodge of Massachusetts, who, during his long years in the Senate, never had a progressive thought except by accident.

From the angle of a European, and especially of a British observer, it is difficult to understand the political attitude of the American working classes. Under both Mr. Gompers and Mr. William Green, the American Federation of Labor has consistently refrained from adopting a coherent political philosophy. It has, so to say, traded the votes of its members, now to one party, and now to another, in the effort to secure particular measures in which it was interested. The party outlook of the Railroad Brotherhoods has not differed very markedly from the party outlook of Main Street. The Congress of Industrial Organizations has, indeed, since its foundation worked hard, above all in 1940 and 1944, for the return of President Roosevelt; though it is notable that Mr. John L. Lewis, the leader of the United Mine Workers, when he left the C.I.O., sought to throw all the influence of his organization against Mr. Roosevelt's re-elections. There has been a good deal of socialism among the garment workers, especially in New York; but, even while this has been the case, a distinction must be drawn between their socialist outlook and their support, in recent years, not for the Socialist candidate for the presidency, but for Mr. Roosevelt. It is notable that Mr. Sidney Hillman, leader of the Amalgamated Clothing Workers, by birth a Russian Jew and by faith a socialist, was, in 1944, the leading figure in organizing the Political Action Committee of the C.I.O., which devoted its energies to getting out, at a very considerable expenditure, the working-class vote for Mr. Roosevelt.

Whereas, in fact, the tendency in Europe has been for the trade-unions to give birth, not always directly, but fairly definitely, to a socialist party, as in Britain, or as in France and Germany and Belgium, to provide the main support for such a party, the American experience has been wholly different. It is true that there have been working-class parties here and there at different periods. William H. Sylvis, the leader of the Molders' International Union, who died while still a young man in 1869, had established connexions with the First International. The National Labor Union, at its first convention in 1866, insisted that the workingmen of America should "organize themselves into a National Labor Party," but the opposition was so strong that the resolution never had more than a paper value, and by 1872 the union was dead. There were bitter labour struggles with the employers after the panic of 1873, but none of them suggested the desirability of independent working-class action. The Greenback party gained some working-class support, but its presidential candidate, James Weaver, secured only three hundred thousand votes in the election of 1880. When Eugene Debs ran on the straight Socialist ticket in 1920, he polled only one million votes; and even the elder La Follette, as a progressive Farmer-Labor candidate in 1924, did not reach five million votes and won only his own state of Wisconsin, the political machine of which was largely in his hands. No one has ever doubted either the intellectual quality or the moral integrity of the Socialist candidate, Mr. Norman Thomas, who succeeded Mr. Debs as the leader of his party; but neither in 1940 nor in 1944 did he manage to poll a tenth part of the votes Mr. Debs was able to gather. And though the Communists have run candidates from the Russian Revolution until the election of 1944, they have not yet succeeded in gaining as many as one hundred thousand votes in an electorate which now numbers some sixty million citizens.

Anyone who analyses the party position in the United States must be careful to realize that the absence of effective parties on the Left does not for one moment mean the absence of Left policies. Certainly Jefferson and, to a limited degree, Andrew Jackson were the sponsors of Left policies in the period before the Civil War; there was a definitely liberal tinge in the conservatism of Theodore Roosevelt and Woodrow Wilson; and the first term, at least, of Franklin Roosevelt saw policies put into operation to which the quality of radicalism may be fairly applied. Yet it is broadly an accurate generalization to say that, historically, a conservative party, by whatever name it called itself, has always been in power in the United States, and that, on the federal plane, no radical party has ever been able seriously to challenge its authority. By what reasons can this curious phenomenon be explained?

We must remember, first, that it is, in fact, a good deal less unique than at first sight it seems to appear. After all, Liberals and Tories in Britain did not dream of really radical measures, except for the purposes of platform rhetoric, until the general election of 1906; and not until 1922 did a working-class party become the official opposition in the House of Commons, while it has only just attained a working majority there, even though it has twice before been the government of the day. There was a large socialist party in Germany after the time of Bismarck; but even after the collapse of the Empire in 1918, though it could form a government, it never possessed the authority effectively to govern. There have been Radical Socialist governments in France, though their policy has never been more than mildly liberal; and the two Socialist governments of which Léon Blum was prime minister in 1936 and 1937 passed measures not unlike the more audacious legislation in President Roosevelt's first term of office. But what really emerges from a comparison of the American party position with that of all Europe, save Russia since the October Revolution, is the central fact that conservatives in the United States pursued a policy which differed in degree, rather than in kind, from the policy of a radical or even a socialist government in any important European state until 1945.

It is not, on this showing, in the policies that the explanation of the difference between the parties in the United States and Europe is to be found. Nor is it easy to assign the difference to the class composition of parties in either continent. For when one examines the social origins of American legislators, including the presidents themselves after the victory of Andrew Jackson in 1828, it is not unfair to conclude that many of them were men whom a working-class party would expect to attract in Europe. Abraham Lincoln endured not less than Ramsay MacDonald all the hardships that poverty involves; and if prime ministers like Gladstone and Salisbury were rich men, so were presidents like Washington and Franklin Roosevelt. The Democratic party sent to the White House men with a modest competence like Cleveland and Woodrow Wilson; but neither Lord Oxford nor Mr. Lloyd George had greater opportunities when they started their political careers.

There is, indeed, a probability, if the evidence of the Gallup polls is valid, that there are two important aspects in which the Democratic party is different from the Republican. It seems to emerge that, on the whole, the supporters of the Democrats are younger than the supporters of the Republicans; and, what perhaps follows from this conclusion, the prosperous voter is to be found among the Republicans, and the voter of modest means among the Democrats. It is certainly, I think, significant that the main sources of hostility to Franklin Roosevelt were among the wealthy classes; and that this has a relation of some permanence is suggested by the fact that the main supporters of "appeasement" at the time of the Civil War were the wealthy manufacturers and merchants of New York and Boston and Philadelphia. It is clear, too, that if one makes a correlation between the census returns and the election results, the drift in the cities is towards a Democratic emphasis among the poorer sections and a Republican emphasis among the more well-to-do. But against this must be set the fact that the large owners of cotton and tobacco are mostly Democrats by tradition, while the farmers of New England and the Northwest are mainly Republican. From this it follows that each party is historically a coalition in which the antagonism of each part to the other emerges as soon as one examines the direction of its economic interests.

One is tempted to conclude from all this that the time is rapidly approaching for a realignment of political parties in the United States. It is significant that the wealthy in both parties combined, after the first few months of Mr. Roosevelt's first administration, to limit his power to secure the passage of radical legislation. It is, I think, still more significant that, with the development of the Congress of Industrial Organizations, the tendency becomes more marked for the unions which compose it to take an increasing part in politics. And this tendency is likely to grow for the simple but inevitable reason that the growth of federal intervention in economic affairs is certain to continue. The coming of social security, the implications of the Labor Relations Act, the federal control of hours and wages, these, to take instances only, involve the need to establish criteria of action in the shaping of which labour is bound to take an increasing interest in order to take an increasing share; the Taft-Hartley Act is likely to strengthen this need. The point at which this development is likely to emerge is set by the experience of Europe. Where the period of economic expansion reaches its limit there emerges always a disparity of opportunity which results, sooner or later, in an antagonism of interest. And where that antagonism begins to take a conscious form the result is always that a party is formed to safeguard interests, on both sides, which feel themselves to be in jeopardy.

No one can examine the main political parties in the United States to-day without seeing quite clearly that they are in essence great coalitions of interests which range from the Left to the Right, though each, no doubt, excludes, if it can, the extreme Left. And that is not merely true of our own day; it has been broadly true at least since the time of Andrew Jackson and, perhaps, even since the time of Thomas Jefferson. Its result is the simple but vital one that, save in periods of momentous crisis, like the Civil War, the policy of each party is acceptable to its rival. Few presidents, I suppose, have been more hated than Franklin Roosevelt; but, in three of his four elections, the platform of the major rival candidate has only been verbally distinguished from his own. We naturally think of Henry Cabot Lodge as the senator who, as chairman of the Foreign Affairs Committee of the Senate, secured the rejection of the Treaty of Versailles and kept the United States out of the League of Nations. But it is important also to remember that, as early as 1916, Senator Lodge was a vigorous advocate of a League of Nations to which the United States should belong and to which full powers should be accorded to deal with any possible aggressor. Both parties have always offered, so far, enough concessions to the forces of Labour to be able to divide the votes of the workers; and it is only in recent years that the trade-unionist in the cities has begun to suspect a special affiliation between the Republican party and business interests which would be harmful to him if a Republican were to reach the White House.

It was easy to maintain this agreement upon fundamentals, as well as this continuity in techniques, until at least some such period as the Great Depression of 1929. No doubt from time to time one could hear the creaks in the party machines as they moved majestically on their way. But, until 1929, the rise of third parties always served to correct any large departure from public expectation among Democrats or Republicans. And, until 1929, there was always sufficient economic elbow-room in the United States to make a third party little more than an incentive to adjustment. Until the nineties there was the frontier; after the possibilities of the land began to be exhausted, there was the immense internal growth upon the industrial plane; while during that growth, and beyond it, there was the continued creation of purchasing power for the little man by the different bonus schemes for veterans of the wars in which America participated. There is, indeed, a real sense in which the bonus secured by the American Legion and similar bodies for its members, from the Civil War down to the present time, may be regarded as inherently another form of that expansion which the frontier symbolized for so long.

But the problem since 1929 has begun to assume a shape quite different from that in the earlier years of the republic. With both the major parties committed to an individualist social policy (which does not, of course, prevent each from accusing the other of betraying traditional American ideas at each election), it becomes ever more dubious whether full employment is available in terms of individualism. The trend of modern economic theory rejects the concepts of free enterprise upon which the main American parties rely; it is, indeed, no exaggeration to say that in the last generation full employment has been attained only in periods of war as a result of the immense orders placed by government with manufacturers. With the cessation of those orders, the pursuit of the historic American policy of free enterprise is likely to result either in mass unemployment or in a grave reduction in the standard of living. To avoid being impaled upon the horns of this dilemma it becomes necessary both for Republicans and Democrats to accept a distribution of purchasing power quite different from anything that America has previously known. But to accept that difference means, quite simply, the recognition that the age of free enterprise has gone. That recognition, in its turn, means a wide extension of federal ownership and control in industry and agriculture and, therewith, a fundamental alteration in the kind of economic privileges which the leaders of American industry have enjoyed. The situation then emerges in which either the political parties are at odds with the leadership of industry, or that leadership refuses to accept the new principles of organization to which political parties seeking an electoral majority are bound to move. At this point, as I think, the organized workers of the United States are faced with the necessity of acting upon postulates which business leaders quite obviously reject. And I do not see how they can accept the necessity of such action within the framework of the existing party structure. American labour, in short, will be driven into independent political action in the post-war period much as circumstances forced the British trade-unions into a similar path. They have been able to play both sides so far much as the British workingmen were either liberal or conservative until 1906. It is even possible that some of the American labour leaders will resist the tendency to independence, as Mr. Ramsay MacDonald did so long as he hoped for a Liberal seat in the House of Commons, or as Labour men like Mr. G. N. Barnes and Mr. G. H. Roberts did at the close of the war of 1914 when they clung to Mr. Lloyd George. But they will increasingly find that the more adamant the demands of labour, the more unified will be the activity of the Republican and Democratic parties; and the more unified that activity, the wider will be the gap which separates capital from labour in the United States. It is difficult, indeed, not to infer from the Political Action Committee which Mr. Sidney Hillman formed in 1944 the first effective emergence of political independence among the trade-unions. Too, while it may be true that the influence of that Committee was overwhelmingly thrown on Mr. Roosevelt's side, it is reasonably clear that the reason for the Committee's decision lay less in the character of the Democratic party than in the policy on labour matters it imputed to Mr. Roosevelt, and, still more, to his opponent Mr. Dewey. It is no more likely to retain what may be termed the habit of coalition than the Labour party in Great Britain was likely to retain the habit of coalition with Mr. Churchill. On this assumption, it is at least probable that American trade-unionism will pass through two phases on the political plane. As soon as a conservative Democrat fights for the presidency against a conservative Republican—and this may well be in 1948—the American workers, like the British workers in 1906, will move swiftly towards independent political action. In the first phase of that independence, no doubt, they will be a relatively minor party on the federal stage, insisting that they inherit the traditions of Jefferson and Lincoln. But, in that first phase also, they will make clear the fact that Republicans and Democrats alike speak for an America from which, in any profound way, the interest of the workingman is excluded on all fundamental matters. They will then be driven to the Left, like the British Labour party; and they will find not only that this movement, whatever name it be given, makes them in fact a socialist party; they will find, also, that their opponents, both Republican and Democratic, will discover that there is little essential difference between them. When this emerges, the American party situation is not likely to differ in fundamentals from that upon the Continent in Europe. It is even possible, moreover, that the arrival of this situation may be quickened by the influence of the Soviet Union upon the industrial and political habits of Western and even Asiatic civilization.

I add that I do not think this view is falsified by the traditional habits of the "Solid South." For it is important to remember that the South is being industrialized at a great speed; that great numbers of its Negro population are migrating to the North and the West; and that the anxiety of the South to attract industry as rapidly as possible will both change its position as a "colony" of the North and make its industrial problems issues which call for federal action rather than for decisions separately made in each Southern state. The next age in American history is more likely than any previous period to dissipate the mythology of states' rights by a growing insistence upon equal and uniform treatment for things that are equal and uniform. It may then well emerge that the classic theory of federalism is obsolete in its historic American form; and there is no plane upon which its obsolescence is more likely to be demonstrated than in its expression in party organization. For an America that confronts relations of employer and employed which have been so long known in Europe may with some confidence be predicted to adjust those relations in terms which, whatever their names, repeat the experience of Europe. It is at least of the higher significance that this is what is happening in the Dominion of Canada.

IV

American Political Institutions:
State and Local

I

WHEN the fifty-five men who met at Philadelphia in the spring of 1787 drafted the Federal Constitution they were, in fact, giving birth to a single commonwealth. The nature of their achievement was concealed from most of the citizens, partly by the illusion which history deposits, and partly because, with the possible exception of Alexander Hamilton, none of the members of the Federal Convention would have dreamed of denying the character of sovereignty to any of the thirteen states which were forming a more perfect union. It required, indeed, four years of a bloody civil war to make it indisputable that the states of which the United States is composed are provinces of a great commonwealth from which they cannot legally secede, and to the political character of which they must ultimately adjust their vital political habits. It is unquestionable that an American state, even when it is as small as Delaware in area or as small as Nevada in population, has, nevertheless, an initiative in law-making to which no English county, and, still less, any French department, can pretend. All of them have features of their own, and some of them can look back upon a history of which they are entitled to be proud. But they are not sovereign states in any effective sense of that complex term. Rather they are provinces, more or less important, which do not need to look to Washington in determining certain aspects of their behaviour, as every area of local government in England and Wales must look to Whitehall and Westminster if it becomes possessed of the desire to embark upon innovations.

The American state is a province in a greater commonwealth, but it is a province in which it is not difficult to distinguish what may perhaps be termed the vestigial remains of sovereign power. Young or old, it has a governor and a legislature, the latter, with the exception of Nebraska, being composed of two chambers. Young or old, it has its own judiciary,

138

which ends in the dignity of a State Supreme Court; it has its own Civil Service, and it is likely to have its own Public Service Commission developing, in an ever-increasing degree, its own state administrative law. It is pretty certain to have its own educational system, which leads to fulfilment in a state university. It will have its own way of giving to or taking from its urban and rural areas the power of self-government. It will have a militia and a state police. In most states there will be an attempt to give reality to the idea of popular sovereignty by the use of the initiative and the referendum and, sometimes, of the recall.

But that is not all. Many of the states are built around traditions which are significant rivulets in the mainstream of modern history. Virginia, Massachusetts, Rhode Island, Pennsylvania, California, Illinois, New York, these states, to take examples only, have a history with an epic quality about it. No one can read the record of the opening of the West without the sense that as that dynamic movement settled down into the channels of constitutional stability, it gave birth both to ideas and to ideals which have made a deep impact upon the rest of the world. It is a great thing to be a citizen of a commonwealth in which Chaucer and Shakespeare, Newton and Dickens, Nelson and Robert Owen, were also citizens. But it is difficult to think that a man can come from Virginia without an analogous pride in that great dynasty which gave Washington, Jefferson, and Madison to the presidential record, or that a man from Illinois can be conscious of his state as an historic memory without thinking of that supreme day in modern history when Abraham Lincoln set out, not only for Washington, but for that road which made the cemetery at Gettysburg the twin sister of Periclean Athens. It is difficult, no doubt, to believe that any resident of Boston ever had a stirring of the heart when he watched the remarkable Adams family look down from the height of their great gifts upon ordinary mankind; but it is, too, at least as difficult to read the work of Emerson or Thoreau, of Theodore Parker or Mr. Justice Holmes, without the conviction that a citizen of Massachusetts knows as well as any Englishman or Frenchman how to dream great dreams. The very fact of being an American is, in an important sense, already a challenge to the Old World; but the additional fact that one inherits the achievement of almost all the original thirteen states gives a colour to life's adventure the more flashing and the more proud the more fully the achievement is known.

The states are provinces of which the sovereignty has never since 1789, been real. But they are provinces which, with all their limitations, have something of the magic of Athens and of Rome, of London and of Paris and of Florence. They breed in most of their citizens an undeniable parochialism; but the states are few in which there is not something akin to loveliness in their parochialism. Anyone who reads, for example, the address of Emerson at Concord that celebrates the memory of the Revolution can hardly doubt that the farmers and shopkeepers and labourers who, with their wives, gathered to listen to it felt that they were sharing in a great tradition which added to the dignity of human nature. And to that sense of participation there must be added the elevation of personality which came to a large percentage of the emigrants who exchanged the poverty and tyranny they had known in Europe for an atmosphere in which, until the beginning of the twentieth century, they had a measure of hope and exhilaration they had never previously known. There are plenty of dark places in the life of every American state, a frustration which often goes deep, the exchange of one wage slavery for another. The democracy of the American states has always been partial and, for not a few of the races they have absorbed, at many points pitiful and incomplete. Above all, as an idea, it is far more complex and interstitial than most of its protagonists, even its European protagonists, have been willing to admit. The elements of which it is compounded in a state, for instance, like Mississippi, or Louisiana, makes the democratic ethos of Sweden or Denmark a thing that challenges comparison with anything these Southern states have known. There has been a harshness to minorities, a suspicion of newcomers, a hostility to those who depart from the uniform line which the past has imposed, which combine to make intolerance in American states a phenomenon as real and as widespread as tolerance itself. The Negro, the Oriental, the Jew, the Roman Catholic, have all tasted of its bitterness; and few people who examine either the Haymarket riots, or the trial of Sacco and Vanzetti, but must be persuaded that no simple formula will explain the working of democracy in American states. And once the formula of democracy ceases to be simple, it raises grave issues which need constant readjustment to a new mental climate if democracy is to hope for a continuing reality.

For democracy in the states does not mean merely that men and women can choose their governors, important though that choice may be. They choose their legislators; they choose, or may choose, a number of officials whose functions may vary from that of the attorney-general of the state to the superintendent of education or the head of the medical service. It is comparatively rare for the governor of a state to have at his disposal any great volume of patronage; more usually, the electorate makes its decision, even though, in general, it is rare for a party to find that there is a split in the distribution of offices. The nomination, as a rule, is decided by the political machine of the state; and the political machine, in its turn, is at least likely to be in the hands of the boss who dominates the machines. Senator Quay in Pennsylvania, Mr. Barnes in New York, Mr. Roraback in Connecticut, will have at least a predominant influence in the choice of the main nominees of their party. When they decide who is to run, they take into account the character of the electorate they seek to dominate. A Democratic state in New England will certainly contain some Roman Catholics of Irish origin; a Republican state in the Middle West will look with anxiety for suitable Germans and Scandinavians. It is rare, in the South, for the Democrats to consider a Roman Catholic as suitable, for the Fundamentalism of the South still looks upon candidates of the Roman persuasion with profound suspicion. In the Harlem district of New York City it is important to appeal to the Negro voters; and in the Bronx a Jewish candidate may well secure votes which transcend any party allegiance.

The outcome is like nothing so much as a crazy quilt in which each party is seeking to maximize the appeal of its list of candidates. Generally speaking, it is unlikely that the men who are chosen, even when they are elected, will go very far. A good governor may reach the Senate; the governor of a critical state, Ohio, New York, Kansas, may well, if he makes a genuine reputation in office, have at least a chance of the presidential nomination. Both Roosevelts, like Grover Cleveland and Al Smith, were governors of New York; Mr. Landon was governor of Kansas; Mr. Coolidge passed through the governorship of Massachusetts to the vice-presidency and then, on the death of President Harding, to the White House. If it is an exaggeration to say that the governance of a state is the high road to a national career in politics, at least it creates the possibility of that adventure. But there is the important limitation that a state position in a state the votes of which are unlikely to raise any questions is not very likely to move a man from the state to the national theatre. Maine and Vermont are always Republican; and there is little reason for their leading men to dream that the final national eminence awaits them. That is true, also, in the main of the Solid South; the depth of its attachment to the Democratic party means, in general, that its outstanding political figures must rest content with the Senate as the final achievement to which they can look forward.

State politics have changed a good deal in the last thirty or forty years. Partly that is due to the superior and growing interest of federal issues; partly to the growing dependence of the states upon assistance from the federal government. The turnover of personalities in state politics is very much more pronounced than in the federal scene; there is less excitement, the issues are less important, the achievement possible is on a narrower basis. No doubt it is true that state government has an importance that it is easy to underrate; but it is also true that it is increasingly less important than before the twentieth century began, because the implications of American federalism are far less significant than they were in the nineteenth century. And if it is true that, every now and again, state government makes possible a great career in federal life, it is still more true that the vast majority of the politicians it attracts have little influence outside the area in which they operate. The capital city of most states is not often the vital metropolis in which the effective life of the state is organized; Harrisburg, in Pennsylvania, for example, is never likely to compete with Philadelphia in importance, any more than Albany is likely to compete with New York. The fact is that, as a general rule, neither the scope of its functions, nor the opportunity it affords, will make the politics of a state significant as Washington is significant. And not a few of the states are deprived of anything that can be called a profound political life for the simple reason that they are dominated by economic interests which transcend all party interests. Montana is in the hands of the great copper interests; Delaware is the bailiwick of the Du Pont family; even North Carolina must operate within a framework defined by the masters of cotton and tobacco; while, in the ultimate analysis, Louisiana is dependent upon the great sugar interests. And where the economic domination is absent, there are alternative forms of pressure of which the parties must take account. The racial elements, in the states like Minnesota and Nebraska, the religious impact which the cardinals can make in cities like Boston and Chicago, the economic authority of a great family in a particular city, like Muncie, Indiana, the determination in the West that white supremacy shall not be challenged by Oriental immigration, all these make for a framework of limitation within which the state parties must find the means of accommodation.

And that accommodation they manage to find. Sometimes it is attained by the decision not to raise an inconvenient question; the treatment of the Negroes is a typical example of this approach. Sometimes it is attained by raising the issue in such a fashion that it is imposed on the parties in the state by influence which normally hold themselves aloof from the ordinary political conflict: an example of this attitude is the attitude of the American Bar Association, in its state organizations, when it presses upon both major parties, as in New York, those candidates for the Bench of whom it approves. It is a fair generalization to say that both Republicans and Democrats assume that they will not, if successful at the polls, so use their power as to make the position of their rivals impossible. There may be a more profound emphasis here or there; but what emerges as fundamental is the fact that the general contour of state politics is rarely very different whether Republicans or Democrats be in office. Few governors of New York State in modern times have done a more cleansing job than Charles Evan Hughes a generation ago; but there was little in his record that would not have been gladly approved either by President Roosevelt, when he was governor, or by his Democratic successor, Mr. Herbert Lehman.

It is, of course, both true and important that, from time to time, state politics take on a special hue either from the character of the machine in power, or from the sources of the support upon which that machine depends. The progressive period in the history of Wisconsin has rarely been rivalled since the Civil War, while the state of Georgia under Governor Talmadge had a peculiar character of its own. It is far from easy for a foreigner to understand why the citizens of Texas endured the era of the Fergusons; and the habits of Louisiana, when Senator Huey Long dominated its life, obviously raise issues which are bound, one day, to assume a pivotal importance in the democratic life of America. There are periods when the governor of a state refuses to take an initiative of any kind; and there are, equally, periods when a governor, like New York under Al Smith, is able to rouse the attention of all politically minded

Americans by the quality of his achievement. There are states where the governor is elected on grounds of which it is not easy to see the political relevance; a candidate who is successful because of his skill in playing the guitar makes one feel that the rivals in Dickens' Eatanswill were dealing with sober and serious issues. Nor would any discussion of state politics in America be complete which failed to note the corybantic excesses of a well-known orchestra leader, Mr. Vic Myers, in Washington, whose success was built on methods which even the famous Barnum might well have envied.

It would not be true to say that the result of a state election can be received with indifference by the voters; for a good governor may make a great difference in the area he seeks to control, and his relations with Washington may make a real impact upon the lives of the citizens he rules. But it is, I think, true to say that the significance of the governor is set in the framework of his federal ambitions rather than of his purposes in the state; and it is still more true that the members of a state legislature are likely to be men of no particular importance who rarely sit long enough in session to work out a programme which arouses deep interest among their constituents. And it is grimly true of at least two-thirds of the states that the effective character of the policies they pursue is determined more by pressure groups and lobbyists outside the category of elected persons than it is by the men whom the voters have chosen to represent them. No doubt there are exceptions to this generalization; but it is not excessive to insist that the real power in Connecticut lay, while he lived, with J. H. Roraback, who was the protector of the public utilities in that state; while the real power in Wyoming was in the hands of the great lumber millionaire, Weyerhaeuser. No one who examined the influence of Mr. Flagler in Florida or of Mr. Mellon in Pennsylvania will need to doubt that their wills were treated with a respect at least as great as that of the official choices of the electors. The party machine in each state is linked to a system of vested interests the views of which it dares to neglect only at its peril. That is well known both to the Republicans and the Democrats; and where the vested interest, like that of Mr. Mellon in Pennsylvania, is really powerful, the effective centre of political importance is only formally in the governor's mansion or in the chambers of the legislature.

It is, of course, beyond all doubt that crisis makes the power of a governor or a legislature of special importance where it occurs. And it is, no doubt, the case that the emergence of crisis pushes the vested interest into the background. A great strike, like the Teamsters' strike in Minneapolis in 1934, invests the governor with a power of choice which it is rarely easy for any vested interest to challenge. On the other hand, it is clear from the unhappy fate of Governor Altgeld of Illinois in the early nineties that where the crisis is big enough to involve presidential action, it is in the White House that the essential decisions are made; and a governor who sought to move in a direction different from that of the president would probably be terminating his political career. This is only one illustration of the general theme that the states are basically provinces of the great American commonwealth and that provincial purposes are always ultimately subordinate to the purposes of Washington.

The American state, of course, has real roots in the affection of its people; and it is upon the habits of the state that their citizenship depends. The area of its potential functions is large, and that despite the immense development of centralization in the last thirty years. Its weakness, as a political organization, is twofold. There is the weakness which comes from the fact that in the interrelations of political and economic power it is usually those who possess economic power who have the final word. Usually, though not always; for the machine so skilfully built up by Huey Long in Louisiana represented the working and lower middle classes, the "poor white trash" of the state, who gave him the possession of its authority in return for the bread and circuses he provided upon so ample a scale. But, so far, the elbow-room for expansion which America has possessed has made the technique of men like Huey Long only rarely successful. The state political machine, whether Democratic or Republican, may reward its supporters with the spoils of power; but it is difficult to see that any state, except Wisconsin during the supremacy of the elder La Follette, moved in any continuous way in a direction disapproved of by those who controlled its main economic interests. Every state, this is to say, has really had an invisible government, to use Elihu Root's effective phrase, which, in one way or another, has set the criteria of action for the formally elected government. It has been the natural consequence of this situation that the policies both of the governor and the legislature of each state are as much an effect as a cause.

The second great weakness of the American state as a political entity lies partly in the large number of offices to which politicians must be elected, and partly in the discontinuity of legislative action, which prevents the operation of a good deal of that criticism of the administration which makes its work effective. That judges should be chosen by popular vote is curious, though intelligible in the light of American historical conditions; and it would certainly be difficult to maintain with any confidence that the judges in those states who are appointed to office by the nomination of the governor, with the approval of his council, have a better record than those judges from states where they are elected by popular vote. Massachusetts may have been given by the nomination of the governor judges of the first order like Shaw and Holmes; but the system of election gave Cardozo to New York in our own day, and Samuel Nelson nearly a century before. And nomination produced the appointment of Judge Webster Thayer to the Superior Court of Massachusetts, a choice as dubious as any produced by popular election.

But the range of popular choice is far more extensive than most Europeans can even imagine. Offices as various as those of the attorney-general, the auditor of state expenditure, the secretary of state, the commissioner for agriculture, the superintendent of education, the superintendent of public lands, the surveyor-general, the state treasurer, may all be filled by persons chosen by popular vote. And to them must be added a mass of city and county officials, the mayor, the coroner, the public prosecutor, the sheriff, aldermen, and councillors, who, like the governor and the lieutenant-governor, are chosen on a straight party ticket. And to all this must be added the complications begotten of that direct primary, which, in its origins, was an optimistic search for means to protect the citizen against the despotism of a party, and the possibilities of the recall, which sought to permit a significant percentage of the electorate to elicit an expression of public opinion against an official whose conduct they regarded as unsatisfactory. There must be added, further, the proviso in a majority of state constitutions that, save in a special session, their legislatures shall not sit for more than forty-five or fifty or ninety days in each year. This provision, in its turn, must be set in the context of the initiative and the referendum, imported, in the first instance, from Switzerland, by enthusiastic citizens from the Western states who believed that direct democracy was the cure for all the diseases of the body politic.

So that in most, though not in all, states, their citizens, on the plane of action by the state, are choosing a large number of officials, about many of whom they know nothing at all save that they are Democrats or Republicans, and in a considerable degree, further, they are voting upon legislation referred to them for judgment, often with little preparation for the judgment they have to make save the propaganda skill of the pressure groups associated with the measures involved. In some states, too, they may be asked to exercise the power of recall against an official, who might be the governor or a judge, over issues which call for both insight into character and skill in weighing testimony. At the back of it all is the unbreakable American faith in the judgment of the people, or, at least, of the people not of African descent. Perhaps, too, there is related to this faith a conviction, fairly widespread, for example, in the states of the Northwest, that the wider the degree of popular participation in government the more closely related to public well-being will be the results achieved.

2

THE results have rarely borne out the simple faith on which they are based. Rather is it true to say that the sheer volume and frequency of the choices a citizen is asked to make tends to intensify, save in rare instances, the power of the party machine in the state. For, when special excitement is absent, the number of citizens who will make the necessary investigations which give their judgment an independent validity is pretty small. They take on trust, for the most part, the advice of a person or an organziation in which they have confidence; or, in many instances, they support the candidate or the issue which they see in a perspective of affection.

An American business man to whom the local Rotary Club president
means a great deal, the veteran of the First World War who finds his
leisure made happy in the evenings he spends at the club house of the
Legion, even the housewife who admires the woman speaker of the
Thursday Luncheon Club and learns from her to follow the counsels of
the League of Women Voters, all of them, where their political views are
not a simple inheritance from an earlier generation, vote by authority
rather than by examination. For the latter, they have rarely the time ; and
though there is much to be said for the view that Americans have better
schooling than any people outside the Scandinavian states, they have not
yet attained the level where public activity seems to them more important
than private interests. So that where they are asked to do so much, they
tend, crisis always excepted, mechanically to accept the judgment which
gives them a feeling of confidence.

It is hard, otherwise, to explain certain continuities of state tradition for which, otherwise, there is no shadow of justification. The Republicanism of Maine and Vermont is an inherited attitude of mind quite
independent of the historical conditions in the United States, just as the
Solid South votes the Democratic ticket on issues which were finally
settled at Appomattox. In cases like these, the candidate who secures the
nomination is virtually elected. A Democrat in Maine has significance
only at the national convention of the Democratic party, just as a Republican in Georgia is merely a vote to be counted when his party chooses
its presidential candidate. And alongside these historic continuities there
are economic emphases which rarely transcend tradition. A voter in
Nevada or Nebraska would find it difficult, as a general rule, to support
a candidate who was hostile to silver coinage. The residents of Beacon
Hill in Boston, or of Milton and Quincy, almost start from the political
postulate that an Irish-American in Massachusetts ought to be a police-
man and not a governor ; just as the Yankee farmers of Connecticut have
a healthy distrust of members of the Yale Faculty or commuters to New
York who are not either of old New England stock or millionaires. There
are areas of California where it is unnecessary even to argue that trade-
unions are a menace to American prosperity ; and a man of radical convictions in some of the steel towns of Pennsylvania must either have a
genius for silence or decide pretty early to search for a place where he
may find less one-sided hostility.

Attempts have, of course, been made, as with the direct primary and
the short ballot, to correct the power of the state machine whether Republican or Democratic. I do not think they can be regarded as more than
very moderately successful. Their inadequacy lies less in the procedures
themselves than in the simple fact, set down nearly two centuries ago by
Edmund Burke, that men are more important than measures. Once a
figure of outstanding ability who has profound ambition emerges, the
destination to which he seeks to move is almost invariably Washington.
In the result, a career in state politics is either no more than a stage in an

ascent, or a means of satisfying the ambitions of second-rate politicians. Al Smith was a remarkable governor of New York; but he looked upon the Executive Mansion at Albany as a halt in his journey to the White House, and when he failed to reach the presidency in 1928, it never occurred to him to return directly to New York politics. After Governor Landon had fought Mr. Roosevelt in 1936 for the presidency he, too, ceased to play a part in the politics of Kansas. An analysis of state politicians, in short, makes it clear that they either use the local theatre as a basis from which to move forward, or regard it as the culmination of their hopes. And if they take this second view, their prospects depend very largely on their relation to the state machine, even, it may be, to the attitude taken towards them by the boss of that machine, the more especially if the context of their political career is set by the rural, rather than by the urban, side of the particular state.

The state machine, a small number of great cities apart, provides the party with all the qualities out of which its character is moulded. It has one single aim—that of victory at the polls; and its interest in policies is given, not by what they are in themselves, but by the contribution they can make to victory. For victory means jobs for the henchmen of the party in the state; it means the chance of lucrative contracts; it means safeguarding its dependents, very often, from the necessity of earning a living in the ordinary way. The successful machine may put its own lawyers on the courts; it may secure the support of powerful business interests; still more, it may prevent those interests from helping the other side. The machine is essentially a broker of ideas; it sets itself the task of finding out what principles of action are most likely to win a majority. It has to find the right candidates for the right jobs; perhaps, even more, it has to prevent the wrong candidates from being chosen. It must make the voters feel that their well-being is directly related to the victory of the party it controls; and to create that feeling it has to have an accurate sense of the influences which count for most in the state. It is not an organization for the discovery of ideas for their own sake; it is an organization of men who come out first for the winning ideas at the right time. Its business is thus to keep its finger on the pulse of public opinion; but it must be able, as it judges public opinion, to work out with precision the weight that attaches to the different elements out of which public opinion is compounded. It reaches out from the state boundaries to the smallest precinct in the area it seeks to capture. Those who control it must know not only how to win the support of the great corporation; they must know as well how to convince a group of poor immigrants, to whom citizenship has just been granted, that their friendship is imperative. They must be able to measure just what volume of reward the support they gain requires without risking, in the gift of that reward, the good opinion of the mugwumps whose vote determines most elections. They must possess every type of political *condottiere,* from an orator like Choate to a drill sergeant like Mayor Hague of New

Jersey. If they can combine supreme ability with what is not very different from the quintessence of corruption, as the Democratic party did with Huey Long in Louisiana, they achieve the ideal at which they aim. What, on the other hand, they must avoid is the type of whom "Boss" Barnes of New York was an important example—the kind of leader whose likes and dislikes threaten the power of the machine to go into action when the battle comes, without risking the division of his forces. And they must avoid, also, entrusting their leadership to men who rapidly create indignation or contempt, either by such open corruption as that of Tweed, or such open stupidity as that of Mayor Hylan of New York.

The state machine must not only seem to have ideas upon which it can act; it must have those ideas. And it must accrete to itself, whether the state be large or small, leaders who have the power to make it significant on the national stage of politics. William Jennings Bryan made the Democratic party of Nebraska a matter of concern to all Americans for nearly forty years; Borah made the small state of Idaho an element no Republican convention, and no Republican president, could possibly overlook. In the generation before the entrance of America into the First World War Ben Tillman achieved a similar result for the Democratic party of South Carolina; and ex-Governor Stassen of Minnesota has, even before he has reached middle age, made his state a power among Republicans, so that great states like New York and Pennsylvania are acutely aware of its significance.

Generally speaking, the political machine of any state must, above all, beware of giving offence to elements of importance in the area that it controls. No doubt there are states in which some vested interest is so powerful that its support is decisive; this is true of the influence of the Du Ponts in Delaware, and of the Guggenheims in Montana. But domination as simple as this is exceptional. New York is far beyond the control of the House of Morgan, just as Pennsylvania is far beyond the control of the Mellon interests. For long years, Connecticut was dominated by J. Henry Roraback, as the servant of Connecticut Light and Power. But he made the fatal mistake of assuming that it was not necessary to be interesting; and the result was that when Wilbur L. Cross, a professor emeritus of distinction at Yale University, interested the electors in his campaign for the governship because, at a time of crisis, he combined honesty with the ability to be a "character" almost in the style of Dickens, the Republican ascendency in Connecticut was overwhelmed in defeat. The experience of Connecticut is not, of course, unique; there is hardly a major state in the Union which has not duplicated it since the Civil War. And there are not a few states in which, even within a single party, the unity of the machine is constantly in jeopardy. When "Len" Small was governor of Illinois, there were as many Republican politicians among his enemies as there were Democrats; and the conflict between Frank O. Lowden and Morton D. Hull for the governorship of Illinois in 1916 revealed much the same position. Senator Byrd of Virginia rose to the governorship by seeking a political issue which would enable him to oust Senator Swanson from the leadership of his party in that state; and it is true to say that, ever since his successful reorganization of the Virginia administrative machine in 1926, he has been fighting hard in his own party to keep the leadership he then won.

Few states, moreover, avoid the political complications which ensue from the fact that their parties have a boss to whom the elected persons, from the governor downwards, must pay obedience. Theodore Roosevelt spoke loudly of his independence when he was Governor of New York; but he was always careful to keep in step as much as possible with Boss Platt and his machine. Lincoln Steffens, in a famous passage, has told us that the "permanent governor" of Rhode Island was blind General Charles R. Brayton; from a room in the office of the sheriff he made the decisions which governors and state legislatures alike accepted.[1] Everyone knew where the real power lay; and his authority was exercised without any effort to conceal it. Even more dramatic is the famous speech of Senator Root to the New York Constitutional Convention of 1915 in which he painted his famous picture of the "invisible government" of New York State. "From the days of Fenton and Conkling and Arthur and Cornell and Platt," he said, "from the days of David B. Hill down to the present time, the government of the state has presented two different lines of activity, one of the constitutional and statutory officers of the state, and the other of the party leaders—they call them party bosses. For I don't remember how many years, Mr. Conkling was the supreme ruler in the state; the governor did not count, the legislature did not count; . . . it was what Mr. Conkling said, and in a great outburst of public rage he was pulled down. Then Mr. Platt ruled the state; for nigh upon twenty years he ruled it. It was not the governor; it was not the legislature; it was not any elected officers; it was Mr. Platt." [2]

The sources from which this "invisible government" drew its power in so many states, Democratic and Republican alike, were far from simple. Some of it was due to the fact that both members of the executive and members of the legislature had so short a period of office; some of it was due to the fact that either law or custom made continuous re-eligibility impossible; some of it, as Root himself said, was due to the division of powers among the executive officers; and some of it was due to the fact that renomination was always difficult, and sometimes impossible, if the elected person had failed to satisfy the "invisible government." The elder La Follette has told us how, in his own state of Wisconsin, "the bosses did not regard the selection of a candidate for governor as a matter in which the voters of Wisconsin were entitled to have any voice. During a recess in the sessions of the convention, Gov-

---

[1] Lincoln Steffens, *Autobiography* (New York: Harcourt, Brace, 1931), p. 465.
[2] *New York Constitutional Convention of 1915* (Albany: New York State Library, 1915), Vol. III, pp. 3387–88.

ernor Upham was summoned before an executive session of the Wisconsin bosses, informed that he would not be given the endorsement of a renomination, and his successor, Edward Scofield, was chosen." [3] This is only a singularly effective description of what has happened, in greater or lesser degree, in most states in the Union at some time in their history. And perhaps the most important comment to be made on Senator La Follette's narrative is that when he broke with the orthodox Republican machine in Wisconsin, he had to build up his own personal machine to protect his authority both in Madison and in Washington.

There is little that is singular to the United States in the habits so revealed except the open and frank admission of their reality. No British prime minister could hold power for long if it were not for the patronage, including the honours list, that he controls; and any careful examination of the British Dominions would show that the habits of their political parties are about midway between the open machine politics of an American state and the technique of delicate concealment which is regarded as fitting in London. The system in France, under the Third Republic, and of Italy up to the seizure of power by Mussolini, differed in expression and method rather than in principle from the character of the American system. It is, no doubt, true that every so often the voters revolted against a boss who went too far, as Mr. Root tells us New York revolted against Roscoe Conkling. It is true, also, that various expedients, like the direct primary and the short ballot, have been tried in order to transfer the centre of effective political power from the boss and his machine back to the electorate. But I do not think any of them can be said to have scored an outstanding success.

The reason for this is, broadly, twofold. In the first place, the machine politician was a professional who devoted the whole of his time to the job; the voter, and, very often the reformer also, was an amateur who was interested for a brief period or else was concerned with some particular change. The only way in which the elector could assert his power in any continuous way was by himself becoming a professional. Woodrow Wilson in New Jersey, Hiram Johnson in California, Charles Evans Hughes in New York, all found that there was no other means of securing the aims they had in view. And when it was obvious that public opinion in their states was moving with some enthusiasm in their direction, there was about an equal chance that they would find that they could count upon the support of the very bosses whose policies they were attacking. We must not forget that Platt made Theodore Roosevelt and Charles Evans Hughes governors of New York, nor that Alfred E. Smith was the political offspring of Tammany Hall. The boss and his machine are the purveyors of a commodity—power—which is, for them, a piece of merchandise for which they want purchasers at the highest price they can secure. If they find that the buyers in the market will not look at

[3] R. M. La Follette, *Autobiography* (Madison: The Robert M. La Follette Co., 1913), p. 189.

one kind of commodity, they regard it as their function to provide another. If the farmers of California are in revolt against the extortionate railroad rates, the Republican machine will provide them with Hiram Johnson, and his slogan "Kick the corporations out of politics" will give the angry farmers the temporary illusion that they have asserted their power as the sovereign people and won a great victory. But the illusion is a temporary one; and its magic fades simply because it represents an incident and not a process.

The second reason for the power of the party machine is its relation to the system of private ownership in industry and agriculture. For the men who run railroads and farms and factories want to run them with the minimum of interference and the maximum of profit. They secure both of these to the degree that the party machine is on their side. It makes all the difference in the world whether there is an eight-hour day rigorously enforced by an appropriate system of inspection or a formal statute which establishes the eight-hour day but provides no machinery for its enforcement. The taxes in Mississippi and Georgia would be very different from what they are if the educational provision for black and white children alike were, say, at the standard to which people are accustomed in Massachusetts or New York. The position of a great corporation like General Motors or Du Pont depends in a high degree on the use that is made of the state police power. And if a state decides itself to own its electricity supply, or to permit one of the cities under its control to own and operate the main means of transportation within its boundaries, the private citizen is excluded from an important area of enterprise. Mining laws, taxation methods, laws relating to riparian rights, laws relating to building, or to the disposal of salvage, or to public health, all these make an immense difference to farmers and factory owners, to bankers and prospectors. Because they make so big a difference, the owner of property is naturally anxious that the party machine should see his case in the most favourable light possible. He is willing either to pay for such an outlook or to refrain from criticism where, though he does not approve, he is not personally concerned. There thus develops an important sense in which the party machine is the intermediary between the power of the state and the protection of owners from invasion by that power. The alternative would be the necessity for every business interest to enter directly and continuously into the process of politics and thus to give up the energies it wishes to devote to profit-making to the pursuit of politics as a profession.

It is from this necessity that the party machine generally undertakes to save the great mass of business men. No doubt the machine is subject to a large number of other pressures, religious, trade-unionist, temperance, educational, and the like. Its members have to judge, on each issue before them, just how far they can go in any particular area without risking their hold on, or their aspirations to, control of the state power. But, granted the conviction that the risk can be safely taken, the machine is the broker for any client who will pay its price. The risk is the danger it runs that it may mistake the public opinion it has to satisfy at election time. For both parties are well aware that public opinion is an incalculable factor which may get out of hand for reasons that not even the most experienced of bosses could have predicted. In the normal way the party machine operates over an area where expectations are pretty obvious and the range of satisfactions capable of fairly straightforward definition. But it is now at least open to question whether, in the field of state politics, any certain meaning is left to the concept of the normal way. It was Alfred E. Smith, a Tammany product, who gave New York as creative and as clean an administration as it has had in years. A member of the house of Vanderbilt was as good a governor as Rhode Island has had since the Civil War. A Farmer-Labor governor of Minnesota, Olson, might well, but for his premature death, have changed the whole alignment of party politics in the states northwest of Chicago. Dr. Wilbur Cross not only captured Connecticut for the Democratic party, but showed in his two terms as governor all the shrewdness of the professional politician, together with a simple humanism from which a machine candidate is usually free. Mr. Upton Sinclair came within an ace of becoming an independent governor of California despite the hostility of professional politicians in both parties. After the economic depression of 1929 there was not only elected a president with an experimental temper; he called to his service a host of academic advisers whom the professionals normally regarded as wholly impractical; and the coming of world war not only put an end to the tradition against a third term, but even made a fourth term seem the natural safeguard of American interests. And despite the split in the ranks of labour, it looked as though, at least in the great industrial states, it was going to prove possible to organize a trade-union vote which would make its decision without any serious regard to the will of the professional politicians. As President Roosevelt began his fourth term, indeed, it was permissible to doubt whether the party machine of any state was quite certain what future lay before it.

The possibility of raising this doubt has an importance of an exceptional kind. From some such time as the presidency of Theodore Roosevelt the balance of power in American government began to shift unmistakably from the states to the federal government. The epoch of Woodrow Wilson gave a new intensity to that shift; and though his term of office was followed by the negativism of Coolidge and the pathetic attempt of President Hoover to walk blindfold towards the gathering storm, the election of Franklin Roosevelt altered with obvious permanence the incidence of the relations between Washington and the states. That alteration was on so vast a scale that it raised new questions to which the professional politicians had no obvious answer. For, on the plane of government, it made Washington the pivotal element in the finances even of the richest states; it even raised the issue of whether a good governor could not be defined as one who knew the art of getting the maximum aid from Washington for his own experiments in his state. And, on the plane of party, it made it fairly beyond question that the state machines were less able to organize voters in a period of experiment and crisis than at any time since the Civil War. Perhaps four or five million workers' votes seemed to pass outside their sphere of influence. The Negro vote was less responsive to them than ever before and far more critical of their habits. Certain pressure groups, above all that of the men in the defence services, began to develop criteria of action quite outside the range of experience which the Republicans and Democrats were historically able to understand. The federal government, moreover, was poking long fingers into the very heart of the state policies, by measures like the National Labor Relations Act, the social security legislation, the help offered to schemes of health and housing and education. Those measures compelled the party machines to begin what was for them the quite novel process of thinking in terms which had a federal context not once in four years, but every day of every year. The alternative was to become the dependencies of the economic royalists, with the certainty that, if this occurred, they would lose their hold on all save the professional ward-heelers in each state.

Nor was this all. The implications of the great power schemes undertaken by the federal government raised the very important issue of whether the state was the alternative governmental area to the United States. The Tennessee Valley Authority was, obviously, the first great stage in a movement in which Boulder Dam and Coulee Dam suggested new and quite vital possibilities. There might be, in the next generation, a Missouri Valley Authority; to what would that be the prelude? Is it not at least probable that the next generation will see a reorganization of the constituent units within the federation? The problems, certainly, with which the United States is confronted cannot be fitted either neatly or precisely into the two main categories of federal government and state government. There is not only the fact that the existence of concurrent power makes co-operation between the two increasingly necessary; there is also the fact that certain areas of function require areas of control which are less than the federal authority can command and more than a single state can provide. The issue is not merely one of grants-in-aid from the federal government, important though the future of this system is, if there is to be a minimum standard throughout the United States in things like housing and health, education and social security.

Beyond the state boundary there looms increasingly the fact of the region. It becomes ever more obvious that the geographical area must be suited to the function performed, and that the states as units fail to satisfy this criterion. The historic antithesis between the rights of the state and the supremacy of the national government becomes utterly unrealistic in the light not merely of technological change, but also of the need to tackle common needs and common opportunities by a joint effort. As soon as one begins to look at American problems in this way, the issues raised by the "Dust Bowl" and the "Great Plains," to take two examples only, transcend the prospect of a satisfactory solution which either halts at the historic boundary of a state or trusts to the hope that politicians will be wise enough to make joint action possible where there are joint problems. And it is important to distinguish between a conception of regionalism on these lines and the famous thesis of American sectionalism associated with the great name of F. J. Turner. Sectionalism by its nature is based on factors of division which are always tending to conflict; regionalism, again by its nature, is seeking to unify interests in an area which has failed to realize its common institutional needs. As Professor Turner saw, sectionalism finds its expression in politics and legislation where the members of Congress, for example, pay no heed to their parties but emphasize their sectional interest. It is in the conflicts of sectionalism, whether of the tariff or of currency, that one sees most clearly those interstices in American federalism which prevent its full use of its natural resources and the completion of its nationalism. The sectionalism of its division by states where the boundaries of these are either traditional merely, or artificial in character, makes America remain a vast sub-continent which is still seeking the means to an effective decentralization.

It is an issue for the specialist in human geography to decide what, on balance, is the form of regionalism best suited to American needs. The point that emerges from the admission that the region is a social necessity is that the division of the United States on the present basis of state organization has at least two wholly evil results, the one economic, the other political, in character, though, of course, they dovetail into each other. The economic evil is the failure to achieve a balanced economic life through the failure to utilize to the full the resources at America's disposal. That is seen in the wastage of timber and oil, in the antagonism between the city and the rural area, in the impact of communication between the centre and the circumference of life in the states. The political evil is the refusal to treat needs that are equal and uniform in an equal and uniform way, very largely because the lack of relationship between the character of the needs encountered and the method of responding to them has the almost inevitable result of giving to political institutions in each American state an interest quite separate from that of the citizen body with which they are concerned. This separate interest emerges in every realm of life. It is seen in comparing the infant mortality rate in San Antonio, Texas, with that of Boston or of New York City. It is seen in the laws relating to labour, in the rates of transportation by rail or by road, in the law concerning the relation of debtor and creditor. Railroad rates have been set in a grain-growing state just at the point where they do not discourage the farmer; and the more powerful the influence of the railroad in state politics, the more likely it is that the farmer will be the prisoner of its capacity for moderation. There is, indeed, an important sense in which any great vested interest in a particular state will compel the adjustment of most elements in the life of that state to its wants and habits. Because the Anaconda Copper Corporation plays so large a part in the life of Montana, the professors of economics at its university must handle the question of mining taxation with exceptional delicacy. And Mr. Henry C. Wallace showed nearly a generation ago that the railway manager discouraged industrial growth west of the Mississippi because "he conceived it to be to the advantage of the railroad to keep the farm and the factory as far apart as possible in order that the railroad might haul their respective products the longest possible distances." [4]

There is no natural relation between the area of an American state and the adequate performance of the functions to which it is committed. The parties which seek the votes of its electorate are bound, therefore, to weigh the interests which operate in its life and to adjust their policies to the volume of that interest. And each interest, in its turn, is compelled, if it can, to secure an influence over party policies lest these use the State power to its disadvantage. The attitude of the Democratic party in the South to the problems of colour and of child labour are a simple illustration of the relation between interest and political power. More complicated examples are not less interesting, as in the interplay of state and federal influence in the Northwestern Pacific states in a matter like the provision of electric power. Who owns power in this realm owns a large part of the economic future of this area. If the ownership is social in character, and if it is able to provide an adequate supply at a cheap rate, the repercussions elsewhere in the United States are certain to be profound. That emerged unmistakably in the conflict between the Tennessee Valley Authority and the Commonwealth and Southern Corporation when it was directed by Mr. Wendell Willkie. The real meaning of that conflict lay in the knowledge, on both sides, that the socialization of electric power was a long step on the road from the negative to the positive state. By taking that step, the Authority was in fact building the foundations of a new organization in American life, intermediate between the state and Washington. And upon its success there might well come to depend a very considerable part of the future of those industries which are vital to public welfare.

For the success of such intermediate organizations has the central and simple result of calling into question the chief basis of party organization in America. Their success means, first, that the principle of individualism, upon which, in the main, both major parties have relied, becomes a matter it is reasonable to doubt; and their success means, in the second place, that the Tennessee Valley Authority is likely to be merely the first of a series of such authorities; and the significance of this de-

[4] Henry C. Wallace, "The Farmer and the Railroads," *Proceedings of the American Academy of Political and Social Science* (1922), Vol. X, p. 65.

velopment in the field of electric power is that it suggests the prospect of parallel developments in other fields of kindred importance, not least in that of transportation.

Under these circumstances, it is not easy to think of the state as the appropriate unit of administration below the federal government. No doubt, as Frankfurter and Landis have argued, the Compact Clause of the Constitution offers the necessary possibilities of transcending state limits; but any careful survey of its achievements, even when it is undertaken, as by Professor Jane Perry Clark, with goodwill towards, and faith in, its opportunities, suggests that the Compact Clause requires something like geological time to achieve the results that are desirable. But the United States, with all its resources, has not geological time at its disposal. On the contrary, the evidence is both abundant and growing that it must seek to make area coincide with function if it is at once to avoid excessive centralization and to be in a position effectively to deal with the social and economic issues before it. Despite the greatness of the traditions to which states like Virginia and Massachusetts, Pennsylvania and New York, can appeal, it is doubtful whether they can meet the problems before them with any confidence that they can solve them. It is, indeed, only too likely that if they attempt to rely upon their own authority, they will be driven to seek federal aid in order to achieve a reasonable standard of performance. But all federal aid, sooner or later, means federal control; Washington will wish to know, and, indeed, is entitled to know, that its grants are spent both wisely and efficiently. It was this fact which made Professor Dicey, the eminent English lawyer, insist, half a century ago, that federalism is only a stage on the road to unity. Yet few observers of the American scene would regard a centralized United States as likely to be both efficient and free. The scale is too large for administrative unity to be possible for a continent with a climate like that of California and like that of Maine, with habits as different as those of the New Englander and the Southerner, with resources so different as those of Nevada and New Jersey, or of Kentucky and New York. Once the frontier had been reached, the historic basis of federalism was administratively obsolete; an experience, it is worth noting, that is true also of Canada and Australia. The American who has reached the frontier enters upon a new world; he needs to adapt the process of its administration to requirements which were unthinkable in the spring and summer of 1787 at Philadelphia. No doubt it will be difficult to make the necessary adaptation; but the longer it is postponed, the more drastic will be its impact when the time for its recognition has arrived.

3

BELOW each state are the counties and the cities which each contains. It is a broad but roughly true generalization to say that they are, both of them, the outstanding failures in American politics, and that their antagonism has been one of the main sources of the failure, also, to transcend that provincialism which marks even great cities like New York and Chicago, and the metropolis of Washington itself. Partly, no doubt, the reason for this lies in the fact that the American tradition still thinks of the individual farmer and his needs as central to the fulfilment of the American ideal. Jefferson's suspicion of urbanization still lingers a century and a quarter after his death. It is echoed in the first report of the Interstate Commerce Commission in 1888; for that body, it was natural to assume that great cities give birth to great social and political evils. Twenty-five years later, the "new freedom" of Woodrow Wilson was nothing so much as a plea for the rights of the "little man" against the giant corporation which was already the major feature of the American economic landscape. And right down to the eve of the Second World War, a jurist as influential as Mr. Justice Brandeis was the leader of a school of thought which preached the "curse of bigness" without any historic insight into the sources from which that philosophy came.

For it is American rural life that, more than any other factor, has determined the character of local institutions. Once the assumption is made that the farmer is simple, God-fearing, and virtuous, it becomes easy to assume that evil is the creation of the cities; and from this there follows the dual result, first, that what Lincoln Steffens called the "shame of the cities" is taken for granted as a natural thing, and, second, that in practically every state of the Union the rural areas secure overrepresentation in the state legislature. No doubt the American farmer can claim that he has been shamefully exploited by such mechanisms as the tariff, and by such interests as those of the banks and the railroads, as well as by the purveyors of electric power. No doubt, also, the tradition and thought of pre-revolutionary America has lingered, in most aspects of life, in the rural areas rather than in the urban, if only because the main body of immigrants has, rather naturally, settled in the cities. Rural America tends to be Protestant, even Fundamentalist, hostile, whether Republican or Democrat, to innovation, uninterested in most social experiments, and inclined to think that anyone who lives in one of the great cities is almost round the corner from sin. It was predominantly rural America which was responsible for the "great experiment" of prohibition; though one must not omit the fact that the brewers were largely of German origin and that big business regarded it as likely to result in more efficient workingmen. It is probably true, also, that the main strength of the Women's Christian Temperance Union was in the rural areas, and, in the South, at least, the main strength of the Ku Klux Klan. It is not an exaggeration, I think, to suggest that xenophobia is endemic in rural America, and that it places more emphasis on historic conventions like the equation of respectability with church attendance than is the case in any considerable urban area. How far the utterly disproportionate political representation of the countryside is the simple expression of the natural lust for power, and how far it is the result of a conviction that the correction of this disproportion would give the sinful city excessive political rights, it is difficult to say.

What is important, in any assessment of American local government, is to realize how incomplete is the work of the melting pot there. Rural America is not only predominantly Protestant; it is also hostile to recent immigrants, not least from Roman Catholic countries, and to Jews. Perhaps that is why the most extreme forms of Evangelical Christianity take so swift and sudden a hold on the rural areas; it is a compensation for the Puritan "folkways" that bids the farmer and his family avoid the seduction of the cities. But, in any event, the farmer has lost his case. The population statistics are all against him. Rural Illinois cannot hope permanently to maintain a situation in which Chicago is bound to be misgoverned, any more than rural New York can prevent New York City from being handed over for long periods to Tammany, or Philadelphia to whatever corrupt interest enables men like Senator Vare to retain power in Pennsylvania. For the fact is inescapable that the overrepresentation of the rural areas in the states is one of the means by which the city boss retains his authority. Many a small farmer is willing to come to terms with the big corporation or the boss of some city machine when he finds that he may have to default on his mortgage or that the zeal with which he emphasizes the importance of political priority is received with a smile of cynical contempt by his neighbour whose income is no larger than his but who is able to drive to the capital in a Buick instead of a Ford.

I am therefore convinced that no small part of the situation which permits the widespread and deep-seated corruption in American cities is due to the framework in which the state legislature is set. No doubt this is only part of the story. Something must be attributed to the large number of immigrants who find the boss and his machine more helpful and friendly than the corporation which employs him or the neighbours among whom he lives. It is the boss who gives him the party or the picnic, who helps him when he is in trouble, who sees that he gets his citizen's papers, who finds a job as stenographer at City Hall for his girl. No one who ever met him will forget Mr. Martin Lomasney, the "Tsar" of the Eighth Ward in Boston. "I think," he said, "that there's got to be in every ward somebody that any bloke can come to—no matter what he's done—and get help. Help, you understand; none of your law and justice, but help." [5] That help, of course, is not a gift offered free of charge. It is rooted in corruption, corruption of men, corruption of the institutions men build. It poisons the legislature, the administration, the courts. It entrenches all sorts of special privilege and vested interests behind walls through which the ordinary man cannot hope to penetrate. It creeps into every nook and cranny of the body politic. And it draws into its net every class in the population, rich and poor alike. It may be a poor pedlar who wants a licence to sell his goods; it may be a street rail-

[5] Steffens, *op. cit.*, p. 618.

road which wants to raise the cost of transportation. I do not think it excessive to say that there is no large city in the United States in which the honesty of the police force is beyond all question. Nor is it excessive to say that there are few great business organizations which have not, at some time or other, availed themselves of the service of the machine to obtain by corruption, whether of fraud or of violence, what they could not have obtained by the direct persuasion of argument.

Nor is the machine system a city product merely. In the cities, no doubt, it is more obvious, more highly coloured, more dramatic in its expression; Tammany Hall in New York, the Thompson and the Kelly–Nash machines in Chicago, the Pendergast machine in Kansas City, these, to take examples only, are part of that American history which is known even to Macaulay's schoolboy. But the county also has its machine. It is less obvious because it is less concentrated. The spoils by which it prospers may be less direct and almost certainly less large. But it would be a great mistake to assume that, proportionately, the county chairman runs a machine that is less real or less effective than the machine of the cities. On the contrary, the fact that there is less news value in the affairs of a county than in the affairs of a town, that the press is likely to be less widely read, and that the residents of the county are less able to meet and talk things over, may well make the rural "boss" more powerful and not less powerful than his city analogue. He may be a banker in a small county town, or the county prosecutor, or a landowner, or a lawyer. His politics are likely to occupy a smaller place in his life than in that of the head of a great city machine; and he may even, like a recent "boss" of Westchester County in New York State, combine the functions of corruption with a genuine and profound ardour for building roads. But the important fact is that the machine in the rural area works on the same lines and for the same ends as the machine in the city. There will be the same trickery in the registration of votes and in the counting of them. There may be the "long ballot" which, in the city of Chicago, means that the hapless elector has to decide whom he wants for one hundred and seventy-eight different offices. And the victor, despite the growth of the "merit" system in the Civil Service, has still at his disposal enough jobs to make it worth the while of his supporters to stand by him; in New York City, for example, there are three thousand jobs at the disposal of the successful machine, and they are mostly the best jobs in the city service. Nor is this limited to the cities; Adams County, Ohio, has a record which compares with almost anything except the supreme urban scandals. And if there is a quarrel within a party machine, as when the Mellon faction could not agree with the Vare faction in Pennsylvania in 1926, the scale of corruption on both sides was something that would have struck a note of envy in even the leaders of the Nazi party in Germany.

The foreigner is bewildered, at first blush, by the scale upon which these machines attempt to function. The reason for that scale goes back, in essence, to the Puritan belief that citizens can be made good by legisla-tion. In the result, almost any subject may be dealt with by legislation or regulation, from the control of brothels to the value of π. And once there is a law which touches a theme from which men desire to escape, it is obvious that they will pay for their liberation. At once, therefore, the machine in power has an asset it can use in trade; it may be the opening of a saloon on Sunday, or the decision to ignore a "red-light" dis-trict in Cicero, Illinois. Whatever the theme, it has the vital elements of blackmail in it, and the boss will rarely have any difficulty in collecting blackmail on any theme where he chooses to announce that the law will be enforced. He has, as Mr. Raymond Fosdick has pointed out,[6] the police at his disposal for this purpose, and they constitute a ladder by which he not only climbs to power, but is able to stay there until some special scandal outrages the electors. A boss who has the services of a pliant district attorney and an obedient chief of police will rarely find any difficulties in following the famous precept of Plunkett of New York and take advantage of his opportunities.

There is, moreover, the chance so skilfully termed "honest graft." The machine has inside knowledge and can buy property for a rise, whether it is for a school or a hospital or a road. And the machine can punish its enemies by assessments which are unduly high, or by insisting that a critic who owns a building has failed to conform to the regulations of the building code. I have myself known the owner of an apartment house in New York City who refused to report a murder which he saw from his own windows because when he had previously given informa-tion of this kind the building department required him to make altera-tions in his property which drove him to the verge of bankruptcy. And there must be few machines of any importance in the United States, whether in rural or in urban areas, which have not had, at one time or another, some great vested interest, a railroad, an insurance company, or an oil corporation, among the best of its customers.

4

So FAR, at any rate, in American history, it cannot be said that the reme-dies urged for this evil have done more than scratch the surface of the system. E. L. Godkin spent half a lifetime in the defence of the Civil Serv-ice system of appointment by merit after examination; and he was proba-bly the main influence who sought to persuade Lord Bryce that this would achieve that end. But the answer is the simple one that they were wholly wrong, and that they were wrong because they assumed, quite mistak-enly, that the wealthy citizen was likely to be interested in good govern-ment. The truth, in fact, has been that no class has done more to main-tain the machine than the wealthy, for the simple reason that they look

[6] Raymond B. Fosdick, *American Police Systems* (New York: Century, 1920), pp. 115–16.

to it to safeguard their privileges from invasion by the poor. If Lord Bryce, indeed, had reflected on the habits of the British aristocracy before Gladstone's famous Order in Council of 1870 establishing competitive examinations for entrance into the Civil Service, he would have seen that his approach was excessively simple. He never understood that admirable distinction drawn by William Allen White between the bosses—the "governing classes"—and the vested interests, or "ruling classes," who used the bosses but were always careful never to have other than political relations with them. Mark Hanna, after all, was no more than a Republican boss on a national scale; just as Tom Johnson was the city boss of Cleveland. And what it is essential to grasp is, what men like Bryce never seem to have grasped, that the millionaire who sought freedom from interference was ready to pay a Democratic boss when he held power and a Republican boss if he defeated the Democrat. The important principle was that enunciated by Lincoln Steffens [7] in the muckraking era that so long as a business man was occupied with his affairs and making money, he was willing, even anxious, to pay for protection; he was a bad citizen just because he felt that he had no time for politics, and left its organization to men like Platt or Croker or Jimmy Walker or Hines. After all, however respectable his public reputation, so well known an orator and lawyer as Chauncey Depew only differed from Boss Platt in the size of the retainer he received from the interests, in his case mostly insurance companies, which he protected from attack in the legislature of New York. What has changed in the machine system since the time of the Civil War is not the system which enables the bosses to levy blackmail, but the different sources from which they draw their revenue. A careful analysis of the career of the late Mr. Samuel Insull of Chicago brings the permanence of the old technique into the full light of day.

There have been, of course, continuous efforts to reform that system. Some good has been accomplished by the introduction of direct government. Still more benefit has been the outcome of the simplification of the old-fashioned and intricate machinery which still exists so widely. The commission plan and the city manager plan, especially the second, have had good results, though not, I think, anything like as good results as were anticipated from them. The city manager—who may be a complete stranger to the city he administers—is an expert in the technique of administration; he has the zeal of the professional; his future depends in large measure upon his efficiency. But so far, at any rate, in American history, it is difficult to feel that any of the methods advocated by the reformers have gone to the heart of the problem. For the real issue does not turn upon questions of machinery. In part it is a matter of eliciting both interest and knowledge from the ordinary citizen—the two qualities most feared by any machine—and in part, also, it is a matter of persuading the great vested interests, whether they are symbolized by a

[7] Lincoln Steffens, *The Shame of the Cities* (New York: McClure, Phillips, 1904).

person like William Whitney or Samuel Insull, or by a corporation like the Erie Railroad or Bethlehem Steel, from seeking the short cut to wealth which the machine can offer them at an agreed price.

It is no use pretending that either of these ends can be easily attained. There are many Americans who still look on politics as the short-cut to wealth and the politician as the broker who trades in the shares of its special stock exchange. And among those many men are not merely the poor and the humble, but also, as the Pujo Committee showed in 1912, and the Black Committee twenty years later, some of the outstanding names in American business life. It never occurred to the business associates of Mr. Richard Whitney to warn him against the practices which led to his conviction. It never occurred to the late J. P. Morgan that his "preferred list" of people, for whom, whether Republican or Democratic politicians, shares were bought on the grand scale instead of on the lesser scale that is usually typical of the city boss and his assistants, was still a method of buying influence, and, therefore corruption. When I taught at Harvard University twenty-five years ago few names were more honoured than that of Henry Lee Higginson. He had given munificent gifts to the University; he was an outstanding patron of the famous symphony orchestra of Boston; and he had a passion for the arts. But he did not hesitate to announce that the "nation and our legislation can safely trust the ruling Wall Street men" [8] even though it is clear that there has never been an investigation of the "ruling Wall Street men" from which they have not emerged with damaged reputations. They have bought judges and legislatures as they have bought old pictures and manuscripts; and they have evaded taxation over their incomes in the same way as they have, when they could, evaded the customs on their return from a tour of Europe. If the men who look upon themselves as the guardians of American culture behave in this way, why should one expect different standards from political bosses in high office.

Nor does the problem of municipal and state corruption end there. For, first, when either of these areas of government has the good fortune to secure men to rule them who are not open to corruption, there is the danger that they will suffer, like Altgeld, for their honesty. And no evidence has yet emerged to prove that the city manager plan or the commission system of government is much more than a pill to cure an earthquake. For while there have been city managers of great ability, Clarence A. Dykstra in Cincinnati, for example, and while there are examples of the successful operation of the commission system, as in Des Moines, Iowa, the proportionate improvement these procedures have effected is pretty small. Few of the great cities have adopted either of them. Where the change has been attempted, an awakening of civic interest has rarely endured after the sense of novelty has worn away; and not a few of the

---

[8] Bliss Perry, *Life and Letters of Henry Lee Higginson* (Boston: Atlantic Monthly Press, 1921), p. 441.

city commissions have seemed to be little more than a new committee of the local Chamber of Commerce, as some, at any rate, of the city managers have been men whom the wealthy residents of the area have been prepared to approve. Nor do I think that any proponent of either of these remedies could honestly claim that they gave better results than did Milwaukee in the long years of its Socialist administration.

And it is here, I suggest, that the clue to the problem of local government in America, whether of state or city or county, will be found. If rich Americans are prepared to use their wealth to buy immunities and privileges, nothing can prevent a machine from coming into existence to sell these to them. So far, with rare exceptions, they have been so prepared. New York and Boston, Chicago and San Francisco, Seattle and Cincinnati, are only the more notable examples of this readiness. The student of a middle-sized town, such as Professor and Mrs. Lynd studied in their remarkable analysis of Muncie, Indiana, will have no difficulty in putting his finger on the root of the problem. Every resident of Beacon Hill in Boston can give one a full account of the sins of Mayor Curley and Martin Lomasney, as every wealthy resident of Seattle can grow hot and angry over the habits of Dave Beck of the Teamsters' Union. But almost all of Beacon Hill was angry when justice was demanded for two anarchist fish pedlars named Sacco and Vanzetti; and there were very few residents of Seattle who fought against the waste and inefficiency of that dual electric power system which its great engineer J. D. Ross strove to end by complete municipalization. Local government in the United States will develop from corruption to honesty as soon as the rich in America are ready to surrender the advantages, sometimes the immense advantages, they have gained from the fact of its corruption. It is not yet evident that, thus far, they have reached that state of mind where they are prepared for the surrender. On the contrary, they are still, in the main and in both major parties, inclined to the view that an honest and efficient government which makes no distinction between its citizens will open the flood gates of radicalism.

The epoch of Franklin Roosevelt has, indeed, made for changes in local institutions by bringing within the ambit of federal regulation matters which were previously the prerogative entirely of a local machine. The old-fashioned boss may remain in Chicago and Jersey City; but he went to jail in Kansas City, and Tammany was unable, for a twelve-year period, to break the hold of Mayor La Guardia in New York. And the assassination of Huey Long removed from the American scene the only figure of this generation who might have rivalled Hitler. It is possible, though it is far from certain, that organizations like T.V.A. and measures like the Social Security Act may be the beginning of a new era in the local politics of America. For the end of the Second World War is not less likely than the end of the first to bring with it a deep and widespread sense of fatigue. Crisis presidents, as Americans have learned to their cost, bring as their successors men, both at Washington and elsewhere, who offer "normalcy" as their programme; and it is in the relief from the pain of thought that the real source of corruption is found. It is significant that most of the newspapers are hostile to the great experiment, federal and local, in adult education which has been perhaps the supreme gift of Mr. Roosevelt to the United States. It is significant, too, that it has been unusual for Hollywood to attempt even to drive home the real lesson he has taught. And though the radio commentator has never been able even approximately to rival the genius which Mr. Roosevelt has brought to this new instrument of propaganda, there is no assurance that his successor will be able to reproduce his technique.

The hope of the next age in this realm lies in the possibility that "freedom from want" may become a living part of the American system. Next to this is the possibility that the political activity of the trade-unions may move with the same vigour to local elections as they operated in the federal elections of 1944 for the presidency. But if they are to exercise an activity as vigorous as that of 1944 they have to make certain that the candidates, in state and city and county, for whom they fight mean as much to them in the tasks of local government as they realized, under the urgent pressure of the C.I.O., that Mr. Roosevelt meant to them. But they cannot make this certain unless they play their full part in the choice of the candidates they are to support; and they cannot play that part unless they actually themselves engage in the choice of candidates. The only way, in short, to prevent a wholesale return to the rule of the boss and the machine is to make the issues of local politics as real and as compelling as Mr. Roosevelt succeeded (not, perhaps, without some aid from Nazi Germany and Japan) in making the issues of national politics. What America needs locally is the ability to choose between conservative policies and radical policies. It has rarely had that ability outside the federal realm, with the result that its local politics have largely been a listless affair with only odd moments of purifying statement. But a listless parochialism is the atmosphere in which the machine is certain to flourish; and once it flourishes the evidence is inescapable that the commodities it has to sell will be bought by those who can afford them. That mattered less in the age when Americans were engaged in the conquest of their vast continent than it does today when they set the international tempo of the world. That is why the epoch has arrived when positive institutions are urgent in matters of local, as well as in matters of federal, concern. Negative institutions in local matters in the second half of the twentieth century will destroy the power of the United States to play that part in world affairs to which it is called alike by its might and by its dignity.

V

American Business Enterprise

I

IT IS no exaggeration to say that in no previous civilization has the business man enjoyed either the power or the prestige that he possesses in the United States. Names like those of Astor and Vanderbilt, Gould and Ford, great merchants like Stewart, great bankers like the two Morgans, vital figures in railroad construction and finance like J. J. Hill and E. A. Harriman, steel magnates like Carnegie and Frick and Schwab, oil kings like the Rockefellers and the Sinclairs, timber millionaires like Weyerhaeuser, these, and men like these, have disposed of an authority which it is difficult not to describe as imperial in nature. Certainly in modern times, the only men who have rivalled them in power have been either political despots, like Napoleon or Hitler, or great aristocrats who exercise the main functions of the state.

The roots of this combination of power and prestige lie deep in the total circumstances of American history. The power is clearly the outcome of the immense resources at the disposal of Americans; whether it be coal or steel, timber or cattle, there has been a spaciousness of opportunity which neither Europe nor Asia has so far known. The important problem has not been the fact of power, since so obviously the resources were there for exploitation. Rather, the important problem has been the factors which have gone to the making of the extraordinary prestige the American business man enjoys, and the degree to which, in ever-increasing measure, every aspect of American life has been adjusted to a perspective he has defined.

In part, no doubt, the foundation of this prestige has been the Puritan gospel of work, which has achieved the identification of success with a state of grace. In part, also, it has been the sheer necessity of completing the conquest of a continent; to the victors were given the spoils in abundant measure. Something, also, must be attributed to the fact that the War of Independence destroyed in large degree the feudal idea, and thus made what Veblen called the "idea of conspicuous waste" different in kind from anything known in Britain or France, in Germany or in Tsarist Russia.

Nor must one omit the significance of the fact that the great hordes of immigrants who came to America before 1914 left Europe to better their fortunes and were willing, even eager, to work with astonishing vitality in order to achieve that end. American immigration has been compounded of what was most remarkable in Europe among those who felt that the Old World denied them the rights to which they were entitled. They had energy, resolution, faith. For the most part this was the capital with which they had to make their way. And the very effort of hewing a civilization out of a wilderness developed and intensified these qualities.

Most of the problems of the United States until quite modern times were problems which called for practical ability. There were the Indians to be resisted, the forests to be cleared, roads to be built, houses to be constructed, harvests to be sown. If early America gave high status to the theologian, the jurist, and, perhaps until the time of Andrew Jackson, to the politician also, it is not easy to mistake the fact that, almost from its origins, increasingly after 1776, and most notably after 1865, the status of the business man has gained upon all of these. And after 1776 the status of vocations which had previously been notable in their own right, as it were, became notable in the context given to them by the emergence of what became almost recognized as the divine right of the business man. The successful clergyman was the man who could attract the millionaire to his church. The successful university president was the man who could most successfully persuade the rich to endow his university. Great scholars like the historian Francis Parkman were held in far less esteem than great practical inventors like Edison. Even the great philosopher, like Charles Peirce or William James, was seeking, even if unconsciously, a metaphysic that would justify the claims of the business man. It had been assumed with astonishingly little discussion that the culture out of which a great civilization is formed emerges in some mysterious fashion as a by-product of material success. It may well be doubted whether any people has given an energy so continuous and so ardent to the faith that truth and happiness are revealed by the conquest of material well-being, and that the man of wealth is the chosen vessel of the Lord.

It may be doubted, further, whether any previous community in history has laid so great an emphasis upon the obligations of the individual citizen to hew his way to success. With, of course, exceptions, and even notable exceptions, the faith of American business has been the simple conviction that a man's failure in life is reasonably attributable to his own faults. No democracy has been less interested in its failures; in an economic sense, no democracy has so magnificently rewarded its successful men or been so continuously convinced that prosperity was always round the corner. It is, I think, significant that so deep is this conviction that it has not yet proved possible in the United States to create a permanent working-class party. The average American does not really doubt either that he himself belongs to the middle class, or, at least, that his children will do so. Aware that his standard of life, if he is a white man, is far beyond the standard attained anywhere save in New Zealand, he draws the inference therefrom that the cause of this success lies in the private ownership and control of property. The state power is there to defend the American way of life against aggression, internal or external; and it may be used legitimately to educate the nation's children, to lay down standards of performance in such realms as food and drugs, or railroads, or the cleansing of streets. But most Americans have a sense of deep discomfort when they are asked to support the positive state. They tend to regard it as a method of eroding the responsibilities of the individual. They tend to feel that what is done by a governmental institution is bound to be less well done than if it were undertaken by individuals, whether alone or in the form of private corporations. The main clue to the understanding of American enterprise is the need to realize that articulate America still looks upon the state as the enemy as soon as it moves from the area of defence or of police. Whatever functions it performs additionally to these are in the nature either of a *pis aller,* or, like the Geological Survey or the Bureau of Standards, something it would not pay citizens to undertake as a private enterprise.

It is important to realize that private enterprise in America has, first of all, become industrial rather than agricultural in its emphasis, and that, in the second place, the individual has given place to the corporation as the unit of production. Moreover, certain other features in American economic life have developed, especially since the Civil War, against which both Jefferson and John Taylor warned their people. Finance capital has become the master of industrial capital, the farmer-owner has increasingly given place to the farmer-tenant, especially in the South and the Southwest; and, as Taussig and Joslyn have shown, there is a growth of nepotism in the direction of business affairs comparable in character to that which has taken place in Great Britain. There is a growing tendency, also, to an increase in the expenses of distribution, especially in the costs of advertisement. Immense as is the productive capacity of American business, as the war has shown so strikingly in the weapons it has demanded, there is not even an approximation to the full uses of its resources, nor is there any serious effort to utilize the total labour power at the disposal of the nation. And, war apart, it is not unfair to say that the distribution of effective demand in the United States bears little or no relation to popular need, and something like four to five million Americans are, in time of peace, akin to refugees in that they have no security of tenure and depend very largely on the accident of casual demand.

Behind all this is a philosophy of economics which is as antiquated as it is unmistakable. It is convinced that freedom of contract is incompatible with equality of bargaining power; and it therefore looks with profound suspicion on all forms of trade-union activity. And since most judges are successful lawyers, and since most successful lawyers are the agents of business men, the courts share the view of business that the purpose of the law is to protect the business man's conception of free contract. And that outlook is not confined to the courts and business man. It is the normal outlook of most professors of economics and sociology, of men like William Graham Sumner, of John Bates Clark, of Thomas Nixon Carver. They assumed that the government was the enemy to be feared, that the major problems of poverty had been solved, that what ex-President Hoover termed "rugged individualism" was the secret of American success. They rarely intervened directly in politics; but, like E. A. Harriman, they were careful to keep on good terms with both of the major political parties and to utilize to the full the mechanism of the machine system in each. They dismissed all radicals as cranks; and by the term "radical" they meant anyone whose views were different in any important particular from those of the United States Chamber of Commerce or of the National Association of Manufacturers. They regarded socialist principles not as the natural reaction from the habits of a capitalist society, but as a foreign importation which no good American could approve; and they were insistent, after 1917, that the October Revolution in Russia was not only a failure, but bound to be a menace to the essential idea of civilized living.

After the Great Depression of 1929 it is probable that at least a faint shadow of scepticism fell across this outlook. But once Mr. Roosevelt sought, in the first, fine careless rapture of the New Deal, to give to organized labour those rights which it had been so long denied, one may doubt whether the scepticism remained. The men whom Mr. F. L. Allen has so admirably termed the "Lords of Creation" did not really doubt for long that the welfare of the United States depended upon their prosperity. Men like Mr. Ford and Mr. Rockefeller were able to adjust themselves to the statutes of the New Deal only because that adjustment was the necessary condition upon which they were awarded government contracts. Most of them looked back to the rule of Harding and Coolidge as to a golden age. They read little; and most of what they read they were willing to have chosen for them by book clubs, which saved them the trouble of trying to find out themselves what was important. If they collected books, like Mr. Huntington, or pictures, like Mr. Frick, they knew nothing about them except that what was expensive must be deemed worth having; and if they assisted research, like Mr. Rockefeller, it was less because they understood its implications than because they were advised by a highly paid public relations counsel, of the type of Mr. Ivy Lee, that the endowment of research would cover up a past they were naturally very anxious to conceal.

No doubt there are occasional exceptions among the ruling class of American business. An eminent banker, like James Ford Rhodes, could devote all his leisure to the production of a good second-rate history of his time.[1] But few men knew that class better than Charles Francis

[1] J. F. Rhodes, *History of the United States from the Compromise of 1850* (New York: Macmillan, 1892–1910).

Adams,[2] the son of the eminent minister to London; and it was his final opinion that he had no atom of desire ever to meet again any of his business associates. When they made speeches, they piled commonplace upon commonplace; when they wrote books, like Mr. Carnegie,[3] it was obvious that they had no notion of the forces which were changing the nature of their time. In general, they acted like Oriental despots to whom any ordered principles of conduct were without meaning so long as they attained their end; and they used men like Ivy Lee in public relations, or Samuel Untermyer in the law, as mercenaries from whom they demanded nothing but success, for which they were willing to pay highly, in their search for wealth and power. I suspect that an occasional figure like J. J. Hill was as interested in the technique of railroads as in the fortune he amassed from his success. But the Vanderbilts, the Astors, the Goulds, the Rockefellers, had really no interest save in wealth and power. They liked, no doubt, to be spoken of with reverence and, for that reason alone, they insisted that they were the stewards of the great fortunes they built up. But they looked upon the masses of America with a mixture of contempt and indignation which they set, like Mr. George F. Baer, in the background of a nauseating religiosity. And their refusal to respect the dignity of ordinary men's lives was displayed on every occasion when, as in the strikes at Homestead, or at Lawrence in 1912, or during the maritime strike of 1934 on the Pacific coast, the workingmen of America sought to translate the purpose of America into the daily round of their effort. The methods of the firm of Pinkerton, the use of machine guns and later of tear gas, their employment of armed guards in their factories, were a sufficient index to their view of human nature once it threatened the vested interests they believed it to be their duty to safeguard.

2

The American business man has certain remarkable qualities in an exceptional degree. His vitality is extraordinary. He lives his business from morning to night; he gives to it the devotion that a medieval saint gave to his religion. He is almost always experimental about it, eager to take a chance, anxious to change from one vocation to another if the latter seems to offer additional opportunities. He believes profoundly in the possibilities of machinery; and he is almost always willing to take the long rather than the short view. He knows, as no other people but the Germans and, since 1917, the Russians know, the value of *expertise* and research. He assumes that success in a business calling is of itself a title to influence, and since there are few men who do not desire influence he agrees with but little difficulty that the successful business man ought

---

[2] Charles Francis Adams, *An Autobiography* (Boston: Houghton Mifflin, 1916), p. 190.
[3] Andrew Carnegie, *Triumphant Democracy* (New York: Scribner's, 1888).

to be respected. There is, indeed, an important sense in which it is true to say that for most Americans the acquisition of wealth is a form of religious exercise; that is why, perhaps, a well-known advertiser could write, in the twenties, of Jesus Christ as a successful business man without the public feeling that there was some incongruity in the thesis.

It might be an exaggeration to argue that the religion of America is business; but in no other country does the direct pursuit of money-making wear a more virtuous air. In no other country, either, is it so simply assumed that the opinions of a successful business man are important. And, at any rate, since the time of the Civil War, the tempo of business life in the United States has been unsurpassed elsewhere. There is a passion for technical change merely for the sake of change. There is an eagerness of mind, a restlessness of temper, which it is difficult indeed to overemphasize. It is striking to notice the absence of status; and the consequence of this absence is an encouragement to effort which is rare indeed in other countries. The American man of business, moreover, has a respect for his customers which is probably unique. In no other country is there so profound an effort to satisfy their wants, even to discover them. If life consisted only in economic relations it would be difficult to find a society in which there was so full an attempt to realize their full implications.

But there is a grave weakness in this mental climate which it is important to emphasize. It has become so important in the United States to be commercially successful that it is rare for business men to look upon their civic duties as important. They are almost tempted to regard them as an unjustifiable interference with the real tasks a man should seek to fulfil. In the result, the political class in the United States is separated from the men who are occupied in business, and, in consequence, the business men are anxious to be left alone by the politicians. They want, of course, security for their property and the maintenance of public order. But where the politicians are driven to action beyond the circle which these objectives trace, the tendency of American business is to suspect that the government is going outside its proper sphere. It then assumes that *laissez-faire* is the right principle of social action, and any departure from its habit a contradiction of political wisdom. They then, as business men, develop a sense of deep alarm as soon as any positive legislation is proposed. The less of statutes the better is almost an axiom in Wall Street and State Street; and they assume that the more ample the area of private life, the wiser is the policy of the State power. But this emphasis on private action as inherently superior to public action is not only untrue, but has the devastating result of persuading business men, first, that they should play no part in politics, and, second, that the more negative the government, the better it is. But since the number of business men who attain success is necessarily small, the outcome of this attitude is an alliance between the political machine and business which corrupts the whole quality of American life.

This is the inevitable result of such an atmosphere. Once the business man assumes that politics are not his affair, a group of men will arise who will make it their function; and since they then have a commodity to sell, they are in a position to compel the business men to purchase it. No one can easily explain the character of American politics except upon the basis that the habits of its business men have been for the most part private and not public in emphasis. And to this must be added that it has not been easy to persuade Americans that bigness is not the same thing as grandeur. A man who has a large business is regarded, *a priori,* as more important than a man whose business is small. And few of even the big business men are willing to assume that the understanding of American culture is their concern. They know the theatre as tired business men. They know music almost wholly in the terms of the reputation a maestro or an orchestra has won from the intellectual *élite* and their own wives. They rarely read, outside the newspapers; the study of books is a vocation either of women or of the universities. They are deeply interested in golf and the life of the country club; that, broadly speaking, is the main source of the interests to which they are devoted. They are deeply interested in their health; and the masseur is almost central to the lives of those who can afford to belong to the important club in a town.

The American business man is also a great "joiner." He is a Mason, a Knight of Columbus, a Rotarian, an Elk, a Buffalo, a Kiwanian. He thinks it vital to be a "booster" and not a "knocker"; and he is deeply hostile to the trade-union movement which he thinks is un-American. In a period of a strike, he is convinced that it is his duty to support a mystery called "law and order," by which he means that any demand for an increase in wages or a diminution in the hours of labour is an attack upon the fundamental ethos he calls "Americanism." He has no hesitation in using violence against the men who go on strike; but he has equally no hesitation in insisting that the striker is the embodiment of violence and, therefore, a threat to government. He knows very little of the history of American labour, and he is still less aware of what is happening to labour in foreign countries. He arrives at his office very early in the morning, and the energy he puts into his work is almost fantastic in its intensity. He knows very little of the life of America beyond the vocation he has chosen; and he looks upon his function with a passionate devotion which it is difficult to exaggerate. That emerges in the curious worship of the conventions of his profession; if he is a realtor, or a mortician, he will not admit that the doctor or the lawyer performs a superior function. He dislikes most politicians; he is willing to admire only the man or men who can do him some personal favour. What is interesting here is the fact that his vocation is his politics and that he rarely understands that his attitude to politics is the chief reason for its failure to achieve a real integrity in persons. For the fact that he refuses to study or to understand the issues that he has to decide is the root of the power by which the political machine is able to operate. In general, he knows the technique of his profession; but the larger issues of American life are something that he has rarely examined and still more rarely understood.

One of the most honourable traditions in American life is the fact that, unlike Europe, there is no calling which is assumed to be dishonourable. And it is only in recent years that there has begun to emerge on any considerable scale a leisured class comparable to that in Europe in that it enjoys privileges without the obligation to perform any function. Indeed, so long ago as Tocqueville's great work, it was already being noted that the wealthy American settled in Europe when he sought to avoid the duty of earning his living; and it still remains true that the American who does not labour is regarded with suspicion in the community to which he belongs. He may have a large inherited fortune; but it is still assumed that does not exclude the duty of proving that he can add to the well-being of the commonwealth. The great business man in the United States has an aristocratic status comparable to that of the land-owner or the soldier or the priest in pre-capitalist Europe. In this sense American democracy engenders an aristocracy of its own in which the return to labour instead of the return to idleness is the criterion of adequacy. And since it follows that labour is in itself a source of dignity, it follows that an American assumes that, as it were, he may hope to carry a millionaire's cheque-book in his luncheon basket.

The outcome of this attitude is complex. In the first place, a very few political positions apart, American ambition is concentrated on the business world and those areas, like the law, which are its dependencies. Money is a vital species not only of political power, but also of social prestige. The opinions of a wealthy man assume an importance merely because he is wealthy. He has a status in the community to which he belongs which sets the perspective of every other type of reputation. He will naturally act as a leader in all charitable and religious activities. The local press will build its outlook round the views that he holds. The kind of house he lives in, the sort of vacation he spends, the manner in which he chooses, as a collector of books or pictures, for example, even the clubs to which he belongs, set the tone and the atmosphere to which most of his neighbours will aspire. And, because he is free from the traditional relationships of his European analogue, he can act with a ruthless experimentalism which few Europeans would dare to emulate.

But this is not all. Since wealth is, as it were, the test of grace in the individual citizen, and since the mental climate is so predominantly set by men of wealth, there follow two conclusions which have a profound bearing upon the nature of American democracy. In the first place, it becomes divided into a very small number of enormously rich families and a vast multitude who, whatever their aspirations, have no hope of attaining wealth. And since that vast multitude appears to the small class of the rich a threat and a danger, the institutions of the multitude assume this characteristic also. As a consequence, the fact that wealth is the main effective source of aristocratic power means that the organization which the masses have built for their protection in Europe, whether trade-unions or co-operative societies or socialist parties, are viewed invariably with disfavour and not seldom with organized hostility. That can be seen in the attitude of the courts and the legislatures to the trade-unions, in the failure of the consumer to protect his interests. No doubt there have developed a number of important producers' co-operatives; but their main purpose has been to create safeguards against consumers' control rather than to serve the consumers' interests.

And to all this must be added the absence, in the relations of employers and employed, of any inherited goodwill; the purpose of each is simply to use the other. Out of this attitude arises a willingness, on both sides, to use violence as the technique by which success is gained. No one can examine the history of a great American strike without the sense that the employers assume that public opinion and the State power will both be on their side, and that the workers depend upon an appeal to some future history about the coming of which they have no sort of certainty. When Theodore Roosevelt appointed his commission on the coal strike in 1904, he secured the acceptance of his nomination of a labor representative, Edgar E. Clark, only by appointing him in the role of sociologist. From a somewhat different angle, the famous steel strike of 1919 and the textile strike of Gastonia are not very easy to distinguish from the habits of civil war; and the blood that has been shed in the coal conflicts of the last fifty years make even the bad relations between the miners and the mine-owners in Great Britain seem almost like an idyll in their quality.

It is, indeed, no longer true to argue, as Tocqueville argued, that there is a division of interest among the employers. On the contrary, the employers form a compact body the strength of which has grown pretty considerably in the last hundred years. They have used every division among their workers—territorial, racial, religious, national—through which they could hope to maintain their power. Since they overwhelmingly own the press, they are able to make a case against their employees which it is not easy for the latter to rebut; and the growth of new means of communication, like the radio, has meant that the employing class has a weapon at its disposal of enormous influence. Nor is that all. Anyone who examines the content of the movies since Hollywood became the capital city of the cinema industry cannot fail to realize that its direction is either to a psychology of escape or to the assumption that a labour leader is naturally a racketeer with whom no responsible man will have any connexion. And since, in the modern community, the continuity of public services is essential to the well-being of the State, whether it be the delivery of the mails or the supply of coal, or the running of the railroads, the workers' right to strike is almost bound to encounter the sovereign power of the community and be beaten or accept a compromise which they could probably have attained without a strike at all.

It may be true that the "yellow dog" contract has been overthrown in recent years. It may be true, also, that with the development of the Congress of Industrial Organizations, there is a growing hope that unskilled labour will, at long last, approximate to a place in the sun. But it is at least open to question whether the split in American labour will not, in the long run, assist the business man rather than endanger his supremacy; it is reasonable to argue that Mr. William Green and Mr. John L. Lewis hate the C.I.O. more than they hate the employers from whom they seek advantages the benefit of which is common to all members of the working class. The workers have been fortunate in the two facts, first, that the New Deal followed on the Great Depression, and, second, that the government moved into the grim epoch of the Second World War which made the worker an essential element in the organization of victory. But the central problem of economic power in time of peace remains; and there has been nothing so far to show that the authority of the employers has suffered any final diminution.

3

THE ordinary American business man must be scrutinized also as a citizen of a mighty commonwealth. It is in this aspect, perhaps, that he appears to least advantage. He is rarely interested in politics, at least in the sense of seeking to influence directly the character of its party life. He is still less interested in literature and the arts in a really serious way. No doubt he will subscribe to the Book-of-the-Month Club—though he is unlikely to read the books it chooses—and he is ready to support the local symphony orchestra. But his life is overwhelmingly wrapped up in his commercial affairs. He wants, of course, to live in the fashionable part of the city; he wants to drive the car which proclaims a secure bank balance; he is eager to belong to all the possible clubs membership in which is an index to social and economic prestige. He will, in his spare time, give to golf or bridge or poker an intensity of interest which far exceeds anything he can be persuaded to offer to the study of most political issues, domestic or international, which America confronts. He will devote immense energy to securing a good education for his children; and he will never be persuaded to doubt the greatness of America's future. That optimism is so profound that it is difficult to make him understand that the history of the world did not begin either in 1492 or in 1776. He is deeply suspicious of trade-unions, and the one reputation he desires to avoid is that of being regarded as a radical. And though a greater proportion of the business leaders in the United States have been to a university than is the case in any comparable country, it is at least probable that in no other country has a university training left so slight an impression.

This does not for one moment mean that he has not a number of great human qualities. His hospitality is remarkable. He is magnanimous wherever his support is enlisted for any good cause, from China to Peru. And his magnanimity is the expression of a vivid sympathy for any people not on the American continent who are struggling to achieve their freedom. Negroes and Jews apart, he is capable of an easy tolerance which assumes that success carries with it all the complex rights which go to the making of the American ideal. His mind is almost instinctively attuned to fashionable change; and his zest for mechanization, whether at home or in his business, if it is equalled in the Soviet Union, is certainly unsurpassed elsewhere. He has not an atom of that pride which makes an Englishman seek, if he can, to avoid the stigma of trade; and he has none of the Frenchman's passion for an early retirement on a modest competence. He has a real faith in the value of the expert, and he believes, almost with passion, that few things are more just than to pay him adequately in the context of a commercial adviser. He works devotedly and for long hours; and his corporation becomes for him almost an object of religious devotion. He is a staunch believer in the validity of republican institutions for the United States; but this does not exclude the power to venerate monarchical institutions in foreign countries. In general, he thinks it an obligation to respect the main forms of the Christian religion; though its rites are significant for him only as conventions since he is rarely aware either of its history or of its theology.

He assumes as a principle of living the general wisdom of convention and conformity; he does not like to be pointed out by his neighbours as a person who is "queer" or "different." He tends to be bewildered by the immensity of the social changes in the last generation of American history; and, once he has attained success, that bewilderment transforms him pretty easily into a *laudator temporis acti* who looks upon the past with a romantic nostalgia. But he is always sure that America will solve its problems and that, however ugly the immediate issues may seem, as they appeared in the years of the Great Depression, nevertheless in some providential way, prosperity is just around the corner. And he does not doubt that the roots of this prosperity lie in the urgency of individual effort, the willingness to face adversity with courage, and the wide recognition that America is not only "different," but, in some magic way, more hopeful in its prospects than any other country. He never forgets that, generally speaking, his fellow business men are better housed, better clothed, and better fed than the business men of other nations. He does not seek to explain why this should be the case; but the fact that it is the case gives him a romantic sense of superiority which he finds it difficult to conceal, above all when he is abroad.

The American business man's optimism is in one sense justified; no other people has a prospect immediately before it that offers so considerable an opportunity to the individual. On the other hand, it is a source of very real danger. For it has been shown in the three terms of President Franklin Roosevelt that it is difficult indeed to persuade the business man to accept the full civic responsibility which is his. He likes to blame the politician or the trade-unions, even the tariff or foreign "agitators." He makes for himself a facile picture of a world in which everything goes

well because the legislature, whether state or federal, is happily inactive
and no union asks for an increase of wages or a shortening of hours. The
slow erosion of the small man in business, the steeper ladder which must
be climbed to security, the growing fear of new ideas, the violent dislike
of any attempt to organize the workers, the use of every means of propaganda, the Churches, the wireless, the press, the cinema, to deter the
workers from listening to the siren voice of the walking delegate, all
lead to a philosophy which still attempts to prove that each man can do
best for himself. It is not an exaggeration to say that the intellectual
principles of all save the most exceptional business men in America are
less those of giant industry, with monopoly capitalism as its outstanding
feature, than those representing the culture of a suddenly enlarged village, almost afraid to examine the changes which it is uneasily aware
are occurring in its life. The business man was symbolic who said to the
Lynds' assistant, "We're not going to have any labour trouble here. Our
mayor was pretty radical back years ago, in his first term, but he is more
co-operative now." [4] Clearly, to the business men of Middletown, "more
co-operative" means more ready to accept the individualist outlook which
they regard as the index to safety.

And that safety, to most of them, is identified with freedom. They assume by freedom a social condition in which property is safe, and the
best way to insure its safety is to have the minimum of legislation. The
rights of a man become the power he has the strength to secure; and if
he has the wit to secure it, he does not think that any politician or judge
should interfere with its possession. So that the chief article of the business man's philosophy is that a citizen is what he has got and that the
State power exists for its protection. In essence, it is an eighteenth-century
philosophy, an outlook which gives little or no heed to the vast changes
in American economic development since the Civil War in general, and
since the First World War in particular. It applies the doctrines of the
simple, agrarian society of Washington and Jefferson to contemporary
America. In Wall Street and State Street it believes with Alexander
Hamilton that "your people, sir, is a great beast." It is, indeed, tempting
to argue that the attitude of American business to the problems of the
modern community combines the methods of Thomas Hobbes with the
accents of the religious revivalists Moody and Sankey. For a history of
men who have been the main factors in the vast economic development
of the last eighty years is like nothing so much as the record of imperial
despots who justify their policies partly by the insistence that it is nature's law that the weaker must go to the wall, and partly by rationalizing their achievement to themselves, or having it rationalized for them
as the expression of Christian principles. So Bishop Lawrence of Massachusetts, for long years a member of the Harvard Corporation, could
urge, with no sense of self-deception, that "in the long run, it is only to

[4] Robert S. and Helen M. Lynd, *Middletown in Transition* (New York: Harcourt,
Brace, 1937), p. 37.

the man of morality that wealth comes. We believe in the harmony of God's universe. We know that it is only by working along His laws, natural and spiritual, that we can work with efficiency. . . . Godliness is in league with riches. . . . Material prosperity is helping to make the national character sweeter, more joyous, more unselfish, more Christ-like." [5] How long the run must be, Bishop Lawrence did not say; but it is at least a matter of reasonable doubt whether Christ would have recognized His gospel in the careers of the men who dominated American economic life.

4

THE fact was that, certainly by the end of the First World War, the economic power of the United States was concentrated, as nowhere else in the world, in the hands of a few hundred men who recognized no responsibility for its use except to themselves. There was criticism of the great power they wielded; there was even, as in the Sherman Act, an attempt by Congress to control this vast empire of which they disposed. Acts like those which established the Interstate Commerce Commission sought to protect the American people from being their subjects; measures like the Federal Reserve Act of 1913 endeavoured to prevent the growth of an immense and centralized money power in private hands; measures like the Clayton Act, by declaring that labour was not a commodity, sought to safeguard the status of labour. Men like Theodore Roosevelt spoke sternly about "malefactors of great wealth" though they were careful to take no action against them. The "new liberalism" of men like Woodrow Wilson offered to American citizens the hope that their sons would be "the head of some small, it may be, but flourishing business" just as the epoch when it began to be certain that the economic destiny of the United States would not in essence be different from that of Europe. The great boom of the Coolidge epoch was followed by the Great Depression which, for a moment, seemed to call into question the business man's imperial power. For something like the first few months of Franklin Roosevelt's first term it looked as though America would indeed have a New Deal in deeds as well as words. Had that occurred the United States might have experienced another revolution as profound as the Civil War.

But what occurred was in no sense a revolution. The Great Depression transformed America into a social service state such as Great Britain had become under the Liberal government of 1906–14. The incomes of the very wealthy were taxed at new levels. Social security, including pensions for the aged, was introduced. The federal government assisted the programme of housing, and came to the aid of the unemployed by providing them with work or relief in various forms. It secured a tighter control of the process of investment when it established the Securities and Exchange Commission. The Wagner Act pushed forward the status

[5] William Lawrence, *Fifty Years* (Boston: Houghton Mifflin, 1923), pp. 13-14.

of trade-unionism to a level beyond even that which had been dreamed of by the Knights of Labor. Nor was it unimportant that the New Deal made the process of government interesting in a way that it had not previously been interesting as a career even in the great days of the Virginian presidents. But when all the results of the New Deal are added up, both ownership and control remained fundamentally in the same hands as before President Roosevelt entered the White House.

And that meant, despite the immense sweep of mass production, that the enterprise of America was founded on the theory of restriction and not of abundance. That is indicated by a number of considerations. America in a world of peace has the choice between three possibilities. It can maintain the levels of full employment brought to it by the Second World War by so altering the distribution of its wealth that its capacity for production is equalled by its capacity to consume. Or it may maintain that level by a great and continuous programme of public works, which would do for the epoch of peace what the requirements of victory did for the epoch of war. Or it may embark upon a policy of foreign investment. This third choice, clearly, is of two kinds. America may attempt the kind of long-term investment which, by raising the standard of life through the capital equipment of backward areas like China and South America and the Balkans, creates a demand, over a period, for its consumer-goods proportionate to its capacity to produce. Or there is the grim alternative of an American economic imperialism seeking a swift return on present investment through the use of its immense strategic and financial power.

It is, of course, a matter of complicated speculation to decide which of these choices America will make. No one who has studied the history of American business enterprise will imagine that it is likely that its leaders will surrender, or even, if they can avoid it, compromise, their authority. Their habit has been to fight for every position that they occupy, and to yield only when, as in the Civil War, the slave-owners were overwhelmed by the forces of the North. Nor is it easy to believe that in a system of state capitalism either the ownership or control of property can pass beyond the stage the New Deal had reached by the time of Pearl Harbor. It is not the habit of property to tax itself on any serious scale except in a crisis. When everything is at stake, as in a great war, property owners may be ready for large-scale sacrifices; but anyone who studies in detail either the pre-history of the Civil War, or the period which preceded Pearl Harbor, will realize how cheerfully most men are prepared to surrender the freedom of the masses on condition that they retain possession of their own property. A crisis as sudden and profound as the Great Depression may lead to a temporary acquiescence in important innovations. But the New Deal if it has shown anything, has shown that the acquiescence achieved by domestic difficulty is of temporary duration; while even an event like the Second World War has called for sacrifices from the workers at least proportionate to the sacrifices of the wealthy. It is significant, in this latter instance, that President Roosevelt was quite unable to secure the acceptance of his programme of taxation and that the system of rationing imposed hardly scratched the normal surface of consumption.

It is not therefore easy for an observer to accept the conclusion even of an economic historian so distinguished as Professor Louis Hacker that the new State capitalism of America "heralds an era of abundance, which is protected by the American tradition of the Enlightenment, the American Revolution, Jeffersonianism, Old Radical Republicanism, Populism." That each of these has contributed an element to the American tradition that is important I am not for one moment concerned to deny. That their outcome will keep Americans, in Professor Hacker's words, "economically secure . . . and politically free" seems to me far less certain.[6] Professor Hacker does not inquire for whom that security and freedom will be retained. He omits the fact that the overwhelming proportion of Negroes in the United States has never enjoyed them. He does not discuss the immense implications of the virtual closure of the United States to European and, still more, to Asiatic immigration. He fails to analyse the bearing of the present system of ownership and control on the number of American citizens to whom security and freedom are part of the normal expectation of daily life. And writing before Pearl Harbor, it is perhaps natural that he should have overlooked the price paid for fatigue by a nation that has engaged in a great war, which its rulers seek to prevent from assuming revolutionary proportions. Yet it is Professor Hacker himself who sees that the significance of the Civil War for the United States lay precisely in the fact that its revolutionary implications enabled the normal fatigue of war to be overcome.[7]

My own conjecture is that after twelve years of exciting innovation, in which are included the immense experiences of the Second World War, it is at least highly probable that the ruling class in the United States will be violently opposed to further domestic experiment of any size in economic matters. It is, no doubt, true that President Roosevelt was elected for his fourth term in considerable degree by the organized political action of the working class. But it is necessary to note here at least two things. In the first place, the central importance of President Roosevelt's fourth term belonged not to social or economic experiment but to the achievement of victory in the field and to the building of a lasting peace upon that victory. But each of these, in their turn, depended upon the ability of his successor, Mr. Truman, to secure the co-operation of exactly those business interests which, at least since 1936, had been mostly concerned to achieve President Roosevelt's defeat. To get their co-operation President Truman's policy must, in the main, be set in a framework which avoids the type of innovation which, like the Wagner Act, was symbolic of the New Deal. And, in the second place, once it

[6] Louis M. Hacker, *The Triumph of American Capitalism* (New York: Simon and Schuster, 1940), p. 435.
[7] *Ibid.,* Chap. 24, *passim.*

was so tragically determined that President Roosevelt should not have a fifth term, it was reasonably obvious that both the major parties would seek for a candidate in 1948 who could be trusted to give the wealthy class a period of peace and quietness after the mounting excitement of the years from 1933.

I do not therefore believe in that economics of abundance upon which Professor Hacker lays so strong an emphasis. He is, I think, confusing mass production with abundance. They are quite different things. A society of which the economic basis is, as in the United States, capitalist, is not concerned with abundance but with the making of profit for those who own and control the instruments of production. Profit comes from the satisfaction of effective demand; and the outstanding fact in the economic life of America is that the distribution of wealth does not make possible the use of its productive resources by American consumers. That grim truth emerges from the fact that if the government of the United States ceased to place orders for the waging of war the number of its unemployed would, at the present rate of production, be counted by millions. And once we effectively re-enter a world of peace there is no reason to expect that the government of the United States will place orders with private industry on a scale which will secure full employment at adequate wages for the mass of American workers. The main preoccupation of wealthy America will be tax reduction, and the obvious high roads to tax reduction are either the socialization of ownership—which is a threat to the heart of wealthy America—or the reduction of the orders placed by the federal government with private enterprise. It is a reasonable speculation to assume that the attention of wealthy America will be directed to the second of these alternatives. It then becomes a fairly safe prophecy that, after a boom period in which the shortage of consumers' goods is replaced, the post-war America of monopoly capitalism will, even with its capacity for mass production, stagger in some zigzag fashion into a new depression.

There is, of course, the possibility that the new America will seek to build up the standard of life in backward countries like China by long-term investments at low rates of interest. America is a generous country, as capable as any other of taking the long view. And, on the long view, certainly the more prosperous the rest of the world, the greater will be the call upon American production. The difficulty of believing that this will happen depends upon many factors. First, it is unlikely that American business men, who lost so heavily on international investments between the two world wars, will be tempted to take that risk a second time on the same terms. And, in the next place, the very nature of the risk will make it hard to persuade the ordinary investor to accept low interest rates on loans about the repayment of which he will feel grave uncertainty. There is also the third difficulty that loans of this character are in fact unlikely to be repaid unless they are directed to satisfactory purposes and under suitable guarantees. But the history of international lending makes it abundantly clear that neither of these ends is feasible unless the borrowing is done on behalf of the masses and the whole financial process operated under the independent auspices of a world authority. It is one thing, to make an obvious comparison, to undertake the kind of loans made by investment houses in the United States to Cuba or to Latin American states with a bribe, as in the case of Peru, of a sum of four hundred and fifteen thousand dollars to the son of its then President for what were euphemistically termed "services" in connection with its flotation; but it is a very different thing to organize loans through a channel like the Economic Section of the United Nations. In the first case, as the inquiries set on foot after the Great Depression made clear, a small number of men amass great wealth without regard to honesty or integrity; in the second, there are honesty and integrity, but there is no hope that American investors will acquire great fortunes with any swiftness. And the larger the degree in which the second method is utilized, the more the world is bound to move towards that planning of its economic life which is in direct contradiction to the philosophy of the American business man.

On this showing, the most likely American choice is the old, if simple and evil, one of economic imperialism, of which it has already had some experience between 1919 and 1939. It is evident that, if this be the choice, it will emphasize each element in the economic life of the United States of which the Depression of 1929 was the logical outcome. There will be an abyss between productive capacity and purchasing power which cannot be bridged. There will be an increasing concentration of wealth and income; in President Roosevelt's special message to Congress of April 29, 1938, he reported that already in 1933 one-tenth of one per cent of all the corporations which returned an annual estimate to the Bureau of Internal Revenue owned fifty-two per cent of the corporate wealth of America and that eighty-four per cent of the net income of manufacturing corporations was owned by less than four per cent of them. Leadership passed in the inter-war period from industry to finance-capital; the House of Morgan alone controlled nearly one-fourth of America's corporate wealth. And ownership, as distinct from earning, brought little to the average American. The concentration was such that, as President Roosevelt said, it had "roughly the same effect as if, out of every three hundred persons in our population, one person received seventy-eight cents out of every dollar of corporate dividends, while the other two hundred and ninety-nine persons divided up the other twenty-two cents between them." And this was in a period when there was not only a gap between production and consumption, but when so conservative a body as the Brookings Institution could conclude that sixty thousand families at the top of the income scale saved almost as much as the twenty-five million families with incomes below five thousand dollars per annum. All of which is to say that, economically at least, America is already a class society in the monopolistic stage, and its foreign trade depends upon its willingness to finance the countries that import from it. Granted the situation the Second World War has brought to Europe and Asia, the development of any further American economic imperialism will sooner or later intensify the same factors which led to the Depression of 1929. The Marshall Plan has not altered this. At some stage, the over-all situation would issue in a crisis incompatible with the traditional philosophy of business enterprise in the United States. For at some stage American capitalists would have to look to the State power to make the economic life of the community a going concern.

From this angle of approach, it is difficult to say that the philosophy of American business has had any coherent relation to its practice. The philosophy has been a system of principles which emphasized individual opportunity, the neutrality of the State, the power of business to rely on its inherent capacity for dynamic expansion. It was hostile to bureaucracy, and its economic character was determined by the direction of its political power. None of these principles had any serious meaning after 1919. What was being created, slowly before 1929 and rapidly after it, was a new mercantilism in which it was ever more difficult to find the real sources of responsibility. The workingman who told Mr. and Mrs. Lynd that he had at first sought to understand the New Deal but had rapidly given up trying because its complexity was too great [8] was, in fact, announcing the abdication of his citizenship. And it is, *a priori,* obvious that a democracy cannot hope to endure if its problems leave its citizens convinced that they cannot understand them. For the next stage is that in which a bewildered multitude is deprived of its political power, is even ready, perhaps, to surrender it. When that stage looms before a nation, it is in serious danger of moving into the epoch of fascism.

For the real issue that American business has still got to examine with genuine intellectual honesty is the question whether so immense a concentration of wealth as has taken place in the United States since the Civil War is really compatible with the maintainance of democratic political institutions. It has proved compatible, no doubt, with the New Deal; but the price of the New Deal has, on any showing, been high. It has made the process of government far less intelligible, because far more complex, to the ordinary man. It has involved America in international power politics, with the knowledge that full employment depends upon the continuance of a budget which can attain the necessary height only by the process of government spending. And this, in its turn, means that the power of government over the lives of citizens is bound, on any showing, to be enormous. Mr. Roosevelt's policies gave a direction to the economic life of America from which it will be very difficult for his opponents to go back. That, after all, is why the Republican programme in the presidential election of 1944 sounded so like an alternative programme for the Democratic party, with the invective hurled at different persons, no doubt, but in essence the same programme with the same promises,

[8] Lynd, *op. cit.,* p. 256.

even though it was suspected that the beneficiaries of a Republican victory would have been very different from the beneficiaries of Mr. Roosevelt's fourth term.

And if the beneficiaries were very different, the procedure through which welfare was extended to them was less different in reality than it appeared upon the surface. The economic royalists may have hated Mr. Roosevelt as perhaps no president has been hated since Andrew Jackson; but whether they approved or disapproved, they wanted the contracts through which he piled up the deficits they condemned, and he, in his turn, especially after Pearl Harbor, needed their co-operation since upon it depended the mobilization of America's full economic capacity. In the result, they were the essential intermediaries through whom the politicians secured the results at which they aimed. And this relationship is the more interesting, even impressive, when it is remembered that its every implication contradicts the pattern of values which almost all Americans are asked to accept unless they wish to incur the charge of being "radical." They believed in the gospel of success through individual initiative, in a kind of Darwinian struggle for survival in which those who proved themselves the strongest in the competition of business would also be those whose victory was best for America. They believed that any man will be successful provided only that he works hard, and they thought American civilization was in danger once the habits of business were interfered with by the politicians. They accepted the thesis that business leaders have wealth because they have exhibited superior fore-sight, that the wealthy, indeed, are both abler and of a higher character than the poor, which is the reason for their wealth. They find it diffi-cult, and even dangerous, to suppose that there is any ultimate dishar-mony of interest between capital and labour, and they regard the trade-union organizer as a troublemaker whose habits are un-American. Above all, they are convinced that a healthy outlook is by nature optimistic, and that few people are more dangerous than the critics of fundamental Amer-icanism. Those critics, indeed, are the men whose refusal to tread the middle way is largely responsible for things like bolshevism in Russia and nazism in Germany. To safeguard America against their poison is the surest way of preserving its greatest traditions as well as to fulfil the promise of its greatest hopes.

The contrast is obvious between the traditional pattern of these values and the actual habits of American business life. It is difficult not to feel that the contrast has reached that point which Tocqueville noted over a century ago as always dangerous in the history of a democracy, the point, as he put it, "where the taste for physical gratifications among such a people has grown more rapidly than their education and their experience of free institutions." That is the point where status is so much the out-come of monetary fortune or of economic power that men are ready to feel that whatever interferes with its acquisition is a source of irritation. But in that mood a nation may as easily lose, as it may retain, its freedom

by confounding the power of property with the fulfilment that freedom
makes possible; and in that mood, also, a people finds it difficult to distinguish between the private interests of a few and the public interest of
the many. Nor is as much done to prevent the distinction from being
made as it is by those few themselves, whose threat is the greater because
they do not realize that it is a threat at all. On the contrary, they act
from a conviction that is pathetic in its sincerity that the maintenance of
their authority is the vital condition of public good.

"I am of opinion," wrote Tocqueville in what is, in some ways, the
most remarkable chapter of his famous book, "that the manufacturing
aristocracy which is growing up under our eyes is one of the harshest
which ever existed in the world; but at the same time it is one of the
most confined and least dangerous. Nevertheless the friends of democracy should keep their eyes anxiously fixed in this direction; for if ever
a permanent inequality of conditions and aristocracy again penetrate into
the world, it may be predicted that this is the channel by which they will
enter." [9] The confinement of which he spoke disappeared with remarkable swiftness after the Civil War, so that the dangers he foresaw have
again cast their shadow over American life. For not only has the
perspective of American politics been set by the will of what Tocqueville
terms "a manufacturing aristocracy," but it is a perspective so set that
there remains a permanent class of workers, growing, proportionately,
in size, who cannot seriously expect ever to climb far beyond the limits
from which they began. And even when they are driven by catastrophic
experience to organize into trade-unions for the sake of self-protection,
they find that they must adapt themselves to the needs of private property, that they seek to live by what social reforms they can wrest from a
State power which is permanently in the hands of their opponents. They
cannot seek a genuine independence of the State power for this is to hand
themselves over to be exploited by its agents. They dare not rest content with its neutralization since that results in the emergence of an economic anarchy which, by threatening law and order, brings the State
power once more into play to assure their safeguard or restoration. And,
in any case, in the epoch of monopoly capitalism the "manufacturing
aristocracy" of Tocqueville cannot accept a trade-unionist policy which
endangers the continuity of production.

For, under modern technological conditions, continuity of production is the necessary basis for an adequate communal life. In its absence,
all the foundations of modern society—power, transport, food, the services of health and housing—are in danger. This is why a prolonged strike
in the mines or on the railroads, at power stations or at the docks, at
once makes government action one of the terms in its equation. It becomes essential for trade-union leaders to hew close to a line of action

[9] Alexis de Tocqueville, *Democracy in America,* translated by Henry Reeve (New
York: Appleton, 1904), Vol. II, p. 649.

which does not compromise them with the government. Experience makes it plain that once they do so the result is to call out against them the police and the army. But the trade-union leaders have also to secure for their followers the satisfaction of that expectation of continuous improvement in material well-being which is, after all, the rationale of their existence. It thus becomes an urgent matter for trade-unions in the United States to persuade the wealthy class to accept the necessity of continuous social reform. This, in its turn, requires an economy of abundance; and this economy is unavailable to the United States under contemporary conditions save upon terms which the state power must itself define. A refusal of those conditions, if it be more than verbal face-saving, becomes immediately a revolutionary act; and since no State power can permit its inherent principle to be called into question—which is what a revolution attempts—American trade-unions must, for their own safety, accept those conditions. In the age of an expanding capitalism this serves to conceal the fact that well-being is available only on the terms of the State power. But when that expansion halts, as in a slump, still more, when it passes into the age of economic contraction, concealment becomes an increasingly difficult objective to attain.

This concealment is the purpose fulfilled by the philosophy of the American business man. By his emphasis upon a system of values which largely represent the hopes and aspirations of an America which no longer exists, he is trying to bridge the gap between the dream and the reality. The system of values is supported by every device that propaganda can suggest. It is the basis of what is taught in school and college. Upon it are founded most of the traditions of which it is customary to speak well in addition to those of which it is customary to speak badly. The log cabin to White House tradition, the faith in the United States as the land of boundless opportunity, the insistence that, unlike European communities, American democracy is real and classless, the confidence in a special American destiny, the conviction that there is work for everyone who is willing to work, the acceptance of the principle that whatever is bigger is therefore better, which is held side by side with the principle that it is the special genius of America to respect and safeguard the little man, all of these form aspects of a pattern of behaviour which the press and the radio and the cinema combine by endless repetition in countless forms to make appear the "natural" pattern of American behaviour. So an ardent Republican like Professor William Starr Myers can fill the columns of a widely selling periodical like the *Saturday Evening Post* with an ardent attempt to prove that the "rugged individualism" of President Hoover had already set the stage for recovery when the New Deal, by insisting upon State action, undid all the good President Hoover had accomplished by his reliance upon the working of natural law.

5

A PHILOSOPHY like this must, if it is to succeed, be capable of summarizing effectively the mass experience upon which it tries to impose itself. The issue before the next generation of Americans is precisely whether this summarization will be proven by the facts of American economic life. It is easy to see how a legend like the career of Abraham Lincoln or the drama of careers like those of Carnegie or Edison or Henry Ford may help to persuade innumerable other Americans of the reality of their right to hold similar aspirations which will issue in similar results. But an increasing number of Americans are likely to discover that the concurrence of the historic conditions and the extraordinary ability of these men is an exceptional thing remarkable for its very exceptionality. It takes a great deal of effort in a people before it can utilize its Lincolns when it has the good fortune to find them. He is not the ordinary man one meets in the smoker of the Pullman train. The danger of the American business man's philosophy is that it assumes that the ordinary man will become extraordinary if the occasion requires it, just as there is usually in the Senate of the United States a body of men whose outlook is mainly shaped by a combination of surprise and disappointment that they, instead of its actual incumbent, are not in the White House. So the routine of American business breeds a class of leaders whose main interest arises from their identification of acquisition with justice. When the acquisition is challenged, it is rare indeed for them to understand that the claims of justice to recognition are not thereby equally challenged. And even if they have a sense of that understanding, it is on the level less of a social right recognized than, as is so typical of an aristocracy, of a benefit conferred out of a conscious magnanimity.

This is why so many business leaders in the United States are, on the one hand, afraid of all new thinking lest it breed a challenge, and, on the other, have an outlook for which it is difficult to find any other word than totalitarian; by which I mean that they seek either directly or through the agents whom they control to allow no important aspect of social life to be beyond the range of their power. That emerges as clearly on the plane of education as it does upon the plane of culture. It seems as natural for wealthy America to control the schools and colleges as it seems obvious to them to regard literature and the fine arts as an escape from reality to which they lend their patronage rather than as a means whereby the life of America may be fulfilled and enriched. Certainly it is true to say that American speculative thought was bolder, more sure of itself, more willing to ask the vital questions and listen to the answers that were given, say, between some such time as that of Andrew Jackson and the end of Grant's second term than at any period since that time. The great epoch of New England, the confidence of Walt Whitman, the remarkable analytic power of men like Calhoun, were met with a pride in the very fact of their quality which contrasts very strikingly with the attitude to work of the first critical order in the period after the First World War. Nineteenth-century America may be almost arrogant in its self-confidence, but at least it is an unafraid America. Twentieth-century America is intellectually timid by comparison. It is not sure what a new idea may not prove capable of achieving; and it is still less sure whether a new idea may not prove dangerous to the established order. It is very anxious to prevent too public a revelation of the things of which it knows it should be ashamed. One does not go to the movies to see a film on the T.V.A., the picture of what the enterprise of government may achieve. One does not like too close a public scrutiny even of Main Street or to brood on the failure of hope in a family like the Joads.[10] A newly appointed dean of the Harvard Law School caused eyebrows to be lifted when he announced his support of President Roosevelt's Court Plan in 1937. A professor of economics was dismissed from a university for asking untimely questions of the evangelist Billy Sunday. Looking for academic heresies is a favourite occupation of the yellow press. The veils which discreetly shroud a figure it is unwise to see from too close at hand must not be unfolded.

Hardly less revealing is the direction taken, after the Treaty of Versailles, by the lunatic fringe in American thought. The revival of the Ku Klux Klan, the ready ear lent by the masses to the doctrines taught by such men as Townsend and Father Coughlin, technocracy in its various shapes, the remarkable rise to power of so able a demagogue as Huey Long, the willingness of Congress, year after year, to continue its subsidies to the committee which has given to the name of a Texas congressman, Mr. Martin Dies, a spurious immortality, the attainment of new levels of intolerance in matters of race and religion, all these are examples only of a temper the rise of which is evidence beyond dispute that America, even before the Second World War, was losing its sense of an inner security which could rise, almost without effort, above the problems it confronted. And to all this it is important to add that there were few observers in the inter-war years who were not impressed by the decline in all forms of religious orthodoxy, in the instability of the younger generation in those issues of morals about which their elders had been so supremely confident, in the danger to the family and its unity represented by the wholesale externalization of pleasures. The philosophy of the American business man was finding the sources out of which it would be challenged even when, under President Coolidge, it appeared to be indulging in a complacent orgy of successful speculation under the impression, as he made clear, that rich men are fit objects of national worship. The thin-lipped, unimaginative officeholder, who seemed to be made of granite as unbreakable as the rocks of his native Vermont, had no conception, when he permitted the nomination of Mr. Herbert Hoover at the Republican convention of 1928, that when he passed out of the White

[10] John Steinbeck, *The Grapes of Wrath* (New York: Viking Press, 1939).

House an epoch came to an end of which he was an interesting and re-markable symbol.

It was the epoch in which the utilitarian expression of native American Puritanism ceased to answer the basic questions which Americans every-where were driven to ask, year in and year out, after the great crash on the Stock Exchange of October 29, 1929. There seemed on that day to have been released forces making for doubt, even for despair, which could not be returned to the vasty deep from which they came. "America," as the poet Archibald MacLeish had written, "was promises." But after the dawn of the Great Depression, it became even more difficult to be certain that the promises would be fulfilled. A hundred years ago, even half a century ago, few Americans ever doubted that a period of stagna-tion would be followed, fairly quickly, by recovery to a new level of prosperity. In the last generation depression has had a background of permanence about it which has given birth to fears which somehow would not die down. Anyone who compares the atmosphere of eager faith of the America from the time of Jackson until the First World War with the complex and artificial efforts, after 1919, to persuade the world that business men had discovered the secret of permanent prosperity can hardly avoid the conclusion that they were afraid and anxious, by an excessive influence of reiteration, to conceal their fear from themselves.

They failed so to conceal it; and it is evident enough that their failure is the cause of the determined persecution of workingmen whose opinions were deemed dangerous. It is important to note that, after 1929, it was hard to find a business man who could face the future with any sense of security. The New Deal was in method nothing so much as a con-tradiction in terms of all the principles upon which they had been accustomed to rely. They therefore hated the New Deal, President Roose-velt, the intellectuals, especially the academic intellectuals, who under-took to act on "theories" which they were brought up to condemn. How could men who knew life only from books possibly dare to explain to men of action that behind their practices there lay a vast body of unex-plored assumptions of most of which they were unaware, not least that they had ceased to have a meaning in the United States of the Great De-pression? They resented the investigations of their behaviour in the Coolidge epoch, and, not least, the obvious applause with which the masses received the results of the investigations and their demand that the be-haviour revealed should have consequences in the courts. They saw their gods reviled and the doctrines they had been accustomed to venerate treated with angry contempt. It was like nothing so much as the experi-ence of a profoundly religious pagan hearing a Christian in the first two centuries insist upon the folly and ignorance of paganism.

What emerged as the outcome of these years of angry debate was the rebirth of the doctrine of a "higher law," which had been at the basis of Calhoun's philosophy. By the "higher law" a minority was justified in its claims against a majority, once reason and experience were on its side. The Supreme Court was striking down each item of the New Deal with a rhetoric which, in judges like Sutherland and McReynolds, could hardly help but remind the historian of Choate's fantastic argument in the Income Tax case.[11] At that stage, the American Constitution seemed to them almost an additional book of the New Testament, and the majority of the judges apostles of a righteousness rooted in reason. When the Court drew back before the volume and intensity of public criticism, the business men of America were uncertain of where they stood. They worshipped a Constitution which was interpreted by their own lawyers, clothed, no doubt, in the majestic robes of the Court, to coincide with their own philosophy. When the Constitution was a body of doctrine which a legislative assembly could control, they fell flat on their faces and shrieked that President Roosevelt was guilty of a deliberate usurpation of power, that he had turned a constitutional democracy into a personal dictatorship.

And this view was the more interesting because of the framework in which it must be set. Partly, it was given by the cult of the lawyer who, in a changing world, was the unbreakable rock upon which their security was founded; and, partly, it was given by the elevation of Lincoln to the place of the supreme hero in American history. That elevation satisfied an important need in the mythopoesis of American life. It gave a basis for the traditional faith in the common man, while it showed, so that everyone could see, that the American Constitution offered the highest political office in the Union to a poor and largely self-taught railsplitter who had nothing to rely on for his advancement save his own character and energy of mind. This elevation of the man who died in saving the Union was a simultaneous elevation of the Constitution through which the Union had its being, and the elevation of the Constitution became, as it was viewed through the mists of time, the ultimate technique of safeguarding the rights of property from "invasion" by the multitude. One can see, at least as far back as the consternation produced by Theodore Roosevelt's advocacy of the recall of judicial decisions in 1912, how the combination of Lincoln and the work of the Supreme Court maintained the continuity of interpretation that property required, how the myth had been born which gave to the wealthy the comforting conviction that their possessions were safe and to the common people the luxury of building their aspirations on the knowledge that the greatest figure in American history was one of themselves.

What gave this work so exceptional an interest were the things omitted from its formulation. Nothing was said to make it plain that, under the American system, the Constitution meant precisely what the Supreme Court desired at any time, and that most of the members of the Court were appointed to it because they were successful lawyers in the sense in which the business man understood success. Still less was said to make it clear either that Lincoln was an extraordinary man, melan-

---

[11] *Pollock* v. *Farmers' Loan Company,* 157 U.S. 690 (1895).

choly, aloof, profoundly ambitious, a political schemer of outstanding ingenuity, or that he handled the Constitution, during the crisis years in which he was president, with a determination that it should be the servant, and not the master, of the purposes he wished to see prevail. For the first fact would have emphasized the heights upon which Lincoln lived, and the uniqueness of his experience in ascending them. And the second fact would have made it obvious that the source of that "higher law" embodied in the Constitution had in fact nothing mysterious or eternal about it but lay primarily in the conceptions of what was necessary to the preservation of the Union as these formed themselves in the daily experience of the war in the mind of a man whose presence in the White House no one would have ventured to predict before he entered it. And among those conceptions, it is important never to forget, was the abolition of slavery without compensation to slave-owners, one of the largest sacrifices of property rights to public necessity that has occurred between the French and Russian Revolutions.

The business men of America operated the myth as practical men concerned to see that it secured the ends they had in view. They could not even imagine, much less concede, that the value of any myth to its age lies in its capacity for adaptation to those needs which its rulers regard as paramount. What they regarded as the historic deposit of a law fashioned in the image of Reason itself was, as Judge Thurman Arnold pointed out, no more than the "folklore of capitalism." But it was hardly less interesting that Judge Arnold himself rejected the business man's conception by arguing in favour of the rise of a "competent, practical, opportunistic, governing class" which will act on the principle that "any governmental creed that is proffered by actual leaders must change to fit the emotional need of their people." [12] It is obvious that this assumes the desirability of an *élite* which takes care of the masses much as a doctor takes charge of his patients; and, indeed, Judge Arnold compares disdainfully the standards of the law with those of medicine. It is clear to his mind that the average citizen is too incompetent to look after himself, and that so long as the men with the expertise necessary to rule do so, they need have no concern with the masses save to organize their emotional satisfaction. The governor of the new American order, as Judge Arnold conceives him, may not unfairly be described as a modern version of Machiavelli's Prince with a specialist's knowledge of psychiatry.

Judge Arnold clearly does not object to the philosophy of the business man on the ground that it makes the few the masters of the many; he merely argues that it is urgent that the business man should really know his job. Since he does not believe that ordinary people can attain to this real knowledge at a level which may be regarded as scientific, the right to rule belongs to the men who are competent. Judge Arnold does not ask, any more than business men have been inclined to ask, competent

[12] Thurman Arnold, *The Folklore of Capitalism* (New Haven: Yale University Press, 1937), p. 21.

for what and competent for whom? From his angle of approach, merely to raise this question is to suggest that some faith or ideal is desirable which transcends the claims of expediency and discovers the necessity of principles of social action which become imperatives because they enable us to satisfy demand on the largest possible scale. That satisfaction depends upon our ability to know demand, and this, in its turn, is a function of the citizen's ability not merely to make his demands articulate, but also to judge rationally the policies which operate to satisfy them. Since rational judgment depends upon knowledge, and since men think differently who live differently, there must be common purposes which enable men to trust one another, and to co-operate with one another, not as end and instrument, but as fellow-adventurers on a voyage of discovery; as Mr. Justice Holmes put it in a well-known sentence, "Every year, if not every day, we have to wager our salvation upon some prophecy based upon imperfect knowledge." [13]

If we approach the central issue in this way there is little left of the business man's philosophy, and, perhaps, even less of the sophisticated version of it for which Judge Thurman Arnold stood sponsor. The philosophy of the business man emerges in its historical setting as simply and as naturally as the philosophy of the slave-owner in the ancient world or the feudal lord who must rarely have doubted that by enabling him to maintain or even increase his well-being, his tenants were adding to their own.[14] The historical setting is given us partly by factors in the material environment and partly by the quest of mankind to become the masters of Nature. There are elements in it which are there because the geographical discoveries of the fifteenth and sixteenth centuries coincided with a successful rebellion against the authority of the Roman Catholic Church; and the coincidence arises from the fact that the explorers set new horizons for men to scan which they could not hope to reach if the system of values they accepted was confined to the modes of behaviour which Rome was prepared to approve. The rebellion became revolutionary in its proportions, and in doing so it dug deep fingers into every aspect of man's relation with the universe. There was a new philosophy, not least a new method of examining philosophical questions. There was a new science, which fought its way, by the seventeenth century, to the need for verifying its principles by experiment. There was a new ethic, which slowly sought to make the conduct of the life we know the test of right and wrong. There was a new approach to politics and to economic issues as men found one way of access to well-being more adequate than another. The unfolding of the new way of life that all this permitted was rarely either coherent or balanced in time and space. Not seldom, indeed, the very innovators themselves were unaware of what they were doing, still less of the scale of their innovation; John Calvin would have found

---

[13] *Abrams* v. *United States.*
[14] *Cf.* my *Rise of European Liberalism* (London: Allen & Unwin, 1932), Introduction and Chap. I.

it impossible to admit that his theology, and the social ethic it implied, was other than a recovery of truths revealed by Christ which had been denied or lost by subsequent generations before him. Out of this reshaping of the foundations of human thought and, hardly less, the transformation of the search after knowledge from a humble waiting on the will of Providence as revealed through his Church, to a hunt after power, with wealth as the vital index to power, there emerged a new attitude to work, to the poor, to property as the mark of grace, to the idea of Nature as an ordered cosmos the laws of which could be discovered by research and thereby make the individual the master of that Nature before which he had, since the exile from Eden, been no more than a helpless rebel.

All these are elements which have gone to the definition of the business man's philosophy in the United States. Inevitably, one epoch has seen one element emphasized more profoundly than others; and each has its rationalizations, both conscious and unconscious, by which it sought to impose them on some particular time and place. The circumstances of New England made its texture there seem very different from its texture in the deep South or in the Pacific states. And those circumstances are made different by the different national inheritances out of which the United States has been formed, German and Slav and Italian, as well as British and French and Dutch, and a Scandinavian element the impact of which is as unmistakable as that of the great Polish emigration. The tacit acceptance of the business man's philosophy as a pattern of values was the result of its association with an expanding economy which brought wider and deeper satisfaction to a larger proportion of the population than was probably ever the case previously in history. It was always challenged, challenged as a pattern of ideas and as a practical way of life. But until the last frontier had been crossed, as the nineteenth century drew to its close, it is broadly true to say that it met each challenge with triumphant success. Its basis seemed to be justifiable not merely to the men who profited by it, but, for the most part, even to those, whether native-born Americans or immigrants from Europe, who knew a life that was always insecure and often harsh. It was able to claim that, under its auspices, America had been transformed from a vast and thinly populated desert into a wealthy continent capable of producing in agriculture and industry more riches and, also, more chances of access to it than any other nation in history.

Its weakness was the decisive one that it assumed the permanent validity of its scheme of values even when the conditions which made the scheme acceptable had begun, quite obviously, to undergo a radical transformation. So that, slowly, from the closing of the frontier to the end of the First World War, afterwards at an astonishing rate, it became a philosophy on the defensive, a method of safeguarding the vested interests of the past rather than of organizing the emerging interests of the future. And the more fully America became involved in world affairs, the more apparent did it become that the higher this business philosophy—like

most great systems when they come to the cross-roads of their history
—pitched its claims, the more difficult it became legitimately to expect
their fulfilment. It was the logical outcome of this habit that it should
make the system seem less attractive, for its function as a barrier against
both adaptation to change and fulfilment of new hopes became more
obvious. The arguments which seemed convincing when New England
manufacturers were building Lowell, Massachusetts, had an aura of grim
unreality about them when they were half-echoed a century later in
Gastonia, North Carolina. The exhilaration which workingmen all over
the United States were able to feel in the drama of a career like that of
Andrew Carnegie or of J. J. Hill, they felt either with difficulty or not
at all when their rulers sought its evocation in the record of Mr. Thomas
Girdler in the steel industry or of the Van Sweringen brothers in the
railroads. The proud consciousness of an imperial position that the elder
Morgan could show when he was examined by the Pujo Committee in
1912 seemed an arrogant superiority to the rights of ordinary Americans in 1934, when his firm attempted to meet the relentless cross-
questioning of Judge Pecora; and there was a widespread sense, outside
the ruling class, that Judge Pecora's clients were more than a special
committee of the Senate; they were the whole people of the United States
who had fought their way to freedom in 1776 that the New World
might redress the balance of the Old. It did not seem easy, as the Black
Committee went on with its work day by day and week by week not to
conclude that the men of property in the United States, more wealthy
than their analogues in Europe and willing to play for still higher stakes,
were the great feudal barons of a vast industrial empire in which they
accorded the worker no proportionately greater rights than the villein
had secured in the dead feudal age.

So that a philosophy which, as late as the First World War, could
afford to take the offensive against all rivals, which, indeed, in terms of
comparative political strength, had no rival about whom it had need to
be anxious, was, at least a decade before the outbreak of the Second
World War, very obviously on the defensive. No doubt its exponents
still repeated, if with a certain shrillness, its historic shibboleths. Bodies
like the Chamber of Commerce and the National Association of Manufacturers described to one another at their annual conventions, first, the
identity of this philosophy with Americanism, and, second, the danger to
the purity of the American idea of "foreign" notions quite clearly unsuited either to American circumstances or to the American character.
New institutions came into being, like the National Industrial Conference Board, to give the formal appearance of scientific "objectivity" to
the old tradition and to deny, as it were, the growing volume of assertion
that the emperor had no clothes on. Academic economists who showed
signs of a disproportionate interest in alternative doctrines were hunted
down in their colleges as angrily as theological unorthodoxy was attacked a century ago by men of the type of Andrews Norton at Harvard;

promotion was deferred, reappointment was discouraged, in the last resort there was even outright and unblushing dismissal. The university president became, increasingly, in part a man who could successfully raise funds for his institution and in part a man who achieved this end by preventing college posts, especially in the social sciences, from being filled by men with "dangerous" ideas. The *Bulletin* of the American Association of University Professors is an illuminating commentary on the fear evoked among business men by any teacher guilty of unconventional ideas. But it is also testimony of the fact that business men are on the defensive about their philosophy and are no longer prepared for the kind of ruthless dissection of its principles which, a century ago, would not have caused them a tremor of discomfort.

It is not, of course, true to say that the wealthy caste in America has become the kind of closed caste that was characteristic of the Hungarian land-owning class or of the Prussian Junkers. It is, however, a fact that access to the seats of power is less easy for certain minority groups, both national and religious, and that there is a tendency to regard these groups as fortunate if they escape from the burden of being hewers of wood and drawers of water. They are groups, also, which are very easily selected as the scapegoats to be punished for sins for which they bear no more responsibility, and through their position, probably less, than most others. It is obviously a symptom of great importance to the understanding of the tensions of contemporary America that there should be an immense growth in anti-Semitism. It is important, too, that Negro success should be far more resented, in the North as well as the South, where a generation ago such success would have been regarded as the proof that the American tradition was solid. And, in this context, it is difficult to measure the significance of Senator Huey Long, who built his extraordinary empire by organizing the "poor whites" of Louisiana against the wealthy business interests of the state. For the basic thesis of his campaign was a demand that "the wealth be shared," a thesis of which the implications were, first, that the existing distribution of wealth in America was unjust, and, second, that the poor had certain claims deserving satisfaction as the first charge upon the income of Louisiana, in the first instance, and, on the larger theatre on which he was beginning to operate at the time of his assassination, upon the national income of the United States, in the second. This is the first stage in the rise of a Hitler.

The philosophy of the American business man worked up to the end of the First World War mainly because, the issue of slavery apart, the continuous expansion of the market made it always possible for a compromise to be reached between the different senatorial sections on the issues which arose among them. Each could see some solution ultimately agreed upon without a sense of profound frustration. After Cleveland's first presidency, the Democratic party was, as it were, restored to the status of national responsibility, and the differences which divided it from the Republican party were no greater than those which divided a Democrat of William Jennings Bryan's outlook from a conservative Virginian Democrat like Senator Carter Glass. It is reasonably obvious, in fact, that, party aside, Senator Glass would have found it easier to subscribe to most of the doctrines which Senator Henry Cabot Lodge, a typical Back Bay Republican of Boston, spent his life in upholding than to those which Senator Hugo Black fought for with such energy and determination in the first administration of Franklin D. Roosevelt. The overwhelming majority of the membership of the American Federation of Labor found it as natural as did most of their employers to vote Republican or Democrat right down to the outbreak of the Great Depression. During all his long years as president of the Federation, Samuel Gompers strove to prevent it from thinking in terms of independent political action, and with success; and anyone who reads the innumerable speeches he made on the fallacies of socialism, or the literature of that curious body, the National Civic Federation, in which a trade-union official, Mr. Matthew Woll, collaborated with a social worker, Mr. Ralph Easley, to keep the workers pure from the contamination of doctrines which insisted that there really is a class war in a capitalist society, would find little difficulty in understanding why dissent from the conventional way of social thought was rare until so very recent a time.

There is little difficulty in understanding its hold in the past. There is, I suggest, a very real difficulty in understanding its hold on the present. A social philosophy must have the capacity to fulfill the expections to which it is pledged if it hopes to survive. It is exactly this capacity in the American business man's philosophy that is in doubt. The hymn to "free enterprise" which its exponents do not weary of singing cannot at some point fail to reveal itself as a hymn to a principle which was long ago outmoded in American economic life. The trusts cannot be chorused away by cheering the Sherman Act, above all when it is apparent that no administration, whatever its party complexion, would seriously hope to do more in a single presidential term than make a kind of standardized genuflexion towards its shade. It sounds admirable, no doubt, in the chief address to the annual convention of the Chambers of Commerce, to call upon the president and Congress to clear the "bottlenecks of business," in Judge Thurman Arnold's phrase, by preventing the curse of bigness from overshadowing the life of President Roosevelt's "forgotten man." The call is one to which there cannot be any effective response: Du Pont, General Motors, Henry Ford, Standard Oil, the American Tobacco Company, these are not Goliaths against whom a new David is likely to advance successfully to the attack, even when he can speak as an assistant attorney-general of the United States. For the technology of modern business requires the large corporation if it is to maintain all the implications of mass production. It is impossible to see that the plant, or the capacity to wait for long-term results, both economic and psychological, or the means to endow research on the necessary scale, or even the capital to retool plant, as Mr. Ford retooled the machinery for his later models—that any of these will be available to the small man. The theory that his future is, as it were, just round the corner, and that with the re-emergence of the framework of laws to prevent the growth of these great industrial empires he will enter into his inheritance, is mythology that ceases even to perform the task of edification.

Yet it is not easy to find that American business men have, on any large scale, the sense that their philosophy is bankrupt. They still produce the values it has been accustomed to endorse as values which ought to commend themselves at once to any reasonable mind. They still think that any able man can make a success of business if he gives his whole mind to it, and that his failure is the outcome either of defects of mind or of defects of character. Their reception of the Taft-Hartley Act has shown that they still have a profound hostility to trade-unions; and they lose no effort which might persuade general public opinion to see in the trade-union the enemy of the American idea. That alert hostility was shown quite remarkably in Texas where the regents of the state university dismissed three instructors in economics for seeking to explain to their students that the forty-hour-week law did not mean that civilian war workers could not do more than this period of work in the plants concerned with war production.[15] It was shown not less profoundly in the passionate opposition to the work of Mr. Sidney Hillman and the Political Action Committee of the Congress of Industrial Organizations in the presidential election of 1944.[16] The undercurrents in that opposition were a significant expression of much that is most ugly in American economic life.

But, perhaps above all, the incapacity of the American business man to see the need for new ideas emerged most clearly in his explanation to himself of what the American effort in the field of war production really implied. He did not grasp the fact that its immensity was due to the orders placed by the federal government with manufacturers, and that when those orders were no longer placed, he and his fellow-citizens would be confronted by an immense problem they were psychologically unprepared to solve. He did not see, either, that the things he resented—high taxation, the control of prices, the very small area in which he was affected by rationing—were all of them a pathetic and futile effort to meet the issues raised by monopoly capitalism with an ideology which was beginning to look old-fashioned even in the Coolidge epoch. His obvious conviction that he is a simple, straightforward fellow who just does his job and does not "play politics," and that he is therefore bound to be at a disadvantage when he confronts the sophisticated and tortuous European, remains unchanged, despite his inner conviction that the course of em-

---

[15] Professor C. E. Ayres, "Academic Freedom in Texas," *New Republic*, December 4, 1944, p. 742.

[16] Cf. Joseph Gaer, *The First Round: The Story of the CIO Political Action Committee* (New York: Duell, Sloan & Pearce, 1944).

pire has taken its sway westwards and that he is the master of an imperial destiny which is backed by a productive power beyond all precedent. He feels confident that the future is his; and it is only very occasionally that he permits himself to reflect upon the meaning of the Russian victories in the war. When he does, he is apt, like the western manufacturer Mr. Eric Johnston, the president, in 1943–44, of the United States Chamber of Commerce, to say with light-hearted ease that Russia goes forward by one route and the United States by another, with the inference that, after all, the general direction is the same. He thinks, though with suspicion, that communism is all very well for the Soviet Union, but that the United States, with its different history and traditions, is firmly set on the road of free enterprise. How that free enterprise can be reconciled either with the dependence of Americans upon an increasing degree of government intervention, or with the position of the people of the Southern states as virtually a colonial dependency of the North and East, he does not ask himself. He concludes that as the past of the United States has been a very miracle of swift expansion, so will its future be a similar miracle. And he is too self-confident by nature to suspect that it is a grave error for any nation to depend upon miracles for its progress.

One final remark about the philosophy of the business man is, I think, worth making. No one with any knowledge of his habits but must admire his amazing vitality, his inexhaustible interest in his vocation, his pride in being recognized as a person of significance in his town or state or among his competitors in the industry in which he is engaged. Nowhere in the world is there a commercial community whose members are more eager to be privately magnanimous, or retain so long the first vivid enthusiasm of the young man who starts out on his voyage of business discovery. Nowhere else, either, is there a commercial world whose members have a greater zest for discussion and information or a more ardent faith in the universal validity of the rules under which it operates. There is a religious intensity about his attitude which has the usual consequence that he is dismayed and indignant when the attitude is challenged.

It is difficult not to suspect that his concentration upon business has had the result of depriving him of a certain maturity of temper, a capacity for a wide-ranging outlook, which are the vital hallmarks of a mind that is fully responsible and civilized. The lack of maturity is shown in various ways. It is exhibited in his curious respect for statistical astrologers like Mr. Roger W. Babson and his kind. It is shown in his inability to play, in his suspicion that whatever is profound, outside the natural sciences, is bound to be heavy and dull, in his conviction that the artist, the poet, the philosopher, and the musician deal with elements to which he can afford to give only his spare time or which are, more suitably, a realm to be patronized by his womenfolk. Not least, he wants to be abreast of the culture of his day without making the hard intellectual effort which has not only gone to the making of that culture, but which he gives as an obvious necessity to his own daily work. That is why he is an ardent consumer of popular manuals which purport to give him in pemmicanized form what he hopes is a clue to the day-after-tomorrow's knowledge.

This temper has been communicated, as is natural in a business civilization, to almost every aspect of American life. It can be discerned in academic research, both in the social and in the natural sciences. In the social sciences, it shows itself in a variety of ways, the subjects chosen, the zest for quantitative examination at immense length of problems that yield their answers to simple analysis in terms of common sense; a good illustration of the first is the conferment of a doctorate in philosophy in home economics for a study of dishwashing in small restaurants, and a good example of the second is a vast piece of co-operative research which established by careful statistical inquiry the result that people with large incomes tend to live in bigger houses than people with small incomes. In the natural sciences, it leads to more emphasis being laid on issues of applied science than on the attempt to go back to re-open the fundamental questions. It is, of course, true, as I shall show later in this work, that Americans have accomplished work of outstanding quality in most of the fields of human knowledge. But it is, I think, also true that there is a passion for that inquiry which shows a quick, dramatic return or for the grandiose type of investigation in which the result is often wholly disproportionate to the size of the effort involved. It is not, I suggest, mere fancy to argue that far too much American research is undertaken by university teachers to prove that they are practical men; and it is difficult not to see in the growth of the vast proletariat of research, through whose ranks one passes to reach the inner sanctum of the professor himself, a form of organization for inquiries which has been moulded, even though unconsciously, upon the upward march of a visitor to a great American business firm, from the junior clerk, through a hierarchy of secretaries, to the great desk, with its massive collection of telephones, at which the managing director is planning his new advertising campaign. It is all full of sound and fury; but the main purpose of a good deal of it is to enable the managing director to believe in himself.

One other illustration must suffice. It is tempting to argue that the impact of this temper on the habits of the American Churches has steadily increased and is still increasing, and that whether they be Protestant or Roman Catholic; the pattern of clerical behaviour, the hearty welcome, the emphasis upon the fact that the Churches do things, the anxiety to use its equipment in the fullest possible way, the movement of interest from dogma to conduct, the eagerness to prove that the minister is a man of the world, the effort to make religion not that aloof and awesome thing that a man searches out in order to be at peace with himself, but a solid and saleable commodity as certain to offer a good return to the investor as a new car or a new refrigerator—all this is unmistakable. The minister is a member of the Rotary Club and of similar organizations; he is concerned with the practical problems not merely of the lives of his congregation, but of the neighbourhood in which he dwells. He feels that he must speak on social problems in such a way that his followers discern in what he has to say the kind of realistic advice that a trusted banker gives to his client. He spends immense effort on making his church an attractive rival on a Sunday to the hundred competing claims which golf and the automobile, the movie and the country club, have made quite different from anything he could have contemplated when he was a boy fifty, or even forty, years ago. He is—more, of course, in the city than in rural America—the salesman of one form of leisure against other forms; and he knows that if he loses his grip upon his art as a salesman his potential customers will go elsewhere. At its extreme, this is expressed in figures like Billy Sunday or Aimee Semple McPherson, who frankly turn their churches into music-halls and get an attendance proportionate to the thrill of the "turns" they can offer.

In the last analysis, the problem of the business man is the gap between the philosophy he professes and the character of the environment to which he has to apply it. He seeks to live by a creed so long outmoded that its recitation belongs less to the realm of thought than of ritual. And he is in the dilemma that the ritual no longer performs the magic which was once the inner secret of his power, and that, with the ritual fading away, the hold of the myth becomes more difficult unless it be transformed. He is coming rapidly to the stage when he must choose between a creed which does not work and a world which can be conquered only by innovations as drastic as those which led to the foundation of the United States of America or those which were the outcome of the Civil War. He will, of course, make the innovations, since adaptation is the invariable price of survival. But he is haunted by the dread of what he may find in the world into which he then enters. He is, above all, haunted by the fear that, when he has entered it, he may have lost the power to control his own destiny.

VI

American Labour

THERE are three fairly clear periods in the history of the American labour movement. There is the period before the foundation of the American Federation by Samuel Gompers; there is the period when, under his leadership, craft unionism seemed the sole concern of the Federation and its constituent unions; and there is the period which opened with the break away of John L. Lewis, Philip Murray, Sidney Hillman, and other leaders, at the Atlantic City convention of the Federation in 1935, to form the Committee for Industrial Organizations. In a sense, each of these periods has its own distinguishing feature. Before the advent of Gompers, the American labour movement is very strongly reminiscent of the Owenite period in British trade-union history. The Knights of Labor, like the Grand National Consolidated Trade Union of Owen, were a rocket shot across the sky, revealing a need but lacking the patience and the resolution to fulfil it. The period of Gompers' rule, with its faint afterglow in that of his successor William Green, is marked by many of the features of trade-unionism in Britain before the famous Dockers' Strike in 1889. With the emergence of the C.I.O., American labour begins to develop very special characteristics of its own of which the two outstanding are the success of the new body in organizing the workers, skilled and unskilled, in the mass-production industries, and its demonstration that the "white collar" workers can be unionized by the same means, and for the same ends, as the man who depends upon manual skill or physical strength for his living.

Broadly speaking, American trade-unionism is naturally marked by certain features which derive from the special environment of the United States. It is marked by violence, by a violence which is not limited to the unions, but may equally be shown by the employers or by the government, sometimes local, sometimes even federal. And, parallel to this violence, is the hostility of the courts to labour organization; the periods in which the courts, including the Supreme Court at Washington, have approached the problems set by the industrial relation in a temper prepared to meet trade-unionism objectively are rare and of scant duration. A third feature is the general unwillingness of the trade-unions to move directly on to the plane of political action. There have been, as, indeed, there are today, working-class parties built upon trade-union support. But they have never been nation-wide either in organization or influence. Though it has seemed, on a number of occasions, that the unions would at long last take the decisive political step of forming a workers' party, in the end they have always preferred to manœuvre between the major parties in the belief that this gives them a bargaining power they could not obtain in a direct way. They have been what Americans like to call a "pressure group," seeking limited and particular objectives rather than expanding into an organic philosophy like that, for example, of the British Labour party. There have been Owenites, co-operators, Henry Georgites, socialists, communists, among their members; but the results of all presidential elections, with the two possible exceptions of the support for Debs in 1920 and for La Follette in 1924, make it plain that the overwhelming mass of workers in America have contentedly voted Republican or Democrat without any obvious sense that such a choice has involved their frustration.

It is particularly interesting to a European observer to note that there is no special tendency in the American labour movement toward socialism; on the contrary, there is rather an eagerness on the part of its leaders, either like Gompers, to dissociate themselves fiercely from any connection with socialism, or, like Mr. Hillman, one of the architects of the C.I.O. and an able and shrewd president of the Amalgamated Clothing Workers of America, to insist that their socialism is a personal conviction which neither involves nor directs their union activities. Eugene Debs, indeed, perhaps the best-loved figure in the history of American socialism, was, in the nineties, an important organizer in the world of railroad trade-unionism; and William Z. Foster, the outstanding figure in the great steel strike of 1919, was an ardent member of the Communist party; but, in neither case, did their political faith ever attempt to permeate their industrial relations. The American labour movement has always operated, in the main, on the assumption that trade-unions exist in a capitalist world the framework of which they do not seek to change; and they have seen their chief functions, first, in maintaining the right of the workers to bargain collectively, and, second, to get the best conditions on the job that their bargaining power makes possible.

Each of these features deserves some special attention. Why is it that, on a large view, the violence attendant on industrial disputes in the United States should be so much more formidable and ugly than it is in Britain or France or Sweden or Belgium? It is not merely that, right down to the present day, there are few of the big unions in America in which events like the Sheffield outrages in Britain—now nearly a century away from us—are not an everyday occurrence. It is not merely, either, that there are few great corporations in American industry which do not possess, or are at least prepared to hire, private armies of their own to beat up overzealous trade-unionists, to spy upon them, even to enter their organizations in order to betray the union's secrets to the employers. It is not merely, again, that famous cases like that of the Chicago anarchists, like that of Mooney and Billings, like the Deportations Delirium of 1920, show a savage hostility to radical ideas which is utterly careless of the evidence available. The great American strikes, Homestead, Ludlow, Paterson, Seattle, Herrin, Gastonia, to name only a few, have been set in a background of brutal massacre in which the employers and the public authorities have been pretty deeply involved, without any obvious need to answer for the action they have taken. Violence, of course, begets violence; and it is impossible not to remember that there have been many cases in which the strikers have fired on the police and the militia, or have beaten up, even killed, strikebreakers, and have compelled men to join a trade-union by the threat, or the actuality, of terror. Figures like William Hutcheson of the United Brotherhood of Carpenters and Joiners, or Dave Beck of the Teamsters Union in Seattle, are capable of exhibiting habits that we normally associate with a body like the Vehmgericht of the middle ages; and it is not an exaggeration to say that the "Molly Maguires" in the anthracite region of Pennsylvania turned that area for a considerable time into a dark valley of fear.

We must see this in its proper perspective. No one can read a document like the Report of the La Follette Committee on Civil Liberties, which, after all, deals not with some distant past, but with events between 1919 and 1939, without a shudder at the things men will deliberately do if they even remotely suspect that their property is in danger. Mr. Pullman in the Pullman strike, Mr. Rockefeller's agents in Ludlow, did nothing worse than the things there revealed. If there are unions into which the racketeer has penetrated, it is important to remember that, as often as not, it is the employer who has paid him to penetrate there. There are still areas of the United States, some of the company-owned steel towns, for example, or the Imperial Valley in California, or the sharecropper country of the deep South, where the very idea of freedom of speech is hardly known, and where, within the last decade, a trade-union organizer has entered at the peril of life and limb. Even a Socialist candidate for the presidency, Mr. Norman Thomas, a nationally respected figure, was deported with threats from Arkansas when he went there as a gesture of approval for the effort to organize the sharecroppers. The record is one of espionage, of blackmail, of perjury, of beatings up, of ugly violence planned by the employers' agents in their hunger to break up trade-unions. There has been a reckless disregard of elementary human decencies for which no words can be too strong. There has been complete contempt for the law; and anyone who judges union violence must always bear in mind that Mr. Henry Ford was driven to accept the authority of the National Labor Relations Board only when he found, with the coming of the Second World War, that he could not obtain orders from Washington except by compliance with its provisions.

What, then, explains the persistence of this violence? It is not a phenomenon to be dismissed quickly and simply by saying that it is a relic of the frontier period of American history. No doubt the habits of the frontier contributed an element to its understanding; no one can read the record of the gold rush in California or of the settlement of Texas without seeing that the frontier bred a type of self-reliant adventurer who had to look to himself for protection and not be too scrupulous about the means he took for his defence. But, after all, the men who run the steel industry, the automobile industry, and a score of others, have not themselves had any experience of the frontier and no longer employ workers who have come back from the frontier to their factories. Something, perhaps, is due to the complicated racial mixture one finds in a city like Chicago or Youngstown; the problems of organizing a discipline which will work in so intricate a pattern as is to be found there makes for an authoritarian attitude in the employer; and this, in its turn, tends to create an atmosphere of rebellion among those upon whom it is imposed. But I incline to the view that the main explanation lies in a different direction. I believe that the basis upon which the concepts of organization are built is the belief in an atomic view of industrial power. The employer, from the millionaire like Mr. Ford to the foreman of one of his shops, thinks of the business he runs as "his" business. He is insistent, therefore, that those whom he employs shall accept his terms. He is not employing partners; he is employing "hands." He has no interest in them save as they enable him to produce profitably. And if he accepts their right to organize, it may well be that he is jeopardizing his power to compete, even, it may be, his ability to pay his way. He is not, in the time-honoured phrase, "in business for his health." He knows workingmen: if they are given an inch they take a yard. The earlier he prevents his workers from being in a position where they can speak to him on equal terms, the less chance there is that they may be able to question his authority. He therefore insists on the fullness of his right to command, out of fear that any moderation or concession on his part might be mistaken for weakness.

And, alongside his outlook, there is the attitude of the workers to be considered. If they are American by origin, they inherit a tradition which tells each that he is a free man than whom there is no superior; and he resents being enmeshed in a mass of restrictions which make that freedom seem to him unreal. If he is an immigrant, he has come to America in search of opportunities which are almost a golden legend in his old country; and when he finds that his access to those opportunities is hedged around on every side with prohibitions and limitations which emphasize his position in all its "insecurity" and subordination, it is as though the dream he had dreamed in Yugoslavia or Greece, in Poland or Italy, is something he will not be allowed to dream. All about him are the evidences of well-being. If he stands alone, it is beyond his reach. If he joins with others to formulate his demands, he finds that what he thought about in those exciting weeks and months when he was arranging his journey to America begins to assume the vesture of unreality. It then becomes obvious to him that the right to associate with others for the improvement of his condition is of the essence of his power to go forward. And the one thing in the deposit of American history that he understands is the fact that the citizen, just because he is an American, has the right to go forward.

In the result, the one clear concept in the employer's mind is his need to be the absolute master of the men in his factory; and the equally clear concept in the worker's mind is the fact that only co-operation with other workers will give him the status which creates his opportunity to go forward. And all this, of course, is coloured by the long tradition of a United States where opportunity is equal and where there is freedom from the half-feudal habits of the Old World. That is why the fight for and against the recognition of trade-unions has been waged so fiercely. The employer, not less than his workers, has seen to the full the meaning of Mr. Justice Holmes' famous phrase that "liberty of contract begins where equality of bargaining power begins." [1] Once he concedes recognition to the workers the discipline he can impose arises out of discussion and not out of authority. His right to hire and fire, his ability to cut the rate, his decision about the additional reward for working overtime, these, to take instances only, no longer remain fully in his own hands. And he has an uneasy sense that once the union has found an entrance into his plant, it can maintain its hold only by eating into his authority. Where he wants to command, he may be driven to persuade; and persuasion means the ability to produce reasons that a trade-union official, who may not be, is indeed unlikely to be, one of his own employees, is prepared to recommend as satisfactory. He knows, too, that the official has in mind not merely the economic conditions of a given plant, but the general economic conditions throughout the industry. He is bound to feel that the price of union recognition is a steady movement towards constitutionalism in industry.

That is why he has fought it with all the resources he could mobilize. And that is why, also, the worker has hit back with every weapon he could use. The one saw in the trade-union a denial of his right to property; the other saw in it the basic safeguard both of his security and welfare. And when argument failed, each was prepared to fight, because he saw without much difficulty how much was involved in surrender. And this readiness to fight, especially in the epoch after the Civil War, was operative in a world where the employer saw that, if he won, the chances opened to him were immense; for it was the age of Vanderbilt and Rockefeller, of Gould and Fisk, of men, that is, to whom wealth was power and power so intoxicating that they were utterly careless of the means by which

[1] *Coppage* v. *Kansas*, 236 U.S. 1 (1915).

they acquired it. But the worker saw, in his turn, first that the Homestead Act gave him an alternative to industrial dependence, and, second, that if he wanted to stay in the city on terms he thought fair, the employer would comb Europe for labour which knew nothing of his standards and was always ready to undercut his demands until it had become domesticated to the American environment; and when that domestication had taken place, a new wave of immigrants restarted the process of undercutting. The Irish were followed by the Italians; the Italians were followed by the Greeks. Then came Poles and Slovaks, Rumanians and Finns. There was even recourse to Mexican labour and, for a period, to the potentially endless stream of Asiatic peoples. Granted the problem created for American trade-unions by the ruthless exploitation of the immigrant in the generation after the Civil War, it is not difficult to understand why American trade-unions entered upon the fight, which culminated in victory after the First World War, to stop the increasing flow of men, and even women, whose main value to the employer was the reserve army against the trade-unions which could be constituted from them.

It is in this background, I think, that the tradition of violence in American economic life must be set. No small part of its colour is provided by the fact that the ruling class knew, and the workers themselves were half-convinced, that America was a classless society in which there was no room for the rigid social divisions of the European continent. To join a trade-union meant to stamp oneself, if not as infected with un-American ideas, at least as betraying the American faith that a man's character and brains and two strong arms would assure him a successful career. It was to risk the chance of losing your job, to mark yourself off as a man with no other ambition than to accept the fate of him who always obeys and never rises to the position of command. America was different; all its citizens had an equal opportunity to rise. The trade-union movement sought to prevent men like Carnegie or Charles M. Schwab from making the best of themselves. So that when the worker gave to his Church the zeal and the subscription he might have given to the trade-union he was acting in the American way. No less a person, after all, than the great president of Harvard University, Charles William Eliot, said that the true American hero is the strikebreaker. Behind him, certainly, was all the power the state could muster. The courts protected him by massive injunctions. The police protected him by clubbing and arresting workers who stood on the picket lines. The state militia and the national guard would, more often than not, be called in to assure owners that if they wished to run their factories no union interference with the rights of property would be tolerated. As one seeks to understand the scene, it is hard not to conclude that all the conditions were set for a drama in which it seemed as natural for the worker to fight his way to recognition as it was for his employer to fight against it.

There was no serious chance for an effective trade-unionism in America until after the Civil War. And when, in the eighties, Samuel Gompers began to build the American Federation of Labor, his only hope of success was a reliance upon men who knew just how far they could safely go with their employers, and who were not too nice about the means of pressure they exerted against their fellow-workers. The unions had to hack their way into a hold upon industry. And once they had won this hold, they had to make it clear to the employers that they could not be overlooked. That meant the formulation of demands which would prove to the members they served the value of their organization. But they had so to formulate them that they seemed to their own members demands it was reasonable to make. And since the average worker was predominantly interested in his own job and, where he was a craftsman, had a real pride in his skill, Gompers, naturally enough, given the period in which he began his task, founded the A.F. of L. on a craft basis. It is true that industrial unionism in certain industries developed within the Federation, the mining industry, for example. But its roots were in the crafts and it was for the improvement of the craftsman's position that Gompers was above all concerned. He sought to find room in the American tradition for a trade-unionism which had no politics save the right of the worker to a secure job at the highest rate of pay for the shortest number of hours of toil.

One has only to read the literature of the employers' organizations, especially that of the National Association of Manufacturers in the period when Mr. David Parry was its president, to see that Gompers had not the remotest chance of securing the peaceful consent of business men to his purpose. To admit that his claim was just was to jeopardize the whole philosophy of the business man. It was to offer security to men whose skill and methods alike became obsolete with a swiftly changing technology. It was to admit into the management of their plants men whom they did not employ and could not dismiss, men whose loyalty to any particular business concern had no roots of any kind. It contradicted the theory, still so passionately held in the United States, that every employer is really a trustee for his workers and hence, by implication, the guardian of the public welfare. Inferentially, it denied the doctrine, hardly less dear, that there is a basic harmony of interest between capital and labour. It offered the professional troublemaker, in the businessman's view, the opportunity to practise his vocation at the business man's expense. Under these circumstances business decided to fight; and it began to operate its decision in what was perhaps the first epoch in which American workingmen attained any full realization of their position. There was a permanent urban proletariat; there were slums as terrible as any in Europe; there was a break in agricultural prices which left the farmer poised between the devil of his mortgage and the deep sea of freight rates which seemed to make profitable production impossible. When the American Federation of Labor set out on its adventure it had no more chance of avoiding conflict than a poor Jew of escaping from

Hitler's clutches. And the vitality and self-respect of the American worker only made the use of violence, on both sides, more certain.

2

GIVEN the social pattern of capitalist democracy in America, the attitude of the courts to labour is its quite logical outcome. In a *laissez-faire* age, in which "Man versus the State" might almost have been the motto of the republic, the courts set out to protect a conceptual person in his right to all property which was legally his, with the insistence that the right to labour where he can find a job on terms that he agrees upon with the employer willing to pay him for his services is a vital part of his right to property. It is this right to dispose of his labour power as he will that, in the eyes of most American judges, makes the American worker a free man. Without that right, to the legal mind, his position begins to approximate that of a slave.

It follows that the courts, almost down to our own day, attacked the fortress in which the workingman sought refuge from two angles. They attacked it in order that the business man might use his legal property as he thought fit; and they attacked it in order that the worker might make what disposition he pleased of his labour power. In order to achieve these purposes the courts used a variety of weapons, of which perhaps the most dramatic was the injunction. They forbade any picketing which was not "peaceful" in character; and it is not an exaggeration to say that, in any important strike, the police assumed that no successful picketing could be peaceful. They forbade the secondary boycott. They used the Sherman Act against a trade-union on the ground that its action was a conspiracy in restraint of trade. They ordered strikers back to work. They ordered them not to approach within a certain distance of a plant involved in a dispute. Chief Justice Taft, when Judge Taft, held that the Railroad Brotherhoods cannot interfere with the duty of a carrier to accept the freight of a connecting carrier, under the Interstate Commerce Act.[2] When Congress attempted to narrow the immense area of threat to union action involved in the application of the Sherman Act to the field of industrial disputes by passing the Clayton Act in 1914, the Supreme Court of the United States so construed it as to make it void of all effectiveness. How effective was the use of the injunction even to prevent any effort at unionizing the coal mines of West Virginia has been told in detail by a careful observer.[3] In the Coronado Coal case [4] the Supreme Court held that a trade-union, though an unincorporated association, may be made liable as distinct from the individual liabilities of its members, as though it were in fact incorporated; a decision which

[2] *Toledo, Ann Arbor & North Michigan Railroad* v. *Pennsylvania Company*, 54 Fed. 730 (1893).
[3] Winthrop D. Lane, *Civil War in West Virginia* (New York: Huebsch, 1921). This was the result of the decision of the courts in the famous Hitchman case.
[4] *United Mine Workers* v. *Coronado Coal Company*, 259 U.S. 344 (1922).

carried the injustice, though not the statutory correction, of the Taff Vale case across the Atlantic. The injunctions issued are, as often as not, all-embracing in their scope; in the Tri-City Central Trades Council case, it was made applicable to "all persons whatsover." [5]

Strikers must not harass or annoy the employers or the patrons of the employer against whom they strike. They must not parade in front of his premises. They must not organize their picketing. They must not persuade customers not to patronize their employer. They must not harass any of his workers who continue at work or induce them to violate their contract to do so. They must not seek to procure a sympathetic strike. They must not penalize any union member who continues to handle their employer's products. They must not even issue a circular in which penalties are threatened in such cases. They must not threaten a boycott. They must not refer to a complainant who seeks an injunction as "unfair." In the Gompers case, the president of the American Federation of Labor was enjoined from "in any manner whatsoever impeding, obstructing, interfering with, or restraining the complainant's business.[6] Words like "scab" and "traitor" must not be used about those who remain at work. Union leaders may even be enjoined against a threatened strike. An injunction has been issued enjoining a union from disbursing funds for court costs or enabling any striker to sublet his house where his employer was also his landlord. An Ohio judge has decided that where persuasion to strike is attempted in the presence of three persons, it ceases to be persuasion and must be prohibited; and he ordered that all pickets shall be American citizens and able to speak the English language even though it was testified that more than ninety per cent of the workers concerned in the strike were "foreign-speaking men." The fantastic injunction issued by Judge Wilkerson in the Railway Shopmen's strike of 1922 almost extended to enjoining the union not to have any hard feelings against the employers. It is not surprising that Mr. Justice Frankfurter should, in his academic days, have described it as a "landmark in the history of American equity"! [7]

To the use of the injunction must be added its enforcement by proceedings in contempt. A picket line may be specifically allowed, but when it is maintained over a considerable period it is held to have violated the injunction and proceedings for contempt follow. So, too, it was held to be contempt for a shopkeeper to put a card in his window to announce that he did not want to deal with "scabs"; this was a violation of the clause against abuse and insult. This view is the more remarkable since the Circuit Court of Appeals in another district held that it was not contempt for a newspaper to call strikebreakers such names as "dirty scabs," "scavengers," and "traitors." In one case the court finds the

[5] *American Foundries Company* v. *Tri-City Central Trades Council,* 257 U.S. 184 (1921).

[6] *Gompers* v. *Bucks Stove & Range Company,* 221 U.S. 418, 420 (1911).

[7] Felix Frankfurter and Nathan Greene, *The Labor Injunction* (New York: Macmillan, 1930), p. 103.

epithets unpardonable after seeing their meaning in Webster's Dictionary; in another case their use is permitted after the court has examined them in the Standard Dictionary. And by constituting itself the judge of the circumstances in which the injunction is functioning, many courts have almost taken charge of the strike by saying how many pickets there can be, where they can be placed, and how they are to behave. Frankfurter and Greene have shown that, in the federal courts alone, eighty-eight persons were convicted and fifteen acquitted in contempt proceedings arising out of injunctions between 1901 and 1929.[8] It is significant that in fifty-eight appeals from these convictions, twenty-one were reversed. It is not impermissible to guess that most of these reversals were simply the outcome of the mitigating effect of time.

It is important to realize what is implied in the willingness of the courts to scatter injunctions to business men as a medieval prince scattered largesse on his royal progress. And here we have the authority of that judge who, in the last generation, probably did more to win back some of the prestige the courts lost by this procedure. Injunctions, said Mr. Justice Brandeis, are not normally sought "to prevent property from being injured, nor to protect the owner in its use, but to endow property with active, militant power which would make it dominant over men." [9] And it has been very hard to persuade American legislatures to pass statutes limiting the power thus conferred. The judicial view of conspiracy has hardly been affected. The preference has gone towards building particular exceptions. A state is free to decide whether or no it will repress a combination of wage-earners; there is nothing in the Constitution to guarantee freedom of association. Twenty years were passed in the long campaign by the American Federation of Labor to withdraw trade-unions from the scope of the Sherman Act. It is interesting to note that when Senator Sherman proposed his legislation it contained a clause which excluded trade-unions and farmers' organizations from its scope. It is still more interesting to note that when the bill came out of the committee to the floor of the Senate, this clause was omitted. It is clear from the speeches, especially that of the well-known senator from Massachusetts, George F. Hoar, that the clause was omitted for the simple reason that no one thought of the bill as anything but a means of curbing the trusts. Its application to labour was a brilliant piece of judicial expansion, and it is significant that while working men have been sent to prison under the Act, no case appears to be known in which any officer of one of the great corporations has ever been imprisoned.

When, after a twenty years' struggle, Congress passed the Clayton Act in 1914, Mr. Gompers at once claimed that this had removed trade-unions from the scope of the Sherman Act; and both the speeches in Congress and President Wilson's own address in accepting renomination for office in 1916 suggest that this was the generally prevailing view.

[8] *Ibid.*, p. 130.
[9] *Truax* v. *Corrigan*, 257 U.S. 312, 354, 368 (1921).

But they reckoned without the courts. *Paine Lumber Company* v. *Neal* [10] already foreshadowed the nullification of the Clayton Act; and *Duplex Printing Press Company* v. *Deering*,[11] four years later, reduced it to the proportions of a farce. The Supreme Court, in substance, used a higher law of its own making by which to read into an Act of Congress an intent which was exactly opposite to the announced purposes of the men who passed the statute. And to this must be added the decision of the courts, cut into pieces by Mr. Justice Holmes in a famous dissent,[12] by which any statute forbidding the discharge of a worker because he belonged to a union was held unconstitutional on the ground that it denied freedom of contract which it was the sacred function of the "due process" clause to protect. And that is not all. It is obvious that the judicial mind which arrived at these results was assuming that the United States was a society in which employer and employed bargained freely on equal terms. The courts saw no reason why a corporation like the Hitchman Coal Company should not make the "yellow dog" contract—the acceptance of the obligation to refrain from joining a union—a condition of employment. Even with all the changes that have occurred in the industrial mind since the Sherman Act, it is difficult not to conclude that, as a general rule, the courts have been, for all practical purposes, the agents of Big Business. And this is in a realm where the doctrines used are the outcome of a hypothetical body of law built upon a hypothetical constitution of which the Supreme Court has constituted itself the guardian.

It is not going beyond the mark to say that the Supreme Court, until the period of the New Deal, built its theory of the Constitution on the predominance of *laissez-faire*. No doubt there have been occasional judges who saw no reason why this should be what Mr. Justice Holmes called the "inarticulate major premiss" of judicial decisions. But it has been generally true that the large majority of the judges thought in this way. That is why, until almost the other day, so much legislative experiment, especially from the states, was stricken into impotence. It might be an attempt to limit the hours of labour; it might be an attempt to establish a minimum wage; it might, in the federal sphere, be an attempt to abolish child labour. Whatever the experiment, the majority of the Court assumed not only that it was the judge of actions taken by responsible legislatures; it probably did more by a kind of pre-natal control of legislative action, through the knowledge in the legislature that certain types of statutes would be stricken down, than it was able to accomplish by positive action. It is true that when it sustained the Wagner Act,[13] it accepted a theory of the nature of liberty of contract which was at variance with an attitude which went back to the Civil War. No doubt the change, from the

---

[10] 244 U.S. 459 (1917).
[11] 254 U.S. 443 (1921).
[12] *Adair* v. *United States.*
[13] *National Labor Relations Board* v. *Jones and Laughlin Steel Corporation,* 301 U.S. 1 (1937).

angle of the American labour movement, was both salutary and important. But it was not less essential to see that the change still marked the fact that, amendment apart, the ultimate meaning of the Constitution was in judicial hands. From 1937 the Supreme Court's influence has generally been tilted in a liberal direction. But it might, just as easily, move back again if the climate of opinion encouraged it to do so.

For the labour movement is bound to remember what, with but rare exceptions, American judges are likely to be. "It is vain," wrote Mr. Justice Miller in 1875, "to contend with judges who have been at the Bar the advocates for forty years of railroad companies, and all the forms of associated capital, when they are called upon to decide cases where such interests are in contest. All their training, all their feelings, are from the start in favour of those who need no such influence." [14] The problem which emerges from this atmosphere is the fact that, unless there is on the Bench a judge who can, like Mr. Justice Holmes, put aside his own private philosophy and accept the decisions of a legislature which is at least as likely as he is to be right on the issue of constitutionalism, judicial review becomes transformed into an instrument where the successful barrister, elevated to the Bench, does for his clients as judge, what he previously did for them as counsel.

This may be put in another way. No one can honestly examine the history of the relations between labour and the courts without seeing that their result is to give the vested rights of property a special place in the American system. That is positively apparent in the ideas of Hamilton and Marshall, of Webster and Taney and Story, and of Chancellor Kent long before the Civil War; it is still more apparent after it. The view of John Adams that unequal property is the necessary outcome of liberal institutions has found a wide echo on the judicial Bench. But once that has been assumed, the next step is quite naturally to argue that laws which seek to invade that inequality are themselves a source of danger to the stability of the commonwealth. The main technique has been to due process of law; and this has been interpreted to mean not what a normal reasonable man would be justified in regarding as just, but rather as a method of protecting the property the wealthy class has acquired and, therefore, the laws under which that property is safe. Due process of law is not a road, but a gate; and those to whom it bars admission are the masses in the community. It is a way of protecting the past legal rights of the few against the present legal claims of the many. And, as Mr. Justice Miller emphasized, the men to whom the task of protection is confided are for the most part the men who, before they reached the Bench, were already trained to insist that the legal rights the few have acquired must be made safe from invasion.

This is why Mr. Chief Justice Waite's advice "to go to the polls and not to the courts" [15] was an evasion of the issue which every democracy

---

[14] Charles Fairman, "Justice Samuel F. Miller," *Political Science Quarterly*, March 1935, pp. 42–43.
[15] *Munn* v. *Illinois*, 94 U.S. 134 (1876).

must confront. For when the masses went to the polls, they found that the will they sought to translate into legislation was just as dependent as before on the outlook of the courts. The Congress might establish a commission to fix railroad rates, for example; but it would still find that the regulation of rates did not mean the power to confiscate property; and when it sought for the definition of confiscation, it found that this depended upon the mind of the judges.[16] And the cumbrous process of constitutional amendment apart, there was no appeal from that mind save its own sense of what was "reasonable." On the historic record, it is hard to deny that the judicial sense of "reasonableness" was built above all on the belief that democracy and *laissez-faire* capitalism are interchangeable terms. No doubt, to speak only of the dead, there were judges capable of sufficient self-restraint to transcend that belief. A conservative aristocrat like Mr. Justice Holmes, Jeffersonian democrats like Justices Brandeis and Cardozo, were able to do so. But anyone who reads the decisions of men like Justices Bradley and Brewer, Peckham and Pitney, will find not merely that such self-restraint is rare, but, even more, that most of the judges are quite honestly unaware that they are acting on premisses which imply this interchangeability. And if we move from the realm of judicial decisions to the realm where the judge speaks as a private citizen, to the orations, for example, of Mr. Justice Brewer, then we find that these premisses are really almost articles of religious faith. And we have the interesting problems in casuistry raised, for example, by the hidden relation between President Coolidge and Chief Justice Taft, in which we learn, though only after the death of Taft, that he had acted as a kind of intriguing elder statesman to the Republican party during the period when his independence of party convictions was of the very essence of his position.[17]

The issue raised by this outlook is one of momentous significance for the American labour movement. For the trade-unions cannot possibly accept the validity of the argument that democracy means *laissez-faire* capitalism and hope to perform any useful function on behalf of their members. Hardly one of the methods by which they seek to give reality to the idea of liberty of contract—the strike, the sympathetic strike, the boycott, the secondary boycott, the closed shop, picketing—but comes up against a body of legal principles which empty it of power and are formed into a framework for the Constitution beyond which it must not move. If it is said that from 1937 onwards the judges have been less rigorous in their hostility to the trade-unions than in the seventy years before that time, the answer, I think, is twofold. It is impossible, in the first place, to set the relaxation of less than a decade, a relaxation, moreover, closely related to economic crisis and to total war in which it has been important to win support from the workers, against the long years of stringency. And, in the second place, the cycle of attitudes to the trade-

---

[16] *Butler* v. *Gorely*, 146 U.S. 307, 331 (1892).
[17] Henry F. Pringle, *The Life and Times of William Howard Taft* (New York: Farrar and Rinehart, 1939), Vol. II, *passim*.

unions through which the American courts have passed, a period of suppression, a period of indifference, a period of limited supervision, and a period in which the machinery of the State power allots a function to the courts which arises from the workers' relation to an administrative agency of the Executive, the National Labor Relations Board, this cycle is not American merely but is typical of all advanced capitalist democracies like Britain or Germany as well as the United States. And the cycle raises the immense issue of whether giant capitalism can admit the existence of autonomous working-class organizations. It suggests that the illegality of the trade-unions at Common Law, the fact that their functioning is a legislative concession, means that they are always likely to operate in the background of a never fully stated doctrine of "public policy," which most judges will use as the House of Lords did in Great Britain in the Osborne case, which sought to hinder political activity by the trade-unions,[18] or as the Supreme Court of the United States has so often done in upholding, as in *Truax* v. *Corrigan,* an injunction granted by a lower court.

The implication of this approach is relatively simple. The Common Law of the United States is, like that of Great Britain, a body of doctrine which has been shaped by the courts to meet the requirements of an owning and managing class. It is a kind of reserve power from which the judges can, and do, draw the weapons which enable them to meet the challenge of legislation to a capitalist society. For this reason it is a very difficult thing for the American labour movement to have confidence in the courts. A trade-union lives by its ability to insist upon removing by legislation the power of the owner or his representative to make his property a militant source of domination over the workers' lives. No doubt there is an area in which it can find common purposes with the employer. But as soon as it reaches the boundaries of that area, the courts are very likely to be hostile to its claims. It is then driven to seek the support of public opinion for legislation which, at the worst, will neutralize that hostility. To this end it must seek to secure in the federal and state legislatures men who are prepared for the arduous task of remaking the foundations of the Common Law.

There is nothing surprising in this antithesis. Historically, every ruling class builds the institutions and the doctrines that will safeguard its supremacy. No doubt there is variation in the fullness with which that supremacy is maintained. No doubt, also, it is rarely that a ruling class in a capitalist democracy like the United States will bluntly admit that the end it has in view is its capacity to safeguard its claims. There are always at hand a mass of rationalizations which can cover up the naked purpose to which the state power is always devoted. "Freedom of contract," "due process," "conspiracy in restraint of trade" are only three of those that have been used to preserve what it appears safe to preserve of economic individualism and all its consequences. The rationalizations

---

[18] *Osborne* v. *A.S.R.S.* (1911) A.C.

may be different in one area of the United States from those in use in another; and time may be a factor, suggesting one rationalization in one epoch and another rationalization in another. Crisis may make a difference; the fear of violence may make a difference; war may make a difference. Normally, I suspect that in the period when American capitalism was expanding with such dramatic swiftness, the law was less concerned to conceal the motives of its decision than when expansion halted. The Supreme Court over which Marshall presided did not even attempt to reach the level of sophistication in defence of the rights of property that was used under Chief Justice Hughes during the first years of the New Deal. Only Mr. Justice McReynolds, in the last generation, would have spoken from the Bench, as in the Gold Clause decision,[19] as Mr. Choate spoke from the Bar in the Income Tax cases.[20] But the sophistication does not mean a change of direction; it means only that greater care must be taken on the journey. So long as capitalist democracy in America is permeated by the philosophy of the business man, that philosophy will be the spinal column of its law. The American labour movement must assume that it can change the law only by building the democracy of the United States on different economic foundations.

3

THOUGH there have been efforts made since the beginning of the nineteenth century to bring the American labour movement into politics directly, none of them has been nation-wide and none of them has been lasting. Naturally enough, every wind of doctrine that has blown through the United States has left some impact upon it. There are influences traceable to Paine, to Robert Owen, to Saint-Simon, and to Fourier. Henry George had a profound effect for a brief period. Since some such time as the Civil War there has been a Marxian thread in the labour pattern; and Fabian socialism before 1917, and Russian communism after it, have had a clearly traceable influence upon its way of thought. Yet, in the end, the real clue to the attitude of American labour to politics lies in the fact that the labour movement is American. It has had Irish leaders, German leaders, Russian leaders, Italian leaders as well as leaders with a long American ancestry behind them. Some of them have been devoted Roman Catholics, some devoted Protestants, some professing Jews. There have been leaders who brought to the movements the habits of British trade-unionism, of German social democracy, of the revolutionary parties of Tsarist Russia. In combination, what has emerged has been, both in outlook and in action, the unmistakable product of the American environment. It is essentially to that environment that it owes all that is fundamental in its character.

This means that, broadly speaking, its approach to politics has been a

[19] *Perry* v. *United States,* 294 U.S. 330 (1935).
[20] *Pollock* v. *Farmers' Loan Company.*

pragmatic one. It has assumed the validity of the American tradition and, within this framework, sought so to act that it could secure the greatest material benefit for its members. After many, and sometimes curious, experiments, it accepted pretty fully, until the Great Depression at any rate, the attitude of Samuel Gompers that there was no place in American political life for a working-class party. Experience rather suggested the wisdom of organizing the votes of trade-unionists so as to reward their friends and punish their enemies. Gompers made the American Federation of Labor essentially a pressure group, a national lobby in Washington, a state or city lobby in other areas of the United States. It was a pressure group which repudiated the doctrine of class war. As a consequence, in its major if less dramatic expressions, it repudiated any alliance with revolutionary ideas. Its members were mostly without any party consciousness at all, or as naturally Republican as Mark Hanna or as eagerly Democratic as William Jennings Bryan. The fluidity of American classes, their mobility, which was an obvious inheritance from the frontier, the frequency with which the labourer of one day was the foreman of the next and stepped thence to the position of superintendent or even manager, made it natural enough for the able and ambitious trade-unionists to assume that they would not remain for ever in the ranks of the wage-earners. They lacked the political solidarity which comes to a class the members of which battle together to win the franchise. They were so diverse in origin, nationally, religiously, linguistically, that it was not easy to make them fully conscious that they were members one of another. They were, indeed, hardly less convinced than their employers that private property was sacred and America more free than any country in the world. And most of their leaders were fully convinced that to go beyond the fight for the right to bargain collectively about the conditions of their labour would only take them down to hopeless defeat. It is even reasonable to argue that, until the Great Depression, they were as suspicious of governmental action and protective legislation as their employers, and it is only in recent times that this suspicion has been overcome. After about 1911, indeed, they approved of workmen's compensation laws, though as recently as 1930 and 1931 the annual conventions of the American Federation of Labor rejected compulsory unemployment insurance.

Local situations apart, it may be said that the American labour movement has still a good deal of confidence in the non-partisan technique. It is true that it worked whole-heartedly for the election of President Roosevelt in 1932. It is, no doubt, important that the C.I.O. subscribed large sums to the Roosevelt campaigns in 1936 and 1940, though it is significant that its support of Mr. Roosevelt for his third term of office cost the C.I.O. the adherence of Mr. John L. Lewis, until then its president, and the affiliation of his powerful and wealthy United Mine Workers of America. It is still more significant that, in the presidential campaign of 1944, the C.I.O. set up the Political Action Committee, under the leadership of Mr. Sidney Hillman, which may well have had a major responsibility for the election of Mr. Roosevelt for a fourth term even in the conditions of war. Its success in the contest has led to the decision to make the Committee a permanent organization parallel with, and growing out of, the C.I.O. This development does not affect the policy of the A.F. of L., which remains non-partisan in Mr. Gompers' sense; in 1944 Mr. Lewis personally supported Governor Dewey, the Republican candidate, though the evidence suggests that most members of his organization supported Mr. Roosevelt.

It is too early to predict whether the P.A.C. has an important future before it. Its task in the election of 1944 was relatively easy; its choice lay between a liberal-minded President who was waging a successful war and a machine-made candidate behind whom there had rallied most of the reactionary forces in the United States. The real test is more likely to come in an election in which neither the Democratic nor the Republican candidate has more than the historic formal interest in trade-unionism, and the workers' vote sends, in a more normal period, a new president to the White House who, if he be a Democrat, represents the unprogressive forces in the party, or, if he be a Republican, is backed by, and will, in all likelihood be responsive to, the pressure of Big Business. Under these conditions the P.A.C. cannot with any ease urge one candidate rather than another. It may play a role in the choice of members of both Houses of Congress; it may seek, even successfully, to influence the mid-term congressional elections in the light of the president's record up to that time; it may even, if it is then influential, acquire a real importance in the choice of the candidate, two years later, who opposes the outgoing president. But it is tempting to argue that the P.A.C. must, unless there is a choice between a liberal candidate for the presidency and the normal nominee of the party machine, either become much more than it has thus far thought of being, or recognize that an election between a new Coolidge and a new John W. Davis is unlikely to enable it to create any real enthusiasm among its constituents. It would then become merely a pressure group which the professionals would have little difficulty in seeing was unable to exercise any pressure; and it is highly improbable, in these circumstances, that it would secure either the money or the men it required to maintain a serious influence.

If, on the other hand, it sought to become much more than it now is, it looks as though there are two courses open to it. It is possible that it may force a realignment of parties. The drive to that realignment dates, in a fundamental sense, from the rise of the Populist movement, which was an effort to rescue the farmer and the small business man from the ruthless grip of the railroads and the great corporations. In the intermediate years there have been ebb and flow in progressivism without its being able to find a permanent resting place in either party. If the P.A.C. were to force upon the Democrats a genuinely progressive candidate after President Truman's term is over, it might well succeed in breaking the Solid South by driving the reactionary elements into the Republican camp. On that basis, the Republican party would become what it has never yet been—a national conservative party uniting that element in all sections of the United States—while the Democratic party would become a national liberal party capable of ending the traditional Republican allegiance of states, like Iowa and Minnesota whose Republicanism has little or no spiritual relation with the Republicanism of Maine and Vermont. And such a liberal party, backed by the P.A.C., would fairly rapidly become an expression of the forces that found meaning in it, so that there would be an end of the present position in which the voter chooses between two parties in neither of which can he find clarity or coherence of principle. This would be the twentieth-century equivalent of the great work done by Jefferson and, a generation later, Andrew Jackson when they organized the revolt of the common man against the forces of property embodied in the Federalist party.

This may not, indeed, prove a possible task. The roots of party allegiance in the United States go deep, not least because the machines in city and county depend for their existence on the present alignments. If it should prove impossible, it is difficult to see how the P.A.C. can avoid the effort, hard though it be, of trying to build a third party, which would arise much as the Co-operative Commonwealth Federation has arisen in Canada, or as the British Labour party has grown out of the radical wing of the historic Liberal party as the latter moved to the conception of the social service state without abandoning its ultimate roots in the defence of private ownership in the means of production. There are many elements which a skilfully directed P.A.C. could organize into both coherence and importance. There is the Socialist party which, with all its limitations, was able under Eugene Debs to poll close to a million votes; the main reason for its decline in the last twelve to fifteen years has been, apart from the folly of its isolationism, the conviction of hundreds of thousands of unattached progressive voters that they must not risk the return of a man like Landon or Dewey. There are the remains of the nominally Republican party of Senator La Follette in Wisconsin; and there is the growing progressive element on the Northwest Pacific Coast. There is the American Labor party which, though its influence is limited to New York and though it has those growing pains which always come from the effort at Communist infiltration, might, properly directed and controlled, become a force of considerable importance in the states of the Atlantic seaboard. What attitude would be taken to a third party by that educational organization into which the American Communist party transformed itself during the Second World War is, of course, quite unpredictable. Its decision would almost certainly depend upon the view taken in Moscow of what development it desired in American politics. If it supported a third party of this kind, that party would, quite obviously, be accused of "un-Americanism," of being paid by Russian gold, and whatever other slogans the older parties thought might do it harm. But since under any circumstances, as the election of 1944 made clear, a new party would, if it were progressive, be attacked as the hireling of Moscow, it seems rational to be hung for a sheep not less than for a lamb.

The real obstacle in the way of an effort by the P.A.C. to form a third party lies in the present schism in the ranks of American trade-unionism. There is the A.F. of L.; there is the C.I.O.; and there are also the four Railroad Brotherhoods which belong to neither federation, in addition to a number of smaller unions whose temper is vitriolic in inverse proportion to their size and importance. A third party that is to make real headway must, at all costs, find ways and means of ending these divisions; for their result is to multiply enormously the confusion and uncertainty in the mind of the American elector. It does nothing but harm to the definition of a clear choice when the leader of the Miners and the leader of the Carpenters are ardent Republicans, the first through the ill-temper of vanity, and the second because his union is essentially a business concern in which he is the managing director with the out-look of an ordinary political boss who has strayed into trade-unionism instead of running a Jersey City or a Boston. It does still more harm when the Railroad Brotherhoods stand aside from the vital political activities of the nation. By so doing they leave their members, nearly a million in number, with attachments in politics that are largely an anachronism in the light of the changing world that is faced by American labour. Unless the P.A.C. can somehow mend these rents and tears in the structure of the trade-union movement, it is not very likely that any attempt on its part to build a third party would have more or longer significance than the Progressive movement in 1912 or the La Follette campaign of 1924. It is always worth fighting at Armageddon, but it is also important to win the victory.

What, by the Gompers technique, has been achieved? Up to 1933 comparatively little. The proportion of trade-unionists to the working population of the United States was not large enough to make the major parties feel that their support was a vital factor in an election. They were even uncertain whether the A.F. of L. had the influence over its members that it claimed. It secured the limitation of hours in a number of states. It obtained the Clayton Act from President Wilson. As early as 1888 Congress made provision for arbitration in railroad disputes. After the institution of the cabinet office of Secretary of Labor in 1913, it was customary, until 1933, to appoint a tested veteran of the Federation to the post; and this was, in some sense, a recognition of the growing status of the labour movement. After a long struggle the Federation secured the eight-hour day in government employment and on public works given out to sub-contract by the federal authorities. After the Debs case, it worked for forty years to limit the use of the injunction in labour disputes and to obtain trial by jury in cases of contempt arising therefrom; the Norris–La Guardia Act of 1932 represented the partial measure of success obtained. It outlawed "yellow dog" contracts; it tightened up the procedure under which injunctions are issued; it enacted that any alleged contempt not committed in the presence of the court must be tried before a jury; and it empowered the defendent, in such cases, to ask for trial before a judge other than the judge who had granted the injunction. There have been a number of union members elected to Congress and to state legislatures; it has seen a miner elected lieutenant-governor of Pennsylvania. It obtained the appointment of the Commission on Industrial Relations in 1913, and the report of that body was, generally speaking, in sympathy with the outlook of organized labour. The threat of a railroad strike in 1916 brought about the enactment of the eight-hour day. In the First World War, it obtained a great enhancement of its status with the government; the attitude of the Taft–Walsh Labor Board and the War Labor Policies Board, of which Mr. Felix Frankfurter was chairman, marks that advance. So, too, does the report of President Wilson's Mediation Commission, which probably had considerable influence in mitigating the worst issues between labour and capital during 1917–18. The Federation, too, was represented on the Council of National Defense and upon a number of administrative boards, such as the War Industries Board, which organized the productive effort of the United States. It also secured, as the price of postponing the steel strike, the calling by the President, in October 1919, of a National Industrial Conference; if it failed, at least the President had sought for understanding between capital and labour on a nation-wide basis. It was, further, a great victory for trade-unionism when the Railroad Labor Board, established under the Esch-Cummins Transportation Act of 1920, announced that it would recognize no "outlaw" organization.

I think it is fair to argue that this is a pretty complete picture of the conquests of the Gompers technique. It must be set in the background of the grave decline of trade-unionism in America after the First World War and until the Great Depression. Company unionism flourished in most private industries. Laws were passed in a number of states enacting heavy penalties against "criminal syndicalism." Scientific management threatened, in industry after industry, the skilled workers' control of their jobs. In the steel strike of 1919–20 the men had a case against the owners as complete as the defeat they suffered. Though there was a passing interest in the nationalization of the railroads when Mr. Glenn Plumb put forward his once famous plan, Mr. Gompers himself opposed it, and support for it petered out. Though there were individual members with a socialist outlook before the Great Depression, there was no sign of any change in basic outlook in the Federation. Not even the fury with which business men pursued the offensive against trade-unionism, nor the hostility of the courts, nor the maintenance of wide areas of the country into which the union organizer dared not even enter, persuaded the Federation that its non-partisan character might bear, if not revision, at least renewed scrutiny. Most of the officers of the Federation, and a

considerable proportion of the officers of its constituent unions, accepted
the philosophy of "rugged individualism" without any serious question.
All that they asked was a chance to gather up some of the crumbs from
the rich man's table.

The theory of Mr. Gompers was in substance the simple one that he
outlined at the convention of the Federation in 1924. "The trade unions,"
he said, "are not inclined towards the Marxian theory of government.
On the contrary, they are manifesting a constantly growing interest and
participation in the institutions dependent upon private and co-operative
initiative, and personal and group adventure." Mr. Matthew Woll, the
"crown prince" of the Gompers regime—though a crown prince who was
denied the throne—said flatly that "industrial democracy cannot come
through the workers alone; we need the help of the employers." Gompers' successor, Mr. William Green, said in his May Day speech of 1925
that the aim of trade-union officials and business men is identical; they
must "unite to fight the Reds." Though the Federation supported the
candidature of the elder La Follette for the presidency in 1924, immediately after his defeat it withdrew from the Conference for Progressive
Political Action which had been formed by the Railroad Brotherhoods;
and these also announced that they were hostile to any attempt at the
formation of a new party. The Gompers technique meant that, so far as
possible, no industrial issue was projected on to the political plane. It
assumed that the state was a neutral power the possession of which was
open to all citizens in equal degree. It opposed the building of a workers'
party since this would imply the acceptance of a class theory of the State.
On the Gompers view, there were no classes in the United States. Capitalism was a thoroughly adequate frame for the political institutions of
democracy so long as the employer recognized the right of collective bargaining.

So that when the Great Depression broke like a tornado upon American economic life the labour movement, on its economic side, was utterly unprepared to cope with its political consequences. Most of its leaders accepted the social philosophy for which President Hoover stood;
they had no alternative philosophy to put against it. For over three years
they watched the rising tide of mass unemployment very much as though
it was a sudden flood bound, sooner or later, to recede. They punished
the "rugged individualism" of President Hoover by throwing all their
influence on the side of Mr. Roosevelt. When he was elected, they supported all his measures of relief, his great programme of public works,
his National Industrial Recovery Act, with its special recognition of
labour and the demand for collective bargaining; but there is little evidence to suggest that they understood that Mr. Roosevelt was, with
extraordinary skill, using the Democratic party in a great emergency
for purposes it did not approve, and would not, as soon as confidence was
restored, be willing to accept, on the plane on which Mr. Roosevelt sought
to take action. Indeed, they learned so little from the first period of Mr.

Roosevelt's first term that the split occurred in the ranks of the American Federation of Labor which resulted in the formation of the C.I.O. They welcomed the Social Security Act and the Wagner Act when they came. But they drew from the New Deal the inference that if the power of the labour movement is thrown on the side of a liberal president, the result will be legislation so valuable to labour that a third party is not only unnecessary, but is even a threat to the prospect of electing a liberal president. The C.I.O. has therefore continued to employ the technique of Gompers; the only difference is the vigour and urgency with which they have used it.

A distinguished historian of the labour movement in the United States has argued that this course is wise on the ground that where, as in America, the power of government to regulate industrial conditions is "restricted by a rigid, organic law," it is a mistake for labour to build a political party.[21] Professor Perlman was writing in 1922, though it is evident that he had not changed his opinion thirteen years later.[22] In his judgment, even where the courts are prepared for a broad interpretation of the Constitution, what the labour movement could obtain through political action would not be worth the energy it would take. Since, further, sovereignty in the United States is built on the division of powers, "to a party of social and industrial reform this division offers a disheartening obstacle." And it seems clear to Professor Perlman that "party differences are considered differences of opinion or of judgment on matters of public policy, not differences of class interest. . . . Class parties in America have always been effectively countered by the old established parties with the charge that they tend to incite class against class." Professor Perlman even argues that if a real labour party were created and persisted in America, the "old party politicians," if they could not destroy it by encouraging divisions within its ranks, would, in the end, join together against "their upstart rival." This is the logical outcome, he thinks, of the special American environment. "The limited potentialities of labour legislation together with the apparent hopelessness of labour party politics compelled the American labour movement to develop a sort of non-partisan political action with limited objectives thoroughly characteristic of American conditions." [23] Professor Perlman even suggests that this indirect approach has given the workers in wartime more than they could have won by a direct share in political power as a party.[24]

It is not necessary to deny that both the traditions of American life and the division of powers under its Constitution make the political activity of labour more difficult than under a more flexible system in order to see that Professor Perlman's case is built on enormous assumptions

[21] Selig Perlman, *History of Trade Unionism in the United States* (New York: Macmillan, 1922), p. 285.
[22] Selig Perlman and Philip Taft, *History of Labor in the United States* (New York: Macmillan, 1935).
[23] Perlman, *op. cit.*, pp. 287–89.
[24] *Ibid.*, p. 290.

none of which he has seriously explored. He assumes that the State power in America functions in the interest of society as a whole and not as the safeguard of the property relations of a capitalist society. He does not ask whether this is possible. He does not even ask why the State power in America should function differently from the State power in any other community. He assumes that the Republican and Democratic parties are not concerned to promote class interests, but operate for the well-being of the whole community. He does not inquire why, in such an America, the class which owns capital is so careful to hold all the key positions in the business of governing, nor does he explain why those who hold these key positions are so set on protecting the interests of capital. He assumes that men who are seeking this reform or that get their ideas considered objectively on their inherent merits. But it is surely obvious that, whether it be the abolition of slavery in the South, or the recognition of the right of a trade-union, in the steel industry, for example, to bargain collectively on behalf of its members, to get a rate for a job increased, or to secure the closed shop, the reformer is trying to function in a society which is penetrated through and through by the fact that it is a capitalist society. If he accepts capitalism as final, he cannot push his reform beyond the point which is considered safe, not for society, but for themselves by the owners of capital. He must then collaborate with them, and the degree to which he pushes his reform is set by the point at which they refuse any further collaboration. He may think the point less high in the scale than is in fact consistent with their safety. But everyone knows that once his first principle is the duty to collaborate, the power to decide is not in his hands. What happens, in these circumstances, is that he either abandons the hope of being able to secure the reform he desires, or he accepts some compromise, the character of which is defined by the owners of capital. And this is true, it must be remembered, even of a man in so pre-eminent a position as the president of the United States himself. How much more it is likely to be true of the president of a trade-union it is hardly necessary to elaborate. It is, at any rate, worth bearing in mind that Judge Gary was not in the habit of welcoming discussions with the leaders of the steel unions, and that the organizers of the United Mine Workers have not always been welcome in the coal towns of Illinois or West Virginia or Pennsylvania.

Once this is clear, two things may be said to follow. Professor Perlman is right in thinking that when capitalists need the co-operation of the trade-unions, as in war, they are more ready to make concessions to them; and he is also right in thinking that American capitalists, in an era of expansion, are more open to argument than when they move into a period of difficulty. But what he does not see, what, even more, the practitioners of the Gompers technique have failed to see, is that so long as the key positions in the economy of American society are held by capitalists, they are not likely to surrender those positions. And from this it follows that if the trade-unions desire to occupy them there is no alternative open to them but to seek to take possession of the State power. But there is no reason in all the past experience of America to suppose that capitalists will agree to so vital a change; a refusal on their part to accept this adaptation is, in Professor Perlman's words, "thoroughly characteristic of American conditions." So that at the point where circumstances convince the American labour movement that a vital change is the condition of its safety, labour must take the necessary steps to capture the State power. It can do this either by organizing a political party which wins an effective majority at the polls, or it can do it, in a quite exceptional situation, by violence. The one certain thing is that it cannot do it by trusting to the magnanimity of the employers and assuming that, when the community welfare demands it, they will gracefully abdicate their power. Above all, it appears reasonably obvious that in the epoch of monopoly capitalism in the United States neither the great corporations nor the historic political parties will embark upon a programme of radical reforms. If they will, Professor Perlman, and those who think like him, must explain, or explain away, why President Roosevelt failed to achieve any significant popularity with Big Business.

The weakness in the approach of American labour to politics is the vital one that it has taken its theory of the State from the employers and asked only for concessions and adjustments on the ground that the American government, as the agent of the State power, is a neutral and mediating force among the different elements in society. And implied in this outlook is the doctrine that the property relations of the United States are eternal and that all labour can do is to persuade the State power to act rationally and objectively. There is not an atom of serious evidence to justify this position. The business of the American government in a capitalist democracy, especially a capitalist democracy moving ever more swiftly to the stage of organized monopoly, is essentially to see that those who own the monopolies are assured of that law and order which maintains the continuity of access to profit. There are, no doubt, degrees of emphasis in the policy pursued. Under President Roosevelt, a tax policy like that pursued by Mr. Mellon, as Secretary of the Treasury under Mr. Coolidge and Mr. Hoover, was hardly thinkable; just as it is difficult to think of a measure like the Wagner Act being pressed upon Congress in the period before the Great Depression. Nor is there any doubt that the State performs all kinds of functions which are in no sense economic or relevant to the relation of classes in society.

But what is undeniably clear is that the State power defines conditions which arise out of the relations given by the fact that America is a society in a fairly definite phase of capitalist development. What is not less clear is that its authority, as State power, is directed to preserving the structure of capitalism as a whole. This piece of legislation or that may injure this or that section of the ruling class in the United States. The threatened dispossession of thousands of farmers by the foreclosure of their mortgages may lead to the Frazier-Lemke Act. The passionate indignation of millions of small investors may result in the establishment of the Securities and Exchange Commission. The agony of the years when frustrated and disappointed men saw that they could not face the future with any confidence may lead to social security legislation. The State power in the United States is not less concerned than elsewhere to prevent ill-fortune from driving men to the point where they can contemplate revolution without repining. It keeps the peace, within the frame of the profit-making system, because continuity of production is impossible without peace, and continuity of production is necessary if profits are to be made. But no one can seriously examine either of the major American parties and conclude from their record that either of them seeks to subordinate the claims of capitalism to the claims of democracy. The fact that the United States is a political democracy set within the categories of capitalist economics only means that the area within which the workers can manœuvre for concessions is far wider than in a dictatorship like Nazi Germany or an oligarchy like the France of Louis-Philippe. Of course this right to manœuvre within a wide area is of high importance; but it leaves untouched the central fact that the Republican and Democratic parties will necessarily operate the State power, federal or local, in the United States on a basis implicit in the fact that it is a capitalist society.

4

AMERICAN labour, this is to say, is operating within a social framework in which it is not only the junior partner, but in which it is not in a position where it can in a profound way control the basic purposes either of industry or of agriculture. And this is true even though there are certain aspects in which there are trade-unions which function on a far higher level of competence than is the case with the unions of any other country. Certain unions, for example, the Amalgamated Clothing Workers, the International Ladies' Garment Workers, which are quite outstanding, the United Automobile Workers, the American Federation of Teachers, the Newspaper Guild, have approached the problems they confront with an insight into their nature that is remarkable. They have understood that, if they are to bargain successfully with the employers in their industries, they must have at their disposal the knowledge which will enable them to conduct negotiations on equal intellectual terms. In the result, they have appointed staffs to take care of their interests which may fairly be said to constitute a civil service of outstanding quality. They employ full-time lawyers; they employ full-time economists; they employ technical specialists where these are required. Hardly less important, they organize the main offices of their unions so that their officials have the assistance necessary to concentrate their minds on their essential function—the grasp of the way in which the industry as a whole operates in which the union is seeking to improve the position of its members.

And what is true of a number of individual unions is also true of the Congress of Industrial Organizations as a whole. Under its present leadership, it is, I think, true to say that as a policy-making body it is better equipped for its function than any other national trade-union organization in the world today.

It has discovered three things, at any rate, of the first importance. It has discovered how to organize the white-collar worker—the clerk, the journalist, the teacher. It has realized that industrial management—the work of the executive class in industry—is something that the unions must know as completely as the employers, and, if possible, better. They must go further, and concern themselves not merely with the pay and other conditions of their own members, but also with their efficiency and with the over-all significance both of national economic policy and of whole industries in the context of the larger policy. The proposals put forward by Walter Reuther for American industry in the war effort are merely an example, though a remarkable example, of the scale on which the new trade-unionist is beginning to conceive his problems. And to these must be added that, especially in recent years, there has been an immense advance in the skill with which the American unions, far more, perhaps, on the side of the C.I.O. than of the A.F. of L., have handled the problem of organizing their power as "pressure groups" in the lobbies of forty-nine different legislatures, each of which has inherent in it separate and complicated problems of its own. It is one thing to seek for influence over a legislature like that of the state of New York; the required pattern across the line in a state like that of New Jersey, dominated by what is largely a personal and malevolent tyranny, raises quite different issues which have to be handled by a quite different technique.

On the other hand, there must be set against the importance of these advances—and they are of very great importance—the realization of two things. The first is the grave danger implicit in the split in the American labour movement, a split which it may take longer to overcome than optimists now imagine. The second is the fact that, basically, the American employer has not willingly accepted the union shop as this was made possible by the Wagner Act, and is therefore pretty certain to exploit the position final victory in the Second World War is bound to create, when anything from ten to fifteen million soldiers, sailors, and workers want jobs that may not exist. This must be set in the perspective of a federal government, even a Supreme Court, not necessarily as favourable as was President Roosevelt to the philosophy of collective bargaining through free trade-unions. Nor must one forget that for the trade-union in America a favourable government in Washington is a new experience to be set over against almost a century of hostility and suspicion. It becomes, therefore, tempting for the English observer to regard American trade-unionism as akin in its basic psychology to the place of nineteenth-century Nonconformity in British political life. The Established Church was to the British State power very much what the

State power has been to the American business man; the guardian of rights, the protector of privilege, it could be looked to in any of the three sources of political authority as a normal rule; where that was not the case, a man like Governor Arnall could always be checked and controlled by co-ordinate or superior power. So that just as the English Nonconformist tended to regard State action with suspicion, as the action which hampered his freedom and was even the main source of his persecution, so the American trade-unionist tended to regard the political authority of the State as the reserve power which the employers brought into play when their own strength was not enough to maintain their domination. That was why Gompers persuaded the A.F. of L. to become a pressure group seeking the right to control of the job in the factory from the political parties; and it is notable that he merely reformulated the conclusion of G. H. Adams when the latter foretold the failure of the Working Men's party in New York City in 1828. They both thought the path of wisdom was to trade votes with the politicians in return for the maximum protection of job control as the empire in which the unions would be sovereign. The one thing the unions did not want was the invasion of their empire by the State power, for they were convinced that State action was only too likely to be hostile action.

Predominantly, the A.F. of L. still thinks in these terms, so that some of its leading figures could, throughout the period of the New Deal, be found quite comfortably in the ranks of the Republican party. Even more notable was the fact that, in 1940, Mr. John L. Lewis, the chief original architect of the C.I.O., supported the Republican candidate, Mr. Wendell Willkie. If, ostensibly, his opposition to the late President Roosevelt was based on his dislike of a break with the third-term tradition, only a little more scrutiny was needed to see that, his vanity apart, Mr. Lewis's opposition was based, above all, on the fact that he regarded the support of the C.I.O. as the consideration in a contract between himself as the president of the C.I.O. and President Roosevelt as the leader of the Democratic party in which he traded votes for concessions. When the level of concession seemed to him inadequate to the strength his organization could bring to the Democrats, it seemed to him quite natural that its votes should be given to the Republican party. It is clear that Mr. Lewis regarded the trade-unions as outside the categories of party politics and only to be tempted into the ground these occupied by an offer proportionate to the strength the unions could display, just as Mr. Philip Murray and Mr. Hillman took the view that on a comparative estimate of experience and hope it was worth entering that political arena from which Mr. Lewis held back. What it is important to realize is the assumption among all trade-union organizations that they must retain their power to pick and choose between friends and enemies by an *ad hoc* judgment made about each candidate in each election. The only difference in principle between the outlook of Mr. Gompers, say, in 1913, and Mr. Hillman in 1944, was that the latter had evolved for the C.I.O. a much more effective organ for political expression in the P.A.C. than anything Mr. Gompers had constructed in his long years of almost unrivalled leadership.

The result of this division of method between what may, I think fairly, be called the politics of policy, to which British trade-unionism was first committed in 1900 in a small way, and in a decisive way in 1918, and what, once more quite fairly, may be termed the politics of manœuvre, on which the American unions rely, is, I suggest, that in a slow and somewhat irregular approach the British trade-unions are moving to the capture of the State power in Great Britain, with a view to the transformation of a capitalist into a socialist community, while the American trade-unions rely upon a pragmatic approach, which, broadly, accepts for the time being the indestructible character of American capitalism and seeks only to get out of it the best possible terms for the organized workers. The Trades Union Congress of Great Britain, in a word, is feeling its way to the fulfilment of a socialist philosophy of which the Labour party is the proposed instrument, while all the major organizations in the trade-union world of America refuse to concern themselves with a doctrinal effort of this kind, which they clearly regard as irrelevant to conditions in the United States.

This attitude is strongly defended on a number of grounds. It is pointed out that American labour has often tried to found a political party and that the effort has always resulted in failure; even the Farmer-Labor coalitions of North Dakota and Minnesota had the most brief of existences. We are told that both Mr. Gompers and Mr. Hillman started as class-conscious Socialists, and learned in the hard school of experience that a socialist outlook was unrelated to American conditions. Still more, they came to understand that the concept of class in the United States has a different content from that in European countries, and that the continental sweep of America gives a flexibility of character, and a looseness of discipline, to political parties that enable well-organized pressure groups to permeate them with an insistence upon particular claims, which are given added strength by the centrifugal tendencies of American sectionalism.

I see no reason to doubt that it is folly in the extreme to seek to apply categories that are valid for European labour history as though they were ready-made for American experience. It is obviously true that the ideas, both of class and of party, are subdued to an environment different in America from that in Europe. It is clear, therefore, that the methods of the American labour movement must take account of these differences if they are to be applied with the hope of success.

But if we are not to underestimate the differences, it is equally important that we must not exaggerate them. I venture to suggest that the argument of those who depreciate the attempt to use European categories to interpret American experience is largely built upon assumptions of which they are gravely unconscious. They believe, first, that America has a special destiny for itself, and that it must follow that its citizens have larger opportunities than the European worker can expect. They infer that the wider social equality of America is related to a similar equality in matters of the functioning of economic classes. They are convinced, since all efforts have failed thus far to form an American socialist party on the basis of a belief that the workers have a special historic mission at a given period of capitalist evolution, that, therefore, in American conditions there is a natural inevitability about the failure. They urge that the diversity of American conditions in so vast a territory makes the notion of a unified and disciplined political party out of harmony with the pluralism of political control involved in the geographical and economic facts. They argue that a political party is less a body of ideas than a group of managers trying to sell more commodities to more interests than their rivals can do in return for the right to operate the State power. They insist, indeed, to quote one learned supporter of this view, that "whether we [Americans] like it or not, the kind of political action that we are obliged to follow is the method of collective bargaining in politics, pressure politics." [25]

I find it very difficult to accept this view. Let us grant that America is a big country rich in diversity, that its social mobility is far greater than that of any European country save the Soviet Union, that its political structure is a hindrance and not a help to the unification of political power. It nevertheless remains true of America that the more profound the centralization of economic control in the United States, the more uniform is the pattern that giant enterprise there imposes upon both industry and agriculture. It remains true, further, that in an increasing degree the number of workers in the United States who may hope to escape from their dependence upon the sale of their labour power is smaller and not greater every year. The quasi-Jeffersonianism of Woodrow Wilson, that "curse of bigness" upon which Mr. Justice Brandeis laid so much emphasis, were already nostalgic anachronisms at the time of their formulation. The real result of the anti-trust movement, from the time of Henry Demarest Lloyd to that of Thurman Arnold, who as assistant attorney-general engaged in the hopeless task of trying to apply the Sherman Act must be so carefully distinguished from the eminent jurist who, as a Yale professor of law, had shown that "trust-busting" was a labour of Tantalus, was merely to give lawyers more income for more ingenuity in devising ways round the law, and courts an economic function that they were always unable, and usually unfitted, if not unwilling, to perform. The first outstanding fact in American economic history is that it repeats, if on a vaster scale, the general character of development in the life of European communities. The differences are more notable before the Civil War; after it, what is most striking is the growing development of the resemblances.

[25] Selig Perlman, *Labor in the New Deal Decade* (New York: International Ladies' Garment Workers' Union, 1943–45), p. 33. *Cf.* his *Theory of the Labor Movement* (New York: Macmillan, 1928).

There is, indeed, little to separate the early history of American socialism from the character of what Marx called "Utopian" socialism in most other countries. America has its community-building idealists like the Brook Farm enthusiasts, and they are mostly contemporary with their European analogues. The New York Working Men's Party is a pretty obvious relation of contemporary working-class radicalism in England. It is clear that a body like the Knights of Labor has unmistakable kinship with Robert Owen's Grand National Consolidated Trades Union. It is also clear that the outlook of Samuel Gompers is not very different from that of the English trade-union leaders from the foundation of the Trades Union Congress in 1872 to the formation of the Labour Representation Committee in 1900; and there is a good deal to be said for the view that the Fabian doctrine of "permeation," supposed to be so characteristically English, was a doctrine indigenously evolved by American labour in the search to fulfil similar purposes. If British trade-unionists clung closely to the Liberal party, in the era of Gladstone and Bright, there was always a significant section to whom the Tory democracy of Disraeli and Lord Randolph Churchill made a special appeal; just as American labour tended, especially after the panic of 1873, to follow the fortunes of the Democratic party, with exceptional Republican emphases when the claimants to its support were men like the elder La Follette, or Theodore Roosevelt in that difficult period when he was, quite mistakenly, supposed to be the standard-bearer of progressive ideals. Nor must we fail to notice that, while both Great Britain and the United States have always had their small Marxist parties, partly composed of intellectuals and partly of workingmen, in neither country did Marxism establish an important intellectual influence until after the October Revolution in Russia. It is always a significant fact to remember that, if Lenin was unknown in the United States in 1917, the number of labour leaders in Britain who knew of him in any serious way could be counted on the fingers of one hand. Nor is it less significant to bear in mind that, both in Britain and in the United States, the relationship of the Churches to the labour movement, not least to the trade-union side in each, has a startling resemblance and a parallel evolution.

For the history of the Churches in both countries is, in the context of labour, essentially an evolution from emphasis upon theological dogma to emphasis upon social ethics. Men so diverse as William Ellery Channing, Theodore Parker, and that remarkable figure, Orestes Brownson, in the earlier part of the nineteenth century, Washington Gladden, George D. Herron, and Monsignor J. A. Ryan at its close, have their parallels in Frederick Denison Maurice and Charles Kingsley, in the earlier period, and in Stewart Headlam and Henry Scott Holland in the later.[26] A document like the Report of the Interchurch Committee on the great American steel strike of the nineteen-twenties is built upon practically the same premises as the documents issued under the leadership

[26] See Charles E. Raven, *Christian Socialism* (London: Macmillan, 1920).

of William Temple after the First World War, and, out of the Malvern Conference, during the Second. The Churches, both in the United States and in England, seek at once to persuade their members that economic power is a stewardship which is abused only at the peril of salvation, and that, where it is abused, those who suffer at its hands should take no step which may have a violent outcome. More than this; it is even true to say of the Churches in both countries that they contained men who resented any attempt to insist that they were concerned with social welfare not less than with individual grace, and that they were institutions which acted as an important reservoir through which discontent could be drained into safe channels. Anyone who compares the influence of Nonconformity in South Wales with that of the sects in North Carolina during the difficult period when the cotton industry was taking root there, cannot avoid being impressed by the striking resemblance between their functions.

I shall deal in a later chapter with American religion as a social gospel. The really outstanding fact is the necessity of recognizing that the impact of the Industrial Revolution was, if with a different time lag, following much the same pattern in America as in Europe. The experience, indeed, is so similar that the same inferences are drawn both by individuals and by organizations. There is felt in both countries, with the emergence of machine technology, the same loss of security, the same severity of discipline, the same increased pressure for the gain of shorter hours, the same disproportion in the respective rewards of labour and of capital. And in both the transition from the position of an independent journeyman to that of a wage-earner confers the sense of psychological degradation. It is these, in combination, which produced not merely the interest of "intellectuals" like Albert Brisbane and Horace Greeley in Utopian socialism; it produced, also, an agrarianism like that of G. H. Evans, and the great westward movement. It is difficult not to feel that an important part of the significance of the frontier in American history is the escape it provided for workers in the eastern states and in Europe from industrial harshness in the one, and poverty combined with political persecution on the other. No doubt the hope of the frontier was strengthened by the magic visions conjured up by the gold discoveries. But the frontier was, in a very significant way, the compensation for the widespread discovery, in the generation before the Civil War, that neither the tradition of political freedom nor that of religious freedom to which America had seemed dedicated could deflect or diminish the immense power of the growing corporation and the ruthless appetites of absentee ownership. A group of skilled workers might gain here and there. But no one can seriously examine the general position of the workers on the eve of the Civil War without the awareness that, with all its courage and with all its dreams, the labour movement had been hopelessly beaten on the field it had chosen for battle.

It is, indeed, difficult not to feel that the vigour and the relentlessness with which, in the period before the Civil War, democracy and *laissez-faire* were identified, the depth of the labour movement's defeat on most fields where it attempted reform, had much to do with determining the mental climate which, ever since, American labour has been seeking to transcend. Practically all the economists were agreed with Henry C. Carey that free economic enterprise was the fulfilment of the Declaration of Independence.[27] Few men of influence, after the Civil War, had an attitude on social and economic problems very different from the view taken, at the end of the eighteenth century, by Edmund Burke when he wrote his *Thoughts on Scarcity* (1795). This outlook seemed to be reinforced by the teachings of science; one must never forget the degree to which the implications of Darwinism in the field of economic relationships were defined for Americans by Herbert Spencer and his disciple, the widely read and widely popular lecturer John Fiske. Nor must one omit the pervasive influence of the log cabin to White House legend and the faith learned by millions from Horatio Alger and his like, stories of poor boys who become millionaires—a legend which almost magical dramas like the careers of Andrew Carnegie or of Thomas Alva Edison seemed to make true beyond the power of dispute. There might be panics like that of 1873; there might be passionate questionings like the angry phases in the long history of the Populist movement. But, by and large, it is pretty true to say that the American labour movement entered the twentieth century with an outlook not in essence different from that of American business men. Certainly it would have repudiated with a good deal of indignation the idea that workingmen had interests which could not be harmonized with those of their employers. Still more strongly would it have denied that there are permanent barriers between classes which only individuals with exceptional ability or exceptional good fortune are able to overpass.

The important inference, I think, that was drawn from this was reinforced by the special character of American experience. Few things were more prevalent in America, until the Great Depression of 1929, than a disbelief in the positive State, except the belief—quite naturally strengthened alike by the growth of America's immense productive capacity and the hunger of the European immigrant to find his chance, denied him in Europe—of a better fortune and a happier life in the United States. All this enabled the American to be confident, self-reliant, optimistic; it convinced him that only the weakling looked to the State for support. And this meant, in its turn, an acceptance, the more deeply rooted because it was so largely unconscious, of Paine's famous aphorism that society is due to man's wants and the State to his wickedness. So that politics was regarded, as Finley Peter Dunne so brilliantly depicted them in Mr. Dooley's conversations with Mr. Hennessy, as, on the whole, an unclean affair from which honest men kept apart, save where they had to inter-

---

[27] See Joseph Dorfman, *The Economic Mind in American Civilization* (New York: Viking Press, 1946), Vol. II, Chap. xxix.

vene to prevent or to punish some particularly noxious corruption. One
has only to compare the inability of a distinguished journalist like E. L.
Godkin to understand the relation between politics and business with the
insight which dawned on Lincoln Steffens, as he investigated municipal
corruption and came to grasp the result of a system in which parties
represented not competing systems of ideas so much as competing stock
exchanges on which favours could be bought and sold, to understand,
also, the approach of labour to the idea of independent party action.

Obviously enough, those are right who claim that a considerable part
of this approach has been determined by sectionalism. Until, as it were,
only the other day, American politics were dominated, by the facts, first,
that the rural population was more numerous than the urban; and, second, as both Jefferson and Jackson so remarkably demonstrated, that
political victory went to the party which knew best how to combine different sectional interests, whether wheat, or cattle, or dairy farming, in
a single appeal. It must be remembered, too, that until the victory of
Cleveland in 1884 the Democratic party was no more than an unsuccessful protest, and since then only once, in 1916, won in its own right until
the great triumph of Franklin D. Roosevelt in 1932, unless there were
cleavages within the Republican party. And since the Republican party
has been, throughout the period, a party largely dominated by the great
corporate interests, which fought urban labour, on one front, mainly
through its hostility to trade-unionism, and the farmers on the other, by
reason of its zeal for the tariff and for "hard" money, it is intelligible
enough that, as the memories of the Civil War faded, labour should have
come, in the main, to think of the Democratic party as the party of minority interests to which, as itself a minority group, it could look for support. This attitude was naturally intensified as the balance of population
began to swing in America towards an urban emphasis, the more especially since trade-unionism was so overwhelmingly an urban phenomenon.
After all, it is historically a fair generalization that, as a rule, the great
American cities have been Democratic in outlook; it was there that the
trade-unions mustered what strength they had.

But I think it is true to say that the general objective of the American
trade-unionist did not seem to him so much political as economic. What
he sought to obtain was the control of the job in the factory or the workshop or the railroad, and to bargain on equal terms with his employer
about the rate for, and the conditions of, the job. He found that, in practice, this meant a struggle to get the closed shop; and, until the end of
the Great Depression, it was usually a struggle in which he was defeated,
in part directly, by the superior strength of the organized employer, in
part indirectly, by the intervention of the courts, on the one hand, and
the massive immigration from Europe as well as the remarkable mobility
of labour, on the other. There is a sense in which more things in American life conspired to prevent the emergence of a common outlook among
the workers than in any country of comparable industrial development.

There was the vast size of the territory; there was the constant movement to the West, as well as the ease with which men could change their
occupation; there was the immense difficulty of welding swiftly into an
organic whole workers, often unskilled, in an era of rapidly changing machine technology, of twenty or more different nationalities, speaking different languages, and barely, if at all, acquainted with the English tongue.
There was the combination of ease and skill with which the employers exploited differences of colour and of religion. There was the failure of
the farmer, even of the farmer in the Populist revolts, to see that the high
road to the defeat of the octopus he was fighting was to make common
cause with the urban workmen. For it has been untrue for many years to
argue that the farmer's real need is a free market in which monopoly
does not threaten his chance of a fair price, so that the agrarian world is
made safe for the little man. If the Great Depression made anything clear,
it revealed that the future of agriculture lay with the great factory farm,
whose owners, whatever their product, have ample capital for the latest
machinery, the most scientific fertilizers, the means of efficient irrigation,
and the power, by co-operation, to stand up to the middle-man in all
problems of marketing and to exact fair treatment from the railroads in
all questions of rates for transportation.

No doubt the number of farmers who saw this was small, and has,
indeed, remained small. But it seems to me difficult to accept the theory
that all is explained when the magic word "sectionalism" has been
breathed either by the historian or by the sociologist. It is, of course, true
that American political parties have always hewn very close to a sectionalist line. That is shown very remarkably in the great presidential election of 1860 when the split in the Democratic party made Abraham Lincoln's election possible; the contrast between the view taken by Illinois
and Upper Ohio of their interests as compared with the view taken by
Lower Ohio and Indiana is a contrast largely set by trade relations with
the South as these were determined by market opportunities set, in their
turn, by railroad development. But it then becomes urgent to remember
that this sectionalism is itself not less a result, than a cause, of a party
organization which left each body, as it were, no more than a group of
brokers selling favours to the highest bidder. The very fact that, after
some such period as that of Clay and Webster, politics became a business
just like any other business, and that men entered upon it and climbed
upwards in it less frequently by zeal for principles of national action than
by shrewdness in dominating men and skill in salesmanship, meant that
the American politician was almost as much concerned in playing sections off against each other as he was in finding the way to integrate their
interests. Federalism encouraged this outlook at almost every point. It
did so before the Civil War because the Southern view of its "peculiar"
institution encouraged and intensified all the centrifugal tendencies inherent in a federal system; and it did so after the Civil War because the
"robber barons," both great and small, naturally found it far easier to

safeguard the privileges they corruptly bought by making their operations at Washington alternatively the climax or the basis of their operations in the different states. That meant that they could conceal from
the public view a considerable part of the range of their manœuvres. They
could, for example, buy vast tracts of land through the federal government, or use it as the source of a tariff increase, while the favours they
were purchasing in local freight rates, or building regulations, or statutes
permitting new methods of incorporation, or a franchise for a street railway, were hardly known outside the area they particularly affected. The
tragedies of corruption in Pennsylvania in the era of the Quay machine,
or of New York in the era of the Tweed ring, affected the state of Kansas as little as the iron despotism of Huey Long in Louisiana affected
New York in the epoch of Franklin Roosevelt, or the long reign of Henry
Cabot Lodge in Massachusetts, when Quay was bringing such dishonour
on the Republican party.

American capitalism dealt with the political parties much as a customer in a department store deals with its salesmen; if the goods he
wants are not there, he goes next door in the conviction that he will get
what he wants for the price he is prepared to pay. When, after nearly
half a century of systematic failure in its search for direct influence,
American labour, under the influence of Samuel Gompers, set out to find
a new basis for action, it naturally enough decided that the immense success of business men in dealing with the politicians justified the close and
careful imitation of the methods of business men. And a whole school of
social philosophers arose to congratulate American labour alike on the
concrete realism of its approach and upon its happy freedom from that
entanglement with "doctrinaire" ideas which increasingly marked the
habits of the European labour movements. What the social philosophers,
the Wisconsin school, for example, elevated into a characteristic example
of American common sense, and, also, into the proof that the American
scene required a quite different kind of political action from anything
suitable in Europe, always on the ground that the conditions were quite
incomparable, was naturally welcomed with enthusiasm by the two major
political parties. For, first, it assured them that the absence of a significant rival left them in assured possession of the field; and, second, until
the epoch of the Great Depression, it left the world of business satisfied
that labour was not scrutinizing with any serious scepticism the philosophy with which it had provided the politicians as a safeguard of its interests. Theodore Roosevelt, as a Republican president, might throw a
sop to the labour Cerberus by declamation against "malefactors of great
wealth"; that, even with an increase in wages, mattered far less than if
he had supported John Mitchell in his demand for union recognition.
Woodrow Wilson, as a Democratic president, might give the American
Federation of Labor the cheering gesture of the Clayton Act; the important thing for the Democratic party, in its coincident dealings with
its business clients, was its right to a high degree of confidence that the

Supreme Court would rapidly find that the Clayton Act left things much as they were before Mr. Gompers asked his legions to cheer its arrival on the statute book.

5

AT FIRST glance it might appear as though the bi-partisan approach to politics of American labour was justified by its experience during the presidency of Franklin Roosevelt. Here was a party leader who legislated in its behalf on the grand scale. He recognized that, in an era of giant corporations, collective bargaining was an elementary principle of industrial action that brooked neither denial nor delay. He went far towards changing the character of the Supreme Court from that of a body hostile to the claims of labour for almost half the life of the Republic into a body dominated by its friends. He transformed the largely negative state of his predecessor, with its simple faith in *laissez-faire* doctrines which had been obsolete in America for at least seventy years, into a social service state in which at least the foundations were laid of insurance against unemployment and sickness and old age. He recognized the obligation of the federal government to come to the relief of the jobless by initiating what was by far the greatest programme of public works the United States had ever known. He agreed to use the federal power to provide an abundant supply of cheap money even at the cost of taking down that Cross of Gold before which, despite the eloquence of William Jennings Bryan, Wall Street had continued to worship; and he was insistent that the small debtor must be protected against exorbitant claims from his creditor, whether the latter was a loan company specializing in hire-purchase or a banking corporation with a grim willingness to call in its notes whenever a wisp of wind seemed to threaten confidence. He stimulated, as part of his programme of public works, not only an advance in the standard of public housing for persons of relatively moderate means; but he also admitted the validity of the principle that federal funds could be used to maintain and to encourage the cultural heritage of the American people. It is not in the least unlikely that, a century from now, the historian will pronounce the experiments in writing and painting, in music and the theatre, by far the most significant part of the Works Progress Administration.

On any showing, the achievement of the New Deal makes the period from 1933 to 1940 one of the most significant epochs in American history. It is in no sense difficult to understand the enthusiasm for, and the loyalty to, the great President who fought for its principles among the overwhelming majority of men in the labour movement. But it would be a great mistake to infer from the achievements of the New Deal that it had altered in any profound way the fundamental characteristics of the American State power. The main body of Democratic members of Congress supported the Roosevelt programme—despite notable devotees—

less because they accepted its principles than because they did not wish to split their party. A majority of the Southern Democrats remained invincibly hostile to any changes which might have led to a renaissance in the South; they prevented the offer of any serious help both to "poor whites," such as the sharecroppers of Arkansas, and to the Negroes. If the South, with its combination of poverty and dependence on the one hand, with privilege and caste on the other, was the outstanding problem confronted by the United States on the domestic plane, no one can seriously claim that the Democrats could face it honestly on the basis which made labour approve the New Deal. It is, indeed, even true to say that labour leaders were as anxious as anyone to leave the issues of the South to the safety of rhetorical declamation rather than to the dangers of congressional experiment. The drive in Congress for the New Deal, even more, the long, daily struggle to maintain it unimpaired, came overwhelmingly from the East and the West, from the cities in contrast to the rural areas; and the public opinion behind it, as, indeed, against it, was more for a man and the policies with which he sought to stem the tidal wave of economic crisis than for a party and its principles. Mr. Roosevelt may have convinced the American labour movement that he was on the right road; he certainly never convinced either the machine of the Democratic party or that curious complex of disparate interests which made up the Republican party.

For what is surely of the first importance is that, as the drift to war changed the usual position of more workers than jobs, there was less and less discussion of any possibility of using the conflict to strengthen the foundations upon which the new policies were based. What seemed mainly to emerge out of the war experiences was the determination of business men, whatever their party allegiance, to continue their fidelity to the traditional business philosophy of America and to argue, like Mr. Eric Johnston, the president of the United States Chamber of Commerce, that this might legitimately be termed, in some mysterious fashion, the defence of the system of free enterprise. Labour fought hard to secure the nomination of Mr. Henry Wallace as vice-presidential candidate in 1944; it could not even secure the support of Mr. Roosevelt himself, who could not risk the loss of machine support even to safeguard ideas with which he was in obvious sympathy. The succession therefore passed to a loyal adherent of the Democratic machine. It is difficult to suppose that this can renew the life of Mr. Roosevelt's domestic policies save as a new crisis creates again the atmosphere of 1932–33. What is then more likely to confront American labour is not a challenge merely to the gains of the New Deal, but, of far more profound importance, a challenge to the idea of American democracy itself.

No doubt the flexible character of parties, the loose and decentralized organization on which they depend, encourages the labour movement to faith in the principle of helping their friends and harassing their enemies. No doubt, also, the election laws of the different states make the emergence of a new party exceptionally difficult. In Nebraska, for instance, a new party can only nominate its candidates in a state convention provided that this is attended by not less than seven hundred and fifty delegates, and that county conventions are held simultaneously at which one hundred delegates are present. Wyoming permits the nomination of candidates from new parties either by convention or by petition; but it prohibits the name of the party from being printed on the ballot paper, and this, obviously, works to the advantage of the older parties. To all this, of course, must be added the fact that under the American system the creation of a new party of nation-wide proportions is an immensely expensive affair, and that it is a process handicapped by the fact that most of the professional organizers look to the patronage which the older parties have traditionally led them to expect. Nor must one omit the fact that the election laws of many states put a premium against novelty by requiring so large a number of voters to petition for its place on the ballot as to open a very wide door to intimidation.

Yet the historic American division into Democrat and Republican presents the labour movement with an upper limit to its effort beyond which it is hardly likely to pass. For, first of all, the machines of both parties are, in state after state, ultimately controlled by the great corporations; the dominance of Delaware by the Du Ponts is only the extreme instance of this control. And, secondly, anyone who examines the composition of Republican and Democratic committees, whether for national or for state action, will note the overwhelming preponderance of lawyers and business men, and the virtual absence of trade-union leaders and small farmers from their personnel. If one examines campaign contributions, it is evident that when, as in 1928, twenty-five persons can contribute over one and a half million dollars to the campaign fund of the Democratic party, in its national context only, and that all of these, of course, were from the great corporate interests of America, they expect a return on their investment. The little man subscribes; but from sixty to seventy per cent of either party's campaign fund comes from the several hundred subscribers who represent the forces of Big Business. And to this must be added the vital fact that these forces are, as a rule, pretty equally represented in the funds and the direction of both major parties.

A further complication is introduced by the distribution of electoral votes in the United States. Frederick J. Turner's famous sentence that "statesmanship in this nation consists not only in representing the special interests of the leader's own section, but in finding a formula that will bring together the different regions in a common policy" [28] must be set in the context not only of the fact that no major section holds enough electoral votes to entitle it to neglect the less populated sections which, pretty obviously, still retain the balance of power; but also of the

[28] See his *The Significance of Sections in American History* (New York: Holt, 1932).

fact that while only slightly over forty per cent of the American population is still rural in character, the distribution of the population gives an urban majority to only twenty-one of the states. The effect of this is that while a party that is predominantly an urban party might hope to control the fight for the presidency, it could not hope, under the present Constitution, to control the elections to the Senate without winning a considerable volume of support from states which are predominantly rural in character. This disproportion is, moreover, enhanced by the general overrepresentation of rural areas, and deeply divided, in its relation to parties, by the kind of farming upon which these concentrate. The great areas of export, like the cotton states, are not likely to share the outlook on federal economic policies of the dairy-farming states, which supply the demands of the home market. The problem which confronts any party which seeks to make the labour movement its basis in America is how it can penetrate the individualist psychology of the rural areas.

Most American observers think that labour would be wasting its time if it were to make the effort. They assume a permanent incompatibility of temper between the outlook of the organized trade-unionist and that of the small farmer. "Emotionally or sentimentally," writes Professor Perlman, "the farmer reacts even more strongly to labour moving in on him as a master than he does to Wall Street; . . . the inspiration may be from the outside, but the bitter feeling is certainly there." [29] No doubt it is; but it is also of great importance to realize what has been happening to American farmers. In 1880 only one-quarter of all American farms were worked by tenants; in 1930 over forty-two per cent were so worked. Tenancy replaced ownership on an increasing scale in the corn, hog, and wheat areas of the North, and in the tobacco and cotton areas of the South; in 1930, nearly three-quarters of the cotton farmers were tenants, and about half of these were sharecroppers. The mortgages on American farms in 1930 made up nearly forty per cent of their value. Foreclosure and inability to pay taxes drove more and more farming families into the cities; the day was passing when the wandering settler, whether a Yankee from New England or an immigrant from Scandinavia, could hope to buy his farm out of his savings. He had decreasing incentive to look after the soil, decreasing incentive to plant any but cash crops, decreasing incentive to improve his buildings, to use machinery, or to stay on a particular farm for any length of time. Of American tenant farmers in 1935, more than one-third had occupied the farms on which they were visited for less than one year; in many regions that proportion was more than one-half. To all this must be added the further significant fact that to the economic insecurity of the farmer and his wife must be joined the educational insecurity, especially in the South and the Southwest, of their children; while many families without their own farms, too often in the tragedy of rural America, suffered also from the sense of being apart from the real civic life of the community. Too few of them

[29] Perlman, *Labor in the New Deal Decade*, p. 10.

voted; still fewer could belong to neighbourhood organizations; fewer still had the chance to follow the movement of affairs, still less to read books. In the great areas of wheat and cotton crops, American agriculture, by the time of the Second World War, had reached the tragic situation where its capacity to produce continually expanded while its capacity to market profitably continually declined. Nor did the New Deal touch the root of the problem; all that it did was to subsidize the farmer at the taxpayer's expense in order to persuade him to reduce his output. Individualism in American agriculture reached the point where an economics of restriction and a growing concentration of ownership looked like its inevitable fate.

At this point in the evolution of American capitalism it becomes ever more difficult to see how the labour movement can accept as permanent the present alignment of parties. To do so is to accept both structures and purposes of which the implications all threaten the future of labour, for they all assume the permanence of an individualist economy in the United States, in which, apart from sudden crisis, as there will be an ever-expanding area of jobs, there will also be an ever-diminishing area of trade-union control. There is no reason to suppose that this will be the case. Not only does this analysis presuppose that an American capitalism is emerging which can operate successfully without requiring that reserve of unemployed which is endemic in the system; it also fails to take account of the massive dynamic of what is today the most swiftly changing technology the machine has ever displayed; it omits to attempt any inference from the nature of the State power in American society; and it shows a singular inability to measure the probable outcome of the immense problems of the transition from a war economy to a peace economy in the United States. Nor does it even seem curious about the fact that, given the present distribution of wealth, there is no prospect that the vast productive machine in the United States can be worked to full capacity unless there is a continuance of government orders on the scale of recent years; but since the maintenance of this scale would mean the maintenance of taxation of something like the present magnitude, it would raise grave questions in the field where the incidence of the State power becomes a matter of primary importance.

The point is that to have any effective power over this incidence the labour movement needs, first, unity within itself, and, second, the discovery of ways and means of penetrating the still stubbornly resistant area of American life. So long as the first is absent, it is fairly obvious that each American labour group spends far too much time, not on the straightforward business of organization, but upon a fierce, internecine competition from which only the employers benefit. That competition even harms the integrity of organizations which, like the National Labor Relations Board, ought to be the protecting rampart of the whole of labour instead of a method of choosing between its various expressions. It encourages industrial warfare, which is obviously futile; and it gives outmoded minority organizations in particular plants or particular industries a chance of perpetuating unnecessarily their obsolescence. I suspect, myself, that no small part of this internal hostility has very little to do with the objective interest of the workers, and far more to do with the vested personal interests of union officials, national and state, who have not only lingered too long upon the historic scene, but have made provision for their successors by appeals to group loyalty which have long since lost any serious meaning. Anyone who goes through the directory of American trade-unions and seeks to fit them into the developing pattern of American business can hardly fail to conclude that it proves how widely, despite the lessons of the last fourteen years, some millions of American trade-unionists have been unable to learn the central lesson —which, after all, the Knights of Labor sought to teach—that the worker is first of all a wage-earner, and then a carpenter or a miner, a textile operative or a dustman or a printer. The absence of the full sentiment of solidarity among wage-earners—a sentiment that Eugene Debs understood at once in the great Pullman strike—is one of the major sources of the business man's strength in the United States.

But hardly second to this in importance is the need to break down the barrier between the urban outlook of most trade-unions and the conviction of the small farmer, the sharecropper, and the farm-labourer that they do not have any kindred interest with the workers in the city. This is not a matter of passing resolutions; it is not even a matter of a temporary interest in active organization, such as that which produced the Southern Tenant Farmers' Union, which was built in Denver in 1937 as a section of the United Tannery Workers of the C.I.O. For, after all, the main facts about that tragic body were, first, that it was an attempt to meet a problem created by nearly a million and a half sharecroppers, Negro and white alike, who, with their families, rarely earned more than two or three dollars a week. Granted all the devoted work put in by the leadership of men like Kester and Mitchell, the two supreme facts were, first, that the new union never reached one-tenth of its potential members, and, second, that the combination of planter supremacy and government-sponsored terrorism were sufficient to keep the great mass of the Southern tenants either frightened or inert. There was a sudden spurt of membership in 1938; there was a promise of aid from Mr. John L. Lewis, through the C.I.O., which came to nothing when Mr. Lewis left the C.I.O. over the issue of Mr. Roosevelt's third term. By 1940, except as precious memories whispered here and there among friends whose bona fides could not be questioned, it was difficult to believe that the necessary unity between labour in town and country had retained much more than a formal programmatic significance.

Yet it is on the achievement of that unity that the major future of American labour depends. If it were living in the epoch of an expanding frontier, its separation would be intelligible. That time has passed. There is less chance for the man on the farm without capital than there is for the worker in the city who has only his skill upon which to depend. The man on the farm is poor, uneasy, too often unhealthy and uneducated; but he knows that he is all of these, even while he feels driven to accept, with but a rare question, the predominant ideology of his Southern master. If he is a Negro, that is to say, he must either passively accept his lot or, if he be energetic, cherish a hope of moving to some city in the West or North where he may find industrial opportunity. If he is a "poor white," he very easily accepts the conviction that it is the Negro's lower standard of life which accounts for his misfortune, and he devotes to achieving social superiority over the Negro the energy he ought to devote to combining with him to attack the plantation owner who exploits them both. It is, no doubt, true that the whole environment forces him in this direction; it is the sublimation alike of his ignorance and of his desire, amid his poverty and his insecurity, to be somebody himself and to have a satisfying sense of superiority to somebody else. And it is also true that the insulation of distance makes talk with neighbours difficult and cuts him off not merely from the world of books and newspapers, but even, through poverty, from the world of radio. It is not an exaggeration to say that the "poor white trash" of the farming tenantry of America are, in a real sense, its "submerged tenth." They too rarely emerge above the poverty line to reflect with any detachment upon the meaning of their condition.

The trade-unionist of urban America has an abstract sense of the need for solidarity with the poor farmer and the agricultural labourer; and, again rather abstractly, he is aware that only a prosperous rural *couche sociale* will create a demand for the consumption goods upon which his own prosperity depends. But he is facing two immense difficulties which, in combination, give rise to a third. He is preoccupied, in the first place, with the need to make his own control of urban industry secure; it is, after all, only since the Wagner Act that he has had confidence that, apart from a very few special cases like the railroads, union recognition gained is likely to be union recognition retained. Secondly, hardly less than the rural American himself, he is held in the clutches of the old Jeffersonian tradition of the farmer as a free man on his own homestead, just as the rural American lives to possess his own farm as the basis of his freedom, and is still suspicious of any movement of which the origins are in the city as a threat to his chance to stand on his own feet. Because the tenant in Georgia or Arkansas has seen so many attempts at farmer-labour cooperation die, whether of inertia or of actual suppression by the combined forces of the planter class and the government, his habit is to approach any new attempt half in doubt and half in fear. He will join it when it has proved its power to succeed; he too rarely sees that it can prove its power to succeed only if he joins it himself. The psychological outcome is the wholly natural one that he keeps the idea of an urban partnership at arm's length. As a result, the trade-unionist in the cities, faced by the immense difficulties of continuous rural organization, above all the problem of maintaining interest and faith after a small initial success, tends to think that the effort is not worth the price, and to abandon it after the first wave of hope has receded. Nor must one forget how rare is the patience in the United States which can wait for some long-term result. It is the historian who can see that the ancestry of tenant organization goes back to the foundations of colonial America, and that one of the most vital strands in the American inheritance, even as early as the Revolution, was the suspicion of democracy as a system of government which placed property in danger because it placed the State power at the disposal of the poor and the uneducated.

And it is just here that the most powerful case is to be found for independent action on the political plane by American labour. Most of the things that are urgent, if it is to organize the mental climate in which the fictitious antagonism between town and country is to be broken down, depend upon State action. Only government action can abolish the vicious poll tax which so widely disfranchises the very class of rural citizens who most need the vote. Only government action, both central and local, can make the necessary provision for proper roads, proper schools, a proper health service, proper service of agricultural *expertise,* proper water-supply and electric power planned for the little man as the T.V.A. plans it, and fair regulation of railroad rates. Only government action, once more, can end the vicious truck-system, by which the poor farmer is not only constantly in debt, but his very purchases are a source, always of considerable, and sometimes of scandalous, profits to the plantation owner. Only State action, above all, can arrest the condition in which the government appears as an armed sheriff with his deputies to uphold the right of a band of vigilantes either to "keep the Negro in his place" or to expel by violence a union organizer from the city as a foreign "troublemaker." Small and exceptional areas apart, the pattern of American rural life is imposed by a party machine which, over the years, has gone far towards using the State power to construct an indigenous feudalism the likeness of which to conditions in Poland or Hungary, Italy or Yugoslavia, it would, of course, indignantly repudiate. But no serious observer can fail to see, behind the mask of American "freedom," the reality of an American peonage.

There is little evidence to suggest that the necessary changes could be made through an effort to influence either of the historic parties. It would obviously break the hold of the Democratic party on the Solid South; and though few people can seriously doubt that a breach in this hold would be an immense blessing to the United States, the resistance it would encounter from the state machines and their bosses could hardly be overcome without a generation of effort. Nor is the Republican party likely to respond to labour overtures on any important scale. Were it to do so, it would risk the support not merely of Big Business, but also of the millions of well-meaning and even lovable small business men who have been disciplined by generations of teaching, from relatively sophisticated exponents like William Graham Sumner to ignorant but raucous propagandists like Westbrook Pegler, into the belief that all State interference is evil and that its most dangerous form is to permit the unions to secure the closed shop and thus prevent the employer from "running his own business in his own way." Despite all the efforts of men like Holmes and Brandeis, a good Republican feels bound to believe that any diminution in liberty of contract is, where labour is concerned, a forerunner of that government paternalism which is the inexorable enemy of the American idea.

Nor must it be forgotten that while Mr. John L. Lewis in his C.I.O. days, and the Political Action Committee under Mr. Hillman, in the election of 1944, gave money freely in support of Mr. Roosevelt, the attempt of the A.F. of L. to remain independent of political parties has always meant that there were labour leaders, like Mr. Tobin and Mr. Hutcheson, who formed "Labour Committees" for the Democratic and Republican parties respectively and received large party funds for their operation. It is not excessive to suggest that the real object of these funds was less normal political propaganda than an attempt to enable appropriate "Labour Tsars" to do whatever a paid machine could do to prevent an effective unity of labour action in the campaign and on election day. Nor is it easy to see how that unity can be attained so long as powerful trade-union leaders are open to influences of this kind.

It may be argued, further, that the history of Mr. Lewis's relations with President Roosevelt indicate other grave weaknesses in the method of indirect approach. Looking over the history of American trade-unionism, it is difficult not to admit that, despite his illimitable vanity, his ruthlessness, and, what was no doubt its main source, his vast appetite for power, Mr. Lewis has been, thus far, the most dynamic figure in its record. He did not seek in the Gompers' way, to win prestige for the trade-union movement by securing the Department of Labor for one of his colleagues in each successive president's cabinet, with a scattering of minor posts for others, but for active support of labour policies in return for large-scale contributions to the presidential campaign fund, and a parallel, even spectacular, drive to get out the labour vote for the nominee of his support. In the election of 1936, for example, the United Mine Workers of America, of which Mr. Lewis was president, gave nearly half a million dollars to the Roosevelt fund. Yet, within a year, the fight over union recognition in Mr. Girdler's "Little Steel" companies, and their use of violence legalized behind the mask of company-dominated local authorities, led not to government support of labour's demands which the President had previously urged, but the well-known "plague on both your houses" speech which was the beginning of Mr. Lewis's hostility to the President and the road to his support for Mr. Wendell Willkie's candidature in 1940. Partly, no doubt, his vanity was hurt; partly, also, Mr. Lewis thought the President's attitude a poor return from the man "who had supped at labour's table."

But the real source of his hostility went, I think, deeper than either vanity or resentment. Anyone who looks at the resolutions of the C.I.O. convention of 1938 at Atlantic City will see that Mr. Lewis, and, no doubt, his colleagues too, were seeking to give the classic conception of the "right to a job" a supporting foundation, in both federal and state legislation, for which neither the Democratic nor the Republican party was even remotely prepared; and some of the resolutions struck at the roots of the police power of the states, as the courts interpreted that power, in the interest of civil liberty. It is clear that civil liberty, in the mind of the C.I.O. convention, was essentially an attack on the alliance between private employers and the State power, and thus an attempt to redefine a relation which had become almost a traditional one since the close of the Civil War. And all this must be set in the context of the convention's alarm at the growth of fascism both in Europe and in Asia, its suspicion of American vigilante associations, its open, and largely justified, attack on the National Guard as a strike-breaking organization, its obvious fear of the press and the wireless as weapons in the hands of its enemies. Mr. Lewis himself showed the uneasy sense in his own mind that all the gains of the previous five years might prove abortive when he spoke of the need for "some power somewhere in this land of ours that will go over and above and beyond those corporations, with all their influence and power, and provide a job and insure the right to live for [the] American."

Yet Mr. Lewis, like Mr. Philip Murray and Mr. Sidney Hillman since, refused to examine his own central problem. Obviously he no longer believed in "the free play of economic law" which he had advocated in 1925. By 1935 he seemed to think that the development of class-consciousness could be avoided in America if the employers would only recognize a community of interest with the workers, though he agreed that the eagerness of the employers to accord this recognition was not very great. But Mr. Lewis had no coherent philosophy of labour. He never wanted to know more than the next step he should take. He had no desire, as he phrased it, "to indulge in philosophical cogitations or academic meanderings about the philosophy or the academic benefits that might come to posterity through the work that you [the delegates at the Atlantic City convention of the C.I.O.] are doing in this pressing day and year." I do not suppose that Mr. Hillman would have spoken differently in 1944; certainly he did not speak differently at the preliminary conference of the World Trades Union Congress in the spring of 1945. Lewis's interesting reference to that "power somewhere in this land of ours that will be capable of protecting the worker against the great corporations" remains as indefinite as his programme. It is, indeed, far from clear whether Mr. Lewis was aware that no other agency could effect the ends he sought for save the State power itself; nor is it clear that he understood that, in an organized community, the State power can be exercised by government alone.

And once this is admitted, the only sure way, in a democratic community, to count upon any coherent and continuous action by the State power in some given direction is to form a political party strong enough in support to form a government able to operate effectively. To rely upon political parties which are, on the one hand, effectively committed to a way of life which, so to say, regards the worker as the ordinary shareholder, to be satisfied only when the owners of debentures and preference shares have been satisfied, is a policy intelligible and defensible only when the economic evolution of a community is not yet mature enough for the mass organization of the workers to be possible as the most important basis for a party of the Left. And, on the other hand, since the political party in the United States is less a party of doctrine than an agglomeration of interests which will try to reward the highest bidder, a labour movement which relied upon the bid it could make to attain an effective response to its claims would always find itself in a twofold difficulty. In any pressure it could exert in the choice of a presidential candidate, its influence would, almost invariably, be negative rather than positive; it might secure elimination of its enemies without being able to secure the choice of its friends. It would be, this is to say, just one more pressure group among many, the interaction of which would overwhelmingly tend to give weight to the doctrine of "availability." It is only in a crisis as profound as 1861 or 1933 that the "available" man is the exceptional man.

The other difficulty is not less real. For reasons that I have discussed elsewhere, under a constitution built, like the American, on the doctrine of the separation of powers, there is always a potentially inherent conflict between Congress and an exceptional president.[30] For not only is it the natural habit of a legislature to be critical of an executive which seeks to direct it, but it is the consequence of an exceptional president that he seems to dwarf the Congress and thus to direct hostility to the proposals he recommends. It is thus not enough for the trade-unions to secure a friend in the White House; they must be sure that Congress will accept the benefits he is willing to confer upon them. The one effective way to be sure of this is to have enough friends in Congress also to assure a firm majority for a favourable presidential lead. How difficult this is of achievement is shown by the experience of President Roosevelt; for not even his overwhelming majority in 1936 was sufficient to secure the acceptance of his Court plan, and there were few of his policies, until Pearl Harbor, in which he was not compelled to follow a technique of agile and sometimes tortuous compromises, now shifting a little to the Left, now shifting a little to the Right, as he could best read the indications of the limits within which Congress would move. And once America entered the war, on December 8, 1941, he had to purchase the immense powers he received by accepting both methods and personnel which

[30] See Chap. III; and my *American Presidency* (London: Allen & Unwin, 1939), Chap. II.

Congress exacted in return for those powers. It was not accident, but grim necessity, which put so large a part of the control of war production, in all its aspects, in the hands of men who, up to the verge of war itself, had been fighting almost every significant principle of the New Deal. Nor, almost as significantly, was it accident that, after the tragic death of President Roosevelt, his powers passed to that vice-president, Mr. Truman, who had been nominated at the Democratic convention of 1944 as the candidate to satisfy those elements in the party which would not accept the "favourite son" of the C.I.O.'s Political Action Committee, Mr. Henry A. Wallace, its assured and outright friend. And that was to say that even if the transition from war to peace was to be in the hands of a loyal party follower of President Roosevelt, it was also to be in the hands of one who satisfied Big Business because he had made no commitments to the labour movement.

Thus although labour made great gains from 1933, the vulnerable flanks of its battle line remained gravely exposed. It had no sort of certainty that a peace economy, or even the transition to it, would not result in large-scale unemployment, sufficient in quantity to threaten the new volume of its strength; and it did not know whether it could influence President Truman to follow, even if at a slower pace, the social principles of the New Deal. Mr. Murray and Mr. Hillman might proclaim their faith in the power of the United States as a capitalist economy to provide jobs for all under good conditions; they did not with their employer co-signatories explain whence that power would be derived. From Munich onwards, the improvement in the American economy was in overwhelming degree the outcome of foreign and domestic war production. It was quite easy to show in principle how war orders could be replaced by peace orders; it was far more difficult to prove that the distribution of wealth in a capitalist society makes continuing consumers' demand a substitute for government demand. They did not seriously attempt to confront their central problem—that the generating motive of capitalist production is profit and not need. Government demand is effective demand because by taxation and in other ways the government can in fact make production possible at rates of return which are profitable. This is not the case with consumer demand unless it is backed by effective purchasing power. No leading figures in the American labour movement have shown how that power was certain to be present. They hitched their wagon to the star of a free enterprise masking a more concentrated business control than at any period in American history. Their reliance upon its benevolence, when the crisis of war passed, was merely a declaration of religious conviction which had little rational warrant in any previous experience, least of all in the sequel to the First World War.

This analysis leads, I think, to two conclusions, the second of which is set by a perspective requiring very delicate delineation. The first is that the pragmatic approach to the issue of State power by labour has concealed the defects of that approach because the economic crisis moved, after 1937, into an international crisis ending in global war; and global war, under modern conditions, means so vast a programme of public works that the demand for labour can hardly be satisfied. The "little depression" of 1937 ought to have convinced the trade-unions that the "benevolence" of capitalist democracy operates, outside the drama of war, under very stringent conditions; and that the way to transcend those conditions is to be as ready as the nature of capitalist democracy permits to control the law-making power. A political party, this is to say, would have been a far more solid protective armament for labour than any it now possesses, since everything now points to a ragged and bitter struggle on the industrial field, and to an effort, on the political, to renew the aims of the New Deal without most of the psychological requisites for success. If it be said that American trade-unions are far stronger than in 1933, that has an important statistical foundation; but it has still to be shown what strength that statistical foundation will reveal if Big Business conducts a merciless campaign for the recovery of the ground it lost in the Roosevelt epoch. That is in large degree dependent on what political expression the economic powers of the trade-unions will be able to find for their principles. Certainly the British trade-union movement would be in a very critical position, after the end of the Second World War, unless it were protected on the political flank by its expression in the drive and strength of the Labour party in the House of Commons.

The second conclusion is more complex. If my argument is right, the United States has reached a stage in its historic development where the objectives of its labour movement are in fact unattainable without the formation of a political party directly concerned with their promotion. It will, of course, have to be more than a trade-union party merely. It will have to find ways and means of eliciting the support of all unprivileged farming groups, most of all, the poor tenant farmers of the South, whether Negro or white, and that tragic mass of migratory agricultural workers who make their melancholy pilgrimage every year from the farms in New Jersey to the fruit fields of Florida and California. It will have to establish its claim to the allegiance of the scientific worker, of technicians like the engineer and the architect, of industrial executives, especially of the younger generation, of lawyers and of members of all branches of the medical profession, of teachers of every type, of journalists, from the "cub reporter" on a small-town weekly in a state like Wyoming or Nevada to the highly expert special correspondent of the daily papers in the great metropolitan cities. It must interest the artists and the technicians in occupations like music and the theatre, the cinema and the radio. It must know—the trade-unions have already shown that they do know—not only the significance of research, but also how to make that research bring home the vastness of the issues involved to the immense American public, a public always more anxious to move on to the next interesting theme than ready to stay for an answer to all seminal questions. It must avoid the mistake made by the British Labour party when, in its constitution of 1918, it gave separate and indirect representation, in its governing organs, to the workers by hand, since, on experience, this makes decisions on priority of issues a matter of intricate, even of conflicting, psychological emphasis. The member of such a party must belong to it in his own right as a person, and because he or she believes in the principles and policies for which it stands.

In the highest sense, also, it must be a party with a comprehensive view of all the problems, national and international alike, which face the United States. It must not be merely a bread-and-butter party, devoted mainly to the issues which seem to promise an immediate return; on the contrary, it must rate very high not only those things which relate to the spirit of the American people, the arts, for example, but also those projects the return upon which lies in the more distant future, as in the scheme for a Missouri Valley Authority, to take an engineering case, or in raising the standard of American medicine to a more even level. It must be national enough to put the interests of the backward sections and the under-privileged groups before the interests of the more advanced and the groups which enjoy a relatively higher economic and social position. It must recognize that it must begin by refusing to allow its purposes to be invaded by any divisions based on colour or national origin or religious creed. The tensions these have already caused, or are, indeed, causing, are the roads along which what Jeremy Bentham called "sinister interests" advance to the destruction of all that is best in the American tradition. That is why, in this age, it is quite especially urgent that labour definitely turn its back on the "Know Nothing" element in American party politics; for not only the original group of that name, but grim transformations like those of natural radicals—Ben Tillman, and Thomas E. Watson, and Huey Long, for example—make it abundantly evident that "Know Nothingism" is, in the middle twentieth century, one of the direct routes to a fascist society, certain to be exploited by what Mr. H. G. Wells has happily termed the "raucous voices" of our time.

Though circumstances dictate the urgency of its action upon the national plane, an American labour party must give proportionate attention to the fact that the United States is a federal commonwealth in which a myriad of issues can be settled only at the circumference and not at the centre of decision. Since it must seek to determine the destiny of what is virtually a commonwealth, it must realize that healthy local government is a primary condition of its success. Influence in state and metropolitan city, in county and in township and village, must seem to it of primary significance; and its leaders must quite consciously abandon the notion that the only ultimate theatre for the display of their talents is in Washington. It must, too, avoid the danger, which neither Great Britain nor France has wholly overcome, of thinking either that a candidature, not least in a safe constituency, is a fitting reward for an eminent trade-union leader who is just beginning to be past his prime, or that the possession of an eminent name in science or in letters is a sufficient substitute for the qualities which make a man an effective member of a legislative assembly; in this latter aspect, the history of university representation in the British House of Commons ought to be a sufficient warning to it. And it is worth emphasizing, in the light of European experience, first, that ample room should be found early for young men and women to begin their political careers before their first energies are exhausted and before middle age has begun to infect them with the normal inclination towards caution rather than audacity, and, second, that the lawyer's natural flexibility of mind does not inevitably combine with glibness of utterance to produce either profundity or straightforwardness.

An American party of this character must, from the very outset, make up its mind that science has produced the world market and that this has already rendered isolationism quite obsolete. Those, therefore, who argue, like Mr. Clare Hoffman of Michigan in the debate on the Fulbright Resolution,[31] that any provision which seeks to make the United States join an international organization for the purpose of maintaining world peace really "means the repeal of the Declaration of Independence," or "the entering of the thin point of the wedge which, when driven home, means the loss of their independence, and the flying above the Stars and Stripes of an international flag," really belong to the Jefferson Brick epoch of American history. So, too, does Representative Jessie Sumner of Illinois, who seems to have regarded any commitment of the United States to a world-security organization as a denial of Americanism and the outcome of a Machiavellian plot of Great Britain to secure "hand-outs across the sea." [32] The simple view which assumes that all other governments play power politics, and have sinister motives behind their policy of alluring American virginity into their den of thieves to deprive the United States alike of its purity and its wealth, must really be exposed as a myth unworthy of a mature people. An American labour party cannot serve American interests better than by insisting that, if their main well-being depends on peace, the preservation of prosperity and democracy abroad by institutions and methods in which the United States itself collaborates is, by all odds, the surest way of safeguarding their reality on American soil.

No foreign observer of American politics is likely to underestimate the scale of the problem the labour movement would confront in seeking to build a party of this character. It would be a frontal attack on powerful vested interests already deeply rooted at the centre of power. It would suffer much from the ebb and flow of all political organizations, which have to learn, in their early history, to prevent the clash of persons from being elevated by confusion into the clash of principles. It would call down upon its head all and more of that fantastic invective which was poured out against Thomas Jefferson when he set out to

[31] *Congressional Record,* September 30, 1943.
[32] *Ibid.*

break the Federalist stranglehold upon the infant commonwealth by organizing, during the presidency of John Adams, the original Republican party. It would be accused of communism; it would be argued that it was seeking to promote class war in the United States; it would be insisted that it was un-American; there would be angry shouts that, since it threatened the "rights" of private property, it would strike a blow at the traditional roots of American prosperity; its leaders would be accused of being bought by "Moscow gold." Attempts would be made to play off one section of the party, geographically, against another section, or one functional interest against another. It would be the "Nigger party," or the "Jewish party"; its secret head would be found to be the dead, like Marx or Lenin, or even Trotsky, or the living, like Stalin and the European leaders of that Third International, which, it would be explained, had never really been disbanded and was now secretly concerned with robbing the United States of its freedom and its wealth for the sake of foreign nations less happily placed in civilization. Many of its members would quite certainly be victimized, some openly, like teachers, and others in more secret ways, as by the use of financial power against a young doctor or industrialist or farmer who had not yet paid off his mortgage to the bank. Quite certainly, I suspect, the higher institutions of learning, on whose faculties its members might be found, would discover that they had the choice between the generosity of the wealthy class of America on the one hand, and academic freedom upon the other.

It is, of course, highly probable that if such a new party were to prove a serious success, it would have the result, as with the success of the Labour party in Great Britain after the war of 1914–18, of compelling a realignment of parties. What form this would take it is not possible to predict with any confidence; one can only emphasize what elements would merge into a new background. It is, I think, reasonable to suppose that it would then be far more difficult for the Republican and Democratic parties to continue pretending that they look back either to founders or to principles which have ceased to have any genuine relevance to their contemporary perspectives; and it would be even more difficult for them to remain organizations of largely similar political complexion, often contradictory within themselves, as when the Democratic party contained both Grover Cleveland and William Jennings Bryan, or the Republican party President Coolidge and Senators Norris and La Follette. Parties would, sooner or later, have to adjust themselves to new ideological criteria; and I suspect that one of the most important outcomes of this adjustment would be the birth, in the United States, of a genuine conservative party.

Professor Brogan long ago pointed out the need of such a party. Not since the days of the Federalists, as he has said, has America had a party "opposed to aggression against property rights, denying the egalitarian thesis of their opponents, and attempting to hold up the American Revo-

lution at the point most convenient to the upper middle classes." [33] I
think he is right in his insistence that the intellectual level at which the
conservative case has been defended since that day has been mostly con-
temptible. "To bring all kinds of pressure to bear," he has written, "and
when that has failed, to indulge in the most violent abuse and rhetorical
excess of language, has been the method of the American 'better classes'
when confronted with dangerous movements among the more numerous
part of the population, the poor." [34] The Homestead strike and the
Pullman strike, the tactics of President Cleveland and Mr. Olney in the
railroad strike of 1894, of Attorney-General Palmer in the "Deportations Delirium" of 1920,[35] are examples of the one; of the other, the concluding speech of Mr. Choate in the Income Tax case,[36] the utterances
of Mr. Justice McReynolds from the Bench of the Supreme Court during the first period of the New Deal,[37] or, perhaps the supreme example,
the speech of Representative Snell, the presiding officer at the Republican
Convention of 1932, who said of the Democratic party's members that
they were a mere chaos of factions and that "the nation is to be asked
to accept confusion as national policy and disorder as a rule of government." [38]

If a real radical party, built upon the mass basis of the trade-unions,
were thus to regenerate American conservatism and transform it from an
oligarchy which denounced where it could not corrupt and hired either
public or private armies to destroy both life and liberty where it could
not coerce by threat, the whole level of the spirit of American political
life would be raised. Certainly there is no other way to remove from that
life the *condottiere,* federal or local, in office or out of it, who are now
hired by those who, in Professor Brogan's phrase, regard themselves as
the "better classes" to do by foul means what they themselves lack either
the trust in reason, or the faith in democratic institutions, to do of their
own volition by means that the general public opinion of America would
hold to be fair. And the longer this removal is postponed, the harder will
it be to accomplish; for nothing has shown more clearly than the fascist
experience of our time, perhaps more decisively in France, where until
1940 the forms without the substance of democracy were maintained,
than in Germany and Italy, where after 1919 their hollowness was patent
even on a superficial examination, that there is a point in the decline of
democratic method where it becomes impossible to arrest the increasing
impetus to dictatorship.

[33] D. W. Brogan, *The American Political System* (London: Hamilton, 1933),
p. 384.
[34] *Ibid.*
[35] *Cf.* Louis F. Post, *The Deportations Delirium of 1920* (Chicago: Kerr, 1923).
[36] *Pollock* v. *Farmers' Loan Company.*
[37] *Cf.* E. S. Corwin, *The Twilight of the Supreme Court* (New Haven: Yale University Press, 1934), for a discussion of Mr. Justice McReynolds' views.
[38] Charles A. and Mary R. Beard, *America in Midpassage* (New York: Macmillan, 1939), p. 124.

It is this which makes the need for rapid renovation so urgent in the United States and which places upon the labour movement there so heavy a responsibility. Labour's main weakness has been its readiness to accept the methods of success which gave American business men their overwhelming authority after the Civil War. The trade-union leaders, like the leaders in finance and industry, were too lightly content to build a loosely federated system of private empires, which dealt with the governments within America, as with the different strata of public opinion, as though they were independent communities with which, in most ways except on the straightforward plane of public discussion, some kind of treaty had somehow to be made. Neither the world of business nor the world of labour has seemed, since 1865, really fully to understand the place of the State power in a democratic community. Above all, each has always failed to insist that majority rule, even more, majority rule through government by discussion, is the one vital way known to us of keeping democratic procedures alive. Each has weakened the procedure by trying, and too often with success, to find ways round it. Daniel Webster was content to be the agent of Big Business of his day; but Webster never failed to operate his agency through the political processes of the Constitution, and he did not fail to note, in his speech to the Massachusetts Constitutional Convention of 1820, that "the freest government, if it could exist, would not be long acceptable if the tendency of the laws were to create a rapid accumulation of property in a few hands, and to render the great mass of the population dependent and penniless. In such a case, the popular power must break in upon the rights of property, or else the influence of property must limit and control the exercise of popular power. Universal suffrage, for example, could not long exist in a community where there was great inequality of property."

The change in the mental climate of America in the half-century after Webster spoke those words has been described in a remarkable passage by Brooks Adams. "They have witnessed," he wrote as early as 1871, "some of the most remarkable examples of organized lawlessness under the forms of law which mankind has yet had the opportunity to study. If individuals have, as a rule, quietly pursued their peaceful vocations, the same cannot be said of certain single men at the head of vast combinations of private wealth. This is particularly the case as regards those controlling the rapidly developing railroad interests. These modern potentates have declared war, negotiated peace, reduced courts, legislators, and sovereign states to an unqualified obedience to their will, disturbed trade, agitated the currency, imposed taxes, and, boldly setting both law and public opinion at defiance, have freely exercised many other attributes of sovereignty." [39] Thirty years later he went even further. The American capitalist, he wrote, "thinks in terms of money more exclusively than the French aristocrat or lawyer before the French Revo-

[39] I owe this quotation to Professor Ralph Henry Gabriel's remarkable book, *The Course of American Democratic Thought* (New York: Ronald, 1940), p. 144.

lution ever thought in terms of caste. . . . If he is restrained by legislation, that legislation is in his life an oppression and an outrage, to be annulled or eluded by any means that will not lead to the penitentiary." [40] Adams noted the capitalist's irresponsibility, the narrow specialism which makes him too stupid to understand social relationships, his lawlessness when he must himself depend upon the protection of a law he never hesitates to outrage in his own interest. "Unless" Adams concluded, "the capitalistic governors of America can make over their mentality, and renovate their policy," the outcome is certain to be the drastic remedy of revolution.

Adams, we must remember, wrote before the revelations of the Pujo Committee, before the epoch of Harding and Coolidge repeated, if with more sophistication, yet on a more imperial scale, the uglier phenomena of the Gilded Age, before the Black Committee's portrait, under the relentless analysis of Judge Pecora, of Wall Street's habits, before the grim picture of democracy which emerged in the testimony given to the La Follette Committee on Civil Liberties; the evidence of all these more than justifies his grave forebodings. His indictment displays the matrix within which American labour developed. It helps to explain the habits of violence in its history, its permeation, as in the New York building trades, by racketeers, its reliance upon courts it yet distrusted, its internal dissensions, its ruthlessness, its suspicion of legislatures, its conviction that the lobbyist could influence political parties best by going to the secret sources of power, its consequent belief that a political expression of its own strength would divide its authority by concentrating the attention of its members on matters outside the industrial field in which it was struggling more often for survival than for control. Granted the forces by which it was confronted, and the methods they were prepared to use, the wonder is not that American labour felt driven to imitate too many of the capitalist techniques, but that, with all its faults and mistakes, it retained any idealism or clarity of vision at all. The trade-unionist who managed to survive in any company town with a free mind and an independent spirit was, on any showing, a good deal of a hero. His leaders, who not seldom took their lives in their hands every time they directed a strike, must pretty often have felt that they were organizing troops on a battlefield. Almost everything that is unsatisfactory in the habits of American labour is directly traceable to the profound contempt for democratic purposes and the reign of law which has been the outstanding characteristic of Big Business in America ever since the end of the Civil War.

Capitalist contempt for politics and the politician has bred in the labour movement a real cynicism about them both. Capitalist manipulation of the State power has led to the conviction in trade-union members that the more free they are from its attention, the more likely they are to be

[40] Brooks Adams, *The Theory of Social Revolutions* (New York: Macmillan, 1913), pp. 208 ff.

safe from attack by its agents in their activities. Like business men, they
have found it easier and cheaper to buy protection from the machines and
their bosses, whether at Albany, New York, or at Springfield, Illinois,
whether at Harrisburg, Pennsylvania, or at Columbus, Ohio, than to
embark on the long, hard road which might lead to their independent
right themselves to exercise the State power. They had so often attempted
this, and so often failed. By the time the Knights of Labor dissolved
into a pathetic shadow of its original hopes, the idea of a political party
came to seem a part of social Utopianism, along with Brook Farm and
scores of similar communities the lives of which had flickered brightly
for a brief moment and then been extinguished. They had seen, moreover,
the failure of so many other groups which had sought, and failed, to found
third parties. The Populists had failed, even with the weight of agrarian
enthusiasm behind them; they had gone on raising more corn, but the
hell they dared to raise made only a spasmodic impression at Washington
until they got paid for raising less corn. They had seen the flaming enthusiasm of Theodore Roosevelt when, amid thundering applause at
Chicago in 1912, he "stood at Armageddon and battled for the Lord";
but they had also seen Theodore Roosevelt, in 1916, not only return to
his Republican allegiance and even recommend an old-line reactionary
like Henry Cabot Lodge as his candidate; but, what was worse, they had
watched the eager young idealists of the Progressive movement shrink
into middle-aged cynics, determined, above all, not to be taken in a second time. What may well have counted most of all, they had observed
long years of effort result in a Socialist party whose impact was hardly
more than a pathetically feeble gesture in a national election; and, after
1920, they had watched Communists and Trotskyists struggle angrily
with the Socialists and with one another, without visible evidence that
they ever did more than provide capitalist-dominated legislatures with a
new excuse for putting still more repressive statutes against labour into
operation, or giving professional witch-hunters like Mrs. Dilling and
John Rankin the chance to set out on new excursions. Even when a
nation-wide effort enabled Senator La Follette to run as a national third-
party candidate in 1924, he could carry only his own state of Wisconsin,
though, no doubt, there was some significance in the fact that, in a dozen
other states, he elbowed the Democratic candidate into third place.

It is intelligible enough that, with this historical pattern before its eyes,
the American labour movement decided that the way of hard-headed
and practical realism was to assume that the politicians knew their own
business best, and that the trade-unions' task was to stick to the things
which made for integration and not to yearn after either institutions or
methods which merely divided the strength upon which they could count.
It is, indeed, highly probable that the experience of the Roosevelt epoch
added more firmness than ever to their conviction; not only did they secure from him more real and concrete gains than in any other comparable
period, but, had they failed to throw all their influence behind him at

the polls, he might well have been defeated, in 1936, by Landon, who was but a pale shadow of Hoover, or, in 1940, by the unexpected Wendell Willkie, who, as the nominee who had beaten the machine, might well have become its prisoner once he got into the White House. And, in 1944, they had to throw all their weight behind Mr. Roosevelt's fourth candidature, not because they would risk the victory of the United States if he were defeated, but because they did not dare to trust the organization of the transition from war to peace to the hands of Mr. Dewey and the ardent Roosevelt-haters upon whose aid his main policies would have depended.

So stated, the decision of American labour to work through the historic parties seems to have logic and some considerable success on its side. For those parties, at election-time, may no more neglect the labour vote than they can neglect the Roman Catholic vote, the farmers' vote, or the Fundamentalist vote in the South. But, on any long-term view, no critical analysis can fail to regard it as a major strategic error. For the economic system has reached that point where not only is it true that almost every serious demand of the organized workers has a background of necessary legislation in which it must be set, but, still more important, the creation of the positive conditions which would facilitate labour's next great steps forward depend on the permanent construction of a positive democracy in the United States, which could only be overthrown by the operation of forces similar in nature and power to those which gave Hitler and Mussolini their backing. These forces exist, and there is plenty of evidence to prove their connection with the darker elements of American reaction. The resentment against Negro pressure for wider opportunity, the rising tide of anti-Semitism, the temper of movements like those of Father Coughlin, of Dr. Townsend, and a myriad of lesser rabble-rousers like Gerald L. K. Smith, all give point and emphasis to the fact that the New Deal was less an achievement of basic changes in the political way of life than the purchase of time to think. It was, as it ought to have been, a supreme lesson in adult education for the American workers, the right reading of which might still mark a turning point in their history.

But, as yet, nothing is less clear than the hope that it has indeed been rightly read. The very scale of the Great Depression brought great gains so swiftly and, comparatively speaking, so easily to the workers, that their tendency, even more, the tendency of their leaders, has been to believe that these are permanent gains. That is a deceptive belief since it fails to take account of two facts. The first is that the gains were held only because the threat to them of the recession of 1937 was masked by the rapid drift of the world into total war; and the second is the fact that, with the war's end, the immense economic problems that it has left may not be answered by strengthening the foundations of the New Deal, and seeking to carry it further. That is not a thing which the Political Action Committee of the C.I.O. could decide. It could not be decided by the labour movement alone even if it were to find the means of healing the divisions by which its effective strength is so gravely weakened. It is decided by the interplay of all the social and economic forces of American life as they seek to mobilize their striking power on the plane of political action. It is, in fact, a battle for the State power in America that is slowly but relentlessly coming into view.

To wage that battle with genuine hope, American labour needs not only to define its immediate aims, but to draw, at least in large outline, the pattern towards which these are to converge. Without that pattern, it will merely fight a series of discrete actions, ill planned in any case, mostly without relevance to one another, yet affecting one another as the ebb and flow of battle is bound to affect the general spirit of a campaign. The weakness of the present position lies in the fact that it is built upon an experience of solidarity which has failed to grow into a philosophy of solidarity. Far too small a proportion of the workers see the intimacy of the connection between what they think and do inside the factory and what they think and do when they have left it. Far too few have been taught to recognize where their fields of hope really lies; they are still living in that state of psychological coma embodied in Horatio Alger and Russell Conwell, in one age, and in Henry C. Link and Dale Carnegie in our own time. Far too few have been made to recognize that the president and Congress at Washington are not far-away men and women on a distant planet, but people whose ideas and purposes they help to shape at each stage of development. Still less have they been made to understand that the thing with which they have to be concerned is not this speech of the president, that executive decision, some Act of Congress, a particularly offensive member of the House of Representatives, like Parnell Thomas, or a determined enemy of all progress, like Senator McKellar of Tennessee; they have to concern themselves with the inner spirit and large-scale direction of all American political institutions. Above all, perhaps, in the next era, they have to grasp the central principle that what the United States is abroad, that, also, is what it will be at home; that, if they want the United States to be an important fact in safeguarding freedom and democracy abroad, they must themselves take a full participating share in making the State power safeguard these same objectives at home. In the American world, freedom and democracy are indivisible parts of a mental climate which cannot be limited any longer to particular regions, or even enjoyed without regard to the fate of other parts of civilization.

6

IT CANNOT be too emphatically insisted that American labour now confronts a crisis which, in the general issues that it raises, is likely to rank with the Civil War as one of the supreme crises of American history. American ideals of democracy and freedom, no doubt, have been threatened before; there have been efforts to limit them to a propertied class, or to the white race, on grounds that could be shaped into a philosophic argument; but the elasticity and expansion of physical America were able to transcend all efforts at limitation. The modern pressure to this limitation, however, has a status different from that of its predecessors. It comes from an American capitalism in decline which must achieve this end if it is to survive; it must do so quickly if it is not to lose its hold upon the State power.

That is why there is a real decline in tolerance in the sphere of economic and political matters. No doubt this is in a great degree masked by the growth of religious indifference and of less rigidity in the criteria of personal behaviour; but this dualism has always marked important epochs of crisis. That is why, also, there is a growing tendency to attack the trade-union movement indirectly as well as frontally; the attempt to remove Mr. Harry Bridges from his leadership of the dockworkers on the Pacific coast by deporting him as an undesirable alien is a good example of this habit. Nor can anyone fail to see that behind the contemporary American doubt of the principle of equality there is a profound anxiety to justify the inequalities which could, in their turn, become part of the defence mechanism of a privileged oligarchy. The depreciation of environment as against heredity, the inferences drawn from half-scientific attempts at intelligence-testing, the revival, so curiously apt, of the notion of superior and inferior races, as well as the stress laid on this notion in the differential race controls on immigration, the popularity of books like those of Pareto and Spengler which make a cult of hostility to the view that political philosophy can be rational, all these are part of a drive against equality as the foundation of American philosophy. So, too, is the growth of scepticism about the possibilities of mass education, a scepticism the more interesting because it so largely emanates from teachers and students in the higher institutions of learning. A more illuminating example of the effort to prevent the extension of the frontiers of knowledge it would not be easy to find.

Nor is it less significant that the development of mass welfare in the kind of social service state which the New Deal brought into being brought a tidal wave of protest against the new levels of taxation, an irritable conviction, not unakin to that of an earlier age, that poverty or unemployment was the result of personal fault, a widespread opinion that relief work and social insurance endangered the workers' sense of personal responsibility. It was of particular interest to note how much of the attack on the growing area of social service embraced by the State power was based on a political philosophy in large part indistinguishable from that of Burke or Hannah More, and how much of it assumed that State intervention would injure the beautiful personal motive of charity, which was believed not only to be invaluable in itself but, broadly, and because of the American genius for organization, to take care of all worthy cases. The complete imperviousness to the facts of the people who held, and hold, these views is one of the most striking phenomena of the time. There are many wealthy business men and their wives, especially in the metropolitan areas of the United States, who regard with horror the taxes they pay to mitigate the sufferings of the poor on the ground that public opinion has already compelled them to pay an annual contribution to the "community chest" of the city in which they live.

Even more important is the shrinkage of opportunity in the second quarter of the twentieth century as compared with any earlier period in the history of the republic. It is not only that the log cabin to White House myth is shown to be a legend with hardly even the power to edify because of the fact that it has no application to any president since the century opened; it is also that proportionately fewer members of the working class than in earlier times either attain the status of business leaders or to have hopes of attaining a moderate private competence upon which to retire. The glowing dream of Emerson's day in a great cultural heritage made available to all faded into a situation where, though wage-earners and clerical workers were some seventy per cent of the employed population, only twenty-four per cent of the students in universities and other college institutions came from working-class families. Nor has the chance of employment ever been smaller for those with a higher training such as is symbolized in the possession of a doctorate in philosophy. Nor must one forget the immense differences in educational opportunity for children in Massachusetts or New York on the one hand, and those, say, in Georgia or Mississippi on the other. A rural school for white children in many counties of the South has to be seen to be believed; but a similar school for Negro children can rarely be believed even when one has seen it. Anyone who reads the history of a great institution like Teachers' College at Columbia University from the Great Depression to the beginning of the Second World War, and compares it with that of the decade before 1914, can see quite decisively that the natural optimism of the American has become a faith which is aware of a threat to its validity that it does not want to see examined in detail.

It is, of course, true that there is still in the United States a far greater occupational mobility than is generally true of European civilization. But it is also not less true that this has grown far more restricted in the twentieth century than it was before the Civil War, as it was more restricted after the Civil War than it was before it. Nor can anyone doubt the emergence in America of the historic lines of class demarcation which have marked the evolution of capitalism elsewhere in any country where it has operated on a major scale. Nothing, indeed, shows this more strikingly than the decline of the farmer from owner to tenant in the last half-century; that is an example of proletarianization, economic, social, and cultural, which marks an epoch in American history. So, too, does the contrast between the eager hopes of the westward movement a century ago, and the dreary pathos of the four million migratory labourers and their families who constitute America's internal refugee problem in our own day. In the one case, we encounter the vivid and unbreakable faith of the pioneer who scans a boundless horizon; in the other, we are watching the increasingly dulled inertia of defeated citizens who suspect the hostility of society, and rarely know, as they are moved on from state to state, where they will be permitted to lay their heads.

And one other thing must be said. No concept has played a larger part in the shaping of the American faith than the conviction that there is a constant upward progress. That led to an experimental temper, which did not believe that there were obstacles in any realm capable of hindering permanently the forward movement of mankind, or, at any rate, of American mankind. It is a temper that one can see at its highest expression in the soaring confidence of Whitman's greatest poems, as in the faith in goodness, even perfectibility, that Emerson can never bring himself to deny. And though there were Americans in whom can be seen a more sombre and questioning spirit, even before and just after the Civil War, Hawthorne, for instance, and Melville, and in his remote, labyrinthine way, Henry James, it has still been generally true, until very recent days, that concealed in most Americans somewhere was a disciple of William Godwin. It is only in the last generation that Americans have begun to see, what Veblen saw so vividly in the generation before the First World War, that at the stage where capitalist enterprise ceases to be capable of a profitable expansion in which the whole community shares, it becomes the enemy of any science or technology which needs relations of production it cannot continue to master, the enemy of a free culture, the enemy. as Webster saw, of all democratic principles which threaten its control of the power it has possessed to use the coercive authority of government as the supreme safeguard of its privileges.

It is in these circumstances that the imperative case arises for American labour to organize for action on the political field. There is no other way now open to it to call into play the central purposes for which universal suffrage was won; there is no other way in which the majority of the American people can shape the ends of government to its own ends. That, after all, is the sure insight that Lincoln had. "A majority," said Lincoln, ". . . is the only true sovereign of a free people. Whoever rejects it, does, of necessity, fly into anarchy or despotism. Unanimity is impossible; the rule of a minority, as a permanent arrangement, is wholly inadmissible; so that, rejecting the majority principle, anarchy or despotism in some form is all that is left." [41] The alternative which Lincoln so decisively posed is the alternative that the American people has again to decide.

And what is, I think, quite clear is that only the labour movement is in a position to choose the majority principle. It can organize around itself the numbers necessary to make the choice effective. It can prove that no other group in American life has now either the interest or, in-

[41] Philip Van Doren Stern (ed.), *The Life and Writings of Abraham Lincoln* (New York: Modern Library, 1940), p. 653.

deed, the strength to choose it. Even more, it can show that, save for brief moments, the whole drive of the constitutional system has been away from majority rule and towards the excessive protection of minority interests. That was true in the period of Federalist rule; and that was why Jefferson was able so successfully to reassert the majority principle. Andrew Jackson went to the White House as the representative of the common man seeking to protect his rights as a person against a minority interest which sought to protect the claims of property against the rights of persons. From 1840 to 1860 the Southern states sought, even to the point of secession, to safeguard their "peculiar institution" as a minority privilege no majority could invade; and that was why Lincoln was so insistent that the alternative to minority privilege is majority rule; why he was prepared to make war on behalf of majority rule. What is perhaps most tragic in the aftermath of his victory is that, from the Gilded Age right down to the present time, what has presented itself as majority rule has been, in fact, a mask behind which a propertied minority has devised rules of law the inherent purpose of which has been to prevent the working of the Constitution in such a way that the equal right of citizens to "life, liberty, and happiness" has not only not been realized, but has been in constant danger. The threat, indeed, has been averted only because the United States for so long had enough power of economic expansion to make concessions to the people; this seemed, at the moment of their achievement, to safeguard the great central purpose of the American dream.

It is at least highly dubious whether that power of economic expansion is now great enough to enable the majority principle to survive another crisis of the magnitude of the Great Depression, unless steps are taken now to make certain that it does survive. And it is worth insisting, once more, that the gravest injury ever done to the labour movement by the influence upon it of capitalist ideology was its permeation by the doctrine that it should strive only in an indirect way for political expression. By accepting the status of a pressure group merely, it declined its obvious historic mission of formulating a political philosophy for that America which had, somehow, to hold fast to democratic principles in politics even while it sought to remake the economic foundations of American life. That refusal cannot be justified by saying that, were another great depression to come, either the Republican or the Democratic party would offer Americans a second, perhaps even a profounder, New Deal. For, first of all, there is no evidence to show that this would be the case; and, second, what evidence there is over most of the world suggests the conclusions not only that any mass unemployment which lasts for a considerable period is incompatible with democratic institutions, but that war alone provides a public works programme large enough in scale to cope with mass unemployment, and too often leaves even the victorious nation less able to safeguard democracy than it was before the war began.

American labour leaders, as it is, enter a post-war world in which all the main engines of political power are outside their control. They do not speak directly to the people on a fully national plane; this is a capacity reserved, on the American scene, for the president, for an occasional senator, for the Supreme Court in its collective capacity, and for a very small number of outstandingly wealthy men who are accorded that curious veneration Americans accord to those whose success has lain in the realm of money-making. It is obvious, for example, that neither Mr. William Green of the American Federation of Labor nor Mr. Philip Murray of the Congress of Industrial Organizations could hope to be impressive on that level. It is still more obvious that Mr. John L. Lewis, so far the most dramatic figure in the history of the labour movement, would arouse instant hostility from an audience at least as large as he would convince. There is no one of independent status, like Henry George some seventy years ago, able to invoke for an idea the mind and conscience of the whole nation. There are many who command respect in special circles; there are innumerable specialists of high eminence in particular fields; but when one compares the attention they attract with the scale of the attention that is required, the conclusion is inescapable that they cannot seriously hope to be heard. Nor is there evidence to suggest that the Churches have either the will or the influence proportionate to a task of this magnitude.

I am arguing that, when the next great crisis threatens American well-being, it is problematical whether a solution can be found for it in harmony with the American tradition of democracy. That is not in the least because I think that the leaders of American business life have ceased to believe in democratic government. I am sure they do; but the important point is that they believe in it on their own terms. And their own terms assume that democracy will not work in such a way as to deny the main principles of the business man's philosophy of life. For such a denial he is even less prepared than were the Federalists of New England in the First generation of the republic, or the Southern slave-owners in the twenty years before the Civil War. But once a democracy permits an economic oligarchy to hold it to ransom in this way, it is bound, rapidly rather than slowly, to cease to be a democracy. It is not accident that many of the outstanding leaders of business enterprise in the United States had great admiration for Mussolini until about 1940; and that the work of Hitler could evoke applause from powerful industrialists who were not sure, as they measured the price of President Roosevelt's New Deal, that American labour did not require a Hitler to deal with its "pretentions." It is not for nothing that, locally as well as nationally, the main standards of political behaviour have been made out of a long worship of what William James called the "bitch goddess, Success." And success does not mean the achievement of Joseph Henry in physics, of Melville or Whitman in letters, of T. H. Morgan in biology. Success means the material fortune of Rockefeller or Vanderbilt or Frick, the

practical and intelligible success of Edison, the swift and dazzling notoriety which converted Lindbergh overnight from an inspired mechanic
to a god in the Valhalla where Washington and Lincoln dwell, in a
majesty capable of being invoked but never possible of formulation.

It is the immense weakness of American labour that it takes for granted
the belief that the foundations of democracy upon which its claims are
built remain something permanently given instead of perceiving their
grave fragility. It has seen vast changes in the whole social environment
in which it functions—in the scale and swiftness of technological adaptation, in the habits of the family, in sexual behaviour, in the influence of
the Churches, in standards of literature. It is not enough to set against
all that these changes imply the plea that since the Great Depression
millions have become sceptical of the claim that the future of democracy
could ever be safe in the hands of business men. It is not even enough for
the contemporary poet, like Archibald MacLeish, to remember, in wistfully rhetorical verse, that "America was promises," and that freedom
comes only to those who make the promises come true. Still less is it
enough to dream that the millions of young Americans who return from
the five continents and the seven seas after winning historic victories
for freedom and democracy from the Arctic to the Antarctic will become passionate crusaders for freedom and democracy at home; mostly,
in sober fact, they will be millions of vital, slightly sceptical young
men, eager to settle down, and profoundly relieved to be back in an
America they will never want to leave again save for a rapid sight-
seeing holiday from which they will return with new satisfaction in the
routine of American life.

I am therefore arguing that America stands on the threshold of its
third great revolution and that the psychological preparation of its people has been declined by the very agency which should be taking the lead
in its making. I am not denying for one moment the immensity of the
task; to change the basic *mores* of this vast, sprawling continent, so infinitely kind and so fantastically relentless, at one and the same time, so
generous and so corrupt, so hostile to tradition in all superficial matters
and so deeply conservative in all fundamental notions, is a task that calls
for qualities which not more than three or four American statesmen in
the record have displayed. Nor am I underestimating how much, in the
next years, Americans will learn from the vast impersonal forces which
shape a nation's experience far more than any conscious leadership can
hope to do. I do not belittle, either, the force of the American past in
holding at bay the dark legions which a privileged oligarchy will always
call to its support when it fears that the inner citadel of its strength
is threatened.

My argument is the different one that the protection of freedom and
democracy can rarely be improvised with safety, and that it calls for
careful and patient organization if it is to hope for success. I am arguing
that those who seek to organize it must be historically fitted for their

task and strategically placed to carry it out. They must be able to elevate the concepts they employ to that level where they are linked to what is most respected in the nation's past traditions, and to the expectations in the emerging future that citizens cherish most dearly. I am arguing that only the American labour movement can provide the effective basis for that organization, and that it can do so only by a direct entrance upon the political scene. It must do so not merely in the interest of trade-unionism as it has conceived it in the past, as a new method of securing a kind of sovereign control of the job in field and office and factory. It must not do so in a sectional spirit, though it must learn how to handle the delicate problems of sectionalism. It must not do so in an exclusive spirit that seeks to replace the loose threads of doctrine which now bind the major parties together by a narrow and rigid orthodoxy, the dogmas of which may, well terrify as much as they inspire. It must learn to persuade millions who now think they are its enemies that they are, in fact, its friends. It must be insistent in its protection of those who come to its support from the threat or challenge by which vested interest will seek to terrorize them into silence and submission. It must learn to beat the machines and the bosses without itself giving birth to them. Above all, it must refrain from offering to its members the kind of career and the kind of reward that turns its leaders into brokers of benefits and political institutions, into a kind of stock exchange where the real influences are safeguarded by their ability to remain invisible at the crucial hour.

If the labour movement needs wisdom for this task, that is not to say that it does not need shrewdness too. Above all, it needs the shrewdness which has learned to think of American problems in American terms, and of international problems in an American context. It does not need to be Quixotic because it is political realism to be magnanimous. It does not need a sacred scripture, though it will suffer nothing from having a precious song-book. Its task is to create the understanding that the American dream is in danger, and that those who join in its ranks are preserving the splendour of the American dream. It would be an immense contribution to American civilization merely to embark upon the task, to take up the work of restating, in twentieth-century terms, that problem of freedom which Jefferson saw so clearly in the first American Revolution and Lincoln so supremely in the second. But it is urgent to remember that time is not the friend of those who put their hands to constructive toil when an economic system has entered upon its final phase. Every day of waiting is a day lost; and, sooner than it is agreeable to contemplate, an undue postponement of the need to start the rebuilding may mean the discovery that its foundations were broken even before men bent their energies to the construction.

VII

Religion in America

I

NO ONE who studies the early history of what was to become the United States can doubt the importance of the Christian tradition in the shaping of its heritage. If that tradition grew with relatively curious swiftness into a perspective distinctively American, so that even the Roman Catholic Church of the New World, while Catholic, is yet different from the Catholic Church of Europe, yet its impact upon the American way of life was, and, indeed, continues to be, in many aspects profound. The very fact that men and women of national origins so diverse, and of ecclesiastical allegiances so innumerable, shared a common Christian cosmology had a vital influence in unifying the values of the way of life that was to be recognized as American; and this, through the reverence in which the early settlers held the Old Testament, applies also to the small but significant body of Jews who settled there. Nor can one omit to emphasize that it was, perhaps above all, the zeal for religion which was responsible for the early American development of educational institutions, from the primary school to that theological seminary which has flowered into Harvard University. It is impossible, on any showing, to overrate the debt that learning in colonial America owes to the many-sided enthusiasm of its clergy.

No doubt, further, the physical environment of America had an immense influence in mitigating the acerbity both of theocratic conceptions on the one hand, and of churches to which colonial governments lent the support of the secular arm on the other. However willing the early settlers may have been to persecute, the New World could not escape its destiny as a haven of refuge. It had to take account of the need for unity in the face of the Indian danger. It was profoundly influenced by the physical fact that distance made any effort at compulsory uniformity extraordinarily difficult to maintain. Within a quarter of a century of the landing at Plymouth, New England antinomianism was already making it clear that the inner light would burn as steadily as the flame of authority which the authority of an historic church might seek to burn; and the writings of Roger Williams suggest that not only the tem-

264

perament of their author—who himself showed the classic dislike of the
innovating preacher for insights different from his own in his exchanges
with George Fox—but the very environment itself was unfavourable to a
continuous and persistent acceptance of the obligation to persecute in
the name of authoritative truth. The Massachusetts Bay Company might
feel, as Winthrop argued, that it was a duty to restrict a full share in
political power to those who accepted the Cambridge Platform of 1648;
and it is no unfair generalization to say that colonial America before 1700
looked with suspicion on unorthodox religious opinion and was willing,
though with some obvious doubts, to suppress any public worship which
sought expression through a different Church from that patronized by
the State power. But once the Privy Council in London had approved the
Rhode Island Charter of 1663 with its insistence that a man might hold
what religious opinions he chose provided that he did not "actually disturb the civill peace," it was clear that no effort to impost uniformity
could succeed.

Toleration was also encouraged on economic grounds. Since population was important, not least as a source of income in the proprietary
colonies, it speedily became evident that there was an antithesis between a persecuting orthodoxy and successful immigration. And since
it became obvious that flourishing colonies, properly controlled, were a
source of wealth to the mother country, it was foolish to discourage trade
by rigorous interference with the faith of the settler who made it possible.
It is true that there was a good deal of ill-will to Roman Catholicism and
deep hostility to any kind of free thought. It is further true that in matters like Sunday observance it was for long difficult to make any important step towards a recognized secular code of behaviour. Even in
Pennsylvania the Quaker refusal to bear arms or to take an oath caused
difficulties throughout the colonial period. Nor is it unimportant that the
Privy Council had both to protect the Church of England, as a minority
group to which a certain hostility always attached, and to prevent Non-
conformist Churches from obtaining a hold on the colonial assemblies,
which might well have proved a barrier to American economic development.

In the result, by the end of the seventeenth century it is pretty true
to say that the main climate of religious influence in America was rapidly
ceasing to be shaped either by any rigour of uniform doctrine or by any
strict alliance between any Church and the secular power. It is evident
from a book like that of John Wise, *A Vindication of the Government of
New-England Churches* (1717), that there was little chance for authority to be centralized in a clerical hierarchy. "An aristocracy," he wrote,
"is a dangerous constitution in the church of Christ." The democratic
outlook he espoused was increasingly spread by a variety of influences.
German Pietists, like the Dunkers, the Mennonites, and the Moravians,
were radical in social, and individualistic in religious, matters. Communities which dwelt on the frontier could rarely afford settled clergy

and even tended to the neglect of religious observance. If American Pres-
byterianism would have suited an oligarchical government, its main membership was drawn from Scots–Irish immigrants with a strong political
sense which resisted any special privilege. Tithe was never a great success
in any American colony; and most Anglican clergy in America were, in
any case, men who had abandoned hope of preferment in England and
had little expectation of bettering their fortunes save by the patronage
of the wealthier classes in colonies like Virginia and South Carolina.
Missionary effort was on a small scale, and the planters were suspicious
of attempts to convert the Negro slaves or the Indians, lest this should
lead to an attack upon their authority. By the time of the Great Awakening, round the second third of the eighteenth century, the foundation had
been laid for a latitudinarian temper which undoubtedly paved the way
for separation between Churches and the State power. That is a notable
thing when it is remembered that Established Churches existed in a
majority of the thirteen colonies.

It is not, I think, excessive to say that the Great Awakening has remained the supreme event in determining the character of American religious history. That is not, of course, because it produced in Jonathan
Edwards the one outstanding theological philosopher the United States
has known: America had already swept beyond him when he wrote.
It is rather because it both summarized and liberated forces the influence of which is still profound. It drew a class line between branches
in many of the sects by its insistence on the need for individual conversion, by its enthusiasm for revivals with their emphasis upon an
emotional grasp of truth and their indifference both to reason and to
scholarship, by its dislike of formal ritual and its acceptance of the old
Puritan doctrine that a minister requires not training so much as the
power to evoke the awakening of the spirit among his followers, the acceptance of what can only be termed a kind of mystic Fundamentalism. In
the hands of a great preacher, as with George Whitefield on his famous
tour of 1739, the spirit of the Great Awakening swept the humbler citizens with the same irresistible power as Methodism in England at the
call of John Wesley. Nor was it lacking in important social result. It
brought new forces to the fight against Negro slavery. It encouraged
some of the more obvious forms of humanitarianism, like the care of
orphans. And, quite unquestionably, it unconsciously stimulated hostility
to authority by making its converts sure that their personal insights into
truth need not be subordinated either to the claims of rank or to the
claims of wealth.

But the vital outcome of the Great Awakening lies in a direction which
Jonathan Edwards dimly realized and regretted, though it swept onwards
with a power quite beyond his control. What, in essence, it claimed to do
was to free men from sin, to make this world, for the converted, no
longer a vale of tears, but the prelude to the coming of the Kingdom of
Heaven where the converted were certain of glory since they had already

given their hearts to God. And once it was possible to transcend the sense of sin, it was obvious that the citadel of Puritanism was in danger. No doubt that transcendence took different forms in different people. Samuel Johnson of King's College became an Anglican; Jonathan Mayhew not only approached, if he did not cross, the frontiers of Unitarianism, but he began to find political expression for his faith in the universal benevolence of God. He began to see the hatred of tyranny and the duty to resist oppression as the natural outcome of true religion. Charles Chauncy was certain, by 1784, that "the whole human race are . . . made for happiness." A generation later the Puritan theology was a backwater in that main stream which, as with William Ellery Channing and Theodore Parker, has in truth become the central American expression of the world-wide romantic movement. And because that expression comes in a period of political victory and economic expansion, it is democratic, self-reliant, optimistic, experimental.

But that is not all. When the rigors of seventeenth-century Puritanism were found too harsh for a free and self-confident America, there poured into the vacuum that was thus being created not merely the emotional revivalism of the Great Awakening, but also that faith in the "religion of nature" which passed with swiftness into deism, and from deism, by a logical transition, into rationalism and free thought. We know not only of the fairly wide circulation of deistic books as early as Wesley's visit to Georgia in 1735; we hear also of groups, like that around the painter Robert Feke at Newport, which discussed the new doctrines. Attacks begin to be published against priestcraft and superstition; there are even newspaper criticisms of revealed religion itself. With great caution, men as well known as Joseph Hawley and John Adams were influenced by this scepticism; and there can be no serious doubt that though, like Voltaire, Benjamin Franklin did not approve of the spread of such ideas among the masses lest "talk against religion" might "unchain the tiger" and cause social unrest, he himself had ceased by the time of the War of Independence to have any faith in traditional belief. There was, indeed, far more likelihood than the evidence permits us to affirm with certainty that, by the end of the eighteenth century, rationalism had made a good deal of progress among the urban masses; it is not easy, otherwise, to account for the popularity of Paine's *Age of Reason,* or of Volney's *Les Ruines.* The circulation of Ethan Allen's *Reason the Only Oracle of Man* (1784)—if indeed he wrote it—may have been small, but it is clear from the attacks to which it gave rise that it had a very considerable reputation. Even better known was the blind deist Elihu Palmer, whose *Principles of Nature* (1802) not only formulated a system of ethics which had no need for any theological sanctions, but also helped to found a whole group of free-thinking clubs and a number of free-thinking journals which, if their circulation was small, still testified to an interest in rationalism far wider than either the clergy or the comfortable classes could contemplate with equanimity.

What emerged was in part the doctrine of progress, founded on the faith of the infinite perfectibility of man, and in part the doctrine that restraint is only necessary for those who are still in the chains of sin. It is only a step from the conviction that restraint is evil in man's religious life to the view that it is no less evil in its effect upon social life. As the first hinders man from reaching God, so the second prevents him from fulfilling himself. As the first begins to look to the coming of the New Jerusalem, with the same passionate conviction as did the Fifth Monarchy Men in the time of Cromwell, so the second leads some, like Emerson, through religion to a kind of transcendental anarchism, and others, like Ripley of Brook Farm, to the Utopianism which looked to social salvation in the immediate future by the formation of self-governing communities. As early as 1818 Joseph Emerson, the cousin of the sage of Concord, was convinced that "the signs of the times proclaim that the Millennial day is approaching." It was faith in the Millennium which gave the Mormons the conviction that, despite all persecution, they would speedily enter that promised land where they would build a New Jerusalem. William Miller made thousands of converts by his argument, dramatically reinforced by the comet of 1843, that the end of the world would come in that year. If his interpretation of biblical prophecy failed, no less a person than Mark Hopkins was, only two years later, insisting that the Kingdom of God must be very near; the evils of drink and war, slavery and oppression, war and sexual licence, were all, he thought, very near their end. Miller no doubt expected a miracle from Heaven; Mark Hopkins was satisfied to believe that the result would be achieved by the change wrought by Christianity in the nature of man. But the common element in their outlooks was far more important than any difference in method which divided them.

And the essence of that common element, the driving force which made a religious belief founded on the despair of man's sinfulness into a conviction of his unlimited prospect of good, was the element of faith in America, above all, of faith in an America to whose destiny no boundaries could be set, through whose democracy all men and all things could be made new. There was little chance for a religion of pessimism in an America which was discovering a new world of amazing riches every day, an America which could take to its bosom all the weary and give them not merely rest, but also hope for themselves. There was still less chance when every species of millenarian utopianism on the frontier not only pushed the pioneer to almost incredible exertions and enabled his family to endure equally incredible hardships, but provided them with psychological satisfactions by which, at some camp revival, their energies were refreshed and their hopes renewed. The democracy of expanding America found in the romantic emotionalism of a great awakening, which hardly ceased until the Civil War, the medium of a teleology through which its citizens could be fulfilled, and, by so doing, fulfil America as well. And it is hard to doubt that, as the covered wagons made their way over unknown or half-known wilderness, each pioneer, and his wife, too, driven on by a faith beyond themselves, had an inner knowledge, compensating for all their trials, that in fulfilling themselves they had looked into the mind of God and fulfilled His purpose too. The conquest of America was, for them, the taking of the Kingdom of Heaven by that special power which God had given to His chosen people, the Americans.

Americans were citizens of a chosen people especially favoured of God; to them was allotted a destiny nobler than that which awaited the old and fatigued world of Europe. For Americans there was salvation, and salvation consisted of freedom, individualism, democracy, success. It was no wonder that they were convinced that all Europe envied their immense hopes, that Europeans, and especially their ancient enemies the British, published book after book in which their hatred and ridicule were clearly born of their longing to win back the vast empire they had lost. Nor need they deem it a thing to wonder at that Roman Catholics, a minority mainly weak and poor, dreamed of conspiring with their brethren abroad to overturn American democracy in the interest of the Papacy and its satellites. Hostility to Roman Catholics, which led to the burning of the Ursuline Convent in 1830 at Boston, to Morse the inventor's conviction of a great Roman Catholic conspiracy against America, to nearly a generation of fantastic secret societies all of whose members were pledged to defend their country against this dark menace, culminated in the Know-Nothing movement of the eighteen-fifties, with its determination to safeguard native American purity against the poison, especially the Roman Catholic poison, of foreign influence. It has never wholly died, as was shown by its revival when Alfred E. Smith, a New York Roman Catholic and an eminent governor of his state, ran as the presidential candidate of the Democratic party. The curious history of his campaign shows, almost as clearly as the crusade of Parson Brownlow eighty years before, that the central principle of Know-Nothingism was, above all, a crude belief that Americanism must be all-absorptive, that whatever might seek for links with European beliefs, whatever, even more, might acknowledge allegiance to a power outside America, was by its nature a threat to American independence and to the American right to shape all creeds in terms of the uniqueness of the American dream.

I do not think it is merely fanciful to suggest that the reconciliation of the Roman Church with Americanism was largely the result of the interplay of three factors. In part it was the adaptation of great numbers of immigrants, above all Irish and Italian, to the American environment: what the first generation might turn away from or fail to attain was impressed upon the second unconsciously but indelibly. In part it was the sheer power of numbers: since the eighteen-forties Roman Catholics, if they remained a minority, remained a minority too vast, as the defeat of Blaine made evident, for a party to insult with impunity. And, in part, a number of converts, of whom the most saintly was Isaac Hecker and the most intellectual Orestes Brownson, made of their Catholicism a powerful social gospel in which the Church became the guardian of the rights and liberties of the people, the more ably stated in Brownson's case since few people were more familiar than he with the main currents of doctrine in his time. Indeed, as Archbishop Ireland recognized, none did so much to acclimatize an immigrant Church to the conditions of a new world. In a sense, there was no greater triumph for the idea of America than that it could thus transform to its own purposes an ancient institution which had for so many centuries been committed to relations, both social and political, in which that idea had found no place.

If one looks, therefore, at religion in America at the end of the Civil War, it seems to have become an outlook capable of emphasizing in theological terms the idea of freedom through a growing individualism which enabled all men to fulfil themselves in a way that the Old World had never known. Revivalism satisfied the starved emotions of the frontier. Unitarianism was a widespread compromise which enabled the comfortable to associate a religion in which dogma was reduced to a minimum with a full recognition, largely born of the lingering fears inspired by the French Revolution, of the social danger of infidelity. The widespread growth of Sunday schools and missions brought children and youth into the mood where religion in some form was the conventional attitude of a respectable status. Even Transcendentalism became a mystical expression of an inner harmony between man and the universe; and where that harmony, by its failure to appear, resulted in spiritual crisis, the Roman Catholic Church provided, as the case of Brownson made evident, a haven of certitude in which the sceptic could resolve all the doubts by which he was assailed. In an important sense, moreover, the profound anti-intellectualism of the frontier, in itself the outcome of a practical versatility which knew little of books, made for a religious outlook which disliked the preacher trained in a formal way since he was likely to speak above the heads of his audience. It is certainly untrue to say that religious indifference was widespread. What is rather the fact is that both the distribution of the people over the vast area and the immense, if diminishing, difficulties of communication made the most acceptable expression of faith that which made the deepest appeal to the easiest emotions the preacher could arouse. No one can read the memoirs of the remarkable itinerant preachers of the first half of the nineteenth century without seeing that, outside the more considerable urban centres, where leisure made possible the luxury of speculation, the hold of religion was profound because it provided the easiest means of satisfying the hunger for a communal life. The camp meeting was as great an event to the scattered settlers as the visit of a famous actress to the troops in a distant theatre during the Second World War.

It is also important to realize that the environment of the first seventy years in the history of American religion has left profound traces upon its contemporary character. It has emphasized emotion at the expense of mind. It has been interested in the social behaviour to which religion lends its sanction rather than in the metaphysical explanation of the universe which it accepts. It has put the main authority of most Churches in the hands of laymen rather than in the hands of a trained clergy; and it has even tilted the main incidence of clerical education towards social influence rather than towards speculative interest. Most significant of all, just because it was the expression of a romantic and individualist epoch, it has facilitated the growth of sects, partly because men and women were so accustomed to identify their emotional convictions with a Divine Revelation, and partly because the submission of that revelation to obedience to an organized Church seemed at once a denial of conscience and an admission of external authority hostile to the self-reliance so widely bred by the conditions of the time. A half-literate population either disliked an intellectual discipline imposed from without or sought for a Fundamentalism ratified by its own emotions. No doubt that "Come-Outism," of which the Shakers are by all odds the most striking example, reflected something of that protest against aristocratic control of which the triumphs both of Jefferson and Jackson were expressions in the political sphere; just as Mormonism was a combination of fervent rationalism and that egalitarian protest against the contrast between the lot of the rich and the poor which has marked Christianity from its earliest epoch.

But no one who examines with care American religious experience in the first half of the republic's history has the right to suppose that its influence decisively shaped the character of that history. It brought immense consolation to many; it helped to organize many important canons of behaviour; it encouraged, in appropriate areas, a considerable number of social and philanthropic causes. But in a world which seemed committed to the principle of *laissez-faire* no Church was seriously able, and few seriously attempted, to do more than mitigate the major tragedies of *laissez-faire*. The real centre of power rested with the wealthy to whom the Churches were a valuable instrument for making the poor contented with their lot. That, indeed, was seen quite clearly by Horace Greeley. "To the conservative," he wrote, "Religion would seem often a part of the subordinate machinery of Police, having for its main object the instilling of proper humility into the abject, of contentment into the breasts of the down-trodden, and of enduring with a sacred reverence for Property those who have no personal reason to think well of the sharp distinction between Mine and Thine."[1] That does not seem an unfair description of the total outcome at the beginning of the Gilded Age. The Churches, in the main, provided a means of escape for emotional drives which might otherwise have been directed into the examining of social foundations, and, at the same time, a means of safeguarding men of wealth by limiting their obligation to that sense of stewardship through which the early Church made its peace with the Roman world.

[1] Horace Greeley, *Recollections of a Busy Life* (New York: Ford, 1868), p. 524.

2

ON NO other showing can one explain the predominant reaction of the Churches to the Gilded Age after the Civil War. It is difficult not to feel that there re-emerged a new Puritanism in which the acquisition of property became a sacred calling, a revival of the old view that no test of God's election is more clear than that of worldly success. "The Moral Governor," wrote D. S. Gregory, "has placed the power of acquisitiveness in man for a good and noble purpose." [2] Mark Hopkins taught that every man ought to acquire property as a means of benevolence to his neighbours, that the right to private property was the basis of all social progress. The Reverend Russell H. Conwell, one of the half-dozen most popular preachers of his time, told scores of thousands of citizens all over the United States that it is a duty to secure wealth and an important test of a man's usefulness to the community. He urged men to enrich themselves and not to be diverted from their purpose by the foolish envy of the unsuccessful.[3] As late, indeed, as 1900, Bishop Lawrence of Massachusetts was preaching a gospel that would not have been repudiated by John Winthrop or Cotton Mather. "In the long run," he wrote, "it is only to the man of morality that wealth comes. We believe in the harmony of God's universe. We believe that it is only by working along his laws, natural and spiritual, that we can work with efficiency. Only by working along the lines of right thinking and right living can the secrets and wealth of nature be revealed. . . . Godliness is in league with riches. . . . Material prosperity is helping to make the national character sweeter, more joyous, more unselfish, more Christlike. That is my answer to the question as to the relation of material prosperity to morality." [4] Seldom can men like Jim Fisk and Commodore Vanderbilt have been given an ampler or a more urgent blessing.

Nor is there any doubt of its accuracy in expressing the view of the wealthy themselves. The elder Rockefeller never doubted that his millions were a personal gift from God. The famous banker, J. P. Morgan, Sr., combined a profound Anglican piety with the most successful private banking house in the history of the modern world. They had no difficulty in securing a Christian ethic which placed behind their millions all the authority the Church could muster. If the world was ruled by a Divine plan, then all that was in it must be part of that plan. Poverty, therefore, was inevitable and arose, in the main, out of personal fault. In a civilization like that of America, where the gates of opportunity were so widely open, poverty meant only that through hard work and frugality every boy could climb into the class of the wealthy. If he did so climb, he ought to justify his success by suitable philanthropy; if he failed, he ought submissively to accept the will of God which had thus judged him

---

[2] Daniel Seely Gregory, *Christian Ethics* (Philadelphia: Eldredge, 1875), p. 224.
[3] Russell H. Conwell, *Acres of Diamonds* (Philadelphia: Huber, 1890), p. 19.
[4] Lawrence, *Fifty Years*, pp. 15–16.

for his sins. No one who fulfilled his duty and watched for suitable opportunities was likely to fail. He must not waste his time; he must not spend money or leisure in idle, much less in vicious, amusement. He must ever seek the means of self-improvement. Granted conduct of this kind, and granted that the driving power of a trust in God was behind the effort, no young man could fail whom God elected for His Divine purpose.

It is obvious that, with a doctrine of this kind, the wheel has come full circle, and that as capitalism began to pass into its first stage of monopoly the old Puritanism reappeared in a new guise. No doubt it was both reshaped and strengthened by a phraseology borrowed from more modern developments in thought. The classical economists provided it with the idea of life as a stern competition in which those who won were obviously the leaders of the economic effort of society. The slow but sure acceptance of Darwinism added the notion that this was a world in which the fittest were selected for survival. Society was thus best served by leaving the fittest to govern the economic universe they had thus come to dominate. To their secular defenders, the wealthy were a natural aristocracy; to their friends in the Churches, they were, not less clearly, the elect to whom, as the powers that be are ordained of God, it was fitting that other men should give obedience. It was even clear that a natural law, which was part of the Divine pattern, willed that the rights of private property should be free from invasion. And this meant, in its turn, that there were realms the State power must not be permitted to invade. It ought not to be permitted to weaken the responsibility of the individual citizen by transferring to him amenities he had not earned at the price of imposing taxation upon the wealthy. Invasion of this kind would not only hinder the rich from practising that gospel of stewardship which was at once their duty and their justification; sooner or later it would tempt a majority, necessarily composed of men both envious and mediocre, to use the State power to evade natural law. Just as economists, like John Bates Clark, were proving that, by a miracle of precision, the impersonal mechanism of the market gave to each man, whether millionaire or weekly wage-earner, exactly what he earned, so clergymen like Bishop Lawrence were insisting that the actual distribution of wealth was not a merely human arrangement, but a means through which the Divine will saw to it that the most worthy and most moral citizens were also the richest. The descendant of one of the founders of the American textile industry must have been sorely troubled when a president of the United States could speak of "malefactors of great wealth." That must have seemed like a criticism of God's pattern for the universe.

Not, indeed, that the new Puritanism went unchallenged. Its historical foundations were riddled with sarcasm by the remarkable oratory of Robert G. Ingersoll, since Paine perhaps the most persuasive of American free-thinkers. If he was not profound, he was everywhere influential, and his militant infidelity was probably the more important because, humanitarian though he was, he did not doubt the general individualist case, he was a stout Republican who had commanded a regiment in the Civil War, and he was, in private life, a successful corporation lawyer. And alongside the flank attack of infidelity there arose, also, a new social gospel within the Churches. A Congregational minister in Massachusetts, the Reverend Jesse H. Jones, sought in 1872 to unite the trade-union movement to Christianity; if he failed, it was because the socialism he preached had not yet any clear message even for an America which was painfully experiencing the grave panic of 1873 and realizing that, under the presidency of General Grant, the federal government was a thing that was permanently on sale to the highest bidder. Ten years later Theodore Munger, the eminent Congregational pastor, was beginning to find considerable acceptance for his view that even if every individual is accountable for himself as a person, nevertheless the elements of that person are shaped by a social inheritance he cannot control by his sole effort. Munger never went so far as a Christian socialism; but at least he grasped the fact that a Christian individualism was, in the contemporary society, a wholly inadequate answer to the problems it confronted. Washington Gladden also avoided a socialist profession of faith. But as early as 1885 he welcomed the growth of labour organization and admitted the right to strike; he even preached co-operation and the public ownership of utilities. He saw with effective clarity that not the will of the wage-earners, but the nature of American society was making class war inevitable. He recognized that the State power was in the hands of the employers and that, in the conditions of the eighties, it was bound to be used against the workers. He did not hesitate, at a period when it took great courage, to denounce the Church as little more than an agency siding on all occasions with the wealthy and therefore untrue to the spirit of its Founder. He even denied the right of foreign missions to accept money from what he regarded as tainted sources like Standard Oil. If his remedy was little more than the cloudy rhetoric that preaches the brotherhood of man and the Fatherhood of God, at least it was in striking contrast to the blissful acquiescence of Bishop Lawrence in the heavenly organization of things as they are.

And Gladden did not stand alone. Ministers like Sheldon of Kansas, like Bliss, who edited the once famous *Encyclopædia of Social Reform,* like George D. Herron, at one stage a professor at Grinnell College, like Walter Rauschenbusch, a professor at the Rochester Theological Seminary, all sought earnestly to achieve something akin to a socialist pattern under the sanction of Christian ideals. It is, of course, important that they rejected the main principles of Marxism; they would not accept either historical materialism or the idea of class war. They disliked strikes, though they often thought the objects of the strikers were just, and they denied fiercely any validity in revolutionary effort which did not confine itself to changing the hearts of men. They tended to accept the notion that all could be brought to find their redemption in the Fatherhood of God, and, thereby, learn to accept the brotherhood of man, and thus be led, by the higher spiritual elements in their natures, to make the changes required in the economic and social foundations of America out of which it would become a Christian order. If they did not profoundly impress even their fellow-ministers, they were mostly comforted by the conviction that they did seriously disturb the serene self-confidence of those who were satisfied with existing conditions.

And to some extent, no doubt, this was true. The fierce attacks of men like E. L. Godkin, William Graham Sumner, and the famous preacher Henry Ward Beecher, against those who stirred up the poor to doubt the sacred character of private property and *laissez-faire* are, in some degree, a measure of their success. It took a great effort, in periods like the depression of 1873 or the panic of 1907, to believe that man has no more power over his own destiny than, as Sumner put it, "by his ignorance and conceit to mar the operation of the social laws." [5] The line of criticism of legislative action on behalf of the underprivileged which argued that their unhappy condition was the necessary outcome of a law of nature as well founded as Newtonianism; or the conclusions, which Theodore Woolsey of Yale University drew from his examination of socialism, that its doctrines threatened individuality, would break up the family, and destroy religion; or the ardent hope of the philosopher William T. Harris, for a period the Federal Commissioner of Education, that, with the spread of knowledge, men would see that socialist thought, even when clothed in a religious garb, would destroy that uniqueness of the individual which modern institutions had set free from the strait jacket of the middle ages; all this was an attempt to quieten doubts which found expression in every Church. Sometimes the answer takes the form of the simple "success story" of men like Edison or Rockefeller, Lincoln or Garfield; sometimes it takes the more sophisticated form of books like those of Irving Babbitt and Paul Elmer More, in which they devote a good deal of learning to prove that democracy means the negation of culture and leadership, and that, as More put it, all civilization depends upon putting the rights of property before the claims of persons. Sometimes journalists like H. L. Mencken sought, by a kind of sophomoric Nietzscheanism, to persuade Americans that belief in democratic values was impossible for anyone who realized that civilized living is, after all, an adventure open only to the few.

The Christian protest gathered momentum from the disclosures of the tawdry revelations during Grant's presidency. It began the formulation of its gospel with that view which, in Rauschenbusch's phrase, regarded capitalism as "a mammonistic organization with which Christianity can never be content." [6] It became as steeped in the social progressivism of its era as was the outlook of the New England renais-

[5] William Graham Sumner, *The Challenge of Facts and Other Essays* (New Haven: Yale University Press, 1914), p. 55.

[6] Walter Rauschenbusch, *Theology for the Social Gospel* (New York: Macmillan, 1917), p. 224.

sance of Emerson's time by the new aspirations of Jacksonian democracy. At its root is a twofold doctrine: the first is a belief that man in himself is virtuous, but corrupted by an evil and invisible empire operated by privilege for its own benefit; and the second is that ideas can of themselves compel action if there is behind them a driving power of sufficient force. This, it is assumed, is provided when the ideas are in conformity with the will of God. For God is a democrat who believes that the power of the people can be used for creative ends if it is organized for that purpose. Since change is inevitable, there must be a teleology to give direction to the change. Given knowledge and goodwill and the faith to collaborate with God, there is no reason to doubt that a just social order can be achieved.

By the beginning of the twentieth century the religious approach looks like a curious compound of Rousseau and of pragmatism set in the perspective of a fundamental moral law which is identified with the Christian ethics. The approach is neither general nor uniform. Its exposition depends partly on the events of American history, partly on the temperament and social relations of the expositor, and partly on whether he took a Calvinist view of human nature in the rich or in the poor. If he was urban and Protestant, he would be influenced for the most part by the congregation to which he ministered; if he was rural and Protestant, his outlook would be shaped by his desire to keep his Church the centre of social life in the area he served. He was always aware of the threat of indifference and of infidelity, and therefore sought to find ways and means through which he could use, if indirectly, the sanctions of power in his community to ward off the threat. He wanted influence and he wanted numbers. He was uneasily aware of the competition he faced from the growing secularization of life, which made even Sunday observance unable to hold its ground against the invasion of amusements purveyed by business men who saw in its relaxation an opportunity for profit. Perhaps the explanation of the hold so interestingly maintained by the Roman Catholic Church is that it offered no concessions to the individual in the realm of belief, while it was always prepared to be charitable to evil conduct for which the sinner did the penance for which it called. Where Protestantism was attacked on all its fronts—whether by science, in the form of a direct scepticism of any supernatural explanation of phenomena brought increasingly under natural control, or by scholarship, which made it increasingly difficult to accept the dogmatic authority claimed by its churches, or by the difficulty of reconciling urban facts like low wages or bad housing or high infant mortality with the professed interest of God in the welfare of the individual—the Roman Catholic Church could confront these challenges with relative equanimity by simply insisting that none of them affected the truths proclaimed in its name.

The result can be seen in the inter-war years. Anyone who compares the defeatism of the social gospel after 1918 with its eager hopes in the days of Gladden and Rauschenbusch can see that disillusion has set in. It is tempting to generalize what occurred by saying that religiosity had taken the place of religion. In the urban areas the clergy were part of a group in which public relations counsel, advertising men, lecture bureaus, organizations like Rotary and the Kiwanis, sought to condition Americans to the new dogma that business, as a practical form of social service, was really in itself a religion; it is a symptom of importance that Churches increasingly adopted the successful techniques of business. It was genuinely held that the gospel of business efficiency was the practical expression of Christian principle; with, of course, the inference that the greater the scale of that efficiency, the more did business contribute a civilizing influence, and thus become a profounder fulfilment of the Christian ideal. And that inference could be drawn not least from the vast drive of the epoch for prosperity through mass consumption. You made your home cleaner when you bought a refrigerator on the instalment system. You used your leisure for health, and you educated your family in the knowledge of America when you bought a car. A correspondence course in anything from memory-training to pemmicanised philosophy enabled you to get promotion in your job by producing the right knowledge just at the moment when the manager required it. Your wife studied the magazines which told her how to dine out with you so that your business associates were impressed by the quiet distinction of her conversation; and the twelve beauty treatments she took out of her savings by the efficiency of her housekeeping made you proud to spend your leisure in displaying her style. She even began to read books and to join a lunch club where a visiting lecturer explained just what the book was intended to mean. The age of the machine, by standardizing consumption, went far towards standardizing religion too; and it was rare to find a dawning suspicion that standardized religion, distributed by a clergy anxious not to be regarded as out of step with the trends of the age, was becoming a kind of undogmatic heartiness concerned with proving to ordinary Americans that God had solved the central problems of their civilization.

I do not think that this interpretation is essentially contradicted by the persistence of Fundamentalism in the South, and by its general resistance to the invasion of the less rigorous standards of behaviour which obtained elsewhere. For, in the first place, the conflict over Fundamentalism was in itself a conflict between an older and a younger generation, and, so far, itself important evidence that the traditional religious pattern was breaking down. The religion of the South, moreover, was held taut by the persistence of a long hostility, of which the revival of the Ku Klux Klan in the years after 1919 is one symptom, to the Roman Catholic Church; it was difficult to relax that tautness without loosening the battle line the Southern Protestants deemed themselves to be holding against an enemy they regarded with even fiercer emotions than they did the new habits of loose religion. And, in any case, the conservative religious *mores* of the South were in large part the outcome of feeling rather than of thought, a compensation for inferior standards of education which made a considerable part of the religious debate uninteresting, if not unintelligible, to most who heard of it. To this must be added the decisive fact that the main foundations of Fundamentalism were, in fact, a complicated mask behind which careful scrutiny reveals economic features in large part hidden from the mass of the population.

Nowhere, to my knowledge, has the basis upon which the Churches of the South were built been more carefully, or more decisively, brought out than in Professor Pope's remarkable study of the cotton towns of North Carolina, and especially those of Gaston County.[7] Here is an area in which the clergy played an important part in both organizing and maintaining the enthusiasm for its industrialization. Few resident mill-owners, and even fewer mill superintendents, have failed to pay at least conventional devotion to one or other of the evangelical Churches. Most of these depended in considerable degree upon subventions from the mills; and most of the clergy received some part, often an important part, of their income from the same source. In many of the mills it was hardly possible even to obtain employment unless the applicant had a recommendation from a minister of whose soundness the management possessed no doubts. The clergy, in their turn, sang hymns of praise to the mill-owners who showed what a combination of "devotion to business and consecration to God" could accomplish. The mill, indeed, was a Church which "gave life to all around and about them."[8] A cotton mill could be dedicated, at its opening, "to Almighty God." That was in 1880; but nearly half a century later a clergyman could write, significantly enough, in the *Southern Textile Bulletin,* that "Southern industry was pioneered by men possessing the statesmanship of the prophets of God. . . . I personally believe it was God's way for the development of a forsaken people."[9]

Ministers have served as directors of the mills, and that as recently as 1938. They have made an alliance with mill-owners to promote Prohibition in the interest of industrial efficiency. Their pastorship has resulted in a more disciplined and submissive body of workers than can be found among men and women who are religiously indifferent. "Church members," says one official, "are more dependable workers."[10] Just as the Churches in the South acquiesced in Negro slavery before the Civil War, so they acquiesce in wage slavery after it. There is a direct correlation between the number of mills and the number of churches; even the proportion of the white population in the mills which goes to church has grown fairly continuously since 1880.[11] There is even a direct correlation

[7] Liston Pope, *Millhands and Preachers* (New Haven: Yale University Press, 1942). I want to acknowledge my deep debt to this important book.
[8] *Ibid.,* p. 23.
[9] *Ibid.,* p. 25.
[10] *Ibid.,* p. 30.
[11] *Ibid.,* p. 44.

between the number of spindles, the value of church property, and the salaries of ministers.[12] There is a growth of class stratification in the churches; workers tend to go to one church, and members of the managerial grades to another.[13] The latter are more ornate, more comfortable, and better built; and their ministers receive a salary which is, on the average, twice as high as that of ministers in the churches attended by the workers. This emerges very notably in the fact that while ninety-one per cent of the ministers serving churches attended by the workers live in company-owned houses, sixty-five per cent of ministers serving churches attended by the managerial group live in houses which they themselves own.[14]

Professor Pope quotes interesting examples of the curious hold of superstition and magic on the workers in their religious attitude. Their attitude to sin makes most of the habits of their economic rulers come within this category. Their services are intended to stimulate emotional excitement and to permit escape from the dull routine of the mill into an atmosphere of other-worldliness. The appetite for revivalism is strong, and it is interesting to note that one of the main themes of the songs there sung is the home waiting for the worshipper "after the last spindle has become wound." [15] In the churches attended by the managerial group, it is not regarded as desirable for religion to touch too closely on the problems of private life. Emotionalism is frowned upon. The minister should be "a good fellow," who "ought to be a leader in all community enterprises, such as projects sponsored by the Chamber of Commerce." [16] Most of the sermons preached there deal with the eternal commonplaces to which their hearers have been accustomed. Innovations are rarely welcomed; the congregation desires to be made confident about the existing social order. While Episcopalians, Lutherans, Presbyterians, and Methodists recruit the main body of their members from among the managerial groups, Baptists and the more esoteric sects are overwhelmingly drawn from the working class; [17] and it is the general rule that the more educated the minister, the less likely is it that his church will have an influence on the mill-workers. Many of those, indeed, who minister to the esoteric cults may well be unable to read, and some may be workers on a period of leave from their normal life in the mill.[18]

One of the most interesting phenomena, among the many Professor Pope has so carefully described in this area, is the continuous emergence of new sects. All of them seem the outcome of some category of frustration; all of them make grace in their members a matter of primary importance; and all of them make abstention from the things they themselves are likely to lack—the wearing of jewelry is a good example—a

[12] *Ibid.*, p. 46.
[13] *Ibid.*, p. 71.
[14] *Ibid.*, p. 82.
[15] *Ibid.*, p. 91.
[16] *Ibid.*, p. 93.
[17] *Ibid.*, p. 100.
[18] *Ibid.*, p. 109.

religious requirement. They tend to stress the insignificance of worldly wealth. They emphasize the need to accept the literal meaning (of course in their own special sense) of the Bible, and their contempt for the more wealthy churches like the Lutheran and the Presbyterian. They exalt the status of those who are "saved," and despise any worldly success that is independent of "salvation." It is significant that the support they receive from the managements of the mills is likely to vary proportionately with the support each of them can command in a particular year from the workers in the mill towns.[19]

It is quite apparent from the evidence that Professor Pope has collected that the mill churches attended by the workers are overwhelmingly dependent upon the goodwill of the managers. It is not only that they contribute to the maintenance of the buildings and to the salaries of the ministers; nor is it that the mill companies may actually own the buildings and be able to prevent their use for any but a religious purpose. It is even more significant that, in 1929, the Annual Conference of the Methodist Episcopal Church of Western North Carolina should have resolved that the manufacturers "should bear at least one-half the burden of maintaining religious worship in mill communities," [20] and this was done in the conscious background of the value of the Churches to the mills when labour discontent results in a strike. There are mill towns where it is the practice to deduct church contributions from the weekly wages of each worker.[21] There are others where the minister is warned not to discuss labour problems from the pulpit. There are others in which any doubt of the validity of the paternalism of mill control is rapidly followed by a change of minister.

Nor do the ministers themselves call the practices of the cotton mills into question. They express no discontent about child labour, or wages and hours, or the stretch-out system. They take the view that they ought not to "meddle" with questions of this kind. Some of the smaller sects tend to be strongly pacifist. While they usually allow their members to join trade-unions, they discourage them from engaging in the activities of agitation. The Churches may support campaigns against slot machines, or pool rooms, or gambling, or prostitution; but the kind of exhortation to the mills is a plea "to join hands in the Spirit of Christ . . . in securing a better industrial order." [22] They will be anxious about Sunday observance, but they seem to remain, both in sermon and in conference, coldly aloof from all economic matters. Their anxiety, they explain, is to extend the influence of the Church and so save souls; this they could not do if they became involved in economic conflict. Their emphasis is upon an individual finding his way to God by cleansing his sins in the Blood of Christ. They think it "radical" to appeal to mill-owners to exhibit "a Christian spirit of co-operation and sharing—that is the answer

---

[19] *Ibid.*, Chap. VII *passim.*
[20] *Ibid.*, p. 149.
[21] *Ibid.*, p. 156.
[22] *Ibid.*, p. 169.

to all the 'isms' of this chaotic day." [23] Even if it be true, as Professor Pope remarks, that most ministers know little about economic matters, it is still startling to find that their place of work does not seem to arouse in them any desire to learn. Once the management of the mill aids the Church, its minister suffers nothing to persuade him away from the path of acquiescence in the habits of the employers. When, in 1939, the mill-owners began what was virtually a compulsory sale of mill-owned houses to their employees, with weekly deductions from wages to pay for them, not even the ministers who saw that these sales, in fact, relieved the companies of a heavy maintenance charge, while it tied the worker to a particular company by selling him what might well be a house in need of repair, made any protest; that was limited to owners who did not sell their houses and were therefore anxious about the virtual wage differential their competitors were obtaining by these means. [24] Despite the famous Gastonia strike of 1929, ministers are either hostile to, or critical of, a really free trade-unionism, so much so that the Textile Workers Organizing Committee of the C.I.O. have found them the worst enemies they have to face; revivalists, said one organizer, regarded them as "agents of the devil, with the marks of the beast on our foreheads." [25] Their main emotion over the strike of 1929 was of relief that the "trouble-makers" had departed. They were glad to return to the ways of behaviour which the years before the strike had made a routine part of their lives.[26]

There is little in the superb analysis Professor Pope has made of Gastonia which is not paralleled, if from a different approach, by the Lynds' remarkable studies of Muncie before and after the Great Depression.[27] In both there emerge three outstanding features. The first is that the Churches are, in the main, a static and not a dynamic influence; their concern is to preserve a culture of yesterday, and not to assist in the emergence of innovations which are apparent to everybody. The second is their conscious inability to hold their own against the obvious forces by which they feel themselves to be challenged, with the sense that the wealthier the source of the challenge, the less likely they are to meet it. The third is that they hope for such influence as they can retain by appealing to the older generation and its memories of an earlier day for their right to attempt to make their impact upon the young. In North Carolina they are uneasily aware that the bond between them and the business community not only grows more loose, but that it is maintained very largely as part of a conventional pattern which has its special sanctions in the social rather than in the religious realm; their real authority is operated, and is expected to operate, over the wage-earner, for whom

[23] *Ibid.*, p. 179.
[24] *Ibid.*, p. 194.
[25] *Ibid.*, p. 202.
[26] *Ibid.*, p. 329.
[27] Robert S. and Helen M. Lynd, *Middletown* (New York: Harcourt, Brace, 1929), especially Chap. VII, and *Middletown in Transition*, especially Chap. VIII.

they provide a source of discipline by their organization of a means of self-expression. They draw the hearts of their followers towards the provision of a religious sanction for the ideal which the English philosopher, F. H. Bradley, called "My Station and Its Duties" by proffering to them an outlet, without which the scale of frustration would result in a long series of strikes instead of in the single protest, as in 1929, in which they were so helpful to the traditional rulers of Gastonia.

The greater resources of Muncie make the pattern more complex in detail though it remains similar in principle. Divisions of opinion are more various; the Churches must co-operate with institutions like the Y.M.C.A. and Y.W.C.A., which seek to reach the younger generation by combining, not without skill, the spirit of the Church with an institution which is part athletic and part social, a more comprehensive and more sophisticated version of the "church social" of thirty years ago. They have to deal with a population large enough for some of its elements to be able to afford to differ from the *mores* the Church offers for acceptance, and others whose connection with these *mores* is pretty discontinuous and tangential in character. Their clergy are better paid, better educated, and in a number of instances far more aware of the world about them. In Muncie, "corybantic Christianity" seems to have a far less natural place than it does in Gastonia; the revivalist theatricalism is looked upon far more doubtfully than it is in the mill towns. Muncie is not devoid of metropolitan pretensions; and its citizens tend to imitate some of the less extreme culture patterns of Chicago or New York or even Washington. More books are read, more questions are asked, political issues on the national plane seem far less remote. Muncie, indeed, has a college and a theatre, and secularization has penetrated far deeper than among the farmers turned industrial workers who are the mainstay of Gastonia. Yet, at bottom, the difference in the culture patterns is less one of kind than of degree. There is the same inability to see what could replace the Church as the source of moral integration; there is the same sense, alike in the ministers and their congregations, that religion, in the Muncie–Gastonia sense, is the protective armament which holds the antique from invasion by the new challenge. There is the same tendency for the sect to express the poor congregation's abandonment of hope, and the same tendency for the Church to express the formal confidence of bigness in the validity of the existing social order. Since Muncie provides a more varied and secular appeal to its citizens' leisure hours than Gastonia has to offer, the Churches in the latter have more social influence than they have in the former; but the gospel in each type of institution is the same. Each pleads that only through grace is salvation to be found; just as each, when it comes to the underprivileged groups, seeks to sublimate their frustrations by the simple expedient of making what is economically difficult religiously heterodox. Each makes conformity to the social code the main purpose upon which the Churches lay their emphasis; and each regards the individual citizen in an atomic way which separates him, with all its power, from the massive collective relations in which he is involved. For it is, supremely, this atomization which makes the ordinary man or woman feel lonely and helpless, and thus makes him ready for direct response to religious appeal.

3

THE temptation is, of course, to interpret phenomena of this kind in terms of rather simple Marxian formulæ, but I think the issues go deeper. While there can, on any showing, be no doubt of the immense impact of economic upon religious phenomena, it is also true that the religious side is itself connected with a whole chain of other factors, political, social, cultural, and psychological, each of which enters into the economic and may be capable of influencing the economic pattern to its needs. Nor must one forget the relation of religion to sex. It is not only that the "corybantic Christianity," as T. H. Huxley termed it, of revivalism feeds on, and is fostered by, emotionally starved or frustrated people; there is also the special influence of religion upon women, especially of single women, and the degree to which, in the *mores* of our civilization, they look, and are encouraged to look, to the Churches as a substitute for husband and home. There is the psychological realm, where the worker who counts for little or nothing in his factory or in the fields finds in the Church the chance to be in the lead, as a deacon, or a member of the choir, for example, that is not open to him when he is the unit on the assembly line; and the same impulse may well drive the lonely or ill-treated wife to find in the activities of the Epworth League of the Methodist Church that oasis she hoped to discover in her own home.

The statistics show that, despite the automobile and the movies and golf and bridge, some fifty-five per cent of adolescent and adult Americans are still, in some sort or another, Church members. They show an institution which, in its different expressions, has property worth some seven billion dollars and an annual income very nearly as large as the total budget of Great Britain before the First World War. There are fewer students in the theological colleges. There are more and more feverish efforts to find ways of making the Churches attractive in the light of competing claims; and, in this aspect, the growing interest of the Churches in athletics, which, with a wealthy metropolitan Church, may even take the form of appointing a director of athletics who is a professional, has obviously great significance. So, too, has the development of "parochial" schools, and the effort to secure a religious hour, with special denominational instruction, in the public schools. It is probable that the attempt to give the clergy some training in sociology has failed, largely because it is just one more element in an overcrowded curriculum; and that may be the reason why, in the great cities, the minister of any well-endowed Church tends to become, more and more, the head of a team of specialists, each of whom deals with one aspect of the

Church's relationships, while he remains in part the director of their activities and the consultant who is called in to deal with especially difficult cases. At the moment, I am concerned only to emphasize the complex nature of the ecclesiastical pattern and the danger of premature generalization. For a European visitor who seeks to understand the American religious scene can hardly escape a sense of complete bewilderment, for he is confronted with two hundred religious denominations all claiming their roots in Christian doctrine; and even if he confines his study to Churches with more than fifty thousand members he will find at least forty-eight in this category. The law separates Churches from the State; but he will find that parochial schools where a particular creed defines the environment of education are at once protected by the law and are growing in number; he will find, also, that all property "used for religious purposes" is immune from taxation. Though he will be told on every side of the growth of religious indifference, especially among the younger generation, he will note that voluntary contributions to the Churches amount, so far as is known, to something between seven hundred and eight hundred million dollars every year; and that if few American denominations have buildings of outstanding architectural importance—for the spirit which produced Chartres and Salisbury no longer survives—numbers of churches are built upon the assumption that a crèche, a car park, a restaurant, and a system of flood-lighting are all part of the "plant" with which a "modern" American Church, if it is wealthy, expects to equip itself.

He would, I think, be astonished at two other general features. The first is the intense preoccupation of most Churches with practical rather than with doctrinal problems; boys' clubs, women's societies, forums for public debate, libraries, playgrounds, even kitchens, are all, as it were, avenues down which the Church member may move in the hope that his interest in the Church may be maintained. He would find that the Churches reach out long fingers into every aspect of the individual's life that they can reach. Through the Y.M.C.A. and the Y.W.C.A.'s they assist in providing most of the facilities of a well-ordered club set in the perspective of a "hearty," even muscular religiosity; and, not seldom, they offer the chance of lodgings and meals for the unmarried younger workers at a reasonable price. He would find that the clergy belong in considerable numbers to business organizations which seek to convince business men that industry and commerce are "callings" which give service, of which profits are a mere by-product, to the community. "Our conception of God," wrote Bishop Fiske, "is that He is a sort of Magnified Rotarian." [28] He would discover that the clergy preach at business conventions and are ready to discuss subjects like "Advertising in Building a Bible Class" and "Advertising the Kingdom through Press-Radio

---

[28] Charles Fiske, "Confessions of a Penitent and Puzzled Parson," *Scribner's Magazine*, December 1927, p. 660.

Service." [29] He will note with interest that the successful preacher is the man who knows how to avoid the danger zone in controversial subjects and arranges his service so as not to cast too heavy a burden on the housewife who is anxious not to be late for lunch. Nor can he fail to regard as significant the type of use to which religious broadcasters, such as Mgr. Fulton J. Sheen, put the time on the air their supporters enable them to purchase.

The other feature is the depth of the contrast between "Liberal" Christianity, and "Fundamentalist" Christianity. In whatever denomination the first is found, it is striving, in general, to do three things. It seeks, above all, to bring its theology into some sort of conformity with those findings of theological scholarship and ecclesiastical history which no person with any serious respect for reason can hope to deny. It seeks, in the next place, somehow or other to come to terms with science, and especially to prove that its doctrines are in no wise prejudiced by the Darwinian revolution, still less by the developments of modern physics or modern geology. It tries to find a body of social doctrine which enables the Churches to be the conscience of the social order so that proper emphasis is given to the need for applying Christian principles to the acquisition and use of property. In the realm of social doctrine, indeed, the range of possible variation is astonishingly wide. A Liberal Christian may devote his main energies to expounding the necessity of pacifism. He may urge that Christianity and capitalism are incompatible. He may think it is enough to renovate the ancient doctrine of stewardship. He may express his outlook by devotion to social reform and plead for better housing, a living wage, the abolition of child labour, insurance against unemployment, or the right to a trade-unionism at least powerful enough to secure agreement from the employers to settle industrial differences by conciliation or arbitration. In the Roman Catholic Church, a body like the National Catholic Welfare Council, building on the social policy of Leo XIII, will seek to take action to mitigate the less admirable features of American industrialism, even while it accepts the doctrinal standards of the unchanging Church. An outstanding example of this outlook was the striking and courageous report on the steel industry by the Inter-Church World Movement in 1923. It was claimed, in 1912, that the overwhelming majority of social workers were provided by the Churches; [30] though it is interesting to note that the same authority, writing fifteen years later, had rather wistfully to admit that most social workers had, in the interval, lost all interest in organized religion. [31] It is not easy to see what exactly is the theological status of Liberal Christianity. Its

[29] J. R. Sprague, "Religion in Business," *Harper's Magazine,* September 1927, p. 431b.
[30] Charles Stelzle, *American Social and Religious Conditions* (New York: Revell, 1912), p. 176.
[31] Charles Stelzle, "Is the Church Slipping—and Why?" *World's Work,* September 1927, p. 512.

doctrines on all fundamental issues are a departure so far from any rigorous precision in theological belief that its exponents seem nearer to a Unitarianism, to which each exponent adds the coloration of those principles upon which he himself feels most deeply, than to Christian dogmas in any historic sense of the term. It often seems, to the outsider, to have arrived at a stage where an acceptance of theism, a conviction that no character in history is more noble than Jesus, and a hope that personal immortality may be true are, together, its whole creed. With some Liberal Christians, the notion of miracles is no longer acceptable, and with this has gone any need for belief in the supernatural authority of the Bible. With others, the deep dissatisfaction with things as they are lends to the insistence that only the creative consciousness of the infinite worth of Jesus' teaching will evoke in men a sense of sin sufficient to subordinate self-interest to the community's welfare. Liberal Christianity has produced many noble men, and not a few thinkers of remarkable distinction. But the problem they raise, not least for themselves, is whether their attempt to build a Christianity in full accord with historical knowledge and scientific research leaves any rational basis upon which a Church can be founded.

Above all, that problem is raised of the relation of their outlook to that of the Fundamentalist. To the Fundamentalist, whether Protestant or Roman Catholic, the basis of belief is authority. For the second, the source of authority is the infallible insight of Rome; for the first, it is the infallible Bible, all the teachings in which are permanently true and universally applicable, while its historical record is beyond any challenge. The Virgin Birth, the Incarnation, the Resurrection, the Atonement, the power of the Holy Spirit to bring man the sinner through faith to grace, the certainty of the Second Coming in the actual sense of the New Testament, the conviction that truth is known by revelation and not by verified experience, all these are essential to Fundamentalism. It looks upon the theological scholarship of the century since Strauss and Bauer as the work of the Devil. It assumes that if science contradicts the Scriptures, it is science which is mistaken. In its crudest form it finds expression in the fantastic attitude of William Jennings Bryan in the notorious Scopes trial in Dayton, Tennessee; but there is much the same outlook, if in a more sophisticated form, in the attacks on Darwinism by men like the Jesuit Le Buffe.[32] Not only have a number of states passed laws against the teaching of the doctrines of evolution; but the Baptists of Texas resolved, in their Annual Convention of 1922, that in none of their "institutions of learning" was anyone to be employed "who denies the Deity of Jesus Christ, or the inspiration of the Bible, or who holds to the Darwinian theory of evolution, or any other theory of evolution which contravenes the teaching of the Word of God." [33] Associations exist, like the

---

[32] Letter to the *New York Times*, March 17, 1922.
[33] Quoted by A. W. Slaten in an interesting article, "Academic Freedom, Fundamentalism, and the Dotted Line," *Educational Review*, February 1923, pp. 65 ff.

"Bible Crusaders" and. the "Supreme Kingdom"—the latter founded
by a former leader of the Ku Klux Klan—whose purpose is, above all,
to destroy Modernism. It is estimated that the Churches with a Fundamentalist membership control the outlook of some twenty-five to thirty
million people. If that is true, they probably outnumber the Liberal
Christians by a very solid majority.[34]

It is important to understand the grounds of this Fundamentalist
achievement. In part, no doubt, it is a peculiarly geographical phenomenon. Most of the areas it dominates are remote from the large
metropolitan centres which rapidly adapt themselves to new ideas; and
most of them show the pattern of a culture which, outside the religious
field, has been toughly resistant to the invasion of concepts which threaten
a jealously guarded tradition. Most of them, too, have been isolated from
the eastern states and the main impact of European immigration—itself
an agent of cultural diffusion—by the Appalachian mountains and by
the ruinous economic and social effects of the Civil War. It is important
that the ten states in which Fundamentalism has made most headway
have an illiteracy rate which, with two exceptions, is from two to five
times as great as that of the United States as a whole. Economic poverty has bred ignorance, and ignorance, in its turn, has deeply resented
the effort to renovate the basic ideas from which comfort has been
drawn, especially where those attempts come from sources in themselves
suspect. Nor is it easy to escape the conclusion that men like Bryan, who
had been thwarted politically by business interests in the great cities, became distrustful of religious changes recommended on rational grounds.
They urged, as a consequence, the need for confidence in the emotions
of the heart and the danger of zeal for the scepticism of the head. He,
like the underpaid and often uneducated ministers of the "Bible Belt,"
could recommend Fundamentalism as, not least, a real compensation for
the dissatisfactions of poverty and of failure. Just as in the seventeenth
century the "inner light" produced its English Fundamentalism, with
great leaders like George Fox, even great writers like John Bunyan, so
an analogous American climate had similar social results. Nor must we
forget how much more the emotional satisfaction of a religion of the heart
is likely to be than one which, like Liberal Christianity, is constantly seeking to revise its own foundations. The Fundamentalist wants in his religious life that security he so rarely achieves in other realms of effort.
Modernism offers him no comparable consolation.

To this must be added the important fact that the Fundamentalist is,
from his own angle, a social reformer as earnest as the Liberal Christian.
No one is more anxious to legislate his neighbour into what he regards as
moral behaviour. Temperance, even to the point of Prohibition, the denial by law of the use of tobacco, the stern repression of the greater sex
freedom of this age, the strict observance of the Lord's Day, the censor-

---

[34] See the discussion by A. C. Dieffenbach in *Religious Liberty* (New York: Morrow, 1927). Dr. Dieffenbach is himself a Modernist.

ship of "immoral" books and films, the regulation of habits like those of
dress and the use of cosmetics, which may so easily become a source of
sexual temptation, hatred of birth-control, the stern punishment of the
prostitute and all concerned in her "evil" profession, on all these the
Fundamentalist feels as earnestly as the Liberal Christian on the living
wage or on better education. It is notable that most of them involve the
repressions we normally associate with asceticism; and it is not a long
step from the practice of asceticism to the identification of its denials
with saintliness. If the outsider sees in this asceticism the sublimation
of the frustrations of handicapped and underprivileged communities, the
answer is, of course, that no other consolation has any comparable power
of satisfaction. Why should the Fundamentalist surrender that consolation to men whose religious outlook is built on wholly different principles? Why, even more, when he sees that the great metropolitan areas
are sunk, as he thinks, in sin and infidelity, should he not conclude that
only a sound religious faith, which stands like a rock against temptation,
can be strong enough to produce sound morals? God and Jesus preside
in person over the destiny of every man, and every man can approach
them in prayer with the sure knowledge of direct response. What gain
is there for him in the erosion of that ecstatic sense of immediate contact, and the substitution, in its place, of some impersonal force, unknown,
and perhaps unknowable, outside his inner and real life, which he may
venture to hope is making for righteousness? His Kingdom, as a Fundamentalist, is not of this world. Why, having won his place in the Kingdom of Heaven, should he surrender it for earthly satisfactions which
are mostly set in the perspective of sin and may jeopardize his conviction
that he is saved?

And underlying all this there is a vivid realization that, at some stage,
the Modernist and the Fundamentalist are likely to come into conflict.
They do not share the same premises; they hardly talk the same language. It is obvious, too, that there is involved in these differences a claim
to property in terms of doctrinal truth. Who are entitled to the Churches,
their charities, their seminaries, their mission funds? Can either side, in
the long run, see them devoted to principles they do not accept, to spread
ideas which they believe to be incompatible with the good life? From a
Fundamentalist standpoint, any compromise with Liberal Christianity
is a surrender to the Devil and thus a threat to salvation itself. The
Fundamentalist looks upon the things the Liberals have given up as the
bastions of the faith. He is convinced that the Modernist has set his
feet on a road that leads directly to atheism. He is already uneasy at the
gulf which yawns between his own conception and the Liberal philosophy. Every surrender to the latter is not only a surrender to the
Devil; it is arming him with the instruments to enable him to wage his
campaign. Just as the Roman Catholic has fought for parochial schools
lest his children be corrupted by secularism, so the Fundamentalist is
anxious to purge all institutions of teaching which undermines the true

faith. "Worse than an assassin who kills the body," wrote a Fundamentalist in Kansas City, "is he who shatters the faith of youth." [35] If the schools and colleges in a state create the atmosphere in which faith is thus shattered, the Fundamentalist naturally feels that he must either change the atmosphere or resist the imposition of taxes devoted to purposes so alien from the central purpose of his own life.

To this must be added that the United States has been the breeding ground of new revelations of a Fundamentalist character. If some, like Mormonism, have had a deep root in nationalism and thus made America, as it were, a new Holy Land, they were also profoundly Puritan and enabled many of their votaries to grow from poverty to wealth by engagement in a calling which made possible the practice of well-chosen ascetic virtues to result in the obvious "election" of success. Others, no doubt, like that in which Aimee Semple McPherson became notorious in Los Angeles, mainly provided a cloak of religiosity in which a skilful exploiter of emotion could use, uninhibited by any scruples of delicacy, the starved impulses of ignorant multitudes to reap a financial harvest. Nor, I think, is the case otherwise with super-evangelists like the ex-baseball player Billy Sunday, who combined massive intellectual ignorance with such brilliant powers of salesmanship that he became one of the outstanding "public relations" experts of Big Business. In return for fantastically high fees, he devoted his skill in transferring mass anger against bad economic conditions to the excitement of religious revivalism. His influence was rarely, perhaps never, permanent; but he was at least skilful enough, as in Philadelphia in 1915, to break an important strike and to be the occasion of one of the most remarkable examples of university interference with academic freedom at the instance of Big Business that there is on record. [36]

But no case is more interesting to examine than that of the most rapidly growing religion in the United States—Christian Science. However remarkable may have been the real founder of Mormonism, Brigham Young, or that simple-minded but moving prophetess from Manchester, England, "Mother" Ann Lee, to whose visions are due those Shaker Communities in whose history only a Philistine could fail to find a certain romantic beauty, it is difficult not to feel that the most typical American contribution to ecclesiastical organizations is the Church founded by Mary Baker Eddy. Here was a woman of humble origin, if sincere, nevertheless without serious intellectual cultivation of any kind, the writer of a new Bible now devoutly accepted as inspired by some millions of her followers in America and Europe, confident that she knew the meaning of books in the Scriptures of the Jews and Christians which had baffled scholars of the first quality for generations, who occupies for the members of her Church a position hardly below that of Jesus Christ.

[35] The Reverend A. Northrop, quoted in Maynard Shipley, *The War on Modern Science* (New York: Knopf, 1927), p. 154.
[36] Lightner Witmer, *The Nearing Case* (New York: Huebsch, 1915), *passim*.

She was not only able to found a Church whose faith and liturgy she prescribed in the most minute detail; she escaped from looming catastrophe into legendary semi-deity in matters where, to say the least, the normal canons of historic testimony would have wrecked the career of most other persons. She had three husbands; she had a son in whom she not only had no interest but out of whose separation she managed to make herself the victim of a conspiracy which never occurred; she got her main inspiration from a self-confident charlatan, Phineas P. Quimby, himself an infidel, from whom she probably took the whole basis of her doctrines; she transformed a fairly simple accident, diagnosed by her doctor as concussion with a possible spinal dislocation, into a glorious and outstanding miracle. She transcended her practice in magnetism, her early hysteria, her poetry—compared to most of which Miss Ella Wheeler Wilcox assumes almost the proportions of William Cowper or John Keble —her facile rhetoric, her careful correlation of the fees she charged with the will of Providence, even the group of her early students who charged her with financial greed, bad temper, and "the appearance of hypocrisy," to end as the half-divine head of a Church in which she held virtually autocratic power, as the owner of at least one internationally known newspaper, and a successful millionaire. It is, on any showing, a record so remarkable as to border on the realm of the incredible.

This is not the place for me to describe, much less to discuss, the tenets of Christian Science. It must suffice to say simply that what they contain of truth has been a central part of medical knowledge—and, indeed, of other religions—long before Mrs. Eddy's time, and that what they contain of her own contributions are a mere mixture of quackery and rhetoric. Only the convinced believer could find her book readable except as a study in one woman's pathological psychology. Only the devout, who by their faith have closed their minds, could accept the fantastic claims made for her outlook and ignore the immense volume of tragedy and suffering for which it has been responsible. We can only note the thousands of Christian Science healers, some of whom are said to earn from ten to twelve thousand dollars a year; their possibly eight million patients in a year's period; the fact that most of the Church's followers are either of the wealthy or of the comfortable classes; that over forty American states make provision for what is virtually exceptional treatment for Christian Science "practitioners"; and that their nursing homes in England have been, since 1927, freed from the normal obligation of nursing homes that they must be under the control of a qualified doctor or nurse. To these facts should be added that, seemingly, one may be a Christian Scientist and yet a member of some other Church, that vaccination is permitted, and that the hold of the doctrine seems, with very small exceptions, to be limited to Anglo-Saxon communities. If it made some small headway in Germany, it had practically no influence in France or Spain or Italy; and its permeation of South America seems to have been confined to American or British residents there.

The real problem is not the doctrine, but the explanation, first, of its general success, and, second, of its main success with people of assured financial status. No doubt it has important links with the vaguer atmosphere of Emersonian Transcendentalism, in the autumn of which it was born. No doubt, also, it began to win its hold in a country which seemed to tolerate without any limit religious novelties of the most remarkable kind. It owes much to the unbreakable tenacity of its founder, the intensity of her conviction, the luxury of submission to a dominion its votaries may not challenge. But I suspect that it owes most to three things. First, the very name of Christian Science was a brilliant inspiration of the first order; it transcends, at a stroke, the hostility between two ways of life which other Churches have not been able to accomplish in centuries of effort. Born in an expanding America, it is an optimistic creed, a declaration that evil is non-existent, that the mind can conquer the ills of the flesh, that there are no fears which cannot be conquered by Divine mind. It makes no serious call upon the intellect; the services of the Church are decorous and simple; there is a sacred book which contains a good deal of esoteric magniloquence laid down in language so imperative, and often couched in terms faintly iridescent with the Biblical memories of childhood; there is the great founder whose faith conquered her own disease and made a great fortune from very modest beginnings. As one looks at it all, and sets it in the context of the rate with which new sects were born in that period, it is easy, given the intense and dominating personality of its founder, to understand its success.

It has, second, a special appeal to women; it gives them high status and a new occupation, for the immense majority of the "healers" are women. It has a special appeal to neurotic people, to whom it brings relief from fear and pain. It appeals to the rich, upon whom it makes no serious demands, for it offers them, in response to their faith, a comforting assurance that the pain of the world is unreal, that they need not, therefore, be disturbed by its appearance, since this is unreal and can be conquered by those who suffer if they will but put themselves in the frame of mind to recognize that they can be liberated by their own effort. Its morality is a fairly simple version of conventional American morals. There is no need to be disturbed by any of the problems of theological exegesis which disturb the world external to the world of Christian Science. It cannot fail unless the victim is lacking in conviction; then failure, obviously, is the victim's own fault. With the half-educated, it is impressive to read a book the writer of which not only has no doubts, but possesses an overwhelming conviction of the supreme importance of what she has to say. And third, it is above all a gospel which says nothing of its failures and can offer, to anyone who has no knowledge of modern psychiatry, a massive list of what seem like miraculous cures. It is, therefore, crowned by the pragmatic test of its truth—the test of success. It has no political and no economic dogmas. It can hardly fear any hostility save that of the medical profession; and most doctors know that a large proportion of

Christian Scientists will combine their faith with a half-ashamed resort to the physician or surgeon or dentist in serious cases. And since Mrs. Eddy, with great acumen, forbade the practitioner to "treat" any patients without their knowledge and consent, and has made most of her Church's propaganda so discreet and unobtrusive as to be utterly inoffensive, it is one of the rarest events to see it arouse either hatred or even criticism. It is a world within a world: to the insider, an object of profound devotion; to the outsider, an object of faintly sardonic contempt. Nothing so far in its history has brought it into important conflict with any single vital feature of the traditional habits of American civilization.

If the English observer is tempted to say that a phenomenon like Christian Science may well be possible in the United States, but hardly likely outside it, there are, I think, several things to be said. The first is that though Christian Science is American in its origin, it is both popular and growing in England; it is notable that few books so easily procurable as Mrs. Eddy's retain so high a proportion of their original price as hers. The second is that it is difficult not to connect the growing interest of the Church of England in a ministry of healing with the experience of the power of Christian Science over its votaries. The third comment is that a multiplicity of sects is common in every country where some special circumstances disturb the traditional values of its civilization. The reader of Thomas Edwards' *Gangræna* (1646), or of Ephraim Pagitt's *Hæresographia* (1644), or of the early anger aroused by the Quakers in the first half-century of their history, will agree that precisely this multiplication took place in the seventeenth century in England; just as a study of the Wesleyan revival in the eighteenth century will warn him not to exaggerate the differences between human nature in Great Britain and human nature in the United States. There is little evidence to suggest that the revivalism of Evan Roberts in Wales, in this century, differed very profoundly from any of its American analogues, or that such differences were of kind rather than of degree. I suspect that the American revivalist operates on a larger scale than in England or in Wales, and I am fairly confident that the technique of salesmanship he brings to his offer of salvation is, as a rule, more outspoken, more dramatic, and more persuasive than that of any Englishman in the last century, with the possible exception of the famous Baptist Charles Spurgeon. In the realm of more sophisticated effort, it is surely significant, also, that Buchmanism, even if American in origin, was far more successful, proportionately, in England and in Scandinavia than it was ever able to be in the United States.

The Registrar-General of Great Britain publishes no religious statistics comparable in character to those of the religious census undertaken every ten years by the director of the American census; we therefore know but little of the esoteric Churches which exist in the United Kingdom, nor even their number. But it is worth while to remember that there are still followers of Joanna Southcott, who failed to achieve her pro-

claimed power to achieve a new Virgin birth, and even relics of the Mug-
gletonian sect; and there is an important sense in which the lay preachers
of the Nonconformist Churches may be said to have found there the main
training on the one hand, and the evangelical spirit on the other, which
they brought to the foundation of the Labour party—a spirit the mention of which is still able to win applause when it is mentioned during a
Labour meeting. If the American development took a different turn,
that is very largely because the geographical problem of its evangelists
made continuity of relation and discussion quite different from anything
known to his English brother after, say, the fifties or the sixties of the
nineteenth century. The men who rode the frontier until almost a half-
century ago in the United States were dealing with scattered populations
on the edge of the frontier, while the English or the Welsh evangelist was
moving by railroad to complete journeys the stages of which had already
become conventionalized. So that while the variation in the character of
British routine varied only in terms of the special individuality of the
British revivalist, his American colleague was combining the call to religious fervour with a social event in the life of the different communities
he might take in as he went on his way. The American was not only
welcome for the salvation he had to offer; he was welcome, also, because
he brought news of a half-forgotten world, the emigrants from which
had to strive hard to remember, while their children knew only by hearsay
the meaning of the ideas interchanged between their parents and the
visitors. The easier access to books in England counted for something
after the establishment of county libraries; that is a problem for the
American the principles of which he has still to state. The engineer, the
miner, the stevedore, in a British port or works or mine, has for the most
part made a bargain with fate he does not propose to reopen; if he is
ambitious, it is through his trade-union or his local party that he hopes
to advance; the American of the same craft is still not yet quite sure that
he need give up the hope of founding his own business, certainly of owning his own car, and perhaps his own home too. The ambitious boy in
England will not look for advancement to the connections he is likely now-
adays to form in his Church; for if his employer has done well, the
chances are that he and his wife, if they remain religious, are thinking of
joining the Church of England, with its superior social status, at the
earliest moment. The ambitious boy in the United States has perhaps half
a dozen Churches to choose from, even if he be a Negro, in each of which,
belief apart, he can find the connections to help him in his career. In England, moreover, it is exceptional, outside the great cities, for either his
parents or his employer to expect him to be a Church member, even if
they have an interest in his welfare; but in great areas of the United
States, he will find that religious indifference may well, at the best,
make him suspected as unsafe, and, at the worst, may brand him as a
"Red." In the latter event he cannot well do better than set out with new
determination for new pastures. Outside perhaps half a score of American

cities, downright infidelity is still not a passport to social regard; it can hardly yet be taken with indifference.

The history of the free-thought movement in the United States forms both an interesting and revealing pendant to the history of religious belief. As early as 1662 Thomas Prince reported that the decay of religion was "very visible and threatening";[37] fifty years later the Associated Churches of Connecticut displayed a similar alarm.[38] At the time of the wars against France, Timothy Dwight complained that Americans became the prey of infidel officers in the British Army who were anxious to make proselytes.[39] No doubt towards the middle of the eighteenth century, especially as the influence of the Great Awakening began to decline, there was a considerable growth in religious indifference and some acceptance, as with Franklin and Jefferson, of deism; it is even possible that deism had a considerable hold upon the richer planters of the South. There is a good deal of evidence to suggest that men like Washington himself, like John Randolph of Roanoke and St. George Tucker, had little religious belief or interest; and there was a good deal of scepticism in some of the Southern colleges. We are even told that a discussion society in North Carolina had a circulating library of infidel works, and it is certain that Paine's *Age of Reason* was widely read. Men like Chancellor Kent of New York were, in the first enthusiasm for the French Revolution, the enemies of priestcraft and religious superstition. William Ellery Channing spoke of scepticism at Harvard, Lyman Beecher at Yale; and there was a good deal of deism at Bowdoin, Dartmouth, and Princeton. "French" ideas were in the air, and a good many students liked to parade their knowledge of Voltaire, Rousseau, and Paine. The first anti-Christian book written in America, *Reason the Only Oracle of Man* of Ethan Allen, was published in 1784. But Allen's book—if, indeed, he was its author—was, by all the accounts we have, nothing like so popular as the work of Paine; and there appears to have been a fairly wide demand for Volney's *Les Ruines*, which was translated from the French by the joint efforts of Jefferson and Joel Barlow.

From books there followed a free-thought press and the organization of free-thought societies. In these there participated a very considerable number of well-known figures, Robert Owen and his son, Robert Dale Owen, Frances Wright, Elihu Palmer, Abner Kneeland, of whom the latter suffered prosecution and imprisonment in Boston. Before 1850 some thirty free-thought journals seem to have been published, seven of them in New York, two in German, though the number of their subscribers was small and it was rare for any of them to last more than a few years. A number of societies existed, some of which, particularly

---

[37] M. Louise Greene, *The Development of Religious Liberty in Connecticut* (Boston: Houghton Mifflin, 1905), p. 123.

[38] William B. Weeden, *Economic and Social History of New England, 1620-1789* (Boston: Houghton Mifflin, 1890), Vol. II, p. 549.

[39] Timothy Dwight, *Travels in New-England and New-York* (London, 1823), Vol. IV, p. 354.

that of Robert Dale Owen and Frances Wright in New York, seem to have attracted, and held, an audience of up to one thousand persons. If there was angry attack, hardly less from the ordinary than from the religious press, there was also a continuing interest, though it is broadly true to say that, publicly at least, the support for a free-thought movement came, in the main, from the urban working class in perhaps half a dozen cities of considerable size; and in the fifties aggressive infidelity was obviously declining. In the latter half of the nineteenth century it was represented by one distinguished exponent, Robert G. Ingersoll, who played in the United States a role not very dissimilar from that of Charles Bradlaugh in England. Since his day, I think it is true to say that no free-thinker has been able to make his creed a matter of national interest. The enthusiasm of the first half of the nineteenth century has either given place to indifference or, over a small field, has been satisfied with the quasi-ecclesiasticism of movements like that of "Ethical Culture," or of "Community Churches," for example, that of Dr. John Haynes Holmes in New York at the present time, where, in the background of a vague and undogmatic theism, an attempt has been made to preach ethical humanism on a basis which has brought the results sought for near in outcome, if different in sanction, to the social doctrine of Liberal Christianity as conceived by men like Gladden and Bliss and Rauschenbusch. A small Comtist church also had a brief existence, though it never took a serious hold.

For two-thirds of the history of the United States, this is to say, the real enemy of the Churches has been indifference and not infidelity. There has been a profound conflict within the religious field, no doubt, in the deep, perhaps growing, antagonism between the Protestant Churches and the Church of Rome. There have been periodical moments of excitement, the revolt of Moncure Conway, the heresy trial of Charles Augustus Briggs, the fight, not yet over in the "Bible Belt" of the South, over Darwinism. But, all in all, the Churches have remained a vast pressure group whose organized hostility it is important to avoid. An avowed and militant atheist could hardly hope to be elected to a political office of the first importance. Though Roman Catholics and Jews have reached positions as high as the governorship of New York, neither, as yet, can hope for a successful candidature for the presidency, though no presidential candidate could succeed if, during the campaign for his election, his supporters gave offence, as during the Blaine campaign of 1884, to a powerful religious group. All the political machines must take care to see that in the distribution of patronage they have regard for the religious composition of their supporters; a foreign observer notes with interest, for example, a number of Jewish policemen in New York and Chicago who successfully passed Civil Service examinations more easily than their coreligionists can do who compete for places in the foreign service. An American president anxious to avoid criticism will take care to attend Church on Sundays with some regularity; and the main political insti-

tutions—Congress, the Armed Services, the state legislatures—will have
their chaplains from the major denominations and will find a place for
brief religious services among their activities. Some state constitutions,
indeed, still exclude from office citizens who are declared atheists; and a
complete survey of the law would show that, though the federal separation of Church and State is complete, there are important traces in the
formal practices of states which would sanction an important departure
from complete neutrality.

All in all, it is true to say that the influence of Christianity in the
United States is everywhere pervasive without being anywhere generally profound. The decline of interest in theological questions which
Lord Bryce noted when he wrote his *American Commonwealth* [40] has
certainly continued, perhaps at an accelerated pace. If the sale of the
Bible is still in millions, a knowledge of the Bible has clearly declined,
above all in the population which has had a college training; and the
style of American writers rarely shows any trace of the influence of the
Authorized Version. If one analyses the reports of sermons in the press
in four great cities for a period of three months, their predominant note
is a social–ethical one, an emphasis on the duties of individual citizens,
with only a vague background of dogma. In periods of national crisis,
during the Great Depression, for example, or upon the outbreak, and
during the continuance, of the Second World War, there has been ardent
effort to explain the problem of evil and an overwhelming conclusion
that this is God's punishment of man for his sins. There is a good deal of
sectarian rivalry, both in the United States itself and in missionary work
abroad; there is the impassable barrier between the Roman Catholic
and the Protestant Churches, which makes co-operation between them
always difficult and sometimes impossible. There are few communities
where a minister of distinction, especially if he be a preacher of great
eloquence, will not be a figure of considerable civic importance; I do not
think it is an exaggeration to say that men like the Reverend H. E.
Fosdick, a New York Baptist, and William Scarlett, Episcopalian
Bishop of Missouri, have something of the nation-wide status enjoyed
perhaps only by Phillips Brooks of Boston in the latter part of the nineteenth century. Nor is it beyond the mark to say that in the borderland
where ethical principles touch upon and cross over into the theological,
only William Temple, Archbishop of Canterbury, has had the kind of
intellectual influence among Christians to whom their faith is more than
an emotional satisfaction and consolation that has been held by Professor
Reinhold Niebuhr of the Union Theological Seminary in New York.

To this, I think, there must in honesty be added the important fact
that the pervasiveness of the Churches, Roman Catholic as well as Protestant, comes in a large degree from the subtle compromise they have made
with the world rather than from a defiant proclamation of their doctrine.

[40] James Bryce, *The American Commonwealth* (New York: Macmillan, 1910),
Vol. II, pp. 781 ff.

They have not been able seriously to compete with the growing secularization of American life. The automobile, the movies, the country club, the not always silent relaxation of sexual habits, shown not least in ecclesiastical sanction, the Roman Catholic Church apart, of birth-control, the overwhelming failure of the moral crusade for Prohibition, the need to make the Church attractive partly by the use of the advertiser's technique and partly by enabling it to compete with the world by making religious membership an avenue to social amenities—all these are evidence, granted their scale, that in the silent treaty between the Churches and the world shaped by the habits and concessions of the last fifty years, it is the Churches and not the world that have yielded. Whatever the sum of individual exceptions, the Churches know either that they must make their peace with modern science, or by-pass it by taking refuge in an authority that reason is not permitted to invade or in a mystic faith that is not verifiable by experience. Whatever the extent to which ministers, here and there, proclaim the need to "Christianize the social order," the overwhelming body of American clergy use that need as a slogan for some indefinable future and not as a criterion to judge an immediate present. They seek every possible route by which to escape the need to take sides on concrete issues. "The Church," they say, "is not in politics." Or their concern is with individual salvation and not with a social order. Or the doctrine of stewardship may throw a garment of morality about the economic behaviour of wealthy men who are religiously inclined, which seems not to extend to wealthy men who are indifferent to religion; the Rockefeller Foundation, the University of Chicago, and a hundred other examples of generosity balance the grim history of Standard Oil and the Colorado Iron and Fuel Company, which revealed its habits so devastatingly in the Ludlow massacre. Mr. Rockefeller's case is perhaps the supreme example of this compromise. But it reveals quite inescapably the point at which the challenge of Christianity is moderated into a hope that, in some mysterious way, evil methods are converted into noble ends by the power of faith.

What, save in the most exceptional cases, is clear is that the Churches have no alternative but to make this compromise, especially in the economic realm, unless they desire to be revolutionary organizations aiming at the overthrow of the whole ethos of American civilization. Once they desire to exist in the world, to employ ministers who must have salaries upon which to support a wife and children, to build churches, to compete with organizations which might otherwise claim the allegiance of their members, to train their ministers, to attract men and women to their service in the face of other careers which are open to them, their power to live depends upon property; and they must adjust their practice to the area within which they can hope that men, and especially rich men, are willing to endow them. That is why Mr. Bernard Shaw was right when he argued that, in the last resort, Churches are bound to be what he called "a sort of auxiliary police, taking off the insurrectionary edge of poverty"; [41] to make the other road is at once to invite conflict with the state power. That is why the first emphasis of the Churches must be on the individual soul to be saved, and that in indifference to whether its possessor be rich or poor. Indifference, because if a given Church believe in salvation by faith, the worldly status of its member is irrelevant if he holds that faith; while if it preaches salvation by works, if its member perform those works deemed adequate to salvation in the view of the Church, that performance must logically result in the acceptance of his membership. The Churches are therefore left in the position that they are bound to preach submission to the powers that be, even while they are urging that no values really matter save those in the Kingdom of God. Indeed, the more they emphasize their view that only eternal values are really important, the more, however unconsciously, they are really preaching submission to the powers that be. That is why Wesleyanism, in the epoch of the French Revolution, was a stabilizing force in English politics. That is why Fundamentalism in the South has tended to divert attention from the evils of the social order and thus, in a real sense, to assist in their consolidation. That is why the gospel of a social Christianity confines itself to large generalizations, such as the need for more brotherhood and mutual understanding, which rarely give concrete direction on particular issues, or makes specialized recommendations; for example, the need for better housing, or a higher standard of education, upon which most people with any social sense have been for long years agreed.

I must emphasize that this is no more a criticism of the Churches than it is of any other institution within a community the habits of which must conform to categories of behaviour which are set by the rules enforced through the use of the State power. Churches must accept those rules or fight them; if they fight, so long as those who operate the State power have firm hold of its authority the Churches have no option but to give way. The Mormon Church was not able, outwardly at least, to continue the practice of polygamy; Christian Scientists were permitted the patent contradiction of accepting vaccination as a civic duty. No Church could evade the obligation to recognize the authority of the civic courts, although those who exercised the state power in the courts might decide, as so often in doctrinal matters, that they would not concern themselves with internal problems which a Church was regarded as itself competent to determine. Since there is no religious establishment in the United States, the legal decisions suggest that no American court would exercise the kind of jurisdiction exercised by the Judicial Committee of the Privy Council in England in the Gorham case,[42] when it found that an infant was not eternally damned if it died before baptism, or by the High Court in R. V. Dibdin,[43] where a lay judge could, obviously rightly, find that an

---

[41] George Bernard Shaw, Preface to *Major Barbara* in *Collected Works* (London, 1930), Vol. XI, p. 287.

[42] 1850.

[43] 1911.

Act of Parliament could bind the Church to the acceptance of a marriage which, in that canon law which Anglicans regarded as binding upon them, was obviously contrary to the Law of God. But it is, again on the decisions, highly probable that if an ecclesiastical dispute turned upon matters of property which were set in the context of doctrine, American courts would regard themselves as bound to scrutinize the meaning of trust deeds in the same way as the House of Lords did in the famous Free Church of Scotland case just over forty years ago.[44] Property and contract certainly, tort perhaps, are vast categories within which an American Church is a voluntary association not less subordinate to the civil power than any other association. It exercises its freedom within limits defined by the State power. Its compulsions are derivative and not original in the eyes of the law.

4

IT IS obvious, I think, from all this that no simple explanation of the interaction between American democracy and religion can hope to be successful, nor, indeed, of the reciprocal influence of the one upon the other. If certain things are clear, other things are so intricate that it is not always evident which of them is cause and which of them is effect. It is fairly obvious, also, that we are rarely dealing, in any division of space or time, with a straightforward correlation between two precise items, partly because neither of the items is an entity with exact boundaries, and partly because each is influenced by, as it acts upon, in its turn, a hundred other things which do not submit to reduction into categories sharp enough for statistical measurement. No one, for instance, can read today the chapters in which Tocqueville discussed the relations between American democracy and religion in his day without seeing that even this most distinguished of all foreign observers of the United States wrote less with his mind than with his heart. With an openness usually absent from one of so reticent a temper, what he described were rather the hopes and imperatives he sought to see fulfilled in the democracy he regarded as inevitable, than the body of factual experiences from which principles might be drawn.

It must, I think, emerge as unmistakable to any detached observer that a number of generalizations can be made which cannot seriously be called into question. Pretty clearly, in the American civilization of the twentieth century the impact of technology on the use of leisure makes religion as a social factor dependent upon its ability to compete with alternatives offered; since these are likely to vary with the size of the community and its scale of living, the influence of religion is generally in inverse proportion to urbanization of the area in which it operates. It will mean least in vast cities like New York or Chicago, Los Angeles or Philadelphia. It will mean something more in the smaller metropolis like Boston or In-

---

[44] 1900–1901. See my *Studies in the Problem of Sovereignty* (New Haven: Yale University Press, 1917), Chap. IV.

dianapolis. It will mean more still in the small cities of less than one hundred thousand inhabitants; and it will mean most of all in the smaller townships and the rural areas. This is simply because the more intimate the community, the less easy it is to depart from the traditional *mores*. In the great metropolis the private habits of the citizen are lost unless he chooses so to conduct himself that his habits become a matter of public discussion; otherwise, it is probable that enough people will behave as he does to make his behaviour an accepted part of the general pattern. But as the community involved is smaller in size, the decrease in the choices offered means that the social sanctions behind the traditional choices remain sufficiently strong to draw attention, with increasing emphasis, to anyone who rejects them for some part of the pattern of behaviour which has not yet won its way to acceptance. This means, I think, that the greater the growth of urban life in America, the smaller is likely to be the hold of any religion which expresses itself through a Church organization.

The second generalization that is, I think, beyond doubt is that the hold of religion as expressed in a Church—Roman Catholics and Jews apart—is likely to be stronger in the South than in the North, stronger in the West than in the East, and stronger in the Southwest than in the Northeast. The main cause of this difference is, quite simply, that each of the first-named of these areas has a lower standard of life than the second. That means less education, less sophistication, fewer choices through which to secure a satisfactory adaptation to the environment. Since few people can get through life without an external standard upon whose authority they can feel a sense of reliance and safety, the Church is, for the vast majority of people who are either unaware of, afraid of, or alien from, the complexities of modern culture, a refuge whose older patterns of belief either give them emotional comfort or act as safeguards against the intrusion of thoughts or conduct which may confuse or challenge them. This, incidentally, is the central reason why Liberal Christianity is mainly urban and middle class, and Fundamentalist Christianity mainly rural and *petit bourgeois*.

The third generalization is that the power of the Churches is in some important degree maintained by the protection they offer to folkways of different immigrant groups which might, otherwise, be unable to find compensation for the inferiority they have felt in their effort to come to terms with America. This is markedly the case with the hold of Roman Catholicism over the Irish, the Italians, the Poles, and the French Canadians. In a lesser, but still important, degree it is true of the Lutheran Church in its impact upon Germans and Scandinavians. It is also true of the group not as immigrant, but as driven to an inferior position from which escape is hard, in cases like the hold of the more esoteric Christian sects, largely Baptist in origin, upon Negroes and "poor whites" in the South. Interestingly enough, Jews in America, who, despite the antiquity of their original settlement, tend to remain exotic everywhere once they are a notable element in a community, depend less upon the synagogue as the source of their inner sense of safety than upon the social, charitable, or, since the Balfour Declaration of 1917, the national institutions they succeed in building in Palestine.

Where, as in Boston or New York or Chicago, a minority group is powerful enough to count in the general life of the community, the bond of religious unity will give it a sense of self-confidence which may make it consciously aggressive against other groups which have formerly refused it access to the fullest opportunities it sought. It is worth while to turn for a moment to a concrete example of this relation. Though Boston has had an Irish and an Italian population from the eighteenth and middle nineteenth centuries respectively, the serious influx of either dates only from the Irish famine of the forties on the one hand, and the late eighties and the nineties on the other. Boston, at that stage, was profoundly Protestant, at least in the sense of a hostility to the Roman Church, fixed in a social structure through which it was very difficult to penetrate, and living by a culture of which it was not only enormously proud but by whose standards it was convinced it had the right to judge all other cultures. In a remarkable way, economic and social power, even, though in a smaller degree, political power, was shared among a relatively small traditional class which resented any intrusion into, or doubts of, its right to exclusive control. It lived in its own part of Boston—Beacon Hill and Commonwealth Avenue; it had its own clubs, admission to which it regarded as the conferment of a superior kind of citizenship; it governed Harvard University and, so far as it could, kept a considerable number of its main academic positions, not least the nationally important presidency of Harvard, very much within its own circle; it dominated the Bar and the Bench, banking and insurance and investment, the historic wholesale trades like textiles, paper-making, the shoe industry, and public institutions like the remarkable Boston Public Library and the Museum of Fine Arts. Both Irish and Italians were poor. They began, naturally enough, by performing the social and economic functions to which least consideration was attached by the classic Bostonians. When they climbed upwards and grew wealthy, they still found an impenetrable barrier that cut them off from all relationships which implied acceptance of their equality; the old Boston families would not recognize their title until they were numerous enough to be a matter of concern to a politician intent on re-election, like the older Henry Cabot Lodge; and even then they were made to feel that, in the eyes of "Back Bay," Senator Lodge was letting the real Boston down. The old families marked with concern the movement of the Irish and the Italians into the better residential districts of the city.

The result was the inevitable result. Each immigrant group built, as it were, a city of its own, and these groups united easily, on the political level, to fight Brahmin exclusiveness and dependencies. They were parties within a party. They developed their own industries, their own charitable and financial institutions, their own schools and their own rival to Harvard in Boston College. By the time of the Progressive movement under Theodore Roosevelt, they had arrived at a point where their place in the life of the community made it impossible for them to be ignored by the daily press, and it is interesting that, while the traditional paper of Back Bay succumbed to the Great Depression, the papers which catered specially to the Roman Catholics grew increasingly prosperous. In the result, historic Boston has not only become a minority, struggling, possibly in vain, to hold its position, but it has been increasingly compelled to yield a main share of the great positions in the state to men whom, if it had the courage, it would still openly despise. And no Bostonian has anything like the general influence, whether in Massachusetts or in the United States as a whole, of the Archbishop of Boston. Perhaps the climax came when Franklin Roosevelt chose a poor Irish boy who had climbed to great wealth, and married the daughter of an Irish political boss, as ambassador to Great Britain. That position, after all, was the supreme mark, seventy years ago, of the high eminence so real a Brahmin as James Russell Lowell had attained.

The fourth generalization I venture to emphasize is the necessity of any Church which seeks for wide influence to remain within the accepted circle of prevailing ideas. An occasional preacher or professor of theology may transcend them, but this is a rare phenomenon. And since the mental climate of the age changes, the framework of the ideas the Church will accept changes too. There will be, for example, far more insistence today, not upon faith in a future life, but upon religion as a help to success. There is a clearly growing distrust of theological systems. There is less emphasis upon dogma, and more on religion as a guide to conduct. There is a growing avenue for the expression of the characteristic "practical idealism" of Americans, which is, perhaps, a special way of emphasizing the "idea of the calling" which finds itself, after it has attained success, in the approval of philanthropy as a way to fulfil social obligation. Save, therefore, in the specially Liberal Churches, the Churches are marked by a fairly static dogma, which is accompanied, though in a form which is careful not to step too rashly, by eager praise of the doctrine of stewardship. This enables them to unite the rich and the poor. They can regard the generosities of the one as the proof of their allegiance, while they use that generosity to persuade the poor that they have a simple method of mitigating the ills from which they suffer. A harsh critic would be inclined to say that, with few exceptions, they are preaching and practising a sophisticated version of the outlook of the "Saints" in England during the evangelical revival.

They have, of course, paid an important price for this. In general—the Roman Catholic Church stands apart from this view—there are two ways in which they have surrendered any hope of making the idea of equality an integral part of their religious practice. The Churches which cater to the rich specialize in forms of service; the Churches which cater to the poor specialize in the offer of salvation. Most Anglicans in America belong to the upper class—Mr. J. P. Morgan was a devout Episcopalian. The Methodist Church tends to attract the well-to-do merchant or manufacturer, to whom the Anglican Church has still too "British" a flavour with a ritualist, even a sacramentalist, outlook, which he suspiciously compares with Rome. The Baptist Church, on the whole, maintains its hold upon the little people—the small shopkeeper, or the clerk, or the workingman in the small town—who adapt its habits to their experience of life and find their satisfaction, above all in its more exotic dogmas, in the conviction that they have found the only true road to salvation; having found the world too difficult to cope with, they reduce its importance to a nullity, or at least to no more than a vestibule to the other life, in which the successful will pay the penalty for straying from the true path in their excessive interest in worldly affairs. And the Churches have lost their hold upon equality because they cannot safely face the grave problems of the minorities, whether racial, like the Negro, or religious, like the Jew; they are not even anxious to confront too seriously the duty of finding accommodation for the poorer members of national groups which are not highly regarded by the "best people" of their areas.

All this, let us note, has had a special effect, in the fifth place, on the Protestant Churches as institutions dedicated to a theology on the one hand, and on the type of clergy they increasingly tend to produce on the other. They have turned from the serious attempt to relate doctrine to contemporary life, to being agents of consolation and social welfare, and to a formal guardianship of the need for individual morality in social relations. This transformation explains why the average minister is today something of a welfare worker, something of an organizer of extra-religious activities, something of a professional "booster" for "civic uplift," as well as a preacher to his congregation and a more or less successful counsellor to such of its members as are in personal difficulties. The test of his achievement is partly the size of his Church membership, and partly his ability, through its growth, to make the buildings of his Church ever more impressive. To attain these ends he must be able so to preach that he is able to stimulate, without any risk of offending, those in his congregation to whom he can look for assistance; above all, he must be careful not to lose them to rival Churches. It is best for him to be fairly young, to have an attractive wife who can please without seeming to demand any social precedence, to be himself dynamic and efficient and practical, to be a good "mixer," to give the impression that his duty to maintain high standards is fully compatible with being a reasonable man of the world, not to interfere with those practical political issues against which the solid pillars of his community take a firm stand, like communism, or strikes, or the "closed shop," or public ownership, and to win such a respect from the non-members of the congregation to which he ministers that the members feel a reflected pride in the esteem felt for him as a safe and sound man. He must not preach to them a theology so scholarly or so mystical that they cannot follow the meaning of his teaching. He must make them uncomfortable about sin in general, without ever doubting that America goes consistently forward. If there are economic difficulties, he must be certain that they can be overcome without the necessity of any serious changes in the principles which the American business world approves.

The next general inference which can, I think, be safely drawn, relates to the lay members of the Protestant Churches. There is, no doubt, an active and energetic core, perhaps ten to fifteen per cent of the total, whose lives are built around Church activities, and whose zeal in their pursuit is the outcome of a simple acceptance of the principle that the way of the Church is a sure path to salvation in that after-life the reality of which they no more doubt than they do their assumption that faith in Christ and the Gospel of the Cross is a necessary part of salvation. The grounds of this outlook vary considerably. For the more intellectual it is a refuge from the haunting and difficult problem of evil in a world where it too often appears that the righteous are forsaken and that their seed must beg for bread. To others, it is a consolation, too deep for rational analysis, which enables them to endure a life here and now that is too frequently harsh and ugly. To others, again, it is a way of fulfilling social impulses without the satisfaction of which they would be starved and lonely people. Where, especially, their outlook is Fundamentalist, attachment to a Church is the one method they have found of preserving their inner integrity of spirit in the wider world so full of temptations to evil; and it is notable that this group tends to show the least interest in, and the main hostility to, the effort of the Church to extend its influence by moving into the field of social welfare. Support for this extension, indeed, is far more likely to be found among Liberal Christians, upon whom rigidity of doctrine sits far more lightly, than among Fundamentalists, who tend to assume that the real mission of the Church is fulfilled when it has led individual men and women to grace. Both types may have that missionary spirit which is the religious expression of the American's practical energy; but whereas, with the Liberal Christian, it will probably lead to a vague social philosophy which seeks fulfilment in general good works, for example, the abolition of child labour, with the Fundamentalist, it is more likely to concern itself, first of all, with bringing friends and acquaintances to a sense of grace through the conviction of sin, and, at a less important level, with a negative support for the continuance of that grace by repression of evil habits like the drinking of alcoholic liquors, smoking, birth-control, and those entertainments the character of which is regarded as "immoral" because they are held to stimulate sexual appetite. It is the outcome of such repression, when it passes all bounds of common sense, that it finds its sublimation in careers so fantastic as that of Anthony Comstock, or activities like those of the

Watch and Ward Society in Boston, a body of which the Mather dynasty seems to be the permanent executive committee.

The rest of the Church membership lives on a very different footing. To many, it is a traditional relation it never occurs to them to break. To many, also, it is the performance of a conventional rite which they accept because friends, or people whom they respect, or the majority of those among whom they live, appear to do so. Some belong because it enables them to find friends; others because it helps them to climb the business ladder or the social ladder. Many join because, since they think it wise to send their children to Sunday school, their own attendance at Church seems naturally to follow and safeguards them from the need to answer difficult questions. A small proportion, mainly women, go because they like the minister, or because attendance leads them into social activities in which they can achieve some needed self-fulfilment. A large proportion goes to Church casually and infrequently, partly because they do not wish to be marked out as unbelievers, and partly because it is a change from the automobile excursion or golf and tennis or the country club. There are others, again, to whom some faint contact seems occasionally desirable because it makes them "feel good." Others can be attracted only by some special, often incredible, revivalist campaign, the excitements of which have either been communicated to them by friends or highly publicized in the press; though here it should be added that, outside the smaller sects, most ministers are fully aware of the narrow religious content in these revivals, and of their use, mainly, as the emotional stimulus to a campaign for a new church building or a new organ, or, it may be, the provision of a lecture hall as an annex to the church.

What is notable in all this is complicated. Americans generally will identify religion with the Churches. They will even value them as an important safeguard of a not very precise body of values which they call "Americanism." They have little critical knowledge of what their Church believes, perhaps the less knowledge when they believe with a strong emotion. What appears even more clear is that they do not want this knowledge and that it is rare for their ministers to offer it them. They feel, in a vague way, that the more the Church keeps to a pretty traditional doctrine and preaches what they regard as a sound "ethic" which strengthens the hold of contemporary America upon its citizens, the firmer will be the sanctions of law and order. They like to hear warnings against "agitators," optimistic insistence upon the greatness or the uniqueness of America, optimistic prophecies about the future of America; they want to be convinced that the Panic of 1907, or the Great Depression after 1929, or, with successful men, the "insanity" of the New Deal, has nothing to do with the nature of American economic institutions but is the outcome of sin or folly or envy on the part of men who have failed to apply the "golden rule" in their daily lives.

It is interesting to observe how little in one way, and how much in others, the Roman Catholic Church has been influenced by the environment of America. Historical circumstances have made the United States so profoundly a Protestant country that it is always difficult not to feel that the Catholic Church is permanently on the defensive; even its aggressive policies, as in Boston in the era of Cardinal O'Connell, or in Brooklyn, New York, in the vulgar attacks of the followers of Father Coughlin, have about them the exaggeration of men who are not quite sure of, or satisfied with, their place in the secular scheme of things. It is not, indeed, beyond the mark to say that Know-Nothingism, the Ku Klux Klan, the political revolt of the Solid South against the candidature of Governor Smith in 1928, are all parts of the important fact that, beneath the surface of things, the Catholic Church is not fully recognized as having achieved a real fusion with Americanism. Partly that is because the history of immigration, much of it an immigration the impact of which is known to many Americans still alive, made the Catholic Church the active defender of minority groups; and partly it is also the fact that, in protecting them, the Church sought to safeguard them against the results of an Americanization which invariably tended to the relaxation of their religious ties. This had the deeply interesting result of giving the Catholic priest an authority over his flock which has remained more living and more intense than any which the ministers of other Churches dare seek to secure. The Irishman or the Italian, the Pole or the French Canadian, who deliberately rejects this authority is rare; that is why the Catholic vote comes nearer to being swung by ecclesiastical influence than that of any other Church; and why the outstanding Catholic prelates in the United States, Gibbons, Farley, Hayes, Mundelein, were men whose opposition no president was likely to seek and whose counsel he was usually glad to welcome. After all, a cardinal in Baltimore or Boston has links, through the Vatican, with interests of importance to America which spread all over the world.

The imperfect fusion of the Roman Catholic Church with Americanism follows, of course, from its theory of the universal claim to sovereignty in this world upon which it is built. It is, in some sort, an *imperium in imperio,* for it seeks to build a kind of citadel for its members entrance into which marks them with an ethos that is permanent. To this end it builds its separate school system, its special training colleges, its special universities; while its School of Diplomacy in Georgetown University at Washington has shown a remarkable power of infiltration into the Department of State in the federal government. It is also fair to say that there is a special Catholic world of literature and of scholarship, the atmosphere of which is permeated by principles and attitudes which a non-Catholic American would have some difficulty in understanding. To all this must be added the vital fact that the Roman Catholic Church stands alone in America in its complete exclusion of laymen from any effective share in the making of its decisions. A Roman Catholic industrial magnate may be asked for advice upon financial matters, or be urged to contribute to the Church funds; but he has no kind of say in the disposi-

tion of its properties, the appointment or promotion of its priests, the
character of its doctrine or its teaching. It is not an unfair comparison
to say that the Catholic laity in America are compelled to play the part
of privates with no hope of promotion in the great army of the Church;
the commissioned ranks are reserved, without challenge, for its priesthood. No other Church would venture to impose so complete a status of
subordination upon its members; nor has any retained, by virtue of the
discipline this implies, so full a respect for the priest from the members
of his Church as one can find in the Roman Catholic communities of
America.

In this aspect the Roman Catholic Church is not only sharply distinguished from other American Churches; it is also felt to be so sharply distinguished by the ordinary citizen. Unlike any other Church, it is the
Roman Catholic Church in America; it is not the American Roman Catholic Church. I do not mean for one moment that the overwhelming
majority of its members, clerical and lay alike, are not as loyal and devoted Americans as the members of any other Church. Undoubtedly
they are. But there is still in them some hardly definable quality which
gives their loyalty and devotion a permanently different perspective from
that of the others. That has emerged, in recent times, in their attitude to
the Soviet Union, to Mexico in the last generation, and to Republican
Spain. In each case the opinion of American Catholics was set in a
frame of reference notably different from that in which the opinion of
any other denomination was set. Even if American Catholics are dubious
about the wisdom of the policy for which their hierarchy decides, they
are less inclined to overt criticism of it, still less to serious opposition,
than would be the case with Methodists or Baptists or Unitarians. It
is as though some impulse from the *Respublica Christiana* of medieval
times makes the relation of the individual Catholic laymen to secular
policy tinged always with the recollection that there was a time when
positive law derived its validity from its conformity with a Divine Law
of which the Roman Pontiff was the appointed guardian.

The Roman Catholic Church, I have suggested, is in America, but
it is an American Church in a sense quite different from that of any
other denomination. It must, nevertheless, apply the body of its social
teaching to an American community in which the great mass of its members are poor men and women dependent wholly upon the sale of their
labour power for their living, a much smaller number who enjoy the
relative comfort and security of a solid *bourgeoisie,* and a very small
number who, like Thomas F. Ryan in the last generation or J. J. Raskob
in our own, are among the outstandingly wealthy men of the time. The
Church in America, from the Encyclical *Immortale Dei* of Leo XIII in
1885, through its related pronouncement in the *Sapientiae Christianae*
(1890), the *Quod Apostolici Muneris* (1878), and the *Libertas* (1888),
down to the Encyclical *Quadragesimo Anno* (1931) of Pius XI, which
was itself both a salute to, and a modernization of, the *Rerum Novarum*

(1891) of Leo XIII—the Church possesses a body of directives which it is the business both of its priests and laymen to apply in concrete detail to the situations they occupy; with, of course, the overriding principle of interpretation that, in the last resort, the validity of any particular application is a matter upon which the finding of the Church itself, that is to say of the Supreme Pontiff at Rome, is conclusive and final.

Here, once more, the Roman Catholic Church in America differs from other American Churches in having a wide-reaching and authoritative code of social action. There is, of course, a considerable range of variation in the inferences drawn from the code; some Catholics of high eminence made it the basis, for example, of their warm support for the New Deal of Franklin Roosevelt; while others saw no incompatibility between its principles and membership in that Liberty League the aim of which was nothing so much as the destruction of the New Deal. It is, indeed, extraordinarily difficult to find a single, unchallengeable, meaning in the code; and it is still more difficult to know what authority it possesses over the minds and actions of Catholic laymen. It is clear that it condemns any social system built upon *laissez-faire;* but it equally condemns socialism and communism. It is emphatic in its approval of private property; but it agrees that certain undefined forms of property must not be left in private hands. It urges employers to pay a just wage related to family responsibility; but it warns the worker not to press for a wage which would inflict injury upon his employer. It appears to approve co-partnership and profit-sharing; there are certain passages in the Encyclical *Quadragesimo Anno* which appear to the outsider to bestow a somewhat cautious blessing upon the corporate state in its Fascist form, as with its prohibition of strikes and lockouts and the provision for compulsory arbitration; [45] it recognizes the need to organize the workers, but having its suspicions of the ordinary unions, perhaps because they act as a source of socialist ideas, it prefers "Christian" trade-unions under episcopal encouragement. It emphasizes throughout, naturally enough, that it is to the improvement of individual character under the inspiration of true religion that the only road to a just social order can be found.

The problem for the outside observer therefore becomes a complicated one. There are many Catholics in the United States who belong to either the Socialist or the Communist party; there are, of course, many hundred thousands who not only belong to what Pius XI called the "neutral" trade-unions, but would resent profoundly any attempt to lessen their strength by introducing into the industries where the "neutral" unions operate the competitive element of "Christian" trade-union; and over the major sector of American industry, trade-unionists, whether Catholic or non-Catholic, would bitterly resent and resist any attempt to

---

[45] I use the edition published by the Catholic Truth Society as a tract called *The Social Order, Its Reconstruction and Perfection* by His Holiness Pope Pius XI (London, 1935). The passages dealing with the corporate state are the paragraphs numbered 91 ff.

introduce the habits of the corporate state. Nor is this all. It is patent that there must be a large number of Roman Catholic employers who pay their workers less than a living wage; nor is there any evidence to suggest that either co-partnership or profit-sharing experiments are more frequent among Catholic, than among non-Catholic, employers. Whether the Roman Catholic Church improves the character of those, employers and workmen alike, who accept its teachings, raises questions which do not admit of any quantitatively precise answer. It is notable that the rate of crime is higher among professed Roman Catholics than among members of other religious denominations,[46] but this, obviously, cannot be attributed either to the principles or to the influence of the Church to which they belong.

What is, I think, beyond all doubt is the fact that the Roman Catholic Church as an organized institution exercises a conservative, even a deeply conservative, influence in all matters of social and economic importance. This is the outcome of its emphasis upon faith, and not works; of its distrust of radical movements it cannot control; and of its historic dislike of any strong central authority with which it is not in special alliance. It is deeply suspicious of any extension of the federal government's power; that has led it, for example, to be one of the outstanding opponents of the Child Labor Amendment. It has rarely spoken forthrightly about outrageous practices by employers, such as were revealed in the findings of the La Follette Committee on Civil Liberties. The educational standards in its schools and most of its colleges do not compare with even the average standards of those maintained by the states or by private endowments such as Harvard or Yale. It is far more anxious when an attack on parochial schools is threatened than when it is shown that the rate of illiteracy is higher, and the school-leaving age lower, in the Catholic Church than among other Churches in the United States. It continues to set its face firmly against birth-control. As the refusal to allow Bertrand Russell to teach mathematical philosophy at the College of The City of New York, on the grounds that he was an unfit person, made clear,[47] even in a neutral institution the Church will use its underground influence to interfere with academic freedom; while the McMahon case at the Catholic University of Notre Dame is an interesting example of the perturbation of the hierarchy at the possibility that a "modern" outlook was creeping into the institution.[48] Nor is it easily possible to dismiss as unimportant the difficulty other Churches encounter in securing official co-operation with the Roman Catholic Church on issues on which interdenominational co-operation between Protestants has been found to be simple and straightforward.

The short way of summarizing the position is, I think, to say that as

[46] This is not, of course, an exclusively American phenomenon.
[47] Cf. John Dewey and Horace M. Kallen (ed.), The Bertrand Russell Case (New York: Viking Press, 1941).
[48] The dismissal of Professor McMahon was explained on the ground that he was "difficult."

an organized institution the Roman Catholic Church shows less direct interest in the problems of the time, save as they touch the interests, and especially the economic interests, of the Church, than any religious organization of comparable importance. I doubt whether its religious leaders feel inwardly anything like the strain that an observer can find in the writings of men like Reinhold Niebuhr, or the long line of his predecessors who go back to the seventies and eighties of the last century. No doubt the Roman Catholic Church can claim one intellectual giant in the field of social analysis in the person of Orestes Brownson; but it is important to realize that all his work of serious stature was done before his conversion. Men like the famous Father Hecker, a century ago, worked hard and nobly at the task of aiding individual men; there is a sense in which he can fairly be described as the American Vincent de Paul.[49] No one can fail to respect the devoted effort of Monsignor Ryan, in the last generation, to work out a Catholic social philosophy which would put the Church squarely on the side of large-scale social reform.[50] I do not think it can be said that he succeeded, and I suspect his influence was greater outside his own Church than it was within it; in any case, it would be difficult to argue that he had got much beyond the position of Theodore Parker, or as far as mild Christian Socialists like Gladden and Rauschenbusch were prepared to go.

If one tries to get at the root of the Roman Catholic attitude to contemporary life, there emerges at once an issue of fundamental importance. By making the conduct of the individual in its relevance to his salvation far more significant than the material standards of the environment in which he lives, and by insisting that the state power is a neutral agency concerned with a social welfare regarded as common to all citizens, the Roman Catholic Church insists that the men who operate this power, no doubt in an imperfect way, reach out beyond the bias and partiality from which few of us are able to escape. Out of this comes the principle that, subject, of course, to ecclesiastical approval, the Catholic layman must broadly live by the Scriptural injunction that "the Powers that Be are Ordained of God";[51] where he wishes to depart from this command the Church is at hand to tell him of his obligation. All of which amounts to saying that while the philosophy of the hierarchy is, in the main, the beatification of the *status quo,* a doctrine that rarely brings it into conflict with the business man's normal philosophy, departures from this norm will be authorized by the authorities of the Church rather than by the clergy in conjunction with the laity.

So that, in the last analysis, however different be the source and origins of the Roman Catholic outlook, its results are not very different

---

[49] See Walter Elliott, *The Life of Father Hecker* (New York: Columbus Press, 1891).

[50] J. A. Ryan and Moorhouse F. X. Millar, *The State and the Church* (New York: Macmillan, 1922).

[51] *Cf.* the brilliant book of Kirsopp Lake, *Paul, His Heritage and Legacy* (New York: Oxford, 1934).

in outcome from those of the major Protestant denominations. Each, so to say, makes its peace with the contemporary character of society in the different generations, partly because any revolutionary teaching on its part might jeopardize the security and stability of the property it has to defend, and partly because of its constant recollection that the kingdom it is striving to attain is "not of this world," which makes it avoid any excessive search to answer the material problems of the here and now. Each proclaims with vigour its concern with a general moral outlook rather than with a particular reflection of that outlook in immediate and specific remedies. Each is emphatic that the social order is the sum of the particular individual citizens who constitute it, and that the improvement of the social order follows, and does not lead, the moral improvement of the individual members who find, with the aid of grace, which the Church enables them to discover, the path to the Kingdom of God. Each has largely changed from emphasis upon doctrinal principle to emphasis on social attitude. Each is deeply hostile to any policy which may lead to a test of relative power between opposing groups, and each argues that, rightly surveyed, there is a higher common interest between them which is founded, no doubt within the frame of moral values provided by the Churches, by those to whom the State power is entrusted. This outlook is even shared by the remoter sects whose beliefs are exotic and whose membership is small. Overwhelmingly, as in Gaston County, North Carolina, they represent the men and women who have passed, or are passing, beyond the chance of worldly success. But what they then do is make a virtue of necessity, and argue the irrelevance of, even the antagonism between, worldly success and salvation. They are then able to maintain that their very failures in material life set them free to devote themselves to those unearthly considerations upon which they build as they ascend into the Kingdom of Heaven.

I have pointed out how immense is the aid given by all this to the protection of the conventional. The Churches are perhaps the most important influence in the social process of stabilizing the behaviour of men and women with little to gain and, not seldom, much to lose by challenge of the ruling ideas the governors of America impose. No doubt the largest Church of all is the Church of the Indifferent; but by choosing not to choose, they enable the opposition to the Churches to be at a minimum. No doubt, also, most cities of considerable size possess small groups of free-thinkers who may, on occasion, raise their voices; but behind the massive chorus of the Churches' claim, it is unlikely that their voice is widely heard. In any case, they rarely fight for political office of importance, and, if they did, the knowledge of their infidelity would be a long step to their defeat. The result is the simple one that whatever be the acerbity, and it is often harsh, of interdenominational rivalry, the vital fact is that the main influence of the Churches is on the side of the business rulers of America. That is expected, and, in general, it is welcomed; even the president of the American Federation of

Labor will prove the regularity of his Americanism by making apparent, like Mr. J. P. Morgan, his loyalty to, and his affection for, the Church of his youth; while Theodore Roosevelt, when he dismissed Thomas Paine as a "filthy little atheist"—a summary which was not only untrue but strangely conflicted with the strikingly different judgment of General Washington who knew what he owed to Paine—must have been well aware that he was sacrificing the duty of honesty to the hope of popularity. The fact that Jefferson's deism and the doubt of Lincoln's religious outlook are things the discussion of which are hardly delicate in America, save in small scholarly circles whose findings do not reach the multitude, suggests that the separation of Church and State has not prevented the former from becoming the moral agent of the latter. Respect for the Churches in America is not merely an act of courtesy from a secular society to religious organizations; it is a profound vote of thanks from a social order with limited objectives to bodies without the influence of which their objectives might have been scrutinized much earlier and their limits vigorously questioned. For even the main critics of the American idea have been mostly men who drew a different inference from the same religious postulates as their opponents. They only lacked the means and the staying power to maintain the work of critical examination.

5

To WHAT conclusions does this examination lead? No one can doubt for one moment the immense power of the Churches in American life. They have inspired a great deal of invaluable social work. They have given immeasurable consolation to millions. Until almost the beginning of the nineteenth century they were the main driving-power behind the demand for wider educational facilities. In Jonathan Edwards they produced one of the outstanding figures in American thought; and in Channing and Theodore Parker, two men who will always have, if a secondary, still a significant, place there. The evangelical work of the Churches on the frontier did much to mitigate the harshness and loneliness of its life, and to temper the rugged individualism it produced to the atmosphere which eases the building of social relationships. They have done something, though less than might have been expected, for learning in theology and philosophy; and they have done something less for history, whether in the realm of American experience or in the wider theatre of the world. They have acted as a kind of aura to give the sanction of tradition to modes of behaviour struggling against the increasing change which is the one permanent feature of American civilization. Of their large-scale missionary enterprise abroad, especially in the Far East and in the Levant, I am not competent to speak; I can note only my own sense that, however it be valued, no one can read the record without being impressed by the heroism and devotion of many of the selfless men and women who gave all their lives to this calling.

Yet the central question is what the main function of the American Churches has been in the complex civilization in which they operate. I do not think this can be answered except by saying that they have been one of the outstanding influences for securing the acquiescence of citizens in the existing social order of any particular time. There are noble exceptions, yet generally they have given support to values which the relations of production made it necessary to impose. They have followed the emergence of those values with their approval rather than sought to challenge them or to transform them. They have adapted themselves to the world about them rather than sought to change it. They have rarely been notable, as organizations, for audacity or experiment. They could be Abolitionists in the North, while they accommodated themselves to slavery in the South. After the Civil War they could accept Negro citizenship, in a fairly genuine way, in the North and the West without seeking to disturb the denial of its reality in the South. They have seen without anger conditions in certain industries which were virtually no different from peonage. There are few evils in American life which they have not either condoned or been anxious to disregard. They have rarely challenged the powerful or fought with decisive passion against the abuse of power. For the most part they have been content to voice high maxims of platitudinous morality, while declaring that concern for their social application in given instances would be to enter a political realm in which they had no place. So that their role, taken by and large, was either service to the existing order by urging devotion to it, or service to it by helping its victims to find consolation in the visions of another world. There has never been that gap between the standard of the Churches and the standard of the secular world which has put the latter on the defensive before its critics.

Nor is there serious evidence that Church principles have produced a higher level of social behaviour in believers than in either the indifferent or the unbelievers. The supposition that the Churches provide a sanction for moral conduct without which the community would suffer grave injury is at no point borne out by American experience. On the contrary, there is a good deal of evidence to suggest that there is no Church in the United States which has not been generally willing to accommodate its habits to the acquisition of temporal power. Where it has been able to secure magnificent buildings, it has explained its pride in their possession as joy in a habitation worthy of its Divine mission; where it has had to be satisfied with a poor and shabby edifice, it has been emphatic that asceticism is the fulfilment of the will of God. The Roman Catholic Church apart, most Churches in America have, in greater or lesser degree, adapted every technique known to the art of advertising as though the commodity they had to sell was an automobile or a wireless set; indeed, the passion to be "up to date" in their method of appeal has been one of the curses with which the Churches have been inflicted ever since the immense potentialities of advertising have been realized. The proportion of the professional personnel in the Churches who have been adequately trained for their work has always, however remarkable the exceptions, been pretty small; and the proportion of their members who really understand their teaching is smaller still. They have had to accept the great limitation of ecclesiastical claims on social leisure in every generation as competing methods of occupation have been introduced; but, in general, rather than risk a conflict in which they feared defeat, they have sought to adapt the new methods to their own use so as to give them some degree of religious tinge. They have not even dared to rival the automobile; and their relation to the movies and to literature has been partly to ask for a share in their censorship—in which the success of the Roman Catholic Church has been remarkable—and partly to use the more serious films as a topic upon which to preach, in the hope that thereby they would draw a larger audience to their sermons in the morning or evening of Sunday. Innumerable discussions at conventions make evident their declining hold on youth; and the Lynds' account of their influence on the youth of Middletown [52] suggests less the ability to arouse interest and attention than the acceptance of a more or less conventional ritual which both sides are aware will largely disappear with the advent of the age of accepted maturity.

In general, though by no means invariably, the Churches accept the secular standards of success. A higher salary is a better index than a lower; a large congregation is better than a small; a big subscriber to Church funds will have more influence in its activities than a small subscriber. Only too well aware of the pressure of the outside world, the Church that can afford it organizes itself as closely as possible on the successful activities of the outside world. The Church social is more like the "junior prom" if it can afford it; the member of social distinction gives a lunch or a reception or a dance to the more suitable of its members, if she can be persuaded to do so; the nationally known lecturer is invited, if his fee can be paid, to its forum in much the same way as a successful lecturer or a novelist or even a poet makes a nation-wide tour of the women's clubs as a regular part of his function. Even prayer becomes directed sometimes to objects it is difficult not to describe as secular, as when its efficacy is tested by being used on behalf of the basketball team of a local school. And the richer Churches foster a whole host of auxiliary organizations, mostly permeated, like the Y.M.C.A. and Y.W.C.A., with the hope that they will prove by their provisions of a cheap hostel and cheap athletic facilities an avenue through which the young man or woman may almost insensibly pass into a half-conscious acceptance of Church membership as the central thread round which he builds his life. If there is pacifism in every Church, sometimes pervasive enough to include a majority of its members, as a rule its dogmas will be compatible both with the attitude of a conscientious objector, pro-

[52] *Middletown*, Chap. VIII.

vided that his conscience is immovable, and the young man who accepts combatant service as a moral obligation.

The type of clergy, moreover, especially in the urban areas, is undergoing a change. He is now, increasingly, someone with whom an average business man will enjoy a good talk. He is unlikely to be a stern dogmatist like Andrews Norton, or a Utopian idealist like Washington Gladden. He regards it as a victory for Christ to be elected to the local country club, if he can afford it, or if some rich member undertakes to pay his dues. He is a Rotarian or a Kiwani. He is interested in the local dramatic society. He confesses to his pleasure in his weekly golfing. He may take his glass of whisky with the rest. He will "boost" his town and its advantages. He will develop a pride in its local men of substance. He will have all the proper suspicions of politicians. He will tell you, with some emotion, how the heaven-sent integrity of his Church member who keeps the local bank enabled him to keep it open despite the depression of 1933. He descries a stranger at one of his services almost as quickly as the manager of a local department store is aware of a new customer. In a fairly small town he tries to know, or be known by, everyone; and he is always anxious to convey the impression that his first anxiety is his service. He feels it his duty to serve on every possible local committee, and to get a name among the more substantial citizens as a really practical man. He "keeps in," so far as he can, with the local editors, for none knows better than he the importance of the quarter-column report of his Sunday sermon, which he takes care to send in on Friday or Saturday. He has, also, far less time for reading than he would wish; parochial duties, civic committees, the social round, take up so much of his time that he is unlikely to have read any difficult book through, unless it is one the discussion of which is expected of him as a guide to others. He agrees that there are many evils still to be cured in the United States; but he is always deeply impressed, first, by the immense advances that have taken place since he was a boy, and, second, by the far greater power and responsibility the United States has won among the nations of the world. The future, he is clear, lies with America; and, if he has a literary turn, he will quote you with some unction Bishop Berkeley's famous line about the westward course of empire.

He is a little disturbed at the indiscipline of the young; he would like to strengthen the ties of family relationship. He may even regret the disappearance of the quiet evenings with one's parents that were usual when he was their age. He deplores the failure of the "noble experiment," but, in a metropolitan centre, is likely to agree that it was breeding disrespect for the law. If he is tolerant and open-minded, he may tell you that he warmly approves of labour unions, so long as they do not make their members discontented or turn their minds to violence. He is likely to deplore all strikes; he is sure that independent arbitration, binding on both sides, would have a far more fruitful result. He agrees that "social justice" is terribly important; but he is not, with incredibly rare exceptions, a socialist, partly because when he went to college he learned to distrust all "isms" in Sociology A, and partly because it seems such a heavy count against socialism either that its devotees tend to be infidels, or that a member of his congregation, one of his trustees, in fact, who is a wealthy industrialist and a "deep student," has told him that it is simply the creed of the unsuccessful who have been made envious by frustration. He speaks with abhorrence of violence, and especially of the Russian Revolution, to whose godlessness he attributes all its mistakes. He is sure that the main clue to a better social order must be, first of all, in the improvement of human nature in individuals. That, he is sure, is the special function of the Church, and he can give you at least half a dozen instances from his own congregation in which, where the recognition of sin has led to grace, a one-time selfish man, who, perhaps, neglected his business and his family for drink and gambling, now is generally recognized as one of the soundest men in town. He feels pretty confident that, if Heaven bless his work, and he is able to make the Gospel more widely known, he could do something real, however small, to prepare the coming of the Kingdom. Then, if his sphere be a small one, he is likely, according to temperament, either to tell you that by reason of its size, he really hopes he is making his influence felt, or that if he only had more far-reaching opportunities, there is so much more he could do. And, once more according to his temperament, he may speak of the pleasure or difficulty he finds in association with his fellow-ministers, in their zeal to co-operate, or in the back-biting by which they take advantage of one another.

"All the American clergy," wrote Tocqueville, "know and respect the intellectual supremacy exercised by the majority; they never sustain any but necessary conflicts with it; . . . they readily adopt the general opinions of their country and their age; and they allow themselves to be borne away without opposition in the current of feeling and opinion by which everything around them is carried along. . . . Public opinion is therefore never hostile to them; it rather supports and protects them; and their belief owes its authority at the same time to the strength which is its own, and to that which they borrow from the feelings of the majority." [53]

I do not think, with certain small reservations, that this could be more admirably put. What is astonishing, however, is the conclusion Tocqueville draws. "By respecting," he argues, "all democratic tendencies not absolutely contrary to herself, and by making use of several of them for her own purposes, religion sustains an advantageous struggle with that spirit of individual independence which is her most dangerous antagonist." Whether religion can, in this simple fashion, be equated with the Churches is obviously an issue upon which differences of opinion will be profound. What is, I think, quite obvious is that the "spirit of in-

[53] Tocqueville, *Democracy in America*, Vol. II, Chap. v.

dividual independence," of which Tocqueville speaks has, in fact, completely conquered the Churches, and what these respect are less "all democratic tendencies not absolutely contrary to herself," than the oligarchical tendencies which are the barrier to the expression of the idea of equality in the economic field. So far, this is to say, from the Churches permeating America with the religious spirit, America has permeated the Churches with the spirit of the successful man. And since the outstanding type of successful man is the business man, it is within the framework of ideas in which he moves that, in general, the Churches move also.

I do not, of course, suggest for one moment that there are not many, and important, individual exceptions to this rule; it is also the fact that the exceptions are individual exceptions. Once the main emphasis of the Churches moved from dogma to behaviour, they had either to accept the general conventions imposed by American conditions or fight those conventions. Individuals once more apart, I do not think it can be seriously denied that the Churches, in fact, accepted them. Nor is it a sufficient reply to this generalization to say that the Churches have built codes of desirable principles in the social field to which they have attached importance. What would have been a sufficient reply would have been the proof that the Churches have been continuously militant about them. That they have never sought to be. Indeed, one may go further and argue, with justification, that the real emphasis of the Churches has always been on the importance of a change of heart in the individual—this is especially true of the Roman Catholic Church—and that the implication of this attitude is an atomistic view of society which is incompatible with the nature of society itself. It is not really very helpful to religion if a Church is proud of Mr. Rockefeller's membership in it, or of Mr. Morgan's, if that membership shows no visible sign of exercising influence upon the social relations created by their enormous power. It is not really helpful, either, if the influence of the Churches, as with the more esoteric sects, is directed to offering salvation in the next world as a compensation for a failure here and now. For that means only that the esoteric Churches are preaching the same gospel of success in a different context and upon a different view of the significance of time. And to this, it may be added, that the Roman Catholic Church is, if indirectly, one of the strongest influences in the United States against any large-scale effort at change. For no Church is more anxious to preserve respect for authority, or more conscious that the collapse of authority in one sphere may lead to collapse in others. So that while no Church in America has more care for the salvation of its members, no Church with any power comparable to that of the Roman Catholic Church is less interested in salvation by works. There is not a great deal of difference between its relation to the government of the United States and the relation between the Empire and the Papacy until the time of Hildebrand. Like the Protestant Churches, the Catholic lays down the principles by which it stands in the social field; but, like the Protestant Churches also, it rarely shows signs of continuous militant concern about their application.

Whatever, therefore, be the weight to be attached to the exceptional men who have made a social gospel the chief concern of the Churches, the objective result of the work of the Churches has been to add an ecclesiastical aura to the American creed of success. No single influence in the United States, save the cinema in the last generation, has had the same authority in conditioning the ordinary American to the acceptance of that creed. In almost all their different roles, that is the real outcome of their functioning. It is true of the sermons; it is true of the social and charitable work of the Churches; perhaps, above all, it is true of their educational work. That is surely why so many of the social workers who begin with membership in a Church, who, not seldom, find in its teaching an inspiration to what begins as a genuinely missionary effort, rarely remain loyal in their allegiance to it. No doubt some of them retain a faith in some personal or impersonal power which works for the victory of justice over injustice in the world; but the vast majority find that allegiance incompatible with their recognition of the magnitude of the problem with which they deal, and the pitiful inability of their Church to play a real part in solving it. They feel, in short, that the Churches have no answer to the problem of evil in the context in which, as social workers, they have to grapple with it, and that the minister is more likely to evade than to accept any commitment which may compromise its position as a Church.

What Tocqueville did not realize when he argued that the Church maintains "an advantageous struggle" with "her most dangerous antagonist" was that he made two immense assumptions, neither of which he proved. The first was the assumption that the "spirit of individual independence" is normally operative in the average American in the field the Church seeks to occupy; and the second was that the "advantageous struggle" meant the spiritual enrichment of the individual in some sense that gave to him or to her the conviction of responsibility for his or her effort in the earthly life. But the truth surely is that most Americans have no more than a purely traditional acceptance of the convention that membership of a Church is a strong thread in the ordinary pattern of American living, that they accept it much as they accept the Constitution, or believe in the Democratic party if they live in Alabama or in the Republican party if they live in Vermont. Granted, as one obviously must grant, that the kind of spiritual enrichment of which Tocqueville speaks is a deep emotional experience the Churches are privileged to offer to many of their members, the overwhelming fact is that the conduct of Church members is not, on the evidence, any different in degree or kind from that of citizens who are not Church members. Any analysis of history outside the United States would, indeed, make it astonishing if the conduct were in fact different.

It seems to me, therefore, that the American evidence merely proves that in a mental climate like that of America, in which, as in most of the world since the French Revolution, the Church is either separate from the State power or its subordinate partner, ways and means will be found to make the Church, in all its forms, adjust itself to the ends which are implied in the relations of production in the United States. It is no more remarkable that an ardent member of a Church, like Theodore Parker, should seek in the name of his creed to build a better world, than that one who, like Paine or Jefferson, dissented from all Churches should engage in the same search in the name of the social philosophy he holds; just as it is no more remarkable that an ardent churchman, like Mr. Rockefeller, should be able to reconcile his business practices with acceptance of his duties as a Christian, than that Stephen Girard's commercial relentlessness can be connected with his profound hatred of the clergy of all denominations. Baptists like Daniel Sharp will speak of the duty of obedience on the part of the poor at the beginning of the nineteenth century [54] as Bishop Lawrence will identify the distribution of wealth with the Will of God at the beginning of the twentieth. An unestablished Roman Catholic Church in America will work patiently, if less obviously, for political influence in the same manner as an established Roman Catholic Church in Spain. American Lutheranism will show, if in less degree, the same kind of respect for established authority as it has shown in Germany. Once an American Church has become an institution which seeks property and hopes to grow in influence by extending its possessions, all the evidence suggests that, even if at one or two removes, it will reflect the habits and the standards of the political society within the framework of whose State power it seeks to move.

On a long-term view, I doubt very much whether the institutional religions of the United States, wherever they are based on some dogmatic interpretation of the universe, are likely to be able to evade decay. They cannot reconcile their claims with a life that grows ever more secular, and ever more remote from the historical results of the criticism which cuts, ever more sharply, the ground from under the foundations upon which any fixed doctrine rests. They find it ever more difficult to come to terms with science. The bareness, even the hollowness, of their metaphysical pretentions becomes ever more surely revealed. No doubt they are still a refuge for many who, unhappy, try to find an unassailable dogma upon which to build their right to consolation. No doubt, also, so long as they devote so much of their attention to those "good works" which are in a high degree the debt owed, but not paid, by social injustice to civil obligation, they will provide a background of emotional satisfaction to all who hope to find in charity an escape from the intolerable burden of thought imposed upon us all by the inadequacy of our civilization. No doubt, again, there will always be men and women who cannot face the universe unless they are convinced that its principles of organiza-

[54] Daniel Sharp, *On the Tendency of Evil Speaking Against Rulers* (Boston, 1828).

tion are not neutral but move under Divine inspiration to the unfolding of an ever greater good.

I venture to think that the American Churches, as a mass expression in American life, produce religiosity and not religion. For if by religion we mean that profound sense of an infinite universe so complex, so mysterious, so certain, as each of its immense problems are explained, to present us with new problems still more immense, its power to elevate is in the highest degree independent of historic dogma and the outcome of lonely meditation. Those who are able to reach beyond the petty cares of today or of tomorrow, who know that if faith gives comfort, reason leaves mystery beyond human penetration, know also, like Spinoza, that the fulfilment of the call to a deeper humility and a more profound elevation of spirit and of mind do not come from a participation in some formal ritual which is produced by some supposed history which, in the end, can never confront a critical analysis, nor from any temporary embodiment in a creed which has always to defend itself against some rival creed. The quality that is of the essence of a religion is the inner and passionate impulse which drives those who possess it beyond and above themselves to an elevation where they can conquer the immediate desire, and the temporary caprice, in their search for a fraternal relation with all who suffer and all who are broken by the tragedy of a pain they cannot face. Religion, in this sense, can never compromise with the world; it must be willing to break it or be broken by it rather than to yield the imperative passion in which it finds its supreme expression. It is not a spirit which makes for personal contentment. It is not even a spirit which believes that fame or knowledge or power can ever compensate for the surrender of that inner vision which persists in those who present it by the fact that its call is never denied.

This religion existed long before any of the historic religions were born, and it will live on long after many of them are dead. It has no institutions, no dogmas, no ritual, no priests; it is a spirit something of which is in the character of those who possess it, something of which, also, breaks into flame as that character meets experience of the world. Its possession is independent of greatness, whether of mental power or of social position, whether of wealth or of official dignity. If it is found in Socrates, it is found in Albert Schweitzer; it is unmistakable in that last supreme utterance of Vanzetti, as it is a light that gleams in the controlled, yet impressive, emotions the careful observer can find in many of the writings of Mr. Justice Brandeis. I do not know how to put it better than in those magic words of the man to whom we owe in its final recension the Book of Proverbs: "Where there is no vision, the people perish." [55] That vision, born of a moral sensitivity that invariably is compelling, will suffer sorrow or prison, exile or death, so long as it can communicate its insight to a world to whose hatred or whose anger it can respond with serenity or tolerance.

[55] Prov. 29:18.

I do not, of course, deny that religious men and women of this quality have been members of all American Churches; my point is the very different one that it has not been the function of the Churches to produce men and women of this kind. There is an earthy Philistinism about them, a regard for prudence, a careful diligence, a willingness to compromise with the powers that be, which are all bound to cloud the religious vision in the sense that I have sought to give it. The reason for this difference is that what William James called "the drift of the cosmic weather" in the United States made the Churches come to terms with the secular world on the terms imposed by that world. Indeed, I do not think it is unfairness or exaggeration to compare them with those curious cults of the later Roman empire which provided their votaries with a sanction at once for acquiescence and escape. Churches are bound to be, for the most part, a method by which their members are schooled to the acceptance of the world. Few of the religious qualities can attain full expression without danger to the secular standards prudence urges them to accept. They make peace with convention as the condition of survival in a world in which material success is the value which permits no rival to challenge its authority.

That is why I believe that the Churches in America have promoted religiosity but not religion. I mean by religiosity the support of the folklore of some specific social order by bringing to its general support the magic aid of an institution which claims its foundation in the will of God. The support can be achieved in different ways; those who rule may be defended as the embodiment of God's purpose. Or those who are poor and unsuccessful may be urged to the duty of submission, perhaps with assurance of compensation in the life to come. Or some given Church may itself be so organized that its interests, as a Church, cannot be separated from those of the secular community within whose boundaries and, therefore, under whose State power it operates. There can be little doubt, I think, that underneath the aid thus rendered there is the immense strength which arises from the traditional superstitions of many thousand years, of a conviction, at once conventional and uncritical in the ordinary member of the Church, that it has a magic power of mediation between the Divine will and human want, which goes back, as Robertson Smith has pointed out, through the worship of saints' relics to the pagan cults out of which that worship was born. No doubt we have moved a considerable distance from the *Respublica Christiana* of the medieval period, in which the conviction was almost universal that the saint could work magic for those who gave the appropriate reverence to him. But we have not lost the sense of authority in the Churches as the instruments through which the pattern of the right and just is woven. When, therefore, they add their power to a political community, they tend to impose on all their members to whom critical analysis, whether historical or metaphysical, is strange, something like the duty of an obedience so habitual and as authoritative as that which they bring to the faith they accept. Political allegiance becomes, as it were, a natural part of, or a corollary from, obedience to the Church. When, after the Reformation, the supremacy of political over ecclesiastical society became increasingly difficult to challenge, the Churches lived by the support of the State power, just as in the medieval world the secular ruler was supported by the sanction which the Church, as the guardian of Divine law, put behind him.

This is, I think, the central dynamic of the function performed by the American Churches when stripped of all but its essentials. They have ceased themselves to make the standards of value for the secular society about them; on the contrary, their own standards of value are given to them by the secular world. They are agents, no doubt powerful agents, in the task of maintaining a social order which is often resented, frequently attacked, and, often enough, so operated as to provoke open challenge from those who are excluded from its benefits. Their real, if half-hidden, function is to repress the critical faculty in their members. They affirm; they dogmatize; they expose a revelation which they insist can be denied only at the peril of salvation. In large degree they seek to divorce reason from experience; and thereby they put the minds of men in a mould or routine of which the result is normally an intellectual passivity before any issue which touches foundations. They create an atmosphere which tends to acquiescence in the habitual; and the outcome of this tendency is a persuasion to identify the habitual with the necessary.

The American Churches are thus a stabilizing influence in the community. But the stability they help to secure is of a special kind. To extend their influence, they must avert their eyes from whatever phenomena might endanger their power to expand. And in a large degree they have accepted the very criteria their theological premises should have compelled them to denounce. They have equated bigness with grandeur; they have made greatness a synonym of success. So that it is not excessive to argue that they have made the philosophy of the American business man an ideal to which they have lent the immense prestige they possess. That prestige has roots so ancient that few men have either the time or, perhaps, the will, to examine the soil in which the tree itself has grown. They inherit it as part of their environment; they look upon it, in Burke's famous phrase, as something they ought to venerate where they are unable presently to comprehend. It provides them with a code of behaviour against which they trespass only with trepidation. It seems to offer a clue to the meaning of life which might, otherwise, be difficult and alien and remote. So that what it approves helps them to decide between right and wrong without having to bear the intolerable burden of thought. Man, who is Nature's rebel, is tamed by the Churches to be the willing slave of the State power. And it is the central secret of their persistence that men are persuaded by its ministers to regard this slavery as the key to their salvation.

VIII

American Education

Nothing, perhaps, is more heroic in the American tradition than the faith in education and the passion to secure it. One can find that faith almost at the beginning of its history, as one can find it, hardly undiminished, at the present day. It has, no doubt, varied in scope and in intensity. Here, it has excluded the Negro from its ambit, there it has excluded the worker. Here, it has been regarded with suspicion and doubt, there it has been regarded as no more than the prelude to the serious business of living. The Americans are a serious and a practical people; to expect a nation which wrested civilization from nature to be interested in education merely for the sake of the play of the mind would be folly. It has been to them an intensely pragmatic matter, which trained citizens to perform adequately functions which were regarded as of significant value in American society. Education has been not the training of a gentleman, as so often in Europe, but the training of a clergyman, teacher, a doctor, later a lawyer or a business man, who could contribute the knowledge of some vocation the importance of which was widely accepted in the new civilization. That is not, of course, to say that education for the decorative use of leisure has ever been completely absent from the American scene, but it has never been its predominant strand, and it has always had to defend itself from a criticism which has never lacked in vividness. The American is fairly entitled to say that even the well-endowed dilettante has, until the twentieth century, been regarded as almost permanently on the defensive in the life of his civilization. Until the twentieth century the question: what has he made of his training? has always seemed a legitimate question to ask of the educated men.

The American passion for education has had one or two significant results from its very nature, and certain results by way of by-product that were also not without their importance. In its origins, it is difficult wholly to separate it from its quite specifically Puritan mould. It was to produce preachers, or to produce men, or even women, who could face life without fear and conquer it. If the aristocracy of New England or the South, the rich merchant or the owner of an imperial estate in New

York, seemed to have taken as their model the English nobleman with his books and pictures, his gardens and his hospitality, his need to have some place, even if a merely local place, in public affairs, his desire to be, if not a man of learning, at least a man of cultivation and taste, we must remember that the American version of the English original underwent an important change as it crossed the Atlantic. There was never a period in American history, until after the Civil War, when the functionless dilettante was a characteristic type. No doubt, though with remarkable exceptions, he was versatile rather than profound. But one usually discovers that there is some practical turn in his versatility; it may be architecture or politics, natural history or agricultural experiment; the strain so inescapably American is there. For he is not a member of a closed society, and he has to understand trade and commerce to live successfully enough to be sure of his ease; and this is especially the case when, as before the Revolution, he was so largely dependent on English production for the luxuries which were the proof of his status.

The American tradition is almost coeval with the provision of schools and colleges; there is the urge to education wherever there is a reasonably sized community with something like a stable life. But we must never forget that, alongside the school and the college, the tradition leaves an important place for men and women who have been trained only by conflict with life; who, because means or leisure or territorial situation were a difficulty, know little of the cultural heritage available. No doubt they absorbed something from the itinerant preachers; a few had access to such parish libraries as the zeal of men like James Blair founded; and there must have been relatively few households where the Bible and the popular almanacs were not read and discussed eagerly, even excitedly.

Out of all this there exists that strain in the American tradition which is easily convinced that respect for education goes much too far, that a man learns much more by what he does than any professional instruction can possibly give him. It is the obviously successful rather than the obviously profound who evoke the higher admiration from the average American. He is inclined to attribute Woodrow Wilson's mistakes to the fact that he was an unpractical university professor. He is not really sure that a man with desire for real distinction could rest content with the teacher's modest income or the sedate and sheltered life the vocation is supposed to imply for those who practise it. It is significant of certain values which remain an intensely American attitude that one of the main grounds against the New Deal of Franklin Roosevelt was the fact that so many of its experiments had their source in the ideas of university teachers who could not, it was axiomatically assumed, know much, if anything, of the problems of real life.

American education, in fact, is set in the background of two principles which it has never been possible completely to reconcile. The first, and perhaps historically the older, is a faith in the social value of the mind disciplined by instruction to understand the world about it; the second, which was given its main emphasis after the Revolution by westward expansion, is the belief that once the adolescent can read and write and has mastered the simple mysteries of arithmetic, life itself is the best school to which he can be sent. The second view has, at the level represented by an age between fourteen and eighteen years, had to give way slowly but persistently to the demand for general and compulsory education for all children; while on the level of higher education, it has been weakened, though by no means destroyed, partly by the growing recognition that a college education can have certain real benefits, both material and immaterial; and partly, perhaps mainly, by the increasing recognition that certain vocations—medicine, for example, or scientific research, or architecture, or, though in a less degree, the law—are better practised by men and women who have behind them training at an academically satisfactory standard than by either the self-taught or by the older apprentice system which, as in all the subjects, especially law, that I have mentioned, lingered and still lingers in the United States.

The persistence of the two principles is quite easy to understand. The first owes its dynamic in part to the psychological inheritance from Renaissance and Reformation Europe, which is a vitally formative element in the American tradition; in part to the deep, almost religious faith in democracy and progress, with its continually growing emphasis upon the right to equal opportunity; and, in part again, especially after the Jacksonian period, to the widening volume of agreement that it was incompatible with American ideals to divide the community into the ignorant many and the cultivated few. So, for example, the eminent inventor S. F. B. Morse denounced in 1828 the unhealthiness of a society in which the artist was dependent on the patronage of the wealthy few; the integrity of American art depended upon making it the outcome of a genuine and widespread popular understanding. So, also, Robert Dale Owen could tell Congress, in 1846, that the zeal for knowledge must reach not "scholars and students alone . . . but the minds and hearts of the masses." There is, after 1830, an amazing growth of the appetite for self-culture. After the famous Massachusetts Act of 1837—which required the state to set up a Board of Education with an official responsible for enforcing and improving the school laws, which, as early as 1827, had required each large town to maintain a free high school—the urgency of men like Horace Mann and Henry Barnard, Calvin Stowe and Caleb Wiley, persuaded state after state to follow the example of Massachusetts. No doubt the progress was slow; state provision for the education of the poor was confined to New York and Massachusetts in 1830; by 1850 it is improbable that more than half of the New England children received free education; while in the North and the West it varied between one-sixth and one-seventh, and in the South and the Southwest it was, naturally, lower still. But if it was still the habit of the rich to send their children to private schools, it is nevertheless true that well before the Civil War state schools were beginning to be institutions in which the children of the poor and the children of the rich could mingle on equal terms. The free school had already ceased to be thought of in terms of charity.

Not, indeed, that the argument for free, much less for compulsory, education, made its way without difficulty. Some of the wealthy men who could provide an education for their own children at private schools saw no reason why they should pay taxes to educate the children of the poor. Sometimes they argued that free education was a form of pauperization which undermined family responsibilities. Sometimes they objected on religious grounds : the school would be a source of infidelity. Sometimes they insisted that a numerous class of educated workmen would, by providing a source of industrial discontent, threaten the prosperity of the nation. Edward Everett, president of Harvard University from 1846 to 1849, was in favour of the free school system. But he wanted it fully understood that he favoured it on grounds of expediency only ; he thought there was no more right to free schooling than there was to free tailoring. Others thought the training a free school could offer would merely breed pride, in proportion to that little learning which would be a contempt for real learning. Others were sure that popular education was the first step on the dangerous road to socialism. Not least important was the attitude of the self-made man like Daniel Drew whose success was won despite the absence of all but a very limited formal education. "I didn't get very much schooling," he told his Boswell. "Somehow never took to it. I always got spelled down the very first time around, but I never minded that very much." [1] Mr. Drew was far from exceptional in his class ; and one cannot even count the books and articles which drew a stern moral from the dramatic facts that Andrew Jackson and Abraham Lincoln were both virtually self-educated men.

Physical conditions added to the problem. Means of communication were for long incomplete. Communities were small, with large distances between the schoolhouse and the farm ; resources were too slender to pay a trained teacher, or any kind of teacher, for more than a few months in the year, and the teacher was only too likely to be in process of passage to another and better-paid vocation ; and the nearer one got to the frontier, the more the child was an economic asset whose time could not be spared for "unnecessary book-learning." Nor must one forget the power of those religious denominations, always with some influence, and sometimes really powerful, which thought education the road to scepticism unless it was in their own hands—this has always been true of the Roman Catholic Church in America—or, alternatively, insisted that what was important was salvation, and that there was nothing to prove, and a good deal to disprove, that the school was the gateway to salvation. If some business men argued that an educated working class was more sober, more industrious, more thrifty, and therefore more dependable than one without

[1] Bouck White, *The Book of Daniel Drew* (New York: Doubleday, Page, 1910), p. 8.

education, there was an equal number of business men on the other side to insist that the better-trained workingman was far less fit than the illiterate for the workshop or the factory or the construction of railroads, and they thought that where, as with foremen, for instance, some smattering of education was needed, the necessary numbers could always be found without laying the burden of a taxation, which was certain to increase, upon industrial enterprise slowly fighting its way to stability. There is even evidence to show that in their eagerness to establish themselves financially a significant proportion of the early working-class emigrants from Europe had no special anxiety to see education too general or too well administered.

In the end, of course, the reformers won; but it is important, at the outset, to realize the partial and fragmentary character of their victory. The American Constitution makes education a matter for the states to plan, and though the federal government has sought, especially in recent years, to give both encouragement and aid to the backward areas, there is still nothing like a national minimum standard of education in the United States. There is usually a big gap between rural and urban education. There are hundreds of thousands of children, especially the children of Negroes, of migratory workers, of sharecroppers, who either get no education at all or an education so interstitial and fragmentary that they grow up hardly possessed of simple literacy, not seldom unable to cross its boundaries. There are states in which the formal provisions for schooling exist on paper, but in which the equipment or the teachers are utterly inadequate. There are states in which teachers' salaries are so low that it can only be by accident that a school attracts a teacher with any proper training. The degree to which this is the case can be seen from the fact that in 1943 more than one hundred thousand teachers left the schools in the Southern states to find work in the war factories of the West and the Northwest. There are the religious complications involved in a parochial school system like that of Massachusetts or of Oregon; in both these states the educational standards fall far below, at least on the average, the standard of the ordinary public schools. And there are, not seldom, grave political complications which result in the schools being made the victims of the dominant political machine in city or state, with the superintendent of education as the instrument of the machine.

Yet there is no doubt at all of the deep enthusiasm for education in the United States, not least among the working class. A high percentage of the children go to primary school, a very large percentage go to high school; while the appeal of the college education is now so great that, as I shall show later, it raises far more problems than most of the institutions of higher learning have been able to solve. The economic factor, of course, remains decisive at every stage. Scores of thousands who would like to get more education leave school because the parental income is too low and they must earn a living. or because there are social standards in matters like dress, or games, or clubs, beyond the reach of that income and entailing unhappiness and frustration in the child unable to conform to them. Children in large families tend to leave school on pecuniary grounds earlier than children in small families. In a sample I have taken in three schools of a city of a northwestern state, amounting in all to over three thousand children, it was clear that Italian, Irish, and Polish children left school at least a year earlier than the children of Scandinavian, German, or British parentage. The Roman Catholic child left two years earlier than the Protestant child. The child of the solid workingman, with the safeguard of a craftsman's skill behind him, usually stayed up to at least a year longer than the child of a clerical worker in one of the lower "white collar" vocations.

As one looks at the public school system of America, the first generalization one is tempted to make is that it is not a system at all and that no generalizations about it are true. There are schools so magnificent that both their architecture and equipment take one's breath away; and there are schools so mean and pitiful, usually in the South and most often deemed good enough for Negro children, that even some of the blacklisted schools of London are admirable by comparison. There are exciting experimental schools, in which teachers and taught alike are infected with the enthusiasm of their innovation; and there are schools where, despite the fact that all the teachers are trained, the atmosphere is dull and faded, the communication of a routine in which the teacher has ceased to be interested. The pupils, whose attention is rarely arrested, show an inner weariness which is always so easy to detect. There are high schools where one feels at once the impressive stimulus of a principal's remarkable personality; where the teachers are a real team, the material used, such as textbooks, vital and stimulating, the environment so alive that one can see the pleasure taken by the students in their own effort. Yet I have visited high schools a small distance away from the type I have just described where the inertia and apathy are obvious alike in the principal and his colleagues; where it is apparent that the attention of the children has rarely, if ever, been arrested; and where the discipline of the classroom is so lax that what there is of it is less the outcome of co-operation between teachers and taught than the outcome of fear. I have seen, on the other hand, a Negro high school in a Southern state where the building was poor, a considerable proportion of the children badly dressed and undernourished, the principal himself, a university graduate, receiving a salary lower than an elementary schoolteacher in the public schools of New York City, where there was no class with less than sixty children, which yet won an ardour of challenging response from its pupils that was only less remarkable than the chorus of praise the school received from the parents of the children who were taught there. I heard a history lesson for the highest grade on the causes of the Civil War which, in its grasp of significant fact and the sheer artistry of its presentation, was beyond all praise. Only twice in my own experience have I heard and seen teaching of comparable quality, or teaching so effective in eliciting so immediate an intellectual excitement from the children to whom it was addressed. They were not hearing about the Civil War, but living in the midst of the confused chaos of tragedy and hope it had meant to the generation which fought it.

In so complicated and confused a scene it is therefore rash almost to the point of folly to reach any large conclusions. New York State alone has 11,400 schools, some 80,000 teachers, and 2,250,000 children in the schools; and this is apart from the great number of private schools in the state. On every schoolday, the taxpayers of New York spend almost two million dollars on its schools. Involved in the wise use of this immense sum is the future behaviour and civic quality of the next generation of New York citizens. Perhaps only two other states, California and Wisconsin, rival New York in the effort it makes on behalf of education. But all the forty-eight states, in their different ways and at their different levels, are engaged in the same task of trying to help their children to face the world in which they will have to live in an adequate way. They seek to provide schools which will enable the children who attend them to acquire some knowledge, but, even more, to learn how knowledge is acquired, to understand the tools and the institutions by which man has sought to adapt the world to his needs and wants. The school seeks to teach the art of living together, the way to evoke the capacity to use one's brains, the building of character, the grasp of that complicated and elusive ideal, the American way of life.

The schools, of course, do not make this attempt alone. There is no element in the community in which the child lives that does not make its contribution. His home, his friends, his Church, the way he uses his leisure, the life about him, the impact on his senses, of things seen and heard, the myriad calls of a great city, the changing changelessness of country life, all these make the same attempt whether it be conscious or unconscious. The child who grew up in the world before 1914 met an experience in school qualitatively different from that of the child who grew up in the world after 1929; he encountered different traditions and different values. It is obviously one thing to fit a child for a world that seems stable, where relatively there are, as a result, a fair measure of security and an expectation that normally one may fulfil one's reasonable hopes. It is, not less obviously, a very different thing to fit a child for a world in which the First World War leads to the Great Depression, and the Great Depression to the Second World War. A child born in 1904 would have encountered the entrance of the United States into the First World War with something akin to the shattering experience of an earthquake; a child born in 1924, might well, given quick intelligence, have realized from the Munich tragedy of 1938 that by the time he would be seventeen years of age he would be marching to a war of which none could measure the consequences. It is obvious that the schools must educate for a changing world, adjust themselves to values which are the outcome of the fact that the cosmos of the generation before 1914 has become something near a chaos today. Certainly there is hardly a vital element in the American tradition which is set in the perspective it possessed for a man or woman who is now fifty years old. Have American schools met this challenge with success?

2

I DO not think most serious observers would deny that, even though there be many and even distinguished exceptions, American education has not met the challenge with a success proportionate to its intensity. Granted all the additional expenditure, granted a teaching force of greater adequacy and generally high devotion, granted far more careful and extensive educational research, granted higher standards of medical care and psychological knowledge of the mind in childhood and in adolescence, most people with knowledge would say that the schools have seriously failed to keep up with life. It is, I think, a matter of common agreement that too large a proportion of the youth leaving school has not been made ready for the world they must enter. They find it too hard to cope with the problem of earning a living, in part because they have too rarely discovered what they are fitted to do, and in part because their training has not made them elastic enough to escape without frustration from their mistakes. Too many who go on to the higher levels of training are not yet mature enough for the intellectual burden it entails, even when they have been certified as so ready. And a disturbing proportion of them enter the period of maturity with a remarkable unawareness of the civic context of their lives and their own deep need to understand it for their own sakes.

These are, of course, large assumptions, for the proof of which I can refer only to the vast critical literature of the past twenty years. No one, certainly, can read the immense and vital discussion which has grown out of the great challenge flung down by John Dewey nearly half a century ago to the American school system without seeing that it has not yet been answered. It is not only that the school curriculum is not flexible enough for the variety of types with which it has to deal. It has not, in addition, undergone that thorough adaptation to new economic and social conditions which is required. It has not yet made a serious training for citizenship the natural outcome of the environment it attempts to create. There has been far too large a gap between the content of what is being taught and the immense body of new knowledge, both of natural and of social science, which has reshaped the contours of our world. And there has been quite ineffective recognition, first, of the changed position, as compared with fifty, or even thirty, years ago, that institutions like the family and the Church, the movie and the motorcar, occupy in the life of youth. Nor, in the age of machine technology, has there been sufficient recognition of the fact that preparation for the creative use of leisure in the middle years of life is, in a sense, one of the most important guides to living the American school can set itself to provide.

Above all, it may fairly be argued, there is no agreement among American educators, still less among American citizens in general, about the end at which the schools should aim. There undoubtedly is a great deal of experiment, often finely conceived and imaginatively carried out, but it is rarely experiment that is clearly envisaged as having a national bearing, still less as needing the test of continuous and widespread application. There are fashionable modes like the Gary plan, which have their brief but crowded hour of glorious life; but when their hour is over, they are rarely heard of again. There are conferences without end, nation-wide conferences, state conferences, city conferences, mixed conferences of teachers and parents, teachers and administrators, parents and administrators; mostly, after a mass of fervent rhetoric, they boil down to the agreement that something must be done. But as soon as a demand is made for precise definition of what should be done, it becomes clear that there are wide disparities of opinion. Men like Kilpatrick and Counts, working under the original inspiration of Dewey, have no doubt that the supreme task of the schools is to prepare the way for a new social order; others look upon this task with a kindly scepticism; others, again, insist that the main function of the schools is to safeguard the tried and tested "American values." Others, once more, taking their cue from the approach to college training of Professor Hutchins and his followers, really doubt whether a genuinely democratic education is possible at all; they restrict their interests to the training of an *élite,* the members of which are alone capable of understanding fundamental issues. Yet others are convinced, like Mr. Thurman Arnold, that all political societies live by their successful mythologies, and that all education can do is persuade a small number to see through these mythologies without repining. Still others, especially in the authoritarian religions, are convinced that the ethos of the whole modern effort is one great mistake, and that the real need is to use the schools to concentrate attention upon "eternal" values. But no one religion is eager to agree with any other about what should be regarded as the eternal values. Certainly they are not the same, nor verified by the same source, in Boston, Massachusetts, as in Memphis, Tennessee.

In England, about ninety-eight per cent of the available children go to school up to the compulsory leaving age of fourteen, with a similar percentage in New York until fifteen. After that age, the English figures are only half those of New York, and in university training only about one-third as large. The growing American tendency everywhere is the same, with the result that, the Soviet Union apart, a larger proportion of youth over fifteen does two more years of school. But, at the high school level, less than twenty per cent either plan, or are able, to go on to college, though the curriculum has nothing so much in view as the preparation for college. The result is, of course, that this curriculum rarely meets the needs of those four-fifths of high school students who are unlikely to have any formal education after high school. Their real need is, first, to learn how to believe in, and to fit themselves for, citizenship in a democratic society, together with some vocational education set in a humanistic background. And this real need is the more intense, the greater the volume of juvenile employment. For if the boy or girl, especially the city boy or girl, cannot find interest in school, and may be, wartime apart, without a job for a period from one to three years, urbanism is a threat to their morale; and it is still more of a threat to the perhaps thirty thousand boys and girls who drift each year from the farm to the unknown city because of the lack of opportunity for work in rural areas. All kinds of attempts have been made, like the Civilian Conservation Camps, the work projects of the National Youth Administration, the 4-H Clubs, and so on, to find that combination of work and training which will keep youth steady and keen. But after a promising initial start they have shrunk to a small proportion of what their founders intended, on financial grounds. The result is a real abyss between drifting away from high school and finding steady work, which no method has yet been able to bridge.

If anyone were to examine the 1930 census of occupations in New York State, of those who were sixteen years and over he would find fourteen per cent were unemployed, and twenty-six per cent were married women looking after their own homes. A bare five per cent were in agriculture, rather more than fifteen per cent in trade, thirty-four per cent in manufacturing, twelve per cent in domestic service, eight per cent in the professions, and sixteen per cent in Civil Service positions or clerical employment. This is not a startling change from the previous census, though opportunity in agriculture has declined, and the chances in clerical work and occupations in which salesmanship is a part have increased. What is the function of the schools in relation to the people who set out for these careers around seventeen or eighteen years of age? They obviously dare not assume an unemployment percentage of fourteen. Equally, they dare not train the children from rural areas for careers that are declining in volume. They have little or no knowledge of what a boy or girl who does not train for a profession will be doing seven or eight years after the school period is over. If they try to build real craftsmen, they are bound to take account of the fact that the whole technological direction is towards the multiplication of the semi-skilled, with the really superior craftsman, if increasingly important, yet increasingly limited in number. Marketable value is coming to mean the power to adapt oneself swiftly to quite unexpected technical changes, the drift of which is to make the rapid learner of a repetitive and routine job the chief type of worker for whom there is a demand. Little in all this represents anything to which the American school system has given close attention; no one can look at its curricula and believe that the teachers who drew them up had more than the dimmest perception, if, indeed, they had any perception, of what the immense industrial revolution since the twenties has meant. And let us remember that this industrial revolution has been remarkably, if devastatingly, accelerated in tempo between 1939 and 1945, without the schools having had any chance of considering either the industrial revolution or the swifter tempo that is the outcome of the war. What are the schools to do?

The answer is given not merely by the critics of the present system, but by the facts themselves. Youth leaving school between fifteen and nineteen does not need, ought not, indeed, to be given some special technique which finds its immediate sale on the labour market and is thenceforward a frame within which it is enclosed until retirement from work. Youth needs a rough map of the universe, a training in the art of living with other people, a realization of what is meant by a world perpetually in flux, and an insight into the art of self-adaptation to the fact of change. Nothing is so ruinous either to mind or to character as premature specialization through an early emphasis on vocational training. Boys and girls are sent to school not to become bricklayers or shop assistants, clerks or typists, but men and women who can help to make democracy a living principle of action. The school has some eight or nine years in which to prepare them for this function. If the rulers are wise, they know that only in the last three or four years is the child likely to grasp the fact that knowledge in itself is interesting when it is significant, and that no educational scheme which aims simply at fitting the child, boy or girl, to earn a living can really communicate the sense that knowledge is significant. The school, therefore, ought not to make the preparation for earning a living anything more than a grasp of the general principles, economic and scientific, which underlie the opportunities to be encountered. The elaboration of the technique a special vocation requires is in part the outcome of its actual practice day by day, and in part the outcome of organized and deliberate post-entry training.

Any careful examination of the American school will show that this attitude is in a high degree exceptional. Either its work more or less stops at the point where youth begins work, before some such age as sixteen to eighteen, in which case its objective aim is the conditioning of youth to the world in which he must fight for his living, or, at its more advanced levels, it is a preparation for some entrance examination into college. But since more than eighty per cent of American youth does not go to college, citizenship training is a by-product of school efforts at a time when its urgency was never more striking. It is not only that knowledge advances at so immense a rate. It is not only, either, that a vast effort is made to "condition" the mind by a thick fog of propaganda which is not easily penetrated. Specialization has done much to increase intensity of knowledge at the expense of its breadth; the result is that it is harder than ever before to obtain a broad picture of the contemporary world which invests it with meaning for the child who, on entering it as an adult, has the hard task of becoming a responsible citizen.

The public schools of the United States have hardly yet begun to confront the implications of this position. The use of the new tools of education—the radio, the cinema, the illustrative chart, the photographic illustration, the gramophone record—are still rare. Teachers' salaries are still too low to attract the able and ambitious into the profession, save in the exceptional instances where they have a vocation that will not be denied. Most of the educational districts in the United States need drastic reorganization; they present immensely different opportunities, they complicate the problem of transportation, and they make far too difficult the problem of teacher-supply. Far too little attention is generally given to the full use of the basic intellectual instruments—reading, speech, writing, and arithmetic; it is, indeed, a fairly common experience for a university teacher to discover that few students at nineteen know how to read a whole book or to write with ease a coherent argument. There is far too little emphasis on the significance of the public library. There is still less attempt to utilize the opportunities of local museums and art galleries or of field excursions. The lack of free provision of such things as textbooks and kindred necessary supplies widely handicaps the poor children in every state. There is still an overcrowded curriculum, less integrated to have common relationship to an agreed objective than composed of bits and pieces added together, sometimes to satisfy some special, it may be passing, interest, and sometimes to placate some well-organized pressure group. There is still a nostalgic faith in the weirdly anachronistic "little red schoolhouse" of a by-gone era, while, alongside, schools are built to a fantastically luxurious plan, in which a good deal of the provision made is half-used or never used once they become going concerns. And state education is only too often either over-administered, so that the teachers are doing a mass of clerical work for which they have neither time nor interest; or under-administered, in which case no real capacity exists anywhere for measuring the efficiency of the school system.

There are other aspects of state school systems which are obviously in need of reorganization. Far too many of the normal schools are quite simply shoddy substitutes for a really adequate college education. Far too little effort is made, even within the boundaries of a single state, to organize the use by one normal school of the specialists from another. There is too little encouragement for the teacher either to improve his or her own standards, or to regard mobility, up to some such age as forty, as not less important than security. The degree, further, to which insecurity of tenure exists is indefensible to the point of outrage; and far too often it is made a means for making the teacher dependent on some special interest or the political machine in power in state or city. It is rare to find that the education departments of most states are seriously engaged in helping teachers to keep up with developments in their own subjects; there is too little communication about new material, too little co-operative effort to revise curricula, too little discussion about good and bad textbooks, or new and old. Nor is there much realization of the immense advantage to the teacher in almost every element of the vocation in working in a reasonable-sized school in a reasonable-sized district; the one-room or two-room school, still so typical even of states like New York, almost always means that the teacher suffers from want of companionship on the one hand, and quite inadequate living conditions on the other. Nor is any full-scale attempt made to give any but the very exceptional teacher either the chance of travel or the opportunity to do research.

To this I must add two other remarks. No one can examine with any care the school system of the average state or city without perceiving pretty quickly how real, if often impalpable, are the restrictions upon the teachers' freedom. The drive, conscious or unconscious, to enforce conformity to the code of conventional behaviour is overwhelming; and, as yet, there is no teachers' trade-unionism strong enough to offer security against its results. The average teacher must be perpetually on guard about his or her religious opinions, political opinions, economic opinions, social behaviour. He must be careful about the books or periodicals he encourages his pupils to read. He must too often be so guarded in utterance, in the common room as well as the school room, that he tends to lose the habit of spontaneity and develops a second self which becomes a mask for his inner personality; and unless he is a very exceptional man, the outward mask, like that of the hero in Max Beerbohm's *The Happy Hypocrite,* becomes the inner character. This is at least one of the outstanding reasons that the teaching profession has become the natural refuge for the shabby genteel; few people of vigorous character or with a passion for ideas will accept the inhibitions imposed by the combined force of administrative power and silent convention, and they tend to leave the world of teaching for a realm in which they can be themselves. What this pressure can be at its worst can be seen by anyone who reads the almost incredible minutes of evidence on teachers' loyalty before the Lusk Committee of the New York legislature after the First World War; and the mental climate revealed there is very far from being confined to New York.[2] Any close examination of material such as this makes it easy to understand the witchcraft trials at Salem in the seventeenth century; with the difference that in the modern state there are far too few who have, like Judge Sewall, the nobility of mind to confess in public the wrong for which they have been responsible.

The other remark that is, I think, worth making is that there is in the United States far too little research into educational problems that is at once co-ordinated and continuous. I do not for one moment mean that there is not an almost bewildering amount of educational research

[2] See Chafee, *Freedom of Speech.*

in the United States; indeed I doubt whether anyone could even hope to keep abreast, in any serious way, of the research undertaken by the members of Teachers College of Columbia University in a single year. I mean rather that there is no real attempt at a common effort to decide upon the problems which call for investigation, or to see that means are available to examine the results of research on the same plane not merely for America as a whole, but even for a region, the Southwestern states, or New England, or the Northwest states, at the same time. Not very much can be gained from a comparison of the annual reports of education boards or of superintendents, for the simple reasons, first, that they are rarely compiled upon the same basis, even the same statistical basis; and, second, that a change in the personnel of a board, or a new superintendent, may well mean a report based on new premises of interest, which makes it difficult and often impossible to follow through, from year to year, what happens in some particular aspect of school work. So that even when the brave and helpful effort of the Federal Commissioner of Education at Washington is borne in mind, it is literally impossible to paint even in the broadest outline a generally accurate picture of the state of American education at any given time. Far too much of the research done, not least in the university departments of education, is what may be termed personalistic research, by which I mean that its subject matter has been determined more by the interests of the would-be doctor of philosophy or his professor than by the inherent importance of the topic chosen; to which must be added that it is curiously rare directly to relate university research in education to the actual work of the city or state administration of schools in the area where the universities are situated. Nor does one often have so remarkable and illuminating a survey as the outstanding Board of Regents' Inquiry of 1940 into the character and cost of public education in the state of New York—a work that compares in quality with the famous Minority Report of the British Royal Commission on the Poor Laws of 1909. But what we really need is a whole series of similar studies for typical states in each region of America.

To this must be appended the note that, with all the general and genuine interest in education in the United States, it remains astonishing that so little is done to associate the public with the work of the schools. There is a gap one cannot fail to notice between the teachers and the public and between the administrators and the public. I do not mean by this an aloofness between the schools and the individual child's parents: that relation is usually good and mostly, I think, more genial and more helpful than it is in either Britain or in France, though less so than in the Scandinavian countries. I mean rather that there is a fund of experience and goodwill that could be mobilized for the protection and improvement of the schools which remains largely unevoked. Whether this is because of the natural tendency of a professional body to look askance at lay co-operation, or whether it is because most teachers' experience of interest from the public arises out of attack or suspicion from the local Chamber of Commerce, or the local branch of the American Legion, or some irate clergyman of a local Church resentful of teaching in some such subject as history or biology, I do not know. I can only note the curious failure to utilize a large fund of profound goodwill in any organized form, and to make the comment that it is a failure that deprives the professional educator of a great opportunity to transform unreflecting, into informed, enthusiasm.

3

FOR the overwhelming majority of American children the high school is the end of their formal education. It is, of course, natural that it should have changed so remarkably in the last half-century, for American life itself has changed very remarkably too. It is today a place for learning things ; but it is also a place which has usurped, in the activities it fosters after school hours, much of the time that was spent at home or in organizations like the Church some fifty years ago. It has made the cult of athletics in its various forms almost a kind of religion, not, indeed, that more than a small proportion of the boys or girls in high school actually play the games themselves. There is a small *élite* who form the school team, an *élite* of whose prowess the rest are applauding spectators, who can count on the right to prestige, whose rivalry with the teams from other schools will absorb not only the eager attention of their own schoolfellows, but of the general citizen body and even the local press. A good baseball or football player, may, indeed, be kept on in his high school by financial support from business men anxious that a school in the town in which they live may wrest a state championship from a rival school in another town. No inconsiderable part of a school's rating in the community will be derived from the athletic status it achieves in some popular game.

A high school may have its fraternities and sororities even though they do not have the formal name. They are social clubs which usually possess a prestige known, with careful precision, by every boy and girl at the school. Those with the highest prestige are bodies in which membership is sought with surprising ardour: perhaps nothing matters as much, except great athletic distinction, to the boys and girls. These clubs do little more than give tea parties in the houses of their members with two or three formal dances, perhaps elaborately staged at a local hotel, at commencement time or Christmas. But they are taken with astonishing seriousness. They are classed as indices of social distinction in much the same way as the clubs frequented by their elders. They enable the boy or girl to get on, to make significant contacts, to find a useful road towards some chosen career. Membership is very largely based on parental social standing, and this, as a rule, is a reflection of parental income. It is not easy for a boy or girl from a poor home to conform to the conventions of a group accustomed to dress well or to spend money freely: the exceptions tend to be those who are prominent in the school for other reasons, athletics, for example, or because their father is a popular preacher in a Church of high standing, or is an important official in the municipal service and therefore regarded as a desirable acquisition. Otherwise, the clubs seem like a premature classification of the adolescent into the groups to which they are expected to belong in adult life. The strata of the community are, as it were, projected into the life of the school.

There will be groups, too, which accrete about the studies taken in the school, science or engineering, a literary society, a debating club, which may well have its special "team" which will formally debate against "teams" from other schools. These manage to secure a diverse patronage, varying, as often as not, with the popularity in the school of the particular teacher who is its specialist in the subject. These groups have nothing like the prestige of the social clubs, though they often try to secure some crowded hour of glorious life by securing a lecture from some writer or scientist of note who may live near or be passing through the town. And most schools are likely to have one or more rather wan religious groups, which rise and fall with parental interest in some religious denomination. It is probable that there will be a dramatic club which puts on plays. There is a high school paper, and the annual year book of the school, the editors of both being chosen by the boys and girls themselves. There is the election of class officers, positions much sought after, especially in the last two years of high school, when a keen campaign is waged between rival candidates, with all the different groups to which each candidate belongs doing the utmost they can to prove their influence by securing the election of their nominee. There will also be groups which go regularly to the movies together and defend with passion the superiority of the film stars of their choice. Or there may be *ad hoc* groups to promote some competition, perhaps within the school, perhaps, with greater keenness, in competition with another school, in any subject from general knowledge to a spelling bee. There is likely to be a glee club and, in a school of any size, an orchestra. So various, indeed, are these extracurricular activities that the outsider is sometimes tempted to regard the studies of the school as just one more activity hastily sandwiched in between the rest.

In all this, there emerge two features which stand out in baffling contrast. There has never been an age in American history when the general belief in education was so widespread or so profound; even fifty years ago there was serious opposition in most states to compulsory education. Yet it does not appear that in any American high school the boys and girls attach importance to the possession of intellectual distinction by one of their number. The real title to importance belongs to the successful athlete; after that, it emerges in part from the impact of the extracurricular groups, and in part also to the fact of having exceptionally wealthy parents, or parents who, for one reason or another, have a socially prominent position in the community in which the school is placed. Nobody seems to attach particular importance to excellence in the subjects which the school is there to teach. Nobody even seems to imagine that the spinal column of the high school curriculum has much to do with life. The study of Greek and Latin, of course, has almost disappeared. The character of language-teaching in the colleges is virtually built on the assumption that the first-year undergraduate begins at very nearly the beginning. The reading of great literature for its own sake is rare; though I ought here to add that I have met boys and girls in the high schools of New York City to whom Melville and Tolstoy and Edgar Allan Poe were objects of a reverence it is difficult not to call religious. Few high school pupils embark upon their life careers with any serious insight into the forces which have shaped American, much less European or world, history. They have their heroes—Washington, Lincoln, Lee, Edison, and at one time Lindbergh. They know who is in the White House, or can say, with as much reason as their fathers, that they are Democrats or Republicans. They read, or skim, the daily paper, at least its sports page and film news, and almost invariably the "funnies"; perhaps they may follow with eager excitement some gangster mystery or notorious murder trial. They are quite likely to have a deep interest in some optional course offered by the school, accountancy or shorthand, home economics or elementary engineering; quite possibly they will really enjoy a course in the appreciation of music, or the hour each week they may devote to painting or modelling. All of them are likely to have had a course of study in civics in which the predominant emphasis was on the immense achievement of America, the width of the opportunities it offers, the duty of patriotism, the sacred right to individual property, and the folly of violence in the United States where every citizen can get what he wants by the use of the ballot-box.

The American parent is rare who knows enough of what his boy or girl is doing at high school to discuss with any intimacy the detailed study programme they follow. They have a fairly clear picture of the personalities of the men and women by whom they are taught; they remember enough of their own school days to be disturbed if the grades awarded are consistently on the border-line of failure. They have pride enough to like to hear of a warmly praised "theme" or essay, which they enjoy showing round to their intimates in the office or Rotary Club or the Kiwanis; they may even like to show a set of verses if only to hear the hoped-for comment: "Why, it's almost as good as Eddie Guest; it ought to be printed in the paper!" They recognize, especially the father, that they will have to advise the boy, perhaps the girl also, at seventeen or eighteen, about the choice of a career. But they know very little about the intimate life of either. A hurried meeting at breakfast, when the father is rapidly scanning the paper; a possible meeting at the evening meal, when both boy and girl are watching the clock anxiously not to be late for an appointment to dance, or go to the movies, or attend some extracurricular activity which enfolds the attention of either, for the wealthier groups a possible three or four weeks of daily contact on a summer holiday, where communion so largely depends on a common interest in golf or fishing or some other diversion, a communion which may be destroyed if—as often happens—the parents belong to the local country club, where they meet and play games by day, and bridge or poker by night, with friends of their own age; this is the normal intercourse of the present day between the two generations. Now and again, there may be a storm between father and son, or between mother and daughter; the children are out too late or too frequently; their home ought to be good enough for them; don't they ever do any work? Are they determined on failure in life? Or sudden crisis may, rather awkwardly but in a way that often proves a landmark in the life of both parent and child, compel them to throw down the barriers and talk like two human beings who recognize the need for a joint search for the right approach, to which affection will provide the key.

They are glad that their girl is good-looking or that their boy is asked everywhere because, by all odds, he is the best dancer in his class. They take pride in the speech he makes, or the violin solo she plays, on Commencement Day. They assume that what the boy or girl learns at school does not really matter very much. High school builds character. It enables their child to make friends who may one day be valuable. It teaches them the terms on which they must mingle with their fellows. They are likely to learn manners, and the importance of not straying too far from the conventional path. With luck, they may achieve enough prominence in school to come to the notice of someone in the life of the community whose later influence may be found valuable when it is sought. They get to know what it means to be an American, and the rough edges of personal idiosyncrasy are smoothed away. As a rule, parents may count upon the likelihood that, if their children have contempt for "highbrows," or think it must be "awful to be a teacher," thirty years after their graduation they will be stammering out much the same commonplaces to their own children as they themselves are painfully seeking to put into words; in short, they recognize with gratitude that the high school has done for their boy or girl about what they felt entitled to expect of it.

But, in fact, their expectation is too low, and it is too low because they have no clear perception of the purpose or the possibility of education. Their expectation is too low because they confuse preparation for getting a job with preparation for life in a democracy; they are satisfied with a half-understanding of what citizenship ought to mean. They consequently allow far too many forces to play upon the school which stunt its real potentialities. There is the force concerned with keeping down costs; that usually means teachers and teaching of inadequate standards. There is the force concerned with making the school an appendage of the existing pattern of economic interests; that too often means timid teaching, teaching that lacks drive and spontaneity and energy, and therefore the power to light a vital spark in the minds of children. And since this force so often has the power to operate through the machine of the party in power, it fails to make for an awareness of the kind of world into which the high school graduate will plunge when he begins to earn his living. There is the force which wants education, at all costs, to be "practical," and that has far too frequently meant the invasion of the curriculum by subjects like dress-making or shorthand or bookkeeping, which do not make for the thinking mind as do the more fundamental subjects. There is, too, the force which insists on judging the school achievement by relations and standards which are really irrelevant to its central purposes. It is a "good" school because the "best" people send their children there, or because its athletic record is remarkable, or because everyone speaks well of its dramatic club.

I think that the result is that the American parent too often mistakes sophistication for maturity. Both father and mother alike are hampered in their judgment by the acceptance on their own part of social values which by their very nature undo what a school, above all in a democracy, should set out to do. They want, in their own life, to "keep up with the Joneses"; they want their children to know the children whose parents they themselves want to know; they regard the real work of learning how to think, and how to begin using the apparatus of knowledge, as peripheral rather than central in importance. In the result, the boy or girl at the high school relies on the same kind of externalization of pleasure for the means to self-fulfilment as his parents. They do not want to be "left out" of things. They want, if possible, to be able to use a car; they want to have seen every movie that is talked about; they want, on their own plane, the kind of social distinction the parents want on theirs. Their conventional behaviour is nearly always considerably older than their intellectual development. They have learned too little to make a continuous effort at intellectual concentration. They are not quite sure that they respect intellectual distinction unless it is associated with material or with social success. Their training has rarely persuaded them of the importance of thinking for themselves, that interesting literature is not necessarily new, or that politics is something more than the efforts of the politicians or a "racket" in which one is necessarily involved if one wants to get something important done. They are too easily convinced that in real life most things are done by "pull," and that, accordingly, knowing the "right" people is one of the most important tasks before them. They are afraid of too much interest in literature or art or music; that leads to their risking the label of "highbrow" or "queer." They want to be known as good "mixers," the kind of person who is thought of as able to make a party a success, or to make some committee "go" which has the kind of purpose likely to be conventionally approved.

They are, so to speak, driven by the combined force of their training and their environment towards the social average, and the outstanding result is the difficulty with which they encounter non-conformity or scepticism in any area where they meet it. They go out into the world with a set of stereotypes which little save an earthquake can persuade them to examine critically. Yet their good qualities are unmistakable. They are kindly, cheerful, full of a diffused goodwill. They like doing things for themselves, whether it is mending a car, or hitch-hiking across the continent, or getting a job on their own, or finding out for themselves the inwardness of some novelty, especially a mechanical novelty, which has aroused their interest. Their vitality is abundant and fascinating. Except in the realm of speculative ideas, they are always willing to try some new experience. It is exceptional to find them without ambition, or pessimistic, or lacking in self-confidence. They have an eager if somewhat naïve faith in America, a pride in its bigness, even a sense of ease about its power. They are individualists in that special sense which the mental climate of America seems to breed; that is to say, they expect life to be a keen competitive struggle in which there is little give and take. They are restless young people, distrustful of equilibrium or serenity or the mood of reflection. They have vivid enthusiasms and an ardent capacity for hero worship. They plunge with vigour into the stream, and they assume that the swiftness of its movement is quite certain to be forward. They rarely, therefore, look backwards. The world began for them when their own memory began. Even the history of America is not so much a tale that is the prelude which explains their own life, as a tapestry on the wall at which they gaze with a certain pleasure because in one part or another they find a flash of inspiration. And, perhaps above all, they have an amazing capacity to weave for themselves the pattern of their life's adventure. They are still convinced that America is a land of pioneers; and they set out on their exploration with a good deal of the spirit of those who made the great western trek in the second third of the nineteenth century.

All of this is really to say no more than that the young people who emerge from the high schools of America are, above everything, a microcosm of adult America. They are moulded to the same ideas, prepared for the same ways of behaviour, trained for much the same careers. It should be added that they are no more moulded in a uniform pattern than the members of any other national community. They will have their eccentrics, their shy and reserved types, the boy with a passion for reading, the girl who wants to make a career of her own, as in any other society. Perhaps the two features in which they differ from other youth is in a certain superficial precocity and a tendency to regard abstract interests as strange. They have a good deal of information in a haphazard and rather ill-digested form. They are somewhat too likely to believe that the more they add to their information, the more they add to their knowledge. They are swift to judge, inclined to divide experience into the pleasant, which they equate with the exciting, and the unpleasant, which they equate with the uneasy mood of not knowing with certainty just what they are going to do next. Above all else, they are interested in today rather than yesterday, and in tomorrow rather than in today.

They have an intense belief in the folly of superfluous effort and in the short cut by which that effort can be saved. They are provided with a kind of realistic good sense, which leads them to come as quickly as may be to terms with a social order they think it a waste of time to challenge. Perhaps the thing most lacking in them is the sense of the need to scrutinize those inward recesses of the spirit deeper than any conventional formula for life. Only the few find that the highest intellectual passion comes to those who, after experiment with the formula of others, decide on the attempt to make their own.

4

HIGHER education in the United States probably occupies a larger place, as it is certainly more lavishly endowed, than in any other country in the modern world. American colleges exist by the hundreds, as students exist by the thousand. There is no end to the variety of type as there is no end to the material they seek to use. There are the great private universities with their several, perhaps many, thousand students, like Harvard and Columbia, Yale and Chicago. There are immense state universities, maintained by public funds, voted, as a rule, annually, by the state legislatures, like Minnesota and California, Wisconsin and Ohio. There are the smaller private colleges like Amherst and Williams in the East or Pomona in the West. There are the special colleges for women, like Bryn Mawr or Smith; there are the colleges maintained by the religious denominations; there are colleges for Negroes, like Howard and Fisk Universities; there are the small colleges attempting to prove the truth of some special educational theory, like Bennington in Vermont, or Antioch in Ohio, or Sarah Lawrence in Bronxville, New York; there are the great schools of technology, like those of Massachusetts, or California, or Pittsburgh. There are the graduate schools in the major universities, the business of which is to train the students in research. There are the professional schools, the law schools, for example, in which America for over half a century has given a lead to the world, the schools of medicine and engineering and architecture. Nowhere else in modern civilization can be found profusion so rich or standards so complex. There is a sense, indeed, in which it can be fairly said that anything is true of some college or university in America, and that nothing is true of them all.

Let me begin by noting certain features in the relation between the United States and its higher institutions of learning which stand out in marked contrast to the customs of Europe. With certain notable exceptions, such as Oxford and Cambridge, few universities can compete with some hundred or more American institutions in amplitude of buildings or in richness of material equipment. A visitor to Harvard or Yale does not know whether to envy more the superb library facilities which each can offer to its teachers, or the attractive accommodations which each provides for the student who is in residence. There are, of course, American colleges the libraries of which are almost bound, unless their professors have private means, to involve an intellectual semi-starvation for something like seven or eight months in the year. But the collections, whether general or special, at Harvard and Yale, at Cornell and Michigan, at Texas and the Union Theological Seminary, are, to take examples only, remarkable by any standard; so, too, is the devotion of the alumni to their old institutions; professorships, scholarships, buildings, research funds, special collections of books or manuscripts, pictures or intruments, these are provided on a scale and with a constancy to which there has hardly been anything comparable in Europe since the seventeenth century. I doubt, indeed, whether there has been in England in the last hundred years anything of the scale and frequency of this form of munificence save the single instance of Lord Nuffield's gifts to Oxford.

Another aspect in which the American university differs widely from the European system is in its attitude to athletics; and here it is difficult not to insist, quite simply, that the American view is fantastic. It assumes a small number of highly trained players, some of whom have what is virtually a professional status, who develop their powers under the control of a highly expert coach; he, in his turn, may be paid as much as the president of the university, and as much as three or even four times more than the ordinary professor. If the member of the team is of exceptional quality, it is overwhelmingly probable that his academic failures will be disregarded; indeed, cases have been known in which the expenses of young men of third-rate intelligence have been paid during their university careers in order that their athletic prowess might be available in football or baseball or some other team. The whole system leads up to a series of monster games in monster stadiums in which as many as one hundred thousand spectators will be watching. Each team will have its organized applause directed to its encouragement by especially appointed cheer leaders. Not seldom, a long run of failures in some series of games to which the alumni attach emotional importance may actually lead to a crisis in university affairs; it often leads to the satisfaction of university needs having a real dependence upon athletic success; and it invariably results in athletics securing a place in the life of the university which is altogether disproportionate to its importance. Few students actually play games; in a remarkable degree these are confined to actual or would-be members of the teams themselves. And surrounding the whole system is a complicated business apparatus, both of university officials and undergraduates, the influence of which on the university structure it would be difficult to justify. I cannot believe that a student who spends his main energies in becoming first a candidate for the post of "manager" of the track team, and then its actual "manager"—pretty nearly a full-time job for a year—is getting the best that a university can give him. If he is, either there is something wrong with the university or the student ought not to have continued to go through the farce of studying on those terms.

It may be said that athletics play a considerable part in the life of English universities. A "Blue" at Oxford or Cambridge enjoys immense social prestige, and an event like the annual boat-race of the two Universities is something like a national social and sporting event. But there is no real comparison between the English and the American situations. The English position is wholly based on an amateur status; there are no professional coaches; the athlete does not enjoy a privileged academic position; and since there are no great stadiums to be filled, financial problems have no effective importance in university athletic life. Their major bearing, indeed, is mostly on the issue of how far provision is made for the student who has no hope of distinction in the game he plays and is interested only in the healthy exercise of his muscles. To all this must be added the fact that, generally speaking, an eminent undergraduate athlete is mostly eminent among his own kind, and that the student who desires distinction in his own generation of a more universal kind must seek for it outside the athletic realm. I think it is true that in most universities, and perhaps more especially in Oxford and Cambridge, teachers will be found who devote special attention to cultivating a well-known "Blue." But, on examination, it will usually be found that this is a psychological sublimation of some defect in the teacher himself rather than a natural recognition, on his part, of some special attractiveness in a temporary friendship with the stroke of the Oxford boat or the captain of the Cambridge cricket team. There is never the febrile atmosphere of American athletics; and I doubt whether, in the period before the war, the continuous loss of the boat-race by Oxford made any difference to its standing in any realm with which, as a university, it needed to be concerned.

The government of American universities, moreover, is in marked contrast to the government of universities in Europe. Most of the former are governed by a president who is responsible to a body of trustees; and his appointment may vary in method from co-option, as in the case of the Corporation at Harvard University, through a mixed body in which members of the usually important alumni association will be represented by elected members, to the usual position in a state university where its Regents will be chosen by the governor with, or without, the consent of the state legislature. There is nowhere—I think wisely—anything like the virtually complete self-government of Oxford or Cambridge, which may fairly be termed syndicalism tempered by the investigations and recommendations of a Royal Commission every thirty or forty years; nor is there much resemblance between the American system and that by which, with variations, the Scottish or the English and Welsh universities are governed; and the resemblance with the methods of France or pre-Hitler Germany, Switzerland or Holland, are faint indeed. The Court of a British university is mostly concerned with the large issues of general policy which usually arise out of recommendations made by its teaching members; and since these mainly control the academic policy and possess, after a period of probation which is rarely more than five years, pretty rigorous security of academic tenure, the ultimate governing body, usually large, on which laymen sit is much more likely to be a source of effective public opinion than one of effective governance. Nor is the principal or vice-chancellor likely to be an effective or successful administrative head unless he accepts the role of *primus inter pares* among his colleagues. I do not agree with the aphorism that in Britain a university administrator is likely to be a professor who has given up hopes of being eminent in his subject; but I think it is true to say that he will invariably find on the academic boards on which he presides a number of teachers at least as eminent, if not more eminent, than himself, and that he will never find it easy to make continuous headway with his proposals against their opposition. If he cannot secure their support, he is more likely to concern himself with building schemes or a prayerful search for more endowments than with the real substance of academic policy. It is, moreover, rare for any but occasional academic appointments to lie even predominantly within his jurisdiction.

The American system of governing universities is very different from this. The trustees are important. They are chosen because they are successful alumni or eminent, that is to say wealthy, men or women from whom direct help for the university may be expected, either from their own resources or from those it is thought they may be able to influence. They meet frequently; they pay careful and continuous attention to the "public relations" of the university; they expect their views about its policies to be closely regarded; they are usually on the watch to see that steps are taken to prevent the university from being undesirably regarded among any important group from whom help may be expected or whose good opinion may be regarded as valuable; they settle major financial matters; they appoint the president of the university and, if necessary, secure his resignation; and they are, all things considered, the most powerful influence in settling the terms of academic appointments and, very often, the choice of important professors, and the general direction within which academic policy must be framed. They rarely know, except by accident, most of the teachers whose lives they govern. As a rule, their view of academic value will be based on the estimate formed of any teacher to be considered by the report upon him furnished by the president. They rarely participate in any discussion of academic problems in which there is an interchange of mind between them and the teachers concerned with those problems. Since, apart from their zest for expansion at all costs, their main concern is that the teacher, especially in any realm about which a vivid public opinion is focused, should not be heard and, possibly, not seen, they tend to be anxious for professional figures who will not arouse discussion in any critical field. They do not mind approving the appointment of an eminent physicist to a chair so long as he confines his radicalism, say, to the nature of atomic energy, or of an eminent classical scholar whose views on the decline of Athens are fiercely denounced by equally eminent scholars in the *Classical Review*. They even accept, without too much repining, a professor of Anglo-American literature who, like William Lyon Phelps of Yale, may make himself, as he bids farewell to scholarship, the darling of the ladies' clubs of America, or, as a temporary visitor, a distinguished poet and critic like Mr. T. S. Eliot, of whom they can be told not only that he is on the side of the angels, but that he is convinced that angels are traditionalists, Catholics, and monarchists. They want, above everything, to safeguard the university from straying, through the habits of its teachers, into paths that may lead to inconvenient discussion in general or to be regarded as "unsafe" by powerful economic interests on matters which those interests believe to be vital to social stability. And they expect the normal American university president to be their executive agent, among other things, in carrying out this policy.

They are mostly successful men; stockbrokers, lawyers, bankers, an occasional bishop, a man of large business affairs, these are, overwhelmingly, the source from which the trustees of American universities are drawn. Often they do not know the university from within; often they do not even take steps to know it intimately from without. The idea that an institution in which many of the teachers have invested their lives ought not to be operated by virtually an autocratic sovereignty from which, in any comprehensive way, the teachers are excluded does not seem to occur to them. They are directors running a "plant," no doubt a difficult and peculiarly complex plant, in much the same way as they become directors of any other enterprises. No doubt, the corporation pays only impalpable dividends. No doubt goodwill, with its consequential endowment, is more important than the standard of efficiency to which they are usually accustomed. No doubt their decision to get rid of an inconvenient employee must be preceded by a somewhat more careful attention to the opinion both of the inner and outer world than if they were dismissing a departmental manager or a minor executive. They cannot wholly forget that the internal politics of a university, especially one of national repute, is likely to be a matter of eager interest to the public, and therefore of vivid exploitation by the press. The public relations of an important college, or even of a secondary one which happens to have a significant figure on its staff, are likely to evoke widespread public discussions; or they may find themselves involved in some undesirable scandal about the wages paid to their charwomen, or about the habits of their fraternities—a form of social organization peculiar to the American college—or about their admissions' policy, especially where it involves the Negro or the Jew. The trustees have usually immense powers, but the materials with which they deal requires careful handling. That is why the wisdom of their activities is so largely a function of the wisdom of the president they have chosen. He is the vital link in the chain they seek to preserve unbroken.

5

THE American college president is a unique institution. No country in Europe has his exact analogue. The rector of a continental university holds office only for a few brief years; so, too, do the vice-chancellors of Oxford, Cambridge, and London. If the newer universities in Great Britain have developed towards a chief executive officer who has permanency, the limits of his discretion are set with considerable rigidity. He cannot control the university curriculum. He is more rarely the controlling factor in appointment or promotion. If he sought to dismiss a teacher on grounds of intellectual disagreement or public clamour, he would find himself opposed by a tradition as tough as any in English life. English university life is rarely, if ever, shaped by the direction of any single man. It takes its character from a mass of varying trends and ideas among which it is impossible to discover with any precision the extent of the individual contribution.

The American scene presents a very different spectacle. To most men the university is largely embodied in its president. They speak of the Harvard of Eliot or Lowell, the Yale of Hadley or Angell, the Chicago of Harper or Hutchins, the Princeton of Woodrow Wilson, the Virginia of Alderman, because the president, in each case, gave a special character to the institution of which he was the head. The president of an important university cuts a big figure in the public life of his day. His announcements are "news" in the technical sense of the term. He has it in his power radically to alter the perspective of his institution. His interest in a particular subject, his zeal for a particular teacher, the emphasis he makes in the always painful choice between buildings and men, may well give special shape or colour to the character the university assumes. When President Eliot chose Langdell as the Dean of the Harvard Law School, when President Lowell decided to institute the Harvard Graduate School of Business Administration, when President Angell set up a system of separate colleges within Yale, they were each embarking upon a crucial experiment. Weak and timid college presidents there have doubtless been in abundance, but the man with a policy, and with a character compounded of strong will and energy, can stamp himself upon an institution with a force that is unknown in the universities of the older world.

Normally the president is the link between a body of trustees, whether publicly or privately appointed, and the teaching body of a university. It rarely happens, save in a very small college, that the trustees are intimately acquainted with the teachers; they are, therefore, largely dependent upon the president's judgment of their value. Upon finance, buildings, size and promotion of staff, new developments, relations between faculties and students, or between the university and the alumni, or the university and the outside world, the president is the essential vehicle of all vital information. No one else has the same access to the trustees. No one else can know the bent of their minds, the best way to win their assent, the things it is inadvisable to attempt in the light of some special obstacle that may be encountered. The important day-to-day business of the university is in the president's hands. Few things of any importance can be considered in any aspect of its life save with his approval, and most things must be discussed through the medium of his personality. He is the responsible pivot upon whom the whole university turns.

No one, of course, can deny that a great president can, with such powers, be a potent force for good. Eliot at Harvard, though he made some disastrous mistakes, showed clearly what a man can do who has a big and imaginative conception of his office and who knows a good man when he sees one. But, in this realm as elsewhere, great presidents are rare. The average president can hardly be expected to be, at one and the same time, a skilful executive, a good judge of academic reputation, sufficiently aware of developments in science and learning as to know what requires financial emphasis, an effective beggar among rich men, and also a person of such standing in the general community as to win respect for the university by his public pronouncements. Yet all these things, at least, a university president is expected to be. The conception is that of a superman, and the evidence suggests that supermen have been the exception among university presidents.

For, once the institution is of any size, the president's knowledge of its inner life is necessarily in large part at second-hand. He depends upon deans, information casually acquired at a dinner party, knowledge gleaned in looking into a problem that has suddenly become urgent. His trustees can rarely be well informed. They can advise about investments. They can warn him against some teacher of heretical views whose presence is a danger to the flow of manna from the wealthy. They can give general encouragement or general warning about the policies placed before them. They can put him in touch with possible sources of fruitful revenue. They may help a little by their private prejudices or particular knowledge of some man or department in the institution. But a wise board of trustees can hardly hope to do more than this without an interference that is bound to result in grave error. For the average trustee knows little about either the personnel of the university or the state of teaching and research into its work. The board needs expert advice on every occasion when it makes a particular judgment; and, in general, it must depend upon the expert advice of the president at every turn.

But, of course, the president is not an expert. He himself depends on what he can pick up as he goes on his way. If there are no outstanding men in his university who have risen from specialist distinction to general wisdom, he must act, for the most part, on hearsay evidence. The more, therefore, he can make his case by methods of objective proof, the safer he is bound to feel. Promotion for A because he has written a book. A laboratory for B because he will otherwise accept an astonishing offer from a rival university. A tutorial system at Harvard because it is successful at Oxford and Cambridge; a society of junior fellows at Harvard because President Lowell had veneration for All Souls'. New buildings instead of better salaries because a particular donor prefers the immediate immortality of stone to the more impalpable values implied in advancing the economic status of professors. A chair in fine arts instead of more money for engineering because some trustee has a belief in the æsthetic value of the genteel tradition. Emphasis upon athletics, with a new stadium if possible, because three football defeats running at the hands of the university's chief rival have persuaded the alumni that their *alma mater* is not what it was. Vast expenditure on geography, even to the point of closing down other departments, because geography is the president's hobby and he hardly knows that other subjects exist.

If the president is a weak man, some trustee or group of trustees will dominate his policy; or he may be the pathetic mouthpiece of an energetic wirepuller on his faculty. If he is a strong man, he may well use his trustees as a screen to secure a special protection for his personal policy. And he very seldom escapes from the illusion of size. Most trustees are business men to whom financial growth is the test of the president's success. He must cultivate the foundations, wealthy men, and the big corporations. If a rival president gets a big endowment, he must go one better. He dare not offend the rich upon whom he depends. He must be interested less in the digestion of experiments than in their extension. Bigger library buildings, larger dormitories, a better stadium, a more spacious chapel, all with appropriate dedicatory exercises, are the key to the ideal. Honorary degrees must be dangled before appropriate persons. Speeches must be made which local public opinion welcomes as the voice of a "sound" man. He must never be a socialist; he must use large abstract words like "liberty" and "justice" sufficiently often to make it evident that he cannot be accused of un-American ideas; he must emphasize his faith in that "American way of life" which has so obviously given the U.S.A. a destiny different in kind from that of other nations. He must lead a blameless private life so that the public has assurance of the soundness of his morals. Without belonging to a particular Church, he must insist in a general way on the worth of Christian values; and it is always a help if, at fairly frequent intervals, he can preach a lay sermon with a vaguely religious background in the college chapel. In personal relations he must cultivate a happy mixture of heartiness and deference. He should invite, if possible, any distinguished foreigners visiting America to the university, so long as they are not too radical, and preferably in important public office; a British ambassador or, before Vichy, a notable French soldier was always a successful choice. And if the president goes abroad, he should meet a sufficient number of the eminent there to be in the news while he is away; a public dinner in Paris or in Rome, so tactfully arranged as to appear spontaneous, may greatly enhance his power with the trustees and his reputation among his fellow-presidents.

Governmentally, in fact, a president is the inevitable prisoner of the special university environment created by American social and economic conditions. They define his purposes and his possibilities, and he will be chosen only if he seems likely to fit into the pattern they involve. No one can imagine William James or Willard Gibbs as a university president. The position demands men who are conservative without seeming reactionary, tactful, prepared to equate bigness with grandeur, able to cut something of a figure, ready to defend liberalism but prepared swiftly to denounce that deviation from the accepted boundaries of liberalism which is known as licence. Such men abound in American universities. They make much the same speeches, especially at one another's inaugurations. They have much the same ambitions. Even the self-conscious postulates of their policies can hardly be distinguished from one another. They even collect about them, so far as they can, much the same type of trustee. The unmistakable result is that decisions must move within a narrow circle. The system is built upon direction from above and not upon co-operation from below. Its structure is a pyramid in which only the apex emerges effectively above the horizon. As a system, no doubt, it can point to overwhelming financial success; apart from Oxford and Cambridge, no university in the British Commonwealth of Nations, and certainly none in continental Europe, can rival the endowments of at least some fifty of the major American institutions. And I doubt whether a professor at Oxford or Cambridge would dare, like Professor Beale of the Harvard Law School, to buy a great collection, the famous Dunn Library of early law books, while on a visit abroad, in the serene confidence that friends of the school would subscribe the funds necessary for its purchase.

Yet the basis of university government is too narrow for effective leadership to be possible. The things it is bound to emphasize are public values, not least those with a dramatic context to them. The things it cares about are the things which push still higher the apex of the pyramid; the glory achieved thus enhances the presidential position. It is, of course, a great thing for the university when one of its teachers gets a Nobel prize, or the Copley Medal of the Royal Society, both of which stand for unmistakable and international distinction; nor is it a small thing when some hitherto obscure member of the faculty, like Parrington at the University of Washington, suddenly achieves eminence by being awarded the Pulitzer Prize. Such an achievement makes the headlines; it can be publicly celebrated; and there can be special eulogy of the recipient —of whom the trustees may quite likely never have heard—in the president's annual report. Certainly it is true that Vernon Parrington had few friends outside a handful of intimates among the faculty and the group of students who took his courses each year until the award of the prize awakened the college authorities to the fact that they enjoyed the privilege of employing an eminent scholar whose value they had never known till it was announced from New York. On a different plane, I have myself seen the startled surprise of college presidents on being informed that some scholar on the faculty had a distinguished reputation abroad; on one occasion, it had the pleasant consequence that the scholar was invited—for the first time—to meet the trustees at dinner and figured in the next list of promotions. It is in facts like these that the presidential system in American universities seems singularly unfitted to bring out what is best in the life of a company of scholars.

This becomes even more true in the context of the relations between the president and his faculties, above all in a large university. There are, of course, exceptions, though these are more rare than most students of university matters would care to admit. But it is, in part, inherent in the very fact of size; there are too many teachers in some of the giants among the colleges for any president to know them in more than the most vague and impersonal way. A great scholar here, a renowned teacher there, may emerge for him as definite characters about whom he has ideas; but, in general, he does not know much about them, least of all when they are young and it is immensely important to judge their promise. And since the university is organized upon the basis of an elaborate system of grading, that means a real difficulty in making either appointments or promotions upon any principle but a hopeful guess unless a tried and tested teacher is involved. They depend far too largely upon the opinion confided to the president by the men who possess his ear, or upon some chance impression he has formed, or the publication of a popular book, or availability for executive work. A man may miss his chance because someone of whom the president thinks well dislikes him or disagrees with the theories he puts forward. Or it may be that he is registered in the presidential mind as lazy, because he has published nothing for five years, or unco-operative, because he insists upon doing his own kind of research when what is required is the kind of research which will interest the great foundations and bring some more endowment to the university.

I am not painting an imaginary picture. I have myself known professors who published only the kind of book they thought likely to interest the president. I have known others, of high intellectual distinction, who were left to stifle for years in the arid backwoods of a second-rate denominational college because the most powerful of the presidential intimates at a large school disliked the tendency of their work. One of the most distinguished American philosophers was left to languish in an inferior position until late middle age because the heads of his department did not understand or were not interested by work which, in its special realm, was famous all over the world. Another university did not invite a famous scholar to its faculty because the president thought it already possessed all the Jews the traffic would bear. In yet another case, a distinguished historian left a great eastern university for an inferior position in the Middle West because he could no longer endure the refusal of the president and his advisers to take the risk of promoting younger men whose radical views in the field of the social sciences were both interesting the students and arousing some measure of public controversy.

The presidential system has three great deficiencies: it makes it difficult to add to the sum of new knowledge in fields where departure from the conventional view may lead to criticism of the university by those it must seek to please; it makes stimulating teaching difficult in any area of contemporary policy where there is vivid public debate; and it makes it difficult for a young scholar, unless he has private means, to get advancement early enough in life to embark, at his own time and in his own way, upon a book that is his life's ambition. The sheer scale of the university is always tending to require publicity for its maintenance. There is thus an almost inherent drive to appoint or promote men with executive competence (since they take part of the load of responsibility off the president's shoulders), or men who get results which can be made the basis of an application to the foundations; long-term values in investigation stand at a discount compared to the values which the world outside can easily understand. When quantitative research is in fashion, it begets quantitative research elsewhere by the bucketful; when Professor and Mrs. Lynd published their classic investigation of *Middletown,* half a dozen universities set out to rival it on a much vaster scale; and one of the studies which resulted devoted elaborate investigation to showing in comprehensive tables, first, that the rich live in larger houses than the poor, and, second, that diet costs less in proportion to the family income among the salaried class than among the wage-earners.

It is not merely that in itself this centralization of authority in the president is bad; it has the not less noxious result of emphasizing to any teacher without security of tenure—and that is the position of the great body of teachers—his sense of dependence. There must be innumerable men in American universities whose promotion has only come from a threat to move elsewhere. One of the most delicate academic operations is for the young teacher to balance the chances that the threat will fail of its effect against the necessity, somehow, of getting an increase of salary. It is not easy to prevent his claims being overlooked unless he has exceptional courage or an exceptional power of salesmanship. Advantage always lies with the man of personal charm who can make himself useful in half a dozen administrative ways, and not with the scholar whose insight makes him sail against the stream or who lacks the gifts committee work requires. Nor can he speak his mind with ease about the president or his intimates. In the lower ranks of the academic hierarchy such criticism simply comes to be looked upon as inability to co-operate effectively; in the upper, it means that the dissidents will find that their recommendations about men or policies are inadequately weighed. If, as in an Oxford college, all members of the staff were on an equal footing, once a period of probation were passed, the whole psychological atmosphere of an American university would be revolutionized.

Presidential centralization makes either for timidity or indifference over the whole range of academic policy among university teachers. Doubtless they explain their silence to themselves by saying that they must not let down the institution; the real fact is their knowledge that the price of antagonism is more than most of them can afford to pay. There are, of course, notable exceptions in every university; but I believe that it is generally true and borne out by the relatively small number who have any part to play in shaping university policy. Outside a remarkably small range of persons, most teachers hardly know what is happening in the university as a whole, and only too often a time arrives when they have lost even the desire to influence it. It is notable, in this regard, that the atmosphere of colleagueship is always more intensive and creative in the professional schools of a university than in the ordinary undergraduate and graduate colleges. That is because the existence of an expert professional opinion acts as a real check upon the president in a way that, mathematics and the natural sciences apart, is hardly open to the non-professional branches of a university. The result upon a professional faculty is an *esprit de corps,* a level of interest, and a genuine independence that are difficult to attain in other branches of university life.

With this exception, effective dissent from presidential policies needs something like organized revolt to be effective. There is rarely faculty representation on the board of trustees; there is thus little chance of any continuous access to them. Finance, for the most part, is an uncharted sea for the teachers since, as a totality, it is regarded as outside their province. The average president, in any case, can govern by dividing. He discusses economics with one set of professors, English literature with a second, the history of science with a third; they do not share in making a co-ordinated whole. Effectively, the controls are all centralized, so that, at the periphery, no one can really gauge the necessity or desirability of a particular line of action. One knows of presidents who do not even consult their faculties about promotions or appointments. One knows of universities in which vast sums are secured in an atmosphere of complete departmental ignorance, and the teachers have them, whether they approve or no, to protect the good name of the university by refusing as best they can not to look the gift horse in the mouth. In any case, the sanctions at the president's disposal, except in the case of a really eminent professor, are always formidable. Good form demands that one does not attack him in the open; and it is unconstitutional to go to the trustees behind his back. The effect on the average dissenter is that he becomes normally content to let things take their course; and he is then assumed to agree with a policy with which his disagreement may, in fact, be ultimate.

The position I have described is not a caricature but the logical outcome of the academic environment developed during the last century. When at the close of the First World War it was decided that the memorial at Harvard to the men who died in France should take the form of a new and ampler Appleton Chapel, I knew at least a score of Harvard teachers who disliked the idea; but I knew none of them who thought it worth while to push his dislike to the point of opposition. Such an attitude is explicable only when some special scheme may be regarded as the vagary of a really great president; and I have ventured to suggest that great presidents are rare. The result is to exalt a man who should be essentially an administrator to a position where he is not only a dictator, open or concealed, but whose success or failure is curiously accidental. He never utilizes the full academic resources at his disposal; he uses only those that are "available" for the special pattern he is seeking to weave. Men and measures alike are subordinated to that pattern. The needs of the university are not assessed in terms of a full and free discussion by academic equals. Needs mean a discussion of the bits and pieces about which the president and the trustees have either not made up their minds, or do not feel so keenly about that they would resent the suggestion of change. These bits and pieces are, as a rule, either remote from a full university policy on the one hand, or too unimportant to evoke any wide or profound interest from the faculty on the other. Presidential authority, in a word, is out of harmony with the kind of power which would elicit a maximum interest in the teachers who must live by its results.

This relation between president and faculty has, of course, a special bearing upon the problem of academic freedom; and this issue has an importance so outstanding in the university life of America that it requires special emphasis. And this is true even though no single comprehensive generalization is possible, even though variations exist with every board of trustees and almost every president. But because certain features of the landscape are common to all colleges, it is, I think, worth while to spend a brief time in their examination.

I begin with the assumption that no teacher can attempt to teach adequately or to embark upon researches with a full mind and heart unless he can speak the truth that is in him without regard to the novelty or the inconvenience of the results he believes himself to have attained. His intellectual activities, therefore, must be unimpeded. He has the obligation, in return, to pursue his task in a scientific spirit; that is to say, he owes it to the university not to leap into utterance without the careful and critical examination of the facts upon which he bases his conclusions. But once he has made that effort, the university, in its turn, can neither penalize him, nor permit his penalization, without destroying the peculiar value upon which its whole value as an academic institution depends.

It cannot be said that this has been the characteristic atmosphere of American universities. An occasional theological dispute apart, academic freedom was hardly a serious issue until the issues of slavery and abolition became matters of burning controversy. There were enforced resignations from Western Reserve University over abolition. Hendrick, of the University of North Carolina, was dismissed in 1856 for supporting Frémont for the presidency of the United States. A number of universities penalized the formation of anti-slavery societies on campus in the Middle West. E. B. Andrews of Brown University resigned its presidency over his views on free silver. It has become a fairly general rule that wherever a subject is a matter of passionate discussion, the university teacher who speaks forthrightly on the unpopular side will find himself attacked. He may be dismissed; his promotion may be retarded; he may be involved in attacks so vicious that they act as a deterrent against any further forthrightness either from himself or from others; or he may turn into that type of frustrated intellectual who is hounded into seeing attack in every criticism, however honest, of his views. No one can even imagine the range of interference who has not studied, year by year, the investigations into university dismissals by the Association of University Professors, or the hearings, in the thirties, before the committee of the Massachusetts legislature on bills to require an oath of loyalty from teachers to the Massachusetts Constitution, or the fantastic proceedings before bodies of the United States Congress, like the Thomas Committee on Un-American Activities and the La Follette Committee on Civil Liberties. The experience of nearly a century suggests that the more sharply public opinion expresses itself, especially that public opinion which the universities desire to placate, the less chance there is that the academic person will be safe if he is heretical. He is more likely, I ought to add, to be safe in an endowed university than in one maintained by a state.

Here, once more, I believe that the centralization of authority in the president is a contributory cause to this position. Partly this is because he has to satisfy his trustees; and the sacrifice of an uncomfortable teacher is one of the most facile burnt-offerings to place upon their altar. Partly he has to make the attitude of his alumni favourable to the point of generosity; and a teacher whose utterances they dislike may easily make his position a difficult one. Partly, also, he has to raise money; and the presence of a notorious socialist upon his faculty may easily become a grave hindrance to that end. It is the very eminence of the president in the academic pyramid that makes him the court of appeal from any of his professional colleagues who arouse dissent by what they have to say. And it is thus the logic of that eminence that he should seek to avoid the prospect of public discussion by securing, so far as he can, the services of men, no doubt so far as possible distinguished men, to whose views objection is not likely to be taken.

"Availability," this is to say, has become an important prerequisite of important academic appointments; but "availability" is also the keynote of mediocrity. Yet mistakes in appointments are made, and the presidential system has developed its mechanism for preventing them from becoming too frequent. One method, particularly favoured in the state universities, is to refuse permanent appointments; teachers are engaged only for limited periods, perhaps as short as a year. If a teacher then becomes obnoxious to some powerful interest, and the danger of a public outcry is small, he can be dropped from the faculty. A very remarkable instance of this kind was the case of Professor Herbert Hutton of Ohio State University, who was dismissed for making a speech at a nationalist meeting in India, to which it is almost incredible that any reasonable human being could have taken exception. And the grounds may not necessarily be political. A president who finds that some teacher raises difficulties for him for causes unconnected with the quality of his work can always invoke the renewal of appointment as a lever against him. Some presidents, like Hutchins of Chicago, who has had long and sharp conflicts with his faculty, have rationalized their quarrels into the principle that security of tenure is undesirable on general grounds; while others, like Conant of Harvard, have invented limitations on promotions that are likely to mean the postponement of security to the future, when the teacher is on the threshold of middle age.

But the issue is not confined to security of tenure; it touches, also, the whole question of promotion. Wherever this is not automatic in its nature, the teacher must tread carefully in an approved path if he wishes to be moved upward. I have known men deliberately to refrain from the expression of deeply felt opinions upon matters where they had special knowledge for fear that their promotion might be jeopardized. I have known others who refused to write books about controversial subjects for the same reason. I have even known men to remain silent upon purely academic issues because they did not want to court presidential disfavour. President Lowell informed one of his faculty in 1919 that he himself would resign if dismissal was the penalty for utterance in a famous dispute of that year; but he also told the lecturer in confidence not to expect promotion from the university. I know well a professor in a famous eastern university most of whose platform utterances outside his lecture room were followed by a presidential inquisition; and the breaking point came when it was suggested to him that he might desirably submit the manuscript of his public lectures to the president for criticism. An eminent professor of law was asked to refrain from discussing the verdict of a famous trial lest he prejudice the fund that was being raised among the alumni of the university. I select illustrations only; but they seem to me to convey the lesson that no teacher can be really free in the presence of such sanctions and such uncertainties, and even less free when he considers the large chance that being "dropped" by one place may mean being blacklisted by all to which he would have wished to go. I know one teacher of high distinction, dismissed during the First World War for non-existent pro-German sympathies, who has never since obtained academic employment; and this although, at his own university, a group of friends offered to found a chair on his behalf.

No one, I think, who is at all seriously informed of the present position can doubt that a high level of academic freedom is not easily compatible with the presidential system. Just as the president is made the prisoner of the interested public, so the professor, unless his tenure is permanent, is the prisoner of the president. He must not be obtrusively radical; that disturbs the trustees and the alumni. He must always be discreet and decorous in what he ventures to say. He can, of course, be extreme in physics or chemistry, or in the Scandinavian literatures; there he cannot be checked by business interests and does not arouse their attention. But he is a nuisance to the president if he publishes unconventional views or conclusions on any matter of social or political concern. No one will worry if he attacks trade-unions, or denounces strikers, or proves that the problem of poverty has been solved in America, or insists on the natural intellectual inferiority of the Negro, or the urgency of a return to *laissez-faire*. But he must be careful about public ownership, the Soviet Union, the limits of American democracy, the relation of the political machines to Big Business; if he is in California, he would be wise to be discreet about the remarkable habits of the Giannini Foundation of the University of California; if he is at the University of Pittsburgh, he should refrain from examining the Mellon interests; if he is at Montana, he had better be silent about the relations between the State Tax Commission and the Anaconda Copper Mining Company. Like Charles Beard, he may find the atmosphere of perpetual friction so irritating that he will decide, to the intellectual loss of hundreds of students, upon freedom outside the university. Or, like Thorstein Veblen, he may wander from university to university in a vain effort to discover a spiritual home.

We do not know the price paid for the present system because we do not know either the extent or the intensity of the suppressions it involves; above all, we do not know what is lost by what may be termed the prenatal control of research, which operates by warning off teachers, especially the younger ones, from entrance into critical fields of inquiry. Most men who suffer from the suppression cannot reveal their suffering; they have to conform because they have no alternative vocation. Presidents, of course, pay lip-service to academic freedom, though a careful search almost always reveals some subtle reservation; and the system as it is can always be explained away by men who have never felt its incidence. The particular heretic was a "difficult" person; he was not a good teacher; he was an exhibitionist; his results were one-sided; important figures in his field of research thought he was lacking in a sound grasp of principle. He has not been dismissed; he has merely not had his appointment renewed, as it has been for some time the policy of the university to make economies in the department he serves.

It is, of course, true that there is a great range of variation in the degree of control that exists. But I do not think any gathering of fifty liberal-minded men would fail to reveal a sense that, increasingly during the last fifty years, they have experienced the need to be silent where their conscience urged them to be forthright; and that the impact of their teaching in the social sciences was scrutinized quite differently from that of their conservative colleagues. No doubt the Harvard overseers were troubled by protests against Professor Chafee's mid-Victorian at-

tachment to freedom of personality; but I doubt whether they received
any protest against Professor Carver's rapturous picture [8]—published
shortly before the Great Depression—of the fullness of American economic democracy. And I should be inclined to guess that Professor Carver
had never felt, in his long academic career, that there was ever a serious
threat to the teacher's freedom. Those who have never experienced inhibition rarely appreciate the protests of others who feel like slaves. Men think
differently who live differently. That is why I have argued that if every
American university teacher were guaranteed security of tenure after
some agreed period of probation, the mental climate of the universities
would change swiftly; it would change still more swiftly if the teachers
abandoned that shabby genteel tradition which, with startlingly few exceptions, has prevented them from organizing in trade-unions to bargain collectively about the conditions of their work. There would then
be not only a far larger number of first-rate critical examinations of
American traditions and institutions; there would also be a far more exhilarating and attentive atmosphere in the classrooms. It is difficult, on
other terms, to explain the disparity between what they say in Europe
and what they write in America; or to account for their profound absorption in the liberal movements of the Old World, or their doubts of,
or their cynical indifference to, the liberal movements in the New. On
vacation in London or Paris they will speak far more strongly than I have
written of the more impossible mandarins of the American academic
scene; in the United States they are either silent or they attempt a defence in terms of the difficult role a university president has to play. I
cannot believe that the need for a constant avoidance of judgment, or so
constant a softening of judgment, on basic social questions is a healthy
frame of mind. It is at least as bad for students as it is for teachers. For
it not only makes the university function under the shadow of vested
interests; it makes innumerable undergraduates feel the gap between the
real world and the picture of its nature that university departments of
social science are permitted to reveal. The student reads Mr. Steinbeck's *Grapes of Wrath;* he finds that a score of government reports document every detail of the portrait it so graphically draws.
Is it seriously a matter for wonder that he should find it difficult
to reconcile the answers of Professor John Bates Clark or William
Graham Sumner, of Rotary Clubs and the Chamber of Commerce, of
the neo-Thomism of Robert M. Hutchins, of the "rugged individualism"
of Herbert Hoover, of the "open-shop campaign" which the National
Association of Manufacturers so euphoniously described as the "American Plan," with the facts revealed by every serious inquiry into social
conditions? If, as Mr. F. L. Allen wrote, "the overwhelming majority of
the American people believed with increasing certainty that business men
knew better than anyone else what was good for the country," how could

[8] Thomas Nixon Carver, *The Present Economic Revolution in the United States*
(Boston: Little, Brown, 1925).

teachers explain significantly in universities dependent upon business men the relation of the latter to, say, the Gilded Age or the Great Depression? And if they failed to explain it significantly to their students, how likely were these to feel in any profound and concrete way the obligations of intelligence? All American university problems centre around issues of this kind.

6

MOST American institutions of higher learning fall into one of two patterns. They are colleges which, like Amherst and Dartmouth, confine themselves to undergraduate teaching for a degree in which the staple subjects of the humanities or the sciences form the backbone, or they add to their main undergraduate teaching special advanced training, usually organized in separate schools, with their own special diplomas or degrees for the professions or business, or for trained research workers (who may also become teachers) in the humanities and the natural sciences. Some of them also undertake adult education and instruction by correspondence courses; many of them run special summer schools in which a teaching staff partly composed of their own instructors, and partly of their colleagues from outside, give intensified, short courses in the different fields of learning. It is a widely spread and interesting custom that large numbers of schoolteachers should regard the university summer school as a "refresher course" in which they can extend and invigorate their knowledge.

Alongside these classical types of higher instruction, there are several others which deserve a word; in most states, and in some privately endowed universities, there will be found teachers' training colleges—the normal school or, as in the well-known Teachers' College of Columbia University, an institution, at the graduate level, which at once does investigation in educational methods and results and trains future educational specialists either for institutions like its own or for educational administration in the field. There is also a small, but growing number of research institutions, the staffs of which, as in the Huntington Library in California, go on with their own researches permanently or for some period for which they have been invited; or, as at the Institute of Advanced Study in Princeton, limit their student body to a small number of exceptionally qualified and mature graduates who are expected to learn from the eminent men with whom they collaborate by discussion and by observing their work as it proceeds. There is also, though on no great scale, a special field of workers' education; a number of trade-unions, very notably in the different branches of the tailoring trades, have made important and illuminating experiments in both general and vocational post-entry training; whilst the Socialist and Communist parties have both had, the former for nearly half a century, their specialized schools of instruction which have been not merely centres for education in doctrine, but also centres, if on a small scale, for research, some of which has been of exceptionally high quality. There is also a number of denominational institutions in which, as in the Union Theological Seminary of New York and the Jewish religious colleges of New York and Philadelphia, work in their fields is done at a level and of a quality which compares favourably with that of any similar bodies outside the United States.

With the large-scale efforts, like the Chautauqua movement, to popularize knowledge in the United States, I have insufficient acquaintance for comment. Here I am concerned with the students in the undergraduate period of university life, and with the graduate student who is either doing graduate vocational work, as in the law school or in the medical school, or training himself to undertake original research in the humanities or the natural sciences. And, here again, it is important to insist on the dangers of generalization. It is easy to say that, almost everywhere, the lecture system is overdone; no one can have heard men like the great medievalist scholar C. H. Haskins lecture at Harvard, or heard what students have to say of how the lectures of William James or Allyn Young, of Parrington or Carl Becker (I mention only the dead), made an epoch in their lives, without seeing that the statement really means that there are too many bad lectures. Or we may be told that the small college has an immense advantage over the large one, since it permits a closer relationship between teacher and student; to which there is the obvious and important answer that it depends wholly on the quality of the teachers in the small colleges, and that many of them would find it difficult to justify their existence to any body measuring their work against a reasonable standard of university instruction. Or we are asked to admire that trend away from President Eliot's free elective system (the system which Professor Morison has called the "greatest educational crime of the century against American Youth" [4]), while we remember that the various forms of concentration of studies, even when accompanied by some form of individual tutoring which has taken the place of the free elective system, still leaves the overwhelming mass of American students without any adequate guide to the complex heritage of culture in our civilization. There are conditions and reservations to be attached to almost every general conclusion about this area of American education.

That said, I must emphasize that there are two conclusions necessary to any perspective of the whole. It has become fashionable to say that far too many young men and women go to the university who can never hope to profit by the training it offers; and, not seldom, the proof is offered in illustrations of their ignorance and incompetence in the broad area in which they should have knowledge. It is, of course, obvious that there are misfits in this category of the population as there are in most others. But a good deal of the criticism is wholly misplaced if it is intended to convey the inference that there is not enough capacity in the

---

[4] Samuel Eliot Morison, *Three Centuries of Harvard, 1636–1936* (Cambridge: Harvard University Press, 1936), pp. 389–90.

United States to deserve intellectual training at the university level. Part of the criticism is a decaying remnant of the genteel tradition; there underlies it the unstated assumption that knowledge for knowledge's sake is the end a university has in view, and this, in its turn, presupposes a leisured class, parasitic on the rest of the community, which has the means to pursue intellectual exploration without the need to trouble about the end of the voyage. There is, in fact, nothing shameful about going to a university to secure, if one can, the means to make more of one's gifts in the kind of world in which we live; what is shameful is the fact that such a motive should be thought shameful. And if one subtracts from the student population those who gain little or nothing from it either because the teaching is poor, or because their economic circumstances leave them no time for that leisurely reflection which is at the heart of the undergraduate years, or because their health needs attention, or because they have psychological difficulties which are unheeded and uncured, or because they have chosen the wrong field of studies and do not discover that they ought to change it, the number of those who waste their own time and that of their teachers is not only relatively small, but is quite disproportionately found in that group of men and women who have assured social position, the prospect of pretty certain economic security when they leave the university, and the means, while they are students, to devote their main energies to an endless round of social activities.

The other generalization I venture to make is built upon a teaching experience of twenty-five years, of which perhaps one-third has been spent in universities in most parts of the United States. It is evident, I think, that there is in every college generation a small number of outstandingly able people for whom the teacher can do relatively little except offer them friendly counsel and see to it that unnecessary obstacles in their path are either removed or made as little a hindrance as possible. It is not always easy to detect this ability; save in the sciences dependent upon mathematics or in poetry, its arrival at maturity is unpredictable. Such intellectual growth as that of Darwin or Emerson or William James is a series of illustrations of what I seek to convey; in another sense, perhaps, Mr. Justice Holmes, whose most creative intellectual years seem to have been reached when he was between thirty and forty. The real business of a university is with men and women whose intelligence, however good, is still below the little group whose members, whatever the university can do to them, will still achieve extraordinary insights. And with those who concern it in this more average way, while the teacher can never do much, what he can do is of real importance. He can explain how principle is hewn from the crude rock of fact, and convey, as he explains it, not only that this hewing of principle is about as difficult an effort as any to which human hands are laid, but also that it is practically always a co-operative effort in which it is impossible to say that some single person was the sole and unaided discoverer; all principles, that is, are a way of explaining how men and women live together in a society they are forever seeking to understand and changing by the fact that they understand it. He can explain to the student the interrelations of things, not merely the direct simplicity of Darwin's cats and clover in Australia, but the more complex relation, say, between the commercial success of Holland in the seventeenth century and the character of Dutch painting in the same period. He can encourage, in the third place, both accuracy of observation and the kind of effort required to detach as much as possible the emotions of the observer from the facts observed. Through it all, the teacher must seek to show his students the danger of habit without philosophy, the need for general principles he can justifiably use to test the claims which press themselves upon him for assistance. And through it all, also, he must seek to convey the inescapable dynamism of life, the need to be ready for novelty and experiment, to refuse to confound the new with the dangerous or the traditional with the beneficent, and, above all in a civilization so dependent upon the division of labour as our own, he must convince them of the curse of specialization, the need for an ever-increasing number of minds able to co-ordinate, to build wholes and not parts merely, if we are to attain that balanced life in which human beings reach beyond frustration to fulfilment.

The teacher, of course, will fail; it is by persuading his students to embark upon what must be a co-operative adventure of this kind that he helps them to use their minds and to strengthen their characters in the process of using their minds. The first real question, at the undergraduate stage in an American university, is how far the methods used are likely to reach towards the ends desired. I do not myself believe that we ought to be melancholy and pessimistic because it is clear that training in Latin and Greek will never again be the spinal column of the arts curriculum. They once held that place for historical reasons in a special environment, and now that the special environment has disappeared, it seems to me quite obvious that the historical reasons for their primacy have disappeared also. What ought, I think, to concern the observer is the broad fact that an American student who has just been graduated from college is about two or three years less intellectually mature than an English or French student at the same stage and of the same age. Why should this be the case?

The reasons, I think, are multiple. In part they reach back into the high school, the standards of which make the entrance requirements to an American college lower and less exacting than those in England or France. In part they result from the fact that the main emphasis in the undergraduate period is less on the individual intellectual effort the student makes for himself than on the effort that is made for him by those who teach him. He goes to far too many lectures, and he is asked to understand them less by thinking and reading about their subject matter than by taking notes of facts retailed and being able, at some later "quiz," to give the illusion that he has retained enough facts in his memory to convey the impression that he has not idled away his time. In most of his discussion classes, especially in a large university, he will not be able to probe the mind of the professor whose lecture he has heard, but the mind of some professorial assistant, who is only too likely to be himself a graduate student to whom the task of taking the classes or marking the twenty minute "test" paper is probably a nuisance necessary on economic grounds while he ploughs his way forward to his doctor's degree. Nor, as a general rule, will the undergraduate read either whole books or great books. He may be given a textbook which covers the whole course and summarizes, more or less well, what seven or eight times in ten he has already heard in his lectures; or he may be asked to read a series of pages in another book, quite possibly a classic, which makes him form the habit of making his mind a receptacle for bits and pieces of books which he is rarely shown how to fit into a pattern, much less a pattern with a significant historical background.

I know that there are universities which seek, by orientation courses, by courses in contemporary civilization, by "majoring" in a special field chosen by the student, who must then write a considerable essay to get high honours in his degree, by the development of the tutorial system and the institution of "reading periods," to correct the belief that learning consists in getting a number of "credits" from examinations in courses attended, with "grades" adequate in standard to justify the conference of the degree. But I suggest that there are several factors which destroy the claim that any or all of these are effective in any but isolated cases. The "reading period" is not only a naïve admission that the student will not turn spontaneously to books during the academic year; it is also an admission that he is not likely to read on his own initiative even in the long vacation. Reading books, that is to say, is a task to be performed and not an adventure to be enjoyed. Nor has the American university been able to make its teachers agree that "tutoring," in the sense the word conveys at Oxford or Cambridge, is a far better method of exciting interest in the students' minds than the vast majority of lectures—that is indicated by the generally inferior status of the tutor to that of the professor—and it has far too seldom persuaded professors that the invention of the printed book has made most purely narrative lectures obsolete, a dissuasion, indeed, from reading. Far too many professors go on giving the same lectures unchanged from year to year, so that Kittredge on Shakespeare, or Babbitt on Romanticism, becomes for his hearers an ancient monument which they visit as an American in London has lunch at the Cheshire Cheese, or, in Paris, makes a hurried tour through the glories of the Louvre. In all this it is important to note that, in spite of the immense energy spent in most colleges in teaching English composition, an undergraduate with a "style" is as rare as one who, on his own initiative, has sought to explore something of that cultural heritage the significance of which the university is supposed to impress upon him.

It may be, as Dr. Capen, the chancellor of the University of Buffalo has argued, that "at least fifty per cent of the work done in [the university] ought properly to be classified as secondary education and rightly belongs to the secondary school";[5] I think myself that this is broadly true of practically all that is taught in the freshman year of an American college. But I think far more is due to the failure to convince the student that hard intellectual effort is really important, and that the achievement of genuine intellectual distinction is supremely valuable. If the student thought the status of intelligence as valuable as eminence in athletics, or the time spent on understanding why the American Revolution occurred as well spent as "making" the editorial board of the college paper or the management committee of the college glee club, he would not leave the university so intellectually immature or so resigned to the conviction that he has been prepared by social relations rather than by intellectual discipline for the battle of life. But it is in that temper that, very largely, he does leave; and it is the acceptance of the values this temper implies that accounts for the mass of decorative or vocational subjects which now force their way into the curriculum, either that the degree may be achieved with the minimum effort or that the student may enter life with one piece of baggage from the university that he does not want to leave behind him. I remember a student in a western university who told me with complete candour that he was far more interested by the effort to get advertisements from local shopkeepers when he was trying to "make" the college paper than he was by any of his lectures or seminars; and he is today a distinguished administrator in Washington.

I think myself that the explanation of this atmosphere has deep roots in American history. In part it is the natural outcome in a nation to which leisured reflection or a zeal for reading were less important than clearing a wilderness or building a house. And in part, especially in more recent times, it is the outcome of the fact that the accepted values of American civilization have been more decisively defined by the business man than by any other figure. His interest is in doing things, not in reflection upon causes. He wants results more than methods, ends rather than means. He has no great admiration for professors; they are abstract rather than practical, they ask curious questions, they are interested in queer and remote matters; above all, they very rarely make a respectably sized income. He understands a mind like that of Edison, which wants to turn a scientific principle into a commodity he can market for profit; he is barely patient with an attempt to explain to him that Albert A. Michelson was much the greater man. He understands why Mr. Chaplin is a great artist—his income stands as the proof of it. But, if he is told to accept Mary Cassatt as a great artist, he can only go by the prices her pictures bring at the sales. He believes in a college education for his son,

[5] Samuel P. Capen, *Inaugural Address* (Buffalo, 1922).

even for his daughter, since the statistics show that the average income of college graduates is higher than that of people who have not been to college. And he is pretty sure that his children's studies are less important than the contacts they make, the friendships they form, the status they gain in extracurricular activities. He wants his son to "make" the best fraternity, the best college clubs, to lead in those realms which he remembers, or has heard, are the really important ones. Where his son visits in his vacation, by whom he is invited to the Junior Prom at the neighbouring women's college, these are the things about which he and his wife will anxiously inquire. Of course, he will tell his boy or girl to work hard; but by "working hard" he does not mean intellectual development so much as being well regarded by classmates who can be helpful to him as a person worth cultivating for his future promise.

It is not therefore remarkable that intellectual values should be profoundly neglected in the undergraduate attitude. On the contrary, it would be remarkable if it were otherwise. Those who are disturbed about the outlook of the American university student, who speak, for example, about his cynicism, his indifference, his detachment, are really approaching the problem they confront from altogether the wrong premises. When Mr. Archibald MacLeish, for example, supposed that the students had been misled into isolationism before Pearl Harbor because they had read the wrong books, his simple diagnosis was a particular evasion of a situation far more complex than he was willing to admit even to himself. For when war actually came, and these students were swept by the hundred thousand into a war that was not of their making, the cynicism and indifference and detachment were as though they had never been. I have myself seen hundreds of these young men, and I have had innumerable letters from them. They are mostly very simple letters. They say little more than that the defeat of Hitler and Japan is necessary to the future of civilization and that when they come home—some of them, alas, never came home—they want to understand why the catastrophe of a world war occurred, and how they can prevent the next generation from having to face so terrible an experience. And as they were thinking these things, perhaps in the jungles of Southeast Asia, or in a foxhole in the African desert, their parents at home had one decisive thought uppermost in their minds: will it end soon enough for our sons to come home to a victorious America? Danger evoked from many of them a sense of proportion about values, which broke through even the hard veneer of what a business civilization sought to impose as a guiding creed upon all whom it encountered. But if, when the danger is over, there is nothing in peace to evoke that sense of proportion, if, even more, we try to suppress what the danger accomplished by an enthusiastic return to conventional ways of behaviour, we ought not to be really surprised if there is a return to the pre-war atmosphere in the colleges. Taken by and large, they cannot be other than a reflection of the society which created them. The limits within which they move are limits set for them by the forces in that society which seek to safeguard it from any search for fundamental change.

How much this is the case emerges from a report of the committee of Harvard professors who were set by the president of that great university the task of discovering what should be the purpose of general education in a free society.[6] What worries the committee is the loss of any central principle, which was what unified the educational effort of the nineteenth century when there was general acceptance of "the Christian view of man and history as providing both final meaning and immediate standards for life." They emphasize the need for "some over-all logic, some strong not easily broken frame, within which both school and college may fulfil their at once diversifying and uniting tasks." An "over-all logic," this is to say, is to release the full expression of individuality, while at the same time it impresses upon the student the need to act and live as a co-operating citizen in a democratic community. What is the formula for this "over-all logic"? The committee suggests the "ideal of co-operation on the level of action irrespective of agreement on ultimates." It does not seem to occur to the committee that this is in fact the evasion of the "over-all logic" they desire to attain. "Co-operation on the level of action" was possible in wartime between nations as different in outlook as Russia and the United States; it is the "agreement on ultimates" that became the vital matter the moment hostilities ceased. Mr. Churchill could lead a coalition government of Tories and Socialists until victory in Europe was won; afterwards, almost at once, "co-operation on the level of action" became impossible simply because Tory "ultimates" and Socialist "ultimates" were too distant from one another. The committee does not seem to realize that this is what always happens in life. They think that education produces the open mind, the reasonable man, toleration, that instincts and sentiments can be made subordinate to the claims of reason. It is pleasant to think so; but one wishes that the committee had some evidence to prove that the subordination has, in fact, been made. The problem of the Negro in the South, the relation of capital and labour in the California fruit farms or in the automobile industry in Michigan, would then be more hopeful than they appear to the outside observer. Nor is it easy to guess why the victory of reason may be expected if all college students at Harvard take a series of general courses in the humanities and in the social and natural sciences. Many universities for many years have given such courses without the result for which the committee looks so earnestly.

The truth is that the committee could not answer its own questions without seeking to probe into the social foundations of American life; and this, of course, would have involved a challenge it dare not make. Average American parents are not going to send their sons and daughters to any college from which they may come back convinced that the

---

[6] *General Education in a Free Society* (Cambridge: Harvard University Press, 1945). The second chapter acts out the general theme of the report.

American way of life needs to be thoroughly refashioned. The parents want their sons and daughters to be kind and gracious and intelligent; but they want them, above all, to know how to "get on" in contemporary America, and to begin by recognizing how rare it is to be at once success- ful and a non-conformist in any regular profession or calling. The com- mittee could not face the fact that the difficulties in the high school and the college merely reflect the difficulties in the United States itself. The "Christian view of man and history" has ceased to satisfy because the values it imposed have ceased to satisfy. There is an inner and profound conflict within the United States which reveals itself on all fundamental matters of social and economic constitution. And since the colleges are overwhelmingly controlled by one party to the conflict, they naturally reflect the artificial compromise made by university teachers who are uneasily aware that Milton was only right in the very long run when he insisted that truth is never worsted in an open encounter. The grave fact is that the encounter has ceased to be open in precisely those realms to which the conflict has moved. The same causes that made theological orthodoxy the centre of conflict a hundred years ago, make the demand for orthodoxy in the social sciences the centre of conflict today. A ruling class in any society will permit discussion of its fundamentals only when it can watch dissent from them with smiling ease. In the United States, as the passionate hatred of President Roosevelt made clear, there is no longer this confident serenity.

But the result of the absence of vital discussion on the mental climate of the American college is obvious. Very few of the central issues which di- vide men in the world outside can be fully and freely debated within its walls; or, if they are debated, the victory of the conventional must be as- sured. So that principles for which men wager their lives, even though they be mistaken, must lose all their ardent vitality as they receive aca- demic attention. The last generation of American students must have been bewildered indeed that the Russians should have made a successful revolu- tion in the name of Marxian doctrine if that doctrine could be refuted so easily in a brief course of lectures. They cannot have wondered less at the passionate antagonism to Wall Street, among farmers and trade-unionists, if the Great Depression of 1929 had no connection with policies so largely shaped by the men who controlled American finance. They may even have been disturbed to discover that an experiment like that of the Tennessee Valley Authority is outstandingly successful, when they have been taught that the public ownership of electric power is always a threat to sound American principles. Or, if they compare the public mythology of the Constitution with its analysis by scholars like J. Allen Smith or Charles Beard, the gap between legend and reality may become disturbing. And all this is much more likely to be the case if they find that a college presi- dent may be driven to resign for the offence of approving birth-control openly, when they know that contraceptives are sold in every drugstore; or that Roman Catholic voters may be able to prevent so eminent a philosopher as Bertrand Russell from teaching mathematical philosophy in the City College of New York because the ecclesiastical hierarchy abhors his social and ethical doctrine.

In this kind of confusion no unifying doctrine can be found for the simple reason that citizens in the community are ceasing to hold the great ends of life in common. There can be unity of action against the external foe; instinct and emotion then unite to make the intellectual judgment simple and straightforward. But unity of action within the community is inhibited in too many areas by the non-existence of unity of thought, since there are so many problems upon which the depth of disagreement prevents any agreement about the issues upon which action is to be taken. Even if a university, like Chicago under Chancellor Hutchins, adopts a kind of neo-Thomism as almost a quasi-official doctrine, some, and those the ablest, students will know either that it is a pathetic escapism or a half-baked and arrogant excuse for rejecting conventional values in America without seeming to threaten the claim to power of the American business man; [7] the few who are attracted to the doctrine usually suffer from some form of inferiority complex which they compensate by the conviction that its acceptance is proof that they belong to an *élite* in the community beyond the reach of the common man.

A unifying principle will be found in the college when a unifying principle is found in American life. But it will not be found in American life until men have rediscovered a common road upon which to travel to an agreed end. In such conditions the full and free analysis of contentious issues ceases to be a threat. The teacher can speak his mind without fear. He need not be appointed because he is aloof, or sound, or an almost professional opponent of unorthodox ideas. Where there are inhibited minds, the student quickly realizes that the result of inhibition is to make the college an ivory tower in which he is offered shelter from dangerous ideas; and since he is just at the age when ideas are interesting because they are dangerous, he quickly forms the conclusion that he need not take too seriously an academic life which he suspects to be, in the social sciences, at any rate, a well-organized technique of evasion. Nor will he be led to a different view even if he takes such new Orientation courses as the Harvard committee recommends. For they, in their turn, will only matter in the degree that he feels that his professors are teaching them so as to confront the contemporary scene in an honest effort to understand the whole of its meaning. He can detect the Westbrook Pegler or the George Sokolsky even in the solemn and sophisticated complexities of a sociologist whose statistics are intended to prove that Lenin should have benefited from the superior wisdom of his teacher.

[7] *Cf.* John U. Nef, *The United States and Civilization* (Chicago: University of Chicago Press, 1942).

7

GRADUATE work in the American university has two major sides. On the one hand it is professional training for a vocation like law or medicine. If the standard of this training inevitably varies from place to place, few serious observers would deny that, at its best, it is far ahead of any similar training in Europe. A great law school, like that of Harvard or Yale, Wisconsin or Columbia, will turn out students who, at their best, are likely not only to know more law than, say, an average law teacher in a British university, but also to have a far more critical mind about the problems of the law. These best students will have helped to produce, with no more than occasional professorial advice, journals of a quality good enough to be cited with respect by the most eminent American judges. Their teachers will naturally be considered for the highest judicial positions. Mr. Justice Holmes was a professor at the Harvard Law School when he was called to the Supreme Court of Massachusetts; so was Professor Felix Frankfurter when Mr. Roosevelt nominated him to the Supreme Court of the United States. Professor W. O. Douglas went from Yale, through the Securities and Exchange Commission, to the Supreme Court as the youngest judge who had sat there since the famous Story; Dean Charles E. Clark and Professor Thurman Arnold went, by way of Yale also, to the United States Circuit Court of Appeals. Dean Harlan Stone of Columbia University Law School went therefrom, first, to be the Attorney-General of the United States, and thence to the federal Supreme Court of which he became Chief Justice. Nor is it unimportant to note that when Mr. Taft ceased to be president of the United States, he became professor of constitutional law at the Yale Law School, and later returned to Washington to become the only ex-president of the United States who also occupied the great post of Chief Justice. These are merely instances of a general habit of mind.

There have, of course, been professors of law in British universities of the highest intellectual distinction. Blackstone and Dicey, Sir Frederick Pollock, and that greatest of all English historians since Gibbon, F. W. Maitland, were all for many years professors of law. But of them all, Blackstone was the only one to reach the Bench, and this was less because he was an eminent Vinerian Professor at Oxford, than because, in between, he was a member of Parliament and Solicitor-General. No doubt it is true that a number of English judges have lectured upon a part-time basis in English law schools, like Lord Wright, who was an early and brilliant lecturer on commercial law at the London School of Economics and Political Science. But they invariably do this only while they are establishing their position at the Bar; it is a temporary financial expedient and no more. And even if, in the last thirty years, there has been a tendency for the Lord Chancellor to offer the dignity of King's Counsel to a few law teachers of exceptional eminence like Dicey, this remains infrequent; and I am, I think, right in believing that between

Blackstone and the present time Sir Henry Maine is the only great jurist
—an English lawyer uses the term to denote a lawyer remote from practical experience—to whom high judicial office has been offered; and it
must be remembered that he had served a full term as legal member of
the Viceroy's Council in India. The main road to the Bench in England
lies, first, through the House of Commons, and next through actual practice; a "writing" lawyer may even find himself at a disadvantage, since
the habit is to think that a barrister is free to publish because his desk is
empty of briefs. England supports one law review of real distinction, and
another, not yet of equal standing, which is still struggling to live. The
Cambridge Faculty of Law produces an annual number of a law review,
and the London School of Economics and Political Science an "Annual
Survey" of judicial and administrative decisions and of statutory en-
actments. Books, mainly textbooks, apart, there are hardly half a dozen
really eminent names in the whole range of its legal literature since Bentham and Maine.

The contrast with the law schools of the United States is startling. It
is startling in the quality of teachers; it is startling in the volume and
distinction of their published work; and it is startling in the light of the
achievement of American students at their best. The big law firm in New
York or Boston or Chicago jumps at the chance of getting one of the
top men from a good American school; so, too, especially in recent years,
has the administration at Washington or New York. It would be easy
to name a score of young graduates who went from Harvard directly to
a post of real significance in the office of the Attorney-General or of the
Secretary of Labor, in the Department of the Interior or the Department
of State; a journey, I suggest, that would be almost unthinkable in
England. The professor of law on a faculty, with a high standing in
the profession, is a man held in high esteem; even his favourite pupils
are sought after. Judges will eagerly canvass his opinion of their decisions; they are not unlikely themselves to write against him in defence
of themselves. In the result, a good American law school is not merely
a place where law is often admirably taught; it is also a place where a
good deal of important law is likely to be made. As a consequence, no
one who knows the dozen or so major law schools can really doubt that
they are far more alive, far more able to elicit eager interest from their
students, far more likely to be engaged in significant research, than all
the English law schools put together. I hazard the guess that Professor
Sheldon Glueck of the Harvard Law School has done more, in his own
department, for the serious study of criminal law in its results upon convicted defendants than all the law schools of England together with the
work of the Prison Commission, the four Inns of Court, and the Law
Society. There is nothing that remotely compares, either in fullness or
precision, with the crime surveys of Cleveland and of Boston, or of
similar studies, like those of procedure and bankruptcy and freedom of
speech, which have been undertaken either singly or in co-operation by

American professors of law. Nor can I omit to emphasize that no generation of students seems to leave the better schools without receiving from their teachers an inspiration to study some problem in law reform.

Of the position of the medical schools I am not, of course, competent to make a judgment in similarly comparative terms. But there is, I believe, no shadow of doubt that American medical education, at its best, is at least as good as that of any other country. It is indeed notable how considerable a proportion of the eminent figures in modern American medicine have bred teachers in the university schools. The fame of the Johns Hopkins Medical School, in the days of Welch and Osler and Adolf Meyer, hardly yields precedence to that of the University of Vienna in its greatest days. It is, moreover, suggestive that, almost a generation before Great Britain, the better American schools had realized the significance of social and industrial medicine, and the value of the history of medicine in its community setting as a clue to the secret of its progress. In this regard, it is not too much to say that the works of Henry E. Sigerist at Johns Hopkins marks something of an epoch in the development of medical education; as those of Bernhard Stern have done at Columbia University. Dr. Sigerist and his colleagues realized, what only an occasional figure had recognized elsewhere, that if medicine is put in its proper historical background, much of its failures and successes begin to be understood. Nor is there much doubt that the policy of whole-time professorships to which medical men of the first quality are called while they are young enough to do pioneering in research has had great advantages in making the university schools of medicine, at any rate at their best, something akin to what the Graduate School of Medicine in London was intended to be.

Broadly speaking, the university professional schools have been a remarkable success. The general standard of their teaching is extraordinarily high; the level of student interest is exceptional; and the schools manage not only to produce research work of outstanding distinction, but imbue a considerable proportion of their students with the sense that an interest in the social responsibilities of the *métier* they follow is part of the obligation they assume when they decide to follow it. The comparison, in this regard, between the law schools of America and the law schools of Britain is all to the former's advantage. The British law school has not yet found any creative place in the system of training either for the Bar or for the solicitors' side of the profession. The American law school has made itself not only the main source from which the best lawyers and the best judges are likely to be recruited, but also a vital instrument in the struggle for law reform. The kind of criticism which judicial opinion and legal administration ought perpetually to encounter is something that the British university law school has hardly even begun to recognize that it ought to undertake as part of its normal function; that function has been primary in the work of an American law school, at any rate of the first rank, for something like fifty years. And if it be said that the British law schools have produced great scholars, Maine, Maitland, Pollock, Holdsworth, to take some outstanding examples, the answer is the simple one that the American schools have produced Holmes, Ames, Thayer, and Pound, quite apart from their additional claim to have set the criteria of criticism in issues of contemporary doctrine in work like that of Thomas Reed Powell in constitutional law, of Francis H. Bohlen in the law of torts, of John Chipman Gray in the law of real property, of Frankfurter, in his academic period, in the vital field of administrative law, of Chafee in the field of civil liberties. And this is quite apart from the work done by the university law schools in the important field of legal administration, which in Britain has mostly been left either to an occasional government committee or to some solitary investigator who, like Sir Edward Parry, was driven to furious protest by daily experience of the urgent need for reform in one aspect of the work of the court over which he presided with such distinction. Lawyers with the deep social responsibility of Parry are as rare in England as jurists with a passion, like Bentham, to adapt law to the needs of a new time.

It is curious to note how different are the habits, and the results, of the non-professional graduate schools from those of their professional analogues. To understand this difference the graduate school must, however briefly, be set in its historical background. It was far from infrequent for American scholars of a century ago, men like Ticknor and Everett and Bancroft, to spend several years in Europe in preparation for the life work they intended to undertake. For the most part they were in comfortable circumstances. They accepted the New England tradition, so finely exemplified in Parkman and Prescott, that private wealth ought to admit its obligations by devotion to the cultivation of knowledge. Not a few of them were deeply perturbed by the mainly English criticism that the American contribution to letters and learning was, compared with its wealth, of relative insignificance; and since many of them were still in thrall to the idea that American scholarship was a minor branch of English scholarship, they were, in no small degree, moved by a desire for intellectual independence. That attitude was emphasized in a famous appeal of William Ellery Channing,[8] and later in the acid but brilliant phrase of James Russell Lowell in which he referred to "a certain condescension among foreigners." The desire for cultural independence coincided with, was even, perhaps, an outgrowth of, the persistent attempt of American economists, especially after the war of 1812, to plead, like Henry Carey, for a new political economy which would suit American conditions and therefore reject the postulates of the classical political economy which the predominance of England had fastened upon Europe.[9] And it was, no doubt, greatly aided by the rise of the new West, and the sense there that neither the habits nor the forms of eastern cul-

---

[8] *Remarks on National Literature,* in *Complete Works* (London, no date), p. 101.
[9] See Dorfman, *The Economic Mind in American Civilization,* Vol. II, Chap. XXIX.

ture, so obviously tied to European, above all to English, models, would suit the circumstances of a new America. Even if they were criticized and disliked, there can be but little doubt that the growth of the West had an immense influence on American ways of thought.

Slowly before the Civil War, but with remarkable acceleration after it, this attitude coincided with the discovery of German university scholarship, with its immense achievements and elaborate organization. Many of the younger students began to visit the German universities and to take their doctorate degrees in Germany. When Johns Hopkins University was founded, research there began to be built around the seminar, with the conception of the professor, surrounded by his band of devoted pupils, working at some problem he thought important in a coherent and systematic way. It began to be the custom to train the student for scholarship by an elaborate discipline in methodology and bibliography, in the proper grasp of the way to handle original sources, in the belief that true learning emerged from the intensive cultivation of a small field of inquiry rather than from embarking, before the student was ripe enough for investigation, on some massive issue beyond his powers and experience. To this, I think, must be added the important inferences that the young scholar's work ought to be worthy of publication, that if he took one part of a field, his neighbour in the seminar might well take a related part, which enabled each to stimulate the other—the real beginning, I suspect, of the modern craze for co-operative research—and that a period of devotion such as this to original research was the necessary prelude to the work of university teaching. The publication in 1883 of the first series of the Johns Hopkins *Studies in Historical and Political Science* was a landmark in the academic history of the United States. Within a decade the doctorate in philosophy had become the well-nigh indispensable passport to the right to teach in an American university.

The popularity of the system grew by leaps and bounds. A university soon became an institution which could take pride in its ability to attract graduate students. Research achieved a status equal with teaching in importance; the tradition became established that there was little or no hope of a permanent university position without the degree of doctor of philosophy. Teachers were appointed in the belief that, where they went, research students would follow; it even became increasingly necessary for the teacher to publish in order that his name might be continually in the minds of students who were uncertain what university to choose for their graduate work. Or, if he did not publish, he needed the kind of influence with his colleagues in other universities which enabled him to secure posts for the students who were registered under his supervision. Once, moreover, the doctorate had become a passport to a college post, it began to be a distinction universally sought. The members of the faculty of a normal school desired it as a means to promotion. A teacher in a high school would regard it as the key which unlocked the door to a principalship. It became necessary to invent ways and means of helping along the young men and women in quest, in ever-increasing numbers, of their Ph.D. Not everyone could be given a scholarship, still less a travelling scholarship. But there could be teaching fellows, who combined some form or other of class work, quarter-time or half-time, with their research; there could be university assistants, who paid their way through college by taking off the professor's hands the laborious work of holding the "quiz" or a class or reading his examination papers for him; or there could be the research assistant to the professor, who hunted down references for him in the library, made notes at his indication of significant material he desired to use but had not the time to go through for himself, read his proofs for printers' errors, and compiled the index to his book. I have even known research assistants who read and digested for their professors books in languages the professors could not read, so that, on publication, they could not be accused of overlooking important foreign work they ought to have known. And in between the performance of such labours the assistant went on with his own researches. First, as a rule, he took the master's degree, an examination in a field of studies connected with the subject on which he thought of specializing. Then he prepared for and took his general examination, an oral examination in which a group of professors "grilled" him, much in the manner of continental Europe, to be sure that his background knowledge was adequate for the work on which he proposed to embark. After this, he would begin preparing his thesis, which might take him anywhere from two to five or six years, according to the time at his disposal and his habits of work.

The range of academic studies, moreover, which now shelter themselves under the wings of a university institution has increased at an almost terrifying speed. There is the vast area of commerce, both territorial and functional; there is the complex called "home economics," which may include the analysis of family budgets or the examination of the machinery most suitable for dish-washing in small restaurants. There is the immense area called "education," on which one student may be working at the history of the methods of teaching elementary arithmetic, another on professional solidarity among teachers in England, a third on tendencies towards centralization in the state educational system of Illinois, and a fourth on what French critics think of the American educational system. The study of Romance philology may take one man to the examination of what Dante has to say about each species of the animal kingdom mentioned in his works, and another to an analysis of the use in French of the infinite, instead of the finite, verb. A group of students may take the problems of reconstruction in the South after the Civil War, and each give attention to their impact upon a particular state. Another group may study the drift to administrative centralization in one or a number of states. As each new specialism pushes its way to university recognition, it is hardly unfair to say that its teachers feel they have won for it its full status when one of their students has received his doctorate in the subject.

The writing of a thesis goes through a physiological rhythm almost as regular as the circulation of the blood. The student chooses his "topic" in consultation with the professor who is to supervise his work. It is curiously rare for a student to know what it is he wants to write about. Far more usually, he accepts the professor's suggestion, and he then decides upon a theme from a list of possible subjects which the wise professor keeps, as it were, in stock; or he works upon some project the material of which may ultimately be the basis of a chapter, or a paragraph, or a footnote in the *magnum opus* the professor is writing. The subject once chosen, the student compiles a bibliography of whatever exists about his subject, with special reference to manuscript material or to remote sources, like old newspapers, not previously used in work upon his theme. He goes through all the obvious material conscientiously, taking careful notes as he reads; if the manuscripts are in Europe, in the British Museum, for example, or the Bibliothèque Nationale, he tries to get a scholarship to London or Paris, or to get a loan against his future, to consult them; or he may be fortunate enough to persuade a wealthy university to have photostatic copies made that he can peruse at leisure in its library. After more note-taking, he begins to arrive at a scheme of work which he will probably amend somewhat in the light of discussion with his supervisor. He then begins the heavy work of writing his thesis, consulting at intervals his supervisor or other professors from whom he may get ideas or counsel. As he writes, he will support each statement he makes with a footnote showing the source from which it is taken, until, not seldom, the text itself seems like a small island, surrounded by a veritable ocean of references. And when the last chapter is done, he will conscientiously add the most comprehensive bibliography he can compile, perhaps classified with a minute precision that would evoke a smile of approval from the shade of that ingenious librarian who invented the Dewey decimal system. The thesis submitted, he is examined upon it by a small committee of professors to whose hands is entrusted the fate of the research and its author.

Not even in Germany has so massive a system been evolved, so intricate and so terrifying, in order to help a young man or woman learn how to write a book. It has evoked an endless stream of protests, of which, perhaps, the acid essay of William James [10] is the most famous. But no criticism has yet proved powerful enough to stay its torrential movement; it has been said that in the year before the outbreak of the Second World War more than three thousand doctorates were granted in the United States. I have myself calculated that in one Midwestern university alone, and that by no means the largest of its area, over six hundred doctorates were conferred from 1919 to 1939. Sometimes the university re-

---

[10] "The Ph. D. Octopus," in *Memories and Studies* (New York: Longmans, 1912).

quires that the theme be printed; most of them today more mercifully ask no more than the submission of several typewritten copies, one of which will remain on file in its library. But few of them are published in the ordinary way; only a minute percentage, when published, ever reach the dignity of a second edition. Out of 459 numbers in the Johns Hopkins' series, which represents the best work of all its graduate students in the social sciences for sixty years, only fifty-four are out of print; and the demand for these is apparently not ample enough to justify reprinting. Out of 380 numbers in the well-known Columbia University *Studies in History and Economics and Public Law,* published between 1893 and 1903, only nine appear to be out of print, and only one volume seems to have gone into a second edition. Much the same is true of similar series published under the auspices of Harvard and Yale Universities.

Obviously enough, statistics of this character tell but a small part of the significance of any volume. Few people would, or could, rightly expect that a learned and heavily documented book could normally expect to have a wide sale. Its author is almost certain to be unknown; his theme is likely to be narrow; nor is he likely to have made any exciting discoveries or put forward any important generalizations. Yet, when all this is granted, the picture remains a disturbing one. A student writes a book not because he feels called to write that particular book, but because he is bound to write a book in order, broadly speaking, to have a certificate of competence which entitles him to begin or to continue teaching in a university. He rarely conceives of the subject he takes as the preliminary study for some great book he has at least the ambition one day to write. He rarely even seeks to approach it in an original way. It is often thorough, often useful, now and again it may shed some new ray of light of real significance upon its subject. It is but seldom that its author finds inspiration or even stimulus in doing it. It is a task that must be got through; it is a means to opening a gate, a possible road to promotion. Rarely, indeed, does he see the bridge between his particular field of study and the next field. Rarely, either, does he inquire whether what he does is important in itself or likely to be the basis upon which some later scholar may build more important work. His anxiety is to get the work done so that he may enter the stage of work where he has become his own master.

I do not want for an instant to paint a picture that is out of perspective. Everyone knows that remarkable books have been written for the doctorate, and that some of them rank as indispensable in their field. But that is not because they were written for the doctorate; it is because they were written by remarkable men and women. The system as a whole holds hundreds of students in bondage every year to an idea that is wholly illusory. Some of them are fundamentally incapable of writing a good book. Others are not yet mature enough to write one. Others, again, have no desire to write a book and learn little or nothing from their effort to write it. And the system develops habits of its own. It begets what the

French call the *fureur de l'inédit*. It begets the obligation not to write upon a topic, however important, upon which someone else is known to be writing; hence the publication every year, in the learned American journals, of long lists of subjects already pre-empted. It begets the passion for footnotes, the conviction that no statement will be believed unless it can be referred to an earlier writer or document, and it gets, perhaps above all, what can only be termed bibliographical elephantiasis. No doubt there are supervisors work with whom is an illumination the light from which will give vision to the student for the rest of his days; no one who worked with Frederick J. Turner, or with Carl Becker, but must have felt the excitement of seeing how the great artist hews from the rough stone a portrait which comes to life, just as no one can have submitted an idea for critical examination to William James, or to Morris Cohen, without the joy of seeing how a great swordsman can cut it to pieces. Quite obviously, a man who is born for thought or learning, whether in the humanities or in the sciences, will find the Ph.D. a hurdle he can take in his stride; and there will always be some for whom the system leads to association out of which solid work, even occasionally inspired work, will emerge.

Yet, granted all this, the system has now become a vast machine which kills the very purposes it was intended to serve. It leads to premature and excessive specialization. It leads to the production of a fantastic mass of minute researches of which but a small part has any special significance either for the author or for the public they are intended to reach. In the social sciences especially, it breeds a race of researchers who cannot see the woods for the trees. But its worst effect is, I think, that in all save the really exceptional scholar, it becomes a form of escapism which makes for unreal thinking and ineffective teaching. It makes for the first because the intense concentration on a small theme seems to breed a type which becomes afraid either of large generalizations or considering issues which reach beyond its boundaries. He becomes unaccustomed to the co-ordination of his specialism with the larger problems of which it is a part. There even comes a time when he resents being asked either to let his mind play freely over a large realm of ideas or to show an awareness that the need to arrive is not less important than the preparation for the journey. And he becomes, only too often, an ineffective teacher, because his training inhibits him from realizing that the one thing his students want to know is how the subject helps to explain the kind of world in which they live. He thinks that the more he detaches himself from such an explanation, the more scholarly his treatment ought to be regarded. He begins by taking no risks because he is uncertain; he ends by taking no risks because he has ceased, by use and wont, to have any convictions at all. He becomes a purveyor of information, most of which is easily available in books, which he retails afresh every year in much the same way as an automobile dealer sells his cars.

It would be an immense boon to American education if the Ph.D., together with the immense administrative apparatus it has come to involve, were got rid of altogether. Most of the labour it involves is not in any real sense, educational. Most of the men and women who have something real to say in their chosen field of study would say it anyhow, whether there were a degree or no; and its existence leads a multitude of people to try to say something when they are uneasily conscious either that they have nothing to say or that what they are asked to examine is not in fact worth, as a problem, the immense effort they have to spend upon it. I think it is reasonable to insist that most of the creative minds in American universities are aware that this is the case; but they shrink from the effort involved in a sustained attack upon what has now become an immense vested interest in the university. Not least among the evils is the fact that it tends to destroy the reflective mind, the mind that broods over a large range of facts until, by a flash of insight, a relation is seen between them from which they come to have a new meaning. In place of the thinker, it puts the card index; in place of the play of ideas, it puts the footnote and the bibliography. Nothing invented since the Inquisition has had so sterilizing an effect upon that habit of free speculation and eager debate of first principles out of which the scholar is most likely to transform information into wisdom.

Two other features of the university system deserve a word. The first derives directly, the other indirectly, from the institution of the doctorate. The first is the use of volume of production as one of the main indices to promotion. Unless a teacher makes his mark early, either by a promising piece of work or by the quality of his personality, there is a constant drive to publish, especially in a large university, lest his claim to promotion be overlooked. The result is that the learned journals of the United States are full of what can only be called machine-made research in which the habits of the aspirant to a Ph.D. are prolonged year after year until the teacher is satisfied he can climb no higher. He is afraid of being labelled as "unproductive," so that, year after year, he will de-devote his leisure to grinding out articles which are only too often dead even before they have reached the printed page. And because most of the scholars who edit the journals are aware that the articles are insignificant, the question of whether to publish them or not tends to become either the presence of some unpublished document or the tabulation of some material, the first of which will only very rarely have importance, and the second of which will give a precision, the labour of which is out of all proportion to its value, to some simple platitude which everyone knew before. It may be a letter, say, of Robert Southey saying that he has received a parcel of books for which he had asked, or it may be a table to prove that in a New England village there are more Packards above the railroad tracks per family than there are below them. The point I am concerned to make is that the whole academic atmosphere tends to lead to the insistent cult of the insignificant, and those who are driven to the practice of this cult are bound themselves, before long, to become insignificant too.

The other feature which needs emphasizing is the cult of the textbook. This depends upon a number of factors. The need for a doctorate tends to make the achievement of a permanent university post something that few teachers will reach before their thirties. By this time they may well be married and have family responsibilities. They find it difficult to live in any real comfort on their salaries. They know that the author of a successful textbook will certainly earn a far greater reward than he is likely to do in the normal way if he gives his time to serious research. His needs are great; the publisher's offer is tempting. He knows that it is, of course, a gamble, but if it is a successful gamble he can buy a new car, or take his family away for the summer vacation instead of spending hot and tiring days in New York City or Chicago, or get someone in "to do the chores or look after the children" so that his wife may have some time in which to call her soul her own. The result can be seen in the catalogue of any educational publisher in the United States. Each has his history of America, his government of America, his geography of America, his principles of economics, his textbook of statistical method, or of accountancy, or of ancient history, or of medieval history, or of modern history. Once there is a large potential audience to whom teachers can address textbooks, they will be published almost beyond computation; and since the appetite grows by what it feeds on, one success is only too likely to lead to another venture, in the hope that it may be repeated. These books vary very little from one another. They usually crowd such a mass of information into their six to eight hundred pages that the student loses himself in their midst. And, worst of all, the need to get the book used in as large a range of colleges as possible leads to the suppression of any ideas that have colour or vitality or a bias that might offend. Nor must it be forgotten that one of the inevitable results on the student is that he expects to find in the textbook all he needs to know about the subject, and he tends to regard with horror the notion that he may reasonably be asked to read the original authorities out of which the subject gained its existing contours.

8

NOTHING in all this detracts from the two outstanding facts that there are great American schools and colleges and great American teachers. What I am seeking to throw into full perspective are four things. There are too many Americans, especially in the South among the migratory workers and among the Negroes, who are either getting no education at all, or not enough education, or education under physical conditions that are fatal to the results it seeks to achieve. There is, in short, far too unequal a distribution of educational opportunity. Up to the high school level, it is generally inadequate in the South, especially in the rural areas, and the salaries paid to teachers are far too low to attract sufficient competence into the profession; too often teaching is merely a halt on the road to a decently paid vocation. And at both the high school stage and the college stage the system suffers, first, from lack of any clear perception of a common and recognized purpose, and, second, from the confusion between the art of thought and vocational instruction on the one hand, and between an intellectual discipline and a social function on the other. To this must be added that there is, in general, a constant tendency to overcentralization, with its inevitable result of exalting the administrator at the expense of the teacher, and to that excessive devotion to graduate studies which so often results in the sacrifice of the wide horizon to a premature and extravagant specialization. What makes the educational work of Dewey, or the classic exhortations of William James, so notable, is their realization that the teacher, whether in school or college, must be in the fullest sense a thinking citizen before the work of any educational institution can be adequate to its high purpose.

It is precisely that power of the teacher to be, in the fullest sense, a thinking citizen that is continually obstructed, and often perverted, by the mental climate of an America dominated by the business man, who is so curiously fearful of the habit of free speculation. This is a temper than which there is nothing more hostile to the real task of the teacher. Because of that fear, half a hundred malign influences play on the school and college under its protection. They are the victims, too often, of the political machines; the "teachers' oath" controversy in Massachusetts is a good example of this. They are swayed this way and that by pressure groups of every kind. Now it is a Church which demands undue influence; now it is some employers' propaganda organization seeking, as in the field of public utilities, direct indoctrination of students; even the publishers have what it is difficult not to call "lobbies," which try, through pressure and even bribery, to get one textbook rather than another adopted in a state. Sometimes it is the press, especially the "yellow" press, which tries to manufacture enough public hysteria over usually nonexistent dangers to terrorize the teacher into submission to its own view of the boundaries of legitimate discussion. Here it may be the local Chamber of Commerce; there it may be the local branch of the American Legion; somewhere else it is the local branch of the Knights of Columbus. All of them think that school and college are the legitimate objects of their interference. None of them seems willing to realize that what matters, above all in lecture room or classroom, is the quality of the teacher's mind and character, and that when they are set on inhibiting these in any direction, they are really cutting away the foundations of creative education. I remember vividly the remark of the able superintendent of education in a Midwestern state, who said to me that the politics of his job left him no time for any serious reflection upon educational matters. "I have," he said bitterly, "been chosen to appease all the interests which want to take over the schools from the community."

The fact is that business men very rarely understand the meaning of education or its purpose; they all believe in a mystic entity called "education"; but they have rarely thought through their mysticism to the point where they can think reasonably about it. They are far too prone to think that the "practical mind" is the one thing of importance, without ever asking themselves what assumptions lie behind the mass production of "practical" minds. They are far too prone, also, to believe that freedom ought to end where their private prejudices begin; and they can rarely be made to understand what little relation there is between their private prejudices and reason. They do not easily accept the dynamic of social life, so that, especially in fields where first principles are being remade, they are likely to equate speculative innovation with actual evil. All of them would be horrified—perhaps the upholders of denominational schools are an exception—if they were told that they were attempting, no doubt on a smaller scale and less successfully, the kind of social indoctrination against which they protested so angrily under the Nazi regime in Germany or in the era of emperor worship in Japan. Yet that is really the case. When Professor Scott Nearing, admittedly both a competent economist and an admirable teacher, states his opinion freely of what T. H. Huxley would have called the "corybantic Christianity" of the notorious evangelist Billy Sunday, he is obviously harbouring "dangerous thoughts," and his contract with the University of Pennsylvania is not renewed. When a president of the University of Michigan explains the necessity of birth-control, it is made convenient for him to resign. These are merely significant illustrations of a general temper which has a profound and pernicious effect on every aspect of American education.

An eminent American educationalist, George S. Counts, once posed the question whether the schools of the United States dare build a new social order. The answer, of course, is in the negative. No educational system, at any level, will ever transcend the general postulates of the community in which it works; and those postulates, in a broad and general way, will be set by the values accepted by the ruling class in that society. There will, no doubt, be occasional deviations from the norm; here and there a non-conformist, especially a non-conformist whose reputation in the world of learning is international, will not only be given a licence to roam at large, but attention will even be directed to his non-conformity in proof of the tolerance of the system. For an educational system does not exist in a vacuum. It exists always within a social system which makes its own nature and purpose the framework within which the nature and purpose of its educational idea must function. Any real discussion of education is therefore a discussion of the society in which it operates, and once we begin to discuss social change, it is obvious that we must discuss a change from one end or principle to another end or principle. The discussion must be conscious and deliberate and thorough: that is to say, it must really be an open and free discussion of a philosophy of life. It must go beyond the changes which happen without our having willed them, to the changes we seek to make happen by social action because we believe them to be desirable in the light of our philosophy of life. But men cannot really debate their philosophies of life— for it is agreed that there no longer exists what the Harvard University committee calls "agreement about ultimates"—without examining the very basis of our civilization.

It is easy to see the difference between the change we consciously make and the change that occurs out of circumstances we have not ourselves willed. The "progressive" schools of America are mostly an example of the first. Some social group, usually people in affluent circumstances in a metropolitan area, are dissatisfied with the educational methods in the community in which they live. They combine to form an experimental school of their own where, with their approval, the teachers seek to apply some new method to a group usually of the founders' children and the children of some of their friends. The fees are likely to be high; the new method is likely to be derived from some inference from a new phase in child psychology which is fashionable at the moment; and, after a time, the original impulse of experiment dies away, leaving the school to function as just one more private school among other private schools, which differs from the ordinary public schools, in the fact that its higher-income-group parents can pay for a larger proportion of teachers to pupils. Some of these schools, like the well-known Lincoln School in New York City, had a considerable body of experience behind them, and they did exceptionally well, for a carefully chosen group of children, much the same things as the publicly owned and controlled schools of the city. No one, I think, has yet sought to found a "progressive" school which is built upon principles outside the predominant American "way of life." "Progressive" means, in the main, a belief that preparation of the child to enter upon that "way of life" can be eased or advanced by techniques the ordinary school system is neither able nor willing to employ.

The other type of private school is simply a variation upon the English principle of the boarding school. A few of them, like Groton, or Andover, or Exeter, are a fairly conscious imitation of the English public school as this was shaped by Thomas Arnold and Edward Thring, save that none of them lays the English emphasis upon the study, from an early age, of Latin and Greek. The rest are privately owned adventures in which the boy or girl is taken off the parents' hands at a fairly high fee and educated for college, or for business, or for "society," or in the hope of entrance to West Point or Annapolis. A large number of them will stress some special feature, like riding or secretarial practice, or the "arts and crafts," and some even take their pupils, with proper chaperonage, for three or six months to France or Italy, where they receive a final "cultural" polish and brush up their French or Italian by contact with its native expression. Obviously the motives which have enabled these schools to grow at so remarkable a rate in the last fifty years are very mixed. The parents have to be in China, or a boarding school makes an impending divorce much easier, or both parents are at work all day, or the child is a difficult one who seems to need special attention. But I think it is not an exaggeration to suggest that the growth of the private school in the United States was the outcome of the sudden increase of the *novi homines* and their wives in the golden days after the Civil War. They differentiated the children of the new wealth by making it no longer necessary for them to go to the same schools as the children of wage-earners; and it was obviously the hope that this would bring them closer, both in manners and in outlook, to the children of parents whose wealth had a considerable pedigree behind it. Nor is this development unconnected with the growth of special colleges for women, like Bryn Mawr, or Vassar, or Smith, which were meant to do for the daughters of the upper middle class what Harvard and Yale and Princeton did for their sons. The "genteel" tradition in school and college was thus differentiated from the older tradition, which emphasized the importance of the common school as an element in maintaining the American principle of democracy.

Nothing has, indeed, ever been able to build up an "old school tie" tradition in the United States which has even the pale shadow of the influence it possesses in Great Britain. It is not a help, but a hindrance, to a political career to have been at Groton or at Exeter. Independent means do not count for very much except in the Foreign Service of America; and they count there because it still remains difficult for an American diplomat, whether in Washington or in a foreign capital, to live that "fashionable" life the official is so curiously required to live on the rather meagre salaries paid by the State Department. But the habit of an education separated from the tradition of the common school is growing. No one exactly set it on foot with any conscious purpose; it merely began and spread because it was found to supply a need in the skilful supply of which there was profit. Nor is it accident that, parallel with this growth, there has, slowly but surely, emerged that cult of the *élite* in the United States which has looked with wistful appreciation to the more "aristocratic" societies of Europe with their "standards," their easy and gracious habits of command, their supposed sense of *noblesse oblige,* their imagined remoteness from the sordid business of money-making. Not even the deadly satire of Finley Peter Dunne could make the heiresses of New York or Chicago doubt that it was somehow more imposing to be the wife of an English peer, or an Italian prince, or even of a French vicomte whom the coming of the Third Republic left without status or function. "Culture" in the life of the new wealthy class, as in the springtime of New England, really meant being like Prescott, or

Parkman, or Tyler, who wrote works of classical quality as a vocation. It meant buying famous pictures at fantastic prices on the advice of an expert, or making collections of rare books which surpassed most collections known outside the great public libraries of Europe. Or one might amass the treasures of early American craftsmanship, as in furniture, or entertain with a magnificence which, if rivalling Imperial Rome in its luxuries, differed from it in that the more exclusive the circle of one's guests, the more distinguished one's entertainment was supposed to be.

The basic philosophy of the small oligarchy which by the eighties of the last century had come to exercise a power in the United States, hardly even threatened until 1933, was stated with candour and incisiveness by Mr. F. T. Martin in 1911. "The class I represent," he wrote, "care nothing for politics . . . [but] touch the question of the tariff, touch the issue of the income tax, touch the problem of railroad regulations, or touch the most vital of all business matters, the question of general federal regulation of industrial corporations, and the people among whom I live my life become immediately rabid partisans. . . . It matters not one iota what political party is in power or what president holds the reins of office. We are not politicians or public thinkers; we are the rich; we own America; we got it, God knows how, but we intend to keep it, if we can, by throwing all the tremendous weight of our support, our influence, our money, our political connection, our purchased senators, our hungry congressmen, our public speaking demagogues, into the scale against any legislature, any political platform, any presidential campaign that threatens the integrity of our estate." [11] Mr. Martin was not exaggerating. He was merely describing with clear-minded accuracy the premises upon which the financial oligarchy did their thinking. And they knew their men. They helped to pick Theodore Roosevelt as the Progressive candidate in 1912 in order to ward off the far worse danger of the elder Robert M. La Follette. They were influential in securing Woodrow Wilson as the Democratic candidate in that year not only because they saw that he was the safest alternative to William Jennings Bryan, but also because they knew that his liberalism, however pungent its speech, worked within well-defined limits which did not touch the heart of the oligarchic power; indeed, in his second victory of 1916, the issues of the European war had already made it unnecessary to threaten the great financial empires of America. Their help was too badly needed to aid in the task of producing war materials upon an adequate scale.

And in the production of war materials they learned how to adapt the propaganda of the war effort to peace. "The war taught us the power of propaganda," wrote Mr. Roger Babson, business "forecaster," in 1921; "now when we have anything to sell to the American people, we know how to sell it. We have the school, the pulpit, and the press." There fol-

[11] Frederick Townsend Martin, *The Passing of the Idle Rich* (New York: Doubleday, Page, 1911).

lowed those years of amazing effort to sell the United States the "American plan," and the immensity of that effort can be judged by the remark of the Senate Committee on Education and Labor in 1926 that after they had all allayed the danger of "radical revolution," the National Association of Manufacturers had "settled back to the quiet enjoyment of the fruits of their efforts during the years of prosperity." [12] Nor were they wholly without justification. Even in the hard year of depression in 1930, the American Federation of Labor preached the need for active cooperation with management. "The overwhelming majority of the American people," wrote Mr. F. L. Allen, "believed with increasing certainty that business men knew better than anybody else what was good for the country." [13] Only the reader who carefully studies Mr. Beale's patient and relentless examination of the pressures to which the teacher is subjected [14] can grasp what that meant; even the American Bar Association declared its anxiety to "reach the mind of the child while it is plastic," while an information committee of the public utilities of Illinois, which expressed, of course, the aims of that dishonourable architect of ruin, Mr. Samuel Insull, sought "to fix the truth about the utilities in the young person's mind before incorrect notions became fixed there"—which is a somewhat subjective way of saying that they were anxious to compel the schools to insist on the benefit of private ownership in the utility field. Business men as well as the main body of economists still speak of American free enterprise even though it is obvious that, ever since the Great Depression, the day of the "little man" has irrevocably gone, and that of the great corporation, partly sustained and partly directed by the federal government, has taken its place. What exactly would be the relation of organized labour to this quasi-partnership remains a quite unknown matter.

When, therefore, Professor Counts asks if the schools dare build a new social order, [15] the answer is to look at the interests with which they would have to debate its desirability. These, as Professor Counts has himself shown, dominate all the governing controls of the public schools; they dominate, not less overwhelmingly, the colleges and the universities; and if they hold the reins a little less loosely in the professional schools, it is with them that the ultimate authority resides. The answer, therefore, to the educational reformers in the United States is that to build a new social order through educational institutions means agreement upon what that new order shall be. There is no such agreement in sight. There is an ebb and flow in the waves of change, but these operate, so to speak, within an inland sea whose boundaries are well defined, as they are

[12] *Report of the Senate Committee on Education and Labor* (Washington, 1926), p. 43.
[13] Frederick Lewis Allen, *The Lords of Creation* (New York: Harper, 1935), p. 222.
[14] Howard K. Beale, *Are American Teachers Free?* (New York: Scribner, 1936).
[15] George S. Counts, *Dare the School Build a New Social Order?* (New York: John Day, 1932).

carefully guarded against the dangers of a storm. There can be significant experiments, of which the Dalton Plan is an interesting example, here and there, notably in the private universities, there may be an atmosphere of exceptional tolerance. To this should be added the important fact that in the past fifty or sixty years a small number of distinguished thinkers in the United States, of whom William James, John Dewey, and A. N. Whitehead are most outstanding, have done remarkable work, to which it is difficult to pay too high a tribute, in making the professional educator aware of the significance, both for school and university, of the simple development of scientific knowledge and its technical application even when this comes into conflict with either the inertia or the hostility of interests and institutions which erect high barriers against the fuller use of the power thus put into our hands.

I cannot put this better than in some remarkable sentences of Dewey himself. "The conflict," he has written, "is between institutions and habits originating in the pre-scientific and pre-technological age and the new forces generated by science and technology. The application of science, to a considerable degree, even its own growth has been conditioned by the system to which the name of capitalism is given, a rough designation of a complex of political and legal arrangements centering about a particular mode of economic relations. . . . Change in patterns of belief, desire, and purpose has lagged behind the modification of the external conditions under which men associate. Industrial habits have changed most rapidly; there has followed, at considerable distance, change in political relations; alterations in legal relations and methods have lagged even more, while changes in the institutions that deal most directly with patterns of thought and belief have taken place to the least extent. This defines the primary, though not by any means the ultimate, responsibility of a liberalism that tends to be a vital force. Its work is first of all education, in the broadest sense of that term. . . . The educational task cannot be accomplished merely by working upon men's minds, without action that affects actual change in institutions." [16]

This seems to say that intelligence in politics is to persuade men to correct the "lag" which prevents our institutions being proportionate to the prospects implied, but not liberated, in the external environment about us. Its defect, as I think, is twofold. It does not tell us, in the first place, how the persuasion is to be effected, nor does it emphasize the degree to which institutions and, with them, the relations, legal, political and economic, which they implicate, are all deeply pervaded by an intense emotional background which exerts an almost religious force over those who have the power to maintain them. That this force should be weakened by the influence of intelligence is obviously desirable. Yet, in general, it is true to say that only the impact of immense events is likely to have this result. The Great Depression showed, if it showed anything, the

[16] John Dewey, *Liberalism and Social Action* (New York: Putnam, 1935), pp. 75–76, 54–62, *passim*.

ignorance and the selfishness of American business leaders in the boom years of the nineteen-twenties; and it is pretty certain that the four elections of Franklin Roosevelt to the presidency were, despite the war, nothing so much as an explicit condemnation of business leadership by voters who felt they had been betrayed by its behaviour. Yet within five years after 1929 American business men began to act once more as if their conduct had never been called into question. By the end of the Second World War commercial and industrial leaders in the United States were speaking as if nothing mattered but the swift restoration of pre-war economic conditions.

"The role of the State," Professor Whitehead has written, "is a general judgement on the activity of the various organisations. It can judge whether they welcome ability, whether they stand high among the kindred institutions throughout the world. But where the State ceases to exercise any legitimate authority, is when it assumes to decide upon questions within the purview of sciences or professions. . . . Of course, whoever at any time has physical power, has control of physical compulsion, whether he be a bandit, a judge, or a political ruler. But moral authority is limited by competence to attain those ends whose immediate dominance is evident to enlightened wisdom. Political loyalty ceases at the frontiers of radical incapacity." [17] It will be observed that, like so many of the liberal approaches to the problem, Professor Whitehead raises more questions than he solves. He thinks of the State as something detached from, almost disinterested about, the organizations which make up the community. In fact, of course, there is no such detachment. The State power is exercised by men who are just as much within the community as those over whom they rule; and there is no *a priori* reason to expect more detachment in them than in others. Nor are we told how to decide what questions are "within the purview of the sciences or professions." Few people, in the light of the last hundred years, would agree that lawyers or doctors, architects or teachers, engineers or accountants, ought to be, for example, the sole judges of the conditions of entrance into their professions; yet those conditions are obviously within their purview. The discovery of how to use atomic energy is obviously, also, within the purview of at least a dozen of the natural and applied sciences; but no one would for a moment suggest that the scientists, qua scientists, could exclude the statesman from decisions about the use of atomic energy. On the political plane, certainly, the only means the scientist has to influence the statesman's decision is in his role as citizen; and his influence there is far less related to his technical capacity than it is to the quality of what civic wisdom he may possess. Nor does Professor Whitehead explain how "enlightened wisdom" determines either the "competence" of statesmen to define ends, or the need for

[17] Alfred North Whitehead, *Adventures of Ideas* (Cambridge: The University Press, 1933; New York: Macmillan, 1933), pp. 71 ff.

their "immediate dominance," or how we know how to recognize those who possess "enlightened wisdom" when they announce the possession of "moral authority" by one set of persons and not by another. Indeed, when Professor Whitehead argues that "political loyalty ceases at the frontiers of radical incapacity," he comes very near to the acceptance of Hobbes' view that political power belongs by right to those who know how to keep it. On this view, a successful rebellion is always justified; as on this view, also, the business man who has so largely shaped American civilization for the last hundred years is entitled to his power because no one has ever challenged him successfully. Yet we know that this is not the principle of State authority which Professor Whitehead approves even though his men with "enlightened wisdom" look perplexingly like a self-appointed aristocracy. If they are this, they make nonsense of every democratic claim; if they are something else, whether appointed or elected, we ought to be told who appoints or elects them, and the criteria by which their "enlightened wisdom" can be seen.[18] The general common sense of mankind seems to insist that no trusteeship exercised by a small group on behalf of the rest of the community ever fails at some point in its history to confound communal welfare with its private self-interest, and that in the quite genuine confidence that the two things are one.

The business man dominates American civilization. His function is so to organize American society that he has the freest possible run of profitable adventure. To do this he must organize the symbolism of that society so that there are no vital obstacles to the performance of his function. And since one of the main avenues through which the symbolism he requires can secure acceptance is the educational system of America, he can relax his control of that system only at his peril. That is why he controls the state power. That is why, also, he sets the boundaries within which scientific discovery may be used. That is why the Churches and the press and the movies all operate "within a framework he approves" as most likely to make his symbolism acceptable and effective. He is not, and cannot be, "interested" in the individual in society as an end in himself. He is interested in individuals who regard society as successful when it creates the atmosphere in which his symbolism produces the largest returns. He does not understand why, or how, people can argue that a world is valid for its citizens only when it can find a place for fulfilment in their lives in that living present which alone has meaning for them. It is this which explains his indifference to the sufferings which attended the birth of industrial America or to those which now coincide with the displacement of the small American farmer by an agriculture based on large-scale capitalist enterprise increasingly tied in with the industrial trust and thus with the financial interests which dominate American life. For if he devoted his mind and heart to the remedy of those sufferings, he

18 *Ibid.*, pp. 345-46, 354, 374.

would, in fact, be promoting changes in social principles and institutional organization which would destroy the symbolism upon which his role depends.

At this point educational reformers in the United States are, in effect, telling him that the art of successful community building consists in an uninhibited ability to move from one set of symbols to another, because life is process, process means change, and those who resist change because they revere the ancient symbols will drive the community either to revolution or to decay. The reformers are entirely right in telling him that he is refusing to accept the nature of the universe. He cannot understand, save in the most rare instances, why there should be people who are outraged when he protests in the name of ethical principle against the revision of symbols he regards as sacred. The symbol may be a currency principle like the gold standard; the execration with which William Jennings Bryan was greeted was a protest made in the name of a religious faith. Or it may be the "simple system of natural liberty" of Adam Smith which leads him to revere the self-regulating market economy, which involves in its turn the classic freedom of contract on the one hand, and on the other, that liberal State which for nearly a century automatically insured increasing welfare until it was destroyed by interventionism and planning. The only good society is that in which State interference is at the minimum compatible with external peace, internal order, and the compulsion on business men to compete with one another. To deny this postulate is to destroy the central principle of the business man's symbolism—his faith in the moral rightness of his function and of his faith.

Yet this is, in fact, what liberal educational reformers like James and Dewey and Whitehead, are really asking the business man to do. From him who has destroyed civilizations, wasted the natural resources of whole continents, and made life a mean and pitiful thing for millions—whether the victim was a Polish steel worker in Pittsburgh, or a Mexican pecan-sheller in San Antonio, or even a native-born American sharecropper in Arkansas or Mississippi—from him they ask co-operation in changing the whole character of one of the key institutions by which the dominance of the business man is maintained. They ask him to permit the inducement of the sceptical mind, instead of the mind trained to accept authority because it is taught to identify the customary with the necessary. They ask him to encourage the free play of doctrine in school and university, so that nothing remains sure but what unfettered intelligence is ready to approve. They insist to him that there is nothing so sacred that it may not be submitted to an examination which strips it of its sacredness. They suggest to him, in a word, that he should co-operate with them in making possible social adjustments the outcome of which can only be the destruction of the supremacy he has enjoyed for so long. The possible worlds they offer him in exchange are all of them built upon a fundamental denial of one or another of the vital articles of his faith.

They regard human beings as ends in themselves with whose demands society must strive to put itself in accord. Institutions therefore must be revised on the basis that the claims of living are satisfied in terms of time ; that would mean, to take one example only, that the outstanding function of the Churches would be criticism of all business activities which separated the worker from his labour power and looked upon the purchase and sale of that labour power merely as a commodity. It would mean the planned State instead of the State which regrets all deviations from the principle of *laissez-faire*. It would even replace the cash-nexus as the basis of economic relations on the ground that it condemns the great majority of human beings to live in a social and cultural vacuum incompatible with the dignity of human nature. They are asking him to subordinate the religion of private property to a collective social purpose which makes joy in work, the adventure of creative living, ever more fully open to the masses of mankind.

I frankly think that historic experience since 1914 makes the liberal educationists' philosophy a simple optimism of which the outcome, in the end, is catastrophe. Its real result is not to convince the business man of its validity but to warn him against its dangers. He then seeks for a defence of his symbolism, and he can always find learned men to devote their energies to its provision, as well as distinguished journalists to popularize the defence so that it can be read with eager satisfaction on Main Street. And when the *Reader's Digest* insistently offers summarized proof that a planned society is a servile society, then the plain business man in Keokuk, Iowa, or Sandusky, Ohio, need no longer trouble himself with the assumptions of the proof or with its omissions, and it is not surprising that employers' associations should circulate millions of copies of the summary all over the United States. Propaganda on this scale hardly looks like the prelude to abdication.

It is more intelligible that a body like the Harvard committee should beg that the discussion of first principles should not prevent "co-operation on the plane of action." It is not a plea likely to achieve any lasting success, for it assumes that the business of living and the art of thought can be kept distinct from one another over a considerable period, whereas the truth is that they continually interpenetrate one another so that thought becomes a call to action, while action perpetually requires organized reflection on its purposes and methods. The Harvard approach, moreover, is an obvious specific for quiet times ; and anyone who looks into the contents of that Pandora's box from which so much involving high passion has been liberated by the Second World War will not be tempted into the belief that the next thirty years are likely to figure as a quiet time in the view of the historian who writes a century from now. The discovery of the atomic bomb alone has revolutionary implications we hardly dare even to measure. The mere fact that it has made men of science everywhere conscious of the international realm of their studies as an exercise in social obligation instead of a delightfully convenient intellectual routine is already an indication that great changes are impending. "Co-operation on the plane of action" has no meaning in an epoch of great changes unless it is built on the principles of a common faith.

It is widely and rightly held, in the United States as elsewhere, that a new education has become urgent because an environment has emerged for which the old education is inadequate. There cannot be a new education without a new society to sustain it. And a new society needs a new philosophy of living which evaluates human beings and social institutions on a scale more proportionate to the new environment. It is not just a matter of altering the curriculum in some more or less drastic way. The need will not be fulfilled by abandoning the elective system or by multiplying orientation courses. It will not even be fulfilled by getting better, or better paid, teachers into the schools and universities so as to raise the level of student achievement. What is wanted is a fundamental change in the spirit by which the present American system of education is permeated to its very foundations. I do not think that change can come save by an alteration in the values of the American way of life; and the only road to that alteration lies in recasting that way of life as part of a reorganization of the principles of Western civilization.

I should myself say that what we have got to learn is the need to discover society, and that this means rediscovering individuality by making power a force that is relevant to freedom and by making the fear of freedom unnecessary and unjustified, even in a society so intricate as that of the United States. In their various ways that was seen by Ruskin and Matthew Arnold and William Morris in Victorian England, as it was seen for the contemporary America by Emerson and the early Orestes Brownson and Walt Whitman. All of them saw that, in Engels' words, freedom is the recognition of necessity, and that you cannot ask for a free world when the spirit of man is chained by the inner principle of a social organization which begins by insisting that the slavery of the many to the few is in fact to be regarded as freedom. Their insight is today becoming more and more the premiss of the faith upon which America has gone beyond disillusion to the recognition that social art must build upon reality. That faith becomes in each year at once more indigenously American and more mature, because it observes the high distinction of the history in which its premiss is set. A foreigner may doubt whether the new faith will persuade the business man to think great thoughts with the imaginative sweep required by the situation of his country. At least he may hazard the guess that the class which turns its back on the sweeping reconstruction that is required will find that it is seeking to arrest the kind of irresistible current the strength of which, as Edmund Burke noted in an age very similar to our own, seems to proceed rather from the decrees of Providence than from the wills of men.

IX

American Culture

I

"LITERATURE," wrote Jefferson to an English correspondent in 1825, "is not yet a distinct profession with us. Now and then a strong mind arises, and at its intervals of leisure from business emits a flash of light. But the first object of young societies is bread and covering." [1] Yet when Jefferson thus implied that a literary profession is the outcome of a mature civilization, with its obvious inference that culture is furnished to a society by a leisured class with the time and the means for its cultivation, he was at once underestimating what America had achieved by the end of the colonial period, and was accepting, probably unconsciously, the Renaissance ideal of a culture in the shaping of which the masses have no share. Only the gentleman, he thought, can afford thorough knowledge of, and cultivation in, the arts and sciences, to experience the full measure of a creative life. It was already then, as it remains today, a mistaken ideal, since it supposed that the product of imagination and refinement was the outcome of freedom from the need to earn one's living. It thus separated the practice of the arts from the categories of life in which the masses could hope to share. More than this: it assumed that fatal separation of art from craftsmanship which tends to make it the subject of patronage instead of an element of civilization which permeates the whole of community living. The arts thus became the field of activity for the exceptional man, and he became dependent upon the patronage of a small, refined class for recognition. This dependence, in its turn, made the artist assume that it was the taste of the few for which he must produce, and that, accordingly, the satisfaction of the many was not a matter with which he need concern himself.

It is highly probable that the first hundred and fifty years of Protestantism did a good deal to emphasize this separation. By throwing the reformed Christian back upon himself, by making his salvation so ex-

[1] Merle Curti, *The Growth of American Thought* (New York: Harper, 1943). See Chap. v for an illuminating discussion of the rise of American intellectual independence.

clusively a matter his own thought or effort could alone decide, he was
tempted to view "worldly" things like the arts with some disdain, as
activities inessential to the real task of living, and to find in the doctrine
of the "calling" the need to scorn delights and live laborious days. As
he was so largely a member, whether well-to-do or poor, of the class
which earned its living by working long hours and intensely in the vocation practised, he tended to put the arts in a large degree outside his
scheme of living. This tended to emphasize the Renaissance view that
arts most truly belonged to the "gentleman's calling," and existed, as they
were developed, for his pleasure. Most of them then became expressed
through forms in which they received a refinement and sophistication by
which it was intended to mark them off from the crudeness and the
earthly realism of what came to be regarded as the "popular arts." Even
the artists themselves became men and women who gravitated, if they
could, towards the court, the aristocracy, and the wealthy *nouveaux riches*
whose patronage was an indication that they had emerged from that
slough of materialism in which they had neither time nor opportunity to
contemplate more than the daily round of exhausting toil. Even education was built upon the assumption that the training to perceive and appreciate the beautiful was something from which the masses were necessarily excluded. "Polite" letters, as with Addison, or the change from
Hogarth's attitude to life to that of Reynolds, exemplified the movement
from a common social experience to an isolation which the arts were
driven to accept by the changing climate of opinion in the century and
a half after 1600.

When Jefferson accepted this view he did less than justice to the
past of America. He was, in fact, accepting a European tradition which,
though it was to have profound influence in the United States, was far
less deep-rooted than he supposed. For though colonial America did not
produce many figures of first-rate significance, Franklin at least excepted,
in the world of culture, there is plenty of evidence of innumerable minor
figures and of a widespread interest in artistic creation. The men who
built Salem and Charleston, Williamsburg and Alexandria, were architects of a quality who bear comparison with any of their contemporaries
in Europe; and if Charles Carroll was a rich man of leisure, he was also
one of many men extraordinary enough to have secured something very
near perfection in the houses they designed for themselves in the eighteenth century. Nor could one easily deny the right to be called great artists
to the men who designed and built those superb clipper ships which are
among the glories of New England. In furniture, in domestic utensils, in
the early school of American portrait painters, there is again the attainment of beauty at a high level. It is, indeed, hardly so in most departments
of letters. Few people save the specialist would read the poetry of Michael
Wigglesworth or Anne Bradstreet; if there is living argument and passionate feeling in the theological writings of Hooker and Roger Williams,
of the Mathers and John Cotton, I do not think there is anything in this

realm notable for the perfect adjustment between style and material until Jonathan Edwards, and relatively little after him until the nineteenth century. What histories there are seem entitled to be regarded as interesting rather than distinguished; we read a work like Captain John Smith's account of Virginia for the interest of its facts rather than for the quality of the narrative. Nor is it less true of writers like John Winthrop, or diarists like Judge Sewall. The fact that they were important men makes what they had to say important because they said it, rather than because they said it with either the power, or the elegance of contemporaries like Clarendon or Cardinal de Retz.

Yet, with the eighteenth century, American literature begins in many fields to find a level of high quality. Not since James Nayler had Quakerism achieved a finer expression than in the exquisite simplicity of John Woolman; while the sermons of Wise and Jonathan Mayhew have a combination of force in argument and gravity in eloquence which put them on a par with any of their contemporaries, Bishop Butler alone excepted. I have already noted the eminence of Jonathan Edwards as a philosophical theologian. What is far more remarkable is the growth of a political literature which, from about the end of the Seven Years' War until the beginning of the Civil War in 1861, represents a century of unsurpassed achievement in this field. Franklin and John Adams, Otis and Paine, Madison and Hamilton, Thomas Jefferson and John Taylor of Caroline, merely to note a handful of the outstanding names who had made their reputation before 1800, are men who are surpassed by only three, or perhaps four, of the greatest European political thinkers of the eighteenth century. Again, no doubt, it is true that there are no great American historians; though an Englishman is bound to remember in how solitary an eminence Gibbon stands in the eighteenth century; there are no biographers to whose work one desires to return; and when Parrington edited his anthology of the "Connecticut Wits" he hastened to emphasize that he was not claiming for them any significant poetic status.

It is different in science. Almost from the beginning there is keen interest, careful observation, and a recognition that the scientific mind has a special place and function in society. Benjamin Franklin takes his place in the first rank of his contemporaries; and men like Rittenhouse, Rush, and Fulton are, even if they stand below him, still names one cannot neglect. There is a wide interest in natural knowledge; William Byrd's *Diary* is one kind of testimony to that interest, as is the veneration in the reception of Joseph Priestley, as a refugee, another kind. Jefferson may have made no scientific discovery of importance; but the comprehensiveness and depth of his anxiety to know are only more notable than his eagerness to assure a general welcome for, and use of, scientific discovery. The lieutenant-governor of New York, Cadwallader Colden, studied with some distinction both botany and physics. The American Philosophical Society, to which Franklin contributed so much in Philadelphia, was an admirable body, whose members were to be found in

Massachusetts and the West Indies, in New York and Georgia. Professor John Winthrop of Harvard was a Fellow of the Royal Society, and eleven papers from his pen were printed in its proceedings.

We need not exaggerate the achievements before 1800; yet it is important to note that they were largely indigenous; in science they had produced Franklin, while in political philosophy their general quality rivalled that of any European country. We have to remember that the American nation which won its independence in 1783 numbered less than three millions and was scattered over a vast area in which internal communication was still very difficult; while the Revolution went far towards disrupting internal trade and brought something like havoc in Tarleton's wake in Virginia. But there were at least six American cities with a vivid appreciation of painting, architecture, and music. There were theatres in New York and Charleston. Salem achieved a dignified beauty when McIntire began to build his beautiful houses and spacious buildings of civic importance. There were many fine portraits on the walls of its houses. There was an assembly room for dances and, after 1780, a subscription library. Salem had also its own philosophical society, and one of its citizens had a private library which only Jefferson's surpassed in all America. When one thinks of the Salem ships which were sent to China and the Indies, bringing back their treasures of silks and spices and tea, it is a little difficult not to think that this little Massachusetts port had become a gateway through which men passed to a vision of the wider universe.

No one would claim that there was great music or great drama in America before 1800; but the interest in each was wide, and even with the influences which come so clearly from France or Germany or England, the traces are unmistakable, sometimes in subject matter, sometimes in treatment, of native American influence. In the plays in which the American Indian, for example, is the central theme, I do not myself believe that the portrait of the noble savage, his dignity, his eloquence, his tragic sense of a fatal destiny, is derived from the reading of Rousseau's *Works;* I believe, rather, that they represent in part the experience of discussions with Indian chiefs in solemn conclave, out of which these qualities became a tradition in the folk memory of America, handed down from generation to generation, and, in part also, a sense of the need to do justice to a wronged people that, as it were, its brooding spirit might be placated by this tribute. Rousseau's noble savage, who is, after all, at least as old as Montaigne and the Jesuit *Relations* and other travellers' accounts, served rather as a *post hoc* justification by philosophy of a trend already there. So, too, the passion for choral singing, already widespread in the eighteenth century, seems to me to come less from devotional practice than from the fact that, in a large number of small and scattered communities, communal singing is one of the most natural forms of enjoyment as well as one of its most unifying forces. It is interesting to note that though the Massachusetts tradition of Puritan severity prohibited a theatre in Boston until 1793, plays were performed there for at least a generation before that, and at the Boston Concert Hall, John Rowe could hear a reading of *The Beggar's Opera* with a musical rendering of some of the songs. It is, I suspect, pretty hard to think that foreign influence turned the sternly pious New England Calvinist into the gay and carefree Yankee, wryly humorous, keenly observant, as shrewd as Sam Adams and as recklessly and merrily unworldly as George Handel Hill—the very name is significant of much—who made his marching song, itself a jig-tune somewhat remote from the assumed kill-joy temper of the Puritan, go round the world. Nor do I think that Tacitus or Livy, Plutarch or Thucydides, had much to do with stamping the classic temper on the revolutionary age. It was Locke and Sidney and Montesquieu and Blackstone that were read by Otis and John Adams, Jefferson and Madison, when they were young men; when, and only half-deliberately, they found themselves committed to the foundation of a free and republican commonwealth, it was as natural a gesture, as in France after 1789, that they should turn to the history of Greece and Rome for the pedigreed decoration which gave background to their attitude. But it was already an Americanism into which the classical theme was woven; it was a colour merely in a pattern which had been designed elsewhere.

I am anxious, this is to say, to make two points which seem to me important for an insight into American culture. The first is that whatever the volume of the baggage imported from Europe in the settling of America—and no doubt it was very large—once unloaded, it began immediately to undergo significant changes; it became, in fact, American. The second is that when all is said that can be said of American indebtedness to European, and especially English, civilization, the debt is less than the contribution brought by America itself to the product involved in the mixture of the European and, indeed, oriental heritage with the American environment. For we must regard the culture of the United States not as the provincial expression on the circumference of civilization of something that can be grasped only at its centre. We must rather regard it as an effort, often groping and uncertain, after a civilization of its own; in the course of which it borrows, sometimes with glad acknowledgement and sometimes with unhappy shame, from the achievements of the older world. We must be careful, too, not to regard American culture as a series of separate categories in which its literature and technology are the most important. The categories are of art and not of nature; the real pattern is indivisible; each aspect of it enters into, and colours, all the others. So that whatever is taken or received from the Old World becomes different as it is adapted to its new home. It is obvious that American furniture of the eighteenth century was greatly influenced by the careful perusal of Thomas Chippendale's designs; but it is not less obvious that the result is not Chippendale furniture. There can be little doubt but that Paul Revere owes much to the great French tradition in silverware design, the art, for instance, of Paul Lamerie; but there can be little doubt, also, that he mixed with that tradition something of his own, and that this was American in character. The same is true of architecture, both in domestic and in public buildings. It is true of things so different as household utensils and of folk-songs. The families of the mountaineers in Kentucky may sing the ballads of seventeenth-century England, but they are somehow adapted to the Kentucky air. It is unmistakable that the Jefferson who wrote the Declaration of Independence was steeped in the constitutional literature of England, less fully of France; but it is still more unmistakable that the final document which emerged is specifically and unmistakably American. So, too, at each phase of his long career, one can see what contribution this writer and that thinker made to the work of Benjamin Franklin; but when all the debts are acknowledged, the final outcome is a man who could not but be recognized as an American citizen.

Anyone, therefore, who writes of the American heritage from European culture must set it always in a perspective emphasized by two important considerations. The first is that it was not a transplantation but an adaptation. The agent of transmission speaks in a different environment to a different audience; and that means that what he inherits, or what he borrows, is never the same thing once it has passed over to his use. The second thing is the danger of thinking of American culture as, so to speak, a minor outpost of European culture from which little could be expected because of its youth, its pre-occupation with the task of wresting a wilderness from nature, the consequential materialism of its outlook on the one hand, and the "lag" in its cultural maturity on the other. All of this is the outcome of a body of emotions and counter-emotions which has meant an attempt to judge the American achievement by European standards, and the assumption that its cultural maturity was retarded until there arrived in the pattern of its social relations that leisured class, typified in the "gentleman" of the Renaissance, with whose emergence culture is supposed to appear on the scene. The truth is that America has never been the home of a materialism in any way more profound than that of Europe; but in Europe the passion for power and security through acquisition has, as is inevitable where the social organization is far more hierarchical, been more carefully veiled.

The attempt to explain American culture in terms of its "youth," with the inference of a natural retardation in the acceptance of intellectual novelty, is a curious phenomenon which deserves more examination than it has received. The explanation was accepted in the eighteenth and early nineteenth centuries by men as eminent and as devotedly American as Franklin, John Adams, and Jefferson. Franklin's stressing of his reasons, and the outlook of John Adams, are especially notable. "All things have their season," wrote Franklin, "and with young countries as with young men, you must curb their fancy to strengthen their judgment;

. . . thus poetry, painting, music (and the stage as their embodiment), are all necessary and proper gratifications of a refined state of society, but objectionable at an earlier period, since their cultivation would make a taste for their enjoyment precede its means." So, too, John Adams must have thought when he yearned for "leisure and tranquility to amuse myself with those elegant and ingenious arts of painting, sculpture, architecture, and music. A taste for them all is an agreeable accomplishment." But Adams was convinced that culture ever springs from luxury, and that its condition is the wealth which, leading to tyranny, is an evil that the young America should avoid.

When one examines this doctrine with care, its source is, I think, unmistakable. It belongs to the conflict between primitivism and sophistication of which Rousseau's first *Discourse,* which won the prize at Dijon, is perhaps the most famous outcome. But this, in its turn, is deeply connected both with the long eighteenth-century debate upon the virtues and the dangers of luxury—a debate in which men so notable as Mandeville and William Law, Voltaire and Hume, took part—and with the famous battle between the ancients and the moderns out of which the doctrine of progress began to take its nineteenth-century shape. Both primitivism and luxury were a framework within which men sought to attack and justify the existing order, just as the quarrel between ancients and moderns is a method, among other things, of justifying alike innovation and the right to make critical inquiry into realms hitherto barred from their entrance. To all of these the theory of a "young" America is related, as it is deeply interwoven with the impact of the "noble savage" on the one hand, and the physical immensity of America on the other.

America as the "young" nation is at once a defensive and a prophetic concept. It is defensive in the sense that it seeks to protect the state of culture from attack and to argue that its roughness and crudity are the outcome of the fact that its citizens are still devoting their energies to fighting battles with nature which more ancient nations fought long ages before. It is prophetic because it argues that, when the battle is won, all the achievements of European civilization will be open to Americans because they will then have the wealth, and therefore the time and the refinement, to cultivate the arts. It is, I suggest, obvious that this is the outlook of men who have the conviction that they are regarded as provincial, that in some sense they feel themselves to be so and resent the accusation. There is no need for me to labour the point that the argument assumes, first, that culture is by nature aristocratic and so not to be looked for from a nation whose traditions are too new to have developed any fixity of form ; and, second, that it comes late rather than early in historical evolution. It is thus a fusion—of which both Jefferson and Adams often show themselves to be afraid—of the concept of the gentleman with the doubt whether, in its European form, it can take root in the United States without the destruction of the American idea. That is why there is the constant insistence in Jefferson's writings of the need for a social order in the New World which will avoid the necessity of paying the price paid for its culture by the Old.

Obviously enough maturity is not required by any society for the production of great painting, or great sculpture, or great poetry; and the history of ancient religions seems to suggest that great ethical precepts are at least as closely related to material primitivism as they are to material sophistication. If we agree that there go to the making of a culture three things which can never be separated—a material background, that is, a body of national resources and a technique with which to exploit it; a body of attitudes, which includes the relations among the men who seek to employ the technique; and a body of ideas and sentiments, which both arise out of and are then projected back into those relations—it is difficult to say more about the "youth" of America and its culture than that the continent of the New World was only fully developed after 1492; for those who developed it brought with them both the attitudes and the ideas which were already deep-rooted in Europe. Almost from the first there is the same social structure, the same common stock of ideas, the same techniques upon which to draw. How deeply all these went down into the American consciousness is shown by any comparison between the conservatism of Europeans in 1800 and the conservatism of Adams or Hamilton. What is, I think, genuinely new in America is, first of all, the unlimited sense of physical spaciousness, with its vision of a potential wealth also without limit; and, second, the resultant sense of boundless opportunity which makes it impossible to give either attitudes or ideas their European rigidity or to demand for them the almost caste-like hierarchy in which so much of Europe was framed until a recent time. And, above all, because this very spaciousness drew to America great waves of immigrants who sought escape from the European rigidity, there was bound to be absent from American cultural life anything like the stability of form in either attitudes or ideas characteristic of Europe. Here was a continent in which millions could for nearly three centuries enjoy the illusion that they controlled their own lives.

What, therefore, I suggest, has given its particular character to American culture is, first, this spaciousness which seemed, as it did not seem in Europe, to give to the ordinary man an unbreakable title to be himself and to stand alone; and, second, the uncomfortable sense that if he turned away from Europe and separated himself from it, he was cutting himself off from the vital stream of civilization. It is thus a culture which is moving away from Europe at the same time as it has a nostalgic longing to be one with the pattern of ideas from which it is derived. It is thus, also, always seeking to be different and always seeking to be the same. It is always anxious to be independent and always conscious that it cannot escape dependence. The emphasis, of course, is different in different periods, even in different places. Interdependence is easier to accept before 1776, and more difficult after it. The classic revival, which swept the South in architecture and painting from the War of Independence to the fifties of the nineteenth century, had a deeper hold on the South than on the North because it seemed to relate the Southern slave-owners to their great predecessors in the Greek city states and in the Roman commonwealth. In the aftermath of the great German emigration of 1848 many American painters went for training to the academy at Munich; but after the Spanish-American War, Paris was almost without competition as a training centre for American artists. Yet at the same time it is almost an exact generalization to say that while there is nothing that can be called an American school of painting, there is no European school the exponents of which in the United States do not express something in their work which is American, and do not depend upon special American conditions to secure acceptance in the United States for some innovating principle to which they have been converted.

This is, of course, an immensely complex subject. I am anxious to bring out the importance of these things as the principal clues to the grasp of American culture. The first is that its intellectual stock is essentially European; and that, granted its history, this could not but be the case. The second is that until the American Revolution most Americans assumed a unified empire of European culture of which the colonies of the Atlantic seaboard were inevitably a province, and they therefore accepted, with little either of doubt or of suspicion, the view that American culture would develop on the same principle as the European; that is, when there was a leisured class wealthy enough to have time to devote to luxuries like the arts, then America would begin to achieve what Europe had achieved. The third is that after 1776 certain doubts began to emerge. Political independence was followed by a desire for cultural independence. America was to be new, or different, to be responsible for achievements attained without the price—luxury, for example, and despotism—which Europe had to pay for its culture. I have argued that this desire makes the vision of American potentialities of vital significance. I have inferred from this an inevitable emphasis on individuality, on the consciousness of America as different, as creating not less a repulsion from, than an attraction to, European civilization; and I have emphasized the fact that the element of spaciousness in American life meant, as it seems everywhere, an absence of a principle of stability, a passion for the mobile and the changing, quite different from anything Europe has experienced in modern times.

But to all this there is one consideration to be added which is only now beginning to assume its full proportions. However more profound the flexibility imposed by historic and geographical conditions in America, the general pattern of social structure which emerged was akin to that of Europe. The central concept of culture was thus ultimately based on the Renaissance ideal of the gentleman, with all the immense consequences which followed from that ideal. This meant that, however much it was attacked, however widely, whether in space or time, there might be deviations from the ideal, there was always a return to that central concept; and therefore the constancy of the return could not but mean, consciously or unconsciously, the acceptance of European standards of achievement. And this must be set in the context of the fact that the immensity of the migration to America was always renewing the interest in Europe, the attachment for Europe, the exploration of its cultural habits, in a way that gave this acceptance new force and refreshment at every turn. More than this. The tradition of provincialism lingered; even the persistent announcement, every so often, that American culture had at last thrown off its European fetters was really only one more proof of the durability of this provincialism. There has never been in American culture anything that even approximates to the kind of autarchy by which French literature, for example, has so largely lived ever since the great classical period of the seventeenth century. I do not myself believe that this provincialism has resulted in impoverishment, even though, as the self-exile of so many Americans has made evident, it has imposed upon many a heavy strain. On the contrary, my own conviction is that, like its reception of so many and such diverse emigrant strains, provincialism has deepened both the vitality and the experimentalism of American culture. It has made America ready for a richer and more various synthesis of its own which has not yet, indeed, found stable frontiers, but is, I think, more likely to find them as the new generation continues its discovery that the essence of America is plurality in unity.

2

THE outstanding achievement of American literature is the swiftness with which it strode from provincialism to half-acknowledged universality. Before 1800 there is nothing, save in the field of politics, which could command, or even deserve to command, a European audience; by 1900 it is true to say that there were few forms of creative effort in which Americans had not done work of the highest quality, just as it is true to say that no country was more sensitive to the changing climate of thought and emotion in Europe than was the United States. Emerson, Hawthorne, Melville, Whitman, these men show that America had moved to the very front of the cosmic stage. Henceforth it might be disliked; it could not be neglected. And behind these four giants there crowded a host of lesser figures, some of them interesting, some of them destined, like Edgar Allan Poe, strangely to influence other cultures, all of them significant. If there is a brooding pessimism in Hawthorne, and a defiant pessimism in Melville, the outstanding fact in all of them is the combination of sweep of vision and depth of penetration. If it be said that Emerson's mind is so unselective in its sensitivity that it is like a mirror, and that there are moments when one is almost fatigued by the lusty optimism of Whitman, the fact remains that here is a vision that faces life, and judges life, not from a remote telescope poised on some lofty tower, but with the swift, shrewd judgment of men who understand their neighbours. Whether it is Emerson in his garden at Concord or Hawthorne in the genteel mansion at Salem, whether it is the Whitman of the hospitals of Washington or the retired Sage of Camden, or whether it is the Melville who, in his office at the Customs House, still dreams of the South Seas—all of them link their understanding of their neighbours to a long historic process which makes their insight a vivid and exciting cosmology.

In the slightly more than a century and a half since the foundation of the American republic the scale of literary creativeness has implied a rich, surging, palpitating life that is, I think, without precedent in the history of the world. Let us agree that the number of writers who have affected the international tradition is small. Let us agree, too, that only too often, as with Longfellow, an obviously second-rate writer has enjoyed an incredible reputation in his lifetime because he was able to put the platitudes of Main Street into pleasant jingles. It is even true that there is an edifice of considerable size in which there dwell the "superior people," who disdain the eager striving of the multitude, sometimes the aloof academic snob, like Irving Babbitt or Paul Elmer More, sometimes the amusing and impenitent snob, like H. L. Mencken, sometimes the merely social snob, like the novelist who is one phase, and a deeply important phase, in the life of John Hay. What matters, I think, in the culture as a whole is not so much the fact that so few in number reach the supreme heights, but that a vast army sets out on the journey to scale them. Every sort of experience is reported; most sorts of experience are vividly reported. There is a devouring curiosity about life in all its aspects. There is an infinite, almost touching, zest for the discovery of what is being done elsewhere. There is an amazing gratitude to, and appreciation for, everyone who can throw light upon America for Americans. I find in this yearning to know what America means, what America is for, one of the central clues to its literature.

And behind that yearning there is, I think, the half-conscious standard which determines the attitude of almost every American writer of significance. It is not easy to miss in the period since the Pilgrim Fathers landed on the rock-bound coast of Massachusetts the deep sense of a mission. America is different. It is opportunity, it is promise, it is experiment. Things there can be so made that the traditions of the Old World do not place their dead hand upon the New. Life, as it were, can begin afresh. There is room for all; there is no reason to put up the barriers against that ache for self-fulfilment which the Old World dare not satisfy lest, in so doing, it disturb the pattern of social relations upon which the stability of its constituent societies depend. That is the oppressive shadow which need not hang, and ought not to hang, over American life. America can offer fulfilment. It has the means of renovation. It is a refuge. It lends its strength and its spaciousness to the weak, to the men and women who have moved within the narrow boundaries of rigid tradition. In this sense, the majestic phrasing of the Declaration of Independence, with its emphasis on liberty, equality, and the right to happiness, is a kind of Magna Charta proclaimed in defiance of one kind of social order and in justification of a new.

This, I venture to think, is the central philosophic theme round which, in one way or another, all American literature, right down to our own day, has been built. It emerges clearly in the writings of men like Franklin and Jefferson. It is the very essence of Crèvecoeur's famous picture. It is the clue that David Ramsay of South Carolina used to explain the success of the new-born republic in the War of Independence.[2] So also, it seemed to Joel Barlow when in his *Vision of Columbus* (1787) he pictured the great explorer seeing religion and science secure their highest fulfilment in America. Professor Morison has recovered for us the unlearned but clear-sighted vision of a New England farmer, William Manning, who wrote: "Larning is of the greatest importance to the report of a free government."[3] It is the *leitmotif* of the somewhat shrill poetic voice of Philip Freneau. And perhaps nothing illustrates it better than the grounds given by Noah Webster of dictionary fame. "This country must at some future time," he insisted "be as distinguished by the superiority of her literary improvements as she is already by the liberality of her civil and ecclesiastical institutions. Europe is grown old in folly, corruption and tyranny—in that country, laws are perverted, manners are licentious, literature is declining, and human nature is debased. For America in her infancy to adopt the present maxims of the Old World would be to stamp the wrinkle of decrepit age upon the bloom of youth, and to plant the seed of decay in a vigorous constitution."[4] It is not an exaggeration to say that in the quarter of a century from the Declaration of Independence to 1800, Americans achieved the firm conviction that, so to say, they had called into being a new world in the realm of mankind which had already begun to redress the balance of the old.

My argument does not, of course, suppose that the promise of America appeared in similar forms to all Americans. It is obvious that Thomas Jefferson's ideal, for example, was different in kind from that of Alexander Hamilton, and different again from the ideal of that tough old conservative John Adams. I am concerned only to argue that to each generation of Americans there has seemed a latent promise, and not seldom an actual fulfilment, of a spaciousness in life beyond anything that men could look for elsewhere, and that it is in the experience of that promise that the American writer finds the mental climate of his effort. In some, as in Emerson and Whitman, it makes for a soaring optimism; even what is evil in the United States is the prelude, as it were, to good, because it is American evil and there is room enough to accomplish its

---

[2] David Ramsay, *The History of the American Revolution* (Philadelphia, 1789), Vol. II., p. 316.

[3] William Manning, *The Key of Libberty* [1798], edited by Samuel Eliot Morison (Billerica, Mass.: The Manning Association, 1922), p. 20.

[4] Curti, *op. cit.*, p. 145.

transformation. With others, like William Ellery Channing and Theodore Parker, the evil of what is evil is the more unpardonable because it has less cause to exist on American soil. The experiments in community-making, like Brook Farm, even the foreign phalanstery of Victor Considérant in Texas, the perfectionist community of John Humphrey Noyes at Oneida, the Shaker communities, all of them, I think, express in their different ways the faith that, somehow, mankind is born anew in America. It is difficult, even impossible, to escape the sense that, until the panic of 1837, perhaps until the sense of impending civil war after the execution of John Brown, there is over all America and in all phases of life a mood of immense expectancy. There is hardly a star to which some American was not willing to hitch his wagon.

But the mood of expectancy has to work in a world in which there are disappointments as well as hopes. While Emerson salutes "Man the Reformer," Orestes Brownson, in those remarkable papers which preceded his conversion to the Roman Catholic Church, is predicting, on lines not very dissimilar from those of Marx and Engels at the same time, the approach of catastrophe through the struggle between classes in America. The clash over slavery, the conflict under Jackson between the agrarian interests of the South and the industrial interests of the North over the Bank and the tariff, the fantastic speculation in land, the emergence at least as early as the twenties of the last century of the labour problem, the housing problem, and that immigration problem whose intensity is shown by the passions which gave birth to the Know-Nothing movement, all these mean that, alongside hope, there is also despair. It is despair which took Isaac Hecker from Brook Farm and transcendentalism to the more restful anchorage of Rome. It is despair that made of William Lloyd Garrison an Abolitionist who thought the republic which tolerated slavery an accursed thing. One can read, too, in the faded pages of labour journals in the generation before 1860, of dreams that have withered and of a promise that has failed. Nor can one fail to note the significance of Thoreau's imprisonment for refusing to pay taxes to an unjust commonwealth. *On the Duty of Civil Disobedience*—the very title is a trumpet call to action. It is worth remembering how it echoed for Tolstoy on the Russian steppe, and for the young Indian barrister in South Africa, who learned from its pages the secret of how to defy an empire.

What, in short, conditions the whole atmosphere of American literature is the economic framework within which it has to work. For that means, as a framework, that with all its spaciousness, its immense resources, the absence of the rigid caste divisions which were the bane of European civilization, the far greater chances of distinction it offered to the native-born American who was poor and had, like Lincoln, to acquire an education in the odd intervals between earning a living, or to the immigrants who came by the thousands to escape hunger in Ireland or despotism in Germany and Italy, the fundamental division in American life was still the division between rich and poor. In this respect the

American Civil War was not merely a turning point in the history of the United States. It was a turning point in the history of the world. It registered not merely the victory of anti-slavery against slavery, of anti-secession against secession; far more important, it was the final step in the march of industrial capitalism to the conquest of world power. Once the American continent was finally enmeshed in the habits of a market economy, with its false confidence in an automatically achieved equilibrium, and its false confusion between technological progress and social well-being, it became inevitable that all national communities which did not directly revolt against the market economy would be swept into its embrace. That was bound to mean a state power the intervention of which was directed, above everything, to keeping the market economy at work almost at any price. The Negro was freed, indeed; but he was freed on the implicit condition that he did not ask for the results of freedom. The South was made a dependency of the imperial North; and it developed those tragic frustrations which still limit its recovery to its use as a weapon against an American working class seeking to escape from the iron consequences of a market economy. It made liberty a function of one's place in the market's hierarchy of power. It ruled out equality as incompatible with the accumulation by the investor of the ever-increasing capital necessary to exploit market possibilities. It made the real boundaries of a community no more than the limits of profitable exploitation by those who dominated the market. It made technological improvement dependent not upon social need, but upon the prospect that it might bring profit in terms of the market. Above all, it made social relationships dependent upon the needs of the market economy, even though it is obvious that in a well-ordered community economic institutions must be subordinated to a system of social relationships which give citizens elbow-room to express and fulfil the whole of themselves. For the market economy, the citizen was a person who was significant only when his influence upon material results was wider than the mere sale of his labour power would imply.

All this was what Tocqueville meant when, almost a generation before the Civil War, he warned the United States against the dangers inherent in an aristocracy of manufacturers; and even though it be true that the market economy which made social relations its helpless appendage was already well established in England before 1865—though there, too, it had taken almost a civil war to complete its triumph—the movement of the United States, in the same direction, built economic categories of action which every nation had to accept if it sought either power or influence. And once it came within those categories, it impressed upon the mass of its population all the characteristics of a proletariat. It not only limited the freedom of citizens—even where it agreed they should have this freedom—to the right to vote; it had to see that the vote was never so employed as to threaten the fundamental laws of a market economy. Whether it was education or housing, whether it was health or leisure, the men who were the masters of the market were the men who really decided what the economy they directed could afford. Positive law thus came to depend upon what was regarded with the reverence due to natural law; though it was rarely seen that what was taken for natural law was, in fact, nothing more than the logical implications of the market economy. And the whole intellectual and emotional apparatus of society had to adjust itself, as best it could, to the perspective of the sacrifices exacted by the strait jacket in which America was encased after 1865.

There were, of course, premonitions of this development. Hamilton foresaw it, and welcomed it, for he worshipped strength and power and had a contempt for the multitude. Jefferson and John Taylor recognized its dangers, but had never the grasp of the means to overcome them. In a somewhat crude way, Jackson and his supporters felt those dangers also; that lies at the root of their struggle with Nicholas Biddle and his financial cohorts. The difficulty was always the degree in which the stark choice being made was obscured by other currents, which made its recognition and observation difficult. The issue of slavery obscured it; so, too, did the rise of groups which, like the Locofocos, concentrated their hostility partly upon the foreign immigrants and customs which were invading their country. It was obscured, again, by the vast free lands, the immensity of which prevented almost everyone from considering what would happen when there was no longer an open frontier towards which men could go on pushing; even Lincoln, whose shrewdness and sagacity were surpassed only by his magnanimity, foresaw an America in which, in unending continuity, the industrious and striving apprentice himself would become a master.[5] Nearly fifty years later Theodore Roosevelt thought the problem could be solved if the government tackled a few "malefactors of great wealth." For Woodrow Wilson the problem was not in essence different from what it was in the view of Lincoln; and while Franklin Roosevelt, in his famous campaign of 1932, seemed to be demanding fundamental change, his policies make it obvious that he demanded changes only so far as these were permissible within the limits of the market economy. He did not think for one moment of transcending those limits.

So that slowly before 1865, and with almost breathless speed after it, American literature was adapted to the requirements of the American economy. I do not, of course, mean that it was a conscious adaptation; on the contrary, many American writers, even writers of genius, wrote in complete or partial unawareness of the environment which set the perspective of their effort. There were, naturally, men who were completely or partially aware of their position and used all their effort to communicate that awareness to their contemporaries. The important thing is that with the arrival of the Gilded Age the promise of American life became a myth which had no chance of fulfilment in real life. The promise was

[5] "Speech at Milwaukee," September 30, 1859, in Stern, *The Life and Writings of Abraham Lincoln*, pp. 559–64.

defined by the Age of Enlightenment; and, like most of the intellectual
constructions of that period, the leaders in that age sought for laws of
nature in the social realm in the confident assurance that they could
there repeat the immense triumphs of physics in the scientific sphere. They
were mistaken, because they built their premisses of action not upon the
idea of a social man to the satisfaction of whose needs the economy of
the community was geared: they built them upon the assumption of an
objective economic world in which trading for profit in the individual's
own interest was the one fixed axiom upon which all else depended. And
since, like Adam Smith, they believed that the harmony between individual interest and social interest was given, they did not doubt the reality
of the "invisible hand." So that, in the presence of a vast continent, massive in resources and, when the nineteenth century dawned, still dimly
imagined and not accurately explored, with a small population which
was always offered an escape from the need to labour in the East for
another by occupation in the new West, it seemed rational enough to
emphasize the promise not as a myth, but as a reality quite simply to
be unfolded by the flux of time.

It did not happen that way; and all American culture has been profoundly influenced by the fact that it did not happen that way. The
change can be seen from every angle and in every realm of thought.
There is the disillusion of the agrarian novel; the sturdy, rural freeman
of Jeffersonian democracy becomes the soured and cynical Biggs in Ed
Howe's *Story of a Country Town* (1884), with his conclusion that "a
man with a brain large enough to understand mankind is always wretched
and ashamed of himself." Even an optimistic temperament like Hamlin
Garland finds it hard to force himself not to permit his inhabitants of the
Middle Border to become as much the creatures of an ironic destiny as
the men and women who dwell in the Wessex of Thomas Hardy. Few
modern novelists of the South any longer seek to satisfy themselves with
the wistful and melancholy romanticism of George Washington Cable's
stories of Louisiana; nor is there any critical audience for the sword-
and-pistol historical romances written, a long way after Scott, by novelists like Mary Johnston. To all the more important figures in the American novel the Southern picture is one of tragedy, waste, decay. This is,
I think, the increasing emphasis of the American novel ever since the
genius for satire of Mark Twain was, almost forcibly, driven by compulsion into a humour which hardly hid his sense of the worthlessness of
life. The well-known phrase of William Dean Howells that Mark Twain
was the Lincoln of American literature expresses a many-sided truth.
For Mark Twain was of the old frontier by birth. He was grown up well
before the great financiers had made the United States the restless and
dissatisfied society in which wealth and corruption had stifled the dynamic optimism of his youth. He saw the free and easy comradeship of
the little town where Tom Sawyer lived turned into an unimportant
and drab unit of that mechanized industrial society where nothing ever

happened save something worse than he had feared. The humorous Mark Twain, who was so happy and so much at ease when he wrote of his days as a Mississippi pilot, or recalled with a spontaneous glow of golden happiness the great moments of his own youth in *Huckleberry Finn,* was, in the end, with all his immense success, broken by the contrast between the simple ideal of social justice the frontier had taught him to revere and the relentless drive of the new industrial America that drove the weaker to the wall without even a moment to spare for regret at the sacrifice.

It is quite clearly the impact of the new bargain with destiny which was the outcome of the Civil War that is responsible for the rise of realism in American literature. That impact was, no doubt, profoundly influenced by the immense advance in the status of science after the publication of the *Origin of Species,* and by the recognition that, as Howells said with characteristic penetration, since only people "with the weak and childish imaginations" want aristocratic heroes and heroines in a country where these correspond to no social reality, the artist must survey and dissect and analyse the ordinary life about him. If he went abroad, he brought back from Turgenev and George Eliot, from Hardy and Dostoevski and Flaubert, a reinforced faith in the need for a simple veracity about the life about him. And this quest for simple veracity, which one can see in that remarkably effective *Hoosier Schoolmaster* written by Edward Eggleston in 1871, differs only from the realism of Theodore Dreiser or of Sinclair Lewis, in the one case as a Dutch interior differs from the angry complexities of a painting by Hogarth, and in the other, as differs the technique of a quickly moving "talkie," in which every gesture is noted and every individual inflection of speech is recorded with flawless accuracy. Nor must one miss the significant fact that, even when William Dean Howells had been taken to the heart of literary Boston and made, as the editor of the *Atlantic Monthly,* the standard-bearer of the "genteel tradition," the hardness of the scene about him drove him to the expression of a social, even a socialist, realism which, for all its quietness and effort at persuasion, was still deeply burdened with an inner heartache. I do not think myself that Howells ever fully escaped from the refinement of that Brahmin Boston whose decaying vitality he increasingly perceived. But he did recognize that he would move among the dead if he stayed there; and his decision to leave the refined gentility of Beacon Hill to immerse himself in the unabashed naturalism of New York was a gesture of real significance in the history of American letters.

In a sense, after the victory of realism in the midst of the Gilded Age, there are only two kinds of novels of any importance in the next seventy-five years, though each kind, no doubt, can be broken down into minor categories. There is realism quiescent or realism flamboyant on the one side, and there is escapism on the other. The University of Chicago teacher Robert Herrick is an admirable and underrated example of the first type of realism, as Stephen Crane and Frank Norris represent the flamboyant school in its beginnings, and John Dos Passos, Ernest Hemingway, and Upton Sinclair represent its contemporary expression. Herrick's *Memoirs of an American Citizen* (1905) seems to me by far the best picture so far drawn by an American novelist of the business man as conqueror of American life. If to his careful etching of an ugly type which allows no peace to Herrick's tormented conscience, one adds the acid portrayal of "society" in New York which makes Edith Wharton's works minor classics of her time, or Ellen Glasgow's ruthless yet delicate dissolution of any claim of Virginia to have done anything since the Civil War but imitate, like a ghost, the ballet of its dead past, there results a portrait of spiritual desolation which is decisive. And the only difference between this type of analysis and what I have called flamboyant realism is that where the first is, as it were, a series of portraits where the artist seems himself almost to weep at what truth compels him to portray, the second type draws attention to the ugliness of the corpse and to the conviction that the only fault was the major indecency of a society which, so disfigured, was yet avid of life. It is here that flamboyant realism joins hands with the primitivism—itself a form of realism—so characteristic of the American novel between the two world wars. For here the characters are in a fundamental way stripped from the outset of any rational relationship to a social context in which discussion leads to conclusions, and thence to actions. They become instead the creatures of impulse, seeking in a blind way the satisfaction of some appetite, so profoundly committed to hatred for the society in which they live that they seem like creatures out of Hobbes' state of nature. They have moments of tenderness only when they perceive a world of being into which they can plunge without the need for shame or forgetfulness or loathing. For all of them America is a dreary wasteland. There is no longer any promise. They even doubt whether the record of past promise is not a myth. Their outstanding ambition is not to make terms with the world, but to proclaim their hatred of the ugliness of all its values.

Nor is the escapist novel any different in its meaning. Sometimes it is cynical, as with Carl Van Vechten; sometimes it is fantastic, as with Elinor Wylie; sometimes it is, as with Robert Nathan, a kind of potpourri of the wistful and the whimsical. Its pose is that it is living in a world of fancy, that there is a delight in the unreal which no exploration of the actual can offer. Its practitioners blow some light soap bubble towards the sun and clap their hands with delight at its iridescence. Or there is the escapism of James Branch Cabell, a fake medievalism which seeks to be coy and intimate and to make a thin thread of philosophic satire run through the whole. There is, too, the escapism of Joseph Hergesheimer, in which lovely women, always faintly perfumed and exquisitely dressed, sit in beautifully furnished rooms, languorously moved by an emotion of faint proximity to sin. There is the escapism of Edgar Saltus, a poor-hearted mixture of Oscar Wilde and Huysmans, in which the author tries to satisfy the jaded appetites of the half-educated by staging a series of what are really strip-tease acts in the scented atmosphere of a lacquered drawing-room. Taken singly, none of the escapists is of any importance; taken together, they show that in a civilization where economics has annexed culture, an audience can always be found for those who have nothing to say.

I have already noted that there is a point where realism touches the primitive. That is the point where thought seems to have lost its meaning and action is itself taken for thought. It does not seem to matter much what the action is so long as it is vigorous and applauds the strenuous life. Anyone who examines its contemporary expression and then traces back its pedigree will see, I think, that it goes back through Rudyard Kipling and Theodore Roosevelt to Dickens and Bret Harte. Partly it is a protest against the decadence of the *Yellow Book* era. But partly, also, and increasingly, it is a revolt against contemporary values in sex and economic life, an attempt to insist that the real is the unconscious and the instinctive, and that we are fulfilled as we act so as to satisfy these. At its greatest, it has produced the plays of Eugene O'Neill; at its most glittering, the novels of F. Scott Fitzgerald; at its most pathetic, the novels of Sherwood Anderson; at its most complex, the writings of Gertrude Stein. In all of them, the great thing is to drink, to have sexual affairs, which are usually brief, and bitter, and end in more drink; one has to live with men and women who are racked by complexes and forever making excursions into the half-world where the millionaire and the bootlegger, the New York sophisticate and the champion boxer of the time, live on the same plane to experience one another's sensations. In a born novelist like Ernest Hemingway, this primitivism culminates in a cynical despair, born in large degree from the experience of the First World War, which seems to imply that the morale of civilization has broken down and that intelligence is bankrupt. And even though, in his remarkable novel of the Spanish Civil War, *For Whom the Bell Tolls* (1940), he has made a noble plea for the indivisibility of freedom, the dominant impression of his work is that, with all its finish of style and power of narrative, it is only in violence that the inspiration to fulfilment can be found.

Primitivism as a form of art is likely to appear either at the beginning or at the end of a civilization. At its end, it is hostile to reason, convinced that emotion is the clue to satisfaction, anxious that the emotions should be lusty and obvious and direct. When Erskine Caldwell makes one of his characters tell us that "it's folks who let their heads run them who make all the mess of living," he is near to the mood of D. H. Lawrence's urgency that we should think with our blood. At that point life ceases to have an organized purpose and becomes no more than a drift onwards from one experience to another. We grope in the dark because we are done with thought. We do not know where we are going. We have lost our way and we know only that to live is to act, and that the more primitive the action, the nearer it is to the heart of life. That can be read, I

think, either as a criticism of our social order as profound and terrifying
as Rousseau's, or as the clearing of the stage for a revaluation of all values.
On either showing it has rejected the promise of American life. What
it portends no one can foresee except that the depth of its indignation
is the measure of its disillusionment. Few things are so fatal to the
economic foundations of a culture as the discovery by its intellectuals
of their meaningless falsity.

To all this must be added at least a note on Henry James, by so much
the most distinguished figure among the literary expatriates of America.
He illustrates, I think, two problems of his time, it may be, two problems
of our own time also. An artist of high seriousness of purpose, he left
America because he missed there the thick soil of a rich culture in which
alone, as he thought, the artist could grow. After some years of Paris,
he settled in London where, save for two brief intervals, he lived for
almost fifty years, dying, indeed, a British citizen. During those years he
wrote criticism and plays and novels, none of which was a popular success; but many of them have come, especially in the inter-war years, to
have an influence upon our generation second only to that of James Joyce
and Proust, the latter of whom may be regarded, at least in part, as
deeply indebted to him. What, from my angle, is important is the fact
that in the almost half-century of his European life the central preoccupation of Henry James' mind is the relation between America and Europe.
In his deliberate, almost microscopic, way he is always seeking to discover how, or whether, an adjustment can be made between the European, with his deep traditions and rigid codes of behaviour, and the
crudely impulsive American, who is usually rich, often the type of successful man as anxious for the life of sophisticated intelligence as most
of the men whom James himself knew at the Saturday Club in Boston,
and generally driven to return to America because he cannot find the
terms of accommodation with the Old World.

There is, no doubt, an important sense in which James' fifty years in
Europe is an illustration of escapism in sensational form. "It behooves
me," he wrote to Charles Eliot Norton in 1870, "as a luckless American,
diabolically tempted of the shallow and the superficial, really to catch
the flavour of an old civilization (it hardly matters which) and to strive
to raise myself, for one brief moment at least, in the attitude of observation." [6] But it is important in noting the escapism of Henry James to remark two things. He took his duty as an artist as a faith; and in the
ugly rawness of the Gilded Age he saw no place for that faith. He did
not think he could practise it in an America made arid by the vulgar
ascendency of business men, and he thought that their relentless passion
for acquisition, even more, their conviction that there was nothing that
money could not buy, destroyed the sense of respect for beauty which
is what justifies the claim to be civilized. I think myself that the propor-

<hr>

[6] *The Letters of Henry James,* edited by Percy Lubbock (London: Macmillan,
1920), Vol. I, p. 12.

tions of his judgment were wholly wrong, and that he attributed to Europe traditions which were, in fact, no more real, and certainly no more interesting, than those he could have found in America. The point is that in post-Civil War America he found himself without roots because he could not accept the values imposed by the new business men who had swept into power with Appomattox. The second thing of interest is that, to the very end of his life, no preoccupation of his mind and heart ever came near his shy devotion to America. He preferred, unlike Mark Hopkins, "the merely contemplative and quietistic life, which has so often been the result or the cause of inefficiency or idleness," even to the great game of being employed in "accumulating property honestly," which President Hopkins thought the best way to discourage "any sentimentalism about the worthlessness of property,"[7] which might so easily prevent appropriate gifts to Williams College. James does not seem to have felt any of Dr. Oliver Wendell Holmes' hatred of labour leaders, nor John Hay's insistence that they were violent and unscrupulous. Rather, he felt what Charles Francis Adams, the son of the famous minister to England during the Civil War, felt about his business associates. "I have known, and known tolerably well," wrote Adams, "a good many 'successful' men, 'big' financially, men famous during the last half-century; and a less interesting crowd I do not care to encounter. Not one that I have ever known would I care to meet again, either in this world or the next; nor is one of them associated in my mind with the ideas of humour, thought, or refinement."[8] Nor did Adams stand alone in this severe view. There is thus a real way in which James might have justified his pilgrimage as the one road to making secure that life devoted to art which might have been overwhelmed in the American scene. Certainly it is notable that the overwhelming majority of the novels about American business men published in his lifetime were severely critical of their ability to understand the historic American values. If James attacked them from Europe, Howells and his successors attacked them from America. They were, in common love of America, co-operators in the same task.

3

THERE is a literature of imagination and a literature of learning; and few aspects of culture indicate more clearly the character of a culture than the harvest that is gathered from the seed sown by the scholars. Quite obviously the field is far too wide for me even to attempt any serious examination of the whole. I can only pick out three areas in that field and seek to estimate the significance for culture of what learned men have achieved. I must note at the outset that the last hundred and fifty years almost divide themselves into two equal parts. There is a period, up to

[7] Mark Hopkins, *Lectures on Moral Science* (Boston: Gould & Lincoln, 1862), p. 104.
[8] Adams, *Autobiography,* p. 190.

some such time as the foundation of Johns Hopkins University, in which the outstanding type is the amateur, like Prescott or Bancroft or Parkman, a man of means who represents in America the same high endeavour as Grote represented in England before the fifties, and Lord Acton after them. In the late seventies the amateur begins to give way to the professional. Overwhelmingly it is upon the academic scholar, who combines research with teaching, that the advance of learning depends; and the amateur with means or leisure becomes either a patron or a collector. The exceptions to this charge are few; in history, for example, the only three names of amateurs who count are Henry Charles Lea, James Ford Rhodes, and Henry Osborn Taylor; and of these, only Lea can be regarded as in the front rank of men who both ask significant questions and answer them significantly. James Ford Rhodes is, at best, the earnest and commonplace mind which hardly sees more in the material than could be seen by anyone who was not very troubled by the habits of James G. Blaine. Rhodes preferred to trust the steering of the State power to a business man's agent like Mark Hanna rather than to a dangerous radical like William Jennings Bryan who had no knowledge of the inescapable laws of the market economy. Henry Osborn Taylor wrote charming books in which much learning was associated with deep appreciation of the pageant of ideas. But he sought too little for the causes of the philosophies he examined ever to penetrate to their foundations. The minor amateurs, George Louis Beer, for example, wrote monographs behind which were solid research and interesting hypotheses; but they did nothing to alter, or even seriously to influence, the major principles of judgment in their field.

I propose to take historiography, literary criticism, and philosophy, and to examine their outcome as expressions of American culture in the last century and a half. I can do no more than sketch the broadest outlines of the survey that needs to be made; for nothing shows the inner essence of a culture more fully or more richly than the close examination of these fields. Above all, the historian makes the character of his age implicitly evident by the canons of judgment he applies to the meaning of another age. Since I believe, moreover, that in the fields of history and the historical criticism of literature American scholarship today leads the world, it is of exceptional interest to discover the criteria by which it makes its judgments. And there is the further interest of the fact that as only the American student of history, in contrast with the student of economics or of politics, has seen the significance of what may perhaps be called total history—by which I mean the interaction of all social influences in the production of the mental climate of a civilization—the result is that the historian in the United States has a deeper awareness of what is happening in our time than scholars in any other field of social studies.

The writers whom I have ventured to call the "amateurs" did, of course, some really admirable work. It is possible, today, to smile at the naïveté with which George Bancroft set out to show that God had taken the United States under his special protection. No one can fail to note how many of the state histories produced by local patriotism are set in the background of the conviction that the world's great age has begun anew, in Massachusetts or Vermont, in Pennsylvania or South Carolina, as the case may be. But Parkman, at least, with indomitable courage, was recovering an epic which challenged comparison with the best European work; while Prescott and Motley painted in their own way gorgeous tapestries in which the massive labour of compilation still left a great narrative adventure to enthrall the reader in the romantic tradition of Sir Walter Scott. The amateur historians, with the one outstanding exception of Richard Hildreth,[9] write almost wholly on the political plane. They are interested in picturesque history; their centre of reference is usually, therefore, some great man or some dramatic movement. They have not yet learned to estimate the importance of the impersonal factors of history; they only rarely see the mutual interaction of ideas and environment. Their statesmen will the events in which they are involved because they have a great character or a great mind. They see, as it were, the front of the stage; they do not examine with any closeness what has to happen behind the curtain to put their hero or their villain in his particular attitude when the rise of the curtain reveals him to his audience. I do not think it is entirely fancy which persuades me that Macaulay was their model narrator, and that their informing principle of selection was the Carlyle-Emersonian concept of the hero, a concept so often verified for them in their own experience since their fathers had told them tales of Washington and Jefferson, and they had themselves seen John Quincy Adams and Andrew Jackson in Washington, and dined with those merchant princes of New England and New York whose unresting enterprise was already beginning to change the face of the American landscape. The largest part of amateur history is a special category of romanticism. It is an epic rather than an analysis, a splendid tale in which we cheer the hero's triumph or weep at his failure or his early death. Mostly, too, we assist at the celebration of a progressive victory, which means that the Protestant or the white man, secular learning or the right to toleration, have advanced a stage further on the road to the survival of the fittest. There may be, as with Parkman or with Prescott, a laurel wreath upon the grave of the vanquished; but it is hardly excessive to say that for most of them history is a majestic procession hopefully culminating in the recognition of the American republic as the end result of civilization.

The serious transfer of historical analysis to the professionals began with the famous seminar of H. B. Adams at Johns Hopkins; as one looks

---

[9] Richard Hildreth, *The History of the United States of America* (New York: Harper, 1849–52), 6 vols.

back, the romantic simplicity of its first phase is now almost a comic episode. The seminar was set in the framework of that mystic Teutonism which the patronage of Bismarck and the widespread fear of French ambitions had persuaded scholars in half a dozen countries to regard as the source of democratic institutions. If Stubbs and Freeman in Britain could reverently worship at that shrine, it is not remarkable that Adams was deceived, and that the first volume of the *Studies in Historical and Political Science* should explain, with due solemnity, the "Germanic origin of New England towns," or the presence of "Saxon tithingmen in America," or even of Norman constables; after all, the first pamphlet in the series was a typically ardent hymn by Freeman to the Teutonic discovery of freedom in the forests of Central Europe. At least the myth did not long endure; and from the eighties onwards there is both a massive sweep in the general conspectus taken, and a skill in supplying new hypotheses for verification, which might be surpassed by a remarkable genius like Frederic William Maitland in England, or an occasional master like Theodor Mommsen in Germany, but was certainly in its total significance rarely equalled and not yet surpassed elsewhere.

I do not mean that the achievement was not purchased at a high price. Excessive specialization has been the curse of the professional historian in America. Far too often he evades the need for the full-scale work or the large generalization, partly because his training tempts him from the outset to timidity, and partly because life has become too short for most men to have the courage to risk a general view when the materials to be known are so vast and so detailed, and each authority in a special field is waiting, like a hidden sniper, to shoot the stranger who ventures into his private preserves. Yet there are remarkable general histories and remarkable special monographs, not merely for American history but for the whole course of man's development. No English work even remotely compares with that superb achievement which Charles and Mary Beard called *The Rise of American Civilization*.[10] Here the trained historian joins with the social philosopher to give meaning as well as colour to the picture that is painted. And though McMaster's work[11] is in part overorganized and in part overwhelmed by its material, his history of the American people broke the ground for our understanding of the process it explains and is superior in depth and insight to the comparable histories of other countries. On the colonial period there are not only admirable general histories, like those of Andrews[12] for the seventeenth, and Osgood[13] for the eighteenth century; there are also special monographs of remarkable illumination—Alvord on the significance of

[10] Its successors, hardly of equal quality, are *America in Midpassage* and *The American Spirit* (New York: Macmillan, 1942).

[11] John Bach McMaster, *A History of the People of the United States from the Revolution to the Civil War* (New York: D. Appleton-Century, 1883–1913), 8 vols.

[12] Charles McLean Andrews, *The Colonial Period of American History* (New Haven: Yale University Press, 1934–38), 4 vols.

[13] Herbert Levi Osgood, *The American Colonies in the Eighteenth Century* (New York: Columbia University Press, 1924), 5 vols.

the Mississippi Valley,[14] Schlesinger on the American merchants [15] Becker on the Declaration of Independence; [16] and in two remarkable articles, one of the younger American historians, Louis M. Hacker, has shown with brilliance how a philosophic theory can make old facts reveal new insights.[17] On the nineteenth century there is a great wealth of first-rate work. The publication in 1893 of Turner's remarkable paper on the influence of the frontier marked an epoch in the study of American civilization.[18] It is, I think, legitimate to say that in the light of fifty years' discussion Turner's hypothesis seems exaggerated and one-sided; if the frontier deeply influenced the outlook of the more ancient areas, these, after all, sent their ideas and institutions to influence the frontier.[19] But Turner produced a theory which fertilized all American historical thinking for half a century; it was a new insight when he offered it, and there has been no illumination of equal distinction in the interval with but one exception. That exception is the work of Professor Beard on the circumstances which shaped the formation and acceptance of the American Constitution.[20] Greeted with indignant fury when it appeared—even Mr. Justice Holmes regarded it as outrageous,[21] and the *New York Times* virtually demanded Beard's dismissal from Columbia University [22]—Beard's explanation has now become part of the settled tradition of historians. What it did was really no more than to humanize the demi-gods who were supposed to have achieved a divine construction in the brief months of that hot summer of 1787 in Philadelphia, by showing from a massive examination of the archives that the Founding Fathers were well aware that the translation of possession into property gives business that sense of confidence without which it lacks the buoyancy essential to adventure. And when Beard completed his explanation by showing the relation of the Federalist approach, with the sanctions discovered by John Marshall for its sure arrival, to the rise and partial triumph of Jeffersonian democracy,[23] it was generally agreed that he had provided the only basis upon which the general character of American history in the nineteenth century could be soundly built upon intelligible foundations.

[14] Clarence W. Alvord, *The Mississippi Valley in British Politics* (Glendale, Calif.: A. H. Clark, 1917), 2 vols.

[15] Arthur M. Schlesinger, *The Colonial Merchants and the American Revolution, 1763–1776* (New York: Columbia University Press, 1917).

[16] Carl L. Becker, *The Declaration of Independence* (New York: Knopf, 1922, new edition, 1942).

[17] Louis M. Hacker, "The First American Revolution," *Columbia University Quarterly*, September, 1935.

[18] See the last chapter of this book.

[19] Nor is there any evidence that the frontier grew original institutions.

[20] Charles A. Beard, *Economic Interpretation of the Constitution of the United States* (New York: Macmillan, 1913).

[21] Mark De Wolfe Howe (ed.), *Holmes-Pollock Letters* (Cambridge: Harvard University Press, 1941), Vol. II, p. 4.

[22] Beale, *Are American Teachers Free?*

[23] Charles A. Beard, *Economic Origins of Jeffersonian Democracy* (New York: Macmillan, 1915).

It is impossible here to survey more than an occasional example of how the professional historian has brought light into obscure places of the past hundred years of American civilization; no choice, in any case, could be just or representative that was not in itself a full history of historical writing. But there are some monographs that almost name themselves. Professor Hansen's study of the Atlantic migration,[24] Professor Curti's account of American educators,[25] the succinct but remarkable history of American democratic thought by Professor Gabriel,[26] Norman Ware's discriminating essays on American labour from 1840 to 1860,[27] Professor Morison's great history of Harvard University,[28] Henry David's incisive account of the Haymarket Affair,[29] and Bernhard Stern's successful pioneer work in showing the historical factors which shaped the progress of American medicine,[30] all these, in their different ways, have been pathfinding research of a high order. As I have said, I think their cost has been high, in the sense that they are representative survivals from a vast literature much of which has perished almost as soon as it has been published. But the price apart, it is difficult to feel that any country has ever before provided so fully the materials for the study of its past or charted so clearly the map by which one finds one's way through their massive abundance.

I dare not even seek to attempt any list of the contributions by American scholars to the understanding of history other than their own; I venture only the general estimate that some of it, not least the work which deals with English history, is of outstanding quality. I must rather try to infer from the work I have so inadequately described the relation it bears to my general hypothesis. No one, I think, can seriously measure the character of the work done in the last seventy years, and particularly since the end of nineteenth-century peace in 1914, without seeing that it has been the half-conscious preoccupation of the historians, above all of those who have sought to explain and not merely to narrate, to discover what went wrong in the development of the American promise. No one now takes seriously the legend of a special American destiny. No one now doubts that an immense price has been paid by the farmer and by the worker for the industrial revolution which has centralized American

---

[24] Marcus L. Hansen, *Atlantic Migration, 1607–1860* (Cambridge: Harvard University Press, 1940).

[25] Merle E. Curti, *Social Ideas of American Educators* (New York: Scribner, 1935).

[26] Gabriel, *The Course of American Democratic Thought.*

[27] Norman J. Ware, *The Industrial Worker, 1840–1860* (Boston: Houghton Mifflin, 1924).

[28] Samuel Eliot Morison, *Tercentennial History of Harvard College and University, 1636–1936* (Cambridge: Harvard University Press, 1930–36).

[29] Henry David, *History of the Haymarket Affair* (New York: Farrar & Rinehart, 1936).

[30] Bernhard J. Stern, *Social Factors in Medical Progress* (New York: Columbia University Press, 1927); *American Medical Practice in the Perspectives of a Century* (New York: Commonwealth Fund, 1945); *Medicine in Industry* (New York: Commonwealth Fund, 1946); *Medical Services by Government* (New York: Commonwealth Fund, 1946).

power economically in so small a number of hands. No one fails to realize the immense dangers inherent in that "invisible government" of which, towards the close of his long career, Mr. Elihu Root spoke such passionate words. The significance of the great "trusts," the problems of the still tragic South, not least of the impact of its poverty upon the relations of the Negro and the white man, the danger latent in the unreal party divisions, the grim fact that social mobility is proving consistent with the emergence of classes which grow slowly more separated from each other, the grave need for, and the even graver difficulty of securing, constitutional reform, the disparity between social need objectively measured and business principles subjectively held, all these are examples merely of the emphasis which modern historical investigation has made the only basis upon which the problems of America can be seen in their full perspective. The implication is the unmistakable one that the future of America is not a necessary progress to greater well-being, but a struggle for the fulfilment of democracy in which the battles to be fought will be hard and long.

4

THE criticism of literature has been a strand in American culture of quite exceptional interest. In a general way it can hardly be said to have had an important and effective place before the Civil War. No doubt there were men of genius, like Emerson, whose insights have the inspiration of the man endowed with the true prophet's gift. No doubt, also, one can see important implications in the attitudes of men like Fenimore Cooper and Nathaniel Hawthorne. But criticism of literature as criticism of life, begins, as a serious matter, with James Russell Lowell, and it then diverges into two main streams. There is the academic criticism which seeks to make literature a "scientific" subject; here the influence of German methods was overwhelming. And there is what I may fairly call "creative" criticism, by which I mean that the critic seeks to make his view of literature express the philosophy of life he holds. Creative criticism has its home inside as well as outside the universities; indeed, it is in the universities that some of its most remarkable work has been done. I shall try to show that a broad view of these eighty years makes this part of American culture a part with increasing value for the understanding of American life.

The central fact about the work of James Russell Lowell is that he was no more than the Harvard professor in the genteel tradition with nothing original or incisive to say. He disliked the uncomfortable and the challenging. He was at home in the outlook of those Boston interiors where nothing unpleasant was discussed and most things unconventional abhorred. He disliked the raw, uncouth proletarian whom massed immigration brought into being. He was made unhappy not by the spectacle of poverty, but by the thought that crude men, by crude methods, were challenging the long-undisputed supremacy of Cabots and

Lowells. He understood the world of the Saturday Club in Boston, genial, witty talk of cultivated men who had reached that happy level where there were no material problems. He agreed with the Irish-American E. L. Godkin, the first editor of *The Nation,* that there ought to be a merit system in the Civil Service, that the corruption of the Gilded Age showed "unforeseen tendencies" in democracy, and that the best kind of government was that in which "gentlemen," in the Bostonian sense of the term, ruled because the masses gladly accepted their guidance; but after the one brilliant flash of his *Biglow Papers,* nothing that he wrote either of politics or of literature suggests anything more than a rich man, with a large library at his elbow, retailing well-turned commonplaces from the utterance of which he derived much satisfaction. Not only did science disturb him; he was even upset by a book like Leslie Stephen's *History of English Thought in the Eighteenth Century.* Its revelation that the free-thinkers and the radicals had an illustrious intellectual pedigree, and had so often got the better of the argument, made him feel as uncomfortable as a man in evening dress who receives guests at dinner in their ordinary clothes.

Lowell's career at Harvard was ending just when, in the late seventies, the "scientific" study of literature was beginning; and it has now spread all over the United States. Some of its results are beyond praise. No one has ever shown more clearly the working of the creative imagination than did John Livingston Lowes in his *Road to Xanadu*—a superb re-creation of each stage in the process of Coleridge's famous poem. F. B. Kaye edited Mandeville's *Fable of the Bees* with a precision and fullness of knowledge that opened new windows onto its subject. Works like Perry Miller's *Orthodoxy in Massachusetts* (1933), or William Haller's *Rise of Puritanism* (1938), or F. O. Matthiessen's *American Renaissance* (1941), remade the field they ploughed not merely with a learning that is wholly admirable, but with an imaginative insight which makes their analyses of the past throw vivid light upon the general problems of civilization. In work of their kind scholarship fuses with wisdom to produce standards of judgment by which one begins to see how the interrelation of forces produces the kind of values men accept. We are made, as it were, to re-live experiences which enrich our own experience by widening it and deepening it. The special combination they effect makes their themes take on relations of universality. They do for their subject what, on an ampler canvas, Sainte-Beuve did in his *Port-Royal.* They not only bring the dead to life, they make us see how the dead are part of a vast tradition in which we also are involved, and they make us conscious of the intellectual obligation we have not merely to accept, but also to reshape, that tradition.

But that is a very different "scientific" approach from that of literary philologists like F. J. Child or Albert S. Cook, or J. M. Manly or George C. D. Odell. Here the effort has been to make a massive collection of material seemingly for the sake of its size. The material is rarely evaluated. There is real difficulty in seeing what principle emerges from its collection. It does not seem helpful to the grasp either of historic evolution in letters or to the setting of literature in the framework of its time. It is more like an immense, indeed, portentous, card catalogue in which good, bad, and indifferent are thrown together with no other aim but size. It is learning for the sake of learning; and it has no power to distinguish between literature as the expression of individual talent and of the mental climate of a period, and literature as linguistic technique, with the replacement of value, aesthetic, or historical, or philosophic, by an attention to philological minutiae which not seldom blinds the scholar to the main purpose for which literature is studied. I venture the guess that if a third of the effort spent on the collection of often fifth-rate ballads, or seventh-rate religious poems, or in the compilation of catalogues of plays that will never be acted again and whose performance at all must remain very difficult to explain, had been spent in the superb kind of work done by men like Moses Coit Tyler in the last century, or Vernon Parrington in this, it would have three times the value. Anyone who looks at the critical apparatus supplied to add to the appreciation of literature by members of this scientific school will see how sadly they misjudged the critic's office.

Creative criticism, on the other hand, has had, especially in recent years, immense achievement to its credit. Parrington, Lowes, Matthiessen, Edmund Wilson, Alfred Kazin, see the artist's work as the expression of what a civilization is seeking to be. Such critics give meaning not only to the man or woman they discuss, but to the significant elements in the environment to which he belongs. They realize that the critic's function is to provide a philosophy of interpretation and to have canons of judgment by which to make his philosophy valid. They see how much of the writer's work is rooted in traditions which he is led to accept, or to seek to modify, by the relation to them in which he is involved. They know that there is a level the attainment of which makes the task of criticism itself a form of creation. That is why their work is set in a background in which historical insight mingles with individual understanding, so as to make for measure and proportion. What men like those whom I have named have made us see is that, with all that American literature has inherited from Europe, it is American life itself that has been the real source of what the writer had to say. The melancholy of Melville, the ultimate pessimism of Mark Twain, the supersession of the Brahmin tradition which, for perhaps half a century, made Boston look upon itself with such admiration, are linked with the realism of the last half-century, the satire, the indignation derived from the discovery, often a sudden and shocked discovery, that the America in which they were living was not the America in which they had been brought up to believe. They saw that no writer of any consequence, and certainly no great writer, is ever simple; they saw that what goes into what he has to say is all that he sees of the relation of man to society. They saw, also, that a book is a social act, that a great book is, as it were, an effort to legislate, and, therefore, that literary criticism is an important part of social history. What, too, is of exceptional importance in their effort is the sense of a civilization, if not in decay, at least in profound crisis, because its great men of letters either lose hope or are full of protest at what they regard as a betrayal of what was once a noble dream. They show us how, whether in the violence of, say, Hemingway or Faulkner, or in the labyrinthine escapism of Henry James, or in Dreiser's bewildered amazement at the crude passions of that acquisitive society he saw symbolized in the febrile Chicago of Charles T. Yerkes, the promise of America was brutally separated from the actuality of America. They felt that in this separation there was born a spiritual sickness which made the search for the foundations of a new America imperative. They got beyond that naïveté which sneered at democratic America as a wasteland in which some corner could be reserved for a few choice spirits who whispered to one another in a language they thought no multitude could hope to understand. They passed from America insurgent to America resurgent by seeing that the inspiration of America must be American, because the hostility to that inspiration was American too. It is difficult to exaggerate the significance of their work for the vital reason that they recognized, first, the greatness of the American promise, and, second, the greatness of the failure to redeem it. If there is better or more significant criticism than this at the present time, I do not know of it.

I recognize, of course, that those whom I have named are but a small platoon in a much greater regiment, and I do not even seek to deny that they made incredible mistakes, or that many who seemed to be marching with them lacked altogether their dynamic sensitiveness and their power to see America in American terms. It is, for example, fantastic that a man of Parrington's stature should have taken James Branch Cabell with seriousness. Only the break-down in the values of a civilization could permit a critic like H. L. Mencken to be taken at his own valuation. For the truth is now obvious that Mencken was simply an irresponsible product of the Harding–Coolidge epoch in the same way as Andrew W. Mellon. He was often right about the things he attacked; he was almost invariably right for the wrong reasons. In the end, there survived in Mencken nothing except the desire to deny the conventional, which meant that he believed that this denial made him an aristocrat. No one can read his attack on Governor Altgeld, or on William Jennings Bryan at the time of the Scopes trial in Tennessee, without the recognition that he was not a serious critic. To himself and his friends the width of his contempt and the gay irony of his attacks on Prohibition, Comstockery, and the rest, made him seem the Voltaire of his age. In fact he was the amusing clown in a ten-year harlequinade, with a glib patter which was rarely amusing enough to make it certain that he was not just another kind of Philistine. For his very attempt to be cosmopolitan and to transcend the experience of America reveals him at bottom as a person who makes cosmopolitanism provincial—like the expatriate who displays his anger against America while he sips his absinth at the Dôme or the Rotonde. It is a proof that Mencken knows too little of his real task as critic to have any deeper desire than to avoid facing the actual America. That he wrote his petty epic of escape from Baltimore makes no difference. He never knew America intimately enough to have the right to attempt its valuation. He was no more than the lively scavenger of the superficial. He tempted the inhabitants of Main Street to believe that they were profound because they shared his prejudices. He was in rebellion; but he never sought in any profound way to understand the thing against which he rebelled. He never realized that the great critic must either be capable of generosity or have the genius of Dean Swift gleaming through even the blackest of his hours. What destroyed Mencken was that he admired his own cleverness so whole-heartedly that he never had time to consider what it was he should seek to be clever about. He appears on the stage like Dan Leno in the English pantomime at Christmas; he never understood that Dan Leno now survives only in a kindly note in the *Dictionary of National Biography*. No mockery is ever creative until it begins to be profound.

It is interesting to note the emergence of a critical approach, which came to be called the "New Humanism," as an expression of profound dissatisfaction with the America which the Gilded Age took first into the noisy glitter of the Spanish-American War and thence into the false dawn of that progressive era in which Theodore Roosevelt disillusioned so many who were young enough to believe that he meant what he said and was more than the cowboy of the Western World. From 1912 onwards there was a real quickening of the pulse of democracy, and from a date which the publication of Van Wyck Brooks' famous manifesto of 1915, *America's Coming-of-Age,* marks clearly, the moral and æsthetic barriers were down. It was no longer possible for America to wear either the mask of youth or the mask of special destiny, to conceal the fact that it was part of an ordinary world, however powerful it might be as a factor in that world. Nobody could mistake the fact that the old standards were gone and that the old values were as much a target as an end at which to aim. There was confusion, anger, bewilderment, a riot of experiment, in which nobody was certain of anything. America gave the impression of a country supremely anxious to exhibit with disillusioned haste all the skeletons in its ancestral cupboards. The adoration of novelty suggested that everything traditional had been found out, and that everyone's experience was significant. Nobody thought the past a safe anchorage; and nobody recognized any faith as possessed of that validity which exacts the obligation to revere. The war of 1898, the epoch of "muckraking," the bankruptcy of Woodrow Wilson's "new freedom," which took the United States into the First World War without its effects going deep enough to act as a full catharsis for half a century of disenchantment—all this was bound to lead to some kind of counter-reformation.

What is important in the challenge to the drift towards a revival of the American promise of the pre-Civil War period is the form in which the counter-reformation came.

There are at least two sides to it, of very different character. There is the profound traditionalism of Irving Babbitt, and in a lesser degree of Paul Elmer More. In one sense, indeed, this form of revulsion from the age can hardly be called American at all. With Babbitt, it is rather an attack on the whole ethos of the American faith. When he traced all the ills of America to Rousseau and romanticism he was, in his own view, pleading for order against disorder, for a standard of values against an anarchy of values, for unity against pluralism, for thought against emotion, for spiritual health against material wealth. It is impossible not to feel, in reading Babbitt, that he is the lineal descendant of Joseph de Maistre, and that he would have been at home with the militant Bossuet, who so inflexibly imposed the principles of the Revocation in his diocese. For almost all that his generation valued Babbitt had contempt. He hated a civilization in which rich men were held to be important because they were rich. He hated its politicians, who angled for the votes of the ignorant mob. He hated scholars who did not see that America, in choosing freedom rather than authority, mobility rather than hierarchy, was abandoning the hope of that rigorous intellectual discipline which accepts the command of its thinkers as its way of life. Babbitt made war on Rousseau because he saw in faith in the common man and his impulses a glorification of a state of nature which, in fact, he thought as evil as had Hobbes two centuries and a half before. His conservatism was not American in its foundations; he did not shrink, like Charles Eliot Norton or James Russell Lowell, from what was a whole-hearted abandonment of the genteel tradition, with its aloofness, its discretion, its reticence, its ability to come to terms with life by evading all its problems. On the contrary, with an obstinate courage he went into the marketplace to denounce with hot fury all the experiments which his epoch attempted because they implied that there were not permanent standards which men examine at their peril. With Maistre, he could have said that the executioner is the cornerstone of society. He was never content to lament; he was happy only when he denounced, and there was hardly anything in contemporary America that he was not anxious to denounce.

Babbitt had immense, even unbreakable, strength of character; and it is to this that he owed his influence. But he nowhere justified the premisses of his thinking. He was a rationalist who exploded with fury as he watched the irrationalism of the common man. He had a contempt for human nature in almost every form of its American expression. He hated the rich because they mainly acquired their wealth in crude and ugly ways; he hated the poor because they were so obviously failures and so clearly ignorant. He thought America the paradise of the average man; and the average man had neither self-control nor the knowledge to distinguish between good and evil. Babbitt had no religion; in a sense, he had no philosophy. It is tempting to argue that there is a real justice in viewing him as a romantic who made his own temperamental disgust with America the source of a fury which he explained to himself as the yearning for a perfection of which his age was incapable. He had not an atom of flexibility in his mind, no sense of curiosity, no capacity to see into the sources which explain the changing historic experience. He was an egotist who identified his private universe with communal good; and his very perversity is the measure of his unhappy disappointment in an America which, for him, was a tragic failure because it was so far removed from the desire to interest itself in the meaning of his private universe.

I doubt whether in any large sense Babbitt, who spent the main part of his life as a professor at Harvard University, had any disciples except Paul Elmer More. No doubt he influenced, in a particular way, some of his pupils, Stuart Sherman, for instance, and T. S. Eliot, and a little set of wealthy æsthetes who persuaded themselves that their dislike of the eager, hungry, infinitely mobile America of the nineteen-twenties was not an anachronistic revival of the genteel tradition, but a yearning for universality. I suspect, too, that he had some remote connection with the curious and rather pathetic revival of neo-Thomism by which the *élite* of Chicago have tried to forget the stockyards, and the Irish, and Al Capone, by assuming that their true genealogy goes back through Aquinas to Aristotle. But Stuart Sherman, when his powers were at their most mature, deserted Babbitt; at the time of his tragic death, he had already found an exciting importance in the New America. T. S. Eliot took refuge from its agonies partly in expatriation and partly by self-baptism in a mental climate so like the habits of the seventeenth century in England that he was obviously disciplining himself to be, if not a member of the community of Little Gidding, at any rate a thinker of devout faith who would have been at home on a Sunday at Great Tew, and who looked back with pious regret at a world in which, for a decade, men like Donne and Falkland and Lancelot Andrewes had been replaced in popular esteem by Calamy and Sibbes and those equivalents of Hollywood fantastics, the Baptists and Fifth Monarchy men. The Chicago school had little to contribute except the ardent insistence that only the best was worth having; and their fiscal agent, President Hutchins of the University of Chicago, procured the funds to prove what was the best from wealthy manufacturers who knew very little of what he was about except that he did not like radicalism, a position they regarded as one pre-eminently worthy of endowment.

But Paul Elmer More, in a more timid and somewhat spinsterish kind of way, stood by his master. He had begun in the school of rigid Calvinist orthodoxy. He moved steadily, despite an occasional lapse like his affection for the poems of Heine and his occasional sense of being haunted by religious doubt, to an Anglo-Catholicism which turned its back on the things of this world, to find his refuge in a creed in which he wedded

Plato to Christ in an effort to build a system in which the principles were
orthodox enough to make him regard trade-unions and social settlements
as indefensible concessions of weakness. He was an orthodox reactionary
in the style of an Oxford don who, before the troublesome era in which
Jowett and Mark Pattison insisted on disturbing the complacency about
them, had stood immovably for Church and King. He worshipped orthodoxy which, for him, defined the boundaries of the central spirit
of tradition; and orthodoxy meant not only the rule of aristocracy,
but the recognition that pity and charity are mere scavengers which
tempt us to risk the defeat of aristocracy. "The rights of property,"
he wrote, "are more important than the right to life"; and, for him, almost
all the great Victorian liberals suffer from their tendency to sympathize
with suffering. He was amazed that John Morley could not see in the
magic towers of Oxford the residence of an exquisite pharisaism the
sheer ritual of which was itself a guarantee of the quest for perfection.
He loved Newman and Burke and Sir Thomas Browne because they
represented a moral code which he would die rather than abandon. He
never even sought to understand the liberal doctrine of his day. One can
see him mourning with that stout-hearted reactionary, Sir Robert Inglis,
the defection of Peel from the good old cause in 1829; one can realize how
his bitter dislike of Milton's opinions was a final barrier to his understanding of Milton's majestic poetry. If he lacked the strident fury of
Babbitt, he yet yearned for salvation; and without any sacrifice of his
inner integrity he would have been the chaplain to a new Archbishop
Laud, who accepted the condemnation of Proust and James Joyce because, though he had to admit the greatness of their talent, he had also
to admit that they never strove to see the vision splendid for which he
was ever searching. He was a man of utter honesty, whose failure is
that, while he had real learning and a hunger for fame, he could never
let himself go, lest out of energy and expansion he might make concessions to standards which tempted men from the narrow path. He spent
his whole life in affirming the need in America for an aristocracy; that
meant its need for property, so that the aristocrat could have the means
for the life of culture; then the society would become safe, because its men
of leisure would be secure enough to devote themselves to the life of the
spirit, and thus prepare themselves for salvation. It would have been interesting to have seen how Collis Huntington, or Rockefeller, or Frick,
prepared themselves for that life, and how Paul Elmer More would have
explained to them the vocation to which they were called. It would have
been still more interesting to have watched him, at one of Mr. Carnegie's
famous house parties in Skibo Castle, explain to Morley why he looked
upon the latter's outlook as a betrayal of the faith, while he saw, or
convinced himself he saw, that men like J. P. Morgan were on the same
spiritual pilgrimage as himself. But there was too profound an uneasiness
in his mind ever to see the boundaries of legitimate experiment more
safely marked than the past traditions had marked them. Nature and

temperament had fitted him to dwell in the home of lost causes; his tragedy was to mistake the little province of his mind for the vast metropolis in which all right-thinking men could find peace.

So the New England Indian summer faded away. Apart from the reactionary traditionalism of Babbitt and of More, there are two other currents of criticism which deserve brief analysis. The first, which began in the nineteen-twenties, though it reached its climax only in the half-dozen years before 1939, was an attempt to explain the American scene in Marxist terms. With at least two periodicals at their disposal, with congresses and book reviews organized, so as to make as plain as possible the division between the sheep and the goats, the Marxists set out to storm their way to leadership of the intellectuals. They had immense difficulties. There were not only the internal troubles within the American party itself, which led to schisms and conflicts which made it hard to know the goat from the sheep; there were the divisions in Moscow itself, above all the division between Stalin and Trotsky, which led to internecine warfare in the United States almost as passionate as the polemic waged in the Soviet Union. It produced books and articles which were as ardently accepted as they were eagerly denied by those who kept the diverse canons of authentic Marxism in their keeping. In a real way, the attempt to use Marxism as a clue to American ideas, whether in books like Granville Hicks' *The Great Tradition*, or James T. Farrell's *A Note on Literary Criticism*, or Bernard Smith's *Forces in American Criticism*, was less an intellectual than a religious exercise. It was too excited and too rigid to have anything but the appearance of a hothouse growth. It tried to make the artist someone who enlisted in an army and ought therefore to write his books by the rules set out in the *Manual of Military Law*. He was to aim at promoting the class struggle. He was to depict the worker as a hero, and show up the futile parasitism of the leisure class. As critic, he was to insist that even if every Marxist did not write a good book, no good book could be written except by a Marxist. His judgment was always to be written on the basis that any book which was not a militant demand for proletarian freedom was reactionary, or escapist, or bourgeois, or petty bourgeois. And, until the Nazi-Soviet Pact of 1939 threw the Marxist writers into mingled alarm and despondency and confusion, the critics slashed relentlessly at every effort which did not follow what they regarded as "correct" principles with the same fervour that the Presbyterian Thomas Edwards put into his arrogant *Gangræna* almost three centuries ago.[31]

The Marxist phase was historically important even if it was largely devoid of critical significance. It showed, in the first place, that the Russian Revolution had universal implications and was the symptom of a disease as wide as civilization itself. No doubt there was something ironical in the militant aggressiveness of critics who were prepared to identify

---

[31] See Max Eastman's brilliant and amusing *Artists in Uniform* (London: Allen & Unwin, 1934).

an incantation with a remedy, if only it was sufficiently dogmatic and violent. But it showed how deep was the frustration for this group of American writers in the quality and the standards of their own culture that they should have been so proud to mistake an anæsthetic for a faith. For it was to find a faith that they were primarily concerned. America, they felt, had failed them; and they turned to Moscow with all the zeal of a Mohammedan who goes to Mecca that he may be purged of sin. They did not see that when they accepted the formulæ and the categories, they were surrendering their imaginative insight and their duty to explore experience. They conducted criticism as though it were a court-martial in which they were at once the judges and the prosecuting counsel. They were not even aware that they rarely criticized the artist as an artist, but rather insisted on judging him by what implications they could find in his attitude to social change. Their very fanaticism was, in truth, a measure of their unhappiness; and their unhappiness was the outcome of their profound conviction that the American promise had been betrayed. They felt themselves being dragged by the relentless forces of the economic oligarchy which dominated American life into a new dark age; and in their fury and bewilderment they turned to the new orthodox church of Moscow because this seemed, by its highly expert power of denunciation, to offer them the deepest emotional comfort for the threat under which they saw themselves living. They were the index to the sickness of an acquisitive society which had not yet recovered the road to convalescence. They drugged themselves into indignation, too often an arrogant indignation, because they were too disheartened by the world about them to have the confidence to attempt creative adventure. They were so disheartened that they forgot that Marx had worshipped Balzac, as Lenin had worshipped Tolstoy, even though by the canon both were obviously reactionaries. That was why, as one looks back at their work, they seem rather like puppets, trying to play the role of Dostoevski's Grand Inquisitor; but they never knew that to have a mood of anger is not to have a philosophy of progress. Yet they have the very powerful defence that both their pathos and their futility were the outcome of an historic failure of which they shared the result but not the responsibility.

Almost parallel with the Marxist movement was the loose and half-organized regiment of Southern reactionaries. The motivation of both groups was the same: profound abhorrence of contemporary America. But while the Marxists were the trumpeters of a messiah who was still to come, the Southern reactionaries were the trumpeters of a messiah who had never been born. John Crowe Ransom, Allen Tate, R. P. Blackmur, Yvor Winters, these, to take the main figures amongst them, had three obsessions: they hated the democratic way of life; they convinced themselves that the South, before the tragedy of its defeat in the Civil War, had been the supreme depository in the United States of all that was richest in the Western heritage of culture; and they believed that the deeper and wider their isolation from the main stream of American life, the more fully they could hope to realize in themselves an imaginative fulfilment. They became the more fulfilled the more distant their private ivory tower not merely from the typical Main Street of America, but from any *cul-de-sac* in which there dwelt some human being with normal appetites and average thoughts. They ceased to have interests in the subject matter of life; it was form alone which mattered. There was no social content in literature, or, if there was, it was not the critic's concern but the historian's. It existed, as I. A. Richards has admirably said, merely for "isolated ecstasies." They had, of course, a cult of order, which meant form and required a ritual. Robertson Smith has shown that, in the twilight zone between anthropology and religion, the ritual begets the myth, and the myth, in its turn, begets a theology. So, precisely, did the Southern reactionaries develop a philosophy which enabled them to live in a South without roots in the past or the present, an abstract South which had no meaning save as a base from which to attack the dominant American culture and all its works.

"The South clings blindly," wrote Allen Tate, "to forms of European feeling and conduct that were crushed by the French Revolution and that in England, at any rate, are barely memories." [32] The main ambition, of course, of most Southerners is for a fuller share of the material well-being enjoyed by the North. But since, to Tate and the rest, this ambition merely proves that Northern vandalism will stay at nothing in its remorseless drive to power, whatever they associate with the North they are compelled to hate. They hate democracy. They hate science. They hate an industrial society. They hate a liberal education. They hate the pragmatism which they associate with the triumph of capitalist materialism. They therefore invent a Southern plantation in which there is an aristocracy with leisured dignity, a feudal relation between master and man, an island of regional cultivation surrounded by an ocean of barbarism. It has great traditions, a noble religion which asks from its votaries the discipline of self-restraint and the recognition that all material values are as futile as they are worthless. If the question of slavery is tentatively raised, they are all prepared to argue that at least it built human relations far better than any made possible under industrial capitalism; and Mr. Tate has even insisted that the ethical mistake of slavery in the South lay in the fact that though the plantation owner gave all that made his life worth while to the slave, from the slave he received nothing in return. They are not, indeed, prepared to be morally troubled about slavery. If it is said that slavery corrupts all those affected by the relation it implies, Mr. Tate is ready to retort that "societies can bear an amazing amount of corruption and still produce high cultures." They think of themselves, so obviously, as the last dying remnant of an idyllic civiliza-

[32] Allen Tate, *Reactionary Essays on Poetry and Ideas* (New York: Scribner, 1936).

tion, tasting the last high ecstasy of their private vision even while the barbarians are breaking down the doors which shelter them from the bitter disillusion of life.

It is difficult not to think of this Southern school—critics, poets, biographers, and the rest—as men who are pessimistic and embittered by the failure of all their hopes. All that they hate is intelligible; nothing that they love has public significance. Like the Marxist school, they are the product of a civilization which has lost its faith and lacks any standard by which to test the values in actual being. They have a tragic sense that all is wrong; and they can comfort themselves only by looking back to a hypothetical golden age, the unhistorical character of which gives it the enchantment of a fairy story. They coerce themselves into the belief that there was this golden age not because they believe in it, but because it enables them, at once, to lash contemporary America with their criticisms and to escape from what they regard as its horrors into a dream world from which all is excluded but the "isolated ecstasies" which this aristocratic remnant can enjoy. They have refined life to a point where living has gone out of it; and they dwell like bloodless ghosts behind the gauze veil which they try to persuade themselves is in truth a wall of unbreakable steel. But, in fact, they have no hope, and they have even lost the vitality which gives life its zest. Their tradition is a synthetic product, their faith a synthetic faith. They have made it out of their fears of what might result from a critical examination of that imaginary South they have called into being. One cannot even say that they are haunted by the dead; for none of those whom they recall so wistfully had any existence in an actual past as they recall him. They are, in a word, cheating themselves into the belief that they have defeated their enemy by turning their backs upon him. With all their passionate intensity of phrase, their vivid rhetoric, their mock-heroic extravagances, their devout zeal for the fantastic paradox, they are actors in a dead play, performed in a theatre where there is no audience. They hear nothing but the empty echo of their own voices; and, in a mood half of anger and half of a lofty condescension, they try to persuade themselves that this echo is the only applause by which the true priest of culture can venture to be satisfied.

So that what emerges from three-quarters of a century of American criticism is the collapse of the unity of a culture. There is no agreement about principles, no agreement about values, no central frame of reference within which the critics can find a common purpose. Only on the plane of action where, as in war, different philosophies are forgotten in the short-term struggle for victory does unity appear. Once the victory is won, the differences re-emerge to become more deep and more vivid because they have become suffused with doubt about the worth of the struggle. And, on the plane of action itself, it is important to realize that the unity is one of coercion and not of consent. Men fight with a self-forgetfulness which gives to many of them a stature of heroic proportions; but it is of the essence of this self-forgetfulness that among the things forgotten are the ideas which alone remain the weapons which can fulfil as well as destroy. The busy speed of modern war, which, overnight, sweeps whole continents into its orbit of influence, gives for a brief moment a false sense of peacefulness because a great decision has been taken. It makes for an artificial order, an artificial hierarchy, even an artificial fellowship, so long as men and women have to act without considering the philosophic grounds upon which they act. But on the morrow of victory they find that their unity has been one of rhetoric and not of relations. They have changed the landscape by their raging torrent of attack; but they find in the ruins the same people who lived there before, with the same appetites to satisfy and the same problems to solve; and there is the same difficulty by which they were driven before they closed their ranks to meet attack that they do not know where to go or even how to start on their journey. The one difference in the new peace is the presence among them of the ghost of another lost generation; and, once again, they make the heart-breaking discovery that unity on the plane of action can save them only if they find a unity about the ultimate values of civilized life. They are left again with the same torturing issue to be resolved, and they have to meet it in that mood of irritated fatigue which makes the search for rational principle so hard. They mistake the tired acceptance of some high-sounding slogan for the supreme opportunity that history offers to malignant men and selfish interests who are ready to turn the triumph into a disaster. They thus make the road to recovery a longer and more bitter search than the swift zest of action had made it possible to imagine. For when a war has been won, men have to decide for what it was that they fought; and it is always difficult to live the reflective life in the aftermath of a Golgotha which seems to deny the very principle of life itself.

5

IN NO country in modern times has philosophy been so intimately related to the foundations of a national culture as in the United States. No doubt the philosophy of the schools has been in large degree both conservative and technical; it originated, after all, in the training of ministers, the sons of gentlemen, and members of the professional classes, by colleges founded and maintained by religious denominations. It had, naturally enough, the main purpose of upholding the traditional way of life both in Church and State. No one can fail to notice how slowly and with what difficulty the medieval scholasticism of the schools began to be influenced partly by scientific change, partly by philosophic innovation, but, above all, by the fact that philosophic speculation was taking place in the new continent of America. Indeed, it is perhaps legitimate to argue that not until the time of Cotton Mather was there any overt inclination to depart from the established bases of philosophic thought. That shrewd conservative, with his keen sense of coming heterodoxy, noted in his *Diary* in 1716 that "there are some very unwise things done, about which I must watch for Opportunities to bear public testimonies. One is the employing of so much time upon Ethics in our colleges. A vile 'Piece of Paganism.' " [33]

The "Vile Piece of Paganism" was, in fact, the natural development of the impact of colonial experience upon the political thought of America. It was the outcome of a slow but inevitable rejection of the Puritan conception of a theocratic world, with its implication that grace had descended to those saints whom God had selected by showing His approval in their arrival at success; whence the theocracy of the spiritual life was, so to say, matched by an aristocracy in the practical.[34] No doubt the "people," when they had property and were members of a Congregational Church, might help in the choice of their governors. That was emphasized by Thomas Hooker in his remarkable election sermon of 1638.[35] But though the forms of government were notably more free in Connecticut than in Massachusetts, even Hooker agreed that citizens must choose their rulers "not according to their humours, but according to the blessed will and law of God," since it was by "the own allowance" of God that they had this power.[36] They did not believe in equality, in democracy, or, for the overwhelming majority, in religious toleration. John Cotton wrote: "Democracy I do not conceive that ever God did ordeyne as a fitt government either for church or commonwealth. If the people be governors, who shall be governed? As for monarchy and aristocracy, they are both of them clearly approved and directed in scripture"; and he goes on to cite Bodin to show that popular election of rulers in nowise constitutes a democracy.[37] And, indeed, that suspicion of democracy, rationalized into the principle that all that is, is of the will of God, was more than proved by the indifference to the social well-being of the poor among the Puritans of the New World. It was not until the time of Woolman [38] and Benjamin Franklin [39] that one begins to detect a tender and sensitive social conscience on the one hand, and a sense that the laws of property are a human contrivance made by the State for social well-being and liable to alteration through its agency on the other.

One can see, in fact, that all American thinking in the seventeenth century is set in the framework of the Calvinist scheme. Even the eager

---

[33] *Diary of Cotton Mather*, June 28, 1716, in Collections of the Massachusetts Historical Society (Boston, 1912), 7th Series, Vol. VIII, p. 357.

[34] See Perry Miller's remarkable *Orthodoxy in Massachusetts, 1630–1650* (Cambridge: Harvard University Press, 1933) and his *The New England Mind* (New York: Macmillan, 1939).

[35] Collections of the Connecticut Historical Society (Hartford, 1860), Vol. I, pp. 20–21.

[36] *Ibid.*; Letter to Lord Saye and Sele, quoted in Perry Miller and Thomas S. Johnson, *The Puritans* (New York: American Book Co., 1938), p. 209.

[37] Cited in Miller and Johnson, *op. cit.*, p. 188.

[38] Amelia Mott Gummere (ed.), *Journal and Essays of John Woolman* (New York: Macmillan, 1922), pp. 424–27; the reference is to his "Plea for the Poor" written in 1763.

[39] Albert Henry Smyth (ed.), *The Writings of Benjamin Franklin* (New York: Macmillan, 1905–07), Vol. IX, p. 138.

plea for toleration in religious matters of Roger Williams is no exception to this, since his real purpose in insisting upon the separation of Church and State was far less a tenderness for men's consciences than a fear that their unity meant the government of the Church by civil men and thus a threat to its purity. Popular control of the Church through elected magistrates he thought evil since it gave the Church "to Satan himself, by whom all peoples naturally are guided." [40] It is not until the eighteenth century, when John Wise, very notably the son of an indentured servant and, though a graduate of Harvard University, deeply permeated by a sense of the claims of the class to which he belonged, that we begin to see the emergence of a "natural reason" which assumes "an original freedom of mankind" and seeks to satisfy the just demands of liberty, equity, equality, and the principles of self-preservation." [41] Wise found his criteria of government in Pufendorf and Locke, and he saw no difficulty in the view that democracy "is as agreeable with the light and laws of nature as any other whatever . . . and more accommodated to the concerns of religion than any other."

Before the eighteenth century was twenty years old the Calvinist framework had lost its grip on the minds of men. And only another generation was to pass before Jonathan Mayhew drew the logical conclusion. He emphasized the necessity of goverment by consent. He argued that utility and happiness are the sole ends of government. He insisted upon the right of revolution against an evil government. "To say," he wrote in 1750, "that subjects in general are not proper judges when their governors oppress them, and play the tyrant, and when they defend their rights, administer justice impartially and promote the public welfare, is as great treason as ever man uttered. 'Tis treason not against one single man, but the state against the whole body politic; 'tis treason against mankind, 'tis treason against common sense, 'tis treason against God. And this impious principle lays the foundation for justifying all the tyranny and oppression that ever any prince was guilty of. The people know for what end they set up and maintain their governors, and they are the proper judges when they exercise their trust as they ought to do it . . . when from subject and children he degrades them into the class of slaves, plunders them, makes them his prey, and unnaturally sports himself with their lives and fortunes." [42] Already, a quarter of a century before the Declaration of Independence, all its teaching was acclimatized among men of standing in Boston.

I cannot even attempt here any account of the revolution in American political philosophy. But it is necessary to note that from the period of the Confederation onwards there are two antagonistic patterns in its

[40] Roger Williams, *The Bloudy Tenent of Persecution* (1644) in Publications of the Narragansett Club (Providence, 1867), 1st Series, Vol. III, pp. 249–50.
[41] John Wise, *A Vindication of the Government of New-England Churches* 1717 (Boston: Congressional Board of Publication, 1860), p. 25.
[42] Jonathan Mayhew, *A Discourse Concerning Unlimited Submission and Non-Resistance to the Higher Powers* (Boston, 1750), p. 40.

unfolding. The one begins with Jefferson and John Taylor and reaches out, through Andrew Jackson, to Lincoln, thence to William Jennings Bryan and the elder La Follette, and from them to Franklin Roosevelt and Henry Wallace. It has, as I see it, three main threads. The first is the emphasis upon the rights of personality as superior to the rights of property; it is the view which comes from the adaptation of Locke's ideas to the atmosphere of the United States. It sees democracy as a process which involves both the individual's active participation in politics and his training to a level where its problems are never so complex that he abandons the hope of understanding them. The second is its suspicions of bigness, especially in industry and finance; for it recognizes that bigness means uniformity and centralization, and that these, whatever gain in efficiency they may imply, always dwarf the individual and tend to overshadow the expansion of political democracy by the growing threat of economic oligarchy. That was why, in the well-known letter to Dupont de Nemours, Jefferson could insist upon "action by the citizens in person in affairs within their reach and competence, in all others by representatives chosen immediately and removable by themselves," as constituting with the vital moral right of revolution the essence of free government.[43] And the third thread is its belief in the positive use of the State power to correct the danger of an excessive concentration of power in a few hands. That principle was admirably stated by Franklin Roosevelt in his Jefferson Day speech of 1932. "I am not speaking," he said, "of an economic life completely planned and regimented. I am speaking of the necessity, however, in those imperative interferences with the economic life of the nation that there be a real community of interest, not only among the sections of this great country, but among its economic units and the various groups in these units; that there be common participation in the work of remedial figures, planned on the basis of a shared common life, the low as well as the high. In much of our present plans there is too much disposition to mistake the part for the whole, the head for the body, the captain for the company, the general for the army. I plead not for class control but for a true concert of ideas." [44]

The other pattern begins with John Adams and Alexander Hamilton. It passes through the tradition imposed by Marshall upon the Supreme Court to the men who fought Andrew Jackson over the Bank and financial centralization, thence to the New York merchants, who sought "appeasement" of the Southern slave-owners on the eve of the Civil War [45] and whose outlook had been effectively presented by Daniel Webster in the previous generation. After Appomattox it is shaped into a theory of

[43] Paul L. Ford (ed.), *The Writings of Thomas Jefferson* (New York: Putnam, 1892-99), Vol. X, p. 246.

[44] *The Public Papers and Addresses of Franklin D. Roosevelt*, Vol. I, p. 632 (New York: Random House, 1938, Vols. I-V; Macmillan, 1941, Vols. VI-IX).

[45] Philip S. Foner, *Business and Slavery* (Chapel Hill: University of North Carolina Press. 1941).

the State by Francis Lieber and his disciples, through whom the State power is made a principle of action both separated from and over the will of the people. This outlook begins to acquire precision of emphasis in the Supreme Court in the epoch of Grant, and is reinforced by that growth of violence between capital and labour which is symbolized by the Haymarket riots and the Pullman and Homestead strikes. It acquires the status of something like a "natural law" as social Darwinism comes to be accepted as the basis of political philosophy and as the cruder theories of government propounded by Herbert Spencer are developed and Americanized by William Graham Sumner. It is, moreover, influenced by experience like the self-reliance of the frontier, the suspicion of the alien immigrant as full of un-American ideas, and the dislike, even though they profited by it, of the corruption and inefficiency of a government based so largely on the power of the bosses and their machines. As Adams, while in theory favourable to popular sovereignty, was at the same time convinced that men are so incapable of self-government that they must be restrained by force and ruled by some power beyond their reach, so, a century later, his successors evolved for the business man a "higher law" to which the legislator must conform, a "law" which involved the Supreme Court in maintaining the right of property as sacred and preventing any interference with freedom of contract. Presently, and especially between 1920 and the Great Depression, the view is emphasized that the successful are an *élite* in whose well-being is contained—as in the "invisible hand" which, with that contemporary of John Adams, Adam Smith, operates the "simple system of natural liberty"—the well-being of the whole community. That explains the popularity of Fascist Italy with business men in the nineteen-twenties, and the avidity with which a mass of publicists read the work of Pareto and depreciated the claim of the ordinary man to share in a governmental process which was quite obviously the function of experts.

"We both love the people," wrote Jefferson to Dupont de Nemours in the letter from which I have already quoted, "but you love them as infants whom you are afraid to trust without nurses, and I, as adults, whom I freely leave to self-government." Nothing illustrates that difference better than the clash on the Supreme Court from the time of Mr. Justice Holmes' famous dissents in the Adair and the Lochner cases down to the transformation of the Court after the attack upon it by President Roosevelt in 1936 to 1937. What that great judge called the "inarticulate major premiss" of the Court became the axiom that the will of a majority, whether in Congress or in a state legislature, is *ab initio* void if it disturbs the security of property rights. The purpose of the Court seemed to be to safeguard business from the interference of legislatures on the political front, and from the interference of organized labour on the economic front. The Court was even prepared, as in the famous Abrams case,[46] to

---

[46] *Cf.* Chafee, *Free Speech in the United States,* not least the citation from Hughes at p. 102.

strike down vital civil liberties if these permit the expression of ideas the majority of the judges dislike. From the Civil War right up to President Roosevelt's Court proposals of 1937, it is not an exaggeration to say that there was usually a coincidence of opinion, between the judges and the business men, that Hamilton was right when he thought of the public as "a great beast." It must be tamed, for its own good by submission to a discipline imposed upon it by masters whose decisions are inherent in nature and beyond the reach of electoral authority.

By a curious fortune, this outlook, which was in essence the adoption and development of the early Federalist outlook, the attitude so frequently given expression by men like Gouverneur Morris and Fisher Ames, was reinforced in its power by the influence of the ideas through which the South sought to defend its "peculiar institution." From Calhoun and Fitzhugh down to the Southern reactionaries, whose critical philosophy I have already discussed, there emerged, first, an insistence on the permanent inferiority of the Negro to the white man; and, second, a contempt for the "poor white trash" of the South, who competed so savagely with one another, especially in periods of depression, for jobs that in the days of slavery only Negroes were thought low enough to perform. Thence came the inference that the unsuccessful were the unfit, and that since the unsuccessful were so obviously the majority of the population, it was indefensible to allow them to rule. From this conclusion came the assumption that democracy was an evil form of government since it put the State power in the hands of men quite clearly incompetent to exercise it wisely. What was required was government by a "natural" aristocracy, which meant in its turn, government by successful men. And since in the business civilization the successful men were by definition, so to speak, the men of greatest fortune, it was right and proper that they should be regarded as the natural aristocracy to whom was entrusted the exercise of power on behalf of the people. Even after the Great Depression President Hoover was able, without conscious intellectual difficulty, to eulogize their "rugged individualism" as the true source of American well-being; [47] and a popular publicist like Mr. Walter Lippmann could, if in a more sophisticated way, urge that the forcible preservation of the "simple system of natural liberty" was the only method by which America could be preserved from the tyranny of a planned society.[48] There were few business men who did not applaud this outlook as they watched the processes by which the New Deal sought to bring into being the positive State.

At almost the beginning of the Federal Constitution John Taylor had predicted this outcome of adherence to the Hamiltonian philosophy; [49] and in the eighteen-thirties Tocqueville had warned Americans that an oligarchy of manufacturers might easily become the worst form of tyranny.

[47] Herbert C. Hoover, *The Challenge to Liberty* (New York: Scribner, 1934).
[48] Walter Lippmann, *Inquiry into the Principles of the Good Society* (Boston: Atlantic Monthly Press, 1937).
[49] John Taylor, *An Inquiry into the Principles and Policy of the Government of the United States* (Fredericksburg: Green & Cady, 1814).

But no one saw either so profoundly or so incisively the full meaning and consequences of this evolution as the economic sociologist Thorstein Veblen, perhaps the most distinguished speculative mind in the field of social philosophy that America has produced since Thomas Jefferson. No doubt the style of Veblen was tortuous and intricate in an irritating way; no doubt, also, there was a constant tendency to satirical detachment, which made it difficult to be sure exactly where he stood on a number of vital matters; and his habit of coining a special and complex vocabulary of his own, though it often resulted in striking and even remarkable phrases which have become part of our own thought, not seldom resulted in a real misunderstanding of his purposes. Yet the very difficulties of Veblen's style are an important index to the times in which he lived. They are part of the defensive armour of a great thinker who knew that if he spoke out fully and freely the whole of his thought, he would have had an even more difficult career than his attitude to the professional *mores* of his vocation created for him. Anyone who examines the precautions taken by Richard T. Ely to explain that his desire for social reform did not commit him to socialism, or notes how William Graham Sumner's hostility to expansionism after the Spanish–American War nearly cost him his chair at Yale University despite his long years of passionate championship of a social philosophy which was nothing so much as a rationalization of the business man's loathing of government regulation, will, I think, understand and forgive Veblen's monumental circumlocutions; as it was, the suspicion of his views went far towards wrecking his academic career; and it was not until the last ten years of his life, when he had gone outside the normal categories of college life, that he spoke out directly without the complex evasions he had imposed upon himself for nearly a generation.

In essence Veblen devoted his main effort to a massive demonstration of the triumph of finance over industry, of the power of the former interest to exact ransom from the latter as a permanent charge upon its productive output. He showed, too, in a remarkable way, how this triumph had both used and affected every element in the national community and had made it essential for the latter to embark on a predatory imperialism which swept the whole world into its net. He brought out with incisive clarity and mordant wit how all the factors of social organization were so shaped by the implications of this victory as to make the outstanding figures of big business the "leaders" of the community, its statesmen the priesthood who performed the ritual required by the doctrine of the business "church," and judge, official, teacher, journalist, the men and women who imposed the appropriate backbone of the business "creed" in school and university upon the children and the youth, and in the courts by the sanction of penalties for any attempt to evade the observance of the "ritual." In particular, he showed how the separation of business from industry developed a conflict between the beneficiaries of the first and the rest of the community, so that whatever interfered with the right of those beneficiaries to the exceptional privileges which resulted from their strategic position—the trade-unions, for example—would seem bound to be regarded as interfering with a "due process of law" which had become so deep-rooted a part of American consciousness as nearly to be accepted as part of the necessary structure of social organization. And since, in general, the community was dependent upon the continuous operation of its essential industries, it followed that government would become an agent for the "business interests" whenever there was a break in continuity of operation which arose from some challenge to the tax levied by finance on production; so Cleveland interfered in the railroad strike of 1894, and business was able to make Governor Altgeld seem an enemy of society. Nor did Veblen fail to show both the disastrous wastage of natural resources which followed from the conflict of interests, and the frustration of technological progress which it both engendered and fostered.[50]

The main burden of modern research has amply confirmed most of Veblen's major conclusions. In particular, it has demonstrated the danger to technological advance,[51] and the fantastic waste and corruption which are necessary to enable the exactions of business to be satisfied.[52] If verification is the test of hypothesis, his prophecies of the farmer's future, of the disappearance, as a type, of the self-made man, of the reduction of the country town to the status of a helpless agent in the chain of influences leading to the satisfaction of the special privileges of business, and of the coming dethronement of the gold standard, deserve to rank among the outstanding insights of modern sociology. His prophecy that the outcome of an ever wider acceptance of business control would result in its reaching, even passing beyond, "that critical point of chronic derangement in the aggregate beyond which a continued pursuit of the same strategy on the same business-like principles will result in a progressively widening margin of deficiency in the aggregate material output, and a progressive shrinking of the available means of life," [53] was amply borne out during the Great Depression; just as his insistence that the subtle alliance between business privilege and national prestige would result in war had its tragic proof in the Second World War of 1939–45. Not, indeed, since Marx had any social philosophy so magistrally depicted the implications of the system which dominated civilization.

There are two things it is worth while to note in the character and outcome of Veblen's work. The first is that its main conclusion was an emphasis that the dependence of American culture on business privilege

[50] For a full biography and bibliography, see Joseph Dorfman's deeply interesting *Thorstein Veblen and His America* (New York: Viking Press, 1934).

[51] See Bernhard J. Stern, "Frustration of Technology," *Science and Society,* Winter 1937.

[52] *Cf.* Lewis Corey, *The Decline of American Capitalism* (New York: Covici, Friede, 1934) ; and Allen, *Lords of Creation,* preamble and especially Chap. 9.

[53] Thorstein Veblen, *Theory of Business Enterprise* (New York: Scribner, 1904), p. 107.

would result in catastrophe; that the demands of business privilege would ruinously abridge that promise of well-being which was so vital an element in the American outlook. It is not, I think, an unfair conclusion that it was as this abridgement began to take place that there emerged the bitter pessimism and disillusion of the literature in the nineteen-twenties and thirties. Nor is it unfair to emphasize that no one did so much as Veblen to evoke and to stimulate that critical and scientific analysis of American civilization and institutions which came to maturity about the same time. What Veblen did so remarkably was to compel his contemporaries, above all his younger contemporaries, not merely to scrutinize the values they had been wont to take for granted and to recognize, as disinterestedly as they could, the causes served by those values, but to begin to think in terms of remedies which might safeguard the United States against the consequences of their application. No one is more responsible than Veblen for the recognition that the immense good fortune of the United States in wealth-getting after 1865 was due to a series of special causes, akin in total result if different in detail, from the special causes which gave to Great Britain its remarkable economic supremacy for the sixty or seventy years after 1815. He made the younger social philosophers aware that even before the age of the aeroplane, still more before the age in which the secret of atomic energy was discovered, the United States was an integral part of a necessarily interdependent civilization, and that it could not hope to be immune for long from the results of that interdependence. He provided the negative case, at least, for the proof that the national sovereign state, which claimed self-determination as its prerogative in all spheres of policy, was not only an obsolete institution persisting to preserve the evils of business privilege, but also an obstacle standing in the way of that *civitas maxima* which, by its transcendence of that privilege, would open prospects which would give technology and workmanship hopes for which otherwise there could be no fulfilment.

It is interesting, and this is the second point, that Veblen's influence on economists should have been less for a generation than upon any other branch of American culture. He has himself explained, at least in part, the reason for this curious fact.[54] The classic economics of America, like that of Great Britain, started by being a passionate defence of a new social order against attack, and continued by assuming that the principles of its defence were eternal truths. That was evident in the philosophy of John Bates Clark. When he formulated it, he had no idea that he was assuming that each citizen in a community like the United States, in which he lived, remained a free man politically with the moral duty of obeying fundamental law so that he might control his own fate. Nor did he see that the equilibrium he desired, with the State as impartial arbiter, was already unattainable because the monopolies he feared were not only

[54] Thorstein Veblen, *The Place of Science in Modern Civilisation and Other Essays* (New York: Viking Press, 1925).

in active being, but were already making impossible the role he assumed that the State power would play.[55] The sincerity of Clark was beyond all doubt. Competition was the rule of the universe of economic life; on a long view of it, the exceptions to the rule were negligible or could be destroyed by the State power. Once the entrance of monopoly was prevented, it was the supreme beauty of the market economy that it gave each commodity its proper price and each citizen exactly the return to which he was entitled. In this approach Clark was merely the most outstanding of the major economists of his time.

It is not difficult to understand that the immense growth of wealth in the United States after 1865 should have dazzled rival philosophers into the same worship of production for profit in the United States as dazzled Nassau Senior and McCulloch in the first half of the nineteenth century in England. In both cases there was such an overwhelming consciousness of new power that men felt, like Burke, that what some called Providence and others Nature, compelled "men whether they will or not, in pursuing their own selfish interests, to connect the general good with their own individual success." [56] This led them to assume that the amazing energy and ambition of these business men would make for a superb culture as a by-product of these qualities; they did not dream of the degree to which they were harnessing all hope of civilizing effort to the service of a crude economic individualism, and that institutions intended for one purpose would be overwhelmingly subordinated to the demands of another. That was what Veblen understood so remarkably; and it is interesting to note how, since the epoch of Harding and Coolidge, the stream of economic thought in the United States has divided. The classical American school, still perhaps predominant, continues to assume a pattern of production in the United States in which there is perfect competition, perfect mobility of labour, an economic man whose behaviour is precisely regulated by the simple calculus of hedonistic psychology; and it has little doubt but that observed exceptions to this pattern are but small deviations quite easily dealt with by a neutral State power which vigorously pushes the Sherman Act to its logical conclusion. That the hypotheses upon which it bases its conclusions are obsolete, and that its conclusions distort the relation of all social and political institutions to the anachronistic abstraction upon which it relies for analysis, are rarely suspected by any of those who still stand firmly by the traditional ways. Not even the momentous experience of the nineteen-thirties has disturbed its conviction that all will be well in the long run if men will refrain from interference with natural laws.

The other school has at least begun the work of restating the postulates

[55] John Bates Clark, *Essentials of Economic Theory as Applied to Modern Problems of Industry and Public Policy* (New York: Macmillan, 1907), especially pp. 55-57, and *Social Justice without Socialism* (Boston: Houghton Mifflin, 1914), *passim.*
[56] Edmund Burke, *Thoughts on Scarcity,* in *Complete Works* (London, edition of 1802), Vol. VII, p. 384.

of political economy. Deeply influenced by Veblen and by Keynes,[57] impressed, too, by the fact that the Great Depression so largely corresponds to the social philosophy of the former and to the new hypothesis of the latter, its pattern of production starts from the principle that imperfect competition is the vital rule of the contemporary economic order in the United States. From this there has followed a wholly different conception of the State, a recognition that the simple hedonism of equilibrium theory is not subtle enough for the problems it seeks to solve, and that the sheer speed of the dynamic of the productive system makes it impossible to assume constancy for the variants, which the classical school held to be mere fictions not greatly affecting the adequacy of the abstract pattern from which the "laws of economics" were deduced. The result has been outstanding, first, in that quite different questions are asked; second, in that the system is seen as a mode of social behaviour which is what it is by human design and not by "natural" imposition; and third, in that a realistic political economy is emerging which derives its character from all the social processes in which men are involved and begins to see how much the coercive power of the State shapes the character of economic policy. It becomes increasingly obvious that the answers we get depend upon the questions we ask, and that within the framework of the older economics these were largely derived from assumptions inherently irrelevant to the modern scene.

Of political theory as a special field of social philosophy it is curious to note how little there has been of first-rate importance since the Civil War as compared with the richness of the tradition which preceded it. Lieber, Burgess, Woodrow Wilson, Goodnow, Bellamy, Herbert Croly, even Henry George,[58] are hardly effective substitutes for men like Hamilton, Jefferson, Taylor, Madison, and Calhoun. With the professionalism of this field, as it passed into academic hands, it is broadly accurate to say that descriptive writing took the place of philosophic evaluation. Indeed, apart from some brilliant but transient journalism, it has mostly seemed the purpose of writers on political theory to evade evaluation. They have sought to be above the battle which raged so fiercely in the days of the Progressive movement up to the First World War, and throughout the New Deal up to the present time. And though some of the descriptive work is of outstanding quality, alike in its fullness and its precision, it is content not to touch upon the main controversial issues which alone give a rich content to political speculation.

In a considerable degree this is true of legal philosophy also. No doubt the first post-war period had in Mr. Justice Holmes a jurist in the great tradition, whose quality puts him alongside men like Savigny and Maitland, as it had in Mr. Justice Brandeis, a legal thinker who refreshed the whole tradition of American law by forcing the courts to relate their

---

[57] John Maynard Keynes, *The General Theory of Employment, Interest and Money* (New York: Harcourt, Brace, 1936).
[58] See Gabriel, *The Course of American Democratic Thought,* Chaps. 18–25.

axioms and postulates to economic and social realities evaluated in the light of an almost Jeffersonian conception of democracy. Mr. Justice Holmes was throughout his remarkable career essentially an open-minded conservative with the deep sense of fair play which distinguishes the aristocrat at his best. His importance lay less in the values of his own social philosophy, where, on the whole, he held a modified doctrine not unakin to that of Herbert Spencer—whom he regarded highly for having given, as he thought, effective expression to the social content of Darwinism —but rather by reason of the method by which he sought to make his judicial colleagues decide their cases. In part it was a sociological approach to the making of law, a refusal to dwell within a narrow jurisprudence of concepts which, even if unconsciously, as with his predecessor Mr. Justice Field or with his own contemporary Mr. Justice Van Devanter, already contained conclusions which made the *ratio decidendi* not in terms of the facts before the Court, but by the end both judges would wish to reach to strengthen the kind of society they thought *a priori* desirable. Partly, it was a pragmatic approach, in that Mr. Justice Holmes sought to reach a result which would ameliorate the situation a legislature sought to remedy; and his juridical pragmatism refused to invoke that "higher law" which has enabled so many American judges to invalidate legislation they happened to dislike. It was also a part of his pragmatic method that he refused to confound antiquity with experience; he denied with vigour that a rule could be regarded as valid merely because it had been made several hundred years ago.

Mr. Justice Holmes' work was epoch-making in American culture because, with the possible exception of Mr. Justice Miller, he alone sought in all his work to see law in the context of a dynamic society. He was a realist not merely because he brought to the world he had to interpret a superb historical sense—which enabled him to see at once how much of Marshall and Kent and Story was the outcome of what he called "inarticulate major premisses" which they mistook for eternal truth—but also because he saw, like the soldier he had been, that those who controlled the State power usually employed its authority to legislate in their own interest. It was at this point that he had both the wisdom and the courage to insist that in a political democracy the right decision is not the decision the judge would like to make in the case before him, but the decision that a legislative majority is empowered to make by the competence it derives from the Constitution which gave it the statute-making authority. "My agreement or disagreement," he wrote in *Lochner* v. *New York,* "has nothing to do with the right of the majority to embody their opinions in law." [59] Perhaps first among the jurists of his time, and certainly with the greatest distinction, he refused to turn either his preferences or his needs into absolutes by which the purposes of other men must be accepted or rejected. "The life of the law," he wrote in a famous phrase, "has not

[59] *Cf.* Oliver Wendell Holmes, *Collected Legal Papers* (New York: Harcourt, Brace, 1920), especially the paper on "The Path of the Law."

been logic, it has been experience. The law embodies the story of a nation's development through many centuries, and it cannot be dealt with as if it contained only the axioms and corollaries of a book of mathematics." [60]

In the later years of Mr. Justice Holmes, what remains remarkable is that, conservative as he was upon almost all matters of social constitution, he remained the passionate advocate of the right to experiment. Only one other effort has been made in the United States to propound the principles of a jurisprudence on foundations not less wide than his. Dean Roscoe Pound of the Harvard Law School brought an impressive volume of learning to defend what he called an "engineering" theory of the law.[61] The student of his massive essays is tempted to wonder whether more than two or three men in the whole history of legal scholarship have brought so formidable an apparatus of learning to the construction of a juristic philosophy. Yet, on close examination, the vast apparatus is not an entrance into new ideas, but a spectacular façade to cover the almost *simpliste* acceptance of an optimistic neo-Hegelianism already obsolete when it was propounded. Anyone who reads the "jural postulates," as Dean Pound calls them, which are the outcome of his analysis, will see that after his long journeys through the immense literature of legal theory he arrives at a framework of principles which are the obvious outcome of his affection for the country town of Lincoln, Nebraska, which in his boyhood was just beginning to push forward to metropolitan status.[62] They assume that men may reasonably rely on their own exertions for their livelihood. They warn the community that neighbourliness is a social duty which they can reasonably be expected to exert themselves to fulfil. They regard it as reasonable that the state should step in to provide the citizens of Nebraska with the amenities and improvements that no man is in a position to provide for himself. They think of the freedom of contract as that power of decision and movement which may reasonably be expected from an independent farmer who has enough land and enough husbandry to confront life without undue fear of the morrow. They are framed, that is to say, for a community of small owners such as the Middle West knew in the epoch just following the Civil War. Few people who read their precedent analysis, in which carefully worked-out categories are provided for all the schoolmen of jurisprudence from the Greeks to Kohler, would infer that their outcome is the postulates of which Dean Pound so enthusiastically approves. It is as though the observation of the whole historic legal system from Plato onwards resulted in the formulation of principles such as a reasonable-minded Republican might have approved between sixty and seventy years ago on the condition that the rulers of America approved the "rugged honesty" of

[60] Oliver Wendell Holmes, *The Common Law* (Boston: Little, Brown, 1881), p. 1.
[61] Roscoe Pound, *An Introduction to the Philosophy of Law* (New Haven: Yale University Press, 1922), and *Interpretations of Legal History* (Cambridge: The University Press, 1923). These are still, I think, the best guides to his outlook.
[62] Arthur M. Schlesinger, *Political and Social History of the United States, 1829–1925* (New York: Macmillan, 1925), Chap. xv.

Cleveland rather than the corrupt slickness of James G. Blaine. For there is nothing in Dean Pound's principles to suggest that he has considered in all their implications the emergence of the giant corporation, the arrival of large-scale and involuntary unemployment, the separation of labour power from the worker, the domination of society by the market economy, the fact that, as he himself puts it, the movement from status, through contract, to relation [63] means that relation is fixed by precisely that dependence of industry upon business in the sense in which Veblen used those terms. Dean Pound is able to be simply and unquestioningly optimistic because he still thinks, by and large, of an America that is an overgrown Nebraska, in which wise judges maintain a decent equilibrium between the big owner and the little owner. That wild jungle of ruthless habits of the business nature "red in tooth and claw with ravin," of which Frank Norris and Robert Herrick and Theodore Dreiser were writing as novelists, or Lincoln Steffens and Henry Demarest Lloyd and Ida M. Tarbell as public-minded journalists, has left no real impact on his legal thinking. One has only to read his attempt to refute the economic interpretation of the history of the rule of vicarious liability in *Rylands* v. *Fletcher* [64] to see that his principles still assume an America just emerging from the sturdy self-reliance of the middle frontier period, where artisans are still individually known to each other and "justice" means that plaintiff and defendant can walk away from court arm-in-arm, satisfied that the judge has fairly balanced their conflicting claims. Dean Pound has built his legal philosophy round the recollection of an idyll, not upon the serious effort to measure the grave abyss which had opened, in the generation after 1870, between the postulates of the courts and the realities of that capitalist America which had left behind the chances of that frontier civilization, with its exciting opportunities and ardent pioneering, for a settled community in which experiment paid to privilege a special fee for the right even to embark upon innovation.

What Dean Pound, with all his learning, failed to see, Brooks Adams recognized with piercing clarity in a book as remarkable in its way as the analysis of John Taylor a century before. Adams, the younger brother of the historian, and the grandson of John Quincy Adams, had a good deal of that sour integrity which was characteristic of the remarkable family to which he belonged. A Boston lawyer, who saw business at work, both at first hand and through the experience of his brother Charles Francis Adams, who played an important part in the history of the Erie Railroad, he recognized the consequences of the capitalist habits, which had come to full maturity, when he wrote: "Modern capitalists appear to have been evolved under the stress of an environment which demanded excessive specialization in the direction of a genius adapted to money-making under highly complex industrial conditions. To this money-

---

[63] *Cf.* his articles in the *Harvard Law Review* of 1911–15, especially "The Scope and Purpose of Sociological Jurisprudence," June 1911, pp. 591–92.
[64] *Rylands* v. *Fletcher*, 3 House of Lords 330 (1868).

making attribute all else has been sacrificed, and the modern capitalist thinks in terms of money more exclusively than the French aristocrat or lawyer before the French Revolution ever thought in terms of caste." [65]

What is the result? The business man—it is clear that Adams' business man has a close resemblance to the business man of Veblen—"conceives sovereign powers to be for sale. He is not responsible, for he is not a trustee of the public. If he be restrained by legislation, that legislation is in his eye an oppression and an outrage, to be annulled or eluded by any means which will not lead to the penitentiary." [66] Like Veblen, therefore, it is clear to Adams that conflict lies at the heart of society. The business man, even without knowing it, is a revolutionist.[67] He cannot grasp any social relations which transcend his own special and selfish interests. Dependent upon a law which he lacks himself the skill or the training to enforce, he yet has to rely upon it for the maintenance of his power. He must, therefore, not only preach without end the need of other people to respect the law, but he must find ways and means of shaping it to his own purposes. So he becomes "of all citizens the most lawless. He appears to assume that the law will always be enforced, when he has need of it, by some special personnel, whose duty lies that way, while he may evade the law, when convenient, or bring it into contempt, with impunity. The capitalist seems incapable of feeling his responsibility as a member of the governing class in this respect, and that he is bound to uphold the law, no matter what the law may be, in order that others may do the like." [68]

What disturbed Adams was his conviction that the combination of business men and lawyers resulted in courts which made themselves into third chambers of the legislature, eager to exercise a veto power over statutes which business men did not like. "I find it difficult to believe," wrote Adams, "that capital, with its specialized views of what constitutes its advantages, its duties, and its responsibilities, and stimulated by a bar moulded to meet its prejudices and requirements, will ever voluntarily consent to the consolidation of the United States to the point at which the interference of the courts with legislation might be eliminated; because, as I have pointed out, capital finds the judicial veto useful as a means of at least temporarily evading the law, while the Bar, taken as a whole, quite honestly believes that the universe will obey the judicial decree. No delusion could be profounder, and none, perhaps, more dangerous." [69] For Adams saw, nearly twenty years before the renewed emphasis of Professor Whitehead,[70] that rulers who concentrated on the function of money-making could not see the over-all needs of the so-

[65] Brooks Adams, *The Theory of Social Revolutions*, p. 208.
[66] *Ibid.*, p. 209.
[67] *Ibid.*, p. 210.
[68] *Ibid.*
[69] *Ibid.*, p. 219.
[70] Alfred North Whitehead, *Science and the Modern World* (New York: Macmillan, 1925).

ciety they sought to guide. "Apparently," he wrote, "modern society, if it is to cohere, must have a high order of generalizing mind—a mind which can grasp a multitude of complex relations. . . . Capital has prepared the specialized mind. . . . Capitalists have preferred the specialized mind. . . . Capitalists have never insisted upon raising an educational standard save in science and mechanics, and the relative over-stimulation of the scientific mind has now become an actual menace to order because of the inferiority of the administrative intelligence." [71]

It was this absence of proportion between the width of imaginative need and the narrowness of the specialized money-maker which seemed to Adams the evidence that the wisdom government required was not forthcoming; it was, he thought, the symptom of a disintegration which is the inevitable precursor of revolution. It meant, he insisted, not only a "universal contempt for law, but a contempt most frankly displayed by the very class most in need of a respect for law." [72] It is obvious that he was not hopeful. He asked not merely for a drastic remaking of the capitalist outlook, but for so great a centralization of authority in the federal government that Washington could discipline the whole nation into unity. This was, in fact, to ask that the government should use the State power impartially without regard to its dependence on the small economic oligarchy upon which, as all the facts were simultaneously showing, its outlook was based. The agent, so to speak, was to become the principal, and he was to force his master to a respectful and unselfish submission of which he had himself declared the business man to be incapable. It is tempting to think of Adams' despairing *cri de cœur* as one more example of the liberal effort to domesticate the tiger by persuading it to take a correspondence course in the habits of self-sacrifice. He forgot that the men to whom he appealed had specialized in the reading of company prospectuses and were uninterested in, as they were untrained to appreciate, the literature of social reform.

The social philosophers of an age are the summaries of its conflict of principles in the theatre of events; and both combine, if not to determine, yet profoundly to influence, its metaphysical outlook. No one can look at the half-century before the outbreak of the First World War without seeing that the problems which plagued Veblen and Holmes and Brooks Adams were those which, on a different plane, cast their shadows over the outlook of Josiah Royce and William James, the two thinkers who, with the exception of their younger but not less remarkable contemporary John Dewey, best mirrored the passion somehow to find terms upon which man might be at peace with the universe. Royce, in effect, sought to solve the problem by giving the idea of loyalty to the great community the driving force of a deep religious faith, which was to emerge from the conviction that the community is a hierarchy of ever-widening loyalties. These, in their highest expression, become the un-

[71] Adams, *op. cit.*, pp. 217–18.
[72] *Ibid.*, p. 227.

changing and eternal absolute in which all human beings find their fulfilment. However the individual may fail, whatever be the evil or the unhappiness he may endure, if he sees his sorrows as part of the process in
which the Absolute unfolds, its immanent self-realization, he may find
his triumph in the sense that his own defeat is an essential part of its victory, his happiness in the fact that, as he suffers, the evil of his pain is
transmuted into the good of the Absolute.[73]

Royce sought in a Hegelian answer the justification of a society in which
men lose their individuality in the coercive subordination imposed by the
State power for the production of that unity which is the essence of
effective group life. Disliking the subordination thus forcibly imposed,
since he thought it made for a uniformity which destroyed individual
uniqueness, he thought that a voluntary discipline, self-imposed in the
service of the ideal, would evoke the spontaneity which made liberty and
authority but different sides of the same shield. For him, clearly, there
is an eternal unfolding of a common good already immanent in the Absolute, and it is by voluntary submission to the will through which that
common good is realized that man, in a full sense, becomes himself. This
is, at bottom, a variant of Rousseau's general will, an effort to discover
a mystic refuge in which a passionately desired faith to believe that the
universe is timelessly good enables one to argue one's self into the position that one is victorious when beaten, happy when unhappy, found
when one's superficial sense perception indicates one is lost.

Despite all the rigor of the logic Royce brought to bear so bravely
on the superstructure of his edifice, it is difficult not to see that its foundations are an emotional longing for an America he has lost. And the very
intensity of the effort to recover it cannot conceal the fact that the search
has failed. It is hard to find satisfaction in the comfort Royce derives from
the emotion he has recollected in his own tranquillity, since both the
comfort and the emotion are, at bottom, a private perception and not a
public intuition with the status of universality. It is a romantic voyage in
quest of the unobtainable, which seeks to be persuasive by an organic coherence that is not in the facts of reality, but in the logic of the assumptions which it has decided shall conceal the starkness of those facts; and it
is this, perhaps above all, that makes the serene optimism which Royce
ultimately attained at once a measure of his inner and utter despair, and
the proof of how deeply he needed to escape from a world about him
which he could not have dwelt in save as a rebel against the discipline
it imposed.

William James found a solution not different in kind but by a different route. Partly he found it in a faith that is not unakin to a sophisticated Manichæism. By the will to believe in a world where a limited God
is always struggling to conquer evil, man can transform his neighbour

[73] Josiah Royce, *The Philosophy of Loyalty* (New York: Macmillan, 1908) and
The Hope of the Great Community (New York: Macmillan, 1916). The metaphysical basis of Royce's social philosophy is set out in his *The World and the Individual* (New York: Macmillan, 1901).

by making him share his ideal. The soldier who believes that the members of his platoon will face the enemy with the same courage as himself lends them that courage and intensifies it by the strength of his will to make them brave. He is then justified in insisting that his faith produced works; its validity is shown by its results. And since this is an unfinished universe in which the actions of each one of us determines the shape of things to come, we can help to mould it not as unfolders of a predetermined pattern, but as builders who change the design as our will is verified by experience. "Mind *engenders* truth upon reality," wrote James. "Our minds are not here simply to copy a reality that is already complete. They are here to complete it, to add to its importance by their own remodelling of it, to decant its contents, so to speak, into a more significant shape. In point of fact, the *use* of most of our thinking is to help us to *change* the world. . . . Thus we seem set free to use our theoretical as well as our practical faculties. . . . To get the world into a better shape, and all with a good conscience. The only restriction is that the world resists some lines of attack on our part, and opens herself to others, so that we must go with the grain of her willingness to play fairly. Hence the *sursum corda* of the pragmatist's message." [74]

There are two comments upon this creed which need to be made. On the one hand, it is an affirmation of faith in the individual, an insistence upon his freedom, a call upon him to act, and a promise that his action will not be in vain. It urges the desirability for experiment and makes the individual citizen the man whose experience validates the need to go on experimenting. It is against acquiescence, and permanence, and stability; it prefers freedom and the new chance to security and the old order. By making the will initiate the act, and centering the will as free in each of us, William James was at once defending the simple Emersonian democracy in which the American reformer helped to change the world, and he was protesting against a doctrine like that of Royce which made the individual insignificant save as a syllable in the speech of the Absolute, predetermined in his destiny, devoid of meaning as he was unique, stripped of power as he stood alone. To enclose the world in an unchangeable eternal pattern was, for James, to turn it into a prison for mankind. It was because man made the design of his own future that he had cosmic significance; it was by willing to push his future in the direction his experience seemed to call for that he found fulfilment.

Yet James, obviously enough, was not wholly able to conceal the grim doubt at the back of his mind which would not give him rest. "The world resists some lines of attack . . . and we must go with the grain of her willingness to play fairly." It is not upon the world that there rests the responsibility for fairness; it is upon each one of us. And we play our own game fairly by "opening the line of attack" which goes with the

[74] Letter to the *New York Times*, November 3, 1907. I am indebted for this quotation to Professor Gabriel's remarkable and illuminating volume, *The Course of American Democratic Thought*, p. 286.

grain of the world. What does this mean if it does not convey the warning that certain doors are closed? What must we do if it is through those doors that will, experience, faith, all bid us pass? Is the *"sursum corda,"* then, of pragmatism's message, an optimism tempered by the warning that our power to create begins only when we have divined the secret of the universe, and that we must travel down the road that secret indicates? If that is so, how do we discover the secret? Is the prior condition of fulfilment an adaptation to the demands of the world about us whatever we think of those demands? And if we accept that adaptation "against our own grain," have we not lost the spontaneity and uniqueness of that personal activism through which, on James's view, we find the medium of individual creativeness? Is not James saying, under his breath as it were, that the right to experiment begins when something like Royce's loyalty to the community is taken for granted? And does it not then emerge that our experiment, in fact, is service to the community's end in which, somehow, we are to find our own end? Is not James driven to admit that we all end in the bosom of the Absolute, even if he permits himself to hope that the Absolute is—if we only will hard enough—perhaps a little less Absolute than Royce had prophesied? And if that be the right conclusion, are we not bidden to find fulfilment less in the arrival at our own end than in the journey down that road which is the way to which the Absolute compels us?

6

I AM not, of course, arguing here that American culture ends in a *cul-de-sac*. Rather, I am seeking to show that the doctrine of self-realization, which the spaciousness of American conditions gave to Americans in a form of special profoundity, was dependent upon the idea of ceaselessly expanding opportunity and could not convey the conviction that the universe existed for man's fulfilment as the opportunity began to find barriers restricting free access to the road. Since liberty is always a function of power, the fewer the men who own or operate that power, the smaller the number of those to whom liberty has significance. The kind of elbow-room freedom demands, not least the freedom to criticize the narrowing down of opportunity, must make those aware of how a culture is preserved demand a democratization of power which enables men to find anew the means for the liberation of creative energy. I have argued here that in the main realms of American thought the sense of openness and expansion diminishes, and that, with its diminution, there emerges the scepticism, even the pessimism, which men reveal when they measure the distance between the promise for which they had hoped and the reality they had found to be possible. That is the source of the road to despair one finds in Henry Adams. He is the victim of the delusion that democracy hastens to disaster because he can see no source from which the spaciousness which made it possible can be recovered.

A further treatment ought, of course, to show the application of this relation of culture to expansion in its expression in music and the theatre, in painting and in architecture. I have not the knowledge to apply the test. I can here argue only that thought is always in time, and that the values thought infers are not abstract forms, themselves imperatives out of time, but practical criteria built out of practical experience in a changing civilization. That is why Dewey can say that "ideas have been in fact only reflections of practical measures that different groups, classes, factions, wished to see continued in existence, or newly adopted"; and he notes that "we live in a money culture . . . that our technique and technology are controlled by interest and private profit." The lesson of American culture is that structure follows function, and that when society puts the business man, above all the specialist in the finance of business, in the centre of power, the culture becomes expressive of that society dependent upon the values arising from the structure which the business man imposes in order to keep his power. American thought is necessarily conditioned to that pattern, whether by attraction or repulsion; that is why it seems less contemplative than practical, less concerned with the ultimate things than with the swiftly changing claims of each moment. But, above all, a society in which the business man is the representative man is bound to look askance at any process of liberation which sets men free from a control to which they have become habituated. The business man seeks to insist that the rebel against his power is a rebel against Nature. He tries, that is, to take his right to power outside the category of time and build its claims upon a *mystique* which is not open to national examination. That is why, also, he is hostile to critical procedures and anxious to preserve those categories of thought which do not challenge the values he has established.

The crisis of American culture is the outcome of the fact that those values are in such obvious decay. Whatever the avenues they opened in the past, their application now evokes in most forms of thought a sense of inadequacy and frustration. They prevent growth; thereby, they belittle man. They are prohibitions against the emergence of those productive relations in society which enable its members to feel that whatever is accessible of well-being they can both explore and use. By the very fact that expansion of well-being has become a threat to the supremacy of the business man, he is compelled to frustrate that expansion; and when he so acts, he frustrates simultaneously the expansion of culture too. For it is not accident that the great ages in the history of culture are also the ages in which the consciousness of culture is most widely shared. Once more the right to share is rigidly limited by a profit-making system, which must impose its discipline ever more stringently as its central objective becomes ever more difficult; the whole of civilized life is bound to be sacrificed to a part of it; and both the quest for happiness and the search for beauty will be sacrificed to its claims. The curse of Midas has been heaped upon the business man in the United States, and he has sought, out of fear, in his turn, to impose its narrowing obligations upon the society he dominates. That is why a fundamental change is needed in the direction of American life; for nothing is more fatal to the greatness of a culture than impotence to translate the mind of man from the relation of past tradition to the relation of emerging creativeness.

X

America and Its Minority Problems

THE AMERICAN problems of minorities exist on three different planes. There is the racial Negro minority, which raises issues of growing rather than of lesser intensity. There is the problem of religious minorities, of which by far the most important is that of the Jews. There is also the very grim problem of the agricultural minority, which, despite all its efforts in Congress, has for effective purposes been largely reduced to dependence upon the financial and manufacturing interests. This problem, though largely bound up with the special problem of the South, now reaches in important ways beyond its boundaries. Though the Negro problem is the outstanding racial problem, the place of the Japanese, the Chinese, and the Mexican, is also of real importance, and the issue of the American-born Japanese has become, in the light of the Second World War, one of the major tests of political wisdom and social tolerance in the United States.

Before I discuss the three different planes in detail, there are certain preliminary observations it is important to make. It is broadly true that the American government and the American people have been unsuccessful on each of these planes. But it is also true that most other governments and peoples have been equally unsuccessful. The record of South Africa in relation both to the Negro and the Indian is a dismal one. The record of Poland in relation to Ukrainians and Jews is one of savage and relentless hostility. It will be many generations before the world forgets the German treatment of the Jews even before the outbreak of war in 1939; for six years after that the German nation acquiesced in methods of barbarism such as no civilized people had attempted at any time since the end of the Thirty Years' War. In the years of conflict, moreover, from 1939 to 1945, the German nation acquiesced also in mass atrocities against Poles, Russians, Czechs, Greeks, and Yugoslavs, on a scale unknown in modern history, and avowedly committed on the ground of German racial superiority, wholly apart from the ferocity inseparable from war. There have been successful multi-national states like Switzerland; but even in Belgium the relation between Walloon and Fleming has rested upon an uneasy equilibrium since the separation of Belgium from Holland in 1830. If little can be said in defence of American relations with the indigenous Indian population of the United States, little can be said in defence of the attitude of invading settlers of any nation toward any racial group of a different colour from themselves and of less military effectiveness. British experience in East and West Africa, Belgian experience in the Congo, Dutch and British habits in Indonesia and Malaya, Japanese methods in Korea, none of these sets a model for imitation or eulogy. France has a better record than most countries in her treatment of the colour problem in France itself; but there is little to admire in her African record, still less in her habits in the Middle East, and almost everything to condemn in her rule over her Indo-Chinese colonies. The records of Spain and Portugal as colonial powers could not be defended by any person who thought civilized habits more important than the making of profit. The Italian colonial effort is far from being the worst; but there is nothing in it to suggest that, confronted by problems of the American scale, the postulates of its policy would have been in any degree superior.

In any thorough-going way, the problem of racial relations, where the issue of colour is involved, has been solved only by New Zealand and Soviet Russia; and where the problem of religious prejudice is deep-rooted, it has been solved by Soviet Russia alone. Since the Dreyfus case the menace of anti-Semitism has been a deep shadow over French politics, and the fact that after the end of the First World War the outstanding French statesman, M. Léon Blum, was a Jew, was one of the forces which added to the strength of reactionary groups. In Great Britain, where even with the tide of refugees from Nazi barbarism the Jews are hardly more than one per cent of the population, anti-Semitism has been intensified in the last generation. It was certainly one of the very few effective propagandist methods used by the Mosley drive to a British Fascist movement. It has been an element, if only a minor element, in British policy in Palestine. It is significant that before the outbreak of the Second World War British statesmen, though repelled by the scale and intensity of Hitler's attacks upon the Jews of Germany, did not for one moment allow that repulsion to interfere with their effort to appease him; there is, for instance, no reason to suppose that Mr. Neville Chamberlain showed any interest in the fate of the Jews who fell into Hitler's hands as a result either of the annexation of Austria or of the sacrifice of Czechoslovakia at Munich. It is, moreover, well known that a veiled, if discreetly organized, discrimination against Jews exists in Great Britain. There are vocations they virtually find it impossible to enter; there are schools and colleges in which a tacit *numerus clausus* operates against them; there are clubs it would be useless for them to seek to join. And in any large city where there is a considerable Jewish population, there is a significant tendency to form a specific Jewish quarter. No one, moreover, who studies with any care the British general election of 1945, can doubt that some of the elements behind Mr. Churchill—though not, I am confident, Mr. Churchill himself nor, I am confident, with either his knowledge or consent—sought carefully, though rarely openly, to stir up anti-Semitic prejudice against the Labour party by exploiting the fact that its chairman—who holds office for one year only and has no special weight or authority—was, by accident of seniority, a Jew.[1]

When, therefore, we analyse the problem of minorities in the United States, it is of vital importance to bear these comparisons in mind. However unsatisfactory British treatment of the Negro, it is better than the treatment he receives in the United States. However indefensible may have been America's treatment of its native-born Japanese in wartime, it was no worse than British treatment of Chinese, provided they were not wealthy, in Hong Kong, or Singapore, in peacetime. With far more Jews in proportion to the whole population than Great Britain, the main difference between American and British anti-Semitism has been that the former was more violent, more crude, and less discreet than its British counterpart. The decline of the American farmer has been both more rapid and more spectacular than the divorce of the British from the land; and the intensity of the sufferings of the American worker on the land has been at once more obvious and more appealing. But it is to be remembered that the divorce between the farmer and his land in Britain has been spread over nearly four and a half centuries, in at least three of which we have only partial records, at peak periods, of what wholesale enclosure involved for the independent yeoman; while it is less than a decade since the agricultural labourer in Great Britain has begun to enjoy either decent wages or access to the amenities of civilization. And this comparison would omit at once the immense sufferings of the Irish peasantry during the period of British domination—sufferings reflected in the large Irish emigration to the United States in the nineteenth century—and the special agony of that period when the "reform" of the poor law in Britain after the passage of Gilbert's Act in 1782 paved the way for the policy of driving the peasant, at any cost, into the factories which were so greedily awaiting his arrival.

There is one other element in the discussion of American minorities which it is worth while bearing in mind. Once any group is at a disadvantage in comparison with the rest of the community, it suffers not only from inferior economic opportunity, but also from, what is often worse, the deterioration of all its cultural contacts involved in its economic relationships. We know this, on a massive scale, from the anthropological investigations of the effect of the white man's invasion on Africa and Polynesia. There is not merely economic exploitation; there is also

---

[1] It is of interest to students of social psychology that, during the election campaign I received ninety-seven letters asking whether Mr. C. R. Attlee, the leader of the Labour party, was a Jew. The only foundation for the question was the existence of a bloc of Jewish voters in his constituency.

the complete break-down in social values caused by the scale of the invasion, and this results in what may be a fatal impairment of vitality. Consequently, as Rivers noted in Melanesia, the native may die simply from the lack of the will to live; or he may acclimatize himself to spiritual and intellectual decadence which, in a community geared to the market economy, is often equated with an inherent inferiority of quality imposed by nature. It is then easily inferred that the degradation so obvious to the observer is biological in its origin, and that an alteration in the environment can do little or nothing to improve the habits of peoples whose defects are the consequence of an unalterable germ plasm.[2]

It is worth noting that this degradation may occur inside a civilized society, the culture of which is also catastrophically destroyed, as well as in a primitive society, whose native culture is destroyed when it is exposed to the overwhelming consequences of a market economy imposed by the white man's invasion of its way of life. No one can read the accounts of English urban life in the first fifty or sixty years of the new machine age without seeing that the Industrial Revolution had the same effect upon the rural workers driven to the towns as the white invasion has had upon the native tribes of the South Pacific or of East Africa. This resemblance has been noted by a well-known American writer. "In England," he says, "where incidentally the Industrial Revolution was more advanced than in the rest of Europe, the social chaos which followed the drastic economic reorganization converted impoverished children into the 'pieces' that the African slaves were later to become"; and he notes that the defence of child labour hardly differed from the defence of slavery and the slave trade.[3] It was this sense of utter degradation which aroused the anger of Cobbett, the passionate crusade of Robert Owen, the despairing judgment of Mill that all the developments of machinery had not lightened the workers' burden by a single hour. It was this sense that started early Tory reformers like Oastler and Fielden and Shaftesbury; and it was at the very heart of William Morris's socialism.

What it meant in essence has never been more supremely stated than in the famous chapter on the "Nature of Gothic" in Ruskin's *Stones of Venice,* and I quote two passages because they are central to the argument I shall want to make at a later stage. "You must either make a tool of the creature," he wrote, "or a man of him. You cannot make both. Men were not intended to work with the accuracy of tools, to be precise and perfect in all their actions. If you will have that precision out of them ... you must inhumanize them." That is why, he wrote again, there "are signs of a slavery in our England a thousand times more bitter and more degrading than that of the scourged African or the helot Greek. Men may be beaten, chained, tormented, yoked like cattle, slaughtered like summer

---

[2] W. H. R. Rivers (ed.), *Essays on the Depopulation in Melanesia* (Cambridge: The University Press, 1922).

[3] Charles S. Johnson, "Race Relations and Social Change," in Edgar T. Thompson (ed.), *Race Relations and the Race Problem* (Durham: Duke University Press, 1939), p. 274.

flies, and yet remain in one sense, and the best sense, free. But to smother their souls within them, to blight and hew into rotting pollards the suckling branches of their human intelligence, to make the flesh and skin . . . into leathern thongs to yoke machinery with, this is to be slave-masters indeed. . . . It is verily this degradation of the operative into a machine, which, more than any other evil of the times, is heading the mass of the nations everywhere into vain, incoherent, destructive struggling for a freedom of which they cannot explain the nature to themselves."

I quote this passage for two reasons. It shows, first, that the minority problem in the United States is only a particular example of what has been going on everywhere and what still is a practically universal problem. It shows, second, not only how a degraded human nature becomes itself unconscious that new circumstances can evoke its humanity, but also that those who are what Ruskin so rightly calls the "slave-masters" become conscious, after a time, of nothing but the degradation of their slaves, and thus impervious to any argument which involves a claim on their behalf for the recognition of their humanity. At different levels this is inherent in the relationship a minority problem involves, even when the majority admits individual exceptions to the rules it imposes upon the minority. The essence of the issue to be met remains what it has always been: the frustration of normal behaviour by special treatment which penalizes the expression of normal impulses in the victimized minority. Nor must one forget that the failure, through this penalization, to express these normal impulses is then taken as the proof that the victimized minority is incompletely human or somehow less capable of civilized sentiment and behaviour than the persons who impose the penalties. That is how, for nearly two thousand years, the Gentile has thought of the Jew. Having barred him, for example, from a number of occupations, as from agriculture, he has then resented Jewish concentration in finance and commerce. Having driven him to live for centuries within the narrow and narrowing walls of the ghetto, at the mercy, only too often, of government whim or mass brutality, he complains that Jews tend to herd together and to be suspicious of their neighbours. Having made the Jew the scapegoat upon whom he has visited the sins of nearly twenty centuries, the Gentile is sometimes angry that the Jew refuses to accept this role and attacks the refusal as arrogance; or he is sometimes angry that the Jew accepts his historic role and sneers at his servility. That Jewish habits are no more than the adaptation of human impulses to a pattern of behaviour coercively imposed very rarely dawns upon the persecutors. They will not stay to think that Jews are, more than they are anything else, what Gentiles have made them since the Diaspora.

It is in this context that we must set the problem of minorities in America. We must take note of a bitter struggle for wealth and power, in which not only do the defeated go to the wall, but, as they go, give to the victors the very characteristics the victors had imputed to the defeated. Hitler persecuted the Jews to prove the folly of their faith in a God who had made them his chosen people and to break the myth of their unbreakable power. But to do so he had to make the German nation itself a chosen people and to proclaim to the world that German might was invincible; he made himself, and the people who followed him, into the image of the thing he thought it his divine mission to destroy. Just as the secure citizen during the depression rationalized his fear for his own safety into the conviction that the unemployed must be unemployable, since he could surely find work if he tried hard enough, so many of the unemployed themselves came, out of their misery, to accept the unceasing reiteration that they were unemployable in truth, and thus to become in fact unemployable, because they were degraded to the level where despair, in destroying courage, destroys also the power of thought. So, also, we must note that when master and slave, employer and employee, Jew and Gentile, are conditioned to behaviour implied in the historic stereotype made customary by time, any departure from the stereotype which makes the relation of power and subordination of dubious validity produces hateful irrationalities in which the man, or group, or class whose privilege is threatened regards those seeking to escape the burden of privilege as persecutor and not as victim. It is themselves they regard with pity; and they are almost as astonished as they are angry when the movement of ideas becomes a stream the flow of which they can no longer direct to their own advantage.

2

THE history of slavery in the United States is too well known to need recounting here. I need only emphasize three elements in its tragic record. It is important that, when the federation was made, most outstanding Americans, including Thomas Jefferson, himself a slave-owner, had little doubt of the self-erosion of an evil system which they did not seek to defend. Nor was there any significant change in this expectation until the invention by Eli Whitney of the cotton gin made the slave's labour a valuable commodity upon the growth of which the whole plantation economy of the South came to rest. This involved not only a complete revaluation of the principle of slavery, but also a demand for free trade, that the South might take advantage of the cheaper world market as against the heavily protected domestic market, and a passionate insistence upon states' rights as the only means of safeguarding the Southern claims against the rationalist industrial capitalism of the North and the West with its ever greater emphasis on free enterprise developed by free labour. No one more brilliantly expounded the Southern view than John C. Calhoun. His work was at once a defence of the plantation economy and an attack on the economic principle of Northern industrial organization. Calhoun argued that wage slavery in the North was the equivalent of chattel slavery in the South. He added, with vigorous emphasis, that chattel slavery was the more preferable. For not only did it give the owner—what wage slavery did not—a direct interest in the well-being of the slave, but, as in the economy of ancient Greece, it set a ruling class free to train themselves for the task of ruling, while it made them the natural trustees for the well-being of slaves whom nature had made for subordination and service. He therefore desired to extend slavery, if possible, but at least to safeguard it from invasion by a federal majority. To this end he reaffirmed the right of a state to nullify a federal law, and its further right, in the last resort, to secede from the Union.

The long and ever angrier debate upon the merits of slavery which preceded the Civil War is far from over; for it is obvious that, if in constantly changing forms, its substance lies at the root of any attempt at imperialist domination of a less powerful group by one more powerful. What is more significant for the understanding of the United States is the fact that the defeat of the South meant the final victory of nationalism and the uncompensated destruction of slavery, together with the reduction of the South to a position of dependent poverty from which it has hardly begun seriously to emerge. It has also meant that a vast legend has been woven about the pre-war South, the implications of which have profoundly affected the status of the Negro in the South in particular, but all over the United States as well. The Southerner not only argued that the slave states had built a civilization nobler and of finer texture than the coarse materialism of the North; he also insisted that the institution of slavery was the cause of this superiority, which was shown in the more aristocratic traditions, the more sensitive manners, and the deeper culture of which the South was the historic guardian. Some defenders even went so far as to claim, with a happy indifference to fact, that the South was the spiritual heir to the seventeenth-century intellectual tradition of the Cavalier cause, and that it was the refugees and the descendants of that defeated aristocracy who had sought to keep alive its ancient splendour in the face of a hostility which sacrificed it to a mean commercialism dependent on the support of an ignorant majority unfit to exercise power.

It cannot be doubted that the catastrophic ruin of the South by the combined effect of war and emancipation had much to do with its defeat and decline. But, on the evidence, it seems unmistakably clear that slavery was only one among many causes for the break-down of Southern economy. It is obvious that, once the downright criticism of slavery began, there was a decline of intellectual freedom in the South which came in part from a growing censorship of all criticism of the institution, and in part from the concentration of intellectual energy upon ideas of which the public expression proved acceptable for its defence. It is also obvious that the Southern planter, especially when he was rich or from an old family, thought that the creative mind ought not to seek to make its intellectual work a profession, but should be content to allow literary effort to be the by-product of a gentleman's habits. Most of the supposed Southern interest in culture in the generation before the Civil War is no more than a polite fiction. There were few literary journals, and most of these did not survive for more than a few years; where, as with the *Southern Literary Messenger,* they did manage to struggle on, their predominant note is their failure to win any serious interest from the ruling aristocracy of the South. The scale of urban life was small, with the result that there were no Southern publishers of repute, few public libraries of any importance, and far less education than in the North. The census of 1850 shows that Southern illiteracy was at least twice as great as in comparable rural areas elsewhere, and about four times greater than in New England. If the Southern aristocrat sent his sons to college in the North, after 1850 he ceased increasingly to do so, because he feared their exposure to anti-slavery ideas; and in the census of 1850 it is shown that only one in ten of the white children went to any kind of school. Nor do the praiseworthy efforts of North Carolina to redeem this weakness compensate for the intellectual inferiority of the whole area. The truth really is that if the South had produced a great literature before 1861—and it is worth remarking that, after Edgar Allan Poe, the best-known writer was William Gilmore Simms, who was always conscious that such interest as he aroused in the South was due less to the intrinsic merit of his work than to the need to recognize the social distinction of his connections by marriage—there would have been no Southern public numerous enough to enable its authors to earn a living. Nor will the reader of the ardent attempts to prove the existence of an audience deeply interested in a liberal culture be tempted to admit more than the fact that in a general intellectual desert there were scattered and interesting cases.[4] Of particular interest is the fact that H. R. Helper, himself a citizen of North Carolina, in his significant *Impending Crisis,* explained the cultural poverty of the South by insisting that slavery was a positive hindrance to intellectual effort.[5] That is indeed the general conclusion of most serious historians in subsequent years.

It is possible to argue that the cultural poverty of the South went deeper than the institution of slavery. With very occasional exceptions the South pinned all its faith to an agrarian economy. It was not merely that less than four hundred thousand out of eight million white Southerners owned slaves at all, and that less than fifty thousand of these owned more than twenty slaves; it was, even more, the fact that the whole outlook of the South was dominated by these fifty thousand men, and that their ambition was the extension of this slave-based estate without much regard to the swiftly changing contours of the American economy. The South never seems to have understood, until its fate was ultimately decided at Appomattox, the consequences of pinning its whole faith to a rural economy, in which the profit-making capitalist simply put his surplus into more

---

[4] *Cf.* Gabriel, *The Course of American Democratic Thought,* Chaps. 9, 10.
[5] Hinton R. Helper, *The Impending Crisis of the South: How to Meet It* (New York: Burdick Bros., 1857).

slaves for the plantation. That simply meant an ever-increasing dependence upon the North, not only for capital loans for agrarian development, but for every sort of commodity which the South itself did not produce. Hence the dependence of the South on, for example, the New York market, and its pathetic belief that, because it was in debt to New York, it could lay down the law to its creditors by the threat of repudiation, which would force upon them a policy of appeasement. It never saw the significance of two things: first, that the West, which was also based on agriculture, was strongly opposed to the institution of slavery; and, second, that its decision to confine its energies to agriculture meant that, without a short and decisive campaign, it altogether lacked the industrial potential to give the threat of secession any hope of success. If to all this there are added soil erosion, through wasteful use, which continually necessitated the expenditure of large sums in the purchase of new lands, the extravagant style of living of the small class of really wealthy planters, and the continuous loss of manpower in the South through the migration of young men who could find no real opportunity there, it is not difficult to see how disastrous the plantation economy was to the very purposes it hoped to preserve.[6]

It is important, for the period after the Civil War, to see how completely the vast majority of the whites in the South were bound up with the plantation system. They were likely to be poor; they were even deprived of economic opportunities by the fact that the Negroes worked mines and factories and railroads. But they seem to have preferred poverty based on the privilege of feeling superior to the Negro than to cut themselves free from a system of which they were hardly less the victims than the Negroes themselves. Helper emphasized this in his *Impending Crisis* in 1857; and he frankly told the middle class and poor whites that their salvation lay in destroying the planter class. They could not believe him. They rated their status as members of the ruling race—even though they had little effective share in its power—as more important than an economic reorganization which would give them a real opportunity of improving their condition. At least, as long as the Negroes were slaves, they could feed on their sense of psychological superiority. They chose to be victims of the plantation system rather than find that there were able black men, in any numbers, from whom they did not receive the recognition servility owes to arrogant indigence.

It was the natural accompaniment of the philosophy of slavery, as this was expounded by its major advocates, that we should be asked to accept the picture of a happy and contented slave population, well cared for, obedient, "almost members of the family," naturally fitted for their environment, and so bound to the plantation where they worked by ties of a mutually affectionate allegiance that there would never have been a

---

[6] *Cf.* Hacker, *The Triumph of American Capitalism,* Chaps. XXI–XXVII, for a brilliant treatment of his subject which embodies the latest research on the issue.

demand for freedom had it not been for agitators from outside. It is admitted, of course, that there were occasional misfits, like a rebellious slave or a cruel master; but we are asked to believe that, as a general rule, the Negro hugged his chains. No one knew so well as he how bitter would be the price of emancipation. It came not at his desire, but as part of the process of imposing upon the South that coloured bondage to the North, which still continues so disastrously.

Practically all of this is sheer fantasy.[7] It is unquestionable that there were many good masters, and many more devoted slaves. But the evidence is quite clear that, for about forty years before the Civil War broke out, there was a widespread and growing undercurrent of fear in the relations between blacks and whites, which had the result of tightening up the rigour of the controls imposed by the owner upon his slaves. It is not only that there were innumerable individual escapes into freedom. It is not only, either, that there were collective plots and widespread revolts, like that of Vesey at Charleston in 1822 or of Nat Turner in Virginia in 1831, which were suppressed with merciless cruelty. There was, for from ten to fifteen years, a widespread slave unrest, fomented, no doubt, by Abolitionist propaganda, by the impact of West Indian emancipation, by the struggle to introduce slavery into new areas, and by the loathsome insistence on the return of runaway slaves from free territory. Historians, especially in recent years, have given massive evidence of an atmosphere of constant conspiracy: rebellions here, murders there of owners and overseers, houses set on fire, the use of troops to put down, or spies to discover, emergent conspiracy before it was ripe. This is the general picture. We cannot only trace the severity with which the offending slave was treated, often without even the pretence of legal procedure; we can even discern the effort of the South to prevent publicity, not least of the measures of repression on which they depended. The Southern whites almost became an army in civilian clothes, and the Negroes a subject people in an unoccupied country under quasi-martial law. Negro schools were forbidden. Negro Church services, and their ministers, were watched as an obvious source of danger. Freedom of meeting was curtailed even among free Negroes, who had to secure passes to permit their movement, and they were not permitted to arm themselves lest they prove capable of resisting the white man's orders. Anyone who is tempted to accept the Southern mythology of a great, happy family disrupted by Northern intransigeance, of a Grecian idyll broken by a materialist commercialism, ought to study with care the legal, and often enough enforced, status of the American slave before his emancipation.[8]

---

[7] Herbert Aptheker, *Negro Slave Revolts in the United States, 1526–1860* (New York: International Publishers, 1939).

[8] W. E. B. Du Bois, *Black Reconstruction* (New York: Harcourt, Brace, 1935) Chap. 1. Nothing in Ulrich B. Phillips' two books—*American Negro Slavery* (New York: D. Appleton, 1918) and *Life and Labor in the Old South* (Boston: Little, Brown, 1929)—does anything to touch the contentions of Dr. Du Bois.

It is beyond all question that, certainly by 1850, the contradictions, economic and psychological, at the heart of the Southern system were beyond the power of compromise to resolve.

Not, indeed, that the effort at compromise was not made. The struggle over the tariff, the struggle over railways, the struggle over a homestead law, the demand for easier immigration laws, the fight for the Wilmot Proviso, the desperate conflict over each item in the Clay Compromise of 1850 and over the Kansas–Nebraska Act of 1854, all show the deepening realization of a desperate position. So, too, does the reception of the Dred Scott decision; it was a veritable preparation for a battle which only exceptional optimists hoped to avoid. No doubt the motives of Senator Stephen A. Douglas were very mixed; but that he really sought to satisfy the South by his doctrine of popular sovereignty seems to be beyond question. But within the framework of the American situation compromise was quite impossible. Costs had begun so to eat into prices that it was only the exceptional man who, by the eighteen-fifties, was effectually solvent.[9] The Southern economy was so rigidly geared to its unique institution that it could no more break with the system of ideas it imposed than France could break with the *ancien régime,* or Russia with Tsarism, without a revolutionary catastrophe. That is why Beard is so inescapably right in insisting that the Civil War was, in fact, the second American Revolution.

3

THE Civil War was a revolution; but to grasp the nature of the contemporary Negro problem, it is necessary to realize that, in a vital sense, it was a revolution that failed. It transformed the productive capacity of America; it did not change in any of its essentials the psychology of the South. It is tempting to compare its results with the impact of the First World War upon Germany. There also a dynasty was overthrown; there also new men came into political office whom it is natural to equate with the men who attempted to administer the congressional theory of reconstruction between the end of the Civil War and the bargain over the Hayes–Tilden election in 1876. The latter had hardly begun to make their efforts felt than wider political necessities made it necessary to abandon them, just as the needs of German capitalists made them throw overboard the men of Weimar in order to maintain their alliance with the army whose officer caste was the bulwark of their privileges. They thus restored to power the same men who had run the Imperial regime. But these men, in their turn, discovered that they were not strong enough, in the new conditions, to rule by the old methods. They therefore turned for aid to those organizations of the unemployed, the *petit bourgeois,* and the *déclassé* adventurers, of whom Hitler was both the symbol and the leader. With their assistance, the custodians of Imperial Germany re-

---

[9] Hacker, *op. cit.,* Chaps. XXII–XXIV. This is the best brief analysis known to me of the central position of the problem.

stored their old world, without the emperor, indeed, but in an even stronger and more arrogant form.

This is, I think, what happened in the South after 1865. There were, no doubt, corruption and inefficiency in the "carpet-bag" regimes. But most of the contumely and scorn which have been heaped upon them is without justification. Few of them even approached the Ferguson standard in Texas, or the Huey Long standard in Louisiana, or the Talmadge standard in Georgia. The normal Southern picture of ignorant and drunken legislators filling their own pockets is far too like the portrait painted of the Bolshevik government in its early days to be accepted by a generation which has learned something, at least, of the habits of professional propaganda. A good deal of the policy which is so often described as the corrupt filling of its members' pockets by the new administration turns out, on close scrutiny, to be akin, as an accusation, to the Bolshevik practice of "nationalizing" women; it is the partisan account of a tax policy which not only placed the burden on the rich for the benefit of the poor, but allowed the representatives of the poor to place the burden there. The first unforgivable sin of the carpet-bag and military governments was that they deprived the men who were accustomed to power of what these deemed their divine title to government. It is not really surprising that, when the men of the old regime returned to power, the main effort of the dependent historians who wrote the record of the temporary rule of new men was to evade the proportions of truth by the sheer scale of their invective.

This has been put in vigorous terms by a Southern historian who has had the integrity to transcend the persuasive fictions of his region. "The worst crime of which they have been adjudged guilty," writes Professor F. B. Simkins about the Reconstruction governments,[10] "was the violation of the American caste system. The crime of crimes was to encourage Negroes in voting, office-holding, and other functions of social equality. This supposedly criminal encouragement of the Negro is execrated even more savagely as with the passing years race prejudices continue to mount. . . . Attempts to make the Reconstruction governments reputable and honest have been treated with scorn, and the efforts of Negroes to approach the white man's standard of civilization are adjudged more reprehensible than the behaviour of the more ignorant and corrupt. Social equality and Negroism have not a chance to be respectable." And if to this we add the fact that, in the early years after their restoration to power, the old rulers of the South had not merely formed an alliance with Northern capitalism for the joint exploitation of their former Empire, but had also persuaded the poor whites to become, once again, their psychological allies by playing on their fears of a black supremacy in the South, it be-

[10] Francis B. Simkins, "New Viewpoints of Southern Reconstruction," *Journal of Southern History,* February 1939, pp. 49–61. I owe my knowledge of this brave and remarkable article to Professor Hacker's valuable book which I have already cited.

comes easy to understand how swiftly and easily their old authority was regained. The Ku Klux Klan rode out in its hey-day in the belief that it was safeguarding the white men's rule in the South. What, in fact, it was doing was protecting the new alliance between the old Southern planters and the new Northern capitalists against the danger that the poor white citizens might recognize that the New Presbyter was but the Old Priest writ large. The failure of congressional reconstruction made possible a successful counter-revolution by those whom the Civil War had seemed to destroy. And it is, very largely, by the ideology of this counter-revolution that the South is still governed in its political and social thinking.

I think this view is justified if one takes the career of any of the typical "poor white" Southerners who arrived at the Senate after the presidency of Grant. It can be seen in Watson of Georgia, in Heflin of Alabama, in Vardaman of Mississippi, of Tillman of South Carolina. All of them were men who accepted the Southern myth without question and then found that, as it operated, it was without a shadow of serious significance for the well-being of the poor white man. All of them sought to marry the Democratic party in their states to a Populism which sought to give the underprivileged some right to hope. With the possible exception of Heflin, I do not believe that any one of these men began as other than a sincere believer in the duty and capacity of his party to do justice to whites whose interests had been neglected. When each of them showed some signs of a successful appeal to the poor whites, he was attacked by so powerful a combination of the "new rich" and their agents that to maintain his hold he transformed himself into an unscrupulous demagogue who held on by appealing to the vilest prejudices and hatreds he could find; and each, of course, found at once that nothing paid so well as attacks upon the Negro.

The career of Watson typifies pretty accurately the transformation to which I have alluded. He emerged in the Georgia of 1880 with the habitual poor white's respect for the "gentleman," for the man with a brave record in the Civil War, and for religion as the embodiment of old traditions it is desirable to respect just because they are old. The "gentleman" he met was Governor Colquitt, a man of distinguished family, with all the habits and manners of his kind and a financial uncleanness that is beyond dispute. He encountered "Southern chivalry" in J. B. Gordon, one of Robert E. Lee's best officers, who had not only been wounded five times, but had led the last charge at Appomattox; and Gordon, thereafter, both as governor of, and senator from, Georgia, was not merely the paid agent of Collis P. Huntington, but his ardent assistant in some of the worst of the large-scale dishonesties by which Huntington climbed to his immense riches. He met religion in the shape of J. E. Brown, who had at one time had relations with the carpet-bag government of Georgia, and had even entered into dealings about the Negro vote. Brown, too, as governor and senator, was the centre of an organized looting of the state treasury which might well have put Boss Tweed upon his mettle. But Brown's deep religious sentiment, his attendance at Sunday school, his passionate devotion to charitable works, his refusal either to drink or smoke, all led to his being looked upon with high regard by the church folk of Georgia.

For nearly ten years Watson stood with the Democrats of Georgia as a "regular" and fought for them with dash and nerve. But when he found that new wealth was everywhere piling up in fantastic leaps and bounds as industry began to develop there, and that the farmer and wage-earner remained as poor as they had been left by the devastation of Sherman's armies, he swung with passionate indignation into the leadership of Georgia Populism, overwhelming the Democratic machine as he burst into Congress. Two years later the Democratic machine had its revenge. It defeated him for Congress in what was probably one of the half-dozen most dishonourable political campaigns in the history of American politics; and it is even possible that, to the dishonesty of the campaign, it added the faking of the result. The effect on Tom Watson was twofold: it made him the representative of the underdog and senator from Georgia for almost a generation; and it brought out in him a vanity, a lust for hatred and revenge, an insatiable passion to gratify a desire for cruelty that can only be described as sadistic; and all of these were set in the background of remarkable energy and of real oratorical powers which, in other circumstances, might have made him an important figure. He fought his opponents so savagely that he became himself the author of corruption and lynching and shooting. Though he had in his early days been a friend of the Negro, he developed into the most revolting type of Negro-hater. He became insane in his attacks on the Roman Catholic Church and on the Jews; in the revival of the Ku Klux Klan after the First World War, he was perhaps the main influence in making hostility to Catholics and Jews an essential element in its programme. No one can say that Tom Watson was a great man; but he might easily have become both an important and a useful man. He certainly began with ambitions that were honourable and purposes that were high. The new pattern of the traditional South turned him into an ugly precursor of the type our generation has seen in all its naked brutality in Julius Streicher.[11]

It is unnecessary to show how much of the pattern of Watson's career is repeated in succeeding generations, above all, how brilliantly it was repeated in the short life of that dangerous genius Senator Huey Long. What I am concerned to emphasize is the point that the counter-revolution in the South after the Civil War was bound to have the results Watson's life exemplifies once it had based itself, on the one hand, on an

---

[11] *Dictionary of American Biography*, Vol. XIX, p. 549; Thomas E. Watson, *Political and Economic Handbook* (Atlanta: Telegram Publishing Co., 1908) and C. Vann Woodward, *Tom Watson, Agrarian Rebel* (New York: Macmillan, 1938) are both very revealing books.

alliance between the old ruling class and the "robber barons" of the Gilded Age; and, on the other hand, on the breach between the poor white—whether small sharecropper or mortgaged farmer, or urban artisan or underpaid "white collar" worker—and the Negro, whose interests were identical but deliberately separated from those of the poor white. A politician was bound either to betray the interests of the tragic class to which he belonged, or to seek the overthrow of the half-feudal masters of the new South; and since both of these were impossible for him, he was driven to exploit the hatreds which would preserve his career. I do not think he ever knew that those hatreds had been deliberately re-created as a safeguard of the privileges the new rulers of the South enjoyed. Nor do I think it ever occurred to him to doubt the assumption of permanent Negro inferiority to the white man in which he had been brought up. For, as a boy and youth, the sense that he was at least above the Negro's level was one of the few compensations for poverty and its attendant miseries that he enjoyed. He could not transcend it without a kind of psychoanalytic examination of the obsessions which drove him on. If he had admitted his obligation to accept the Negro as his equal and ally, either he would have had to leave the South, since there would then have been no place for him in politics, or he would have had to try to build up a revolutionary party, which would quite certainly have been premature, and, as certainly, would have been broken in pieces. The necessary framework of his activity was thus conditioned by an environment which compelled him to choose between being the poor creature of a class whose hostility to his own he saw with clarity at first-hand, or he had to be the evil kind of hate-monger he became. He chose the latter, I think, not for the sake of the wrongs he wished to right, but out of the frustration he felt about wrongs about which he could do nothing. And that frustration was depressed to a pathological level in the ugly and angry effort to maintain himself against his enemies. He shows in remarkable and precise clarity the background in which the minority problems of the United States must be set.

Watson lived into the Harding–Coolidge epoch; and it must be noted that there has since been no essential change in the situation he confronted. There have been prosperity and depression, recovery and recession, total war and the immense problems of adjustment which attend the transition from war to peace. The Negro has moved in great numbers to the North since Watson first entered Congress; he has forced his way, above the Mason and Dixon Line, into careers and professions on a scale that would have been unthinkable fifty years ago. He has fought with courage in two world wars. He has done scientific work of high quality, and work in literature and music second to none in the same period. Even in the South one can perceive a deeper wave of resentment at the treatment meted out to him than at any time since his arrival in the United States. It is not a sullen resentment, though, of course, there are Negroes in whom this is the uppermost emotion. In a deeper degree than ever

before, it is a creative resentment, since its main roots lie in a sense of
qualities searching for, but denied, fulfilment, and the conviction that
these qualities are not only valuable in themselves, but of high importance
to America and beyond its boundaries. The resentment has, no doubt,
evoked some polite assurances of goodwill and an occasional gesture of
nobility, such as Mrs. Roosevelt's offer of the White House grounds to
Miss Marian Anderson when she was denied the use of Constitution
Hall because of her colour. We hear from optimistic journalists, like
Virginius Dabney, of tolerant kindliness in the South, of a new outlook
there which gives the right to new hope; we must examine the actual
situation in the light of the possibilities which reveal themselves.

4

THE student of the Negro problem is fortunate in that he has today the
most comprehensive and significant survey of the issues raised by race and
colour within the boundaries of a white community that has ever been
made. Professor Gunnar Myrdal's analysis is based on personal investigation and collective expert research. It has the advantage of being made
by someone detached from the actual complexities of the scene who is
at the same time a specialist and public figure of high eminence. His
book [12] is so outstanding a landmark in the study of its subject that the
only thing those who come after him can do for many years to come is to
note his conclusions and to discuss the implications for action to which
they give rise. He paints a grim picture; I do not believe it is more grim
than the facts themselves warrant.[13] If they tempt the humane reader to
passionate condemnation, above all of the attitude in the South to the
Negro and his problems, they also make clear that passionate condemnation will do as little as the Civil War itself to solve the grave issues before
the United States. It is only in a positive approach that the hope of any
progress can be found.

Let us begin by realizing that we confront a condition and not a
theory. Whatever be the small improvements made here and there in the
treatment of the Negro, he is, in general, as ruthlessly exploited as the
contempt and ingenuity of the South permit. He is exploited as citizen,
as consumer, as producer. Whatever institutions can be so operated as
to effect his being driven to a consciousness of inferiority and a sense
of hopelessness, they are so operated. Even for the educated or wealthy
Negro the South is a prison. Attempts by liberal-minded men and women
to mitigate the barbarity of the present situation are always timid and
utterly disproportionate to the scale of the problem. There is no real
evidence to suggest that the Negroes can hope, even by a fully united
effort, to secure any reasonable recognition of their claim to be recognized

[12] Gunnar Myrdal, *An American Dilemma: The Negro Problem and Modern
Democracy* (New York: Harper, 1944).
[13] St. Clair Drake and Horace R. Cayton, *Black Metropolis* (New York: Harcourt, Brace, 1945).

as American citizens without the alliance of a section of the white people
in America big enough to compel the South to a revision of its basic attitudes. There is no prospect of a successful revolt by the Negroes; not
only are they too small in numbers, but revolt would lose them what small
sympathy and support they at present receive from outside their own
ranks. Nothing in the evidence suggests a biological inferiority in the
Negro as compared with the white man. When the barriers are down,
his faculties are capable of making the same kind of contribution to civilized life as the white man. But the fact is that he is oppressed or repulsed
at every turn. If he asserts his rights, he is arrogant; if he accepts humiliation, he is servile. Whether it be education or health, the place where he
lives or the place where he works, whether it is justice in the courts or
justice in the legislature, the assumptions of Southern action are destructive of the very basis upon which the Negro can hope for fulfilment as a
human being. There is no single vocation in which he does not suffer
from being a Negro; there is no single environment in which he can hope,
quite simply, to give expression to his own personality. Even so tolerant
and humane a president as Franklin Roosevelt hardly dared do more
than pay occasional verbal homage to the Negro claim to be treated as a
rational human being.

No doubt there have been real and noble attempts to improve conditions—journalists, social workers, teachers, clergymen, trade-unionists,
have made such efforts. No one can look at the results and say honestly
that they do more than touch the fringes of the problem. The only effective protection the Negro has lies in the fact that there is a chance
of escape, and that the peculiar psychology of the South has not been
able, in any comprehensive way, to penetrate other areas of the United
States. That is not to say that he is not victimized politically, socially,
and economically outside the South; he is so victimized in ways that
are often conscious and shameful. But that victimization in the North
has neither the universality nor the intensity of Southern victimization. It is not a social philosophy that has political value and measurable
economic consequences. It is less the deliberate dehumanization of a
whole race than the vicious exploitation of an individual here or a group
there. There is not the same continuous and determined effort to use
the power of the state to keep the Negro from improving his position.
There is not the same fantastic expectation that the Negro will be
content, and ought to be content, to accept a status of permanent inferiority. There is not the same shadow of contingent disaster hanging
over Negro life whenever, in the South, it challenges the *mores* imposed by Southern ideas. The white man or woman who is friendly
to Negro aspirations does not run the risk of boycott or worse. The
judicial courts do not assume that there is one law for the black and
another law for the white; nor is there a gap of the same width and depth
in their treatment at the hands of the police. Negro success does not
arouse the same resentment, and social discrimination, while it is still

real, and often important, is not an organized framework of policy to which the white man, as well as the Negro, must adjust himself.

It would serve no useful purpose for me to document these generalizations; Professor Myrdal and his associates have done this so fully and decisively that it does not need to be done again. I desire only to draw certain inferences, which are, I think, of real importance, from the facts these generalizations summarize. (1) There is no basic difference between nazi racial theories and those, in general, of the South. When the Southerner talks of freedom and democracy, *a priori*, he excludes the Negro people from their benefits. (2) The treatment of the Negro in the South induces in the white citizen all the evil characteristics of a *Herrenvolk*. It makes brutality, violence, exploitation, arrogance, all seem natural. It encourages lawlessness, and this disrespect for law extends to those whose business it is to enforce the law and to promote respect for it. These qualities easily, and perhaps only half-consciously, become extended from treatment of the Negro to treatment of the poor white. The depressed condition of the poor white is in large part the outcome of the fact that to grind down a group in a subordinate position has become part of the habitual strategy of Southern whites in a position of power. (3) The treatment of the Negro makes the Southerner who seeks to aid him a condition that verges on the impossible. He risks too much by continuity of friendly action; nothing but continuity of friendly action is likely to be of any avail. The fatal consequences of this dilemma in Southern life can be seen by anyone who compares the governors and senators from the South, up to some such time as the Missouri Compromise, with their successors in the period since the Civil War. I think it is true that some of those successors were the victims of the very system they helped to impose; but there can be no doubt that they helped to lower the standard of American political life in general, and of Southern political life in particular. (4) That lower standard is reflected in the behaviour of American political parties to this vital test of the reality of American ideals. At no time since the Civil War has the Democratic party, even in the Northern states, dared to face the implications of Southern treatment of the Negro, lest it lose the political, and especially the electoral, advantage of the "Solid South"; and this is as true of presidents so liberal as Woodrow Wilson and Franklin Roosevelt as of a conservative president like Grover Cleveland. Nor is the Republican record different in any vital way. While it has often denounced the behaviour of the South, it has always consistently avoided the obligation to act about the consequences of that behaviour. When Republicans are in office, Negroes get a somewhat larger share of the patronage than they receive from the Democrats, but there is no other decisive difference.

The evil consequences do not end there. The United States has a long and honourable record of protest, as in the case of the Jews in Tsarist Russia and in Nazi Germany, of protest against the ill-treatment of minorities abroad; but there can be no doubt that the sincerity of its crusades has been called into doubt, and their effectiveness seriously weakened, by knowledge of the American record in the case of the Negro. This was especially notable in the reception of American criticism of British policy in India; and there were signs that a tendency was growing in the United States towards a better "appreciation" of that policy as a kind of *quid pro quo* for British silence about the American problem. These crusades also raise the interesting question of whether they are a a sublimation of the guilt felt by innumerable Americans outside the South, and by some inside it, for their acquiescence in the deliberate exclusion of millions of their citizens from any real share in the major amenities of civilized life. The treatment of the Negro has its repercussion, if in a lesser degree because they are fewer in number, upon the attitude towards Mexicans, Chinese, and Japanese in the United States. Mexicans have a slightly better chance than Negroes, but the usual Southern practice is still wholesale exploitation on the ground of racial inferiority. There has been a barrier between the Americans and their oriental communities ever since the stoppage of immigration from the East. Though nothing like the intensity of the Negro issue is involved, there have been invisible, yet formidable, impediments in the way of the Chinese or Japanese who sought, as American citizens, for equality of treatment. The removal, after Pearl Harbor, of thousands of Japanese from the Pacific states to what were virtually concentration camps, even where they were American-born, may, in particular instances, have been justified as a security measure in time of war. But, on the evidence, it must be said that the ruthless and wholesale fashion in which the removal was carried out was a cynical violation of the civil rights of American citizens, which is an ugly precedent. I must add that the record of American-born Japanese in the Armed Forces of the United States offers no justification for the scale of the measures used against civilian persons of the same type; and the effort of states and areas to prevent their return to their homes, after the defeat of the Japanese, bears all the marks of an organized exploitation of popular, and mainly ignorant, emotions by interests concerned to profit in the uprooting. If it was possible to apply selective internment to suspicious German-Americans or Italian-Americans, the same method could have been applied to Japanese-Americans whose loyalty was in doubt. That it was not was the result of colour prejudice; and this was rooted in the habits engendered by the treatment of the Negro.

The problems involved are obviously an inheritance from the era of slavery. They cannot be approached, much less solved, except upon the basis of an understanding that the South has maintained all that it was legally possible to retain of the slavery system before Emancipation, and that, after the brief interlude of "Black Reconstruction," it has been able to do so by the tacit acquiescence of the federal government and the careful inertia of Northern public opinion; the grounds for this maintenance are, I think, clear. In part it was a compensation for defeat. It enabled the South to convince itself that even if it was defeated by superior force on the field of battle, it was still able, in a fundamental way, to win the peace by forcing the military victors to accept the formal principle of abolition while retaining the substance of racial domination. In part it was an economic manœuvre by the old leaders of the South, in alliance with Northern capitalists, to turn the South into virtually a semi-African or Indonesian colony to be exploited by the typical methods of economic imperialism. The pattern of Negro subordination, moreover, has served as the basis upon which to treat the poor whites, both in industry and agriculture, with much of the same ruthless disregard for freedom and civil liberties, to obtain the maximum profit from their exploitation. That is shown by the virtual peonage of the sharecroppers and by the unhappy economic condition of the workers in the cotton towns; and it has been brought out with striking clarity in the joint relations of industry and government in their attitude to trade-unionism and to strikes. The continuation, after the Civil War was over, of the social and economic isolation of the poor whites from the Negroes has meant a deep division among the wage-earning class of which the employers, both in agriculture and in industry, have taken full advantage. In the general result, it is difficult to see any fundamental change in the vital relationships of Southern society. There is far greater tension. The Negro, in spite of all handicaps, has advanced in a remarkable way; he is more conscious of his powers, more confident of his achievements, less willing to accept the relation of servility than at any previous time. His leaders—and he has had remarkable leaders—are fully aware that Southern liberalism is an extraordinarily sensitive plant, more likely to wither than any other effort to be tolerant in the whole United States. They know, too, that whatever issue there is about which the South is prepared to be reasonable, it shows no greater understanding of the need for equality of status than it did thirty years ago.

I do not deny that there are exceptions, some of them outstanding exceptions. No one who has read the decisions of Mr. Justice Black in civil liberties cases affecting the Negro which have come before the Supreme Court, or the speeches of Senator Lister Hill of Alabama, or the journalistic efforts of men like Mr. Virginius Dabney and Mr. Jonathan Daniels, without the conviction that, Southerners though they be, they are deeply disturbed by the insistence of the South on clinging to its traditional pattern of social life. But it is only honest to say that they, and the small number of men and women like them, are exceptions. The liberal in the South is permanently on the defensive. He lives in an atmosphere which, because it is contemptuous of his liberalism, always compels him to protest his love of the South, his recognition of its special position, his realization that the particular case which has made him rise to protest is an exceptional case. He must never be too insistent;

he must be careful not to give the impression that he is making a general indictment.[14] It is only the very occasional man of national reputation, like President Frank P. Graham of the University of North Carolina, who is strong enough to resist the impact of the mental climate without risk to his position or his reputation. Nor do the Southern intellectuals generally avoid that betrayal of their function which is the final sin against the light. On the contrary, far too many of them either evade their responsibility altogether, or take refuge in strident paradoxes, like Allen Tate, or in pathetic clichés like the insistence that Northerners cannot understand the South, or that, if the outsider would not meddle in what is not his concern, the relation of Negro and white would not be a problem, or that only citizens of the South can readily know the inner reality of the problem. The observer must either see the tragic situation in the Southern states himself, or hear Southern senators opposing, for example, congressional legislation intended to make the franchise for the Negro real by abolishing the poll-tax, or intended to establish decent standards in Negro wage rates, to realize what the system breeds.

"The interest felt by the non-slave-holders of the South in this question," wrote a Kentucky editor in 1860, "is not prompted by dollars and cents. Their zeal for their social institutions does not rest upon a pecuniary calculation, nor does it arise from an apprehension of loss of property. It is emotional and deep-seated. They believe slavery to be right and socially beneficial. Instead of degrading labour and destroying its reward, they believe it elevates and enhances labour. Its effect is felt in society, and brings a condition of public sentiment, taste and life, entirely congenial to their taste and feelings. . . . The strongest pro-slavery men in this state are those who do not own one dollar of slave property. Go to the mountains and find there thousands of as true Southern men as tread the soil of the cotton states, yet comparatively few own slaves. They are sturdy yeomen who cultivate the soil, tend their own crops; but, if need be, would stand to their section till the last one of them fell." [15] If slavery has gone, the pattern of social relationships which is implied in this quotation has fully remained. So, too, has Fitzhugh's argument that the opponent of this pattern has socialism as his real objective. He thought that if only Jefferson's liberal ideas could be removed from the principles of the Democratic party, it would protect the true conservative order that was in the making; otherwise the drift of events would be bound to move towards a revolution which would end in a military dictatorship.[16]

This fantastic dream-world has merely adapted itself, where the Negro in the South is concerned, to a situation where the legal principle of chattel slavery has gone. But the romantic idyll which was written for its

[14] *Cf.* Virginius Dabney, *Liberalism in the South* (Chapel Hill: University of North Carolina Press, 1932), for a Southern liberal's defence.

[15] See William B. Hesseltine, *The South in American History* (New York: Prentice-Hall, 1943).

[16] George Fitzhugh, *Sociology for the South* (1854).

defence—an idyll which Mark Twain, himself a Southerner, thought traceable to the influence of Sir Walter Scott's novels [17]—still persists. When an eminent Southern novelist like Ellen Glasgow strips the romanticism which forms a protective mask off Virginia, she is charged with looking at the society she describes with "un-Southern ideas," and she is told that "she has understood the weakness of the Southern tradition more than its strength, and has often warped strength to look like weakness." [18] Mr. W. T. Couch, who is himself a liberal Southerner, can actually agree that "the intellectual who fights against the exclusion of the Negro intellectual from eating places, hotels, and social gatherings of whites . . . , who limits his fight to discrimination against the Negro intellectual, is of extremely doubtful service to the race"; and he gives the extraordinary defence of this view that segregation forces Negroes who might otherwise isolate themselves "to take up the cudgels for their people." [19] He insists that there is "sound reason, at least for the present time," for the practice of educational segregation.[20] He suspects that the majority of Negroes do not overcome their handicaps because they lack the necessary ability and that "it is entirely possible that most of them would not improve a great deal even under the best conditions." [21]

Mr. Couch, I think rightly, argues that the "conception of Southern economy in terms of cheap and servile labour is the main source of most of the Negro's (and the poor white man's) disabilities, and that this conception and the system which gives it effect must be changed before the genius of the Southern people, white and black, can find its full expression." [22] He yet thinks that it could be argued—and with much truth in his opinion—that "bad as conditions are for the Negro in the South, with a few exceptions . . . his condition in the South is generally better than anywhere else on the face of the earth." He agrees upon the difficulty of change in the Southern white mind. "She [the South] scornfully rejects expert diagnosis and treatment, and she persistently fails to treat herself or even to recognize that her energy and genius are paralyzed by a malady which could certainly be rendered less burdensome, which with careful, persistent treatment might even be transformed into another of her charms." [23]

The assumptions which underlie what Mr. Couch calls the "faith" of a Southern liberal are of fascinating interest. I venture to believe that his attribution of Southern difficulties to Southern dependence on "cheap and servile labour" is right. But behind that view are further assumptions which Mr. Couch, herein a typical Southern liberal, does not explore. The South, for him, is a woman; the removal of the source of her

[17] A view not wholly without foundation.
[18] Donald Davidson, "The Trend in Literature," in W. T. Couch (ed.), *Culture in the South* (Chapel Hill: University of North Carolina Press, 1934), p. 200.
[19] W. T. Couch, "The Negro in the South," in *ibid.*, p. 470.
[20] *Ibid.*, p. 472.
[21] *Ibid.*, p. 476.
[22] *Ibid.*, p. 477.
[23] *Ibid.*

difficulties would be the restoration of "her charms"; here is already the implied acceptance of that easy romanticism of which Mark Twain spoke. It rests upon the illusion that the citizens of the South are really a special people, that if one could only get back to the older South, all the virtues which enabled it to breed statesmen, and loyalty and chivalry, and the kind of feudal obligation to dependents which was so general and so touch-ing before the Civil War, would, somehow, re-emerge. He already be-lieves that the Negro fails because he has not the capacity to overcome the handicaps placed in his way; and this is an inference drawn from the fact that since a very few Negro intellectuals in the South have been able to overcome them, this is the obvious proof that the fittest have survived. Mr. Couch does not mention that, outside the Negro colleges in the South, practically all the Negro intellectuals who have "overcome" the handicaps were already Northerners, or else had to leave the South to overcome them; and when he "suspects" that, even if the handicaps were removed and the "best conditions" created in their place, "most of them would not improve a great deal," it is obvious that, though unconsciously, he accepts the Southern view of the permanently inferior biological endowment of the Negro which could never rise high enough to take ad-vantage of the "best conditions."

There is, in fact, as Professor Myrdal has demonstrated in his monu-mental study, no evidence to show that Negro inferiority, in any particu-lar, has any source other than the environment which is forced upon them; and there is no evidence to suggest that the historic "idyll" of the South was ever available to more than two-tenths of one per cent of all the white population in the South before the Civil War; that is, if we assume that the leisured aristocracy which gave content to its civilization was com-posed of those who owned at least one hundred slaves.[24] The "Virginia dynasty" of men like Jefferson, John Taylor, and Madison apart, there is no literature and no science in the old South which is comparable to the quality of what was achieved in the North without the advantage of the "peculiar institution." The legend of Southern culture is, in a high degree, nothing more than another example of that fertile source of con-fusion between leisure and culture which has its roots in the Renaissance tradition of the "gentleman"; it identifies elegance and what Veblen called "conspicuous waste" with a high quality of civilization; the "new" South is somewhat overwhelmed as it looks back on the eighty years since the Civil War and notes, above all in the textile industry, the im-mense progress it has made in manufactures. The result is a profound complacency which grows angry at an attempt to discover the causes of its wealth. "The whole attitude of the section," writes Professor Mitchell, "reaches back to the agricultural South of Slavery, the fighting South of the Civil War, and the punished South of the Reconstruction."[25]

---

[24] Beard, *The American Spirit*, p. 279.
[25] Broadus Mitchell, *The Industrial Revolution in the South* (Baltimore: Johns Hopkins Press, 1930), p. 5.

The truth is, as Professor Mitchell has emphasized, that after the Civil War the South had an industrial revolution, to the understanding of which it brought the state of mind by which it had been possessed since the days of Calhoun. The immense growth of its cotton industry was the cause of the plantation owner being replaced by the capitalist as the dominant figure in its economy. Sometimes with honest ingenuousness, most often with that shrewd cunning which he insisted was the special vice of the Northern manufacturer, he preached industrial development as the source of Southern salvation. The clergy. were his allies, so were the journalists, so, if less directly, were the economists and sociologists of the universities. The cotton town was to be the plantation. It was to be distinguished by the same paternalism, the same self-sufficiency, the same sense that the economic relation between employer and wage-earner was not a cash-nexus merely, as in the North, but a mellow and kindly fellowship in which both co-operated to put the South on its feet once more. The hours might be long; the work might be intense; communal social services might be replaced by company philanthropy; child labour might be normal; a good deal of family life might have to be sacrificed to the need for women to work to augment the poor wages of the husband; trade-unionism might have to be discouraged, even fought, with the aid of the state militia, the police, and private guards, lest the most evil of Northern agitators, the walking delegate, set in operation from outside those forces of discontent which could so easily lead through things like strikes to delay in Southern recovery. All this was the natural price to pay for giving back to the South the great primacy it once enjoyed in the life of the American nation.

It is not difficult to understand why this appeal came with such force to the poor whites. They had the common memories, with their new masters, of comrades who had fought side by side in a great war. They were ready to regard the free Negro as their enemy since, after all, it was for his emancipation that the Northern armies had broken the South into pieces; and it was in the name of the Negro's elevation that the legion of carpet-baggers had descended like locusts—so the legend ran—upon the South, to line their own pockets at the expense of humiliating, after defeat, Southern citizens whose only offence was their willingness to risk their lives for their country. After all, the leaders in the industrialization of the South were in considerable part the men whom the poor whites had been accustomed to follow before 1861. They were grateful for the effort which gave them regular wages and a good deal of social welfare instead of the mean economic life on soil-eroded farms where the owner was in debt and the tenant could escape from his landlord only by leaving his half-derelict farm and moving on to new lands where there was rumour of hope. They were grateful; and their first concern was that this opportunity of a livelihood, which, if it was hard, was still steady, should not be snatched from them by the mass of Negroes only too eager to take their place and to work for wages even less than the white man's, since, as hardly human, their needs were less. To translate this situation into the familiar categories of the slave tradition of Southern economic and social relationships must have seemed to them, who had shared the pre-war faith with their new masters, a right and natural thing.

That, I think, is how the present pattern of social thought began in the South after the surrender of Lee. It was an obvious response to immediate opportunity, perhaps even to immediate necessity. Few of those who made the response were in a situation to take long-term views of it. Their wants were urgent; they sought to defend them by adapting to their service the one philosophy they knew. So that even when, by the First World War, factors like the movement of the Negro to the North, and the general stoppage of European immigration into the United States, had enormously altered the situation in the South and thus rendered the traditional philosophy and the relations it implied so obsolete that they were a massive obstacle to further progress in the South, the persistence of the traditional philosophy could be shaken but not broken. Indeed, there is an important sense in which its very obsolescence gave it a hold. It had about it the kind of nostalgic pathos which made Jacobitism retain its hold long after it had become irrelevant to reality. The consequence of this is that the Negro future is bound up with a series of vicious circles from some of which he can never hope to escape merely by his own effort. The Negro is held down because it is to the interest of the Southern white—a real interest in the case of the Southern capitalist, a psychological compensation in the case of the poor white—to keep him from a share in political power; and the North does not interfere, partly because the power of capitalism in the South is a reinforcement of Northern capitalism in the industries of which it has large investments, and partly because it has no desire to fight over again the battle of the Negro. And the Negro is held down economically because, once he began to rise, the whole economic structure of Southern industry, would be in jeopardy and the issue would be set in the perspective of a threat to white supremacy there. For an economic rise would mean a strong Negro trade-unionism, which, as it was successful, would obviously lead to a similar development among white wage-earners; and the obvious answer to such an effort on the part of Southern manufacturers would be to use the fear of Negro domination so that racial hatred could offset class struggle. Nor can one look for any serious advance in social status for the Negro except in terms of greater economic well-being. He must be held down socially, since that is the tribute paid by Southern capitalism to its white wage-earners in return for an economic submissiveness which, despite occasional strikes of some magnitude, and spasmodic attempts by the American Federation of Labor or the Congress of Industrial Organizations, is in startling contrast to the workers' outlook in other parts of the United States. The compulsory prostration of the Southern Negro is the foundation upon which the whole superstructure of the South's social economy has been built. To change the one is necessarily to compel vast changes in the other.

Those changes will be slow in coming. It is significant that the benefits distributed by the New Deal in the South gave least to the Negro who needed them most. It is still more significant that, not even under the profound and dramatic pressure of a war in which one of the things made unmistakably plain was the tragic evil of racialism, was there any sign of a Southern effort to revise the pattern of its social action. Only when large-scale economic pressure forces the workers in the South to recognize that they are themselves the victims of Negro victimization, that those whom they have helped to repress are, in fact, their natural allies, will that revision be undertaken. It is even a matter for serious doubt whether it can be attempted under anything like the existing capitalism of the South. For that capitalism, behind the mask of a well-meaning paternalism, is a domestic form of American imperialism in which the workers are divided from one another, the better to be exploited, in much the same way as the British government in India played off Hindu against Moslem the better to protect its own power from invasion. The walls of that American imperialism are still strong; and the Negroes have no trumpet whose sound could be the signal for their destruction. Yet a wise South would be aware that it cannot permanently maintain its "peculiar institution" in an epoch when, all over the world, the coloured peoples have begun to resist subordination, and when there is growing proof that historical forces no longer make it compatible with the emerging future. That is clear from India and China, from Indonesia and French Indo-China; even more, it is clear from the experience and teaching of Soviet Russia. The tragedy of the South is likely to be that in the next age, as in 1861, it will lack both the knowledge and the imagination to recognize for its own sake how urgent it is to be wise in time.

5

THE growth of anti-Semitism in the United States is, as a public phenomenon, a matter of comparatively recent growth. There have been Jews in the American colonies from the seventeenth century; they played a useful part in the Revolution. But until the middle of the nineteenth century their numbers were so small that they hardly impinged with any seriousness on the popular mind. The failure of the German revolution in 1848 brought a number of exiles to America, for the most part members of solid professional and business families, from whom there have come American Jews of eminence in the twentieth century, the most distinguished being Mr. Justice Brandeis, who has an outstanding position in the history of the Supreme Court. The great wave of Jewish immigrants began in the eighties, when persecution began to sweep like a plague over Russia and Southeastern Europe. They came in their thousands from the old Austro-Hungarian Empire, from Poland, Rumania, Russia, Lithuania. Overwhelmingly they were poor; they could not speak English; they were mostly orthodox in religious outlook. Since historical circumstances in Europe had confined them to a relatively small number of occupations, for the most part urban in character, it was into these they crowded, starting in the great cities and spreading out, as they became established, into the smaller towns. The clothing industry, cigar-making, the restaurant trade, the travelling pedlar, these mostly absorbed them at the outset. As they settled, they sent for their families, and the driving ambition of their lives was to see their children, in the fullest sense, educated Americans. They made almost incredible sacrifices to send their sons to college, and then into the professions, like law and medicine. As some of them became wealthy, they founded important banking houses, they built great department stores, they became predominant figures in almost every form of the entertainment industry. The love of scholarship was deep in their tradition, and many of them sought an academic life or, in the larger cities, became schoolteachers. On the whole, a considerable proportion of the first generation remained wedded to an orthodox religious outlook; in the second generation there was a large scale drift to various forms of a Judaism more adapted to American conditions, and a still larger drift to a religious indifference which made the Jewish element in their lives of minor importance. And that Jewish element became even less in significance as they began to intermarry with non-Jewish Americans, perhaps more largely than the Jews of any other country except pre-Hitler Germany.

The evidence is overwhelming that they were law-abiding, that they loved America with the passion of people who had found a refuge from persecution, that they were more rapidly "Americanized" than most other immigrants, and that they responded with remarkable zeal to the claims of the American way of life. They worked hard; they helped one another with that lavish generosity which only members of a people historically habituated to persecution are likely to show. Many of them were passionately interested in politics; and in most cities with a Jewish population of any size they became an important element in the local party machines. As workers, they were increasingly devoted to trade-unionism; the American Federation of Labor was the creation of Samuel Gompers, a Jewish cigar-maker from London. In the garment industries, they built trade-unions which, from small and difficult beginnings, have become outstanding in the quality both of their organization and leadership among trade-unions anywhere in the world. The Jewish intellectual and the Jewish worker were, and still remain, a vital part of the small, yet not insignificant, socialist movement of America; after 1917 they played an important part, also, in the Communist party, which the Russian Revolution brought into being. They went into Congress; Theodore Roosevelt appointed a Jew, Mr. Oscar S. Straus, as Secretary of Commerce and Labor. A considerable number of them were put on the judicial Bench. They played a great role, from the close of the nineteenth century, in almost every aspect of American culture. They had increasing significance in American journalism; Joseph Pulitzer and Adolph S. Ochs were both men who mark a turning point in the history of the American newspapers.

I think it is true to say that, broadly speaking, there was little organized anti-Semitism in America before 1914. There were undefined, but understood, barriers. There were unpublished limitations upon the number of Jews who could enter a particular university at the same time. There were well-known clubs from which it was a tradition that Jews should be excluded. There was an occasional hotel, especially in the South, which would not let its rooms to Jewish visitors. Real estate agents became increasingly aware that too high a percentage of Jewish tenants in a building or a street or a district would tend to send non-Jewish tenants in search of alternative accommodation. They could expect only an occasional political nomination of first-rate importance; Colonel House, in 1913, significantly advised President Wilson against making Brandeis the Attorney-General in his cabinet. The time remains distant when a political party would have the boldness to nominate a Jew as its presidential candidate. In the medical profession, everybody took it for granted that certain hospitals would refuse an appointment to a Jew, however eminent as a physician or surgeon. And, with rare exceptions, the universities preferred not to have more than a very few Jewish members on their faculties at any single time. For what it was worth, not even outstanding wealth, like that of the banker Jacob Schiff, or of the copper magnates of the Guggenheim family, could hope to penetrate the most exclusive social circles; and it has been said that the banker Otto Kahn, though he paid most of the deficit on the Metropolitan Opera House in New York, was never permitted to rent one of those boxes in the first circle which was one of the recognized marks of social distinction. A Jew might be a vital adviser in the entourage of a president or of a governor; there was yet a certain line beyond which it was agreed, on both sides, he should never attempt to cross.

Yet, on the whole, before 1914, it is difficult to say that, in any general way, the American Jew felt inhibited or insecure. Particular Jews might suffer much because they were Jewish; on the whole, in America an unstated *modus vivendi* had been reached which left the Jew satisfied with the opportunities opened to him, and the non-Jew broadly convinced that the professional Jew-hater must be a pathological human being. No one can read of the American reaction to the Dreyfus case, or to Russian outrages like the pogroms of the Tsarist period, the Kishineff massacre, or the Beiliss trial for the old and infamous blood accusation, without seeing that, if the Jew was regarded as somewhat different, there was no organized drive towards anti-Semitism, nor would there have been much response to one if it had been attempted. There was often deep business rivalry, as between Lazard Frères of New York, or Kuhn, Loeb & Co., with J. P. Morgan & Co. of the same city. Now and again one notes in the press the hint of an excessive Jewish element in radical movements, not least in their literary or artistic expression. One can find a remark here, or a warning there, against the "clannishness" of the Jew: let one in "and they all want to come," "give one a house in X Street and they all take houses in X Street." But, for the most part, before 1914 I should have said, on both written and oral evidence over a wide area, that any Jewish sense of frustration was exceptional rather than normal, individual rather than collective. The American Jew felt that he was accepted into the American community at least as fully, and probably more fully, than the Roman Catholic of either Irish or Italian origin. Above all, he was unlikely to be told that he was a type permanently unadaptable to the conditions of American life.

One begins to detect a change during the First World War; thenceforward, the emergence of new orientations has been extraordinarily rapid. It is not only that old barriers have become more definite. Still more striking has been the open organization of anti-Semitic activities the scope of which must have revealed to any disinterested observer how fragile was the basis of the tolerance extended to Jews. There were barely concealed limitations upon the entry of Jews into some of the best-known colleges of the East; neither President Lowell of Harvard University, nor President Hopkins of Dartmouth College, was at pains to deny the careful operation of a *numerus clausus* in the institution each controlled. There was another *numerus clausus* in both the appointment to, and promotion in, academic posts. Jews had great obstacles to overcome in securing medical appointments, especially in the junior grades, in hospitals. There were even townships, like Litchfield, Connecticut, where there was a tacit agreement not to sell them either houses or the land for their erection. In the South especially, they were increasingly excluded from hotels. The late Mr. Henry Ford devoted a large sum of money not only to financing an anti-Semitic paper, the *Dearborn Independent,* but also to the distribution of that well-known and infamous forgery, *The Protocols of the Elders of Zion.* The rabble-rousing priest, Father Coughlin of Detroit, not only broadcast and preached against the Jews week after week, but made an anti-Semitism modelled pretty directly on Nazi doctrine a vital feature of his weekly journal. The Ku Klux Klan, in its revival of the twenties, made anti-Semitism a plank in its platform; and it was only one of at least a dozen organizations which were devoted to the same propaganda. There were a number of anti-Semitic outbreaks in Brooklyn, New York, and in the environs of Boston, serious enough, in the latter case, to force the governor to set up an inquiry. Both congressmen and senators lent their names in support of the movement. President Roosevelt's use of Jews in the administrative machinery of the New Deal was one of the central themes in anti-Roosevelt propaganda. The influence of Mr. Sidney Hillman was attacked on the ground that he was a Jew. The supposed prominence of Jews in the Russian government was used to prove that Jews were communists and therefore hostile to the American way of life. Until the entry of the United States into the Second World War it is not an exaggeration to say that the isolationists did not hesitate to employ anti-Semitism as a weapon of high psychological importance in their attempt to maintain the neutrality of America.

I do not doubt that American anti-Semitism must be set in its proper proportions. The mass of American citizens disliked its overt expression, and no one protested more strongly against Nazi treatment of the Jews than President Roosevelt and the greater part of leading American citizens, whether in public life or in private. Americans in general gave warm and continuous support to the Jewish effort to build up a "homeland" in Palestine. But it still remains the fact that American anti-Semitism after 1914 was both wider and more intense than ever before, that its exponents had less compunction than ever before in shouting their intolerance from the housetops, were more able to secure funds for their activities, and were more successful in securing an audience for their propaganda. Certainly they made American Jews as a whole far more deeply conscious that they were still widely regarded as an alien element in the United States than at any previous period. The anti-Semitic campaign had a ferocity and vulgarity about it which might well remind an observer of the methods by which Hitler let loose his atrocities in Europe.

What was the ground for this new campaign with its virulence of spirit and its widespread ramifications? Three things about it were, I think, notable. The first was its use as a political weapon. Here the Jew was the medium through which to attack radical ideas in Europe, as in the attack on Russia, or in the United States itself, as in the assumed radicalism of the New Deal. The second was its use as an economic weapon: the Jews either controlled finance and were therefore responsible for the Great Depression, or they controlled the new forces of trade-unionism, like the Congress of Industrial Organizations, and were therefore responsible for industrial unrest, which, by preventing recovery, was an attempt to attack the economic foundations of American well-being. The third was the degree to which, mainly, it appears, through the influence of Father Coughlin, Roman Catholics, especially Irish-Americans, both in Brooklyn and in Boston, were associated with the anti-Semitic campaigns. And though there was a period during which, as a result of his attacks on President Roosevelt, Father Coughlin's episcopal superior, Bishop Gallagher, secured the cessation of his broadcast addresses, he was able to commence them again in the familiar anti-Semitic strain, and he continued to publish his propaganda uninhibited in his weekly journal, *Social Justice,* without interference of a public kind, or at any rate, from his Church. Negatively, the Roman Catholic authorities in America permitted a priest of their Church to play, if in a minor way, the role played by Goebbels in Germany. It was the federal government which finally put an end to Father Coughlin's major adventures.

It must be observed that, in any active way, almost all the purveyors of anti-Semitism in this period were cheap and raucous demagogues whose main interest was in the money they made out of it; and there were intricacies in the finances of their propagandist apparatus which raise important, but not fully answered questions.[26] There was the outstanding exception of Mr. Henry Ford; and among the political figures who lent themselves to an anti-Semitic approach, Senator Burton K. Wheeler of Montana, an ardent isolationist and therefore the almost frenzied critic of Mr. Roosevelt's foreign policy, was the only figure of any real standing. There was an obvious expression of anti-Semitism by Colonel Lindbergh, the well-known Atlantic flyer, who became a strong opponent of America's entry into the Second World War and a convinced believer in both the weakness of Russia and of Hitler's invincibility. These apart, nearly every instrument of anti-Semitism who sought positive action was a mean and second-rate person; and the followers each attracted were, overwhelmingly, narrow, ill-educated fanatics, of the same type as Hitler was able to attract to his movement at its beginning.

The real questions are three. Why did the kind of negative anti-Semitism, like that in the colleges of the United States, both as regards the students and the faculty, increase? Why did the main emphasis of positive anti-Semitism derive its strength from the attention it drew to the supposed power of Jews in the worlds of finance and labour? Where, finally, were the real sources of the money upon which the anti-Semites were able to draw?

I think the first question is fairly answered by saying that the causes were much the same as on the continent of Europe. Anti-Semitism grew in France after 1919, and it had its academic repercussions there also. It was rife in Eastern Europe, especially in Poland and Rumania. It existed in Britain, as the Mosley movement showed in the thirties, though it did not seem openly to affect British academic life in more than an occasional and superficial way. It was rife in Eire, after 1939, and was openly avowed in Dublin, not least in Roman Catholic circles near to the Eire government. Nor must it be forgotten that there was some attempt to exploit its possibilities in the British general election of 1945. Looked at under this head, it seems to me reasonable to conclude that negative anti-Semitism in the United States was a part of the counter-revolutionary wave which swept most of the world after the October Revolution of 1917 in Russia. It was more frank and open in the United States largely because, at any rate on the academic side, the life of the college possessed a greater "news value" than it generally had for the popular press of Europe, apart from nazified Germany. Men became everywhere more conscious of Jews, more awkward, as they are always awkward, about those whom they have grievously wronged, and more anxious to evade the issues their

<hr>

[26] See an interesting series of articles by J. L. Spivack, "Plotting the American Pogrom," *New Masses,* October 2 through November 27, 1934, and Gustavus Myers, *History of Bigotry in the United States* (New York: Random House, 1943).

presence raised, by limiting the need to meet these wrongs, by limiting their contact with Jews. As is usual in such cases, quasi-private discrimination became public knowledge, and became more difficult to handle by reason of the fruitless attempt at evasion or secrecy. A good example of this was the vehement discussion of President Lowell's decision—which deeply divided his own faculty—to limit Jewish entrance into Harvard by compelling every applicant to submit his photograph when he sought admission to the college. I ought to add, for the honour of Harvard, that President Lowell was compelled to go back on his decision, at least so far as this particular innovation was concerned.

Positive anti-Semitism was, I think, mainly stimulated by economic strain and distress. Fear of the Soviet Union counts for something; until 1927 the best-known name, after Lenin's, was that of Trotsky, and not only did he become a means of identifying Jews with communism outside Russia, but his views reinforced the conviction that all poor Jews in the United States were not unlikely to be agents of the Communist International. Old suspicions of Jewish radicalism were then strengthened by the remembrance that not only was Marx a Jew, but that a number of the outstanding members of the Socialist and Communist parties in America were Jews. From this it was only a step to the conviction that the Jews were a menace to Americanism. This conviction easily became, after the collapse of 1929, the source of a dual mythology. Rich Jews were a menace to general American well-being because they were regarded—though this was wholly untrue—as being the men responsible for the breakdown of its finances. Intellectual Jews were an analogous menace because they were held to supply President Roosevelt with the most dangerous theories with which he experimented in the New Deal. After 1936, when this aspect of the myth broke down badly, poor Jews became the substitute menace, since they organized "radical" trade-unions to fight the classic theory of the American business man on "freedom of contract," as he interpreted it to mean legislative non-interference with industrial and commercial enterprise; though few men can have seriously thought, if they examined the C.I.O., that John L. Lewis, Philip Murray, and R. J. Thomas were the names of typical Jewish trade-union leaders. The rationality of a belief, however, is obviously less important than its existence. It is fairly clear from the nature of the fight between the supporters and the critics of President Roosevelt's policy that what Americans call "smear tactics" were used to depict him, as far as possible, as the deluded victim of siren Jewish voices. Certainly this went so far as to persuade the more timid Jews, especially among the wealthier members of the Jewish people in America, to protest as strongly as they could in private against any attempt by the President to place eminent Jews in key positions in his administration.

We do not know who paid for all this propaganda. It is probable that, in its early years, a good deal of the financial backing came from Mr. Ford. It is still more probable that, after 1933, a good deal more came indirectly from Hitler through the good offices of German officials in the United States. It is at least possible that there were substantial subsidies from business men and business organizations to the purveyors of anti-Semitic propaganda, some part of it, at least, being provided by wealthy but timid Jews who thought that, after the manners encouraged by the Nazis, they were purchasing immunity by blackmail of this kind. What is clear in it all was the determination to "sell" a stereotype of the Jew as the alien source of social and economic disturbance: on the one hand, the sworn agent of the Jewish conspiracy to dominate the world; on the other, the instrument, through Russian gold, of the effort to make Washington the slave of Moscow. The propaganda, even after Pearl Harbor, had obviously gone deep, for I have myself met in Britain a considerable number of American officers who had no doubt of its truth; they were even ready to assume that American sympathy for the Jews of Europe and of lend-lease to Russia were decisive proof of the Jewish hold on the President's mind. It is still more notable that this sentiment persisted among men who had themselves seen the unsurpassed infamies of Belsen and Buchenwald. Nor was this sentiment confined to the non-commissioned ranks; it reached even to the level of the general officer.

Again, I think, sober consideration requires us to examine positive anti-Semitism in the United States as a phenomenon which was part of a world counter-revolution. The same characteristics appeared in France and, in a less degree, in Great Britain; it had, of course, deep roots in Poland and Austria, and it appeared, though less strongly, in the new succession states of Czechoslovakia and Yugoslavia. Two features about it are notable. It is, in the main, and in its full expression, proportionate to economic adversity. It rises and falls with depression and prosperity. It is also more likely to be swift, in the rise from an awareness of difference to a high state of tension, in a Catholic country than in a Protestant, once there is any considerable Jewish population engaged either in the professions or in commerce. And since the proportion of "intellectuals" among Jews is likely, for historical reasons, to be higher than in the community as a whole, Jews are more likely to be critical of tradition, eager for innovation, bearers of cultural experiment and therefore more likely to be regarded with hostility by those who stand by the ancient ways. The Jews are always vulnerable, first, because their complete assimilation is rare; they therefore appear at once as separable from the environment about them. They are especially vulnerable, second, not only because a small proportion of them is rich, but also because that proportion is likely to be concentrated in a relatively small area of production; this has the effect of making the proportion seem many times greater than in fact it is. And they are especially vulnerable, in the third place, because the twin facts of their interest in ideas and the poverty of their masses, a poverty so often allied to physical and political insecurity, gives them an exceptional zeal for all radical movements which attack, among other evils, the age-long intolerance of anti-Semitism. In the result, they are the natural objectives of counter-revolutionaries, who want a scapegoat upon whom to concentrate the hate and anger they wish to arouse; and this has, for them, the additional advantage, that in the earlier phases of counter-revolution it is always possible to ruin them, to create new openings by their ruin, and to represent this outcome as a "victory" for its authors. In the United States this effort, of course, will always be represented as the defence of "Americanism" against "alien and subversive influences."

I think it likely, therefore, that anti-Semitism will persist in the United States in the more positive form it has assumed since 1914 so long as the social and economic equilibrium, which, after the Civil War, gave the business man his remarkable supremacy in its civilization, continues to remain in jeopardy. It will be a technique for drawing attention away from the real problems before America to illusory dangers which have a long and half-familiar history behind them, which will be steadily purveyed to those who have neither the knowledge nor the intelligence to confront an intricate situation. I even think it likely that those who protest most loudly against anti-Semitism in the general American community will be in indirect and complicated relations with those who promote it. I suspect that the hierarchy of the Roman Catholic Church in the United States, while formally regretting its existence, will not be inwardly averse to it, partly because it diminishes the recurrent tendency to anti-Catholicism in the United States, and partly because it assists in the retardation of those attacks on tradition which the Church knows, by the most ancient of its intuitions, is the main safeguard for the preservation of its social power. Upon the Jews themselves it is likely to have three main effects. With some it will quicken and intensify, mainly through intermarriage, the process of assimilation. With others it will revive and strengthen the renaissance of Jewish nationalism, which now centres itself round the creation of a "homeland" in Palestine, the more so since American responsibility for the success of that "homeland" will be greater and more direct in the future than in the past. There will be some who seek escape from the consequences of this positive anti-Semitism by becoming what may, not unfairly, be called the "protected ward-heelers" of their persecutors. They will regret that Jews accept important public positions. They will urge that acquiescence in a kind of second-class citizenship which is the highroad to safety. I think it is a little unfortunate that a Jew should appear as prosecuting counsel in a case like that in which Bertrand Russell, in an obviously deplorable action, was declared morally unfit to teach the philosophy of mathematics in the City College of New York.[27] So, too, there can be found Jews who will agree that some popular resort, a country club, a restaurant, a seaside community, is getting spoilt because so many Jews go there; or they will give money to rebuild a church, or provide it with a new organ, as a form of protective

---

[27] Dewey and Kallen, *Case of Bertrand Russell*. In England a barrister is of course bound to accept a properly tendered brief—provided he is not already briefed for the other side.

colouration. And some American Jews will stand up as proudly to the anti-Semitism they encounter as the men and women of the Warsaw ghetto in that last supreme defiance of the Second World War.

I think that anti-Semitism is thus likely to remain an important alternative to the persecution to the Negro until either the American business man has so assured a supremacy in the national life that he does not need fear and hatred as weapons wherewith to assure the diversion of his critics from the challenge they are making; or the pattern of American economic life has so changed that neither anti-Semitism nor Negro oppression is a weapon that a ruling class needs to keep in reserve either to divide its enemies or present them with a kind of scapegoat in the sacrifice of which their sense of failure can be sublimated. In this context the experience of Soviet Russia and of Poland is of extraordinary interest. In the first, the reign of the business man has been brought to a close; and in hardly more than a generation there is a virtually complete disappearance of both anti-Semitism and colour prejudice for the first time since the rise of Christianity in the one case, and since at least the renewal of the slave trade in the sixteenth century in the other. Poland received its freedom, after being suppressed as an independent nation-state for nearly two hundred years, at the Peace of Versailles; thereafter, until the outbreak of war in 1939, Jew-baiting was one of its major industries. In the period of Nazi conquest and occupation the Jew and the Pole shared an agony it is beyond the power of words to describe. They fought side by side, and were tortured and murdered side by side. Yet, when liberation came in the spring of 1945, Jews coming back to Poland from the horror of concentration camps in Germany fled back to them for safety rather than endure the recrudescence of Poland's ancient industry. It becomes difficult not to infer that, in liberated Poland as in the United States, the Jew is the scapegoat of the interests which seek to protect a declining social order which has no longer the inner strength or self-confidence to preserve itself by the clear virtue of its own merits. Anti-Semitism is the child of waning hope and of fear.

6

AMERICANS have always been a mobile people. From New England on to the Middle West, from Virginia to Texas, over the snowbound Sierras into California, the legend of America is of restless energy and of ceaseless pioneering. Names like those of Kit Carson and Daniel Boone still echo with the thrill of adventure, and it was in the spirit of one seeking salvation on the migrants' road that Abraham Lincoln himself pressed on through Indiana from Kentucky to Illinois. There is a romance in the restless pressure of millions crossing the whole continent to which no one has ever failed to respond. The frontier and the driving pressure to push it ever forward, the hardships overcome, the courage displayed, the ingenuity and the good fellowship, the zest for new lands, the conquest, almost each decade, of territory so vast that it seemed to reduce Europe, which had not yet forged the final link with Russia, to almost a province alongside an empire, all of this, with its fierce energy and its reckless ebullience, its ready mixture of unlimited vice and unbreakable virtue, is part of that American epic of discovery which rivals in fascination, as, indeed, in influence upon the history of mankind, the greatest voyages of the sixteenth and seventeenth centuries.

In the century from 1820 [28] forty million people entered the United States; in 1930 more than twenty-five million were living in a state other than that in which they were born. It is hardly an exaggeration to suggest that few Americans, as they pass out of the stage of adolescence, feel the definite conviction that they have made their final geographical bargain with fate. They move on to find a better future. They go to their new homes with zest and some inner sense of a new world to conquer. They like the sense of having to try themselves out against strange people and a community with different ways. They taste a real triumph when the moment comes at which they have the sense of being accepted, of becoming a person whose part in the life about them is at least taken on their own terms. There is, indeed, something akin to magic in the way in which the America of the nineteenth century took its new children to its heart. Carl Schurz was a refugee from the broken German revolution which failed in 1848. Within five years of landing in the United States, he was a candidate in Wisconsin for the office of lieutenant-governor, though he had not yet been naturalized; and he had been barely a decade a refugee, seeking to establish a new home, when he was appointed American minister to Spain.

It is all like a fairy tale, but one in which there are episodes as grim as the "horror" novels of the last thirty years of the eighteenth century. The immense horde, perhaps as many as five millions, of migratory workers and their families who today haunt the highways of America have a tale to tell not of optimism realized, but of tragedy fulfilled. In part they are the victims of an agrarian revolution as deep as that which changed the foundations of English life in the sixteenth and, again, in the nineteenth century; or as that of Soviet Russia in the grim years when the peasant was forced to accept collective farming; or of those which the aftermath of the Second World War is enacting before our eyes in Southeastern Europe. In part, also, they have been paying the price of that massive soil erosion the gravity of which is only now beginning to impress the American mind. The migratory workers are a random sample of all that has gone into the making of America—descendants of New England, pioneers, grandsons of sturdy Scandinavian immigrants, defeated Negro sharecroppers from the South, Mexicans hurriedly imported to save some threatened crop. Some of them have a pattern in their wanderings. They move in seasonal stages, in some battered car

[28] To be precise, from 1820 to 1926 there were thirty-seven million emigrants from Europe to the United States.

piled up with their belongings, right across the continent from New Jersey to California, harvesting one crop here, and another there, their only home being the road on which they travel, or the labour camp where they stay while they pick the particular crop in the state in which they have arrived. Others may be part of the two million farmers who, in the first five years of the Great Depression, had to work outside their own farms because these did not provide them and their families with the bare needs of subsistence.

What is characteristic of this tragic minority, whether they are on the road or are the sharecroppers of the South and the Southwest—though their problems grow more real as they grow larger in Middlewestern states like Michigan and Indiana, or in Eastern states like New Jersey—is quite unmistakable. They are, in overwhelming proportion, disinherited people. Their standard of life is below the peasant level of Europe. If they are emigrants on the highways, they have no homes, rarely a book, never a week's access to the news of what is happening in the world about them. They work in a seasonal industry, so that they never know security or certainty. The power of their employers, backed by the strong and often ruthless hand of the police, is too overwhelming to offer any real chance of enduring success to a trade-union which might seek to organize them. They live too near the margin to attempt anything but the sudden, feverish strike against their omnipotent masters, which, usually dying almost as soon as it flares up, rarely does more than give the names of their leaders to their enemies, so that, next year, they may be refused a job as undesirable "agitators." Where they camp, their conditions of life, with rare exceptions, lack all the major elements of sanitation or comfort. A water supply is rare; still more rare is decent medical service or proper disposal of sewage. There is no prospect of any continuity of education for their children. Once the particular crop, for the picking of which they have been engaged, is harvested, they must be driven relentlessly away, lest their poverty make them a relief charge upon the locality in which they are working; it is not, indeed, an exaggeration to say that they experience, at its worst, all the inherent harshness of the Elizabethan "settlement" law. If they make a little money over and above their keep on a job, they are mostly certain to spend it either on getting to, or waiting for, the next job. Not seldom, as they move on their way, they must sleep on the roads, without any shelter but the outworn automobile they possess, through storm or oppressive heat. If they are imported Mexicans, hired wholesale through an agent for use, for example, on the sugar-beet farms of Colorado, it becomes hard to distinguish their status from that of persons watched with hostility by the poorer workers about them, lest permanence mean that they bring the bottom of the wage level even lower. When it is remembered that the average annual income of a whole Mexican family working on the sugar-beet farms is likely to be less than six hundred dollars, given the size of Mexican families, this is an attitude that is completely intelligible. But its result, of course, is to favour the employer by driving a wedge between American labour and Mexican labour, which has the same effect as the abyss between the Negro and poor white in the South.

It is a grim picture; but the fate of the family-sized farm is not less grim. Soil erosion, the development of the machine, the operation of great land companies who made large-scale factory-farming indistinguishable in habits from urban industry, the difficulties of marketing, have all combined either to drive the owner of a family farm off the land altogether, or to reduce him to the half-helpless condition of a tenant-farmer battling hard against remorseless debt and semi-starvation. By the onset of the Great Depression the number of wheat farmers in Montana had dwindled from thirty-five thousand in 1917 to fourteen thousand. In the generation from 1900 to 1930 the number of live-stock farms in the United States had more than halved. The scale of this agrarian revolution is enormous, and despite all the efforts of the federal government, especially since 1933, nothing has seriously arrested its progress. Indeed, the outstanding result of the New Deal programme to help the farmer has been to accelerate the catastrophic process of consolidation rather than to slow it down. The movement from the land, said Mr. E. A. Willson, the executive director of North Dakota's Public Welfare Board, "is caused by the farmers, mostly tenants, being forced off the land by owners and large operators who are able to increase the size of their farm-units very profitably because of the benefit payments of the Agricultural Adjustments Administration program." [29]

It is hardly beyond the mark to say that within a decade there will not be a single crop in the United States in which the small farmer will not be driven even more closely to the wall. Mechanization and the scientific treatment of soil, packing and canning, transportation and marketing, oblige him to sell, and the more concentrated ownership becomes, the less chance there is left for the small farmer to preserve his position. The evidence is literally overwhelming that, year by year, the man who had a prosperous farm at the end of the First World War is now a migrant looking for some crop-picking job, frequently, from 1929 to 1939, in competition with a bewildering variety of skilled men, from urban America, who had taken to the roads in desperation; or else he has become a sharecropper on whose horizon there is little to be seen except the dark shadow of an ever-deepening poverty. No one can really grasp the pitiful character of the small farmers' tragedy who has not seen how the Dust Bowl was changed from a rich agricultural area into a rival of the Gobi Desert. It destroyed the land. It ruined the health of large numbers since the dust caused respiratory diseases. It sent up the number on relief. It hit the towns because it reduced agricultural purchasing power. There is no element in American life which has not felt the impact of the agrarian revolution.

[29] Henry H. Collins, *America's Own Refugees* (Princeton: Princeton University Press, 1941), p. 51. I owe much to this admirable book.

The conditions under which large numbers of the sharecroppers live have to be seen to be believed. Most of them dwell in a cabin of two or three rooms built with rough boards of a single thickness. Perhaps a third of them have no windowpanes or sashes. The roofs are leaky in two-thirds, while screening or paint exists in less than ten per cent. Sanitation is abominable; it required the effort of the Works Progress Administration to bring the number of fly-proof toilets to one in every fifty of these houses. Few of them have ever seen a doctor; they depend on the help of the midwife or a kindly but unskilled neighbour when a child is born. Most of the diseases from which they suffer are the outcome of defective nutrition. Their cash income is so small that they have too often to live on the credit afforded to them by the plantation owner, mostly buying at excessive prices and paying a high rate of interest. The women wear old gingham dresses; the children rarely have shoes and often are clothed in a contrivance made from the sacks of flour or feed. Sheets or mattresses, shirts or underlinen, are rare commodities in the richest cotton-growing country in the world. If the family income is seventy-five cents per day, with the labour of women and children in the rush season included, it is above the sharecropper's average. Their furniture is usually a pitiful collection of odd, often broken, furniture, inherited from the past, or a system of contraptions made out of wooden boxes. They get a little comfort from the Churches, but, almost invariably, it is the comfort of escape. Their children can rarely hope for as much as six months' schooling in a year; and even this is likely to be intermittent not only because of the rain and the cold, but because of the fact that the sharecropper is only too grimly likely to move on to another tenantry the next year. In any case, a schoolteacher in the cotton country will get about thirty dollars per month as salary, and is unlikely to have had more than a hurried and superficial training; and the county superintendent shows few signs of insisting on an adequate standard of school accommodation and equipment. And the defects of what is provided for the white sharecroppers' children are, in general, virtues, compared with the provision with which the Negro children must rest content.

Few white, and no Negro, sharecroppers have any part in the government of the communities in which their lot is cast. The Negro, of course, is rarely permitted to vote; and the combination of the poll-tax, apathy, and fatigue, makes an election in which there is a fifty per cent poll of white sharecroppers an event. Both are at the mercy of local administration wherever they turn. The owner of their land is likely to be part of the machine which picks the officials, whether in relief, in the sheriff's office, or in the courts. The shape of their working is adapted to the landlord's will or convenience. The hearing of a case is set to "oblige" him. Relief may be suspended when he wants more labour. Deputy sheriffs may round up considerable numbers at the week-end, to release them on the conditions that they go early into the fields. It is always hard, and often impossible, for the tenant to enforce his rights. Not only does he face a hostile judge, but he will probably be unable to afford a lawyer, and he will be baffled by the niceties of legal procedure. If he is a "trouble-maker," a local vigilance organization may pay him a threatening visit. The "uppity" Negro sharecropper faces the even more desperate position of knowing that an endeavour on his part to secure his rights at law may lead to his being hunted across the swamps at night by a mixed group of white owners and their tenants, the latter finding some ghastly compensation for their own miseries in feeling that at least there is a group below them to which, at the call of their master, they may show by cruelty their superiority.

It is a system at its worst, as in the deep South, where it combines all the evils of an obsolete feudalism in social relations with a penalizing inefficiency which drives men down to a level of ill-fortune where even understanding is an effort. But it is still evil in areas to which it has spread, in areas which never inherited the pattern of living imposed by the South's "peculiar institution," in Oklahoma, in Colorado, in Missouri. As it deepens, it has two grave political consequences; it strengthens the power of the new economic oligarchy—the real authority which may well be away in Chicago, or San Francisco, or New York—over the local administration, from governor and state legislature to some local sheriff and county board. But the direct effect of this is, in its turn, to make the relations between the economic oligarchies and the state political parties closer too, so that it begins to have an important impact upon federal politics as well. That impact, of course, increases with the growing industrialization of agriculture, and with the consequential capitalization of agriculture by the great urban financial interests. Out of this there emerges, without any doubt, an agriculture at once more efficient and more prosperous to the few who can stand the strain of revolutionary change than at any of the earlier phases in its history. But it makes plain that the price of this change is paid for by the moral and material degradation of millions of human beings.

The federal government, especially during the first two terms of Franklin Roosevelt, worked with passionate energy to arrest this degradation. The great power and irrigation projects deserve the highest praise. Housing, rural education, relief, medical care, protection of the mortgaged farmer, help in co-operative marketing, direct subsidy, effort at price stabilization, aid and advice upon fertilizers and machinery, even aid in buying them, both the plans for these and their performance probably represent a scale of assistance beyond anything that Mary Lease, or William Jennings Bryan, could have hoped for, when they sought victory for the Populist movement, from the eighties of the last century to the eve of the First World War. Yet even the vast scale of this effort has mitigated only a small part of the territory affected by the change, and has not seriously altered its direction. I think it is clear that there must be a complete change in the social relations of American agriculture, and, therefore, in the laws of property upon which it is built, or the prole-

tarianization of the farmer will go on irresistibly until the small independent farmer, upon whom men like Jefferson and John Taylor placed
their reliance as the real source of health in American society, will become a historic memory. Migration from poor areas to good areas solves
nothing; it may even sharpen the problem. It leaves whole areas struck
into impotence and debt by leaving them with a population too small
to support the institutions prepared for better days. For migration is
almost wholly an unplanned effort by one broken family or a little group.
It moves without adequate means or adequate knowledge. "Rural migrants," says Mr. Carey McWilliams in his remarkable book, "are unlikely to move in the wrong direction, but they are apt to move at the
wrong time." [30] Migration from farms to cities, which is accelerated during periods of prosperity, transfers wealth to the cities, and during periods
of depression, it transfers poverty and dependency to the farming areas.
If the migration of farm families to the city continues, it will result only in
the transfer of still more rural capital to urban areas and in a further retro-
gression of rural life. More land will pass from the ownership of farmers,
and eventually more than half of the entire agricultural income will be
diverted to the cities. Reluctance to incur expenditures for rural schools
and churches may be expected from many urban landowners; reluctance
also to engage in efforts to retard erosion of the soil and depletion of
natural resources.[31]

The result is in no doubt. If the great empty spaces of the West were
filled with men who might, otherwise, have crowded into the factories of
the East, and were thus the famous "safety valve" against industrial discontent, the duration of the "safety-valve's" power was, at most, two generations. Now, the inherent conditions of the American economic position
have deprived it of that power. The small farmer has no future. He is
destined to see himself either driven to the cities to become part of the
urban proletariat, or kept on the roads, or as a poor tenant if he continues to work on the land. Agriculture is increasingly sucked into the
vortex of the market economy. It is now dominated by industrial power;
thence it will pass into the phase where its conditions and habits are
controlled, as in the major industries, by the great financial interests.
The programme which agrarian reformers seek to apply in mitigation
of this result—trade-unionism in agriculture, rural public works, public
employment agencies, a great scheme for rural housing, health and education, assistance, as under the Bankhead–Jones Farm Tenant Act, to
the sharecropper so that he may become an owner—mostly belongs to
utopian realms.[32] There is more hope in the idea of large-scale co-operative
farming under federal supervision to cope with some part of the problem;

[30] Carey McWilliams, *Ill Fares the Land* (Boston: Little, Brown, 1942), p. 197.
The book is written with incomparable knowledge and forms by far the best introduction to this problem.

[31] The last two sentences are Mr. McWilliams' citation of testimony given before
the congressional investigation of 1940, presided over by Mr. Tolan.

[32] See McWilliams, *op. cit.*, pp. 207 ff. where all these projects are discussed.

but the opposition it would arouse from existing interests would make its progress far too slow to forestall the ill-effects of the changes which are already taking place. Even if the federal government were to purchase and reconstruct whole communities for resettlement, the title to ownership remaining in whatever authority was set up for its administration, it would be many years before its fulfilment could hope to meet the size of the issue before America. Nor is it likely that such an effort would secure the necessary political backing on a major scale. Within the existing pattern of American economic life, it has little place except as a show piece, like Williamsburg in its reconstructed form.

That, indeed, is the conclusion to which all serious investigations are bound to come. The rights of these tragic victims of the agrarian revolution cannot be protected in any adequate way within the framework of a market economy, any more than they could have been in England during the relentless application of steam power to industry from 1780 to 1848. Just as it was necessary to destroy the peasant villages of England to feed the endless appetite of the new factories, so it is necessary in the United States to destroy the small farmer-owner to secure the economies and the profits which are the outcome of mass production in factory-farming. Each revolution has had to create a landless proletariat in order to fulfil itself; and each created the instrument it required with determination and without pity. Each resulted in a vast increase in productive power without ever pausing to consider the price paid for its achievement. The literature of protest in the early nineteenth century in England reads strangely like the far-off echo of the Populist protest in America; and the reports of the La Follette and Tolan Committees will be used one day to assail the masters of early twentieth-century capitalism, as similar reports were used to assail the masters of early British capitalism. Social obligation was as rare among the British pioneers as it has been among the American.

That absence of a sense of social obligation in the economic oligarchy of America is more difficult to justify than in their European precursors. They had a wider experience upon which to build. They worked in a political perspective of democracy and freedom. Yet they denied the economic implications of both. In the result, the problem of their minorities has been quite insoluble, since they would have to surrender their possession of the State power to make a just solution possible. "Our industrial and economic order in all its phases," writes Mr. McWilliams, "is not democratic. It is neither owned nor administered nor directed democratically. It functions in an automatic manner. It is at variance with our social and political ideals. Its prime objective seems to be the concentration of wealth and power in the hands of a constantly decreasing number of individuals. It breeds poverty and want, scarcity and insecurity, not by accident but by necessity. It can no more eliminate unemployment than an engine can run without fuel." [33] I do not think this is an excessive

[33] *Ibid.*, p. 231.

emphasis. The minority problems of contemporary America require a
new America for their solution. As they stand within the present framework, governments of a generous disposition can put ointments upon their
wounds; they cannot heal them. Indeed, it is perhaps the supreme tragedy
of the present position that the wounds are necessary not only to maintain the present economic order, but also to divide its victims in such a
way that one group may glean some comfort in its suffering by the knowledge that it can aid its rulers in the oppression of another group. America
will not go forward to the solution of these grave and growing issues until its citizens have displaced the business man as the idol to be worshipped
in its marketplaces. That time is not yet, although it will come. It will
come because America nears in each decade the stage in which it will be
driven to the realization that it can have either finance capitalism or democracy, but not both. Even its rulers will then be surprised how deep-
rooted in its soil is the tradition which makes democracy the parent of
freedom.

XI

America as a World Power

AFTER just over a century and a half of independent history the United States has emerged from the Second World War as by far the most powerful State in our civilization. The small community of some two and a half millions, overwhelmingly agrarian, of 1789, whose main ambition was to avoid being involved in world affairs, has become a great community of one hundred and thirty-five millions with an industrial capacity greater than any other community has ever possessed. Other nations, Russia, for instance, China and India, have larger populations; it is even possible that China and perhaps Russia have greater potential industrial resources. But it does not seem likely that any other nation can hope, in the next thirty, perhaps even the next fifty, years, to rival the United States in the power to produce or in technological skill. And since it is upon these, above all other, factors that the modern nation-state depends, it is highly likely that, for at least the next generation, no power will have greater authority or greater responsibility in shaping international development.

Anyone who observes the anxiety of the United States in its early history to emphasize the extra-European status it sought to enjoy, the emphasis of its early statesmen upon the danger of "entangling alliances," the eagerness with which it sought, by the Monroe Doctrine, to be free from the impact of foreign nations in the hemisphere in which the pioneer leaders believed its destiny to be set, the profundity of that isolationist tradition which is still so widespread among its people, can hardly help remarking upon the irony of its present position. A situation has developed in which it is safe to say that every major European decision and every major Asiatic decision has repercussions about which America must make up its mind to have a policy. Paine's famous warning that "it is the true interest of America to steer clear of European contentions" is now so impossible a basis of policy that it has ceased to have any meaning. It was perhaps true, until the latter years of the nineteenth century, that the combination of American power and British interest was strong enough to make the Monroe Doctrine a principle that the rest of the world was compelled to respect. It was also true, as a consequence, that American expansion, north, west, and south on the new continent, was achieved with an ease and directness the nations of Europe and Asia must envy. What it desired, it secured, either by purchase, as with Louisiana and Florida, Alaska and the Virgin Islands, or by wars, the scale of which, like those with Mexico and Spain, was at no point a serious test of its strength. Its purposive abstention from the quarrels of Europe it was able to maintain until the First World War. It had difficulties with Great Britain, as over the Oregon boundary and the Venezuela issue; with France, as over the Bonaparte-supported tragedy of Maximilian in Mexico; and with Germany, as over the prospects of the war with Spain. Yet none of these can be regarded as of first-class importance. Until the First World War the twofold policy of neutrality in all European problems and acceptance by Europe of the Monroe Doctrine enabled America to avoid any serious concern about its international position.

Partly, no doubt, this was the outcome of geographical fact and technological status. Until the age of the bombing aeroplane, the sheer distance of the United States from any other nation willing, or able, to threaten it rendered it invulnerable for all serious purposes. Canada was too thinly populated to be a threat from the north; no South or Central American republic was ever developed enough industrially, or effective enough politically, to threaten it from the south. The Civil War apart, the United States was never compelled to maintain large defensive forces. That was not because there was an implied reliance upon the naval power of Great Britain for American safety. It was because European divisions made an attack upon the United States a perilous adventure, and because, also, the easiest road to imperialist expansion lay for the European powers in Africa and Asia, and not on the European or American continents. It was the fixed principle of European diplomacy until 1914 that none of the rival powers could take the risk of seeing America allied to one European nation at the expense of the others. That was what enabled the ideal of "no entangling alliances" to remain so long fulfilled. That was why, also, the European nations watched the United States establish what has been hardly less than a virtual suzerainty over the countries to its south without interference, though not always without indignation. It is obvious that the long immunity from any serious international interference which the United States has enjoyed is the outcome of a small number of quite simple factors, even though its results have been very important. It has not made the international outlook of the United States different in kind from that of other nations, though it has stressed certain factors in a different way than did Germany or France, Russia or Britain. The ends of American foreign policy have been much the same as the ends of foreign policies in other communities. Its elements have been similarly compounded. The weighting has been different here, the emphasis has been different there, because the position and history of the United States have been set in a different perspective. But the fundamental objectives have been the same as those pursued by other nations. To grasp this is the first essential in any attempt to judge the implications of America's world position. Like other nations, the United States has aimed at self-preservation through security as its first objective in international relations. Like these, also, it has sought economic expansion both internally and externally. It has been no different from them in that inner sense of pride in itself, expressed in the search for prestige, which has led it to assume at once that it has a special historic destiny, and that the use of opportunities to increase its influence and power is the road to the fulfilment of that destiny. It has had the same faith as other nations in the validity and worth of its own special moral values, even the same difficulty in believing that their rejection can ever have been either justified or sincere. All these drives to action have combined to form the pattern of American policy in each successive age. From Washington down to Franklin Roosevelt they have been the basis upon which policy has led to action. Jefferson purchased Louisiana out of the realization that if it were to form the basis of a French empire in the New World it would be dangerous to the United States, just as Franklin Roosevelt saw the threat to American security involved in a conquest of Europe and its colonies by Hitler. Behind the Spanish American War there lay almost a century of conviction that the Caribbean would be safe only when none of its territory was held by a strong European power. Men so different as John Quincy Adams, Henry Clay, and James Buchanan all insisted, when they were Secretaries of State, that both Puerto Rico and Cuba must be regarded as what Adams called "natural appendages to the North American continent"; all of them were prepared to make war in defence of that view.

It is important, further, to recognize that the isolationism so often regarded as a uniquely American characteristic has no such status and never had. On one side, it has been nothing more than an ardent desire not to be involved in European disputes; therein, it has a partial resemblance to the constant British tendency to keep apart from the Continent to which it is obviously inseparably attached, and, still more, to the remarkable determination of Switzerland and Sweden to maintain their neutrality even under pressure which involved suffering almost as great as the abandonment of neutrality would have involved. On the other, American isolationism has been the expression of the psychological gulf which separated, and was felt to separate, the way of life of the United States from that of the rest of the world. No one can read the literature up to the present time of travellers from Europe to the United States without discovering their awareness of that gulf and the fact that they have seen, more or less clearly, that it is a challenge to the way of life in Europe. It is a challenge because its outlook, ever since the Declaration of Independence, has always given a status to the principle of equality which the European tradition has rejected except in the rare moments of revolutionary activity. It is a challenge because the class structure of American society has never had the rigidity of the European, and this has made individual opportunity greater, and the chance, consequently, that social pressure would not frustrate the fulfilment of the claims of personality. Nor has it been unimportant that, save for the four years of the Civil War, American citizenship was a safeguard against the claims of almost all the European nations to impose some period of military service upon their youth.

The psychological foundations of isolationism go even deeper than this, if in more subtle ways. The ordinary American accepted it because he felt that his tradition and its habits made for a directness and simplicity of living which were preferable on any showing to the decadent sophistication of Europe; and he tended to regard the Europeanized American much as the "Italianate Englishman" was regarded in sixteenth-century Britain. The European observer, on the contrary, feared that the drive of American civilization was not only towards a dangerous materialist approach to life, but also towards the enforced imposition of a uniformity of thought and conduct fatal to the rich diversity of European culture. That can be seen in the criticisms of men like Tocqueville and Dickens and Georges Duhamel. Americans feared European influence as the source which threatened the uniqueness of their experiment. The governing classes of Europe feared American influence as likely to undermine the social structure upon which their privileges depended. This comes out very clearly in the attitude of those governing classes to the Civil War. In England, for example, the sympathy of the aristocracy for the South, and of the working class for the North, was essentially the outcome of a realization that the principle of democracy was at stake, and a repulsion from, or attraction to, its survival which reflected pretty directly the strains and stresses of the internal situation. In much the same way, the modern French traveller in the United States, of whom André Siegfried is typical, fears that the sheer power of mass production will have the result on Europe generally, and on France in particular, of sacrificing distinction to comfort, and the exploring opinions of the few to the conventional opinions of the many. The converse of this is the American conviction that the future of the United States can be healthy only if its creative genius finds its inspiration in American soil and escapes from the exotic bonds which have limited and deformed its possibilities.

Isolationism, so regarded, is thus at once a search for security, in which cultural separation helps and influences political separation, and a means, closely connected with security, of remaining unaffected by clashes of interest which lead to war. It is notable that isolationism has always been consistent with the American claim to the fullest right to trade with other nations on equal terms. That is why America has been the protagonist of the doctrine of freedom of the seas in wartime, and of the Open Door in China; that is also the reason why Commodore Perry was permitted to compel Japan, by the use of naval power, to desist from its hostility to foreign trade. In effect, in all these directions its movement was a purely economic one; political doctrine followed, and did not lead, the trader's effort to do business wherever he could. The tradition of the United States was that of neutrality; it adopted doctrines which would minimize any abridgment of its commercial opportunities if other nations went to war. That was why it resented the use by Great Britain of its naval supremacy in the struggle with Napoleon; that is why it protested so strongly, both to Britain and to Germany, against their interference with American shipping from 1914 to 1917; that is why, within two years of the Anglo–Chinese Peace of 1842, the United States signed the Treaty of Wang-Hia with China by which it obtained, as it has preserved, "most favoured nation" treatment. It may, indeed, be fairly said that American opposition to the partition of China, which has so often seemed imminent since the eighteen-nineties, has been essentially the result of its perception that if China were to be carved up, as Africa had been, the open door to equal trading opportunity would be shut by the tendency of each partitioning power to convert its special area into a monopoly for its own citizens. When Japan sought, indirectly at the time of the Nineteen Demands, and with brutal directness after 1937, to reduce China to the status of a colonial dependency, the riches of which Japanese business interests would exploit, to assure political mastery in Asia, America moved with but little hesitation to accept the challenge. Pearl Harbor was not merely the commencement of a war; it opened a new epoch in the history of the world.

2

THE history of American foreign policy follows, if with shifting emphasis, the same pattern of development as that of any other great power. It has, no doubt, been less continuously involved in relations in which conflict was implied; from this danger it was safeguarded by nearly one hundred years in which its main energies were involved in the discovery and exploitation of its own massive resources. The confidence implied in the knowledge of these, the assurance it has had since the Civil War of well-nigh inexhaustible strength, the absence from its social structure of a military class with significant power, these have probably made prestige politics less important for the United States than for any other community of comparable significance. There is no more disinterestedness in the American record than in that of any other country; this is clear enough from its determined insistence on having its own way in Latin America. When a distinguished American scholar writes "that America has acted politically on a higher moral level than other countries is hardly to be denied. . . . And it has stood generally for loftier principles of international conduct than other powerful countries. This is reflected, sometimes movingly, in the instinctive trust in America, the implicit belief in the disinterestedness of American motives that one finds almost everywhere in the world," [1] it is difficult not to be a little bewildered. It is true that Professor Peffer excepts Latin America from this claim. It is true, too, that he makes this affirmation the outcome of the safety and detachment of America's international position. But he still insists that "in general America has not been a participant in the imperialistic struggle, the rivalry of expansionism that has given the spirit and content to modern international relations." [2]

It is certainly true that American territorial expansion is modest alongside the relentless appetite of the main European powers and of Japan. It is also true that the United States has generally been sympathetic to the cause of oppressed peoples, and more than generous to a nation which has suffered from such calamities as earthquakes or tidal waves. But Professor Peffer has supplied the appropriate commentary on the limited character of American territorial expansion when he says that "no territory has been sought, principally because none was required." The domain of the United States occupied its main attention and absorbed the overwhelming proportion of its accumulated capital until the turn of the twentieth century. What territory it required it took as relentlessly as any other power. It protected the Latin American investments of its citizens with the same ruthless efficiency as any European power; the histories of Bolivia and Nicaragua, of San Domingo and Cuba, leave that beyond doubt. Most of its sympathy with oppressed nations has been confined to the passage of rhetorical resolutions in Congress, and these, in their turn, were as often inspired by the complicated possibilities of domestic politics as by zeal for the oppressed nation. In the test case of Republican Spain, even President Roosevelt accepted the "appeasement" policy of non-intervention lest active support for the republic should jeopardize his hope of Catholic votes for Democratic candidates in the congressional elections of 1938. Its actual relation to the policy of imperialist expansion has been governed by the factors, geographical, economic, and political, which gave it the immunity of immaturity by which it was freed from the major contradictions in which other nations were involved. Year by year, since 1900, that immunity has grown smaller. Year by year, since 1900, American destiny has become more closely involved in all major changes in international relations. In each of the two world wars its political leaders have tried hard to preserve American neutrality. The moral case against the aggressor, the sense that important values were in jeopardy, came after American entrance into the war, and not before. In each of the world wars the public opinion of the United States demanded a full-scale effort at appeasement before Congress accepted the President's advice to declare war; in neither case was the certainty that a negotiated peace would be the prelude to an-

[1] Nathaniel Peffer, *America's Place in the World* (New York: Viking Press, 1945), p. 45.
[2] *Ibid.*, p. 47.

other war given the weight it deserved to receive in the period before America became an active participant.

In other words, the place of America in international relations, while it has been different from that of the other powers, has not been different because the American philosophy of international relations has been different, but because the situation of the United States called for a different application of the same philosophy. But it is important that the philosophy has been the same. America wanted certain things; if its government could not get them by negotiation, it got them by force, if it declared them important enough to justify that force. Historically it has been more fortunate than most other great nations in that it was usually in a position to get what it wanted by negotiation; and not the least reason for this fact was the inability of any opponent to rely with any hope on dealing with the United States as an equal. This is still more the case today, in the age of air power and all the new weapons it has made possible, than it was even a generation ago. For, since modern war is total war, and since total war depends upon productive capacity and technological skill, the United States is, for the present age at any rate, likely to carry more decisive weight in total war than any other power. So long, therefore, as it is a commercial nation which proposes to trade in wartime, the parties to any conflict will either desire its active participation as an ally, or try to find ways and means of obtaining access to its industrial potential. That it will somehow manage to trade in wartime emerges clearly from a study of the periods preceding each of the two world wars. In the first period, during the three years before its entrance into the struggle in 1917, it traded in munitions of war with Great Britain and France upon a massive scale, and only British sea-power prevented it from trading with Germany too; in the second, it provided Japan with many of the materials of war for the attack on China; it assured the defeat of Republican Spain and the victory of the fascist satellite Franco by its acceptance of non-intervention; and it assisted Germany directly until 1939, and indirectly through its shipments to Spain until 1941, as it similarly assisted Italy both in the war with Abyssinia and in the twilight of Italy's neutrality between September 3, 1939, and the Italian entrance into the Second World War. In this last war also, the scale of its industrial assistance to Great Britain was of paramount importance in the critical year of 1940 when Great Britain stood alone. The description of the United States as the arsenal of armaments is a literal description of the function it has performed as a neutral in the periods before its entrance into each of the two world wars.

This is to say that, for all practical purposes, America is now bound to be a vital factor in every war of importance, unless it were to decide not to engage in any foreign trade which might have relevance to war once there is reason to believe that war is on the horizon. It has no longer the power to be neutral even if it has the will. At some stage it has to decide to which group of powers it will give its full assistance as an ally. The experience of the nineteen-thirties makes it clear that even the most vigorous measures designed to prevent American entrance into a war have little hope of success. All the principles of the so-called Neutrality Acts failed to take account of the impact of total war upon the American economy. They also failed to take account of the fact that, in a large-scale war like that of 1914 or of 1939, American interests and American emotions will be not less deeply engaged than those of the belligerents themselves. After the First World War, had America kept aloof both commercially and militarily, it would have had to confront a Germany able to mobilize all the resources of Europe and its colonies; after the Second, it would have had to confront a Hitlerite Germany with a mastery of Europe, the Middle East, and Africa, and a Japan which had subordinated to its expansionist purposes all the resources of Asia and the Southwest Pacific. It did not, indeed, it could not, be impartial before such a choice. The economic injury to itself during the war period would have been profound; the strategic position it would have occupied after a German, or, still worse, a German–Japanese, victory would have been disastrous. It had, in both cases, to choose a side which it would eventually support by force of arms, unless it was ready to take the risks of confronting victors who would choose their own time to settle their accounts with an America in a far worse position than when the action of America itself could choose its allies. Whatever the will of the United States, in short, a war of the first order is bound to affect America so profoundly that the only elbow-room in policy it possesses is to make its choice of allies coincide with what it thinks and feels to be the interests it is right and wise to support.

America, then, is now of necessity a pivotal factor in any major war of which one can see the possibility. It does not matter that the transcendant power of Germany and Japan has been destroyed for the time being. It does not even matter that their recovery from wholesale defeat will be a long and difficult process. The end of hostilities has not made for an assured peace. The forces which led the United States into war in 1917 and in 1941 have not been permanently overcome; they have merely changed their direction. Mankind has had a reprieve; it has not had more. America has still to make up its mind whether it will organize positively to co-operate in peace, or whether, as in 1919, having helped to impose terms upon the vanquished, it will then wash its hands of any continuing responsibility for their application. And one ought to realize that it will not be easy for Americans to make up their minds. A deep-rooted tradition, now reinforced by the consciousness of immense strength, will impress the warning that continuous responsibility deprives the United States of a free choice in international affairs, that it really puts American sovereignty into a control not exclusively American. It is at least probable that most Americans returning from the different theatres of war will be hostile to experiments which threaten their assumption that victory means escape into privacy. And so much of the wide-ranging reconstruction for which the aftermath of this war will call will depend upon the scale of the American contribution to its achievement that millions of Americans will have that angry xenophobia which comes from the constant strain of bearing the world's burdens in an epoch when the domestic problems of the United States will be heavy, and the attention given to the international scene will seem, at least superficially, like the diversion of effort from problems which require every ounce of energy American statesmen possess.

Anyone can see that, in the light of its past, the drive to isolationism is likely to be as strong in the next few years as it was after 1919. Yet its strength must not allow the observer to be diverted from perceiving the stark fact that isolationism is no longer a workable policy for the United States. As a sheerly practical fact, international affairs are now an inextricable part of its domestic affairs. It is bound to have foreign trade. It is bound to be both emotionally and intellectually involved in the direction of world events and to influence them profoundly as it will be influenced by them. The real choice for Americans is not between withdrawal and participation. The real choice for them is between an aggressive nationalism which seeks safety by domination, and honest participation in a new world effort both to outlaw aggressive war and to create the conditions which no longer make one nation or another think of war as an instrument of national policy, in the last resort, to be regarded as a legitimate gamble for which preparations may be made.

It is no use to deny that there is a considerable body of American opinion which looks to an aggressive nationalism as the better and more practical way. Its adherents are deeply impressed by the scale of American power; we are now entering, they say, upon what is, in fact, the "American Century." Great Britain is fatigued, its economic position is parlous, it will have all it can manage in the effort to preserve its imperial authority. France has become a second-rate power. Its recovery even of its pre-war position will take many years, and its industrial potential is too low to make it a serious opponent. In the next generation, the three major powers of the Axis will have all they can do to achieve a status of reasonable economic and political self-respect. Nor is it likely that, in this period, either China or India could achieve either the industrial power or the technological efficiency which are necessary to challenge American hegemony; both of them, indeed, are likely to depend upon American capital for any large steps towards effective modernization. The one power which raises any question in the minds of Americans who think in this way is Russia. They dislike the social principles for which it stands; and they are aware that these principles awaken a growing interest in Europe and in Asia. They look with suspicion on the immense internal expansion of Russia and the new strength it has acquired by its transformation from an agricultural economy into an industrial economy the potential capacity of which grows by leaps and bounds. Even though Russia has suffered deeply from the war, they have an uneasy sense that economic developments in the Urals and in Siberia may well compensate within a decade for its war losses. Russia is the one power quite certain not to tread the path to Washington either with pleasure or with humility. The exponents of the idea that this is the hour for consolidating American supremacy are, therefore, divided. Some of them think that it would be wise to settle the issue of American hegemony while Russia is still licking its wounds. Others argue that the better course is to build, under American leadership, so strong an alliance against Russia and its ideas that it becomes obvious from the outset that any challenge to American world leadership is doomed to overwhelming failure.

It is unlikely that the proponents of this outlook have ever really tried to measure the costs its acceptance would involve. It would involve a permanent and large-scale militarism in the United States to which all other aspects of its life would be necessarily subordinated. Not only would that make for the emergence of a permanent and powerful military caste—an emergence which would call for the sacrifice of one of the main traditions Americans have sought to defend—but it would compel the subordination of labour to the necessary implications of the industrial programme this militarism would make inevitable. Nor must its strategic implications be overlooked. In the age of air power, the defenders of an active American militarism would be driven to demand the control of bases all over the world the situation of which exposes the United States to the risk of attack. In the Arctic, on the Atlantic coast of Africa, in the Pacific, air bases would become instantly urgent; and the situation of Alaska would involve land defences on an enormous scale. To all this must be added the changes that would be required in the dispositions of the American economy, and of the social habits that economy has produced. A welfare economy is rarely compatible with a military programme which seeks to secure invulnerability against the possibility of totalitarian war; for the latter involves the acceptance of values which not only alter customary priorities, but even subordinate that market economy which is the main principle of the American economic system to its imperative demands.

I do not myself believe that Americans generally would accept adjustment to all this without a strain which might threaten the unity of the United States. Once that unity was threatened, moreover, either such a programme would have to be abandoned, or differences of opinion about its desirability would have to be suppressed. Aggressive nationalism, in other words, would not be easily compatible with the theory of American democracy. It would lead then to a partnership between the leaders of the Armed Forces of the United States and the leaders of Big Business, and the State power would be used for what might well be termed the safety of the United States, but would, in fact, be the subordination of labour to financial power. And since no one supposes that the trade-unions would accept this subordination without a struggle, the out-

come would be either incompatible with aggressive nationalism or fatal
to American democracy. The situation, moreover, would be exacerbated
by the pressure of other influences. One of these would be the attitude of
the State Department. For though there is a small group of genuine progressives in the Department, its general outlook is reactionary. That has
been seen in its South American policies; as a general rule, it has always
been willing to support the rich, semi-fascist cliques, who have merely
rung the changes on different degrees of dictatorship, so long as these have
not sought to interfere with American economic penetration. That has
been shown, also, in its policies towards the Soviet Union.

The Roosevelt period apart, the State Department has been one of
the major sources of hostility to the Russian experiment; and even in
the Roosevelt period a good deal of its outlook was determined by the
conviction that a socialist community was an inherent threat to the safety
of American standards of well-being. Nor was there any general benevolence to the nations seeking, like Spain or Italy, to free themselves from
the yoke of dictatorship; it was the support lent by the United States to
the policy of non-intervention which, at least as much as any other factor,
led to General Franco's victory. We have not yet been given the materials upon which to make a full judgment upon Franco–American relations during the Vichy period; but at least we know enough to feel uncertainty as to the motives of the American diplomats who so long sought
for a *modus vivendi* with some of Vichy's most sinister figures. Nor is
it easy to follow the urgency with which so many of the State Department's specialists in Far Eastern affairs have always insisted that "stability" in Japanese life can be attained only by preserving the imperial
throne, with the related emphasis that the more moderate supporters
of Japanese expansionism could be regarded as a helpful factor in Asiatic
renovation. It is, indeed, difficult to find any evidence of an effort by the
State Department, either in Japan or in China, to know, much less to
support, the movements and the men seeking to build a real democracy
in Asia. Rather, it remained amply contented to put its faith in men whose
outlook was hardly distinguishable from that of Big Business in the
United States.

The other influence of a profoundly undemocratic kind is that of the
Roman Catholic Church in the United States. The day has long since
passed when men like Archbishop Ireland sought to make its policies
accommodate themselves to the American atmosphere. It has now become the relentless and undeviating supporter of ultramontanism in
foreign, and reaction in domestic, affairs. All its weight has been thrown
on the side of hostility to Russia, hostility to Republican Spain, and hostility to the new Mexico. It was sympathetic to Mussolini's Italy. It
saw little to condemn in the outlook of Vichy France. It is still friendly
to the Poland of Pilsudski's colonels and of the great landowners. It
makes propaganda with enthusiasm for Salazar Portugal, which differs
only from Franco Spain in being able more effectively to conceal its

barbarism, as it made propaganda for the clericalist Austria of Dollfuss. Nor does its outlook differ in domestic matters. It has been from the first a vigorous opponent of legislation against child labour. In education, especially in the last thirty or forty years, it has sought to build a religious *imperium in imperio* within the American system; and it has taken almost fantastic precautions to prevent any winds of liberal doctrine from blowing through the halls of its universities. So far, moreover, as its clerical hierarchy has been able, it has sought to unify the Catholic vote, city by city, and state by state, as well as on a national basis, to use it as a pressure group in support of policies which the Vatican approves. It is, indeed, difficult not to regard the great mass of Roman Catholic voters as constituting, on all matters of major importance, a colony of the Vatican and organized by agents *in partibus infidelium* on behalf of interests of which the Vatican approves.

It is significant, surely, that the approach to foreign relations of the State Department and of the Roman Catholic Church resembles closely that of American finance-capitalism, and that they are all concerned with setting limits to democratic fulfilment in those nations in which the power of a small privileged class has for long been used to exploit the poverty and ignorance of the masses. They would all support an aggressive American nationalism if it prevented any threat to the stability of privilege in foreign countries. They have never been troubled by reaction in Poland or Hungary, in Austria or in Yugoslavia. When Mussolini was overthrown, their influence was devoted to support of a monarchy which, for over twenty years, was the principal collaborator of Fascism, and in no small degree the source of its respectability. It is significant, also, that both in Germany and in Italy, as well as in Japan, American Army leaders have tended, on the whole, to come to terms with interests that were either the direct supporters of dictatorship, or prepared to collaborate with it. Certainly the evidence suggests that a large proportion of the Military Government officers in the Armies of Occupation were suspicious of any Germans or Italians with Left convictions, and were inclined to accept as true the insistence of Nazi officials who were not well-known outside their local area that they had joined the Nazi party only as a way of keeping their jobs; and when men like General Eisenhower or General Clay insisted on denazification, these officers chose supporters of the old Centre party. Many of them had so venomous a hatred of communism that they regarded any progressive-minded German as a communist; and they were even prepared to believe that Nazis were at any rate men who could be relied upon to assist in preventing a communist revolution in Europe.[3]

It is obvious that if the United States becomes aggressively nationalist it must organize its military and naval resources upon a scale commensurate with the interests it seeks to protect abroad. It could not rely

[3] See two important articles by Dr. Saul K. Padover, in *The Nation*, October 6 and 13, 1945.

upon improvisation in an emergency, for, in the age of air power and its new weapons, still more, in the age of the atomic bomb, to trust in improvisation is clearly to jeopardize the chance of mobilizing successfully the industrial potential upon which modern war depends. This obviously means not merely general conscription; it also means large professional defence forces, and large stockpiles of the latest weapons of war, which are constantly renewed and replaced as the outcome of research. Once this stage is reached, the foundations have been laid for an alliance between the naval and military leaders on the one hand, and big business on the other; and that alliance is bound, in its turn, to have a profound effect on the programmes and policies of political parties. Not only would it have to drive them into securing bases all over the world—whether with or without the consent of interested powers—but it would also have to make the politicians accept the necessity of establishing a psychological authority great enough to make its decisions accepted without question. This involves, of course, the classic politics of prestige; and the way of life which any nation must then follow is historically given by the experience of Germany and Japan in our own era. The degree is large to which it would mean a complete reversal of the historic traditions and the historic values of the United States. Above all, it would breed the kind of professional *élite* at the apex of American social life to the consummation of whose power all other opportunities would have to be sacrificed.

An aggressive nationalism of this kind would have to put itself beyond the possibility of challenge. This would mean that it could not accept alternative empires in a position to challenge its prestige. Nor could it accept any policy which sought the acceptance of racial equality, especially in matters where colour is concerned. And the very fact that it would be a new phase of American history would mean a direct challenge to all existing interests, a challenge which would lead, first, to a revival of the struggle for armaments, and then, quite certainly at some stage, to war. An America that had made itself powerful enough might, of course, win that war; but on any showing it would have become in the process a different America. If it won, the major problem it would then confront would be how to combine the preservation of its supremacy with the acceptance of the typical habits of the police State this kind of prosperity would entail. If it lost, the problems it would present can be judged in some measure by the scale of the issues the world confronts in fitting Germany and Japan once again to take a reasonable place in the community of nations.

It is no use saying that the adoption of aggressive nationalism by the United States is unthinkable in the light of its traditions. The traditions of a nation are set by the purposes to which its rulers are able to persuade or to force the masses to lend their support; and those purposes are, in part at least, the outcome of the impersonal drive of the economic and social system. The relations between the United States and Latin

America show that this result is possible; necessity would give the prospect of such a result a theatre for wider operations. And, unless special care be taken, the economic position of the United States may easily create that possibility, for its productive capacity has so far outstripped the power of its people, given the present distribution of wealth, to consume what is profitably available in the market, that at its present technological level there must either be exports on a massive scale, or unemployment of a size that might well exceed the unemployment of the Great Depression. No doubt the difficulty might be transcended by a vast redistribution of wealth in the United States, which would increase the grimly low purchasing power of those whom President Roosevelt called the "underprivileged," perhaps one-third of the population of America. But there are no signs that American business men would accept a redistribution of such magnitude. There are no signs, either, that they would accept the taxation implied in a programme of public works which sought, like the programme of the National Resources Planning Board, to abolish slums, to provide decent schools, to give universal access to cheap electricity, and to help the small farmer out of his present insuperable difficulties. The choice seems to lie between long-term investment, at very low rates of interest, in the great backward areas of the world in which, with reasonable capital equipment, there are immense potential markets, and straightforward economic imperialism of that more modern type which does not physically dominate a country, but achieves the same effect by penetration to the point where the result is indistinguishable. The first is a policy compatible with the slow building of a world organization to cope with the causes of war. The second is a policy which makes any attempt at a world organization inevitably futile and leads, quite certainly, to a third world war.

There is no real certainty which of these policies America will choose. The Second World War has brought into being the United Nations, to which, differently from its attitude to the League of Nations in 1919–20, America has committed itself. But the organization is hardly born; and it is already clear that, before its ability to function is even evident, the major powers, and not least the United States itself, have found terms of common agreement only on that plane of verbal rhetoric where words are used as counters to conceal ideas and purposes. The ideological abyss between Russia and the United States is profound. It is an abyss which has intense repercussions on every aspect of their relations. It makes each suspicious of the other's policies on armament, on foreign investments, on public loans, even on scientific research. Americans watch with resentment the development of a Southeastern Europe very largely penetrated by Russian influence and increasingly hopeful of Russian protection. Perhaps even more, they are suspicious of the growth of Russian influence in Asia, its patronage there of nationalist movements, the developing interest in its economic methods displayed by China and India. The Russian attraction in the Far East is paralleled by its drive through the Middle East towards the Mediterranean, which, so obviously, is regarded with grave uneasiness by Great Britain as well as by the United States. The United Nations has begun its labours in a world in which there is far less clarity of purpose than seemed possible in 1919. Then, even though the United States had refused to join the League, there had been everywhere a conscious and genuine hope that "a war to end war" had been waged. In 1945 the San Francisco Charter was drafted on the eve of one of the most overwhelming victories in the history of mankind. It had been a war "for freedom and democracy." Every regime which had linked its fortunes to the Berlin–Rome–Tokyo Axis had been broken into pieces. Yet it became uncertain whose freedom and victory had been won even before the cheers for the statesmen, who had planned the victory, had died away.

3

WHY is this? What is it that has left all thinking men and women in doubt whether the problem of peace has been solved? It is, no doubt, true that there is a deeper horror of war among the masses of the world than at any previous time. It is even true that few statesmen would dare to proclaim that they are embarking on an offensive war, or even that they seek objectives which are ultimately unobtainable except by means of war. Yet not even the depth of the will to peace is able to secure peace. Hardly anyone wanted war in 1914; hardly anyone wanted war in 1939. Above all, no one can study the policies of Woodrow Wilson and Franklin Roosevelt, both before and during the early part of the first two world wars, without the conviction that forces outside themselves drove each of them into a war that was not of his making. Now the Second World War has been won on the battlefield, and the United States has to find ways and means, in association with other nations, of avoiding the drift to a third catastrophe.

I have given reasons why I do not believe that this drift could be arrested by the return of the United States to isolationism. I have sought to show that no major war could now occur without an effort by some of the belligerents to draw upon the productive capacity of the United States for munitions of war; and that no American government would be strong enough to resist the pressure of its citizens to engage in trading activities with one or more belligerent nations, any more than it could avoid being affected by an outcome of the struggle which would seriously alter the *status quo ante bellum*. More than this: I have argued also that an attempt by the United States to protect itself through a world hegemony which relies upon its own strength would ultimately become incompatible with the maintenance of democratic institutions in its civilization; and in the light of historic experience this suggests that the abandonment of democracy would lead directly to American territorial adventures, which would lead to the very war it was desired to avoid because these adventures would cut right across the basic interests of other powerful nations which would fight rather than abandon them.

I therefore believe that the deliberate militarization of the United States, so that it confined security in its own strength, is no guarantee of international peace; on the contrary, it would in all probability make pretty certain a rapid drift to war. I do not, moreover, accept the view that a working military alliance between the United States and Great Britain would have in it the real assurance of peace. For while it is no doubt true that there are objectives which the two countries would agree to secure, whatever the cost, each has important objectives which the other could not be counted upon to support by force of arms. Certainly the United States would not support any effort by Great Britain to maintain its suzerainty over the West Indies and Hong Kong, or over the Malay States; and it follows from this that only an expansionist United States is likely to regard itself as having a paramount interest in defending whatever conditions, especially territorial, the British government may regard as fundamental to its suzerainty there. It is conceivable that Great Britain would protect Turkey if Russia sought direct access to the Eastern Mediterranean by assuming control over the Dardanelles; it is unlikely that, in such circumstances, the United States would pledge its resources to the automatic support of Great Britain save for the interests concerned in the politics of oil. Nor do I think it probable that the government of Great Britain would guarantee unconditional military support to American policy in the Far East, in Latin America, or in Alaska, especially since American policy in Alaska might raise issues of such profound strategic import for Russia that British public opinion would insist upon the retention of freedom of action by its government to make possible a judgment upon the circumstances in each case.

I believe, therefore, that a general alliance involving automatic military support by the two countries would be difficult to attain. At the most, a mutual agreement for common action would have to be limited to special spheres of common interest, the Caribbean, for example. This means that the only way America can hope to throw its weight behind a peace-preserving procedure is by membership in a body like the United Nations; to this the Congress of the United States has agreed. It has accepted the consequential implication that where the Security Council of the organization agrees on measures to prevent or stop aggression by any nation, the consent of Congress will not be necessary to the fulfilment of any obligation the Security Council may impose upon the United States. This is really to say that if the members of the Security Council are really determined to see that collective action is taken against actual or potential aggression, they have the power to do so without seeking further authority from the elected legislatures upon which their governments are likely to depend. On any showing, it is a big step forward in American thinking that Congress should have agreed that this vital part of the right to declare war should be transferred from the legislative to the executive branch of the American government. For practical purposes, this is to say, the authority to use the power of the United States against aggression is vested in the president of the United States.

No one who compares this decision with the determined refusal of membership in the League of Nations in 1919 can fail to see that experience has persuaded the government of the United States to set its will to peace in a new institutional perspective. That does not make it possible to evade the fact that the will to peace does not exist in a vacuum. It is important to remember that the responsibility of the Security Council is likely to be effective only in the degree that its members, who while they are permanent have each a veto upon action, have either an equal interest in the maintenance of peace, or, alternatively, the conviction that the prevention of aggression is, in all circumstances, the highest interest of the members. It is not mere cynicism, but solid experience, which compels the insistence that it will not be easy to attain this level of responsibility. It was evaded in every major test that the League of Nations confronted during its tragic career. It was evaded, notably, in the Italo–Abyssinian dispute when the fact of aggression was beyond discussion; on that occasion, the half-hearted attempt to impose sanctions on Italy was dismissed by Mr. Neville Chamberlain as "midsummer madness." It was evaded again in the Sino–Japanese dispute, despite the overwhelming evidence of the Lytton Report and the willingness of the United States to be associated with any action the League might take. On that occasion, not only did the British Foreign Secretary, Sir John (later Viscount) Simon brush aside contemptuously any idea of collective responsibility; but in the House of Commons Mr. Leopold Amery, who had previously been, and was soon to be again, a cabinet minister, defended the right of Japan to aggression in China on grounds which assumed that evil practice in the past justified evil practice in the present. All the major aggressions of Hitlerite Germany, moreover, were either not dealt with by the League at all, or were dealt with by specially devised procedure outside its framework, as in Munich in 1938, mostly with the purpose of preventing Russia from having any say in the decisions reached. And it is perhaps a part of the fantastic illogic of the League's history that what was virtually its death-bed act was the expulsion of Russia from its membership for the invasion of Finland, an expulsion which was probably one of the few instances in its record in which the members of the League acted with a full heart.

It is thus evident from the inter-war years that the will to peace requires something more than a formal institutional apparatus if it is to function successfully. And, indeed, in the brief period that has elapsed since the defeat of Germany and Japan, the manœuvres for position that are taking place are not a good augury of success in this field. No one can honestly feel that British policy in Greece, or Italy, or the Middle East, sets concern for peace above strategic and imperialist considerations. No one, either, can argue with confidence that the Russian transformation of Poland, Hungary, Rumania, Bulgaria, and, in a lesser de-

gree, Czechoslovakia and Yugoslavia, into something like satellite powers, whether on strategic or on economic grounds, is more than a series
of steps in exactly the kind of power politics which preceded the Second
World War. This, certainly, is the American view. American policy
in China, however nobly its motives are explained in presidential mani-
festos, has the objective result of building a China in which the foreign investor will have full elbow-room for profitable speculation and
concessions. American policy in Japan may seek to destroy the more
aggressive forms of its militarism; but it makes no serious attempt to
discover and unleash, much less to support, the popular forces there,
lest the intellectual outlook of such a Japan prove more sympathetic
to Russian than to American ideology. American policy in the Middle East looks as though its basic motive is to safeguard a full share
for its own vested interests in the development of the oil resources
of that region. There is even a good deal to be said for the view that
American diplomacy is using the immense economic power of the United
States to arrest, not least in Britain and France and Italy, the drift of opinion and experience to the Left. This brings out, with increasing clarity,
the abyss between the ideology of the American economy, with its emphasis on the private ownership of the vital means of production, and the
emphasis of the European economy upon a public ownership of these
means, which is based upon an increasing acceptance of socialist principles.

I do not for one moment suggest that these grave divergencies of view
are in themselves any warrant for refusing to attempt the United Nations
experiment. Without it we are quite certainly doomed to a large-scale
battle for power which must end in war. With it, there is a chance that
we may have time to resolve enough of the major contradictions in the
present situation to make possible the slow growth of confidence in international institutions, and the slow but decisive acceptance of their
authority in all matters that concern the preservation of peace. But we
ought to embark upon the experiment with a far clearer insight into its
difficulties than we had in 1919. The optimism which surrounded the birth
of the League of Nations was as ill-founded as the confidence which assumed that it could work in isolation from the attitudes and interests of its
members. That optimism and that confidence led public opinion to look
for results quite outside the premises which limited the possibilities of
action, especially on the points of critical importance. We ought to be
quite clear that similar limitations obtain at the present time.

There is the grave limitation set by the American fear that its economic
power would be abused by being employed to assist in the growth of
socialist experiment abroad. It was evident during the financial negotiations over the loan to Great Britain in 1945–46 that American business
men and American politicians regard with deep distrust the existence
of a Labour government in Britain. Their stereotype of wisdom is set
by their own system which they so curiously call "free enterprise." They

watch with suspicion and fear the prospect of a successful socialism in Russia and the growth of a large sphere of government-owned and government-controlled industry elsewhere. They dislike the emphasis in China on the need to evolve a system of social relationships which would by-pass the long struggle between capitalist privilege and the general interest. They are aware that the growing intensity of intervention by government in the economic area limits the opportunities of American penetration, and that the intellectual repercussions of this on their position in the United States itself are growing profound. They are therefore tempted either to refrain from economic assistance altogether, or to give it on terms which strengthen the survival power of class privilege, in the country which needs aid. The inescapable result of this policy, in the long run, would be to make Washington and Moscow the focal points in a future struggle for economic independence in which the world would be even more grimly divided into American and Russian spheres of influence.

But any division of this kind makes disarmament at least difficult, and perhaps impossible. For no country which is the focal point of a sphere of influence can afford to leave itself open to successful military challenge; and every step it takes to safeguard itself from that danger involves a similar step on the part of its rival. More: once this frame of mind is the basis of policy, economic relations become transformed into military alliances, with the need in the greater powers to see that their satellites are able, if not to defend themselves successfully, at least to stave off disaster until the power of their patron can be brought into the field. No one can read the history of the critical year 1940–41 without seeing that the shape of United States neutrality was determined by the necessity of safeguarding its own interests by large-scale assistance to Great Britain. No one, either, can help seeing that the future of any country in which, as in Greece or Hungary, there is a profound cleavage between a small group of privileged capitalists and the great mass of the people will be largely determined by the degree to which that small group can count upon external aid in its struggle to retain ascendency and, to that degree, will be encouraged to go on struggling to restore the *status quo* from which it derived advantage. So long as there is the hope that American ideology will permeate the use of American economic power abroad, it is difficult to make the United Nations a system in which any important drive to aggression can be regarded objectively.

We can go further than this. One of the main reasons for the failure of the League of Nations was its refusal to take seriously its vital function of assisting in the revision of treaties. The contrast between the concessions made to the Weimar Republic in the period before 1933, when everyone knew that Germany was unable to back its demands by force, and those made to Hitler after 1933, when everyone knew that he must gamble on securing by force anything he could not secure by consent, is notorious. So, alas, was the tenderness of the League to aggressive powers like Japan and Italy. There was a persistent refusal, during the history of the League, to face squarely the implications of Litvinov's famous phrase that "peace is indivisible." And even if we agree that part of this refusal was the outcome of a deep hatred of war, of a fear that its cost would always be disproportionate to its results, it is no less certain that part of the refusal was based on ideological considerations. Mussolini was virtually condemned for his attack on Abyssinia; but the central reason for the abandonment of sanctions was the fear among British and French statesmen that his overthrow by the use of sanctions would leave a communist Italy as the residuary legatee of his broken power. Japan also was virtually condemned after the Manchurian "incident" of 1931; but nothing else followed from the condemnation, mainly because Great Britain was more willing to see China sacrificed to Japanese imperialism than to join in a full-scale war for the destruction of Japanese imperialism. In each case it is clear that, behind the decision arrived at by the League, the powers directly concerned were anxious about the social consequences of sanctions—an anxiety which prevented the procedure against aggression from ever having an objective character. And the powers indirectly concerned were anxious not to become involved in a situation in which they felt themselves materially indifferent to the outcome.

Exactly this situation will be repeated in the United Nations. The great powers have insisted upon retaining the right of veto in the Security Council; they even retain that right where they are themselves directly involved in some particular case with which they are concerned. This is to say that they have begun by loading the dice against the kind of judgment which it is, especially in the early years of peace, imperative that the organization should make swiftly and decisively if its authority is to become real. It is impossible to doubt that this right of veto is retained because of the depth of mutual suspicion among the powers. How deep that suspicion goes is shown by their inability to agree upon a common policy about the future of Germany and Japan. It is shown again by the extent to which ideological prepossessions enter into their attitudes to the changing equilibrium of authority within their States and in their colonial possessions which have been affected by the war. Americans are deeply disturbed by the prospect that British concern for "law and order" in the Middle East may easily result in the maintenance of its citizens in the misery of feudal exploitation; but they refuse to agree that their policy in China, also pursued in the name of law and order, has precisely the same result from a different angle. They refuse to see that their policy in China has the inevitable effect of maintaining those interests in power in China which are favourable to the historic policy of the Open Door, which means, in effect, the opportunity for American investment in China on America's terms.

It is, indeed, a matter of common agreement that only unity among the great powers will enable the United Nations to work. The moment that unity breaks down, there will be a scramble not only to form alliances within its framework, but also to remobilize the latent power of Germany and of Japan as a factor in the creation of a new balance of power. This danger makes it obvious that the kind of peace imposed on Japan, for example, is a matter of supreme importance to the United States, Russia, and China. It is one thing to leave the essential possessions of Japan, the Kuriles, for example, and the Pacific Islands, and Southern Sakhalin, as Japanese possessions; it is another thing to give them as air bases to one or more of the powers; it is another thing, again, to use them as the basis of an international security force maintained in these territories as a safeguard against the revival of Japanese aggression. In the same way, it makes a large difference to the whole future of the Far East whether the control of Japanese industry is left in the hands of the Zaibatsu, or whether a Japanese State power is created which is able to control the vast corporations the Zaibatsu have built up. With this question is intimately bound up the future of the Japanese imperial monarchy as an institution. The American temptation is obviously to try to maintain the Emperor as a puppet through whom the State Department makes known its decisions; equally clearly, the interest of China and of Russia is to get rid altogether of an institution which was used, and could be used again, as a source of indoctrination of the Japanese masses in that combination of feudalism and capitalism of which the imperialistic policy of Japan was the outcome. But if the imperial throne is abolished, it is highly probable that the essential Japanese outlook will turn towards friendship with Russia. This reorientation would obviously have a profound effect, negatively, upon American influence in the Far East.

A good deal of the outcome of American policy towards Japan is decisive of its policy towards China; and this, in its turn, influences in a high degree the relations of the United States with Russia and Great Britain. If America keeps a relatively strong Japan in existence, it leaves in being a strong threat to the Chinese future, and that threat, in its turn, requires the swift advance of China towards industrialization and democracy. But the very need for swiftness is, in the circumstances of the next generation, a temptation to American finance-capitalism to preserve conservative interests in China and to make major Chinese economic concessions to Americans the price of this preservation. In this is implied, almost *ipso facto,* Russian encouragement of "Communist" China to balance the threat of an American-dominated China, which is, in its turn, protected by a new Japan schooled to dependence on American patronage. And behind these immense issues lie the problems of the future of the colonial peoples in Asia and of the valuable raw materials which are at once a source of profit and of power. The successful working of the United Nations will very largely depend upon whether, in the first instance, America can reach a *modus vivendi* with Russia about the answers to these problems, and, in the second instance, a *modus vivendi* with Great Britain.

But the *modus vivendi* is not an operation in a vacuum. While it is true that the historic policy of the United States, so well exemplified in its treatment of the Philippines, has been on a higher plane than that of any European nation with colonial interests, it is also true that this historic policy was in large part the outcome of an internal economic situation in the United States which changed slowly between 1900 and 1914, and ever more rapidly after the end of the First World War. The end of the Second World War marks two vital changes in the character of the issues the nations face. First, it has made Asia central and no longer peripheral to the problems of Europe and America; second, it has made them central at a time when the export both of capital goods and of consumers' goods by the United States is vital to the maintenance of a stable economy of its own. And these two changes have become urgent just at the moment when Russia is not only the second strongest military power in the world, but when its military strength supports a way of life which business leaders in the United States regard with unconcealed hostility. The Russian way of life, moreover, seeks as clearly to prevent external economic exploitation as the American way of life inherently drives its business leaders at once to seek for that exploitation and to regard its critics as dangerous stumbling blocks in the way of the fulfilment of America's "manifest destiny." There is, to put it shortly, a grave contradiction between the objective purpose of the United Nations and the impersonal drive of economic forces in America.

I am not suggesting that this contradiction is confined to the United States; it obviously is also true of Great Britain, and it would be gravely true both of Germany and Japan if they were permitted to return to normal international relations merely as impoverished editions of their former selves. But the contradiction is supremely important in the United States simply because the economic power of the United States will be the outstanding factor shaping the life of the United Nations. If we agree that American isolationism is now no longer a practicable policy, or, rather, that even an attempt to return to it on the part of the United States, would begin, inevitably, a new race for empire, which would render it imperative for all the great powers to take what precautions they could against the almost explicit threat to their own interests of American expansionism, then we have to discover ways and means of shaping the power of the United States so as to transcend the contradiction with which it presents our age. Just as war was necessary to deny the right of Germany and Japan to begin a new epoch of aggressive expansion, so this discovery is necessary to prevent the implications of the American economy being found, perhaps fifteen or twenty years from now, incompatible with the working of the United Nations. For that incompatibility has already begun to show signs of opening a new epoch in which there is developing a search for a new balance of power in which the parties will do all they can to shift its incidence to their advantage; and this will ultimately have the same disastrous effect on the United

Nations as it had upon the League of Nations. In international politics it is not only necessary to will what is right; it is also urgent to know what it is right to will.

4

THE first great urgency is to bring wisdom to bear upon the making of American foreign policy at that point in its constitutional framework where the power to make decisions has been placed. The traditional working of the system has had three major results. The power, first, of actual diplomatic negotiation with foreign countries has been, for practical negotiation, what Jefferson declared it must inevitably be, "executive altogether." Sometimes the president has invited one or more senators, or other figures of eminence in political life, to participate in the making of executive decisions; thus President Roosevelt invited Senator Vandenberg of Michigan, and ex-Governor Stassen of Minnesota to be members of the delegation he sent to San Francisco to assist in making the draft charter of the United Nations. No doubt, on most occasions, there has been some preliminary consultation with senators; few presidents have been foolish enough not to take soundings in the legislature before they actually submitted a treaty for a ratification which demands a two-thirds vote for approval. Even Woodrow Wilson, who tried his opponents high, attempted some small degree of mediation by taking with him to Versailles Mr. Henry White, whose affiliations were wholly Republican. But the decision is the president's alone; and this is perhaps why Charles C. Pinckney, when he explained the mechanism of the Constitution to the South Carolina Convention, argued that "political caution and republican jealousy rendered it impossible for us to vest it in the president alone." [4] Davie of North Carolina offered a view which perhaps explains more precisely what Pinckney meant by "republican jealousy." He showed how difficult it was to reconcile the divergent outlook of the big and the small states on the one hand, and the states with and without an interest in foreign trade on the other. This division, he said, "made it indispensable to give to the senators, as representatives of states, the power of making, or rather ratifying, treaties. Although it militates against every idea of just proportion that the little state of Rhode Island should have the same suffrage with Virginia or the great commonwealth of Massachusetts, yet the small states would not consent to confederate without an equal voice in the formation of treaties." [5]

It is worth noting that attempts were made in the Federal Convention at Philadelphia to associate the House of Representatives with the treaty-making power. They were rejected by large majorities, and the opinion expressed by Roger Sherman that the need for secrecy would be violated if the consent of the House had to be obtained seems to have been the

---

[4] Jonathan Elliot (ed.), *The Debates in the Several State Conventions on the Adoption of the Federal Constitution* (Washington, 1821), Vol. IV, p. 265.
[5] *Ibid.*, p. 120.

central factor in their rejection.[6] No doubt the major reason for the final compromise was the desire to limit the power of the executive; and no doubt, also, the traditions of the period of Confederation counted for much in the decision. There is no reason to suppose either that the ratification of the Senate was regarded as a method of democratic control, or that the Convention was disturbed by the prospect of possible conflict between the Senate and the president. That prospect was touched upon; but the remark of James Wilson to the ratifying convention of Pennsylvania that the check of the one upon the other would "produce security for the people" most probably represented the general opinion.[7] That no inherent struggle for the balance in the treaty-making power was widely expected is, I think, shown by the surprised indignation of George Washington when the Senate insisted upon the private discussion of his Indian treaty. We can see from the diaries of John Quincy Adams and of William Maclay how immediately the argument began which has lasted down to the present time. The president has always resented the exercise of its discretion by the Senate; and the Senate has equally resented any effort by the president to make the exercise of its power a purely formal matter.

From the first active years of the Constitution the conflict between the president and the Senate has been one of the most vital and discussed of its features. To win the assent of the Senate to a treaty has probably caused more agony and resentment among presidents and Secretaries of State than any other problem save that of appointments. It has caused much confusion and profound irritation among foreign powers; they have never been able quite to understand why, after a long and careful negotiation with the State Department, the Senate should be able, often on grounds that are largely withheld frrom the public view, to make the whole of their labours sterile by the direct rejection of a treaty or by insistence upon amendments which either the President or the other party to the treaty felt unable on various grounds to accept. Since, especially, the rejection of the Treaty of Versailles, with the consequential refusal of the Senate to permit American membership in the League of Nations, a furious campaign against the Senate's participation in the treaty-making power has been waged. That the Senate should take seriously the powers conferred on it by the Constitution has seemed indefensible by the critics on a number of grounds. Sometimes it is argued that the main motive of senatorial interference is either personal or partisan or both. Sometimes exception is taken to the fact that a minority of the Senate can undemocratically hold up a treaty which the majority approves by the hard necessities of the two-thirds rule. Sometimes the criticism is built upon the ground that the separation of powers tends to make the Senate anxious to obtain credit at the expense of the president, and thus to make it amend or reject treaties on institutional grounds un-

[6] Max Farrand (ed.), *Records of the Federal Convention* (New Haven: Yale University Press, 1911), Vol. II, pp. 392-94, 538.
[7] Elliot, *op. cit.*, p. 507.

connected with the substance of the actual treaties themselves. The determination of the Senate to make its power to ratify a real power is beyond question; and there must have been few presidents who have not felt, often with bitterness, that it represented, above all, a deliberate attempt of senators to encroach upon the proper sphere of the executive authority in foreign affairs.

Certainly it is the determination of the Senate which has led to the emergence of that twilight world in American diplomacy which is the third traditional outcome of the constitutional position. The Senate must confirm the major diplomatic appointments, and it must be persuaded to ratify treaties. Since the exercise of these powers causes great embarrassment to the president, especially when he belongs to a different party from that of the majority in the Senate, he seeks to evade its compulsions by the use of special envoys who have no official status, or by the use of "understandings" with foreign powers, which are not regarded as treaties or are made by virtue of his position as commander-in-chief of the Armed Forces of the United States; by these means he evades the need to secure the co-operation of the Senate in carrying out a policy upon which he has decided. Under President Wilson, Colonel E. M. House acted in this capacity; though House did not hold any official position, he toured Europe, where he discussed with prime ministers and foreign secretaries matters of the highest moment, some of them involving decisions which gave the President the power to present the Congress with a *fait accompli* which it had hardly any alternative but to accept; and President Franklin Roosevelt used Mr. Harry Hopkins during the Second World War in a similar way. One has only to note the supreme example of an "understanding"—the exchange arranged between President Roosevelt and Mr. Churchill in 1940 of the fifty destroyers for the bases leased to the United States on the Caribbean territory of Great Britain—to see how far-reaching can be the outcome of an "understanding." Nothing, indeed, shows more clearly that, subject to the extreme contingencies of impeachment, a president who is determined to have his way in foreign affairs is unlikely to find the Constitution a decisive barrier against his will.

It is unnecessary to deny that the present powers of the Senate in foreign affairs are an unquestionable handicap to the case of foreign relations with the United States; quite obviously they are. But the rhetorical passion which has accompanied most criticism of the Senate's jurisdiction is not borne out by the careful measurement of the position. The State Department has published a list of the treaties submitted to the Senate by the president between 1789 and 1934; there are nine hundred and sixty-nine of them. Of these, six hundred and eighty-two were ratified in the form in which the president submitted them, and fifteen were rejected. Of the others, one hundred and seventy-three were amended, and ninety-nine were either withdrawn by the president, or allowed to lapse, with no pressure for final action; and it should be added that no treaty was rejected until 1860, that is, for almost half the life of the United States. In the case of the rejected treaties, it would be difficult for any detached observer not to agree that the Senate was wise in refusing to approve General Grant's very dubious attempt to secure the annexation of San Domingo in 1869–70; while if the Senate's treatment of the Peace of Versailles is difficult to defend, it is difficult not to admit that its view was consistently upheld by the voters of America in election after election. The rejection of the Olney–Pauncefote Treaty of 1897 is explicable and, I think, justified by the fact that its effect would have been largely to deprive the Senate of any say in the making of Anglo-American policy. Large numbers of the amendments which presidents have been asked to make were attempts either to secure additional benefits to the United States, or to emphasize traditional American doctrines to which insufficient weight had been allowed by the negotiators; or else they concerned quite trivial matters which caused no difficulty. The average time which has elapsed, moreover, from the submission of a treaty to its ratification has been two months. I do not think this can be regarded as excessive if the Senate is to take its function of ratification with any seriousness, since it includes both the hearings and discussion by its Foreign Relations Committee, as well as the full debate in the Senate as a whole.[8]

"The fate of the Treaty of Versailles," Professor Holt has written, "turned the attention of thoughtful people to the treaty-making power of the United States. They saw that the exercise of that power had produced such bitter conflicts between the president and the Senate, and had so increased the opportunities for political warfare unconnected with the merits of the question, that many treaties had been lost. They knew that the ratification of nearly every important treaty had been endangered by a constitutional system which, instead of permitting a decision solely on the merits of a question, produces impotence and friction."[9] These are strong and, I think, unjustified words. There is little evidence to show that the material interests of the United States have suffered seriously by the form given to the treaty-making power by the Constitution. There is a good deal of evidence to prove that much of the conflict it has engendered has been at least as much the fault of the president as it has been of the Senate. The rejection of the San Domingo treaty in 1870 was based on well-founded suspicions that it was the result of corrupt agreement between the president's advisers and a dubious clique in San Domingo. Most of John Hay's difficulties with the Senate were the outcome of his sheer ineptitude in handling the members of the Foreign Relations Committee; he blamed on their obstinacy what was at least as much the outcome of his curious combination of weakness and insolent contempt. Henry Cabot Lodge organized the defeat of the Treaty of

[8] Royden J. Dangerfield, *In Defense of the Senate* (Norman: University of Oklahoma Press, 1933), is a full-scale and careful discussion. See also my *American Presidency*, Chap. 5.

[9] W. Stull Holt, *Treaties Defeated by the Senate* (Baltimore: Johns Hopkins Press, 1933), p. 307.

Versailles; but it is equally important to realize that he owed his victory, at least in part, to the lofty disdain with which the Senate was treated by President Wilson, both in the making of the Treaty and in his passionate campaign to secure its ratification.

It is, I think, pertinent to add here that there is little evidence to suggest, despite enthusiastic advocacy on the other side, that the history of the League of Nations would have been very different if the United States had joined it in 1920. For the period up to 1932 at least, the temper of American public opinion was strongly in favour of avoiding any serious commitments abroad, and the presidents in office equally strongly upheld that view. In the same period the influence of the United States would have been thrown against any effort to come to an understanding with Russia; while the great Morgan loan of the nineteen-twenties to Mussolini does not suggest that it would have been a liberal influence in the handling of fascist nations. Nor do we know of anything in the record to suggest that the membership of the United States would have helped in any way to prevent the accession of Hitler to power. In all the major policy-making of the League there was usually close, if unofficial, contact with American observers and with the State Department. The great Chicago speech of President Roosevelt in 1937 on the need "to quarantine aggressors" would not have had any greater effect on a mind like that of Mr. Neville Chamberlain had it been made in Geneva; and it must not be forgotten that the evil agreement of Munich in 1938 was received with at least as much satisfaction in the United States as in Great Britain. Taken as a whole, it is difficult to feel that the history of international relations between 1920 and 1939 would have been very different if the Senate had ratified the Treaty of Versailles without amendment. If it might have been more willing, through Secretary Stimson, to arrest Japanese aggression in China by the use of sanctions than was Sir John Simon, as British Foreign Secretary, there is no reason to suppose that it would have been any more anxious to impose sanctions on Italy during Mussolini's war against Abyssinia, or over the Nazi militarization of the Rhineland, or over the invasions of Austria and Czechoslovakia which were its aftermath. And since all the negotiations which led to the outbreak of the Second World War in 1939 were made without regard to the League, the early neutrality of the United States, and the very intelligible desire of President Roosevelt to maintain it up to, perhaps even beyond, the point of actual danger to its interests, surely make it plain that in the degree to which the League sought to involve America in European affairs, to that extent the president and the Senate alike would have been compelled by the public opinion of the time to refuse obligations which a large majority of Americans felt to be unnecessary and unjustified.

It will be noted that Professor Holt, in his condemnation of the Senate's power in foreign affairs, objects to opposition to treaties on party grounds where these do not touch the merits of the treaty involved, though he himself agrees that foreign policy may legitimately be made the ground of party difference. British citizens who look back on the inter-war years are not likely to dissent from this second conclusion. The foreign policy of any government is a basic index to the general policy it seeks to fulfil; and if there is a real difference between the philosophy of the party in power and the party in opposition, it is nowhere more likely to be evident than in foreign affairs. If, as in the United States, the difference between parties is as difficult to discern as it there is, *in abstracto* there is a real basis for Professor Holt's view. But it is a counsel of perfection when the fight for office is as deep and bitter as it is in America. It is inevitable that a party out of power should, in normal circumstances, do what it can to discredit its opponent; and the corrective must be supplied by the working of public opinion. So long as party politics exist, every subject is necessarily within its boundaries. To ask politicians to act like saints in a realm where they see advantage in acting like politicians is hardly a counsel of wisdom. The remedy for this difficulty must be found in another direction.

Let us remember first that no one has ever seriously proposed that the president should have uncontrolled authority in foreign affairs. There thus emerge two questions to be solved, one of procedure and one which goes deeper into substance, even though its form be that of procedure. It is sometimes proposed that the control of treaties should be given to the Congress as a whole. In defence of this, it is argued that there is nothing sacrosanct about the present arrangement, that the conditions under which it was made have altogether altered, and that the transference of the treaty-making power from the Senate to the whole Congress would prevent a small number of states, with a small proportion of the population, from exercising what is virtually a veto power over the representatives of states in which the majority of Americans live. Certainly it is impossible today to justify the two-thirds rule; and joint resolutions of both Houses have already been the basis of vital decisions. It was by joint resolution that America annexed both Texas and Hawaii; the same process was used to end the war with Germany in 1920 and to ratify the entrance of the United States into the International Labour Office. On general grounds there is no reason to suppose that the extension of this practice would result in any additional weakness not now inherent in the American system.

But this would not meet the central problem in the American Constitution. That problem consists in the fact that American foreign relations are conducted at two levels, one of which involves direct contact between America and some foreign power or powers, with decision resulting from the direct contact, and the other, which also involves decision, being outside any area in which direct contact is possible. To meet this situation two proposals, not necessarily incompatible, have been made. The first is the regular appearance of the Secretary of State before the Foreign Affairs Committees of the two Houses of Congress. There, it is suggested, he should give information when required and, if necessary, submit himself to cross-examination; when secrecy is desirable, the Committees would be in a position to enforce this, as they are at the present time. The second and more complex proposal is to associate a permanent congressional body with the president and the Secretary of State in the making of foreign policy. Professor Peffer proposes that it should consist, apart from the president and the Secretary of State, of the Secretaries of War, the Navy, and the Treasury, and the chairman and two ranking minority members of the Committees on Foreign Affairs in the Senate and the House of Representatives; no doubt he would now limit the two services to representation through the Secretary of Defense. "This body," writes Professor Peffer, "would meet regularly with the President, not as at present, when the President calls in such members of both Houses as he chooses, if and when he chooses, and informs them of whatever he wishes them to know, principally in order to induce them to win congressional approval of some specific act. It would meet regularly under the chairmanship of the President and with him survey the whole state of world politics and its bearing on American interests. It would take up specific issues that arise and demand decision, thrash out a decision with the President, and sponsor it thereafter. It would be a participant and an active agent, not just a listener. It would be in effect a cabinet for foreign affairs, a recognized arm of the government functioning on an equal plane with the President." [10]

I do not myself believe that either of these proposals is practicable. It is one thing for the Secretary of State to appear on some special occasion. But regularity of appearance would raise issues of his relation to the president, of the revelation of documents, of the problems created when the Congress is of one party complexion and the president of another. It is not only that the position of the Secretary would be impossible, both when the president is unwilling to have information disclosed, and when the Secretary gives answers unsatisfactory to the president to whom alone he is constitutionally responsible; there is the further difficulty that almost all presidents have kept some parts of foreign policy in their own hands and carried it out through agents of their own. The position of a Secretary of State who appeared before the committee and was questioned on some issue about which he had no knowledge would be one which compelled him to forfeit either the confidence of the committee, by showing that there were areas of policy in his own Department from which he was excluded, or the confidence of the president, by committing him to policies about which, in a fundamental way, he was bound to be uninformed. Under President Wilson, for example, neither Mr. Bryan nor Mr. Lansing could have undertaken the function envisaged in this proposal; and under President Roosevelt it could hardly have been performed either by Mr. Hull or Mr. Stettinius. This proposal altogether omits consideration of the intensely personal relation between a presi-

[10] Peffer, *op. cit.*, p. 216.

dent and his cabinet, and, above all, of the important fact that most great presidents have, to a large extent, been their own Secretaries of State. Any institutional process which sought to disturb this relation would either rapidly break down, or make a basic alteration in the character of the president's office quite disproportionate to any gain which might result from its operation.

This is still more true of the larger proposal. Whether its status be that of a convention of the Constitution or of a change made by formal amendment, the subordination of the president implied would make his position intolerable. He could not, in any case, sit in a "cabinet of foreign affairs" where four of his cabinet officers, all of whom owed their appointments to him, were able to argue against him, to intrigue against him, even to vote against his views; very early in the evolution of this committee he would clearly require from its cabinet members, as a condition of their appointment, that they act solely under his direction. Nor is it easy to see how colleagueship of an intimate kind is possible on executive matters between two chairmen who may conceivably be members of the party opposed to the president, or even of a section within his own party opposed to his outlook, and who will almost certainly have attained the positions they hold on grounds of seniority alone. It is, further, highly unlikely that any president would be willing, while delicate negotiations were pending, to trust the knowledge of all their details to two important members of the opposing party; and the more vital the issues of policy involved, the more difficult would be the matter of confidence.

But the difficulties do not end there. There is no reason to suppose that this committee would always agree upon the decisions it made; as an election drew nearer, indeed, the smaller would be the chance of agreement. Where there are differences of outlook, is the final decision to be left to the president, subject only to the overriding power of Congress? Are the dissenting members of the committee to reveal their dissent and to utilize in their discussion of it the confidential material which has been disclosed to them? Can any guarantee be adequate, first, of necessary secrecy, and, second, against the danger that the congressional members of the committee may be subject to undue external pressure? Nor is it easy to see how the minority members of the committee could be of value unless they were able, supposing they were in agreement, to carry their party with them on the stand they took. There is, moreover, the special difficulty of personal relations. A "cabinet" presided over by President Grant, with Senator Sumner attending as the chairman of the Senate Committee on Foreign Relations, hardly seems made to secure either coherency or swiftness of decision. It is not even easy to conceive such a "cabinet" working smoothly with President Franklin Roosevelt as its chairman and the isolationist Senator Borah as the ranking minority member from the Republican party.

The truth, I think, is the very simple one that it is impossible to graft odd bits and pieces of the parliamentary system on to the congressional system. The British method works, in part because the conduct of foreign affairs is, as in America, "executive altogether," and in part because both the prime minister and the foreign secretary are by normal constitutional practice directly responsible to the House of Commons. The unity of policy comes from the fact that the alternative to parliamentary approval of foreign policy (or, indeed, any other cabinet policy) is either a different government or a general election, with the high possibility that, normally, the first involves the second. The essence of the British method is to make the executive at once a part of the legislature and, in all ordinary circumstances, its master. The cabinet tells parliament just as much as it considers desirable; the only effective way in which Parliament, if it so desires, can register its disaffection with what it is told is by turning out the government or making the prime minister feel that his position there is so insecure that it is better to seek the refreshment of his power through the hazards of a general election. No one from the Opposition in either of the Houses of Parliament could share cabinet responsibility without destroying the inherent principle of the British system.

Since the American Constitution is built upon the separation of powers, this second proposal would completely alter the balance of authority to which it is directed. A weak president would be at the mercy of the committee because he would not dare to dissent from it; and a strong president would reinforce all the opposition to him in Congress unless he was able continuously to dominate its work. The proposal would change the whole relation between the president and his cabinet by dividing the latter into members who were on the suggested committee and members who had no place on it. Nor is this all. The categories of foreign policy are of art and not of nature. Where a treaty, for example, has financial consequences, it would be difficult for members of the Appropriations Committees in the House and the Senate to be left outside; so, also, where it touches a subject like commerce or agriculture or the conditions of labour. Nor would the president be able to secure a direct and simple separation of foreign from domestic policy; for the interplay of the one upon the other is central to the problems he confronts. The whole basis upon which his authority rests would be jeopardized by the fact that in a vital aspect of power his independence would be controlled by men the basis of whose power is sectional, and not national like his. If the president himself were directly responsible to Congress, the whole nature of the Constitution would be changed, but at least his position would be easier and more intelligible than under a proposal which makes him subject to the constant interference of a committee which could not even guarantee him that the result of their co-operation would be the acceptance of his foreign policy by the legislature. For it is certainly hard to believe that because the president makes foreign policy in conjunction with four members of Congress, even granted that they are important members, the legislature would abdicate from its right of independent decision.

If the purpose of the proposal is somehow to democratize foreign policy, in part on the British model of making the prime minister and the foreign secretary answerable to Parliament for their policy, the answer, of course, is that the control of foreign policy in Great Britain is in no effective sense democratic. There is no obligation in the Crown to submit treaties to Parliament for ratification; where this has been done, as when Arthur Henderson was foreign secretary in the Labour government of 1929–31, it is not a decision by which his successors have been bound. There is no right in members of Parliament to receive any information the appropriate ministers do not think fit to disclose; their only remedy is a vote of censure upon the government. Every cabinet, moreover, has consistently refused to accept even an advisory committee on foreign affairs on which members of the Opposition have seats. The one element in the system that has any sort of democracy about it is the fact that by convention the government is bound to submit to the ordeal of debate whenever the Opposition demands it. I do not doubt the importance of his convention, not least the significance it has in illuminating the public mind on international affairs.

Nor does the proposal for the United States to accept the parliamentary system make any serious contribution to the solution of how to democratize foreign affairs. It replaces the check of the Senate on the power of the president by the check of the "cabinet on foreign affairs"; or, rather, it imposes an additional check on the president's discretion which there is a bare chance may be now and again of positive value. And it still leaves totally untouched two major problems: first, of interesting the voting community as a whole in the international process, so that its members may make their views count at the centre of power; and, second, of some proportionate relation between executive negotiation and legislative decision in the field of foreign affairs. I think it is probably true that no other country has been more successful than the United States in its effort to solve these problems, perhaps it is legitimate to say that none has been even so successful. For if one adds to the Senate's role in the treaty-making power the right of the two Houses of Congress to make investigations, with the far-reaching results obtained by the authority to subpœna witnesses and records, the outcome is the ability to dramatize international relations on that plane where their interest begins to assume some proportion to their importance. There is, no doubt, a good deal to be said against the Nye Committee on Armaments,[11] but if anyone seriously compares both the quality and range of its inquiries with those of the British Royal Commission held almost at the same time,[12] there cannot be any serious question that the Nye Committee, from every point of view, did a far more effective job. And whatever the weakness of the Nye Committee, it brought home to a wide group of Americans

[11] Though it was a far better investigating committee than its British analogue.
[12] The British Commission had no access, in fact, to the serious material it should have examined.

the grimly sordid nature of modern war, the deterioration it breeds in the relations it creates between the leaders of the defence forces in the modern community and industrial interests, which is of very high sociological value.

On the first procedural issue, then, I conclude that the simplest and most effective reform would be to leave the power over treaties where it now is, in the Senate, but to replace the two-thirds rule by the requirement of a simple majority. I see no significant advantage in bringing the House of Representatives into discussions of this kind; though I agree that there are no substantial arguments, save those of tradition and the undesirability of additional complexity, against such an association. But I think there would be serious dangers in any attempt to create a "cabinet on foreign affairs" of the type I have examined. Not only would it gravely impair the balance of power in the American Constitution; it would also threaten that prospect of presidential leadership in this area, which America, so far, has mostly been fortunate enough to enjoy in most of the serious emergencies by which it has been confronted. Nor do I think that one area of the Constitution could be reorganized in this way without important repercussions on other parts. If reorganization is to be attempted—and I do not doubt that it is necessary—it ought not to be a patch-work and half-conscious process, but one which is deliberately undertaken over the whole field of the Constitution in the light of a full discussion, and in which the nation is fully prepared for large-scale changes. A renovation of the American Constitution is too vital a task, upon which far too much hangs, to be done in any hole-and-corner way. If it is to be done, nothing less is necessary than the gravity and wisdom of that Philadelphia Convention of 1787 which still remains unsurpassed as a model exercise in the art of making a government.

The second essential issue, I have argued, though procedural in form, cuts deeper into matters of substance. If the United States is to choose membership in a body like the United Nations in preference to a return to isolationism or to a military alliance with another great power, it can play its proper part in such an international body only by accepting the limitations membership must involve. That means at present two things; at a later stage it may mean more. It means, first, that the distribution of powers in the American Constitution must not act as a barrier against the fulfilment of its obligations by the United States. The men of 1787, naturally enough, were planning for a small agrarian society, relatively homogeneous in character, and they did not have, and could not have had, any prevision either of the coming of giant industry or of the necessary uniformities in certain spheres of action that this evolution would require. The most obvious example is that of labour conditions, the control of which, save where they enter into the full-scale habits of interstate commerce, is still left to the separate states. It is, I think, obvious that any decisions taken by the United Nations, and accepted as binding by its members, must be taken to bind all units of American government, and thus cannot be limited to the federal area alone. If, for example, the United Nations General Assembly accepts a recommendation from its Economic Council to abolish all child labour below a certain age, that must become the law in Georgia and Mississippi, and neither state can be permitted so to operate the abolition that, while it applies to its white children, there is a tacit agreement to neglect its application to Negro children. In the light of experience it is even necessary to insist that the federal government take steps to make that application effective, and to answer for its effectiveness to the international authority.

Even more important is the prevention of aggression and its consequences. Early in the history of the United Nations its Security Council will have to organize ways and means of preventing aggression and of dealing with it immediately should it occur. This will certainly mean the acceptance of the responsibility to place certain armed forces, aeroplanes, ships, perhaps even bombs, at its instant disposition; it will mean that Congress has accepted, beforehand, their use for purposes of which the Security Council approves; and it may well mean an automatic right in the officers of the Security Council to carry out thorough-going inspection, military and civil, both of the armed forces of member nations and of the industries within them and their employment. This means that Congress as a whole, and the Senate in particular, must register a self-denying ordinance against any interference in this realm which might prevent or slow down the working of collective security. In a greater degree than in the past, the representatives of the United States on the different organs of the international authority must be empowered to record American decisions without the possibility of a subsequent refusal to implement them by the federal government on the instructions of Congress.

In one way this is an immense change in American policy; though there are angles of importance which, when analysed, put the change involved into its proper perspective. It means, formally the surrender of that power of final decision that we term sovereignty, and sovereignty is one of those frightening words round which men's emotions gather passionately. There is no escape from this surrender if the United Nations is to have the chance of practical effectiveness; for once a great nation refuses to abide by the obligations it has undertaken, the world is only too certain to lapse into the kind of power politics of which the nineteen-thirties present so complete and devastating an example. It therefore becomes essential that whatever undertakings are officially given by the representatives of America to the different organs of the United Nations, they shall be automatically accepted by the federal legislature. The legislature must therefore seek to make its mark on American policy in the United Nations by the influence, or, indeed, the authority, it can exercise before American assent or refusal is proffered to the international authority. So, also, with the public opinion of the United States. It cannot seek to reverse a decision after the process has begun of executing it, even if it should emphasize its view by a complete reversal of political power in the presidency or in Congress. For such an outlook would so undermine the central fabric of the international authority that once again it would be impossible to maintain it as a going concern. Like that of the other great powers, the price the United States must pay for a policy of collective security is the acceptance of an inherent incapacity to attempt to undo major decisions on policy.

With one major exception, which I shall discuss presently, the historic tradition of the United States ought not to make the task of promulgating its defence policy incompatible with the direct implications of collective security. Unless the psychological and economic results of the Second World War elicit among Americans a passion for territorial expansion—and of this there is little evidence—it may well be expected to become one of the main influences for stability among the United Nations, not least by the possibility that it will be sympathetic in its attitude to the nationalist aspirations of colonial peoples. The problem of bases will prove troublesome; and there are issues of frontier adjustments in Europe and the Near East which are fairly certain in the next twenty years or so to make for a revival of American isolationism; and this may well be intensified if America resumes a generous immigration policy in the next few years. I do not think that an isolationist revival would be either deep or wide. For as soon as its implications are seriously scrutinized, it becomes obvious that they involve American militarism on a scale which would make the conditions of peace resemble pretty grimly the conditions of war. Nor could that revival hope to achieve any serious influence, as I have said, without disaster to any system of mutual security, or without being the prelude to a new world conflict in which America would be inevitably involved. But that, of course, is the one thing the isolationists seek to avoid. It is paradoxical, but true, that their ideal is capable of fulfilment only when the principle of collective security has overriding authority which compels the surrender of national ambition to its demands.

The real problems the United States will confront by its acceptance of collective security are economic and ideological. The economic problems are set by the principles put forward by the United States, at the height of its economic power, as the basis for international trade. With the exception of one important point—the emphasis upon non-discrimination —the principles are, broadly speaking, a reaffirmation of the classic theory of the market economy as this was expounded in the hey-day of *laissez-faire*. If the Bretton Woods agreement is not a return to the gold standard, it has not proved easy for its defenders to explain wherein the difference consists. There is no way in which any nation can be secure in the possession of either steady sales or of steady supplies. State trading is set solely in the context of commercial considerations. Creditors of Great Britain in the sterling area are to receive no payments until 1951; that means, to take a single example, that India cannot use her sterling balances in London for five years, and that is, in effect, to deny to India any large-scale industrial development save as America is willing to assist India with loans. Nor can the sterling creditors of Great Britain be paid after 1951 except in gold or dollars; that makes the likelihood of large-scale repayment look very small indeed. And since Great Britain is prohibited, even within the Commonwealth, from accepting any long-term loan on less advantageous terms than its American loan until 1951, it follows that Britain could not buy, say, the Australian wool clip on credit except on conditions which, in effect, America has determined. This is really a prohibition upon international economic planning of any kind; and it may well prove to be the enthronement of American finance-capitalism as the master—Russia apart—of the world's commerce, which will settle its character upon terms which the United States approves.

That is the logic of the economic situation bequeathed to us by the Second World War. The difficulty it creates is one of immense proportions. It re-creates the circumstances of *laissez-faire* as between all States, without regard to their unequal bargaining power or productive capacity, or the degree of recovery from the effects of war, in the struggle for world markets. No doubt it gives a real chance of development to those nations which, like the United States or Russia, are really living upon the basis of a continental economy, within which there is a domestic market as big as Europe itself. But it makes the position of the smaller nations hard and precarious—especially where they have suffered severely from the war—unless they lower their standard of living considerably or are allowed to penetrate the American domestic market upon conditions easy enough to enable them to accumulate enough investment capital to embark upon large-scale development. If they borrow from America, they become chained to its economic chariot as dependencies and not even the effort of the Marshall policy can directly prevent such dependence.

It is, I think, obvious that this position cannot last. The world will not agree to have the character of its economic life, the standards, therefore, of its material well-being, set by the imperative of the American business system. It is not only that the conditions exclude the possibility that the competition for markets could conceivably be on equal terms. Even more, it excludes any serious chance of trade arrangements between two or more nations without American approval. Still further, it limits the advantage any nation may believe itself to secure from the adoption of socialist measures in any realm by which international trade is affected. Monopolies of private character may develop as competitors of similar monopolies elsewhere, but are certain sooner or later to come to an agreement about the division of the international market, like the treaty between I. G. Farben and Du Pont, or between I. G. Farben and Imperial Chemicals in Great Britain. The result of such agreements is to make the State power in either country something like an annex to the great industrial empires which are thus created; and since these industrial empires are ultimately driven to make treaties of agreement with that financial power which Veblen so rightly called "predatory capitalism," the productive relations of a society are set by the concessions to the workers in any country which the masters of its productive capacity think they can make without jeopardy to their mastery of the State power.

It is at this point that the ideological differences of which I have spoken become important. For the situation we occupy resembles very much the struggle between the Roman Catholic Church and the rebellious sects at the time of the Reformation. Implicit in the American system is a body of economic values which beget, in their turn, a body of social values; and these become a philosophy, the historic roots of which, while explicable in terms of past American conditions, are today quite obviously obsolete. It is a philosophy based on a view of the relation between individuals in society which makes almost complete abstraction of the fact that the main differences in their position are not the outcome of natural laws, but of rules made by privileged men to maintain their privileges. It naturally judges all other philosophies, as the Roman Catholic Church in the sixteenth century judged all other sects, upon the assumption that it alone possesses the real truth, and that freedom for the individual is unobtainable if its postulates are not accepted. It is, therefore, suspicious of all State intervention in economic life unless it is the kind of intervention, a tariff, for example, which business men expect to receive from the organized community in their search for their own economic security against external competitors. How deeply this philosophy has taken hold of the American business man I have already discussed in an earlier chapter. Here it is only necessary to affirm that it differs in degree only, and not in principle, from the central ideas of the Nazi economy and of the quasi-feudal capitalism of Japan. This raises the issue whether it can successfully be made the basis of an international political policy which looks to peace through collective security.

I frankly do not think it can; and I do not think it can because it has become the philosophy of an economic civilization in contraction and not in expansion. If foreign trade were unnecessary to America, its position would be different; but that would be the case only if the income of the American people were able to absorb its full productive capacity. Since it is very far from being able to do so, the profitability of the American system, especially at its present technological level, has the hard choice between the capture of large-scale foreign markets and the growth of mass unemployment at home. This is a choice which, as the safeguards inserted in the Anglo-American loan make clear, American business has already made. The outcome is therefore a battle with other nations for markets, in which neither can afford to fail. Indeed, as I have said, the system to which America has led the world is workable only upon the condition that American business finances the advance of its rivals on terms those rivals can accept. At the moment, it is not easy to see that either its industrialists or its financiers are ready to make the sacrifices such financing would entail. Committed as they are to the principles of the market economy, they are bound to think of international lending in the simple but deceptive terms which the nineteenth century, from perhaps 1830 to some such period as 1880, was able to approve. But those terms are today devoid of meaning. They impose a burden on the borrowing State which leads quite directly, as we saw in the inter-war years, to repudiation or to fascism or to both; and any of these saps the very foundations of collective security. An international society, this is to say, has not enough of a common outlook unless its members have an equal interest in the operation of its economic system; and the weakness of the American position is its insistence on using its unexampled economic power to prevent the emergence of that equal interest.

And it is, moreover, attempting to do so when the success of the Russian system and the slow emergence of territories like India and China into full nationhood offer alternatives to the American position. Their effort is nothing so much as a determination to free themselves from that dependence on the market economy in which America alone has confidence. The implications of this contrast are very far from satisfactory on any showing, for they offer a choice between methods of economic organization of which the social consequences are immeasurable. In a world dominated by a market economy the battle is ever to the strongest, and the race to the swiftest of foot; and the price paid for weakness is a low standard of life, poor cultural opportunities, and political dependence in precisely those fields where a nation is most justified in seeking an independent way of life. The community that has transcended the market economy has entered a world where it can plan its production in terms of its needs. It is unlikely to be cursed by the social consequences of a system in which the capacity to make profit is the supreme test of worth; and it can offer cultural opportunity to all its citizens without fearing that their intellectual development will be construed by its ruling class as a threat to the privileges they possess by reason of their capacity to make profit.

On the other hand, experience suggests that transcendence of the market economy does not secure political independence, even to the strong nation, so long as another strong nation is striving to maintain the market economy. Where this situation exists, the danger is great that the smaller nations should feel compelled—or actually be compelled—to take shelter beneath the protection of a strong nation with the material means at its disposal to defend its way of life. A wide ideological abyss between the major members of a collective security system is in any event a strain upon its power to operate with ease. If the abyss is made even more wide by the weakness of a nation whose economic life depends upon the functioning of the market economy, the strain may quickly become too heavy for a system of collective security to bear. That is the supreme difficulty which the economic policy of the United States now intensifies. It is trying to compel the rest of the world to adjust its economic institutions to a theory of what its business men call "free enterprise" just at the time when a large part of the rest of the world is increasingly rejecting it, in the light of its results upon them. On any showing, it is bound to be difficult to find the means of a satisfactory compromise between outlooks so different as these. For such compromise always means accepting principles which alter the way of life of those nations which accept it, and, in particular, it alters the power of any strong nation, even more, of a privileged class within a strong nation, to exploit its strength. This raises the question of how far an America dedicated to the preservation of free enterprise will co-operate in aiding the economic and cultural organs of the United Nations to mitigate, even, possibly, fundamentally to alter, the consequences of the market economy upon international relations. It is not an area in which, so far, the world has had any experience of American habits. So far as they are known, it seems legitimate to make a careful distinction between the remarkable, if somewhat impulsive, generosity of Americans in their capacity as private citizens, and the ruthless grasp of what is wanted by the United States in its public capacity. And in this latter aspect, the very claim that even informed citizens may make that the United States "has stood generally for loftier principles of international conduct than other powerful countries," [13] is interesting evidence of how easily the ruthless grasp of self-interest may be rationalized into a deep regard for the common welfare. It is not beyond the imagination to conceive a situation where the United States might withdraw from an international authority to safeguard some principle the protection of which it regards as "a sacred trust" for mankind. Certainly in this context we must remember how America's desire to trade as fully as possible with other nations, alike in war and peace, evolved into the doctrine of freedom of the seas and made the defence of that doctrine, not least in the hands of Woodrow Wilson, a great moral crusade. Yet it is the same United States which, when it has itself been at war, has used its naval power to enforce the right of search and seizure with an amplitude and directness which has never caused its leaders to feel the pang of conscientious scruple.

Nations must realize, moreover, that while the Second World War has stripped the rest of the world of its major foreign investments, it has left the United States not only with immense interests abroad, but with important gaps in its own supplies which it could fill only by driving other countries into the orbit of its power. It depends on Bolivia for its tin, on Peru for its vanadium, on Canada for its nickel and its wood pulp. It would be easy to extend the list into a long and varied catalogue. And to its influence must be added that the enormous production surpluses of the American economy, together with the sheer volume of its savings, seeking for outlet in investments abroad, changed, between the First and Second World Wars, the whole impact of the United States on international economic relations. It is hard to measure the responsibility of the American tariffs, particularly of 1922 and 1930, for the economic

<hr />

[13] Peffer, *op. cit.,* p. 45.

difficulties of Europe. It is certain that the restrictions on immigration after the First World War gravely prejudiced the chances of European recovery. It is probable, too, that the ability of American manufacturers to build factories and produce goods in foreign countries whose commodities were not permitted by the American tariff to enter American markets, while the main profits of these external establishments went back to extend the American home market, did a good deal to disturb the effort in Europe and Asia to secure a more balanced economy. What is certainly beyond dispute is that the growth of these interests abroad compelled the American government actively to intervene on their behalf whenever steps were taken which threatened them. One has only to examine the vigorous attack of Mr. Hoover, as Secretary of Commerce, against any artificial price-fixing unfavourable to American buyers—of Egyptian cotton, or Brazilian coffee, or Chilean nitrates, or Malayan rubber, to take examples only—to see that the sudden and vast push by the United States of the market economy into the international field gave the old policy of the Open Door a new meaning of far wider significance than in the past. It meant not merely "most favoured nation" treatment in the old sense; it meant also that while the American market was largely closed against foreign competition, the investment bankers demanded equal access to financial opportunity abroad, and restraint upon the price-fixing habits of foreign monopolies as soon as Americans wanted raw materials. It was not accident, either, that the State Department began to interest itself directly in the consequences of foreign investment upon the international position of the United States.

Only a detailed picture of the immense American stake, direct and indirect, in foreign countries can convey any adequate notion of its scale and intricacy. It is probable that, by 1939, American corporations had two thousand branch factories outside the boundaries of the United States, and that these employed upwards of three hundred thousand workers. Nor is it beyond the mark to estimate that, at the same period, American investments abroad, direct and indirect, amounted to fifteen billion dollars. In fact, though the export trade was only a little more than ten per cent of the total American production, the dependence on it of some of its vital industries was very large, notably (apart from food and raw materials) in refined copper, in agricultural machinery, and in aircraft and their spare parts. It is important, also, that whereas in the four years before 1900 over seventy-five per cent of American exports went to Europe, in the four years before 1935 the percentage was only forty-seven; exports, in the same periods, more than doubled to Canada and South America and the African Continent, and multiplied almost five times to Asia. The emphasis of American foreign trade after the First World War, that is to say, was directed strongly to the undeveloped countries from which America could derive a large part of the vital new materials upon which its industrial strength depended; this is true of metals like chromium and manganese, nickel, platinum, and tin, where over ninety per cent of

American consumption was dependent upon supplies from foreign countries.

The position reached on the eve of the Second World War can, I think, be fairly put by saying that the interests of American agriculture were being sacrificed to the interests of American industry. This was only in part the result of Mr. Cordell Hull's attempt to rebuild the idea of the international division of labour through the mechanism of reciprocal trade agreements. Far more, it was the outcome of the fact that America was, after 1919, a creditor and not a debtor nation, that it had embarked upon a vast programme for a national mercantile marine, and that the greater the size of its agricultural production, the less easy would it be for the foreign debtors of America either to repay their old loans or to secure new ones. It therefore paid America to restrict agricultural development at home to make possible industrial conquest abroad. The twofold result of this decision was to increase the dependence of agricultural countries upon American manufactures and to prevent any large-scale rise in their standard of living, since a country mainly producing raw materials is bound to live at a lower standard than one which has begun seriously to enter the industrial field.

It is unnecessary for my argument to prove that, by 1939, the economic side of American foreign policy was oppressive either in Europe and Africa or in Asia; it is enough if I have shown that in the evolution of its character, the search for American well-being involved the imposition of a way of life upon the less powerful nations with whom the United States dealt. And to maintain the relations of this way of life, it became increasingly necessary for the government of the United States to regard interference with those relations as aggression, which, in the final outcome, could only be solved by war. American finance-capitalism reached a stage where it was in alliance with its government for the promotion, through the use of the State power, of American prosperity. It had the resources; it had the manpower; it had the armaments; the combination of these produced what was like nothing so much as a new mercantilism. While it is largely true that this mercantilism was of the first importance to what it has become customary to call the "satisfied powers," since it meant an American intervention that was essential to their victory, the question remains of the purpose it will fulfil when all nations except Russia and its dependent States are, at the end of the Second World War, dependent upon the United States for renovation and development, and when the United States can gain access to Russia only on Russian terms. Particularly is the question important when the United States and Russia approach the theory of renovation and development for purposes which it is difficult to reconcile easily. How, in these circumstances, can collective security work?

That seems to me the overwhelming problem once regard is paid to the immense excess productive capacity of the United States and the unwillingness of its manufacturers and bankers to pay wages to the Ameri-

can worker which would enable him to make domestic consumption a
source of investment as profitable as the penetration of foreign markets. It is hard to see that any nation, except Russia, is in a position
seriously to resist the power of this penetration. The goods offered are
cheap; the technique of salesmanship, if aggressive, is remarkable; and no
small part of the necessities of life, in the kind of world bequeathed to us
by the Second World War, depends upon its victims having a swift and
wide access to them. In the degree that this happens, all these nations
are drawn within the orbit of American power. In the degree that it does
not happen, either they remain economically primitive, or they must
wait until some other power is in a position to extend them long-term
credits to assist their development. Obviously enough, to refuse to be
drawn into the American orbit is to choose the hard way to improvement
in well-being; from the history of the great Russian experiment something of its cost is known. To choose the hard way, moreover, as Poland
and Hungary, and in a lesser degree Rumania and Bulgaria, made clear,
means to break the vested interests with which American finance-
capitalism is accustomed to deal; and in cases like Yugoslavia, and, again,
in a less degree, China and Italy and Czechoslovakia, the hard way seeks
to promote purposes in development far more akin to Russian than to
American principles. If the terms on which America is prepared to assist
in the recovery of Great Britain without recourse to what Sir Stafford
Cripps has called "austerity methods" is the soft way, the issue arises
of just how America would treat a semi-developed nation, with a low
standard of life, investment in the development of which is a far greater
risk for American bankers and their clients than was investment in
Great Britain, which still has great assets from its past predominance to
put forward as collateral, and could not, without psychological strain, be
treated as a client power. Is it illegitimate to declare, in the light of all
this, that collective security means for the United States an international
agreement which insists that no aggressions should be used against the way
in which its business men choose to deploy their economic supremacy?
And is it not the natural question to ask in relation to the preceding question whether, Russia always apart, the economic well-being of other peoples would be the residue America is prepared to leave them after its own
major interests have been satisfied?

It is not enough to reply to this that the classic theory of international
trade, upon which the defence of the American outlook depends, assumes
that prosperity, like peace, is indivisible; a nation cannot injure its neighbour without injuring itself. That is true under conditions of universal
free trade, where the partners to a bargain are of equal strength, and one of
them has an alternative nation with which to bargain if it so desires.
But these are not the conditions which in fact obtain. The United States
is not a free trade power, but a strongly mercantilist country, and there
is no apparent reason to suppose that it proposes to abandon mercantilism
in the foreseeable future; and none of the partners to an economic transac-

tion under present circumstances, especially if the United States be one of them, can usefully be considered as bargaining on equal terms. On the contrary, few nations today have any freedom of contract that is substantial, first, because their needs are too great, and, second, because the war has made it very likely that a considerable time must elapse before alternative sources of supply are available. Most of them, therefore, are less purchasers of, in the ordinary sense of the term, than petitioners for, both capital and consumers' goods. In this position, the United Nations, always with the exception of Russia, becomes an organization, granted the available premises of American action, for creating the character of permanence for the economic supremacy of the United States.

It is that exception of Russia which makes the second great problem to which I referred earlier. That problem is the use to which the immense discovery of atomic energy is to be put in the next ten or fifteen years. There is already a wide basis of mutual suspicion among the United Nations. Russia is suspicious of the attitude of the great capitalist powers to a socialist people; the great capitalist powers are suspicious of the influence upon their masses of any striking advance in the success of the Russian experiment. The Russians suspect the deep interest of Britain and America in the Middle East; they cannot but be aware of the attraction of the oil deposits of the Caucasus, which are so difficult to defend; Britain, and in a less degree America, are disturbed by the growth of Russian influence in the Middle East, by Russia's hostility to Iran, its pressure upon Turkey to make possible full Russian access to the Mediterranean, its interest in Aegean bases, its suggestion of a possible entry into the African colonial field. There is the problem created by the very different view taken of China's future by socialists on the one hand, and the exponents of free enterprise on the other. There are vital decisions to be taken on the place of Germany and of Japan in the world economy of the next generation; and it is not hard to see that the approach to these decisions will not easily be made from common premises. Agreement about these issues can emerge only in an atmosphere in which the nations primarily concerned are clear in their own minds that peace is their major interest and that nothing any of them can gain by the use of war as an instrument of national policy would compensate it for the loss of peace.

It is at this point that the implications of atomic energy become so vital for international relations. By chance and determination, combined with geographical location, Anglo-American scientists were able to make, and the United States to use, the first atomic bombs. Their incredible power was demonstrated not only by the destruction they wrought in Japan, but also by the speed with which they proved that an enemy nation, with no comparable weapons, has to choose between the grim alternatives of swift surrender and catastrophic destruction. Since the bombs were of American manufacture, and the plant to make them dependent upon technological knowledge available only to a small group of American, British, and Canadian scientists, it was announced by President Truman that this knowledge would not be made public, but would be held by the United States as a "sacred trust" on behalf of mankind. This must be read in the context of the fact that, so far as we know, all other atomic bombs so far manufactured are in the possession of the United States, and that, as yet, no other nation has the plant necessary for their manufacture.

The general principles of atomic fission are, of course, the common possession of the world of science; like most universal discoveries, they have been the outcome of long years of effort by the men and women of many nations. It is accepted that, as we learn to apply these principles to the problems of industry and agriculture, wholly new vistas will be opened up in the organization of human welfare. It also appears to be the case that in the exploration of how these principles are to be applied, it is certainly difficult, and perhaps impossible, to distinguish between the achievement of knowledge which has a bearing on peace, and that which has a bearing upon war.[14] It is for this reason that all personnel engaged in work upon atomic fission were sworn to secrecy, with liability to criminal prosecution if they made any of their knowledge public. Scientific papers were withdrawn from publication, and scientists were prohibited from taking part in a friendly visit to Russia if their special field of research was directly related to the atom bomb. Though the scientists became aware, as perhaps at no date since the seventeenth century, both of the social significance of science and the urgency, if it was to be fully devoted to the service of man, of permitting no barriers to separate scientific workers in one nation from scientific workers in another; though, still more, they organized to bring home to public opinion the significance of open knowledge and full freedom of debate, statesmen, administrators, and the leading figures in the defence services combined to insist upon secrecy. Congress hurriedly discussed the ways and means of maintaining American primacy in this field. The Prime Minister announced that a government-sponsored centre of atomic research would be built without delay in Great Britain. If the Russian government was officially silent, it allowed it to become known that some of its outstanding physicists and engineers were already devoting their energies to atomic problems, and, in 1947, it claimed to be able to make the bombs. Perhaps as dramatic a sense of what it all implied was given when, at the order of the American authorities, the main Japanese apparatus for atomic research was deliberately dismantled and destroyed.

The demonstration of what the atomic bomb could do was soon reflected in international relations. President Truman's decision to keep the technological aspects of its manufacture a secret was largely responsible for the breakdown of the Foreign Secretaries' Conference in London in the autumn of 1945; Mr. Molotov, the Russian Commissar of Foreign Affairs, made it clear that as long as a policy of secrecy was maintained

---

[14] On all this, *A Report on the International Control of Atomic Energy* (U.S. State Department Publication 2498, 1946)—the Lilienthal Report—is the fundamental authority.

there could be no agreement about any major issue involving peace. This deadlock Prime Minister Attlee sought to break, by a conference in Washington with President Truman, at which he pressed for a policy which would enable the "secret" to be shared with Russia. He was at least partially successful, for he secured assent to a procedure which might ultimately lead to the secret being shared. The United Nations, it was agreed, should be asked to set up a commission to study the handling of this and kindred problems. It would report to the Security Council of the United Nations upon ways and means of sharing all scientific knowledge of use in the making of peace. It would explore how to build safeguards against the use of atomic energy for the purposes of war; and it would, for this end, be the effective agent of the United Nations in every area, both of production and use, where fissionable materials were involved. Obviously, to carry out these tasks the right to inspect atomic plants in all States would be essential. It is not less essential that the veto power should not be used against these activities.

To most observers the proposals of the Lilienthal Report have seemed to offer a really constructive solution of the problems it considered. Yet it is evident, from the discussions which have followed upon its publication, that it has failed to quieten, at any rate, the suspicions of the Russians. They set the Report in the context of an American foreign policy which, to them, seems at every turn an attempt to contain Russia within limits which maximize American power, and especially American economic power. The American offer, on this view, leaves America, so to say, the sole judge in what is an international cause. The result is a grave deadlock, which offers little hope that ideas which look to the future will be presented to the statesmen who have to make the final decisions in the temper of experimentalism and audacity which the subject requires. But the central consideration is the fact that a weapon to which, at present, no answer is known, and to which, at present, many experts believe no answer is possible, is the monopoly, for the time being, of a single nation, and that it is guarded as a monopoly because that nation is not satisfied that it should risk the possession of the atomic bomb by another nation from whose policies it gravely differs. Since the United States realizes that these differences may not be capable of resolution by discussion, it has clearly decided to set the problem of continued secrecy in the background of a possible war. It is, therefore, naturally anxious, because it is thinking in terms of an age that is already outmoded, to retain as long as it can the exclusive use of a weapon the employment of which would probably be decisive. It thus deems of secondary importance the two facts, first that its monopoly has no more than a short-term value—perhaps three or five or ten years—and, second, that since its monopoly is a matter of public knowledge, an atmosphere of suspicion is created which permeates all the major differences to be discussed by a general sense of ill-will and insecurity.

5

THE main assumptions which appear to lie behind most American thinking on its future as a world power are three in number. There is the assumption that American economic supremacy, and the physical power
that goes with it, will be used in an ethically better way than other predominant nations have used it in the past. There is the assumption that
the combination of goodwill towards peace and fear of war will, especially
while the United States has a monopoly of the atomic bomb, be sufficient
to maintain the peace, especially when these are backed by the principle of
collective security embodied in the United Nations. There is the third
assumption that compromise is possible, given goodwill, between social
systems built, like that of the United States, upon the market economy,
and systems, of which that of Russia is the outstanding example, which
reject the market economy and its social implications. Each of these assumptions deserves separate consideration.

Broadly speaking, the record of the United States as an international
power is better than that of most other great nations. It has not, indeed,
been an especially good record in Latin America; there it has continuously used authority backed by force to impose its will upon States with
which it has disagreed; and while it is true that the settlement with
Mexico over the latter's oil nationalization policy was an admirable example of what President Roosevelt called the attitude of the "good
neighbour," the attitude is new, and it is far too early to assume that it has
become a permanent part of the American outlook. The major reason for
the good record of the United States outside Latin America is the fact
that, until only the other day, all its inquiries were devoted to discovering its own resources and developing them. Now that the general pattern of this process is complete, the American economic system compels
it to look abroad for new sources of profit, just as, a century ago, the
repeal of the Corn Laws in Great Britain forced its manufacturers to
think in terms of exports, visible and invisible, as the source of their
well-being. Since the American economy is directed by the same causal
circumstances, there is no reason to suppose that it will not be faced by
the same effects. This is bound to mean larger-scale imperialism, the
evolution of which it is always necessary to protect by the contingent use
of armed power.

About the second assumption, two recent experiences are obviously relevant. Goodwill is, no doubt, important; but that it is not of itself decisive
is shown by the fate of the Kellogg–Briand Pact signed by sixteen states
at Paris in 1928, and ultimately adhered to by sixty-one in 1930; Ar-
gentina and Brazil were the only two important States which refused to
sign. The pact was a solemn pledge to abstain from war as an instrument
of national policy. There were no sanctions behind it, and there is no
evidence that it had any other effect than the award of the Nobel Peace
Prize to one of its authors, Mr. F. B. Kellogg, who was at the time the

American Secretary of State. The second experience is that of the League of Nations. It was, as Lord Cecil has shown in persuasive detail,[15] a failure due essentially to two causes. First, the ambition of powers like Germany, Italy, and Japan, all defeated or disappointed in the First World War, was greater than their will to peace; and, second, the great nations, especially Britain and France, had never, at the great turning point in its history, enough faith in the importance of the experiment either to give a genuine lead to the smaller nations, or to take the risk of what might happen if authoritarian regimes, like those of Mussolini, Hitler, and Japan, were broken by the use of the sanctions not merely permitted, but actually enjoined, by the Covenant.

That lack of faith was a complex matter. Part of it was the outcome of the traditional diplomatic dislike of accepting commitments independently of the circumstances in which they have to be made good; that same dislike made for an important, possibly fatal, lack of clarity in British foreign policy, in the two or three years before the outbreak of the Second World War. Part of it was the sense of deep alarm at the growth of Russian influence over so large a part of the world. British and French statesmen, especially if they were conservative, dreaded the prospect that, if the dictators fell, their place would be taken by parties likely still further to strengthen Russian influence. This, they feared, might shatter the whole basis upon which capitalist civilization is built; in particular, they were convinced that any growth in Russian influence would reinforce the drive to colonial action which threatened the durability of the imperialism so necessary to maintain capitalism as a going concern.

Obviously the most important question before the United Nations is whether, after the break-down of the League, and the catastrophe of the Second World War which followed upon it, the chief members of the new body have learned the clear lessons they teach. Keeping the peace is not merely a question of goodwill; it is a question of whether the conditions can be enduringly built in which that goodwill is continuously sustained; it is not a matter of profound hatred for war; in every civilized nation there exists a profound hatred for war. Mr. Ramsay MacDonald, Lord Baldwin, and Mr. Neville Chamberlain all hated war; they sacrificed so much of their power to that hatred that they helped to unloose a far vaster conflict than any they hoped they were avoiding. It is, indeed, an inescapable lesson from the inter-war years that once the members of an international body begin to pick and choose between applying and evading the principles they are pledged to operate, the whole body begins to disintegrate. The disintegration is cumulative; for those members who have been restrained from taking action outside those principles begin to speculate upon ways and means of successfully throwing off the re-

---

[15] Lord Cecil, *A Great Experiment* (London: Cape, 1941). Lord Cecil's book has quite exceptional value, because it records the views of a statesman who was at once one of the main architects of the League, and, throughout its history, one of its most devoted supporters, at different periods in high office in the British Government.

straint. Once the dread of war persuades a great power to condone aggression, it is certain that a number of the smaller powers will follow its example. The moment that breach in collective security against aggression has been made, faith in its workability dissolves, and the old policy of power politics once again takes the feet of the nations down to the abyss of war.

How deeply all this has penetrated the American consciousness it is difficult to say. No one can doubt the reality of the American aversion from war, nor that this aversion is intensified by the whole weight of American history and ideals. But, as I have said, aversion from war is not enough. It degenerates all too easily into that tragic willingness to appease which not only lengthens the chance of aggression, but also begins to find grounds to justify the aggression. Mr. Neville Chamberlain's attitude to Czechoslovakia in the Munich period grimly illustrates this process of degeneration; he obviously resented the Czech refusal to be enthusiastic over its own victimization.

And while the vast majority of Americans are averse from war, we must not forget that, alongside this aversion, there has grown, above all since the Spanish-American War, the consciousness of great strength, and the sense that destiny has called the United States to fulfil a high mission to mankind. It is here that the American enthusiasm for a "business civilization" becomes so significant. For, to the American, the "gentleman" who is the historic type symbolical of British civilization and its supremacy is now in final retreat before the "business man" who is symbolical of American civilization. The feeling is widespread that, with victory over Germany and Japan, the great hour of the business man has arrived; and it must be remembered that no other type so profoundly shapes the character of American thought or has done so much to mould the American way of life. That is why we have to take into account so heavily his preference for practical common sense over philosophy. However kindly he may be in personal relations, he is massively energetic in action, convinced that if a man does not look after himself, no one will look after him. He reserves his main admiration for success, for the ends achieved rather than for the means chosen; and it is not unreasonable to argue that, of course without knowing it, he has adapted to his *métier* the main doctrines of Machiavelli's *Prince*.

I have already sought, in an earlier chapter, to analyse the business man's outlook upon life. Here I can only say that, for him, the world is a market which the combined power of high pressure salesmanship and cheap mass production will open to him as Pistol's sword could open his oyster. He has seen how swiftly the Americanization of the world has proceeded in the last twenty-five years. He knows how remarkable are his achievements in improvisation. He is aware that he has no rival in taking the gambler's chance, or of ruthlessly scrapping expensive means which do not seem to promise the end for which he is reaching. With his remarkable vitality and his endless zest for novelty, he thinks of Europe, for the most part, as an interesting antiquity on which the sun is setting. He thinks of Asia as an inexhaustible market which he has the supreme chance now to organize and control.

He takes his ideas from the literature of the American Chamber of Commerce and the National Association of Manufacturers. He mainly thinks of "politics" as a wanton interference with the natural laws by which business men govern society either by elected amateurs, who only too often are corrupt, or by "bureaucrats," who, in the last dozen years, have been "impractical" college professors with curious and unsafe "notions" in their heads.

He is certain that all other countries are behind America in efficiency and are jealous of its strength. He is, a little curiously, firmly convinced that all other countries seek to take advantage of American simplicity and generosity.[16] His test of Russia is the quite fixed one of whether its rulers will do business with Americans on American terms; for not even Mr. Joseph E. Davies has convinced him that the Russian experiment can succeed, even though he is a little troubled by the resolution of Russia and the unbreakable heroism of its armies in the field. He agrees that nothing must permit another depression like that of 1929; but since, for him, history always begins tomorrow, he has managed with astonishing success to forget the degree to which his habits and methods were responsible for the Great Depression. He is willing to admit that government control must be far-reaching in wartime; but that it is simply a hindrance to the potential achievements of free enterprise in peace is an article of faith that he holds with an intensity of conviction so passionate that it is difficult not to call it religious in nature.

I venture to think that American business men will do more than any other group to shape the "stereotype" of America's place and function in the United Nations. No other group has comparable power. There is no comparable national organization among farmers, whose isolation and dispersal over the continent prevents their having an effective power of centralized pressure. The strength of organized labour is partly dissipated by its own disunities, and partly by the fact that it lacks an effective organ of political expression. Women's organizations have shown, as in the Prohibition campaign, the power to exercise considerable influence, but they have been concerned mostly with single and particular objectives rather than with a line of general policy. The Federal Council of Churches of Christ is also an influential body; but its very nature limits it to the kind of general pronouncement which receives respect but does not secure authority. So that, in any fundamental way, the great organizations of business men are largely without serious competitors, and their stereotype has the wider attraction because so much in its character is compounded of ideas and purposes which have a familiar and recognizable place in the American pattern of thought about international relations.

[16] For an interesting comment on this conviction, see Lord Cecil, *op. cit.*, pp. 144–45.

The business man will agree without difficulty that, so long as the Monroe Doctrine is respected, the principles for which it stands are applicable to Latin America; he might even support the adaptation of the Pan-American Union into one of those regional organizations envisaged as possible in the discussions at San Francisco. He can see, too, how necessary it is to curb the continual drift of Europe into war, since he has learned that European war interferes with American commerce, and even, before long, puts its grim fingers deep into his own emotional life. He is convinced of the need to prevent any great power except his own from seeking to dominate the Asiatic continent while China and India go through the long and painful process of industrialization; no one is more aware than he that any such successful domination would be fatal to his own hopes of finding an immense market there. I doubt whether he will agree to scale-down the American two-ocean Navy. He will insist on a standard of air strength comparable to the pre-1914 British naval practice of outbuilding its two nearest rivals. Any maintenance by Russia of large-scale military and air forces is bound, perhaps even while the United States has the monopoly of the atomic bomb, to break down America's long tradition of refusing to impose military service on its citizens. It is, therefore, within this framework that the Security Council of the United Nations will have to move in all proposals it may make which look towards a disarmed world.

There are other elements in this stereotype that we must take into account. He will naturally keep the bases he has leased for ninety-nine years; that is a closed issue he would not agree to see reopened on the basis, say, of their transfer, after suitable financial compensation, to the United Nations itself. In the light, indeed, of the Japanese war, and the new possibilities of air attack, he is more likely to demand further bases in the Pacific and Africa, perhaps also in the Azores and Greenland, and to support the demand of the Naval Affairs Committee of the Senate that a power incapable of defending some vital strategic point of its territory, from which the United States might be attacked, shall lease it, on the Caribbean model, to the United States as a necessary sacrifice to international security. He will, I believe, find difficulties about any proposals from the Social and Economic Council, or from the parallel Scientific and Cultural Council, if these are incompatible with what he will call "sound American principles." He will even become quickly uneasy about the assumption of responsibilities in the quarrels of distant peoples in whose fate he has little interest and little belief that he need be seriously concerned. He may even become profoundly uneasy where he finds that United Nations action arrests what he believes to be his "natural rights" to attain success, where he can, by the "business methods" to which he is accustomed.

This is, I think, the background in which the whole problem of atomic energy must be set. There are two major sides to it which require discussion. If I take the economic side first, it is only because, by so doing, the military side is set in a clearer perspective. Here, while it is no doubt true that we are only on the threshold of the atomic age, its possibilities are not open to doubt. They offer the prospect of an endless supply of energy at almost incredibly low cost in terms of human nature. They set the problem of poverty everywhere in an entirely new context. Whether it is utilized to restore the barren wastes of Asia and Africa, whether it is for irrigation to bring vast deserts into livable condition, or whether it is for making life tolerable by air-conditioning which would remove the burden of climatic extremes of heat and cold, in those areas of human life atomic energy brings new hope of abundance for mankind. But it brings this on the condition that nations are institutionally prepared for its application. For in most large industrial societies the disproportion between the power to produce and the power to consume is so great that any great technological discovery makes new unemployment by adding to productive power, and thus the need for manpower grows ever more small. That is why a free enterprise society is able, on the historic evidence, to secure full employment only by imperialist expansion; and this, as we know, has been the main prelude to war. That is why, also, it is impossible to leave the control of its development for peaceful purposes either in private hands, or, as Congress attempted in the May–Johnson bill in the autumn of 1945, in the hands of a control commission whose sole concern would be military security. The latter would obviously stifle independent research in the name of security, on the ground that it complicated the problem of inspection; and its desire would be to put scientists into uniform, in laboratories under the domination of the military, with the results that research would be given a special emphasis, freedom of publication would be impossible, and a barrier would be erected between scientists engaged in this work and other scientists, both in America and outside it, which would destroy the great international republic of science; or such a control commission would, for cheapness and convenience, centralize research in the finely equipped laboratories of the great commercial corporations like those of General Electric or Du Pont. The second alternative would, I think, inevitably subordinate the pace at which the public enjoyment of the peaceful implications of atomic energy was possible, to that which would safeguard the vested interests of industries and financial institutions the value of whose capital apparatus would otherwise be jeopardized. We have already heard rumblings from the oil and coal industries about the danger of developing too fast the industrial potentialities of atomic energy. They put the danger, of course, on "social" grounds; what they mean is that they could not face a loss on their investment, which is no more than the inherent outcome of the pattern of industrial organization and the laws of property by which it is sustained. There is no way to meet this danger except by public ownership of the whole process and public operation of the research involved, and it is clearly necessary for some government criteria to be evolved to set the standards of use and cost in the life of the international community. The alternative is a series of private monopolies, safeguarded by all the devices legal ingenuity can discover, and linked together in different nations by the kind of agreement which, in the inter-war years, I. G. Farben was accustomed to make with Imperial Chemicals in Britain or with Du Pont in the United States. That is the sure road to a new and devastating servitude to monopolies, which have never yet shown their power to overcome the problem of unemployment. Here, if anywhere, it is surely clear that private ownership of basic processes and materials and private control of research are alike incompatible with full employment.

If this be so, the free enterprise system to which the American business man pins his faith becomes at once a threat to the public good and to international peace. For it is bound to retain outmoded methods in the interest of safeguarding its capital investment, and this means insisting on poverty where the road to abundance will lie increasingly open. It is difficult to doubt that this will lead to grave internal strain, even, possibly, to social convulsion. History has shown how slowly and painfully a mainly agrarian population was acclimatized to the demands of machine technology during the Industrial Revolution in Great Britain and in the United States; and we have seen with our own eyes the price of disciplining a vast horde of individualist peasants in Russia to the same demands in a much briefer space of time. In private hands, the atomic age would be inaugurated by the emergence of this problem once more, and, very rapidly, on a far larger scale. And, as it so emerges, it becomes indissolubly linked with international relations, since the more difficult the domestic scene, the more urgent it becomes to mitigate that difficulty by increasing the power to penetrate foreign markets. At this point the threat to peace, democracy, and freedom becomes an unmistakable one. The free enterprise system—the American business man's euphemism for a capitalism from which most of the world is seeking to free itself— leads, by inexorable stages, through crisis to war.

It is at this point that the economic aspects of the problem set up by atomic energy link up with the military problem. The American business man is formally favourable to a United Nations organization. He has approved the decision of Congress to ratify, by a large majority in both the Senate and the House of Representatives, the President's signature of the San Francisco Charter. The United States is a member of the new international authority. But the Charter was drafted before the first atomic bomb was dropped on Hiroshima; and very few of the delegates to the conference which drafted the Charter had any knowledge that the bomb existed, or any insight into the momentous changes it would involve in the relationships between nations. They therefore drew up a constitution for the new organization which not only preserved the full sovereignty of its members, but, largely at the instance of the great powers, entrusted the major function of preventing aggression to a Security Council, in effect controlled by the great powers, since all of them were members of it, and could keep their seats even when a case in which one of them was involved was under discussion, and could veto any decision by the other members of the Council to take action against itself. In the new phase of history into which the world has entered, this is clearly inadequate protection. For its reliance is upon the good faith and the goodwill of the members of the United Nations. That method was tried both in the Kellogg–Briand Pact and in the Covenant of the League. The nations learned, as they ought to have learned, that, though good faith and goodwill are indispensable instruments in preventing aggression, they are moods of mind and heart which a nation that is desperately sick within itself will disavow relentlessly if it believes that there is any reasonable chance that a policy of aggression will cure its disease.

Obviously, therefore, the first step to be taken is to include in the Charter of the United Nations the rule that there shall be no further manufacture either of atomic bombs or of other weapons of mass destruction; and to this must be added, very decisively, that the stock of bombs in possession of the American government must be destroyed. That rule cannot remain merely a pious aspiration. If the United Nations is to enforce the rule, it must be equipped with the power to do so. What technical methods are necessary to the effectiveness of that power is a question for the technical experts, scientific and military. All that I need to affirm here is that it must include the right to inspect freely, whenever such manufacture is suspected, the right to put sanctions into operation against a refusal to permit inspection, and the right to define what may not be manufactured in such a way as to keep pace with changing scientific discovery. At once it becomes necessary to provide the United Nations with bodies capable of making and enforcing these rules, and none could hope to work if unanimity were necessary among its members. For here unanimity would mean, for all serious purposes, that enforceability, or non-enforceability, in each instance would be a separate political decision of the Security Council, which would deprive the rule-making of that certainty of operation without which it has no meaning. I think, further, that the task of enforcing the rule cannot be left to the government of the nation in which it has been decided that the offence has occurred, but must obviously be the function of what Americans have termed a "task force" acting under the orders of the Security Council as, for this purpose, the executive body of the United Nations. It would, I think be impossible to wait for the decision of a permanent court of international justice upon the issue of whether a rule has been broken; for by the time it met, heard evidence, and rendered judgment, it is only too likely that the conflict would be well under way.

Two things are, I suggest, clear in their analysis. If, in the first place, the use of atomic energy and other weapons of mass destruction is to be outlawed, the United Nations must logically become a rule-enforcing, as well as a rule-making, body; and, because no optimistic reliance upon goodwill is adequate. it must be equipped with the executive power neces-

sary to swift and instant action against an offender. This has both a negative and a positive side. Negatively, it means preventing the manufacture
of such weapons in the light of possible conflict; positively, it means the
power, when conflict does break out, to prevent their manufacture and
to operate sanctions against any party to such a conflict which seeks to
evade the rules in order to secure a swift victory. Anyone who reflects
upon the exercise of this executive power will see that it is necessarily
far-reaching. It makes the rule of unanimity completely unacceptable.
It requires a full ability to inspect, which will bring the inspecting officials
into direct contact with the nationals of all countries involved. It may
require the international ownership, perhaps, also, the international control, of all basic raw materials which may be used to manufacture "weapons of mass destruction." To achieve this adequately, it may well require
the international ownership of the actual territory in which the raw materials are found; the United Nations may thus come to have its own
"bases" in all parts of the world. It will require, further, full and precise
statistical material about the use to which any nation is putting the raw
materials, together with the right to demand explanations for any significant change either in imports or exports. Nor can one doubt that in
any attempt to carry out this function effectively the United Nations will
have to employ scientific and military experts to its own, with access to
all industrial and defence installations, which clearly include the chemical and aeroplane industries, engineering and electric plants, and all government possessions such as aerodromes, naval stations, depots for the
store of war materials, and so forth, which may be regarded as relevant
to its work; and the executive body under the United Nations must,
quite inevitably, have the power to subpœna and examine the personnel,
books, and papers of any authority, public or private, which operates in
this field, if necessary without the consent of the government of the
nation to which they belong.

That this is not only a far-reaching programme, but also a profound
limitation of what has been historically regarded as the sovereign power
of national governments, is, I think, impossible to deny. It is no more
than the logical conclusion to which any disinterested observer of the
problem is drawn. And since the alternative is to take the grave risk of
trusting to goodwill alone, it follows that if the American government
were to decide to place all its reliance upon the method of goodwill, it
would have to make immense adaptations in its defence programme to
safeguard its citizens, its military and naval installations, and the factories which are central to its war potential; it would have to take power
to direct the necessary personnel, at least the scientists, the technicians,
and the skilled craftsmen, where they are required. Freedom of publication would have to be limited; and it is at least open to question whether
the vital corps of workers in any of these categories would be allowed to
change their jobs without permission.

It needs no lengthy argument to prove that neither the conference of the necessary powers of control upon the United Nations—powers of control which are enforceable by swift executive action—nor reliance merely upon good faith can be made to suit the free enterprise system in which American business men have confidence. Anyone who scrutinizes the clauses of the May–Johnson bill will see how vast were the powers it was proposed to entrust to the federal government, before the Attlee–Truman conversations resulted in the Attlee–Truman proposals for the possible transfer of the whole subject to the United Nations. If we suppose that, after suitable inquiries, the transfer is made, then two possibilities arise. The control may presuppose executive direction, in which case State sovereignty is everywhere limited. If executive direction is withheld, on the ground that the time is not ripe for so vast a change, then I believe that the United States will have to adopt the kind of safeguards I have described. It would then become necessary to adapt the free enterprise system to their implications, and its assumptions would obviously undergo profound changes in the process.

It is said that the peoples of the great powers, and particularly those of the United States and Russia, are not psychologically prepared for an international authority with wide powers of executive direction in this vital field. Wisdom, it is argued, demands that we proceed by stages, so that the government which consents to any wide transfer of power from itself may be sure of the necessary support before it commits itself to so grave an experiment. I do not think there is much substance in this view. It omits any regard to the fact that all the major governments have already taken decisions of immense importance in this field without thinking it necessary to consult their peoples. President Truman's original declaration was made on his own initiative, and without prior discussion of any kind in Congress; the Truman–Attlee statement was made not only in the same way, but in the background of a debate in the House of Commons in which both the Foreign Secretary, Mr. Ernest Bevin, and Mr. Winston Churchill obviously deprecated any public discussion of the issue. We have no real knowledge of what is in the minds of the Russian leaders, except Mr. Molotov's emphatic declaration that his country has this secret and many others, and a declaration about the importance of what atomic energy may achieve when applied to peaceful means. Indeed, it may generally be said that, apart from private initiative,[17] no government has made any effort to inform, much less to educate, its citizens about the choices that are open to them.

Is it not proper to conclude that this governmental attitude arises from the fact that none of the political leaders is ready to see popular demand forcing them into decisions for which they are not themselves prepared?

[17] Such as that taken by *The Nation* Associates Forum in a conference at New York, December 1–3, 1945. See the special supplement to *The Nation*, December 22, 1945. For another effort, see the discussion on the Chicago Round Table program between President Hutchins and his colleagues on November 11, 1945, published in pamphlet form as "Peace and the Atomic Bomb." In February 1947 the B.B.C. devoted a week of remarkable broadcasts to the general theme.

It is difficult otherwise to explain the official curtain of silence which is at present maintained. The President of the United States speaks of the "sacred trust" in his keeping; with the British and Canadian Prime Ministers, he has affirmed his sense of grave responsibility, and the three political leaders have made an offer on terms of future collaboration with other governments. None of them has taken the really critical step of saying what the choice really is, and to go on to the insistence that his government is ready to risk the experiment of entrusting the United Nations with the power of executive direction in co-operation with other governments, and to make the consequential alterations both in the San Francisco Charter and their own constitutional powers. And this, after all, is the acid test. No one really knows what any national opinion is ready to accept if it is not given the choice of acceptance or refusal. Indeed, there is a disinclination to make the problem a matter of public concern. This seems far less related to governments' views of popular feeling than to their suspicions of one another's policies so clearly reflected not only in the making of the San Francisco Charter, but, still more, in the international conferences that have been held since the defeat of Japan in August 1945.

For sovereignty, it must be emphasized, is not a mere metaphysical abstraction, the debates about which have interest only for jurists and political philosophers. It is a concrete reality which gives the government of any independent nation the power to be bound only when it chooses to be bound, the right, therefore, to subordinate the good of mankind, if it thinks fit, to the self-interest of its own people, as itself alone it interprets that self-interest. To limit this power is, obviously, to deprive itself of the right to make and to apply its own criteria of wisdom and unwisdom in policy in whatever categories of action the limitation is accepted. No one would, I think, seriously argue that the common people of any country ever benefits when its government exercises its sovereign power to make war to attain some objective that it cannot win by peaceful means. Resistance to aggression, like that of the dictators in the Second World War, is rather an act of elementary self-preservation than an act of sovereignty; for the refusal on the part of any government concerned to defend its territory against aggressive attack would very rapidly deprive it of the power to make any decisions.

We are concerned with the reservation of sovereign rights to a government which has, at the back of its mind, at least the possibility that it may have to make war to secure some end which it declares vital to its interests. It refuses mediation, conciliation, arbitration; it declares that it must be the judge in its own cause and that it will brook no interference with the judgment it decides to make. In all such instances in modern times the common peoples have had no interest in a decision of this character, nor, indeed, have they ever been consulted. I do not think it can be seriously claimed that the common people of Great Britain had any interest in the Chinese Opium War of 1843, or in the bombardment of Alexandria in 1882, or in the South African War of 1899–1902. I do not think, either, that it can be argued with any force that the common people of Tsarist Russia had any interest in either the Crimean War or in the Russo-Japanese War; and I think that Lenin was right when he insisted, in the First World War, that it was to the interest of the common people in Russia that its government should be defeated in the field to make possible the successful revolutionary overthrow of the Tsarist regime. Nor did the common people of the United States have any interest in the Mexican War of 1846, or in the Spanish–American War. In all these cases—themselves typical of many others—each government used its sovereign power to protect vested interests and to enhance its own prestige; and these were so closely connected with one another that their mutual relations were inseparable. Sovereignty, in fact, is always the covering behind which the connection between vested interests and government is concealed from the common people. It is the process through which the emotional drive of a nation is mobilized behind a government' which would be impotent without its evocation. It is in the passionate excitement of war-making of this kind that ordinary men and women are led to refrain from a national examination of the purpose they are asked to support. Once the struggle has begun, it is normally an easy thing to make opposition, and even criticism, seem a seditious attack upon the unity of the nation.

I believe myself that the half-conscious background in which the thought of the American government about the atomic bomb is set is deeply related to the determination of American business men to push forward their interests at a moment when they think their hour of destiny has arrived. Acceptance of any serious form of international control would inhibit the unfettered exercise of their power; and since they shape, as no other interest shapes, the foundations of American policy, they are not anxious to limit the immense opportunities they see before them. They hate and fear the growing power of Russia. They think of Great Britain as the "weary Titan" no longer able to carry its heavy burden. I do not for one moment suggest that this is due to ill-will, or a lust for power, or unreasoning nationalism. It is, in the main, the outcome of the economic position in which the United States finds itself at the present stage of its development. The sovereign power is used, as it is always used, to protect a given set of productive relations, which their beneficiaries seek to justify by proving that their private advantage is the public good. They do not make this identification out of a merely selfish approach to the problems before them. The social content of their outlook is determined by the position in which they find themselves; and the men and women are rare who can transcend the boundaries of their position. We can understand why the productive relations of the Southern states led the plantation owners to see the merits of Negro slavery, but not its vices. We can understand, too, why the productive relations of the big corporations in America today make them resist with indignation the idea that trade-unions should have the power to compel inspection of their books so that the public may be informed whether some demand of the workers is financially justified; what appears to the workers a direct method of making public opinion an effective factor in industrial disputes appears to the corporation executives as a wanton interference with the right of the owners of private property to manage it in their own way. Nor is it less natural that the rulers of American business enterprise, needing a profitable market for their immense productive power and convinced that they can defeat any rivals in the race for its possession, should resent any restraint upon their access to victory, the more so when the domination of a foreign market helps greatly to assist them to overcome, or to evade, disturbing pressures they might otherwise encounter at home.

That is why so large a proportion of American business men look with such deep suspicion on Russia. They recognize that the decisive challenge to the free enterprise system comes from the socialist mode of ownership. They recognize, further, that in the degree that a socialist society is able at once to abolish unemployment and to raise the general standards of living among its citizens, it becomes a challenge to a society based on free enterprise unless the latter can outdistance the achievement of the ideas to which it is opposed; for they rightly understand that achievement which relieves the workers of one country from the major material evils of capitalist civilization is bound to infect the workers of another country in which those evils remain with the new ideology, and thus to weaken the hold of traditional authority. This, in the final analysis, is preserved for them by a government which, by maintaining its sovereignty, has the supreme coercive power in the community, at its disposal. If the weight of that coercive power did not maintain the social values implicit in the free enterprise system, its stability would be fatally undermined. They know, too, that this is more likely to be the case in a country where, as in America, the tradition of political democracy goes deep; and they are haunted by the constant fear that the common man may use his electoral power first to abridge, and then to destroy, the privileges which accrue to a small number, where the means of production are in private hands. That is the ghost which has haunted the American business man ever since the Federal Convention of 1787; and his mingled fear and hatred of its shadow has been greatly intensified by the evidence of the common man's consciousness of this power, as it was displayed in the nineteen-thirties in the New Deal of Franklin Roosevelt.

Internal policy must always be related to external policy. If the internal equilibrium of economic forces and their social results are to be maintained in the next generation, America must find the means of external economic expansion. The greater the degree to which it submits to limitations upon those means, the greater must become the internal pressure to decisive change. It is, therefore, intelligible enough that American business men should view with dislike limitations upon their sovereignty at a moment when they feel that their opportunity is supreme. It is the more intelligible if we remember that, in the United Nations, not only will the view of Russia carry weight only less decisive than that of America itself, but it will be one which is likely to receive wide support from nations whose social systems are set increasingly by a pattern of which Moscow, and not Washington, is the inspiration. The problem would, no doubt, be there by the signature of any effective system of collective security; but in the form in which it was signed in San Francisco, American sovereignty remained unabridged and unfettered. The sense of moral obligation could always dissolve into the knowledge of juridical freedom.

All the major influences of American business today are striving, with all their power, to keep unchanged the international institutions of the age before the discovery of atomic energy, after its implications have become clear. Save for the scientists themselves, and a number of unorganized intellectuals and social reformers, whose influence is in any case spasmodic and interstitial, they have on their side most that is powerful in American life; not least, they have the War and Navy Departments at the moment when their chiefs enjoy the great reputations they have made out of a victorious war. All the main instruments of publicity are largely in their hands. It is therefore not surprising that the first reaction of President Truman was to suggest that the "secret" be kept safely in American hands. That, at least, gave a period in which American supremacy could not be called into question; and that period might suffice to enable American business to lay the foundations of the external economic expansion it required. Even when he was persuaded to make the conditional offer of collaboration through the new international authority, the offer was timidly conceived, in terms of an approach hardly touched by the vastly changed environment in which all men's social thinking, especially on the international plane, is bound to be done. Nothing, frankly, is to be gained by denying the grave disproportion between the problem nations are set and the new offer President Truman was persuaded to make to its solution. It may temporarily postpone the crisis that is bound to come when a nation of great power lives by an ideology no longer relevant to its situation; the more so when it stands in the presence of another nation of great power which lives by an ideology whose relevance to the time is dramatic and direct. For it is as true of the international community as it is of the national that, as Lincoln said, a house divided against itself cannot stand. American business needs to retain American sovereignty at a time when the concept is obsolete for America and dangerous to the peace of the whole world. It will require statesmanship of the highest order to transcend this contradiction. Statesmen have to be very clear that the alternative to transcendence is catastrophe.

6

THERE is a curiously interesting curve of development in the first and second centuries of the history of the United States as a world power. In the first century, its statesmen are mainly concerned with internal consolidation and expansion, with security against the possible results of European ambitions on the American continent, and with the free development of its external trade. In the second period, expansion and security become merged and are tied in close relation with the policy of freedom for American commerce. The western movement illustrates consolidation and expansion; the acquisition of California and Florida, of Louisiana and Texas, of Cuba, the Phillipines, and Puerto Rico, have a deep tinge of expansion, but are, all of them, hardly intelligible except as safeguards against a Europe which, as Jefferson's correspondence shows so well, it regards with mingled feelings of strategic fear and social superiority. The constancy of the demand for "the freedom of the seas," in 1914 as in 1812, makes it a permanent part of the foundation upon which American foreign policy has been built.

After the Civil War the consolidation of America was internally complete, and no subsequent effort of importance has ever thought in terms of its disintegration; nor has any challenge been made to the Monroe Doctrine, save in diplomatic intrigue, like that of Germany in the First World War, or in the frenzied hopes of the wilder Nazis and Japanese fanatics in the Second. Nevertheless, because the technological basis of security has been rapidly changing in the last fifty years, the second century of American history has seen the emergence of a strategic expansion, as evident in the purchase of the Virgin Islands from Denmark during the First World War as in the acquisition of bases on lease from Great Britain during the Second. We do not yet know how far the principle of strategic expansion is likely to be pushed in the coming years; but it is a new and significant form of the interests of America as a world power. But the great feature of the new time is the contrast between the American effort to open up its own continent in the nineteenth century, and its effort to open up the Asiatic continent in the twentieth. Both efforts resulted in wars—with Mexico and Spain in the nineteenth century, with Japan in the twentieth. The difference is the outcome of the change in the processes of American economic life. In the first period, America needed, above all, to discover and exploit its own resources; security apart, international affairs were a matter of secondary importance. In the second period, the dynamic of the American economic power had made a vast hinterland essential to American business and finance, since, without far-reaching changes in the distribution of wealth in the United States—changes which would involve profoundly different relations of production—there was no prospect of maintaining the standard of life to which the American people had become accustomed. That is why the Open Door in China was laid down as a pivotal principle of

American foreign policy from the first, and that was why vital American interests were involved as soon as Japan exhibited her intention of dominating Asia as a Japanese hinterland. The rival ambitions could not have been compromised. Only war could have settled the outcome.

But what that outcome may mean is still a secret beyond our power to penetrate. The Asiatic hinterland is a very different area, as we move into the second half of the twentieth century, than it was even in the first quarter of this period. Revolutionary nationalism has swept over it with a force to which even greater concessions will have to be made; there are no European possessions there the foundations of which will not have to be largely reorganized in the next decade. And there is increasing realization among the peoples of Asia that to end the long and hard epoch of colonial subjection they require both industrialization and freedom. To make that combination, their leaders are insistent that foreign economic relations shall not result in replacing direct government by a European power, like that of Great Britain in India, of Holland in the Dutch East Indies, or France in Indo-China, by the indirect government which has played so large a part in the American penetration of its Latin neighbours. They realize how widely different are the two procedures in form, but they have a growing suspicion that an investment banker in New York can achieve the same substantial results as a colonial secretary in London or Paris or the Hague. That suspicion is emphasized by the impact upon them of the results of the Russian Revolution, above all in the relations built by Moscow with the backward peoples among the citizens of its own vast continent, and the swift pace of economic development from the Urals across to Vladivostok. There is already on foot an immense battle between the American way of life and the Russian way of life for the possession of the soul of Asia. It will, no doubt, be a long and complex struggle, with results very different from any our own generation can anticipate. As we seek to understand its meaning, it is important to bear in mind that Asiatic nations which achieve industrialization with freedom will present to America problems as grave for its own economy, as they may do to Russia if their development is shaped to a pattern in conformity with American economic needs. In the resolution of this difference lies a good deal of world history for the next hundred years.

The passage of supremacy from Europe to America was inevitable once Europe remained a divided continent, apparently incapable of unity, and America achieved its massive industrialization. The maintenance of divisions meant not only a serious misuse of economic resources and the subordination of general well-being to the rapacious appetite of national power; it meant also that the rivalry division involved was extended beyond the boundaries of Europe to a competitive imperialism which none of its national States had the ultimate power to sustain. Europe has been wasted and impoverished by two wars in the last generation, which have left it dependent for its future upon the goodwill of America or the influence of Russia. That dependence would not disappear, even with economic recovery, if the divisions which characterized the earlier period still remained; it might, on the contrary, make it more profound. That is the importance of Mr. Attlee's warning in the autumn of 1939. "We must," he said, "federate or perish." [18] But it is far from clear whether the conditions of possible federation exist, either psychologically or politically. There is no common tradition of living together; the passion for self-determination, largely begotten by the French Revolution, has lost little, if anything, of its intensity, and the absence of a common tongue is a grave barrier to common thought. Even if all these difficulties could be overcome, there remains the complex question of where the boundaries of the federation are to be drawn. It is certain that a West European federation from which Russia was excluded would be difficult to build, partly because it could have no meaning until both Spain and Portugal were democratized, and partly because the British position, both as a member of the Commonwealth and as a power with great Mediterranean and Asiatic interests, would make a coherent foreign policy impracticable. If all of Europe were to be included, then all of Russia must enter it, since a breach in the unity of the Russian economic system could be made only by its defeat in war. And since Russia regards a West European federation as a threat to its security, it is doubtful whether the Scandinavian countries would take the risk of joining it. If there is some small advantage, on economic grounds, in trying to form within the framework of the United Nations a system of relatively small economic federations in Europe, it is improbable that this would compensate, by its result, for the labour of its building; nor, in any case, would the advantage begin to emerge for some considerable time. Above all this, there is the outstanding fact that there exists in Europe no common system of values to bind men together, no single faith by which they could live.

The future of Europe, therefore, seems to me to depend upon the future of the United Nations; permanent well-being is permitted to it only on condition that this organization is successful. But success, in its turn, depends upon the ability of America and Russia to find the terms of a working compromise. Without that compromise, each of the organs created by the United Nations will become, even if slowly, an arena rather than a forum, in which America and Russia will seek to secure the support of each European member whose strength or strategic position makes its alliance of importance. As soon as one begins to inquire what terms make possible a working compromise, it becomes apparent, I think, in the light of historical evidence, that it is made possible only by a common interest in peace. If it is said that Americans and Russians quite obviously possess that common interest, I should agree at once; I have already argued that ordinary people everywhere do not benefit by war. But to admit this is not to say that the United States and Russia have a com-

[18] Speech at the Caxton Hall, *The Times of London,* October 8, 1939.

mon interest in peace. Rhetoric apart, that depends as much upon the inherent purposes to which the State power of each is made by its economic system to lend itself, and these purposes are only in part the conscious production of men. That does not mean for one moment that men and nations are the blind instruments of a destiny beyond their control; on the contrary, the ideas of men shape the purposes of the State power just as the State power of any government wields shapes the purposes to which men lend the drive of their energy and emotion. The common interest in peace in both America and Russia, which Europe needs for its self-preservation, is not, as it were, out there; it has to be made by the effort of them both, and the behaviour of Europe itself will either help or hinder that effort by the judgment made upon it by the two great protagonists. If they find, in their international relations in those fields of action they regard as vital, that no difference in policy is serious enough to justify conflict, the United Nations is likely to work well enough to give Europe the security in which there is time for recovery and renovation. It would also make it highly probable that America and Russia had come to share a faith in values wide enough to make their common interest in peace the central factor in international relations. But if the makers of policy in either nation become convinced of a decisive incompatibility of interest, it does not seem to me possible to avoid a third world war, in which both the geographical position and the productive capacity of Europe will unite to make it stand in relation to that war much as Belgium has stood to the European wars of the last three centuries.

I do not accept the views of writers who argue that, in the past, capitalist America and socialist Russia have always found that their "national interests have coincided at the most critical moments of [their] history." Mr. Starobin, from whom I quote, explains this coincidence on the ground that "the fundamental American interest was to prevent the rise of any one power in Europe and Asia to world hegemony. The destruction of fascism would guarantee this objective. The collective security of Europe, which is decisive for the Soviet Union, becomes the decisive measures of the future peace for the United States." [19] But Mr. Starobin is far too sensible to suppose that the defeat of the Axis powers, three years after he wrote, would produce of itself a static condition in which, *eo nomine*, the common interest in peace of the two major powers forthwith would transcend all ideological considerations. We are to assume, he tells us in the preamble to this confident prophecy, that while the United States remains a capitalist nation, it is one in which "the pro-fascist and appeasement forces shall be at least as limited as they are today." He thinks "we may even assume a larger participation of labour in the affairs of government, as a result of their indispensable contribution to the war effort, or at least a continuation of the relationship of class forces as ex-

[19] Joseph Starobin, "The Prospects of American–Soviet Relations," *Science and Society*, Summer 1942, p. 207.

pressed in the New Deal." [20] He may assume that; but even in the brief period since the victory over Germany and Japan it is clear that a bitter struggle will take place in the United States before the assumptions are verified. He deals with an anti-Russian critic, who "suggests that only by a return to a modified capitalism would the Soviet Union qualify as a factor in determining the peace," by arguing that it is more realistic to take the view of Professor Ralph Barton Perry that "we must come to an understanding not with a Russia founded on our own model, but with a communistic Russia." If this is accepted, Mr. Starobin suggests that "a basis for agreement between the two countries can be shown to exist from the expressed war and peace aims of both countries." [21] To this he adds one further assumption. "From the American viewpoint," he writes, "the needs involved in the reconstruction of Europe and the development of Asia offer opportunities of an exchange of goods and investment of capital. So long, as for instance in China, as this exchange of goods and investment of capital proceeds on the basis, not of subverting the sovereignty of the peoples involved, but under their jurisdiction, for so long will America realize its potentialities without returning to the conditions of the nineteenth century." [22]

I do not believe that Mr. Starobin really deceives himself. If, he says in effect, the post-war relations of capital and labour in the United States broadly accept the New Deal as their basis; if, further, American business men do not seek to come to an understanding with the Russia they desire, but with the Russia that is; and if, finally, their investments abroad, as in China, for example, leave the sovereignty of the people unimpaired in whose country the investments are made, there is no reason to expect disagreement. But Mr. Starobin knows that he is here saying only that if the United States becomes friendly to labour at home, and non-imperialistic abroad, after the war, there is every reason for us to expect peace with Russia. Of course there is. If we begin by making premisses which assume the validity of the results we desire, it is not very difficult to show that, given the premisses, precisely these results will follow. But it is precisely the question whether we are entitled to make these premisses about which the core of Mr. Starobin's analysis should have centered. What evidence there is does not suggest any anxiety among American business leaders to safeguard the gains of labour from the New Deal; on the contrary, it points to a resolute will to keep the trade-unions in a permanently subordinate position. And so far as we can interpret the activities of the United States' Armies of Occupation, both in Europe and Japan, whatever may have been their directives, the application of these has been a somewhat half-hearted attempt to purge Germany and Japan of their fascist elements. Certainly the revival of a neo-fascism in Italy after the winter of 1945, the picture of the widespread

---

[20] *Ibid.*, p. 205.
[21] *Ibid.*, p. 206.
[22] *Ibid.*

acceptance of Nazi co-operation in Germany, together with a lack of any
zeal for bringing known anti-fascist leaders into positions of authority,
are not very hopeful signs that "appeasement" belongs to a closed era.
Nor is it without grave significance that General MacArthur, the American soldier in charge of the occupation in Japan, has insisted on working through the Emperor—despite protests from both Chinese and American experts in the Far East—and has displayed a sullen hostility to the
agreement for a Russian share in the making of policy in occupied Japan.
If to these indices to the American outlook there is added the uncomfortable fact that, simultaneously with the plea of President Truman for
unity in China, and the Moscow Agreement of December 1945 that American and Russian troops should be withdrawn from Chinese territory
at the earliest possible moment, aid from the United States to the Chung-
king government proceeds upon an increasing scale, there is not very
much left for the right to the assumptions Mr. Starobin was optimistic
enough to make in 1942. The simple truth is that we have knowledge
of the direction American policy will take, as in Greece and Turkey,
which is alarming. With that knowledge, the fate of Europe, thus poised
uneasily between one new world, which feels its strength, and another,
which has begun to move from adolescence to maturity, is something
which does not lend itself to hopeful prophecy.

7

THE vital danger inherent in the American position is the simple one
that its drive to expand may come to be regarded as a mission—the "manifest destiny" of the United States—at this turning point in the history
of civilization when the power and authority of America are at their
zenith. No student of the history of the United States can afford to omit
this element from his assessment of the future. It is not only that it has
been the rationalization by which America has justified expansion to itself whenever the situation has justified expansion in its own eyes, perhaps, most remarkably in the brief negotiations between Secretary Lansing and Denmark over the purchase of the Virgin Islands; [23] it has
enabled the acquisition of the desired objective to be attained on biological grounds, sometimes on the ground that self-preservation makes
acquisition necessary, sometimes on the ground that it is the "law of
nature" for a people to expand, sometimes on the ground that when
expansion ceases, death supervenes. Or the ground may be shifted to
"natural right," which covers claims to expansion by propinquity, to expansion for security, or even to expansion lest one be given, as a neighbor,
a dangerous nation without one's own consent. Or the ground may be
moved to the right to the pursuit of happiness; and this has entitled Amer-

[23] Albert K. Weinberg, *Manifest Destiny* (Baltimore: Johns Hopkins Press, 1935).
I cannot adequately express my debt to this remarkable and indispensable book. All
the quotations which follow are from Dr. Weinberg's anthropological discoveries.

ica, in its own eyes, to the navigation of rivers, the command of ports at their mouth, and to the control of North American destiny. There has been expansion for reasons inferred from the facts of geography, not seldom coupled with an inferred knowledge of "the great Purpose of Human events." Or expansion has been based, as, notably, when the Indians were dispossessed, on the superior ability of the American to use the territory he has coveted, and this has been put forward as the justification of the claim to California and to Texas. It even justifies the right to economic imperialism where the occupying country hinders the development of the waste places. "The right to occupy a portion of the earth's surface," wrote the well-known investment banker, Mr. G. E. Roberts, "is . . . qualified by a proper consideration for the general welfare"; [24] and William H. Taft, when president of the United States, could speak of the need to bear in mind, when thinking of the Caribbean, that "it is essential that the countries within that sphere shall be removed from the jeopardy involved by heavy foreign debt, and chaotic national finances, and from the ever-present danger of international complications due to disorder at home. Hence, the United States has been glad to encourage and support American bankers who were willing to lend a hand to the financial rehabilitation of such countries." [25]

Nor is this all. "Manifest destiny" may mean a geopolitical theory of international relations; from at least the time of Benjamin Franklin, the assimilation of Canada has been in the American consciousness. So, too, have been not only the West Indies, but, at one time or another, all European possessions which border on the Caribbean. And to these ambitions must be added the interest in Cuba, in the Phillipines, and in Hawaii. The need to bring them into the orbit of America's power had become, by the eighteen-nineties, when Captain Mahan began fully to exercise his remarkable influence, an unconditional imperative; "whether they will or no," he wrote in 1890, "Americans must begin to look outward." Three years later the American export trade seemed to him to involve an American sea power strong enough to realize that "it is imperative to take possession, when it can be done righteously, of such maritime positions as contribute to secure command." [26] The limitation of "when it can be done righteously" seems to mean when the ruling opinion in America thinks that this step has become inevitable. We must not, however, omit the influence, at the end of the nineteenth century, of the doctrine of the "white man's burden." It becomes the obligation of the United States to civilize the backward peoples, to spread Christianity, to hinder the sacrifice of native peoples to barbarism like the actions of Spain in the Phillipines. And even if the "backward peoples," like the Filipinos in 1898, refuse to be civilized, then America must impose civilization upon them lest opposition injure its prestige among the other great powers.

[24] *Ibid.*, p. 95.
[25] *Ibid.*, p. 432.
[26] *Ibid.*, p. 259.

Alternatively, the United States must regard itself as the trustee of native welfare and act on its behalf whatever the opposition it may encounter.

Two other elements in the pattern of "manifest destiny" deserve some annotation. The first is the theory of the United States as the wielder of an international police power by which it preserves law and order within the general sphere of its interests, and, of course, especially within the area to which the Monroe Doctrine applies; it even appears that, in the Western Hemisphere, America must regard itself as responsible to Europe for the fulfilment of this obligation. As an international police, the United States may quell revolution, restore governments of its own choice, reorganize a country's financial arrangements, and insist upon the fulfilment of what President Wilson called "certain moral values of Pan-Americanism" [27]—values which it appears to be the duty of the United States, as more advanced and experienced in their understanding than other American powers, to define. It is, perhaps, a little curious that President Wilson was able to combine this view with a passionate belief in self-determination, and that he was convinced that such interventions as he made in Mexico, or Haiti, or San Domingo, were no more than the creation of the necessary conditions of "constitutional liberty," and, therefore, only formally in conflict with the doctrine of self-determination. For, since the government of the United States remains the final judge, it might well appear not merely to the country in whose affairs America intervenes, but even to an external observer, that "constitutional liberty" means something very like the acceptance of those principles of political behaviour and institutions which are regarded with most favour in the United States. Franklin Roosevelt, indeed, repudiated the idea that the United States must act alone in the exercise of this authority. He urged that, "when the failure of orderly processes affects the other nations of the continent . . . it becomes the joint concern of a whole continent in which we are all neighbours." [28] But Mr. Roosevelt was not then president; and he gave no guide to the institutional method by which he would have translated his approach into action.

The final aspect of "manifest destiny" to which I wish to refer is the view that America is fated to be the leader of the world. Many diverse streams have contributed to the formation of this outlook. From the sense, at the outset of its national history, that America is not like other peoples, comes the conviction that it is superior to them. From that superiority has come the ardent faith of men like Senator Albert J. Beveridge, in the last generation, that God had "marked the American people as His chosen nation to finally lead in the regeneration of the world." [29] Sometimes this faith is expressed by a belief like that of William Jennings Bryan that the whole world would accept America as the natural arbiter

[27] *Ibid.*, p. 435.
[28] *Ibid.*, p. 446.
[29] *Ibid.*, p. 459.

of its disputes. Sometimes, as with President Taft, the finance-capitalism embodied in "Dollar Diplomacy" is different from all other finance-capitalism because America's motive is "international philanthropy." Sometimes, as with both Woodrow Wilson and Franklin Roosevelt, it actually rejects territorial expansionism in order to secure international co-operation against aggression, above all to secure stability in the relations between States. Certainly a wide difference has emerged in the last thirty years between the idea of "manifest destiny," as Theodore Roosevelt and Henry Cabot Lodge conceived it—the simple idea that the nation should prove its virility by using it—to the idea which Woodrow Wilson and Franklin Roosevelt have sought to win acceptance for—the idea of leading the world to a rational scheme of organization by which collective power shall be mobilized against the nation which invokes war as an instrument of its ambitions.

Yet it is far from easy to be certain that this is any more than a temporary stage in America's view of its place in the world. We may agree at once that there is no single aspect of the way in which America has approached its international problems that cannot find its equivalent in the history of other great powers, even, indeed, of small ones. We may agree, most particularly, that expansionism has always clothed itself in the rhetoric of high ideals, if only because, otherwise, it evokes from men and women that hatred of war that is as old as war itself. Perhaps, on the whole, the moral record of the United States has been better in the last century and a half than that of the great European powers or of Japan. It still leaves unsettled the central and vital issue which is the test of the American claim to world leadership. If the historical analysis of "manifest destiny" shows anything, it shows the almost unlimited power of the human mind to equate what it ought to do with what it wants to do, to throw, in all sincerity, the protection of ethics over the nakedness of desire. I do not suggest for one moment that, in this, America differs from any other nation, though it is perhaps possible that the Puritan background of the American tradition, like that of England, makes the discovery of a moral foundation more urgent to action it is proposed to take, than is true of other nations.

In any case, the argument I have made seems to me to lead to the conclusion that America's activity as a world power will depend, as much as anything, upon its ability to overcome the stresses and strains of its domestic life. Foreign policy is never, in any nation, an outlook capable of being separated from its internal position. Each enters into the other and influences it. What America will be in the next half-century as a world power depends most profoundly upon what it does to its own citizens. The America of the Gilded Age, the America, even, of Harding and Coolidge, could not give that development its character without making the reality behind the appearance of international relations one which is incompatible with any long-term programme of peace, and that the more because of the new conditions set by the discovery of atomic fission. For a considerable period this is going to introduce a sense of fear and insecurity into foreign affairs. An America at peace within will be in a position to mitigate the insecurity that will result. But for an America that is unable to attain a satisfactory equilibrium in social relations, especially in the fields of labour and of race conflicts, the temptation will be to look abroad to "foreign ideas" for the source of American troubles; and there will be a mass growth of mushroom organizations permeated by that "red hysteria" which marked the fantastic performances of Attorney-General Palmer in 1919–20. The situation is serious enough in the winter of 1947. A mental climate has been created from which may grow, all too easily, the demand that America display its strength; a weak government might well accept the temptation to yield to the demand. For nothing is more dangerous to any nation than the possession of great resources without the ability to use them wisely, which, almost invariably, is the outstanding quality of a weak government.

It is here that so much of the use to which America puts its outstanding authority in the next epoch is going to turn upon whether great leadership is not only available, but also succeeds in convincing the nation that it is both great and available. That was done slowly in the Civil War by Abraham Lincoln; it was done swiftly after the Great Depression by Franklin Roosevelt. In each of these cases the great president was able to mobilize public opinion for great ends; in each case public opinion agreed that great ends required instruments of proportionate power for their fulfilment. But in each of these cases the background in which that leadership was set was provided by the fact of crisis; the tensions were already there which it was urgent to ease, the problems to be solved were so great that no man could dare to disregard them. At the close of a great war a national society is anxious, above everything, for rest from the fatigues it has endured; it is hungry for the normal; it seeks for relief from the hard effort of new thought. That is, of course, the kind of age when thinking government, as Bagehot termed it, is at a discount, because both its innovations and its energy are resented as invasions of the right to tranquillity. And the very resentment fatigue engenders gives opportunity to reaction, since it is able to put its plea in terms of a past era of peace to which men look back with longing. That is the first great danger America will face as it seeks to find the action that is comparable to its strength. We can be very certain that, unless it overcomes this danger, there is little hope of peace in our time.

XII

The Professions in America

IT IS part of the deep-rooted social egalitarianism of America that the idea of a profession is far more inclusive than it is in Europe. The lawyer and the doctor, the architect and the engineer, the teacher and the clergyman, the journalist, the banker, and the accountant, these, with commissioned officers in the Armed Forces, with civil servants, and with artists and men of letters, practically exhaust the categories of professional men and women in Europe. We do not mean by a profession a vocation the entrance into which depends upon the achievement of a qualification of the right to practise it, since this is untrue of artists and men of letters, of journalists, of bankers, and of the clergy in many, usually small, religious denominations. But we are accustomed to expect, not always justly, standards of behaviour in professional people more exacting than those we apply to business men, or farmers, or workers in industry and agriculture. We assume standards of performance which make money-making subordinate to their attainment. We look to the professions for some degree of research into the subject matter with which they are concerned. We argue that each of them has a tradition and a moral code within which the particular practitioner must normally move and have his being. Perhaps the full-time politician whose service to civic life is the main career to which he devotes his energies falls also within this rubric. Most people, I think, would agree for example, that Jean Jaurès and Sir Henry Campbell-Bannerman were fundamentally professional men.

The area of occupations to which the American normally applies the term is far more wide. I think it would be strongly argued that it includes the advertising specialist, the publicity expert, the real estate agent, who sought so earnestly to be known as a "realtor," the publisher, the undertaker, who in the last generation has been elevating himself to the grim dignity of a "mortician," the "naturopaths" in all their manifold variety, the business "consultant," the insurance agent, the confidential secretary, the host of men and women engaged in broadcasting, hotel proprietors, a large number of the men and women in the cinema industry

564

—script writers, directors, producers, photographers, to name but a few
—investment counsellors, tax consultants: the list might almost be extended indefinitely. There is much to be said for the view that all Americans, the *rentier* apart, who do not earn their living by the manufacture of some commodity in a factory, or by farming, and do not normally belong to the wage-earning class, either because they receive individual fees from a client, or because they receive a monthly salary, or because they are paid in some form of percentage basis, regard themselves, and are widely regarded, as members of a profession. If that status is in jeopardy, nothing is more likely than the emergence among them of an organization which will appoint officers, hold at least an annual convention, and adopt a body of rules which will probably be called a "code of ethics." Even business men seek professional status. It is, moreover, characteristic of American business men that they continually seek to use their associations, even where their policies are so well-known as those of the National Association of Manufacturers or of the Chamber of Commerce, as policy-making bodies. It is assumed that the safe-guarding of the public interest by a prohibition against "unethical practices" is a matter of primary concern. It then becomes wholly natural for bodies like the Rotarians to develop, in which business is set within a vaguely defined frontier of moral, and even religious, principles. And an organization like the National Industrial Conference Board, or the Chemical Foundation, or the National Electric Light Association, will give the appearance of solid and detached research to publications the only object of which is, in fact, of a strictly commercial character.[1] Labour groups apart, every vocation in the United States is seeking for grounds upon which to justify its status as a profession.

It is not, I believe, merely fanciful to argue that this constant effort to extend the area of occupations which have been recognized as professions is historically the outcome of the Puritan doctrine of the "calling." It began as an emphasis upon the virtue of work as a medium through which the claims of religious duty could be fulfilled; it then led inferentially to the views, first, that success in work was proof of God's grace and that failure was the punishment for sin. This led, in the second place, to the conception of poverty as the punishment for sin, and to the new conceptions of idleness and the poor which began to be general in the second half of the sixteenth century. With the decline of religious conflict and the growth of toleration—partly the result of economic, and partly the result of intellectual, influences—the doctrine of the "calling" was reshaped by the effort to find social laws governing the universe as wide and as compelling as the physical laws discovered by Kepler and Copernicus, by Galileo and Newton, and other great men of science. The result can be seen in the seventeenth century in the attitude to the poor

---

[1] *Cf.* the remarkable materials in Beale, *Are American Teachers Free?*, especially Chap. XVIII *et seq.;* and Robert A. Brady, *Business as a System of Power* (New York: Columbia University Press, 1943), Introduction and Chaps. VI and VII–X.

taken by economic writers like Thomas Mun, and John Cary, and Laurence Bradden. It emerged in the eighteenth century in writers so different as Daniel Defoe and Bishop Berkeley, Arthur Young and Edmund Burke.[2] Much the same outlook is characteristic of the American writers; they began with glosses upon the canonist doctrines of the middle ages and swiftly adapted them to colonial conditions. If John Cotton and Increase Mather, John Winthrop and Judge Sewall, found a theological basis for wealth, by the eighteenth century this was replaced, as nothing shows so well as the writings of Benjamin Franklin, by a rationalist utilitarianism, hardly different from the contemporary doctrines of European, and especially British, economic speculation.

But in a new country like America, where labour was scarce and where wealth was so much more the return to actual effort than was the case in more settled and stratified Europe, it was very difficult, at least before the last years of the eighteenth century, to make social distinctions in terms of men's occupations. No doubt the clergy always had a place apart, though many of them laboured with their hands. No doubt the ownership of, and speculation in, land made a small number of men wealthy and powerful. But it is significant that not until the epoch of independence did the lawyer and the physician secure a status of distinction; and it is clear, as I have sought to show in an earlier chapter, that there was relatively little admiration for the artist or the man of letters, much less for the actor or for the musician, once the performance of his function had a mainly secular setting. This is especially true, even beyond the Revolution, of the teacher's status; the regard in which he was held depended in a high degree on the proximity of his work to preparation for an ecclesiastical calling. What America wanted was men and women who would make it great by exploiting its natural resources; and there is little evidence of a distinction between one occupation and another except in its capacity to secure wealth for the men who produced it.

The difference, I think, began to emerge in the closing years of the eighteenth century and became more strongly emphasized as the nineteenth century developed, though the relation between status and occupation has never been so direct or so influential as it has been in Europe. It was the outcome of the growth of a leisured class in America; its wealth enabled its members to travel and to educate their sons in Europe. It led them to import European fashions and ideas and standards, and increasingly to accept the ideal of the gentleman as the criterion which measured the status of an occupation. This outlook was reinforced by the disrepute into which manual labour fell, partly through the inference of its association with slavery and with the habits of the Southern plantation owners, and partly because it became ever more clear that the manual labourer could not hope to rise to wealth if he continued to labour with his hands. It was reinforced, further, by the grateful recognition of the part played

---

[2] *Cf.* my *Rise of European Liberalism;* and Edgar S. Furniss, *The Position of the Laborer in a System of Nationalism* (Boston: Houghton Mifflin, 1920).

by the lawyer in defining the American case in the Revolution, and by the increasing need of his services, with the growth of industry and commerce, after independence had been won. With the closer alliance, moreover, between science and medicine, the doctor attained a new eminence; and since a leisured class, as well as the men with newly made fortunes, became anxious for both amusement and what Veblen has termed "conspicuous consumption," the arts and literature began to be patronized upon a scale which the ideal of the gentleman required. At this stage, which is clearly mature by the time of John Adams' presidency, the separation of business from the professions began to follow the European model.

But it was never so complete as in Europe, and Americans have never grown so accustomed to the separation as Europeans. The tradition of the need for effort, the attitude to all work as a "calling," the consequent suspicion of the leisured life, have all been a vital part of the inheritance of American civilization, and they have made it difficult for the values implied in the concept of the gentleman to have any influence comparable to their authority in Europe. That difficulty has been enhanced by at least three other factors peculiarly American. The first, and most important, is the absence of the rigid class structure which still has so large a part in European society; the second is the remarkable mobility of the American, both occupational and territorial, which has inhibited that rigidity of values typical of more static communities like Great Britain; and the third is the degree to which positions of honorific significance are open to men and, increasingly, to women, without regard to the occupation they follow. It may be membership in the cabinet; it may be appointment to an embassy or legation abroad; it may be, in the case of an academic lawyer, appointment to the Bench, even including the Supreme Court;[3] it may be one of a variety of special posts, as when a social worker, like Mr. Harry Hopkins, was selected by President Franklin Roosevelt, first, as head of the Works Progress Administration, then, if for a brief period only, as Secretary of Commerce, and, finally, as his main personal adviser on international affairs. In Great Britain, I think, it is true to say that Sir William Blackstone was the first academic lawyer to reach the Bench and also the last; though even he had a period, after his tenure of the Vinerian professorship at Oxford, when he was a member of Parliament and solicitor-general. I do not think there is any case in which anyone outside the narrow ranks of the professional diplomats and the politicians de carrière has ever been appointed to a British embassy, or to a colonial governorship, with the special exception of Lord D'Abernon's mission to Berlin, until a railwayman, Sir F. J. Burrows, was made governor of Bengal in the early winter of 1945.

To the British way of thinking, the ideal of the professional has been that of the gentleman with ample means, who could devote his energies to

[3] In 1946 four of the nine members of the Supreme Court had been full-time university professors of law.

politics at Westminster, or, as a landowner, become a great figure in the life of the county where he dwelt. The assumption—for which the evidence is far smaller than is generally believed—was that his private means made him free from the danger of corruption; he could, therefore, take a detached view of the public welfare. Professions were occupations as nearly as possible related to that ideal. Those who practised them must be their own masters. They must be able to possess the culture of which the British ruling class believed themselves the guardians and the patrons. They must have the social manners that class displayed to the outside world. Intermarriage between them and their children on the one hand, and the aristocracy and its children on the other, must not seem outside the wonted routine. Entry into a profession, and qualification as the test of entry not less than competence in practising it, must not, normally, be open except to those behind whom there is considerable financial support; even today, as Professor Ginsberg has shown, [4] the degree to which the barrister's side of the legal profession remains hereditary, and is dependent, for the average entrant, on influential connection, is remarkable. The outstanding trait of the professional man, so notable in the lawyer and the doctor, is the maintenance of the elaborate pretence of a very remote interest in the financial return for his work; and much the same outlook is preserved by fixed salaries for the clergy and the civil service and university teachers. None of these, at least directly and openly, will bargain about salaries, or, in the higher categories, think of a trade-union affiliated to other workers' organizations for the protection, by collective bargaining, of their main standards of life. Part of the conventions of their behaviour is the assumption that, because they are professional men, monetary reward is a secondary consideration. It is, in fact, their outward indifference to money that enables them to be accepted as gentlemen, and to embody in their lives the values which that character imposes. The famous visit of Voltaire to Congreve tells its own story. Both Scott and Dickens used their immense success to symbolize their entrance into the "calling" of a gentleman; and the first impulse of the lawyer who obtains great wealth is, like Mansfield or Eldon, to buy a country estate and play in the county the part of the noble landowner.

It is, I think, a significant fact that none of the outstanding professions in Great Britain has made any serious inquiry in modern times into the terms upon which its members perform their functions; and, still more significant, that, with the partial exception of the Law Society, none of them has any standing organization directly concerned with the improvement either of its own knowledge of its own working, or of its relations to the public. Both the Bar and Medicine have immensely powerful professional bodies to protect the privileges of their members; and I know of no body in Great Britain with authority comparable to that of the General Medical Council. There is a General Council of the Bar, over which the Attorney-General presides; but it is not an exaggeration

[4] Morris Ginsberg, *Studies in Sociology* (London: Methuen, 1932).

to say that it has never concerned itself with the improvement of the law or gone into the difficult problems involved in the semi-direct relation between barrister and client. The Inns of Court control admission to the Bar; but their attitude to legal education is more like a social function than an intellectual discipline. The solicitors have been more social-minded, especially in the last thirty years; but even they have concerned themselves with the problems of justice peripherally rather than directly. Nor is it, I think, unfair to say that the drive to greater public responsibility in the British medical profession has come from outside rather than from inside its ranks; while the clergy of the Established Church in England are still too deeply tied in with the character of the British system of property, especially in the rural areas, to make the consideration of capacity for social service the main basis upon which its normal habits, or its methods of promotion, have been built. Only in the national and local Civil Service, in the Armed Forces, and in the public teaching profession is it frankly admitted that monetary considerations are really important, and that what are often called "professional ethics" usually begins to be real where income offers some chance of an adequate life, and its recipient must seek promotion by standards of achievement in which there is some pretence to objectivity.

In all this, the great contrast with the United States lies largely in three directions. First, and most striking, is the open way in which the American profession examines its own behaviour and sets out directly to improve its character as a public service, as compared with the reticence and complacency of British professions. Second, it is notable that an American rarely has special standing by reason of the profession he pursues; there must be something notable about the performance of a lawyer or a doctor to make his status different from that of a business man of about the same level of income. And, third, though American doctors rarely change to another occupation, changes in other professions are frequent, and it is a common occurrence that their members should have paid for their training by earning their living in almost any other sort of occupation. No doubt there are other differences. The American professional man is far less averse to methods of publicity by which he may become known; the more careful reticence of a British professional man is, in this respect, much nearer the aloofness of the gentlemanly ideal than is the American habit of mind. A far larger percentage of Americans who acquire a professional qualification utilize it as a way of earning their living, especially in the law; in Britain, it is far more common for a man who does not propose to practise to secure a qualification much as one takes a university degree. Professions are far less likely to be hereditary in the United States than in Great Britain, and, apart from medicine and, in the East and Middle West, the law, entrance into them is both cheaper and easier. It is, perhaps, due to the persistent heritage of frontier life that the American professional man is, from one angle, far less specialized, while, perhaps as the outcome of the more complete technological conditions of the United States, he may well be far more specialized than is the case in Great Britain. Geographical conditions probably explain the fact that, while in Britain the outstandingly successful men in most professions tend to gravitate to London, in the United States, not only has Washington no pre-eminence of this kind, but there are at least a dozen centres which offer greater prospect of success.

There is, moreover, an interesting psychological factor of difference which is not without its significance. The whole apparatus which makes up the professional man's physical environment resembles that of the business man in the United States in a degree that is just beginning to be known in Great Britain. The lawyer's "chambers" are his "office"; so, too, is the doctor's "surgery." Both of them will use, and be far more dependent upon, a secretary, a dictaphone, a modern filing system, and similar aids to what is either "efficiency" or "excessive overhead costs," according to one's habit of mind. An American professional man is likely to have more books, and more of them in the latest edition, than his opposite number in Britain. Unless he has been a failure, his office is more likely to be emphatically modern in design than the lawyer's chambers or the doctor's study in Britain, which seem to exhale a faint odour of antiquity not wholly undeliberate. I remember the astonishment of a distinguished American lawyer, who was seeing England for the first time, when I took him to see the Attorney-General in his room at the Royal Courts of Justice; he talked long afterwards about the difference between its faded disorder, its rather mean furniture, and its lack of distinction, as compared with the amplitude and opulence amidst which the American Attorney-General did his work. He was, perhaps, even more impressed at the difference between the rooms of the Law Lords in the House of Lords and the magnificent apartments provided for the justices of the Supreme Court in their recently built palace in Washington. It is a feature, I think, which distinguishes the two approaches to the professions at almost every turn. One is tempted to think that the English lawyer, for example, does his work in surroundings far more like those of an American provincial town, like that Springfield from which Abraham Lincoln went to the White House more than eighty years ago, than the suites of offices in the modern skyscraper in which the American lawyer of today performs his mysteries. Certainly few law clerks or secretaries of an eminent lawyer in the United States would accommodate themselves, without difficulty, to the little poky foreroom which the English barrister or solicitor offers to his subordinates. Nor can an observer fail to note that a patient who sees his specialist in Harley Street or Wimpole Street is essentially looking at the comfortable drawing-rooms of the late Victorians of wealth, furnished with inherited late eighteenth-century furniture; in New York or Chicago or Philadelphia, he would not be quite certain, some medical apparatus apart, whether it was his doctor or lawyer whom he was consulting.

It is impossible for me here to discuss in any detail more than two of the professions in the United States. I select, as the outstanding examples, the legal and medical professions. I do so partly because they are at once the most important and the best organized; and partly because there is a wealth of material about their conditions at once more extensive and more profound than exists about any of the others. Though some of these have been the subject of careful studies, the engineer, for example, far more is known of the conditions under which the workers by brain actually function, literary people, for example, or artists, than is known in any thorough way either of their organization or of their economic problems. This is even true of the teaching profession; no one has yet drawn a full picture of the American teacher on all the different planes of his life. The importance of such studies is, indeed, recognized; and a series of notable accounts of the doctor, the engineer, the nurse, and the social worker have been published by one of the great American foundations. But they do not approach the completeness with which the legal and the medical professions have been studied; nor, indeed, have their own members been so interested in self-analysis. It may well be that this is the outcome of a climate of opinion in America generally which has been more conscious of an inadequate relation between these services and public need than is the case with other professions; though the inadequacy has been just as great in Britain without the result of compelling either public inquiry or self-analysis. However that may be, nothing shows the American professions so clearly, in a society like the United States, than the law and medicine, since none has so fully provided the model on which others work. The analysis of their characteristics is an index to a very considerable and growing area of American life.

2

I TAKE the legal profession first; and it is worth remarking, at the outset, that the lawyer was not highly regarded in the American colonies until well into the eighteenth century.[5] They were relatively few in number, and if the citizens looked upon them with suspicion, that was probably a reflection of the attitude to them of innumerable Englishmen of the seventeenth century, not least of the formidable John Lilburne; though lawyers like Selden and Prynne and Oliver St. John played an honourable part on the popular side in the English Civil War, and Coke atoned for much of his earlier career by his discovery of Magna Charta after his dismissal from the Bench. It may be, as Mr. Charles Warren has argued, that the rigidity of the Common Law, the difficulty of obtaining law books, and the type of man who became a lawyer, were responsible for this view.[6] A brief scrutiny, moreover, of such a book as William London's *Catalogue* suggests that law books were no more difficult to

[5] Beard, *The Rise of American Civilization*, p. 100.
[6] Charles Warren, *A History of the American Bar* (Boston: Little, Brown, 1911), Chap. I.

obtain than theological writings, which were imported in considerable numbers; while the career of Judge Sewall in Massachusetts shows that men of standing and character did not hestitate to enter the legal profession. It is, I think, far more likely that the lawyer was an unnecessary luxury in a colony until its affairs were on a settled footing and urban life and mercantile pursuits had become normal features of its existence.

For from the beginning of the eighteenth century lawyers began to multiply. They were more likely to attend college than any other profession but the clergy; and they went over in considerable numbers to the English Inns of Court. They repeated, moreover, that tendency to combine the legal profession with political interests which has so long characterized West European civilization in general, and that of England in particular. Professor and Mrs. Beard have told us that thirteen out of twenty-four members of the Albany Congress of 1754 were lawyers; in the first Continental Congress twenty-four of the forty-five delegates were lawyers; in the second, which was responsible for the Declaration of Independence, lawyers numbered twenty-six out of fifty-six members; while at the Philadelphia Convention, thirty-three of the fifty-five delegates were lawyers.[7] Obviously they had become, by the time the Constitution was launched, a pivotal element in the community; and after 1789 there was a rapid growth of organized Bars, the beginnings of law schools, and the emergence of men like Marshall, Story, Wilson, Kent, and Livingston, each of whom, in his way, did by decision or by writing all, and even more than all, of the work comparable to that of Mansfield when he adapted the English Common Law to new economic conditions, as much by the sheer weight of his intellectual authority as by any other method. No one, certainly, is now likely to argue that the great John Marshall was deeply learned in the precedents of the law.[8] It is not really important that there was a deep dislike of the lawyer after the Revolution; the position of poor debtors, the currency situation, and land speculation, in all of which the lawyer was mainly the agent of the rich, and especially of the creditor class, sufficiently accounts for the unpopularity noted by contemporary observers. What is far more important is the fact that, from 1800 onwards, almost every new factor in the development of American civilization, land settlement, canal building, banking, railroads, the growth of corporations, the development of public utilities like gas, electricity, road transport, the telegraph and the telephone, all these, with their inevitable concomitants, first, of statutory regulation, and, second, of commission control with a consequential administrative law, have brought the legal profession into an ever closer relation with the life of the United States.

One has to remember that more than two-thirds of the men who have held the American presidency have been lawyers. That is true of over seventy per cent of cabinet officers. It holds for fifty-eight per cent of

[7] Beard *op. cit.*, p. 10.
[8] Oliver Wendell Holmes, *Speeches* (Boston: Little, Brown, 1913), p. 87.

state governors since 1865. Since that date, also, seventy-two per cent of the Senate and sixty-four per cent of the House have been lawyers; and, taking ten states as a sample, seventy-one per cent of their legislatures were composed of lawyers. If to these are added the judicial bodies in the federal government, the states, and the cities, the attorneys-general, the district attorneys, the legal members of government departments, state and federal, the immense place held by the lawyer in American life becomes clear. He is at the centre of almost all sources of public decision.

It is far from easy to be certain about the statistics of lawyers in the United States. The Census returns classify them by age, colour, and sex, and for each city of more than twenty-five thousand people as well as for the whole Union. But even when one knows that in the nineteen-thirties there were about 160,000 lawyers in the whole Union, it is difficult to be certain just what this implies. It is not really known whether they are adequately distributed, whether the profession, as so often claimed, is overcrowded, whether the distribution has any proportionate relation to the need for legal aid, and so on. It must be remembered that lawyers are admitted to the Bar of a particular state, and that they do not often, appeals to Washington apart, move outside its boundaries. It has been shown that some 7200 enter practice annually, and that this is a figure more than sixty per cent higher than is needed to keep the number of American lawyers stable; but it is not known whether this is because social and economic changes imply a need for more lawyers, or because people are more anxious to avail themselves of legal advice. The Census of 1850 showed that, in all branches of the legal profession, there were 103 lawyers for every 100,000 of the population: in 1880, for every 100,000, there were 128 lawyers of every kind; in 1900, there were, on the same basis, 151; in 1920, there were 125; and in 1930, there were 140. In the decade before 1930 lawyers increased in number twice as fast as the general population; but in Massachusetts they increased four times as fast, and the same is true of the District of Columbia; in Florida, while there was an increase in population of fifty-two per cent, the increase in the legal profession was one hundred and thirty per cent. These are exceptional, however, for a number of reasons. In eighteen states, either the proportion of lawyers declined, or the population increased in ratio faster than the profession. Indeed, if one takes all the figures since 1850, the number of lawyers per hundred thousand of the population was higher in 1930 than in any of the intermediate decades.

But this is not the whole story. Mr. P. J. Wickser [9] has shown that in 1930, on the basis of population and wealth, the profession was overcrowded in five states, among which was New York. Since, overwhelmingly, the lawyer is an urban creature, it is interesting to note that in Akron, New Haven, Boston, New York, and Washington the increase in numbers varied from twenty to forty per cent. It is, I think, reason-

---

[9] Philip J. Wickser, "Law Schools, Bar Examiners, and Bar Associations—Cooperation versus Insulation," *American Law School Review*, April 1933, p. 734.

able to suppose that the increase in the federal capital was mainly due to the growth of government work, while that in New York and Boston was due to their position as metropolitan cities serving, in legal matters, areas far wider than their own boundaries. This is brought out by the fact that, in the Census of 1930, the ninety-three cities with more than 100,000 persons contained twenty-nine per cent of the American population, but almost fifty per cent of its lawyers; while cities and rural areas under 25,000 persons, with some sixty per cent of the population, contained less than forty per cent of the lawyers. While there was one lawyer for every 146 people in Washington, one for 351 people in Seattle, one for 379 in New York, and one for 371 people in San Francisco, in some of the Northern states, like Maine, there were 1045 citizens per lawyer, in Pennsylvania, 1190 citizens, in South Carolina, 1532, in Mississippi, 1609, and in Alabama, 1656. While the average number of persons to each American lawyer throughout the United States is over 750, in small cities and rural areas it is 1200, in cities with a population of over 100,000 it is in the ratio of one lawyer to 470 citizens. And this contrast is heightened by the fact that, as students of rural social life have shown, in those areas the lawyer is overwhelmingly likely to live in a county seat, and very rarely outside such a place.[10] It thus becomes likely that agricultural America must go, as a rule, to a big urban centre for anything in the nature of specialist legal advice.

Dean L. K. Garrison, in a deeply interesting study, has shown that in the State of Wisconsin there has been, in the fifty years since 1800, a growth not only in legal business, but also in the chance of a successful career for the lawyer.[11] On a narrower statistical basis, the same result has been reached in an inquiry by Professor J. E. Brenner into the California Bar.[12] Judge Clark has shown by a careful survey of an effectively representative sample of Connecticut citizens that there is in that state a need for substantial legal aid in relatively simple matters which might well, if rendered at the outset of a claim or grievance, do much to save a great deal of public litigation and, perhaps even more, personal unhappiness.[13] On the evidence, it seems highly doubtful whether anyone is entitled to say that there are too many lawyers.

It is true that legal incomes are low. In New York in 1938 an inquiry revealed that the average income of over three thousand practising lawyers was under three thousand dollars a year, and that, in the sample examined, the thirty-four lawyers who earned more than fifty thousand dollars a year earned, among them, more than did the lower fifty per cent of the sample; the inquiry also revealed that in 1935—which was still a period

[10] C. Luther Fry, *American Villagers* (New York: Doran, 1926), pp. 119 f.

[11] Lloyd K. Garrison, "A Survey of the Wisconsin Bar," *Wisconsin Law Review*, February 1935, pp. 145–46.

[12] James E. Brenner, "Ratio of Population to Lawyers," *Case and Comment*, April 1936, pp. 6–8.

[13] Charles E. Clark and E. Corstvet, "The Lawyer and the Public," *Yale Law Journal*, June 1938, pp. 1272 ff.

of depression though its peak had been passed—about ten per cent of the members of the Manhattan Bar were qualified for relief under the poor law. For the United States as a whole, the Department of Commerce estimated that the average annual income of the lawyer dropped from fifty-five hundred dollars in 1929 to forty-two hundred in 1934.[14]

There is no evidence to show that the law is an overcrowded profession for the simple reason that no one has any idea of the relation between numbers requiring legal aid and the numbers available to serve them. It thus becomes futile to argue that fewer people should be admitted to the Bar; or that the entrance to law schools, or examinations for admission to the Bar held by the state boards, or the level of character required, should be made more stringent. Still less is there any sense in arguing, as some lawyers did during the depression, that there should be a ban on admissions to the Bar for a term of years.[15] These proposals have no other objective than to raise the income of the legal profession by spreading work over a smaller number of its members; they envisage the creation of a quasi-monopoly for those lawyers on whose behalf the restrictions are made operative. The argument that this is justified by the determined way in which the American Medical Association has reduced the number of new entrants to the medical profession has really no validity at all, since it merely raises the question of whether the trade-union of the American doctors was, in its turn, justified. A profession cannot honourably argue that it should close the door on newcomers in order to increase the earnings of those who, at some given date, were authorized to practise, even if the real purpose is concealed by the promise that, when the door is opened, the new members will have had a more effective training. That is a denial of all the criteria by which a profession is known.

I shall deal a little later with the problems raised by American legal education and its relation to admission to the Bar. It is more helpful, first, to consider the difficulties faced by American lawyers in convincing the public that the legal system of the United States, including its judicial institutions, which are, of course, also manned by lawyers, is adequate for the problems with which it has to deal. It is not enough to say that there have always been complaints about the administration of the law;[16] what is important is the fact that no attempt to remedy the complaint has ever seriously approached success. There is still delay in the courts; there is still a massive uncertainty; there is still the high cost not only of litiga-

---

[14] *National Income in the United States* (Department of Commerce, 1936), pp. 203 ff.

[15] *Cf.* discussions by Sidney Teiser, "A Proposal for a Limited Bar," *American Bar Association Journal,* January 1935, pp. 42–46; and Robert F. Maguire, "Social Effects of Overcrowding," *American Bar Association Journal,* February 1937, pp. 85–87.

[16] Roscoe Pound, "Causes of Popular Dissatisfaction with the Administration of Justice," an address delivered at the annual convention of the American Bar Association in 1906, reprinted in *Journal of the American Judicature Society,* February 1937, pp. 178–87. Dean Pound draws a grim picture of the position.

tion, with its possibilities of appeal, but even of consultation before a case is heard in the courts. Now, as always, the number of practising lawyers who can be aroused to an interest in legal reform remains pitifully small. Now, as always, it is incredibly difficult to get a lawyer disbarred for inefficiency or unprofessional conduct. Now, as always, the conflict over technicalities, mostly procedural, between judge and lawyers, takes more time than is occupied by the actual evidence. And, as a rule, where swift justice is most badly needed, in the lower courts which decide small cases, both civil and criminal, there is the least ability on the Bench, and the least ability at the Bar. Every judge knows that he is sitting on cases which ought never to have been brought, or in which the resources of some little man who is fighting a great corporation make it almost impossible for him to hope to carry on to the highest court against the resources of his opponent.[17]

Nor is it possible to acquit the legal profession of a high share of responsibility for evils which quite plainly can be tackled. The considerable literature which now exists not only on the law and the poor, but upon what may fairly be termed the underworld of the legal profession, shows that the problems involved are important. It is, no doubt, true that the main causes of disbarment are relatively few in number, and that, to take an example from the large Bar of the City of New York, nearly twenty-three thousand cases of complaint were received by its Bar Association. But of these, less than one thousand were fully investigated by the Committee on Grievances of the Association; and, of these, only one per cent were prosecuted before the appropriate division of the Supreme Court of New York.[18] The record of the New York City Bar, moreover, is, in all probability, a very good one; it is said, on very good authority, that in perhaps ninety per cent of the cases the only result is a warning to the offender.[19] The difficulty goes far deeper than the formal complaint which admits of evidence and investigation.

Its roots lie in three things. First, and above all, in the apathy of the legal profession. Far too few of its members are interested in maintaining its standards; and far too many are anxious not to incur the trouble and unpopularity which is the usual lot of anyone who attempts to crusade for reform; how deep that resentment may go was grimly exhibited before the Senate Judiciary Committee when President Wilson nominated Mr. Brandeis to the Supreme Court of the United States in 1917.[20] The

[17] Robert H. Jackson, "The Bar and the New Deal," *American Law School Review,* April 1935, p. 154.
[18] Esther Lucile Brown, *Lawyers and the Promotion of Justice* (New York: Russell Sage Foundation, 1938), p. 213. I should like to express my debt to this very valuable book.
[19] *Ibid.*
[20] *Cf.* the immense volume of testimony, *Hearings before the Sub-Committee of the Committee on the Judiciary, United States Senate, on the Nomination of Louis D. Brandeis to be an Associate Justice of the Supreme Court of the United States,* 64th Cong., 1st Sess., Sen. Doc. No. 409, which accompanied the Committee's Report to the Senate.

second factor is the outcome of a situation in which the successful lawyer is overwhelmingly the lawyer of the great corporations; and it is no inconsiderable part of his function to find a barely justifiable road to the ends desired by his client. "I have had many lawyers," Mr. J. P. Morgan is reported to have said, "who have told me what I cannot do; Mr. Root is the only lawyer who tells me how to do what I want to do." [21] The nature, indeed, of the relation between lawyer and client, not least at the highest levels, encourages the former to specialize in technicalities of procedure, delay, and appeal. It is not easy to think of Mr. Andrew Carnegie's personal lawyer becoming, as Philander C. Knox became, an effective Attorney-General enforcing the Sherman Act; [22] and it is not very surprising to see him a little later, as senator from Pennsylvania, urging the inclusion of a provision for judicial review of railroad rates in the Hepburn bill, lest sacred rights "painfully won from the tyrannies of the past . . . be forfeited." [23] The atmosphere of the issue is set out, as well as anywhere, in that classic report of Herbert Knox Smith, Theodore Roosevelt's Commissioner of Corporations, in which he told the President that "no moral grounds for attack" against the powerful Morgan-controlled International Harvester Company existed, though there might be technical grounds. Mr. Smith then went on to say that "while the administration has never hesitated to grapple with any financial interest, no matter how great, when it is believed that a substantial wrong is being committed, nevertheless, it is a very practical question whether it is well to throw away now the great influence of the so-called Morgan interests, which, up to this time, have supported the advanced policy of the administration." [24] Theodore Roosevelt decided that it would be foolish to throw the support away. He refused to explain why he had discontinued the investigation; and he refused to allow Mr. Smith to show the papers in the case to a Senate Committee. If this is the attitude on the highest plane, it is not easy to expect men on a lower plane who seek to climb upwards to risk their careers, as they ascend upwards, by doing what the leaders of their profession have so rarely attempted to do.

It is sometimes argued that the standards of the legal profession would be higher if American judges were permitted a wider control of their courts than is now the custom. That might well be so, not least since a relatively high percentage of the judiciary have either little experience of practice in the court room, or have engaged in the type of advice or actual litigation in which the greater the skill in the use of procedural distortions, the more successful the lawyer is expected to be. Yet it is difficult to accept the view that an extension of judicial control is a decisive clue.

[21] Philip C. Jessup, *Elihu Root* (New York: Dodd, Mead, 1938), Vol. I, p. 183.
[22] It was he who advised President Theodore Roosevelt on the Northern Securities case.
[23] *Congressional Record,* May 18, 1906.
[24] Herbert Knox Smith, 62nd Cong., 2nd Sess., Sen. Doc. No. 7, p. 694, and H. F. Pringle, *Theodore Roosevelt* (New York: Harcourt, Brace, 1931), p. 445.

The federal Supreme Court has about as swift a procedure as any major court in the world; the standard of argument before it is often remarkably high; yet all the central issues remain. Nor is there much evidence to suggest that American judges as a group have been deeply concerned with the quality of the legal profession. There have been great scholars on the Bench, Kent and Story and, above all, Holmes. There have been judges, like Shaw on the Supreme Court of Massachusetts, and Learned Hand on the United States Circuit Court of New York, and Brandeis on the Supreme Court at Washington, with a passion for social justice. There have been ardent politicians like Marshall and Taney, Field and Taft. Yet it is very difficult to see that any or all of them succeeded in altering the direction or the level of the profession.

There is, I believe, much more to be said for the view so cogently argued by Professor Llewellyn [25] that the character of the profession has changed because the greatest rewards it can offer now come not to the eminent advocate, nor to the general practitioner who looks after the little client in the little case on one day and the interest of a great railroad on the next, as Abraham Lincoln did in Springfield, but to the lawyer who devotes himself to advising the vast corporations and combines which now dominate American economic life. The result of this devotion is unquestionably to shape the whole contour of American institutions in general. Lawyers have been the guardians of immense vested interests. They have organized the major offensive weapons employed in the fight against any group, whether a trade-union or the League of Women Voters, which sought to promote any kind of social legislation. They have, indeed, built a partnership between themselves and Big Business which has often seemed a barrier to all social change. They are rarely interested in the law, and still more rarely in its relation to justice. Their business is to protect Big Business against the trade-unionist, the reformer, the semi-organized farmers, and even the general public when, for some brief hour, as during the "muckraking" epoch, it is aroused to anger at the habits of predatory capitalism. No doubt the actual number of the lawyers devoted to this branch of legal work is small in proportion to the total number of lawyers; but anyone who studies the handling of the trust problem under Theodore Roosevelt, or the hearings before the Temporary National Economic Committee set up by Congress in 1938, will see without difficulty that the "corporation lawyers" are nothing so much as the engineering troops of reaction.

And this seems to be the view of Chief Justice Stone, who has had experience of the law as dean of a great law school, as a practising lawyer, and as Attorney-General of the United States. "At its best," he has written, "the changed system has brought to the command of the business world loyalty and superb proficiency and technical skill. At its worst, it has made the learned profession of an earlier day the obsequious servant

<hr>

[25] K. N. Llewellyn, "The Bar Specializes—With What Results?, *Annals of the American Academy of Political and Social Science*, May 1933, pp. 177–92.

of business, and tainted it with the morals and manners of the market-place in its most anti-social manifestations." [26] It is almost inevitable that the habits of a profession should be set by its most successful members; and the social results are serious. For the lawyer with a "cause," whether it is justice for the poor in some dull but vitally human realm, like the law of hire-purchase, or civil liberties, or the defence of the Negro, is pretty certain to be regarded either as politically suspicious or a crank. That, certainly, was the view taken of Professor Felix Frankfurter when he embarked on his noble campaign to save the lives of the two unjustly convicted Italian anarchists, Sacco and Vanzetti; [27] it was assumed at once that he had Communist affiliations, that he was undermining respect for the Massachusetts courts, that he would injure the prestige of the law school on whose faculty he served. The eminent corporation lawyer of Boston, Mr. W. G. Thompson, who was dragged into the case in its final stages, himself told me of the bad impression his action made on most of his colleagues at the Boston Bar and of the decline his normal practice suffered. Mr. Justice Brandeis was never forgiven for daring to expose the fraudulent practices of the New Haven Railroad under the presidency of Mr. Mellen, nor for having secured a savings-bank insurance system for Massachusetts, which drove the private insurance companies, with their fantastic costs of administration and the consequent exploitation of their thousands of poor clients, to the defensive; the hatred he earned for the public service he rendered still lives in the incredible attacks upon his character made before the Judiciary Committee of the Senate when he was nominated to the Supreme Court. I have myself known lawyers whose association with the Roosevelt government during the New Deal brought threats of later ruin to themselves or to the firms with which they were associated by business leaders or their "corporation lawyers"; and there has been an eminent figure in the political life of the Roosevelt epoch who severed his formal connection with the law firm to which he belonged lest his partners be penalized for his political convictions. Nor is it unimportant that in this period not a few of the younger lawyers of distinction who went to Washington straight from their law schools with an anxiety to serve the public were, when their ability proved outstanding and inconvenient, cajoled or bullied into leaving the government service lest they prejudice their careers when the political pendulum began to swing the other way.

There are two other tests, I think, of the influence which go to make a profession worthy of the title it claims. The first is what it does for the poor who, normally, cannot afford to avail themselves of its services at the regular fees; and the second is the scale upon which it embarks upon the effort necessary to adjust the law to the needs of the time. I do not

---

[26] Harlan F. Stone, "The Public Influence of the Bar," *Harvard Law Review,* November 1934, p. 7.
[27] Felix Frankfurter, *The Case of Sacco and Vanzetti* (Boston: Little, Brown, 1927).

think it is possible to doubt that, in both these tests, American lawyers, on the whole, have a better record than the lawyers of Great Britain. That is not high praise, since in neither field have the two branches of the British legal profession any outstanding record; it is, indeed, no exaggeration to say that there has been no really great reforming influence in English law since Jeremy Bentham, and, as everyone knows, he did not practise law. That is not the case in the United States where there is a wide and constant stream of criticism of the law within the legal profession itself. But I do not think it could fairly be said that the results of the criticism in legal reform can be regarded as in any way proportionate to the effort involved in the attempt at reform.

For more than half a century, for example, the National Conference on Uniform State Laws has sought to get acceptance of model statutes in order to bring uniformity into a field where there is a fantastic chaos. In the realm of business law, for example, the law of negotiable instruments, it has secured real improvements in half a dozen matters. But where it has sought to iron out differences in the divorce laws, in child labour laws, even in laws governing the compilation and publication of vital statistics, little interest has been aroused; it is, indeed, not unfair to say that only the draft statute which deals with narcotic drugs has been widely adopted in state legislation. The American Law Institute, a body composed of many of the most eminent judges and lawyers, both practising and academic, has laboured since 1923 to simplify the law, to adapt it to modern conditions, and to assist in the improvement of its administration. Its work is enshrined in many stately volumes, to the making of which it is obvious that immense labour and thought have been given. Yet an outside observer who examines its work will be tempted to conclude, I think, that the timidity of the result is in striking contrast to its size. With one exception, it has not touched the field of improvement either in procedure or in the administration of justice. Its "restatements" have carefully avoided discussion of how the law might be reformed, and have concentrated their attention upon what the law is. There has been no attempt at the vital task of comparing the direction of case law with the direction of statute law in the fields that have been surveyed; and this is of especial significance because of the obvious divergence between the two directions from the period when the Institute was founded in 1923 until the effort—an indirectly successful effort—of President Franklin Roosevelt to change the social emphasis of the Supreme Court's decisions in 1936–37. Nor have these massive labours produced any institutional insight, any criticism of the materials out of which law is made, any attempt to assess the bearing of comparative experience on American legal habits. With all its learning, it is difficult not to feel that the real outcome is a sterile skeleton map of the existing law, so bare of content that it does not even provide a basis for that discussion of change which is so long overdue.[28]

[28] Dean William Draper Lewis, then the director of the Institute, has dealt with

It is, of course, true that proposals have been made from within the profession for drastic institutional reform. In 1921 Mr. Justice Cardozo, one of the most loved and distinguished figures in the last half-century of American legal history, pleaded eloquently and earnestly for the creation of Ministries of Justice in the forty-eight states,[29] much along the lines of Lord Haldane's proposal of 1918 for a similar change in England.[30] Thirteen years later an interesting step towards this end was taken in New York where a Law Revision Commission was set up. Its work, as its annual reports show, has been slow in effecting change, but valuable in making clear its urgency. But no other state has yet followed the example of New York; and though less wide-ranging institutions, like the Judicial Councils which exist in more than half the states, have done important work in matters like the rationalization of the courts and the reform of their rules, they have not been permitted the power relevant to their work, nor have they been able to win much interest from the profession.[31] Indeed, it may be argued that the immense growth of arbitration, as an alternative to litigation, and the even greater development of administrative tribunals, are nothing so much as the result of dissatisfaction with the ordinary courts of law. That, certainly, was the strongly expressed view of Mr. Justice Jackson when, as solicitor-general, and later attorney-general in President Roosevelt's cabinet, he discussed the relation of lawyers to the New Deal.[32] He said with emphasis that lawyers and Bar associations were the main obstacles to reform. And it must be noted that the main basis upon which administrative tribunals have been attacked in the United States is the rather ironical one that they defeat those ends of justice to attain which they very largely came into existence. Certainly it becomes an amusing spectacle, in the light of the legal history of the United States, to read that the American Bar Association is suspicious of these tribunals on the ground of their tendency to yield to political pressure.[33]

No one who studies the immense literature on the law and the poor can doubt that the problem of "equal protection of the laws," which

these and similar criticisms in the *American Law School Review* for May 1936, where there is an interesting symposium on the subject. I think he has entirely failed to meet them.

[29] Benjamin N. Cardozo, "A Ministry of Justice," *Harvard Law Review*, December 1921, pp. 113 ff.

[30] *Machinery of Government Report* (London, 1918).

[31] For an account of them see Charles E. Clark and William O. Douglas, "Law and Legal Institutions," in *Recent Social Trends* (New York: McGraw-Hill, 1933), Vol. II, pp. 1462 ff.

[32] Jackson, *op. cit.,* p. 156.

[33] "Report of the Special Committee on Administrative Law," *Annual Report of the American Bar Association,* 1938. This was, of course, the theme of Lord Hewart's famous attack on English administrative law. *Cf.* his *The New Despotism* (London: Benn, 1924), and Carleton K. Allen, *Law and Orders* (London: Stevens, 1945). On the other side, I think that the Lord High Chancellor's *Committee on Ministers' Powers Report* (London: H.M.S.O., 1932), Cmd. 4060, and Cecil T. Carr's brilliant *Concerning English Administrative Law* (New York: Columbia University Press, 1941), have effectively disposed of these charges.

formally occupies so large a place in the constitutional history of the United States, is generally omnipresent over a considerable area of the legal profession. It has not, indeed, been solved. The system of assigning counsel to the poor person has been overwhelmingly confined to criminal cases, and it is usually a task given to a beginner at the Bar or to a lawyer of a small practice or of dubious reputation. The system of the Public Defenders has had very considerable success, both under the ægis of a government authority, as in Los Angeles, or under private auspices, as in New York; and the United States Circuit Court judges, under the chairmanship of Chief Justice Hughes, approved the idea of such an office in criminal cases. But, so far, the scale on which it is operated is so small that it has hardly made any impression on legal institutions. To this must be added the grim conclusion that, despite special courts, like the small claims courts and matrimonial courts, the first type of which has done work of great value in many industrial areas, or the juvenile courts, in which, as with Judge Mack in Chicago and Judge Lindsey in Denver, law was given a breadth of human understanding which has been rare, the popular need for legal aid has far outstripped the popular provision for it. And this is true even when the private legal aid bureaux, in all their varied forms, provide the context in which public legal aid is set. For the private bureau tends to be either a brief period in the life of a young lawyer at the beginning of his career, or a special enthusiasm of a small group of older lawyers, who bear the burden of a duty which ought to fall upon all the members of the legal profession. The observer is bound to be impressed by the devotion of the men and women who give their time and energy to this aspect of legal administration. He is bound, also, to note that the area they cover, not least on the side of advice and prevention, hardly begins to coincide with the vast jungle in which men and women of no means, or of small means, wander unhelped and bewildered. Nor are there yet any serious signs of a drive within the legal profession to devise institutions which bring law into any serious relation with need. Each decade seems to produce its crop of ardent and selfless proponents of reform; here and there they secure an attempt at this experiment or that. But I think it is no unfair judgment to say that, despite islands of interest in the great ocean of indifference, lawyers generally remain unconcerned; they regard the public as a source of income and not as an object of obligation; and it is especially notable that the more successful the lawyer, the less likely is he to be alert to the social relations of his profession. That is even the case where some sudden wave of public opinion searches for an adjustment in those relations. Too often, where that occurs, the successful lawyer is more likely to oppose change than to forward it; and a list of the grounds for his outlook would read almost like the famous catalogues of reasons for resisting reform which Bentham set out so brilliantly nearly a century and a half ago.[34]

[34] Jeremy Bentham, *The Book of Fallacies,* in *Collected Works* (London, 1843), Vol. II, pp. 374 ff.

3

THAT is not, I must add, because the education of American lawyers compares unfavourably with that of lawyers in other countries. Though, quite naturally, admission to the Bar is a matter under the control of each state government, the law schools of the United States are, at their best, among the major achievements of its educational system.[35] There are normally, if we take the five years from 1935, some forty thousand law students in the professional schools in any year; of these, about fifteen thousand attend full-time institutions and the remainder part-time institutions of one kind or another. The part-time school may be a serious institution within a university, or it may be a proprietary institution run by men whose major concern is the profit they can make out of it. The part-time schools have been very severely criticized, and, from a good deal of personal knowledge of their working, I think most, if not all, of the criticism has point. They too often have defective equipment and inadequate staff. They are too often, also, mere bodies attempting to "cram" their students with just enough knowledge to pass their Bar examinations. They lack the ability to evoke interest in the principles of law, or, even more, the problems of its administration, or its relation to the other social sciences. And it is, in general, true that too many of the students in the part-time school, especially the part-time evening school, are, like the lawyers who teach them, tired people who, after a day's work, lack the energy to do either the thinking or the reading required for the serious study of the law. They have their successes, and, at their best, they have the very real justification which cannot be denied to any serious form of adult education. But they suffer in that they do not seek to do more than provide the quickest road to a qualification for the practice of the law. They rarely mix philosophy with the information they impart.

The important element in American legal education consists of the nearly one hundred institutions which the American Bar Association puts in the first class of its list of approved law schools. Nearly all of them are the professional schools of a college or university, and nearly eighty of them operate not only upon a full-time basis, but require at least three years of undergraduate work as a prerequisite to admission; all the outstanding schools demand an actual degree. Three-quarters of them also require three years of study before the final examination for the law degree can be taken, though in some, the Law School of the University of Chicago, for example, that period can be shortened by taking courses in the summer session. It is important to note that the outstanding law schools are confined to fourteen out of the forty-eight states, so that

---

[35] The outstanding authority on American legal education is Alfred Z. Reed, whose two books, *Training for the Public Profession of the Law* (Carnegie Foundation Bulletin No. 15, 1921) and *Present-Day Law Schools in the United States and Canada* (Carnegie Foundation Bulletin No. 21, 1928), are as admirable as they are useful.

their students either come from the wealthier strata of the population, or depend upon scholarships and loans and the ability to work their way through, especially in the long vacations. All the major institutions have a full-time staff the members of which, though not debarred from practice, make teaching and research their primary obligation. Many of them are equipped with law libraries of outstanding range and quality; that of the Harvard Law School, for example, is unquestionably the most superb collection of books on law there is anywhere in the world today. Most of them, further, do not seek to teach the law of some particular state, though they may have one or more special courses about the special rules of the state in which they are situated; since they draw their students from all over the United States, it is with the general field of law that they mostly concern themselves. Generally speaking, there is no standardized curriculum in these schools, though it is usual to have a fairly rigid prescribed course in the first year and to permit "electives" later. The concentration of students appears to gather about two focal points: the first is the courses which fit directly into the state Bar examinations, and the second is the courses which relate to the work of the great firms of corporation lawyers, who look largely to these schools for the younger members of their staffs. It should, perhaps, be remarked that since 1933 there has been both increased attention to, and increased interest in, courses in public law which might be relevant to work in one of the agencies of the federal government.

It is well known that a new epoch dawned in American legal education when, in 1871, C. C. Langdell, then the newly appointed dean of the Harvard Law School, introduced the "case method" of teaching law; though it is perhaps only fair to say that James Barr Ames, his successor as dean, was only slightly less influential in determining the character of that epoch. They had a hard fight to replace the dogmatic lecture on what the law was, obediently written down by students in their notebooks, by the critical analysis of vital cases, in which the basic principles of the law were found by the exchange, not seldom the vivid, even angry, exchange, of ideas between teacher and student. But they won a victory so complete that today perhaps eighty per cent of the outstanding American law schools build at least their main work upon this method. If it has been less successful in penetrating other countries in which the Common Law rules, I think it can, in the broad view, claim that it makes for a far higher standard of legal education. In Great Britain or the Dominions, where the case method has made relatively small headway, the British schools have produced no law journals which even approximate in critical power to at least a score of law school periodicals in the United States; and, their remarkable quality apart, one must remember the admirable training in the grasp of legal principles that a student gains by his membership of an editorial board—no doubt confined to a small group of the ablest students which is judged in large part by the quality of its comment upon contemporary decisions. To this I would venture to add that the best students in the law schools of at least a dozen American universities seem to me, at the end of their training, to be far ahead of a really good student at Oxford or Cambridge or London who has taken a higher degree in law. They have a deeper grasp of principle; they have a wider range of interest; and they are more willing to attempt an independent valuation of judicial decisions than is true of most first-rate law students in Great Britain. Indeed, I think that few young English lawyers would deny that a year or two of graduate study at Harvard or Yale, at Columbia or at Northwestern University in Chicago, is a far greater intellectual stimulus in the normal way than anything a British university law school can offer.

No judgment on the case method is more authoritative than that of the late Josef Redlich, an eminent Austrian lawyer who was one of the few European scholars with a thorough grasp of the Common Law. The case method, he wrote, "laid the main emphasis upon precisely that aspect of the training which the older textbook school entirely neglected: the training of the student in intellectual independence, in individual thinking, in digging out the principles through penetrating analysis of the material found within separate cases: material which contains, all mixed in with one another, both the facts, as life creates them, which generate the law, and at the same time rules of the law itself, component parts of the general system . . . The concepts, principles, and rules of Anglo-American law are recorded not as dry abstractions, but as cardinal realities in the inexhaustibly rich, ceaselessly fluctuating, social and economic life of man." [36] I venture to believe that Professor Redlich was wholly right. But I venture to think, also, that the judgment he made must be kept within a narrower framework than appears from his eulogy. It is not merely that the case method requires an exceptionally high level of teaching, and that it makes a more exacting demand upon the average student than it does upon the student of exceptional ability. My own experience is that to be really effective it requires far smaller classes than are now usual, at any rate until the year of graduation, in the best American law schools. Once there is a big class—and at the Harvard Law School I have seen between two and three hundred students studying the law of torts or the law of contract—it becomes either a monologue by the teacher tempered by occasional questions from a specially audacious student, or an exchange between a teacher and a dozen or so among his audience, while the rest listen and write down in their notebooks what the teacher announces as the result of their discussion of the case.

There are, I think, other problems to which the case method has not yet found an answer. By its overwhelming emphasis upon judicial decisions as the source of law, it tends to set the purpose of law in a wrong per-

[36] Josef Redlich, *The Common Law and the Case Method in American University Law Schools* (Carnegie Foundation Bulletin No. 8, 1914), pp. 39-40. Professor Redlich, as is well known, was the author of classic works on English parliamentary procedure and English local government. The report from which I quote was a special investigation made at the request of the Carnegie Foundation.

spective. It gravely depreciates the significance of statutes and of administrative regulations; indeed, it tends to make them appear as the raw material for judicial interpretation rather than as activities which are valid in themselves. And it tends to make the student assume that the normal outcome of legal difference is litigation in a court of law, instead of giving litigation its proper weight as one of a number of ways in which legal difference is resolved. By giving undue pre-eminence to fundamental legal principles of the Common Law, it fails adequately to convey any real sense of the scale upon which, in the law of torts, for example, trade-union legislation and statutes on workmen's compensation and employers' liability have made historic principles an anachronism. So, too, with the law of property, the very basis of which has now been profoundly altered by statutes relating to housing or to procedure where ownership raises issues related to public health. It is not, I think, unfair to say that the case method may well tend to train students to look at the law statistically and not dynamically. One of the obvious results of this approach is the assumption that normal law is judge-made law, and that law made outside the ordinary courts is a diversion from the main stream. That this attitude will generally lead to profound juristic conservatism, and, therefore, to at least a scepticism of the validity of change by legislation, is the clear lesson of experience.[37]

There is a further and, perhaps even deeper, difficulty in the case method. The law student who reads the report of a case, even more, the report of a case as printed in a case book, is given very carefully selected material upon which to judge the outcome. If the report is printed in full, what he is given is the materials selected by the judge from all the facts before him as relevant to the decision he has decided to make; and if these materials are further summarized by the law teacher who has compiled the case book, what the student really studies is the relation between the *ratio decidendi* of the judge and the facts that he has chosen to prove the validity of his arguments.[38] He does not, therefore, see either the facts or the result in the rich and multiform context which life gives to them, but only in the narrow framework within which the judge wishes to keep them confined. He cannot, from such an approach, even begin to understand all the sociological implications of a decision like that of Lord Abinger in *Priestley* v. *Fowler*,[39] or of Mr. Justice Holmes in the Danbury Hatters case.[40] And, once that understanding is absent, the law student is not concerned, as he ought to be concerned, with a law which functions in society as a method of social control which has to be evaluated, but rather with law as the application of a *corpus* of fixed principles

---

[37] *Cf.* my note in the *Committee of Ministers' Powers Report,* pp. 135-37. The citation there from Sir Frederick Pollock is of special importance in this connection.
[38] *Cf.* Edward S. Robinson, *Law and Lawyers* (New York: Macmillan, 1935), a deeply interesting study by a psychologist of high distinction who was not a lawyer.
[39] *Priestley* v. *Fowler,* 3 M. & W. 1, 7 (1837).
[40] *Loewe* v. *Lawlor,* 208 U.S. 274 (1908) and 235 U.S. 522 (1915).

which are not made by judges but discovered and rediscovered by them. This tends, of course, to legal habits of mind which refuse to confront the law in terms of its total relations with life; even more, it breeds the kind of lawyer to whom only "pure" law, which does not look beyond its own boundaries for its validity, can properly be regarded as relevant to his judgment. The outcome is pretty certain to be a jurisprudence of artificial and mechanical concepts which always limp behind the actual world it is their business to serve.

No doubt many eminent American teachers of law have seen this danger and sought vigorously to build safeguards against it. No one who knows the early work of Dean Pound, that of Mr. Justice Frankfurter, of Professor Sheldon Glueck at the Harvard Law School, of Judge Charles E. Clark and Judge Thurman Arnold at Yale, of Professor Joseph P. Chamberlain at Columbia, or the impressive call for change which Dean Hains sounded to the alumni of the Law School of the University of Illinois, can doubt that there is real awareness of the need to give the prospective lawyer some insight into the working of law in the structure of social institutions as a whole; none of them, I think, would argue that the case method alone produces lawyers who understand the relation between the courts and social processes. No doubt, too, all kinds of interesting experiments have been made, like the combination of the Yale Law School with the Harvard Graduate School of Business Administration, or the cooperation between the University of Denver and the University of Colorado for the study of the bearing of psychiatric knowledge on law, together with the prospect of actual observation of clinical experience. New units of legal study have appeared, such as family law and business law; and there has been an expansion from the study of the case itself into wider social material which bears upon its meaning.

Yet, proportionately, it still leaves the case method the overwhelming master of the field. So that, despite changes in the curriculum and the emphasis given to those changes by a very different social climate from that of a generation ago, the perspective of legal training is, in my own judgment, set by principles of a law that is becoming obsolete as it is being taught, and of a law that is primarily conceived in terms of the judge rather than of the legislation or administration. If it be said that there is a growing tendency for the better law schools to provide courses in statutory interpretation and in the role of Congress or the state legislatures in the making of the law, there are, I think, at least two important answers: first, that the number of students who take such courses is small, and that most of these look forward to teaching work in law and not to practice; and, second, that these courses are usually taken either in the student's final year or as a post-graduate subject. This means, in fact, that for the great majority of law students good law is judge-made law; and, on the evidence, judge-made law is almost always concerned to slow down the pace of change by adapting judicial results to a framework of principles the main explanation of which more often lies in the past, perhaps even in the distant past, than in the problems of the contemporary scene. Since law is conservative in its normal attitude to social relations, I believe that the case method is more likely to reinforce the conservatism of the entrant into the legal profession than to interest him in the amendment of the results it seeks to impose. The case method may well make for a more alert and logical conservatism; but it looks to traditionalism rather than to progress by the means upon which it relies.

It is probable that some corrective of the traditionalism is supplied by the growing tendency of the best American law schools to rely upon the full-time teacher rather than upon men who spend most of their time in actual practice. No one who is aware of the high prestige enjoyed by the great legal teachers since Langdell's time can doubt that this has been an important and salutary change. The names alone of men like Ames, Thayer, Hohfield, John Chipman Gray, J. H. Wigmore, to mention the dead only, represent an achievement of high importance. They disprove the notion that the good lawyer can be bred only in practice of the law day by day. American professors of law have been the equal of any advocates in the occasional great cases they have taken; they have been among the most outstanding figures on the Bench; and their work in government agencies, like the Securities and Exchange Commission, or the National Labor Relations Board, or the Department of Justice, can challenge comparison with that of any comparable group in this important area. The great law teacher exercises an influence it is almost impossible to overestimate; he shapes the way of thought of his students for a lifetime of effort. And it is important to recognize how much the great law teachers in the United States have been responsible for adapting the law to the solution of problems their colleagues in practice either overlooked or would not face.

Yet one must be careful not to exaggerate the extent of this corrective. For, first of all, the number of great law teachers at any time is small, and it cannot be said that a great law teacher is more likely to be a reformer than a conservative. The legal profession, moreover, has no more enthusiasm for the law teacher as reformer than for the practising lawyer as reformer. Certainly Roosevelt's nomination of Professor Frankfurter to the Bench caused many misgivings and some angry criticism, as had the earlier offer to him by Governor Ely of a seat on the Supreme Court of Massachusetts. The legal reception of Mr. Justice Frankfurter's appointment was mixed because he had fought hard and courageously for reconsideration of the outrageous verdict in the Sacco-Vanzetti case, and, rather curiously, he was supposed to be a "radical." The quite simple truth that, in fact, Mr. Justice Frankfurter was, like his great predecessor Holmes, a liberal conservative who retained an open mind and a suspicion of the famous maxim *boni judicis est amplificare jurisdictionem* did not dawn upon those who criticized his nomination. And hardly less interesting was the sober warning issued by the *Boston Herald* to Dean Landis when, shortly after he had been appointed successor to Dean Pound at the Harvard Law School, he announced that he favoured President Roosevelt's plan for reforming the Court. That important New England journal was apprehensive lest the solid foundations of the Harvard tradition be shaken by the choice, as its guardian, of a man who proclaimed his sympathy for a change which the legal profession overwhelmingly condemned. Dean Landis, in truth, like his predecessor, was fundamentally a conservative seeking to safeguard the legal system from its stubborn resistance to the mildest social change. Yet that was enough to create the sense that he might not be "safe and sound," and so give a dangerously innovating atmosphere to the climate of Harvard.

This brings me to the central point in any discussion of training for the legal profession in the United States. At its best, as in the famous law schools of the major universities, there is no sort of doubt that it provides an admirable intellectual discipline. At its best, also, the level of the teaching is remarkably high; and it is often combined with great administrative capacity. But these merits, even when there is added to them the clear evidence of great scholarship and wide discussion of legal matters, do not mean that the best law schools produce among their students generally an abiding desire to adapt law to life. They cannot venture to go far beyond the general legal habits the profession approves. They have to recognize not only that they train less than half the men and women admitted to the Bar; they have to recognize also that a considerable proportion of those whom they do train, among that proportion some of the very ablest, become corporation lawyers whose main function is to protect the great vested interests against statutes which invade their privileges. They have to recognize, further, that, despite scholarships and the American habit of earning one's way through college, the bulk of their students come from families with a comfortable income who want to see their sons maintain the economic status they have inherited; the lawyer who can make a large income at the Bar and, like Mr. Justice Brandeis, maintain a passion for legal and social reform, is a very exceptional person; experience is all the other way. All in all, training for the law brings out that passion in the very exceptional person by providing him with the weapons to meet his critics, as Brandeis did, on their own ground. I know no evidence to suggest that it does more than inform and deepen impulses already there; it does not seriously appear that it has any noticeable power to evoke them.

There is one further point in legal training which deserves some little emphasis. It is probable that, in the last generation, there has been a growth in America, either during the years of training or immediately thereafter, of a practical training for the young lawyer not unlike the English system in which a young lawyer reads in the chambers of some barrister of repute; and in many cases, notably at Harvard and Northwestern Universities—in the latter every third-year student not on the editorial board of its review must spend eight weeks in this way—the Legal Aid Bureau is made a method by which the student unites the lesson of the classroom to the experience of living law. No doubt this is a valuable thing. But it leaves unsolved the important question of how to bring the mature lawyer into touch with the developments of the law. Taken by and large, the law schools seem unsuited to this purpose; they have, at any rate, failed pretty completely to make provision for it. Nor, despite discussion in the American Bar Association [41] and similar bodies, has very much been done. Here and there courses have been provided on the practice of the law, and a lecture, or series of lectures, held on some special subject like taxation, or labour law, or the civil aviation. But, in general, only the fringe of the problem has been touched, or even examined, and it is a very small proportion of the profession that is interested in the experiment.

Yet it is as important for the lawyer as it is for the doctor or the teacher to stop routine practice every so often and look at his work in a wider perspective than he can gain from immersion in the daily round. It is particularly important since the wider the area of government intervention in the life of the community, the more specialized the lawyer becomes. Not only is this the case, but it is largely to the specialist that the great awards in the profession—the federal Supreme Court apart—are likely to go. Still more, they go to the specialist who wins the confidence of the great corporations in the economic life of America. Now specialism itself makes for conservatism; and specialism that is devoted to the service of the great vested interests rarely wins or keeps the confidence of its clients if its outcome is an enthusiasm for the reform of the law. What those clients like to hear from their counsel is passionate rhetorical attack on innovation hostile to the claims of property. This is to say that the leaders of the American Bar are almost bound by their relationships to be in the van of the opposition to reform. And so largely do they set the general temper of the Bar and, even of the Bench, as Mr. Justice Miller noted in a classic protest, that the legal profession is driven to make changes by public clamour rather than to attempt them out of an interest in, let alone a zeal for, the advancement of justice.

"In the past," Whitehead has written, "professionals have formed unprogressive castes. The point is that professionalism is now mated with progress." [42] But, in the law, the marriage is one in which the legal partner is forever trying to arrest the change which the social partner is trying to achieve. I do not for one moment suggest that the American position is different from the English, or the French, or the Italian; and I do not argue that it is more hostile to change today than it was in the nineteenth century or in the eighteenth. I note only that it is general historic experience that the legal profession has no inherent impetus to progress, that it views innovation with scepticism, and that it too often regards with indignation the men who attempt that adaptation of law to life which

[41] *Cf.* Harold P. Seligson, "Post Admission Education for Lawyers," *American Bar Association Journal* (1934), p. 231.
[42] Whitehead, *Science and the Modern World*, p. 235.

is an inevitable part of the social process. There has never been a Jeremy Bentham in the history of American law; if there had been such a man, there is no reason to suppose that there would have been any greater eagerness to further his ideas, in his own age, than Bentham encountered in England in almost a half century of effort at reform. And anyone who examines with close care the attitude of the Bench and the Bar to the first few years of the New Deal, in the nineteen-thirties, will see that the interests largely responsible for the grim years of the Great Depression looked, and looked successfully, to the lawyers, to protect them against the social, especially the fiscal, consequences of public indignation. This was only a new stage in a process which, from the foundation of the United States, has made the legal profession the essential mercenaries of the propertied class. For it is the lawyers, above all, who have provided the arguments which have identified the interests of the American people with those of the small economic oligarchy in whom there has rested an ever-growing monopoly of power. If there should ever come an epoch in American history when that oligarchy prolonged beyond endurance its resistance to necessary change, it is upon the shoulders of the legal profession that the main burden of public anger will rightly fall. It is still unmistakably clear that not even the outcome of the Dred Scott decision [43] has taught the lawyer the lesson that if necessary change is not made by persuasion, there is no alternative but to enforce the change by methods of revolution. That was the emphasis Abraham Lincoln stated with such remarkable power.[44] But it is an emphasis to which his own profession gives little heed and still less reverence.

4

THE history of the American medical profession is, in its way, almost as startling as the history of the United States itself. Until the first part of the nineteenth century, almost until the forties, it is not unfair to call it a scientific dependency of Europe. Most of its few eminent figures were trained in Europe; most of its important textbooks were European, or American adaptations of European work; and most of its doctors were trained by apprenticeship to a practising physician who may, or may not, have given them good value for their fee. Hospitals were very rare; the doctor's equipment rarely exceeded half a dozen instruments and a few drugs and procedures, which, like bleeding of patients, went back to fanciful beliefs as speculative as astrology and as fantastic as the most curious sects of the seventeenth century. Anyone, indeed, who reads such a list of those sects as the *Boston Medical and Surgical Journal* published in 1936 might well think that he was reading an extract from such an attack as Ephraim Pagitt published on the more extreme Puritans in

[43] *Cf.* J. M. Beck, *The Constitution of the United States* (New York: Doran, 1923).
[44] P. Stern (ed.), *Life and Writings of Lincoln*, p. 665.

his *Hæresographia* in 1646.[45] Certainly, despite a handful of really distinguished figures, like Oliver Wendell Holmes, the famous father of a still more famous son, and the discoverer of the cause of puerperal fever, the combination of ignorance, quackery, and incredible sectarianism made the practice of medicine, even as late as the Civil War, one that the public did not find it easy to respect. The right to practise was far too easily given by the different states; and very little of the medical literature published was of any serious scientific importance.[46]

It is, of course, obvious that a good deal of this situation was the outcome of the confused and rapidly changing conditions of American society. Some of it, no doubt, was due to the ghastly results of an incredible use of the lancet, and an almost unlimited reliance upon strong drugs, which must, at the best, have been a terrible strain upon the patient. Some of it was due to the public dislike of "body snatching"—the use, frequently the use by theft, of corpses for dissecting purposes. There was widespread, often superstitious, hatred of dissection. There was deep clerical distrust of the basic principle that disease has no connection with religion but falls within the category of science. There was the traditional belief in the old housewife's remedies to be overcome. Perhaps, above all, there was the horror of operation in the ages before the use of an anæsthetic made it bearable. Medical men had few reliable vital statistics by which to defend themselves. They had to fight the "quack," and the charlatan, and something it is not easy to refrain from calling an age-long belief in magic. And, after all, until the mid-nineteenth century few American doctors knew very much, and even fewer had access to scientific training. The small number of medical schools, even those attached to universities like Harvard and Yale, made their way slowly, and not without serious internal conflict. It looked as though, almost up to the Civil War, there was no direct method by which medicine could win the status appropriate to its importance in society.

Yet the history of the profession in the second half of the century completely altered this position at an ever-increasing rate. Mainly the result was due to an immense advance in clinical diagnosis, in which the large-scale observation of disease in life was followed by the ever more exact verification of conditions in post-mortem examination. This made for far greater exactitude; and it was in part parallel with, and in part the outcome of, scientific advances, symbolized in names like those of Pasteur and Koch, which permitted advances in their medical application, almost as striking as those in physics and chemistry. Specific identification of disease, the irresistible claim of anæsthetics, antisepsis, and then asepsis, the increasing victory of the public hospital over the private home, the

---

[45] B. J. Stern, *American Medical Practice*, pp. 23–24. My whole discussion of the medical profession owes much to this illuminating and suggestive book. Henry B. Shafer's, *The American Medical Profession, 1783 to 1850* (New York: Columbia University Press, 1936) is an interesting preface to Professor Stern's book.

[46] Stern, *op. cit.*, p. 27.

emergence of public health practice, with its inevitable consequence of preventive medicine, the general technological developments of society which permitted new instruments, new procedures of treatment, and ever higher standards of training—all these made the doctor as highly regarded at the end of the nineteenth century as he had been lowly regarded at its beginning.

The immense changes of standards in this half-century both required and facilitated specialization. The refinement of method and of instruments began to require a technique which was beyond the reach of the general practitioner. No doubt the specialist has been pretty closely limited by economic possibilities to the metropolitan areas; but hardly a year has passed in the last thirty years when specialization has not claimed new fields for its own and won recognition for its claims from the recognized agencies of the medical profession. Professor Stern has estimated that whereas in 1928 only twenty-six per cent ranked as specialists, by 1942 the percentage had risen to forty-nine.[47] The change, very clearly, is a startling one, and it has had startling consequences. It means that specialists are concentrated in cities, where alone, in a normal way, the private patient can afford their services, and that the major part of their work is among the rich rather than the poor; and since the rich can afford higher fees, the income of the specialist is about twice that of the general practitioner. So much more attractive, indeed, is the career of a specialist to a medical student today that his tendency is increasingly to start as a specialist as soon as he has finished his medical training, with the result that he by-passes the wider and more human experience that the general practitioner obtains. To this must be added the fact that, as specialization becomes intensified, there is likely to be both an increase in the cost of medical care and a far less intimate knowledge of the patient and his psychology. The patient, indeed, may become no more than a sheet of paper in which a chemical analysis of gastric secretions is the basis upon which his pain is dealt with by the specialist to whom his family doctor has sent him.[48]

We are, in fact, in the middle of a medical revolution. The whole framework of the medical profession has become so complex that its effect is to diagnose an objective condition in the patient and to ignore his personality. In the metropolitan areas, the family doctor, whose very presence was a step to cure because it relieved the strain of anxiety, is being replaced by a series of specialists before whom the sick person passes like a motorcar on an assembly-line. And this impersonality is increased by the administrative aid of nurse and receptionist, by the immensely increased resort to the hospital and its private wards, and the absence of any more than a formal relation between specialist and patient. No doubt this is not the situation in rural areas nor in the small towns; there the family doctor still reigns supreme. But the problem of medical income

[47] *Ibid.*, p. 50.
[48] *Ibid.*, pp. 51–53; and *cf.* Michael M. Davis, *America Organizes Medicine* (New York: Harper, 1941), pp. 56–60.

tends to mean a drift of the better-trained personnel to the areas where the rewards are greater.

Nor is that the only difficulty. Anyone who studies the ratio of doctors to population will note that the poorer the area, the smaller is the medical ratio it secures; and he will note, also, that the poorer areas were worse off in 1940 than they had been in 1920.[49] This is true not only of the doctors' services; it is grimly true also of access to hospital services. It is also the case that the younger doctors turn increasingly to the richer areas, so that, in general, the latest effects of training are less available to the poor who need it most. The effective centres of medical research are also concentrated in the wealthy areas. The effect, moreover, of the war has been at once to train the young medical graduate in the latest techniques, and to rush the medical student through a shorter course of training. Each of these consequences is likely to cause a deterioration in the supply of medical care to poor communities. The trained army doctor, who has had an income in wartime well above the average for his status, is likely to search for a place in which he does not sacrifice that gain; while his less well-trained colleague is likely to return for more education to a good medical school, which, once more, means his movement to an area which can afford a first-rate medical training. To this must be added that, in a general way, the patient-load of a doctor shows that where the need is greatest, the service is most likely to be poor.[50] It is of obvious importance, also, that it is generally where the educational level of a community is lowest that the call on the doctor is lowest as well.

Investigation has also shown that doctors take a very small part in the service of preventive medicine when they are in private practice. It has shown that the sharp, sudden disease is given greater care than the chronic disease.[51] No doubt the main responsibility for these results lies in the defective realization of its needs by the lay community; but this, in its turn, is the outcome of a failure on the part of the doctors to make the relation of health to medical care fully known. I do not think it is unfair to argue that no small part of this failure is due to the burden of medical education. Few doctors can begin to practice before some such age as twenty-six years. It will normally take them at least three years before they earn an annual income of eighteen hundred dollars. They will have spent four to five thousand dollars on their training, perhaps a thousand dollars more on the equipment of their offices. In all probability, the young doctor will try to add to the income from his private practice by working for some public organization which gives medical relief, or for an insurance company or a trade-union. The statistics of medical incomes,[52] though they are complicated and mostly based on relatively small samples, make it clear that while about one in eight earns more than ten thousand dol-

49 Stern, *op. cit.*, p. 64. .
50 *Ibid.*, p. 77.
51 *Ibid.*, p. 86.
52 *Ibid.*, pp. 90 f.

lars a year, one-quarter earns less annually than two thousand dollars; and the rural physician, as is to be expected, earns less than the urban, the Southern doctor less than either his Northern or his Western colleague. It seems, too, to be largely the fact that the poorer the community the doctor serves, the greater will be his loss from unpaid bills; and it is the specialist who suffers least under this head. The Farm Security Administration, in a study made of forty-three thousand families in Texas and Oklahoma in 1941, found that unpaid doctors' bills amounted to over half a million dollars; and the physician in poor urban districts is probably in much the same situation.[53] It is not, therefore, really unexpected that doctors often refuse their services to the more destitute families, and that these, in their turn, are ashamed to ask for those services because their unpaid bills are a load upon their minds.

Granted this situation, it is not surprising that there is a good deal of evasion of announced codes of medical ethics and immense difficulty in their application. Many doctors, for example, get a commission from workmen who have received compensation for injury, in much the same way as the lawyer who takes a risk in the same kind of case. Nor is it surprising that, despite the strong denunciation of the American Medical Association, the growth of the salaried doctor, both in public health work and in private hospitals and industrial practice, increases rapidly; on the public health side, there was an increase in the number of salaried posts from five thousand eight hundred in 1928 to nine thousand in 1941.[54] It is, no doubt, true that the full-time salaried doctor will never earn the great prizes which come to a renowned consultant or an eminent surgeon. But he has at least the assurance of a steady income, with none of the pains of collecting it; he has few overhead charges; he has annual vacations and the constant chance of promotion; and while only fourteen per cent of this full-time salaried class earned more than six thousand dollars a year in 1929, only three per cent had less than two thousand dollars, where the comparable percentage among private practitioners on a fee-paying basis was twenty-four.

Anyone who analyses the problem of the private costs of medical care in the United States has the basis for ample generalization in the remarkable study published by the National Resources Planning Board in 1941.[55] A sample of sixty thousand families, representative of all types of communities in the nation, was the basis of the inquiry. It showed that American families spent nearly two billion dollars every year in medical care, which is some four per cent of the national income of the nation. But it showed, also, that urban families spent sixty-five per cent of this great sum, while families in rural areas spent only thirty-five per cent. It showed, also, that three-quarters of all American families paid half the total cost of medical care; and that a poor family, with an annual income

[53] Ibid., p. 98.
[54] Ibid., p. 101.
[55] Family Expenditures in the United States (Washington, 1941).

of less than five hundred dollars, paid one-tenth of what is spent by a family with an income of three to four thousand dollars. The poorer family, the poorer area, the farmer as against the non-farmer, the Negro as against the white, all suffer in their inability to obtain the necessary service. If we take the figure of twenty-five dollars per annum as the "reasonable minimum cost" per person for all types of medical care—and this assumes group purchase of service instead of individual cost—it is clear that this minimum, even in urban areas, is reached only by families earning two thousand dollars annually; while among families who live by farming, it is not reached before a per capita income of at least five thousand dollars.

It would be wearisome to recount the results of many inquiries which all emphasize the same central principles. The facts are, first, that disability through illness, infectious and respiratory diseases apart, is anything up to nine times as frequent in American families with less than three thousand dollars annual income than in families above that level; and, second, to enable the lower income groups in the United States to have adequate medical care, there would not only have to be a large-scale redistribution of wealth in the United States, but a large-scale change in its standards of living. But that is not all. Even granted all the free medical services available to lower income groups, they go but a small way to meet the problem; for only two per cent of American cities with a population of less than ten thousand persons are in a position to provide any such service. Access to the private doctor is also more difficult by reason of the unplanned distribution of practitioners. The correlation, moreover, between high mortality and low income is marked; the death rate, for example, is about twenty-five per cent higher for skilled workers, and for unskilled workers more than one hundred per cent higher, than it is for those engaged in labour by brain instead of labour by hand.[56] And it is, of course, inevitable that the poorer the area, once the metropolitan areas in the United States are put on one side, the less chance there is of effective public medical care. There are thirteen hundred counties in the United States more than fifty miles from a public hospital; and the treatment of illness in a hospital is four times more frequent in the big cities of the Eastern seaboard than in a poor Southern state like Georgia. The same kind of comparison holds for services like those of nursing, sanitary inspection, and public health control. Malnutrition is more frequent; medical care in childbirth takes place only in thirty-three per cent of cases; in Texas and Oklahoma federal investigation showed that of sixteen thousand cases of serious illness, over half were without any medical treatment of any kind.

Whatever is here said of the general population of America, is, of course, still more emphatically true of the Negro. His health is worse; and he suffers more from epidemic disease, and from nutritional diseases like pellagra, and diseases directly related to poverty, like hookworm.

[56] Stern, *op. cit.*, pp. 11 ff.

There are relatively few Negro doctors; and they increasingly practise in areas outside the deep South. There is discrimination against Negro patients in the hospitals; and there is similar discrimination against Negro medical students seeking hospital training. In most of the Southern states, apart from North Carolina and South Carolina, there is not a single modern hospital which offers them such facilities.[57] The Negro death rate for males is fifty-seven per cent, that of females seventy-four per cent, higher than that of whites of either sex. The Negro male's expectation of life is eleven years less than that of the male white, and of the Negro woman twelve years less than that of the white woman.[58]

If these facts reveal anything, they reveal the astonishing degree to which the pattern of the medical profession and its outcome reflect the general pattern of American life and its results. Where the needs are greatest, there their satisfaction is least organized. Where there is most social and economic discrimination, there the problem of medical care is at its worst. Where preventive medicine could do the greatest good, it is most conspicuously absent; where curative medicine could have its most spectacular success, it has the least chance of displaying the remarkable advances it has made in the last sixty years. It is not an exaggeration to say that access to the benefit of those advances is, outside the great cities, in large degree limited by the means of the citizen. He suffers if he is poor; he suffers if he lives in a rural area as compared with an urban area; he suffers if he lives in the small town as compared with the great city; above all, he suffers if he is Negro instead of white. And the greater the degree of a specialization in medicine, the greater are likely to be the prevalent disparities under the present system. Nor is this the whole case. The impact of a technologically advancing civilization brings with it such changes in the cost of medical equipment that the relation between doctor and patient is increasingly based upon the hospital rather than the home, so that full advantage may be taken of technical improvement. But the more that treatment centres round the hospital, the less chance is there that the poorer areas, urban and rural, will, apart from the great cities, be able to bring its benefits to those who most need them. Medical costs rise, and the more they rise, the more doctors move to the areas where they can themselves hope for a decent standard of life. Medical practice in the United States moves in a vicious circle from which there is now no escape save in the government planning of all health services.

It is here, I think, that the mental climate of the American medical profession most clearly reveals itself. For there is perhaps no more sternly individualist body in the United States than the American Medical Association, unless it be the National Association of Manufacturers. Against socialization of medical services in any form or, indeed, in any realm save that of the care of the insane, it has always fought steadily, and sometimes even recklessly. Like the lawyers, it has a high-sounding code

[57] *Ibid.*, p. 127.
[58] *Cf.* Myrdal, *An American Dilemma*, Vol. I, pp. 171–75 and *passim*.

of ethical principles for the profession; like the lawyers, also, most of
its assumptions are completely irrelevant to the terms of life in a modern community. For underlying those principles is an unconscious picture of a small American town in the eighteen-eighties where most people have their family doctor, and he has seen perhaps a quarter of the
town grow up to manhood since he first settled there. All the Association's habits of mind begin at the point where a patient has a doctor who
helps him not least because an intimate knowledge of his psychology is
part of the equipment the doctor brings to his cure. That the picture is
fantastically out of date seems to make no difference to the fierceness with
which its truth is defended. That the system of competitive individualism among doctors injures alike their income, and their ability to keep
abreast of new knowledge, seems to count for little with the Association.
That the stereotype it is defending results in maldistribution of doctors,
nurses, hospitals, clinics, of all the personnel, in fact, and the institutions
upon which the progress of public health depends, leaves the bureaucracy
of the Association quite unmoved. The America for which, in the medical
realm, it may almost be said to be a legislative assembly is the America
of Grant and Hayes rather than the America of today; and the speeches
of its officials in the annual conventions of the Association sound, both
in the nation and state, more like Mr. Huntington's fantastic complaint
to his partner, Mr. Colton, in 1877, that it was becoming excessively
expensive to buy off the governmental regulation of railroads, than the
examination, by minds scientifically trained, of overwhelming evidence
that ought, by the nature of their calling, to put them in the van of the
demand for fundamental reform.

It is a startling phenomenon for a number of reasons. It is startling,
first, because it is probable that, the South apart, the standard of American medical training is now the best in the world; there are few nations
whose great hospitals can compare with those of America either in service, or in equipment. It is probably true, also, that no other nation has
so fully or so devotedly studied things like the cost of medical care, the
pattern of medical services, or the sociology of medicine. There are in the
United States bodies, like the New York Academy of Medicine, which
have done work which can only be called superlative in organizing research into the social and economic relations of the doctor and the community. And there are, of course, among American doctors innumerable
instances of men whose selfless devotion to the improvement of the
national health is a superb instance of the dedicated life. Women like Dr.
Alice Hamilton did much to make industrial medicine a vital part of its
development. Men like Welch and Adolf Meyer at Johns Hopkins were
unsurpassed in their demand that the training of the medical student
should be rigorous and scientific. If an Englishman can count Sir John
Simon among the great figures of the nineteenth century, assuredly an
American can count Surgeon-General Gorgas among their own great
figures of the twentieth. And, not least, when the American contribution

to medical advance is measured, it becomes obvious at once that it has been overwhelmingly made by men and women working in some public institution, a big hospital, a university laboratory, a research institute, rather than by those engaged in private practice. The achievements of the pioneers have, in all save a few spectacular instances like the use of insulin and penicillin, to creep into general acceptance by the slow permeation of a new generation which goes out to practise.

Some of the causes of this situation are obvious enough. Professions are, in general, occupations which tend to breed conservatism in their members. The American doctor has to be particularly careful because, if medicine were socialized, he would have numerous competitors to face whom, from the herbalist to the Christian Science practitioner, he would be bound to regard as charlatans, and often dangerous charlatans; in few countries, I suspect, are there so many varieties of quackery offered as magic roads to health, and that not seldom in the setting of religious obligation. American medical men, moreover, naturally share the general temper of their social environment. They are optimists, at least when they begin; and when they look at dramatic careers, like those of the Mayo brothers, they start with some inner impulse which tells them to be hopeful that they, too, may have a like good fortune. They are individualists because they do not know how obsolete the philosophy of free enterprise has become in relation to actual conditions. They repeat with real conviction the outmoded insistence that the "soul" of medical practice will be killed if its habits are determined by an impersonal bureaucracy. They speak of socialized medicine as the replacement of freedom, both for doctor and patient, by regimentation. They point to improvements, like the group practice of medicine, they have themselves made. If they live in the South, they mostly do not doubt the validity of its racial discriminations; and, if they did, they mostly realize that it would ruin their chance of success to be known at all widely as a sceptic about them. And since most of their patients are individualists too, the more wealthy, as a rule, the more hostile to socialized medicine, they rarely encounter that constant flow of lay criticism which drives them back to first principles.

Yet, when all this is said, it does not explain the position. The simple fact is that, on economic grounds alone, the private practitioner would be better off under a system of socialized medicine than he is under present conditions. No doubt a small handful of doctors in every generation would cease to make the large, and often fantastic, incomes of some outstanding specialists in cities like New York or Chicago, or of the fashionable psychoanalysts of the hour. The general result, however, would be all to his advantage. He would have security. He would be free from the difficult problem by which he is faced in collecting fees, having adequate equipment, recommending resort to the specialist, arranging for hospital treatment, and so forth. He could contribute far more than he is now able to do to the development of preventive medicine, and to the creation of an effective public opinion about housing, nutrition, the social cost of low wages, and to meet the need for better training of doctors, whether general practitioners or specialists, and to organize proper relations between medicine and related natural sciences on the one hand, and medicine and social institutions on the other.

Yet, broadly speaking, the American Medical Association remains adamant. It is much the most powerful body in its field; for it has not only nearly one hundred thousand members, but it employs itself some five hundred persons as its own civil service. I should not for one moment deny that it has done much admirable work, especially in the improvement of the standards of medical education. Its *Index Medicus* is probably the best guide to information about developments in medicine that there is in the world today. If it is permissible to doubt whether its *Journal* reaches the standard of either the *British Medical Journal* or of the *Lancet*,[59] it is nevertheless a periodical of high utility and merit. The Association has done valuable work in its attacks upon fraudulent patent medicines; and its Bureau of Hospitals is not only creating better standards of equipment, but it is also persuading hospitals of the importance of being of that quality which enables them to give the post of intern a far higher value as a source of medical experience than in the past. These are, no doubt, but a small part of the admirable achievements the Association has to its credit. No one could examine their outcome without recognizing that they are of major social importance.

Yet, when all this is granted, the fact remains that, in the context of public health, the Association is an instrument of reaction and not of progress. It is not merely that it has been strongly opposed or carefully cold to every attempt which looks to better medical provision for the American people. It has fought group practice, and, in some striking instances, has assisted its constituent bodies in the expulsion of medical men for organizing this form of service, or for association with different public health clinics supported in part, or wholly, from public funds.[60] It has been, at best, dubious about schemes for voluntary health insurance; and it has been fiercely and continuously hostile to any form of compulsory service of this kind. Indeed, it may be said that no body has been so influential in securing the rejection of state legislation for this end. It has insisted on this attitude openly, though the history of compulsory health insurance is that, after a relatively brief experience of it, most medical opposition disappears and the public becomes anxious for its extension. Anyone who examines the record of this conflict from 1916 until 1939 as set out by Dr. I. M. Rubinow, who played so large a part

[59] I am, as a layman, obviously quite incompetent to judge; but I say this after discussion with some dozen eminent medical men, among whom I may name the late Sir Arthur Newsholme, in Great Britain, and the late Professor Harvey Cushing in the United States.

[60] Esther Lucile Brown, *Physicians and Medical Care* (New York: Russell Sage Foundation, 1937), pp. 160–62. I have been greatly helped by this admirable summary.

therein,[61] will find it hardly consistent with the assumption that the standards of public health are a major consideration in the minds of those who shape the policy of the American Medical Association.

It is difficult to understand this continued hostility in the face of the famous Report of the Committee on the Costs of Medical Care. Yet no one can examine the inferences drawn from that Report by the Association without seeing that they constitute an anachronistic mixture of syndicalism and individualism.[62] In particular, the Association lays down principles about the cost of medical service and its incidence, which are matters of high social policy it is quite incompetent to decide, and seeks to enforce standards of service which assure the groups with comfortable incomes, or more, that they are not to be included within what it clearly regards as essentially a "charitable" scheme. It even demands that any qualified physician shall be used in the scheme if he chooses to offer his co-operation. It is, no doubt, true that some of the Association's constituent bodies have gone further than the central society; California, for example, voted, though in the face of strong hostility, in favour of compulsory insurance for all employed persons with incomes less than three thousand dollars a year; when it is remembered that in 1933 the annual income of half the families in California was less than one thousand dollars, it is not difficult to see that the California recommendation was as much an assurance of an income to doctors as of investment to patients. President Roosevelt's Committee on Economic Security, which reported in 1935, made strong recommendations in the same direction as the California State Medical Society. It asked, further, for actual plans from doctors, dentists, and hospitals to implement the insurance proposals. It is not difficult to see from the President's own statement [63] that he was unable to secure the necessary organized co-operation from the medical profession. There is evidence, indeed, of a continuing and bitter struggle in the note he himself wrote upon a later message, safe-guarding himself against the charge that the great schemes of joint federal and state aid for medical care that he proposed could be regarded as "socialized medicine." [64] How cautiously he had to move can be seen from his recommendation to Congress,[65] and the pains he took at a press conference in 1940 to emphasize the difference between federal aid to public health and a State medical service.[66]

It must be noted that already at least one-sixth of the public health services of the United States are financed out of taxation. The federal and state governments pay the greater part of the costs of the fight against tuberculosis and syphilis, and for maternity care, child welfare, and the care of the mentally afflicted. The hospitals are dependent upon public

[61] I. M. Rubinow, *The Quest for Security* (New York: Holt, 1934), pp. 207 f.
[62] Brown, *op. cit.*, p. 179.
[63] *Public Papers and Addresses,* Vol. IV, p. 45.
[64] *Ibid.*, p. 461.
[65] *Ibid.*, Vol. VIII, p. 99.
[66] *Ibid.*, Vol. IX, pp. 528–29.

payments for their patients; and in the state of New York—admittedly one of the best organized in this regard—one-quarter of all medical costs of every kind is paid for out of taxation. One eminent physician has urged that the taxpayer should at least support better obstetrical care, better hospital care, more opportunities for precision in diagnosis, a wide extension of home nursing, and more assistance on a much wider scale for those who suffer from chronic disease.[67] He visualizes the obligation to pay doctors for many services, those in clinics, for example, that are now performed without charge. He restricts his proposals to the lower income groups; but, as he rightly points out, since these are the groups which now either do not go to a doctor at all, or are frequently unable to pay his fees when they do, not only would more doctors be needed, but existing practitioners would have a higher and more assured income.

The simple fact is that once it is admitted that the health of the community is a matter with which the government, whether central or local, must necessarily concern itself, the opposition to a State medical service becomes, in fact, a demand for subsidies, whether from voluntary subscription or the taxpayer makes no difference, to the income of doctors. And this explanation has, in fact, been accepted by one of the best-known medical sociologists in the United States. The American Medical Association, said Dr. J. A. Kingsbury in 1908, is "a handful of selfish men who presume to represent the profession." Thirty years later he repeated the same indictment. He termed the Association, in 1938, "the most insidious and irreconcilable of all the professional groups in the country— the organized medical politicians, and indeed, merchants, under the leadership of [its] inner circle." [68]

Obviously this is far too simple an explanation. Much of the character of the Association is the outcome of the fact that a very large proportion of its members are too busy professionally, and too inert or too tired intellectually, to take an active part in its political decision-making; nor, indeed, could a considerable number, especially in the rural areas, afford to do so for financial reasons. The Association, moreover, is by its very nature in the hands of the older members, who are conservative in their habits of mind and therefore distrustful of change. The very nature of its constitution, again, emphasizes this control. It is complicated to the verge of the fantastic; most of its committees are dominated by doctors from cities of over one hundred thousand citizens, who are therefore likely to have the larger incomes; and of the Board of Trustees and the Judicial Council, over ninety per cent are specialists who, once again, are likely to have larger incomes than the average general practitioner. It is these men who choose the committees which deal with such special topics as health insurance. And it is their supporters who edit the publications of the Association. It is not, therefore, very surprising that they report

<hr>

[67] Brown, *op. cit.*, pp. 195 ff.
[68] Quoted from Oliver Garceau, *The Political Life of the American Medical Association* (Cambridge: Harvard University Press, 1941), p. 24.

agreement rather than dissent, and that they bury in committee any matter which is likely to divide the Association. Nor need anyone who knows the functioning of interest groups be very surprised either that it becomes "bad form" to make public a desire for change which a majority in some committee has rejected, or that the public discussion of differences should be looked upon as "washing dirty linen" before outsiders who are only likely to make things worse by their comments. This happens, after all, in every executive experience of the political world.

Nor is there anything novel in the fact that there is wire-pulling for office in the Association; what would be remarkable would be its absence where the offices are regarded as honourable. The centralization of finance in the hands of a relatively conservative body of trustees is far less remarkable than the affirmation, in the course of the automobile strike of 1945–46, by the directors of the immense firm of General Motors that they would not even permit the inspection of their books by share-holders in the corporation. There is far more realism in the comment of another well-known student of the social aspect of American medicine. "As a group," Dr. Bernheim has written, "doctors rarely take time to think; and since they associate almost exclusively with each other, they know little else but medicine and have no other interests." [69]

It is more serious that the Association can, through its *Journal*, largely control the social thought of the medical profession. It not only refuses to print any news the burden of which is hostile to its policy; it even weights its reporting of British news in the medical world to adapt it to the official line.[70] More: it is suspected that the grading of proprietary medicines is influenced by the advertising space pharmaceutical houses take in the *Journal*.[71] It has, as a body, powerful sanctions at its disposal to compel acceptance of its policies. It can refuse services of which the doctor stands in need. It can discipline him. It can boycott him; in the final issue, it can expel him, in the knowledge that a doctor is fatally compromised by loss of membership in his local society. It can, by delaying action on applications for group membership, deny the use of hospital services. It can shape the public mind on medical matters with an authority which few lay people can attempt to examine critically; it does so already, not only by wireless talks and pamphlets, but by articles supplied to the press, and even by motion pictures. Nor does the central government of the Association fail to watch carefully the movement of local medical opinion. Its advertising in state and other local journals of the profession is important to their finances. Its conferences of secretaries of local societies, with speakers of national reputation in the profession putting the official point of view, serve both to give a lead to local societies and to bring to the notice of

---

[69] *Ibid.*, p. 96.
[70] *Ibid.*, p. 99.
[71] *Ibid.*, p. 171.

the leaders local doctors interested in the "politics" of their profession, who may be kept on the right lines by tactful encouragement of further advancement. Anyone who reads an extract from the "engagement book" of Dr. Morris Fishbein, for many years the outstanding leader in American medical politics, would find it difficult to say that he was not just one more of that genus in which Mark Hanna was the supreme museum specimen.[72]

Granted the general inertia of doctors, their fairly widespread ignorance of the social context in which their problems are set, and the contempt the Association encourages in them for any lay opinion on either the economic or political aspects of their profession, the outlook of the Association has nothing unexpected about it. Its leaders know that they are fighting to prevent an invasion of their monopolistic control by public authorities which have not only little sympathy for their syndicalist outlook, but also the capacity to mobilize against them an opinion every whit as expert as their own. That is why, at critical moments, they show a certain dexterity in changing the policies they support; they have done so over federal aid to children, over public grants for medical assistance to the needy, even to group practice and health insurance. It is even whispered that there is powerful support for the quiet "elimination" of one of their most outstanding "political" figures on the ground that, in the technical sense of the term, he has become "unavailable"; he evokes public suspicion instead of public confidence.

But, in the main, the American Medical Association is the main instrument of reaction in the profession. Its major thesis is the incredibly naïve one that socialized medicine will undermine the democratic form of government; the Philadelphia Society has even issued posters for doctors to use which announced that "socialized medicine [is] our present greatest menace to liberty." "Liberty" here means, quite simply, that there shall be no public interference with the right of doctors to organize the practice of their profession in their own way, with no public control of any kind. It assumes a number of principles which it wholly fails to examine. It assumes that the present relation of doctors to the problems of medical care is adequate; and, alternatively, it insists that if changes are to be made they must be made by doctors themselves. "Liberty," therefore, is not the freedom of the sick person to receive proper treatment; nor is it the freedom of the community to be safeguarded from the threat of disease by organized preventive medicine. "Liberty" is a doctor's property right in his profession; he is to be safeguarded against any alterations in the doctor–patient relation, financial or otherwise, which are not made with his consent.

Quite patently, if doctors were asked their view of a syndicalism of this kind in any other occupation, they would reject it with indignation as "un-American." Why is it, when they can see the mote in the eye of others, that they cannot see the beam in their own? I suspect that there

[72] *Ibid.*, p. 128.

are several major reasons for the intellectual confusion in the medical mind. The first, and the most obvious, is the political ignorance of doctors. Little in their professional training makes them feel the need for social understanding. They live within the confines of a full but narrow curriculum while they are training; they live a hard life, after they have begun to practice, at least until they are securely established; and their main anxiety, when security has been won, is not to see it disturbed by "innovation" or "experiment" urged by men who do not think, as they have been accustomed to think, that the well-being of the medical profession is also the well-being of the community itself. I think this outlook is fostered by the "political" policies of the American Medical Association. On that plane it does their thinking for them. Though it speaks only for some sixty per cent of the profession, it is an instrument of immense power, highly centralized, with wide sanctions at its command, and with a propaganda machine hardly less persuasive to those who manipulate it than to those whom it is intended to influence. The opposition to its ceaseless activity is mostly interstitial, and rarely either durable or co-ordinated. No other voice, therefore, comes so clearly from the welter of opinions to the ordinary doctor with anything like the same persuasive force; and behind the persuasion there are techniques of coercion which very few doctors feel in a position to resist with safety.

The second reason, I suggest, is the direct relation between this professional psychology of the doctor and the mental climate of American business life in general. It is an individualist psychology; it suggests that "liberty" means freedom from State control; it tells the medical man that under free enterprise, his career is his own to make or man in terms of his own capacity. It offers him freedom from "bureaucratic" interference; and he has rarely been quick to see that he has, thereby, exchanged the interference of lay officials for the interference of medical officials, most of whom exercise an authority no less pervasive than any upon which lay officials would venture. And since the implications of this attitude fit in with the general American suspicion of government action, the belief that whatever is done by government is likely to be less well done than when it is accomplished by private enterprise, he accepts them, mostly unthinkingly, as valid because they are usual in the general environment to which he belongs. He is, in fact, the prisoner of a tradition the relevance of which to contemporary American conditions he takes for granted. He could not be expected to be aware that almost every examination of that tradition in the setting of the last twenty or thirty years shows not only that it is obsolete, but also that it does direct damage to necessary adaptations, even if it protects a status and its habits which have long exhausted their utility. To ask a busy medical man, often at work for fifteen or sixteen hours a day, whose vacations are brief, whose chance of reading even about medical developments is small, to embark upon a critical estimate of changing principles of American social organization is, quite obviously, to ask for the impossible.

Nor can the doctor help being aware that the advance in the status of his profession is comparatively recent, and that it is by no means definitively beyond check. He has to compete with a score of quasi-medical practitioners who have the legal right to apply their therapeutic nostrums to a credulous public without, in most cases, undergoing a training either comparable with, or as costly as, his own. He has to note the special privileges won from state legislatures by Christian Science practitioners, and, not least, the hold these have obtained upon a significant section of wealthier Americans in most of the great metropolitan areas. Amid the fierce competition to which he is thus subjected, the ordinary reaction of the average doctor is to look upon the conservative policies of the American Medical Association with much the same approval as the Musicians' Union looks upon the restrictive practices of their president, Mr. Petrillo, when he seeks to safeguard the living player against mechanical music on the radio or in the cinema. The doctor tends to assume that the higher the walls built about the monopoly to which he belongs, the safer will be his income on the one hand, and the surer his status on the other. Once he gives way, he is inclined to feel that, though it may be contended that he is merely surrendering the outworks, his advisers may well be right in their insistence that he is in fact admitting the enemy to the central citadel of his security.

There is one other argument by which, reasonably enough, he is influenced. There are few doctors who do not give a considerable portion of their time and effort to public service of a medical kind; it may be the free treatment of poor patients, the acceptance of a consulting post in a hospital, or, at a higher level, the free gift to the community of some new treatment or new surgical method the value of which is beyond all price. The ordinary doctor is inclined to the conviction that, in return for what he thus brings to the community, he has at least the right to be left alone. He has a traditional dislike of a fixed routine built without regard to his individual way of doing things. He suspects that socialized medicine means that not only must he "clock in" and "clock out," as though he were a worker on an assembly-line in the Ford factory at Detroit, but, even worse, that he will be driven to a standardized treatment of patients every departure from which he may have to justify before some committee of officials. And, worse still, he is afraid that his rise in his profession may then become less the outcome of his own skill and effort than of a judgment pronounced upon him by an authority which can rarely estimate in any really intimate way the thought he puts into his work or the skill with which he threads his way to the solution of his problems. He feels a kinship between himself and the artist; neither can yield his essential personality to an official discipline imposed from without. He does his best work when he is most his own master. Constrained to the obedience of rules, he loses the secret of his individuality.

It would, of course, be absurd to deny that there is not some substance in this argument. But the discount which must be made from it before it deserves serious consideration is obviously very large. There is no serious evidence to show that doctors in the federal or state medical services have any less sense of freedom as a normal rule than doctors in private practice. There is no serious evidence, either, to show that full-time teachers of medicine or surgery in the American university medical schools feel an inhibition or constraint because their claims to promotion are assessed by their senior colleagues, and not by the impersonal mechanism of patients' idiosyncrasies. At the level where the doctor departs from pretty standardized rules of treatment to experiment with new methods, the proportion of the profession involved is small indeed; and, at that still higher level where the great doctor, like Osler and Mackenzie, is also a great artist, no suggestion has ever been forthcoming that the gift of his individuality should be abridged by fitting him to the Procrustes' bed of bureaucratic uniformity. It is worth remembering, too, that a very large number of American doctors submit to the rules laid down by the officials of their Medical Association without even being conscious not only that these constitute a bureaucracy, but one they are far less able, in real life as distinct from the paper constitution, to control than they could control the officials of a public department.

It needs, finally, to be said that astonishingly few of the doctors who cry out against the dangers of socialized medicine have more than the haziest notions of what the problem of medical care in the United States actually is, nor of the social relationships in which that problem is so intricately involved. One may even fairly doubt whether more than a few realize how large is the amount of public money now spent on medical care, nor how much larger that would have to be if proper standards both of curative and of preventive medicine were to be erected with resolution and swiftness. More than this. Because most doctors are so pathetically devoid of insight into that hinterland where medicine touches the frontiers of vested interests in social and economic life, they do not adequately grasp the kind of effort that has to be made to break down the barriers vested interests erect against progress in medicine. Few of them have any serious training in social history, even in the history of medicine; work like that of Sigerist, or of Bernhard J. Stern—himself, very notably, a layman—seldom arouses keen interest in the profession. The subscribers to the journals which link medicine to the social sciences would not keep them alive if it were not for subsidies of one kind or another and the sale to public libraries; even a remarkable series of books like Professor Stern's distinguished *American Medical Practice in the Perspectives of a Century,* is the product of an effort subsidized by the collaboration of the New York Academy of Medicine and the Commonwealth Fund, a well-known foundation. It is not, I think, out of the way to suggest that the doctors, textbooks and a journal like that of the American Medical Association apart, read as much, or as little, as the average business man;

and they offer the same explanations of fatigue and the desire for distraction from the daily routine as justification for their unawareness of the world about them.

The truth is that the private practitioner, strongly entrenched though he may believe himself to be, generally hostile to change as he undoubtedly is, now fights a rearguard action in which defeat is obviously inevitable. Medical care in schools, the growth of industrial medicine, the necessity to organize public action on a continuous basis to deal with tuberculosis and venereal disease, public medical relief to the needy, the growing maintenance, at public cost, of the chronically sick and the mentally ill, the growing recognition that federal and state governments must unite to take care of infirm old age, the increasing provision of nurses paid by state or county or city, set in the context of the obvious impossibility of leaving the condition of the community's health dependent either upon the patient's ability to pay or upon the beneficence of private charity, show that the field of medical care is increasingly a matter in which all the vital controls will move to public hands. It is, indeed, probable that the next half-century will come to see medical organization resemble ever more closely educational organization. There will be an immense sector under public operation at public cost—preventively at the cost of the taxpayer, curatively by way of compulsory health insurance. Alongside it a small sector may still survive in private hands. Some of it will fall to the quasi-medical practitioners—the osteopaths, the chiropractors, the naturopaths, the Christian Science healers. Another part may well be an area of experimental medicine, perhaps organized in specialized bodies like the Rockefeller Medical Institute, which, if private in direction, is fundamentally public in objective. A small number of doctors may be permitted private practice, more, perhaps, as a check on the salaried doctor at a community clinic than as a normal institution in the profession; or, as is still more likely, the doctor of the future will be predominantly a salaried officer in a public service permitted to devote a defined proportion of his time to private patients whom he attracts through some special gift or skill. Pretty certainly, nevertheless, the vast majority of the outstanding medical men and women are likely to be, or to become, full-time public servants.

It is difficult to scan the emerging pattern of public health services in all the major countries without seeing that it is around such principles as these that the character of the profession will be shaped. It is surprising to note how little the American Medical Association has bent its mind to preparing the doctor for psychological adaptation to its implications. On the contrary, it has used its immense influence overwhelmingly not only to retard this adaptation, but, even more, to persuade the doctor that the emerging pattern is evil, that he can prevent it being unfolded, that, in seeking to arrest its evolution, he is fighting the battle of democracy and freedom. It is not merely that its outlook plainly contradicts a mass of facts the implications of which it either evades or seeks to misinterpret; what is worse is that its outlook runs directly counter to the personal interests of doctors themselves. Socialized medicine would give them a security they do not now possess in their working life, and it would enable them to confront old age without fear. It would make possible a direct relation between skill and reward, a power to put the man fitted for research and the man fitted for general practice in their proper spheres of action, an ability, every so often, to take leave of practice for the acquisition of new knowledge, or for a rest from the pressure of a hard and absorbing routine. Even more, it would facilitate the proper geographical and functional planning of medical care, and the development of the right proportion between preventive and curative medicine. Nor is there any more satisfactory way in which the art of medicine can find its proper roots in the biological and natural sciences upon which so much of its progress depends.

Of all this, in any serious degree, the American Medical Association takes little or no account. A sense of the emerging future is left either to some figure in the public health field, to the social historian who, like Professor Stern, realizes that the measure of the medical profession is, after all, set by the community's development, to a special body, like the famous Committee on Medical Care, to a foundation, like the Milbank Fund, which endows the undertaking of inquiries into results and tendencies, to exceptional groups like the recently formed Committee on Medicine and the Changing Order of the New York Academy of Medicine,[73] and to the very rare rebel among general practitioners or specialists who has the courage to break through the walls of prejudice and ignorance with which the Association surrounds a profession which ought, by the very nature of its function, to be in enlightened touch with the realities of the world about it. Even if we grant that a number of the by-products of the Association's activity have important social value, its major objectives are, for the most part, dangerous stumbling blocks in the path of progress.

5

ANY full-scale study of the professions in America would, obviously, have to take account of at least half a dozen other types to arrive at conclusions of unquestionable validity. It would have to deal with the engineer and the architect, the civil servant and the officers of the defence forces, the journalist and the teacher. It would need, also, to deal with the twilight world of professionalism where dwell the advertising agent and the public relations counsel, the realtor and the interior decorator. It would need, also, to seek to discover the place in American life of the artist and the craftsman, whether writer or painter, sculptor or musician, the new specialist in radio commentary or reportage, the actor and the public

---

[73] This committee has projected a series of eleven volumes on this theme, varying from studies on medical education and medical research, to studies on nursing, dentistry, public health, and preventive medicine. Three volumes were available in Great Britain by the spring of 1946.

lecturer, whose life is a long round of brief visits to Rotary Clubs, Leagues of Women Voters, and the like, where he makes a brief speech on any subject from the international situation to the latest best-seller, from an account of his month in Russia to an explanation of surrealism.

I cannot here even attempt a partial examination on this scale; it is in itself rather a theme for co-operative research, carefully planned, from which conclusions may be arrived at only after long discussion between those who have been engaged in the effort. I can venture only upon some tentative conclusions implicit in the evidence I have sought here to analyse. It should be noted, indeed, that, apart from a small body of men and women in the sciences and the arts, the two professions I have analysed are outstanding among all others both for the exacting training they require before their practice is permitted, and the standard of social service that is expected from their members. They show the professions, in short, at their best; and this is very plainly seen by anyone who examines the twilight zone between business and the professions as in advertising or in real estate.

What it is first essential to understand is that the professions are operating in what Veblen has so happily termed a predatory culture in which the incentive to work is, as he pointed out, pecuniary gain rather than social service ability.[74] In a civilization dominated by the business man as its outstanding type, it is, in Veblen's words, inevitable that "both in his own estimation and in the eyes of his fellows, the man who gains much does well. . . . To 'do well,' in modern phrase, means to engross something appreciably more of the community's wealth than falls to the common run." [75] In this type of civilization the ethic of any profession is almost compelled to dualism. On the one hand it is almost bound, like the priesthood of old, to a certain disdain for the sordid struggle for gain, and thus to develop, unlike the business man, a code of conduct which is not merely the minimum standard below which a man may not fall without the penalties of the law. Thus one pays one's doctor or one's lawyer in a spirit quite different from that displayed when one makes a purchase in a shop. There is a ritual in the function of payment more akin to the offering of a tribute to the Church, which it is agreed neither priest nor donor shall regard as precisely a business transaction made in part purchase of a commodity of an incommensurable kind which the Church alone can give, namely salvation. So health and the lawyer's advice have come to possess some measure of this incommensurability.

But, at the same time, the professional man wants not only security and comfort; he wants also to stand well with his fellows. Some part of this standing he can attain by exceptional distinction in his vocation; a great doctor like Osler, a great lawyer like Holmes, a great philosopher like James, a great scientist like Willard Gibbs, a great man of letters like

---

[74] Thorstein Veblen, *The Instinct of Workmanship* (New York: Viking Press, 1937), Chap. IV.
[75] *Ibid.*, p. 349.

Nathaniel Hawthorne or Emerson, will have this standing independently of the pecuniary results of their work. But since exceptional men of this stature are extremely rare, success in a profession, like success in business, is likely to be judged by the income it brings, and, thereby, the standard of living it makes possible. That is why the "great" lawyer usually means the lawyer who makes an immense income by safeguarding the interest of the large corporations, and why the "great" doctor is, for the multitude, the doctor whom it has become fashionable for the wealthy to patronize; I have met people in New York who had the same satisfaction in being a patient of Mr. J. P. Morgan's doctor as people in London had when they were able to say that they were operated upon for appendicitis by Sir Frederick Treves, who had recently performed the same operation on Edward VII. The pecuniary element in professional success is, in short, for all except a small group of remarkable people, essential to their recognition by the community of which they are a part. It enables them to mix with the "best" people, to send their children to the "best" schools and colleges, to see them married into the "best" families without any sense of displeasure or degradation in the latter. They can have about them all the characteristics of success—a finely furnished house or apartment, two or three cars, with a chauffeur always at hand, enough servants to make menial duties an amusement rather than a task, well-made and attractive clothes, the ability to afford expensive hobbies, the expectation of belonging to the best clubs as of right. Their names are decorations on the letterheads of all well-regarded civic activities even if, not infrequently, there is a half-seen and underpaid secretary who is really doing the work.

The exceptional few in each profession always apart, the result of this tendency to measure success by pecuniary standards is that the professional man is always being driven, often only half-consciously, to make more and more money, if he can, to convince himself and his community that he is successful. He then begins to esteem from the outset of his career the same virtues which make the business man successful—energy, thrift, the desire to please, the swift appreciation of a patient or client (with its obvious relation to the judgment of market movements), the knowledge of when to be cautious and when to take a risk. But just as the business man has, as he becomes wealthy, an inner desire for aristocratic status, which makes him combine the claims of industry with the pleasures of a functionless class, so the professional man yearns for a status which gives him significance apart from his wealth. The lawyer desires a senatorship, an embassy post in one of the great European capitals, a place in the cabinet, at a lower level the presidency of a Bar association, even, if he can afford it, the important ease of a place on the Bench. The doctor is more limited in his range. But, when he is successful, he seeks something more than money. The presidency of a great medical society or institution, the trusteeship of a distinguished university, the honorary degree that is reserved for the select few, or an eminent position in which it is plain that his name in his profession more than compensates for his virtual irrelevance to its objective. It is by these means that the medical man seeks to attain a status irrelevant to the pecuniary success that has attended his effort; and if this type of recognition comes from a foreign country, so much the better. No one, to take an obvious example among lawyers, would have put Professor James Brown Scott among the really eminent international lawyers. But among the well-paid "promoters" of his subject, few men were, by reason of his position, more sought after or more powerful. And upon few men, accordingly, were lavished more academic honours in proportion to his actual achievement. The key position he held enabled him to exact the tribute that scholarship pays to power.

If all this is carefully considered, it becomes a very illuminating example of the persistence of culture traits from a civilization where they are relevant into one where they have no real meaning. The leisured gentleman of the sixteenth and seventeenth centuries in England is, in the main, the feudal lord of the Middle Ages transformed, largely by Italian influence, into the dilettante aristocrat, like Horace Walpole in the eighteenth century and Lord Houghton in the nineteenth. He may do something, even something of importance. His vital characteristic is that he does nothing obviously for money, and that his position is, above all, fixed, because his status in itself enables him to be something. If I may use a paradox, he has no concrete function even while the fact that he merely *is* has itself functional significance. In a pecuniary civilization the principles of its culture have preserved his importance, even while it has permitted the fusion of his type with that of the successful business man. Mr. Morgan, Mr. Frick, Mr. Huntington have their collections even while they continue as banker, steel magnate, or railroad king. The gentleman blends into the business man by achieving a status of distinction unrelated to the central function he performs.

The same standard is imposed upon the professions by their adjustment to the climate of a business civilization. It is, of course, rare for the blend to be effected at so high a pecuniary level, since the rewards of professional success are so very much smaller than those of business life. But, with, as always, the small class of really exceptional men apart, the principle is the same. And what is of exceptional interest is the degree to which those elements which distinguished a profession from a business get blurred in the result. The acceptance of the principle is, indeed, defended as "realism"; it proves the ability of the professional man to adapt his habits to those of the type which sets the main standards of our civilization. Lawyers and doctors alike organize their vocations upon assumptions which involve great rewards for a few and permanent pecuniary mediocrity for most; they organize them, indeed, by methods which are continually making it doubtful whether the objectives of their profession can be adequately fulfilled. They sacrifice, to put it briefly, the maximum value to society of each profession as a whole, to the competitive scramble in which a small proportion become pecuniarily successful. And having made the success of that proportion the main principle round which both the institutions and the codes of ethics of these professions are built, they are bound to look askance at any innovations which endanger the operative validity of that main principle. That is why, despite endless and even passionate discussion, the lawyers move so slowly to the achievement of methods which give reality to the ideal not merely of justice, but even of equality before the law; that is why, also, doctors allow medical individualism to be so persistent an obstacle to achievement of a uniform and reasonable standard of medical care. The use in each profession of words like "freedom" and "democracy" as the slogans under which they fight all progressive change are, of course, merely rationalizations intended to bring comfort to those who are uncertain or hostile; just as terms like "bureaucracy" and the "annihilation of individuality," or the nightmare of "doctors in uniform," or the "destruction of the personal relation between lawyer and client," are intended to arouse fear of a soulless and uniform corps, too vast to be interested in the "little man," and so to elicit on the side of the *status quo* the public opinion which has been led to believe that the virtue of both professions consists in the ability they offer to patient or client to unbare their inner confidence to doctor or lawyer. The preservation of an obsolete professional mythology is at once a safeguard against the normal fears of change and an evocation of that simpler, less confused, and unhurried America which is now being so carefully clothed, like all dead periods, in the attractive panoply of a golden age.

Any effort at the social improvement of professional standards depends upon the recognition that the members of a profession are important not by reason of what they have, but by reason of what they do. That functional criterion is largely destroyed in any civilization whose cultural habits are permeated by the business man's way of life. Since it is property which, for the most part, secures honour, comfort, respect, and access to status, and since all these are naturally enough objects of ambition, even professional men go on accumulating property until it becomes an end in itself and not a means. A lawyer will become a specialist on contributory negligence, and go on examining cases in which that issue is the main feature not because there is something of real delight in a life devoted to the study of contributory negligence, but because a reputation for outstanding eminence in that field means the chance of a higher income since it has special importance for big employers and insurance companies. A doctor will go on repeating the same operation on countless patients not because he finds satisfaction in its repetition, but because, once it is known that he does the particular operation with a special skill, he is likely to attract the wealthiest patients who have need of such a service. That is why, for an overwhelming proportion of professional men, the pecuniary context of their effort in a predatory culture, to use Veblen's term once more, is an explicit denial of the profession's ethics.

It attacks the individuality professionalism is intended to evoke by making what is important not inside the mind of the professional man, but what is outside his character. He accepts the judgment of superficial appearance and not of inner reality.

I must add that I do not suggest for one moment that the situation is peculiar to the United States; on the contrary, ever since the bourgeois revolution which began to transform our civilization at the close of the fifteenth century, it has spread all over the world. It has even been able to transform the habits of the ancient East as this area has been penetrated by the technique of industrialism. The one significant thing about the professions in the United States is that, being more recent in origin, and less obscure at the margins of their habits, they display so much more clearly the consequences of the compromises to which they have been driven. The English lawyer is not, in fact, very different from the American, nor is the French, nor is the Spanish; the English doctor has a close resemblance to the American, as do his confrères in Paris or Berlin or Vienna. It merely happens that the antiquity of the ritual he observes gives his professional practice a greater elegance of form and a more profound skill in concealing its conditioning to the pecuniary principle. It is perhaps an advantage that where the professions are more recent in origin and less rigid in their ceremonies, it should be easier to detect the degree of difference between the outward claim and the inner reality. It is perhaps because of their youth that they may be able to revise their foundations more swiftly and with greater determination.

XIII

Press, Cinema, and Radio
in America

I

THE WORLD in which the contemporary American moves is a far more complex one than when Jeremy Bentham thought that with public opinion formed by the combined impact of universal suffrage and a free press the safety of representative democracy was assured. The change, indeed, is in quality and not in quantity. The American does not now leisurely wait to hear of events in most of which he feels certain he is unlikely to be involved. In the forefront of his consciousness there is bound to be the knowledge that so immense is the impact of his government on the distribution of international power that it cannot be significantly altered without the assumption of American acquiescence in the result. The view at which he hesitatingly arrives is an equation in which, quite literally, an immense number of variables is present. In part it may be shaped by his national origin, or by that of his ancestors; it makes a difference whether he is English or Irish, French or German, Italian or Yugoslav, Russian or Polish, Norwegian or Dutch. His religion is an element of importance; so is his occupation; so is his income. He is influenced by the sentiments and opinions of the people with whom he works and plays, the politicians for whom he feels admiration or hate, the desire not to be regarded as unconventional, or, it may well be, the pleasure he experiences in following a line of his own. He may think one way rather than another because he likes or dislikes his employer, or because he cannot bear to share the outlook of some rival in his business. He may be a Republican because his grandfather lies buried in the cemetery at Gettysburg, or a Democrat because the boss of the ward in the city where he lives got his boy out of trouble with the police, or a Communist because the habits of Mayor Babcock of Pittsburgh, as shown during the steel strike of 1919, threw a sudden and decisive light for him on the character of the State power. Whatever his outlook, it is the deposit of a labyrinthine process in which it is never possible either for him or for us to measure the proportions in which reason and sentiment and emotion enter into the action he takes. It is important always to remember how frequently the decision to remain aloof from action is itself action that may be critical in its impact at a significant time.

He has to decide what the world is like, and, negatively or positively, form an opinion upon the basis of what facts he may encounter. His major trouble is that few of the facts at his disposal come to him unweighted or uncoloured by a mass of competing interests which seek to make him think one way rather than another. If he seeks his guidance from the press, he will find that the number of journals to which the famous aphorism of the great English editor, Mr. C. P. Scott of the *Manchester Guardian,* that "facts are sacred, comment is free," appears a moral imperative is, on all critical questions, pitifully small. If he goes with any constancy to the "movies," he will, even if he does not know it, be the prisoner of tendencies which are intended to create in him a fairly specific mental climate the character of which will permeate his judgment. He may listen with assiduity to the radio commentators without being seriously aware, as they themselves are frequently unaware, that they are helping him to form his judgments without, only too often, disclosing to him the unstated assumptions which are the framework within which their reports are made. He may prefer the full-scale book in which he hopes to find not merely the writer's interpretation, but all the objective materials out of which the writer shaped his interpretation. But he will find that this is a simplification in which he can put no confidence. Mr. Walter Duranty will draw for him a Soviet Russia which he finds unrecognizable in Mr. W. H. Chamberlin's bitter pages;[1] the character of the Supreme Court in Mr. Charles Warren's monumental history[2] bears little relation to the Supreme Court as seen by learned observers like Mr. Louis B. Boudin[3] or Professor E. S. Corwin.[4] Some memory of his schooldays may surround the name of Governor Altgeld with indignation as a man who pardoned the evil anarchists who threw the bomb which killed seven policemen and wounded sixty others round Haymarket Square in Chicago on May 4, 1886; and he may discover later, to his surprise, that the modern view of Altgeld is of an upright man who sacrificed his career to truth.[5] He may be a Southern white convinced that one of the urgent principles upon which his safety depends is to keep down the "uppity" Negro by every means in his power; and yet he may, perhaps on a holiday with a friend in New York, find the results of his outlook so relentlessly probed by Professor Myrdal that he returns home troubled and ashamed by what he is compelled to confront in that remarkable analysis.

[1] William Henry Chamberlin, *The Russian Revolution, 1917–1921* (New York: Macmillan, 1935).
[2] Charles Warren, *The Supreme Court in United States History* (Boston: Little, Brown, 1922).
[3] Louis B. Boudin, *Government by Judiciary* (New York: Godwin, 1932).
[4] Corwin, *The Twilight of the Supreme Court.*
[5] W. R. Browne, *Altgeld of Illinois* (New York: Viking Press, 1924).

The environment out of which there emerges that intricate and half-conscious complex of emotions, sentiments, and convictions we call public opinion is always a weighted environment. The instruments which shape the minds of citizens are not freely at the disposal of anyone who wishes to operate them. They are controlled, for the most part, by men or bodies who can afford either to create or to employ them. And, for the most part, they are controlled by the vested interests which dwarf altogether the individual and leave him helpless, save as he can find some other association which makes it possible to express his experience of life. It is open to Mr. Eugene Meyer or to Mr. Marshall Field to buy or to start a newspaper like the *Washington Post* or the *Chicago Sun;* the best the ordinary citizen can hope for is to creep into the correspondence columns. The cinema has become Big Business in almost every aspect of its organization; without immense capital at his disposal, the ordinary man must content himself with being no more than the spectator of its operations. The radio in a system based, like that of the United States, on the sale of time to those who can afford its purchase means the virtual exclusion of any voice which has nothing to offer but the quality of what it has to say.

For, broadly speaking, just because each of these three media is a branch of Big Business, its object is not the communication of truth, but the making of profit; and the truth it can afford is rarely the whole truth, but so much of it as is compatible with profit-making. I do not mean for one moment that each of them continually distorts the picture it paints for the purpose of profit. That has, I suspect, never been true even of the worst of American newspapers. Nor do I underestimate the checks, both direct and indirect, that the consumer of these commodities has upon their producers. Quite obviously, a newspaper whose editors are frequently caught out in falsification of news will, in a country like the United States, risk the loss of its readers, and the loss of circulation is reflected in the revenue from advertising, upon which the power to make profit almost wholly depends. Nor is it less clear that the film producers must, in the last resort, depend upon their power to please the public, and that this is a risk of no small proportions. It has, further, been shown again and again that the advertiser who "sponsors" an unsuccessful "feature" in a radio programme will pay pretty heavily for his mistake. And, over and above all this, there are issues upon which, from time to time, the public develops a mind of its own which no amount of specialized propaganda can alter. That was notably the case in the two re-elections of President Roosevelt in 1936 and 1940, when, despite the overwhelming influence of the press, he won with comparative ease. It is, moreover, normally true that where the workingman in America has to choose between the picture of events painted for him by the leaders of his trade-union and the picture painted by the massive instruments of propaganda at the service of his employers, he chooses the former with a high degree of confidence.

The instruments of propaganda are immensely important in American society, but they are never finally decisive. There is frequently an experience beyond the pattern they trace, the power of which they cannot alter. There are *mores* they are bound to respect; there are people whom they dare not denigrate; there are policies and motives which can only be attacked indirectly and not directly. There are types of propaganda which suit one region of the United States and not another. There are circumstances quite outside the control of the instruments of propaganda to which these must adjust themselves. War is the supreme example of this; but so, also, is the impact of swift and observable technological change. New habits may rapidly compel attention and achieve so firm a hold that even the most traditional opposition to their influence must begin by accepting their permanent influence as the basis from which to start their analysis. Anyone who compares, for example, the Southern attitude to Negro slavery in Jackson's day and in that of Polk will see that the press rather adapted itself to a climate of opinion than was responsible for it. In the same way the change in the traditional American attitude to sex, and especially to birth-control, has driven the instruments of propaganda to new attitudes rather than been itself produced by those instruments.[6] There is, in short, an action and interaction between conscious and unconscious influence in the formation of public opinion which it is always vital to bear in mind. Professor Hart has pointed out,[7] for example, that while there were no magazine references to birth-control in 1914, and one reference only in 1918, in 1929, 1930, and 1931 the number of references was forty-eight, forty-two, and seventy-one respectively. This particular change is a function of many variables: it is the outcome of a breakdown in traditional religious influence; it has been influenced by the changing character of family relations; and these, in their turn, as Professor Hart rightly notes,[8] are not only the result of industrial changes like the growth of cities, but, perhaps even more, of technological developments like the motorcar and the invention of far more effective birth-control devices by the combined efforts of scientist and technologists. Nor must one forget either the influence of the First World War upon sexual habits, or the immense growth, after 1918, of forms of collective entertainment, like the dance hall, the road house, and the cinema which, by externalizing pleasure, reduced the influence of the home, as it was conceived even as late as 1914, to pretty narrow proportions in all but the rural areas and those small towns in which change is looked upon with suspicion merely because it is change.

America, again, is not merely a gigantic continent geographically, with the resultant need for careful attention to regional habits; it is also a complex labyrinth of groups—political, religious, economic, social, sport-

[6] Consider the good work of Margaret Sanger and Mary Ware Dennett in education on birth-control.

[7] Hornell Hart, "Changing Social Attitudes and Interests," *Recent Social Trends*, Vol. I, p. 415.

[8] *Ibid.*, p. 422.

ing—each of which must be catered to in a special way. It is not only pretty certain that a Southern Democrat in Georgia would not dream of reading regularly a Republican newspaper even if it were printed in the town where he lives; it is also true that it is practically impossible to establish a strongly Democratic newspaper in such "rock-ribbed" Republican states as Vermont and Maine. It is equally true that few practising Roman Catholics will read a paper hostile to their Church, and no movie corporation would dare to make a "radical" the hero of one of its films. Since, moreover, the purpose of the instruments of propaganda is to make profit which justifies the capital outlay, the larger the outlay, the less possible it becomes to cause offence to any large source of profit; few men or corporations are therefore able to go crusading for any length of time upon an unpopular issue, or to give it a big display without offsetting it by some alternative attraction. Colonel McCormick may devote part of the *Chicago Tribune* to his special passion for isolationism and his special hatred for Great Britain; but he has to compensate for these by the excellent sports-reporting and the skill of the "comic strips" by which his paper is chiefly known. Everyone knows that a film would be overwhelmed with indignant attack, if, indeed, it survived the censorship of Mr. Eric Johnston, as head of the Motion Picture Association, if it offended Catholics or Methodists, the American Legion or the United States Chamber of Commerce. And I doubt whether any of the larger radio circuits, like Columbia or National or Mutual, would allow the purchase of a weekly half-hour of its time by an association of agnostics which sought, however reverently, to present the evidence against the historic validity of any of the major forms of organized Christianity. I am not, indeed, sure that any of them would allow the American Medical Association to conduct a weekly examination of the evidence upon which a faith in Christian Science is built.

In any discussion, therefore, of the major instruments of American propaganda, it is important to recognize the boundary—always shifting, it is true, but still a boundary—within which they work. First, and above all, they must interest people; failure in this regard means overwhelming failure. Second, they must be careful not to offend powerful groups which may join battle with their clients from an equal, or nearly equal, plane of power and influence. Third, what they have to say must not be susceptible of easy contradiction, or shown to be built upon monstrous error incompatible with obvious common sense. Fourth, they must avoid tiring people by incautious repetition; they must, therefore, either crusade for their particular cause for a relatively short space of time, or, alternatively, they must vary the methods of their crusade. Fifth, they must always remember the need for discretion if they seek to challenge traditional *mores* to which great importance is attached; this is particularly true of widely held religious principles, national myths, deep-seated impulses. Sixth, they must never forget that, once they outrage the consumer upon whom they rely, it is likely to take them a long time to recover his attention or belief. Seventh, they must build their activity upon the basis that the concrete is always more illuminating than the general, the appeal to emotion and sentiment usually far more convincing than the appeal to reason. And, not least, they must always bear in mind that the vaster the audience it is desired to influence, the more direct must the character be of the appeal. Most people are wrapped up in their private affairs; most of them, also, have little energy of mind left to spare to examine argument addressed to them on a high level; and most of them regard their leisure as a period in which they are entitled to rest and be amused rather than driven into the discomfort of thought. The makers of propaganda must, therefore, normally seek to please those whom they address, and they must recognize how important it is for them to have always before them the reality of a consumer's sovereignty which they outrage at their peril.

All this is significant because it shows that the American business man, whose domination of the instruments of propaganda is overwhelming, has not yet attained a position in which he can use them in a totalitarian way. He may, with men like him, have a well-nigh unchallengeable power in the cinema industry; but there are vital things he dare not say directly in the films he produces, and, even indirectly, he must handle them with caution. He owns, with his fellow business men, all the major daily news-papers and most of the national magazines of wide circulation; even so, he cannot afford to neglect the impact of a small newspaper, like William Allen White's *Emporia Gazette,* once its owner-editor has won for him-self a national respect and a small but affectionately devoted following; and he must watch with constant care the effect of the "high-brow" week-lies and other journals of relatively small circulation simply because they are addressed to the readers who themselves, in a considerable degree, have an influence to which prestige and authority attach in the making of public opinion. So, too, with the radio. At certain levels, and over certain problems, there are groups with sufficient influence to be able to bring a pressure to bear upon the big networks that it is difficult to resist, to secure, in all normal controversy, the right to answer most of the challenges which are made to them.

Nor must one forget the effect of the spoken word. No people has ever enjoyed the spoken address or discussion more than the American people; with no other is its influence so great. The countless leagues and clubs and forums which, for some six or seven months in the year, will listen with infinite patience to a long succession of speakers eminent or half-eminent, serious or amusing, talking well, or even talking badly, who say their say and answer questions, are one of the most remarkable features of American life. Few of the thousands who have heard Mr. Maurice Hindus describe the daily life of the peasants on a Russian col-lective farm will easily believe again the fantastic generalizations of Mr. Westbrook Pegler or Mr. George E. Sokolsky. A great meeting in Madi-son Square Garden to protest against the barbarism of Franco Spain can-not be dismissed just as communist propaganda when it is presided over by an eminent and devoted Roman Catholic layman like Mr. Bartley Crum. And there is an important sense in which the investigating work of congressional committees has important results. Judge Pecora's brilliant handling of the Senate's investigation of Wall Street in 1934 evoked a public opinion in support of the bill establishing the Securities and Exchange Commission against which all counter-propaganda was powerless. It was the massive evidence collected by the La Follette Committee on Civil Liberties that prevented the large-scale offensive of Big Business by which it was hoped to destroy the effectiveness of the National Labor Relations Act. It was the unshakable testimony of Mr. Harold Ickes before the Senate Committee on Naval Affairs which, in March 1946, compelled the withdrawal of Mr. Edwin Pauley's name as President Truman's nominee for the under-secretaryship of the Navy; the discussion evoked memories of the Teapot Dome scandal too bitter to make Mr. Pauley's acceptance possible, and there are many similar examples.

There have been moments, too, when books and articles have shattered the defences of vested interests with the crashing effect of a bomb. Paine's famous *Common Sense,* at the very outset of the War of Independence had a decisive effect upon men's outlook; it is not an exaggeration to say that it was worth an army in itself to the sorely beset Washington. Mrs. Stowe's *Uncle Tom's Cabin,* crude and sanctimonious though it seems to a later generation, marks a real stage in the drift to civil war; it deepened emotions on both sides to a degree one can appreciate only by reading contemporary discussion of its truthfulness. Henry George's *Progress and Poverty* (1879) was the first definitive sign that the Gilded Age was linked to principles in essence incompatible with the American way of life. In that remarkable epoch of the "muckrakers," which led, if in a circuitous way, through "progressivism" to the reign of Woodrow Wilson in the White House, and thence, after the flamboyant nihilism of the nineteen-twenties, to the New Deal of Franklin Roosevelt, the relentless exposures of Lincoln Steffens and of Upton Sinclair put both the boss system in the cities and the great trusts on the defensive; and though each of them emerged from the attack successfully, they were not wholly unscathed by the ordeal. Indeed, I do not think it is an exaggeration to say that it was the exposure of the methods of the Rockefeller empire by Miss Ida Tarbell in her *History of the Standard Oil Company* (1904) which led Mr. Rockefeller to accept the advice of his public relations officer, the notorious Ivy Lee, to seek to regain by public benefactions the moral loss his reputation suffered as the ugly story of the corruption, brutality, and dishonesty upon which his fortune was founded came to be a matter of public knowledge. Mr. Rockefeller set a fashion which has had many imitators. Foundations like those established by Carnegie and Guggenheim, by Harkness and Mellon, great public gifts like those of Frick and Widener and a hundred others, were all, in considerable part, the outcome of a desire to win a kindly word from history, and a reward in heaven, as a footnote to their general description as "robber barons." And I venture the guess that, half a century from now, Edmund Wilson's *The American Jitters* (1932) will be regarded as having caught, with the precision of a great surgeon, that glimpse of what America at the height of the depression seemed like to the bewildered sufferers who swept Mr. Roosevelt into power.

All of this adds up to the conclusion that there is no simple formula for defining the boundaries within which the major instruments of propaganda exercise their influence on the American mind. It is quite clear that there is no real sense in which they can fairly be called instruments of a totalitarian kind. Each of them is, overwhelmingly, in the hands of owners who exploit them for profit. Many of those owners are both cynical and unscrupulous in the use of their power. Few of them would desire to see any basic changes in either the political or economic foundations of American life; and most of them are far less concerned with truth than with the protection of their interests from the scrutiny of truth. Their power to resist change is collectively enormous. Their ability to fix the stereotype of an ideal America in the mind of the ordinary citizen, which retains the shining contours of the Horatio Alger epoch, is sometimes startling. And they start with the immense advantage of seeking to influence a people who have, perhaps, the most remarkable enjoyment of uniformity and conventionalism for their own sakes as any people in modern times. The uniformity and the conventionalism are, no doubt, regional rather than national in their range; the enjoyment is taken very differently by a Vermont farmer and by the owner of a cotton plantation in Georgia; and it will be taken very differently, again, by a fruit farmer in California. Yet the zest for being like, rather than unlike, other people is there as an unmistakably American passion. They may join different orders, be Elks rather than Moose, Knights of Columbus rather than Kiwanians; the point is that they join. They largely accept the same indices of well-being—a second car, the latest model of refrigerator, the newest combination of television and phonograph. No other people can be so easily persuaded to read the same books, to play the same games, to have the same friendly extroversion in human relations. No other people feels more keenly the same pain in the sense of separation in outlook from his neighbours. No other people is less troubled by the subtle and pervasive danger of mass production; and I doubt whether any other people, save one which, like the Germans under Nazi rule, is driven to dumb acceptance of orders, has ever been so slogan-minded. The American people, at a superficial glance, seem almost predestined victims of the kind of soulless nightmare of unending sameness that Mr. Aldous Huxley has depicted in his *Brave New World*.

And yet the power of those who own and operate these major instruments of propaganda is always being challenged and is never as effective as, superficially, it might seem that it ought to be. There is something in the psychological climate of America which resists any ultimate regimentation of behaviour or opinion. Something always escapes the net which is thrown about the people. Non-conformity is an element in American life which is always called into being by the spectacle of conformity. There is what Emerson called "this din of opinion and debate." It is often crude, sometimes fantastic, sometimes self-stultifying. But what Thoreau, in his noble essay *On the Duty of Civil Disobedience,* argued for in the political sphere is something of which account must be taken in almost every sphere. The enjoyment of dissent almost equals the enjoyment of conformity. It is aided by the restless zest for change which infects at some time almost all Americans. The result is, that with all this power, none of the major instruments of propaganda can hope for the total possession of the minds they seek to influence. They are always trying to complete a circle which is always being broken. And the break always takes place at points on the circle which, as often as not, are quite different from anything that the oracles have expected.

For the significant fact must not be overlooked that the function of propaganda is hardly less to reinforce or to destroy some opinion already formed than it is to create an opinion. The daily column of Mr. Westbrook Pegler may make reactionaries more satisfied with their reactionism because he so persistently makes their outlook seem to them in a special degree "true" American opinion; I doubt whether it has ever produced any other feelings than indignation or contempt in any liberal mind. A film like *The Farmer's Daughter* may give a great deal of gratification to a large number of people who feel that something "ought to be done" to make politics "cleaner"; I am certain that it never caused a single boss of any political machine in city or country or state a sleepless night. The power of radio is immense in a crisis or in an issue the interest in which is already dramatic enough to make the listener eager for information and commentary; in the critical year from May 1940 to June 1941 there is no sort of doubt that the clear and courageous broadcasts of Mr. Churchill from London kept millions of Americans who hated nazism at ease about the power of Britain to survive. But it is also interesting to note that neither the knowledge that nazism was a threat to socialism all over the world, nor that a German invasion of Britain would mean death or the concentration camp for most of its labour leaders, made the American Socialist party reconsider the isolationist principles which were the basis of its approach to the war. It seems to require an overwhelming transcendence of habitual experience for propaganda aimed in one direction to change the outlook of people who are steadfastly devoted to marching in another.

I am, this is to say, doubtful whether the popular belief that the citizen is the prisoner of an environment made for him by vested interests through the propaganda at its command is more than a half-truth in any except the closed totalitarian society. It cannot have suited those interests, for example, that there should have been an immense decline of interest in religion, and an immense increase of interest in science, as shown by the attention devoted to each in periodical literature and books;

the decline of interest in the Bible is shown by Professor Hart to be over fifty per cent in twenty-five years,[9] and there was a steady growth of criticism of, and opposition to, traditional Christian dogma and the work of the clergy.[10] In the so-called "boom" years from 1920 to 1929, the press was able to insist on the evil of communism, the failure of the Russian experiment, the necessity of leaving industrial management to the exclusive control of the employer, and the undesirability of "outside" interference between a corporation and its workers; its attitude after 1929 was one of careful "reasonableness," a rather bewildered search for compromise. Nor was the passionate isolationism which followed the First World War ever able to gain so deep a hold on the general public as to prevent a ceaseless recognition, often perhaps, an uneasy recognition, that it belonged to a past epoch; and it was upon this recognition that President Roosevelt was able to build his policy of assistance to Great Britain after the overrunning of Norway, Belgium, and Holland, and the surrender of France in the summer of 1940.

I am not denying, for one moment, the power of these major instruments; still less do I deny that their influence is overwhelmingly in one direction. I seek only to affirm three things. First, no public report is likely to seem decisive if it contradicts an intimate experience which results in strong private convictions. Second, the impersonal forces of the American scene shape what propaganda has to say at least as much as it is shaped by those who make the propaganda. Third, the very babel of voices which compete for the citizen's attention goes no inconsiderable distance towards distracting, rather than clarifying, the public mind upon any significant issue; and this has the result of giving the propaganda which is built upon relation to a special group a greater weight than the propaganda which is built upon relation to an undifferentiated mass of citizens. The pamphlets and leaflets of the Political Action Committee of the C.I.O. had far more influence with its members than did, say, the *Chicago Tribune* or the *New York Daily News*. The *Wall Street Journal* could work up emotion more easily among the members of the New York Stock Exchange than it could hope to do among the officials of the American Federation of Labour. Mr. D. W. Griffith's well-known film *The Birth of a Nation* would seem far better history when it was shown south of the Mason and Dixon line than it would when it was shown north of it. Mgr. Sheen's radio acerbities sounded far more convincing in South Boston and Brooklyn than they could ever have done in the small towns of Maine or among the cotton-mill operatives of Gastonia, North Carolina. It is only the very rare man or the very outstanding event that commands the attention of the whole public mind for any length of time, or is able to make any considerable section of it reconsider the primary, and often unconscious, assumptions of its basic attitudes. Propaganda follows almost as much as it leads.

[9] *Ibid.*, p. 401.
[10] *Ibid.*, p. 403.

To this it is necessary to add certain other affirmations, which Americans who are impatient either of the wide variety of views their society exhibits, or of their own inability to impose the particular regimentation of ideas or conduct for which they are anxious, often fail to see in any full perspective. That there are propagandists in the United States without an atom of interest in truth is beyond all question. Again, there are men and women who lie because they are avid of power; there are men and women who lie because they are anxious to make money; there are men and women who lie because they are, quite selflessly, so devoted to some particular end that they are unaware of the assumptions they adopt in order to reach that end, or of the degradation involved in the methods they employ for that purpose. I think that Mr. William Randolph Hearst belongs to the first category. I think that Mr. Ivy Lee belonged to the second. Few people can read the history of men like the Mather family in seventeenth-century Massachusetts, or the exponents of the positive case for slavery, especially in the period between the rise of Calhoun and the outbreak of the Civil War, or of the Roman Catholics who have, in the last eight or ten years, given their eager support to Franco Spain, and fail to see that the great body of propagandists belongs to this third class; and many of them belong to this class less because they want consciously to destroy either tolerance or the open mind, than because they are genuinely unaware of the conditions upon which the discovery of truth depends. A good deal more than we like to admit of propagandist effort is the outcome of fanaticism, and the fanatics are not confined either to one class or to one creed in the United States.

It is, of course, true that the major instruments of propaganda are mostly in the hands of wealthy people concerned, above everything, to maintain the economic *status quo*. But it is also true that a good deal of their power is based upon the inertia of Americans in the realm of public thought, an inertia that is the more startling when one remembers the speed and decision with which they act when once they are aroused. It is tempting to attribute this characteristic in part to the individualism of the frontier, the sense it bred that a man depends more upon himself and his energies than upon concerted and collective action, and partly, also, to the fact that, after the fierce political discussions from the foundation of the republic to the end of the Civil War, there was a decline of the sense of the State in America which lasted almost to the emergence of the Progressive movement. That decline still has deep roots today. It can be seen in the distaste of the trade-unions for direct political action. It can be seen in the considerable number of men who are elevated to important political office without any political experience, and not seldom for but a brief period of time. It can be seen, not least, I think, in the still widespread feeling in the United States that politics is a series of discrete issues unconnected by a thread of general philosophy which makes a man have, for example, fierce emotions about the reform of the Supreme Court, or Russia, or the place of the Negro in American civilization, without any thought of the nexus which binds each of these things to the general contours of American civilization.

There is, moreover, one American habit of mind which, as I venture to think, makes Americans more susceptible to propaganda than the people either of Britain or of France. They are at once a practical and experimental people in the things of everyday life and enjoy innovation in that realm, while they are a curiously conservative people in the realm of fundamental ideas. They accept a revolution like the coming of the motorcar or the aeroplane without any difficulty as a natural change. To require, on the other hand, that they adapt themselves to a new assumption about the Constitution, or the character of slavery as a Southern institution, or the pathetic fallacy of Liberal Christianity, is an extraordinarily difficult matter. There is an interesting example of this outlook in the mind of even so distinguished a sceptic as Mr. Justice Holmes. Open-minded as he was, he found it difficult to be patient with the realism of Professor Charles Beard in his famous *Economic Interpretation of the Constitution*. [11] The acceptance of Beard's analysis would have compelled him to re-examine a part of his thinking that, so to say, he had inherited from the environment into which he was born; his acceptance of it went so deep that he was emotionally inaccessible to new ideas in this realm. I suspect, too, that it was a similar unexamined affection for the Supreme Court of Massachusetts, which had played so large a part in his own life, that enabled him to persuade himself that no injustice had been done by the decision of the Court not to interfere with the conviction of Sacco and Vanzetti.[12] Anyone who reads the once famous manual the *Pro-Slavery Argument*,[13] which shut the minds of Southerners to the earlier optimism of men like Thomas Jefferson that the system would ebb swiftly to its close, can still find the traces of its influence in works like Ulrich B. Phillips' *Life and Labor in the Old South* (1929), or Professor Avery Craven's *The Coming of the Civil War* (1942). In both of these it is virtually taken for granted that the real issue of this immense problem was only what took place in the minds of white men on either side; for while they seem aware of an outstanding incident, like the Turner revolt of 1831, the significance of the immense mass of evidence of what Negro slaves were thinking, now so admirably assembled by Mr. Herbert Aptheker,[14] plays little or no part in their narrative. It is unexamined because its analysis would disturb the symmetry of the narrative they are anxious to get accepted.

"No one knows what blasphemy is, or sedition is," wrote Walter Bagehot, "but all know that they are vague words which can be fitted to any meaning that shall please the ruling powers." The principle which underlies this aphorism bears profoundly upon the uses to which propa-

[11] *Holmes-Pollock Letters*, Vol. II, pp. 222–23.

[12] *Ibid.*, p. 205; and see the opinion of Holmes in refusing the writ of certiorari in *The Sacco-Vanzetti Case* (New York: Holt, 1928), Vol. V, p. 5532.

[13] *Pro-Slavery Argument* (Philadelphia: Lippincott, 1853).

[14] Aptheker, *American Negro Slave Revolts*, especially Chaps. 12 and 13.

ganda is put in the United States. There are few persons in America today who do not look back on the habits of Anthony Comstock with a smile. Yet the power to maintain the ban on "indecent" books persists over a wide area. Petronius and Ovid, Voltaire's *Candide* and Rabelais, have all suffered the attentions of censorship in recent years. The Watch and Ward Society of Boston secured a ban on the sale of Judge Lindsey's *Revolt of Modern Youth*—a frank and common sense discussion of companionate marriage—and of Mr. Sinclair Lewis's well-known novel *Elmer Gantry*. In 1928 the Motion Picture Commission of New York ordered more than four thousand cuts in films because they were regarded as "tending to incite to crime," or because they were "indecent" or "inhuman." [15] There is, of course, a censorship, both negative and positive, in the newspaper world and in the radio world. But we must be careful not to argue that this censorship works only one way or that it has a simple and straightforward result. There are suppressions of necessary information, as there are distortions of truth, on the Left as well as on the Right. The *mores* of American society may lead to restrictions on discussion of sex or religion at different levels in different parts of society; Nebraska, North Dakota, and Idaho by statute prohibit smoking in public restaurants; Kentucky, in 1922, prohibited "the appearance of persons clothed only in bathing costumes upon the public highways of this Commonwealth." [16]

Propaganda, in a word, cannot simply be divided into "legitimate" and "illegitimate." It is always set in a frame of reference which needs the closest possible analysis before it is capable of being judged. It is used for very different motives and applied to very different ends. It is propaganda when a body of eminent signatories takes a page of the *New York Times* to urge Americans to give generously for the relief of famine in China; it is propaganda when American journals put the sins of the trade-unions on the front page, or "play up" the findings of the House Committee on Un-American Activities, and put the evidence and findings of the Senate Committee on Civil Liberties obscurely at the back. All advertisement is propaganda, some of it so unashamed that bodies like the Federal Trade Commission have to regulate the claims of many manufacturers for the protection of the public. Almost all the work of pressure groups is propaganda, some of it selfless, some of it a grim mixture of deception and delusion. And there is the special form of propaganda which is based upon an indirect emphasis upon a man or an idea, as when, for example, a statesman is given a national "hook-up" at the peak time of listening, or when a newspaper selects the information it presents upon a predetermined pattern, or when the films are always careful so to tell their stories that the minister of religion appears in a favourable light.

[15] Peter H. Odegard, *The American Public Mind* (New York: Columbia University Press, 1930), p. 273. The whole book is an illuminating and amusing account of the vagaries of public controls of opinion.
[16] *Ibid.*, p. 263, where many other fantastic illustrations are given.

My point is the important one that, while it is undeniable that, in a society like the United States, the categories of living are generally shaped by the major instruments of propaganda to the principles which protect and nourish a business civilization, they are limited in their effectiveness by two considerations. The first, and the more vital, is that they are constantly checked and measured against principles which deny the validity of a business civilization; it is only in "boom" times, or in crisis, that it is difficult to challenge the outcome of "predatory culture" in this field. The second is that these major instruments are themselves departments of Big Business and have thus, somehow, to make a profit. This means a more considerable degree of conformity to public demands than appears on the surface. America is a very variegated civilization, in which, save under grave stress, there are innumerable currents and cross-currents of opinion which it is usually necessary to take into account. This interest, positively, must be pleased; that interest, negatively, must not be offended. There are necessary eulogies which the *mores* of America demand, almost as a ritual, should be made; just as there are necessary taboos which must be respected. Beacon Hill must often have writhed under the pronouncements of the late Cardinal O'Connell; but there was no paper in Boston that would have dared, while he was alive, to have said openly that he was as much a "boss" in his activities in Massachusetts as was Tweed while he controlled the City of New York. In the same manner, Alexander Graham Bell became one of the legendary heroes of American life in the nineteenth century; he became the typical embodiment of the American genius for applying scientific principles discovered by other men to practical purposes. But to the general American public he was the "scientist" *par excellence;* a thousand people knew about him where one knew about Joseph Henry, or Edward W. Morley, or Albert A. Michelson. The one serious discovery Edison made in basic science was put aside by him and its later development was due to the work of Sir Ambrose Fleming. His biographer agrees that it will take something like fifty years before the fact and the myth are separated.[17] In the meantime, every schoolboy will continue to read and think about him as the great scientific genius of his time.

Nor must one forget that all the major instruments of propaganda must subdue themselves, if they wish for success, to the general mental climate in which they have to work. That is admirably illustrated by the course of newspaper opinion in the South from the time of Jackson to the outbreak of the Civil War. Until the time of Jackson the economics of the different sections of the country were complementary to each other rather than antagonistic. It was not until close on the fifties that the fate of the South began to depend upon its ability to maintain slavery by keeping its hold on the federal government lest the growth of industrial capitalism in the North and West—an economic system built upon free labour—hinder its chance of expansion. Economically its "peculiar institution"

---

[17] *Dictionary of American Biography,* Vol. XXI, p. 280.

was already an obsolete interest when the South began to fight for it. The South sought secession because, if it lost control of Washington, it would have to alter the whole foundation of its economic life. So the whole tone of the Southern press began to change, and, both in relation to slavery and to secession, it became almost as blind as was the aristocracy in France before 1789, or in Russia before 1918, to the fact that its institutions were in decay. And that blindness led to a militancy of temper, a reckless, even arrogant, self-confidence, which made it ever more fully the victim of its own propaganda. It had no real sense of the resources massed against it, whether in numbers, in productive capacity, in accumulated capital, in ease of transportation, both internal and external, and, not least, in business capacity. Yet anyone who reads the newspaper editorials Professor Dumond has so usefully collected.[18] can see the fantastic way in which the journalists who wrote them became the victims of the premisses the South had persuaded itself were right and just; even as late as 1862, when the crumbling economic structure of the South began to reveal inevitable defeat, *DeBow's Review* could write that "the North is bankrupt. Her people must migrate or starve." Its well-known editor could not realize that chattel slavery was a survival of a dead epoch the attempt to preserve which has made the South a colony of the North right down to the present time.

The premisses of obsolete interests have living reality long after the interests themselves have perished. Perhaps it may even be said without exaggeration that they do more mischief in the aftermath, when the reality to which they corresponded has disappeared, than they were able to do in their lifetime. Certainly the major instruments of propaganda, as they operate in the South today, are constantly being affected by their linkage to premisses devoid of meaning. Just as William Gregg sought before the war to persuade the rulers of the South to diversify its economy, both to safeguard their own interests and to prevent the poor whites from discovering the extent of their exploitation, so, decade by decade, the poverty of the South has been perpetuated by building its ideology upon principles outmoded by the economic evolution of the United States. What H. R. Helper said nearly a century ago of the poor whites still remains largely true. "They have never yet had any part or lot," he wrote, "in framing the laws under which they live. There is no legislation except for the benefit of slavery and slaveholders. . . . To all intents and purposes, they are disfranchised and outlawed, and the only privilege extended to them is a shallow and circumscribed participation in the political movements that usher slaveholders into office." [19] Slavery, of course, has disappeared, and large-scale capitalism has taken its place. But the poor whites are much in the same position as before 1861; and

---

[18] Dwight L. Dumond (ed.), *Southern Editorials on Secession* (New York: American Historical Association, 1931). This is an invaluable anthology which ought to be compared with the companion volume, *Northern Editorials on Secession* (New York: Appleton-Century, 1942) edited by Howard C. Perkins.

[19] Helper, *The Impending Crisis*. An annotated reprint of this is badly needed.

careers like those of Tom Watson, Ben Tillman, and Huey Long illustrate the price that is paid when an ideology irrelevant to conditions is
supported by a propaganda which is ceaselessly compelled to ignore the
realities with which it has to deal.

There is nothing surprising in this persistence of worn-out ideals, but
it makes all attempts to explain in a simple way the forms which propaganda assumes a major error. The media of communication in the United
States are as complicated as the United States itself. There enter into the
stereotype each citizen forms for himself emotions and ideas and sentiments fashioned by geography, by family tradition, by occupation, by
religion, by the thousand strands of personal experience too subtle to be
conveyed in words. I do not doubt that the basic pattern of this stereotype is moulded by the opinions necessary to justify the general supremacy of the business man in American life. But just as I believe that he
is continually finding it more difficult to maintain that basic pattern in
the atmosphere of political democracy, so I suspect that the major instruments of propaganda have more of timidity than of certitude in their
outlook because they constantly fear to lose their hold upon the public
from whom their profit is derived. I should, indeed, argue that this is made
evident by the three major characteristics of the American press, above all
in the metropolitan areas. It is often arrogant, like the *Daily News* of
New York, the *Tribune* in Chicago, and the now defunct *Transcript* in
Boston. But, if it is arrogant, it is always seeking to placate its readers
by the offer of compensating attractions. The *Daily News* depends upon
the lure of sensation-mongering in crime, not least in the exploitation of
sex crime. The *Tribune* maintains a high standard of sports news. The
Transcript sought to atone for having the outlook of the Blaine era in the
days of Woodrow Wilson by appealing to the considerable public in
the Boston area interested in books and genealogy and the arts, and,
not least, in the past glory of New England achievement. The *New York
Times* and *New York Herald Tribune* tread a line in which, alongside a
cautious editorial view, there is offered to the reader the most remarkable body of foreign news in the world today, a commentary on current
issues by a specialist with a virtually free hand to say what he likes, as
well as a book-section and a magazine-section on Sundays. The *Chicago
Sun* offsets the witch-hunting isolationism of its rival, the *Tribune,* not
only by the careful examination of the relation of American interests to
each phase of the international situation, but also by setting alongside its
editorial policy dispatches from Europe, which, in the hands of Mr. Frederick Kuh, its chief correspondent, are probably the most authoritative
interpretation of the events they describe and dissect to be found in any
American newspaper. Anyone who examines with care the general tendencies of the American press is bound to observe that, when all allowance is made for its general devotion to "business ideals," it is usually
seeking, within its own pages, to provide ways and means of retaining

those readers whom, otherwise, it might be likely to lose by its general outlook.

I do not for one moment contend that the resultant stereotype of what propaganda imposes ever diverges very far from the business man's requirements; that would, after all, be as remarkable as if, under Hitler or Mussolini, the inadequacy of fascist principles had been consistently emphasized. The "American way of life" is, overwhelmingly, set in the perspective of the business man's view of what it should be. But whether it is the press, or the radio, or the cinema, each of these instruments is always struggling to play for safety. Each is aware that criticism has to be met, and that, in the long run, it suffers if it cannot meet the criticism that is made. Each, also, is aware how large a proportion of its public has alternative allegiances it can call into play at will. The newspaper may truckle to its advertisers; but these, in their turn, can get their profit only if the newspaper retains its readers. Commercial radio may live by its sponsored programmes; but the programme which "listener research" proves to be a failure makes the audience, and not the sponsor, the ultimate judge of its adequacy. The magnates of Hollywood may seek to impose their curious combination of opulence and ideas which assume the rarity of the adult mind; they find that a film into which there have gone intellectual integrity and imaginative vigor has a power of appeal and survival far beyond their anticipation; *The Cabinet of Doctor Caligari* and *Potemkin* live on while a thousand more expensive rivals are forgotten in three months' time; and the great film leaves a permanent impact, where the film which reflects the limit of what the magnates of Hollywood think "the public" will understand is, for its audience, as passing an experience as breakfast or the normal crowded journey in the New York subway to the workers who live in Brooklyn or the Bronx.

We must recognize, this is to say, that there is a self-corrective mechanism in each instrument of propaganda as it operates in the American atmosphere. The correction is rarely complete; it is still more rarely made with whole-heartedness; its action is always delayed, and the delay is usually organized. What is important is the existence of this corrective mechanism. I believe that its roots in the American tradition are profound, and that they are the supreme safeguard of its democracy. They are the outcome of that spirit of equality in American life which, often attacked and sometimes repressed, has, so far, always managed to survive the antagonism it has encountered. It is, no doubt, a complex spirit into the making of which many things have gone—the absence of a real aristocracy, the decentralization of discussion, which means that there is no simple centre from which opinion can be shaped, the individualistic habits begotten by the frontier, the conviction that America has a peculiar quality which levels the claim of one man to the obedience of another, even the lawlessness which has been made indigenous in American life as men hacked their path to the ways of civilization through what must have seemed to the early pioneers an endless desert. But, above all, I think, equality has been born from the fact that the vestigial remains of feudalism had little influence after 1776, and that there was, accordingly, no fixity of status. Equality has been the safeguard of a freedom which, though incomplete, has always prevented the final dictation of an atmosphere beyond which men cannot move. Because that dictated atmosphere is never completely pervasive, the major instruments of propaganda have, so far, never been completely effective.

2

BY 1815 there was already a greater circulation of newspapers in the United States than in Great Britain, though it was not until the establishment in 1833 of the New York *Sun* as a penny newspaper that the press began really to attract the attention of the masses. Previous to that time the newspaper was written to appeal mostly to the professional man and the merchant, and though, no doubt, it was read by all classes in the tavern, regular subscriptions outside the middle class were pretty rare. Not, indeed, that the significance of the newspaper was underestimated. Not only the famous trial of John Peter Zenger (1735), but, from the earliest days of the republic, the care with which the able journalist was cultivated by the political parties on both sides makes it clear that the importance of the newspaper was well understood. For it is beyond doubt that the newspapers played an important part in stimulating, during the War of Independence, a wide realization of the common purposes for which Washington's armies were fighting; and they were one of the major sources by which the discussion of the Constitution was made widely accessible. That is shown not only by the fact that the authors of *The Federalist* published their articles in the *Daily Advertiser* and in the *Independent Journal* some time before they were issued as a book, but also by the fact that, within six weeks of Washington's assuming the presidency, Hamilton had chosen John Fenno to edit the *Gazette of the United States* as a paper intended to support the government.

The early newspapers can hardly be called exhilarating, though some able men, like Fenno, Freneau, Noah Webster, Tom Paine and William Duane, made the practice of journalism a career. By 1800 there were one hundred and fifty papers, and their staple commodity was politics. Their news was scant and irregular. The central feature became the signed editorial, which was backed by verse and skits, few of which recognized any limits to general invective or to personal abuse. It was this scurrility, perhaps emphasized by the fact that some of the bitterest critics of the Federalist party were foreign-born, which led to the passage of the Alien and Sedition Acts of 1798. It is possible that the deep unpopularity of these Acts had a large part in establishing the tradition of comment that hardly knows the idea of personal libel, which remains a widespread feature of the American press down to the present time.

What is astonishing is the speed with which newspapers multiplied, and the self-confidence of their owners in making their growth almost parallel the expansion of the westward movement. There were probably twice as many newspapers in 1810 as in 1800, and more than twice as many in 1840 as in 1810. By the middle thirties of the nineteenth century they had appeared in Ohio and Missouri, in Michigan and Wisconsin and Texas. Mostly they appeared only once a week, and the printing was usually as vile as the writing was poor. But we must not underrate their influence in two vital fields: they gave Washington news of local opinion; and they gave local opinion a sense of contact with Washington, not least when they printed the speeches of their own congressman or senator, or some letter from these. Dailies were more rare, though Philadelphia had one in 1784 and New York in 1785; a quarter of a century later there were twenty-seven in the whole country, and as early as 1835 Detroit, then virtually a western outpost, had its daily *Free Press*. If the eastern daily press was, in the main, a series of administration organs, conducted by men who, like the most effective of all editors before the Civil War, Francis P. Blair, combined journalism with a direct hand in political action, that only gave their comment all the more importance.

By the end of the Jackson epoch, and with the growing use of the steam press, the American newspaper began to assume something more relevant to its present form. First of all, the content began to be more varied; politics no longer remained the spinal column, with oddments of news looking rather like vestigial vertebrae. The signed article began to give way to the anonymous editorial. Editors like Thomas Ritchie of the *Richmond Enquirer* began to show that pungency did not need to be scurrilous in order to be effective. Partisan spirit, no doubt, remained intense and continued to be fed with personalia in the vilest taste. But the very fact that editors were coming to regard dependence on politicians as less important than interesting the public made for improvement. Not a little of this was due to the experiments—they were not innovations— of James Gordon Bennett when he founded the *New York Herald*. He realized that the cheap paper must have mass circulation, and that this, in its turn, demanded lightness of tone, the power to amuse, an interest in the daily lives of ordinary people. He subordinated the political devotion of the older papers to the concept of news as a commodity the value of which was dependent upon its ability to satisfy demand. He was one of the pioneers in the idea that "news" must be distributed as speedily as possible after the occurrence of the events it described. With some of his competitors, he helped to create, in 1848, the Associated Press of New York, with the aim of co-operative gathering of news. European information, sometimes from "our special correspondent abroad," became a popular feature. The literary columns began to give Americans a deep interest in a great period of European writing.

Two other features of importance before the Civil War made a great difference. The first was the impact of the telegraph on the daily press;

it is not too much to say that, after the Mexican War of 1846, the speed of information it made possible removed any danger that the newspapers would have to compete with the weekly; thenceforward national papers began to occupy quite different fields of activity, and to free the local press, as in Chicago, or St. Louis, or New Orleans, of any dependence on Washington or New York. The second was the rise of the foreign-language press, very notably stimulated by the European immigration, especially from Germany, after 1848. Not a little of the improvement in taste and standard of the American newspaper of the fifties can be traced to the high principles and eager tolerance of that band of German refugees who left their own country for the United States in search of freedom. And since the Jacksonian epoch was one of intense discussion, in great part due to industrial unrest, men turned to the journals from about 1840 onwards in the eager search not merely for news, but also for guidance in an epoch where every sort of novel experiment was being advocated and attempted.

Before the Civil War four men stood out in the newspaper field. Bennett had immense power from his sheer genius in getting news quickly and getting unexpected news. Horace Greeley in the *New York Tribune,* Henry J. Raymond in the *New York Times,* and, perhaps foremost of all, Samuel Bowles, Sr., in the *Springfield Republican,* provided a full supply of news—political, economic, international, and literary. Even more, they made their editorial columns an influence unsurpassed, down to the present time, in their impact on public opinion. They were open-minded, they wrote with dignity and restraint, they had what may fairly be called a philosophy, and they were known to be independent of party control even when they supported rather constantly particular measures or particular politicians. James Ford Rhodes has pointed out that Greeley made the *Tribune* the "political bible" of the Adirondack wilderness. Raymond made the *New York Times* superior to any previous newspaper in the honesty of its reporting and the dignified courtesy of his comment. Compared to Greeley, he was no doubt cautious to the point of timidity, and he had little of the former's emotional vigour. But, like Greeley, and in a somewhat different way Bennett, he gave his readers from the outset a quality in the reporting of foreign news which has not been surpassed in almost a century of later experience. And one has only to read the remarkable articles which Engels and, now and again, Marx wrote for Greeley on the European situation to realize the remarkable standard of knowledge and insight that were placed at the disposal of American readers. It is not to be wondered at that Mazzini and Kossuth, Palmerston and Garibaldi, were as living to the Americans of the mid-nineteenth century as were most of their successors of the mid-twentieth century to a later American public with far greater means of communication available to them.

Two features are outstanding in this journalism. The first is the incredibly small capital on which it was founded; Bennett started the *Herald* with no capital at all; Greeley had one thousand dollars when he started the *Tribune;* and Raymond raised one hundred thousand dollars from his friends to found the *Times.* All of them were independent of advertisers; each won through to success by the sheer quality of what he offered his audience; and if all three were ardently cultivated by politicians and business interests, all were throughout in a position to take their own line on each issue with which they dealt. Each, moreover, made his audience feel that what it read, both in the news columns and on the editorial page, was significant and mature. It is perhaps true that Raymond's anxiety for a political career made him too anxious to please the powerful business leaders of New York. His famous aphorism that "there are few things in this world which it is worth while to get angry about, and they are just the things anger will not improve," indicates his desire not only to distinguish his paper from that of Greeley, but, even more, to commend it to the cautious and well-to-do class which always fears the influence of theory, of innovation, and of radicalism. Yet, with all their defects, these men, with Bowles, made journalism in America a profession which, at its best, compared favourably with the standards of any other occupation of their time. They thought in terms of the public want and the public interest. It did not occur to them to subordinate their effort to money-making on the one hand, or to organized misrepresentation of fact on the other.

The Civil War created a revolution in the American newspaper, as it did in so many other aspects of the national life. It enormously increased circulation. It made millions of people news-conscious in an entirely different way; and it thus brought the skilled reporter and the special correspondent into exceptional prominence. If some of the editors after the Civil War continued the remarkable tradition Greeley and Raymond had established—Henry Watterson, in the *Louisville Courier-Journal,* carried it into the twentieth century from the sixties, and William Allen White, in the *Emporia Gazette,* brought it right down to the virtual end of the Second World War—it is generally true to emphasize the fact that editorial significance declined almost everywhere. The increase of business enterprise in the Gilded Age brought an immense development in advertising. By the last decade of the nineteenth century it was upon advertising that the major newspapers depended for their revenue. To get this advertising, they had, perforce, to adopt the means which would increase their circulations; and this, in turn, meant, first, a much more extensive service of news, and, second, the ability to attract an ever greater public by exciting its appetite for news, which, in its turn, meant sensationalism. By 1900 most newspapers were so largely dependent upon advertisement that the editor had become less important than the business manager, and the latter's chief function was to sell the paper at almost any cost in order to get the profit from advertisements. And, since 1900, when the Associated Press was established in its present form, that body, with perhaps two of its chief competitors, has been the source of most of the news printed by most of the papers; the special Washington correspondent became important only under Theodore Roosevelt's presidency, and the foreign correspondents did not win their standing as an exceptional group among journalists until the First World War.

With advertisement as the main source of revenue, sensationalism in news became the chief medium of circulation. If its invention was mainly due to the younger James Gordon Bennett, its development was given entirely new vistas, first by Pulitzer in the *St. Louis Post-Dispatch,* which he bought in 1878, and then in the *New York World,* which he bought as a failure from Jay Gould in 1883 and turned into one of the most profitable newspapers in the United States. But of Pulitzer several things must be said: he made the editorial pages of papers a remarkable platform for the defence and advocacy of progressive ideas; he attacked privilege and monopoly; he demanded Civil Service reforms; and he was instant in the exposure of corruption, though it is true that he specialized in a form of reporting which exploited evil and suffering as sensationally as possible to grip the emotions of his readers. When his methods were followed, in the eighties, by William Randolph Hearst in the *San Francisco Examiner,* purposive sensationalism, in the political sense, was followed by the discovery that there was a vast and untouched audience interested in sensationalism with no purpose but its own emotional thrills. As Hearst extended his journalistic empire, he extended the range of his methods. He was willing, no doubt, to attack political corruption where it was unpopular and had reached the proportions of scandal; but his real interest lay in the profit that he made, and he never failed to exploit his power, as over the *Maine,* and over intervention in Mexico, in the interest of profit.

His supreme discovery was the vast audience which was too fatigued or too busy to think, but ready to be amused or thrilled. Hence the comics, the cartoons, the photographs, the devotion to crime, the emphasis on gossip, the passion for scandal. He bathed everything possible in an ocean of sentimentality. To get the more recondite gossip, he paid no regard whatever to the normal respect for privacy. To secure sensation, he did not hesitate to distort facts, or even to invent them. Convinced that few people wanted more than the superficial, he often omitted the discussion of serious matters, congressional proceedings, for example, or so summarized them that their significance could rarely be seen. He seldom printed an important speech, or, if he did, he managed to make it insignificant if he was hostile to it, and trivial and incoherent even if he approved it. If he kept the editorial page, he gave the major article the same character of combined sensationalism and triviality as the rest of the paper, and filled up the rest of the space with everything from sketches of the home life of the eminent or the notorious to articles about marriage and doctors and crime, which might serve to assist the business manager in his quest of circulation.

There can be no doubt, first, that the method of presentation was a great success; and, second, that it has shown the existence of a kind of

Gresham's Law in the newspaper field. The editorial page, in all save the outstanding journals, was reduced to a mere annex of the news and special features. And since the news-gathering agencies, like the Associated Press, began to pour in their material on an overwhelming scale, the selection of the news became vitally related to the newspaper as a great business concern anxious to earn profit. That meant, in a general way, two important things : first, that the principle upon which the selection was made sought, perhaps above all, to satisfy the outlook of the large-scale advertisers, since they were the principal source of revenue ; and, second, such a presentation of the news that the clientele upon whom the advertisers mostly depended for the sale of their goods would not be offended by what they read. The outcome was twofold. Externally, the newspaper was mainly concerned to satisfy the higher income section of its readers ; that meant, at the best, an unmistakable scepticism about labour movements, socialist principles, revolutionary change, anything, in short, that disturbed the *status quo*. Internally, it meant that most journalists with a passion for social justice were either out of place on a newspaper, or, like Fremont Older, suppressed their crusading zeal and became the cynical observers of a scene they ceased to believe it was their purpose to criticize, much less to modify. I suspect that in the first twenty years of the present century more young enthusiasts for social improvement lost their pristine ardour in the early years of their careers as journalists than in any other profession in the United States.

The real effect of the development given by William Randolph Hearst to the new emphasis of Joseph Pulitzer was to suppress all values completely, or to make the values approved those which added to, or at least did not detract from, the supreme purpose of increasing circulation, in order to build up advertising revenue, in order to maximize profit. That is why there has grown up around the daily press the immense mass of weekly and monthly journals of opinion, like the *Nation* and the *New Republic,* the *Survey Graphic* and the *New Masses, Harper's Magazine* and the *Atlantic Monthly*. That is also why journals associated with an outstanding personality, the *Commoner* of William Jennings Bryan, *La Follette's Weekly Magazine,* the *Outlook* in the days when Theodore Roosevelt made it the special vehicle of his opinions, have had such exceptional importance. That is why, further, the journals of special interests—religious, labour, educational, even the learned periodicals— have an exceptional influence upon those elements among the American people who are themselves significant in helping to form the climate of general opinion.

I cannot attempt here to write even an approach to a general history of the American press, but there are certain central factors in that history which are outstanding. In the middle nineteenth century, for example, the daily newspaper seemed not unlikely to become the supreme platform of public opinion. It seemed likely to combine the service of fact with the function of commentator in a degree that would leave it without rival in the field of journalism. Its supremacy became increasingly dubious in the feverish years of expansion up to the early years of the twentieth century. The standards were then made far more by the weeklies, like *Harper's* when, in the evil days of the Tweed ring, it published the remarkable cartoons of Nast, and later by the monthlies, like *McClure's Magazine,* in the days when such remarkable reporters as Lincoln Steffens, David Graham Phillips, and Upton Sinclair were relentlessly dissecting that political corruption which operated under the patronage of business, and especially Big Business, enterprise. For perhaps fifteen years before the end of the First World War the supremacy over opinion was in doubt. After 1919 the daily newspaper made an immense effort to restore its authority. It sought to lead in the attack upon gangsterism; it began to give its readers personal advice upon every subject imaginable from legal difficulties through the mysterious code of etiquette to the problems of marital relations. It began to promote good causes. The *New York Times* asked for special aid for exceptionally deserving cases at Christmas time; the *Chicago Daily News* ran series of free lectures; the *New York Herald Tribune* promoted an annual symposium by eminent persons upon the leading themes of the day. One newspaper had a holiday camp for poor children, another campaigned for free milk; another deliberately refused to accept advertisements of the truth of which it was uncertain. An outstanding feature was the development of the signed column in which a writer not directly connected with the paper, sometimes, like Mr. Lippmann, of real distinction, at other times, like Mr. Westbrook Pegler or Mr. George Sokolsky, making up in vehemence what he lacked in distinction, was given the opportunity—usually syndicated throughout the United States—to make his comment on affairs three or four times a week. The effort of the newspaper was to hold its public at all costs. Its outstanding desire was to convince its readers of its singular devotion to the public good, at the same time as it consolidated and extended its hold upon the expanding stream of advertising revenue.

Yet it is not, I venture to believe, an exaggeration to say that the daily press has failed in this purpose. In part this has been shown strikingly over long years in the revision history has made of its judgments upon collective bargaining and strikes. In part it emerged in the conflict, especially in 1937, between the press and the American Newspaper Guild—a constituent union of the Congress of Industrial Organizations—when the opposition of the newspaper proprietors to the unionization of journalists revealed their overwhelming subordination, as a body of owners, to the interests of Big Business. It came out again in the examination of the public utilities by Congress in 1934, where massive evidence was made available to prove the wholesale corruption of the daily press by direct bribery. There was not only the suppression of "uncomfortable" news, but it was difficult to resist the conclusion that articles were "planted" upon many newspapers which were in fact advertisements for the utilities and were printed by the newspapers as independent investigations. There is far too much reason to believe that the policies of outstanding newspapers were influenced by their proprietors' ownerships of shares in corporations whose activities, in a strike, for example, brought them into the news. On the record, it is certainly difficult not to believe that Mr. Chandler, the owner of the *Los Angeles Times,* used the pages of his journal to protect his vast empire in agriculture and real estate, in oil and in banking, from invasion by the forces of labour. Again, it is still more difficult not to believe that William Randolph Hearst's enthusiasm for the "rights" of the Roman Catholic Church in Mexico was related to his horror lest his immense holdings there in land and in minerals should be taken over by the State in the future interest of the Mexican people.

The dependence of the newspaper press upon the advertiser was alarmingly revealed in its attitude to the Tugwell bill, which sought to control the vicious patent medicine business in the public interest. The element of fraud in its claims was overwhelming, and most of its advertising gave prominence to its claims. Yet because many scores of millions of dollars were a source of newspaper revenue, the Convention of the American Newspaper Publishers Association opposed the bill with indignant fervour, and not only helped to defeat it, but also compelled the President to move Mr. Tugwell to another office. To this must be added, once more, the fact that when the Federal Trade Commission issues its "cease and desist" orders to patent medicine proprietors, even though their content is privileged, the press either does not publish the orders or relegates them to a small and obscure place in its pages. Hardly less striking has been the dishonesty of the newspapers, above all the Hearst press and the *Chicago Tribune,* in placing the responsibility for violence in an industrial dispute upon the shoulders of the union. Anyone who compares, for example, the *Tribune's* account of the Memorial Day massacre of 1937 at the Republic Steel Corporation's plant in Chicago, not only with that laboriously pieced together by the La Follette Committee on Civil Liberties after the exhaustive examination of witnesses, but also with Paramount Pictures' film of the tragic events of that day, is bound to conclude that the *Tribune's* story was a deliberate falsification. The journalists whose evidence against the police was most decisive were the men on the basis of whose reports the newspaper had turned a wanton and outrageous massacre of strikers by the police into an heroic attempt on the part of the latter to preserve the peace even at the risk of their lives.

What is true of Colonel McCormick's *Tribune* and of the Hearst papers is also true of hundreds of other daily papers throughout the United States. No doubt the manner of falsehood and misrepresentation is different; even, to some extent, the matter round which turn the sins of omission and commission differs also. No Northern paper would justify, still less praise, the lynching of a Negro in the South. Few Southern papers would show the deference to the politics of the Vatican that is usual in the press of New York and Boston. Misrepresentation may be direct and brutal here, as there it may be indirect and even decorous in tone. It may be a rule never to attack a man, as Mr. Mellon was never attacked in a Pittsburgh newspaper, or to be silent about the frequency with which the American Legion acts, through its branches, as a strikebreaker,[20] and, from its central headquarters, as a constant menace to civil liberties.[21] There are newspapers which specialize in attacking all trade-unionists as "Reds"; there are others which confine that now accepted term of opprobrium to men and women on strike. There are newspapers which invariably misrepresent the character and achievements of the Soviet Union; others have added Great Britain and Republican Spain to their list of "hates." Few American daily journals attacked the regime of Mussolini until he began his war on Abyssinia. So far as I can find, none of the great New York papers attacked General MacArthur for issuing, when Chief of Staff, a pamphlet which it is difficult not to describe as an incitement to violence to soldiers called in to restore order in periods of civil disturbance.[22] Few of the greater journals have ever seriously and consistently defended academic freedom; they are too cautious to commit themselves permanently. Or if one compares the nation-wide publicity given to Governor Coolidge's supposed handling of the Boston police strike in 1919 with the detailed exposure of his claims by the then mayor, Mr. Andrew J. Peters,[23] which received, outside of Boston, hardly any notice at all, it becomes obvious that the weighting of the scales is a conscious effort.

I do not suggest for one moment that all American newspapers act in this way all the time. Some of the most important have long and honourable records of fighting for great causes; some of the smaller papers have shown notable courage and forthrightness. There are papers in the South, for example, that have risked their existence by fighting prejudice against the Negro, and especially by fighting against lynching. But these are exceptional cases. In general, the big papers are so much a branch of Big Business that, in the main, they are bound to follow in its wake; its standards are bound to be their standards, and its prosperity is the condition of their power to make profit. The smaller journals, with but few exceptions, could hardly survive as paying propositions if it were not for advertisements on the one hand, and for the free publicity provided by the propaganda associations of different industries. Few of them could stand up to the local Chamber of Commerce, or to the local branch of the American Legion, or, in rural areas, to the organized farmers. There is an effective sense, indeed, in which most American newspapers are nothing so much as the collective organ of the great pressure groups which

[20] Marcus Duffield, *King Legion* (New York: Smith, 1931).
[21] Walter Wilson, *The American Legion and Civil Liberty* (New York: American Civil Liberties Union, 1936).
[22] See the pamphlet published under his signature as Chief of Staff and dated August 1, 1935, which was sold by the Government Printing Office. It seems to have been withdrawn after criticism begun by Mr. George Seldes early in 1936.
[23] Report of the Mayor on the Police Strike (Boston, 1920).

exercise their power by giving or withholding their advertisements. They do not dare to go beyond the general lines of action upon which their ability to make profit depends.

This is not to say that American newspapers do not do certain things superlatively well. Their chief American correspondents abroad, both in Europe and in Asia, are unsurpassed, alike in their energy and in their capacity to penetrate to the heart of a situation. There are at least four American newspapers which give more foreign news of a higher standard than any in Europe; and the quality of this reporting is shown by the very considerable number of journalists who have won international reputations. It may be that an occasional journalist in Europe, like J. D. Bourchier, the Balkan correspondent of the London *Times,* or H. N. Brailsford of the *New Statesman,* has surpassed most of his American colleagues in knowledge of a particular area or in philosophic insight into the principles of international relations. But I think the American correspondents, by and large, are providing today, as they have done since 1919, about the best foreign news of any national press in the world. And to this must be added two things: no other press can compete with papers like the *New York Times* in the completeness with which they print essential documents in full; in this respect they resemble the British press in the days of Bright and Gladstone rather than our own. The other remarkable feature is their willingness to publish without pretence at concealment the kind of inner gossip which, in London, a minister may retail in confidence to a specially favoured journalist on the understanding that he uses it not as direct news but only as general background. A careful reader of the major American papers can get a clearer view of what is happening in Washington than an English reader can learn about Westminster and Whitehall from even the greatest of English newspapers. There is a greater frankness, a certain pleasure in well-planned indiscretion, which is notably different from the sleek and well-groomed hints by which the British press indicates the possession of knowledge without revealing its content. Most of Fleet Street was well aware for many months of the incidents which led to the abdication of Edward VIII; but, without compulsion, it maintained a discreet silence about the whole problem until Lord Baldwin, then the prime minister, was ready to take the necessary parliamentary action. That silence would, I think, have been impossible to preserve in the United States. It would have been too great a story to conceal; each news editor would have been afraid of being anticipated by some rival. It would have been accompanied by a mass of detail and a wealth of speculation that would have given the whole affair the air of a Hollywood film. Compared to the swift excitement of an American narrative, the British reports of the abdication read almost like a sermon.

One thing more must be said. No doubt there are many journalists in the United States whose subordination to the views of their papers are the honest result of thoughtful conviction as well as the necessary accept-

ance of conditions which make their livelihood possible; few men have
been more instinctively conservative, for example, than Henry J. Raymond, the founder of the *New York Times*. Many more are made middle-
of-the-road men by the impact of daily experience; they see too much of
the inner workings of political parties and the great business corporations,
of the professions and of union "racketeering," to have much positive
faith left in any large general principles. They become too aware of the
poison of power to be anxious that anyone should win an unlimited victory. But there are also two other types of journalists whose characters
have been thrown into a vivid perspective by the dramatic evolution of
the last fifteen years. Nothing defines them so clearly as the activities
of the American Newspaper Guild under the vivid leadership of the late
Heywood Broun. Many of its members displayed, once they had developed some sort of collective protection, not only a zeal for great causes,
but a determination to get at the facts which it is difficult to praise too
highly. In a slightly earlier period I think this was true of Frank Cobb
of the *New York World;* in our own day it was true of men like Heywood
Broun. He spoke his mind with full freedom, always aware of the risks
he took; and few men did so much to compel the acceptance of the Wagner
Act, in its full implications, by the newspaper industry. On the other
hand, the changes of the inter-war years have also thrown up a type of
journalistic *condottiere,* sometimes attached to a single paper, more often
writing a syndicated column which may sell to several hundred daily papers and be read by an audience of from fifteen to thirty million people,
whose methods resemble those of the racketeer at the height of his glory
when the Volstead Act was still on the statute book. He has his paid
sources of information in government departments. He uses the public
interest in gossip about the rich or the eminent to invade with pitiless
determination the most intimate aspects of private relations. He can put
an untruth deliberately invented into the form of an innocent-looking
question for which he evades all responsibility. He may protect himself
from the law by having his private counsel to advise him on all his "copy";
and he may fortify that protection by heavy insurance against the danger
of being involved in court proceedings. He may even reach the eminence
when people in the public eye, the politician, the millionaire, the film star,
have to placate him in order to secure or to avoid mention in his column.
And since he addresses millions of readers every week, the advertising
value of his name becomes of considerable importance to the makers of
any commodity who wish for the aid of personal authority behind their
effort to increase its sale.

But this is not all. There are some half a score of nationally known
columnists in the United States of whom, perhaps, the late Arthur Brisbane was the most notorious, who act as what it is difficult not to call
the permanent gangsters of Big Business. Their task is the continuous
and violent attack upon any men or any proposals which might lead to
any change in the *status quo*. They have to maintain a permanent barrage

against social reform. They have to create an environment in which trade-unions, government ownership or regulation, Russia, Republican Spain, the Labour government in Britain, the Chinese Communists, and so forth, are all represented as incompatible with the well-being of ordinary people, as a menace to decency, and as a threat to that impalpable but vital good, the American way of life. Their methods are extraordinarily simple. They repeat incessantly, in different contexts, any evil or mistake made by the object of their attack without ever mentioning any good it may have achieved. They compare the prospects it offers at their worst with the best achieved in a similar realm in the United States and thus warn their readers against the threat to their comfort and security. They eulogize the freedom of the United States with its unimpaired tradition of log cabin to White House, or the poor boy who delivers newspapers and ends up as the president of the great corporation. Their America is a place where all would be well if it were not for bureaucratic interference and the propaganda of foreign ideas by aliens, or the descendants of aliens, who do not understand American principles or American ideals. There is, indeed, an important sense in which the major undertone of the reactionary columnist has an atavistic resemblance to the angry prejudices of the Know-Nothing movement of a hundred years ago.

The major weapon of this journalistic group is their insistent resort to personal attacks upon men and women as individuals, and upon groups, who are asking for change. They create a private stereotype of Marx and Lenin, or of strike leaders, and try to link their supposed "crimes" with the contemporary activities of Generalissimo Stalin or Mrs. Eleanor Roosevelt, of Mr. Justice Frankfurter or the American Civil Liberties Union, of Sidney Hillman, the late president of the Amalgamated Clothing Workers of America, or, indeed, of any group which supports the right of labour to organize. Some they attack because of Jewish associations—anti-Semitism is always an essential card in the reactionaries' hand. Others, they hint, are in the pay of Moscow, or part of its conspiratorial network, or, at the least, directly influenced by someone affiliated with the "Reds." The late President Roosevelt was, at critical moments in his administrations, either "communist" or "fascist," as seemed most likely to do him most injury. He was under the control of "wild-eyed" and theoretical professors who knew nothing of practical life. Or he was in the hands of the Jews, since Mr. Henry Morgenthau, Jr., was his Secretary of the Treasury, Judge Samuel I. Rosenman and Mr. Benjamin Cohen among the closest of his advisers; and the withdrawal of the American ambassador from Berlin after the anti-Semitic excesses of November 1938, was used as the proof of the association. The Russian Revolution was, and remains, for them a vast Jewish conspiracy, one of the long-term purposes of which is to disintegrate and destroy the great American tradition of individual enterprise and freedom. As a general rule, they are ardently individualist; and they were enthusiastically in favour of Mussolini as the man who brought "law and order" to a distracted Italy. If they do not defend, at least they usually excuse, all lawless attacks, whether by the police or some vigilante mob, against Negroes, or strikers, or investigators of some local situation who are either themselves known for their Left opinions or who represent some journal whose views are admittedly liberal.

The pattern of this journalism has been permanently fixed in this age by the classic chapter on propaganda in Hitler's *Mein Kampf;* [24] in the campaign of 1932, indeed, when the Nazis lost, Goebbels announced that he would use "American methods on an American scale." "Propaganda," wrote Hitler, "must always address itself to the broad masses of the people. . . . Its purpose must be exactly that of the advertisement poster, to attract the attention of the masses." [25] Anyone who follows with attention the work of Arthur Brisbane and his like will have no difficulty in seeing that they wrote on the same principle. "All propaganda must be presented in a popular form," wrote Hitler, "and fix its intellectual level so as not to be above the heads of the least intellectual of those to whom it is directed. Thus its purely intellectual level will have to be that of the lowest common denominator of the public it is desired to reach. When there is a question of bringing a whole nation within the reach of its influence . . . too much attention cannot be paid to the necessity of avoiding a high level." [26] That this attention has been given by these journalists is obvious from the crude associations they seek to establish in their readers' minds. The aim of the journalist of this type is, like Hitler's, not "to dispense individual instructions to those who have already an educated opinion on grounds of objective study . . . ; it must appeal to the feelings of the public rather than to their reasoning powers." Anyone can verify from a dozen articles of this group how faithfully they follow this formula. They do not argue: they affirm. They are never moderate: they lash themselves into a fury of indignation at those whom they attack, so that to their uncertain readers a mild and tolerant liberal like Mrs. Eleanor Roosevelt may become a "bolshevik," a negrophile, a "pacifist," a friend of the Jews, impractical, a person who abuses her husband's position, a sower of discord, even anti-American because she opposes child labour and supports social reform—whichever may be the special stereotype which suits the journalist's purpose in the particular thousand-word article he is writing. And, above all, the gangster-journalist believes, like Hitler, that "slogans should be persistently repeated until the very last individual has come to grasp the idea that has been put forward."

This last principle is, perhaps, the one most in favour with the journalists of reaction. It could, I think, quite fairly be said of several of the most eminent practitioners among this group that all their attacks are

---

[24] Adolf Hitler, *Mein Kampf* (New York: Reynal & Hitchcock, 1939), pp. 715 f.; *cf.* Edmond Taylor, *Strategy of Terror* (Boston: Houghton Mifflin, 1940).
[25] Hitler, *op. cit.*
[26] *Ibid.*

really one article upon a single theme. They may vary the illustration; the villain (it is usually a villain) or the hero may be changed from time to time. But the *leitmotif* never varies. It is through individual energy and free enterprise that Americans became a great people. Anyone who does not accept this is a "Red," or "anti-American," or an "agent of Moscow." It is time to deal with the "Reds." They are a hidden and subtle conspiracy, spreading sedition and discontent throughout the nation. Every right-minded citizen must be on guard against their noxious influence. It is not enough to feel in a negative way that they are dangerous. There must be stirred up against them every primitive emotion of suspicion and hate. And this, too, is the nazi technique. "The great majority of a nation is so feminine in its character and outlook," wrote Hitler, "that its thought and conduct are ruled by sentiment rather than by sober reasoning. This sentiment, however, is not complex, but simple and consistent. It is not highly differentiated, but has only the negative and positive emotions of love and hatred, right and wrong, truth and falsehood. Its notions are never partly this and partly that." [27] Practically all the reactionary propaganda of the daily columnist is built upon this view. Once he has found the effective formula, his sole purpose is to discover how best to repeat the formula until it has almost become a part of the unconscious background in which his readers' thinking is set. It is the literal creation of prejudice on his part, the validation of a judgment emotionally made before reason can come into play.

Men like Mr. Brisbane are the inevitable end result of making the American newspaper itself a branch of Big Business, the proprietors of which have come themselves to have a heavy stake in the preservation of the *status quo*. Dependent upon advertisers, who are themselves a part of Big Business, the newspaper owners must work within a framework which the advertisers largely define. The real guardian of their interest in the paper is then shifted from the editorial to the business side; and a stage is presently reached when the news columns of the journal differ from the advertisement columns only in that they have a different commodity to sell. It then becomes curious to note how there is almost a self-adjusting balance between the character of the advertisers and the character of the papers. In a daily which caters to Park Avenue in New York or Beacon Hill in Boston, "radical" ideas evoke a solemnly virtuous indignation which corresponds to the solidity of its readers; in a daily which circulates in the Bronx or the poorer districts of Brooklyn, the attack is likely to be hysterical, but brief, with its main emphasis upon the theme that the pillars of the Constitution are being pulled down, while the main theatrical effects are produced by the columnist who identifies the criminals who have persuaded the president to embark upon so un-American an experiment.

In general outline this is what has happened to the great newspapers since the close of the Civil War. It has only in part been a conscious evolu-

[27] *Ibid.*

tion; and it is only pretty slowly that the journalist has come to realize how much he is the prisoner of an impersonal colossus he has helped to create. That slowness of realization partly explains the rarity of public protest by the newspapermen themselves. A figure like William Randolph Hearst may be the subject of elaborate dissection; [28] but no one has ever attempted to do for the press as a whole what Lincoln Steffens did for municipal corruption or Henry Demarest Lloyd for the Standard Oil Company in the first phase of its career. It must be remembered, moreover, that the very range of the newspaper enables a good deal of variety of outlook to be included within the general frame—work that is essential if profit is to be made. The *New York Herald Tribune,* for example, is a profoundly conservative paper which traditionally supports the Republican party; but it prints three or four times a week throughout the year the column of a very able and sophisticated journalist, Mr. Walter Lippmann, who is skilful enough to combine a general devotion to traditional principles with a deceptive air of cool detachment. Or the *New York Times* will atone, after the exposure of its anti-Russian bias by Mr. Lippmann and Mr. Charles Merz, then in their crusading phase, first, by sending as its correspondent to Russia Mr. Walter Duranty, whose reports were, on the whole, pretty favourable; and, some years later, by making Mr. Merz himself its editor. Even the most vehement critic of a newspaper like the *New York Times* is bound to admit that however careful it may be to remain conservative both in news reported and comment of its own upon that news, it makes itself indispensable to the serious student of affairs by the sheer volume of information it makes available and the importance of the correspondence it admits to its pages.

Nor must one omit the relatively limited area of influence of the average American newspaper. To some extent this is changing through the growth of large-scale ownership by chains like the Scripps-Howard organization; it is limited, further, by the reliance the overwhelming proportion of the dailies must place upon the great news-gathering agencies like the Associated Press and the United Press; and it is mitigated, perhaps still more, by the fact that, purely local news apart, most American papers, even in the relatively small communities, are being streamlined increasingly to a uniform pattern. The foreign news comes from an agency; so does the syndicated column; so, too, does the vital comic strip; and this is more likely to be true than not of the main content of the woman's page and the article from Washington. A remarkable editor here, an outstandingly distinguished leader-writer like Mr. James Morgan of the *Boston Globe,* a humorist of sheer genius like Finley Peter Dunne, or a cartoonist of the power of Fitzpatrick of the *St. Louis Post-Dispatch,* may enable this uniformity to seem insignificant beside the impact of their talent. But the uniformity is, nevertheless, on the increase; and the influence of the aeroplane in speed of delivery, and of the teletypesetter in

[28] Ferdinand Lundberg, *Imperial Hearst* (New York: Modern Library, 1937).

enabling what is written in New York or Washington to go straight to the linotype machine in the composing room in a remote town, is only too likely to make men of the type Mr. Sinclair Lewis has depicted in *It Can't Happen Here* more rare in the future than they have been in the past. The Doremus Jessup he drew with such affection had something like his counterpart in real life in Mr. Emerson Jennings, who so fittingly worked in Wilkes-Barre, Pennsylvania. What is most significant, however, in the career of Jennings is that not even the combined effort of eminent counsel and the American Civil Liberties Union could prevent him from being convicted of a grave charge despite the absence of evidence, and that he was clearly the chosen victim of the interests and institutions he attacked.[29] What Mr. Jennings endured is not very likely to encourage other men to emulate that ideal of fair play which seemed so obvious to Doremus Jessup.

3

In 1910 there were some 2600 daily newspapers read by over ninety million people in the United States; in 1940, there were 1988 daily newspapers, and about one hundred and thirty million readers. In the ninety-two cities with a population of more than a hundred thousand citizens, there were 368 newspapers; thirty years later there were only 239. In 1910 about forty per cent of the press was distributed in towns with a single newspaper; in 1940 this had more than doubled, to almost eighty-six per cent. Only fourteen per cent of all American towns had, therefore, more than one newspaper. In 1910 sixty-two papers were controlled by thirteen chains; a generation later there were fifty-one chains which controlled nearly three hundred papers.[30] The owner-editor is thus a vanishing type. More and more, the chains dominate the scene. That is to say, absentee ownership increases, the news, local gossip apart, grows more uniform, readers see, on an ever wider-scale, the writings of the same columnists, the same comic strips, the same "woman's page," and the papers become fixed within the contours of a similar central direction of policy. Increasingly, also, the relations between the big proprietors of newspaper chains and the great advertising interests are the basis upon which the difference between profit and loss is built; the result is that the likelihood grows that the same people or the same corporations will be able to avoid unfavourable discussion or to secure the kind of support which enables their lobbies in Washington or the state capital to warn members of the legislatures to maintain "a decent respect for the public opinion of mankind."

Not, of course, that this phenomenon is peculiar to the United States; it plays a growing part in British life as well, and in countries like Spain, and Nazi Germany and Italy under Mussolini, the organization of uni-

---

[29] See the very moving account by Victor Weybright, "It Happened in Wilkes-Barre," *Survey Graphic*, February 1937.
[30] Morris L. Ernst, *The First Freedom* (New York: Macmillan, 1946).

form opinion by the careful selection of news it went even further. In Soviet Russia, also, the directive to the press assures, and is intended to assure, that any variety of outlook will be the reader's contribution, and will be kept, so far as the daily press can keep it, within the narrowest possible bounds. In the United States and Britain, moreover, apart from a small number of papers, the major purpose of the press is to keep the reader's mind on the personal and the trivial. If they cannot avoid the "big" news they do not like, methods of presentation and techniques of display are available which, combined with a form of editorial comment which fits the news given into the effect it seeks to produce, try to hold the reader prisoner in a mass of detail in which his sense of proportion is consciously perverted and his ability to separate fact and opinion in a large degree nullified.

It is a dangerous situation for the simple reason that, without accurate information, it is difficult to be an effective citizen; and most people have neither the time nor the means to explore for truth in the news. Some corrective might be looked for in the weekly or monthly reviews or in the special periodicals. But the last reach a very small way, since their purpose is to serve the special interest from which they emanate. No one would look for an attack on craft trade-unionism in the *American Federationist*, the organ of the A.F. of L., any more than he would look for the support of labour in *American Industries*, the organ of the National Association of Manufacturers, or the bulletins of the different Chambers of Commerce. Indeed, the trade journals generally make a speciality of attacking "radicalism" in all its forms, and watch with devoted attention lest "dangerous" textbooks or "dangerous" teachers creep into the schools.[31] And when to this there is added the fact that many of the smaller papers regularly print the articles freely provided for them by the trade associations, some of which, especially in the field of public utilities, are able actually to pay for, or secure the amendment of, textbooks used in the schools and colleges, it is obvious that they do not enlarge the frontiers of accurate knowledge.[32]

Of the learned journals I do not speak, though some of them, like *Foreign Affairs*, the distinguished quarterly edited by Mr. Hamilton Fish Armstrong, and the *American Political Science Review*, like the *Quarterly Journal of Economics*[33] and the *Public Administration Review*, as well as, among a smaller audience, journals like those of the Law Schools of Harvard and Yale, have a real, though long-term, effect in shaping American opinion. In the field of journalism it is to the general weekly and monthly press that we must look for a more measured view. This, broadly

[31] Beale, *Are American Teachers Free?*, p. 538.
[32] *Ibid.*, pp. 552 f.; and note the amazing case of Professor Martin G. Glaeser's textbook on public utility economics, written at Professor Ely's research institute at Northwestern University, itself the recipient of large funds from the National Electric Light Association, *ibid.*, p. 556.
[33] Published by Harvard University.

speaking, may fairly be divided into two classes: there are the weeklies and the monthlies which cater to the "intellectuals," and there are those which seek to attract a reading public large enough themselves to have become a part of Big Business. Each of these needs quite separate consideration.

There are today two independent weeklies and a Communist one in the United States that really count intellectually for something; they are the survivors of frequent, often distinguished, experiments, the *Freeman,* for instance, and *Reedy's Mirror,* which flickered for a few brief years and died. Of the three, the oldest is the *Nation,* founded in 1865 by E. L. Godkin, an Irishman who combined something of the crusading zeal of his people with a good deal more of that Spencerian liberalism linked to the Puritan tradition which is seen at its most complete in Harvard University in the second half of the nineteenth century, and was, perhaps, most fully incarnate in President Charles William Eliot. After a somewhat difficult start the paper became linked with the *New York Evening Post,* then in the ownership of Henry Villard, a railroad magnate. It is not excessive to say that Godkin made the *Nation* one of the two or three best weekly journals in the English-speaking world. He was widely read; he had a clear and incisive style; and he was relentlessly honest. He not only made his paper an illuminating commentary on the policies of his time; he also made it a real source of influence. On Civil Service reforms, in the fight of the mugwumps against the attempt of the orthodox Republicans to make the able but corrupt James G. Blaine president of the United States, in the effort—a failure, but a gallant failure —to arrest the drift of America towards the imperialism in which the war with Spain was so important a landmark, Godkin made the *Nation* an expression of much that was finest in the social mind of his time. But that was not all. He was a man of wide friendships, and some of the most interesting of the pages he edited came from James Bryce and Leslie Stephen and Albert V. Dicey. The friend, moreover, of men like William James and brother Henry, of the Adams family, as well as of what was best in the intellectual life of New York and Boston, he made the *Nation* the outstanding source of criticism of scholarship, literature, art, and music. When he retired after an editorial career of nearly forty years, he had given his paper a status no such journal had ever had before. No doubt he addressed a small circle; but he made the *Nation* a weekly which shaped the minds of most centre-minded intellectuals and of other editors in a position to think for themselves. He had no originality; he dwelt, in most of his thinking, within the boundaries of that solid upper middle-class social philosophy which, in Britain, swore by the *Spectator* of R. H. Hutton and John St. Loe Strachey. He was a good deal of a snob; and his general support of democratic government still kept it within the framework of an economic individualism which saw only a little way into the changing nature of American society. Godkin's

Nation limited its grasp of most social problems to the purely political plane.[34]

From his retirement until the end of the First World War the *Nation* had much of intellectual interest and little of intellectual continuity. The editorship was taken over in 1918 by Oswald Garrison Villard, the grandson of the Henry Villard who had come to Godkin's aid some forty years before. Villard made it more liberal in outlook, deeply pacifist and international in temper, full of zeal for good causes, but permeated with a certain peevishness of temper, an irritability which limited its influence. Nor could he adapt himself to the tempo of social change; he seemed to combine the remains of the spirit of Theodore Roosevelt's Progressivism with a sympathy for the objectives of Bryan's Populism, always with a hope that nothing excessive be done; one can see in the paper during the years of his control a contempt for the Coolidge epoch combined with a real fear of the age of Roosevelt when he found himself confronted by changes the scale of which he really preferred to welcome in Europe rather than in America. Villard's liberalism was the rich man's compassion tempered always by fear that it might go too far. The paper entered on a much richer phase of influence when, in the middle thirties, he sold it to Freda Kirchwey. If it lacks, perhaps, the value it had, under Godkin, as a critical medium in the field of the arts, and has still to learn the urgency of making science an integral part of the culture it surveys, on the political side Miss Kirchwey and her colleagues have made the *Nation* as impressive a journal as at any period in the eighty years of its history. It is particularly notable for two things: it examines foreign affairs with knowledge that is first-hand and from a fixed base of socialist principle; and it watches the tangled complexities of politics in Washington with a skill that makes it an indispensable guide to the observer of that labyrinth.

The *New Republic,* which was founded by Herbert Croly in 1914, was born of the lingering optimism which still flickered on the Left Wing of what was not yet dead or cynical of Theodore Roosevelt's abortive Progressive movement. Few weekly journals anywhere have started with so remarkable a body of colleagues. Croly himself was a liberal after the manner of L. T. Hobhouse in England; in American terms, he sought to use the nationalism of Alexander Hamilton to secure purposes that Jefferson might well have approved had he lived a century later. He wanted a strong and positive federal government which would use its power to bring Big Business to heel, and use the full power of Washington to experiment so as to mitigate the consequences of social inequality. With him were associated Mr. Walter Lippmann, until 1917–18 the outstanding influence with the public possessed by the journal, Walter E. Weyl, a *Manchester Guardian* liberal of considerable talent, and Pro-

[34] Rollo Ogden (ed.), *Life and Letters of Edwin Lawrence Godkin* (New York: Macmillan, 1907); Gustav Pollak, *Fifty Years of American Idealism: the New York Nation, 1865-1915* (Boston: Houghton Mifflin, 1915).

fessor Alvin Johnson, an economist of high distinction who probably has sacrificed what might have been a great reputation as a scholar to his selfless devotion to great causes; on the literary side he had Francis Hackett, a critic of tact and style and taste, and Philip Littell, whose work resembled a good deal a kind of porcelain Augustine Birrell.

The *New Republic* had great influence during the First World War. Both President Wilson and Colonel House admired it, and no small part of their approach to the war was shaped by it. One can see, indeed, from its pages that, after 1917, it was as natural for Mr. Lippmann to become the *éminence grise* of Colonel House as it was for the latter to play the same role to Woodrow Wilson. It was in the light of his first years on the *New Republic* that Mr. Lippmann became one of the vital authors of the President's famous Fourteen Points. But the journal lost Mr. Lippmann shortly after the war was over. After Versailles, Croly found himself with an almost wholly new staff, partly through death and partly through resignation. Having had some real, if indirect, share in securing America's entrance into the war, he was bitterly disappointed with Versailles, even to the point, which showed his rare combination of honesty and courage, of opposing its ratification by the Senate. When the age of Harding and Coolidge came, he was to edit the paper for nearly ten more years without the journalistic qualities necessary to maintain its influence. He was a slow thinker with a heavy style; he had none of that ease of relationship which enables a journalist to get swift insights into situations and persons. There was a certain brooding melancholy about him which seemed to make him see life in an aloof way which prevented him from attaining immediacy of contact with it. In the age of Coolidge the only effective role for such a journal as he had founded would have been a combination of careful muck-raking and light but devastating invective. He was incapable of either; and the paper lost both influence and circulation rapidly until the coming of the New Deal. But by then he was dead.

Under his successors there has been much that has been remarkable in its pages. For a period it had as literary editor Mr. Edmund Wilson, one of the first critics of our times writing in the English language; and in the last fifteen years the literary pages have rarely failed to be among the most illuminating in America, not least in the period of Mr. Malcolm Cowley—who had come back from the classic American exile in Paris, at once healthy in spirit and perceptive in mind, to look for the newly significant in letters—and of Mr. Alfred Kazin, to see the critic's task as the sensitive historical adjustment of the subject to the period. Croly's central successor, Mr. Bruce Bliven, had a fine and rugged honesty, as well as an eye for the significant in the news. Mr. George Soule, its economic specialist, had a wide-ranging mind, if one with a constant tendency to oversimplification. Since the New Deal the *New Republic* has often published articles of outstanding influence and quality upon particular themes; and it has specialized both in the massive analysis of the Washington scene and the publication of carefully detailed supplements on things like the voting records of congressmen and senators which have done yeoman service. In attitude, both internationally and nationally, it has given warm support to President Roosevelt's policies from an angle a good deal to the Left of his own. But it suffered up to 1945, and it seems likely to suffer still more in the post-Roosevelt epoch, from the fact that it represents a mood rather than a philosophy. It is interstitial; it is discontinuous in the sense that it rarely sticks long enough to a theme to drive it home; and it has no permanent frame of reference which provides it with stable criteria of judgment. It seems to feel that the world is too much with it; and the result is that it follows most of its analysis with an incantation rather than a remedy.[35]

The *New Masses* is now an official organ of the Communist party. In this form it is the second reincarnation of the gay and brilliant *Masses,* in which, before the First World War, Mr. Max Eastman let the wind of socialism blow through the somewhat studied Bohemianism of Greenwich Village. In this first phase, which lasted until Mr. A. S. Burleson, the postmaster-general in the Wilson administration, refused it the mailing privilege,[36] it was the most interesting expression of the intellectual's revolt against a business civilization that America had so far seen. Reorganized by Eastman from a formless radical paper already limping, within a year of its foundation, to the grave, he made it amusing, exciting, creative, and intelligent. It was, he said, "a revolutionary, not a reform, magazine." But its revolutionary note was less any formal body of doctrine than a happy, brilliant, dashing attack on all the conventions of its time. Eastman kept open house for any writer who sought to shoot at the respectable and the wealthy. He had poems from Vachel Lindsay and Carl Sandburg; there was the moralism of Upton Sinclair; there was the bewildered mysticism of Sherwood Anderson. Anarchists, socialists, disciples of Henry George, ardent feminists, poets of revolutionary temper like Arturo Giovannitti, satirical artists like Art Young and John S. Ivan, everyone was there so long as he laughed or sneered at the existing order, insulted or defied it. Eastman himself wrote a brilliant weekly editorial; and William English Walling, as yet free from Germanophobia, wrote a chronicle of the socialist movement. It was all a little mad and joyously incoherent and unsolemn; the Left movement in America had never had such a weekly before, or since.

The second phase of the *Masses* began after the indictment of its editors under the Espionage Act of 1917 compelled its transformation into the *Liberator*. The old carefree recklessness went with the war. The

[35] In December 1946 Mr. Henry A. Wallace, after his resignation as Secretary of Commerce under President Truman, became the editor of the *New Republic*. To some extent it has become his personal organ and has attempted a higher degree of popularization. In December 1947 he resigned to become a candidate for the presidency in the 1948 election.

[36] *Masses Publishing Co.* v. *Patten,* 246 Fed. 24 (1917); but see the remarkably distinguished judgment of Judge Learned Hand in the court below, 235 Fed. 535; and see Chafee, *Freedom of Speech,* pp. 42 f.

shadow of the censor changed wit and happiness into satire and sting by indirection. The paper was in chains; John Reed continued to write for it, but he asked for release from the editorial board; and one can see in the issues of the summer of 1917 that the winter came steadily nearer. By the time the war was over the remarkable group Eastman had collected round him was scattered; he himself went to Russia, where he fell under the historical spell of the Revolution and the personal fascination of Trotsky. When, with peace, the paper was born again as the *New Masses,* it seemed to be born in middle age, and it was not long before, as the conflict between Trotsky and Stalin began, it passed into orthodox Communist hands. There it has since remained, shedding now one distinguished contributor, now another, as they failed to accommodate themselves to the party line. In recent years it has not seldom had articles of great ability. But it has altogether lost the quality that made its early history a unique episode in American journalism. It is now solemn; it pontificates; it divides the world into the three simple categories of Communists, fellow-travellers, and the enemy. Soviet Russia is good; all other countries are good or bad in proportion to their relations with Soviet Russia. Even books have merit only if they are written by members of, or sympathizers with, the Communist party; otherwise their value consists in their ability to further the cause. Mr. Earl Browder is a remarkable social philosopher until he is expelled from the party; then, suddenly, he becomes an ignorant infamy. Mr. Granville Hicks is a remarkably promising critic until he fails to see, in October 1939, that Great Britain and France are waging an imperialist war. The lightest word of Stalin or of Molotov becomes a text from Holy Scripture. To set the old *Masses* alongside its present incarnation is rather like seeing Heine rewritten in the style of Samuel Rogers.

The liberal weeklies—I use the term in its special American sense—have been a phenomenon of extraordinary interest in the period since the Civil War. They represent an intellectual approach not only detached from mass opinion, but, save in the Communist period of the *New Masses,* detached also from party connection of any continuous kind. They draw their publics mainly from two classes: the first, and the larger, is the professional class, especially teachers and university students; while the second is made up of the mostly self-taught trade-union leaders or the socialist intellectuals in or near the big cities. They work out their policies interstitially; like Croly's *New Republic,* they may support the war of 1917 and fight against the peace which ended it, or, like Villard's *Nation,* they may be strongly anti-Nazi and yet equally strongly isolationist at the same time. They have strong loyalties to particular political leaders, but more to the measures these stand for than to the men in themselves. They thus tend to irritate the good party man because he feels that he can rarely count with any continuity on their support. No doubt there is a long-term sense in which they influence the influential, the people with ideas, and thus make a real impact upon public opinion. But they are mostly on the periphery of power, and not at its centre. This tends to put into their comments a certain sense of aloofness from the real, to make them seem to the man in the White House or a senator seeking not perfectionism, but the compromise for which he can get a majority, irresponsibly idealistic. They express a temper of mind; they do not support an organized movement. They are therefore spectators of, rather than actors in, the battle they are commenting on; for those whom they influence are not organized for action in any direct and coherent way. Croly was for Theodore Roosevelt, and Woodrow Wilson, and Al Smith; the very nature of his views made him an inevitable mugwump. Villard was for Smith and for the Franklin Roosevelt of the first two terms; but he had a passion against the third term which verged on the eccentric, and he was so permeated by muddled and unrelated subjectivities that it brought him into relations with all types of Roosevelt-haters from whom, normally, he would have turned away with horror.

This place at the periphery of power has another, and deeply interesting, result. The men and women who run the weekly journals of liberal opinion are, in a real sense, isolated from the main stream of action; they even have an uneasy awareness of this isolation and seek anxiously to find a compensation for it. Almost always it takes the form of deep interest in, and high expectations of, movements of the Left abroad. A member of the staff of the *Nation* has, in principle, far more in common with the Labour party in Britain, or with the Socialists in France, than he can possibly have with either of the major parties in the United States. He may even feel this so deeply as to seem, almost unconsciously, a member of the one or of the other, to whom distance and nationality are unimportant. Its mistakes then become his mistakes; its failures become his failures. He is bound, therefore, to urge upon it the realization of its principles in that spirit of perfectionism which, three thousand miles away, enables him to forget that politics is a philosophy of the second best. All Americans are devoted to "causes"; the liberal journalist is an American devoted to all liberal causes all over the world. He fights for them—Indian independence, the liberation of Greece, the restoration of the Spanish republic, the overthrow of the Italian monarchy, or the return of the Jews to Palestine—with a devotion that can even become ferocious. He has a deep envy of an Englishman who can be in the battle he can only observe, or of the Frenchman who is actually building the Fourth Republic. Out of it comes the ardour which a visitor to America can see if he watches one of the great football matches and notes how the immense audience is so much at one with the players that there is always an intense and muffled roar as it shouts its advice to the men in the field. And if it is defeated, its members go home irritated, and even angry, sure that victory would have been won if only their advice had been taken at the critical moment, sore that they have been deprived of a vicarious fulfilment.

I think it is this sense of "not belonging" which accounts for a good deal of what is said of the European, even the Asiatic Left, in the American weeklies of a liberal outlook. For that Left achievement partly sublimates their sense of frustration in domestic politics, feeds their capacity to overcome their sense of disquiet at lack of power at home. I suspect that this explains the depth of their devotion to Franklin Roosevelt. He was the first president since, perhaps, Andrew Jackson, in whom they could see the living embodiment of a "cause." They closed their ranks behind him, partly because they knew he would be "knifed" by his own party if it could, and partly because for the first time since the earlier Roosevelt had led his followers into the wilderness and then told them that they had reached the promised land, they had this sense of "belonging." He was friendly, eager for ideas, open to advice and consultation; they felt that they counted, that they were helping the experiment and not merely watching its demonstration. That was why they could be so angry with the deserters from the New Deal, even more than with those who were hostile to it from the start. No president of modern times has given so full or so lengthy a sense of fulfilment, of a life of thought completed by action, as Franklin Roosevelt gave the liberal journalists from 1933 until his death. And I think this explains as well as anything why, in those years, there was a glow in their pages that no one else evoked, from the tragedy of the Gilded Age to the squalid epoch when President Coolidge stood awestruck at the glory of rich American business men.

I digress here for a moment to discuss an issue upon which this analysis, as I think, throws some considerable light. In his remarkable book, *Democracy and the Organization of Political Parties*,[37] Ostrogorski, after a careful examination of their working in Britain and America, insisted that they were evil and urged their replacement by temporary groups of people who supported special objectives and dissolve as each objective is obtained; in no other way, he thought, could the pathology of caucus rule be avoided. The American liberal movement is very much the fulfilment of what Ostrogorski desired. It is a discrete system of groups, each aiming at obtaining some particular end, but never a party aiming to become the government of the United States. It has not prevented the operation, side by side with its efforts, of the two major parties; but it has done a good deal to denude these of doctrine, and to make the party machines, as it were, brokers of ideas, leaning now to the Right, now to the Centre, now to the Left, in an effort to pick the doctrine which, at the electoral moment, will enable them to keep the spoils of office for their supporters. The political party in America does not think; it has no vital philosophic doctrine. It buys the doctrine from one group or another on the gamble that the sum of the doctrines it buys will add up to

[37] M. Y. Ostrogorski, *Democracy and the Organization of Political Parties* (New York: Macmillan, 1902), translated from the French with an introduction by the Right Honourable James Bryce.

enough votes to keep it in power, nationally or locally. That is why it never proceeds directly to a defined goal, but is always weighing pressures against one another in the effort to see where and how it can make the best bargain. That is why, also, its best candidate is, in all normal circumstances, the most "available" one. That is why, again, it finds men of strong general principles, like the elder La Follette, or George W. Norris, so uncomfortable, and why it adjusts itself with so much difficulty to a president like Franklin Roosevelt. For it chose him, as Mr. Walter Lippmann caustically said, because it believed, in 1932, that he was just "a pleasant man who wished to be president." When it discovered that, however pleasant, he had a clear set of purposes which he proposed to drive to the statute book, it felt that all the rules of the game, as the game had been played since the Civil War, had been unfairly broken by a man who had not lived up to the expectations a party is entitled to look for from its candidate.

The weekly journals of liberal opinion in America seem to me to reflect the incoherence of the liberal groups. They support particular aims; they do not fight for general power. They cannot, indeed, so fight, since there is no liberal party, in an organic sense, for them to support. They can form a group to protect civil liberties, or to abolish child labour, or to improve the condition of the Negro, or to fight for the restoration of Republican Spain. But this atomization of a general movement (which, for effectiveness, requires a party seeking power) into a series of groups, even overlapping groups, is bound to put the liberal journal in a difficult position. Save at a special moment, like a presidential election, it has normally no over-all purpose which gives its support a character of constant importance to the politicians. It may be of help to them on some occasion when public opinion is deeply divided and the view of the intellectual Left has a special importance. But, in a general way, the liberal weeklies impress a small group with no profound party affiliations; they are in the background, rather than in the foreground, of the opinion-making factors which are weighed with care in making the final decisions.

4

THE mass circulation weeklies and monthlies require special discussion. Generally speaking, they are divisible, specialist journals apart, into three broad categories. There are the journals like the *Saturday Evening Post, Colliers',* and *Look,* which seek to combine much entertainment with dramatic narrative, the interpretative portrait, and political discussion. There are the journals like *Time* and *Newsweek,* which seek to paint a rapid sketch of the historic panorama of the week before, written mainly in personal terms and with the swift, polished, half-cynical swing of a chorus dancing on a Hollywood film. Then there are the digests, scientific, religious, and so forth, the *Reader's Digest,* with its circulation high in the millions, at their head. There is an important difference between each of these categories; but it is also important to note that they are all built on the same foundation. They are all of them Big Business in a really big way. To achieve this position, they must all (except the *Reader's Digest*) have vast circulations in order that they may have the costly advertising which elevates them to the rank of Big Business. They must, therefore, pay homage to the conventions of dominant America, that is to say, of the fairly successful business man and his wife, and those, not so successful, who nevertheless accept the outlook and the standards of the fairly successful business man. In their different ways they are all written as variations upon a single theme: Traditional America needs no fundamental changes. It is healthy. It is progressive. It still offers great opportunities to those who are thrifty and hard-working. The great industrialists were patriots to whom America owes its power and glory. The little industrialists always have a chance in America. Every workingman has a chance in America. The threats to American well-being come from communists, socialists—and from these especially when they are allowed to poison the minds of the young in school or college—and trade-union leaders, who want to destroy the freedom which is the American heritage. The politician ought to know his place; if he begins putting his fingers into economic life there will be bureaucracy and corruption. A Christian citizen is an American who respects religion, the Constitution, President Eliot's five-foot bookshelf, the rugged honesty of Grover Cleveland, who recognizes the great scientist in Thomas A. Edison, who gives his wife and children a better house every ten or twelve years and a new car every year, and who subscribes conscientiously to the community chest. He does not understand art but he knows what he likes. He rarely reads more than the daily paper and one of these weeklies. He is friendly to everybody on his own level, and fiercely critical of troublemakers. If times are good, he is confident that we have learned how to conquer unemployment; and if times are bad, he is pretty certain that prosperity is round the corner. A realist in business, he is incurably romantic about life. Profoundly patriotic, he never returns from London or Paris or Florence without the sense that there is in America something he cannot define which is beyond the reach of other national cultures.

It is upon these assumptions that the weeklies like the *Saturday Evening Post* are built. A romance which provides a way of escape, some effective reportage, the written portrait of some figure in the news—malicious, or savage, or eulogistic, according to virtue in conduct and, even more, in opinion, as virtue was measured by Mr. Edward Bok—a pretty brief editorial on the theme that America is different or that socialism is born of the hate of the failures for the successful, or an assurance that the Russian experiment must fail because it is contrary to human nature or that Russian "imperialism" is a threat to the world, or an insistence that trade-unionism is the real brake on greater production, or the need for a better standard of living for all—these are its central themes. Ex-President Coolidge may be persuaded to lend his name to the denunciation of "Red" professors. Now and again the journal shows its tolerance by permitting some mild liberal to hope for a more rapid social improvement, or a clergyman of note is allowed to regret the materialism of our time and call for a return to a simpler and saner America. Nor is the claim of the farmer and the small town forgotten. Each receives an accolade at least once each year. The farmer, so long as he has not joined some Populist organization, becomes, whether in article or story, the backbone of America; and, every so often, there is a hymn of praise to the small town which in this age of bigness has kept the democratic habits of an America where rich and poor alike are neighbours on first-name terms.

The *Saturday Evening Post* is written for simple people who believe most of what they are told; but it has the sophistication of organized simplicity. It combines a skilful emphasis upon the theme that all life in America is romantic adventure with the constant warning that "radicals," both domestic and foreign, want to destroy the pattern that makes this quality possible. Its heroes are always, whether in story or in article, simple, straightforward men, who, if they sometimes stray from the narrow path, find their way back in the end; they symbolize the generous-hearted, hard-working young American who is to be successful, or his senior who has become so because he showed the same qualities when he was young. It detests the sceptic and the man who thinks that big changes are needed in the United States. It likes the workingman who is so proud to be an American that his mind is never troubled by problems about the "closed shop" or wages or hours of labour. It is for sound things —a healthy literature, religion, a vigorous out-of-doors life, the wife who knows how to make her house into a home, parents who have the art of understanding, and being understood by, their children. It lives by flattering the "commuter" and his family, the small business man with a car he can replace every year with a slightly better car, whose banker calls him by his first name, who hopes before he is fifty to join the country club, and even, if things go well, to send his daughter to Vassar and his son to Williams. It is built on the provision of escapism on the one hand, and the soothing assurance on the other that, however difficult things are now, they are bound to turn out all right if they are only left in the hands of "sound" men. J. P. Morgan was a "sound" man; so was President Taft; so was Henry Ford. If all is not right with the world, that is largely because agitators inflame the discontented and drive them to break the natural laws of the universe. What should reassure Americans is the tested strength with which the Constitution toughly rejects all rash innovation, and the knowledge that, after all, God is in his heaven.

No one can measure the appeal of the *Saturday Evening Post* who has not read the autobiography of the man who made it, Mr. Edward Bok,[38] or realized that he found in himself the fulfilment of all the Amer-

[38] Edward Bok, *The Americanization of Edward Bok* (New York: Scribner, 1920).

ican legends. There is something in him of Horatio Alger; there is something, also, of the one-time famous message of the Reverend Russell H. Conwell, there is a good deal of the idea that wealth is a stewardship in that curious way which enabled Andrew Carnegie to live for a generation after the Homestead strike without being haunted by its memory.[39] The magazine assumes, with a skill in evading discussion which is noteworthy, that honest and energetic poverty is necessarily in America a halting place merely on an upward march. Of course, it is less simpleminded than Horatio Alger, and far more stream-lined than Conwell's turgid rhetoric. Where Carnegie had the blunt directness of a practical man to whom success lends so authoritative an air that he does not even know the assumptions upon which his credo rests, the outlook of the *Saturday Evening Post* is insinuated rather than spoken out loud, emerges by indirection rather than by express statement. Where it is strident, it is either following a public opinion which has already become so, or the stridency is contributed by some important public figure who bears its responsibility. Its serious function, and its effective importance, is its power to cushion a few million families in the United States, who have just crossed the frontier of the territory where there are doubts and dangers, against the threat of new ideas. It seeks to be, and has largely succeeded in being, an insurance against the disease of disquieting thought.

A visitor from the moon who examined a dozen numbers of the *Saturday Evening Post* would be tempted, I think, to conclude that it was produced by a staff of quiet, middle-aged people who love the America of their childhood and seek, above everything, to safeguard their special class. That is not the conclusion he would form from what are, in some ways, the most representative weekly publications of America in the fifth decade of the twentieth century—the *Time* and *Life* which Mr. Henry Luce and his collaborators, but above all Mr. Henry Luce, have so swiftly and so remarkably constructed. They are more symbolic of the epoch, which Mr. Luce himself has, perhaps prophetically, called the "American Century," than any other journals of their time. Where the *Nation* or the *New Republic* ask their readers to participate in a carefully delimited after-dinner conversation, Mr. Luce invites them to a quick-lunch restaurant where every discussion seems to end with a snap and a flourish before the reader is fully aware that the argument has begun. Where the two "journals of opinion" assume in their readers a general familiarity with the contour of affairs from which their editors make a selection for comment on a basis with which their readers have been long familiar, the technique of the Luce journals is a swift, incisive summary of all the news, so treated that the news itself is comment, and what further comment is provided is mainly there to drive home the point the reporter knew he was to make before ever he began to fire off his story. It all goes with the crackling insistence of a machine-gun. It is always

[39] Andrew Carnegie. *The Empire of Business* (New York: Doubleday, Page, 1902).

precise, though precision and accuracy are two different things. It is always written so as to convey, sometimes to convey with brilliance, the idea that the central figure in the story stopped just after the significant moment to tell Mr. Luce's representative that inner truth to be found in no other journal. We are always meant to feel that, through the enterprise of Mr. Luce, we see, not the formal persona of the man who does things, whether in the United States or Britain, in Russia or China, in Italy or the Argentine, but the man as he really is in his private self, as he looks at his face in the mirror while he shaves. Mr. Luce's business is to persuade his public that, with his aid, they can peer behind the mask all public figures wear to the inner essence of the personality it conceals.[40]

Mr. Luce is a phenomenon of importance; and it is worth examining the technique by which he has attained success. He owes something to his being an American; something to his college training; a good deal to the era in which he was born. His Americanism gives him his surface friendliness, his infinite, though never profound, curiosity, his endless appetite for information, his quick, darting power of observation. He gained at Yale not only the self-assurance which is the secret of material success, but the realization that half the world will take you at your own valuation if you only insist sufficiently upon its doing so. And, coming to maturity in the Coolidge era, he was deeply infected with its cynicism about ideals, its fear that high purposes were no more than the rhetorical fig-leaves by which the pursuit of wealth and power hid itself from the public gaze. Like most of those who grew up in this period, he has never become really mature; there is a sophomoric streak in him which makes him identify notoriety with success, power with greatness, pleasure with happiness, extension of view with intensity of insight, the speed of the journey with the rate of progress. He is shrewd, in the sense that a speculator on the Stock Exchange is shrewd. He has the American notion that, at some point, the by-product of bigness is grandeur. Like so many Americans, he is a facile extrovert, who, at the first meeting, is ready for the exchange of intimate confidences.

Time, of course, owes much to the giant army of his collaborators at home and abroad. Most of them are young and unaccustomed to reticence. Most of them believe that history virtually began when Mr. Luce founded *Time;* and all of them feel that once anybody is in the news, he has ceased to possess the right to privacy. So that Mr. Luce has constructed, with their aid, a journal of immense range, full of that atmosphere of "being in the know," which gives his readers in Peoria, Illinois, or Mobile, Alabama, the sense of a ringside seat at the making of history.

In the result, there is something for everyone, done always with gusto and spice, easy, quick, vivid, and familiar. Few things or people are treated without a touch of sauciness; and the solemn man, whether of the Right or Left, is made to pay for his stuffiness. Every subject is

[40] See Wolcott Gibbs, "Timenterprise," *The New Yorker,* November 28, 1936; and A. J. Liebling, "The Wayward Press," *The New Yorker,* October 11, 1947.

treated as though its inner secrets had been quite specially whispered to the reporter from *Time;* and most of its pages, save where religion generally, and the Roman Catholic Church in particular, are treated, are painted over with a veneer of gay irreverence which often gives the appearance of wit without really involving the hard effort of mind by which wit is achieved. Everything is done in terms of personalities, with photographs which are often brilliantly employed to drive home the point the Left is seeking to attack. There is no abstract discussion. The commentary is always in the method by which the news is reported. The trivial is always cheek by jowl with the important. The style is always a combination of the speed of an O. Henry story with the wise-cracking of Will Rogers as its climax. Every page has its glitter; every issue of the journal is like a swift piece of jazz music written by someone who knows everybody, has seen everything, and has learned that the only people who are ever deceived are the people who persist in enthusiasms.

Time is the logical paper for those who have lost their faith and yet still want to see from the inside what is happening in the Church. Nobody, save the eminent ecclesiastic, is permanently a hero, no cause is sacred, nothing really matters. Even the grim approach of starvation in Europe and Asia can be reported with a background of flippancy which is skilfully worded so as at once to give some facts and to convey the impression that public opinion in the United States is not prepared for drastic measures about food.[41] Behind the façade it erects of hard brilliance in reporting, though an occasional bow is made to tolerance by the exhibition of contempt for men like Bilbo or Talmadge, the real emphasis is always a reactionary emphasis. Most Big Business men always emerge in heroic proportions; they are always energetic; they always do a real man's job; they are always full of new ideas. If some weakness is known about a labour leader, it is sure to be there, given a greater prominence than Cromwell's wart. There is usually a sneering undertone in any report of congressional proceedings. Most government action is shown in the light of its mistakes. No opportunity is missed of attacking Russia, or of hinting that "practical men" found out long ago the follies of socialist enterprise. Science, of course, is news, and a great scientist will be described in much the same way as a remarkable conjurer at a music-hall. Religion is mostly discussed in the forcibly friendly spirit of an Oxford Group house party in which an intimacy with God permits its members that uneasy flippancy an Anglican curate displays when he tries to make himself at home in the public house of his parish. Educational news is reported with an amused disdain which suggests the folly of taking its problems seriously. Even the arts are chronicled as incidents in the lives of the artists rather than as an element still of some significance in the quality of our civilization.

I have discussed *Time* in some detail because I think it has relevance to something of real importance in contemporary America. It is signifi-

41 *Time,* April 8, 1946, pp. 7–8.

cant, first, that it is immensely successful; no one can travel on an American train for a two-hour journey without seeing a dozen men and women absorbed in it. It is significant, second, because the mental climate in which all its reporting is set is one which annihilates all values by a disillusioned cynicism which assumes that principles are the last relic of a dying Puritanism, and that what matters in life is money, power, and the chance of being amused. *Time* has no reticence; it can even luxuriate in lush sentimentality over some act of wartime courage, or the death of a favourite journalist like Ernie Pyle. It wants to encourage all its readers to believe that life is in fact a tale told by an idiot, and that they cannot really be wiser than to sit back and enjoy the spectacle of the noise and fury which signify just nothing. It knows the passion for gossip, and it provides the gossip in abundance. It knows the American love of wisecracking aphorisms, and every page is littered with these. It never forgets the American interest in an approach to intimacy with the great or near great. It knows what Mr. Churchill said on his return, in the spring of 1946, from his American holiday; even more, it knows what the soldier and sailor said who happened to see him walk down the gangway of the ship. It always reveals the large-scale alimonies; it always runs amok in Hollywood; it never forgets the marriages and divorces, the births and deaths, of the rich or the notorious, with a special pleasure in the chance of emphasizing any complexities in marital relationships. A careful reader of *Time* might easily be tempted to believe that Miss Dorothy Parker had written it in one of her most inspired moments as a satire upon what the world—especially the United States—seems like to a body of permanent undergraduates who are, more than anything, afraid that they may be thought not to have shed their last illusion.

Time is for the reader of some sophistication. The *Reader's Digest* is for the tired business man who has almost forgotten how to read.[42] It gives him, in pemmicanized form, brief summaries of articles which have had some success, of articles it has "planted" for its purposes, even of books which are being widely discussed. Since few of its readers have the time or mental energy to think outside their hours of business, the *Digest* helps them not only to have a vague idea of names that may crop up at a dinner party, but even to know what answers are being made to radicals and intellectuals so that they may be ready to defend America from the onslaught of the Left. It is the staple reading of the commercial traveller, the basis of the discussions he initiates in the smoking-cars of countless Pullmans in that decisive hour of the journey when the Negro attendant, with his unending courtesy and flawless skill, is making up the beds for the night. There is always one such devotee of the *Reader's Digest* in every Pullman smoking-car; and his confused summary of some summarized article he did not quite have the time to

---

[42] See John Bainbridge's remarkable *Little Wonder* (New York: Reynal & Hitchcock, 1946), originally a "Profile" in *The New Yorker*, a magazine which is itself perhaps the outstanding achievement in modern American journalism.

finish before he left the diner is perhaps a fitting prelude to that masculine moment when discussion limps and, on the principle of Sir Robert Walpole, the exchange of anecdotes begins.

One must not, of course, exaggerate the influence of these mass circulation magazines any more than one must exaggerate the influence of the daily press. They play a real, though never a decisive, part in creating that "average American" and his wife, in comfortable circumstances, whom Robert Herrick depicted so accurately in his novels. They are people mostly absorbed in keeping up with the tide, anxious to do the right things and think the right things, immensely respectful of those who have reached the apex of the pyramid of wealth and power, immensely resentful of those who criticize their idols. They want the complex made simple; they want a sense of agreeable proximity to the men who make history; they want to be told "smart" things they can repeat, and, even more, they want information about things they can exchange; they want to be amused; and, perhaps more than all else, they want to be assured that they still have the right to that unbreakable optimism which is part of the cultural inheritance of America, hardly challenged, on a serious scale, before the Great Depression of 1929. They know that their fathers, as in 1907, or their grandfathers, as in 1873, faced moments of serious crisis. Some of them vaguely remember evil things like strikes and the scandal over air-mail subsidies, or dangerous men like William D. Haywood and Vincent St. John of the I.W.W. A few of them can even remember the depth of their relief when Theodore Roosevelt rode back from the grim dangers of Armageddon to that less obnoxious salvation that is found in the Union League Club.

It is for these and their grandsons that Mr. Luce's staff does its work. *Time* makes it possible for them to talk; it gives them a conviction that all may yet be well; it puts into phrases that they like the thoughts they are seeking to shape. It makes the news more vivid by colouring its content as the readers would wish to see it coloured. And the readers are grateful for the labels of identification which enable them to know just who are their friends. They like the brief glimpse they get, as through a half-shut door, of science and art, of the latest radio gadget, and the real inside story of the Communists in China. It gives them a sense that they have a map of the universe in their minds; and even if they do not travel farther from New York or San Francisco than Muncie or Lexington, they nearly believe that they could talk about Picasso, or explain the difference between an orchestra led by Toscanini and one directed by Duke Ellington, or even tell Mr. Ernest Bevin how much he has done, since the socialists came to power, to make Americans feel that the Britain of Winston Churchill is still alive. The weeklies of mass circulation are nothing so much as prescriptions to secure a pleasant mental inertia in Mr. Babbitt and the millions like him who work hard, and play hard, are good husbands and devoted parents, who desire nothing but to move on an even keel and to be protected against dangerous thoughts. They do not even know that when they feel deeply, they are usually not thinking at all. And they are certainly unaware of the vital truth that Mr. Luce and his colleagues know so well—the truth that a pleasant mental inertia is the supreme safeguard of the *status quo*.

5

THE cultural magazines have played a significant part in American intellectual life even before, in his Knickerbocker period, Washington Irving may be said to have begun the period of an independent American literature. And some of the early magazines, for example, the *Southern Literary Messenger* when Poe was seeking to impose serious standards of criticism in his book reviews, or the *Dial* when transcendentalism seemed to make New England the meeting place of the Ancient East and the civilization inspired by Athens and Rome, or that astonishing quarterly of Orestes Brownson which, at least before he joined the Church of Rome, seemed to have grasped all the motive forces which strain the balance of a capitalist democracy—all these have a permanent significance in American intellectual history. It is astonishing to note the speed with which the great caravans of immigrants that moved west were followed by a printing press, and the press by little reviews which evoked the essay and poetry, the description of travel and the record of life. Few of them lived long, and still fewer of them were important in themselves. Their significance lay much less in what they had to say than in the zeal for self-expression—even if, too often, an imitative self-expression— which they represented. A frontier Felicia Hemans is, a century and a quarter later, even more fatiguing than her reedy original, and the combination of Leigh Hunt and D'Orsay that N. P. Willis tried to domesticate in the Hudson River country has hardly today more interest than to fill a few pages with those delicate conversation pieces in which Mr. Van Wyck Brooks seeks so wistfully to evoke the spirit of the past.

These magazines, monthly and quarterly, often stilted in style, usually reflective of the fashionable European modes of the moment but without any real inspiration, too rarely aware, as men of genius like Fenimore Cooper were aware, that the maturity of the American mind depended upon its passion for intellectual self-exploration, were nevertheless important because, with all their obvious frailties, they revealed the unity of America with the rest of civilized thought. It is, I think, worth making the point that they reveal in an important way how dangerous it is to push too far F. J. Turner's famous hypothesis of the frontier. For even if ideas were modified, as habits were modified, as the covered wagons rolled on in endless procession and permanent settlements began to be established, in the realm of the mind what rose to the surface and found expression on paper had roots which went so far back that, in the end, their historian would have to emphasize that their sources lay in the doctrines which constituted the common stock of all European civilization. America, no doubt, was searching for a cultural independence long before it was achieved; and perhaps it did not in a decisive way achieve it until the end of the First World War. But the America of Audubon and Fenimore Cooper, the America of John Lloyd Stephens and William Gilmore Simms, were using old forms with a content so new that it was plain to all with eyes to see that they were at once original and as devoid of provinciality as those of Scott or Dickens, Victor Hugo or Balzac. The American continent was establishing its letters of credit by the time that Andrew Jackson entered the White House.

The outstanding monthly magazines in America, reviews like *Harper's,* the *Atlantic Monthly,* and, at an earlier period, the *North American Review,* the *Century, Scribner's,* and the *American Mercury,* have, collectively, played a very considerable part in the intellectual development of America. They have been deeply interesting in three different ways. All of them have been essentially American in their central emphasis; but all of them have devoted serious attention to the perspectives of international affairs, and both *Harper's* and the *Atlantic Monthly* have shown a generous hospitality, especially in the last thirty years, to European contributors. The two last, moreover, have been edited with exceptional insight and skill. With a point of view that may broadly be described as a little right of centre, they have sought to offer their readers an effective cross-section of the social and cultural life that is common to Europe and to the United States. The *Atlantic Monthly* may not unfairly be said to be influenced by the special climate of that Boston which is its spiritual home. It conveys the sense that, in general, there is a self-conscious restraint in what it displays to its readers. It has been a little obviously superior, deliberate partner in the "genteel tradition." When it has published an article like Professor Frankfurter's famous attack on the judicial proceedings in the Sacco–Vanzetti case,[43] it has been with the air of one who insists that the breadth of its tolerance be noticed, since it is aware that it courts the disapproval of the "best people" in Boston. It has, one may not unfairly say, an air comparable to what Harvard feels about the lesser American colleges. But it has always had, too, a very real distinction and an illuminating skill in its editorial power to select those topics for treatment which have more than a passing interest.

Harper's Magazine, on the other hand, has been very distinctively a New York product. It has been cosmopolitan in the sources on which it has drawn. It has mingled the traditional and the radical, unpolitical literature and the fiercely contentious political essay, with remarkable skill. It has had investigations made, like Mr. G. R. Leighton's admirable studies of American cities,[44] which were first-rate contributions to the sociological understanding of urban life in the United States. *Harper's,* I think, has been less inhibited than the *Atlantic* in what it has felt able to publish. It has never had to satisfy, like its Boston rival, an almost

[43] Felix Frankfurter, *Law and Politics* (New York: Harcourt, Brace, 1939).
[44] George R. Leighton, *Five Cities* (New York: Harper, 1939).

hereditary literary circle which watched a little jealously any excessive departure from the tradition of which it was the guardian. The *Atlantic* is ever diminishingly the organ of Beacon Hill; but one feels that its choice of material is always made with half an eye on what the mind of Beacon Hill may say in judgment upon its habits. The editor of *Harper's* has always been able to find protection in the viscous anonymity of New York. He has never been tethered to a post which has limited the range over which he may wander. This is not to say that he wanders far; the magazine keeps mainly to the broad highway of general intellectual traffic. Its sudden excursions into the by-paths of opinion are, as it were, always announced as occasional and irregular picnics about which the reader need not be alarmed. But its central outlook has been consistent with a high standard of information and a genuine receptivity to new ideas. It has, in particular, done a great deal to familiarize the public with that half-known but vital America which is as little realized, and perhaps less understood, in Chicago or Philadelphia or New York, as it is by a foreign visitor who finds in Bloomington, Indiana, or Greensboro, North Carolina, an older but toughly persistent America the influence of which it is fatally easy to underestimate.

The *American Mercury* was in its hey-day in the years from 1920 to 1930, when its pages expressed the vogue of Mr. H. L. Mencken's idiosyncrasies for those who wished to be regarded as sophisticated without the effort it requires to be profound. The *Mercury,* indeed, was less important than significant; it was the organ of a mood which it is worth while to understand. There was in Mencken, as his *American Language* shows, a real scholar, with power of genuinely novel observation. But the Mencken of the *Mercury* was a knock-about clown, sharply cynical, with a slick and pretentious scholarship intended to impress the half-learned; he made irreverence his pretension and sought to sneer his generation out of its respect for past American values partly by violence and partly by the gaiety of his sneers. He was taken at his own valuation of himself by that undergraduate mind which Sinclair Lewis has so skilfully drawn in his portrait of Carol Kennicott in *Main Street*. If there had been anything permanent in Mencken's outlook, he might have lasted beyond the new Gilded Age of the nineteen-twenties. But the real truth is that he had no sense of values. He was a literary exhibitionist, anxious, above all, to be noticed; he was delighted to find that he had only to attack the less literate prejudices of his day—Fundamentalism, Prohibition, Comstockery, the politicians—to equate these with the essence of American democracy and to announce that he belonged to the race of supermen and had gone beyond the last illusion, to persuade many half-literate readers who had yearnings for a wider fulfilment than they could find that he was, in some sort, a combination of Petronius and La Rochefoucauld. He tried to give them the passport to a small, but rich, garden of culture within an America that was beyond hope; and the immense energy with which he paraded his theatrical impudence suggests that he was able without much effort to persuade himself that they were right in being persuaded so to view him.

There are, in fact, two simple proofs of the futility of the *Mercury* as it was shaped to his acrobatics. The first was the very simple one that when, in 1929, crisis came to America, both the *Mercury* and Mencken, its prophet, dropped into an insignificance which showed that he was irrelevant save as a casual entertainer. The other was the fact that the Americana he collected month by month—amusing excerpts from the newspapers of provincial follies—to prove that America was incapable of civilization could be paralleled by the follies he himself was willing to perpetrate in order to be recognized as different. This was shown plainly when he called the Civil War a third-rate war because only two hundred thousand soldiers died in its four years, and when he sneered at Governor Altgeld for "taking the college yells of democracy seriously." It was shown at its lowest level when he denied that the American pioneer had any significance. "What lies beneath the boldness," Mencken wrote, "is not really an independent spirit, but merely a talent for crying with the pack." He suited the age of Coolidge in which, in the aftermath of the disillusion created by the First World War, a restless and dissatisfied generation was prepared to pull down all the idols it had previously worshipped. Mencken persuaded it that the antics of his wholesale cynicism were the last word in modernism. When, with the crash of October 27, 1929, grave problems of a new order had to be faced, it became clear that he had no sort of permanent significance.

It would require a separate and special treatise to attempt to describe the range of the American periodicals, weekly and monthly and quarterly, which compete for the attention of the American public; and I cannot attempt here more than a general judgment upon their value. Some of them in the general field, the *Yale Review,* the *Kenyon Review,* and the *Virginia Quarterly,* for example, have a consistently high level of quality, and, more seldom, articles of quite exceptional distinction. There is also a great mass of "learned" journals which are remarkable in the range of discussion they cover and the permanent value of the new material or the innovating outlook they exhibit. Of these I would like to name two which are relatively newcomers in the field. The first is the *Journal of Negro History,* of which I do not think it is excessive to say that it is slowly but surely altering the whole perspective of our knowledge in its speciality, and has managed, to an exceptional degree, to combine the ability to be scholarly with the power to be of general interest. The other is *Science and Society,* a quarterly journal devoted to the analysis of civilization from a Marxist angle. Like all journals which express a special point of view, it is sometimes narrow and dogmatic and sectarian. But I think it deserves to be said that rarely has any journal gathered in its pages so much genuinely new knowledge in so short a space of time, or so many fresh insights into old themes which seemed unlikely to yield new understanding upon re-examination. It is, moreover, important to note how many of these specialist reviews, of comparatively limited circulation, are "free," in the sense that they offer their readers an outlook and an analysis which have the merit of being the genuine inner convictions of the group which produces them. They are part of the rich variety of American culture which is there waiting for the chance to permeate the national life more intensely, and on a wider scale, than a superficial acquaintance with its louder voices is easily able to perceive. They make their way slowly, and as a rule rather painfully. But they leave the impression that there is in the United States a real possibility of swift advance to high standards of knowledge and of commentary if the chance is given of effective self-expression to the masses of the people. A source of creative leadership is there if its quiet wisdom is not drowned by the "raucous voices" of the mass circulation papers, which have hardly any other objective than to safeguard a dying tradition from that post-mortem examination which would finally free the living generation from a dead past which prevents the fullness of its self-expression.

6

At this point, the temptation to predict the defeat of this creative leadership is profound. How can journals which are read by perhaps half a million people all told hope to compete with the influence of men like Mr. Hearst or Colonel McCormick or, at a somewhat higher level, Mr. Henry Luce? Few journals have a more careful or a more illuminating analysis of the social-economic problems of America than the *Survey Graphic;* if it is liberal in outlook, few of those who share its opponents' view would deny the pains it takes to be scrupulously accurate in its ascertainment of fact and nicely balanced in its judgment. Yet, compared to the mass circulation weeklies, the number of those who are directly influenced by the *Survey* is pitifully small. The major keynote of the press generally has been given its expression by a well-known figure in the American advertising world, Mr. Bruce Barton. "I say, encourage the Interests," he wrote. "Let them go ahead and make more products at lower prices. Let them make profits because that will enable them to pay high taxes and high wages. Let the government stand as an umpire and insist that the game be played fairly." [45]

It is this picture of the American purpose that, in a hundred different ways, the press seeks to drive home to the American public as the ideal at which it ought to aim. There are, of course, important exceptions. The editorial page of the *St. Louis Post-Dispatch* has never attempted to make its readers devotees of the cult of prosperity; and there are perhaps a score of journals with influence which have refused to be taken in by the values born of the passion for material success or the theory that the Big Business man is necessarily a servant of the community. But the ex-

[45] Curti, *The Growth of American Thought,* p. 697, cited from the *Woman's Home Companion,* November 1924, p. 12.

ceptions are small in number and small in influence. The general basis, both of news and comment, is the assumption that success comes to the man who deserves it, and that he deserves it because he combines efficiency with service to the public.

It almost follows from the affirmations which are the inarticulate major premisses, as Holmes would have called them, of the American press that it sees, again with small but always important exceptions, that what is attacked is everything that denies the affirmative stereotype it is sought to impose. There are certain radicals whom one can praise because they are dead, like Thomas Jefferson. But there must always be reservations about Tom Paine and Altgeld and the elder La Follette. Foreign radicals, of course, above all Marx and Lenin, must always appear as obsolete in outlook or wrong-headed, even if the passage of time permits them to be depicted as idealists who lost their way. Contemporary radicals are always dangerous; and among them are always union leaders who have called out their men on strike, or college professors who call into question the "American way of life," or foreigners who draw attention to the contradictions in the American scene. Few strikes are ever justified; and where violence occurs, it must always be attributed, at least until the strike is over, to the baleful influence of the "Reds." It must be assumed that American wealth and American power are envied only by those who have not observed that the well-being of Europe and Asia is a by-product of American expansion. Organizations like the C.I.O. or the American Civil Liberties Union must always be set in a perspective which somehow suggests that they are not quite American. Freedom of speech, when it assumes the right to befriend Russia, or to insist on the "closed shop," or, in the South, to demand a fair deal for the Negro, becomes at once licence. Even an Army Training Manual, in use from 1928 to 1932, told American soldiers that democracy "results in mobocracy. Attitude towards property is communistic, negating property rights. Attitude toward law is that the will of the majority shall regulate, whether it be based upon deliberation, or governed by passion, prejudice and impulse, without restraint or regard for consequences. Results in demagogism, licence, agitation, discontent, anarchy." [46] And this attitude is not a wholly unfair description of the reaction of at least eighty per cent of the American press to militant trade-unionism, socialism, Bryanism in its popular phase, even a considerable part of the very moderately liberal New Deal of which Franklin Roosevelt was the sponsor. It followed, of course, that the men and women who defended these outlooks deserved and received a profound and persistent condemnation. Repetition suitably timed is one of the methods by which the radical is transformed by the press into an enemy of the American public.

I do not suggest that the press has an unchallenged victory. The power of the press to form and lead public opinion depends, in great

[46] *Army Training Manual*, 2000–25 (Washington, 1928), p. 91, cited in George Seldes, *You Can't Do That* (New York: Modern Age, 1938), p. 200.

measure, on the uncertainty of mind to those whom it seeks to direct. A trade-unionist in Oregon who reads that strikes in North Carolina are threatening the well-being of the country sets that claim in the background of an experience which gives it no serious authority. A Negro in New York who reads about "uppity" Negroes in Mississippi in a speech by Senator Bilbo in Washington knows that this curious figure has never been even vaguely interested in a rational discussion of the colour problem. It is, at the lowest, extremely unlikely that the vast majority of teachers are moved by the assertion that this college or that is a factory for turning out "Red" students. The real power of the press comes from the effect of its continuous repetition of an attitude reflected in facts which its readers have no chance to check, or by its ability to surround those facts by an environment of suggestion which, often half-consciously, seeps its way into the mind of the reader and forms his premisses for him without his even being aware that they are really prejudices to which he has scarcely given a moment of thought. When he finds that men whom he greatly respects because they have position, or wealth, or power, share the same prejudices, these tend to assume for him the status of convictions for the safeguard of which he is often prepared to make great sacrifices of time and effort.

A good example of this influence can be seen in the third election of President Roosevelt in 1940. The prospect that he would run as the Democratic candidate for a third time began to emerge during 1938, and was made more vivid by his refusal to state his intentions with any precision. The Republicans were aware that he was the strongest opponent they would have to fight; and they began a long-term campaign to prevent the danger of his candidature. They appealed to history: the traditions of Washington and his immediate successors ought to be regarded as controlling. They hinted strongly that a president who secured a third term would be virtually a dictator. They urged the danger to a democracy of a position in which any man could be regarded as indispensable; to hold office for three terms was, thus, an egoistic assertion of indispensability, since it meant that Mr. Roosevelt thought himself entitled to honours which even General Washington had not sought to claim. They pointed out how immense and dangerous a third-term president's power would be in the realm of patronage; such a president might build up for himself a power that might make him president for life. They insisted that a dangerous precedent would be created the implications of which might bode ill for the whole future of American politics. They urged that, after eight years in office, any president had exhausted his energy and initiative and was entitled to a rest.[47]

What they did not emphasize was that the Washington tradition of two terms only was largely the outcome of the first president's deep dislike of criticism and political opposition, and that had he wanted a third

[47] Charles M. Stein, *The Third-Term Tradition* (New York: Columbia University Press, 1943), is an admirable account of the realities behind the myth.

term, he would have been given it without any serious opposition. They did not explain that almost all presidents, during their second term, have cast about for support for an extension into a third. They either played down, or did not discuss at all, the fact that the Republican party would have been willing, had the circumstances been propitious, to give a third term to Grant; that the major figures in the party machine were anxious to secure for Calvin Coolidge a third term of office, and that, almost certainly, he himself meant those famous words which were interpreted as a refusal to mean that he would be willing to run if he were strongly pressed; nor did they analyse the tortures of philological exegesis by which, in 1912, Theodore Roosevelt justified to himself the view that since McKinley had been elected in 1900, the first part of his presidency could not be regarded, as almost half the Republican party agreed, as a period in which he had functioned of his own right. They did not mention that the strong medical advice of his physicians alone prevented Woodrow Wilson from considering seriously a third term in order to justify and safeguard his part in the making of the Versailles Treaty. And though the opponents of a third term were unsuccessful, they undoubtedly led many who approved of Franklin Roosevelt's policies to vote against him, as they enabled still more who disliked his policies to conceal that dislike by putting their opposition on the ground of a historical tradition the veritable insubstantiality of which was never really made plain to the general public.

Two other examples of the part played by the press in giving the citizens of the United States less than the information to which they were entitled deserve some emphasis. The first is the attempt made by Franklin Roosevelt to reform the Supreme Court of the United States. Whether his particular proposals were wise, or whether the method he adopted of commending them to the American public was skilful, I am not concerned with here. What is important is the way in which the press generally handled his proposals. The Court immediately became a holy institution, the supreme guardian of American well-being. The "nine old men" became sages, the lineal descendants, as it were, of Moses, and Lycurgus, and Solon. The President was trying to "pack" the Court. He was trying, that is to say, to turn an objective and impartial body that was above the heat and stress of the struggles in the marketplace into an obedient instrument of his political purposes. Because, in the honourable performance of its purely judicial function, the Court had declared important parts of the President's programme illegal, he was seeking to make it no more than an annex to the legislature in which he controlled large majorities. He was accused of being a dictator. He was told that he was subverting legal principles to political expediency. Everyone who opposed his plan became, as it were overnight, not only an "impartial" citizen, but a thoughtful person whose views carried weight. President Conant of Harvard University, for example, who was by profession an organic chemist, suddenly became an expert on the politics of the judiciary. Democratic Senator Burton K. Wheeler, a small-town lawyer of no particular juristic distinction, assumed the proportions of a Marshall or a Mansfield when, in the Senate Judiciary Committee's hearings on the bill, he led the opposition to it. Every professor of law who opposed it suddenly became a great jurist. A great blare of press trumpets impressed on public opinion how significant it was that all the major college presidents of New England were united in hostility to the suggested reforms; they did not explain that it was highly improbable that any of these eminent men had given a full day's thought to the issues involved in the conflict. And when, as the outcome of a rather complex intrigue, the then Chief Justice of the United States, Mr. Charles Evans Hughes, was tempted into the arena—it is true on a minor issue—by way of a letter to Senator Wheeler, the press worked up his statistical half-truths into a contrast between the calm of judicial objectivity and the passion of presidential partisanship.

What was interesting in the Court fight was the small number of journals which gave their readers the real perspective of the problem. Most of them were left to suppose that nine was a sacred number in the context of the Supreme Court; few of them were told either of the numerical changes in the past, or the reason for them. Fewer still were told how often the Court had been "packed" before, and how close the connection had always been between presidential purposes and judicial nomination. Hard and bitter experience at any rate had made the officials of the trade-unions and the main body of social reformers only too well aware that, as Mr. Justice Holmes had said, once the Court began to strike down legislation it happened to dislike, there was "no limit but the sky" to the range of its possible interference. A wholly false distinction was drawn between the categories of judicial action and political action; and endless effort was expended to persuade the public that a quasi-mythical entity, "the Court"—which might mean six justices against three, or even five against four—had come to purely legal conclusions in an atmosphere of imperturbable calm into which political considerations could not enter. There was no discussion of the famous calm of Mr. Justice McReynolds, for example, in his opinions during the New Deal period;[48] there was no explanation of that lyrical enthusiasm for a *laissez-faire* society which was the keynote of most of the decisions of judges like Field and Brewer and Harlan[49] in the last third of the nineteenth century. That politics had coloured the approach of chief justices like Marshall and Taney was never suggested. The public was, so far as possible, given the impression that the President was seeking to change a tribunal, into the mind of which political values were never permitted entrance, into a subordinate arm of the executive power. Yet the evidence, for well over a century, has gone to the massive proof that

---

[48] *Perry v. United States,* 294 U.S. 330 (1935).
[49] *Cf.* their notices in the *Dictionary of American Biography.*

the judges were, in fact, hardly less ardent defenders of the Interests on the Bench than they had been when at the Bar.[50]

My point is the very simple one that most of the press watched with joy the effort of the Court to hamstring the New Deal; and when President Roosevelt sought the means of overcoming its opposition, it was rare, indeed, for the papers hostile to him even to attempt to give their readers a balanced statement of the issue. If it be said that this was a complex problem which could not be explained simply to the uninitiated, there are plenty of other instances to prove that the public is allowed to know only what newspaper proprietors think it good for them to know. Mr. George Seldes has shown how the *New York Herald Tribune* failed even to report a strike of the workers in five cities against the National Biscuit Company for deliberately breaking its contract with the union because its owner had large investments in that corporation.[51] Many of the newspapers have fought the Child Labour amendment on the ground that it was an attempt at "sovietizing American youth"; they did not tell their readers that a report of the Children's Bureau of the Department of Labor showed that, on the average, "unsovietized" American youth earned in 1934 eighty-two cents for eighteen hours each week selling newspapers.[52] Nor did the press even attempt to tell the truth about the fight of Mr. Rexford Tugwell, as Assistant Secretary of the Department of Agriculture, against the gross and deliberate frauds practised on the public by the vendors of patent medicines. The advertisements they gave to the newspapers may well have reached the astonishing figure of four hundred million dollars a year; this was sufficient to line up nearly all the press against the Tugwell bill. Nor is this all. I have already noted that when the Federal Trade Commission has used its powers to order some drug company to cease from claiming for its product a quality it does not possess, the press, with a few honourable exceptions, has either wholly refrained from publishing the order—though publication is privileged—or hidden it away in some obscure corner of the paper where it is unlikely to be seen. When it is realized that this concealment assists in the continued sale of products which falsely claim to cure headaches, or constipation, or baldness, or eczema, to take but a few examples, it becomes obvious how dangerous is the result of this conspiracy of silence. Since the passage of the Pure Food and Drugs Act of 1906—the Harrison Law—more than twenty-two thousand orders have been issued against manufacturers in this field. Most of them remain unknown to the public because the press would not risk the loss of so rich a source of advertising revenue by giving them publicity.[53]

---

[50] *Cf.* the remarks of Mr. Justice Miller in Charles Fairman, *Mr. Justice Miller and the Supreme Court, 1862–1890* (Cambridge: Harvard University Press, 1939), pp. 373 ff.
[51] Seldes, *op. cit.,* pp. 86–87.
[52] *Ibid.,* p. 90.
[53] *Ibid.,* pp. 90 f.

The press of the Pacific coast, and the Hearst newspapers in particular, has a heavy responsibility for the maltreatment there of Japanese, even when these are American citizens, and of Mexicans. For years before the Second World War, papers like those owned by Mr. Harry Chandler and Mr. Hearst urged the invasion of Mexico—a course which would enormously add to their economic power. To this end, there has been no device they have not used to paint the Mexican, both in Mexico and as an immigrant labourer in America, as violent, ignorant, lazy, shiftless, and dirty. Their procedure has had the effect of stirring up racial hatred against him, of creating the impression that he is a menace who must at all costs be controlled. And hostility to the Japanese has gone so far that not even the exemplary courage of the American-born Japanese who fought in the armies of the United States has overcome the prejudice created against their return from the internment areas to the areas and businesses they owned in the Pacific states. Many of them, or their parents, have suffered disastrous losses by having to abandon the work of a lifetime, or by having to sell their possessions at a fraction of their real value. And it is rare for the press to make clear how both the police and the American Legion are used by Big Business to attack labour until the purpose of the attack has been fulfilled. That can be seen by anyone who examines the grim history of terrorism in Centralia, Washington, on November 11, 1919; and the earlier record, which is one of lawlessness deliberately organized by the lumber millionaires of the Northwest to prevent the unions from securing a rise in wages, shows the American Legion as a body of organized strikebreakers, using violence as their main weapon, and certain of a pretty effective press silence until the point is reached where its behaviour is too public a scandal to be concealed any longer. But by that time, as a rule, the employers have had their way. The *Chicago Tribune* has not hesitated to support the police force of that city even when it has known that the police were in fact, as in the Republic Steel strike, deliberately acting as agents of employers whose policy was to prevent the enforcement of federal statutes.

It has been said by a New York newspaper, the *Evening Post,* that eighty per cent of the press are anxious to distort any news which touches the origins of violence in labour disputes. It is usual to blame some mysterious people called the "Reds"; there is always a note on the forbearance of the police under provocation; and no one who examines the two volumes of the Wickersham *Report on Law Observance and Enforcement,*[54] and then compares the findings with the contemporary accounts in the press, can doubt that the purpose of the latter is to support, even to encourage, the police in taking the law into their own hands. Indeed, the ease with which the press generally reports without hostility incite-

[54] George W. Wickersham, *Report on Law Observance and Enforcement* (Washington: G.P.O., 1930–31). See also the testimony of Ernest Jerome Hopkins, an investigator for the National Commission on Law Observance and Enforcement, *Our Lawless Police* (New York: Viking Press, 1931).

ment to violence, or the actual use of it, in support of the principles which Big Business happens to approve, is a disquieting fact in its habits. It must be remembered that what matters in this realm is not merely what the big metropolitan newspapers say, but the outlook of the hundreds of small-town journals which are, only too often, the major opinion-forming agencies in their localities. They may praise the lawless violence of vigilantes in parts of California and Arkansas; even a New England trade journal can write of the strikes in the cotton mills of the South during 1929–31 that "a few hundred funerals will have a quieting influence." [55] There are some millions of workers in the South whose conditions are hardly removed from peonage; but with, perhaps, a dozen honourable exceptions, the main attitude of its press to any attempt at escape from peonage is one of gratitude to the mill-owners for having brought their industry to the South, and of praise for the vigilantes who make unionization impossible and for sheriffs who turn a blind eye to their campaign of terrorism against underprivileged groups like the sharecroppers. In a less degree, the alien, especially the alien of "liberal" views, the coloured man, and the devotee of freedom, have little chance of receiving from most American journals the kind of approach to fair treatment which is granted to a big employer or an ardent reactionary, even, before 1939, to a man like Mussolini, or to a distinguished man of science who is disturbed at the "materialism" of our age.

Anyone who surveys the American journalistic scene from that important day, August 19, 1896, when the thirty-eight-year-old owner of the *Chattanooga Times,* Mr. Adolph S. Ochs, took over the proprietorship of the *New York Times,* can see both loss and gain. There is far better reporting from a far wider area of news. The special correspondent is able to give a much more intimate and inside view of the way in which history is made. There is probably a good deal less of the wild and directly personal invective which often disfigured even the most influential papers of the earlier period; few modern editors, would, like Charles A. Dana, expect either to be horsewhipped by an indignant reader or to publish the fact as a piece of news. There is much more specialist information, clarified by writers who are expert in their particular themes. There is, generally, a much more sober effort to assess the situation in the editorial columns than was the case fifty years ago. There has been a decline in the devotion to half-eccentric causes, such as that of Horace Greeley in his crusade, a century ago, for Albert Brisbane's adolescent support of Charles Fourier's phalangism. As a whole, American journalism is more staid, less adventurous, and less personal, more careful in checking its facts, more intelligent in its grasp of international relations, and, in the more responsible papers, more aware that public issues cannot be depicted in simple terms of black and white, or of unbreakable at-

---

[55] Quoted from the New England trade journal *Fibre and Fabric,* in *Sharecroppers All* (Chapel Hill: University of North Carolina Press, 1941) by Arthur F. Raper and Ira De A. Reid, p. 173.

tachment to a party cause, than were the journals which described the assault of William Jennings Bryan on the power of Wall Street in the days when Mark Hanna was the uncrowned despot of the Republican party.

That does not mean for one moment that the changes have all been advantageous. "I see in the near future a crisis approaching that unnerves me," wrote Abraham Lincoln, "and causes me to tremble for the safety of my country. . . . Corporations have been enthroned, an era of corruption in high places will follow, and the money power of the country will endeavour to prolong its reign by working upon the prejudices of the people until the wealth is aggregated in a few hands, and the republic is destroyed." [56] With that simple directness of insight that is characteristic of genius, Lincoln had a prophetic vision of the dangers the last half-century has revealed. Much of the individuality of the press has gone; it has become, effectively, a branch of giant industry, closely co-operating with, because largely dependent upon, its advertisers. Its general principle is the defence of the *status quo*. It is hostile to anything, at home or abroad, which disturbs the self-confidence of business men. It rarely equates success with social vision, and it is disturbed by social experiment. It conceals the dishonesty of the wealthy, or postpones the full revelation of that dishonesty for as long as it is possible; but it is relentless and swift in its denunciation of labour leaders and their supporters who think in terms outside the static pattern which business men approve.

There are important deficiencies in its attitude to international affairs. If the European press generally errs in the fantastic inadequacy of the information it offers upon foreign countries, the American press suffers from two defects proportionately not less important. The first is its quest for the dramatic, and the second is the degree to which its reporting is adapted to the sensitiveness of special groups for whose hostility or criticism it is excessively concerned. A curious example of the first was the illimitable curiosity it displayed over the marriage of the Duke of Windsor to Mrs. Simpson; the second is exemplified in its fear of offending Roman Catholics, which makes any forthright criticism of Vatican policy one of the rarest of its features. Editorially, except during the tense years from 1941–45, it has never really sought to probe, much less to understand, the policies of Soviet Russia. Few of the newspapers have ever had a long-term foreign policy, and too many of them have, though in a lesser degree, reflected the ignorant prejudices of men like McCormick and Hearst. While it is true, as I have said earlier in this chapter, that the American journalists in foreign capitals are a corps of observers unsurpassed in quality, the editorial attempt to drive home the meaning of their dispatches has been very incomplete. There is too much emphasis on simple slogans—power politics, or British imperialism, or the Open Door in China—which are used to evade the necessity of thought. Too often,

[56] P. Stern, *Life and Writings of Lincoln*.

also, the approach to foreign affairs is moralistic, with the government of the United States featured as a disinterested knight in shining armour who has no objective save the just solution. And too often, once more, the undercurrent of all comment on foreign affairs is built upon a hardly concealed conviction that the duty of other nations is to attain, as the economist T. N. Carver had no doubt that America was seeking, "the Kingdom of Heaven and righteousness." [57] It was by no means a lone view when one of the mass-circulation weeklies triumphantly proclaimed that "there is only one first-class civilization in the world today. It is right here in the United States." [58]

Nor is any assessment of the American press complete without some emphasis upon its effort to draw attention away from reality by a massive journalism of escape in which an ounce of fact is mingled with a ton of excitement and success dreams. Sex, crime, adventure, sport, mysticism, the proof that the old Puritan virtues of self-reliance and energy and thrift are, in the context of religious faith, the highroad to well-being and prosperity—these have been formulæ of major importance to the press in safeguarding the public from an interest in the experimental mind. For every article which praised the effort of the New Deal to speed the difficult task of recovery, there must have been at least a score which attacked it as a threat to true Americanism, and fifty which sought to prove that the socialist experiment in Russia was a vital index to the collapse of civilization. Nor has this outlook been confined to the press with a mass circulation; in their more sophisticated way, the historic monthlies, like the *Atlantic,* have found room for a similar outlook. With millions of unemployed, *Harper's* has urged upon its readers that the age of the "economic man" has passed; that technological possibilities now leave nothing but the problem of distribution to be solved. The thesis that the search for social security is the proof of social decadence is preached in every sort of journal, by millionaires and college presidents and economists. There has been an enthusiastic reception for the notion that the real problem in the United States centres round the moral principles of the individual, and not upon the economic behaviour of the business system.

That is why, in general, bigness is still equated with grandeur, why the volume of productive capacity is still confused with the amount of individual happiness. The contented man, General Wood of Sears Roebuck, Mr. Henry Kaiser, who broke into the news by a successful gift for shipbuilding, President Conant of Harvard University, who thinks that the Report of his Committee on Education in a Free Society has solved the problem of making American citizens fit for democracy when it urges men to co-operate for action even if their philosophies are widely different [59]—these are the types whose proclamations arouse

---

[57] Carver, *The Present Economic Revolution in the United States,* p. 65.
[58] Curti, *op. cit.,* p. 688, cited from an editorial in the *Ladies' Home Journal.*
[59] *Annual Report, 1945–46,* of the President of Harvard University (Cambridge: Harvard University Press, 1946).

the press to enthusiasm. The vital basis of it all seems to be an effort to prevent the ordinary American from confronting the dangers involved in the general dislocation of our civilized life. There is approval for all social adventure on the traditional lines; there is fear of experiment where it departs from those traditions. Little effort is made to reveal how deep must be the crisis in our civilization when it results in two world wars within a generation. The attempt to bridge the gap between social thought and technological necessity is frowned upon as a dangerous threat to existing interests. The American press is anxious to persuade its public that there is the chance of entering an epoch in which quite fundamental readjustments are called for with the institutions and ideas which were suited to the civilization of the early nineteen-hundreds. It seeks to prepare for the "American Century," during which the influence of the United States is bound to enter the lives and thoughts of people everywhere, with the mental pattern in which, forty years ago, Theodore Roosevelt found such intense excitement. Like him, it is compelled to be adult while being too often uncertain how to become mature. The press is always emphatic; it does not always know about what to be emphatic. It gives the impression of always being in a hurry, without having really decided upon the direction of its journey. It is full of advice and enthusiasm and warning without ever being sufficiently aware that the condition which would make its outlook impressive depends upon the responsibility which accompanies its expression. It gives the world the impression that it is full of, and overwhelmed by, its obligations, without having given to either any scheme of priorities in value. Its one fixed determination is its insistence that the new realities must somehow square with the old pattern.

It is, I think, this attempt to adjust life as process to institutions as static which is the real weakness of the American press in its effort to domesticate the United States in a civilization so rapidly changing as ours. That is why I suggest that its examination gives the impression of confusion rather than clarity, of incantation rather than of diagnosis, of reliance upon slogans rather than upon philosophy. I am not sure that it is not legitimate to argue that a good deal of the noise and clamour with which the press assails its readers, both at home and abroad, is due to a lack of inner self-confidence. The adventure of explanation in so chaotic a universe implies responsibilities that are evaded and principles that, so far from having been found, have not yet begun to be sought. Something remains of the old American faith in "manifest destiny"; but no one is quite sure of what the destiny is or in what direction it may be fulfilled. The one thing about which the press is certain is the danger of the sceptical mind. It is sure that the right answers are here in the possession of its citizens; it is troubled by the growth in numbers of those who question the answers they receive. It is like a traveller who surveys a new territory with a map constructed on data that are inadequate or obsolete; he grows angry with those of his companions who suspect that he has missed the way. It is this anger which makes it so difficult for the press to give Americans the kind of intellectual leadership they desire. The interests it serves are too widely separated from the implications of its future for it to be able, with a full mind and a full heart, to go forward with a sure step in the resolute conviction that it is on the right road. It does not dare to face the ultimate problems of America with a public measurement of their proportions. It is facing the future in a mood of doubt and fear; and it communicates those emotions to the audience it is anxious to convince that its prophecies and counsels are true. That is why it is read more for its news than its comments. That is why, also, often without knowing it, it is really following those whom it pretends to lead.

7

EVERYONE knows the enormous place the cinema has come to fill in the life of the international community. Scores of millions of people visit the "movies" each week. The films probably do more than any other medium to acquaint one people with the life of another. The leading film stars are more widely known than anyone in the world save three or four leading statesmen; and it was perhaps only during the years of war that this handful of politicians could hope to compete in interest with some score of the well-established favourites of the screen. Their lives are lived in a blaze of unending publicity. Their houses, their husbands or wives, their clothes, their interests, the books they read—when they read a book—their hobbies, what they do on holiday, all these are retailed in minute detail to an audience which seems to have an endless appetite for any scrap of information vouchsafed to it on these themes. In 1921, when Mr. Charles Chaplin revisited London for the first time since he had become a world-famous star, it was almost impossible to control the vast crowds which greeted him at the railway station. When Miss Mitchell's *Gone with the Wind* was about to be filmed, the choice of the actress who should play its principal part began to look as though it might assume the proportions of an international incident. Books that have been classics for a century and more become known to millions of new readers not in their own right, but because a film has been based upon them; and they may even be reissued by enterprising publishers with a special wrapper explaining to a public which knows the name of the actor or actress who took the principal part that this is "the book of the film." It is not, indeed, an exaggeration to say that far more people are aware of the chief artist in the filmed book than were ever aware of the writer to whom the story was due. Nothing, in fact, makes so universal an appeal as the films except a few types of sport; and the appeal begins in the school room and, for most, is still wholly unexhausted in old age. The president of the United States knows that he can make a dinner-party a success by showing privately a new film before it is open to the public instead of depending upon the hazardous enterprise of conversation with his guests. The modern passenger-boat is always equipped with the apparatus for showing films, as are some of the long-distance trains; and a beginning, at least, has been made in the use of the cinema on aeroplanes to break the monotony of long hours in the air. During the Second World War few methods were more successful than free film shows, undertaken at government cost, to persuade evacuees from places in danger of being bombed to refrain from returning to their homes. I doubt whether even the motorcar has effected so striking a change in the habits of using leisure as has the cinema in the last generation.

Everyone knows that Hollywood is the capital city of the film industry and that, though ardent efforts have been made to challenge its preeminence in its economic aspect, no rival so far has even come near to the hope of success. Russia, France, Great Britain, Weimar-Germany, have swept the world with occasional films they have produced. There is good authority for the view that the level of the documentary and educational films in Great Britain surpasses a good deal the level that Hollywood has attained. Many of the most famous stars, perhaps half of the most famous producers, are of non-American origin. Yet, despite every effort to overcome the predominance of Hollywood, an effort which includes legislation, for example, the British Act of Parliament compelling every cinema in Britain to show a quota of British films, the mastery of Hollywood remains virtually complete. Every so often it is announced that plans are under way to rival its power. Millionaires in Europe, the government in Soviet Russia, have entered the field in the belief that, with a world audience at their disposal, they could break the Hollywood spell. They have never come even within sight of success. The Russians, despite superb achievements like *Potemkin* and *Three Songs for Lenin,* have never been able to do much more than attract audiences already deeply interested in the Revolution and its historic environment, or technicians who have realized that in the handling of great mass effects Russian producers have no superior. Where the British film has been intended for a universal audience, it has had to be outstandingly exceptional to hold its own with American productions. Nor is there any serious evidence to suggest that Hollywood is likely to lose its predominance in the foreseeable future. A shattered Europe is unlikely to put the development of a great film industry high on the list of priorities for capital investment; and there is no part of Asia which has even approached the stage where this form of large-scale enterprise can seriously be contemplated. Climatic conditions, moreover, give Hollywood an advantage which is of real importance.

Hollywood has a history into the details of which I cannot here enter. Nothing quite compares with it except the record of some place where gold has been suddenly discovered. Reputations are made and lost with astonishing speed. A few people make fabulous fortunes. Round the public mask of the famous star there is gathered a veritable army of specialists—script writers, directors, producers, make-up men, camera men, lighting technicians, experts in "fake" effects, and a score of others, be-

side the great army of actors and actresses to whom a couple of days in
the week as walkers-on may make all the difference between starvation
and that poverty which is just bearable because it still contains some
faint ray of hope. There is, indeed, an inescapable sense in the visitor to
Hollywood that it is a mixture, in ever-changing proportions, of Big
Business, an artists' colony, a system of imitation palaces, a slum, an
endless series of restaurants, and a lunatic asylum. One meets there
strange people, strange professions, strange religions, fantastic ideas,
and incredible finance. It lures the great novelist, the great dramatist, the
great musician, and the great specialist in the theatre. But it lures also
an unending army of small-town youth, male and female, who stake their
whole future on the conviction that personal appearance, the ability to
dance well, some trick of voice, even some idiosyncrasy like extreme fat-
ness, or skill in riding, or the power to skate well, is the high road to fortune. The glory of the successful star surpasses anything the great statesman or the great soldier or sailor can hope to know except in the first
brief, dizzy hours of success. No modern monarch commands a devotion
so absolute as the important director who is about to make a film and
is rumoured to be still uncertain about his choice of persons for the principal roles. And since it is a world even more inexplicable than the theatre in its moods, the unexpected and the unpredictable happen every day.
A casual pose of a girl in a restaurant may so impress one of the rulers
of this fantastic republic that she may become a household name if she
screens well and is adept in accepting the orders of her producer. A
chance word about a novel in the ear of some magnate who is looking
for a new subject may make a fortune for an author whose life, up to
then, has been passed in wondering whether he could get an advance
royalty from his publisher. One can see in the same restaurant the fulfilment in the star and the failure in the waitress who supplies her wants.
It is a world in which the artificial has become the natural, and in which
most of the normal standards of daily life have ceased to have any meaning. If the visitor can abstract himself for an hour to watch the unfolding
panorama of Hollywood life, it is itself one vast film which epitomizes a
whole world. Nothing that mankind can experience is absent from Hollywood in some shape or form; and, a small number of technicians apart,
nothing is ever experienced there with any profundity except upon the
plane of the emotions. It is full of romance and comedy and tragedy, of
big-heartedness and mean-heartedness, of fantastic success and unintelligible failure. It is a place where most people who have work, work quite
incredibly hard; where, also, most people who have no work, work even
harder in the effort to find it. All its imagination is compounded with
folly, and all its intelligence is permeated by stupidity.

Hollywood is a mass of unfathomable contradictions, where men who
know nothing of anything act upon the assumption of their omniscience.
It is a world where ignorance does not matter, and where time and space
may have no meaning. It is also a world where, without warning, some

specialist knowledge may be fabulously rewarded only to remain unused after it has been called for. If William James was right in esteeming highly the habit of breaking habits, Hollywood would have entranced him, since the basis of its life seems to be the principle that no one should have any habits at all. Yet in its amazing rise to influence certain facts emerge of which the bearing is unmistakable. It is, first of all, a branch of Big Business. It employs more than three hundred thousand people, and the greater part of these are now employed—though only after a long struggle [60]—under conditions settled by collective bargaining between employers and trade-unions. A capital of well over two billion dollars is employed in making over five hundred films every year. There are over twenty thousand cinemas in the United States, with accommodation for some twelve million people; and it is estimated that more than one hundred million persons go every week to the films.[61] And while it is, no doubt, true that the main purpose of the cinema is to entertain, it is also true that few influences in American life are indirectly more important in shaping people's attitudes and behaviour. It is not only that the stars become heroes and heroines to hundreds of thousands of people, and that, as such, their habits, their clothes, their tastes, their opinions, deeply affect the public mind. It is also because the subjects filmed, the events selected for the screen in news-reels, the manner, further, of their presentation, are all subtly, often unconsciously, affecting public opinion. And the use of films for advertising, as well as for educational and religious purposes, grows by leaps and bounds. They played an immensely important part in the training of the Armed Forces in the Second World War. They are coming to be an increasingly significant factor in political elections; the moving-picture van, equipped with a loud-speaker, is likely to be a vital means of "selling" the personalities of candidates in a campaign. It has become, in fact, impossible to doubt that the range of influence of the industry as an element in shaping behaviour is likely to be ever wider as the years go by.

The major objective of the film industry is, of course, profit; that is why the film made for entertainment is the outstanding feature in its life. But even in the non-entertainment side of the industry, it must be realized that a high proportion of the films made aim at "selling" an idea rather than at making an objective presentation of its subject matter. Propaganda, in the sense of persuading an audience to accept some values and to reject others, is implicit in most of the films that are made. It is, no doubt, true that a limit to propagandist emphasis is set by the necessity of respecting important *mores* of the community which it would be dangerous to offend. That is why the industry appointed Mr. Will Hays, who had been President Harding's postmaster-general, as the supreme

[60] Murray Ross, *Stars and Strikes* (New York: Columbia University Press, 1941).

[61] Malcolm M. Willey and Stuart A. Rice, "The Agencies of Communication," *Recent Social Trends*, p. 208. The figures represent admissions rather than persons since many people go more than once in each week.

internal censor of what is and what is not permissible in a film; and it explains why Mr. Eric Johnston, who had been president of the United States Chamber of Commerce, and a widely discussed candidate for the presidency of the United States, was chosen to succeed him. There are limitations upon what may be shown or said about sex and religion and crime; a powerful committee of Roman Catholics, for example, watches the treatment, directly and indirectly, of its Church, so that the film treatment of a novel like Mr. Hemingway's *For Whom the Bell Tolls* must be adapted to the service of the committee's scruples before it is shown to the public. There is also a careful relation between the films and the climate of public opinion. A film like *Mr. Smith Goes to Washington,* in which the brave but naïve young reformer triumphs over the vested interests of corruption in the legislature, could be made in the Roosevelt epoch, but would hardly have been thought of in the age of Coolidge. Mr. Orson Welles can attack a wealthy newspaper magnate when it is pretty universally accepted that his influence is thoroughly evil; again, it is doubtful whether he could have embarked upon so bold a criticism ten years earlier. In an era of depression Mr. Steinbeck's famous *Grapes of Wrath* is widely acceptable; it would have remained unfilmed in an era of prosperity. If, as Mr. Dooley said in an historic aphorism, the Supreme Court follows the election returns, the magnates of the film industry accept current values as the basis of their activities as much as they seek to shape them. From 1941 to 1945, for example, Soviet Russia was treated with a goodwill that it had never previously received both in newsreels and in entertainment films; and its future treatment, as also the character assigned to Russians in films generally, will depend almost entirely upon the course of Russo-American relations. If these go smoothly and well, the Russian has a good chance of being the hero on the screen; but if they go badly, it is pretty certain that he will be assigned the villain's role.

Very careful estimates have been made of the content of films, and the outcome is very revealing.[62] In 1930—and there has yet been no effective change—out of a careful sample of five hundred films produced, twenty-seven per cent dealt with crime, fifteen per cent with sex, and twenty-nine per cent with love, as their principal themes; only comedy, with sixteen per cent, approached those figures. There was less than five per cent about war, less than two per cent about history, and no film that investigation could describe as "social propaganda." [63] This is to say, that in 1930, seventy-one per cent of the films produced dealt with crime or sex or love; and it is notable that this represents an important increase over the figures of 1920. It is interesting, also, to note that the locale of the films was, in over fifty per cent of those shown, wholly American, and over half of these were set in New York or a similar large American city; while the scene was placed in the

[62] Edgar Dale, *The Content of Motion Pictures* (New York: Macmillan, 1935).
[63] *Ibid.*, p. 17.

eastern states of America more than twice the number of times that it was placed in a foreign country, and almost twice as often as in other parts of the United States.[64] If the interior setting of a film is considered, forty-three per cent of films had a bedroom scene; and it is significant of much that where the setting of a film is in a library, those examined by Mr. Dale gave no example of any character reading a book.[65]

An index of real importance to what the films are doing is shown in the type of house in which the characters reside. Mr. Dale, in his admirable survey, rates these as twenty-two per cent ultra wealthy, forty-seven per cent wealthy, twenty-five per cent moderate, and four per cent poor; he leaves one per cent indeterminate.[66] Out of eight hundred and eleven leading characters in one hundred and fifteen films, thirty-three per cent of the heroes, and forty-four per cent of the heroines are wealthy, while forty-four per cent of the heroes are of moderate economic status and eleven per cent are poor; the corresponding percentages for heroines are forty-four and thirteen respectively. The villain male is wealthy in fifty-four per cent of cases, and poor in four per cent; the villain female is wealthy in sixty-three per cent, and poor in five per cent.[67] Not less significant is the occupation followed by the chief characters in the sample of films surveyed. It is rare for any of the leading characters to belong to the working class; they are professional people and their wives, industrialists, members of the Armed Forces, wealthy people generally, not seldom "society" people with nothing to do but kill time. The Mexican, the Negro, and the Chinese are rarely shown in a favourable light; even the Frenchmen and Frenchwomen on the screen are either comic or unattractive. Nor is it unimportant to note the close, but indirect, connection between the film and the clothing industry; there is a real effort to make the women who go to the movies think of what they see in terms of planning to spend.[68]

There are two other elements in the cinema which deserve a special emphasis. While the main ambition of the chief characters is success in love, it is closely followed by financial success in some form or another; but revenge or rivalry, whether in love or business, are also very frequent. Even when the idea of fulfilling some social obligation is the major theme of a film, it appears to be stressed as an individual fulfilment in which what is important is not the outcome for the community, but the outcome for the hero or villain of the piece. The overwhelming major theme is the principle of individualism—the idea that everyone works for his own advantage and that "success" means attaining this result. The successful lover, the man who wins his way to wealth, the girl who makes a successful marriage, the detective who "gets" his man, these are the ideas round which the industry builds the stories it translates into pictures.

[64] Ibid., p. 27.
[65] Ibid., p. 37.
[66] Ibid., p. 39.
[67] Ibid., p. 47.
[68] Ibid., Chap. V.

The man who builds up a successful business has a good chance of being the hero of a film; there would be no such chance for making a hero out of a man who built up a successful trade-union. An occasional scientist, like Pasteur, may win the approval of Hollywood as a subject; but little or nothing emerges in the film story of what science and its methods are, still less of what fundamental research means; the Pasteur of the film is the combination of a success story with a background which leaves the impression that scientific experiment is rather like a "flutter" on the stock exchange by an honest and simple-minded person who is warmly congratulated by his friends for having hit on an investment which turns out well. Most films which are built round scientists show that the producers still think of scientists as men who, with a white coat and some complicated apparatus, hit upon a miracle unexpectedly. There is no sense of the long chain of history out of which discovery emerges, and still less sense of science as a social factor in the life of a community in which there are no international boundaries and no achievement which is not a link in an endless chain of investigation.

The other theme of importance is the content of the news-reels. Here the film-makers seek to give the audience a glimpse of some passing event. There is little that it will not include. It may be the President launching a new battleship. It may be a fashion show. It may be a brief scene from a football match. It varies in content from an eruption of Mount Vesuvius to a brief interview with a visiting statesman as he steps out of his plane at Washington, from a few moments showing the arrival of a group of G.I. brides in New York to the inauguration of the new head of a well-known university. What is outstanding is the emphasis given in the subjects treated by the news-reels, first, to sport—which over any considerable period comes easily first in frequency—and, second, to those aspects of international relations connected with the making of war. There is an occasional glimpse of the movement towards peace, as when Mr. Arthur Henderson was shown at the inaugural session of the Disarmament Conference at Geneva in the thirties. There is attention given to economic conditions, though it is usual in these not only to describe strikers as "a mob," but also to portray the police in a strike as zealous only for peace and order; it is rare indeed for the labour side of a news-reel to be presented fairly. What is most characteristic of the contemporary events recorded on the screen is the overwhelming triviality of the material chosen for presentation. Less obvious is the thread of propaganda which results either from the frequency of items which are, in fact, a half-hidden eulogy of the existing order, or from emphasis upon the undesirable nature of men or ideas which, explicitly or implicitly, criticize it. A convention of the Chambers of Commerce will be featured, with perhaps a few lines from the presidential speech on the satisfactory economic conditions of America; but the conferences of the National Association for the Advancement of Colored People will go unnoticed. Mr. Andrew W. Mellon will get favourable publicity; Mr. Sidney Hillman, will, at best, be treated neutrally, and at a critical time may well appear as a menace to the political independence of working-class voters. A mayor in some town where there is a strike may be seen and heard pleading for peace; but no labour leader will be given the chance to explain on a newsreel why the strike has occurred. And it is far from infrequent to put in the picture of some radical figure in a situation which creates—and is intended to create—emotions of anger or ridicule against him; while the commentary of the announcer is built upon the assumption that those who suggest that all is not well with the United States are in general hostile to its well-being.

8

It is probable that the film is one of the two or three outstanding instruments which shape the habits of mind and thought of the average American, and especially of the younger generation. What are the uses to which the owners of this instrument put their power? The answer, obviously, is to make a profitable return upon their capital investment. To achieve this end they operate upon certain assumptions the validity of which they infer from the revenue earned by films of different types; and this view is confirmed by the speed with which a successful film in some particular *genre* is followed by others upon the same theme, if with slight differences, made by competing companies.

The first assumption is that the overwhelming proportion of the vast cinema audience desires to escape from the drab reality of life into a make-believe world where it can identify its own longings with their fulfilment in the hero or the heroine of the film. That is why sex and romantic love are the main themes upon which endless variations are played. That is why, also, the lives depicted are usually those of people at least in comfortable, and usually in wealthy, economic surroundings. That is why, again, the hero so frequently becomes wealthy after the manner of an Horatio Alger story, and the heroine either advances through love from poverty to wealth, or, if she begins by being wealthy, by her skill in knowing the true gold of virtue from the false glitter of vice. These themes admit the means whereby the producers can surround their stars with an atmosphere of glamour; they live in "wealthy" houses, they are surrounded by servants, they use the best automobiles, their "home life" is a constant round of luxurious pleasure. Ugliness is associated with poverty; and as it is rare for poverty to be the outcome of conditions from which the individual cannot escape, the persistence of ugliness tends to be emphasized as the consequence of individual fault. Large numbers of other films may be devoted to crime, to melodrama, to pure entertainment, as where the skill of a brilliant dancer, or the voice of a popular singer, is made the basis of some kind of story which permits his fullest exploitation. So, in wartime, the film evokes the simple emotions—admiration for the heroes who are fighting our war by recording some special act of courage, for example, the man who ferrets out enemy secrets at the risk of his life, or the brilliant woman spy who deceives the most cunning Nazi agents; or it evokes hatred for the enemy, as in any film depicting Germans or Japanese. There the German general is always the stern and unbending Prussian, the Nazi spy is always hard and treacherous, the Japanese always inscrutable and snakelike. The unhappy ending is rare; the audience must leave the cinema with their yearning for fulfilment almost lusciously, if vicariously, satisfied. They must enter a world in which, for two or three enchanted hours, they are drawn out of themselves and feel that their dreams come true.

The second major assumption of the producers is that the "American way of life" is in itself sound and objectively indisputable. Where, therefore, it goes wrong, it is not the fault of the system, but of some evil man or men who fail to observe its rules. It may be an ambitious and corrupt politician; it may be a dishonest millionaire; it may be an envious and dangerous "Red" who is trying to destroy peace and order, usually by leading simple and honest workers astray to feather his own nest. If in the rare cases where a politician is made the hero he is "successful," that usually means that he either breaks a corrupt "boss" and his machine, or secures the passage of some mild social reform which a few corrupt opponents seek to prevent from passing into law. All the commercial conventions of the capitalist system are respected; the poor are always permitted to hope without ever being told upon what their right to hope is based. All the ecclesiastical conventions are always respected; no Church is ever shown as the enemy of social progress, of science, or of tolerance. Only very rarely are issues like the prejudices against Jews or Negroes confronted; and the status of the Negro as the "natural" underdog is emphasized by casting Negro actors and actresses for roles which indicate their inevitable subordination. There is even a clear thread of nationalism, wherever the foreigner and the American are cast for opposite roles in the same film; there, in a general way, the American is simple, energetic, straightforward; the foreigner is usually complex, lazy, and devious in purpose, the alternative being his appearance as a comic figure who expects to have his living earned for him. Most American history on the screen, moreover, seems to search for means of satisfying the standards devised by the Daughters of the American Revolution, while foreign history, especially European, is filmed at an intellectual level below that of the boy or girl in an American high school. No one who saw Mr. George Arliss in *Alexander Hamilton,* for example, would have any idea why there was a Federal Convention or what it was about; just as no one who saw *Gone with the Wind* would have any serious conception of the causes and consequences of the Civil War.

I do not mean to suggest that there are not serious films, some of them films of genius. Mr. Chaplin, for example, in *Modern Times* succeeded, as only he can succeed, in combining high comedy with a brilliant commentary on the industrial system. And it is undoubtedly the fact that the film industry will make a film in which ideas and art are fused into an impressive unity when it believes that the combination will capture the box-office. But this is not its usual assumption. In general, the industry is afraid of all established institutions, afraid of social experiment, afraid of criticism of the contemporary *mores* of America. It is for the capitalist against organized labour, though it is careful not to be hostile to the industrious and individual workingman. It rarely suggests the importance of social change; or if it does, desirable social change is never much more than private benevolence would seek to effect. Its main social principles seem to be that one must, at all costs, be successful in love, and that the individual pursuit of wealth is not only praiseworthy but likely to bestow benefit upon the community; no industry more assiduously preaches the validity of Adam Smith's "invisible hand." Nor is the industry likely to touch political issues; its model "good citizen" seems to be a streamlined edition of Charles Dickens' Cheeryble brothers in *Nicholas Nickleby,* and, for the most part, life is deemed desirable in the degree that it is not invaded by political issues. Wealth and ability are usually correlated where the business man or the eminent lawyer is the hero; the doctor is either the great specialist who performs a miraculous operation, or the ordinary practitioner who, in a small country town, builds his life in terms of devoted self-sacrifice. The central principle, in short, on which the American film is based is threefold. It is partly an implicit defence of the *status quo.* It is partly an insistence that progress is the outcome of individual improvement. Most of all, it is the triumph of emotion over intelligence, even to the point where emotion is exploited with an intensity that hardly gives intelligence any chance of active expression.

Out of all this there emerge, as it seems to me, certainly obvious conclusions as well as questions quite clearly connected with them. The first is the refusal of the industry to believe that its audience can be treated as though it consisted of adult minds. Is this because that conclusion is, in fact, the truth? Or is it the expression of a Gresham's law in this sphere of leisure, the bad money, as it were, driving out the good? Or is it the natural habit of those who rule the industry to use their immensely powerful instrument to soothe their vast audience into a kind of social somnolence? Is the general stress on individualism the inherent outcome of building all major films around the activity of one or two stars to whom all other actors in the film must be subordinated? Is the virtual evasion of vital themes in politics or economics the outcome of a tested experience that there is no profit in them? Or does the film simply reflect, and not mould, the existing values of contemporary American life? Why does the office which Mr. Will Hays used to fill exercise its censorship upon the special lines he has been able successfully to impose? Is, this is to say, the social immaturity of the American film the implicit outcome of a carefully imposed purpose, or is that purpose imposed upon the industry by the nature and demands of the audience to which it addresses itself?

These are not easy questions to answer; and the more carefully experience is searched for the answers to them, the more complex do those answers become. There can be little doubt that, apart from the desire to make profit, there is no clear purpose in the minds of those who rule the film industry. There is a real sense in which it is not paradoxical to say that they seek to lead their public by following it. There are subjects they will not touch out of fear of the hostility of particular pressure groups; there are other subjects they will touch only in a favourable way; there are others in which they feel bound to deal unfavourably. They want to exploit impulses like sex and pugnacity to the maximum without offending a significant body of Puritan or pacifist opinion. They are always "patriotic," and they extend that term to include hostility to any criticism of what are conventionally known as "American principles." They will not risk attack from the South by dealing forthrightly with the Negro question. They will not risk attack from the big vested interests in agriculture by an insistence on the tragedy of its sharecroppers and its underpaid migratory labourers. They attack the trade-union leader as such, but not the trade-unions. They attack an imaginary politician, but neither the institutions nor the conditions which make him possible. They attack a large newspaper proprietor whom anyone can identify; but they avoid discussion of the degree to which he is characteristic of many lesser figures in the newspaper industry. Their concentration upon the film of entertainment is so overwhelming that the specialized film, educational, scientific, social, is mostly left to the promotion of special interests with a small opportunity of exhibiting it to other than a specialized public. It is notable, for example, that, even with its unparalleled opportunities, little has been done by Hollywood to publicize the great government achievements of the United States, like the Tennessee Valley Authority, or to explain how the work of the Departments at Washington vitally affects the lives of American citizens. There is no serious effort to show the different level of opportunity for a poor boy born in the State of New York and a poor boy born in the State of Mississippi.

The anxiety of Hollywood is to be impartial about politics, in the largest sense, by avoiding political themes. It is anxious also, under all circumstances, to avoid even to seem to criticize the Churches. Hollywood is not, I think, to be regarded as anti-social so much as asocial. Its attitude is so largely governed by box-office considerations that, beyond the conviction that entertainment pays, Hollywood can hardly be said to have any other convictions. It not only operates under a strict code, in the enforcement of which the Roman Catholic Church plays an important part; it has also to remember that all the forty-eight states of the Union have each their official or unofficial censorship. It is influenced by the fact that an important part of its revenue comes from foreign sales; and it has to do a good deal of adjustment lest it offend an important foreign customer. In Greece, for example, during the Metaxas dictatorship, it was forbidden to show the *Prisoner of Zenda* because of scenes in which royalty was ridiculed.[69] Egypt, in 1939, banned the *Song of Revolt* because it showed the French Revolution.[70] Finland agreed to accept *Idiot's Delight*, but for adults only, and with the omission of scenes unsuitable on the ground of their "political tendencies." [71] The French censorship demanded changes in the film of *Marie Antoinette*,[72] and would not permit, in another film, an offensive reference to Napoleon; it also banned *East Is West* on the ground of its offensiveness to the Chinese people, since the Chinese minister had protested against its exhibition.[73] The British censorship is voluntary in character, but it objects to films in which there are cruelty to animals, religious incidents like the representation of the sacrament and the recital of the Lord's Prayer, or a reference to the royal family; thus, in 1938, the exhibitors of *Boy Meets Girl* were asked to delete the word "Buckingham" from the phrase "Buckingham Palace." [74] Hungary banned the film *Juarez* because of its political implications, and *Marie Antoinette* because of "mob scenes and disrespect for the ruling classes." [75]

It is, indeed, interesting to note that any exported film must conform to the habits of the government of the country it enters. Mussolini's Italy would not allow a film in which men were on strike, since Il Duce had prohibited strikes; and its censor deleted a section of a film entitled *Conquest* in which Napoleon is made to explain to Walewska the folly of war and his desire for a United States of Europe built upon democracy.[76] Japan banned all films either disrespectful to royalty or to the soldier.[77] Poland, in 1938, banned the *Life of Emile Zola* on the ground that it contained scenes "detrimental to military honour." [78] In the spring of 1939 *Marie Antoinette* was banned for fear that the revolutionary scenes might affect the attitude of the Rumanian people to their government.[79] Russia bars films showing either the yellow or the black races in an unfavourable light; but it also bars any films which praise royalty, religion, or capitalism.[80] Australia, before the outbreak of war in 1939, insisted on deletions in a March of Time film which remarked on the decline of British prestige in the Far East and on Palestinian riots where British police attacked Arab mobs; [81] and, in 1938, Ontario sup-

---

[69] John Edgar Harley, *World-Wide Influences of the Cinema* (Los Angeles: University of Southern California Press, 1940), p. 142.

[70] *Ibid.*, p. 121.

[71] *Ibid.*, p. 125.

[72] *Ibid.*, p. 127.

[73] *Ibid.*, pp. 128–29.

[74] *Ibid.*, pp. 138–39.

[75] *Ibid.*, p. 147.

[76] *Ibid.*, p. 151.

[77] *Ibid.*, p. 153.

[78] *Ibid.*, p. 176.

[79] *Ibid.*, p. 178.

[80] *Ibid.*, p. 179.

[81] *Ibid.*, p. 99.

pressed references to the Cliveden set and to the Duke and Duchess of Windsor.[82]

In the admirable survey by Professor Harley from which I have taken these illustrations, it is made decisively clear not only that Hollywood must respect the taboos of the United States, but also that each country into which it seeks to push its wares will accept them only subject to respect for its own taboos. It is clear, further, that the main purpose of this respect is to prevent the established order from being subjected to criticism or ridicule, and, especially in non-democratic countries, to prevent any suggestion that a regime may be overthrown by violence. All this must be set in the background of a vast propaganda machine seeking to drive home the urgency of seeing the film. Thus the Warner Brothers' *Dodge City* had its opening night in Dodge City itself, and a special train took from Hollywood to Kansas a small army of stars, radio commentators, film critics, film columnists, which was met by the governors of Kansas, Colorado, and New Mexico, as well as by the "leading citizens" of Dodge City. When *Tom Sawyer* was filmed, a nine months' search for a boy who would fit the leading role was conducted all over the United States, and twenty-five thousand children were examined and five hundred tested on the screen. There were requests over the radio and in the newspapers for a boy of twelve, with curly hair and freckles and the famous grin. There was an inspection march of two thousand Boy Scouts in one place; in Chicago and St. Louis the help of all the teachers was sought. By the time that the film was actually made millions of people must have been aroused to interest in it.

The use of the star's popularity is itself almost a national industry. There are "Madeleine Carroll Clubs" and "Bing Crosby Clubs." We are told about the stars' incomes. We are given pictures of their homes. We are told about their personal habits. They must be built up so as not to be too remote from their adoring public. They have their vast incomes and their vast houses, but they all have a yearning for the simple life. The child stars must be like ordinary children; Shirley Temple made mud-pies and Freddie Bartholomew liked swimming and football and dogs. We are told of Mr. Gary Cooper's humility, and of Miss Bette Davis's courage in the face of difficulty. Mr. Robert Montgomery, after the depression, became a specialist in social and political questions. Miss Durbin reads more than thirty books a year, and Mr. Ronald Colman has a large library to which he can instantly turn for proof of any facts he uses in argument. There are three hundred film journalists in Hollywood; even the Vatican has a press representative there. It is said that the "fan mail" of Hollywood amounts to over a quarter of a million letters a month; and a star of the first eminence may receive as many as three thousand in a week. When the shift in the community's interest is towards social reform, the interest of most stars will move with it. Some of them help

[82] *Ibid.*, p. 108.

Republican Spain; others work for the "closed shop" for movie actors; one runs a co-operative ranch; another is interested in hospitals and houses. There are, of course, very notable exceptions of famous stars who have fought for freedom with sincerity and devotion. But, with most, it is the public mood that counts. At all costs, the public must be made to feel that their problems are issues to which their favourites on the screen give devoted attention. Miss Deanna Durbin, for example, was converted to pacifism by reading President Nicholas Murray Butler's estimate of the social benefit mankind could have secured by devoting to peace the enormous sums spent on war.

The eminent poet, Mr. Archibald MacLeish, has emphasized very directly the problem of making Hollywood socially conscious.[83] He insisted that the industry deal with the living issues of our time, and argued that otherwise the film would remain of necessity a kind of artistic and spiritual abortion incapable of life. To criticisms of this kind Hollywood has responded with some eagerness. It has helped the government to make propaganda for the idea of a big navy.[84] It has co-operated with the State Department in improving the relations of the United States with the Latin American republics. The government itself, indeed, has made propaganda films about farming, housing, the Dust Bowl; *The Plow that Broke the Plains* and *The River* have both been admittedly great technical achievements of great educational value. The direct entrance of the federal government into film-making, of course, raises important political questions. American government is party government. Can the line be drawn between films which are good for the nation in themselves and films which give special support to the party in power? The Beards obviously suspected, in 1938, that government-aided film was used for partisan propaganda. Problems obviously arise about where the films are to be shown, and whether, if they do not get a proper welcome from the circuits, the government will not have to lease or build theatres for its own propaganda. If the government-sponsored films become controversial, it is inevitable that the interests opposed to government will make their own films in reply. It is certainly true that it would help the understanding of the processes of democracy to tell the people what the government is doing.[85] But it is not less true that much of what a particular government does may arouse fierce hostility among its critics. This raises the question of the plane upon which government film-making is to operate.

It raises it the more because the big industries are going into film-making on a large scale. This is true of General Motors, of the United States Steel Corporation, of the Westinghouse Company, of the advertising agencies, of the National Association of Manufacturers.[86] The

[83] Archibald MacLeish, "Propaganda in Hollywood," *Stage,* January 1939.
[84] Beard, *America in Midpassage,* p. 596.
[85] E. Hearon, *Journal of Educational Sociology,* November 1938.
[86] See a remarkable article by S. H. Walker and Paul Sklar, "Business Finds Its Voice," *Harper's Magazine,* February 1938.

last of these has made a series of five films which attack socialism and defend the consequences of changes where men are replaced by machines; it protests against increased government expenditure, explains that the American Constitution is intended to protect free enterprise, and seeks to persuade the American workingman to be contented with his standard of life. Special groups exist which make films on behalf of causes in which they are interested—Republican Spain, Franco Spain, China, the Nazis. A body exists called the American Film Foundation in which organizations like the Daughters of the American Revolution, the Society of Mayflower Descendants, and the Military Training Camps Association participate. It is non-profit-making, and its purpose is to defend the American Constitution against "alien philosophies." So far, its main energies have gone into films glorifying the Constitution and seeking to show that the interests of capital and labour are identical. These "propaganda films" made by special groups are not, as a rule, likely to reach the general film audience. They are shown to special groups or by owners of theatres who think that they can afford to risk an experiment without arousing undue animosity.

But they have an indirect effect on Hollywood which is worth noting. If the film with an idea is successful, the industry makes a stream-lined version of the idea. When the Federal Theatre—that remarkable outcome of the Works Progress Administration's effort—made its success with the play *One-Third of a Nation,* which argued the need for action by the government to cope with the problem of poverty, it was filmed in Hollywood; but whereas the play sought to show that only the government could deal with an evil so vast, the film solved it by the magnanimous conversion of one man. So, too, when the industry noted the huge success on Broadway of Mr. Sidney Kingsley's attack on the slums and their influence on children, it made films about "dead-end kids" who are reclaimed by the individual understanding and the personal charity of the wealthy. With the coming of the Second World War, Hollywood sought to make the British better liked and understood in America by filming *Mrs. Miniver;* and the growth of dislike for Germany enabled it to produce *Confessions of a Nazi Spy* in 1939, and *The House on 92nd Street* in 1945. Both of the anti-Nazi films are interestingly connected with the glorification of that Federal Bureau of Investigation the methods of which have not always commanded the approval of Americans concerned to protect the freedom of the citizen.

When Mr. MacLeish, therefore, demanded that the industry devote the use of the film to the development of ideas about the problems of our age, he was raising, I suspect, a far more complicated issue than he knew. A small group can make a special film to show, in its own movie theatre or in one hired for the occasion, to a specialized audience. It is at least doubtful whether a highly monopolistic industry, ultimately dependent on the great financial interests—as the history of Mr. William Fox made so clear—can be impartial about, much less attack, the way of life those interests are anxious to defend. An "idea," in Mr. MacLeish's sense, usually oozes out, in the hands of a Hollywood producer, into the thesis that democracy is a good thing, or that rich people can do good with their money, or that an honest and determined young man can, with sufficient resolution, break a corrupt political machine. Hollywood will film a great pacifist novel, like Remarque's *All Quiet on the Western Front,* but it will just as eagerly make *Submarine D-1,* which is a hymn of praise to the American Navy. And it is a very illuminating thing that, in the films which deal with the duty of the Armed Forces of the United States, Hollywood can always count on assistance from Washington to obtain the use of aeroplanes or warships or troops with such massive equipment as tanks and artillery. And since the warship, the aeroplane, and the big gun in action suit to a nicety the medium of the movies, a tale built round their use is pretty certain to be popular because it is pretty certain to be spectacular.

Nor, on the evidence, does it seem very likely that a government can hope, without widespread opposition, itself to make seriously controversial films. It can make the documentaries; it can propagate simple ideas or facts about health, or housing, or agriculture. Once it advances beyond the frontiers of common agreement, it faces three major problems. There will be passionate opposition in Congress to spending the taxpayers' money for "partisan" objectives. There will be pressure from the vested interests adversely affected by the controversial treatment of the subject. And, perhaps most important of all, in the face of criticism from these two sources no government will be able to persuade the main circuits which own the theatres to display controversial films to general audiences. Anyone can see at once how many subjects this makes it impossible for a government to choose. It could not depict the facts about the treatment of the Negro, especially in the South. It could not speak out its mind on the conflict over child labour. If it protested against the treatment of Mexicans, or even American-born Japanese, in the Pacific states, it would hand votes to its opponents at the next election. I do not think it could secure the general display of a film which sought to expose the patent medicine racket; and an attempt to dramatize, say, the fantastic gymnastics of the Thomas–Rankin Committee, would be stifled even as it sought to be born. In all but a small area, this is to say, the government must accept a situation in which its power to use one of the vital instruments of propaganda on behalf of purposes to which it is passionately committed is, in a large degree, a power it may not use. The contemporary nature of American society, therefore, leaves this instrument overwhelmingly in the hands of commercial interests.

In the total result, the cinema is thus bound to be a weapon that, in all normal circumstances, is used to preserve the *status quo.* It is not a challenge, but an anodyne. It finds that entertainment is the main source of profit, and, since it exists for profit, it sets out primarily to entertain. Its values are those of the *status quo.* Its censorship is imposed to protect the *status quo*. The immense creative purposes to which it could be devoted—as in the educational field—are largely put on one side because few communities will incur the expense involved in making those purposes a source of profit. I venture to doubt whether the critics are right who attribute to the cinema a heavy responsibility for things like juvenile delinquency; it seems to me far more likely that this judgment mistakes association for causation. But I think the movies are one of the major factors in American life which arrest the process of thinking and make reason the slave of emotion. Partly it does this by its wholesale encouragement, both primary and secondary, of escapism. Partly it does this by its fantastic distribution of emphasis and the confusion of values to which this leads. Nothing, perhaps, illustrates this better than the fact that those responsible for the publicity of Mr. Bernard Shaw's *Pygmalion,* while they allowed Mr. Shaw's name as author to appear, made their main selling point the opportunity the audience would have to see how a street girl selling flowers in London could be transformed into the perfect lady. No comment on the movies is even remotely as significant as the list of books compiled by the public libraries of Cleveland under the title of "Books Eliza should have read." It would have been interesting to have Mr. Shaw's own comment on the view of the Cleveland bibliographer that those who wanted to emulate Miss Doolittle should read works like *Give Yourself Background, Well-Bred English, Individuality and Clothes.*[87] For anyone other than Mr. Shaw, the better part is silence.

9

HARDLY less influential than the cinema is the radio, which, within scarcely a generation, is now an industry employing over one hundred thousand persons. It is said, quite credibly, that over eighty million Americans listen as a matter of course to radio programmes, and that there are approximately twenty-five million receiving sets in the United States. The radio, moreover, is only at the beginning of its evolution; it is not easy to prophesy what its power will be when the ability to listen to an event that is taking place thousands of miles away is accompanied by the power actually to see the event as a spectator. Television may be an influence for good or ill; what is certain, at least, is that its outcome will have consequences of the first importance to mankind.

No one can have passed through the immense experience of the Second World War without a sense of the power of radio. Englishmen listened to the speeches of Franklin Roosevelt, Americans listened to Mr. Churchill, as though the voice of history was speaking in their own room. An eminent American judge has told me how, when in the early evening during each day of the Battle of Britain, he heard the clear and

---

[87] I owe my knowledge of this remarkable list to a former student of mine, Joseph P. Kennedy, Jr., who was killed in the Second World War on a mission which evoked from him the courage that was typical of his character.

calm voice of Mr. E. R. Murrow begin his broadcast with the historic words "This is London," he felt an emotional stimulus it was beyond his power to put into words. M. E. Anseele, the Belgian Socialist, who played an heroic part in the resistance movement there, said, at the annual conference of the British Labour party at Blackpool in 1945, that he could never hope to hear poetry more exquisite than the voice of a British announcer, speaking from London, to whom he listened at nine o'clock each evening while he was in hiding from the Gestapo. Perhaps I may add that few things in my own life have moved me more than when Léon Blum, on his liberation from the German concentration camp at Buchenwald, told me how he and his brave wife had suddenly been cheered one night when they heard me speaking from London, at the instance of the American Office of War Information, and paying tribute to the nobility of his stand. And I think that few people who heard the few words spoken at the end of the broadcast in honour of his ninetieth birthday [88] by Mr. Justice Holmes will ever forget the sense they aroused of ancient history being made to live. Of the immensity of the power implicit in radio both the Berlin of Hitler and the Moscow of Stalin have, in their different ways, borne incontrovertible testimony.

With the technique of radio as a method of propaganda I am not here concerned. Certain elements in its nature, however, need a brief emphasis because they make it a medium so different from any other instrument we have. For the most part, it is a technique which has a private or family relationship, rather than a public or crowd relationship; there are, of course, exceptions to this, as when a speech or a news announcement is broadcast to a waiting audience in a hall or out-of-doors, but, generally speaking, the private context is more significant than the public. Its influence, thus far, is one of sound, and not of sight; the effective broadcaster must, as a rule, get his effects into his voice, and realize that his appearance, so far, has had little importance. It is a medium of communication, moreover, in which the broadcast must, normally, make an instant appeal to its audience; for, with a flick of the finger, the listener may banish it from his attention. It is, moreover, in comparison with both the printed word and the movie, a profoundly impermanent influence. Overwhelmingly, the broadcaster must make his point at once or it has gone for good.[89] That means that the broadcaster must be simple, direct, and straightforward. A pretty definite time is at his disposal; what he wants to convey, he must convey with a precision which leaves no time for afterthought or correction. He is bound to concentrate on the essentials of his theme; to wander down the side roads is almost certainly to fail to make his point. In all matters of social constitution, moreover, he must aim at an average listener whose interest he must know how to hold; for there is always an alternative programme, in the United States many

---

[88] March 8, 1931.

[89] Save, of course, where the broadcast is repeated, or where, as in a small percentage of cases, it is printed after delivery.

alternative programmes, with which he is competing. He can rarely afford to be subtle; he is unlikely to be effective if he is too "highbrow"; and he must never forget that the better known he is, the more diverse, and, therefore the more difficult, is likely to be his audience.

In the United States, as elsewhere, the ultimate control of the radio is vested in the federal government; it operates through a commission the members of which are appointed by the president with the approval of the Senate. But, with a very few exceptions, like the municipal radio station of the City of New York, all the transmitting stations are privately owned, most notably the four big systems, those of the Columbia, the National, the American, and the Mutual Broadcasting Companies, which are, for practical purposes, unique in that they can provide a "national hook-up," have world-wide connections, and are able to cover, whether by offering their facilities on some great occasion or by using their own "radio commentators," practically the whole civilized world. The United States has not only more than six hundred stations; its citizens have at least half, and perhaps more than half, the receiving sets in the world to-day. The stations seek to pay for themselves by selling "time" to anyone who is willing to buy it—there are, of course, exceptions—usually in units of one quarter of an hour. The purchaser may buy time on a local or on a national station; that depends almost wholly on the commodity he has to sell and the amount of money he can afford to use in advertising it. What, as a rule, he does is to "sponsor" a programme which he is persuaded will interest the public to which he seeks to appeal, the virtues of his particular commodity being insisted upon by the announcer at intervals during the course of the sponsored programme. Some forty per cent of radio time is thus sold—naturally at the "peak," and therefore the most expensive, listening hours—and the remaining sixty per cent is filled up with programmes for which the corporation which owns the station bears the expense.

The programmes put on by the broadcasting companies themselves are valuable to them for a number of reasons. They serve the general purpose of increasing public interest in radio. They make the particular station known, and thus increase its advertising value. They enable the station to gain status and prestige, and thus, once again, enhance their value to the advertiser. They maintain the station's right, under the "public interest" clause of its licence, to be allotted its wave length; and they enable it to do enough work of high quality in music, or drama, or education to prevent any systematic outcry against its commercialism. But the essential theme of the American programme is broadcasting for profit. Whatever the station may itself contribute or invent, it is the advertiser whom it has in mind. The commercial programme has usually the best hours of the day. It is devised either to reach the largest possible variety of audience, or to maintain a stable appeal to a special public large enough to convince the advertiser that he is getting value for his money. The commercial programme is usually the outcome of joint planning by the

broadcasting company and some advertising agency, and it may well
be built on the prestige value of sponsoring an important opera company or a well-known theatre group. The non-commercial programme
is, as a rule, the work of the broadcasters themselves. They will give
time to speakers on education, on science, on art, or on literature; they
will arrange special broadcasts for children; they will make a broadcast
version of a play, or an opera, or even arrange with a famous symphony
orchestra to play classical music, or with a well-known jazz band to play
dance music.

The American system of broadcasting involves both a censorship and
a propagandist art. The censorship is indirect in the sense that the Federal
Communications Commission is forbidden to "interfere with the right of
free speech by means of radio communication." A station, moreover,
which permits the candidate of one party to speak on the air, must give
the same permission to other parties. But this is, in truth, a nominal freedom. For few of the smaller parties can afford the immensely expensive
luxury of purchasing the same amount of time as the major parties, and
it is at least doubtful whether the great broadcasting companies would
allow a small party, for instance, the American Communist party, to have,
two years after the campaign had ended, unpaid debts of over one hundred thousand dollars for time allotted. And the fact that the Federal
Communications Commission not only decides upon the advisability of
granting or renewing a licence, but may also "determine" whether "the
public interest, convenience, and necessity" is served by its so doing,
really means that the members of the Commission are an ultimate court
of appeal against any effort to prevent a licence from being granted or
renewed. On this basis, the opinions held by members of the Commission,
quite apart from the utterance of "obscene, indecent, or profane language"
which they must prevent, become a matter of outstanding importance.[90]

It is clear that the Commission takes its functions of warning pretty
seriously. It urged all those to whom it granted licences to refuse the air
to advertisers who did not accept the codes established under the National
Recovery Act; and it warned them against the "greed" or "lack of patriotism" on the part of "a few unscrupulous advertisers." [91] It has denied a licence to a station which permitted an attack on the Roman
Catholic Church.[92] It was only after a long struggle that the Socialist
radio station was allowed a renewal of its licence; and to secure the renewal a campaign had to be waged in the liberal press to secure the
reversal of the examiner's report to the Commission.[93] It is, in fact,
pretty clear that a broadcasting station which gave any considerable place
to radicalism in politics, to criticism of, at any rate, the major religions

[90] Cf. an illuminating comment in the Harvard Law Review, April 1933, pp.
987–93.
[91] Mr. H. A. Lafount, of the F.C.C. as quoted in the New York Times of June
18, 1934.
[92] F.R.C. Order No. 1043, November 13, 1931.
[93] The station is WEVD; the facts are in F.R.C. Order No. 919, 1932.

in the United States, or to controversial discussions over matters like birth-control or the treatment of the Negro might quickly find itself in difficulties with the Federal Communications Commission through the influence of pressure groups upon the Commission's members. Playing for safety is the natural line of a body which may, at any moment, find itself attacked in Congress or in the press.

Indirectly, therefore, the censorship which Congress forbade the Commission to exercise is, in fact, a quite real element in broadcasting. But it is not, of course, anywhere near so influential as the censorship the stations exercise over themselves. None of them can afford to displease, at least in any continuous way, either their audiences or, still more, their advertisers. The result is that the National Association of Broadcasters has agreed that no programme shall "offend public taste and common decency"; that it shall not attack the American government, its officers, or its basic principles; and that it shall not offend any racial or religious group in the community. Its clients, it further agrees, shall have access to an audience only when they are not "dishonest, fraudulent, or dangerous" people.[94] This obviously opens the way to a very wide censorship. It leaves the broadcasters to define what the Constitution means, and what is an attack upon it; it leaves them to define also whom they consider a "dangerous" person; and it enables them to prevent any free discussion of a controversial question which might disturb or offend a Roman Catholic or a Fundamentalist or a Jew. Yet it is difficult to understand exactly how these principles permit the broadcasting of what has been virtually the typical Nazi propaganda, or why a clergyman named Hahn was not allowed to urge that it was desirable to impose higher taxes on large incomes, and to increase the purchasing power of the workers.[95]

In a careful examination of the issues involved in radio censorship, Mr. James Rorty [96] has painted a portrait of the position which, though it is more than a decade old, still seems to me a pretty accurate diagnosis. A fair amount of political criticism, even of radical criticism, will be permitted, especially at election times, though the amount will depend upon the funds at the disposal of the parties, and the attack on the fundamental principles of the "American way of life" will be ruled out. To this must be added the freedom permitted on the programmes, like those of the Chicago University Round Table, for example, for which a respectable organization is sponsor. There is no real criticism either of those who advertise or of the advertising profession. All criticism of the electric power industry is both moderate and carefully controlled. It would be very difficult to secure permission to defend a trade-union engaged in an important strike. It would, similarly, be difficult directly to advocate birth-control, or freely to attack the hostility of the Roman

94 National Association of Broadcasters, *Broadcasting in the United States* (Washington, 1933), p. 16.
95 Lilian Hurwitz, *Radio Censorship* (New York: 1932), p. 44.
96 James Rorty, *Order on the Air!* (New York: John Day, 1934), p. 25.

Catholic Church to birth-control. No radio station, moreover, would permit the use of its facilities to broadcast any matter which it regarded as "obscene," or "tactless," or "controversial."

These are, of course, serious limitations, and it is only fair to say that most professional broadcasters would indignantly deny their validity. They would insist that the outstanding American broadcasters have rarely hesitated to say exactly what they thought even on the most controversial subjects; certainly they could point to a remarkable denunciation from London, in the face of bitter hostility from the American Army's headquarters, of the attitude to Admiral Darlan taken by the government of the United States. They would quote the massive volume of letters the broadcasting companies have received from trade-unions and their leaders thanking them for radio facilities during strikes. They would emphasize, too, the deep respect for freedom of utterance which characterizes the broadcasters in general. And they would insist that federal inquiries have brought together a remarkable body of testimony in support of these propositions with virtually no comparable volume of evidence on the other side.

There is an important sense in which all this is true, yet it is only a part of the whole truth: the too-outspoken commentator may not last. It is important to measure the relative volume of time given to the conformist and to the critic, and the size of the audience each type is permitted to address; nor does it allow for the way in which what is in fact conformist propaganda creeps into the news. If, for example, a strike like the railway strike of 1946 is called off, the broadcaster, alike in tone of voice and form of words, represents the outcome as a victory for the forces of "law and order" against a disruptive influence. A station, in any case, selects its material; and the principle of selection turns on how to reach the largest number of listeners rather than on the attempt to evaluate the material broadcast. Anyone who has listened to radio talks in which the broadcaster seeks to explain some current issue will have little difficulty, if he knows the technique of broadcasting, in knowing just what result the commentator is seeking to achieve. He assumes the "suggestibility" of his audience and uses words or phrases that are weighted for this purpose; he can, by skilful repetition, drive home the suggestion he is anxious to get accepted. And in few "sponsored" programmes is the effect of association likely to be neglected. If several million listeners always expect a particular programme at a particular time, and this has achieved widespread popularity, it is unlikely that a competing programme put on, either locally or nationally, at the same hour, will have much chance of being heard.

The very content of programmes, moreover, shows that commercial radio seeks to avoid discussion of a controversial kind. Nearly seventy per cent of all programmes are musical, with an immense predominance of popular over classical music; and the industry pays special tribute to the character of Sunday in the national life of America by broadcasting more classical music on that day than on any other day of the week. After music, the drama is the second most important type of broadcast. The educational broadcast represents about six per cent of all programmes; it is rare at the week-end—the heaviest listener period—but this may be accounted for by the fact that the schools are then closed. I have myself analysed the programme of a New York station for over a month. Dance music was the largest item, with comic music-hall "turns" coming second; sports, both news and description, came sixth in the list; news reports came seventh; drama came eleventh; religious services came fifteenth, ranking just below cookery and household hints; discussion of national policies ranked twenty-first, and was accorded just over one per cent of the whole radio time, while political speeches were at the bottom of the list and did not even reach one-half of one per cent of the schedule.

Anyone who studies the programmes of the different systems will note that, though with a fairly continuous experimentalism, they have certain patterns. Programmes for children, important orchestras, great international speeches, like those of the president or of the British prime minister, immediate reporting of events like the opening of the United Nations, dance music, Negro spirituals, are all likely to secure a national hook-up. Nearly eighty per cent of the commercially sponsored programmes run for about fifteen minutes, and radio time is mostly sold between six and ten o'clock in the evening, the hours from nine to ten o'clock achieving the maximum commercial value with nearly seventy-five per cent of the time sold. But it is also evident that eleven to midday, and three to four in the afternoon are fairly popular, since nearly forty per cent of this time is filled by programmes of commercial sponsoring.

Over half the radio sets in the world are in the United States; and nearly three families in four own one. But the distribution of this ownership varies enormously. In Washington almost every household has a set; in Arkansas and Mississippi less than one-third of the homes are so equipped. Generally there are nearly three times as many sets in urban as in rural areas; and families with an income of less than one thousand dollars own slightly less than half the number of sets owned by those with an income of ten thousand dollars. There is, of course, an important difference between owning a set and listening to it with any consistency; and the analysis of listener research give no straightforward statistics by which to analyse this difference. It does, however, appear that women listen more than men, and that the time spent in listening is in inverse proportion to the amount of education a listener has had. Nor is there agreement on the length of time spent daily in listening; estimates vary between two and a half hours and five hours in each day. But that does not, of course, tell us whether the listener's whole attention is given to the programme, or whether it is a half-heard accompaniment to the performance of other work; the housewife may let the radio run on all the morning while she is dusting and cooking the mid-day meal.

Listener research has told us a good deal about the choice of programmes made by listeners. Men seem to prefer sports reporting first, then favourite old songs, then music, then news, in that order; their eighth preference is for serious talks on politics or science or history, and, among fifty categories of preference, they put political speeches as the fortieth and sermons as the forty-second. Women put music first, with news in the seventh, serious talks in the twentieth, political speeches in the forty-fifth, place; but they put listening to sermons in the thirty-fifth place, a notable difference from the men's attitude. It ought to be added that, sex apart, both age and occupation make a great difference in listening habits, and that a relatively small number of people listen regularly to more than three or four stations. It appears, further, that older people choose the programme to which they will listen more carefully than younger people, and that a "network" programme is overwhelmingly preferred to one that is purely local. More people like to hear the news broadcast than to read it in the newspaper; and music is at least five times as popular as the spoken word. In the latter regard, it is significant that about half the listening audience is bored by the subject of a talk, and about one-third find the attention it requires to follow a talk excessive. Nor is it unimportant that in any considerable sample of listeners two-thirds are ready at once to give up the variety of programmes available to them for an improvement in the quality of what is provided.

There are some characteristics of listeners of obvious political importance: that people like the news better on the radio than in a newspaper; that they like a speech about six times better as something they hear than as something they read; that they prefer attending both lectures and political meetings to hearing them over the air; that church attendance is hardly affected one way or the other; and that most people prefer commercial radio without a licence fee, as in the United States, to non-commercial programmes with a licence fee, as in Great Britain, even while most listeners want less advertising; all these have their lessons. On a sample of one thousand American soldiers stationed in Great Britain, and coming from forty-two states in the Union, I found that just over ninety per cent listened, while in the United States, to a talk by President Roosevelt, if this was possible, and over ninety-four per cent while they were abroad. Over ninety per cent listened to some or all of the presidential conventions of both major parties in 1944; but while eighty-six per cent listened to one or more of Mr. Roosevelt's campaign speeches in 1940, and over eighty per cent to Mr. Wendell Willkie's, only sixty-seven per cent listened to Governor Dewey's speeches (one or more) in 1944. It was also, I think, illuminating that while eighteen per cent listened to a speech by Mr. Churchill before May 1940, over eighty per cent listened to him during 1940–41, and seventy-four per cent in 1944. Only four per cent listened to Mr. Ernest Bevin in 1940–41; in 1944, this had risen to thirty-four per cent. During a two-year stay in Great Britain, ten per cent had been to hear a debate in Parliament, which was three hours away; four per cent had, while at home, visited their state legislature, and not quite one per cent had visited Congress. Fourteen per cent made it a regular habit to listen to the weekly "American Commentary" on the B.B.C. programme from London.

About ten per cent of broadcasting time is given to educational programmes; and there are nearly one hundred stations owned by educational bodies. At least half the state departments of education use radio regularly in the public schools; while Oregon, Iowa, and Pennsylvania have their own departments with stations exclusively used for this purpose. Both the Columbia and the National Broadcasting Companies not only have educational sections, but arrange important programmes of this type; though it is very rare for any commercial interest to sponsor such a programme. The content of these is largely musical, though literature, history, and, in a lesser degree, current events, all play a real part. It is estimated that over one-quarter of American schools have radio sets, and that some six to seven million children in the schools can be reached by the programmes. These have certain important advantages, even though, music apart, they often suffer, especially in talks, from their impersonality. They help greatly in training children in music appreciation. They dramatize the historical event. They give reality to people—President Roosevelt, for example—whom it is important for children to feel as living persons. Travel talks, moreover, as well as the careful discussion of current events, are a safeguard against a parochial outlook; and a good teacher who uses the radio as the basis of later discussion finds that it is a genuine aid to broadening the mind of any child whose interest has been aroused. If, moreover, it is not used in a routine way, there is no doubt that the radio is a very helpful change from the ordinary work of the classroom. Out of the thousand American soldiers to whom I have referred, seventy-nine per cent had experience of, and enjoyed, educational broadcasting, and nearly fifty per cent of them (49.3) liked discussion between two people as the best way of eliciting their interest. In detailed talk with twenty-five soldiers, they all made the point that the effect of radio in the schoolroom depended, first, upon what the teacher did with its content afterwards, and, second, on their chance, fairly quickly, to be given some interesting book to read about what they had heard.

It hardly needs any proof, from what has been said, that in the last generation the place of radio in American life has been one of growing importance. But just what that place is no one will find it easy to define. Its first significance is as entertainment; if it fails in that area, it fails altogether. It is a useful, even an important, adjunct to education; but no sign suggests that, at any level, it is likely to replace the personal relation between teacher and student. It has done great things for the appreciation of music; and it is, indeed, very tempting to say that this is, so far, its outstanding achievement. It has obviously, especially during the Second World War, done a superb job in the actual and realistic reporting of its events. It can influence international relations: Hitler had few more dangerous enemies, especially in 1940–41, than some remarkable broadcasters, who, by convincing a really vital section of their fellow-countrymen in that critical year, not only of the British will to live, but also of its power to do so in the face of what looked like overwhelming defeat, did much to overcome the isolationist trend in American international policy.

There can be no doubt, I think, of the immense importance of radio as political propaganda. That has been illustrated by the profound influence of President Roosevelt's "fireside chats"; possibly nothing else gave him so strong a hold on the great mass of undecided political opinion. It was illustrated, not less remarkably, in the last few weeks of the presidential campaign of 1940, when a series of broadcast speeches by him were probably decisive in turning the hesitant voters for him and against Mr. Willkie. Political propaganda over the air, indeed, requires a special art of its own. The speaker must have the right kind of voice; he must, as a rule, know how to be at once incisive and intimate; he must time his effect so as to get the impact he wants in not more than half an hour; [97] he must not try to cram a great mass of indigestible matter—statistics, for example—into a radio talk; being unseen, and thus unable, either by gesture or by facial expression, to give his points that special atmosphere which a man like Mr. Lloyd George could give them at a meeting in some great public hall, he must never sacrifice directness to eloquence. He must get a warmth into his voice which gives his listeners the sense of an individual relationship to them; and he must never give the impression of making a set speech from the manuscript through which he is working his way. If he can fulfil these conditions, his use of the radio may be a supreme instrument for his purposes. But he may destroy its value as an instrument if he is merely negative and critical, or if he makes wild charges so unexpected by his listeners that he has no time to persuade them to direct the general drift of their thinking in a totally new direction, or if he devotes himself to screaming invective, like that of Hitler, or to the monotonous repetition of vague generalities, like Governor Dewey in the presidential campaign of 1944. The major value of the radio as a propaganda instrument lies in the speaker's power to arouse an alert eagerness in the minds of those who listen to him. If he fails in that, he may harm his cause and himself rather than help them.

That is why, in my own view, the value of radio as political propaganda lies less in speeches by men and women of political eminence—listener research shows clearly they are unlikely to draw a large audience save in exceptional circumstances—than in news bulletins, in commentaries, and in radio discussions. Here the speakers are likely to know the real technique of their job as broadcasters. They know the arts of emphasis and omission. They can give to their reports the skilful twist, sometimes by the art of timing or placing an item of news, or an argument in a commentary, which compares with the ability of the experienced journalist

---

[97] President Roosevelt got his best effects in a twenty-minute talk.

to make his news-story do all the work of an effective editorial without seeming to the reader to depart for one instant from the factual story he has to tell. Here, as I think, the major incidence of radio propaganda is all on the side of the *status quo*. For, first of all, the purpose of those who run the major stations is to make profit, and they must derive their profit from the sale of sponsored programmes to advertisers. They must, therefore, be careful not to offend unduly the interests of those who are likely to advertise, and few things are deemed more hostile by the big advertisers than a "radical" emphasis in news or commentary or discussion by some station or network. Thus there is very rarely any abundance of goodwill for a strike which interferes with the normal flow of business ; and a settlement of such a strike is always greeted with at least relief, and not seldom enthusiasm. Both before and after the Second World War, the volume of criticism on, and hatred for, the Russian socialist experiment was continuous and profound. The defeat, entirely unexpected in America, of the Conservative party in the British elections of 1945 was reported dismally both as a repudiation of the American favourite, Mr. Winston Churchill, and as an important attack on that "American way of life" of which free enterprise is the cornerstone. It is rare to hear any direct attack on the foreign policy of the United States over the air, still less an attack on the objectives or the methods of its Armed Forces. Where there is presidential intervention in industrial conflict, as in the railroad strike of 1946, it is taken for granted that it is the duty of the strikers to accept the president's proposals. On the other hand, where, as with the Securities and Exchange Commission Act, or the National Labor Relations Act, or the Office of Price Administration, the attitudes of Big Business and the government are different, the main emphasis of the radio will be on the side of Big Business. The government, as such, does not buy time ; and anyone who listened to the description of the coal strikes of 1946 would have thought that they were less the result of long years of bad conditions in the mining industry than of the wilful vanity of Mr. John L. Lewis, the miners' leader. Mr. Lewis may well have been both wilful and vain. But it was not these qualities which made his union give unhesitating loyalty to his orders ; and the almost complete neglect of this aspect of the strikes was about as effective propaganda for the mine-owners as could have been devised.

That is one aspect of the inevitable incidence of commercial radio towards the side from which its profits are drawn. The other is, of course, the fact that since in a commercial system time is a purchasable commodity, the poorer interests cannot hope to compete with the richer interests. It is not merely, indeed, that they cannot afford to buy as much time. They cannot buy it regularly, and they can rarely buy it at peak hours of listening. They cannot, only too often, buy more than an occasional national hook-up. They can rarely use the services of the nationally known commentators—even when these are, as they often are, sympathetic to their cause—since a commentator with a wide following is only too likely to

be "sponsored" by some commercial advertiser who will not allow, quite
naturally, any infringement of his rights to a more or less exclusive service from a name associated with his programme by its application to a
purpose he is very likely to regard with hostility. This, in its turn, throws
the poorer interests back upon either broadcasters whose names are not
likely, as a general rule, to mean very much to listeners, who do not, therefore, give any special attention to such programmes, or to men in the
public eye, like Mr. Lewis himself, whose very statement of a case will
arouse an hostile attitude from most of those who are not already his supporters. And were Mr. Lewis to broadcast on behalf of the miners, not
only would he be followed, in all likelihood, by someone on the other
side; it is equally probable that what he said would be relentlessly attacked, both in radio speeches on stations addressing local audiences, and
through other media of propaganda, like the press, which would leave
the balance of spoken or written argument overwhelmingly against him.
And it must be remembered that Mr. Lewis is the head of a wealthy
union which can afford, on special occasions, to embark upon a pretty
expensive campaign over a short period. His position in this field is far
more advantageous than that, say, of a small group like the socialist
League for Industrial Democracy, or the American Civil Liberties Union. If the latter could regularly pay for a half-hour broadcast at a peak
period on a national hook-up, one could feel reasonably certain that
the general standards of justice in cases which touch personal freedom
would be far higher than they are.

There is one further aspect of this position which requires some emphasis. Any station in the United States would be glad to broadcast a
great artist like Mr. Paul Robeson in a concert of Negro "spirituals"; and
probably a majority of commercial advertisers would be glad to sponsor
him in a programme intended to push the sale of their product. But I
do not think that Mr. Robeson would be allowed to broadcast nationally
on behalf of his own people, to speak the sober truth about the "American
dilemma"; I do not think a body like the National Association for the
Advancement of Colored People would be able to secure that right, even
if it paid for it; and I suspect that if even an eminent white friend of
the Negro sought to buy time to explain over a national network how
Negro soldiers were treated by the administration in the last war, or to
discuss the forces behind the Southern opposition to the Fair Employment Practices bill which, in 1946, died a slow, painful death, caused by
a handful of prejudiced Southern Negro-baiters in Congress, he would
not be allowed to do so. Fear of the South and the pressure of the War
Department would make any exposure of Army practices impossible;
and fear of the South would suffice to make even the bravest representative
of one of the big chains decide that discretion was the better part of
valour. Nor, after careful inquiry, do I think that the national use of radio
facilities would be permitted to American-born Japanese, even those
who fought so superbly in the Second World War, to state their case for

their return, with their families, to the Pacific coast. It is possible that a
single broadcast, preferably by someone of eminence, like Mrs. Franklin
Roosevelt, might be made on their behalf; the kind of general plea for
charity rather than the demand for justice which irritates those who wish
to deny the charity and humiliates those who are denied justice. But even
if the American-born Japanese could afford it, they could not hope to secure regular broadcasts on this topic; and it is, of course, quite certain
that no station on the Pacific coast itself would give them these facilities.

The radio world, in short, is one in which the battle is to the strongest, and the race to the deepest in purse. Most sustaining programmes are,
pretty inevitably, made up on the principle of maximum inoffensiveness,
since that is the best way of commending radio facilities to commercial
advertisers who sponsor the paid programmes at such immense cost. None
of this means, for one moment, that the specialists in broadcasting are
themselves narrow or reactionary or careless about great ends; of many
of them the very reverse is true. But, overwhelmingly, they are bound
to put their private feelings on one side, even if they take the risk of
an occasional excursion into the danger zone. Their job is the sale of
radio time. The masters of the great radio interests are not in the industry for truth or justice or beauty; they are in it for profit. They
cannot, therefore, afford to offend the interests which buy radio time,
especially those who buy it at the peak listening hours. They cannot
afford to offend the listening public; for the price they can charge for
the radio time is, of course, directly proportionate to the size, interest,
and regularity of the audience they secure for the sponsored programme.
No doubt this is in part the outcome of the attention aroused by the content of the programme itself; but it is also closely connected with the
goodwill achieved by the sustaining programmes. In large part, this goodwill must be based on negative, rather than on positive, grounds. It is rare
for a sustaining programme which is really good to be widely discussed,
even more, to arouse interest in the press, unless it offends some interest
powerful enough to make its voice heard. Important business and religious
groups will expend immense effort to protect themselves from criticism,
even from indirect criticism; and, of course, the most important weapon
they have is the pressure they can bring to bear on the commercial sponsors of programmes.

That is why it is so very rare to hear, for example, a frank discussion
of Lourdes and its miracles on a sustaining programme; that would offend
the Roman Catholics. That is why, also, there is no likelihood of a direct
attack upon the politics of the Vatican; the Pope is surrounded by either a
radio conspiracy of silence, or his utterances are recorded with the assumption that he is politically neutral. That is why, further, most of the major
American Churches can have time both to preach their gospels and to attack infidelity; but no infidel would be given time to attack any Church
with a large following, the Methodists, for example, or the Roman Catholics. Nor would it be possible, in a series of educational broadcasts, to ex-

amine the present state of our knowledge about Christian origins. All American radio must work upon the assumption that the salvation of the world depends upon the universal adoption of the Christian ethic. What is true of the Churches is true also of business. It may well be that, a generation from now, some broadcaster on a sustaining programme will be allowed to tell the truth about the profession in which the late Mr. Ivy Lee was so successful, or about the habits of the power lobby in Washington, or the full story of those shipping scandals of the Second World War which, in their scale, are almost entitled to rank with the famous Copper Purchase scandal in the First World War.[98] It is not the fear of libel or slander which promotes the principle of maximum inoffensiveness. It is the very simple fact that the less the association of a network or a station with "crusades" of any kind, the less likely it is to become unpopular with its listeners; and that absence of unpopularity is one of the major criteria by which the advertisers test the value of radio for their purposes. For, after all, they are seeking the attention of average America, and the major fact about average America is the fitful and fleeting interest it has in crusades. If it is forced to heed them with any regularity, it becomes irritated and bored; and listener research will quickly report to the sponsor that, in view of his diminishing radio audience, it would be wiser, because more profitable, to expend his advertising budget in a different direction.

10

PRESS, cinema, radio—amid the feverish efforts of all these to colour the environment a more or less rose-tinted hue, to warn their clients against fundamental change, to insist to him on the good fortune that has made him an American, to make him feel that no destiny will compare with the American destiny, to convince him that his future is of his own making, it is amid all these efforts that the ordinary citizen has somehow to find an equilibrium of his own. He is asked to accept—even if he is unconscious of the request—a number of dogmatic principles that are woven into the texture of the pattern of which he is supposed to be part. There is political equality in America; and there is, of course, a large amount of social equality, though few Negroes or Jews or Mexicans or French Canadians or Poles will share in it unless they are very rich or so specially gifted artistically that they dwell on the borders of the American Bohemia. There is virtual economic equality of opportunity in America; and this although for almost half a century there has been a growing leisured class, and the price of climbing high in the economic scale is ever greater because the ascent is ever more steep. There are good trade-unions and bad trade-unions in America; the first recognize that the employer is just the senior and more experienced partner in a joint enterprise and do not attempt to

---

[98] For details, see three articles by Allen Zeinard in the *New Republic* for May 13, 20, 27, 1946. On the copper scandal see House Report No. 1400, 66th Cong. (The Graham Committee).

cause trouble by strikes which would be detrimental to both sides; the second insist, with the mistaken and reckless support of John Stuart Mill, that "all privileged and powerful classes, as such, have used their power in the interest of their own selfishness," [99] and that, therefore, "the theory of dependence and protection will be more and more intolerable to them, and they will require that their conduct and condition shall be essentially self-governed." [100] What Mill, and the "bad" unions failed to understand, was that America was not Europe, and that every worker, granted thrift, intelligence, and effort, may rise to the highest positions in finance, commerce, and industry. Only in the American propagandist scene is the philosophy of Samuel Smiles still a living body of precepts upon which the good citizen is supposed to act.

There are, of course, other principles, too. The stereotype of the United States assumes that there are "good" and "bad" politicians. The latter are corrupt hirelings who enter politics for what they can get out of it; they interfere with the legitimate activities of business men by compelling them to buy necessary opportunities at the expense of bribes and dishonourable connections; and they are defeated only because, every so often, a "good" politician enters the arena and compels them to stop their nefarious practices. There are, of course, grave problems in the United States, but almost all of them are soluble by goodwill, which produces the necessary change of heart in all concerned. The main factor in producing goodwill is the Church; but the clergy of all denominations must keep out of politics and realize that their chief function is ministering to human souls in the sphere of private life. By thus improving the character of men and women, social relationships are sweetened, and social problems solved, without the necessity of governmental action; the poor are taught a wise patience, and the rich learn the creative happiness of a timely benevolence. Great emphasis is laid on the importance of safeguarding the "American way of life" from foreign attack. Few foreigners, indeed, ever quite succeed in penetrating the secret of that way; and where they challenge its wisdom, it will usually be found that they are themselves immigrants or first-generation Americans who have not yet become properly acclimatized to their new environment. It is, too, an inherent thread in the pattern of propaganda that socialism is in itself un-American, a foreign importation the character of which is wholly irrelevant to American conditions. Sometimes this is explained by the persistent failure of the Socialist party to become a significant factor in American politics; it is thus obviously out of tune with the national character. Sometimes, by the convenient repression of names like Evans and Skidmore in its first phase, like William H. Sylvis and Debs, in its second, it is noted that the leadership of men like Victor Berger and Morris Hillquit shows the un-American char-

---

[99] John Stuart Mill, *Principles of Political Economy with Some of Their Applications to Social Philosophy* (London: Longmans, Green, 1909), edited with an introduction by W. J. Ashley, Book IV, Chap. VII, Sec. 1, p. 754.
[100] *Ibid.*

acter of socialism, even though Mr. Allan L. Benson and Mr. Norman Thomas were their contemporaries in the leadership of the party.

Propaganda emphasizes the difference between the vital democracy of America and the effete aristocracy of Europe, though anyone who reads the pathetic autobiography of Ward McAllister,[101] and the almost fantastic pages of Colonel William d'Alton Mann's paper, *Town Topics*,[102] and compares with them the contemporary drawings of Charles Dana Gibson,[103] would, I think, not unreasonably conclude that if the United States from the eighteen-eighties onwards did not have an aristocracy, at least it was doing all it could to get one. Indeed, one of the most interesting phenomena in contemporary America is the fantastic interest in genealogical studies, and the large number of privately printed family histories by which the *élite* seek to convince themselves that they are not like the common herd. While Mr. Carnegie was writing about "triumphant democracy,"[104] the American steel workers were living in conditions not very different from those of the vassals in a great feudal empire; and those conditions have a grimly reminiscent flavour of the environment in which the textile worker of North Carolina, or the sharecropper of Arkansas, live at the present time. And propaganda also seeks to persuade the average American that wealth and its possessors are no longer important. "It is no longer a distinction to be rich," Mr. Henry Ford has written. "As a matter of fact to be rich is no longer a common ambition. People do not care for money, as money, as they once did. Certainly they do not stand in awe of it, nor of him who possesses it. What we accumulate by way of useless surplus does us no honour." Yet, fourteen years later, President Roosevelt, in accepting the Democratic nomination for the second time could explain how "out of this modern civilization economic royalists carved new dynasties. New kingdoms were built upon concentration of control over material things. . . . There was no place among this royalty for our many thousands of small business men and merchants who sought to make a worthy use of the American system of initiative and profit. They were no more free than the worker or the farmer. . . . The privileged princes of these new economic dynasties, thirsting for power, reached out for control over government itself. They created a new despotism and wrapped it in the robes of legal sanction. In its service new mercenaries sought to regiment the people, their labour, and their property. . . . The savings of the average family, the capital of the small business man, the investments set aside for old age—other people's money—these were tools which the new economic royalty used to dig itself in. . . . A small group had concentrated into their own hands an almost complete control over other people's property, other people's money, other people's labour —other people's lives. For too many of us life was no longer free; liberty

---

[101] See the *Dictionary of American Biography*, Vol. XI, pp. 547-48.
[102] Dixon Wecter, *The Saga of American Society* (New York: Scribner, 1937), p. 339.
[103] *Ibid.*
[104] Mr. Carnegie actually published a collected edition of his works.

no longer real; men could no longer follow the pursuit of happiness." [105]

If the pattern presents itself as reality so differently to Mr. Ford and to Franklin Roosevelt, the general purpose of the instruments of propaganda becomes clear. They are not intended to prevent change; almost everyone in America not only realizes the inevitability of change, but is almost prepared to welcome it. The purpose is to delay the coming of changes which the owners of these instruments believe to be undesirable, and the changes they believe to be undesirable are, roughly speaking, those that strike at their continuing supremacy. That is why the key-word in their effort is the word "un-American." There accretes about it now the sense of a simpler and happier tradition when the United States was a unique experiment in civilization. In our own age of insecurity and the fear that it breeds there is a nostalgia for that past when opportunity was unlimited, when the frontier still seemed endless, when almost everything remained to be discovered. Beyond the Civil War there lies the golden day; and whatever may threaten the existing framework of things prevents the chance that the golden day may return. For some it is trade-unions, for others the declining hold of the Churches, for others, again, the disintegration of the family, for yet others that decline in morals which they identify with the reckless pursuit of pleasure. With whatever they identify the threat, it at once becomes un-American; and the effort of propaganda is to make its un-Americanism convincing to the great majority of citizens.

It is illuminating for two reasons. It is illuminating, first, because, as one can see, above all in the writings of James Fenimore Cooper, of Emerson, and of Whitman, there was an idea that certain forms of behaviour were evil, because un-American, before the Gilded Age. But the idea of what is un-American before 1861 lays stress on hope, adventure, excitement, the spirit of a new creativeness, the sense of living in a springtime in which the sun is always rising. In our own day the idea has changed. It is built on fear; it is too often cynical and disillusioned. Because it is sophisticated, it believes itself to be mature. It pioneers in bigness, and not in grandeur. Where it hears complaint, it suspects conspiracy; where it encounters grievance, it assumes the offensive. Un-Americanism was a positive thing before 1861; it meant enthusiasm for Jefferson and Jacksonian democracy, dislike of the tight little oligarchies in New England and New York and Philadelphia, which thought that the shrewd old soldier in the White House was handing over the future to the mob. Un-Americanism after 1865, and especially after the rise of Populism, became a negative thing. The men who defined it were the financial magnates whom Mr. Josephson has so admirably termed the "robber barons." [106] They could not see that it was as much pioneering to build the Knights of Labor, or the National Grange, or the American Federation of Labor, as it was to build the Northern Pacific or the Steel

---

[105] Roosevelt, *Public Papers*, Vol. V, p. 232–33, *passim*.
[106] Matthew Josephson, *The Robber Barons* (New York: Harcourt, Brace, 1934).

Corporation. They feared the men who, like Henry Demarest Lloyd and Lincoln Steffens, exposed their patronage of that boss-system they so unctuously condemned. They even feared Theodore Roosevelt, whose permanent but energetic intellectual adolescence they mistook for an ardent experimentalism. They feared Woodrow Wilson for the belated individualism in which they detected the Jeffersonian streak. They hated Brandeis, who saw no purpose in the bigness they admired merely because it was big. Their ideal was Calvin Coolidge, a kind of Woolworth-made follower of Alexander Hamilton, who worshipped rich men in the confident faith that they were also virtuous by reason of their wealth. So that Franklin Roosevelt terrified them not because he was profoundly radical, but because, being himself a very great gentleman, he refused to accept the wealthy buccaneer as the end product of the American adventure. And they feared Franklin Roosevelt because his unexpected interest in the play of mind led him to gather around him young and intelligent men who were anxious for adventures in social and economic pioneering.

That is one reason why the attack on experiment as un-American throws a flood of light on the place of propaganda in the national life. The other, which is less conscious, is yet not less profound, and was foreseen over a century ago by Tocqueville when he sat down to write the second part of his great book. It was the fear of individuality, a fear which transformed the natural desire of a people for unity into an urgent demand for uniformity. The change enforced by technology—when it came to imply the need for mass production as a means of satisfying the demand for profit and for increased material well-being—no doubt formed a basis upon which the confusion of unity with uniformity could easily be made. The growth of a centralized political power to match the growth of centralized economic power was—with a time-lag always in its operation—another vital source of the same confusion. Only half-conscious, also, was the fear, slow in its emergence after the Spanish–American War, but swift beyond measure in its progress after the First World War, that with the end of isolation and the appearance of the United States at the centre of world power, differences in thinking were dangerous to unity in action.

The weakness of this attitude was twofold. It assumed, without discussion, that the right premises of thinking were those of the business men, or, rather, of the economists and lawyers, journalists and theologians, who made explicit what business men were too busy to formulate themselves. It then inferred from the refusal to accept those premises the conviction that men who denied them were socially dangerous. One has only to note the incredible "security" measures of the State Department in 1947 to be assured of this. Since few business men were accustomed to intellectual speculation, they knew the results they wanted to reach, but not the questions they ought to ask. The more insistently they received answers they did not expect, based on premises the very formulation of which seemed to them to threaten the foundations of the republic, the more urgent was their clamour for intellectual uniformity, the greater their fear of that individuality which appeared in the passion for social reform.

The second error was their massive underestimation of the living strength of the revolutionary tradition in the American people. All its experience went to make it self-reliant and self-confident. All its tradition was of experiment and innovation. It was a people inherently restless and adventurous, easily tired of the habitual, anxious to move on to something new. When it had reached the limit of the external frontier, it merely turned, as though by instinct, to explore that internal frontier which technological skill and supreme adaptability made infinitely vaster than any experience to be gained from the conquest of territorial space. To seek the imposition of uniformity upon such a people, whether by press or film or radio, was impossible so long as it was a democracy. For as fast as the instruments were devised to this end, there appeared men and women to warn their fellow-citizens of its dangers. And it is notable that almost every aspect of the uniformity the instruments of propaganda were able to impose was in essence a superficial one. They have never yet been able to touch the great secular characteristics which give to the American people their outstanding uniqueness. Mr. Babbitt, no doubt, voted for Harding in 1920, and for Coolidge in 1924, and for Mr. Hoover in 1928; but he did not hesitate to turn to Franklin Roosevelt in 1932. Not all the instruments of propaganda combined could persuade most Americans that the precedent of General Washington's self-denying ordinance was part of the law of nature. That, under democracy, is the rock upon which all propaganda which seeks to make American opinion stable and uniform is ultimately bound to break. At some point, some inner drive tells the American citizen to be wholly himself or to be less than nothing. And when he seeks to be wholly himself, the tradition to which he feels himself bound is that of a man who acknowledges no master. That was the quintessence of Americanism in 1776; and it will never be destroyed without fighting for its right to live.

XIV

Americanism as a Principle of Civilization

I

THE end of the Second World War has found the United States the most powerful nation in the world. If it is outstripped by Russia, India, and China in population, none of them even approaches it in effective productive capacity, and its speed of technological adjustment has made it the primary parent, in recent years, of something that can only be called a new industrial revolution. In a number of ways the United States is beyond all possible chance of successful rivalry within the next few years, perhaps within the next two generations, granted the absence of internal economic or political catastrophe. It has been physically untouched by the war. Its industrial potential has been greatly increased by the fact that it was, in a remarkable measure, the arsenal of the Allies. It has an important lead in knowledge of the technology of atomic energy, in the capacity to manufacture aeroplanes and all other forms of transport, in its ability to feed its citizens at a higher level of nutrition than any other nation except Denmark, and in the machine-mindedness of its workers. It has absorbed within its scientific *élite* many of the outstanding names among the refugees from Axis tyranny —Einstein, Franz Oppenheimer, Szilard, Fermi, to mention only the most eminent. It has learned, as perhaps no other nation save Russia has learned, the value of long-time investment in research on a vast scale, as well as the use of team-work in the tasks of investigation.

All this is important enough; but it is far from being all. The number of American institutions which offer a unique equipment both to the scientist and the scholar is remarkable from any point of view. It is, I think, legitimate to argue that no American laboratory has to its credit so remarkable an achievement as that which the University of Cambridge named after that eccentric genius, Henry Cavendish. But the Mount Wilson Observatory, with its incomparable telescopes, the Eastman Laboratories at Rochester, the Smithsonian Institution so superbly organized by Joseph Henry, the provision both for pure and applied research made by the General Electric Company, the Rockefeller Institute of Medicine, the equipment of the Institutes of Technology both of Massachusetts and California, the provision under way for research into nuclear physics at Chicago and Harvard Universities—nothing that we know of either in Europe or in Asia even begins to rival these; and they are only scattered examples of what is available. Nor is the humanistic side of research neglected. There is nothing outside the United States even remotely equal to the Huntington Library, or to the facilities offered to scholars at universities like Harvard and Yale, or by the Library of Congress. No other effort at co-ordination approaches in quality that of the National Council of Social Research. There is no comparable opportunity of publication open to the European scholar, whether in history or politics, in economics or in sociology, even in the study of literature. In smaller but still vital matters, like leave of absence, the provision of research and secretarial assistance, the offer of grants-in-aid for travel, or computation, or photostatic copies of necessary books and documents, in brief, at least in the major institutions, in the possibility of relief from time-consuming duties of petty routine, the American scholar is at an immense advantage over the European. So, also, is the young man of promise on the threshold of a career devoted to learning. His chance of travel, his opportunity for free time, his knowledge that he can count on the aid and advice of men and women who have already made themselves masters of their fields, all these are organized at a level to which the systems of few other nations even begin to approximate. And to these must be added the important fact that in the realms of administration and public law an able young graduate of an outstanding law school is likely to have a far better chance of doing really important work at an age when he can absorb the full meaning of significant experience with the zest and eagerness of youth than is the case elsewhere. I take one example only. It was the custom of Mr. Justice Holmes and Mr. Justice Brandeis, when they were on the Supreme Court at Washington, to take as their law clerks two outstanding members of the graduating class at the Harvard Law School. Anyone who examines the list of these and relates them to their subsequent careers in the public service will note at once what a very remarkable training ground this experience must have been. The work of the Supreme Court, no doubt, makes it an exceptional institution, and the two justices were, with Cardozo, the three great figures in American jurisprudence since Chief Justice Taney, perhaps since Chief Justice Marshall. But if it is an exceptional institution, exceptional use has been made of it by exceptional young men. I know of no judge in any European system who has offered a newly fledged barrister an experience of similar magnitude.

The outstanding capital of the United States lies in the restlessness which leads to experimentalism. The characteristic American is always on the move. He is always willing to try something new. He is always more interested in tomorrow than today. He is sceptical of anything that expresses itself as permanent or absolute. He changes his job with an ease and self-confidence that appear startling to European experience. The variety of Abraham Lincoln's experiences before he became a moderately successful lawyer in Illinois is well known. President Truman wanted to be a professional soldier. He has been an assistant in a drugstore, a paper wrapper for the *Kansas City Star,* a bank clerk, a farmer, a would-be professional pianist, an officer in the Field Artillery in the First World War, the partner in a haberdashery shop which went bankrupt after a year, a road overseer, a judge of the Jackson County Court (an administrative, not a legal, position in Missouri), a follower of the notorious boss of Kansas City, Thomas J. Pendergast, through whom he was chosen as senator for his state, then vice-president as the compromise candidate in the Democratic convention of 1944, and, through the tragic death of Franklin Roosevelt, on April 12, 1945, the president of the United States. Up to the age of thirty-seven, he had done nothing but fail, save in his minor military role. His work in Jackson County was solid and clean, without being in any way notable. As a senator, he was hard-working, competent, pleasant, and, not least, a good party man. It is not easy to see why President Roosevelt agreed to his nomination for the vice-presidency against half a dozen other possible candidates. The record is that of a man who, until almost forty, showed not a sign of being different from any random sample of the small bourgeois American, and, after forty, moved directly, with giant strides, to the greatest elected political office in the world.

We are accustomed to this in Europe during revolutionary periods, like the English Civil Wars of the seventeenth century or the vast upheaval which began in 1789 and ended in the lonely squalor of Saint Helena. We are accustomed to it as the outcome of that even greater earthquake which brought the Bolshevik party to power in 1917. It is intelligible, again, both in Europe and in Asia, as the aftermath of wars which, like those of 1914 and 1939, destroy the whole social structure of a regime and are themselves part of a revolution, like the epoch of the Renaissance and the Reformation, which gave Western civilization a new world outlook. But thus far the United States has been accustomed to the existence of a ruling *élite* admission to which has never been impossible, save for a special minority group like the Negroes, and the ascent to whose doors has rarely been a steep one. It is impossible to think of a career like that of Wendell Willkie in Europe, save as the outcome of the breakdown in a social system. The advent to power of the first Labour government with a majority in the House of Commons echoed over the whole world; but there was not a member of the cabinet formed by Prime Minister Attlee who had not, if sometimes with brief intervals of electoral defeat, been a professional politician for close on twenty years. The American system reveals a capacity for the discovery of new men, an anxiety to test new things, an interest in absorbing new experience, which remain notable even when all allowance is made for a visible loss, here and there, of important fluidities. What is involved is not due to the frontier, though, no doubt, it has been affected by the frontier; for it is always important to remember that whatever the psychological importance of the frontier, it never possessed an institutional significance. Nor is it due to individualism, or to free enterprise, or to the roots of America in the Puritan tradition. It is useless to speak of either individualism or of free enterprise in a society which, like that of America, has always, on the economic level, been neo-mercantilist in character. If the Puritan tradition postulates religious beliefs which give special encouragement to self-reliance and energy and resolution to those who hold them, the fact, of course, is that these qualities have been abundantly displayed by societies wholly dissociated from religious beliefs and which do not have the remotest resemblance to, or connection with, the Puritan tradition.

There are, I think, three things it is urgent to bear in mind in any attempt to understand the American personality. First, that the War of Independence was a revolution in that it broke the hold of feudalism in America; with all the limitations that precise historic analysis may require, the United States, after all, began as a bourgeois republic in which the masses, as Shays' Rebellion makes clear, were already staking their claim to a share in political power; and by the time of Andrew Jackson the claim was broadly conceded. The same is hardly true of Britain, in one sense until at least the government of Mr. Gladstone in 1868, and in another sense until the government of Sir Henry Campbell-Bannerman in 1906; and even then there remain, forty years later, important vestiges of feudal and aristocratic power which reach down to the foundations of society. Save for a fleeting moment in 1848, it was not true of France until well after 1870. Neither Germany nor Italy has yet known democratic institutions in any effective way; the Weimar Republic was hardly more than a fading hope battling against growing conspiracies. The social structures of Holland and Belgium bear a much closer resemblance in their development to Great Britain than to America. Perhaps the social structure of the Scandinavian countries in the last century, and especially since 1900, is the most akin to that of the United States. But, even here, there is absent a good deal of the sweep and the romance which characterize the American scene. There is less emphasis on the glory of ordinary people. There is a certain tinge of smugness—perhaps thickness is the better word—quite different from the exciting vitality of American democracy.

It is in the length of time that American democracy has maintained its hold on the foundations of the national life that the inner secret of its acceptance of equality may be found. There are plenty of oligarchies in America, economic as in Wall Street, social as in New York and Boston, political as in the circle about the State Department in Washington.

There is hardly a town of any considerable size which does not possess its little cohort of "leading families," and its massed proletariat which lives on the wrong side of the railway tracks. From the first days of the republic there has been a continuous effort to keep the masses in their place. Sometimes this has been derived from the fear that the rise of the masses may limit the power of property; sometimes from the fear that the swelling tide of immigrants from Europe might overwhelm and destroy the original essence of America; sometimes it has been the outcome of an imitative administration imported from the predominantly hierarchical social structures of European civilization. But whatever the source or the intensity of the denial, no one has yet been able to make a successful frontal attack on the idea of equality. From the time of John Adams, who had such difficulty in justifying his doubts to Thomas Jefferson in that enchanting correspondence of their old age, social theorists in America have sought ways and means of undermining its place in the American tradition; they did not even hesitate, like J. Laurence Laughlin of the University of Chicago, so to bowdlerize John Stuart Mill's *Principles of Political Economy* [1] that it was turned into a defence of that type of financial tycoon whose portrait Theodore Dreiser and F. Scott Fitzgerald drew in successive generations. Even as late as 1914 John Bates Clark tried to make the mechanism of the market—the vital source of inequality—an expression of the Christian ethic in social life; [2] and between the two world wars there was a curious interest in the fascist social theories of Pareto. But, in the end, the strength of the egalitarian tradition has been profound enough to leave it as the central thread in the American tradition.

The third reason is at once the simplest, as it is the most important, of all. The individualism Tocqueville discovered in America was emphatically different from his description of it. For him, it was an anarchist conception, man versus the community and its laws, man concerned only with himself, man waging that "beneficent private war" which, fifty years after Tocqueville, Sir Henry Maine contemplated with such complacency. I am not sure that it was not that mythical individualism that F. J. Turner postulated as the outcome of frontier influences, the dauntless and self-reliant pioneer who hacks his way to success unaided by the help of social institutions. The truth, of course, is that there never has been such an American individualism. There have been greedy individualists who sought wealth and power and who were also Americans; but their behaviour can be paralleled from any other place or time. In its essence, American individualism, as Tocqueville encountered it, was a sense of freedom born of the knowledge that no barriers denied the citizen's right to move forward. That sense of freedom gave him hope and energy and that faith in ever-widening horizons which bespeaks the capacity of adaptation to change. No doubt the hold of this idea of equality has waxed

[1] Dorfman, *Thorstein Veblen*, p. 79.
[2] Clark, *Social Justice without Socialism*, p. 49.

and waned at different periods in American history. But the permanent reality it has thus far implied is as evident in the letters of Crèvecœur at the beginning of the republic's history as in the poetry of Walt Whitman or in that remarkable speech of Franklin Roosevelt when he accepted the office of the president for the first time. It is the affirmation that no American need fear anything save fear itself; and the real safeguard against fear is the principle of equality. It is surely a significant thing that each party in the history of the United States, the Communist party included, has always claimed to inherit this tradition; and it cannot, indeed, die so long as there are Americans, men and women alike, who seek to enforce its reality in each successive age.

I am not arguing that there is, as the outcome, an unchanged, or unchanging, national character in America. No one, indeed, who knows America would refuse to recognize the multiformity of Americanism. It is one thing in its Vermont expression, and another and a very different thing in Texas or California. It is one thing in the immigrant Jacob Riis, who found in the environment of the New World the right to fulfil dreams he could hardly have dared even to imagine in the Old. It is another and a very different thing, again, as it finds fulfilment in the Americanism of a conservative aristocrat from Boston like Mr. Justice Holmes. It seeps through the characters of men so different as Jefferson and Andrew Jackson, John Quincy Adams and Abraham Lincoln, Woodrow Wilson and Franklin Roosevelt. Partly it is the unbreakable conviction that man is the master of his own destiny. Partly it is the faith that there is something unique in America. There is an element in it of exciting resiliency, of men who gain new life from contact with life itself, as Antæus gained new strength from contact with the earth. Nor can one omit the remarkable spirit of civic enterprise which has about it, at least in its architectural expression, a quality reminiscent of the pride of an ancient Greek in the external beauty of his city. For whatever may be said—and much may be said—against the sprawling ugliness of Chicago or Pittsburgh, the regard for beauty is always breaking out in public structures, as in the great George Washington Bridge in New York, or the open-air theatre built by relief-aided workers during the Great Depression for the University of Colorado at Boulder.

Americanism is multiform, and it is also, at its very roots, nonconformist. No one can fully shape it the way he wants it to go—no president and no millionaire, no labour leader and no intellectual; and it is not even shaped by all the objective consequences of its mass production system. Something is always escaping to be itself; something is always emerging to protest that things must be done another way; there is always an ardent clash between traditionalist and reformer which makes the consequential Americanism different from what either of them dared both to hope and to fear. No doubt there are elements in Americanism that jar on the foreign mind. There is sometimes an undue vanity, a tendency, as Emerson once said, for the eagle to be too much the peacock. There is an excessive love of the rhetoric of rights and a too easy belief that their declaration is their fulfilment. There is sometimes too much of a hard-headed materialism which too readily measures the object aimed at in terms of the immediate return it will bring. The energy of Americanism sometimes lacks that power of repose which alone makes for profundity of mind and heart. And, in the absence of repose, Americanism too easily tends to exalt success over wisdom, and thus to mistake prosperity for insight. It identifies the philosopher king with the man who has made a fortune by the shrewdness of a Carnegie, or the rapacity of a Rockefeller, or the patient ingenuity of a Henry Ford, rather than with Lincoln, whose mind is built in that character of granite which, applied to politics, elevates the moral quality of the whole community. It suffers also from a certain levity, a desire to get things done more quickly than the nature of the universe permits. It drives the people one way with such ardour and such speed that they hasten to act too often before they have reflected. A body social is too delicate and too intricate an organization to be experimented upon by men who have won the temporary eminence of material power; and Americanism has too often been less than just to itself in the mute admiration it has offered to men of this kind.

Intellectually, I think, there have been two phases in the last century of Americanism. Until at least the nineties it was excessively sensitive to European opinion—European books, European houses and furniture and gardens, European fashions, even the manners of European society set the standards which far too many Americans accepted as valid criteria of taste and behaviour. Even as late as the Great Depression of 1929 Americans could be found in Paris, or Florence, or London, convinced that people with creative talent in the arts were spiritually outcasts in America. Or, in this first period, if they found themselves in America itself, they were too often ostentatiously acclaimed, so that over their possessiveness of its immense hopes there seemed to hover a miasma of arrogance without cause. No doubt they encountered a large-scale European offensiveness; Sydney Smith's "who ever reads an American book?" betokened an incurious superiority it is impossible to defend. Tocqueville apart, indeed, it is almost true to say that the first century of United States history was permeated by that "certain condescension in foreigners" of which James Russell Lowell spoke. It appeared not only in the travel books of European visitors; it was retailed with unction by the novelist and the poet, the politician and the critic. For them, America was numbers and materialism, a kind of democratic cesspool into which were drained the failures of all European countries. It was significant that most European rulers sympathized with the South in the Civil War; one has only to read the actual day-by-day dispatches that Charles Francis Adams sent from London to realize how narrow was the gap which separated England in those critical years from war with the North. Few people lost the chance of drawing attention to the defects of Americanism, the ostentation of its millionaires, the corruption of its politics, the harsh lot of the poor in its economic life, the endemic violence of its life in frontier and metropolis; fewer people still studied its institutions, or recognized how, year by year, an art which in all its forms bore the stamp of native American creation was adding a new category to civilized living. It is, indeed, worth noting that within the last generation so eminent a French observer as André Siegfried has, in effect, warned Europe against the destructiveness of American influence upon France,[3] and that two of the most ardent of the younger intellectuals published, in the decade preceding the Second World War, an attack upon Americanism as a cancer in the body social of our civilization.[4]

It would be easy to show that while Europe luxuriated in emphasis upon these defects, there was hardly one of them it did not share. There was ostentation enough alike in the aristocracy and the bourgeoisie of its mid-nineteenth century; Anthony Trollope's *The Way We Live Now* and the novels of Balzac and Flaubert are not an index to a quiet self-confidence. The difference between the corruption of politics in America and its analogous habit in Europe was that the one was open and avowed while the other was cynical enough to pretend to conceal itself behind a profession of devotion to the public welfare. There was violence, and to spare, among the vigilantes of California, the gangs of New York, and the "Molly Maguires" of Pennsylvania. But Mayhew's picture of mid-Victorian London,[5] the accounts we have of the *lumpenproletariat* in Berlin, the grimness of Paris upon the ugly details of which Zola lavished so much care, suggest that one of the main differences between violence in America and violence in Europe was that in Europe it was regarded as an indecency to reveal its horrors, and that in America it was openly discussed as one of the dangers for which a remedy must be found. The lot of the poor was harsh enough, in all conscience, in America; but Dickens and Carlyle, Engels and William Morris, do not suggest that it was a bed of roses in England, while in France the June insurrection of 1848 and the Paris Commune of 1871 tell their own tales. The vital fact is that of the vast army of immigrants who entered America until 1914 to search for an ampler life, only a very few felt a nostalgia for Europe strong enough to desire to return. And there were many hundred thousands of families in Ireland and Italy and Scandinavia to whom the frequently sent subsidy from the emigrant to America was the sole hope of relief from that condition of *la misère* which meant so deep a mingling of squalor and hopelessness.

The antagonism between Europe and America, which is still far from ending, is an important fact in the history of modern civilization. It has given Americanism some of the worst features it possesses, above all, the desire of wealthy Americans to transcend their Americanism and thus to impose European criteria and habits on their country, and the desire

[3] André Siegfried, *America Comes of Age* (New York: Harcourt, Brace, 1927), especially Chap. XXVII.

[4] Robert Aron and Armand Dandieu, *Le cancer américaine* (Paris: Rieder, 1931).

[5] Henry Mayhew, *London Labour and the London Poor* (London: Griffin, 1861).

of poor Americans, in the mass, to turn their back on Europe and thus to become the victims of the professional purveyors of isolationism, which, where the level of culture is low, is so easily degraded into an arrogant parochialism. The root of the antagonism, I think, is partly the fear of an old and decaying society for a new and vigorous rival—intelligible enough to anyone who reflects for a moment upon the influence of the War of Independence upon the French Revolution—which may threaten the status of all the values it is struggling to preserve. But partly, also, it is the absurd and wilful ignorance of American institutions and culture which characterized the European approach until the outbreak of the First World War. One can number on one's fingers the Europeans who, before 1914, approached the diagnosis of America with sympathetic understanding. With notable exceptions, like Fenimore Cooper and Whitman, Edgar Allan Poe and Mark Twain, American literature was little read, let alone absorbed into the central stream of civilization. Few people, the scholars included, knew much of American history save that George Washington made a successful revolution and that Abraham Lincoln was assassinated at the end of the long and bloody Civil War. There was not even a serious effort to teach American history in the universities, let alone the schools, until American aid helped to prevent the domination of Europe by Germany after 1917; and even then the conditions under which it was studied did little to make it seem an inescapable part of the cultural apparatus a citizen requires if he would understand the universe around him. It would be fair, I think, to say that Bryce was the first man who directly studied America with sympathy and for its own sake; Tocqueville, though he wrote a very great book, was more concerned to discover in American conditions the means to analyse the future of France than to understand the United States on its own terms.

The result has been that when Europe awoke to the fact that America was of momentous significance, America was already a vast colossus for which dependence upon the Old World was already a past tradition. It was so overwhelming in its productive power as to be the decisive factor for many years in world affairs. It had developed a distinct culture of its own which, though vital influences from Europe and Asia and even Africa were notable, was nevertheless unmistakably New World, and not Old World, in character. If in the search for fundamental scientific truth it had still to follow rather than to lead, in the important matter of technological adaptability its people had no rival anywhere. It offered bigger advantages on fewer conditions to men and women of talent than any other society. Having completed its bourgeois revolution by the end of the Civil War, when the resources which awaited exploration remained overwhelming in their abundance, it was not so deeply riven by those inner tensions which are always evoked in the aftermath of a crisis whenever a European bourgeois revolution is incomplete, as in Britain or France, or has failed seriously to emerge, as in Germany and Spain and most of Southern Italy. And, differently from America, no major European power, save Russia after 1917, could resolve its inner tensions save by imperialist exploitation, at a time when that exploitation had produced a nationalism everywhere which threatened in greater or less degree the power to use a people and its land as a *latifundium* worked for the benefit of absentee proprietors.

To this there must be added the important fact that in the century of American history when its significance was, for all serious purposes, ignored by Europe, Americans drew upon all the resources of European civilization for their own development and often brought to their use a vital energy that was all their own. In literature that can be seen, mature and self-respecting, as early as Emerson's return from his first visit to Europe; in scholarship and scientific work it was already so by the end of the Civil War. And in the next three-quarters of a century provision was made for training a larger proportion of its citizens at the highest level, both scientific and humanist, than in any other country in the world. Nor must one forget that in the making of this cultural independence there were immense contributions by the refugees who had poured from Europe into America, not least by the several million Jews through whose historic experience of nearly two thousand years as the intermediaries between cultures the new developments greatly profited.

So that when Europe rediscovered America effectively during the course of the First World War, it discovered an equal and not an inferior. So much an equal, indeed, that the discovery of weaknesses in the colossus was due less to European insight than to the full and frank criticism by Americans of themselves. Some of it was profoundly imaginative in its vision, like that of Henry James; some of it was really irrelevant, like George Santayana's famous attack on the "genteel tradition" in New England, because it rejected one set of values to accept another, or, like that of the American refugees in Paris and in London, because it was, in truth, an escapism which lacked the courage to act in America itself. Mr. T. S. Eliot has said no more of post-1914 America than he had learned from Irving Babbitt and Paul Elmer More before he came to England; and the new faith he sought to construct to replace the Americanism he had lost had already been rejected by all save a remnant who sought in lamentation the excuse for evading the obligation to make analysis the parent of action.

By the end of the Second World War the two capitals of world ideas were in America and in Russia; and the thick veil of the future hides from us the outcome of their interaction. What is at least certain is that Americanism will never again be an outer province, as it were, of the European idea, for, first of all, America has discovered its own past with passionate interest; and that has made the traditions of European culture fall into their place as but a source, however important, from which the stream of Americanism takes its rise. The American knows full well, and proudly admits, the debt he owes to Shakespeare and Rousseau and Goethe, and, from them, through Montaigne and the splendour of the

Renaissance to the central wellspring of all Western civilization in ancient Greece. He knows, too, that he has enriched the heritage of everyone with contributions so distinctively American that none but he could have brought them; and that, increasingly in the last century, American culture has attained a richness and a variety that are unsurpassed elsewhere. If I may so phrase it, having lived intellectually until the time of Andrew Jackson in a house built with the cultural capital of Europe, he has now enough of his own accumulation at his disposal not only to live in a house of his own making, but to find it spacious enough to give to European guests both peace and inspiration.

In the complex relationship between the European tradition and Americanism, the European has found it hard to surrender his right to patronize the American. He has had, therefore, to find some way of rationalizing this right, and he has found it in three directions. The first is in the simple affirmation that in contrast with the aristocratic principle which still, Russia since 1917 apart, underlies the whole social structure of Europe, America is a sternly materialist country given over to the pursuit of the "almighty dollar," a society, indeed, where, as Tocqueville said, everyone has ambitions but where all ambitions are petty in character.[6] Europe, one is to assume, is safeguarded from that materialism since the aristocrat or, as in England, the gentleman, as the accepted highest social type, is above the interest in money-making by the mere fact of being what he is. The second is the affirmation that the only original philosophy America has produced is pragmatism, and that pragmatism is the typical and inferior product of a civilization whose deepest concern is with wealth. The third is the conviction that American life has been so standardized by the uniformity inherent in mass production based on large-scale mechanization that all American art lacks both profundity and creativeness when compared to that of Europe. That is why, to take a simple example, the Nobel prize for literature was awarded to Mr. Sinclair Lewis. The members of the Swedish Academy found in *Babbitt* exactly the criticisms of America that were standard form among Europeans; they were crowning America's own warning to itself to turn aside from the road down which it was marching. They were affirming, amid widespread applause outside America, the implicit superiority of European standards. They were really arguing that the creative work of art cannot, on the showing of a brilliant American novelist, be expected from a society the character of which makes Mr. Babbitt its average type. The American work of art was really not art at all, but a sociological document the knowledge of which enabled Europe to protect itself from the ravages of Americanism.

None of these grounds is seriously capable of defence. Yet each of them must be examined because they lie at the root of the difficulties in unifying the European tradition with Americanism, and thus perpetuate a kind of intellectual separation which does grave harm to a common

[6] Tocqueville, *Democracy in America*, Book III, Chap. IX.

cause. The view that America is more materialistic than other peoples is a myth that is not even edifying. It could hardly be maintained by Great Britain, the "nation of shopkeepers," whose aristocracy founded its fortunes by its rapacious ingenuity in pillaging the revenues of Church and State, or by the determined zeal with which its members went into the City, or by refreshing the family fortunes through marriage with the daughter of some American millionaire. It is completely inconsistent with the unresting avarice of the French peasant, or the passion for thrift which is outstanding not only in the French bourgeoisie, but in the whole range of material habits exhibited by all classes in France during the Second Empire and the Third Republic. The passion for wealth in America has certainly not been greater than that which any observer could find in the Prussian Junker or the builders of the great German industrial combines after the alliance was sealed between Bismarck and the liberal bourgeoisie; and the main characteristic of the *haute bourgeoisie* was its contempt for the *petit bourgeois* because of his failure to make money. Both groups alike embraced Hitler as a saviour, partly in the conviction that he would safeguard them from the threat of increased working-class power, and partly in the hope that they would gain by a policy of expansion new opportunities in which they would have their share. And if, as Marx said, the ruling ideas of an age are the ideas of its ruling class, the American preoccupation with wealth-getting has been no different either in trend or in degree from that which dominated the minds not only of the aristocracies of Spain and Italy, but of that Roman Catholic Church with whom they shared their power that they might exploit the credulity of the masses for their self-protection.

But that is not all. The money-mad American has shown a magnanimity to Europe of which there is no comparable example in history. One's view may vary about the dangers, as well as the benefits, of the princely gifts from wealthy men to the universities of their own country, as about the foundations and the part they play in the organization of American research. But the aid given, especially after 1914, to rebuilding European learning, to the endowment of large-scale experiments, of which the medical Yale University in China is merely one distinguished example, is not more remarkable than the many hundred thousand donations, small and great alike, which have enabled the American Red Cross for at least a generation to be the outstanding example of international generosity in the whole world. I do not think anyone is entitled to speak of the material-mindedness of Americans unless he can produce an instance of comparable and continuous generosity from European experience.

The argument that pragmatism is the one philosophy America has produced and that it is no more than a gospel of success is, of course, both unhistorical and unfounded. Pragmatism, like all other metaphysical doctrines, is no more American in origin than idealism is German; and it would be far more legitimate to charge Hegel and his right-wing successors with the worship of what William James called the "bitch goddess Success" than it would be to charge the American pragmatists with that view. As a matter of historical truth, pragmatism, like all the major tides of philosophic doctrine, is international in its origins and, in its temporary success, as much a reaction from idealism as idealism was from utilitarianism in the sixties and seventies of the nineteenth century. The real cause of the sudden interest in pragmatism was the impact of scientific method and its immense social consequences upon a pure metaphysics which, in the cloistered atmosphere of academic life, made a futile distinction between thought and deed, between theory and practice. Pragmatism was an attempt at their integration. It urged the need to recognize that thought is an instrument of life, and that in life the process of which thought is a part seeks to verify hypotheses which are expected to prove capable, as they are applied, of satisfying the demands men make out of their experience. Whatever the limitations of pragmatism as a metaphysic, it has had two results of exceptional importance. It drew attention to the need for seeing that thought is a social process not less than an individual one, and that, for whatever other purposes it is used, its fundamental purpose is successful adaptation to life. The famous phrase of William James that "good is the maximum satisfaction of demand" throws a real light upon what there is specifically American in the idea. Its connotations are active, experimental, social, democratic. It implies a citizen in a community doing something upon a hypothesis which adds to the total social satisfaction achieved. It makes philosophy an activity for the marketplace and not a debate upon definitions confined to the cloister. Indeed, it may well claim that it has the immense merit of insisting upon the importance of philosophy to ordinary people instead of depriving them of its instruction by transforming it into a monkish vocation for a handful of scholars. In its essence it urges upon the philosopher the need, if he would find the meaning of truth and good, to find them in the experience of daily life.

I venture the guess that no small part of the angry debate which centred around the discussion of pragmatism forty and fifty years ago is set in a social framework of very considerable interest. The major exponents of pragmatism, William James in the first place, and John Dewey in the second, were both Americans who so restated the central problems of philosophy that for the first time since the great debate between official theology and the Darwinians they commanded the interest and attention of the whole civilized world. They were a disturbing element in a complex academic game in which, remote from life, the professors of philosophy sought to discuss the ultimate nature of reality in terms that enabled them to avoid the perplexing issues of a tormented world. The professors restrained themselves from such explanations as might cast doubt on the general validity of things as they are. They had, in part, a fear of putting their own thoughts plainly before the people because they did not know what might be the consequences of popular understanding. They maintained what Heine called the "granary" of their thought as a closed building to which the people were denied the key. That is why, as doctrine, it either yielded society no results at all, or became like Royce's in America, or Bosanquet's in England, part of the defensive mechanism of a privileged order. How fully this was the case the philosopher Collingwood has expressed in a notable passage of his autobiography.[7]

No one can examine the immense impulse to concrete and practical thinking that the pragmatic revolt gave to all the social sciences without seeing that its historic significance lay in the fact that it foreshadowed that breakdown of a social order which began to be explicit in 1914. And the fury of the assault upon pragmatism, especially in Europe, sent a high wind through the lecture rooms of professional philosophers who had never really felt the fresh air since official approval had been given to Hegelian ideas. I think the contemptuous dismissal of pragmatism, sometimes as American and sometimes as no more than the typical philosophy of a business civilization, had its source in three deep-rooted causes, each of which had, by 1900, become part of the half-conscious make-up of the European mind. One was the defensive conviction that European civilization was more creative and more profound than anything that could originate in America. The second was resentment at a practical philosophy which called for results and refused to be satisfied with the pleasure of contemplation which did not result in an hypothesis upon which action could be based. The third, which is obviously in close alliance with the second, was that pragmatism was social, experimental, and democratic; it thus presented exactly the same challenge to official philosophy as America had presented to Europe from 1787 until the defeat of the revolutions of 1848; it was the challenge of a metaphysic which grew out of an egalitarian democracy to a metaphysic which, by its emphasis upon thought for thought's sake, revealed itself as the symbol of a society in which philosophy was the appanage of a leisured class. That challenge was resisted just as utilitarianism was resisted; for utilitarianism, in the hands of Bentham and his disciples, was a weapon in the service of a new order seeking to break down one that it regarded as old and outworn. In a sense, the manner in which pragmatism was resisted represented nothing so much as a dismayed recognition that American civilization was not only mature, but demanded a respectful treatment on its own terms.

In the same way the European refuses to take American art, in all its forms, at the value he attaches to his own arts because he cannot bring himself to accept this blow to his self-esteem. There is a deep, perhaps subconscious, satisfaction that, at least until the early years of the nineteenth century, the inspiration of all American culture was European, and that no American achievement, save perhaps that of Benjamin Franklin in physics, could be seriously compared with the masterpieces of Eu-

[7] Robin George Collingwood, *An Autobiography* (London: Oxford University Press, 1939), p. 147.

ropean creation. It is still broadly true that the interest of Europeans in
America is far smaller, both in width and depth, than the American interest in Europe. It is still more true that an American work which
criticizes America is likely to arouse more attention, to be received with
more satisfaction, than one which is written upon the assumption that
American creative talent no longer looks to Europe either for stimulus
or for standards. So intense, indeed, is this emotion that it is pandered to
by the self-exiled Americans who bluntly affirm, often with satisfied applause from European critics, that the psychological atmosphere of the
New World is unfavourable to the artist; just as it is strengthened by
the curious anxiety of most wealthy American collectors to specialize
in amassing almost anything outside the American tradition.

I believe myself that this European attitude is explicable only in sociological terms. Partly it is due to a sense of indignation that the major
cultural values in America are no longer, for most Americans, a matter
to be determined by European standards; American intellectual independence has created an inner irritation like that felt by most parents when
they find that the child whose mind had been formed by their own beliefs
begins to take a line of his own. Partly, I think, it is an inheritance from
the early nineteenth-century refusal to believe that American democracy
could have either criteria of, or achievement in, the creative arts without
a leisured aristocracy upon whose patronage their development depended. One can see in a good deal of Henry James's writing, as in that
of George Santayana, much more than half a conviction that this European attitude is justified; and it is curious to note how often even so
truthful a novelist as Anthony Trollope will write upon the assumption
that Americans are likely to be crude creatures who learn in Europe the
standards to which a civilized person is expected to conform. Partly,
too, especially since the close of the First World War, there has been
a good deal of resentment in Europe at the growth of power and vitality
in America as compared with their decline in Europe. It is even tempting to suggest that there is a real likeness between the attitude of Europe,
east of the Vistula, to America, and its attitude to Russia since 1917.
In both cases new criteria have arisen out of new experience in which
the older European experience had a relatively minor place; and the
conclusion is reached that the new experience cannot be of comparable
importance with values which, until almost the other day, the whole
world seemed to accept without discussion.

A difference in values goes, also, with a difference in psychological approach. The tendency of the European is to resent the easy expansive-
ness with which the American confronts life, his zest for change, his
willingness to put on one side traditions the Old World finds compelling,
the intensity of his power to concentrate, his conviction that the fact of
arrival is more important than the method of the journey. He dislikes,
too, the American passion for speed, the conviction, so evidently losing

ground in Europe, that the chances are enormous that tomorrow will be better than today. I think that a good deal of all this is the outcome of the relatively small part religious emotion plays in American life, compared with European, and the immensely greater part played by interest in technological advance. For though it is true that the American colonies were founded by men steeped in the doctrine of original sin, who accepted, as a general rule, a universe conceived within the historic Puritan framework, it is pretty obvious that by the time of Jonathan Edwards the sense of this world as a vale of tears and the acceptance of the doctrines of grace and election were speedily losing ground before the conviction, so evident in the rise of innumerable socialist communities and in the Emersonian doctrine of self-reliance, that man saves himself by his own effort and that he accomplishes his salvation in the world of here and now. Religion becomes a form of similar satisfaction; it is pushed to the periphery of life, and the very atmosphere of human relations does not permit either that passionately ascetic life so characteristic of Pascal, or the sublime mysticism we find in St. John of the Cross.[8] To make one's faith centre on this world, to reject historic dogma and the immemorial rituals of classical religions, is, after all, the central principle of Emerson's famous address to the Harvard Divinity School in 1838.[9]

I believe that there is a close connection between this attitude and the American passion for the material comfort that technology can devise. Even more, I think they are closely connected with the natural romanticism of the American spirit, which, very differently from that of Europe, puts its golden age in the future and not in the past. European romanticism, after all, withered into the escapism of Newman, the conservative pantheism of Wordsworth, and the emphasis by Hegel and Schelling and Coleridge that the world is, as it were, a transient thought in the mind of the Absolute. None of this was in the American mode; and none of it squared with the American experience of life. Americans saw themselves the masters of an immense domain, its conquerors, who battled with Nature only, in the end, to master it. They had no sense of freedom as an elusive phantom ever vainly pursued. They were invariably reaching out to the conviction that man was by nature good, and that, in the environment of America, there was being evoked a quality of civilization wholly lacking in the Old World. The early pattern of American political economy, for instance, shows none of that poignant and despairing acceptance of a society in which, as J. E. Cairnes remarked of Ricardo and his followers,[10] "a substantial improvement in the condition of the mass of mankind was impossible." On the contrary, the

---

[8] This was in large part seen over three-quarters of a century ago by Ernest Renan in his essay on Channing. See his *Etudes d'histoire religeuse* (Paris, 1862), fifth edition, p. 357.

[9] Ralph Waldo Emerson, *Works* (London: Bohn, 1913), Vol. III, pp. 392 ff.

[10] Alexander Bain, *John Stuart Mill* (London: Longmans, Green, 1882), Appendix.

ardent confidence in the certainty of immense improvement has been—
at least until the Great Depression of 1929—one of the outstanding characteristics of the American scene.

This element of utopianism in the United States differed from that of
Europe in two distinct ways. First, there was the widespread conviction
of the uniqueness of America; and this conviction impressed not merely
Americans themselves, but, as nineteenth-century emigration to the
United States makes obvious, a large part of Europe as well. And, second, the utopianism of America seemed far more realistic than that of
Europe, since the material basis upon which it could be built was not
exhausted until about a century after the foundation of the republic.
The struggle over slavery apart, almost all the principles to gain which
most of Europe engaged in bloody conflict came to America out of the
natural relations of the economic environment. There was no long struggle for the overthrow of feudalism; there was no bitter relation between
Church and State; there was no angry denial, at least in the North or the
West, of the right to popular education; there was no bureaucracy; nor
was there a large standing army with a special officer caste which enjoyed a special position of privilege in the community; and, not least,
there was no hereditary aristocracy with a special claim to a place in
the American government. In a sense that no other country knew, America was a political democracy based on universal suffrage; and this at
a time when most of Europe was either afraid of universal suffrage
or passionately opposed to democratic institutions.

No doubt America had, until about 1890, the advantages of what Marx
called a "colonial economy," [11] which made the contrast between the opportunities it offered and those Europe offered almost startling. The
point is that the contrast was taken as a challenge at some time during
the century by every ruling class in Europe; even in the Vatican the
"Americanism" of Archbishop Ireland virtually assumed the proportions of a heresy. It is the contrast as challenge that has created the European tendency to look askance at American art in its different forms.
For the admission of its validity as art is not merely the recognition of
American maturity in culture, but the admission that in the making
of values the European vision must be fused with the American before
it is valid. And this involves the agreement to accept the open society
where man is not imprisoned in a set hierarchy and can thus transcend
its privileges. As much of European theology and philosophy has been
world denying or pessimistic, so much of the American, since some such
time as the failure of Jonathan Edwards, has been both world affirming
and optimistic; and the permeation of the European outlook by the American ideal is as revolutionary an experience as the need for America to
come to terms with the new ideal of Soviet Russia. What is in question
is the whole social foundation upon which European culture has been

[11] Karl Marx, *Capital* (New York: Dutton; London: Dent; 1934), Everyman's
Library edition, Chap. xxv, pp. 448 ff.

built, with its deep social divisions, its tragic social and national frustrations, its fear of the socialization of knowledge, its use of all the major Churches as instruments of repression, seeking to reconcile the vast majority to a life of hard toil in which not even the leisure of men and women could normally contain either dignity or fulfilment. The use of American self-criticism as an instrument for denying the validity of American art was a brilliant technique for denying to a Europe, which, as 1830 and 1848, as 1870 and 1914 and 1939, made evident, was restless to the point where, somewhere, stability was always in process of being undermined. And despite all the immense changes in the American scene, those who undermined that stability had always inspiration, and sometimes help, from the dream of the New World. An independent American culture helping to shape world history seemed to an uneasy Europe much as the Revolution seemed to Guizot or to Metternich. Europe lived in the fear of its own shadows.

2

I SHOULD not deny that, amid all its immense achievements, the promise of American life has not been fulfilled. There are elements in the alchemy which has produced Americanism which are ugly and brutal and raucous; they still appeal to, and are applauded by, important sections of the nation. If an anthology were made of the speeches, in the Senate and out of it, of Senator Bilbo of Mississippi, it would bear a fairly close resemblance to the outlook of the Nazi Streicher. It might not be impossible to show that the newspapers of Mr. Hearst and Colonel McCormick and the late Joseph Medill Patterson flourished by their appeal to everything that was the denial of Americanism as it was affirmed by Jefferson, or Lincoln, or Franklin Roosevelt. Nor does it seem fantastic to say that the proceedings of Congress since the defeat of Germany and Japan in the summer of 1945 prove the urgency of large-scale constitutional reform in America.[12] It is hard to say which is worse—the campaigns of some of the candidates or the behaviour of the officials when elected. A great people ought to be educated by its legislative assembly. It ought to be able to look to it for leadership and understanding. No one can seriously claim that this has been true of the Congress since Franklin Roosevelt died.

But politics, whether national or international, is, after all, only an end result. What there is in it of error or misjudgment or of deliberate wrong represents those things that, in the conflict of men and social forces, have pushed themselves to the plane where recognition is either given or denied. The most unhappy thing in the pattern of Americanism must be sought in a different quarter. There were long years in which the integration of art and life were impossible in America. The principles of behaviour were too narrowly imprisoned either through the dog-

[12] As Americans themselves have recognized. See the report of the joint congressional committee presided over by Senator La Follette in the spring of 1941.

mas of a harsh Puritanism or through the grim, physical battle with the frontier. Each made deviation from the norm a danger and punished any challenge to nature by evoking cruelty alongside courage and moral degeneration alongside moral distinction. No one can read American literature until some such time as the publication of Franklin's *Autobiography* (1791) without the conviction that the forces making against any such integration were immensely strong. How strong, one realizes by remembering that the same elements which gave the joyless Mather dynasty its power were those which made possible in the late nineteenth century the massive area controlled by various forms of censorship. To express life fully still seems to a very large number of Americans something like a defiance of heaven, or a fall from grace, from which the whole community must suffer.

From about the time of the Progressive movement the integration which the Puritan tradition had so long inhibited in America began to win its battle. It is easy to see why its victory had taken so long. The Puritan virtues—self-denial, thrift, respectability, rigour, earnestness, the fear of ease and grace and light-heartedness—were exactly the virtues necessary for the achievement of that immense conquest. The life of art, the interest in things of the mind, the freedom of the spirit which can postpone affirmation until it has conquered doubt, these could hardly win their way to general acceptance until there was a sense, widely diffused, of spacious serenity among the people; and it must be remembered that for at least a generation after the Civil War the immigrant had hardly less need of the Puritan virtues than the settler of colonial times. But when the integration began to be effective, there was a new enemy to be encountered. After the Civil War the economic system of America began that feverish development of industrial power which brought with it so many of the urgent dangers that men like Jefferson and John Taylor of Caroline had foreseen. There emerged a *mystique* of commercial success which did not assuage the will to power, but infected those who attained it, and, even more, those who watched its attainment, with a passion, not for the conquest of nature, but for a new sovereignty over those who had been the human instruments of their success.

The world witnessed in the United States, from the end of the Civil War until the Great Depression of 1929, something that it is difficult not to call the decomposition of democratic institutions. The formal government was not the real government; the political parties lacked any genuine differences of principle; the boss and his machine on the one hand, and the lobbyist at Washington and the state capitals on the other, became ever more closely interlocked with the men who dominated the economic life of the nation. Since the old religious orthodoxies had been put aside, save as they were found to be a means of sublimating what might have been profound discontent, their power to restrain behaviour in the economic realm meant little; the more so because they depended, as Churches, upon the very men who regarded the State power as nothing but an instrument for securing the fantastic fortunes which lay open to them. If there were occasional moments of rebellion, the Populist movement, for example, or the I.W.W., they had never the power to stand up to their successful rivals.

There is a whole literature of revolt against the annexation of America by the "Lords of Creation." Sometimes it is a gracious but timid voice, as in William Dean Howells; sometimes it is flamboyant and shrill, as in Jack London and Upton Sinclair; sometimes it is solid but confused in the depth of its rejection of the conquerors, as in Theodore Dreiser. The rebels can document their protest with massive statistical support. They can secure men with some real capacity for leadership, the elder La Follette, for example. They can build temporary organizations to fight with courage and tenacity for this reform or that. And it is even clear that from time to time there emerges a native and profound American radicalism which explains why ideas like those of Robert Owen and Fourier evoked so interested a response a century and a quarter ago. It is, I think, especially significant that after 1933 the shift in interest in both literary and historical studies was towards the men and the ideas previously outside the major trends which interested the scholar. Men like Sylvis and Altgeld are given a new respect; the myth of bolshevist responsibility for the steel strike of 1919 is exploded; the price in human suffering paid for the wealth of the Vanderbilts and Rockefellers and Goulds is brought out with remorseless power; not least, the incredible legend of the Old South as a golden oasis of culture and hospitality and eager friendliness between masters and slaves is shown up for the folklore that it is. No one who studies carefully the half-century before the election of Roosevelt in 1932 can fail to see how new criteria of valuation struggled desperately to emerge. The underprivileged want, equally desperately, to claim their title to the possession of the Americanism which should be their inheritance, and they win a wide support which goes far beyond the confines of a class.

Three times, indeed, they have reached right out for the possession of the State power. They did so with the nomination of William Jennings Bryan for the presidency in 1896. It is easy to ridicule Bryan; he was often absurd, he was usually ignorant, and he had the narrow outlook of a man who has failed to sublimate inhibitions devoid of meaning. But when all is said against Bryan that can be said, his alliance with the silver interests, for example, the fact remains that he was the voice of the authentic American yearning that the forgotten man should be remembered. The same search was embodied in that ardent impatience with the traditional outlook of parties which resulted in the nomination of Woodrow Wilson as the Democratic, and Theodore Roosevelt as the Progressive candidates in 1912. In a fundamental sense, indeed, the sentiments and emotions which led to the choice of both men were mistaken in the persons through whom they sought fulfilment. Woodrow Wilson was a liberal conservative who had very much the outlook of

Gladstone. He was inherently a moralist, who saw the working of politics in terms of "good" or "bad" men at the helm. The America he sought to safeguard was already obsolete when he embarked on its protection; and once he became involved in the First World War, the intensity of his concentration upon international affairs was incompatible with the continuance of even the very modest effort he made towards social and economic reform. Theodore Roosevelt never felt with any profound continuity the social principles he improvised with such vigour. He was really a weak man, who shouted at the top of his voice in the hope that its loudness would drown his own sense of doubt at being separated from the normal line of his party. He showed that in relying on Mr. G. W. Perkins, a partner in J. P. Morgan & Company, as the real manager of his campaign. He showed it also both in his ardent zeal for American imperialism and in the zeal with which he permitted himself to be influenced by Senator Henry Cabot Lodge, the rich and aristocratic lackey of Republican reaction. Perhaps he showed it most of all in the complex intrigue by which he stole the nomination in 1912 from the elder La Follette, who would have been the natural standard-bearer of Progressivism. In the result, the real outcome of the election of 1912 left much the same forces in power as before it had taken place.

The third revolt was the nomination of La Follette as the Progressive candidate in 1924. This was a real challenge, embodied in a man who genuinely represented the effort of the little man, alike in farming and industry, to hold his own against the growing authority of concentrated economic power. La Follette carried only his own state of Wisconsin, though he polled over four million votes throughout the country. His candidature showed unmistakably that the power of the machines in the traditional parties, aided and strengthened by the support of Big Business, was overwhelmingly stronger than any alternative power which could be mobilized against them. And this was the more significant because the philosophy of La Follette was in no real sense an attempt to do more than limit by federal action the predominance of Big Business over Washington. He remained, though a Republican, essentially an individualist seeking to mitigate the excesses of giant capitalism; he was afraid of bigness, he was not afraid of capitalism. He still believed that the State power was a neutral factor in the community which could be swung by the electoral impact of universal suffrage in whatever direction the voters might please. The very scale of his defeat illustrated the weakness of the central principle upon which he and his supporters depended. They looked upon the forces symbolized in the Harding era with a sense of moral outrage; but their proposed remedy was really no more than a passionate plea for a return to a simpler America which was already an anachronism.

It is, no doubt, true that the persistent tradition of hostility to giant capitalism, so clearly formulated by Bryan in the historic election of 1896, was a major factor in enabling Franklin Roosevelt, in the overwhelming circumstances of the Great Depression, to drive legislation to the statute book which would have been deemed impossible five years before; above all, he effected something like a momentous change in the politics of American economic life by giving trade-unions a new and greatly enhanced status in the Wagner Act, which has not yet, by any means, exhausted its original impetus, and shows remarkable vigour even in the face of as strong a challenge as the Taft-Hartley Act. It is also important that the operation of the Wagner Act made it clear that a wide range of white-collar workers, lawyers, journalists, actors, had learned the necessity of collective bargaining and were ready to take advantage of its possibilities; one has only to read the story of the organization of the film industry in Hollywood to see that new factors were entering the American social outlook. Nor, as I think, must one underestimate the new attitude to federal experiment as shown in the successful establishment of the Tennessee Valley Authority and the Coulee Dam, in the acceptance of social security legislation, and, in one sense, the most important of all, in the emphasis upon deficit spending by the federal government on a scale which sought to be proportionate to the volume of unemployment. And it was a new and significant America which made provision, under the Works Progress Administration, for assistance to the arts in a period of economic crisis. The endowment of the theatre, of painting and music, and of literature—one of the most successful aspects of the experiment—may well come to be regarded as marking an epoch in the concept of public welfare as this has been defined by the federal government.

It is, of course, impossible to say what would have happened to the New Deal if the shadow of war had not fallen directly across its effort soon after President Roosevelt's second term began. What is obvious is that for all practical purposes he had to surrender the prospect of radical legislation in order to secure the fulfilment of his rearmament programme and the acceptance of his international policy, at least from the time of Munich until his death. Under his successor, President Truman, within a year of the war's ending, the relationship between the major political parties had practically swung back to what it was before 1933; and if there was any desire in the White House to continue the Roosevelt approach, it was effectively checked by what was virtually an alliance between the Southern Democrats and the great bulk of the Republican party to destroy any prospect that Mr. Truman might revive Franklin Roosevelt's conception of presidential leadership. That had been built upon an alliance between the President and progressive public opinion, which, with remarkable skill, he mobilized on vital occasions against a hostile Congress. It was helped, also, by the way in which he made the atmosphere of Washington so exciting experimentally that it became the Mecca of most able young men and women who felt the need for a new day. They had mostly begun to depart before the surrender of Japan; and, within a year, of those who had originally assisted President Roosevelt in formulating the policies of the New Deal, only Mr. Henry Wallace and Mr. Harold Ickes were left, though but for a short time, without any evidence that they exercised anything like the influence or the inspiration they had previously been able to do. The Washington scene, indeed, may have lacked the depth of cynical corruption it displayed after the First World War under President Harding; but the resemblance was beyond question. Federal leadership had passed from the White House to the Capitol. Step by step, the progressives were being pushed back to a condition of "normalcy"; and it was evident to all who had eyes to see that Big Business was searching for ways and means to regain the positions it had lost under the Roosevelt regime.

This brief summary holds the key, I think, to the real *malaise* of Americanism in the half-century since Bryan's appearance as the Democratic candidate in 1896. There were many American liberals, but there was no organized liberal movement. The Socialists and the Communists were two small sects with hardly any influence on the great mass of the population. All efforts to create an effective third party ended in complete failure. The attempt of the Political Action Committee of the C.I.O. to mobilize labour opinion behind a ticket it approved was important when the electors had a choice as real as that between Franklin Roosevelt and Governor Dewey; it was unlikely to be effective if no such choice presented itself; and there was no evidence to show that the committee had power enough to stand up to the normal authority of the party machines in the election of senators and congressmen in the forty-eight states. In the result, it is not excessive to say that the liberal American was as frustrated fifty years after Bryan, as he was when Bryan emerged as the nominee of the disinterested. He looked for hope to Russia; but he could not, just because he was an American, give whole-hearted support to its rigorous dictatorship. He was eager to be sympathetic to the Labour government of 1945 in Great Britain; but since his liberalism was abstract and ethical and disinclined to consider the concrete problems of power, he was irritated by the slowness with which the Labour government tackled its responsibilities, and almost wholly utopian in his conviction that the responsibilities of power could be met simply by disavowing them. He refused to admit that a government can create a vacuum and trust to its being filled by the forces of progress. He refused, even, to see that to urge the necessity for a policy is to incur responsibility for assisting in its implementation. Most American liberals acted upon the assumption that British labour must accept the reality of one world; but they shrank from accepting the implication that their own acceptance of that reality was not less important. Their own major activities hardly allowed for the fact that they were actors, and not spectators, in a vast drama in which the main theme to be unfolded was quite precisely the purposes to which the United States would put its material leadership of the world.

All this is to say, I think, that liberals viewed Americanism less as a concept of power than as a concept of ethics. They still thought, as they had thought in the time of Emerson, that there was a natural law, expressive of a natural order, which man breaks at his peril; and the defeat of Nazi Germany and Japan reinforced this conviction. They still laid, again like Emerson, far more emphasis on the free individual than upon the free society. They retained the illusion of a security for the American which could be enjoyed by all other peoples if they would only exercise the virtues of reason and goodwill. And there was an inner conviction, inevitably strengthened by their sense of overwhelming power, that it was their mission to lead the world to righteousness. They still had, despite the experience of two world wars, what Emerson called "the disposition to trust a principle more than a material force." "I think *that*," he wrote, "the soul of reform; the conviction that . . . [what is needed] is reliance on the sentiment of man, which will work best the more it is trusted; not reliance on numbers, but, contrariwise, distrust of numbers, and the feeling that then are we strongest, when most private and alone. The young men, who have been firing society for these last years with regenerative methods, seem to have made this mistake; they all exaggerated some special means, and all failed to see that the Reform of Reforms must be accomplished without means." [13] And Emerson quoted the Swiss, Pestalozzi, who shared with all ardent spirits the hope of Europe on the outbreak of the French Revolution, and, after witnessing its sequel, recorded his conviction that "the amelioration of outward circumstances will be the effect, but can never be the means, of mental and moral improvement." [14]

There remain, this is to say, two central elements in Americanism which, though obviously outmoded, retain, as yet, a deep hold upon its substance. The first is its attitude to the time factor; its unit of measurement is born of its own swift evolution and tends to make it view progress in organization as multiplication of numerical complexity. Its own history, therefore, makes it overestimate the speed with which social change can be accomplished; and the failure to accomplish it is attributed to the weakness of human nature and leads too easily to pessimism. The second is the fallacy of abstraction. The individual is not seen in his context as a member of a particular society at a particular time; he is seen as an individual standing outside society who can by an act of will, sometimes called faith, assure his own regeneration. I suspect that this is the outcome of that tradition in Christianity which certainly goes back to neo-Platonism, and is, perhaps, the outcome of its fusion with the pessimism of religions like that of Buddha. It identifies concentration on the self with other-worldliness, and it argues that from other-worldliness there is the hope of saintliness. It therefore either stands altogether apart from politics, viewing this apartness as a religious principle, or it abandons this world as hopeless in the belief that the Kingdom of God is unrelated to any earthly achievement. With the

[13] Emerson, "Lecture On the Times," December 2, 1841, *op. cit.*, p. 478.
[14] *Ibid.*, p. 480.

growth of a general secularism, a neo-Platonic attitude leads, pretty swiftly, to a social quietism which takes the evil of life for granted and the passion for planned reform by co-operative action as a snare which leads to the annihilation of freedom.

Just as the anti-intellectualism of our time, whether preached by an ardent liberal like Reinhold Niebuhr or by a sophisticated official of great learning like Professor E. H. Carr, tells us, above all else, to beware lest we identify the realm of ethics with the realm of power, so there is a duality in Americanism of a similar kind. This Americanism so decisively associates moral conduct with the individual that it approaches politics with the conviction that politics is concerned with a power that is inherently amoral. It is dubious about the chance of moralizing power, and it is therefore suspicious of the State as the brightest embodiment of power. Yet it is usually nationalist enough to put the State power of the United States in a different category from that of other nations, to transfer to it the national virtue of America's unique destiny; with the danger, always, that when it co-operates with other nations it tends to drift to isolationism lest its uniqueness be destroyed by contact with them. Washington's warning against "entangling alliances" was born of a deep sense of the uniqueness of America, and, therewith, of the concept of Americans as a chosen people. From this the step is easy to a distrust of other peoples, an inner and uneasy conviction that an association with them may stain or pollute the special purity of America. It is not accident that, to so many Americans, Europe seems old and evil, a temptation to sin which the wise American will avoid. Nor is it accident that, in each of the two world wars, American participation has seemed to some millions of its citizens not a necessary policy of self-defence, but a genuine act of charity, in which the president and Congress were deliberately casting their vote for right against wrong.

I am arguing that Americanism, in all its aspects, is inherently dualistic, and that its constant tendency is to shrink, whether internally or externally, from collective action on the ground that because collective action must involve coercion, it destroys that power of self-regeneration in man without which no reform is ever fully achieved. In Americans of a religious temper this leads, as a rule, to other-worldliness, so that the things of this life become relatively unimportant compared to the problems of their personal salvation; while in Americans without the religious temper it leads, as with Emerson, to what is almost a philosophy of inaction, even, as with Thoreau, to a separation of the self from social relations, in the belief that some inner faculty of reflection prepares a condition of regeneration. Both attitudes, as I think, go back to the neo-Platonic sources of Christian doctrine, which, in their Puritan form, so largely shaped the ethos of Americanism. But this attitude, however emotionally satisfying in the less complex society of Emerson's day, raises problems for our own that are of a different order of magnitude.

For in modern America, dominated so largely by the technology of the machine, a philosophy of inaction is a philosophy which begins by admitting failure. The American who says, with Dr. Niebuhr, that "a realistic analysis of the problems of human society reveals a constant and seemingly irreconcilable conflict between the needs of society and the imperatives of a sensitive conscience" [15] is really arguing that society is a self with its own laws which are different from, and lower than, the laws by which the individual must regulate his behaviour. But this is to omit the vital fact that society can act only through individuals who can bring to the service of their fellows ways of behaviour that are built out of their experience. Now experience in a vast society like the United States is not universally the same; nor are the "imperatives of a sensitive conscience" the same in Alabama as they are in New York. It is easy for an ardent reformer in Alabama to conclude that it is hopeless to attempt improvement of the Negro's status; just as it is easy for the ardent reformer in New York to conclude that, do what he may, he cannot ultimately prevent the return of Tammany to power. But the truth in each case is that the evidence for these conclusions is not evidence of their impossibility, but only of their difficulty. For Russia has solved the problem of race in its treatment of the national problem; and there is no large British city in which an organization like Tammany Hall has had any hold for something like the past century. At the bottom of Dr. Niebuhr's argument there lies the conviction, of which I have already spoken, that time is a category of thought devoid of value. The world and its problems then become for him not a matter to be rationally examined and met by the methods which reason may indicate, but a place in which the "sensitive conscience" has the chance to test out its imperatives, even while it must despair of success.

I do not need to point out more than the fact that an approach like this is, for all but men of the strongest character, a species of fatalism which tempts to a passive waiting upon events. And this attitude is, of course, a species of inertia which is, in its way, the strongest protective armament any given injustice possesses in society. The reformer is always a nuisance to the orthodox; and if the reformer can be persuaded that his objective is, *a priori,* beyond his attainment, the shield with which he protects the orthodox is indeed a powerful one. It would be interesting to speculate, for example, upon what would have happened to the ideals of Jefferson or of Lincoln if they had accepted the argument of the Russian theologian Berdyaev and told themselves that "when societies begin to hanker after equality, any kind of renaissance and harvest of creation is at an end. For the principle of equality is one of envy, envy of the being of another, and bitterness at the inability to affirm one's own. The passion for equality is a passion for nothingness." [16] That is, of course, the angry affirmation of one whose life and hopes were shattered by the Octo-

[15] Reinhold Niebuhr, *Moral Man and Immoral Society* (New York: Scribner, 1932), p. 257.
[16] Nikolai A. Berdyaev, *The End of Our Time* (London: Sheed & Ward, 1933), p. 54.

ber Revolution; but transferred to the American scene and widely accepted there, it is nothing so much as an insurance policy for the economic royalist. It becomes so easily transformed into the complacent beatification of things as they are, which is a denial of one of the central principles of American history, the right of Americans to change the substance of their social constitution and the directions they may seek in their voyage through life.

Here, I believe, is the source of that *malaise* in Americanism of which I have spoken. Logically the whole of its historic drive ought to have been towards the development of an egalitarian society. And in both the Jefferson epoch and in those remarkable twenty-five years between the victory of Andrew Jackson and the emergence of slavery as a crucial issue, no observer can miss the deep sense of a kind of chiliasm among ordinary Americans. It was a sense which evaporated quickly after the Civil War and has never in any full sense reappeared. Yet, so long as it is absent, the American artist is bound to feel frustrated by the atmosphere in which he lives. That is why, so far, so much of American humour has had that particular note of wryness about it that one finds in Mark Twain and Finley Peter Dunne, and the mordant satire of Ed Howe in one generation and of Sinclair Lewis in another. That is why, too, there is the European escapism of Henry James and the religious escapism of Willa Cather. It explains the savage sense of failure as triumph which is the real meaning of the provocative defiance of such Southerners as Tate and Ransom. It accounts for the deep pessimism of Melville and the wraithlike sadness of Hawthorne. Above all, perhaps, it is this *malaise* which lies at the heart of that tragedy which Henry Adams called his education, when the dream was lost of an America in which men might hope to avoid the ugly schisms and separations of Europe, and when there was driven into Americanism a poison to which no one, as yet, has found the antidote.

Many, no doubt, have tried; some of them, like Bancroft the historian, with the simple faith of an unsophisticated child; even after the presidency of General Grant, Bancroft could write with touching confidence that America "had prepared a Constitution which, in the union of freedom with strength and order, excelled every one known before." [17] To accept this facile announcement must have been difficult for anyone who thought of the attitude of both Jefferson and Jackson to John Marshall, of Abraham Lincoln to the Dred Scott judgments, or of the curious history of the habits of the Supreme Court during the course of the Greenback cases.[18] But the acceptance of Bancroft's buoyant Americanism was given a basis at once more profound and scientific by the remarkable work of F. J. Turner, one of the half-dozen outstanding figures in American historiography. Turner, in a sense, provided the grounds for defending

[17] George Bancroft, *History of the United States* (New York: 1884), Vol. VI, p. 474.
[18] *Hepburn* v. *Griswold*, 8 Wall. 603 (1870) and *Knox* v. *Lee*, 12 Wall. 457 (1871); see also Fairman, *Mr. Justice Miller*, Chap. VII.

the thesis of a native and independent American culture which Emerson had demanded in his famous address on the "American Scholar." [19] He was not merely writing history; he was also justifying the American claim that the United States was, in a special degree, the guardian of democratic civilization. If this were done, he thought, it would contribute to "awakening a real national self-consciousness and patriotism." [20] He was convinced that American democracy had an autochthonic quality about it which it owed, not to Europe, but to its own uniqueness; and he found the source of that uniqueness in the frontier. What it had done was ever to refresh and renovate democracy by the fact that it made America perpetually mobile and brought civilization from some settled habitation to a new wilderness. But because the new wilderness was always different from the old, the experience it offered, the change it effected, gave a dynamic quality to American democracy which was passed from West to East, and thence, if less fully, to the nations of Europe. "American democracy," he wrote in a now classic phrase, "was born of no theorist's dream; it was not carried in the *Susan Constant* to Virginia, nor in the *Mayflower* to Plymouth. It came out of the American forest, and it gained strength each time it touched a new frontier." [21]

The frontier, in Turner's view, remade a man. It bred, as no other influence bred, the sense of freedom, the concept of the citizen who depended upon himself and called no man master. The immense mobility of the frontier, the numerical volume of the pioneers it attracted, its power to awaken ambition and to stimulate hope, all these were different in kind from any experience open to the Old World. And the ambition of the pioneer was no merely selfish ambition. As he battled with the massive forces of nature arrayed against him, he dreamed of a new society which, out of the frontier's natural freedom, would be both inescapably a democracy and devoted to the welfare of the common man. The clue, I think, to this eloquent analysis of Turner lies in the insistence that frontier democracy was natural. It evoked "the fierce love of freedom, the strength that came from hewing out a home, making a school and a church, and creating a higher future for his family." [22] He contrasted this democracy which nature evoked with the older pattern. "This conception," he said in 1903, "has vitalized all American democracy and has brought it into sharp contrasts with the democracies of history and with those modern efforts of Europe to create an artificial democracy by legislation." [23] Thus, in America, democracy is naturally a condition implicit in the mental climate born of the physical environment, whereas, in Europe, it is an artificial contrivance imposed on that environment and not planted there by nature. His conclusion emphasizes the wide difference

[19] Emerson, *op. cit.*, p. 371.
[20] Fulmer Mood, "Turner's Formative Period," introduction to *The Early Writings of Frederick Jackson Turner* (Madison: University of Wisconsin Press, 1938). I owe a great deal to this brilliant essay.
[21] Turner, *The Frontier in American History*, p. 293.
[22] *Ibid.*, p. 267.
[23] *Ibid.*, p. 266.

in character between democracy as American and democracy as European. "Other nations," he wrote, "have been rich and powerful, but the United States has believed that it had an original contribution to make to the history of society by the production of a self-determining, self-restrained, intelligent democracy. It is in the Middle West that society has formed on lines least like Europe. It is here, if anywhere, that American democracy will make a stand against a tendency to adjust to a European type." [24]

I must resist the temptation to examine the validity of this argument in the detail it deserves. If Turner's argument is valid as he stated it, the lack of any serious institutional originality traceable to frontier experience is almost inexplicable. So, too, is the ease with which the frontier, as it became settled, developed the same characteristics and the same stratifications as the Atlantic seaboard of the United States. The Black belt of Chicago does not seriously differ, either in its internal or its external relations, from Harlem in New York.[25] There is little to suggest that the psychological foundations of a Midwestern metropolis can be distinguished, in its maturity, from those of a metropolis in the East. It is far from obvious that the faith in democracy goes deeper in a mature Omaha than it does in a mature Providence. What, rather, the evidence seems to confirm is merely that men and women respond differently to different conditions, and that it is far more difficult to maintain the niceties of class and status, and the separation and aloofness they breed, in a frontier settlement that is just laying its foundations, than in an old city about whose characteristics strongly rooted traditions have already begun to accrete. A frontier township, being new, is pretty certain to have more flexibility, more restlessness, more obvious results from the energy of its citizens, than an old city like Boston or New York or Philadelphia; it is therefore likely to offer more opportunity, which, in its turn, produces more optimism. But, on the evidence, it is difficult not to feel that Turner's theory is a brilliant attempt to find an *ex post facto* justification for that proud claim that American democracy was unique and imperishable which, among others, Emerson and Whitman advocated so eloquently. That emerges especially, I think, in its reference to "those modern efforts of Europe to create an artificial democratic order by legislation." Turner, one suspects, would have been hard put to it to explain just why he regarded the Levellers and the agrarian communists of Cromwell's time as men pleading for "an artificial democratic order," or Babeuf and his later socialist followers in that Europe where Marx and Engels turned a utopian dream into an organized movement. Nor was he very clear about what he meant by "a democratic order by legislation." For where democracy has built itself firmly in Europe, legislation has been merely the climax of a long process of democratic urgency to which it at length became impossible to deny a formal legal sanction.

[24] *Ibid.*, p. 281.
[25] *Cf.* the superb study by Drake and Cayton, *Black Metropolis*.

That is not, in substance, very different from what has been the constant experience of American life.

And these issues are closely related to the central problem that the advocates of Americanism as "unique" are bound, sooner or later, to have to face. Frontier America was essentially colonial America, freed from the necessity to submit to the control of a mother-country whose attitude to colonies followed without hesitation the mercantilist pattern. Primarily it was democratic, as Jefferson so clearly perceived, because it was agrarian; in Turner's sense, the settled city, built upon commerce and manufactures, is the natural enemy of democracy. If I may adapt an admirable phrase of Marx, how can the "anti-capitalist cancer" of the frontier be preserved? How, particularly, can it be preserved after the last frontier has been reached, when, as Marx said, there are "a colossal national debt, with the consequent increased pressure of taxation, the creation of a financial aristocracy of the meanest kind, the handing over of an enormous proportion of the public lands to speculative companies for exploitation by means of railways, mines, etc.—in a word, the centralization at a headlong pace. No longer is the great republic the promised land for emigrants. Capitalist production is there advancing with giant strides." [26] Marx saw clearly in 1867 what Turner did not see in 1893, nor even twenty years later. Marx argued that as capitalist advance devoured the independence of the individual American, it would create relations between him, as an industrial employee, and the great corporations upon which he was dependent, which would transcend, in their psychological implications, all the traditions to which an agrarian community of peasant farmers owning their own land would give rise. Turner obviously imagined that the frontier tradition would survive the disappearance of the economic relations which gave it birth. Even if we admit that in the Populist era, by which he was so clearly influenced when he wrote, the farmers fought fiercely in the name of the frontier democracy they knew against the extortion of the middleman, the extortion of the railroads, and the extortion of the banks, the fact is that they were beaten by the march of capitalist production; and where they procured some brief delay before their capitulation, they protected their democratic ideas by exactly the kind of legislation which Turner described as artificial. For no one can explain the measures by which, in the first years of the New Deal, Mr. Henry Wallace arrested the growing spirit of revolt among the farmers—the denial of the right to foreclose mortgages, the payments to farmers not to grow their crops, the state-created loans at special rates of interest, the immense schemes of irrigation carried out at the cost of the general taxpayer—except as the rescue of democracy, in Turner's sense, by means of legislation. By 1933 even in the Middle West that was least like, so he had thought, the old Europe, there was becoming evident that accumulation of wealth, and decadence of men, that was characteristic of the older world.

[26] Marx, *op. cit.,* Chap. xxv, p. 457.

This is the contradiction at the heart of Americanism which none of its thinkers has yet been able to resolve. Jefferson feared the emergence of the contradiction; but, with all his insight, what he offered was less a remedy than an incantation. For he knew that the concentration of economic power in a small number of hands threatened the security of the democratic idea, and foreshadowed the danger that wealth and government would become interchangeable terms. It was upon that issue that he had fought Hamilton and the Federalist party; and he had been urgent for the restriction of governmental action to the narrowest possible bounds. In that way, he thought, the pure democracy of a classless America might be preserved. It is man the individual whom he sought to safeguard, and it is therefore in the social voluntarism of John Locke that he found the key to democratic well-being. A mainly agrarian America, in which farmers owned and tilled their own soil, and the independent mechanic applied his own tools and skill to the craft he practised, these, for him, were the primary constituents of democracy. Men such as these had little need of government, save for the maintenance of order and defence against oppression. Yet within a decade of Jefferson's death the validity of his individualism was doubtful. Not only were American workingmen, like Skidmore and Evans, urging that America might well repeat the tragedy of the European proletariat; but Emerson and Channing and Parker were warning their readers against a materialism which might destroy the free individual by destroying social equality. The American builders of co-operative communities were trying to side-step the danger of a struggle between classes. Theodore Parker saw quite clearly the psychological consequences that followed from the emergence of a proletariat which had nothing to sell but its labour power.[27] Orestes Brownson insisted, with a power that becomes the more remarkable the more fully it is known,[28] that the class struggle was already the central fact in the American issue, and that the problems it postulated were insoluble on the plane of political democracy.

The Jeffersonian ideal ceased to have any decisive relevance to American conditions round about the time of the depression of 1837. But what Turner called the "pioneer ideal of creative and competitive individualism"[29] enjoyed a kind of prolonged Indian summer of romantic influence until the last frontier had been reached. Then, as Turner himself suggested, legislation began "to take the place of the free lands as the means of preserving the ideal of democracy." He thought that a regrettable change. "It would be," he wrote, "a grave misfortune if these people, so rich in experience, in self-confidence and aspiration, in cre-

[27] See Henry Steele Commager's admirable book, *Theodore Parker* (Boston: Little, Brown, 1936), and Parker's own article, "Thoughts on Labor," *The Dial*, Vol. I (1840), p. 479.

[28] On Brownson, see the excellent monograph of Arthur M. Schlesinger, Jr., *Orestes A. Brownson* (Boston: Little, Brown, 1939), and the important paper by Helen S. Mims, "Early American Democratic Theory and Orestes Brownson," *Science and Society*, Spring 1939, pp. 166–98.

[29] Turner, *op. cit.*, p. 307.

ative genius, should turn to some Old World discipline of socialism, or plutocracy, or despotic rule, whether by class or by dictator." [30]

It is a long and complex story to explain how this devotion to the idea of the American democracy as unique was turned to the limitation of that democracy. Partly it was achieved by the aid of myths like that of Turner, of which the real effect was to maintain, long after it had ceased to have validity, the idea of a negative State power. Partly, also, it was achieved by the Supreme Court, which invoked, or invented, a "higher" or "fundamental" law which was, for all practical purposes, in the keeping of the judges and was used by them to prevent any legislative interference with the swift progress of large-scale capitalism. Nor must one forget that Locke's ideal of the free citizen, with inherent rights that existed before any organized society came into being, was used by men like William Graham Sumner virtually to give the doctrine of *laissez-faire* the status of an eleventh commandment. And when all this seemed to be reinforced by the authority of Darwin and Herbert Spencer, suspicion of governmental intervention in social processes was nearly as axiomatic with labour leaders like Samuel Gompers as with the great leaders of capitalist enterprise themselves.

The faith in this individualism, which by avoiding legislative action was to maintain the uniqueness of American democracy, has had many sacrifices made upon its altar. It is at least some part of the explanation of that unwillingness in Emerson to confront the problem of evil which perplexed and troubled John Morley.[31] It is revealed again, even in our own time, by the conviction so strongly held by Mr. Hoover, for example, that things left alone right themselves, but that where government intervenes to protect the helpless, or to organize opportunity for those who have neither the chance nor the power to seize it, the result is to depress character and to injure effort in those on whose behalf the intervention is made. Clearly there is a good deal of the Puritan spirit left in this outlook. It is related to the belief that success is a test of character, and that the man who fails is the man who has not tried sufficiently hard. It is deeply Protestant in its insistence that man should stand alone, and that he is tempered, like steel, in the furnace where the weak are destroyed. Historically it is an anachronistic deposit from the days when almost all men saw immense horizons open before them, when, for example, as they listened to the vivid rhetoric of William Ellery Channing, they could hardly doubt that the world was theirs for the taking.[32] And perhaps nothing in this aspect of the American faith is so clearly illustrated than by the advice of Channing. He started from the active maxim "anything but slavery; poverty sooner than slavery," [33] yet he was emphatic that the destruction of slavery must come from the moral conviction of

[30] *Ibid.*
[31] *The Works of Lord Morley* (London: Macmillan, 1921), Vol. VI, pp. 40-41.
[32] William Ellery Channing, "Lecture on the Elevation of the Working Classes," *The Complete Works of W. E. Channing* (London: Routledge, 1873), p. 35.
[33] Channing, *Works*, p. 690.

the South that it is evil, rather than from the use of constitutional power against it by the Northern states. And this, once more, was the outcome of a social analysis which separated men from their environment, so that they believed that they could overcome the power of deep-rooted customs and strong interests by an act of will. Channing, like his successors in the next generation, Emerson and Theodore Parker, had little sense of the nature of the State power and the degree to which his assumption of the inherent virtue of human nature was—even supposing it to be true— dependent upon the maintenance of a social equality continuously weakened by the growth of capitalist power. Broadly speaking, all the major social reformers before the Civil War were hostile to the use of the State power as a means of enforcing change.

That hostility can be seen quite clearly in the sharp antagonism, until almost the fifties of the nineteenth century, drawn between the idea of society and the idea of government. Almost all of these reformers had immense faith in the voluntary principle; and it is, of course, this principle which led to the fervour for community experiments like that of Brook Farm. Almost all of them, too, believed that there were immense reserves of good immanent in human nature which could be evoked when the Divine spark was struck by some golden-voiced teacher, Parker, for instance, or Channing. Even when they saw that self-interest predominated over justice, they were still ready to believe that an effort of will could reverse the process and give to justice the victory. They disliked the idea of resort to compulsion; Channing, for example, spoke with enthusiasm of the cause of popular education, but his indignation was not less profound at the notion that this end could be fitly attained by the taxation of the rich.[34] No one can read the literature of the period from Jefferson until the emergence of the Southern attack on equality without seeing how widespread was the conviction of a special virtue in the American people, different from anything known in Europe, which safeguarded American democracy and fulfilled it through a voluntarist individualism.

It is really as the crisis over slavery developed, and especially after 1850, that the contradiction latent in Americanism began to be overt and to cause some anxiety. One can see that growing sense of fear in the discussions over the absorption of the Republic of Texas, and the emergence of a significant expansionism in the drive towards the annexation of Cuba. Thenceforward the *malaise* of which I have spoken became both wider and more profound. Not only this. After the victory of the North it is not an exaggeration to say that the new capitalists of the Gilded Age applied, for all practical purposes, the doctrines by which Calhoun and Fitzhugh had justified Negro slavery to the claims of the growing proletariat. There was still deep hostility to interventionism; there was still even an anxiety to insist that American uniqueness was not affected by industrialization. But it was ever less easy to persuade either the masses or the thinkers that the new capitalist society was relevant to the simple

[34] Channing, "Lecture on the Elevation of the Working Classes," p. 39.

principles of agrarian democracy. External expansion, even when covered by the prayers of President McKinley, began to look suspiciously like Old World imperialism; and the enthusiastic welcome it received from men like Theodore Roosevelt disturbed both the philosopher, as with William James, and the old-fashioned type of business lawyer, as with Moorfield Storey.

Nor could expansionism stop once it had begun. "Dollar diplomacy" began to be clothed with missionary purpose and missionary zeal pretty much as in Europe; there was an American edition of the "white man's burden." "Our wealth and our power have given us a place among the nations of the world," said Theodore Roosevelt in 1909. "But worldwide influence and power mean more than dollars, or social, intellectual, or industrial supremacy. They involve a responsibility for the moral welfare of others which cannot be evaded." [35] It is evident enough that this outlook was an effort to develop a justification for activities no different in principle from those of the European powers in Africa, and the Monroe doctrine made the pursuit of those activities less likely to involve the danger of competition than, for example, the European penetration of Morocco. As I have sought to show in an earlier chapter, this is a logical part of the philosophy of "manifest destiny." But anyone who examines the American mission as that was conceived by Jefferson or Channing or Emerson would feel some surprise at the change it underwent in hardly more than three-quarters of a century. "They are nations," wrote Jefferson to Monroe, "of eternal war. All their energies are expended in the destruction of the labour, property, and lives of their people. On our part, never had a people so favourable a chance of trying the opposite system, of peace and fraternity with mankind, and the direction of all our means and faculties to the purposes of improvement instead of destruction." [36]

It was not a conscious choice by Americans that the ideal they chiefly defined as Americanism in the first sixty years of the republic changed with the victory of the North in the Civil War. The balance of the American economy changed from agriculture to industry; the concentration of wealth in a small number of hands developed at a fantastic speed. Technological change, above all, the developments in mass production and in the methods of communication, led to social transformation by 1939 which no ordinary man could have dreamed of even in 1900. What happened to Americanism was what happened to the medieval ideal as a result of the immense discoveries of the sixteenth century. A great body of new opportunities lay open; the men who were set on taking advantage of them secured the adaptation of the national *mores* to the purpose just as their predecessors had done in Europe some three hundred years before. There is no more reason in this for blame than there is for surprise.

[35] *The Works of Theodore Roosevelt* (New York: Scribner, 1923–26), Vol. XV, p. 291.
[36] Thomas Jefferson, *Democracy*, selected by Saul K. Padover (New York: Appleton-Century, 1939), p. 204. The letter was written in 1823.

Americanism is bound to be more intricate, perhaps even more confused, when it enshrines the principles of a complex civilization embodied in the life of the most powerful nation in the world, than when it stood for those of a relatively primitive community of less than three million people, with no city comparable to London or to Paris, with few manufactures, and largely convinced that its destiny was bound up with the well-being of the farmer who owned his own land. Contemporary America seems as distant from the Jefferson who became Secretary of State in 1790, as Lancashire would seem today to a man whose life ended, like that of Adam Smith, in 1790. Ideas are the children of their environment; and a new America meant, inevitably, a new Americanism.

What is important in the change is that the intellectual basis of the new Americanism has been incapable of the swift adaptation achieved in its economic life. Men's behaviour, indeed, was adapted; but the content of their minds and, therefore, the character of their expectations underwent no proportionate change. The gap meant frustration; and the wider it grew, the deeper the frustration became. Nearly all the effort to explain the social purposes of the new order was irrelevant to its character; it remained, in large part, at least half a century behind. The children of the eighties, like the children of the early nineteen-hundreds, were the victims of a dead mythology which gave them no real clue to the life that lay before them. One can see the outcome of that frustration in most social surveys. People are bewildered, suspicious, afraid. They have passed through Indian Wars, the great Civil War, depressions like those of 1873 and 1907; always they have emerged from them convinced that they were but temporary halts in the fulfilment of the American dream. But there is a difference in quality between the frustrations before 1929 and the frustrations after it. It then became evident that the body of values, moral and intellectual, must be adjusted to the scale of material change; that Americanism, in a world of socialized production—for even if it is individualistically controlled, the productive process is still socialized—must be directly related to the spontaneous activity which a democratic society requires if it is to survive as a valid ideal. And it was clear, even before the United States entered the Second World War, that the problem of these values could not be considered in abstraction, but had to be set in the context of the whole process to which they belonged.

It is one of the difficulties involved in the explanation of Americanism that the rulers of the United States seek to define an experimental and adventurous civilization in terms of principles which no longer express its main qualities. As a result, it is failing to adapt its moral to its material environment. It is, in fact, pretending to itself; and it is only a question of time before the pretence is exposed. As this exposure begins, its symptoms reveal themselves, first of all, in literature; and the main notes struck by the writer of creative power are the notes of satire and disillusion. It is important that these are outstanding among the features of modern American literature. From William Dean Howells to that troubled Chicago school of James Farrell, Meyer Levin, and, on a remoter level, Robert Herrick, in most of the novelists of the Middle West and of the South, in Sinclair Lewis, in Ellen Glasgow, and in William Faulkner, there is an outlook that seems to betoken the erosion of faith and of hope. The same is true, in a large degree, even in the social sciences, and that despite the shadow of the plutocracy under which they have had to do their work. Of the major economists who wrote after 1900, only the work of Thorstein Veblen seems seriously relevant to contemporary America; in political science it is work like that of J. Allen Smith;[37] in history that of Charles Beard and the remarkable school that he founded; in sociology it is the work of Mr. and Mrs. Lynd in one field, and of Bernhard Stern in another, that seems alive and actual and significant. Anyone who compares the contemporary accounts of the Haymarket riots, for example, with those of Henry David[38] or of Samuel Yellen[39] will see how disillusion has taken the place of confidence. Or he can compare the account in a historian like James Ford Rhodes—the Mark Hanna of American historiography—of the efforts of New York business men to find terms of compromise, right up to the surrender of Fort Sumter, with the slave-holding South,[40] with the analysis of the same efforts in Philip Foner's brilliant narrative,[41] to watch the emergence of a savage irony into the texture of the record. Nor is it uninteresting to note the vigour and eagerness of the first two volumes of Parrington's classic work set over against the sense of decay and fatigue in the third.[42] Up to the Civil War Parrington was recording the victory of his principles; in his treatment of the later literature he was trying, not very successfully, to avoid confession of defeat. Where outworn ideas are used as the norm of civilization the artist turns to satire as his protest against a decay the coming of which he foresees.

I am not, of course, arguing that decay is a swift process; the history of Byzantium and of Tsarist Russia is clear evidence that this is not the case. I am arguing only that when the material environment of a civilization has far outstripped the values through which it has been able to satisfy demand, it is bound to be in danger. And that danger is likely to be enhanced in an age of such revolutionary technological advance as our own. For it is not enough to have change in a material environment. It must always be change that is permeated by a purpose which not only can be defined, but can also be made acceptable to those affected by the new environment. Without that purpose, a nation either, like Spain, falls into an insignificance from which it is unable to recover, or, like France in the eighteenth century, requires the excitement of revolution to reawaken

---

[37] J. Allen Smith, *The Spirit of American Government* (New York: Macmillan, 1907).
[38] David, *History of the Haymarket Affair.*
[39] Samuel Yellen, *American Labor Struggles.*
[40] Rhodes, *History of the United States,* Vol. II.
[41] Foner, *Business and Slavery,* especially Chaps. IX–XI.
[42] Parrington, *Main Currents in American Thought.*

its power of creativeness. What has happened to Americanism is that the disproportion between appearance and reality is increasingly too great to put behind the American idea the emotion that gives drive to its intelligence. Many authorities have noted that, despite the energy and power in Nazi Germany, there was an increasing decline in the quality of its science and art,[43] and that was the outcome of the gap between the appearance announced and the reality experienced. In the same way, an Americanism so largely irrelevant to present reality can live for a long time on its past inheritance; but a failure in adaptation means, at some stage, that it must prove to the mass of its citizens its ability to help them to individuality—which is the same thing as fulfilment—in their own right. Without this proof it ceases to have validity for them; and there comes a point where it can no longer support the institutional superstructure that has been built upon its supposed validity.

There is another aspect of this gap between appearance and reality which profoundly affects the values implicit in Americanism. The great ages of society are those in which men do not need to be preoccupied with themselves, when fear of the morrow is never so intense that material energy is concentrated on personal acquisition. Where this occurs, there is a power in the society to devote its effort to the elevation of its general standards, and to be confident that the safety and welfare of each citizen is the by-product of the sense of general welfare. America had that sense in the early years of the New Deal. It had not only the conviction that it was participating in a great debate, in which a renovation of values was taking place; but it also had the sense that it was setting its history in a new perspective, and that, by its analysis, it was refreshing at the source of its original inspiration its methods and its purposes. It could feel, in the drive of great action, the power to move beyond the narrow boundaries of self-gratification. It had the excitement of feeling that the social impulse was being renewed, and that the taint of hard and conspicuous egotism, which was the outstanding feature of the Coolidge epoch, had been magically transcended. The really striking fact about the first years of the Roosevelt experience was the degree of intense public interest it aroused, and, born out of that interest, the feeling in so many millions that they were themselves participating in a life larger than the parochialism of their everyday concerns, a life in which their devotion to the future transcended their sense of being imprisoned in a dead past from which there was no escape.

It was the ability to evoke that transcendence—the very essence of Americanism—which made Franklin Roosevelt a great president. From the Compromise of 1850, it had not been felt very often; twice, perhaps, under Lincoln, when he made the Gettysburg speech and when he spoke the unforgettable purposes of his people in the Second Inaugural

[43] See the remarkable lecture of Dr. Joseph Needham, "The Nazi Attack on International Science," in his *History Is on Our Side* (London: Allen & Unwin, 1946); and V. J. McGill, "Notes on Philosophy in Nazi Germany," *Science and Society,* Winter 1940, pp. 12–28.

Address; fleetingly under Woodrow Wilson; and, once more, in the acceptance speech of Franklin Roosevelt, in his First Inaugural, and in that great discourse in which, on the eve of his second election, he defined the issues which America was searching the means to resolve.[44] The atmosphere seemed to presage at once the renewal and the transformation of American democracy. With all the differences of method and of time, these seem like moments akin to those one can still feel in the speeches which Thucydides has preserved for us from his memories of the great statesmen he heard in Athens.

"It is not," says Jaeger, "a post-mortem report, but a last attempt to preserve the State. . . . All the dangers which he sees threatening . . . spring [he believes] from the internal structure of the . . . State. By good luck, or by the genius of one man, he says, we have at times won great successes, but we have been unable to keep our winnings." [45] Isocrates speaks of the contradiction between the thought and conduct of the Athenians. They regarded the State as a convenience, what Jaeger calls "a sort of equipoise among the many individual selfishnesses," but it is beyond its power to change the nation as a whole, and, like its philosophers, it "withdraws into the cloistered life of school and sect." Isocrates understood that the central problem of politics is to change men's behaviour, and he is certain that only a change in the State constitution can correct their "exaggerated individualism." [46]

Isocrates, rather like Woodrow Wilson, looked back to the renewal of an earlier Athenian constitution as the source of hope; he did not see that such a renewal had become an anachronism no longer relevant to a new world. It was Demosthenes who, from the time of his great speech *Against Aristocrates,* first showed what might have been the road to a new life for the city-state. He was fully conscious of the great Athenian past. But, with the shadow of Philip of Macedon falling darkly over the city, he knew both that the day of appeasement was over and that nothing was so important as to train the people to a new outlook. He was done with the politicians who were satisfied to be important, and at ease, and pretended to the people that their own isolationism would leave them sheltered from the storm which attacked others. He told the Athenians with direct, even brutal, frankness that the responsibility for their fate rested upon their own shoulders. He warned them not only against the fatal folly of inertia, but against the low ambition of small-minded men and the corruption of the soul in the professional politician whose sole concern was to remain in power. He did not ask for a return to the past; but he called for a renewal of that spirit of courage which had enabled an earlier Athens to destroy the Persian foe. He was not asking, as he thought, for some wild effort beyond the utmost imaginable powers of the great city; he was insisting that, where a people is made to

---

[44] Roosevelt, *Public Papers.*
[45] Werner Jaeger, *Paideia* (London: Oxford University Press, 1939–44), p. 110.
[46] *Ibid.*, p. 112; and see the *Areopagiticus* itself, especially Sections 16–20.

understand the full extent of a supreme danger, there somehow emerges an additional energy and courage which enables the impossible to assume the nature of the possible. He realized that the gap even between rich and poor could be bridged if each class made some significant sacrifice for an end higher than its own self-interest. Not even in the great Funeral Speech of Pericles, as it is reported to us by the supreme historian of all, are there words to rival those marvellous sentences in Demosthenes' *Oration on the Crown* in which he pleads with them, in pride and not in fear, to desire no other purpose than the one which their own history compelled them rightly to desire.[47]

To adapt Americanism to a new epoch needs nothing less than the spirit in which Demosthenes confronted the Macedonian threat. It is not enough to appeal to the spirit of the past; it is urgent to create the environment in which that spirit can have a new birth. An Americanism which allows the gap between appearance and reality to grow ever wider, even while it pretends that it is, in fact, being bridged, runs the risk of the same fate as the Hellenistic world. The routine goes on; the old gestures are made; the old formulæ are repeated. It is only the subsequent historian who is able to show that the organization was, in truth, running down, that the fatal flaw was the inability, or the unwillingness, of its rulers and the classes by whom they were supported to resolve the antinomy between the rich and the poor. In America, as in ancient Greece, far too many of the peasants and workmen had little save a life of toil. They had a small say in the politics of the Hellenistic world; they had a smaller place still in its culture; from time to time their masters entertained them, but it was never thought a continuous obligation so to instruct the workers that they grasped the political issues upon which their fate depended. Even the Church, while it may have attacked the cruelty and corruption of the rulers, had no advice to offer to the underprivileged save the duty of subordination; no one can find the effective elements of a positive doctrine in its teaching. The Stoic sought only an escape by preaching the unimportance alike of wealth and poverty. The Epicureans, as is shown by one of the illuminating fragments that have survived, preached generosity rather than justice. "Free life," wrote the Epicurean philosopher, "does not tolerate the accumulation of goods in large quantities since this is difficult without serving either mobs or rulers. But the free man possesses all things in unfailing abundance; and if by chance he acquires large means in addition, he will readily give a large share in them to those near to him in order to win their benevolence." [48] Obviously, in the Hellenistic world,

---

[47] See the moving book of Werner Jaeger, *Demosthenes* (Berkeley: University of California Press, 1938), *passim,* and especially pp. 217–19, 129–38. The vital passage in the *De Corona* is on pp. 202–208.

[48] *Epicurus, the Extant Remains,* translated and with notes by Cyril Bailey (Oxford: Clarendon Press, 1926), p. 67; and see Bailey's illuminating *The Greek Atomists and Epicurus* (Oxford: Clarendon Press, 1928), p. 501; see also Benjamin Farrington, *Science and Politics in the Ancient World* (London: Allen & Unwin, 1939), *passim,* but especially Chaps. IX–XIV.

the Greek idea of a community in which the character of power enables the best faculties of man both to be evoked and trained, and to find a field of self-expression, had ceased to have meaning; and the distinction was increasingly drawn between public and private life. Service to society being no longer the supreme end, the citizen made his own measure of good and evil and saw less and less of an objective purpose he shared with others. Under the authority of Rome, the *immensa pacis Romanae majestas,* he might feel more secure; but he purchased his security by the surrender of active citizenship within a society unified only by the compulsion of military and legal power.

It is a similar issue which confronts Americanism, even if the context is different and the character of the problem more obvious. But it is difficult not to feel a real resemblance between the philosophies of the Hellenistic period in Greece, and the fortunes that awaited them, and the Americanism of our own day. Particularly is it notable that while Americanism spreads its influence all over the world, as did the ideas of Greece after the Macedonian conquest, it was never able to find the secret spring which refreshed its inner life. The importance of Americanism until the end of the Civil War was as a faith, or a principle of faith, which insisted on the elevation and fulfilment of the ordinary man. If it left an undemocratic Europe unconvinced, at least that principle left it profoundly disturbed. But the importance of Americanism to Europe since the Civil War has lain in principles like industrial combination, scientific management, mass production, competitive power. The failure to revitalize Americanism has reduced it from a moral principle to a technological one. It has deprived it of a purpose which achieves in a community a new level of spiritual integration. In its new phase Americanism has transferred the centre of its speculative effort from the issue of what a man is to that of what a man has. It was the failure of this transference to renovate the foundations of Americanism which aroused the widespread interest in Franklin Roosevelt's effort to centre the activities of the State power about the "forgotten man." [49]

If one asks why President Roosevelt failed in that effort, there are, I think, two sufficient explanations. The first is his own insufficiently profound diagnosis of the problem he had to solve.[50] Franklin Roosevelt had very great qualities, imagination, a sense of humour (a supreme need in a democratic statesman), an inner self-confidence born, no doubt, of his own triumph over physical difficulty, the gift of magnanimity, the power of direct approach, the great art of working in co-operation with others, and creating in them, by his own inner generosity, the sense of high adventure. He could take criticism without repining; he was not deterred from policy by temporary defeat; he enjoyed, and, indeed, encouraged, the closest contact with his fellows. But he was never convinced that

---

[49] Roosevelt, *Public Papers,* Vol. I, p. 624.
[50] I have here adapted some sentences of mine from an article in the *University of Chicago Law Review,* December 1938, p. 31.

the foundations of the Americanism he inherited were really inadequate to the demands made upon its institutional expression. A large part of his approach to the problems of his time was conditioned by his belief that the pathology of American life, especially of its economic life, was occasioned by the malpractices of evil men; and from this he drew the inference that it is in the power of legislation, within the existing legal framework, to correct those malpractices, if it is wisely administered. Americanism, he seemed to say, was, in itself, wise in conception; his function as president was that of a physician whose art restores a healthy metabolism. But it was always his assumption that restoration, and not innovation, was his major task.

The second explanation is the grim one that during more than half his period of office as president he was compelled to prepare, or actually to wage, war on a scale the United States had never before confronted. To fulfil that duty he had to give the best of his mind not to the foundations of Americanism in the future, but to their defence in the present. To fulfil it, too, he had to co-operate, largely on their own terms, with men who were mainly hostile even to the minor reforms he deemed so necessary. He had, further, to watch, in the process of the full employment involved in building the immense war-machine which circumstances required, a loss in the millions to whom he had appealed because of their sense of insecurity and dismay. This sense had enabled him to win their assent to the changes he drove forward. War always gives the immediate issues priority over the ultimate purpose; and it is only when the peace comes to be made that there is a chance of fulfilling the announced purposes of war. It is, moreover, rarely more than a chance; for it is seldom, indeed, that the men who wage a great war are either able or fitted to make a great peace.

In the light of the impact of the Second World War I think it unlikely that the interplay of social forces would have enabled even so skilled a political strategist as Franklin Roosevelt to achieve the end he had in view in 1933. But even if he could have made the war an instrument of his purpose, I think, nevertheless, that his attempt to renovate Americanism would have failed, because it was built upon a faulty diagnosis. The President made a separation between theory and practice for which there was no logical validity. Any national system is judged by what it actually does and not by the purposes it announces. The malpractices against which Mr. Roosevelt inveighed so eloquently were less the work of evil men than the essential logic of their inherent nature. Competition did not give place to combination because a few wilful men wished it to be so; it was outmoded because, thereby, the logic of the capitalist process was fulfilled. On its own plane, the answer of capitalism to a government which seeks to use the State power for its control is either sabotage or a demand that no intervention be made against its habits which threatens the self-confidence of those who run the system. For any interventionism which seeks to maintain at once private ownership in the means of production, adequate living conditions for the masses, the power to make profit in national and international competition, and to use the State power as a neutral authority standing, without bias, between contending parties in the intricate, often antagonistic, complex of relationships in the modern community, is doomed to fail. Nothing the President could do had any prospect of relieving permanently the difficulties of commercial agriculture in America. For the fact that the United States had become a creditor country meant that its interests in foreign trade went deeper than its interests in re-establishing a prosperous farming population. That is why, despite all his eager goodwill, the President was unable to do much more than sympathize with the sharecroppers of the South. American capitalism, since the Civil War, has become monopolistic by as determined a drive of predatory finance-capitalism as the modern world has seen. There were fantastic tariffs; there was hardly any barrier to immigration left unbuilt; there was a pathetically weak trade-unionism; and there was wholesale governmental assistance to industry, as well as large loans from most of the investing countries of Europe. Agriculture pushed forward to the Pacific coast just so long as the transformation of the economic structure of America was being completed. When that stage had been reached, the choice opening to America was between a closed domestic economy to preserve the independent farmer, and an open domestic economy which would enable American finance-capital to exploit those immense foreign markets, like China, which lay ready for its profitable penetration; granted the comparative power of the farmer and the investment banker, it was obvious from the outset that victory was in the banker's hands.

I have taken one instance only of the result necessarily implied in President Roosevelt's view that what was inadequate in Americanism was not a matter of principle, but the result of its abuse by a relatively small number of men. It is a typical instance in the important sense that it arrives at a temporary *modus vivendi* in the present by making an immense mortgage on the assumed resources of an unknown, and largely incalculable, future. And it does so by accepting the refusal of the business man to co-operate in such a planning of that future as would ensure that the fulfilment of individuality has an increasing chance of success. Without planning, the destiny of America lies clearly in an increasing concentration of wealth, a growing need to penetrate the foreign market—of which, in one sense, even the Marshall Plan is an expression—and the increasing diversion of its revenues to the defence services, by which it can protect its access to the sources of the trade it believes itself to require. None of this is logically compatible with ideas constructed for an America such as that in which Lincoln grew to manhood. And the massive contradiction which divides an Americanism so firmly rooted in an ideology which the facts have long transcended, makes for both moral and intellectual confusion. It breeds a cynicism, a desire to "get on" because no other criterion seems real in terms of the facts. This attitude does grave harm by its always implicit, and sometimes explicit, aid to the conviction that the politician is no more than the successful broker for the group which exercises the biggest pressure upon him.

The conclusion to which this leads is, in its essence, simple. It is that the peculiar complex of qualities we call Americanism is now subject to much the same forces as the peculiar complex we call Europeanism. Those forces will have a retarded effect in their American expression, partly because America is so much more vast and wealthy than Europe, so that it is able to withstand crisis for a longer period; and partly because these forces have to make their way against the resistance of ideas inherited from an earlier America, just as social forces in Europe have to make their way against ideas inherited from an older civilization there. I admit at once, and gladly, that the content of Americanism, in its earlier phase, was more liberal and more democratic than anything in the analogous European heritage. I am not wholly sure that this is an advantage. It enables the proponents of reaction to fight necessary changes with conceptions that once had the power to stir men's minds to resistance in the name of progress; the new purpose conceals itself beneath the old idea. In Europe, on the other hand, the renovation of an old idea as a fighting conception has little power to deceive anyone about its real character. When General Franco talks about democracy in Spain, no one but a small handful of his supporters is deceived by his terms; even when the Pretender, Don Juan, speaks of creating a constitutional monarchy in the place of Franco's tyranny, everyone knows that a member of the House of Bourbon cannot create a constitutional monarchy. This is also true of the Hapsburgs and the Hohenzollerns. They represent a closed chapter in the history of Europe. The principles of their historic type of monarchy are no longer able to deceive men and women by a false magic.

But it is precisely this false magic which clings to the concepts of Americanism. People still vote for the Republican or the Democratic party in the belief that they stand for separate philosophies and separate interests. That was not, at any rate, Lord Bryce's view. "Neither party," he wrote, "has anything to say on . . . [vital] issues; neither party has any clean-cut principles, any distinctive tenets. Both have traditions. Both claim to have tendencies. Both have certainly war cries, organizations, interests enlisted in their support. But those interests are, in the main, the interests of getting, or keeping, the patronage of the government. Distinctive tenets and policies, points of political doctrine and points of political practice, have all but vanished. They have not been thrown away, but have been stripped away by time and the progress of events, fulfilling some policies, blotting out others. All has been lost except office or the hope of it." This judgment becomes the more significant if it be remembered that it was quoted by Mr. Justice Frankfurter as one of the main reasons why, in 1924, he proposed to support La Follette, the candidate of a third party, rather than the nominee of either of the traditional parties.[51] "Neither of the two parties," Mr. Justice Frankfurter himself commented, "faces the issues. Neither has a conception of social aims through taxation. The Republican party is frankly standpat—things are all right. To the Democrats, also, things are all right, only those who administer them are not. The Republican and Democratic parties do not face the issues because there are no differences in realities cutting across the two parties. They each represent unreal cohesions, because they are both organized appetites, kept alive by the emotional warmth of past traditions." [52] Nor were Mr. Justice Frankfurter's strictures confined to the domestic scene. "Both parties," he wrote, "have an identic record of economic imperialism. This country, under the guidance of both the Republican and Democratic parties, has proved itself an exploiting neighbour because of the false emphasis of our international policy." [53]

It is of real interest that Mr. Justice Frankfurter, who thus felt himself impelled to vote for a third-party candidate in 1924 because the older parties were merely "organized appetites, kept alive by the emotional warmth of past traditions," felt himself able to vote for the Democratic candidate, Governor Alfred E. Smith, in 1928.[54] What reasons did he assign for this change? A vote for Governor Smith, he thought, would be a vote against religious intolerance; [55] his election would have been the "rejection of a recurring attempt in the United States to attach false values to social distinction"; it would have "registered the profound conviction that . . . the practice of true experimentation in government will be furthered, and candor and honesty in public life promoted"; it would have been "a recognition that government itself is an art, one of the subtlest of arts. Government is neither business nor technology, but the art of making men live together in peace, with reasonable happiness"; it would have given "decided momentum to the liberalizing tendencies in American social economy"; it would have been a "recognition that the sanitation of American politics requires a stern reminder of party responsibility for the most extensive scandals in the history of the national government," even while it enabled the American people to separate the honesty of Governor Smith from the dishonest attempt to smear him with the corruption of Tammany Hall, under whose auspices he entered political life; and it would have shown that "the conduct of foreign relations does not require technical equipment or foreign cultivation." "It was," wrote Mr. Justice Frankfurter, "the cultivated Seward who tried to push us into war with England, and the untravelled Lincoln who kept us out." [56]

---

[51] Frankfurter, *Law and Politics*, pp. 314–15.
[52] *Ibid.*, p. 316.
[53] *Ibid.*, p. 317.
[54] *Ibid.*, pp. 320 ff.
[55] Governor Smith was a Roman Catholic, and much of the campaign against him was based on this ground.
[56] Frankfurter, *op. cit.*, p. 328.

Mr. Herbert Hoover defeated Governor Smith for the presidency by a large majority. In 1932 Mr. Justice Frankfurter once more supported a Democratic candidate, this time Mr. Franklin D. Roosevelt.[57] He did so because he disapproved of Mr. Hoover's economic policies which, he thought, "must bear a heavy share of responsibility for our national plight," for, that is, the Great Depression, and its effect both on America and the world. To Mr. Hoover, wrote Mr. Justice Frankfurter, "depressions are like the old epidemics, afflictions which come and go. The task of modern statesmanship is to devise social inventions in order to deal with the maladjustments of our economic life in the spirit in which sanitary science has been dealing with epidemics." He thought Mr. Hoover incapable of that spirit; he judged him incapable of realizing that a "new economic order" had come into being, and that "the essence of modern statesmanship" was "to understand its new problems, to devise ways of dealing with these new problems, and not persist in the old ways of an obsolete society."

I cite the attitude of Mr. Justice Frankfurter because it is, I think, typical of the effort of a modern progressive in the United States to escape from the limitations of traditional Americanism. The implications of his effort must be carefully analysed. Like Lord Bryce, he has no belief that there is any virtue left in the old party divisions. He therefore votes for a presidential nominee in whose honesty, and vision, and courage he has faith. He assumes that a new social order is necessary; and given a partnership between public opinion and the candidate of his choice, he thinks that the victory of the candidate he supports in the election will bring into power the new spirit which creates the new social order. On two out of three occasions public opinion rejects the candidate of his choice. But, on the third, in the midst of an economic typhoon, Mr. Roosevelt is swept into power. It is significant—though Mr. Justice Frankfurter neglects to say so—that Mr. Roosevelt is supposed to create the new social order with that old party the obsolescence of which Mr. Justice Frankfurter had joined Lord Bryce in noting. It is significant, also, that Mr. Roosevelt himself meant—or said he meant—by the New Deal, not "a new social order" so much as the safeguard of the old against the malpractices of evil men. And with all Mr. Roosevelt's remarkable and courageous experiments, with all his amazing hold upon public opinion, it was tragically evident, after his death, that if he had influenced the ordinary man's conception of Americanism, he had been unable so to transform it that there was any general perception of the need for a "new social order." His successor, President Truman, as well as his Republican opponents, returned, almost without knowing it, to the ideology of that Americanism from which, as they seemed to assume, the New Deal had been simply a temporary deviation.

It is an irresistible temptation to compare the impact of the Roosevelt idea during its twelve years of world-wide influence with that of the

[57] *Ibid.*, pp. 329-33.

men, who, since the days of Lenin, have really created that new social order they believed to be necessary; and it is of exceptional interest to make the comparison because it emphasizes the resemblance I have noted between the Americanism of the post-Civil War period and the Hellenistic age which began with the failure to arrest the imperial visions of Philip of Macedon. In both cases men knew that the world had become a smaller place—one world—in which it was increasingly important to recognize the need for the unity of mankind. In both cases the central problem was the deep gulf between rich and poor, and the spectre of revolution it created. In both cases, also, the rich in any city or country, as the poor, felt it to be the implication of a single world that, as revolution anywhere threatened the first, so, in like fashion, counter-revolution threatened the second. It is hardly an extreme analogy to say that, in this unhappy society, Lenin, like Epicurus, urged its citizens to "free themselves from the prison of business and politics." He, too, like his precursor, felt that men were afraid "and through their fear were led to actions most likely to create fear." Like Epicurus again, Lenin insisted that "by means of occupations worthy of a beast abundant riches are heaped up, but they lead to a miserable life." The jungle lay so near that *homo homini lupus* was less a phrase than a grim account of actual relations. Men failed to see, said Epicurus, "that he who has learned the limits of life knows that whatever removes the pain due to want, and gives a fulfilment to the whole of life, is easy to obtain, so that there is no need of that activity which involves competition." That, after all, is what Lenin saw, as Marx had seen it before him. Both of them denied the maxim, upon which both Plato and Polybius had insisted, in the phrase that the great conservative historian made famous, that "the masses in every State are unstable, full of lawless desires, of irrational anger, and of violent passion." [58] It was by reason of this denial that Lenin and his supporters built a new social order, and fought for it with revolutionary passion in the conviction that any alternative social philosophy might well bring leisure and grace and distinction to the few, but that, in the process, it would be compelled to bind the masses to a servitude out of which they would have to fight their way.

That fear of the masses which lay at the root of Plato's doctrine, as of that of Polybius, was also deeply rooted in the mind of Daniel Webster at the very time when Americanism was in its springtime of expansion. "The true principle of a free and popular government," he wrote in 1820, "would seem to be so to construct it as to give to all, or at least to a very great majority, an interest in its preservation; to found it, as other things are founded, on men's interest. . . . The freest government, if it could exist, would not be long acceptable if the tendency of the laws was to create a rapid accumulation of property in few hands, and to render the great mass of the population dependent and penniless. . . . Universal

---

[58] Polybius, *Histories* (Cambridge: Harvard University Press, Loeb Classical Library), Vol. VI, p. 56.

suffrage, for example, could not long exist in a community where there was great inequality of property." [59] Webster, of course, immensely exaggerated the effect of universal suffrage; at least since the time of Napoleon III, we have known not only that it is an instrument peculiarly suited to the purposes of counter-revolutionary dictatorship, but also that there are other, and more subtle means, of checking the threat of universal suffrage to a "rapid accumulation of property in a few hands." The danger of an unlimited franchise is not, in fact, a real danger. The true crisis of a community comes when its members have to learn to regard its traditions from a new angle, and to anticipate its future with a new emotion, and to do both of these upon premises sufficiently alike to enable them to discuss their implications peacefully in terms of reason. For persuasion, and not force, is the real safeguard, where it can be had, of civilized living.

That is why, some eighty years after his death, the question that Lincoln put to his people becomes all-important once more. It was at the Republican State Convention at Springfield, Illinois, that Lincoln, on the 16th of June, 1858, put the issue in phrases that have never been surpassed since he used them. "If we could first know where we are, and whither we are tending, we could far better judge what to do and how to do it; . . . agitation has not only not ceased, but has constantly augmented. In my opinion, it will not cease until a crisis shall have been reached and passed. 'A house divided against itself cannot stand.' . . . I do not expect the Union to be dissolved. I do not expect the house to fall—but I do expect it will cease to be divided. It will become all one thing or all the other." [60]

Americanism must come to mean the same thing for the sharecropper of Arkansas as for the stockbroker on Park Avenue in New York City, for the steel worker in Pittsburgh as for the corporation lawyer in Wall Street, for the senator from a Southern state like Alabama as for a senator from a Northern state like Vermont, if, indeed, the house is to stand. There may be multiformity in unity about the significance of Americanism to all Americans, but there must, at least, be the agreed and unbreakable obligation to accept free debate, with its corollary of free change, where there is a majority will for free change, as the technique by which the content of Americanism is defined.

It is no use pretending that this will be easy. It is not excessive to say that the internal problems of the United States are at least as difficult as they were between 1850 and the outbreak of the Civil War. It is merely platitudinous to insist that its external problems are not only new and immense, but that their very scale is related to the exercise of a power that gives the American people responsibilities with which is bound up the fate of world civilization. In Russia, Lenin cut the Gordian knot of

---

[59] Daniel Webster, *Journal of Debates and Proceedings in the Convention of Delegates Chosen to Revise the Constitution of Massachusetts, November 15, 1820–January 9, 1821* (Boston, 1821).

[60] Stern (ed.), *Life and Writings of Lincoln*, p. 429.

passionate disagreement upon first principles by embarking upon a violent revolution, the momentum of which is still very far from being exhausted. He succeeded in seizing the State power on behalf of the masses ; but the dream he dreamed, with all its nobility, is still far from fulfilment, and it still exacts an almost overwhelming price from those on whose behalf he had his vision. It was far easier to use Lenin's method in agrarian and illiterate Russia, with its major resources undeveloped even when known, and its bourgeoisie of little significance in the national economy, than it would be in a United States so deeply dependent upon a highly developed technological system which, in its turn, largely influences the economic fortunes of the whole world. Social disaster could not, as the Great Depression made plain, descend upon America without every other nation being involved in that catastrophe.

The destiny of America is still in the melting pot ; but it would be dangerous, indeed, not to remember that it is a problem in time. World history is more likely to be shaped by American history for the next half-century than by any other element in its making ; but how it is to be shaped depends on how Americanism is shaped, and that is still a question to which no answer has been given. It is difficult to see how the world can meet its problems squarely without the moral and material leadership which only America is in a position to provide ; it is still more difficult to see how this leadership can be provided until there is a new plane of agreement which enables the full inspiration of Americanism to be used in its service. Twice in the last forty years American presidents have made noble efforts to mobilize this inspiration at a higher level than at any time since Abraham Lincoln. The attempt of Woodrow Wilson was defeated ; and it is very far from clear that the attempt of Franklin Roosevelt will meet a different fate.

How urgent it is that there shall be no failure in this realm will be the more fully grasped, the more the power and weight of American possibilities are really known. Something, no doubt, Europe can achieve, in part by a fuller understanding of America, in part by preparing itself for unity with the best of American purposes at the highest level it can attain. Without that understanding and that preparation the future is dark indeed. Injustice within each national society, and a sense of general insecurity brooding over the chaos of international relationships, might well confront our civilization with that sense of disaster which goes too deep for recovery to be possible. That would be an infinitely tragic fate for mankind at a moment when the possibilities before us are so great of a conscious mastery over the alien forces of Nature. Something in Europe, I say, men can achieve by understanding and self-preparation. But it is within the United States that the final issue is bound to be decided ; on nothing else, perhaps, does the outcome depend so much as upon its ability to conquer both inertia and fear. It is in the degree that America's citizens transcend these dangers that the immensity of their power will redeem the greatness of their historic promise.

passionate disagreement I upon first classified by enchanting upon a so-
lent rejection the promotion of which is still very far from being exhausted. He searches in search a desperate power on behalf of the masses;
but the decline be dreamed, well off its nobility, faced it far from fulfilment; and it still exist in almost overwhelming price from those of
whose behalf he had his visions; it was far easier to use; it must stand
to patrician and different Russia, with its major resources underpinned
even with known, and its byproducts of little significance in the rational economy, than it would be in a United States so deeply dependent
on a highly developed technological system which, in on, more largely
enhances the economic fortunes of the whole world. Such changes could
not as the Great Depression made plain, develop upon America, without every other nation being involved in that catastrophe.

The destiny of America is still in the melting pot; that it would be
dangerous, indeed, not to remember that it is a problem in time. World
history is more likely to be shaped by American history for the next
half-century than by any other element in its making; but how it is to be
shaped depends on how Americanism is shaped, and that is still a question to which no answer has been given. It is difficult to see how the
world can meet its problems squarely without the moral and material
leadership which only America is in a position to provide; it was still more
difficult to see how this leadership can be provided until there is a new
plane of agreement which enables the full integration of Americanism
to be used in its service. Even in the last forty years American presidents have made noble efforts to mobilize this inspiration at a higher
level than at any time since Abraham Lincoln. The attempt of Woodrow
Wilson was defeated; and it is very far from clear that the attempt of
Franklin Roosevelt will meet a different fate.

How urgent it is that there shall be no failure in this realm will be
the more fully grasped the more the power and weight of American
possibilities are really known. Something, no doubt, Europe can achieve
in articulate a fuller understanding of America, to that by preparing itself
for unity with the best of American purposes; for the higher level it
can attain. Without that understanding and that preparation the future is dark indeed. Injustice within each national society, and a sense
of general insecurity hanging over the ideas of international relations,
make them, well I inform our civilization with that sense of disaster
which gives too slim our recovery to be possible. That would be an infinitely tragic conclusion to a moment when the possibilities for
peace are are so great of a conflict is about ready over the alien forces of its
time. Something, in Europe, I say, men can achieve by understanding and
self-preservation. But it is within the United States that the final issue
is bound to be decided; on nothing else perhaps does the future of the
period so much depend its ability to conquer both the rise and fear. It is in
the degree that Americans can, on transmuted those images that the immensity of their power will reckon the greatness of their historic purpose.

Index

Index

Abinger, James Scarlett, Baron, 586
Abolitionist movement, 313, 461
Abrams v. *United States,* 20, 111, 113, 435–36
Absolute, the, in Royce's philosophy, 447, 449
Academic freedom, and Catholic Church, 309, 368; and the press, 187, 640; in schools, 335, 381; in universities, 355–60, 369, 382
Academy of Medicine, New York, 598, 607, 609
Acheson, Dean G., 97, 104
Action, as essence of American spirit, 42, 55–56; as substitute for thought, 411, 412
Acton, Lord, 62, 414
Adair v. *The United States,* 435
Adams, Alvin, 47
Adams, Brooks, 252–53, 444–45
Adams, Charles Francis (1807–1886), 62, 106, 720
Adams, Charles Francis (1835–1915), 168–69, 413, 444
Adams family, 6, 649; *see also* Adams, Brooks, Charles Francis, Henry, John, John Quincy
Adams, Henry, 12, 40–41, 449, 740
Adams, Herbert B., 415–16
Adams, John, 8, 9, 26, 211, 267, 395, 397, 398–99, 400, 434, 435, 518; and Jefferson, 249–50, 404, 718
Adams, John Quincy, 106, 122, 415, 497, 719
Adams, Samuel, 4, 28, 397
Adaptation, in American spirit, 43; of European culture, 398
Addison, Joseph, 394
Advertising, 167, 627, 631, 635, 639, 657, 673, 692, 697
Against Aristocrates, 751
Age of Enlightenment, 9, 407–408
Age of Reason, 10, 267, 294
Agriculture, as a minority, 452, 454, 486–94; prospects of, 535, 755; and trade-unionism, 233, 238, 240–42, 492; *see also* Farmers
Air bases, U.S., 504, 544
Alaska, U.S. policy in, 510
Alcott, Bronson, 41, 42
Alderman, Edwin A., 348
Aldrich, Nelson W., 18
Alger, Horatio, and Bok, 659; epitomizing an epoch, 622; influence of, 231, 256
Alien and Sedition Acts of 1798, 632
Allen, Ethan, *Reason the Only Oracle of Man* by, 267, 294
Allen, Frederick L., 168, 359, 386
Altgeld, John Peter, attitude to, 162, 438, 616, 669; and federal power, 143; Mencken's attack on, 422, 667; rediscovery of, 733
Alvord, Clarence W., 66, 417

Amalgamated Clothing Workers of America, 224, 643
American Bar Association, 142, 386
American beliefs, "America is different," 5; in education, 5; effeteness of Europe, 710; equality of opportunity, 708; failure fault of individual, 166; making citizens good by legislation, 160; political equality, 708; in progress, 39; solubility of problems by good will, 709
"American Century," 503, 659, 678
American Civil Liberties Union, 647, 669, 706
American Commonwealth, The, 16, 61, 63, 296
"American dilemma," 44, 122, 467–74, 706; *see also* Negroes
American dogmas, 157, 708–11
American Federation, The, 648
American Federation of Labor (A.F. of L.), 131–132, 200, 206–207, 209, 215, 216, 218–19, 220, 226, 243, 476, 478, 624, 711
American Federation of Teachers, 224
American Film Foundation, 693
American Industries, 648
Americanism, discussion of, 714–61
American Jitters, The, 622
American Labor party, 217
American Language, The, 666
American Law Institute, 580
American Legion, 135, 336–37, 619, 640, 674
American Medical Association, 575, 598–609; and Christian Science, 619; Kingsbury on, 602
American Medical Practice in the Perspectives of a Century, 607
American Mercury, The, 665, 666–67
American Military Government, 506, 558
American myth, the, 52, 53, 189, 421
American Newspaper Guild, 224, 638, 642
American Newspaper Publishers Association, 639
American Philosophical Society, 395–96
American Police Systems, 160
American Political Science Review, 648
American promise, 82, 403, 404, 407–18, 422, 439
American Renaissance, The, 420
American Revolution, *see* War of Independence
Americans, characteristics of, 16, 39 ff., 61, 715–716; as a chosen people, 269, 415, 561, 738
American Tobacco Company, 109
American tradition, action *v.* theory in, 12, 39, 542; and Babbitt's conventions, 22; belief in progress in, 8, 34, 39; caste postulates, absence of in, 5, 403; change in, 5; Christian heritage in, 7, 264; and Communist party, 719; com-

American tradition (*Continued*)
pared with European, 25, 34; conservatism in, 4, 10; craving for special status in, 5; dignity of man in, 8; dignity of toil in, 7, 34; dynamic civilization and, 5, 54; education and, 5, 23, 34, 324; empiricism in, 12; English influence on, 4; enlightened self-interest and, 15; equality in, 631–32, 708, 718–19; expansionism in, 3, 5; experimentalism in, 4, 8, 34, 403; feminism in, 10; foreign strains in, 3–4; and Great Depression, 34–35; hope, role of in, 6–7, 403; immigrants' contribution to, 13; and the law, 31–33, 55; in literature, 14–15; and majority rule, 17; mass production's effect on, 13–14; and minorities, 24; and negative state, 115; opportunity and, 6, 18, 403; pioneer in, 6 ff.; of political democracy, 81–82; religion and, 3–4, 7, 30, 36–40; pragmatism in, 12; priority of practical man over thinker in, 5, 15, 66, 166, 365, 722; property rights and, 10; radicalism in, 4–5; Reformation and Renaissance heritage in, 325; revolutionary thread in, 10, 713; in rural areas, 157; self-confidence in, 3, 4, 8–9; self-fulfillment in, 403; self-reliance in, 4, 40; shaped by ordinary men, 9; suspicion of, 38; test of, 36, 38; and totalitarianism, 37; unlimited horizons and, 5, 34, 53–54, 400; veneration for law in, 31–33, 55; versatility in, 8
"American way of life," 167, 480–81, 535, 555, 631, 669, 687, 699, 709
America's Coming-of-Age, 423
Amery, Leopold, 511
Ames, Fisher, 9, 436
Ames, James Barr, 113, 373, 584, 587
Ames, Nathaniel, 8
Anaconda Copper Mining Company, 19, 155, 358
Anarchists, Chicago, 64, 202, 616
Anderson, Marian, 467
Anderson, Sherwood, 50, 411, 652
Andrews, Charles McLean, 416
Andrews, Elisha B., 356
Angell, James R., 348
Anseele, M. E., 696
Anti-intellectualism, 270, 738
Antinomianism, 26, 42
Anti-Semitism, 71, 194, 255, 452–54, 456, 477–86
"Appeasement," 134, 500, 559
Appleby, Paul H., 101
Appointments, confirmation by Senate of, 85
Apprentice system in education, 325
Aptheker, Herbert, 626
Architecture, 45, 394, 396
Aristocracy, in America, 710; its cultural theory, 399–400; More on, 426; "natural," 436; and the presidency, 59; and theocracy, 432
Armstrong, Hamilton Fish, 648
Army, U.S., overseas censorship and 1944 elections, 108; treatment of Negro soldiers, 706
Army Training Manual, on democracy, 669
Arnall, Ellis G., 226
Arnold, Matthew, 49, 58, 62, 392
Arnold, Thomas, 383
Arnold, Thurman W., 119, 195, 228, 370; and philosophy of business man, 190–91; on social mythology and education, 331; on social processes and the law, 587
Art, American, attitude of Europe to, 398, 721, 724, 727–28, 730; in colonial period, 394; frustration of, 740; integration of, 731–32; self-consciousness of, 45; snobbism to, 728
Arthur, Chester A., 149
Asceticism, in American religion, 13, 288
Asia, 505, 544; balance between U.S. and U.S.S.R. in, 515; influence of Russian Revolu-

tion in, 555; U.S. penetration of, 554–55
Asquith, Herbert H., 93, 733
Associated Press, 633, 635, 637, 646
Astor, John Jacob, 23, 33, 41, 109, 165, 169
Astor, Vincent, 129
Atheism, 29, 76, 295, 296
Athletics, school, 16, 337, 350
Atlantic Monthly, The, 637, 665, 666
Atomic energy, and international relations, 537–553
Attlee, Clement R., anti-Semitic attacks on, 454 n.; and atomic bomb discussions, 539, 549; composition of his cabinet, 716; "federate or perish," 556
Audubon, John J., 665
Australia, 35, 156, 690
Austria, 506
"Availability," in academic appointments, 356–357; *v.* fitness, 56, 756; of political candidates, 76, 83, 118, 140

Babbitt, 21–22, 424, 713
Babbitt, Irving, 65, 275, 364, 403, 424–25, **723**
Babcock, Edward V., 615
Babeuf, François Emile, 742
Babson, Roger W., 197, 385
Baer, George F., 169
Bagehot, Walter, 12–13, 23, 563, 626
Baker, Newton D., 93, 94
Balance of power, international, 516–17; state *v.* federal, 152–54
Baldwin, Stanley, 541, 641
Balfour Declaration, 301
Ball, Joseph H., 129
Balzac, Honoré de, 428, 665, 721
Bancroft, George, 373, 414, 415, 740
Bankhead-Jones Farm Tenant Act, 492
Bank of the United States, 69
Baptists, 286, 303, 425
Barlow, Joel, 8, 10, 294, 404
Barnard, Henry, 325
Barnes, G. N., 136
Barnes, Thurlow Weed, 140, 148
Barton, Bruce, 85, 668
Baruch, Bernard M., 120
Bauer, Bruno, 23
Beale, Howard K., 386
Beard, Charles A., 52, 66, 692, 749; and academic freedom, 358; and economic origins of Constitution, 22, 368, 417, 626; on lawyers of revolutionary period, 572; *Rise of American Civilization* by, 416
Beard, Mary R., 416; *see also* Beard, Charles A.
Beck, Dave, 163, 202
Beck, James M., 85, 113
Becker, Carl L., 361, 378; *Declaration of Independence* by, 66, 417
Beecher, Henry Ward, 275
Beecher, Lyman, 294
Beer, George Louis, 414
Beerbohm, Max, *The Happy Hypocrite* by, 335
Beiliss, Mendel, and Kishineff ritual-murder trial, 479
Belgium, 453, 696
Beliefs, American, *see* American beliefs
Bell, Alexander Graham, 628
Bellamy, Edward, 441
Bennett, James Gordon (1795–1872), 633–35
Bennett, James Gordon (1841–1918), 636
Benson, Allan L., 710
Bentham, Jeremy, 66, 103, 371, 373, 580, 591, 615
Berdyaev, Nikolai A., 739–40
Berge, Wendell, 119–20

Berger, Victor, 709–10
Berkeley, Bishop George, 315, 566
Berle, Adolf A., Jr., 97
Bethlehem Steel Corporation, 161–62
Beveridge, Albert J., 561
Bevin, Ernest, 549, 663, 702
Bible, 296, 624
Biddle, Nicholas, 54, 407
Biglow Papers, The, 420
Bilbo, Theodore G., 661, 670, 731
Billings, Warren K., 202
Birth-control, 618, 698–99, 699–700
Birth of a Nation, The, 624
Bismarck, Prince Otto von, 62, 133, 416
Black, Hugo L., 79, 86, 114, 195, 471; and investigation of Wall Street, 89–90, 162, 193, 253
Blackmur, Richard P., 428
Blackstone, Sir William, 30, 112, 370, 371, 397, 567
Blaine, James G., 80, 94; and *Boston Transcript,* 630; campaign of E. L. Godkin against, 649; as representative political figure, 64, 443–44; J. F. Rhodes on, 414; and Roman Catholics, 269
Blair, Francis P., 633
Blair, James, 324
Blasphemy, Bagehot on, 626; laws on, 29
Bliss, William D. P., *Encyclopædia of Social Reform* by, 274; social gospel of, 274, 295
Bliven, Bruce, 651
Blum, Léon, 133, 453, 696
Board of Regents' Inquiry, 336
Bodin, Jean, cited by John Cotton, 432
Bohlen, Francis H., 373
Bok, Edward W., 657–59
Book clubs, 168, 174
Borah, William E., 14, 59, 74, 86, 91, 148, 524
Bosanquet, Bernard, 727
"Boss," and men of wealth, 162; in municipal government, 32, 120, 158, 159; origin of, 32; in rural areas, 159; source of his power, 59–60; in state government, 140, 147
Bossuet, Jacques Bénigne, 424
Boston, 11, 50, 154, 301, 397, 409; anti-Semitism in, 480, 481; and *Atlantic Monthly,* 665; and Catholicism, 142, 302, 306, 639; politics in, 158, 163; Watch and Ward Society of, 304–305
Boston Evening Transcript, 630
Boston Globe, 646
Boston Herald, 589
Boston Medical and Surgical Journal, 591
Boston Quarterly Review, 664
Boudin, Louis B., 616
Boulder Dam, 102, 153
Bourchier, J. D., 641
Bowles, Samuel, Sr., 47, 634
Bradden, Laurence, 566
Bradlaugh, Charles, 295
Bradley, Francis Herbert, 282
Bradley, Joseph P., 212
Bradstreet, Anne, 394
Brady, Mathew, 45
Brailsford, H. N., 641
Brandeis, Justice Louis D., 97, 320, 477, 715; Colonel House on, 479; and "curse of business," 157, 195, 228; eminence as a judge, 19, 112, 715; exposure of railroad corruption, 579; hated by financial magnates, 712; and Jeffersonian democracy, 212, 441–42; and legislative experimentation, 30; on liberty of contract and labor unions, 243; nomination to Supreme Court of, 31, 576; passion for social justice of, 578, 589; and standards of political conduct, 65

Brave New World, 622
Brayton, Charles R., 149
Brenner, James E., 574
Bretton Woods agreement, 529
Brewer, Justice David J., 212, 672
Brick, Jefferson, as characterization of period in American history, 16, 249
Bricker, John W., 98, 131
Bridges, Harry, 257
Briggs, Charles Augustus, 295
Bright, John, 23, 62
Brisbane, Albert, 230, 675
Brisbane, Arthur, 642, 644, 645
British Medical Journal, 600
Brogan, D. W., on need for labour party in U.S., 250, 251; on spoils system in U.S. Civil Service, 103
Brook Farm, 46, 51, 229, 254, 268, 405
Brooks, Phillips, 296
Brooks, Van Wyck, 423, 664
Broun, Heywood, 642
Browder, Earl, 653
Brown, J. E., 464
Brown, John, 405
Browning, Elizabeth Barrett, 54
Brownlow, William G., 269
Brownson, Orestes A., and *Boston Quarterly Review,* 664; on class struggle, 744; conversion to Catholicism, 269–70, 310, 405; on dangers in American development, 51; on freedom, 392; kinship to Marx of, 405; on motive forces in capitalist democracy, 664; social ethics of, 229
Bryan, William Jennings, 148, 195, 215, 235, 250, 422; belief in America as arbiter of the world, 561–62; as editor of the *Commoner,* 637; hostility to, 390; place in political philosophy of, 434; and Populists, 58, 130, 491; press on, 676; J. F. Rhodes on, 414; and Scopes trial, 286; as Secretary of State, 106, 523; as voice of "forgotten man" in election of 1896, 733–34, 736
Bryce, James, *American Commonwealth* by, 16, 61, 63, 296; on Civil Service as cure for corruption, 160–61; compared with Tocqueville, 16–17, 63, 722; contributor to *Nation,* 649; on decline of interest in theology, 296; on differences between two major parties, 756, 758
Buchanan, James, 74, 497
Buchmanite movement, 36
Bulletin of American Association of University Professors, 194
Bunyan, John, 287
Bureau of Standards, 20, 101–102, 167
Burgess, John William, 441
Burke, Edmund, and attack on social service state, 257; economic views of, 10, 231, 566; on individual success and general good, 440; on irresistible current of history, 392; on men and measures, 146; and Paul Elmer More, 426; *Thoughts on Scarcity* by, 231
Burleson, Albert S., 652
Burrows, Sir F. J., 567
Business, and use of American Legion, 674; and bureaucracy, 21, 543; and communications media, 21–22, 173, 176, 620, 634, 638, 640, 647–648, 668, 705; critical position in world of, 531–537; critique of, 165–99; and culture, 438–39, 450; and economic welfare, 116; and education, 13, 22–23, 186, 194, 381–82, 383, 386–91, 535–37; faith of, 166; and foreign investments, 178, 180–81, 534; and foreign policy, 542–43, 544, 546, 551; and the Great Depression, 438, 543; habits of, 444; influence on professions of, 18, 214, 567, 599, 610–14, 605, 607; key positions of, 222–24; and labour, 202–203,

Business (*Continued*)
204, 206, 214, 246, 247, 252, 253, 261; and political machines, 32, 59–60, 120, 168, 170–71; practice *v.* philosophy in, 182, 183–84, 185, 199; and prohibition, 157; and reform, 222; and religion, 198–99; Republican party as instrument of, 80; *see also* Business Man

Business Man, F. L. Allen on, 359, 386; Brooks Adams on, 252–53, 444–45; Charles F. Adams on, 168–69, 413; characteristics of, 50–51, 171–72, 174–77, 365–66, 382; and the courts, 189, 190; hostility to Russia, 516, 543, 551, 552; and Locke's political philosophy, 114; outlook of, 166–72, 174–77, 436, 542–43; prestige of, 165, 169–172, 437–38, 450; Tocqueville on, 184; *see also* Business

Butler, Nicholas Murray, 113, 692
Byrd, Harry F., 78, 129–30, 148–49
Byrnes, James F., 120

Cabell, James Branch, 65, 410, 422
Cabinet, in U.S. government, 73–74, 92–99, 108, 117–18
Cabinet of Dr. Caligari, The, 631
Cable, George Washington, 408
Cairnes, John Elliott, 62, 729
Caldwell, Erskine, 411
Calhoun, John C., 46, 49, 74, 86, 91, 93; and doctrine of "higher law," 187; justification of slavery, 457–58, 746; as political theorist, 441; reaction of contemporaries to, 186
California, contrasted with Maine, 156; "EPIC" movement in, 131; and political democracy, 19; Republican machine in, 151; significance of Pearl Harbor on, 35; Sinclair's campaign for governorship of, 152; State Medical Society of, 601; and trade-unions, 146; Vigilantes and the press in, 675
"Calling," Puritan doctrine of the, 565–66, 567
Calvin, John, 191–92
Calvinism, 425, 432–33
Cambridge Platform of 1648, 265
Campbell-Bannerman, Sir Henry, 564, 717
Canada, 35, 137, 156, 560
Canterbury, Archbishop of, *see* Temple, William
Capen, Samuel P., 365
Capitalism, contempt for politics of, 253–54; and democracy, 70; of the North and Southern ruling class, 405, 463, 465–66; and world power, 406; *see also* Finance-capitalism, Monopoly capitalism
Capitalist democracy, benevolence of, 247; identified with *laissez-faire*, 212–13, 230–31
Capone, Al, 32, 425
Cardozo, Benjamin N., election to New York bench of, 144; eminence as a judge, 19, 112, 714; as Jeffersonian democrat, 212; on legislative experimentation, 30; on "masquerade of privilege," 31; plea for Ministries of Justice, 581
Carey, Henry C., 231, 373
Carlyle, Thomas, 62, 415, 721
Carnegie, Andrew, 109, 165, 186, 193, 231, 426, 719; and P. C. Knox, 577; as philanthropist, 621–22; philosophy of, 205, 659, 710; *Triumphant Democracy* by, 169; *see also* Homestead strike
Carnegie, Dale, 256
"Carpet-bag" regimes, 463, 475
Carr, Edward H., 738
Carroll, Charles, 5, 394
Carson, Kit, 486
Cartels, international, 530–31, 546
Carver, Thomas Nixon, 168, 359, 677

Cary, John, 566
Cassatt, Mary, 365
Cather, Willa, 740
Caucus rule, 655
Cavendish, Henry, 714
Cecil, Lord Robert, 541
Censorship, 108, 619, 627, 682–83, 688, 689–91, 695, 698–700
Centralia massacre, 64, 674
Century Magazine, The, 665
Chafee, Zechariah, Jr., 358, 373
Chamberlain, Joseph P., 587
Chamberlain, Neville, attitude to Czechoslovakia, 542; hatred of war, 541; and "quarantine the aggressors" speech, 521; relations with Churchill, 93; relations with Vansittart, 108; unconcern about fate of Jews, 453
Chamberlin, William Henry, 616
Chamber of Commerce of the U.S., 168, 193, 336–337, 359, 543, 565, 619, 640, 685
Chandler, Albert B., 127
Channing, William Ellery, 26, 51, 53, 229, 267, 312, 744, 747; on American intellectual independence, 373; on evil, 405; on French Revolution, 10; and Kneeland case, 29; Puritan spirit of, 745–46; on scepticism at Harvard, 294
Chaplin, Charles, 21, 365, 679; *Modern Times,* 687
Chase, Salmon P., 117
Chastellux, François Jean de, 9
Chattanooga Times, 675
Chauncy, Charles, 26, 267
Cheeryble brothers, 688
Chicago, and anarchism, 64; politics in, 120, 142, 159, 163; provincialism of, 157; rural Illinois and, 158
Chicago Daily News, 638
Chicago Sun, 617, 630
Chicago Tribune, 619, 624, 630, 639
Child, Francis J., 420–21
Child labour, 30, 52, 111, 304, 309, 528, 673
Childs, John L., 131
China, 495, 503, 532, 537, 550, 555; U.S. policy toward, 512, 515, 559
Chippendale, Thomas, 397
Choate, Joseph W., 19–20, 111, 147, 189, 251
Christian Science, 289–92, 298, 619
Christian socialism, 229–30, 274, 275–76
Church and State, 7, 26, 27, 29, 266, 319, 433
Churches, 2–8, 29, 71, 157, 264–322 *passim,* 709, 752; business influence on, 198–99, 305; and communications media, 689, 707; and education, 326, 382; and labour, 229–30, 274; in Southern mill towns, 278–81
Churchill, Lord Randolph, 229
Churchill, Winston L. S., 131, 367, 454; naval base deal with F.D.R., 519; on public discussion of atomic bomb proposals, 549; and radio, 623, 702, 705; relations with Chamberlain, 93
Cinema, *see* Films
Cities, elective offices in, 145; government of, 156–60; growth of, 47; Leighton on, 665; political machines in, 120, 158–64
Citizenship, Christian creed as basis of, 26; education for, 333, 340
City manager plan, 161, 162–63
Civil liberties, 179, 470, 471, 647, 669, 706
Civil Service, 20–21, 72, 139, 649; Bryce on, 160–161; critique of, 99–110
Civil War, 4, 5, 34, 44, 61–62, 134, 138, 406, 462, 498, 635, 667
Clark, Charles E., 370, 587
Clark, Jane Perry, 156

Clark, John Bates, 18, 168, 273, 359, 439–40, **718**
Class postulates, 5, 24–26, 39–40, 61, 498
Classless society, myth of, 185, 205, 220, 221, 223, 231, 258
Clay Compromise, 462
Clay, Henry, 46, 49, 74, 84, 93, 497
Clay, Lucius D., 506
Clayton Act, 207, 209, 210, 218, 234–35
Clergy, in American tradition, 7, 26; as business men, 284–85, 289, 315; as chaplains, 295–96; characteristics of urban, 315–17; and cotton interests, 475; criteria of success among, 166; decline of, 28; and labour, 281, 315–16; in mill towns, 278–81
Cleveland, Grover, 66, 77, 118, 130, 141, 232, 251, 438, 469
Closure in Senate debate, 86
Coast and Geodetic Survey, 101–102
Cobb, Frank, 642
Cobbett, William, 455
Cohen, Benjamin V., 104–105, 643
Cohen, Morris R., 70, 378
Coke, Sir Edward, 30, 112, **571**
Colden, Cadwallader, 395
Coleridge, Samuel T., 729
Collective bargaining, 220, 222, 225, 235
Collective security, 127, 528–30, 532, 535, 540
Colleges, 13, 47, 67; critique of, 343–48, 360; for women, 384; *see also* Education
Colonialism, in American attitude to Europe, 63; and cultural maturity, 45
Colorado Coal and Iron Company, 297
Colquitt, Alfred H., 464
Columnists, 638, 642–43
Comedy, in films, 683; in radio, 701
Come-Outers, 28, 271
Commentators, radio, 616, 700
Commission plan, 161, 162–63
Committee of Industrial Organizations (C.I.O.), 122, 134, 200, 215–16, 221, 225, 244, 669; *see also* Political Action Committee
Committee on Medicine and the Changing Order, 609
Committee on the Costs of Medical Care, Report of, 601
Commoner, The, 637
Common Law, 30, 110, 213
Common Law, The, 66
Common Sense, 621
Commonwealth Federation, 131
Commonwealth Fund, 607
Communism, 80, 624
Communist party (U.S.), 81, 131, 132–33, 217–18, 254, 308, 360, 719, 736
Compact Clause, of the Constitution, 156
Company unionism, 219
Competition, in classical economics, 440; in contemporary economic order, 441
Comstock, Anthony, 305, 627
Comstockery, Mencken on, 422, 666
Conant, James B., 357, 672, 677
Conference for Progressive Political Action, 220
Confessions of a Nazi Spy, 693
Congress, 20–21, 157, 158; critique of, 82–92; and the presidency, 73–77, 128, 245, 517–27; and the U.N., 510; *see also* Senate, House of Representatives
Congressional Record, 83–84
Congreve, William, 668
Conkling, Roscoe, 149, 150
Connecticut, 140, 143, 146, 148, 152
Connecticut Light and Power Company, **148**
"Connecticut Wits," 395
Conservatism, 4, 10, 130, 599, 626

Conservative party, British, 705
Considérant, Victor, 405
Constitution, 17, 18, 72, 189; foreign affairs and the, 522–23, 525, 527; need for reform of, 731; Supreme Court and the, 110–12, 189, 210–11, 435
Constitutional Convention, 72, 138, 417, 552
Constitutional Limitations, 114
Contemplation, American attitude to, 15, 55–56
Contempt proceedings, 208
Contract, freedom of, and bargaining power, 167; as weapon against legislation, 31, 435
Conventionalism, 622
Conway, Moncure D., 295
Conwell, Russell H., 256, 272, 659
Cook, Albert S., 420–21
Cooley, Thomas M., *Constitutional Limitations* by, 114
Coolidge, Calvin, 18, 74, 116, 130, 212, 216, 250, 657–658, 712; awe of business men, 655, 712; and Boston police strike, 640; on "business of America," 46; era of, 64, 168, 187–88, 253; as governor of Massachusetts, 141; policies of, 73, 89, 90, 152; and the Senate, 75, 76, 86; and third-term tradition, 119, 121, 671; as vice-president, 97, 98; Villard's attitude to, 650
Cooper, James Fenimore, 11, 45, 419, 664, 665, 711, 722
Co-operative Commonwealth Federation, 217
Co-operative societies, 173
Copper Purchase scandal, 708
Corcoran, Thomas G., 97, 104–105
Cornell, Alonzo B., 149
Corn Laws, 540
Coronado Coal case, 207
Corporations, 157, 551–52; and party machines, 19, 32, 60, 143, 147, 151, 161–62
Corruption, of cities, 158–60; of courts and legislatures, 32, 158; of politics, 721; *see also* Political Machines
Corwin, E. S., 616
"Corybantic Christianity," 282, 283, 382
Cotton, John, 394–95, 432, 566
Couch, W. T., 473–74
Coughlin, Charles E., 36, 67–68, 187, 306, 480, 481
Counter-reformation, cultural, 423–27, 428–31
Counties, corruption in, 159; elective offices in, 145; failure of government in, 156–57
Counts, George S., 331, 382, 386
Course of American Democratic Thought, The, 252
Courts, 19–20, 30–33; Brooks Adams on, 445; business influence on, 189, 190; critique of, 110–16; and "due process" clause, 30–31; and labour, 31, 173, 200–201, 207–14, 219; *see also* Supreme Court
Cowley, Malcolm, 651
Cox, Eugene, 84
Crane, Stephen, 409–10
Craven, Avery, *The Coming of the Civil War* by, 626
Crèvecoeur, 9, 404, 719
Cripps, Sir Stafford, 536
Criticism, of America by Americans, 723, 724; critique of literary, 419–31; forces in, 427; *see also* Culture
Croker, Richard, 60, 161
Croly, Herbert, 441, 650, 651, 654
Cross, Wilbur L., 148
Crowley, Leo, 120
Crum, Bartley C., 621
Culture, 5, 45, 162, 400, 401, 402, 728, 740–41; American search for independent, 10, 665, 722, 723–24; and business, 438–39, 450; as by-product of material success, 46, 166; Channing on, 373;

Culture (*Continued*)
  crisis of American, 450; European attitude to, 62, 778; European influences on, 11, 63-64, 397-98, 723; and expansion, 449-50; judged by European standards, 398; in the South, 62-63, 458-59, 474; "youth" theory of, 398-99
Cummins, Albert B., 219
Curley, James, 163
"Curse of bigness," Brandeis on, 157, 195, 228
Curti, Merle (Eugene), 418
Cutting, Bronson, 79
Czechoslovakia, 536, 542

Dabney, Virginius, 467, 471
Daily Advertiser, The, 632
Dalton Plan, 387
Dana, Charles A., 675
Daniels, Jonathan, 471
Darlan, Admiral Jean François, 89, 700
Darwin, Charles, 362, 745
Darwinism, 56, 273, 286, 435, 442
Daugherty, Harry M., 64, 89, 95
Daughters of the American Revolution, 687, 693
David, Henry, *History of the Haymarket Affair* by, 418, 749
Davie, William R., 517
Davies, Joseph E., 105, 543; *Mission to Moscow* by, 106
Davis, John W., 216
Davis, Norman, 97, 105-106
Dawes, Charles G., 105
Dearborn Independent, 480
Debate, freedom of senatorial, 90; level of senatorial, 92; between Webster and Hayne, 91
DeBow's Review, 629
Debs, Eugene V., character and insight of, 51; injunction case against, 218; as presidential candidate, 132, 201, 217; repression of, 709; as trade-union leader, 201, 240
Declaration of Independence, 114, 404, 433
Declaration of Independence, The, 66, 417
Defoe, Daniel, 566
Deism, 10, 27, 267-68, 312
De Leon, Daniel, 51
Democracy, 70, 80, 140, 717-18; Army Training Manual on, 669; decline in institutions of, 732-733; distrust of, 62, 432; effect of wealth concentration on, 182-83, 183-84, 744; public opinion in a, 615; in theory and practice, 21, 748-49, 750, 752-53; *see also* Capitalist democracy, Political democracy
Democracy and the Organization of Political Parties, 655
Democracy in America, 16-17, 29; *see also* Tocqueville
Democratic party, 72, 78-80, 129-30, 140, 194-95, 217, 220, 222, 232, 236, 250, 756-57; and Bryan, 148; and Clayton Act, 234-35; contradictions within, 250; and the Negro, 155, 469; Populism and, 464, 465; support of, 78, 129; Tillman and, 148; *see also* Political parties
Demosthenes, on danger of appeasement, 751-52
Depew, Chauncey M., 161
"Deportations Delirium," 202, 251, 563
Depression, *see* Great Depression
Derby, Lord, 105
Detroit Free Press, 633
Dewey, John, 70, 446; and Committee of Forty-Eight, 81; and education, 330, 331, 387, 390; philosophy of, 450, 726
Dewey, Thomas E., and F.D.R., 255; and independent voters, 217; and John L. Lewis, 216; and P.A.C., 136; and presidential campaign of 1944, 120, 130, 704, 736
Dial, The, 664

Dicey, Albert V., 156, 370, 649
Dickens, Charles, 5, 411, 568, 665, 688, 721; on America, 16, 498; *see also* Brick, Jefferson
Dickinson, Emily, 54-55
Dies, Martin, 78-79, 84, 187
Dilettantism, 323-24
Dilling, Elizabeth, 254
Disarmament, 513
Discrimination, against Jews, 5, 140, 456, 479-481, 484-86; against Negroes, 5, 13, 24, 29, 34, 44, 111, 140, 323, 328-29, 380-81, 453, 454, 461, 466-67, 468-69, 476, 596-97, 716; against Roman Catholics, 5, 76, 118, 140, 158, 295
Disraeli, Benjamin, 229
Distribution, 161, 167
Doctorate degree, 374, 376-79, 380
Doctors, *see* Medical profession
Dodd, William E., 105, 106
Dogmas, American, *see* American dogmas
"Dollar diplomacy," 562
Dollfuss, Engelbert, 506
Dos Passos, John, 65, 410
Dostoevski, Feodor, 428
Douglas, Stephen A., 462
Douglas, Justice William O., 370
Drama, 48, 396
Dred Scott decision, 112, 462, 591, 740
Dreiser, Theodore, 52, 409, 422, 444, 718, 733
Drew, Daniel, 326
Dreyfus case, 453, 479
Duane, William, 632
"Due process" clause, court interpretation of, 30-31; property rights and, 114, 211; Supreme Court concept of, 115; and trade-unions, 437-438
Duhamel, Georges, 498
Dumond, Dwight L., 629
Dunkers, 265
Dunn Library, 351
Dunne, Finley Peter, on American heiresses, 384; exponent of American humour, 48, 646, 740; on politics, 231
Duplex Printing Press Company v. *Deering,* 210
Dupont de Nemours, Pierre Samuel, correspondence with Jefferson, 434-35
Du Ponts, and atomic research, 545; and I. G. Farben, 530, 546; influence in Delaware of, 18, 19, 85, 140, 148, 237
Duranty, Walter, 616, 646
Durbin, Deanna, 692
"Dust Bowl," 154
Dwight, Timothy, 10, 11, 294
Dykstra, Clarence A., 162

Eastman, Joseph B., 20
Eastman, Max, 652, 653
Ecole Normale, 59
Economic imperialism, 82, 181-82, 508
Economic Interpretation of the Constitution, 626; *see also* Beard, Charles
Economic philosophy, 439, 440, 441
Economists, Veblen's influence on, 439
Economy, American, 512, 747, 755, 756; of abundance, 179-80; distribution in, 161, 167; individualism in, 68; of restriction, 178; *see also* Business, Market economy, Wealth
Eddy, Mary Baker, 289-90, 292
Eden, Anthony, 74
Edison, Thomas A., influence of his career, 186, 231; reputation of, 12, 166, 365, 628; "success story" of, 262, 275, 339
Education, 5, 23, 69, 146, 257, 258; adult, 163-64; business influence on, 13, 22-23, 194, 381-82, 383, 386-91, 535-37; Churches and, 326, 382; confusion on aims of, 330-31, 332, 369; critique of,

Education (*Continued*)
323–92; Dewey on, 387; in England, 331, 370–71, 372–73, 715; and federal aid, 153; inadequacy of, 330–35; legal, 370–71, 372–73, 715; medical, 372, 594, 598; in New York State, 329; parents and, 339–42, 365; radio and, 701, 703; state systems of, 139; status of, 66–67

Edwards, Jonathan, 27, 42; eminence of, 266, 312, 395; philosophy of, 729, 730; and Thomas Paine, 10

Edwards, Thomas, *Gangræna* by, 28, 292, 427

Eggleston, Edward, 409

Einstein, Albert, 37, 714

Eire, 79, 482

Eisenhower, Dwight D., 506

Eldon, John Scott, Earl of, 4, 568

Elections, of judges, 144; laws governing, 237; machine politics in, 159; sectionalism in, 237–238

Electoral college, 72

Eliot, Charles W., 205, 348, 361, 649

Eliot, T. S., 347, 425, 723

Elite, 9, 435; characteristics of, 384–85; minority groups barred by, 716

Elmer Gantry, 627

Ely, Joseph B., 588

Ely, Richard T., 437

Emerson, Joseph, 268

Emerson, Ralph Waldo, 29, 41, 45, 46, 49, 71, 126; address on Revolution, 139; appraisal of, 15, 362, 402–403, 419, 611; compared to Franklin, 55; and Harvard Divinity School, 48, 729; on native culture, 740–41; on philosophy of, 259, 268, 392, 404, 415, 711, 719, 736–37, 738, 744, 745, 746, 747

Emotion and primitivism, 411

Empiricism, 12

Employment, *see* Full employment, Unemployment

Emporia Gazette, 620

Encyclicals, papal, 307–308

Encyclopædia of Social Reform, 274

"End Poverty in California" movement, 131

Engels, Friedrich, 392, 405, 634, 721, 742

England, 7–8, 24, 35, 439, 440, 632; anti-Semitism in, 453–54, 482, 484; and atomic energy, 537–39; attitude to Civil War of, 61–62; Civil Service in, 99–100, 102–103, 108; education in, 331, 370–371, 372–73, 715; eighteenth-century conditions in, 721; and films, 680, 690; foreign policy of, 88, 511, 512, 541; Foreign Service in, 23, 105–107; government in, 74, 88; Industrial Revolution in, 536; jurisprudence in, 66, 371, 373, 567; professions in, 568–71; U.S. press and, 640

"Entangling alliances," doctrine of, 67, 495, 496, 738

Epicureans, philosophy of, 752

Epicurus, 759

Equality, 57, 717–18; and accumulation, 406; in American tradition, 631–32, 708, 718–19; Churches and, 302, 303; in Declaration of Independence, 404; destroyed by materialism, 744

Erie Railroad, and machine politics, 161–62

Escapism, in the novel, 409–11; in journalism, 677

Esch-Cummins Transportation Act, 219

Espionage Act, and *Abrams* v. *U.S.*, 111; and *The Masses*, 652

Ethical Culture movement, 295

Ethics, of early America, 27; medical, 595, 613; non-theological, 267

Europe, attitude of U.S. business man to, 542–543; attitude to Civil War of, 61–62; attitude to U.S. of, 720–29 *passim;* economy of compared to U.S., 512; impact of Americanism on, 730–31; influence on U.S. of, 11, 43, 63–64, 397–398, 401, 720–21, 723; post-World War II position of countries in, 503; problem of federation in, 556; professions in U.S. compared with those in, 564–65; sophistication of *v.* American crudity, 62; and the U.N., 556

Evangelical Christianity, 158

Evans, George Henry, 230, 709, 744

Everett, Edward, 49, 326, 373

Evolution, hostility to doctrine of, 286; *see also* Darwinism

Examinations, Civil Service, British and American compared, 99, 102

Expansionism, 3, 5, 496, 497, 500, 509, 510, 552–563, 746–47

Ex parte Milligan, 113

Experimentalism, 4, 14, 15, 54, 157, 169, 712

Fabian socialism, 214

Fable of the Bees, The, 420

Fair Employment Practices bill, 706

Fall, Albert B., 95

Farley, Cardinal John Murphy, 306

Farmer-Labor parties, 81, 131, 152

Farmers, 18, 58, 167, 543, 658, 640; conditions among, 238–39, 247; dominated by railroads, 32, 157; as a minority group, 486–94; and trade-unionism, 233, 238, 240–42, 247, 492; Veblen on, 438; *see also* Agriculture

Farmer's Daughter, The, 623

Farrell, James T., 427, 749

Faulkner, William, 50, 65, 422, 749

Federal Bureau of Investigation, 693

Federal Communications Commission, 698–99

Federal Council of Churches of Christ, 543

Federal government, and film-making, 692–94; and minorities, 452; and the Negro, 470; political institutions of, 72–137; protest against persecution abroad, 469–70, 481; radio and, 697; and the states, 109, 152–56; Supreme Court and, 111–12

Federalism, 50, 121

Federalist, The, 632

Federalist party, 217, 417

Federal Reserve Act of 1913, 177

Federal Theatre, 693

Federal Trade Commission, 627, 639, 673

Federation, European, 556

Feke, Robert, 267

Feminism, 10

Fenno, John, 632

Fenton, Reuben E., 149

Ferguson, James E., 142, 463

Ferguson, William Scott, 66

Fermi, Enrico, 714

Feudalism, 34, 165, 632

Field, Marshall, III, 129, 617

Field, Justice Stephen J., 113, 442, 578, 672

Fielden, John, 455

Fifth Amendment, 30–31

Filibuster, 87

Films, 21, 37, 173, 617, 619, 620; critique of, 680–95

Finance-capitalism, 78, 506, 515, 530, 535, 562; *v.* industrial capitalism, 167, 437–38

Finland, 690

First International, 61–62

Fish, Hamilton (1808–1893), 109, 129

Fish, Hamilton (1888–), 85
Fishbein, Morris, 604
Fisk, Jim, 272
Fiske, Bishop Charles, 284–85
Fiske, John, 231
Fitzgerald, F. Scott, 411, 718
Fitzhugh, George, 46, 436, 746
Fitzpatrick, Daniel R., 646
Flagler, Henry Morrison, 143
Flaubert, Gustave, 62, 721
Fleming, Sir John Ambrose, 628
Foner, Philip, 749
Ford, Henry, 12, 23, 39, 64, 165, 186, 720; anti-Semitism of, 480, 482, 483; on distinction of wealth, 710; and N.L.R.B., 202–203; and New Deal, 168; and retooling of plant, 196
Foreign Affairs, 648
Foreign policy, U.S., 409, 495–563 *passim;* in Alaska, 510; atomic energy and, 537–39; in Far East, 498, 512, 515, 534, 554–55; neutrality in, 499, 500, 501–502, 505, 513; press and, 676–677; radio and, 705; Roman Catholic Church and, 505–506; Senate and, 87–89, 126–28, 518–28
Foreign Service, 23, 70, 134, 384; business men as diplomats in, 284–85, 289, 315; U.S. compared with British, 105–107
Foreign trade, U.S., 529–37, 546, 755; in wartime, 501, 502, 509; *see also* Free trade
For Whom the Bell Tolls, 411, 683
Fosdick, Harry Emerson, 296
Fosdick, Raymond B., *American Police Systems* by, 160
Foster, William Z., 201
Four Freedoms, 38, 164
Fourier, Charles, 46, 214, 733
Fourteen Points, 651
Fourteenth Amendment, 30–31, 115
Fox, Charles James, 4
Fox, George, 265, 287
Fox, William, 693
France, 8, 24, 40, 503, 541, 570; anti-Semitism in, 453, 482, 484; attitude to Civil War of, 61–62; colour problem in, 453; fall of, 35, 37; film censorship in, 690; governments of, 133; materialism in, 725
Franco, Francisco, 108, 501, 505, 620–21, 756
Frank case, 111
Frankfurter, Felix, 97, 108, 219, 373, 579, 587, 643; on Compact Clause of Constitution, 156; on injunctions, 208, 209; nomination to Supreme Court of, 370, 588; political creed of, 756–57, 758; on Sacco-Vanzetti case, 579, 588, 665
Franklin, Benjamin, 4, 41, 67; *Autobiography* by, 732; character of, 39; compared to Emerson, 55; on culture, 398–99; eminence of, 6, 8, 12, 394, 395, 396, 727; philosophy of, 267, 294, 403–404, 432, 566; shaping of religion to environment in, 27
Fraternal orders, 622
Frazier-Lemke Act, 223
Freedom, of contract, 31, 167, 435; of Senate debate, 90; of the seas, 498, 554; of speech, 667–68, 669, 698–700; *see also* Religious tolerance
Free enterprise, 21, 60, 136, 546, 645; critique of, 165–99
Freeman, Edward A., 416
Freeman, The, 649
Free thought, 265, 267, 273–74, 294–95, 420
Free trade, 498–99, 536–37
Frémont, John C., 355

French Revolution, 10, 429
Freneau, Philip, 9, 404, 632
Frick, Henry Clay, 14, 109, 165, 168, 261, 426, 612, 621–22
Friendliness as American tradition, 39, 56–57
Frontier, the, 17, 34, 27–28, 57–58, 156, 407, 417, 664; and labour, 203, 257; and Mark Twain, 408–409; Marx on, 743; and mobility of workers, 215; and social Darwinism, 435; Turner's theory of, 64, 417, 644, 718, 740–44, 745
Frost, Robert, 65
Full employment, in free-enterprise society, 545; and individualism, 136; means of achieving, 178
Fulton, Robert, 395
Fundamentalism, 79, 157, 277–89 *passim,* 298, 300, 304–305, 666

Gabriel, Ralph H., *The Course of American Democratic Thought,* by, 252, 448
Gallatin, Albert, 106
Gandhi, Mohandas K., 405
Gangræna, 28, 292, 427
Gangsterism, 32, 82
Garfield, James A., 275
Garland, Hamlin, 50, 52, 408
Garrison, Lindley M., 93
Garrison, Lloyd K., 574
Garrison, William Lloyd, 405
Gastonia, N.C., compared with Muncie, Ind., 281–82; sociological analysis of, 278–81; strike at, 51, 70, 173, 202, 281
Gates, "Bet a Million," 64
Gazette of the United States, 632
General Council of the Bar, 568–69
General Electric Company, 545
General Medical Council, 568
General Motors Corporation, 151, 692
"Genteel tradition," and *Atlantic Monthly,* 665; and Babbitt, 424; and Howells, 65; and Lowell, 419–20; revival of, 425; and Santayana, 46
Geological Survey, U.S., 20, 101–102, 167
George, Henry, 51, 214, 261, 441; *Progress and Poverty* by, 621
George, Walter F., 79
Georgia, 120, 142, 146, 151, 528, 629
Germany, 4, 88, 107, 133; decline in science and art in, 750; extermination of Jews in, 452, 453, 457; influence of its cultural methods, 63, 314, 419; materialism in, 725; place in world affairs of, 537; treatment of minorities by, 452, 481
Gettysburg Address, 17, 49, 139
Giannini, A. P., 358
Gibbon, Edward, 395
Gibbons, Cardinal James, 306
Gibbs, Willard, 64, 351, 610
Gibson, Charles Dana, 710
Gilded Age, 18, 45, 64, 116, 272–73, 407–408, 409, 412, 420, 423, 635, 666
Ginsberg, Morris, 568
Giovannitti, Arturo, 652
Giraud, Henri Honoré, 21, 89
Girdler, Thomas, 193, 243
Gladden, Washington, 229, 274, 276–77, 295, 310, 315
Gladstone, William E., 62, 717
Glasgow, Ellen, 410, 473, 749
Glass, Carter, 195
Glueck, Sheldon, 371, 587

Godkin, Edwin L., 232, 275; career on *Nation* of, 649–50; and Civil Service reform, 160, 420

Goebbels, Joseph P., 481, 644

Goethe, Johann Wolfgang von, 723

Gold Clause decision, 214

Gold Rush of 1849, 31

Gold standard, 77, 529; Veblen on, 438

Gompers, Samuel, and A.F. of L., 200, 206, 215, 219, 226, 229, 478; compared with Hillman, 226–27; on effect of Clayton Act, 209, 235; philosophy of, 131–33, 216, 234, 745; and political action, 195, 201, 215, 216, 219, 220; restrained by injunction, 208

Gone with the Wind, 679, 687

Good citizen, concept of, 39–40

"Good neighbor" policy, 540

Goodnow, Frank Johnson, 441

Goodwill, principle of, 540–42, 547, 709

Gordon, John Brown, 464

Gorgas, William C., 598

Gospel, of business efficiency, 277; of hard work, 15, 165; of success, 53–54, 68, 165, 166, 669, 684–685; *see also* Social gospel

Gould, Jay, 33, 60, 109, 165, 169, 636, 733

Government, 18, 19, 43, 60, 68, 69, 223, 436, 438, 746–77; *see also* Federal government, State government, Local government

Governors, 141, 142–43, 143–44

Graduate schools, non-professional, 373–80; professional, 370–73

Graham, Frank P., 472

Grand Coulee Dam, 153

Grand National Consolidated Trade Union, 200

Grant, Ulysses S., 12, 41, 46, 62, 119, 524, 671

Grants-in-aid, 153, 156

Grapes of Wrath, The, 21, 359, 411, 683

Gray, John Chipman, 373, 588

Great Awakening, 266, 267

Great Depression, 13, 17, 19, 21, 35–36, 77, 89, 135, 188, 220, 255, 260, 305, 667

Great Tradition, The, 427

Greece, 689–90

Greeley, Horace, 230, 271, 634–35, 675

Green, William, 131–32, 200, 220, 261

Greenback cases, 740

Greenback party, 132

Greene, Nathan, 209

Greenland, 544

Gregg, William, 629

Gregory, David S., 272

Gresham's Law, 636–37, 688

Griffith, D. W., 624

Grote, George, 414

Guest, Eddie, 64, 339

Guggenheim family, 148, 479, 621–22

Guizot, François P. G., 731

Guthrie, William D., 113

Hacker, Louis M., 179, 180, 417

Hackett, Francis, 651

Hadley, Arthur T., 348

Hæresographia, 292, 591–92

Hague, Frank, 120, 131, 147–48

Haldane, Richard Burdon, Viscount, 94, 581

Halifax, Lord, 105, 108

Hall, Basil, 16

Haller, William, 420

Hamilton, Alexander, 4, 6, 92, 395, 632; attitude to people, 9, 176; philosophy of, 10, 138, 211, 407, 434, 441; *v.* Jefferson, 404

Hamilton, Dr. Alice, 598

Hand, Judge Learned, 30

Hanna, Mark (Marcus Alonzo), 18, 64, 66, 79, 95, 161, 215, 604; and J. F. Rhodes, 414, 749

Hansen, Alvin H., 131

Hansen, Marcus L., 418

Happy Hypocrite, The, 335

Harding, Warren G., 73, 86, 90, 94, 98, 168, 253

Hardy, Thomas, 408

Harkness, Edward S., 62

Harlan, Justice John M., 672

Harley, John Edgar, *World-Wide Influences of the Cinema* by, 690–91

Harnden, William F., 47

Harper, William R., 348

Harper's Magazine, 637, 665–66

Harper's Weekly, 638

Harriman, W. Averell, 105

Harris, William T., 275

Harrison, William H., 12

Hart, Hornell, 618, 624

Harte, Bret, 411

Harvard Divinity School, 48, 729

Harvard Law School, 187, 648

Harvard report on education, 367–68, 369, 391–92

Harvard University, 16, 22, 40, 162, 665

Harvey, George, 105, 106

Haskins, Charles Homer, 66, 361

Hawley, Joseph, 267

Hawthorne, Nathaniel, 15, 27, 45, 259, 402, 403, 419, 611, 740

Hay, John, 41, 87, 109, 403, 413

Hayes, Cardinal Patrick Joseph, 306

Hayes, Rutherford B., 462

Haymarket riots, 140, 435, 616

Hayne, Robert Young, 91

Hays, Will H., 682–83, 688

Haywood, William D., 663

Headlam, Stewart D., 229

Health insurance, 600–601, 608

Hearst, William Randolph, 646, 668, 676, 731; misuse of press by, 625, 636, 637, 639, 674

Hecker, Isaac T., 269, 310, 405

Hedonistic psychology, calculus of, 440

Heflin, Tom, 464

Hegel, G. F. W., 56, 725–26, 729

Hegelian philosophy, 12, 56, 447

Heine, Heinrich, 425, 727

Helper, Hinton R., *The Impending Crisis of the South* by, 459, 460, 629

Hemans, Felicia D., 664

Hemingway, Ernest, 65, 410, 411, 422; *For Whom the Bell Tolls* by, 411, 683

Henderson, Arthur, 89, 94, 526

Henderson, Leon, 119

Henderson, Nevile, *Failure of a Mission* by, 106

Henry, Joseph, 261, 628, 715

Hergesheimer, Joseph, 410

Herrick, Robert, 52, 409–10, 444, 663, 749

Herrin strike, 202

Herron, George D., 229, 274

Hicks, Granville, 427, 653

Higginson, Henry Lee, 162

"Higher law," doctrine of, 187, 188–89, 190, 435, 745

Hildreth, Richard, 415

Hill, David B., 149

Hill, James J., 165, 169, 193

Hill, Lister, 86

Hillman, Sidney, 120, 200, 201, 244, 246; and Gompers, 226–27; hostility to, 196, 480, 643, 686; and P.A.C., 132, 136, 215–16, 227, 243

Hillquit, Morris, 709–10
Hindus, Maurice, 620
Hines, Frank, 161
Historiography, 395, 414–19
History of American Literature, 66
History of English Thought in the Eighteenth Century, 420
History of the Haymarket Affair, 418, 749
History of the Standard Oil Company, 621
Hitler, Adolf, 37, 76, 127, 163, 255, 261, 513, 703–704; anti-Semitism of, 453, 457, 483–84; *Mein Kampf* by, 644–45
Hoar, George F., 209
Hoare-Laval Treaty, 88
Hobbes, Thomas, 176, 410, 424
Hobhouse, L. T., 650
Hoffman, Clare E., 249
Hogarth, William, 394, 409
Holdsworth, Sir William, 373
Holland, Henry Scott, 229
Hollywood, 631, 680–81, 682, 683, 688
Holmes, John Haynes, 295
Holmes, Oliver Wendell, Jr., 19, 112, 144, 362, 370, 373, 441, 578, 610, 696, 715, 719; and Abrams case, 20; in Adair and Lochner cases, 115, 210, 435; and Beard, 417, 626; *Common Law* by, 66; and Danbury Hatters case, 586; judicial philosophy of, 30, 191, 210, 211, 212, 243, 442–443, 672; and Spencer, 56, 115, 442
Holmes, Oliver Wendell, Sr., 45, 413, 592
Holt, W. Stull, 520, 521–22
Homestead Act, 205, 462
Homestead strike, 169, 202, 251, 435, 659
Hooker, Thomas, 42, 394–95, 432
Hoosier Schoolmaster, The, 409
Hoover, Herbert C., 35, 76, 78, 93, 94, 95, 152, 187, 255; Frankfurter on, 758; policies of, 220, 534, 745; "rugged individualism" of, 43, 168, 185, 220, 359, 436
Hopkins, Ernest, 480
Hopkins, Harry L., 95, 519, 567
Hopkins, Mark, 268, 272, 413
Houghton, Alanson B., 105
Houghton, Lord, 612
House, Edward M., 95, 97, 479, 519, 651
House Committee on Un-American Activities, 187, 356, 627
House of Commons, 88, 89, 92
House of Morgan, 90, 148, 479
House of Representatives, 72, 76, 83–85, 90, 517–518, 523, 527
House on 92nd Street, The, 693
Howe, Ed, 52, 740; *Story of a Country Town* by, 408
Howells, William Dean, 45, 50, 52, 408, 409, 413, 733, 749
Huckleberry Finn, 409
Hudson, Robert, 88
Hughes, Charles Evans, 76, 95, 142, 150, 214, 582, 672
Hugo, Victor, 665
Hull, Cordell, 96, 105, 523, 535
Hull, Morton D., 148
Humanitarianism, 10, 266
Hume, David, 399
Hungary, 506, 690
Hunt, Henry, 5
Huntington, Collis P., 14, 426, 598
Huntington, Henry E., 14, 598, 612
Huntington Library, 360, 715
Hutcheson, William, 202, 218, 243

Hutchins, Robert M., 348, 425; on academic tenure, 357; on democratic education 331; neo-Thomism of, 359, 369
Hutchinson, Anne, 7, 26
Hutton, Herbert, 357
Hutton, Richard H., 649
Huxley, Aldous, *Brave New World* by, 622
Huxley, T. H., 283, 382
Huysmans, Joris Karl, 410
Hylan, John F., 148

Ickes, Harold L., 78, 93, 94, 621, 735–36
Idaho, 148, 627
I. G. Farben, 530–31, 546
Illinois, 86, 139, 143, 148, 158
Immigrants, 6, 18, 158, 166, 269, 300–302, 405, 435, 721
Immigration, 13, 17, 53, 158, 179, 205, 400, 405, 462, 476, 477–78, 487, 529, 533–34, 718, 755
Immortale Dei of Leo XIII, 307
Impending Crisis of the South, The, 459, 460, 629
Imperialism, 496, 509–10, 515, 555; Veblen on, 437; *see also* Economic imperialism, Expansionism
Income tax, 30, 111, 114, 189, 214, 251
Independent Journal, The, 632
Index Medicus, 600
India, 503, 529–30, 532, 654
Indians, American, 396
Individualism, 7, 27–28, 43, 49, 114, 135–36, 643, 684, 745, 746
Industrial capitalism, 167, 437–38
Industrial Revolution, 53, 63, 418–19, 546
Ingersoll, Robert G., 273–74, 295
Initiative and referendum, 145
Injunctions, 207, 208, 209, 218
Insull, Samuel, 161, 386
Inter-Church World Movement, 229, 285
International Ladies' Garment Workers Union, 224
Interstate Commerce Commission, 157, 177
"Invisible government," 52, 144, 149, 419
Ireland, Archbishop John, 270, 505, 730
Irving, Washington, 45, 664
Isocrates, 751
Isolationism, 249, 496–509 *passim,* 516, 624, 722
Italo-Abyssinian dispute, 511
Italy, 453, 506, 514, 558–59, 690, 725
It Can't Happen Here, 647
Ivan, John S., 652

Jackson, Andrew, 6, 12, 49, 54, 95, 130, 217, 326, 415, 434, 719, 740; policies of, 133, 407; significance of, 59, 69, 77, 260, 271
Jackson, Patrick Tracy, 47
Jackson, Robert H., 581
Jacobitism, 476
Jaeger, Werner, 751
James, Henry, 14, 15, 34, 49, 52, 63, 259, 412–13, 422, 649, 723, 728, 740
James, William, 49, 351, 361, 362, 378, 387, 449, 610, 649, 747; and education, 376, 390; philosophy of, 166, 261, 321, 446, 447–48, 682, 726–27
Japan, 37, 453, 499, 505, 512, 514, 515, 537, 538
Japanese-Americans, 453, 470, 674, 706–707
Jaurès, Jean, 564
Jay, John, 4, 520
Jeffers, Robinson, 65
Jefferson, Thomas, 4, 6, 9, 12, 13, 18, 34, 38, 41, 69, 71, 92, 93, 106, 130, 137, 217, 263, 319, 395,

Jefferson (*Continued*)
404, 415, 437, 441, 474, 650, 669, 719, 731, 739,
740; and Adams, 249–50, 404, 718; and agrarianism, 241, 492, 743, 744; on American aim,
747; on culture, 271, 393, 398, 399–400; and economic development, 157, 167, 407, 732, 744; and
foreign policy, 62, 67, 87, 126, 517, 554; influences on, 397, 398; letter to Dupont de Nemours,
434–35; and Louisiana Purchase, 39, 497; and
religion, 9, 27, 294, 312; revolt against Feder-
alists, 9, 58, 249–50, 260, 774; on slavery, 46; as
translator, 294
Jehovah's Witnesses, 111, 113
Jennings, Emerson, 647
Jersey City, 19, 82, 163
Jews, 5, 29, 76, 140, 158, 264, 300–301, 452, 453,
456, 457, 477–86, 687, 723
"Jim Crow" laws, 114
Johns Hopkins University, 63, 413–14, 415
Johnson, Alvin S., 650–51
Johnson, Andrew, 97
Johnson, Hiram, 150, 151
Johnson, Samuel, 267
Johnson, Tom, 161
Johnston, Eric A., 197, 236, 619, 683
Johnston, Mary, 408
Jones, Jesse, 120
Jones, Rev. Jesse H., 274
Josephson, Matthew, 711
Joslyn, Carl S., 70, 167
Journalism, 675–79; *see also* Press
Journalists, 635–36, 637, 641, 642, 654, 655, 676
Journal of Negro History, 667
Journal of the American Medical Association,
600, 603
Jowett, Benjamin, 426
Joyce, James, 412, 426
Judicial review, doctrine of, 31, 111–16
Judiciary, appointment v. popular election of,
144; of states, 138–39; as third chamber of leg-
islature, 20
Jurists, criteria of fitness of, 31; as legislators,
19–20; status of, 166, 571–76; as successful law-
yers, 167

Kahn, Otto H., 479
Kaiser, Henry, 677
Kansas City, Pendergast machine in, 32, 120, 159,
163
Kansas-Nebraska Act, 482
Kaye, F. B., 420
Kazin, Alfred, 421, 651
Kellogg-Briand Pact, 540, 547
Kellogg, Frank B., 540–41
Kelly, Edward J., 120, 159
Kendall, Amos, 95
Kennedy, Joseph P., 105, 302
Kent, James, 19, 211, 294, 442, 572, 578
Kentucky, 79, 86, 156, 627
Kenyon Review, The, 667
Kester, Howard, 240
Keynes, John Maynard, 441
Kilpatrick, William H., 331
"King-makers" in American politics, 95
Kingsbury, Dr. John A., 602
Kingsley, Charles, 229
Kipling, Rudyard, 411
Kirchwey, Freda, 650
Kishineff pogrom, 479
"Kitchen cabinet" of Andrew Jackson, 95
Kittredge, George L., 364

Kneeland, Abner, 29, 294
Knights of Labor, 178, 200, 229, 240, 254, 711
Know-Nothingism, 29, 248, 269, 306, 405, 643
Knox, Philander C., 577
Kohler, Josef, 443
Kuh, Frederick, 630
Ku Klux Klan, 29, 157, 187, 277, 287, 306, 464,
465

Labour, 77, 167, 173, 405, 543; courts and,
31, 114, 173, 200–201, 207–14, 219; critique
of, 200–63; dignity of, 172; and political
action, 131–32, 134, 136–37, 164, 216–18, 219, 220,
227, 243, 247–52, 259–60, 262–63, 625; press treatment of, 637, 643; *see also* Trade-unionism
Labour party, British, 136–37, 201, 217, 227, 247–
248, 250, 643
La Follette, Robert M., Jr., 129, 639
La Follette, Robert M., Sr., 65, 74, 86, 91, 229,
250, 656, 669, 733; philosophy of, 69, 434, 734;
presidential candidacy of, 80, 132, 201, 218,
254, 734, 757; and T.R., 385, 734; and Wis-
consin, 19, 131, 142, 144, 149–50, 150, 217
La Follette's Weekly Magazine, 637
La Guardia, Fiorello H., 163
Laissez-faire, 18–19, 170, 210, 212–13, 230–31, 271,
530, 672
Lancet, The, 600
Landis, James M., 156, 588–89
Landon, Alfred M., 78, 141, 147, 217, 255
Lane, Franklin K., 95
Langdell, C. C., 348, 584, 588
Lansing, Robert, 95, 108, 523, 559
Latin America, U.S. record in, 540, 562
Laud, Archbishop William, 426
Laughlin, J. Laurence, 718
Law, 30–31, 55, 66, 69, 70, 139, 214, 442, 446; *see
also* Law reform, Lawyers, Legal education,
Legal profession
Law journals, 648
Law professors, 588–89, 648
Law reform, law schools and, 372; legal profes-
sion and, 581, 582, 590–91
Law, William, on luxury, 399
Lawrence, Abbot, 41
Lawrence, D. H., 411
Lawrence strike, 169
Lawrence, Bishop William, 176–77, 272, 273, 274,
319
Lawyers, 30, 110, 167, 189–90, 575, 577; *see also*
Legal education, Legal profession, Law reform
Lea, Henry Charles, 414
Leadership in American policy, critique of, 116–
126
League of Nations, 511, 512, 513–14, 517, 541, 547
Lease, Mary, 491
Le Buff, Francis Peter, 286
Lee, Ivy, 168, 169, 621, 625, 708
Lee, "Mother" Ann, 289
Lee, Robert E., 339
Left-wing parties, 131–33
Legal education, 370–72, 583–91, 715
Legal philosophy, 441–42, 443; *see also* "Higher
law," Holmes
Legal profession, 571–82; *see also* Lawyers, Le-
gal education
Lehman, Herbert H., 142
Leighton, George R., 665
Leisure class, 14, 15–16, 172, 566–67; and culture,
393, 399, 426; and education, 362

Lenin, Nikolai, 250, 369, 427, 483, 643, 669, **758–759**, 760–61
Leo XIII, Pope, 285, 307–308
Les Ruines, 10, 267, 294
Levellers, 57
Levin, Meyer, 749
Lewis, John L., 200, 261; and C.I.O., 215, 240, 244, 483; hostility to, 261, 705; politics of, 216, 218, 226, 243, 244
Lewis, Sinclair, 65, 409, 724, 740, 749; *Babbitt* by, 21–22; *Elmer Gantry* by, 627; *It Can't Happen Here* by, 647; *Main Street* by, 666
L'Histoire de Port-Royal, 420
Liberal Christianity, 285–89, 300, 304, 626
Liberal party, British, 217, 229
Liberal party, New York, 131
Liberals, 37, 654, 655, 736–37, 756–57; in the South, 471–72, 473–74
Liberator, The, 652
Libertas of Leo XIII, 307
Libraries, 324, 360, 715
Lieber, Francis, 435, 441
Life and Labor in the Old South, 626
Lilburne, John, 51, 571
Lilienthal, David E., 92, 539
Lilienthal Report on Atomic Energy, 538, 539
Lincoln, Abraham, 71, 86, 130, 133, 137, 233, 263, 486, 570, 578, 716, 757; Americanism of, 719, 731, 750–51; in American tradition, 6, 23, 46, 47, 54, 186, 189, 275, 339; on concentration of wealth, 676; European attitude to, 61–62; on majority rule, 259; philosophy of, 15, 38, 407, 433–34, 591, 739, 740, 760; qualities of, 13, 39, 55, 189–90, 326, 563
Lindbergh, Charles A., 262, 339, 482
Lindsay, Vachel, 652
Lindsey, Benjamin B., 582; *The Revolt of Modern Youth* by, 627
Link, Henry C., 256
Lippmann, Walter, 69, 436, 638, 646, 650, 651, 656
Literary criticism, *see* Criticism
Literature, 4, 14–15, 45, 49, 50, 65, 70–71, 394–95, 733, 748–49; critique of, 402–13; Jefferson on, 393; political, 395, 396
Littell, Philip, 651
Litvinov, Maxim M., 514
Living standard, *see* Standard of living
Livingston, Edward, 572
Livy, 397
Llewellyn, K. N., 578
Lloyd, Henry Demarest, 52, 228, 444, 646, 712
Lloyd George, David, 93, 100, 133
Lobbyists, 84
Local government, political institutions of, 156–164
Lochner v. *New York*, 111, 113, 115, 442, 435
Locke, John, 30, 114, 397, 433, 444, 744, 745
Locofocos, 407
Lodge, Henry Cabot, 41, 60, 79, 135, 195, 234, 301, 562; and T.R., 31, 131, 254, 734; and Versailles Treaty, 87, 88, 135, 520–21; and Wilson, 91
Logrolling, 91
Loisy, Alfred F., 23
Lomasney, Martin, 158, 163
London, Jack, 733
London, William, 571–72
Long, Huey, 67–68, 92, 142, 144, 148, 163, 187, 194, 234, 248, 463, 465, 630
Longfellow, Henry Wadsworth, 41, 403
Look, 656

Los Angeles Times, 639
Lothian, Lord, 105, 106
Louisiana, 140, 142, 144, 148
Louisiana Purchase 39, 496, 497
Louisville Courier-Journal, 635
Lowden, Frank O., 148
Lowell, Abbot Lawrence, 348, 350, 357, 483, 480
Lowell, Francis, 47
Lowell, James Russell, 45, 302, 419–20, 424; *Biglow Papers* by, 420; on "condescension in foreigners," 373, 720
Lowes, John Livingston, 420, 421
Luce, Clare Booth, 85
Luce, Henry, 659–64, 668
Ludlow strike, 51, 202, 297
Lusk Committee, 335
Lutheranism, 319
Lynching, 640
Lynd, Robert S. and Helen M., 50, 163, 176, 182, 281, 314, 749; *Middletown* by, 21, 353; *Middletown in Transition* by, 71
Lytton Report on Sino-Japanese dispute, 511

McAllister, Ward, 710
MacArthur, Douglas, 640
McClure's Magazine, 638
McCormick, Robert R., 619, 668, 676, **731**
McCulloch, John R., 440
McCulloch v. *Maryland*, 110
MacDonald, Ramsay, 94, 133, 136, 541
McIntire, Samuel, 396
McKellar, Kenneth, 92, 256
McKinley, William, 59, 112, 118, **747**
MacLeish, Archibald, 65, 188, 262, 366, 692, 693–694
MacMahon, Francis, 309
McMaster, John B., 416
McNary-Haugen farm relief bill, 122
McPherson, Aimee Semple, 199, 289
McReynolds, Justice James C., 19–20, 189, 214, 251, 672
McReynolds, W. H., 100–101
McWilliams, Carey, 492, 493

Macaulay, Thomas Babington, 415
Machine politics, *see* Political machines
Mack, Judge Julian, 582
Mackenzie, Sir Morell, 607
Maclay, William, 518
Madison, James, 93, 395, 397, 441, **474**
Magna Charta, 113, 404
Mahan, Alfred T., 560
Maine, 78, 129, 141, 146, 619
Maine, Sir Henry, 371, 373, **718**
Main Street, 666
Maine, U.S.S., 636
Maistre, Joseph de, 10, 424
Maitland, Frederic W., 66, 370, 373, 416, 441
Majority rule, 17, 116, 252, 259–60, 435
Mandeville, Bernard, 399, 420
"Manifest destiny," 516, 559, 560, 561–62, 678, 747
Manly, John M., 420
Mann, Horace, 325
Mann, Thomas, 37
Mann, William d'Alton, 710
Manning, William, 404
Mansfield, William Murray, Earl of, 112, 568, 572
Man versus the State, The, 115
Marbury v. *Madison*, 113

Market economy, 406–408, 414, 440, 504–16, 529–37
Marshall, John, 19, 30, 112, 214, 417, 443, 572, 672, 715; and *McCulloch* v. *Maryland*, 110; philosophy of, 17, 434; and property rights, 3, 10, 211
Marshall Plan, 182, 530, 755
Marshall, Thomas R., 99
Martin, Frederick T., 385
Martineau, Harriet, 52
Marx, Karl, 214, 229, 405, 428, 438, 483, 730, 742, 759; on centralization, 743; hostility to, 250, 643, 669; as journalist, 634; on "ruling ideas of an age," 50, 725
Marxism, 214, 229, 427–29, 667
Massachusetts, 19, 79, 139, 141, 144, 146, 156
Massachusetts Act of 1837, 325
Massachusetts Bay Company, 265
Masses, 717, 718, 725, 759–60
Masses, The, 652–53
Mass production, 47, 56; effect on American art, 724; effect on American civilization, 13–14; *see also* Production
Materialism, 724, 725, 744
Mather, Cotton, 26, 42, 394–95, 431–32
Mather dynasty, 305, 625, 732
Mather, Increase, 506
Matthiessen, F. O., 45, 421; *American Renaissance* by, 420
Maurice, Frederick Denison, 229
Mayhew, Henry, 721
Mayhew, Jonathan, 26, 267, 395, 433
May-Johnson bill, 545, 549
Mayo brothers, 599
Mead, Elwood, 102, 103
Medical care, 595–602, 608
Medical education, 372, 594, 598
Medical ethics, 595, 613
Medical profession, 591–609
Mein Kampf, 644–45
Mellen, Charles S., 579
Mellon, Andrew W., 18, 64, 94, 105, 106, 116, 223, 422, 621–22, 640, 685
Melville, Herman, 15, 45, 259, 261, 339, 402, 403, 421, 740
Memoirs of an American Citizen, 410
Memorial Day massacre, 639
Mencken, H. L., 403, 422–23, 666–67
Mennonites, 265
Mercantilism, 30, 535, 536–37
Merz, Charles A., 646
Methodism, 266, 303, 619
Metternich, Prince Klemens von, 731
Mexican minority, 453, 470, 488, 674
Mexico, 62, 89, 307, 540, 636
Meyer, Dr. Adolf, 372, 598
Meyer, Eugene, 617
Michelson, Albert A., 365, 628
Middle East, 35, 537
Middletown, 21, 353
Middletown in Transition, 71
Migratory workers, 380–81, 487, 488–89; *see also* Minorities, agricultural
Milbank Fund, 609
Militarization, 510
Mill, John Stuart, 62, 455, 709; *Principles of Political Economy* by, 718
Millennium, belief in, 268
Miller, Perry, 420
Miller, Justice Samuel F., 111, 211, 442, 590
Miller, William, 268
Millerites, 268

Milton, John, 368, 426
Milwaukee, 81, 163
Ministry of Health, 100
Minnesota, 79, 142, 148, 152
Minorities, 5, 24, 124, 140, 141, 303, 452–57, 716; agricultural, 486–94; Chinese, 453, 470; Japanese and Mexican, 463, 470, 488, 674, 706–707; Jewish, 477–86; Negro, 457–77; *see also* Farmers, Jews, Negroes
Mission to Moscow, 106
Mississippi, 129, 140, 151, 528
Missouri Compromise, 86
Missouri Valley Authority, 153
Mr. Smith Goes to Washington, 683
Mrs. Miniver, 693
Mitchell, Broadus, 474–75
Mitchell, Charles E., 90
Mitchell, H. L., 240
Mitchell, John, 173, 234
Mitchell, Margaret, *Gone with the Wind* by, 679, 687
Modernism, 287, 288–89
Modern Times, 687
Moley, Raymond V., 95
"Molly Maguires," 51, 202, 721
Molotov, Vyacheslav M., 653; and atom bomb, 538–39, 549
Mommsen, Theodor, 416
Monopoly capitalism, 18, 60, 180, 184, 223, 439–440, 546
Monroe Doctrine, 495–96, 544, 554
Montaigne, 396, 723
Montana, 19, 22, 85, 142, 148, 155, 358
Montesquieu, 397
Moody, Dwight L., 176
Mooney, Tom, 202
Moore, George Foot, 23
Moore, John Bassett, 103
Morant, Sir Robert, 100, 108
Moravians, 28, 265
More, Hannah, 257
More, Paul Elmer, 65, 275, 403, 425–27
Morgan, James, 646
Morgan, John Pierpont, 14, 49, 60, 129, 162, 165, 612, 658; and corruption, 162; investigation of, 193; on lawyers, 577; and loan to Mussolini, 521; and religion, 272, 303, 310, 317
Morgan, Thomas Hunt, 261
Morgenthau, Henry, Jr., 94, 101, 643
Morison, Samuel Eliot, 361, 404, 418
Morley, Edward W., 628
Morley, John, 426, 745
Mormons, 28, 268, 271, 289, 298
Morris, Gouverneur, 9, 435
Morris, William, 392, 455, 721
Morrison, Herbert S., 74
Morse, Samuel F. B., 269, 325
Mosely, Edward, 20
Mosley, Sir Oswald, 453, 482
Motion Picture Association, 619; *see also* Hays, Johnston
Motion Picture Commission of New York, 627
Motley, John Lothrop, 45, 66, 415
Movies, *see* Films
Muckraking era, 423, 621; *see also* Demarest, H. L., Steffens, Tarbell
Muggletonians, 28, 293
Mun, Thomas, 566
Muncie, Ind., 20, 142, 281–82
Mundelein, Cardinal George W., 306
Munger, Rev. Theodore T., 274

Munich Agreement, 88, 542
Murphy, Robert D., 106
Murray, Philip, 200, 224, 226, 246, 261, 483
Murrow, Edward R., 695–96
Mussolini, Benito, 108, 255, 261, 521, 640, 643
Myers, "Vic," 143
Myers, William Starr, 185
Myrdal, Gunnar, 44, 122, 467–74, 616

Napoleon III, 62, 496, 760
Nast, Thomas, 638
Nathan, Robert, 410
Nation, The, 420, 637, 649–50, 653, 659
National Association for the Advancement of Colored People, 685, 706
National Association of Broadcasters, 699
National Association of Manufacturers, 122, 168, 193, 206, 359, 386, 543, 565, 597, 648, 692–93
National Biscuit Company, 673
National Catholic Welfare Council, 285
National Conference on Uniform State Laws, 580
National Council of Research, 715
National Grange, 711
National Industrial Conference Board, 193
Nationalism, 11, 503–505, 506–508
National Labor Relations Act, 134, 153, 177–78, 179, 221, 223, 225, 241, 705, 735
National Labor Relations Board, 202–203, 213, 239–40
National Resources Planning Board, 21, 508
Natural law, 407, 408, 440
Natural rights, doctrine of, 8, 114
Naylor, James, 395
Nazi-Soviet Pact, 427
Nearing, Scott, 187, 382
Nebraska, 142, 146, 148, 627
Negative state, belief in, 121, 170
Negroes, 24, 29, 44, 67, 71, 78, 140, 142, 155, 194, 236, 240, 255, 453, 454, 687, 689, 706; discrimination against, 5, 13, 24, 34, 111, 716; and education, 67, 323, 328–29, 367, 380–81; and medical care, 596–97; as a minority group, 457–77; revolts of, 461, 626
Nelson, Donald M., 120
Nelson, Judge Samuel, 144
Neo-Hegelianism in legal theory, 443
Neo-Thomism, 425
Neutrality, doctrine of, 496, 500, 501–502, 513
Nevada, 86, 146, 156
New Deal, 20–21, 68–69, 77, 80, 97, 98, 115, 119, 129–30, 177–78, 182–83, 188, 189, 235–36, 246, 247, 255, 257, 324, 436, 621, 669
New England, 26, 45, 54–55, 140, 156, 265
"New freedom," 17, 157, 177, 228, 423, 621, 733
New Humanism, 423–27
New Jersey, 19, 120, 147–48, 156
Newman, Cardinal John Henry, 426, 729
New Masses, 637, 652–53
New Republic, The, 637, 650–52, 653, 659
Newsboys, average earnings of, 673
Newspapermen, see Journalists
Newspapers, see Press
Newsreels, 685–86
Newsweek, 656
Newton, Sir Isaac, 565
New York, 19, 79, 86, 140, 141, 142, 144, 148, 156, 159, 161; education in, 329; "invisible government" of, 149; Smith as governor of, 141, 142–43, 147, 152
New York City, 50, 109, 154, 157, 639; Harper's

Magazine and, 665–66; machine politics in, 14, 150, 152, 158, 159, 163
New York Daily News, 624, 630
New York Evening Post, 649, 674
New York Herald, 633, 634
New York Herald Tribune, 630, 638, 646, 673
New York Times, 417, 630, 634, 635, 638, 641, 646, 675
New York Tribune, 634, 635
New York World, 636, 642
New Zealand, 166–67, 453
Niebuhr, Reinhold, 296, 310, 738, 739
Norris, Frank, 52, 409–10, 444
Norris, George W., 65, 74, 79, 86, 92, 250, 655
Norris-La Guardia Act, 218–19
North Africa, 35, 89
North American Review, The, 665
North Carolina, 142, 710
Norton, Andrews, 193, 315
Norton, Charles Eliot, 412, 424
Note on Literary Criticism, A, 427
Notes on Virginia, 9–10
Noyes, John Humphrey, 405
Nye, Gerald P., 127, 526–27

Oastler, Richard, 455
Occupations, census of, 332
Ochs, Adolph S., 479, 675
O'Connell, Cardinal William H., 628
O'Connor, Feargus Edward, 5
Odell, George C. D., 420
Older, Fremont, 637
Oligarchy, 385, 717–18
Olney, Richard, 251, 520
Olney-Pauncefote Treaty, 520
Olson, F. B., 152
Oneida community, 46
O'Neill, Eugene, 411
One-Third of a Nation, 693
On the Duty of Civil Disobedience, 405, 623
Open Door policy, 498, 534, 554
Oppenheimer, Franz, 714
Optimism, 39, 708; religion of, 267–69
Oration on the Crown, 752
Oregon, 35, 496, 703
Origin of Species, 409
Orthodoxy in Massachusetts, 1630–1650, 420
Osborne case, 213
Osgood, Herbert L., 416
Osler, Sir William, 372, 607, 610
Ostrogorski, M. Y., Democracy and the Organization of Political Parties by, 655
Otis, James, 395, 397
Outlook, The, 637
Owen, Robert, 5, 10, 200, 214, 229, 294, 455, 733
Owen, Robert Dale, 294, 295, 325
Owenites, 200, 201
Oxford, Lord, see Asquith, Herbert H.
Oxford Group, 661; see also Buchmanite movement

Pacific Coast, 35, 169, 674
Page, Walter Hines, 106
Pagitt, Ephraim, Hæresographia by, 292, 591–92
Paine, Thomas, 3, 9, 10, 43, 214, 231, 273, 294, 312, 319, 395, 495, 632, 669; Age of Reason by, 10, 267, 294; Common Sense by, 621
Paine Lumber Company v. Neal, 210
Palmer, A. Mitchell, 251, 563
Palmer, Elihu, 294; Principles of Nature by, 267

Palmerston, Henry John Temple, Viscount, 62, 93, 634
Pan-American Union, 126, 544
Panic of 1837, 53, 405
Panic of 1873, 132, 663
Panic of 1907, 305, 663
Paramount Pictures, 639
Parents and education, 339–42, 365
Pareto, Vilfredo, 257, 435, 718
Parker, Theodore, 29, 51, 53, 229, 267, 310, 312, 319, 405, 744, 746
Parkman, Francis, 45, 66, 166, 373, 384–85, 414, 415
Parrington, Vernon L., 52, 351, 361, 395, 421, 422, 749
Parry, David M., 206
Parry, Sir Edward A., 373
Party system, 78–82
Pascal, Blaise, 729
Pasteur, Louis, 592
Patent medicines, 639, 673
Paterson strike, 51, 70, 202
Patronage, in the arts, 393–94; political, 91, 93, 140, 150
Patterson, Joseph Medill, 731
Pattison, Mark, 426
Pauley, Edwin W., 621
Peace Treaty of Versailles (1783), 5
Pearl Harbor, 35, 36, 126, 127, 499
Peckham, Justice Rufus W., 113, 212
Pecora, Ferdinand, 90, 193, 253, 621
"Peculiar institution" of the South, 44, 53, 233, 260, 436, 628–29; see also Slavery
Peel, Sir Robert, 12–13, 426
Peffer, Nathaniel, 499–500, 523
Pegler, Westbrook, 242–43, 369, 620, 623, 638
Peirce, Charles S., 166
Pendergast, Thomas J., 32, 98, 120, 159, 716
Pennsylvania, 28, 85, 86, 140, 143, 146, 148, 156, 158, 159, 703
Penny press, 48, 632
Penrose, Boies, 32
Pepper, Claude, 86
Pericles, 49, 752
Periodicals, 620, 637, 677; cultural, 664–68; learned, 648; liberal weekly, 649–56; mass circulation, 36–37, 656–64; trade journals, 21, 648
Perkins, Frances, 93, 94, 120
Perkins, George W., 121, 734
Perlman, Selig, 221–23, 238
Perry, Matthew C., 498–99
Perry, Ralph Barton, 558
Pessimism, 268, 402, 430, 439, 449
Pétain, Henri Philippe, 108
Peters, Mayor Andrew J., 640
Petronius, 627, 666
Peyrouton, Marcel B., 21, 89
Phelps, William Lyon, 347
Philanthropy, 13, 33, 725
Philip of Macedon, 751, 759
Philippines, 516, 560
Phillips, David Graham, 638
Phillips, Ulrich B., Life and Labor in the Old South by, 626
Philosophy, critique of American, 431–49; of Edwards, 729, 730; of Epicureans, 752; see also Hegelian philosophy, Legal philosophy, Political philosophy
Picketing, 207, 208, 209
Pinckney, Charles C., 517
Pioneers, 6–8, 12, 33, 42, 46, 82, 667

Pitney, Justice Mahlon, 212
Pius XI, 308
Plato, and Christ in creed of Paul Elmer More, 425–26; his fear of the masses, 759; in Pound's theory of law, 443
Platt, Thomas C., 32, 149, 150, 161
Plow that Broke the Plains, The, 692
Plumb Plan, 219
Plutarch, 397
Poe, Edgar Allan, 45, 49, 339, 402, 459, 664, 722
Poland, 506, 690; treatment of minorities in, 452, 482, 484
Political Action Committee (P.A.C.,), 132, 136, 215–18, 226–27, 243, 246, 255, 624, 736
Political democracy, 17, 19, 82, 115, 436, 552
Political machines, 19, 59–60, 120, 151; business and, 32, 59–60, 120, 168, 170–71; critique of, 140–164
Political parties, 18, 70, 236–37, 655–56; Bryce on, 756, 758; critique of, 78–82, 129–37; and labour, 222, 227, 232, 242–43, 247–52, 262–63; realignment of, 134–37, 216–17, 239, 250; see also Democratic party, Republican party
Political philosophy, 114, 397, 403–404, 433–36, 441, 625–26; see also Franklin, Hamilton, La Follette, Lincoln
Politics, 14, 59, 142, 161–63, 625–26, 632–33, 665, 721, 738, 751, 752; business and, 19, 32, 60, 168, 171; geographical pattern of, 83, 116, 619; as a profession, 150–52, 171, 233; racial elements in, 79, 141–42; trade-unions and, 131–32, 136–37, 201, 206, 214–24, 227–63 passim, 625
Pollock, Sir Frederick, 373
Polybius, 759
Poor whites, 44, 144, 194, 236, 240, 242, 460, 461, 463, 466, 471, 475–76, 629–30
Pope, Liston, 278–81
Population, growth of, 47
Populists, 51, 58, 69, 115, 130, 231, 233, 254, 464, 465, 493, 650, 733
Portugal, 88, 453, 556
Positive state, 69, 77, 81, 98, 116, 121, 155, 164, 167, 434, 436, 441
Potemkin, 631, 680
Pound, Ezra, 65
Pound, Roscoe, 373, 443–44, 587, 589
Powell, Thomas Reed, 373
Pragmatism, 12, 56, 148–49, 323, 442, 448, 725–27
Prescott, William H., 45, 66, 373, 384–85, 414, 415
Presidency, the, 59, 72–78, 87, 95, 116–29, 163, 186, 245, 517–27
Press, 21, 48, 76, 163–64; critique of, 615–48, 668–679, 708–13; see also Periodicals
Priestley, Joseph, 395
Primary, direct, 145, 150
Prince, The, 542
Prince, Thomas, 294
Principles of Nature, 267
Principles of Political Economy, 718
Private property, 29, 167, 284; accumulation of, 13–14, 53–54, 406; rights of, 10, 30–33, 114, 205, 207, 211, 214, 215, 242, 252, 426, 434, 435, 552
Production, 167, 180, 535–36, 714, 722
Professions, 69–70; critique of, 546–71, 609–14; see also Legal profession, Medical profession
Progress, doctrine of, 259, 267–68; faith in, 8, 34, 39
Progress and Poverty, 621
Progressive movements, 69, 81, 115, 131, 217, 218, 220, 224, 441, 650
Prohibition, 32, 157, 279, 297, 422, 543, 666, 642

Propaganda, 710–12; Hitler on, 644–45; Holly-wood and, 692–95; against Jews, 480–81, 483–484; media of, 617–28 *passim*
Pro-Slavery Argument, 626
Protestantism, 157, 158, 276, 295, 296, 303–305, 393–94
Protocols of the Elders of Zion, The, 480
Proust, Marcel, 412, 426
Provincialism, 157, 402, 423
Prynne, William, 571
Public Administration Review, 648
Public opinion, 90, 152, 510, 512, 528, 615, 617–18, 669–70, 683
Public ownership, 22, 151, 153, 187, 368, 545–46, 735
Pufendorf, Baron Samuel von, 433
Pujo Committee, *see* Senate Banking and Cur-rency Committee
Pulitzer, Joseph, 479, 636, **637**
Pullman, George M., 202
Pullman strike, 202, 240, 251, 435
Pure Food and Drugs Act of 1906, 673
Puritanism, 15, 26, 27, 32, 42, 44, 188, 267, **272–73,** 289, 323, 431, 565–66, 567, **717,** 732
Pygmalion, 695

Quadregisimo Anno of Pius XI, 307, 308
Quakers, 7, 292
Quarterly Journal of Economics, 648
Quay, Matthew S., 140, 234
Quod Apostolici Muneris of Leo XIII, 307

Radicalism, 29, 42, 51, 53, 133, 163, 168, 265; communications media and, 619, 645, 669, 698–699
Radio, 21, 173, 616, 617, 627; critique of, 695–708
Railroad Brotherhoods, 132, 218, 220
Railroad Labor Board, 219
Railroads, 18, 32, 48, 155, 157
Railroad strike of 1894, 251, 438
Railway Shopmen's strike of 1922, 208
Ramsay, David, 404
Randolph, John, 294
Rankin, John E., 254
Ransom, John Crowe, 428, 740
Rappites, 28
Rationalism, 267–68
Rauschenbusch, Walter, 274, 275, 276–77, **294,** 310
Raymond, Henry J., 634, 635, 642
Reader's Digest, 391, 656, 657, 662–63
Realism, 409–10, 411
Reason the Only Oracle of Man, 267, 294
Reconstruction governments, Simkins on, *463*
Redlich, Josef, 585
"Reds," 563, 640, 643, 657–58, 669, 674
Reed, John, 653
Reedy's Mirror, 649
Religion, 10–11, 13, 82, 142, 157, 187, 729, 732, 737–38; in American tradition, 26–30; com-munications media and, 619, 623–24, 661, 699, 701, 702, 707; critique of, 264–322; *see also* Bap-tists, Christian Science, Christian socialism, Fundamentalism, Methodism, Modernism, Protestantism, Puritanism, Revivalism, Ro-man Catholic Church
Religious tolerance, 7, 9, 28, **111,** 113, 264–65, 292, 433
Renan, Ernest, 62

Report on Law Observance and Enforcement, 674
Republican party, 72, 78–80, 129–30, 148, 194–95, 216–17, 222, 232, 236, 250, 670, 756–57; *see also* Political parties
Republic Steel strike, 639, 674
Rerum Novarum of Leo XIII, 307–308
Research, atomic energy, 538, 545; business and, 22–23, 169; in education, 335–36, 360–61, 372, 374, 715; medical, 607, 608
Reuther, Walter P., 225
Revere, Paul, 397–98
Revivalism, 47, 266, 270, 279, 282, 292, 305
Revolt of Modern Youth, The, 627
Revolution, in American tradition, 10, 434, **713;** effect of incomplete, 722
Reynolds, Sir Joshua, 394
Reynolds, Robert R., 129
Rhode Island, 28, 59, 149, 152, 265
Rhodes, James Ford, 168, 414, 634, 749
Ricardo, David, 729
Richards, I. A., 429
Richards, Theodore W., 39
Richberg, Donald R., 93
Richmond Enquirer, 633
Rights of property, *see* Private property
Riis, Jacob A., 719
Ripley, George, 268
Ripon, Frederick John Robinson, Earl of, **73**
Rise of American Civilization, The, 66, 416
Rise of Puritanism, The, 420
Ritchie, Thomas, 633
Rittenhouse, David, 395
River, The, 692
Rivers, W. H. R., 455
Road to Xanadu, 420
"Robber barons," 621–22, **711**
Roberts, Evan, 292
Roberts, George E., 560
Roberts, G. H., 136
Robeson, Paul, 706
Robinson, Joseph T., 78–79, **92**
Rockefeller Foundation, 297
Rockefeller, John D., Sr., 23, 32, 33, 49, 55, 109, 165, 168, 169, 202, 261, 272, 275, 319, 426, 720, 733; philanthropy of, 168, 621–22; and religion, 272, 297, 317
Rogers, Lindsay, 86
Roman Catholic Church, 5, 79, 140, 264, 269–70, 276, 295, 296, 319, 531, 725; and anti-Semitism, 481, 483; and birth-control, 309, 699–700; com-munications media and, 619, 661, 676, 689, 698, 707; critique of, 305–11; and education, 283, 288, 309, 368–69; and foreign policy, 122, 307, 505–506, 625; hostility to, 29, 158, 265, 269, 277
Romanticism, 415, 416, 424, 729–30
Roosevelt, Eleanor, 122, 467, 643, 649
Roosevelt, Franklin D., 15, 29–30, 59, 94, 121, 133, 152, 370, 524, 621, 639, 731, 751; address on sec-ond nomination quoted, 710–11; advisers to, 95, 104–105, 120; and agriculture, 491, 755; and anti-Semitism, 480, 481, 483; and business, 181, 182–83, 388; and Catholic vote, 122, 500; and education, 164; elections of, 119, 124–25, 130, 215–16, 232, 736; on equality, 719; and foreign policy, 89, 517, 519, 521, 523, 540, 561, 562; and Four Freedoms, 38, 71; as governor of New York, 141, 142; greatness of, 124–25, 563, 750; and Hopkins, 95, 519, 567; hostility to, 68–69, 134, 135, 179, 183, 187, 368, 643, 712; Jefferson Day Address, 1932, quoted, 434; and labour,

Roosevelt (*Continued*)
132, 164, 168, 215–16, 220, 225, 226, 235, 243, 255, 735, 736; Lenin compared with 758–59; and medical care, 601; and party politics, 119–20, 122, 130, 235–36, 469, 656, 716; philosophy of, 68, 433–34, 753–55, 758, 761; policies of, 81, 90, 125, 407, 508, 509, 624, 734–35; and the press, 76, 617, 655, 670–73; and radio, 21, 76, 704; and Spanish Civil War 89, 122, 500; and State Department, 70, 95, 96, 105, 523; and Supreme Court, 112, 115, 187, 435, 436, 580, 671–72; tax policy of 78–79, 223; and third-term tradition, 119, 670

Roosevelt, Theodore, 31, 59, 77, 90, 97, 98, 189, 411, 423, 478, 712, 733, 734; and Big Business, 121, 122, 385, 562, 577, 578, 663, 734; editor of *Outlook*, 637; and foreign affairs, 89, 747; and labour, 173, 234; and Lodge, 31, 131, 254, 734; and "malefactors of great wealth," 33, 122, 177, 234, 407; in New York State, 141, 149, 150; on Paine, 312; and the press, 650, 664; and progressivism, 69, 80, 81, 121, 122, 133, 229, 254, 663; and third-term tradition, 119, 671

Root, Elihu, 52, 95, 144, 149, 150, 419
Roraback, J. Henry, 140, 143, 148
Rorty, James, 699
Rosenman, Judge Samuel I., 643
Ross, J. D., 163
Rousseau, Jean Jacques, 276, 294, 396, 399, 412, 424, 447, 723
Royal Commission on the Poor Laws, Minority Report of, 336
Royce, Josiah, 446–49, 727
Rubinow, Dr. I. M., 600–601
"Rugged individualism," 43, 80, 168, 185, 436
Ruling class, 34, 161, 165–69, 405–406, 463, 725
Rumania, 690
Rural government, 157–60
Rush, Benjamin, 395
Ruskin, John, 392, 455–56; *The Stones of Venice* by, 455
Russell, Bertrand, 309, 368, 485
Russell, Lord John, 69, 93
Russia, Tsarist, 62, 479, 551; *see also* Soviet Union
Russian Revolution, 3, 13, 168, 368, 427, 555
Ryan, Msgr. John A., 229, 310
Ryan, Thomas Fortune, 307
Rylands v. *Fletcher*, 444

Sacco-Vanzetti case, 70, 140, 163, 579, 588, 626, 665, 666
St. John, Oliver, 571
St. John, Vincent, 663
St. Louis Post-Dispatch, 636, 668
Saint-Simon, Claude Henri de, 214
Sainte-Beuve, Charles Augustin de, 420
Salisbury, Robert A. T. G. Cecil, Marquis of, 88
Saltonstall, Leverett, 59
Saltus, Edgar, 410–11
Sandburg, Carl, 65, 652
San Francisco Examiner, 636
Sankey, Ira D., 176
Santayana, George, 46, 723, 728
Sapientiae Christianae of Leo XIII, 307
Saturday Evening Post, 21, 656, 657–59
Savigny, Friedrich Karl von, 441
Scandinavia, 24, 140, 556

Scarlett, Bishop William, 296
Schelling, Friedrich Wilhelm Joseph von, 729
Schiff, Jacob H., 479
Schlesinger, Arthur M., 66, 417
Schools, 324–27, 329–39, 383, 384; *see also* Education
Schurz, Carl, 487
Schwab, Charles M., 165, 205
Schweitzer, Albert, 320
Science, 5, 22–23, 54, 254, 395–96, 420, 429, 623–24; theoretical *v.* applied, 39, 66, 166, 722
Science and Society, 667
Scofield, Edward, 149–50
Scopes trial, 286
Scott, C. P., 616
Scott, James Brown, 612
Scott, Sir Walter, 408, 415, 473, 568, 665
Scribner's Magazine, 665
Seattle, 163, 202
Secession, 138, 628–29
Secretaries of State, 106–107
Sectionalism, 83, 116, 154, 233–34, 237–38
Securities and Exchange Commission, 90, 99, 177, 223–24, 370, 621, 705
Sedition, Bagehot on, 626
Selden, John, 571
Seldes, George, 673
Senate, 72, 76, 109, 117, 186, 621; critique of, 85–92; and foreign affairs, 126–28, 518–28
Senate Banking and Currency Committee, under Black, 89–90, 162, 193, 253, 621; under Pujo, 162, 193, 253
Senate Committee on Armaments, 526–27
Senate Committee on Civil Liberties, 202, 253, 627, 639
Senate Committee on Foreign Relations, 76, 127
Senate Committee on Naval Affairs, 544
Senior, Nassau W., 61, 440
Seventeenth Amendment, 86, 92
Sewall, Judge Samuel, 335, 395, 566, 572
Seward, William H., 757
Shaftesbury, Anthony Ashley Cooper, Earl of, 455
Shakers, 28, 46, 271, 405
Sharecroppers, 13, 236, 240, 242, 471, 487, 490–92, 689, 710, 752, 755; *see also* Minorities, agricultural
Sharp, Daniel, 319
Shaw, George Bernard, 297, 695
Shaw, Judge Lemuel, 19, 144, 578
Shays' Rebellion, 10, 57, 69
Sheen, Msgr. Fulton J., 285, 624
Sheldon, Charles M., 274
Sherman Act, 177, 207, 209–10, 228, 440
Sherman, John, 86, 94, 209
Sherman, Roger, 517
Sherman, Stuart P., 425
Sherman, William T., 465
Sidney, Algernon, 397
Siegfried, André, 498, 721
Sigerist, Dr. Henry E., 372, 607
Silliman, Benjamin, 11
Simkins, Francis B., 463
Simms, William Gilmore, 459, 665
Simon, Sir John, 598
Simon, Sir John A., 511, 521
Simpson, Wallis Warfield, 676
Sinclair, Harry, 165
Sinclair, Upton, 131, 152, 410, 621, 638, 652, 733
Skidmore, Thomas, 709, 744
Slattery, Harry, 104

Slavery, 29, 46, 278, 313, 407, 429, 457–62, 472, 625, 626, 628, 745–47

Small, Lennington, 148

Smiles, Samuel, 709

Smith, Adam, 35, 390, 408, 435

Smith, Alfred E., 150, 654, 757; as governor, 141, 142–43, 147, 152; as presidential candidate, 24, 118, 269

Smith, Bernard, 427

Smith, "Cotton Ed," 79, 86

Smith, Gerald K., 67–68, 255

Smith, Herbert Knox, 577

Smith, J. Allen, 52, 368, 749

Smith, Robertson, 429

Smith, Sydney, 720

Smithsonian Institution, 101–102

Smoot, Reed, 92

Snell, Bertrand H., 251

Social Darwinism, 56, 273, 435, 442

Social gospel, 274–75, 276–77, 295, 298

Socialism, 13, 17, 68, 80, 81, 131, 132, 133, 137, 163, 168, 201, 227, 228, 229, 254, 512–13, 552, 637, 669, 709–10; see also Christian socialism

Socialist party, U.S., 81, 131, 173, 217, 254, 360, 623, 709, 736

Socialized medicine, 599–607 passim

Social Justice, 481

Social philosophy, 446–49

Social security, 98, 134; legislation, 153, 163, 215, 221, 224, 235

Social service state, 69, 177, 217, 235, 257

Social Statics, 30–31, 115

Society v. government, 746–47

Sociology for the South, 46

Socrates, 320

Sokolsky, George E., 369, 620, 638

Solid South, 44, 137, 141, 146, 216–17, 469

Soule, George, 651

South, the, 44, 53, 62–63, 156, 277, 400–401, 405, 406, 428–30, 459–76; analysis of cotton towns in, 278–81

Southcott, Joanna, 292–93

Southern Democrats, 120, 236, 257, 462, 628

Southern Literary Messenger, 664

Southern Tenant Farmers' Union, 249

Southern Textile Bulletin, 278

Sovereignty, 138–39, 435, 550–52

Soviet Union, 16, 23, 29–30, 36, 37, 137, 214, 307, 368, 495, 532, 546, 680, 739; and atomic energy, 537, 538; communications media and, 620, 624, 640, 643, 657, 661, 676, 683, 705; in world affairs, 503–504, 505, 508, 510, 511–12, 515, 516, 537, 541, 543, 556, 723

Spain, 453, 556, 560, 725, 749; Franco, 122, 620, 625; Republican, 89, 307, 640, 643, 691–92

Spanish-American War, 423, 497, 542, 551, 649

Speaker of the House, 76

Spencer, Herbert, 30–31, 231, 435, 442, 745; and Holmes, 5, 6, 442; Social Statics by, 30–31, 115; The Man versus the State by, 115

Spengler, Oswald, 257

Spoils system, 93, 103, 144, 147

Springfield Republican, 47, 634

Spurgeon, Rev. Charles H., 292

Stalin, Josef, 250, 427, 643, 653

Standard of living, 53, 82, 166, 552, 714

Starobin, Joseph, 557–59

Stassen, Harold E., 148, 517

State, Church and, 7, 26, 27, 29, 266, 319, 433; Greeks on the, 751–53; see also Negative state, Positive state, Social service state

State Department, 70, 306, 692, 712; foreign policies of, 21, 108, 505, 506, 515

State government, 138–56, 162

Steel strike of 1919, 173, 219, 229–30, 285

Steffens, Lincoln, 149, 157, 161, 232, 444, 621, 638, 646, 712

Stein, Gertrude, 65, 411

Steinbeck, John, Grapes of Wrath by, 21, 359, 411, 683

Stephen, Sir Leslie, 62, 420, 649

Stephens, John Lloyd, 665

Sterling area, 529–30

Stern, Bernhard J., 372, 418, 593, 607, 609, 749; American Medical Practice by, 607

Stettinius, Edward R., Jr., 523

Stewart, Joseph, 101

Stimson, Henry L., 74, 521

Stone, Justice Harlan F., 370, 578

Stones of Venice, The, 455

Storey, Moorfield, 747

Story, Joseph, 211, 370, 572, 578

Story of a Country Town, The, 408

Stowe, Calvin E., 325

Stowe, Harriet Beecher, Uncle Tom's Cabin by, 621

Strachey, John St. Loe, 649

Straus, Oscar S., 478

Strauss, David Friedrich, 23

Streicher, Julius, 465, 731

Strikes, 51, 70, 143, 169, 173, 202, 208, 219, 229, 240, 251, 281, 285, 297, 435, 438, 476; communications media and, 673, 674, 675

Stubbs, Bishop William, 113, 416

Students, university, 361–69 passim

Studies in Historical and Political Science, 416

Success, criteria of, 41, 46, 166, 169–70; gospel of, 53–54, 68, 165, 440, 669, 684–85

Suffrage, universal, 28, 44, 759–60

Sumner, Charles, 524

Sumner, Jessie, 249

Sumner, William Graham, 18, 168, 242–43, 275, 359, 435, 437, 745

Sun, 632

Sunday, Billy, 187, 199, 289, 382

Supreme Court, 30, 72, 235, 434, 580, 671–73, 745; and the Constitution, 189, 210–11, 435; critique of, 110–16; nominations to, 31, 370, 576, 588; proposed reform of, 73, 76, 187, 435, 436

Survey Graphic, The, 637, 668

Sutherland, Justice George, 189

Swanson, Claude A., 149

Swift, Jonathan, 423

Sylvis, William H., 132, 709, 733

Szilard, Leo, 714

Tacitus, 397

Taff Vale case, 208

Taft-Hartley Act, 134, 735

Taft-Walsh Labor Board, 219

Taft, William H., 93, 95, 109, 122, 207, 212, 219, 370, 560, 562, 578, 658

Talmadge, Eugene, 142, 463, 661

Tammany Hall, 14, 150, 152, 158, 159, 163

Taney, Justice Roger B., 211, 378, 672, 715

Tarbell, Ida M., 52, 444; History of the Standard Oil Company by, 621

Tariff policy, 87, 129, 533–34, 755

Tate, Allen, 428–30, 472, 740

Taussig, F. W., 70, 167

Taylor, Henry Osborn, 414

Taylor, John, 17, 18, 51, 395, 474, 492; on eco-

Taylor (*Continued*)
  nomic development, 167, 407, 436, 732; philosophy of, 434, 441
Taylor, Myron C., 105, 129
Taylor, Zachary, 12
Teachers, 334, 335, 336–37, 348, 351–60, 374–75, 379, 380, 588; university, 346–47, 348, 349, 356; *see also* Education
Teapot Dome scandal, 89, 621
Temple, William, Archbishop of Canterbury, 229–30, 296
Tennessee Valley Authority, 21, 74, 92, 109, 153, 155–56, 163, 187, 242, 368, 735
Texas, 32, 142
Thayer, James Bradley, 113, 373
Thayer, Judge Webster, 144
Third party movements, 81, 131, 135, 137, 216–18, 247–63 *passim*, 736; *see also* Progressive movements
Third-term tradition, 119, 121, 125, 152, 670–71, 713
Thomas, J. Parnell, 256, 356
Thomas, Norman, 132, 202, 710
Thompson, W. G., 579
Thompson, William, 159
Thoreau, Henry David, 15, 41–42, 56, 71, 405, 738; *On the Duty of Civil Disobedience* by, 405, 623
Thoughts on Scarcity, 231
Three Songs for Lenin, 680
Thring, Edward, 383
Thucydides, 397, 751
Ticknor, George, 373
Tilden, Samuel J., 462
Tillman, Benjamin R., 148, 248, 464, 629–30
Time, 656, 659–62, 663–64
Tobin, Daniel, 243
Tocqueville, Alexis de, on American ambitions, 316–17; on American application to business, 48; on the American clergy, 318; on American fear of individuality, 712; on American individualism, 724; compared with Bryce, 16–17, 63, 722; on danger to American democracy, 718; on dangers in manufacturers' aristocracy, 184, 406, 436; *Democracy in America* by, 16–17, 29; on division of interests among employers, 173; on problem of American spirit, 52; on religion and democracy, 29, 299; on second term for presidents, 121; on uniformity of values, 49, 498; on wealthy Americans in Europe, 172
Tolan Committee, Report of, 493
Tolstoy, Leo, 339, 405, 428
Townsend, Francis E., 187, 255
Town Topics, 710
Trade, *see* Foreign trade, Free trade
Trades Union Congress, British, 227, 229
Trade-unionism, 13, 17, 31, 51, 64, 68, 80–81, 131–32, 136–37, 146, 152, 164, 167, 173, 177–78, 184–85, 188, 308–309, 315–16, 335, 360, 426, 437–38, 492, 552, 625, 643, 669, 708–709, 711; critique of, 200–63 *passim*
Transcendentalism, 270, 405
Treaty-making power, 85, 87–89, 126–28, 517–27
Treves, Sir Frederick, 611
Tri-City Central Trades Council case, 208
Triumphant Democracy, 169
Trollope, Anthony, 728; *The Way We Live Now* by, 721
Trollope, Mrs. Frances, 16
Trotsky, Leo D., 250, 427, 483, 653
Truax v. Corrigan, 213

Truman, Harry S., and atomic bomb, 537, 538, 539, 549, 550, 553; career of, 98, 246, 715, 716; policies of, 179–80, 621, 735–36, 758
Trustees, university, 346–47, 348, 349, 356
Tucker, St. George, 294
Tugwell, Rexford G., 639, 673
Turkey, 510
Turner, Frederick J., 378; on American culture, 740–41; frontier theory of, 64, 417, 644, 718, 740–744, 745; on sectionalism, 154, 237
Turner, Nat, 461, 626
Twain, Mark, 15, 45, 48, 50, 408–409, 421, 473, 474, 722, 740
Tweed, William M., 148, 234, 465, 628
Tyler, John, 97, 122
Tyler, Moses Coit, 66, 384–85, 421; *History of American Literature* by, 166

Uncle Tom's Cabin, 621
Underprivileged, 68, 81, 733–34; *see also* Masses
Unemployment, 35, 60, 68, 69, 70, 80, 99, 167, 257, 546, 552
Uniformity, 49–50, 622, 646–47, 712–13
Unions, *see* Trade-unionism
Union Theological Seminary, 361
Unitarianism, 10, 267, 270
United Automobile Workers, 224
United Mine Workers, 222, 243
United Nations, 508–29 *passim*, 546–51, 556; Security Council of, 510, 511, 514, 528, 539, 544, 546–47, 556
United Press, 646
United States Steel Corporation, 692, 711–12
Universities, 67, 480, 483; academic freedom in, 355–60, 369; compared with European, 59, 343–348, 351, 353; conditions of promotion in, 379–380; level of teaching in, 362–69; non-professional schools of, 373–80; the presidency of, 166, 194, 348–60; professional schools of, 370–373; *see also* Education, Teachers
University of Chicago, 297, 348, 359, 369, 425
University of Montana, 22
Untermyer, Samuel, 169
Upham, William H., 149–50
Utopianism, 229, 268, 730

Vandenberg, Arthur H., 76, 517
Vanderbilt, Cornelius, 23, 33, 50, 60, 64, 165, 261, 272, 733
Vanderbilt, William H., 59, 152
Van Devanter, Justice Willis, 442
Vansittart, Lord, 108
Van Sweringen brothers, 64, 193
Van Vechten, Carl, 410
Vanzetti, Bartolomeo, 320; *see also* Sacco-Vanzetti case
Vardaman, James K., 464
Vare, William S., 158, 159
Vatican, the, 23, 506, 639, 676, 691, 707
Veblen, Thorstein, 70–71, 358, 567, 749; Brooks Adams' ideas similar to, 445; on "predatory culture," 259, 610, 613; his term "conspicuous waste," 45, 165, 474; his work discussed, 437–441
Venezuela dispute, 496
Vermont, 78, 129, 141, 146, 619
Versailles Treaty, 87, 88, 135, 518, 520–21
Vesey, Denmark, 461
Vested interests, 21, 87, 158–59, 160; *see also* Business, Corporations

Vice-presidency, 72, 97–99, 124
Villard, Henry, 649
Villard, Oswald Garrison, 650, 654
Vindication of the Government of New-England Churches, A, 265
Vinson, Justice Fred M., 110
Violence, in American tradition, 31–32, 55; in labour relations, 51, 169, 173, 202, 240, 281, 297, 435, 674
Virginia, 139, 148–49, 156
Virginia Quarterly, The, 667
Virgin Islands, 554, 559
Vision of Columbus, The, 8, 404
Volney, Comte Constantin de, *Les Ruines* by, 10, 267, 294
Volstead Act, *see* Prohibition
Voltaire, François Marie Arouet de, 267, 294, 399, 422, 568
Voters, 130, 134, 140, 201, 617

Wagner Act, *see* National Labor Relations Act
Wagner, Robert F., 78–79, 129
Waite, Justice Morrison R., 211–12
Walker, Mayor James J., 161
Wallace, Henry A., 78, 93, 94, 735; philosophy of, 38, 433–34; sacrifice of by F.D.R., 36, 98, 119, 236, 246; as Secretary of Agriculture, 101, 102, 743; as vice-president, 72, 98, 99
Wallace, Henry C., 78, 155
Walling, William English, 652
Wall Street, 18, 45, 89, 162, 621
Wall Street Journal, 624
Walpole, Horace, 612
Ward, Artemus, 48
Ware, Norman J., 418
War Labor Policies Board, 219
War of Independence, 9, 621, 632, **717**
Warren, Charles, 571, 616
Washington, 19, 35, 131
Washington, George, 4, 6, 25, 39, 46, 133, 294, 339, 415; foreign policy of, 67, 738; and Paine, 312; and Senate, 518; and third-term tradition, 670–71
Washington Post, 617
Watch and Ward Society, 304–305, 627
Watson, Thomas E., 248, 464–67, 629–30
Watterson, Henry, 635
Wealth, 17, 31, 33, 399, 724; concentration of, 52, 177, 182–83, 183–84, 676, 744; distribution of, 178, 180, 508; as a stewardship, 42, 169, 659; *see also* Business
Weaver, James B., 132
Webb, Sidney, 103
Webster, Daniel, 49, 74, 86, 91, 434; on government, 252, 759–60; on property rights, 111, 211
Webster, Noah, 9, 404, 632
Weimar Republic, 513, 717
Welch, Dr. William H., 372, 598
Welles, Gideon, 95, 108
Welles, Orson, 683
Welles, Sumner, 95, 96, 105
Wells Fargo, 47
Wells, H. G., 248
Wesley, John, 266, 267
Wesleyanism, 292, 298
West European federation, 556
Weyerhaeuser family, 143, 165
Weyl, Walter E., 650
Wharton, Edith, 52, 410
Wheeler, Burton K., 78, 482, **672**

White, Andrew D., 80
White, Henry, 517
White, William Allen, 217, 620, **635**
Whitefield, George, 266
Whitehead, Alfred North, 387, 390, 445, 590; on role of the State, 388–89
Whitman, Walt, 34, 45, 49, 64, 65, 186, 259, 261, 392, 402–403, 404, 711, 719
Whitney, Eli, 12, 457
Whitney, Richard, 162
Whitney, William C., 161
Wickersham, George W., *Report on Law Observance and Enforcement* by, 674
Wickser, Philip J., 573
Widener, Harry E., 621–22
Wigglesworth, Michael, 394
Wigmore, J. H., 588
Wilcox, Ella Wheeler, 290
Wilde, Oscar, 410
Wiley, Caleb, 325
Wilkerson, James H., 208
Williams, Roger, 7, 26, 265, 394–95, **433**
Willis, Nathaniel Parker, 16, 664
Willkie, Wendell, 130, 702, 716; fight against T.V.A., 155; and F.D.R., 76, 78, 255, 704; presidential candidacy of, 79, 118, 120, 121, 226, 243
Willson, E. A., 489
Wilmot Proviso, 462
Wilson, Charles E., 120
Wilson, Edmund, 65, 421; *The American Jitters* by, 622
Wilson, Justice James, 518, 572
Wilson, Woodrow, 12, 15, 59, 95, 108, 150, 152, 324, 348, 407, 441, 469, 523, 651, 654, 712, 719, 751, 761; appointments of, 106, 479, 576; and foreign affairs, 87, 561, 562, 734; and House, 95, 97, 479, 519, 651; and labour, 209, 219, 234; and Lodge, 91; and "new freedom," 17, 157, 177, 228, 423, 621, 733; policies of, 77, 89, 122, 133, 509; and third-term tradition, 119, 671; and treaty-making power, 87, 517, 521
Winant, John G., 105, 106
Windham, William, 3
Windsor, Edward Albert, Duke of, press treatment of, 641, 676
Winters, Yvor, 428
Winthrop, Governor John, 265, 395, 566
Winthrop, Professor John, 396
Wisconsin, 19, 69, 131, 142, 144, 149–50, 217
Wise, John, 26, 42, 395, 433; *A Vindication of the Government of New-England Churches* by, 265
Woll, Matthew, 131, 195, 220
Women's Christian Temperance Union, 157
Wood, Robert, 677
Woolman, John, 395, 432
Woolsey, Theodore Dwight, 275
Workers, 53, 178, 184, 752; education and, 323, 326–27, 327–28, 360; mobility of, 215, 258, 716; skilled, 200, 219, 247; unskilled, 174, 200, 247; white-collar, 200, 225, 247, 735
Working classes, political attitude of, 131–33, 136–37
Working class parties, 133, 166, 201, 215
Workingmen's party, 226, 229
Works Progress Administration, 235, 693, **735**
World affairs, responsibility of U.S. in, 128, 495, 502–503
World-Wide Influences of the Cinema, 690–91
Wright, Frances, 10, 294, 295